THE OXFORD HANDBOOK OF

CITIZENSHIP

THE OXFORD HANDBOOK OF

CITIZENSHIP

Edited by

AYELET SHACHAR

RAINER BAUBÖCK

IRENE BLOEMRAAD

MAARTEN VINK

OXFORD

UNIVERSITY PRESS

Great Clarendon Street, Oxford, OX2 6DP,
United Kingdom

Oxford University Press is a department of the University of Oxford.
It furthers the University's objective of excellence in research, scholarship,
and education by publishing worldwide. Oxford is a registered trade mark of
Oxford University Press in the UK and in certain other countries

First published 2017
First published in paperback 2020

Published in the United States of America by Oxford University Press
198 Madison Avenue, New York, NY 10016, United States of America

British Library Cataloguing in Publication Data
Data available

Library of Congress Cataloging in Publication Data
Data available

ISBN 978-0-19-880585-4 (Hbk.)
ISBN 978-0-19-880586-1 (Pbk.)

ACKNOWLEDGMENTS

....

It takes a village, the saying goes, to raise a child. It takes a transnational community coupled with local support to seamlessly bring together scholars from various disciplines and different countries to advance our thinking about one of the world's most pressing issues—the current state of citizenship, its past, and potential future—the remit of this Handbook.

The editors would like to acknowledge the editorial assistance provided by Naama Ofrath, Ayelet Shachar's doctoral student at the University of Toronto Faculty of Law, who played a significant role in ensuring that the manuscript was submitted in record time and in mint condition. We would also like to thank Dagmar Recke of the Ethics, Law and Politics Department at the Max Planck Institute for the Study of Religious and Ethnic Diversity, who, together with Monika Rzemieniecka of the European University Institute's Department of Political and Social Sciences, flawlessly helped us organize the Oxford Handbook of Citizenship Authors' Workshop, which was generously hosted by the Robert Schuman Centre for Advanced Studies at the EUI in June 2016. Over the course of three intense days under the Tuscan sun, the workshop's participants had the opportunity to tighten the overarching thematic coherence of the Handbook and to sharpen their own respective chapters by reading, commenting, debating, and interacting with other contributors. We are grateful to the Max Planck Society for its financial support of this event, which enabled its success.

At Oxford University Press, Alex Flach, senior commissioning editor, sparked the idea for this Handbook and provided sound guidance throughout the gestation of this project and its early life, fully supporting our vision of adopting a multidisciplinary and comparative perspective. The final stages of submission and production were overseen by Jamie Berezin, who shared the same enthusiasm and commitment to the project as we did. Eve Ryle-Hodges patiently responded to our various requests and helped secure, along with Oxford's design team, the cover image which brings to the fore themes of multiple meanings, overlapping affiliations, and changing scales of membership that are central to the inquiry in this Handbook.

Last but not least, we are grateful to four anonymous reviewers and to our dedicated authors, who endured the extensive feedback provided by the editors in several rounds of commentary throughout the writing process.

TABLE OF CONTENTS

PART III   MEMBERSHIP AND RIGHTS

PART IV   CONTEXT AND PRACTICE

PART V MEMBERSHIP IN THE STATE AND BEYOND

PART VI TOMORROW'S CHALLENGES

LIST OF ABBREVIATIONS

....

AFDC	Aid to Families with Dependent Children
ART	Assisted Reproduction Technologies
ASEAN	Association of Southeast Asian Nations
CJEU	Court of Justice of the European Union
ECHR	European Convention of Human Rights and Fundamental Freedoms
ECOWAS	Economic Community of West African States
EU	European Union
GCC	Gulf Cooperation Council
HNWI	high-net-worth-individuals
ICERD	International Convention on the Elimination of All Forms of Racial Discrimination
ICJ	International Commission of Jurists
IDEA	Institute for Democracy and Electoral Assistance
IDP	internally displaced person
ILO	International Labour Organization
IOM	International Organization for Migration
IRO	International Refugee Organisation
MIPEX	Migration Integration Policy Index
NAFTA	North American Free Trade Agreement
NGO	non-governmental organization
OAU	Organization of African Unity
OCI	Overseas Citizens of India
OECD	Organization for Economic Co-operation and Development
OSCE	Organization for Security and Cooperation in Europe
PNR	Passenger Name Records
RSD	refugee status determination
STC	safe third country
TCN	Third Country National
TPS	Temporary Protected Status
UDHR	Universal Declaration of Human Rights
UHNWI	ultra-high-net-worth-individuals
UI	Unemployment Insurance
UKC	UK and Colonies
UNCRC	UN Convention on the Rights of the Child
UNCRPD	UN Convention on the Rights of Persons with Disabilities
UNHCR	United Nations High Commissioner for Refugees
WTO	World Trade Organization

List of Contributors

Ryan K. Balot, Professor of Political Science and Classics, University of Toronto.

Rainer Bauböck, Chair in Social and Political Theory, European University Institute.

Irene Bloemraad, Professor of Sociology and Thomas Garden Barnes Chair of Canadian Studies, University of California, Berkeley.

Linda Bosniak, Distinguished Professor of Law, Rutgers University School of Law.

Erin Aeran Chung, Charles D. Miller Associate Professor of East Asian Politics, Johns Hopkins University.

Michael Collyer, Professor of Geography, University of Sussex.

Cathryn Costello, Andrew W. Mellon Associate Professor in International Human Rights and Refugee Law, University of Oxford.

Don J. DeVoretz, Professor of Economics Emeritus, Simon Fraser University.

Alexander C. Diener, Associate Professor of Geography, University of Kansas.

Sue Donaldson, Affiliated Fellow, Animals in Philosophy, Politics, Law and Ethics, Queen's University.

Costica Dumbrava, External Research Associate, Maastricht University Centre for Citizenship, Migration and Development.

David Scott FitzGerald, Professor of Sociology and Theodore E. Gildred Chair in U.S.-Mexican Relations, University of California, San Diego.

Chaim Gans, Professor of Law Emeritus, Tel Aviv University.

Matthew J. Gibney, Elizabeth Colson Professor of Politics and Forced Migration, University of Oxford.

Kirsty Gover, Associate Professor of Law, University of Melbourne.

Iseult Honohan, Senior Lecturer, School of Politics and International Relations, University College Dublin.

Nahikari Irastorza, Willy Brandt Research Fellow, Malmö Institute for Studies of Migration, Diversity, and Welfare.

Engin Isin, Professor in International Politics, Queen Mary University of London.

Christian Joppke, Chair of General Sociology, University of Bern.

Will Kymlicka, Canada Research Chair in Political Philosophy, Queen's University.

Noora A. Lori, Assistant Professor of International Relations, Pardee School of Global Studies, Boston University.

Willem Maas, Professor of Politics and Jean Monnet Chair, Glendon College, York University.

Liav Orgad, Associate Professor, Interdisciplinary Center Herzliya; WZB Berlin Social Science Center.

David Owen, Professor of Social and Political Philosophy, University of Southampton.

Kamal Sadiq, Associate Professor of Political Science, University of California, Irvine.

Ayelet Shachar, Director, Max Planck Insitute for the Study of Religious and Ethnic Diversity; Professor of Law and Political Science, University of Toronto.

Jo Shaw, Salvesen Chair of European Institutions, University of Edinburgh.

Oxana Shevel, Associate Professor of Political Science, Tufts University.

Rogers M. Smith, Christopher H. Browne Distinguished Professor of Political Science, University of Pennsylvania.

Peter J. Spiro, Charles R. Weiner Professor of Law, Temple University.

Francesca Strumia, Lecturer in Law, University of Sheffield.

Kok-Chor Tan, Professor of Philosophy, University of Pennsylvania.

Joel P. Trachtman, Professor of International Law, Fletcher School of Law and Diplomacy, Tufts University.

Bryan S. Turner, Professor of Sociology, Australian Catholic University.

Maarten Vink, Chair of Political Science, Maastricht University.

Leti Volpp, Robert D. and Leslie Kay Raven Professor of Law in Access to Justice, University of California, Berkeley.

Neil Walker, Regius Chair of Public Law and the Law of Nature and Nations, University of Edinburgh.

Daniel Weinstock, James McGill Professor, Faculty of Law, McGill University.

PART I

OPENING PAGES

CHAPTER 1

INTRODUCTION: CITIZENSHIP—*QUO VADIS*?

AYELET SHACHAR, RAINER BAUBÖCK,
IRENE BLOEMRAAD, AND MAARTEN VINK

CONTRARY to predictions that it would become increasingly unimportant in a globalizing world, citizenship is back with a vengeance.[1] Politicians worldwide stress its importance, and policymakers debate how best to reinvigorate its meaning in an age of global economic and communication flows, international migration, and intensifying security pressures. Legislatures have introduced more exacting citizenship tests and restrictive admission criteria for certain categories of migrants while selectively opening up access to others. Constitutional and high courts have become embroiled in citizenship matters as activists call upon them to articulate the boundaries of membership in debates over definitions of the family or the place of religion in the public sphere, and to address foundational questions concerning the constitutional limits of state power. Should, for example, the indefinite detention of non-citizens be legally sanctioned? Under what conditions, if any, is it legitimate for immigration law to be a tool of anti-terrorism law?

Scholars, too, have turned their attention back to citizenship after years of neglect. A search in the corpus of Google books reveals that, from 1800 onward, published usage of the term 'citizenship' rises gradually, to peak in the 1920s, as seen in Figure 1.1. Usage

---

[1] Catherine Dauvergne, 'Citizenship with a Vengeance', *Theoretical Inquires in Law* 8 (2007): pp. 489–507.

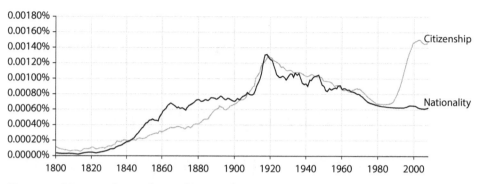

Figure 1.1 Ngram—Citizenship and Nationality
Source: https://books.google.com/ngrams/, original graph

then declines steadily through to the early 1980s, a pattern that also characterizes the term 'nationality.' However, while use of 'nationality' in English language books remains constant from 1980 onward, reference to citizenship has exploded, reaching an all-time high in the early twenty-first century.[2] This renaissance has involved vibrant scholarly debates about emerging postnational, supranational, transnational, and multicultural conceptions of membership, as well as critical discussions of core socio-legal, political, and comparative aspects of citizenship.[3]

This Handbook provides a state-of-the-art roadmap to help us think creatively and level-headedly about some the most pressing and defining issues of our time: the future of citizenship in a turbulent world of growing migration anxieties, marginalization of native-born minorities, and resurgent populism. Our contributors, who are amongst the most knowledgeable senior and emerging scholars in their fields, were asked to synthesize the key debates and questions on their topic. But while this

---

[2] See Ngram Viewer online: https://books.google.com/ngrams/graph?content=citizenship%2C+nationality&year_start=1800&year_end=2008&corpus=15&smoothing=3&share=&direct_url=t1%3B%2Ccitizenship%3B%2Cco%3B.t1%3B%2Cnationality%3B%2Cco [last accessed 25 January 2017]. For the methods behind the search, see Jean-Baptiste Michel, Yuan Kui Shen, Aviva Presser Aiden, Adrian Veres, Matthew K. Gray, William Brockman, The Google Books Team, Joseph P. Pickett, Dale Hoiberg, Dan Clancy, Peter Norvig, Jon Orwant, Steven Pinker, Martin A. Nowak, and Erez Lieberman Aiden, 'Quantitative Analysis of Culture Using Millions of Digitized Books', *Science* 331 (6014) (2011): pp. 176–182.

[3] The literature is too vast to cite. For concise overviews, see Will Kymlicka and Wayne Norman, 'The Return of the Citizen: A Survey of Recent Work on Citizenship Theory', *Ethics* 104 (1994): pp. 352–381; Irene Bloemraad, 'Citizenship and Migration: A Current Review', *Journal of International Migration and Integration* 1 (2000): pp. 9–37, doi:10.1007/s12134-000-1006-4; Linda Bosniak, 'Citizenship Denationalized', *Indiana Journal of Global Legal Studies* 7 (2000): pp. 447–509; Randall Hansen and Patrick Weil (eds.), *Dual Nationality, Social Rights and Federal Citizenship in the U.S. and Europe: The Reinvention of Citizenship* (New York: Berghahn Books, 2002); Bryan S. Turner, 'Citizenship Studies: A General Theory', *Citizenship Studies* 1 (2007): pp. 5–17, doi.org/10.1080/13621029708420644; Sarah Fine and Lea Ypi (eds.), *Migration in Political Theory: The Ethics of Movement and Membership* (Oxford: Oxford University Press, 2016).

volume is labeled a 'Handbook', we envision it as much more than a reference volume. We aim to set an ambitious agenda for both theoretical and empirical explorations of citizenship. The volume's authors were tasked with offering an analysis of silences or missing questions, and to elaborate their own, original understanding of the main challenges and prospects informing citizenship in today's world. The resulting chapters provide an invaluable entry point to students new to these debates, as well as original views that will pique the interest of seasoned scholars.

The Handbook is motivated by the belief that to provide a comprehensive account of the multifaceted and protean dimensions of citizenship, we must adopt a multidisciplinary and comparative approach. Legal academics, political scientists, economists, sociologists, geographers, policy analysts, and philosophers have brought their unique perspectives to bear on illuminating the universe of citizenship contained in this volume. Given the diversity of perspectives, the Handbook does not articulate a single definition of citizenship, which would be either a hopeless task or a sectarian project given the proliferation of meanings and uses of the term.[4] Instead, contributors are attentive to the manifold dimensions of citizenship: as legal status and political membership; as rights and obligations; as identity and belonging; as civic virtues and practices of engagement; and as a discourse of political and social equality or responsibility for a common good. There is widespread agreement among the contributors that we are witnessing momentous changes in the conception and practice of citizenship. But we are far from a consensus about how to interpret these transformations and what to make of their major causes and consequences. While the chapters are largely directed to an academic audience, they have been written in such a way as to be legible to anyone, from members of non-governmental organizations to courtroom officials, interested in cutting-edge knowledge in this highly topical area.

Citizenship, or its lack, is often felt most sharply by those who move across borders, as individuals and families run a gauntlet of passports, visas, technological scans, and officials tasked with enforcing borders. Crossing borders and staying on the other side also raises questions about migrants' relations to the state where they reside and the states they left, and even to the states where their parents or grandparents were born or their spouse holds nationality. But citizenship historically and today is also about those who never traverse an international border. From Black Lives Matter in the United States to the situation of 'untouchables' in India, from the membership of Aboriginals in Australia to locally born Russian speakers in Latvia, citizenship raises questions of what we owe to whom. Is it possible to articulate membership obligations in civic terms, avoiding the slide toward ethnonational and nativist interpretations of 'homeland'-first which are sweeping many parts of the world? Are such special obligations to fellow citizens and co-residents,

---

[4] See W.B. Gallie, 'Essentially Contested Concepts', *Proceedings of the Aristotelian Society* 56 (1956): pp. 167–198.

grounded in place, trust, historical injustice, sharing in a society or partaking in its democratic decisions-making, compatible with duties—local or global—toward all human beings, irrespective of membership status?

Humanists and other visionaries of a global village have advocated freedom of movement across borders and rights based on personhood, not membership in socially and politically constructed nations. But even in today's age of increased globalization and privatization, the authority to govern borders and citizenship resides primarily with independent states and governments, not a world parliament or global demos. In our world, some enjoy significant freedom of movement—such as European citizens do both within the Schengen area and around the globe—while others risk their lives as they escape hunger, violence, or environmental disaster in countries in which 'chance, not choice, has placed them.'[5] Public debates typically presume that states have a moral and legal right to grant or deny entry to their territories, while drawing sharp lines between economic migrants and political refugees, documented and undocumented entrants, citizens and non-citizens. Are these stable distinctions? In today's world, do they constitute a just order or a form of indefensible stratification? And what about hierarchies within a citizenry? How does the ideal of citizenship, or its articulation in fundamental rights or civic engagement, mitigate inequalities based on social-class origins, gender, ethnoracial background, sexual orientation, or other bases of inequality? Is the ideal of social citizenship as a mechanism of inclusion still robust today or has it been superseded by a neoliberal citizenship contract that shuts out those who are classified as unproductive or undeserving?[6]

Contributors to this Handbook shed light on some of the most complex and still-unresolved puzzles in the field. A first set of questions is of a conceptual or normative nature. How can we envision the relations between semi-bounded political communities and more fluid and fluctuating conceptions of membership? Does citizenship entail only rights, or also responsibilities? In a globalizing world, who ought to determine the scope and scale of membership, and according to what criteria? What about the status of non-citizens, semi-citizens, precarious members, and other 'in between' categories? Which requirements are legitimate, or illegitimate, in acquiring citizenship through naturalization? Can citizenship expand beyond the family of humanity to include animals as full and equal members? How

---

[5] This phrase was famously coined by Thomas Jefferson in early American revolutionary thought. See Thomas Jefferson, 'Summary View of the Rights of British America,' in *The Writings of Thomas Jefferson* (New York: Viking Press, 1984), at 4. For further discussion in the context of comparative citizenship laws, see Ayelet Shachar, *The Birthright Lottery: Citizenship and Global Inequality* (Cambridge, MA: Harvard University Press, 2009).

[6] See Margaret R. Somers, *Genealogies of Citizenship: Markets, Statelessness, and the Right to Have Rights* (Cambridge: Cambridge University Press, 2008); Wendy Brown, *Undoing the Demos: Neoliberalism's Stealth Revolution* (Cambridge, MA: MIT Press, 2015).

should we rethink some of the basic assumptions about 'who belongs', or who ought to belong, within the circle of members we call citizens?

A second set of questions arises from comparing and contrasting different citizenship regimes across space, over time, and between different groups of individuals in the same society. Such comparisons draw attention to the variety of historical and current experiences in political communities ranging from the city to the region, and from the domestic to the international level. They also encourage the identification of broader trends detached from local, regional, and national idiosyncrasies. What variations in the relationship between citizenship and nationalism are wrought by globalization and the counter-responses to it? This question has gained new urgency in the era of Brexit, 'America First', and Hindu nationalism, to mention but a few examples. What are the best methods to compare different citizenship regimes? What insights and observations open up when citizenship is studied beyond the traditional Euro-centric focus? Under what conditions are states likely to adopt citizenship policies that permit expanding and diversifying their citizenries, and when and why do they, conversely, attempt to reinforce pre-existing social, gendered, and racialized inequalities? What difference does citizenship make, for whom, and under which membership regimes? Is there a universal notion of citizenship, or multiple and multiplying understandings, depending on the national, regional, and historical context explored? Are we witnessing a march of progress toward ever more inclusive conceptions of democratic participation, or a disintegration of any meaningful sense of membership and solidarity? How can we account for dramatic transformations in recent years, such as the rise of dual nationality, the surge in citizenship-for-sale programs, the innovation of new technologies of bordering and reproduction, and the revival of denationalization powers? How are we to conceptualize the relationship between refugeehood and citizenship in a crisis-ridden world? Given all this variety, how should we capture and reflect the multidimensionality of citizenship, with its ever-changing kaleidoscope of legal status, rights, obligations, participation, and sense of belonging, to name but a few core components? The chapters that follow address these very questions, and many more, as they challenge, explore, and revisit familiar distinctions, unsettling some of the core assumptions that are frequently taken for granted by canonical accounts of citizenship.[7]

In the interest of analytical clarity and succinctness, the Handbook is divided into five separate sections; the headings are organizing heuristics rather than airtight compartments. Wherever feasible, we have encouraged the breakdown of traditional disciplinary divides and the referencing of ideas across sections to highlight the value of interdisciplinary and comparative research. The chapters thereby strive to provide accessible and nuanced syntheses of and reflections on the scholarly

---

[7] A similar effort is advanced, in the context of migration, by Fine and Ypi (n 3).

literature on key topics in the field—and to highlight the most significant challenges that still lie ahead.

Part II, 'Approaches and Perspectives,' presents a gamut of viewpoints through which to conceptualize and investigate citizenship. From revisiting the classic distinction between Greek and Roman citizenship to economic theories of the value of citizenship ascension, the breadth and scope of exploration is sweeping. Historical, republican, feminist, and critical race theory perspectives reexamine liberal constructions of citizenship, revealing how despite the promise of equality, considerations of race, gender, ethnicity, national origin, and related discriminatory grounds have long played a role in deciding who can be a citizen, and who is deemed unfit for inclusion. A panoramic view of the shifting geopolitical scales of citizenship over the last two and half millennia provides a useful reminder of the temporality of our current international system of territorial states. The tools of contemporary political theory are used to shine light on the relationship between political membership and democratic boundaries, the challenges of diversity and transnational interdependence, and the search for reconciliation between citizenship and nationhood. Comparing and contrasting different countries' citizenship regimes—the formal and informal norms that define access to membership and its associated rights and duties, variably regulated by states, sub-state, and supra-state communities—raises new theoretical and methodological challenges.

Part III, 'Membership and Rights,' engages with some of the oldest quandaries in the literature on citizenship, which have gained renewed salience in contemporary politics. In a world of greater mobility and instability, can human rights regimes come to replace the function of citizenship as a source of legal status and basic protection? How do we square purportedly universal human rights norms with the principle of the democratic self-determination of peoples? If citizenship denotes legal status, rights, identity, and a range of distinctive activities and practices, does it require some degree of 'shared values,' however difficult to define? Whose points of view ought to inform such decisions—those of current, or also prospective, citizens? What about those seeking to get in? What dark corners of citizenship's exclusionary past get lost and what is revealed about its emancipatory potential by investigating citizenship tests and other civic integration thresholds used in naturalization? What do these policies tell us about the construction of a national 'us' (and, implicitly, 'them')? The situation of non-citizens, who lack both legal status and (often) the right to vote, is another powerful prism through which to analyze modes of citizenship denial or marginalization. Citizenship exclusion is, however, no longer only manifested in blocked access but also in the revival of powers of denationalization in the context of the 'war on terror.' This raises haunting questions about how the use of denationalization can facilitate atrocities against targeted groups, as occurred in the twentieth century when stripping citizenship from Jews and others led, as Hannah Arendt famously put it, to a denial of the 'right to have rights.'[8]

Part IV, 'Context and Identity,' highlights variations in citizenship regimes practiced in different countries, from immigrant states to 'non-western' citizenship, from settler societies to newly independent states. These investigations reveal competing justifications and logics for configuring the boundaries of political community. In whose name is it constituted? What are the implications of different citizenship rules for political and economic power of different groups, external actors, and other states in the region? What factors explain policy variations, across countries and over time, and how does studying citizenship beyond the traditional 'western' context provide a distinctive understanding of membership? Tensions between civic and descent-based definitions of citizenship have been thoroughly explored in the context of the history and politics of national regimes, but their centrality to debates about how to define tribal membership rules in settler societies is a topic that has only recently gained attention. Further destabilizing familiar categories, the similarities and differences between secular and religious institutional frameworks of membership are considered. Does citizenship matter for lawful, settled immigrants who are already on the territory, such as 'green card' holders in the United States, in terms of their political engagement, socio-economic participation, and civic integration? If so, why and how? Theorizing about the mechanisms linking citizenship status to life experiences opens up new avenues for future research.

Part V, 'Membership in the State and Beyond,' shifts the gaze from the state-centered Westphalian system to new terrains and referents of citizenship. Notions of territoriality as a constitutive feature of citizenship and statehood loom large in the modernist political imagination, but this principle is now under pressure. How far can we venture from the territorial principle in accounting for, or promoting, the idea of citizenship as equal membership? How does it relate to emerging notions of performative, plural, multilevel, supranational, transnational, and cosmopolitan citizenship? In a world of more diverse and fluid common commitments, need one remain a member of a fixed and stable community to enjoy basic rights, protection, security, and solidarity? What is the role of countries of origins and emigrants themselves in facilitating diasporic and transnational communities, especially in relation to economic development and remittances? Is the change in the way citizenship is perceived—moving away from a unitary and exclusive relationship between an individual and a sovereign state—merely interest-driven or genuinely principled? Does it matter? New forms of multiple and multilevel citizenship now span the world, bringing with them developments of various forms of membership both 'above' and 'below' the state. Unlike cosmopolitan citizenship, supranational

---

[8] Hannah Arendt, *The Origins of Totalitarianism: New Edition with Added Prefaces* (San Diego: Harvest Book, [1951] 1985).

citizenship—of which citizenship of the European Union is a prime exemplar—remains bounded in a particular, territorial space. What should, could, and would it mean to speak of, and act, as a world citizen? These are some of the most foundational questions occupying the field in the early twenty-first century.

Part VI, 'Tomorrow's Challenges', ventures into the unknown. How will technological innovation affect the future of citizenship? Will we see the rise of digital communities that enhance democratic participation or, conversely, will new surveillance techniques allow governments to monitor protest and undermine the capacity of citizens to challenge political power? The disposition to identify and classify people is characteristic of the modern state, especially as it has become concerned with governing diverse populations and security risks.[9] Will automated 'smart borders' come to determine access to our communities, enhancing mobility and opportunity for the world's trusted travelers, most of whom hail from affluent and stable countries, at the expense of immobility and exclusion of individuals and groups that are singled out on account of their religious affiliation, country of origin, lack of self-sufficiency, or algorithmic risk profile? Identifying, monitoring, and assessing the legal, ethical, political, social, and cultural implications of these new governance techniques is a task that scholars of citizenship studies are well positioned to carry out.

As sophisticated as new technologies of bordering are, they cannot hermetically seal all gates of entry. The recent wave of migrants desperately reaching Europe's shores in search of refuge serves as a fresh reminder. As governments try to balance their international commitments to human rights protection with domestic pressures to cap and limit such obligations, what guidelines may scholars of citizenship and migration offer in the face of mass influx? The goal of refugee protection is to find durable solutions that enable refugees to live safely and rebuild their lives. These solutions are usually associated with permanent settlement, whether in the host country, a third country or the country of origin. In practice, however, many gain only temporary or conditional protection, if any at all. Perhaps we should think about refugees as potential holders of world citizenship. Today, the harsh reality on the ground is that many governments place refugees, unauthorized migrants, and minority populations in a 'pending' or 'in-between' status that makes it impossible for them to gain access to citizenship as a legal status. This situation of 'precarious citizenship' may linger for years—in some cases over generations—generating vulnerabilities and injustices that often go unnoticed in debates that presuppose that states will act benevolently toward those residing on their territories.

---

[9] See e.g. John C. Torpey, *The Invention of the Passport: Surveillance, Citizenship and the State* (Cambridge: Cambridge University Press, 2000); Ulrich Beck, *Risk Society: Toward a New Modernity* (London: Sage, 1992).

More generally, to whom do we owe membership and based on what criteria? As countries form regional partnerships, they increasingly accept dual or multiple national citizenships, and grant certain rights to non-resident citizens outside their boundaries and to non-citizen residents within their territories. Is it time to also rethink states' duties to their regional partners, to their former colonies, and to those who hold forms of 'quasi-citizenship'? Do constitutional democracies owe special membership obligations toward those outside their borders whose identities and aspirations they have substantially shaped through their coercively enforced policies? In various countries, the super-rich can purchase citizenship with the speed of an international wire transfer. Should citizenship merely be treated as a commodity to be purchased and sold on the market? As the frontiers of citizenship cover an ever-growing array of groups and claims, are we stretching the concept too far and too thin, losing sight of some of the essential features that make the ideal and practice of citizenship meaningful and valuable? Alternatively, can and should full, equal citizenship be extended beyond the parameters of the 'capacity contract' to also include children, persons with cognitive disabilities, and domesticated animals we brought into our society to live and work among us? Does the political community have built-in limits, relating to space, size, place, territory, habitual residence, or species?

With such a dense and pressing agenda, understanding the transformation of citizenship requires multiple angles as we revisit foundational questions about how we organize our lives together as members of shared political communities in a world of growing diversity and complexity. In asking, *quo vadis* citizenship?, we wish to stretch and test the boundaries of existing categories in search of better answers than a return to Rome or Athens. Unlike those anticipating its demise into the dustbin of the history of the ideas, we remain confident that citizenship will remain a core organizing principle and political and moral ideal in the twenty-first century, even if its specific contents and contexts are likely to be transformed. This Handbook aims to explore whether, how, and under what conditions inclusive and egalitarian citizenship can still provide political legitimacy in a turbulent world of exploding social inequalities and dire human need for protection and belonging.

PART II

APPROACHES AND PERSPECTIVES

CHAPTER 2

REVISITING THE CLASSICAL IDEAL OF CITIZENSHIP

RYAN K. BALOT[*]

MOST contemporary theorists hold that the task of political theory is to guide political practice in our own historically specific circumstances.[1] Theorists of citizenship have tended to focus, for example, on the injustices and harms suffered by refugees, the stateless, and migrant workers, often with a view to proposing remedies or to

[*] This piece is dedicated to my colleague Edward Andrew, who will discern in my approach the fruit of many conversations.

I am grateful to Ayelet Shachar, Rainer Bauböck, and Daniel Weinstock for their helpful comments and suggestions on an earlier draft. I would also like to thank the other authors in this volume, particularly Erin Chung and Linda Bosniak, for their provocative comments during the OUP authors' conference.

[1] On different styles of theorizing about this question and others, see Joseph H. Carens, *The Ethics of Immigration* (Oxford: Oxford University Press, 2013), appendix.

advocating specific state policies.[2] Others strive to improve liberal democratic citizenship by re-conceiving of the 'liberal virtues,' or by substituting a conception of freedom as 'non-domination' for the standard liberal ideal of 'non-interference.'[3] A potential worry, though, is that this approach will lead theorists to rest content with only minor amendments to current ideas whose desirability goes unquestioned. Those ideas themselves typically carry with them ambiguities and undercurrents that deserve to be laid bare. Moreover, to the extent that theorists range themselves closely alongside practice, they also foreclose opportunities for wider philosophical speculation informed by diverse historical practices and utopian ideas. The narcissism of the present may cause us to neglect the unsettling or even subversive opportunities offered by broader philosophical inquiry.

A more radical approach would go beyond ordinary practices, even beyond the tyranny of 'Western' perspectives and presentism, to investigate the possible forms, activities, and ends of citizenship altogether.[4] A return to Greek and Roman citizenship is especially promising in this regard, because the ancient Greeks and Romans were both 'non-Western' and 'non-presentist.'[5] At the same time, their 'otherness' gains in significance because of the stubbornly authoritative place they hold in our own ideologies and self-understandings. J. G. A. Pocock has provided an influential reconsideration of Greek and Roman citizenship along these lines.[6] After putting his readers in mind of the 'haunting' Aristotelian ideal of 'political' citizenship, which stresses the goods inherent in active political reasoning and public participation, Pocock concentrates on the Romans' juridical models, according to which the

---

[2] For an overview of contemporary discussions, see, for example, Dominique Leydet, 'Citizenship,' Edward N. Zalta, ed., *The Stanford Encyclopedia of Philosophy* (Spring 2014 Edition), <http://plato. stanford.edu/archives/spr2014/entries/citizenship/>. For specialized and engaged scholarship on such questions, see, for example, David Miller, *Strangers in Our Midst: The Political Philosophy of Immigration* (Cambridge: Harvard University Press, 2016); Matthew J. Gibney, *The Politics and Ethics of Asylum: Liberal Democracy and the Response to Refugees* (Cambridge: Cambridge University Press, 2004); Kiran Banerjee, *Rethinking Membership: Statelessness, Domination, and the Limits of Contemporary Citizenship* (Ph.D. Dissertation, University of Toronto, 2016) (on file with author).

[3] On liberal and republican paradigms, see Honohan in this volume. The major studies of 'liberal virtues' include Stephen Macedo, *Liberal Virtues: Citizenship, Virtue, and Community in Liberal Constitutionalism* (Oxford: Clarendon Press, 1990); William A. Galston, *Liberal Purposes: Goods, Virtues, and Diversity in the Liberal State* (Cambridge: Cambridge University Press, 1991). The seminal 'republican' treatments are Philip Pettit, *Republicanism: A Theory of Freedom and Government* (Oxford: Oxford University Press, 1997) and Quentin Skinner, *Liberty before Liberalism* (Cambridge: Cambridge University Press, 1998). See also Maurizio Viroli, *Republicanism*, translated by Anthony Shuggar (New York: Hill and Wang, 2002). A refreshing set of alternatives is provided by the essays collected in Ronald Beiner, ed., *Theorizing Citizenship* (Albany: State University of New York Press, 1995).

[4] I follow Stephen Salkever in taking 'Western' to refer to the 'cultural world that historically emerges from and is the secular successor to European Christendom': see Stephen Salkever, 'Aristotelian *Phronêsis*, the Discourse of Human Rights, and Contemporary Global Practice,' *Polis* 33, no. 1 (2016): pp. 7–30 at 9, n 1.

[5] On non-Western citizenship in the contemporary world, see Chung in the present volume.

[6] J. G. A. Pocock, 'The Ideal of Citizenship since Classical Times,' *Queen's Quarterly* 99, no. 1 (1992): pp. 35–55.

Roman citizen was a 'subject' and a property-owner. Our current understandings of rights, of citizens as subjects of power, and of the material reference points for citizenship are based on this Roman legacy—particularly, for Pocock, the legacy of the jurist Gaius, who divided the world into persons, actions, and things. Multiple reinterpretations of that legacy led eventually to our own conception of the modern 'subject' as less a citizen than an individualistic, Lockean property-owner with juridically defined rights. Having put Roman 'right' (*ius*) and 'property' (*res*: literally, 'thing') to selective and self-interested uses, modern theorists made 'possessive individualism' (to use the expression normally associated with C. B. Macpherson)—and its postmodern discontents—the unsurprising outcome of the classical legacy.

Pocock's contrast between participatory and materialistic citizenship has a critical edge that I build on in the present essay, with a view to furthering the critique of unexamined contemporary assumptions. Since the goal is not to provide a historical synthesis but rather a philosophical reinterpretation, it will be useful first to investigate the Roman model as a set of dark possibilities that reveal the unconscious of current ideals, and then to explore Athenian democratic citizenship as a provocation to think again about liberal democratic citizenship. Either way, this new archaeology will not resolve practical quandaries. Rather, it will motivate us to see our own questions more sharply, instead of, *per impossibile*, answering them for us.

Roman Citizenship, Republican Theory, and the Contemporary Political Unconscious

Pocock's account of Aristotelian engaged citizenship has helped to give rise to what is now called the 'civic humanist' approach, which, as I indicate later, places political activity and its associated virtues at the center of human flourishing.[7] Although Pocock's approach would broadly qualify as 'republican,' most contemporary republican theorists, such as Skinner, Pettit, and Viroli, have traced their normative paradigms back to ancient Rome.[8] Pettit has provided the most influential account of this 'neo-Roman' model, which emphasizes the rule of law and freedom construed

---

[7] On the ideas of 'political unconscious' and historicization, see Fredric Jameson, *The Political Unconscious: Narrative as a Socially Symbolic Act* (Ithaca: Cornell University Press, 1981).

[8] Cf. the critique of these paradigms in my essay 'Polybius' Challenge to Republican Triumphalism,' *Political Theory* 38, no. 4 (2010): pp. 483–509.

as 'non-domination.' 'Non-domination' implies a condition of independence from arbitrary power, in which citizens pursue their own conceptions of the good life against the backdrop of laws that they have had a hand, at least, in constructing. My aim is to unsettle this optimistic and thoroughly liberalized picture by laying bare the militarism and hierarchies that informed ancient Roman citizenship— darker features that have arguably been fossilized in the Roman and 'neo-Roman' tradition.[9] The rule of law typically disguised the workings of unaccountable elite power; non-domination was idealized only because domination was so pervasive, beginning with the freedom/slavery dichotomy; and citizenship was a civil religion that rendered the people, the *populus Romanus*, fit for grandiose military expansion. These features explain why the ancient Romans were attractive not only to the mainstream constitutional tradition, but also to authoritarian leaders (Mussolini) and to fascist ideologues (Schmitt). They also focus attention on certain problematic features of contemporary republican theory.

Within the ancient historiographic tradition, at least, citizenship first came to sight when the Romans expelled their quasi-tyrannical kings, following Tarquinius Superbus' rape of Lucretia. The freedom (*libertas*) implied by Roman citizenship was construed as emancipation from tyranny and depended on the pugnacious courage of Roman men, their protection of female honor, and their desire to rule themselves (Livy, 1.58–60, 2.1; Cic. *Rep.* 2.45–46). But domination continued to be an omnipresent feature of Roman political life, because Romans made sense of the status of citizens by contrasting it with the status of women, slaves, and non-Romans. Moreover, domination was endemic to the category of citizenship itself: the Roman citizenry was known as the SPQR, or *senatus populusque Romanus* ('Senate and Roman people'), a term that signified an idealized unity of two hierarchically arranged groups, rather than a homogeneous or egalitarian demos. Hierarchy based on birth, class, gender, legal status, membership, and function was central to the Roman experience of citizenship.

Hence, although this republican regime was defined by the rule of law, we are forced to acknowledge that law itself is typically an instrument of, and a disguise for, social power. The law-code of the Twelve Tables (451–449 BC), the city's founding legal document, reveals a small-scale agricultural society in which freedom, domination, and constraint were tangibly intertwined among citizens. On the one hand, all citizens enjoyed legal rights to private property, and they were entitled to seek redress for cases of bodily harm. On the other hand, the code gives evidence of an ambient brutality toward and lack of respect for non-citizens. For example, specific provisions gave the father and head of household (the *paterfamilias*) absolute power, including the power of life and death, over his children (Table IV, 2.a).

---

[9] To recognize the stubborn liberalism of contemporary republican theory, consider that the Romans themselves would have been surprised at the individualistic, egalitarian, and anti-traditional frameworks in which contemporary citizenship theory now finds a home.

The code prohibited intermarriage between aristocratic 'patricians' and lower-class 'plebeians.' It also mandated that women should be under the constant surveillance of male relatives, including their husbands, because of their supposed feeblemind-edness. Slavery was taken for granted; the only questions were how to separate slave from free in religious practice and the extent of owners' liability for their slaves' delicts.

If Roman citizens were privileged, property-owning men who embraced traditional hierarchies, then the Roman ideal of non-domination grew up in an environment saturated by both formal and informal practices of domination. The Roman—and perhaps neo-Roman—inclination to interpret freedom as non-domination reflects the (understandable) fear of subjection to arbitrary and unaccountable power. In light of contemporary income inequalities and global oppression, it makes sense that our own theorists would appreciate precisely this element of republican free-dom. Yet wouldn't a more admirable approach to freedom point citizens in the dir-ection of solidarity and self-development and remove the necessity of persistent conflict and vigilance? Shouldn't the genuinely free citizen be able to enjoy social and civic goods that amount to more than simply the absence of domination?[10] Not being dominated may, in fact, be a quintessentially masculine concern that disre-gards the fluidity and context-dependence of actual relationships.[11] At all events, 'non-domination' constitutes a distinctive, and distinctively unambitious, starting-point for theorizing about the prospects of citizenship.

Romans were familiar with more idealistic possibilities. In Cicero's *Republic*, for example, Scipio argued that a 'people,' properly understood, is not a random collec-tion of individuals, but rather a free association undergirded by shared beliefs about justice and dedicated to pursuing the common good (Cic., *Rep.*, 1.39). Cicero himself held that Rome's classes could and should be characterized by harmony or concord (*concordia ordinum*: Cic., *de Catilina*, 4.15; cf. Augustine, *City of God*, 2.21, 19.23–27). Yet such a perspective was wholly unrealistic in Republican Rome, where citizens typically viewed themselves as agonistic stakeholders. Whether advanced by Cicero or modern theorists, the vision of Rome as a concordant and law-governed commu-nity of equals obscures not only the city's hierarchical, militaristic culture, but also the turmoil, disorder, and internal conflict that characterized relations between rich and poor. As Polybius explained, Rome's incorporation of the people, the Senate, and the consuls in its distinctive 'mixed regime' came about through 'many strug-gles and difficulties' (6.10, tr. Scott-Kilvert). That is why, arguing against his rever-ential humanistic contemporaries, Machiavelli praised the tumultuous character of

---

[10] For a feminist critique of republican 'independence' and non-domination that supports and extends these arguments, see Jennifer Nedelsky, *Law's Relations: A Relational Theory of Self, Autonomy, and Law* (Oxford: Oxford University Press, 2011).

[11] Cf. Marilyn Friedman, 'Pettit's Civic Republicanism and Male Domination,' in Cécile Laborde and John Maynor, eds., *Republicanism and Political Theory* (Oxford: Blackwell, 2008), pp. 246–268.

the Romans' mixed regime as most suitable for survival and expansion (*Discorsi*, 1.2, 1.5–6). Playing the part of a Roman citizen required constant vigilance, a willingness to assert and to defend the rights of one's own group, and continual maneuvering to resist oppression or to extend rights and equality. Legal stability and political rights had to be maintained through fear, violence, and conflict, often following attempts by the nobility (the *patres*—'fathers' or *nobiles*—'nobles') to entrench their own power either in social practice or in law.

Since the lower orders had always fought Rome's wars and thus enjoyed particular immunities and rights to appeal, it was widely accepted that they were stakeholders in the city's success; but the members of Rome's traditional wealth-based elite continually aspired to dominate political life, which in turn meant that ordinary citizens had to fight in order to assert and extend their rights. Historians have often used the phrase 'Struggle of the Orders' in order to capture these conflicts and contingencies.[12] To be a citizen meant to struggle with other groups in the city in order to maintain stature and power. Among the elite, individuals competed with one another as military commanders and as statesmen who strove to extend the Senate's political power; the populace, in their turn, sought to resist elite encroachments and to maintain their dignity. These conflicts lasted several hundred years, during which the people revealed themselves to be assertive and self-conscious about their political rights and about the fair distribution of social advantages and burdens. In 495–494 BC, a famous case, the plebeians were severely distressed by poverty and debt, which led them to withdraw (*secessio plebis*: 'withdrawal of the people') to the Sacred Mount. Their refusal to enroll in the army or to obey the consuls opened the city to attack and put pressure on the nobles (Livy, 2.32; cf. 3.44–54 with Machiavelli, *D.*, 1.44). Fearing violence both externally and internally, the Senate agreed to establish a board of new magistrates called the 'tribunes of the plebs' (*tribuni plebis*), to be filled only by plebeians. The tribunes were considered 'sacrosanct' and 'interceded' in order to defend the people's rights, even to the extent of vetoing the consuls' proposals as they saw fit.[13]

While assertion and secession were politically meaningful in this way, the plebeians' 'citizenship' often amounted to nothing more than occasional revolutionary gestures, combined with the continual need to serve in the army. On a day-to-day

---

[12] Despite the evidentiary difficulties in reconstructing this process of conflict and compromise, it is crucial to understand the basic pattern in order to grasp its impact on Roman citizenship; see Henrik Mouritsen, 'The Incongruence of Power: The Roman Constitution in Theory and Practice,' in Dean Hammer, ed., *A Companion to Greek Democracy and the Roman Republic* (Oxford: Wiley-Blackwell, 2015), pp. 146–163.

[13] Drawing on the class conflicts witnessed in the Roman Republic and discussed by Machiavelli, John P. McCormick argues that the pugnacity of the lower orders can be re-appropriated for modern democratic purposes (John P. McCormick, *Machiavellian Democracy* (Cambridge: Cambridge University Press, 2011)). For a different interpretation of Machiavelli and Rome, see Ryan K. Balot and Stephen Trochimchuk, 'The Many and the Few: On Machiavelli's "Democratic Moment"', *The Review of Politics* 74 (2012): pp. 559–588.

basis, ordinary citizens did not exercise meaningful participatory judgment. Despite revisionist efforts to highlight Rome's populism, Roman republican citizenship was far from democratic, because most substantive decisions were taken by elected officials and magistrates, by the Senate as a corporate body, and by military commanders. Even in popular assemblies (*contiones*), where a kind of populist rhetoric was dominant, few alternatives were presented, and the substance of decisions was taken mostly by the aristocratic magistrates controlling the meetings.[14] In fact, even if Rousseau qua democrat admired the Romans' systems of election and voting, the city's principal assembly (the 'Centuriate Assembly') was both intensely hierarchical and plutocratic, as well as implicitly militaristic, since votes were taken according to 'centuries', which doubled as military units.[15]

If the people asserted its power through refusing to mobilize for war, then the upper orders stage-managed their power continuously, through manifold formal and informal means—a feature of the Roman system that Machiavelli particularly admired (e.g., *D*, 1.13). The more benign face of Rome's hierarchical power relations was epitomized by the patron–client relationship, which gave members of the elite wide-ranging informal power or 'influence' (*auctoritas*); conversely, it made the vast majority of Roman citizens into dependents, in ways large and small.[16] Clients (*clientes*) were required to show their patrons (*patroni*) various forms of deference and respect, and to act as their bodyguards as they carried them in retinue throughout the city. As Quintus Cicero mentioned in a pamphlet on electioneering, an elite individual's status (*dignitas*) would be displayed and magnified through the size and diversity of his retinue (*comitatio*) in the Forum—a retinue made up of his clients and slaves (Q. Cic., *Comm. Pet.*, 34–37).[17]

Contrary to Pocock's presentation of the Roman citizen as an individual with unimpeachable rights, 'individualism' was perhaps enjoyed by the great members of wealthy families; other citizens were plebeians, retainers, and de facto servants. Against this background, it is difficult to discern the republican 'independence' and

[14] The question of Rome's democratic features has been hotly debated: for entry-points into the debate, see Fergus Millar, *The Crowd in Rome in the Late Republic* (Ann Arbor: University of Michigan Press, 1998); Fergus Millar, *The Roman Republic in Political Thought* (Hanover: University Press of New England for Brandeis University Press, 2002); Henrik Mouritsen, *Plebs and Politics in the Late Roman Republic* (Cambridge: Cambridge University Press, 2001); W. J. Tatum, 'Roman Democracy?', in Ryan K. Balot, ed., *A Companion to Greek and Roman Political Thought* (Oxford: Wiley-Blackwell, 2009), pp. 214–227. The view expressed in the text is indebted both to Tatum and to Robert Morstein-Marx, *Mass Oratory and Political Power in the Late Roman Republic* (Cambridge: Cambridge University Press, 2004), on which see also the review of Andrew M. Riggsby, *Bryn Mawr Classical Review* (10 March 2005), http://bmcr.brynmawr.edu/2005/2005-03-10.html.

[15] See Cic., *Rep.*, 2.38–42 for an ancient philosophical reflection on the elitism of this assembly, along with Mouritsen (n 12), pp. 152–153 for a recent account.

[16] See, for example, Richard Saller, *Personal Patronage under the Early Empire* (Cambridge: Cambridge University Press, 1982).

[17] See Shadi Bartsch, *The Mirror of the Self: Sexuality, Self-Knowledge, and the Gaze in the Early Roman Empire* (Chicago: University of Chicago Press, 2006), pp. 121–123.

'self-rule' that so many canonical authors, right up to the present, have highlighted as the keys to the Roman model of citizenship. Rome was an oligarchy characterized by deference and dependence.[18] Instead of providing an admirable model, therefore, Roman citizenship brings to consciousness similar features in the national 'republics' of modernity, perhaps particularly the United States, where deference, hierarchy, differential access, and plutocratic politics have decisively belied the system's egalitarian and democratic ideology. The counterpart of 'neo-Roman' theorizing is our own neo-Roman political culture.

For those accustomed to use the modern vocabulary of individual rights and dignity, one of the most alien dimensions of the Roman experience is civil religion, used as a strategy to manipulate and control the ordinary citizenry. The Senators could, for example, invent military emergencies in order to counteract movements toward greater equality or limitations on elite authority; often they used the people's willingness to swear oaths and to believe in supernatural portents in order to destroy their opposition (Livy, 3.10, 3.15–21; cf. 5.14; Machiavelli, *D.*, 1.13). Livy and Machiavelli agreed that the general Papirius had skewed the interpretation of sacred chickens before a critical battle with the Samnites, both for his own benefit and that of his troops (*D.*, 1.14; Livy, 10.40–41).

Is Roman citizenship the path to a liberal, constitutional order or to authoritarian nationalism?[19] The question comes to a head in the Roman office of *dictator*, which was created at a very early period to enable the city to respond to emergencies. This theoretically short-term office was ideally held by men such as Cincinnatus, who relinquished command (*imperium*) and returned to his small farm after a successful two-week campaign (Livy, 3.26–29). A good citizen can respond to a 'state of exception' (to use the term favoured by Carl Schmitt and Giorgio Agamben) by conforming to the demands of the law and the common good. Or, alternatively, he could seize power like a great many dictators of the Late Republic—and refuse to relinquish it. That pattern typified the authoritarian politics of men like Sulla and Caesar; the idea of a 'state of exception,' of course, took on special meaning for ideologues such as Carl Schmitt, yet it also informs the 'prerogative' of the modern executive, as Locke understood (*Second Treatise*, ch. 14). As usual, Machiavelli pinpointed the ways in which this office was located at the crossroads of beneficial and harmful uses of power (*D.*, 1.34). Both routes from Rome to late modernity traveled through Machiavelli's influential presentation of the ancient Romans in his *Discourses on Livy*.[20] Either way, Rome itself is often a

[18] On Roman oligarchy in a comparative context, see Jeffrey A. Winters, *Oligarchy* (New York: Cambridge University Press, 2011), who, however, distinguishes among 'oligarchs,' 'elites,' and 'the wealthy' in a more technical way.
[19] See W. R. Newell, *Tyranny: A New Interpretation* (Cambridge: Cambridge University Press, 2013).
[20] On Machiavelli's role in laying the foundations for these twin 'corridors' of power in modernity, see Newell, ibid.

study of thoughtful constitutional ideas embedded in a culture where they were likely to prove harmful.

When we turn to external relations, the key is that Roman citizens thought of themselves as a company of men who prized a distinctive culture of 'Romanness' (*Romanitas*), and who subordinated themselves entirely to their 'fatherland' (*patria*), chiefly for the sake of conquest and power. History remembered Romans who chose single combat and certain death for the city's good—for example, Horatius Cocles (Polybius, 6.55)—as well as those, such as Titus Manlius Torquatus, who executed his son for disobedience on campaign (Livy, 8.7). As Machiavelli appreciated (*D.*, 3.1, 3.9), filicide was a critical instrument of the Romans' maintenance of their pugnacious regime (cf. Polybius, 6.54), which required the harshest discipline along with an aggressive attitude toward enemies of the regime.[21] The goal of this brutality was supposed to be a civilizing mission, a goal of spreading justice among nations or peace throughout the world, as in the celebrated example of the 'peace of Augustus.'[22] In Rome's national epic, Virgil's *Aeneid*, the eponymous hero visits his father in the Underworld and learns that whereas others (presumably the Greeks) will excel as artists and natural philosophers, the Roman character will be defined by ruling over others, he says, for the sake of peace; specifically, Aeneas is told, Romans must always make it their mission 'to spare the conquered and to vanquish the proud' (*parcere subiectis et debellare superbos*, cf. *Aeneid*, 6.847–853).

Yet domination did not stop at the city's borders. Military success was so crucial to establishing political credentials that leaders—to take the most notable example, Julius Caesar, in his campaigns against the Gauls—were eager to invent justifications for wars that contributed little to the welfare of Rome. Equally, if the SPQR did not welcome the active deliberation of ordinary citizens, it was able to use the ideal of citizenship as an ideological mask that kept Rome's armies powerful and that made possible an unusual level of self-sacrifice. These toxic cultural conditions were combined in practice with an attitude of hostility toward outsiders. Despite its sporadic tolerance of the foreign, Rome did not embrace the Abrahamic religions or foreign cultures that it viewed as decadent or corrupting. Livy and Sallust both traced Rome's decline to the influx of Greek and Asiatic wealth into the city, which corrupted Rome's simple and austere foundations (Livy, 39.1–9; Sallust, *BC*, 10–12).

[21] On filicide in Machiavelli, see Ronald Beiner, *Civil Religion: A Dialogue in the History of Political Philosophy* (New York: Cambridge University Press, 2010).
[22] For the Emperor Augustus' altar to the 'peace of Augustus,' or *pax Augusta*, see *Res Gestae*, 12; for similar ideas, cf. *Res Gestae*, 3, 12–13, 26–30. For a postmodern appreciation of imperialism based on the models of Rome and specifically Polybius, see Michael Hardt and Antonio Negri, *Empire* (Cambridge: Harvard University Press, 2001). For the argument that the spread of *Romanitas* and Roman 'hegemony' was an early effort at state-building, see Ian Morris, 'The Athenian Empire (478–404 BC),' Princeton/Stanford Working Papers in Classics, <https://www.princeton.edu/~pswpc/pdfs/morris/120508.pdf>.

Cato the Elder ridiculed the Greeks for their fancy and insincere rhetorical techniques, which he contrasted with Roman bluntness and honesty (Plut., *Cato the Elder*, 12.5).

At the same time, the Romans were distinctive in their capacity to integrate outsiders in order to serve in their army. From early on, in fact, the 'point' of Roman citizenship was to provide a dedicated body of soldiers, whether from the Roman plebeians or from newly conquered 'allies.' Unlike the Greeks, who jealously guarded their citizenship even from other Greeks, the Romans recognized early on that incorporating outsiders through grants of citizenship provided manpower and proved to be diplomatically useful. Although scholars have likened this process to 'state-building,' it is preferable to think of Rome's projection of power as an aggressive, even if not pre-planned, project of global hegemony.[23] The Romans' most important tool of hegemonic power was the incorporation of defeated enemies through the strategic use of the privileges of citizenship.[24] The United States has used capitalism and popular culture for these purposes; the Romans used citizenship and 'Romanization.'

Machiavelli particularly commends Rome (by contrast with Sparta and Athens, which took on direct subjects, and by contrast with the leagues of ancient Greece and Italy, which were entirely equal partnerships) for acquiring external 'partners' and allies, while still occupying the seat of power. While the Romans kept power for themselves, he said, 'its partners came to subjugate themselves by their own labors and blood without perceiving it' (Machiavelli, *D.*, 2.4, tr. Mansfield and Tarcov; cf. Machiavelli, *D.*, 3.49). In carrying out these objectives, the Romans extended specific but limited privileges of citizenship, as well as citizenship *tout court* in certain cases, to the different regions of Italy, and then to the wider Mediterranean world. Rome impressed the conquered states with titles such as the 'Latin right' (*ius Latinum*) and references to their status as 'allies' (*socii*), all with a view to burdening foreign peoples with taxation and military service. The Romans were highly successful in using these 'privileges' to spread *Romanitas*; the Romans often became 'patrons' to their foreign 'clients.'[25] Although Roman citizenship conferred benefits on a range of people (e.g., St. Paul, who asserted his Roman citizenship, and ultimately made an appeal to the emperor on that basis, in response to threats of flogging: cf Acts of the Apostles,

[23] See Morris (n 22); W. V. Harris, *War and Imperialism in Republic Rome, 327–70 BC* (Oxford: Clarendon Press, 1979).

[24] See, for example, Michael P. Fronda, 'Why Roman Republicanism? Its Emergence and Nature in Context,' in Dean Hammer, ed., *A Companion to Greek Democracy and the Roman Republic* (Oxford: Wiley-Blackwell, 2015), pp. 44–64; T. J. Cornell, *The Beginnings of Rome: Italy and Rome from the Bronze Age to the Punic Wars (c.1000–264 BC)* (London: Routledge, 1995).

[25] See E. Badian, *Foreign Clientelae, 264–70 BC* (Oxford: Oxford University Press, 1958).

16: 37, 22: 25–29, 25: 10–12), it also operated as an instrumental means of subordination and manipulation. Through their practices of citizenship, the Romans achieved a blend of cosmopolitanism and imperialism that is as striking as it was historically unprecedented.

The spread of Roman citizenship through colonization and conquest was, of course, the original form of 'colonialism,' in both concrete and extended senses. Like their modern European counterparts, the Romans may have thought of themselves as conferring the benefits of civilization on less successful peoples, as in Tacitus' depiction of the barbaric peoples of Germany and Britain in his *Germania* and his *Annals*. Equally, like those counterparts, they have been criticized for destroying a variety of native cultures and local social forms in the process of 'Romanizing' the world, a process that has been likened to the spread of racist ideology.[26] However we evaluate the use of citizenship as a tool of imperialism, it is impossible to deny that Roman citizenship—from the 12 Tables of 451 BC to the 'Edict of Caracalla' (*constitutio Antoniniana*, the grant of Roman citizenship to all free adult males in the Roman Empire) in 212 AD and beyond—constituted a legal status and a set of activities that belonged to a highly traditional, militaristic, aggressive, and occasionally barbaric ancient people.

Three points have by now come into sharper focus. First, ancient Rome does not provide an attractive ideal of citizenship for contemporary theory or practice. Second, the ideals that contemporary theorists have cherry-picked from the ancient Roman world are, upon reflection, closely linked to machismo, militaristic aggression, imperialism, and political manipulation. Finally, the ancient Roman experience of citizenship teaches us not through providing ideals for imitation, but rather through forcing us to recognize our own *Romanitas*. A state with an ideology of independent citizen stake-holders who were free from domination because of the rule of law, with elite theorists who emphasize just these ideals, amidst the workings of an actual plutocracy, in which oligarchs manipulated law, religious belief, and patronage for their own benefit: this scenario should constitute a disturbing reminder to contemporary readers that their complacency is unwarranted. After all, when individual members of the Roman elite grew too powerful, they attacked the city with their own soldier-clients, transforming the office of *dictator* into a permanent military dictatorship, held by men that we now call the 'emperors.'

---

[26] See Benjamin Isaac, *The Invention of Racism in Classical Antiquity* (Princeton: Princeton University Press, 2004).

THE GREEK IDEAL OF CITIZENSHIP:
PLATO, ARISTOTLE, AND
THE DEMOCRATIC ATHENIANS

By contrast with the Roman and neo-Roman models, Greek thinkers, above all Aristotle, presented the citizen as an individual entitled to 'share in' (*metechein*) the regime (*politeia*). As this particular vocabulary reveals, the citizen was a stakeholder who both benefitted from and took responsibility for the city. Correspondingly, and revealingly, the Greeks had no terminology to capture the notion of 'right.'[27] Although the power of office-holders was limited by the law, the citizen did not stand apart from the community or assert rights against it. He was an equal member of the *polis* ('city-state' or 'citizen-state').[28] Instead of rights, Aristotle stressed deliberation (*boulê*) in the Assembly and rendering judgment (*krisis*) in the courts as the central activities that defined citizenship. The contrasts with Roman hierarchy and elite manipulation could not be sharper.

The Aristotelian citizen has often provided a standard of active, participatory engagement that the modern nation-state cannot match—one that, as Wolin has argued, the modern state, with its peculiarly rationalistic, bureaucratic, and administrative systems of power, was specifically designed to eliminate.[29] In the work of Arendt, Pocock, Sandel, Wolin, and others, the 'neo-Athenian' model of citizenship (particularly as expressed by Aristotle) held that civic engagement and participation, along with their associated virtues, are the chief constituents of the good life.[30] From this perspective, Greek citizenship should 'nag' contemporary theorists—for example, theorists of deliberative democracy—because the Greeks' activities

[27] On 'sharing in' the *politeia*, see Martin Ostwald, 'Shares and Rights: "Citizenship" Greek Style and American Style,' in Josiah Ober and Charles Hedrick, eds., *Dêmokratia* (Princeton: Princeton University Press, 1996), pp. 49–61; on rights specifically, compare Josiah Ober, 'Quasi-Rights: Participatory Citizenship and Negative Liberties,' in Josiah Ober, ed., *Athenian Legacies: Essays on the Politics of Going on Together* (Princeton: Princeton University Press), pp. 92–127; Paul Cartledge and Matt Edge, '"Rights", Individuals, and Communities in Ancient Greece,' in Ryan K. Balot, ed., *A Companion to Greek and Roman Political Thought* (Malden and Oxford: Blackwell, 2009), pp. 149–163.

[28] On this egalitarianism, see Ian Morris, 'The Strong Principle of Equality and the Archaic Origins of Greek Democracy,' in Josiah Ober and Charles Hedrick, eds., *Dêmokratia* (Princeton: Princeton University Press, 1996), pp. 19–48.

[29] Most clearly in *Tocqueville between Two Worlds: The Making of a Political and Theoretical Life* (Princeton: Princeton University Press, 2003).

[30] See J. G. A. Pocock, *The Machiavellian Moment: Florentine Political Thought and the Atlantic Republican Tradition* (Princeton: Princeton University Press, 1975) and Sheldon Wolin, *Politics and Vision*, 2nd edition (Princeton: Princeton University Press, 2004), both influenced, of course, by Hannah Arendt, *The Human Condition*, 2nd edition (Chicago: University of Chicago Press, 1998), and both attempting to reverse Constant's normatively inflected opposition between the 'liberty of the ancients' and the 'liberty of the moderns.'

effectively modeled the ideals of civic engagement, judgment, and public discourse that are now so distressingly absent from our public life.[31]

We should hesitate, however, to endorse the Aristotelian model without hesitation, because Aristotle's political science is fundamentally elitist.[32] Many Aristotelian virtues, such as *megalopsuchia* ('greatness of soul') are clearly inappropriate to democratic politics, while Aristotle's emphasis on leisure as a practical necessity for citizens renders his theory inaccessible for democratic societies, whether ancient or modern. A return to the Athenian democracy, as opposed to Aristotle, proves to be both more illuminating and more unsettling.[33] While Aristotle was highly critical of democratic freedom and equality, the Athenian democrats prized freedom, equality, and democracy, as we do. Yet, at the same time, they located those ideals within a different, but highly compelling ethical framework.

In Pericles' Funeral Oration we discern an argument, expressed in the rhetoric appropriate to its genre, that democratic citizenship is a quasi-Tocquevillian, associative project of taking responsibility for one's own ideas, institutions, norms, and life-plans. In the vision offered by both Tocqueville and Thucydides' Pericles, it was crucial to democratic citizens that they embrace these responsibilities as a shared undertaking that took place within a network of relationships for the sake of the common good.[34] The most tangible element of the 'common good' in both cases was freedom, construed both as self-government and as the privilege of thinking and acting independently.

By contrast with Tocqueville's Americans, however, Thucydides' Athenians dedicated themselves to a goal or 'end' (*telos*) that went beyond even freedom itself— that is, to 'flourishing' or 'happiness' (*eudaimonia*). In its modes of deliberation and judgment, Athenian citizenship was responsive to the standards of nature (including human nature), rather than implicitly based on or dedicated to the pursuit of the Kantian-style freedom of self-legislation.[35] This responsiveness explains why the

[31] A certain confusion besets current discussions of 'republican' theory, because 'republican' theorists derive ideas both from Roman antiquity and from Greek antiquity, and the so-called 'neo-Athenian' model, as expressed in the work of Arendt and her followers, itself constitutes a paradigmatically 'republican' theoretical position. See Honohan in the present volume, who rightly stresses that modern republican theories are already thoroughly liberalized. The term 'neo-Athenian' tends to be reserved for criticizing others: cf. Pettit (n 3) pp. 285–286, discussing Michael Sandel, *Democracy's Discontent: America in Search of a Public Philosophy* (Cambridge: Harvard University Press, 1996).

[32] On the distinction between Aristotelian and democratic ideals of citizenship, see my essay 'The Virtue Politics of Democratic Athens,' in Stephen G. Salkever, ed., *The Cambridge Companion to Ancient Greek Political Thought* (Cambridge: Cambridge University Press, 2009), pp. 271–300; on Aristotle's elitism, see also John Wallach, 'Contemporary Aristotelianism,' *Political Theory 20*, no. 4 (1992): pp. 613–641.

[33] Equally, however, we should avoid assimilating the Athenian democracy to the ideals of contemporary liberalism; cf. Ryan K. Balot, 'Recollecting Athens,' *Polis 33*, no .1 (2016): pp. 92–129.

[34] Cf. Ryan K. Balot, 'Transformations of "Manliness" in the Democratic Republic,' in Geoffrey Kellow, ed., *Republicanism: Ancient and Modern* (Toronto: University of Toronto Press, 2015).

[35] On this contrast, with specific reference to Aristotle's 'natural questions,' see Stephen G. Salkever, 'The Deliberative Model of Democracy and Aristotle's Ethics of Natural Questions,' in A. Tessitore, ed.,

Athenians evoked by Pericles regarded the democratic city, and in particular its political activities, as providing the best and most flourishing lives for its citizens: 'In sum, I say that our city as a whole is a lesson for Greece, and that each of us presents himself as a self-sufficient person, disposed to the widest possible diversity of actions, with every grace and great versatility' (2.41, tr. Woodruff, adapted). Pericles' idea is that living in Athens, participating in its public deliberations, playing an active role in its civic and religious rituals, and so on, cultivates the citizens' highest and most worthwhile natural capacities, with the result that they become fully realized individuals. In this sense, at least, the Athenians developed a 'virtue politics' or a 'eudaimonistic politics', which anticipated the educational visions of the classical philosophers.

Yet, in making these points, Thucydides' Pericles clearly distinguished Athenian democratic citizenship from the oligarchic or 'republican' models of citizenship most common throughout the Greek world—not to mention the philosophically informed citizenship imagined by Plato or Aristotle. Athens was not only educational to others, but also superior to them in granting its citizens the freedom to live their lives and to think their thoughts as they thought best, while still respecting the need to give an account of oneself and one's ideas to fellow citizens. The key to Athens's eudaimonistic politics was that the citizens' frequent deliberations on issues of public significance (e.g., war and peace, public expenditure, the naturalization of non-Athenians, etc.) gave their expressions of justice, courage, civic friendship, and political prudence a level of self-consciousness and wisdom that was largely unavailable to citizens of other regimes. As Pericles said:

In this too we excel over others: ours is the bravery of people who think through what they will take in hand, and discuss it thoroughly; with other men, ignorance makes them brave and thinking makes them cowards. But the people who most deserve to be judged tough-minded are those who know exactly what terrors or pleasures lie ahead, and are not turned away from danger by that knowledge. (Thuc., 2.40, tr. Woodruff)

Pericles then goes on to detail the Athenians' superiority to others, for this very reason, in generosity, friendship, and leadership (Thuc., 2.40). Even prior to the Socratic quest to 'render an account' of himself or to achieve self-knowledge, the democratic citizenry of classical Athens had mobilized just such ideas by using a remarkably similar vocabulary, with a view to living the best lives, as they argued, of which human beings were capable.[36]

Aristotle and Modern Politics: The Persistence of Political Philosophy (Notre Dame: University of Notre Dame Press, 2002), pp. 342–374.

[36] Cf. Ryan K. Balot, *Courage in the Democratic Polis: Ideology and Critique in Classical Athens* (New York: Oxford University Press, 2014). On giving an account of oneself, see also J. Peter Euben, *Corrupting Youth: Political Education, Democratic Culture, and Political Theory* (Princeton: Princeton University Press, 1997).

The model evoked by Pericles—which is also reflected throughout Athenian ideology[37]—differed considerably from the Roman, the Aristotelian, and the neo-Athenian models of citizenship. Democratic citizenship was government of, by, and for the people, an egalitarian body that included all citizens of free birth and Athenian descent. Because of their extensive political equality, the virtues of the democratic citizen, as theorized by Pericles and others, were goals to which all citizens, rich and poor, could aspire; there was no Roman 'Struggle of the Orders,' in part because citizens were all members of a single order. Contrary to Aristotle's theory, excellences of character and intellect were not reserved for a precious elite, nor did they depend on especially lucky circumstances or a privileged education. Instead, they were cultivated by the experience of living in the democratic polis, thoughtfully furthering its ideals, participating in politics, and enjoying a rich private life. By contrast with the neo-Athenian theories, finally, democratic Athenian orators did not vehemently push their fellow citizens into an exclusive focus on or privileging of the 'public sphere,' but rather understood that social and private life, while connected to the polis, were dignified spheres of individual exploration and enjoyment.

Like the Romans, however, the Athenians were slave-owners who operated within a patriarchal world and an international anarchy of independent states. What mitigates the undercutting of their ideals—by contrast with the Romans—is not only that we have reason to believe that they lived up to those ideals in some measure, but also that they created institutions in which to reflect on their own lives and their own shortcomings. They lived lives of self-criticism—a virtue less familiar at Rome and neglected within the Aristotelian and neo-Athenian traditions. One principal site of self-criticism was the Theater of Dionysos. In this theater, Athenian playwrights dramatized for audiences of citizens the tragic (or comic) ambiguities that beset democratic political life. Why should citizenship be subject to a 'birthright lottery,' to borrow Ayelet Shachar's evocative phrase,[38] and what were the consequences of the contingencies and seemingly arbitrary histories that determined inclusion or exclusion in a particular political community? What were the disadvantages of excluding women from political life? Did the Greeks' 'barbaric' enemies have any title to respect or even compassion? Like philosophy in the Socratic tradition, tragedians such as Aeschylus and Sophocles forced their audiences to confront these and other fundamental political questions, without offering specific answers or even guidance in addressing them. The democratic Athenians paid for the production of these works out of the public treasury, even though the plays themselves usually interrogate and even destabilize the Athenians' own norms, beliefs, and principles. Arguably, at least, this surprising and potentially paradoxical level of introspection is explained by the Athenians' desire for self-knowledge: a deeper understanding of

---

[37] This argument is the burden of Balot, ibid.
[38] Ayelet Shachar, *The Birthright Lottery: Citizenship and Global Inequality* (Cambridge: Harvard University Press, 2009).

their own lives as citizens, which helped to explain the worth of citizenship along with the shortcomings of even the Athenians' own practices of citizenship.[39]

In attending the Theater of Dionysos, the Athenians were explicitly participating in a religious celebration of the god Dionysos. Even in a democracy, Greek citizenship had an inescapably religious dimension, as Socrates arguably learned to his cost in 399 BC. Yet, although the Athenians engaged in shared ritual practices, their city was far from a theocracy. No particular separation between religion and politics was deemed necessary, because the Athenians did not base their political reasoning on religious omens, sacred texts, or revealed truth.[40] The religious manipulation that characterized Rome's hierarchical and agonistic model of citizenship was impossible within the egalitarian and rationalistic culture of democratic Athens. Animating the public discussions of Athens's free and equal citizens was the consideration of practical reasons for or against particular policies, construed within the larger framework of the city's democratic virtues and ideals. What would elsewhere have been taken for granted as 'revealed religious truth' was subjected to political interpretation and revisionary debate in ancient Athens.[41] An excellent example is the 'Themistocles Assembly': on the eve of the Persian Wars, the Athenians received an oracle that the city's 'wooden walls' would protect them from invading forces. Through a protracted public discussion, Themistocles effectively argued that 'wooden walls' referred not to the rickety wooden fence surrounding the Acropolis, but rather to the Athenians' navy—which did, in fact, triumph over the Persians at the Battle of Salamis (480 BC). In the absence of clear divine guidance, high priests, or sacred authorities, practical rationality proved to be the Athenians' salvation and the highest virtue of Athenian citizenship.

CONCLUSION: ANCIENT LEGACIES, MODERN AMBIGUITIES

Because of its introspection and its elaboration of a eudaimonistic framework, Athenian democratic citizenship constituted a proto-philosophical species of

---

[39] For further reflections on these themes, see J. Peter Euben, *The Tragedy of Political Theory: The Road Not Taken* (Princeton: Princeton University Press, 1990); J. Peter Euben, *Corrupting Youth: Political Education in Democratic Culture* (Princeton: Princeton University Press, 1997); J. Peter Euben, *Platonic Noise: Essays on the Modernity of Classical Thought* (Princeton: Princeton University Press, 2001); and Balot, 'Recollecting Athens' (n 33).

[40] Cf. John Gould, 'On Making Sense of Greek Religion,' in P. E. Easterling and J. V. Muir, eds., *Greek Religion and Society* (Cambridge: Cambridge University Press, 1985), pp. 1–33, 219–221.

[41] See J. P. Vernant, *The Origins of Greek Thought* (Ithaca: Cornell University Press, 1982) and G. E. R. Lloyd, *Magic, Reason, and Experience* (Cambridge: Cambridge University Press, 1979). On the 'Themistocles Assembly,' see Balot, *Courage in the Democratic Polis* (n 36), chapter 4.

democratic citizenship. While Aristotle influentially developed this eudaimonistic paradigm and applied it to citizenship in general, however, much of the ancient philosophical canon—from Plato's *Republic* to St. Augustine's *City of God*—was anti-civic. Within polytheistic Greece and Rome, the good life was reimagined as the fulfillment of philosophical *eros* (Plato) or as a rejection of the city's conventions (the Cynics) or as 'withdrawal' and pleasurable tranquility (Epicurus) or as cosmopolitan rationality (the Stoics). Whereas Pocock stressed the role of property and law in reducing the quality of political relations, it is evident that both philosophical transformations and the rise of pan-Mediterranean empires (such as that of Rome) also helped to make alternative, non-civic lifestyles both possible and attractive to a wide range of people—including those, such as women and slaves, who had once been disenfranchised.

These processes culminated in an entirely new and metaphorical notion of citizenship—namely, Augustine's idea of spiritual membership in the 'city of God' (*civitas dei*). The changes wrought by the predominance of Christianity in pre-modern Europe are the most striking omission in Pocock's wide-ranging account. But it is necessary to keep these transformations in mind, at least in broad outline, if we hope to make sense of the ambiguous, path-dependent developments of post-Westphalian citizenship. The ideals of Augustinian Christianity, reinterpreted by Thomas Aquinas and then Martin Luther and their successors, firmly and widely entrenched the belief that human fulfillment was best sought outside politics, often through religious activities and associations.

The Christian sensibilities of pre-modern Europe, and the post-Christian attitudes of early modern Europe, had two major political consequences. First, Christian doctrine was the predecessor of the human rights regime that is now integral to our understanding of citizenship (see Owen, this volume). Contrary to the beliefs and practices of ancient polytheists, Christianity taught that each individual, however humble or different, possesses a unique and equal dignity in virtue of God's rendering of humankind in his own image. Second, the post-Christian inhabitants of Europe were deeply inclined to obey political authority and to accept a sharp division between political life and private life. This inclination strengthened the tendency of modern individuals to identify themselves as subjects instead of citizens and of theorists to think of them as rights-bearing individuals rather than as stake-holders, as Pocock has emphasized. For entirely understandable reasons, modern thinkers took on the project of establishing a framework in which individuals could be physically secure and increasingly unwilling to participate in grandiose military ventures.

In our own time, political theorists voice many complaints about citizenship, complaints that often work at cross-purposes: for example, that citizenship is too exclusive and that nation-states are unjust, on the one hand, and, on the other, that citizenship is weak or lacks energy and that democratic self-government is no longer viable. Those who express no complaints tend to worry that an overemphasis on citizenship will compromise the private freedoms that the liberal state was founded to protect. The theory and practice of citizenship in classical antiquity cannot provide practical solutions; nor should ancient political theory be asked to do so. Its task, rather, is to deepen our conversations about these questions, not in a spirit of lament or nostalgia, but instead with a view to enriching our philosophical interpretations and understandings. Through studying the Greeks and Romans on citizenship, we acquire a more variegated and subtle vocabulary for discussing political difficulties of our time, and of all time; and we make ourselves more self-conscious about the ambiguities and trade-offs implied by our own regimes of citizenship.

Both the Romans and the Greeks have left a legacy of understanding citizenship that resonates deeply with our own concerns, and perhaps with the permanent concerns of political life. On the one hand, the Romans' elitism and imperialism (whether 'soft' or 'hard') might appear regrettably familiar to the citizen-subjects of our liberal-democratic states: modern citizens are more subject than they recognize to the manipulations of their elite leaders, who often resort to projects of civil religion (as in the American Religious Right) or to the exploitation of xenophobic hostility to foreign gods (as in the declarations of a civilizational war against Islam). Equally, they may be unaware of the colonializing implications of their hegemonic culture. Americanization is as hegemonic as Romanization, and with a much greater degree of self-consciousness and success. We can know ourselves through studying the Romans, but that self-knowledge will be as disturbing as it is enlightening.

On the other hand, if we liberate ourselves from both the Arendtian and the liberalizing vision of the ancient Greeks, then we can also grapple with novel possibilities that inhere in democratic citizenship. Those possibilities are centered on *la vie politique*, to be sure, but their importance lies in the new forms of ethical and intellectual self-realization that they make possible. The Athenian vision—to which Athenian practice approximated to varying degrees—remains embedded in a particular time and place, one that makes its own exclusions, limitations, and defects all too clear to the modern consciousness. Yet the Athenian citizens' own articulation of the growth and human development that democratic citizenship makes possible is relevant to all human beings. This vision is not a utopian fantasy. Alexis de Tocqueville showed that the New England townships of the 1830s educated citizens not only in political rights and duties, but also in how to take responsibility for their ways of life. The goods internal to their experiences of citizenship went well beyond not being dominated or interfered with. Even if their experience, too, is now lost forever, the philosophical appreciation of citizenship demands that we continue to speculate about the highest and most worthwhile goods that the activities of citizenship offer us.

Bibliography

Arendt, Hannah, *The Human Condition*, 2nd edition (Chicago: University of Chicago Press, 1998).

Badian, E., *Foreign Clientelae, 264-70 BC* (Oxford: Oxford University Press, 1958).

Balot, Ryan K., 'The Virtue Politics of Democratic Athens,' in Stephen G. Salkever, ed., *The Cambridge Companion to Ancient Greek Political Thought* (Cambridge: Cambridge University Press, 2009), pp. 271–300.

Balot, Ryan K., 'Polybius' Challenge to Republican Triumphalism,' *Political Theory 38*, no. 4 (2010): pp. 483–509.

Balot, Ryan K., *Courage in the Democratic Polis: Ideology and Critique in Classical Athens* (New York: Oxford University Press, 2014).

Balot, Ryan K., 'Transformations of 'Manliness' in the Democratic Republic,' in Geoffrey Kellow, ed., *Republicanism: Ancient and Modern* (Toronto: University of Toronto Press, 2015), pp. 136–156.

Balot, Ryan K., 'Recollecting Athens,' *Polis 33*, no. 1 (2016): pp. 92–129.

Balot, Ryan K. and Stephen Trochimchuk, 'The Many and the Few: On Machiavelli's "Democratic Moment",' *The Review of Politics 74* (2012): pp. 559–588.

Banerjee, Kiran, *Rethinking Membership: Statelessness, Domination, and the Limits of Contemporary Citizenship* (Ph.D. Dissertation, University of Toronto, 2016) (on file with author).

Bartsch, Shadi, *The Mirror of the Self: Sexuality, Self-Knowledge, and the Gaze in the Early Roman Empire* (Chicago: University of Chicago Press, 2006).

Beiner, Ronald, ed., *Theorizing Citizenship* (Albany: State University of New York Press, 1995).

Beiner, Ronald, *Civil Religion: A Dialogue in the History of Political Philosophy* (New York: Cambridge University Press, 2010).

Carens, Joseph H., *The Ethics of Immigration* (Oxford: Oxford University Press, 2013).

Cartledge, Paul and Matt Edge, ' "Rights", Individuals, and Communities in Ancient Greece,' in Ryan K. Balot, ed., *A Companion to Greek and Roman Political Thought* (Malden and Oxford: Blackwell, 2009), pp. 149–163.

Cornell, T. J., *The Beginnings of Rome: Italy and Rome from the Bronze Age to the Punic Wars (c.1000-264 BC)* (London: Routledge, 1995).

Euben, J. Peter, *The Tragedy of Political Theory: The Road Not Taken* (Princeton: Princeton University Press, 1990).

Euben, J. Peter, *Corrupting Youth: Political Education in Democratic Culture* (Princeton: Princeton University Press, 1997).

Euben, J. Peter, *Platonic Noise: Essays on the Modernity of Classical Thought* (Princeton: Princeton University Press, 2001).

Friedman, Marilyn, 'Pettit's Civic Republicanism and Male Domination,' in Cécile Laborde and John Maynor, eds., *Republicanism and Political Theory* (Oxford: Blackwell, 2008), pp. 246–268.

Fronda, Michael P., 'Why Roman Republicanism? Its Emergence and Nature in Context,' in Dean Hammer, ed., *A Companion to Greek Democracy and the Roman Republic* (Oxford: Wiley-Blackwell, 2015), pp. 44–64.

Galston, William A., *Liberal Purposes: Goods, Virtues, and Diversity in the Liberal State* (Cambridge: Cambridge University Press, 1991).

Gibney, Matthew J., *The Politics and Ethics of Asylum: Liberal Democracy and the Response to Refugees* (Cambridge: Cambridge University Press, 2004).

Gould, John, 'On Making Sense of Greek Religion,' in P. E. Easterling and J. V. Muir, eds., *Greek Religion and Society* (Cambridge: Cambridge University Press, 1985), pp. 1–33, 219–221.

Hardt, Michael and Antonio Negri, *Empire* (Cambridge: Harvard University Press, 2001).

Harris, William. V., *War and Imperialism in Republic Rome, 327-70 BC* (Oxford: Clarendon Press, 1979).

Isaac, Benjamin, *The Invention of Racism in Classical Antiquity* (Princeton: Princeton University Press, 2004).

Jameson, Fredric, *The Political Unconscious: Narrative as a Socially Symbolic Act* (Ithaca: Cornell University Press, 1981).

Leydet, Dominique, 'Citizenship,' *The Stanford Encyclopedia of Philosophy* (Spring 2014 Edition), Edward N. Zalta, ed., <http://plato.stanford.edu/archives/spr2014/entries/citizenship/>.

Lloyd, G. E. R., *Magic, Reason, and Experience* (Cambridge: Cambridge University Press, 1979).

Macedo, Stephen, *Liberal Virtues: Citizenship, Virtue, and Community in Liberal Constitutionalism* (Oxford: Clarendon Press, 1990).

Mansfield, Harvey C. and Nathan Tarcov, trans. *Niccolo Machiavelli: Discourses on Livy.* (Chicago: University of Chicago Press, 1996).

McCormick, John P., *Machiavellian Democracy* (Cambridge: Cambridge University Press, 2011).

Millar, Fergus, *The Crowd in Rome in the Late Republic* (Ann Arbor: University of Michigan Press, 1998).

Millar, Fergus, *The Roman Republic in Political Thought* (Hanover: University Press of New England for Brandeis University Press, 2002).

Miller, David, *Strangers in Our Midst: The Political Philosophy of Immigration* (Cambridge: Harvard University Press, 2016).

Morris, Ian, 'The Athenian Empire (478–404 BC),' Princeton/Stanford Working Papers in Classics, <https://www.princeton.edu/~pswpc/pdfs/morris/120508.pdf>.

Morris, Ian, 'The Strong Principle of Equality and the Archaic Origins of Greek Democracy,' in Josiah Ober and Charles Hedrick, eds., *Dêmokratia* (Princeton: Princeton University Press, 1996), pp. 19–48.

Morstein-Marx, Robert, *Mass Oratory and Political Power in the Late Roman Republic* (Cambridge: Cambridge University Press, 2004).

Mouritsen, Henrik, *Plebs and Politics in the Late Roman Republic* (Cambridge: Cambridge University Press, 2001).

Mouritsen, Henrik, 'The Incongruence of Power: The Roman Constitution in Theory and Practice,' in Dean Hammer, ed., *A Companion to Greek Democracy and the Roman Republic* (Oxford: Wiley-Blackwell, 2015), pp. 146–163.

Nedelsky, Jennifer, *Law's Relations: A Relational Theory of Self, Autonomy, and Law* (Oxford: Oxford University Press, 2011).

Newell, W. R., *Tyranny: A New Interpretation* (Cambridge: Cambridge University Press, 2013).

Ober, Josiah, 'Quasi-Rights: Participatory Citizenship and Negative Liberties,' in Josiah Ober, ed., *Athenian Legacies: Essays on the Politics of Going on Together* (Princeton: Princeton University Press, 2005), pp. 92–127 (= *Social Philosophy and Policy* 17, no. 1 (2000): pp. 27–61).

Ostwald, Martin, 'Shares and Rights: "Citizenship" Greek Style and American Style,' in Josiah Ober and Charles Hedrick, eds., *Dêmokratia* (Princeton: Princeton University Press, 1996), pp. 49–61.

Pettit, Philip, *Republicanism: A Theory of Freedom and Government* (Oxford: Oxford University Press, 1997).

Pocock, J. G. A., *The Machiavellian Moment: Florentine Political Thought and the Atlantic Republican Tradition* (Princeton: Princeton University Press, 1975).

Pocock, J. G. A., 'The Ideal of Citizenship since Classical Times,' *Queen's Quarterly* 99, no. 1 (1992): pp. 35–55.

Riggsby, Andrew M., 'Review of Robert Morstein-Marx, *Mass Oratory and Political Power in Late Republican Rome*', *Bryn Mawr Classical Review* (10 March 2005), <http://bmcr.brynmawr.edu/2005/2005-03-10.html>.

Salkever, Stephen G., 'The Deliberative Model of Democracy and Aristotle's Ethics of Natural Questions,' in A. Tessitore, ed., *Aristotle and Modern Politics: The Persistence of Political Philosophy* (Notre Dame: University of Notre Dame Press, 2002), pp. 342–374.

Salkever, Stephen G., 'Aristotelian *Phronêsis*, the Discourse of Human Rights, and Contemporary Global Practice,' *Polis* 33, no. 1 (2016): pp. 7–30.

Saller, Richard, *Personal Patronage under the Early Empire* (Cambridge: Cambridge University Press, 1982).

Scott-Kilvert, Ian, trans. *Polybius: The Rise of the Roman Empire* (Harmondsworth: Penguin, 1979).

Shachar, Ayelet, *The Birthright Lottery: Citizenship and Global Inequality* (Cambridge: Harvard University Press, 2009).

Skinner, Quentin, *Liberty before Liberalism* (Cambridge: Cambridge University Press, 1998).

Tatum, W. J., 'Roman Democracy?,' in Ryan K. Balot, ed., *A Companion to Greek and Roman Political Thought* (Oxford: Wiley-Blackwell, 2009), pp. 214–227.

Vernant, J. P., *The Origins of Greek Thought* (Ithaca: Cornell University Press, 1982).

Viroli, Maurizio, *Republicanism*, translated by Anthony Shuggar (New York: Hill and Wang, 2002).

Wallach, John, 'Contemporary Aristotelianism,' *Political Theory* 20, no. 4 (1992): pp. 613–641.

Winters, Jeffrey A., *Oligarchy* (New York: Cambridge University Press, 2011).

Wolin, Sheldon, *Tocqueville between Two Worlds: The Making of a Political and Theoretical Life* (Princeton: Princeton University Press, 2003).

Wolin, Sheldon, *Politics and Vision*, 2nd edition (Princeton: Princeton University Press, 2004).

Woodruff, Paul, *Thucydides on Justice, Power, and Human Nature* (Indianapolis: Hackett, 1993).

CHAPTER 3

....

RE-SCALING
THE GEOGRAPHY
OF CITIZENSHIP

....

ALEXANDER C. DIENER

INTRODUCTION

....

WHEN David Hollinger[1] famously posed the question 'How Wide the Circle We?' he probed the changing scope and salience of citizenship in social, epistemic, and

---

[1] David Hollinger, 'How Wide the Circle of the "We"? American Intellectuals and the Problem of the Ethnos since World War II,' *The American Historical Review 98* (1993): pp. 317–337, doi: 10.2307/2166835.

geographic terms. The reflex response of most people (scholars and 'the public' alike) to such a query would likely be the 'Nation-State.' This accords with a particular concept of citizenship, which over the last 250 years has been reinforced by constitutions, laws, and jurisprudence. World maps reinforce this concept by depicting a colorful collage of seemingly, rigidly bordered political entities within which socially cohesive, distinct, national communities reside. Recent decades, however, have seen arguments—among scholars and in public fora—about the changing spatiality of citizenship. A variety of processes under the broad category of globalization (neoliberal capitalism, migration, communication technology, transnational human rights regimes, etc.) challenge national citizenship in important ways.[2] This chapter approaches citizenship through the lens of territory,[3] exploring the processes of re-scaling political belonging, legal rights, and civil beneficence.

Many works on citizenship begin with a proviso that the term is multifaceted. Even a cursory review of the literature presents citizenship as a legal category, a claim, an identity, a tool in nation building, and an ideal. One scholar of political geography characterizes debates on the subject as 'a lot like a *Where's Waldo?* book,' in which one finds Waldo 'has different names and different features in different parts of the world ... The incessant search for him makes him seem simultaneously illusive and ubiquitous.'[4] Such a characterization bespeaks the complexity and variability of citizenship in space and time. It is this variability's relation to political territories that this chapter seeks to unpack.

The literature on citizenship provides a number of key elements that might be fruitfully enumerated for the following discussion. These include (1) the notion that citizenship is multi-scalar, being embedded in relationships that construct places as well as link particular places to broader networks, and (2) that citizenship also varies in meaning, taking on certain aspects and significance for people in different circumstances. Finally, (3) citizenship seems to be defined, as much by what it *is not* as by what it *is*.[5] While its capacity for reinterpretation, reformulation, and nuancing is fairly well established,[6] its location has often been linked to specific scales of place or types of places. As shall be outlined below, these tend to be the dominant political organizational units of specific eras and suggest an evolving geographic optimality for citizenship. This chapter considers a growing literature that problematizes the

  [2] Arjun Appadurai, *Modernity at Large: Cultural Dimensions of Globalization* (Minneapolis: University of Minnesota Press, 1996); Lynn Staeheli, Patricia Ehrkamp, Helga Leitner, and Caroline Nagel, 'Dreaming the Ordinary: Daily Life and the Complex Geographies of Citizenship,' *Progress in Human Geography 36* (2012): pp. 628–644, doi: 10.1177/0309132511435001.

  [3] See also Walker in this volume and Maas in this volume.

  [4] Lynn Staeheli, 'Political Geography: Where's Citizenship?,' *Progress in Human Geography 35*, no. 3 (2010): pp. 393–400, doi: 10.1177/0309132510370671.

  [5] Ibid., p. 393.

  [6] Suffrage movements have expanded citizenship periodically to include new components of population.

notion of citizenship possessing an optimal territorial scale and considers prospects for citizenship wholly untethered to territory.[7]

While much of the discussion in this chapter and in this volume speaks to the relationship between citizenship and States, it is imperative to acknowledge that the narrative of rescaling citizenship is *not* linear. Citizenship does not originate with the polis and culminate in the Nation-State. While this chapter outlines various manifestations of human socio-spatial organization including the polis, the empire, and the Nation-State, it makes clear that other definitions of citizenship have manifested in relation to varied modes of political territorial organization and also in rejection of geographic limitation. Towards the latter point, it suggests that communities of belonging and obligation have existed outside and across the dominant politico-territorial structures of all eras. Varied ideals of belonging and civil responsibility may be more prominently visible or articulated today, but have existed throughout world history, and thereby perpetually formed alternative scales of citizenship. As shall be demonstrated below, a cosmopolitan geographic imaginary has long coexisted with (and often in opposition to) State-based citizenships, offering an alternative to spatial fetishism and the 'banality of geographic evils'[8] such as the 'birthright lottery.'[9]

LOCATING EARLY CITIZENSHIPS

The earliest forms of human socio-political organization involved small, nomadic bands of hunter-gatherers. Governance was largely traditional with relatively egalitarian strata of kinship. Elder members, especially older males, probably enjoyed higher status and authority within the band. Merger or division of such groups was likely catalyzed by various contingencies including food shortages, water issues, or intra-group conflicts. Larger tribal associations would occasionally take shape, adopting systems of chiefdom-governance and limited degrees of social stratification. Membership in such bands was rather fixed and the demands of the hunter-gatherer lifestyle placed severe restrictions on the scale and duration of these arrangements.

---

[7] See Gans in this volume, Tan in this volume, and Gibney in this volume.

[8] David Harvey, 'Cosmopolitanism and the Banality of Geographic Evils,' *Public Culture* 12, no. 2 (2000): pp. 529–564, doi: 10.1215/08992363-12-2-529.

[9] Ayelet Shachar, *The Birthright Lottery: Citizenship and Global Inequality* (Cambridge: Harvard University Press, 2009).

The advent of agriculture and the domestication of plants and animals, known as the Neolithic Revolution (circa 10,000 BCE), heralded sweeping changes for humanity, including the emergence of writing, permanent settlements, social-economic specialization and stratification, codified law, monumental architecture, long-distance trade, and the definition of community membership by residency rather than kinship. Technological and social innovations of this sort catalyzed the development of new, more durable institutions of political organization, namely small-scale States or poleis.

Poleis manifested independently in a variety of regional settings. They are, however, most commonly regarded as originating in ancient Mesopotamia and somewhat later in the Indus, Nile, and Yellow river basins, Mesoamerica, and the northern Andes. These poleis consisted of relatively small urban cores and their immediate agricultural hinterlands. The integrated economic systems they supported compelled scholars to refer to them as city-states, launching a long-standing relationship between urban settings and concepts of citizenship.

City-states usually emerged in clusters within a region dominated by a linguistically related people. Examples include the Sumerians, Phoenicians, or Greeks. Cultural affinities notwithstanding, inter-polity warfare was rather common. Subjugation of one polis by a stronger neighbor constituted the basis for Ethnic-States, in which the governing elite and other privileged classes—warriors, priests, scribes, merchants, etc.—shared common cultural traditions. In circumstances where Ethnic-States extended their scope of conquest beyond an immediate and readily accessible territory, the term Empire may be applied. Centralized governance was the norm within Imperial States, commonly institutionalized following the integration of other cultural-linguistic groups. In short, although ruling elites were generally drawn from the dominant ethnic group, the concept of citizenship acquired a relatively multi-ethnic character.

The sustained appeal of Empire formation is evidenced by political histories of the Tigris-Euphrates' and Nile's basins, in which the succession of Akkadian, Babylonian, Assyrian, and Achaemenid Empires, as well as millennia of Pharaonic Dynasties perpetuated complexly inclusive but still stratified socio-political memberships. Beyond the broader Fertile Crescent region, tribal, city-state, and Ethnic-State variants of socio-political organization held sway. This said, the ancient world presents an ebb and flow of State powers, wherein alternation between strategies of centralization with direct territorial control and systems of decentralization and vassalage were common.

Citizenship within city-states, Ethnic-States, and Empires was intimately tied to the spatiality of power or the spatial structures of both affective and contractual authority. While all three forms of political territorial organization had distinct advantages and proved remarkably durable under the right circumstances, they were also vulnerable to internal divisions and external threats. Given that chroniclers of human history have overwhelmingly lived within and operated on behalf of

States, it is not surprising that the narrative of citizenship and political history tends to omit the vast majority of people who remained 'stateless' and pursued a variety of alternative strategies of political organization and membership.[10] These include hunter-gatherers, mobile pastoralists, or small-scale agriculturalists. Such groups are commonly portrayed as the antithesis of their State-based contemporaries[11] but should be regarded as enacting alternative citizenship ideals.[12]

Contrasting the citizenships of these historic groups is significant to current debates on the subject. For many scholars the direction of causation for citizenship holds 'community' as the starting point of 'sameness' (e.g. common values, shared experiences, common concern for place).[13] Other scholars, by contrast, posit that institutions of citizenship (e.g. public education, military, bureaucracy, bordered territory) lay the groundwork for imagined communities beyond the local and by consequence establish networked sites for the distribution of civil beneficence and standards of responsibility. Such 'social contract theories' of citizenship reflect a particular epistemological positionality pertaining to both the organization of political space and the criteria of civil membership. The former advocate that communal relationships of citizenship may be affective rather than contractual. Current debates about the viability of de-territorialized citizenship reify these schools of thought.

Those living outside of poleis, Ethnic-States and on the frontiers of Empires, like those outside the Nation-State structure today, were in a complex relationship with 'citizens' of political territorial entities for resources, land-use, and power. While resource, technological, and cultural exchanges between State-based and non-State-based citizenries were probably more nuanced and reciprocal than is commonly assumed, the fact remains that early State-citizenship, much like today's, requires an 'other' against which membership might be defined. This suggests that the geographic imaginary of citizenship is founded on bounded spaces of responsibility and limitations of moral concern. This should not however be regarded as the only perspective on humanity.

Articulating an ideal of cosmopolitanism, ancient Greek philosophers like Diogenes the Cynic proclaimed himself a 'citizen of the world' (*kosmou polite*, or citizen of the comos) defying the polis as the source of identity construction.[14] The

---

[10] J. G. A. Pocock, 'The Ideal of Citizenship since Classical Times,' in Ronald Beiner, ed., *Theorizing Citizenship* (Albany: SUNY Press, 1995), pp. 29–53.

[11] Plato, *The Republic*, translated by Desmond Lee (New York: Penguin Press, 2003).

[12] James C. Scott's, *The Art of Not Being Governed: An Anarchist History of Upland Southeast Asia* (New Haven: Yale University Press, 2010) (exploring contemporary strategies of groups of people seeking to avoid control by governments).

[13] Lynn Staeheli, 'Citizenship and the Problem of Community,' *Political Geography* 27, no. 1 (2008): pp. 5–21, p. 8, online http://dx.doi.org/10.1016/j.polgeo.2007.09.002.

[14] Laërtius Diogenes, *Lives of Eminent Philosophers*, translated by R. D. Hicks (Cambridge: Harvard University Press, 1972).

Stoics also put forth a mode of moral responsibility based on concentric circles of compassion in which larger webs of mutual obligation extend from self and family to community, region, and ultimately the world.

CITIZENSHIPS THROUGHOUT CLASSICAL ANTIQUITY

With material technologies moving from Bronze to Iron, human prehistory moves to human history and chroniclers emphasize the rise, fall, and churn of successive empires on a global scale. Manifestations of the State and related concepts of citizenship either diffuse from the Eurasian central hearth (Fertile Crescent writ large) or represent independent occurrences. The emergence of urban-based civilizations in the Americas suggests the latter—but in the varied regional settings in which the related concepts take hold across the Eurasian-African landmass the truth could very well be a combination of indigenous innovation and acculturation.

Regardless, the concept of the State as Empire came to dominate broad swaths of land from the Mediterranean basin to the plains of east-central Asia. The Parthian and Sassanid Empires replaced their Fertile Crescent predecessors but were bookended to the west and east by the Roman Republic/Empire and the dynasties of Imperial China, especially the Han Dynasty. These Empires contributed their own technological and administrative innovations to the evolution of the State as Empire. To varying degrees, both also asserted claims of universal sovereignty and divine sanction.[15] Often credited with forming clear divisions (e.g. Hadrian's Wall and the Great Wall) between their territories and those of 'others' (citizens and non-citizens), in practice, they relied on a range of territorial and social strategies often producing 'fuzzy boundaries.' Sovereignty and the assignation of belonging were less than absolute. Yet for later generations, these Empires came to represent the epitome of territorially integrated, centrally administered States, while citizenship claimed a new status in the spatialities of power manifesting through the concept of 'rights.'[16]

Yet again, the narrative of citizenship and territory lacks a linear arc. Perhaps never more famously than in the case of these two Empires is the presence of 'non-citizens' or 'stateless' people more poignant. To the north and south of Rome and

---

[15] Thomas Hobbes, *Leviathan*, edited by R. Tuck (Cambridge: Cambridge University Press, 1991).

[16] Pocock (n 10); Thomas H. Marshall, *Citizenship and Social Class and Other Essays* (Cambridge: Cambridge University Press, 1950).

China, as well as across most of the Americas, hunter-gatherer, pastoral, and small-scale farming societies predominated. Their impact on history is profound as one considers the fall of Rome at the hands of the Huns and the accession of the Yuan (Mongol) Dynasty in China. This said, the concept of the State as Empire appeared well on its way to becoming the irresistible logic of socio-political organization and the defining characteristic of 'civilization'. While the idea may be argued to have assumed its place among the 'natural order of things', it is nevertheless revealed to be mutable as geographic expansion required integration of new groups. Also evident at this time were voices of cosmopolitanism such as Plutarch who advocated, 'we should regard all human beings as our fellow citizens and neighbors'.[17]

State-Citizenships
and their Competitors

While imperial State structures were regarded as increasingly palpable and inexorable from the perspective of those at their centers, as well as, for many residing in their hinterlands, competing visions of the State and ideals of membership soon upended these assumptions. Jockeying for position alongside, against, and within the idea of the State as Empire was a variety of alternative concepts of political organization and standards of group membership (e.g. Hanseatic League, Turkic Khaganates and other nomadic confederations, Papal authority, etc.). For reasons that remain subject of much debate, this period witnessed a surge in large-scale migrations out of the vast Eurasian steppe region by semi-nomadic groups governed by tribal lineages, personal oaths of loyalty, and cavalry-warrior ethea. The Scythian, Hunnic, Germanic, Turkic, Slavic, Tartar, and Mongol tribes, to name a few, seemed the antithesis of the more settled notions of the State as Empire.

Moving in a generally southerly vector, these Eurasian nomads soon encountered the sedentary imperial societies of China, the Middle East, and the Mediterranean. The resulting encounters are too commonly characterized as a 'clash of civilizations'. In fact, they frequently involved accommodation and the provision of sanctuary from more powerful rivals back on the steppe. At other times, of course, they earned their 'clash' moniker as events of plunder and conquest. A slightly different dynamic propelled Arab armies surging out of the Arabian Peninsula, as religious conversion provided an additional impetus.

---

[17] Quoted in Martha Nussbaum, 'Patriotism and Cosmopolitanism', *Boston Review 19*, no. 5 (1994): pp. 3–16, p. 13, online http://bostonreview.net/martha-nussbaum-patriotism-and-cosmopolitanism.

The seemingly ascendant imperial structure of the period was nevertheless shown to be fragile. In many cases already debilitated by internal strife, famed Empires fell, sometimes amid dramatic invasions and other times through more piecemeal crumbling. The nomadic victors commonly assimilated to the cultural and political structures of the vanquished, co-opting the State as Empire but with their group assuming the role of new ruling elite. Though some, such as the Umayyad Caliphate, Seljuks, Ottomans, and the Yuan Dynasty, achieved considerable success, power eventually fragmented and devolved into a loose and shifting assortment of petty States and feudal systems.

It should be noted that the ideal of Empire persisted even as the pretense of imperial authority was undermined. For example, the notion of a caliphate ruling over all Islamic lands remained a powerful force among Muslims, despite more or less independent reign of a range of lesser emirates and sultanates. A similar system emerged in Europe where Frankish and later German emperors claimed absolute sovereignty as the rightful successors of Rome, but lesser nobles quickly turned their fiefdoms into independent bases of power and acquired broad autonomy. This new spatiality of power quite often brought them into confrontation with their nominal lord; a situation further complicated by Catholic Popes claiming universal sovereignty over religious matters, which invariably entwined with secular affairs. These types of feudal arrangements of lord and vassal were hardly unique to medieval Europe, so there was little to suggest that the groundwork was being laid for a new manifestation of the State and ideal of communal membership.

FORMING MODERN
NATION-STATE CITIZENSHIPS

Medieval Europe would seem an odd birthplace for new forms of political territorial organization and ideals of membership. [18] Constituted by a bewildering collection of quarreling, petty States, trade was limited, science and technology lagged, and living standards were abysmal compared to other civilized regions. Yet, feudal Europe saw monarchical rule strengthen in alliance with a burgeoning urban-based merchant class to incrementally garner power from the lesser nobility and church. While claims of divine mandate for absolute rule can be found throughout history, European monarchs gradually developed the capacities to establish and maintain more direct rule over their subjects. It was this notion of the absolute

[18] See Gans in this volume.

monarchy, bolstered by the growing capacity to precisely demarcate land and identify people as belonging to one State or another that laid the foundations of the modern States.[19]

A system of Statehood was gradually codified in international agreements, most notably the Peace of Westphalia in 1648. These agreements mutually affirmed (1) that each State possessed absolute territorial sovereignty and the concordant right to govern that territory free from outside interference; (2) that States would be regarded as equals and the only legitimate actors in international affairs; and (3) that States would refrain from interfering in the domestic affairs of other States.[20] Obviously, violations of these precepts were common, but this specific scale of statehood and its commensurate ideal of membership gained standing on practical, as well as, a normative grounds. This served to naturalize a system of socio-spatial organization that ultimately became the international system regarded by many as currently under threat.

Centralization of political power by Europe's kings and princes was soon challenged by demands for greater popular representation. This is most dramatically exemplified by the French Revolution and its precept that sovereignty lies with the people and their consent to be governed.[21] Over time notions of popular sovereignty combined with rising nationalist sentiment to challenge, weaken, and eventually topple or dramatically modify the power vested in Europe's monarchies. The State's role would be recast in service to the nation rather than the opposite. Despite voices calling for more universal conceptions of human community,[22] the notion of citizenship also changed to encompass a group of people with a shared cultural identity, normally embodied by a primary language. Nationalists posited that political

---

[19] Stuart Elden, *The Birth of Territory* (Chicago: University of Chicago Press, 2013); Charles Tilly, *Coercion, Capital, and European States, AD 990-1990* (London: Wiley-Blackwell 1990) (suggesting that States arose because of war, and preparation for war).

[20] John Agnew, *Globalization and Sovereignty* (Lanham: Rowman and Littlefield Press, 2009).

[21] Jean Jacques Rousseau, *On the Social Contract with Geneva Manuscript and Political Economy*, translated by J. R. Masters (New York: Bedford/St. Martin's, 1978). See also Alexis de Tocqueville, *The Old Regime and the Revolution*, edited by F. Furet, F. Mélonio, translated by A. S. Kahan (Chicago: University of Chicago Press, 1998).

[22] Examples from the period include German philosopher Christoph Martin Wieland who in 1788 argued that all the peoples of the earth are members of single family and should be treated as such (Kwame Appiah, *Cosmopolitanism: Ethics in a World of Strangers* (New York: W.W. Norton, 2006), and Immanuel Kant's 1795 essay 'Perpetual Peace' which argued that 'the peoples of the earth have entered in varying degrees into a universal community, and it is developed to the point where a violation of laws in one part of the world is felt *everywhere*.' (Immanuel Kant, *To Perpetual Peace: A Philosophical Sketch*, translated by Ted Humphrey (Indianapolis: Hackett Publishing, 2003), pp. 107–108. Outside the European context one may note the rise of the Baha'i faith in nineteenth-century Persia, whose founder Baha'u'llah proclaimed 'the earth is but one country, and mankind its citizens' (Baha'u'llah, *Gleanings from the Writing of Baha'u'llah* (Wilmette: Baha'i Publishing Trust, 1983)).

borders of the State be congruent with the cultural-linguistic borders of their nation, thereby giving rise to the ideal of the Nation-State.

Europe's wars of the nineteenth and twentieth centuries aided in the conflation of national identity and State sovereignty in a mutually reinforcing cycle of State formation and reformation. The French government may have initiated a process of governmental efforts to transform peasants into French citizens, but parallel ventures soon took shape across the continent (e.g. German nationalists demanded a German State encompassing all Germans). Europe's patchwork quasi-feudal principalities, absolutist monarchies, and multi-ethnic Empires soon gave way as the logic of the Nation-State. Beginning with US President Woodrow Wilson's 14 Points and the World War I peace settlements, international law sought to reconcile—however imperfectly—the basic principles of Westphalia with the new realities of nationalism. This process should not however be viewed as *natural* or part of an inevitable evolution of human socio-spatiality. Efforts to enshrine this new norm met with protestations of anarchists, Marxists, and internationalists of the period and, though often denied, have continually coexisted with trans- and sub-national economic, political, and communal practices.[23]

COLONIALISM AND NATION-STATE CITIZENSHIPS

As the notion of Nation-State coalesced in Europe, advances in military, industrial, and mobility technologies facilitated the embarkation of those same nascent Nation-States on wide-ranging imperialist endeavors abroad. The annexation of territory during this colonial period was however *not* commonly coupled with the extension of full citizenship to non-European populations. This worked in concert with the denial of State status to extant polities, except when serving European interests. 'Explorers' commonly issued grand pronouncements claiming the entirety of that landmass—of which they knew little more than what they could see from the coast—as sovereign territory of their patron monarch. Maps were

---

[23] Vladimir Illych Lenin for example stated: 'The full equality of nations; the right of self determination; the merger of all workers of all nations—this is what our national program, informed by Marxism and the experience of the whole world and of Russia teaches to the workers' (Vladimir Illych Lenin, *O prave natsii na samoopredelenie O Srednei Azii i Kazakhstane* (Tashkent: Gosudarstvennoe izdatel'stvo Uzbekskoi SSR, 1960). Albert Einstein described nationalism in 1929 as an infantile sickness: 'It is the measles of the human race' (quoted in Helen Dukas and Banesh Hoffman, eds., *Albert Eistein: The Human Side* (Princeton: Princeton University Press, 1979), p. 38.

regularly drawn to reflect such de jure claims but the de facto establishment of European colonial control was much slower, contingent, and uneven than commonly assumed.

Great variance is also evident in the processes of European colonization.[24] Some cases saw the establishment of direct rule and an influx of settlers, while others enacted indirect rule through local clients and a negligible European presence. While some regard abuse of indigenous peoples as a byproduct of the era's sensibilities, it is important to acknowledge that alternative perspectives existed. Sixteenth century Dominican Friar Bartolomé de las Casas, for example, advocated on behalf of Native Americans and against Spanish genocidal practices. Such voices were almost universally rejected in European colonial ventures in favor of economic gain and imperial competition.

Evidentiary of trans-national dynamics amidst nationalist ideals, many of the earliest colonial actors were joint-stock trading companies—what we might now call public-private partnerships—that enjoyed broad autonomy while establishing and governing overseas colonies in the name of their State sponsor (e.g. East India Trading Company, Dutch East Indies Company). Regardless of style of colonial governance, indigenous territorial practices and political structures were circumvented, pushed aside, or plowed under to make way for European preferences and ambitions. Such practices reached an apex during the so-called Scramble for Africa during the late 1800s, where European rivalries threatened economic progress, compelling the main colonial powers to partition Africa amongst themselves. Despite constituting the majority populations of territories claimed by European powers, Africans were not represented during these negotiations. The negotiators' relatively limited knowledge of the places and peoples that would live under this superimposed map resulted in the crosscutting and division of groups possessing longstanding ideals of community and membership. A similar but less dramatic process unfolded across much of Asia.

Having managed to absorb nearly every part of the world by the early twentieth century, notions of empire seemed ascendant, but in reality, direct European colonial rule was relatively brief in world history. For example, Spanish rule over their American colonies was sustained for about three centuries—roughly from the early sixteenth century to the early nineteenth century, British rule over what would become the United States lasted about 175 years,[25] and most of Africa was not colonized until the late 1800s but gained independence during the 1960s. This is not to suggest the colonialism had negligible impacts.

---

[24] See Gover in this volume.

[25] Britain retained some other territories much longer but granted them significant autonomy over domestic affairs as part of the British Commonwealth. Other colonies were much shorter in duration.

European colonialism may be fairly attributed with fostering profound demographic, economic, and social change in the regions it encompassed. Even in areas that were never officially colonized, such as most of East Asia such changes soon manifest. In respect to rescaling citizenship, colonialism provided the main mechanism for disseminating, operationalizing, and institutionalizing modern notions of territorial sovereignty and the ideals of nationhood associated with the Nation-State. The United Nations founding charter in 1945 and subsequent iterations of international law reaffirmed the basic Nation-State principles as a global norm.[26] By the 1970s, most colonies, with few exceptions, had transitioned sometimes through revolution and sometimes by attrition to sovereign States.

Yet in contrast to Western Europe, where violence of war, forced migration, territorial revisions, and even genocide, produced relatively homogeneous nationalized populations and political liberalism (i.e. democracy) offered 'voice' as an integrative modality for even those possessing identities outside a given State's national ideal ('integration' being a relative term—e.g. Basques, Galicians, Catalans, Catholics of Northern Ireland, Scottish, Welsh, Roma), many newly independent States inherited colonial-era borders that in no way conformed to the notion of the Nation-State. This remains a fundamental contradiction within the modern Nation-State system. The charter of the United Nations, for example, endorses friendship among nations and self-determination of peoples, but it is really an association of States. Nations cannot become members. Moreover, the advent of citizenship has proven interminably complex in most States, having been created from the machinations of colonial powers often lacking knowledge of the cultural, political, economic, and social geographies of the lands they claimed. Such is the Janus face of nationalism—at once possessing a progressive emancipatory function that ultimately requires exclusivity and erasure to remain sustainable.[27]

---

[26] Links between the institutionalization of sovereignty and the growth of the international system can be found in the Covenant of the League of Nations' reference to 'the dealings of organized peoples with one another' which leaves out *un*organized peoples (e.g. those subject to imperialism and colonialism) and the Charter of the United Nations holding the 'principle of equal rights and self-determination of peoples.' As noted by Willem Maas, 'both statements make clear that each "people" is entitled to membership in the international community, as long as it is organized into statehood' (Willem Maas, 'Varieties of Multilevel Citizenship,' in Willem Maas, ed., *Multilevel Citizenship* (Philadelphia: University of Pennsylvania Press, 2013), pp. 1–24, p. 3).

[27] Some would go so far as to assert that nationalism is by nature xenophobic, parochial, militaristic, compassion-limiting, and through its bordering process a moral abomination (see Barney Warf, 'Nationalism, Cosmopolitanism, and Geographical Imaginations,' *Geographical Review 102*, no. 3 (2012): pp. 271–292, doi: 10.1111/j.1931-0846.2012.00152.x; Timothy Brennan, 'Cosmopolitanism and Internationalism,' *New Left Review 2* (2001): pp. 75–84, online https://newleftreview.org/search/multi_parameter?author=Brennan&title=Cosmopolitan%20vs%20International).

FROM MODERN
TO POST-MODERN CITIZENSHIPS

The challenges, alternatives, and prospects of citizenship amid post-modernity and globalization are myriad.[28] Time-space compression may be regarded as a byproduct of advances in technologies of mobility and communication, as well as capitalism's advancing global supply/demand network. Similar technological advances (e.g. roads) and commensurate geographic proliferation of power and influence gave rise to the Stoics' varied realms of compassion during Rome's expansion, Kantian universal ethics during the era of Enlightenment/Colonialism, and State-centered integrative dynamics of nationalization during the nineteenth century. As Anderson[29] suggests, communities extending not only horizontally across space but also vertically across social class were 'imagined' during that period in a manner theretofore largely unique in the world. This too was a product of time-space compression functioning in conjunction with new technologies of power (e.g. measurable space, newspapers, political parties, rising literacy rates, national currencies, national bureaucracies and services like postal systems and standing armies).[30] Today, prospects of scaling-up communities of belonging are made eminently plausible by accelerated flows of people, resources, and ideas across international borders. Foreign investment, transnational firms, and international trade combine with new communication technologies (e.g. cell phones, internet and the varied forms of social media it supports) to form networks that transcend limitations of not only space-time but also (to greater and lesser degrees) the human constructs of national territoriality.[31]

Both markets and production increasingly require trans-State mobility of goods, capital, and people. [32] The scaling up of governance to facilitate this takes form in the new regional organizations to which many States concede a measure of sovereignty. The European Union stands at the forefront of this 'new regionalism' by hybridizing

---

[28] See Lori in this volume; Shachar in this volume; Spiro in this volume; Strumia in this volume; Vink in this volume; Volpp in this volume; Honohan in this volume; Donaldson and Kymlicka in this volume; Costello in this volume; Chung in this volume; Bosniak in this volume; Shaw in this volume.

[29] Benedict Anderson, *Imagined Communities: Reflections on the Origin and Spread of Nationalism* (London: Verso, 1983).

[30] Anthony Giddens, *The Nation State and Violence* (Cambridge: Polity Press, 1985).

[31] Of the world's population, 32.7 percent now uses the internet; though enormous social and spatial discrepancies in access to it exist, this portal to a global system of communication and knowledge is expanding (Internet World Stats, Internet Usage Statistics, www.internetworldstats.com/stats.htm).

[32] Peter Dicken, *Global Shift: Mapping the Changing Contours of the World Economy*, 7th edition (London: Sage, 2014).

national with a supra State European identity.[33] Though imperfect and rightly questioned as to sustainability in times of crisis (see the recent economic downturn and Syrian refugee flows), the ideal of a European citizenship is something few would have considered possible in the first half of the twentieth century.

Akin to the early twentieth century's scaling up of laws to combat the social and environmental abuses of unrestrained capitalism and to level the field for civil development across national territories (e.g. counter spatial inequalities that could threaten national unity), recent efforts to establish a global legal infrastructure constitute an expanded ideal of citizenship.[34] Examples include the 1948 Declaration of Human Rights, humanitarian interventions by the United Nations, and the establishment and function of the International Court of Justice and International Criminal Court.[35] While imperfectly applied and still generally requiring Western benefit for sustained engagement, the mere existence of these bodies and the ideals of universal ethics and justice upon which they are based suggests a less bounded conception of humanity (i.e. a departure from the Westphalian ideals of sovereignty and the 1789 Declaration of the Rights of Man which held 'The principle of all sovereignty resides essentially in the nation. No body nor individual may exercise any authority which does not proceed directly from the nation').

Though much attention is paid to supra State regional organizations, the Westphalian system's ideals of rigidly bounded communities of belonging, compassion, and responsibility are also undermined from below.[36] A global civil society movement includes trans-border institutions like religious organizations, charities/ non-profits, environmental groups, human rights advocates, professional organizations, and trade unions activists.[37] Moreover, Global Cities and sub-State regions have carved out unique trans-border economic linkages while fomenting cosmopolitan identities akin to Medieval Free Cities. These identities stand in distinction to the politico-territorial ideals of Westphalia.[38] Along these lines and partially in

---

[33] See Maas in this volume; Strumia in this volume; Vink in this volume.

[34] Brubaker suggests that higher jurisdictions in which citizens can press claims may foment instrumental notions of citizenship in which rights are prioritized over identification, obligation, and responsibility (Rogers Brubaker, 'The Return of Assimilation? Changing Perspectives on Immigration and its Squeals in France, Germany and the United States,' *Ethnic and Racial Studies* 24, no. 4 (2001): pp. 531–548, doi: 10.1080/01419870120049770).

[35] Tom Farer, 'Cosmopolitan Humanitarian Intervention: A Five Part Test,' *International Relations* 19 (2005): pp. 211–250, doi: 10.1177/0047117805052814.

[36] Will Kymlicka, *Multicultural Citizenship* (Oxford: Oxford University Press, 1995); Will Kymlicka, 'Citizenship in an Era of Globalization: A Commentary on Held,' in Ian Shapiro and Casiano Hacker-Cordon, eds., *Democracy's Edges* (Cambridge: Cambridge University Press, 1999), pp. 112–127.

[37] Pippa Norris, 'Global Governance and Cosmopolitan Citizens,' in Joseph S. Nye and J. D. Donahue, eds., *Governance in a Globalizing World* (Washington: Brookings Institution Press, 2000), pp. 155–177.

[38] Rainer Bauböck, 'Reinventing Urban Citizenship,' *Citizenship Studies* 7, no. 2 (2010): pp. 139–160, doi: 10.1080/1362102032000065946; Rogers Smith, 'Modern Citizenship,' in Engin F. Isin and Bryan S. Turner, eds., *Handbook of Citizenship Studies* (Thousand Oaks: Sage Publications, 2002), pp. 105–116.

response to the increasingly competitive nature of international trade and business, governments around the world have bestowed extra-territorial privileges upon favored businesses and workers. For example, export processing zones and other types of liberalized economic spaces allow for certain workers to possess special citizenship or visa policies. Commonly lumped together under the rubric of globalization, these trends pose substantive challenges to the basic foundations of State-citizenship.

Relatedly, the 'new Argonauts,' comprised of corporate executives and professionals of various global industries including education, resource extraction, development, music, and sports, represent a fluid spatiality that resists borders and restrictive definitions of national/State citizenship.[39] While this group represents a rather thin stratum of elites, some 15 percent of the world's population crosses national borders annually as tourists. Far greater numbers exist outside their States of birth and/or citizenship as diasporic communities, guest workers, visiting students, refugees, remittance communities, and immigrants.[40] In response, more than ninety countries have embraced dual or multiple citizenship, and in 2006 more than forty states allowed non-citizen voting.[41]

The effect of these dynamics on citizenship is multifold and at times contradictory. In one sense, mounting human connections across space catalyze a scaling up of identity. Using data from the World Values survey in 2000, Schueth and O'Loughlin[42] suggest that upwards of one fifth of the world's population self-identifies with the 'global community' as a primary or secondary identity. This same survey data also reveals that primary identities overwhelmingly remain linked to Nation-States and local settings.[43] One may argue that the 'local' and the 'national' provide something putative through which dimensions of citizenship policy are expected. Their naturalization as 'rightful' scales of political spatiality over the last 200-plus years affords both territorial scales a normative and legal basis for belonging, rights, and access to civil beneficence.

[39] Annalee Saxenian, *The New Argonauts: Regional Advantage in a Global Economy* (Cambridge: Harvard University Press, 2006).

[40] See Joppke in this volume; Trachtman in this volume; Gibney in this volume.

[41] Tanja Sejersen, '"I Vow to Thee My Countries"—The Expansion of Dual Citizenship in the 21st Century,' *International Migration Review 42*, no. 3 (2008): pp. 523–549, doi: 10.1111/j.1747-7379.2008.00136.x; Sarah Song, 'Democracy and Noncitizen Voting Rights,' *Citizenship Studies 13*, no. 6 (2009): pp. 607–620, doi: 10.1080/13621020903309607.

[42] Sam Schueth and John O'Loughlin, 'Belonging to the World: Cosmopolitanism in Geographic Contexts,' *Geoforum 39*, no. 2 (2008): pp. 926–941, online http://dx.doi.org/10.1016/j.geoforum.2007.10.002.

[43] Peter Furia, 'Global Citizenship Anyone? Cosmopolitanism, Privilege and Public Opinion,' *Global Society 19* (2005): pp. 331–359, doi: 10.1080/13600820500242415.

THE STATE REMAINS

Increased trans-State dispersion of peoples (migration) in combination with the dynamics of de-territorialized democracy, neo-liberal capitalism, environmentalism, and new geographies of global justice/human rights are regarded by some as heralding the ontological foundations of cosmopolitan citizenship.[44] Yet only roughly 3 percent of people will change their citizenship from their place of birth.[45] Where transnational corporations may engage with global supply chains and lack definite State allegiances, outside of the 'new Argonauts,' these institutions are peopled by human beings for whom communities of local belonging and ideals of State citizenship remain significant. Though many cosmopolitan elites (both of the neo-liberal and the human liberalist ilk) regard patriotism, nationalism, and, by extension, the very notion of 'loyalty' as carrying negative connotations pertaining to limiting seizure of competitive advantage through transfer of patronage/service or irrational commitment to a defined ideology and/or community, these ideals nevertheless continue to resonate amongst the majority of human beings.[46] The bounded political and identity structures of the Nation-State show little sign of eroding into the dustbin of history.

Even a cursory review of contemporary headlines reveals the continuing role of nationalism, as demands by minority groups for Nation-Statehood represent a major challenge to some States. Far from systemically undermining the assumptions of the modern State, they seek to revise the territorial framework of States to better reflect the ideal of the national self-determination.[47] Kurdish nationalists, for example, do not wish to overturn the State system but rather seek a place within that system through the creation of a fully sovereign Kurdish Nation-State. The collapse of Yugoslavia and the USSR gave rise to new states that, twenty-five years on, still host complex negotiations of citizenship with respect to Westphalian ideals.[48] As suggested by Staeheli,[49] to date 'post-national, transnational, cosmopolitan, and global citizenships ... are not alternatives to citizenship-in-the-state but instead are constructed through and in relation to it.'

One could read the above historical narrative of citizenship as an ongoing pursuit for an optimal territorial scale of socio-political organization. The fact that primacy

---

[44] Warf (n 27), p. 279.

[45] Ayelet Shachar, 'Citizenship,' in Michel Rosenfeld and Andras Sajo, eds., *The Oxford Handbook of Comparative Constitutional Law* (New York: Oxford University Press, 2012), pp. 1002–1019, p. 1009.

[46] Schueth and O'Loughlin (n 42).

[47] Alexander Murphy, 'Territory's Continuing Allure,' *Annals of the Association of American Geographers 103*, no. 5 (2013): pp. 1212–1226, p. 1212, doi: 10.1080/00045608.2012.696232; Staeheli (n 4).

[48] Alexander Diener, 'Diasporic and Transnational Social Practices in Central Asia,' *Geography Compass 2*, no. 2 (2008): pp. 956–978, doi: 10.1111/j.1749-8198.2008.00101.x.

[49] Staeheli (n 4), p. 396.

of scale has evolved with technology and in relation to different social, political, economic, and cultural contexts stands as evidence against a stable, fixed-location of citizenship.[50] The Nation-State nevertheless retains a powerful allure relating two primary roles. First, territorialized forms of citizenship and particularly the Nation-State have long been regarded as the 'most feasible way to regulate citizens for particular ends and to create institutional forms that citizens can access to make claims.'[51] As the previous sections of this chapter suggest, improving technologies allowed for recalibration of the territorial scale for better coherence with the enactment of power and capacities for provision of civil beneficence.

Second, the State's allure relates to its instrumentality in the 'construction of sameness.' The optimal territorial scale of citizenship is commonly regarded to be located in 'sites where commitments to the polity and to other citizens and self development can best be encouraged.'[52] Given that citizenship has both political and social aspects, expansion and contraction of territorial scale link to instrumental definitions of belonging. For advocates of social contract theory—citizenship leads to community. This is embodied in Anderson's notion of 'imagining,' which advances the Lockean premise of State rule legitimatized by consent of the citizen. The varied institutions (public education, standing militaries, civil bureaucracies, public symbols—flags, statuary, maps, etc.) that channel the national imagination toward a particular political form and territorial scale reflect an elite-driven shaping of citizenship. Well-founded interventions by Feminist theorists reveal the non-universal aspect of such citizenship (e.g. gender, racial, ethnic, and regional marginality) and how attributes deemed necessary for citizenship have varied throughout history in accordance with circumstantially contingent criteria.[53]

For example, defining the territorial limits of belonging is both an exercise in inclusive identity politics and part of a larger dynamic of exclusion and *othering* in which Nation-States deploy discourses of fear and pride to reinforce the value of the State.[54] Borders are commonly represented as a means of protecting citizens within a State from those who would do them harm. But 'harm' may be defined in a variety of ways, including economic threats (illegal immigrants taking jobs or imposing burdens on taxpayers), challenging socio-cultural norms, or outright violence.[55]

Where inclusion may be passive or a result of some historical cartographic anomaly, exclusion tends to be more often deliberate.[56] This presents the notion of *tolerance* of an 'other' (however defined) as a scaled-up version of the domiciliary ideal

---

[50] See Dumbrava in this volume.   [51] Staeheli et al. (n 2), p. 637.
[52] Ibid. See also Rainer Bauböck, *Transnational Citizenship: Membership and Rights in International Migration* (Cheltenham: Edward Elgar, 1994); Gerard Delanty, *Community* (New York: Routledge, 2003).
[53] Staeheli (n 13), p. 9. See also Volpp in this volume; Fitzgerald in this volume; Weinstock in this volume.
[54] Warf (n 27); Staeheli (n 4); Rachel Pain, 'Globalised Fear? Towards and Emotional Geopolitics,' *Progress in Human Geography 33*, no. 4 (2009): pp. 466–486, doi: 10.1177/0309132508104994.
[55] Staeheli (n 4), p. 394.   [56] Staeheli (n 13), p. 9.

of *hospitality*. Hospitality reflects the power of the legal resident of a given abode/ host (see citizen as insider) over the visitor/guest (see domestic 'other' or denizen as outsider).[57] In such a relationship, the power to designate appropriate ways of being/ behaving is implicit and at the State-scale commonly couched within terms like 'multiculturalism' and 'recognition.'[58] As noted above, 'others' need not be newcomers to the territory. They are often long-time, if not indigenous residents. Hence the notion of re-scaling has purchase in the complex social geographies of the modern era that gave rise to Post-Modern Turn and efforts to perform new or reify varied 'circles of we.'[59]

Despite or perhaps because of challenges leveled at national-scale identities, institutions, and ideals, many States have reinforced their borders, more tightly bounding their territories and enacting policies of control on populations within them (e.g. internet censorship).[60] Processes of securitization and regimes of protectionism engender from 'fear'—whether justified or concocted.[61] But rather than solidifying the margins and facilitating spaces of true acceptance or at least *tolerance* (as referenced above), new technologies have redeployed border enforcement throughout national territories.[62] Rather than focusing on a particular territorial scale of citizenship relating to *group* inclusion or exclusion, legal innovations enhanced by biometric technologies make the body of the individual the site of the border and discipline.[63] In short, borders of citizenship are everywhere—at the physical boundary of the national territory—in the political practices and policies[64]—in social norms (gender, sexuality, etc.)—and embodied in individuals (non-citizens and citizens carry the border).[65] An internationalized anxiety common at the margins

---

[57] See Bosniak in this volume; Owen in this volume.   [58] Staeheli (n 4), p. 395.

[59] On the divisions of citizenship formed by capitalism within State societies see Neil Brenner, 'Open Questions on State Rescaling,' *Cambridge Journal of Regions, Economy and Society* 2, no. 1 (2009): pp. 123–139, doi: 10.1093/cjres/rsp002; Michael Keating, 'Introduction: Rescaling Interests,' *Territory, Politics, Governance* 2, no. 3 (2014): pp. 239–248, doi:10.1080/21622671.2014.954604.

[60] Reece Jones, *Border Walls: Security and the War on Terror in the United States, India, and Israel* (London: Zed Books, 2012).

[61] Iris Marion Young, 'The Logic of Masculinist Protection: Reflections on the Current Security State,' *Signs* 29 (2003): pp. 513–538, doi:10.1093/0195175344.003.0002; Warf (n 27); Pain (n 54).

[62] New border zones have been created within countries through provincial agencies that hold power over the documents and technologies of the mundane. See Jamie Winders, 'Bringing Back the (B)order: Post 9/11 Politics of Immigration, Borders, and Belonging in the Contemporary US South', *Antipode* 39 (2007): pp. 920–942, doi: 10.1111/j.1467-8330.2007.00563.x; Joseph Nevins, *Operation Gatekeeper: The Rise of the Illegal Alien and the Remaking of the US-Mexico Boundary* (New York: Routledge, 2002); Mathew Coleman, 'Immigration Politics beyond the Mexico-US Border', *Antipode* 39 (2007): pp. 54–76, doi: 10.1111/j.1467-8330.2007.00506.x.

[63] Louise Amoore, 'Biometric Borders: Governing Mobilities in the War on Terror', *Political Geography* 25 (2006): pp. 336–351, doi: 10.1016/j.polgeo.2006.02.001; Mathew Sparke, 'A Neoliberal Nexus: Economy, Security, and the Biopolitics of Citizenship of the Border,' *Political Geography* 25 (2006): pp. 151–180, doi: 10.1016/j.polgeo.2005.10.002.

[64] Keating (n 59), p. 239.

[65] Staeheli (n 4), p. 395. See also Volpp in this volume; Weinstock in this volume.

of the State is, thereby, transferred to the daily life choices in re-scaled bordered zones of securitized State territories.[66]

With this said, re-scaling of citizenship is and has always been part of the human effort to organize political space and set limits on the scope of civil beneficence, rights, and responsibilities. The 'circle of we' is not now, nor has it ever been, rigidly delimited by concepts of territory. It is socially assigned in relation to a series of contingent processes, events, technologies, and shifting values that are multivalent and polilocal.[67]

Re-scaling citizenship is a reality of the twenty-first century, brought about by increasing mobilities that extend well beyond tourism and 'guest worker' migrations.[68] Advances in communications technology facilitate connections between individuals, families, and groups across space in a manner unprecedented in human history. The result is, for lack of a better term, *hybridity* of belonging and perceptions of personal and group investment within different polities.

Where such polilocality may have been relatively common within States (e.g. living in a municipality in one province but employed in another), it now prominently exists across international borders. As noted in many studies, long-term migrant communities within a given city may possess a sense of investment and belonging at the urban scale but lack allegiance and sense of responsibility to the 'host' State.[69] In this sense their citizenship ideal 'jumps scales' in accordance with their respective homeland conceptions that link to the 'local' and to a distant State.[70] It is therefore imperative to understand the 'ways in which the institutions supporting those new citizenships are constructed and sustained by nation-level institutions and how the citizenships blend loyalties and affinities that draw from the national state, from other institutions, and from experiences that are not bound by the national state.'[71]

---

[66] Staeheli (n 4), p. 396.

[67] Helga Leitner and Patrica Ehrkamp, 'Beyond National Citizenship: Turkish Immigrants and the (Re)Construction of Citizenship in Germany,' *Urban Geography* 24 (2003): pp. 127–146, doi: 10.2747/0272-3638.24.2.127; Staeheli (n 13); Staeheli (n 4); Staeheli et al. (n 2).

[68] Michael Peter Smith and Matt Bakker, *Citizenship across Borders: The Political Transnationalism of El Migrante* (Ithaca: Cornell University Press, 2008); Yasemin Soysal, *The Limits of Citizenship: Migrants and Postnational Membership in Europe* (Chicago: University of Chicago Press, 1994).

[69] Rainer Bauböck, Albert Kraler, Marco Martiniello, and Bernhard Perchinig, 'Migrants' Citizenship: Legal Status, Rights and Political Participation,' in Rinus Penninx, ed., *The Dynamics of International Migration and Settlement in Europe. A State of the Art* (Amsterdam: Amsterdam University Press, IMISCOE, 2006), pp. 65–98; Helga Leitner and Patricia Ehrkamp, 'Transnationalism and Migrants' Imaginings of Citizenship,' *Environment and Planning A* 38, no. 9 (2006): pp. 1615–1632, doi: 10.1068/a37409.

[70] Robert Kaiser and Elena Nikiforova, 'The Performativity of Scale: The Social Construction of Scale Effects in Narva, Estonia,' *Environment and Planning: Society and Space* 26, no. 3 (2008): pp. 537–562, doi: 10.1068/d3307; Alexander Diener, 'Negotiating Territorial Belonging: A Transnational Field Approach to Mongolia's Kazakhs,' *Geopolitics* 12, no. 3 (2007): pp. 459–487, doi: 10.1080/14650040701305658.

[71] Staeheli (n 4), p. 396.

While processes of naturalization[72] have been employed by States for centuries, efforts to accommodate recent 'globalized realities' manifest in a variety of unique and innovative forms. These include dual citizenship, citizenship-by-investment, deprivation (revocation), *jus domicile, jus nexi,* and e-citizenship/residency.[73]

Bauböck's[74] ideas of vesting people in place at different, not necessarily nested scales, would evoke elements of belonging, legitimize dual citizenships, affirm borderland identities, and promote 'scale-jumping.' While potentially fruitful in terms of promoting affective and communal bases for citizenship through elemental facets of social familiarity and quotidian spatiality, these processes are 'not easily accommodated within nation-centric theories of citizenship and ideals of democracy.'[75]

This chapter suggests that this ongoing negotiation of the optimal scale for citizenship is complicated by historical transition from religious-monarchial sovereignty to popular-territorial sovereignty. The latter was facilitated by the 'unity of the peoples' (real or imagined) and their sanction (real or imagined) of the State to represent them (e.g. social contract theory). The rapid proliferation of this framework over the last two centuries solidified the relationship between democracy and territory, whilst demarcating the borders between contemporary Nation-States. These linkages have become so embedded that criticizing the notion of territorial sovereignty is commonly interpreted as challenging the rule of 'the people.' As noted above, standard political maps support this relationship by portraying the world as a collection of discreet territorial units and naturalize a particular 'circle of we.' Yet, this obscures the complexity of supra and sub-State citizenships, as well as cross-border relationships and the daily practices of integration that pervade the contemporary processes of human life.

---

[72] Marc Helbing, *Practicing Citizenship and Heterogeneous Nationhood: Naturalisation in Swiss Municipalities* (Amsterdam: University of Amsterdam Press, 2008).

[73] For dual citizenship see Sally Marston and Katheryne Mitchell, 'Citizens and the State: Citizenship Formations in Space and Time,' in Clive Barnett and Murray Low, eds., *Spaces of Democracy: Geographical Perspectives on Citizenship, Participation and Representation* (Thousand Oaks: Sage, 2004), pp. 113–127. For citizenship-by-investment see Jelena Džankić, 'Investment-Based Citizenship and Residence Programmes in the EU,' EUI Working Papers no. 8 (Florence: RSCAS, 2015). For deprivation (revocation) see Rainer Bauböck and Vesco Paskalev, 'Citizenship Deprivation: A Normative Analysis,' CEPS Paper in Liberty and Security in Europe no. 82 (2015), online http://www.ceps.eu/book/citizenship-deprivation-no. For *jus domicile* see Bauböck (n 38); Herald Bauder, 'Jus Domicile: In Pursuit of a Citizenship of Equality and Social Justice,' *Journal of International Political Theory* 8, no. 1–2 (2012): pp. 184–196, doi: 10.3366/jipt.2012.0038. For *jus nexi* see Shachar (n 9); Ayelet Shachar, 'Earned Citizenship: Property Lessons for Immigration Reform,' *Yale Journal of Law & the Humanities* 23, no. 1 (2011): pp. 110–158, online http://digitalcommons.law.yale.edu/yjlh/vol23/iss1/2. For e-citizenship/residency see David Trimbach, 'Scales of Estonian Citizenship: Implications for Russophone Political Incorporation,' *Civitas: Journal of Citizenship Studies 3* (2014): pp. 1–18, online http://www.nwosu.edu/Websites/NWOSU/images/nwics/Civitas_2014.pdf.

[74] Bauböck et al. (n 69).   [75] Staeheli (n 13), p. 10.

BIBLIOGRAPHY

Agnew, John, *Globalization and Sovereignty* (Lanham: Rowman and Littlefield Press, 2009).

Amoore, Louise, 'Biometric Borders: Governing Mobilities in the War on Terror,' *Political Geography 25* (2006): pp. 336–351.

Anderson, Benedict, *Imagined Communities: Reflections on the Origin and Spread of Nationalism* (London: Verso, 1983).

Appadurai, Arjun, *Modernity at Large: Cultural Dimensions of Globalization* (Minneapolis: University of Minnesota Press, 1996).

Appiah, Kwame, *Cosmopolitanism: Ethics in a World of Strangers* (New York: Norton, 2006).

Baha'u'llah, *Gleanings from the Writing of Baha'u'llah*, translated by Shoghi Effendi (Wilmette: Baha'I Publishing Trust, 1983).

Bauböck, Rainer, *Transnational Citizenship: Membership and Rights in International Migration* (Cheltenham: Edward Elgar, 1994).

Bauböck, Rainer, 'Reinventing Urban Citizenship,' *Citizenship Studies 7*, no. 2 (2010): pp. 136–160.

Bauböck, Rainer and Vesco Paskalev, 'Citizenship Deprivation: A Normative Analysis,' CEPS Paper in Liberty and Security in Europe no. 82 (2015), online http://www.ceps.eu/book/citizenship-deprivation-no.

Bauböck, Rainer, Albert Kraler, Marco Martiniello, and Bernhard Perchinig, 'Migrants' Citizenship: Legal Status, Rights and Political Participation,' in Rinus Penninx, ed., *The Dynamics of International Migration and Settlement in Europe. A State of the Art* (Amsterdam: Amsterdam University Press, IMISCOE, 2006), pp. 65–98.

Bauder, Herald, 'Jus Domicile: In Pursuit of a Citizenship of Equality and Social Justice,' *Journal of International Political Theory 8*, no. 1–2 (2012): pp. 184–196.

Brennan, Timothy, 'Cosmopolitanism and Internationalism,' *New Left Review 2* (2001): pp. 75–84, online https://newleftreview.org/search/multi_parameter?author=Brennan&title=Cosmopolitan%20vs%20International.

Brenner, Neil, 'Open Questions on State Rescaling,' *Cambridge Journal of Regions, Economy and Society 2*, no. 1 (2009): pp. 123–139.

Brubaker, Rogers, 'The Return of Assimilation? Changing Perspectives on Immigration and its Squeals in France, Germany and the United States,' *Ethnic and Racial Studies 24*, no. 4 (2001): pp. 531–548.

Coleman, Mathew, 'Immigration Politics beyond the Mexico-US Border,' *Antipode 39* (2007): pp. 54–76.

Delanty, Gerard, *Community* (London: Routledge, 2003).

Dicken, Peter, *Global Shift: Mapping the Changing Contours of the World Economy*, 7th edition (London: Guilford Press, 2014).

Diener, Alexander, 'Negotiating Territorial Belonging: A Transnational Field Approach to Mongolia's Kazakhs,' *Geopolitics 12*, no. 3 (2007): pp. 459–487.

Diener, Alexander, 'Diasporic and Transnational Social Practices in Central Asia,' *Geography Compass 2*, no. 2 (2008): pp. 956–978.

Diogenes, Laërtius, *Lives of Eminent Philosophers*, translated by R. D. Hicks (Cambridge: Harvard University Press, 1972).

Dukas, Helen and Banesh Hoffman, *Albert Eistein: The Human Side* (Princeton: Princeton University Press, 1979).

Džankić, Jelena, 'Investment-Based Citizenship and Residence Programmes in the EU,' EUI Working Papers no. 8 (Florence: RSCAS, 2015).

Elden, Stuart, *The Birth of Territory* (Chicago: University of Chicago Press, 2013).

Farer, Tom, 'Cosmopolitan Humanitarian Intervention: A Five Part Test,' *International Relations 19* (2005): pp. 211–220.

Furia, Peter, 'Global Citizenship Anyone? Cosmopolitanism, Privilege and Public Opinion,' *Global Society 19*, no. 4 (2005): pp. 331–359.

Giddens, Anthony, *The Nation State and Violence* (Berkeley: University of California Press, 1985).

Harvey, David, 'Cosmopolitanism and the Banality of Geographic Evils,' *Public Culture 12*, no. 2 (2000): pp. 529–564.

Helbing, Marc, *Practicing Citizenship and Heterogeneous Nationhood: Naturalisation in Swiss Municipalities* (Amsterdam: Amsterdam University Press, 2008).

Hobbes, Thomas, *Leviathan*, edited by R. Tuck (Cambridge: Cambridge University Press, 1991).

Hollinger, David. A., 'How Wide the Circle of the "We"? American Intellectuals and the Problem of the Ethnos since World War II,' *The American Historical Review 98*, no. 2 (1993): pp. 317–337.

Internet World Stats, Internet Usage Statistics, online www.internetworldstats.com/stats. htm.

Jones, Reece, *Border Walls: Security and the War on Terror in the United States, India, and Israel* (London: Zed Books, 2012).

Kaiser, Robert and Elena Nikiforova, 'The Performativity of Scale: The Social Construction of Scale Effects in Narva, Estonia,' *Environment and Planning: Society and Space 26*, no. 3 (2008): pp. 537–562.

Kängsepp, Liis, 'Estonia to Offer "E-Residency" to Foreigners,' *The Wallstreet Journal*, 21 October 2014.

Kant, Immanuel, *To Perpetual Peace: A Philosophical Sketch*, translated by Ted Humphrey (Indianapolis: Hackett Publishing, 2003).

Keating, Michael, 'Introduction: Rescaling Interests,' *Territory, Politics, Governance 2*, no. 3 (2014): pp. 239–248.

Kymlicka, Will, *Multicultural Citizenship* (New York: Oxford University Press, 1995).

Kymlicka, Will, 'Citizenship in an Era of Globalization: A Commentary on Held,' in Ian Shapiro and Casiano Hacker-Cordon, eds., *Democracy's Edges* (Cambridge: Cambridge University Press, 1999), pp. 112–127.

Leitner, Helga and Patricia Ehrkamp, 'Beyond National Citizenship: Turkish Immigrants and the (Re)Construction of Citizenship in Germany,' *Urban Geography 24*, no. 2 (2003): pp. 127–146.

Leitner, Helga and Patricia Ehrkamp, 'Transnationalism and Migrants' Imaginings of Citizenship,' *Environment and Planning A 38*, no. 9 (2006): pp. 1615–1632.

Lenin, Valdimir, *O prave natsii na samoopredelenie O Srednei Azii i Kazakhstane* (Tashkent: Gosudarstvennoe izdatel'stvo Uzbekskoi SSR, 1960).

Maas, Willem, 'Varieties of Multilevel Citizenship,' in Willem Maas, ed., *Multilevel Citizenship* (Philadelphia: University Pennsylvania Press, 2013), pp. 1–24.

Marshall, Thomas H., *Citizenship and Social Class and Other Essays* (Cambridge: Cambridge University Press, 1950).

Marston, Sally and Katheryne Mitchell, 'Citizens and the State: Citizenship Formations in Space and Time,' in Clive Barnett and Murray Low, eds., *Spaces of Democracy: Geographical Perspectives on Citizenship, Participation and Representation* (London: Sage Publishing, 2004), pp. 113–127.

Murphy, Alexander, 'Territory's Continuing Allure,' *Annals of the Association of American Geographers 103*, no. 5 (2013): pp. 1212–1226.

Nevins, Joseph, *Operation Gatekeeper: The Rise of the Illegal Alien and the Remaking of the US-Mexico Boundary* (New York: Routledge, 2002).

Norris, Pippa, 'Global Governance and Cosmopolitan Citizens,' in Joseph S. Nye and J. D. Donahue, eds., *Governance in a Globalizing World* (Washington: Brookings Institution Press 2000), pp. 155–177.

Nussbaum, Martha, 'Patriotism and Cosmopolitanism,' *Boston Review 19*, no. 5 (1994): pp. 3–6, online http://bostonreview.net/martha-nussbaum-patriotism-and-cosmopolitanism.

Pain, Rachel, 'Globalised Fear? Towards and Emotional Geopolitics,' *Progress in Human Geography 33*, no. 4 (2009): pp. 466–486.

Plato, *The Republic*, translated by Desmond Lee (New York: Penguin, 2003).

Pocock, J. G. A., 'The Ideal of Citizenship since Classical Times,' in Ronald Beiner, ed., *Theorizing Citizenship* (Albany: SUNY Press, 1995), pp. 29–53.

Rousseau, Jean Jacques, *On the Social Contract with Geneva Manuscript and Political Economy*, translated by J. R. Masters (London: St. Martins Press, 1978).

Saxenian, Annalee, *The New Argonauts: Regional Advantage in a Global Economy* (Cambridge: Harvard University Press, 2006).

Schueth, Sam and John O'Loughlin, 'Belonging to the World: Cosmopolitanism in Geographic Contexts,' *Geoforum 39*, no. 2 (2008): pp. 926–941.

Scott, James C., *The Art of Not Being Governed: An Anarchist History of Upland Southeast Asia* (New Haven: Yale University Press, 2010).

Sejersen, Tanja, ' "I Vow to Thee My Countries"—The Expansion of Dual Citizenship in the 21st Century,' *International Migration Review 42*, no. 3 (2008): pp. 523–549.

Shachar, Ayelet, *The Birthright Lottery: Citizenship and Global Inequality* (Cambridge: Harvard University Press, 2009).

Shachar, Ayelet, 'Earned Citizenship: Property Lessons for Immigration Reform,' *Yale Journal of Law & the Humanities 23*, no. 1 (2011): pp. 110–158.

Shachar, Ayelet, 'Citizenship,' in Michel Rosenfeld and Andras Sajo, eds., *The Oxford Handbook of Comparative Constitutional Law* (New York: Oxford University Press, 2012), pp. 1002–1019.

Smith, Michael Peter and Matt Bakker, *Citizenship across Borders: The Political Transnationalism of El Migrante* (Ithaca: Cornell University Press, 2008).

Smith, Rogers, 'Modern Citizenship,' in Engin F. Isin and Bryan S. Turner, eds., *Handbook of Citizenship Studies* (London: Sage Publishing, 2002), pp. 105–116.

Song, Sarah, 'Democracy and Noncitizen Voting Rights,' *Citizenship Studies 13*, no. 6 (2009): pp. 607–620.

Soysal, Yasemin, *The Limits of Citizenship: Migrants and Postnational Membership in Europe* (Chicago: University of Chicago Press, 1994).

Sparke, Mathew, 'A Neoliberal Nexus: Economy, Security, and the Biopolitics of Citizenship of the Border,' *Political Geography 25* (2006): pp. 151–180.

Staeheli, Lynn, 'Citizenship and the Problem of Community,' *Political Geography 27*, no. 1 (2008): pp. 5–21.

Staeheli, Lynn, 'Political Geography: Where's Citizenship?', *Progress in Human Geography 35*, no. 3 (2010): pp. 393–400.

Staeheli, Lynn, Patrica Ehrkamp, Helga Leitner, and Caroline Nagel, 'Dreaming the Ordinary: Daily Life and the Complex Geographies of Citizenship', *Progress in Human Geography 36*, no. 5 (2012): pp. 628–644.

Tilly, Charles, *Coercion, Capital, and European States, AD 990-1990* (London: Wiley Blackwell, 1990).

Tocqueville, Alexis de, *The Old Regime and the Revolution*, edited by F. Furet, F. Mélonio, translated by A. S. Kahan (Chicago: University of Chicago Press, 1998).

Trimbach, David, 'Scales of Estonian Citizenship: Implications for Russophone Political Incorporation', *Civitas: Journal of Citizenship Studies 3* (2014): pp. 1–18.

Warf, Barney, 'Nationalism, Cosmopolitanism, and Geographical Imaginations', *Geographical Review 102*, no. 3 (2012): pp. 271–292.

Winders, Jaime, 'Bringing Back the (B)order: Post 9/11 Politics of Immigration, Borders, and Belonging in the Contemporary US South', *Antipode 39* (2007): pp. 920–942.

Young, Iris Marion, 'The Logic of Masculinist Protection: Reflections on the Current Security State', *Signs 29* (2003): pp. 513–535.

CHAPTER 4

....

POLITICAL MEMBERSHIP AND DEMOCRATIC BOUNDARIES

....

RAINER BAUBÖCK

INTRODUCTION

....

DEMOCRATIC polities have boundaries that distinguish them from each other. These boundaries are of two different kinds. Geographic borders separate territorial jurisdictions and membership boundaries determine who is a citizen of which polity. Political theorists have recently been quite busy discussing the 'democratic boundary problem'. In a nutshell, the problem is that the democratic legitimacy of decisions affecting the boundaries of a 'demos' (i.e. those citizens who are eligible to participate in democratic self-government) presupposes that the demos by whom or on whose behalf a decision is taken is already composed in a way that makes its boundaries legitimate. In the first section I claim that this problem is not merely a philosophical puzzle but has implications for citizenship boundaries in the real world. I then discuss general conceptual properties of membership boundaries and structural characteristics of political ones. The final section considers the political challenges that arise if citizenship boundaries do not match territorial ones. The conclusion reflects on the need for contextualizing the boundary problem.

This chapter examines citizenship primarily from the perspective of democratic theory. Its scope is therefore generally restricted to democratic states. This is not meant to ignore that the external function of citizenship as 'nationality' in the international state system applies to all modern states independently of their internal political regimes. I also acknowledge that democratic practices of citizenship exist in non-democratic states.[1] My focus here is on the normative idea that democracy is a form of collective self-government in which citizens authorize governments and hold them accountable.

The Boundary Problem
in Political Theory

Should a citizenship acquired at birth determine people's right to access economic opportunities or political liberties in other states' territories?[2] Do those who have settled outside their country of citizenship have a right to retain that status forever and pass it on to their children? Should they also be allowed to determine the future of that country through casting absentee votes in elections? Does the right of states to determine who their own citizens are include a power to bestow their citizenship on populations in other states and to claim subsequently personal jurisdiction over them? If a majority of citizens residing in a part of a state territory desire to form their own state or join a neighbouring one, do they have a right to unilateral secession? These are only some of the normative questions about citizenship boundaries that arise in the real world of contemporary democratic states. In spite of the bewildering complexity of these questions, political theorists have tried to come up with general normative principles that aim to address the boundary problem.

---

[1] See Isin in this volume.
[2] Ayelet Shachar, *The Birthright Lottery: Citizenship and Global Inequality* (Cambridge: Harvard University Press, 2009).

Most theorists agree today that the problem cannot be resolved if we understand democracy merely as a set of procedures such as majority voting. As Robert Goodin points out: 'It is simply incoherent to constitute the electorate through a vote among voters who would be entitled to vote only by virtue of the outcome of that very vote.'[3] This does not mean, however, that there is no democratic answer. Instead of searching for solutions in democratic methods, we need to examine substantive conceptions of democracy and their underlying values and principles.[4]

Initially, the most widely discussed and endorsed principle was that all those whose interests are affected by a political decision ought to be included in the demos that takes this decision. In a seminal essay Fredrick Whelan already pointed out that 'the question of who is affected by a given law or policy depends on which law or policy is enacted from among the available alternatives' and concluded that the 'all affected' principle is 'a logical and procedural impossibility'.[5] Robert Goodin's defence of the principle bites the bullet: 'Membership in the demos ought to extend to every interest that would probably be affected by any possible decision arising out of any possible agenda.'[6] His conclusion is that the only legitimate demos is a global one that includes everybody. Including all affected interests requires a democratic world government. As a second-best solution, a federal world state might delegate some of its power to states and, as a third-best, independent states ought to offer compensation where their decisions affect external interests negatively.[7]

In an influential early statement of the boundary problem Robert Dahl proposes a somewhat different principle: '[T]he demos should include all adults subject to the binding collective decisions of the association.'[8] Although Dahl remains ambiguous about whether he considers this principle as different from including 'all affected interests', a majority of contemporary theorists endorse a principle of 'including all subject to coercion.'[9]

The disagreement between the two schools is rooted in different conceptions of democratic legitimacy. For Goodin, the task of democratic government is

---

[3] Robert Goodin, 'Enfranchising All Affected Interests, and Its Alternatives', *Philosophy and Public Affairs* 35, no. 1 (2007): pp. 40–68, p. 43.

[4] David Miller, 'Democracy's Domain', *Philosophy and Pulbic Affairs* 37, no. 3 (2009): pp. 201–228, pp. 203–204.

[5] Frederick G. Whelan, 'Prologue: Democratic Theory and the Boundary Problem', in J. R. Pennock and J. W. Chapman, eds., *NOMOS 25: Liberal Democracy* (New York: New York University, 1983), p. 19.

[6] Goodin (n 3), pp. 61–62.   [7] Ibid., pp. 64–67.

[8] Robert Dahl, *Democracy and Its Critics* (New Haven: Yale University Press, 1989), p. 120.

[9] See, e.g., Sofia Näsström, 'The Legitimacy of the People', *Political Theory* 35, no. 5 (2007); Nancy Fraser, *Scales of Justice: Reimagining Political Space in a Globalizing World* (New York: Columbia University Press, 2009); Seyla Benhabib, *Dignity in Adversity: Human Rights in Troubled Times* (Cambridge: Polity Press, 2011); David Owen, 'Constituting the Polity, Constituting the Demos: On the Place of the All Affected Interests Principle in Democratic Theory and in Resolving the Democratic Boundary Problem', *Ethics and Global Affairs* 5, no. 3 (2012): pp. 129–152; Michael Blake, 'Immigration, Jurisdiction, and Exclusion', *Philosophy and Public Affairs 41*, no. 2 (2013) , no. 2 (2013): pp. 103–130.

'protecting and promoting people's interests'.[10] With other utilitarian philosophers he regards government as a device for enabling the broadest possible satisfaction of individual interests. By contrast, most liberal and republican authors emphasize that governments (including democratic ones) are inherently coercive. Their legitimacy depends on securing individual and collective freedom through representing all those coerced in the making of the laws that will bind them.

At first glance, a principle of including all who are subjected to coercive government power seems to lead to a much narrower range of inclusion. Since the principle starts from existing territorial jurisdictions, it appears to justify the inclusion of all current residents in a polity and only these. In other words, it lends prima facie support to universal *jus domicilii*, as opposed to birthright citizenship or naturalization for which immigrants have to apply. Immigrants should be automatically included in the demos[11] while emigrants should lose their right to vote and arguably also their citizenship status.[12]

However, as Arash Abizadeh points out, immigration laws are coercive towards those who are not admitted; potential immigrants (i.e. the rest of the world) should therefore be included in the demos that adopts these laws. This move could be understood as a *reductio ad absurdum*, but Abizadeh's conclusion is instead similar to Goodin's: a demos is only legitimate if it is in principle unbounded.[13]

David Miller attacks this conclusion by challenging the idea that immigration control is coercive as long as people have opportunities to enter elsewhere.[14] Alternatively, one can escape the paradox that exclusion at the border is a coercive act that requires prior inclusion by specifying that only *persistent* subjection to coercive government makes people interdependent and creates a potential for domination that counts as relevant for purposes of democratic inclusion.[15] This still leaves another problem unresolved. Why did colonialism not result in claims for inclusion but for independence? There must be a prior reason why certain populations have a right to territorial self-government[16] before one can determine whom they ought to include in their citizenry.

---

[10] Goodin (n 3), p. 50.

[11] Ruth Rubio-Marín, *Immigration as a Democratic Challenge: Citizenship and Inclusion in Germany and the United States* (Cambridge: Cambridge University Press, 2000).

[12] See Claudio López-Guerra, 'Should Expatriates Vote?', *The Journal of Political Philosophy* 13, no. 2 (2005): pp. 216–234 for an early defence of this conclusion.

[13] Arash Abizadeh, 'Democratic Theory and Border Coercion: No Right to Unilaterally Control Your Own Borders', *Political Theory* 36, no. 1 (2008): pp. 37–65. For a similar conclusion see Näsström (n 9).

[14] David Miller, 'Why Immigration Controls are Not Coercive: A Reply to Arash Abizadeh', *Political Theory* 38, no. 1 (2010) pp: 111–120.

[15] See, e.g., Iseult Honohan, *Civic Republicanism* (London and New York: Routledge, 2002).

[16] Anna Stilz, 'Nations, States, and Territory', *Ethics* 121, no. 3 (2011): pp. 572–601; Cara Nine, *Global Justice and Territory* (Oxford: Oxford University Press, 2012); Oliviero Angeli, *Cosmopolitanism, Self-Determination and Territory: Justice with Borders* (Houndsmills, Basingstoke: Palgrave Macmillan, 2015); Margaret Moore, *A Political Theory of Territory* (Oxford: Oxford University Press, 2015).

More generally, it is not clear how the 'all subjected to coercion' principle can escape the circular reasoning at the core of the democratic boundary problem. Just as an election cannot determine who ought to be enfranchised in the very same election, it seems also incoherent to say that the legitimate demos includes all subjected to coercion by a government that must itself first be authorized by the very same demos.

Some theorists resolve the problem by pointing to a pre-political social community that provides historically given boundaries for the citizenry. Nations are the obvious candidates for such a view.[17] One problem with this view is that it provides justification for different standards of inclusion in democratic states depending on their history of nation-building; settler nations may regard immigrants as future citizens while those that have emerged from the breakup of multinational empires do not. Joseph Carens proposes 'social membership' as an alternative criterion for determining the claims of immigrants to citizenship inclusion,[18] but here again the boundaries of society are essentially those of residence within a given territorial jurisdiction, so the problem how to justify these boundaries vis-à-vis emigrants' claims to remain included and separatists' claims to change the borders remain unaddressed.

I have proposed that including all affected interests and all subjected to coercion call for taking affected interests into account in policy decisions and for providing equal protection of the law to all subjected to it. However, these principles are misapplied when considered as solutions of the boundary problem.[19] As a distinct principle for citizenship inclusion I have proposed that those and only those individuals have a claim to membership in a self-governing political community whose autonomy and well-being depend on the collective self-government and flourishing of a particular polity. This 'citizenship stakeholder' principle assumes a relational correspondence between the normative reasons why individuals have a claim to membership and those why political communities have a claim to self-government. In order to apply it to real-world contexts, we need to match the links that tie individuals to a particular polity with the conditions under which that polity can be self-governing. These ties and conditions differ for independent states, local municipalities, and supranational political unions and their citizenship rules must vary accordingly. Before exploring such variation, we need to establish first what all these different contexts have in common that makes it possible to compare them. In other words, we need to clarify conceptually what we mean by a citizenship boundary before examining how such boundaries differ across types of polities.

---

[17] David Miller, 'Immigrants, Nations, and Citizenship', *The Journal of Political Philosophy* 16, no. 1 (2008): pp. 371–390.

[18] Joseph H. Carens, *The Ethics of Immigration* (Oxford: Oxford University Press, 2013).

[19] Rainer Bauböck, 'Morphing the Demos into the Right Shape. Normative Principles for Enfranchising Resident Aliens and Expatriate Citizens', *Democratization* 22, no. 5 (2015): pp. 820–839.

CITIZENSHIP AS MEMBERSHIP

Citizenship is a membership-based concept. It means many other things too, but all interpretations of citizenship need to rely (explicitly or implicitly) on its conceptual core, which is membership in a political community.

Membership is a categorical and relational concept. From the internal perspective of a group, membership has a binary quality—it serves to distinguish insiders from outsiders.[20] From the external perspective of an observer or the wider society, it serves to distinguish not merely individuals but also membership groups of the same kind by marking their boundaries.

As a relational concept membership necessarily relates an individual or group to a larger social entity. This relation can be described as inclusion. Membership is semantically different from concepts such as belonging or identity that are not inherently categorical distinctions but are generally used to express the strength of an attachment or of an individual or collective characteristic. Like membership, belonging is a relational concept but it can also be used to express an attachment to something that is not a social entity: one may have a sense of belonging to a natural environment but cannot be a member thereof. Identity is a concept that serves primarily to draw a contrast. Identities allow people to categorize themselves and others but the concept need not imply *affiliation* to any particular entity: hermits form an identity category but are not affiliated to any corresponding group or community. Membership is thus not just a formal relation between an individual and a social category but a *status* that individuals or groups enjoy within an entity that has some 'social life' of its own. Membership status can only be generated through (formal or informal) recognition by others. I cannot be a member of a group none of whose members recognizes me as a member.

Membership is a binary concept only with regard to the internal relation between one individual and one social entity at one point in time. It does not imply singularity. Individuals can be serially or simultaneously members in many different social entities, each of which maintains a clear binary distinction between members and non-members. Rogers Brubaker has characterized citizenship as an 'international filing system, a mechanism for allocating persons to states'.[21] A filing system operationalizes categorical *and* singular relations: each item is sorted into one file and one file only. This reflects, however, a peculiar 'Westphalian' conception of citizenship and is not implied when we characterize citizenship as a membership concept. Individuals can be citizens of several polities over the course of their lives, they can

[20] Rogers W. Brubaker, *Citizenship and Nationhood in France and Germany* (Cambridge: Harvard University Press, 1992).

[21] Ibid., p. 31.

be multiple citizens of independent polities and they can be multilevel citizens of polities that are nested within other polities like Russian dolls.

The criteria for distinguishing members from non-members are not always entirely internal ones. Political membership boundaries have often been defined in class, gender, ethnic, religious, or racial terms, i.e. by referring to non-political boundaries that serve as reference frames for determining who can be a citizen and participate in politics.[22] Such intersectionality is a frequent feature of membership boundaries but not a necessary one. For example, it is certainly true that in the current international system citizenship serves to preserve huge social inequalities between states by attaching membership to circumstances of birth and by giving states the power to exclude non-citizens from their territory.[23] However, this is not an inherent feature of birthright citizenship but rather a political effect of global social inequalities. In the European Union weaker disparities and political integration have created conditions for free movement while citizenship remains firmly anchored in the member states' birthright regimes.

Categorical membership also does not entail that the boundary separating members from non-members is a hard one. Some memberships may be difficult to obtain whereas others are easily accessible; some memberships are attributed automatically at birth or to those who deliver a service or take up residence in a territory while in other cases, individuals must express their consent or apply actively.

Finally, categorical membership boundaries can also be blurred through statuses of quasi- or semi-membership. This may seem incoherent, but it is not as long as there is a core membership that can be distinguished from the quasi- or semi-statuses. Designating someone as a *quasi-member* does not turn membership itself into an ordinal concept that expresses degrees of a quality (of membership); it serves instead to maintain a binary distinction between members and quasi-members.[24] The latter are often those who enjoy some of the benefits or bear some of the duties associated with membership without being recognized as members. Conversely, we can call individuals *semi-members* if they are formally recognized as members but deprived of some rights and obligations that are otherwise shared by members.[25] Non-resident citizens are mostly semi-members because they cannot enjoy those citizenship rights that presuppose residence, whereas non-citizen

---

[22] For a discussion how the categorical distinctions of citizenship, gender, race, ethnicity, and religion interact with social inequality see Rogers Brubaker, *Grounds for Difference* (Cambridge: Harvard University Press, 2015).

[23] Joseph H. Carens, 'Aliens and Citizens: The Case for Open Borders', *The Review of Politics 49*, no. 2 (1987): pp. 251–273; Shachar (n 2); Brubaker (n 22), pp. 19–21.

[24] See Smith in this volume.

[25] Elizabeth F. Cohen, *Semi-Citizenship in Democratic Politics* (Cambridge: Cambridge University Press, 2010).

residents are quasi-citizens (or 'denizens')[26] if they enjoy most of the rights of citizens without sharing their legal status.

Because of its categorical nature, membership serves to create and maintain a boundary between a social entity and similar ones in its environment. Membership boundaries are soft or hard depending on how easy it is for individuals to *cross* them by taking up a new membership. This is obviously a matter of degree, but that does not affect the categorical nature of the distinction—just as territorial borders can be open or closed for migration without this affecting the territorial jurisdiction of the states that they separate. Plural and intersecting memberships, quasi- and semi-memberships are a stronger challenge since they *blur* the boundary between a social entity and other entities of the same kind in its environment.[27] Yet, as I have argued above, even in these cases an internally binary distinction continues to provide the hard core without which the very concept of membership loses its purpose.

The final feature of membership boundaries that is highly relevant for those of citizenship is their stability over time. Stability is again not about how hard a boundary is, but about whether the criterion of distinction and scope of inclusion remains the same over time and whether the members perceive themselves as a group that retains a distinct identity over time. Unstable boundaries are those that *shift* through shrinking or expansion, illustrated by secession or unification of political territories but also by fundamental changes in citizenship rules that include or exclude broadly defined categories, for example through newly introducing *jus soli* in a country of immigration.

POLITICAL COMMUNITY AND THE VARIETY OF POLITIES

In all respects discussed so far, citizenship is not essentially different from membership in organisations, associations, congregations, corporations, and other kinds of

---

[26] Tomas Hammar, *Democracy and the Nation State. Aliens, Denizens and Citizens in a World of International Migration* (Aldershot: Avebury, 1990).

[27] See Rainer Bauböck, 'The Crossing and Blurring of Boundaries in International Migration. Challenges for Social and Political Theory', in Rainer Bauböck and John Rundell, eds., *Blurred Boundaries. Migration, Ethnicity, Citizenship* (Aldershot: Ashgate, 1998), pp. 17–52; Aristide Zolberg and Long Litt Woon, 'Why Islam is like Spanish: Cultural Incorporation in Europe and the United States', *Politics & Society 27*, no. 1 (1999): pp. 5–38; Richard Alba, 'Bright vs. Blurred Boundaries: Second-Generation Assimilation and Exclusion in France, Germany, and the United States', *Ethnic and Racial Studies 28*, no. 1 (2005): pp. 20–49. Andreas Wimmer, *Ethnic Boundary Making: Institutions, Power, Networks* (Oxford: Oxford University Press, 2013).

social entities that populate 'civil society'. What is specific about citizenship is that it is about membership in a *political community*.

The notion of 'citizenship' is often also used in a loose sense when referring to rights, obligations, virtues, or practices of individuals or organizations in relation to other social entities. But all such uses are parasitical on a core idea of membership in a political community. They attribute to an entity qualities similar to those of political communities—for example, 'citizenship' in an academic institution refers to the idea that universities have a degree of collective autonomy, that faculty members have equal standing in collective decisions, and that academic institutions pursue a common good to which its members are morally obliged to contribute. Alternatively, citizenship may also be metaphorically attributed to organizations, i.e. to legal rather than natural persons, who have ethical duties to contribute to the common good of a wider society, as the notion of 'corporate citizenship' suggests.

Political communities are organized around coercive political institutions that govern their members or they aspire to establish such institutions. The concept of 'political community' refers to members and their horizontal relations with each other whereas the term 'polity' focuses on the vertical relation between political institutions and those whom they govern. Citizenship normally entails both horizontal and vertical relations, but, as pointed out by Jean Bodin, a political community or 'commonwealth' may survive the destruction of its political institutions and loss of its territory as long as its members maintain their customary laws and aspire to achieve self-government as a distinct polity.[28] In the absence of government institutions, however, 'citizenship in exile' is reduced to membership without legally guaranteed rights and enforced duties and membership itself becomes then a matter of individual choice between assimilation into the wider society and preservation of a diasporic identity.

Where citizenship is institutionalized, however, it is quite unlike membership in a voluntary association. All polities establish rules for an automatic attribution of citizenship that is independent of individual choice. These rules are of three kinds: membership can be derived from circumstances at birth (*jus sanguinis* or *jus soli*), from residence (*jus domicilii*), or from another citizenship. The 'citizenship clause' that opens the 14th amendment to the U.S. Constitution illustrates these three attribution mechanisms: 'All persons born or naturalized in the United States, and subject to the jurisdiction thereof, are citizens of the United States and of the State wherein they reside.' Birthright citizenship in the U.S. is based on unconditional *jus soli*. There is an additional rule of *jus sanguinis* for the second generation born abroad to an American citizen parent that is not included in the 14th amendment. The Constitution does, however, specify that Americans are not only citizens of the federation, but also of one of the fifty states. This latter status is derived from

---

[28] Jean Bodin, *Six Books of the Commonwealth*. Abridged and translated by M. J. Tooley (Oxford: Blackwell, 1576/1955), Book 1, Chapter 6.

federal citizenship and the state of which they are citizens is determined through residence. All these modes of acquiring citizenship (*jus soli* and *jus sanguinis* for federal citizenship, *jus domicilii* and derivative citizenship for federal state citizenship) apply automatically. The only way of becoming a citizen that depends directly on individual choice is naturalization.

To a marginal extent individuals are still able to 'choose' citizenship indirectly by putting themselves in a position that entails automatic attribution. Birthright tourism in countries with unconditional *jus soli* is the best-known illustration. In *ius sanguinis* regimes, some migrant couples decide that one of them should naturalize so that their child will be a dual citizen by descent. *Jus domicilii* combined with free internal movement allows federal citizens to choose where to take up residence in order to benefit from a lower regional tax rate or better social welfare and public services.[29] Derivative citizenship in the supranational European Union creates a strong incentive for third country nationals to acquire the citizenship of a member state in order to benefit from freedom of movement throughout the Union.

Global interdependence and technical innovations in transportation and communication have enhanced opportunities for individual choice driven by unequal instrumental value of citizenships within and across states.[30] Yet it remains true that overwhelming majorities acquire their citizenship statuses without ever exercising individual choice. Why is that so? One explanation is that contemporary states have an interest in securing not only the stability of their territorial jurisdiction, but also of populations over whom they exercise power. They may be happy to admit tourists, travelling business people, and temporary migrants to their territory if these provide them with economic benefits, but they need to distinguish sojourners from citizens in order to claim a stable population base and be recognized as states. Automatic attribution of citizenship provides functional stability in this respect. The other reason has to do with the conditions for democratic self-government. If citizenship were predominantly a matter of individual choice, it would not only be difficult for governments to maintain coercively binding solutions to collective action problems but also for citizens to hold governments accountable. This imperative of boundary stability is characteristic for modern democratic states. The

[29] For economic models promoting competition between local jurisdictions on the basis of individual membership choice, see Charles Tiebout, 'A Pure Theory of Local Expenditure', *Journal of Political Economy* 64, no. 5 (1956): pp. 416–424; James Buchanan, 'An Economic Theory of Clubs', *Economica* 32, no. 125 (1965): pp. 1–14; Bruno Frey and Reiner Eichberger, *The New Democratic Federalism for Europe: Functional, Overlapping, and Competing Jurisdictions* (Cheltenham, UK: Edward Elgar, 1999).

[30] Peter Spiro, *Beyond Citizenship. American Identity After Globalization* (Oxford: Oxford University Press, 2008); Christian Joppke, *Citizenship and Immigration* (London: Polity, 2010); Ayelet Shachar, 'Picking Winners: Olympic Citizenship and the Global Race for Talent', *Yale Law Journal* 120, no. 8 (2011): pp. 2088–2139; Yossi Harpaz, 'Ancestry into Opportunity: How Global Inequality Drives Demand for Non-Resident European Union Citizenship', *Journal of Ethnic and Migration Studies* 41, no. 13 (2015): pp. 2081–2104.

territorial borders of empires were rarely stable and their governments were not accountable to their subjects.

Yet even in the contemporary world, states are not the only polities and citizenship exists at different levels. Federations, such as the U.S., provide one illustration for institutionalized multilevel citizenship.[31] It does not matter whether a federal constitution officially recognizes a distinct citizenship of its constitutive polities (variously called provinces, regions, cantons, republics, or states). Democratic federalism entails that both federal and constitutive level legislatures are directly elected and thus need to determine a respective demos whose members are eligible to vote. The same is true for local level self-government, which is exercised through locally elected municipal councils. At the supranational level, the European, the Andean, and Central American Parliaments are also directly elected and member states of Mercosur are currently moving from nominating national parliamentarians to direct elections for the Mercosur Parliament. Unlike the latter three, the European Parliament has extensive legislative powers. The political world is thus populated by a variety of territorial polities of different kinds, each of which should be understood as a potential or actual space for citizenship.

The rules for determining citizens vary between these types. In contemporary states, citizenship is initially determined by birthright (i.e. some combination of *jus soli* and *jus sanguinis*) and can then be changed subsequently through naturalization, voluntary renunciation, or involuntary withdrawal. Citizenship at the substate level is derived from federal level citizenship and determined through residence. EU citizenship is similarly derivative but in a bottom-up way from citizenship in the member states.[32] As a legal status it is independent of residence and can also be held outside the territory of the Union, but many of the rights associated with the status can only be activated through cross-border movement or activities inside the EU.[33]

Local citizenship is somewhat harder to pin down because it is rarely constitutionalized as a legal status. Let us therefore consider how it differs from regional citizenship in federations. One striking finding is that many democratic states have

---

[31] See Maas in this volume.

[32] The only other contemporary case of bottom-up derivation seems to be Switzerland where citizenship in the confederation is formally derived from cantonal citizenship. However, in terms of substance, federal citizenship law alone determines acquisition of Swiss citizenship through birthright and loss through renunciation and withdrawal. The autonomy of the cantons is reduced to setting conditions for naturalization and federal law determines the minimum requirements. By contrast, EU law leaves member states fully free to regulate access to the common status of EU citizenship. Some constraints have been imposed by jurisprudence of the Court of Justice of the EU (CJEU) that required member states to recognize citizenship awarded by other such states (in Judgment of 7 July 1992, *Micheletti v Delegación del Gobierno en Cantabria*, C-369/90, ECR, ECLI:EU:C:1992:295) and to take EU law into account when withdrawal of nationality leads to a loss of EU citizenship (Judgment of 2 March 2010, *Rottmann v Freistaat Bayern*, C-135/08, ECR, ECLI:EU:C:2010:104).

[33] See Strumia in this volume.

disconnected voting rights in local elections from national citizenship by either extending the franchise to the nationals of specific other countries or to all residents independently of their national citizenship.[34] Including non-citizens in the regional demos is, by contrast, rather exceptional.

A second relevant consideration is how local and national level self-government relate to each other. Federal systems are characterized by a combination of shared rule and divided rule between the nested polities.[35] Their substate polities are not only self-governing but also involved in federal government (often through representation in a second chamber). Local self-government is instead generally just about divided rule through devolved powers over local matters. Moreover, local governments provide local public services and develop a local infrastructure, i.e. public goods that benefit all local residents and only these. Distinguishing between residents who are citizens and non-citizen serves no useful purpose for local governments that can neither control immigration into their territory nor provide diplomatic protection for their emigrants. *Jus domicilii* is therefore the appropriate rule for determining who are the local citizens. Normatively speaking, a requirement of national or European citizenship for exercising the local franchise is an arbitrary restriction of the proper composition of the local demos imposed by higher level governments.[36]

A final distinction which most political theorists fail to draw is between the demos and the citizenry. As suggested at the beginning of this chapter, the demos includes those who are entitled to participate actively in the self-government of a polity. For practical purposes, we can say that all individuals who enjoy active voting rights are members of the demos. In nineteenth-century democracies, women were considered dependent or passive citizens without voting rights. Today, there are three main categories who remain excluded from the demos: children below voting age in all democracies, and mentally disabled citizens or criminal offenders in many. Apart from these, the distinction between citizenry and demos is still salient for special territories or citizens residing abroad. U.S. citizens residing in the District of Columbia can vote in presidential elections but not for Congress; those in Puerto Rico, Guam, American Samoa, and the U.S. Virgin Islands do not have voting rights in any national election. Until the mid-twentieth century, citizens living abroad were nearly universally disenfranchised, whereas most democratic states include them now in the electorate.[37] This global trend represents a significant

---

[34] See Shaw in this volume; Jean-Thomas Arrighi and Rainer Bauböck, 'A Multilevel Puzzle. Migrants' Voting Rights in National and Local Elections', *European Journal of Political Research*, online first, DOI: 10.1111/1475-6765.12176 (2016).

[35] Daniel Elazar, *Exploring Federalism* (Tuscaloosa: The University of Alabama Press, 1987).

[36] Rainer Bauböck, 'Reinventing Urban Citizenship', *Citizenship Studies 7*, no. 2 (2003): pp. 139–160.

[37] IDEA and IFE, eds., *Voting from Abroad. The International IDEA Handbook* (Stockholm and Mexico City: International Institute for Democracy and Electoral Assistance and Instituto Federal Electoral de Mexico, 2007); Michael Collyer, 'A Geography of Extra-Territorial Citizenship: Explanations of External Voting', *Migration Studies 2*, no. 1 (2014): pp. 55–72.

recent shift of demos boundaries and it goes hand in hand with a simultaneous blurring of the boundaries of citizenship through toleration of dual nationality.

It seems obvious that excluding citizens from the demos needs to be justified. The case of minor children is least problematic, but even in this respect, some scholars and advocacy groups have suggested including them either through age-specific participation rights or vicariously through additional votes for their parents.[38]

This question takes us back to the heart of the democratic boundary problem. Since the demos cannot determine its own boundaries through democratic procedures, we need to imagine the citizenry as a self-reproducing political community with a stable identity across time. Human societies reproduce themselves through the sequence of generations and through co-residence in a territory. Minor children and mentally disabled persons are not merely individuals in need of protection by the state; they are members of a self-reproducing political community who share experiences of political membership with their parents and with others of their birth-cohort living in the same polity. National and local polities differ in how they reproduce themselves through birthright and residence but the imperative of including minor children as citizens is the same. If children and the mentally handicapped had to pass a citizenship test or decide at the age of majority whether they are interested in acquiring voting rights, then the demos would turn into a separate association of those who share cognitive abilities and a desire to participate in politics and these citizens would rule over the rest of society.[39] Such a demos would not only lack stability, since it cannot guarantee its own reproduction over time, but also democratic legitimacy. Instead of conceiving of the members of the demos as the only full citizens, they should be regarded as trustees who represent not merely themselves but also those citizens who lack capacities for participating in elections.

The Mismatch between Territorial and Membership Boundaries

Where borders are stable and people are sedentary, there is no mismatch between territorial and personal jurisdiction.[40] But when people move across borders or when borders move across people, discrepancies emerge that raise questions about

---

[38] See Donaldson and Kymlicka in this volume.

[39] For an argument that citizenship should generally be acquired at majority, see Costica Dumbrava, *Nationality, Citizenship and Ethno-Cultural Belonging, Preferential Membership Policies in Europe* (Houndmills, Basingstoke: Palgrave Macmillan, 2014), pp. 141–157.

[40] See Walker in this volume.

the membership status of non-resident and non-citizen migrants, as well as about that of former citizens in now external territories and of previous non-citizens in newly independent or incorporated territories.

If membership is based on *jus domicilii*, the potential discrepancy is minimized and the problem largely disappears. Citizenship is then simply determined by current residence in a territory. Immigrants are no longer distinguished from natives and emigrants are treated as if they had never been members. In case of moving borders the membership of those who stay put follows the change of status of the territory after whatever period of residence is used for implementing *jus domicilii*. Personal jurisdiction will also rarely overlap between polities since only few people have multiple residences between which they frequently move back and forth. Even if they do, a criterion of principal domicile can identify the one polity that has a stronger claim to count the person as a citizen than any other.

Jus domicilii is therefore a rule that maintains a stable criterion of membership (even if individuals move in and out of this status) and avoids jurisdictional conflicts by constantly adapting citizenship boundaries to territorial ones. It seems uniquely suited for a world where individuals are highly mobile across territorial borders and where political borders can be easily modified. This may sound like a global utopia but it is an empirical generalization applying to local level polities in contemporary democratic states.

The international system of states is very different in this respect. Citizenship acquired at birth is normally maintained over a whole life, also by migrants who cross international borders. Conversely, immigrants do not automatically acquire the citizenship of their country of residence but need to apply for naturalization. Mostly they also have to meet other criteria apart from residence, such as income, criminal record, language, and civic knowledge tests.[41] The strong global trend towards toleration of multiple citizenship in both sending and receiving countries greatly facilitates retaining citizenships of origin and allows emigrants to pass these on to children born abroad—in many cases even beyond the second generation. Because the basis of citizenship in independent states is birthright, enhanced mobility and accommodation thereof by states leads to outcomes that are entirely different from those for local citizenship. Instead of adjusting citizenship to territorial borders, the trend goes in the opposite direction of increasing mismatch, a tendency that is reinforced when liberal states disconnect rights from citizenship status and grant them to permanent residents who lack then instrumental incentives for naturalization. First generation immigrants often prefer such quasi-citizenship even to dual citizenship, especially if the institutions and public culture of the receiving country do not encourage them to become full citizens. Source countries of emigrants, on the other hand, encourage these to retain their citizenship status and

[41] See Orgad in this volume.

some offer their former citizens a status of external quasi-citizenship with rights to return and to own property.[42]

This increasing mismatch between territorial and membership boundaries is problematic for 'world state cosmopolitans'[43] for whom independent states should be transformed into local provinces of a global polity whose borders are open and whose citizens pick up local memberships wherever they settle. If one accepts instead that states are and will remain those polities where self-government powers are most densely concentrated and that require birthright membership in order to stabilize their political communities, then the mismatch appears as a liberal blessing in disguise. Internal migrants who move between municipalities and provinces can rely on the protection of their rights by the higher level government of the state. International migrants must instead rely on dual protection by governments of origin and destination.[44] In this context, migrants' rights are enhanced through opportunities to combine a nationality of origin with denizenship or full citizenship in the country of settlement.

Moreover, free movement across internal borders within states is a universal human right,[45] whereas free movement across international borders depends on citizenship. In the international state system, the asymmetry between a universal right to emigrate and a citizenship right to return to one's own country can be reduced through increasing toleration of multiple citizenship or through agreements between states to open their borders for each other's citizens—from visa waiver agreements to full access to settlement and employment, as in the EU, Mercosur, or the Trans-Tasman Travel Agreement between Australia and New Zealand. Extending the geographic range and material scope of national citizenship rights seems thus the most promising route towards global free movement.[46]

Territorial boundary shifts are comparatively rare in the contemporary state system, where all territories apart from Antarctica have been demarcated as under one state's jurisdiction.[47] Internal borders change more often when they are of mainly administrative nature but where they mark the territorial jurisdiction of a polity with self-government powers, changes are often politically contested precisely because they impact on regional or local citizenship boundaries.

Current international law does not recognize a right to unilateral secession from existing states. The principle of self-determination of people that is enshrined in the

---

[42] See Collyer in this volume.   [43] See Tan in this volume.

[44] EU citizens who migrate inside the EU are a mixed category in this respect. The protection of their rights by the higher level EU citizenship reduces their incentive to acquire dual citizenship.

[45] See Universal Declaration of Human Rights Art. 13 (1), International Covenant on Civil and Politial Rights Art. 12 (1).

[46] Rainer Bauböck, 'Migration and the Porous Boundaries of Democratic States', in Stephan Leibfried et al., eds., *The Oxford Handbook of Transformations of the State* (Oxford: Oxford University Press, 2014).

[47] See Walker in this volume.

UN Charter and the human rights conventions has been generally interpreted as a right to self-government for the whole population of legitimate states rather than as a right of nations to their own independent states.[48] After World War II, when colonialism came to be considered illegitimate, this principle grounded a right of colonies to independence within borders previously drawn by colonial administrations. After 1989, the break-up of European socialist states that had formally federal constitutions reinforced the principle of *uti posseditis iuris*, i.e. the maintenance of previous territorial borders that became transformed from federal into international ones.[49] Independence for Kosovo and South Sudan, however, did not fully fit this pattern and was mainly justified on grounds of loss of legitimacy by central governments that engage in attempted genocide against a part of their population.

The fact that international law is conservative with regard to changes of international borders is unsurprising since it is based on agreements between and customary practices of existing states. It can therefore not be taken as a sufficient response to the normative question whether and on which grounds unilateral secession can be justified. Political theorists have debated this question intensely since the mid-1980s. The answers that have emerged can be broadly grouped into three schools of thought. The first one regards democratic polities as voluntary territorial associations and suggests that any group of citizens who want independence for a specific territory has a primary right to secession if they win a majority in a plebiscite within that territory, as long as they are ready to grant the same right to any other group that challenges the integrity of the secessionist territory.[50] A second school sees cultural nations rather than state peoples as the subjects of self-determination claims. Liberal nationalists ground this idea in the value of national membership for individual autonomy and well-being and in the support that a shared national identity provides for democratic and social solidarity among citzens.[51] Inspired by John Stuart Mill's verdict that 'free institutions are next to impossible in a country made up of different nationalities'[52] some liberal nationalists believe that democracy requires a sense of shared nationhood. This does not rule out stable plurinational states if all national groups see themselves as sharing an overarching national identity but it does provide an argument for breaking up multinational states with

---

[48] Antonio Cassese, *Self-Determination of Peoples. A Legal Reappraisal* (Cambridge: Cambridge University Press, 1995).

[49] Steven R. Ratner, 'Drawing a Better Line: Uti Possidetis and the Borders of New States', *American Journal of International Law 90*, no. 4 (1996): pp. 590–624.

[50] Harry Beran, 'A Liberal Theory of Secession', *Political Studies 32*, no.1 (1984): pp 21–31; David Gauthier, 'Breaking Up: An Essay on Secession', *Canadian Journal of Philosophy 24*, no. 3 (1994): pp. 357–371.

[51] David Miller, *On Nationality* (Oxford: Oxford University Press, 1995); Will Kymlicka, *Politics in the Vernacular: Nationalism, Multiculturalism, and Citizenship* (Oxford: Oxford University Press, 2001). See also Gans in this volume.

[52] John Stuart Mill, 'Considerations On Representative Government', in H. B. Acton, ed., *Utilitarianism, Liberty, Representative Government* (London: Everymans Library, 1972), p. 392.

a recent history of violent ethnonational conflict.[53] Finally, a third group of theorists defends a 'remedial-only' right to secession if a state loses legitimacy because of oppression and discrimination of a territorial minority.[54] On some accounts, grievance-based secession claims may not only be triggered by serious infringement of individual rights of minority members, but also by persistent violation of territorial self-government rights at substate level.[55] On the one hand, this makes otherwise stable plurinational democracies vulnerable to potentially legitimate secession claims if they fail to recognize a historic minority's political autonomy. On the other hand, this argument supports also a duty of national minorities to respect the territorial integrity of a state that enables their self-government. In this view, national minorities need not share a common national identity with the rest of the population, but they must be able to see themselves as full citizens of both their self-governing territory and of the larger state.

The focus of this debate has been on justifications for secession rather than on its consequences, one of which is the need to redraw also the boundaries of citizenship. Even more than migration, which presupposes existing territorial citizenries and demoi whom migrants leave or join, territorial boundary shifts demonstrate that the democratic boundary problem does have practical relevance. There are two questions that secession raises in this respect: who should be the members of the demos that decides in a secession plebiscite or on behalf of whom secession is decided by a legislative body? And if secession is the outcome of such a decision, how should the citizenry of the newly formed state be determined? There is a body of international legal norms concerning the determination of citizenship in cases of state succession,[56] but political theory has so far paid little attention to the difficult question of how citizenship ought to be reallocated when borders change.

With regard to the first question, there are three possible answers: the relevant demos could consist of all citizens of the current state that would suffer a loss of territory, of only those citizens who reside in the territory the status of which is being decided, or of all persons who have an immediate stake in the decision since they might lose their current citizenship or would potentially become the citizens of a new state if secession is the outcome. The current Spanish government and Constitutional Court endorse the first view, which allows national majorities to block secession. The Quebec and Scottish independence referendums were based on the second view. In the latter event, some scholars defended the third view, according to which those who might have become citizens of an independent Scotland

[53] David Miller, *Citizenship and National Identity* (Cambridge: Polity Press, 2000), pp. 125–141.
[54] Allen Buchanan, *Justice, Legitimacy, and Self-Determination. Moral Foundations for International Law* (Oxford: Oxford University Press, 2004).
[55] Alan Patten, *Equal Recognition. The Moral Foundations of Minority Rights* (Princeton: Princeton University Press, 2014), chapter 7.
[56] See, e.g., European Convention on Nationality, chapter VI (CETS 166/1997).

should have been entitled to vote.[57] I will not attempt to provide an answer to this normative puzzle here because, unlike theorists defending a plebiscitary right to secession, I do not think there is a general answer that would be the same for secession inside a state (as in the creation of many new states in India since 1947 or the separation of the canton Jura from Berne in 1978/79), secession from a state, or secession of a state from a union (as in the case of Brexit). The context and level of citizenship matters for the composition of the demos also in decisions about the territorial shape and status of the polity.

The second question has again three possible answers the choice of which depends on context as well as normative considerations.[58] If a new state is formed in a territory that has never previously enjoyed self-government, the only defensible solution is to grant citizenship to all those who have a right of residence when the polity becomes independent. This is sometimes called the 'zero solution' and it has been applied in most successor states of the Soviet Union. Estonia and Latvia chose, however, a different approach of 'citizenship restoration' which included those who had been citizens of the independent states before Soviet annexation and their descendants, but excluded internal migrants who had settled in the Baltic Soviet republics.[59] Finally, the successor states of socialist Yugoslavia and Czechoslovakia referred to the previously merely nominal citizenship of the federal republics and converted them into citizenship of the newly independent states.

These three rules echo to a certain extent the general principles for determining individual citizenship. The zero solution could be interpreted as a version of *jus domicilii*, with the important difference that citizenship so acquired is not lost through subsequent emigration. It could therefore also be regarded as a form of *jus soli* that refers to the birth of the state rather than that of the individual. Restored citizenship harks back to the principle of *jus sanguinis*, especially if descendants of the original citizens are automatically included. And the upgrading of a substate citizenship relies on multilevel derivation—with the twist that it is now the derivative citizenship that gets elevated to the top. Finally, there is also an analogue to naturalization. The zero option is normally combined with option rights for individuals to choose a different citizenship than the one initially assigned to them. The important observation is, however, that the choice of rule for initial determination of citizenship does not predetermine the rules that characterize the subsequent regime for individual acquisition and loss of citizenship. Inclusion principles applied when constituting the polity are not necessarily the same as those for the

[57] Ruvi Ziegler, Jo Shaw, and Rainer Bauböck, 'Independence Referendums: Who should Vote and Who should be Offered Citizenship, EUI Working Paper RSCAS 2014/90', in *Robert Schuman Working Paper* (Florence: EUI, 2014).

[58] See Shevel in this volume.

[59] Rogers W. Brubaker, 'Citizenship Struggles in Soviet Successor States', *International Migration Review* 26, no. 2 (1992): pp. 269–291.

ongoing determination of its membership and citizenship allocation in contexts of secession or migration follows different logics.

While secession and the formation of new states have remained relatively rare events, we need to be aware that internal mismatches of territorial and membership boundaries occur also short of full secession when territories have special status that entails restrictions of citizenship rights within the larger polity (as in the case of lack of federal voting rights for Puerto Rico or Washington D.C.) or special self-government rights not enjoyed by citizens residing in other parts of the state (as in the case of the Finnish Aland Islands or South Tyrol/Alto Adige in Italy). Asymmetries of this kind diminish equality of citizenship but may still be justified as an (often unstable) equilibrium between secession and oppressive denial of historic minority self-government claims.

Conclusions

This chapter has focused on citizenship as membership in a political community. I started with a critical discussion of attempts by political theorists to resolve the democratic boundary problem through a single principle of democratic inclusion that applies to all stages of the democratic process and all types of polities. I then investigated conceptual properties of citizenship, arguing that as a form of membership citizenship creates categorical distinctions but not necessarily impermeable, stable, or bright boundaries. Citizenship boundaries are exposed to processes of crossing, shifting, and blurring in contexts of migration, secession, and supranational integration. The third section examined the variety of democratic polities and identified birthright, residence, and multilevel derivation as the characteristic membership rules for independent states, for municipalities, and for subnational or supranational regions. The last section discussed the mismatch between territorial and membership boundaries in the international state system as the main reason for the increasing complexity of citizenship relations in the current world, but also as a potential source of protection and opportunities for those individuals whose lives connect them to several independent states. My conclusion is that normative inclusion principles need to be sensitive not only to the diversity of interests, beliefs, and values in liberal society, but also to the plurality of self-governing polities and of individuals' relations to these.

My discussion has relied on an implicit background assumption. It took for granted that both territorial borders and individual patterns of residence are relatively stable. It is this background that constitutes migration as the crossing of territorial borders of relatively sedentary societies and that makes it possible for these societies to adjust their political membership in response. In a hyper-mobile world where large majorities of people are only temporary residents in any political territory for most of their lives, the boundaries of citizenship would have to be radically reconstructed.[60] We can imagine that such a world would have to combine universal *jus domicilii* in territorial jurisdictions with the constantly shifting boundaries of issue-specific non-territorial demoi whose composition is determined by individuals opting in and out according to their perceived identities and interests. It would be difficult to maintain the idea of citizenship as membership in a self-governing political community in such a world. We might be gradually moving towards it, but this does not entail that reforming democratic citizenship has become a futile task. Instead, democratic theorists and politicians would just have to think harder about how to internalize mobility within larger democratic polities such as supranational unions of states and how to involve immigrants and emigrants in today's territorially based democratic politics.

BIBLIOGRAPHY

Abizadeh, Arash, 'Democratic Theory and Border Coercion: No Right to Unilaterally Control Your Own Borders', *Political Theory 36*, no. 1 (2008): pp. 37–65.

Alba, Richard, 'Bright vs. Blurred Boundaries: Second-Generation Assimilation and Exclusion in France, Germany, and the United States', *Ethnic and Racial Studies 28*, no. 1 (2005): pp. 20–49.

Angeli, Oliviero, *Cosmopolitanism, Self-Determination and Territory. Justice with Borders* (Houndsmills, Basingstoke: Palgrave Macmillan, 2015).

Arrighi, Jean-Thomas, and Rainer Bauböck, 'A Multilevel Puzzle. Migrants' Voting Rights in National and Local Elections', *European Journal of Political Research* (online first, October 2016, DOI: 10.1111/1475-6765.12176).

Bauböck, Rainer, 'The Crossing and Blurring of Boundaries in International Migration. Challenges for Social and Political Theory', in Rainer Bauböck and John Rundell, eds., *Blurred Boundaries. Migration, Ethnicity, Citizenship* (Aldershot: Ashgate, 1998), pp. 17–52.

Bauböck, Rainer, 'Reinventing Urban Citizenship', *Citizenship Studies 7*, no. 2 (2003): pp. 137–158.

Bauböck, Rainer, 'Temporary Migrants, Partial Citizenship and Hypermigration', *Critical Review of International Social and Political Philosophy 14*, no. 5 (2011): pp. 665–693.

---

[60] See Rainer Bauböck, 'Temporary Migrants, Partial Citizenship and Hypermigration', *Critical Review of International Social and Political Philosophy 14*, no. 5 (2011): pp. 665–693.

Bauböck, Rainer, 'Migration and the Porous Boundaries of Democratic States', in Stephan Leibfried et al., eds., *The Oxford Handbook of Transformations of the State* (Oxford: Oxford University Press, 2014), pp. 516–531.

Bauböck, Rainer, 'Morphing the Demos into the Right Shape. Normative Principles for Enfranchising Resident Aliens and Expatriate Citizens', *Democratization* 22, no. 5 (2015): pp. 820–839.

Benhabib, Seyla, *Dignity in Adversity: Human Rights in Troubled Times* (Cambridge: Polity Press, 2011).

Beran, Harry, 'A Liberal Theory of Secession', *Political Studies* 32, no. 1 (1984): pp. 21–31.

Blake, Michael, 'Immigration, Jurisdiction, and Exclusion', *Philosopy and Public Affairs* 41, no. 2 (2013): pp. 103–130.

Bodin, Jean, *Six Books of the Commonwealth*. Abridged and translated by M. J. Tooley (Oxford: Blackwell, 1576/1955).

Brubaker, Rogers, *Grounds for Difference* (Cambridge: Harvard University Press, 2015).

Brubaker, Rogers W., *Citizenship and Nationhood in France and Germany* (Cambridge: Harvard University Press, 1992).

Brubaker, Rogers W., 'Citizenship Struggles in Soviet Successor States', *International Migration Review* 26, no. 2 (1992): pp. 269–291.

Buchanan, Allen, *Justice, Legitimacy, and Self-Determination. Moral Foundations for International Law* (Oxford: Oxford University Press, 2004).

Buchanan, James, 'An Economic Theory of Clubs', *Economica* 32, no. 125 (1965): pp. 1–14.

Carens, Joseph H., 'Aliens and Citizens: The Case for Open Borders', *The Review of Politics* 49, no. 2 (1987): pp. 251–273.

Carens, Joseph H., *The Ethics of Immigration* (Oxford: Oxford University Press, 2013).

Cassese, Antonio, *Self-Determination of Peoples. A Legal Reappraisal* (Cambridge: Cambridge University Press, 1995).

Cohen, Elizabeth F., *Semi-Citizenship in Democratic Politics* (Cambridge: Cambridge University Press, 2010).

Collyer, Michael, 'A Geography of Extra-Territorial Citizenship: Explanations of External Voting', *Migration Studies* 2, no. 1 (2014): pp. 55–72.

Dahl, Robert, *Democracy and Its Critics* (New Haven: Yale University Press, 1989).

Dumbrava, Costica, *Nationality, Citizenship and Ethno-Cultural Belonging, Preferential Membership Policies in Europe* (Houndmills Basingstoke: Palgrave Macmillan, 2014).

Elazar, Daniel, *Exploring Federalism* (Tuscaloosa: The University of Alabama Press, 1987).

Fraser, Nancy, *Scales of Justice: Reimagining Political Space in a Globalizing World* (New York: Columbia University Press, 2009).

Frey, Bruno, and Reiner Eichberger, *The New Democratic Federalism for Europe: Functional, Overlapping, and Competing Jurisdictions* (Cheltenham, UK: Edward Elgar, 1999).

Gauthier, David, 'Breaking Up: An Essay on Secession', *Canadian Journal of Philosophy* 24, no. 3 (1994): pp. 357–372.

Goodin, Robert, 'Enfranchising All Affected Interests, and Its Alternatives', *Philosophy and Public Affairs* 35, no. 1 (2007): pp. 40–68.

Hammar, Tomas, *Democracy and the Nation State. Aliens, Denizens and Citizens in a World of International Migration* (Aldershot: Avebury, 1990).

Harpaz, Yossi, 'Ancestry into Opportunity: How Global Inequality Drives Demand for Non-Resident European Union Citizenship', *Journal of Ethnic and Migration Studies 41*, no. 13 (2015): pp. 2081–2104.

Honohan, Iseult, *Civic Republicanism* (London and New York: Routledge, 2002).

IDEA, and IFE, eds., *Voting from Abroad. The International IDEA Handbook* (Stockholm and Mexico City: International Institute for Democracy and Electoral Assistance and Instituto Federal Electoral de Mexico, 2007).

Joppke, Christian, *Citizenship and Immigration* (London: Polity, 2010).

Kymlicka, Will, *Politics in the Vernacular: Nationalism, Multiculturalism, and Citizenship* (Oxford: Oxford University Press, 2001).

López-Guerra, Claudio, 'Should Expatriates Vote?', *The Journal of Political Philosophy 13*, no. 2 (2005): pp. 216–234.

Mill, John Stuart, 'Considerations On Representative Government', in H. B. Acton, ed., *Utilitarianism, Liberty, Representative Government* (London: Everymans Library, 1972).

Miller, David, *On Nationality* (Oxford: Oxford University Press, 1995).

Miller, David, *Citizenship and National Identity* (Cambridge: Polity Press, 2000).

Miller, David, 'Immigrants, Nations, and Citizenship', *The Journal of Political Philosophy 16*, no. 1 (2008): pp. 371–390.

Miller, David, 'Democracy's Domain', *Philosophy and Pulbic Affairs 37* (2009): pp. 201–228.

Miller, David, 'Why Immigration Controls are Not Coercive: A Reply to Arash Abizadeh', *Political Theory 38*, no. 1 (2010): pp. 111–120.

Moore, Margaret, *A Political Theory of Territory* (Oxford: Oxford University Press, 2015).

Näsström, Sofia, 'The Legitimacy of the People', *Political Theory 35*, no. 5 (2007): pp. 624–658.

Nine, Cara, *Global Justice and Territory* (Oxford: Oxford University Press, 2012).

Owen, David, 'Constituting the Polity, Constituting the Demos: On the Place of the All Affected Interests Principle in Democratic Theory and in Resolving the Democratic Boundary Problem', *Ethics and Global Affairs 5*, no. 3 (2012): pp. 129–152.

Patten, Alan, *Equal Recognition. The Moral Foundations of Minority Rights* (Princeton: Princeton University Press, 2014).

Ratner, Steven R., 'Drawing a Better Line: Uti Possidetis and the Borders of New States', *American Journal of International Law 90*, no. 4 (1996): pp. 590–624.

Rubio-Marín, Ruth, *Immigration as a Democratic Challenge: Citizenship and Inclusion in Germany and the United States* (Cambridge: Cambridge University Press, 2000).

Shachar, Ayelet, *The Birthright Lottery: Citizenship and Global Inequality* (Cambridge: Harvard University Press, 2009).

Shachar, Ayelet, 'Picking Winners: Olympic Citizenship and the Global Race for Talent', *Yale Law Journal 120*, no. 8 (2011): pp. 2088–2139.

Spiro, Peter, *Beyond Citizenship. American Identity After Globalization* (Oxford: Oxford University Press, 2008).

Stilz, Anna, 'Nations, States, and Territory', *Ethics 121*, no. 3 (2011): pp. 572–601.

Tiebout, Charles, 'A Pure Theory of Local Expenditure', *Journal of Political Economy 64* (1956): pp. 416–424.

Whelan, Frederick G., 'Prologue: Democratic Theory and the Boundary Problem', in J. R. Pennock and J. W. Chapman, eds., *NOMOS 25: Liberal Democracy* (New York: New York University, 1983), pp. 13–47.

Wimmer, Andreas, *Ethnic Boundary Making: Institutions, Power, Networks* (Oxford: Oxford University Press, 2013).

Ziegler, Ruvi, Jo Shaw, and Rainer Bauböck, 'Independence Referendums: Who Should Vote and Who Should be Offered Citizenship?' *EUI Working Paper* RSCAS 2014/90' (Florence: EUI, 2014).

Zolberg, Aristide, and Long Litt Woon, 'Why Islam is Like Spanish: Cultural Incorporation in Europe and the United States', *Politics & Society 27*, no. 1 (1999): pp. 5–38.

CHAPTER 5

LIBERAL AND REPUBLICAN CONCEPTIONS OF CITIZENSHIP

ISEULT HONOHAN

INTRODUCTION

THIS chapter compares and contrasts two influential contemporary conceptions of citizenship, located in the liberal and republican traditions respectively. While liberalism is the dominant political philosophy of our time, republicanism has brought to the fore a new focus on citizenship.

As well as significant differences, the two theories have much in common. Furthermore, each of these traditions is composed of multiple strands, so that what constitutes the core of liberal or republican theory is internally contested. Rather than stipulating one of the rival accounts, I adopt a capacious interpretation in each case, noting certain characteristic concerns that distinguish them. As republican-ism is likely to be less familiar, and is still in the course of articulation, it may need more detailed exposition here. I do not attempt to analyse fully the complex rela-tionship between the two theories, but outline them insofar as this is relevant for comparing and contrasting their more sharply distinct conceptions of citizenship.

It is important to bear in mind that, in becoming the dominant political per-spective, liberalism has been effective in absorbing elements of other traditions—including the historically earlier republicanism—and claiming them as its own. As Duncan Bell puts it, 'Most inhabitants of the West are now *conscripts of liberal-ism*: the scope of the tradition has expanded to encompass the vast majority of pol-itical positions regarded as legitimate.'[1] Thus contemporary republicans have had to establish that the perspective they represent is both distinctive and attractive.

Liberal and republican theories offer more or less systematic alternative accounts of the problem that politics addresses, the values that are significant, and the ways in which these can be realized. It is these theories that are examined here, rather than popular ideological or partisan uses of the terms 'liberal' or 'republican' that may share historical origins and elements with the theoretical expressions: these include for example, the position supporting government spending and redistributive tax-ation measures identified as liberal in the USA, the US Republican Party, the mili-tant separatism of the Irish Republican Army, or the anti-monarchist movement in Australia.

In the specific context of citizenship, we should note also the significant distinc-tion between political liberalism, which focuses on the freedom and equality of citizens, and economic liberalism, which focuses mainly on the independence of property and the market from government control, and is not centrally concerned with citizenship at all. Thus, although economic libertarian arguments may be part of the family of liberal theories, they do not feature prominently here.

Liberalism starts from the problem of potential conflict arising from individuals' different interests and divergent moral perspectives; it addresses this through the creation of authoritative political institutions to maintain peace while treating all citizens fairly. Liberal political theory may be understood broadly as a commitment to freedom and equality, though in its neutralist versions this entails constraints on state promotion of any particular vision of the good life or set of comprehen-sive values. Indeed, while needed to moderate conflict, the state itself may present a threat of oppression. Thus liberalism has a particular focus on the relationship between the individual and the state, and what the state may or may not do. Liberal citizenship, then, is primarily a formal, and in principle universal, legal status pro-tecting individuals.

---

[1] Duncan Bell, 'What is Liberalism?', *Political Theory* 42, no. 6 (2014): pp. 682–715, doi: 10.1177/0090591714535103, p. 689.

Republicanism identifies the fundamental problem of politics differently in the fact of interdependence, and the resulting possibility both of domination—subjection to the arbitrary will of others—and of collective self-government, which realizes freedom and other common goods that individuals cannot achieve alone. While some republicans define freedom more in terms of the status of secure non-domination, and others as participation in decision-making, in each case freedom is related to self-government and concern for the common good. But this does not come naturally, and may be undermined by sectional interests. Citizenship is constituted as both a legal status and intersubjective recognition of equality, and entails the active commitment, or civic virtue, of citizens.

The primary focus of both liberal and republican theories of citizenship (and thus of this chapter) is on specifying its *content*, rather than providing criteria to establish its *boundaries*, although that content has potential implications for inclusion and exclusion.

From this brief initial characterization, it should already be evident that liberalism and republicanism are not so much diametrically opposed theories as alternative perspectives on the problem of politics, which share certain values, but interpret, organize, and prioritize them differently. It becomes easier to understand the common elements and continuing tensions between their contemporary expressions when we consider their historical evolution (the next section). The following section analyses the contrasting conceptions of citizenship. Subsequently, I outline the challenges for liberal and republican citizenship in the face of diversity and globalization. I conclude with some considerations on the future of liberal and republican citizenship.

THE HISTORICAL EVOLUTION OF LIBERAL AND REPUBLICAN POLITICAL THEORY

Liberalism and republicanism are not abstract, static positions, but evolving traditions that arose in different historical and political contexts of European history.

Emerging in the early modern period in Italian Renaissance city-states, and developing in seventeenth century England, the Dutch Republic, and eighteenth century Europe, republican theory was first articulated by political figures trying to defend self-governing citizen polities under pressure from princes and kings attempting to concentrate power in emerging European states. The most notable thinkers in this tradition include Niccolò Machiavelli, James Harrington, Jean Jacques Rousseau, Mary Wollstonecraft, and James Madison. These thinkers looked back to ancient antecedents in Athenian democracy and the Roman Republic, where freedom was defined in contrast to slavery or subjection to a master (rather than as the absence of interference in individual choices), and was guaranteed in part by the legal status of citizen, the rule of law, mixed or balanced institutions. But it also required a citizenry who actively participated and displayed political and military virtue to preserve the fragile republic from internal corruption and external threats. In this respect it seemed suited to small states where it was possible to envisage active participation by a significant proportion of the population. In addition, to be a citizen it was required not to be dependent on others, so it required property, although excessive wealth was seen as undermining equality and commitment to the common good. It thus excluded women and those who were not property holders. With the increasing size of states and the growth of commerce in the eighteenth century, to some a civically virtuous and active citizenry came to seem variously impossible, unnecessary, or undesirable. In response, two distinct emphases emerged. One looked to the Roman model, seeing participation as an instrumental means to freedom; thus Madison reworked republicanism for a large modern state in America, arguing for institutional balance and representation (rather than direct participation). The other looked to the Athenian model, seeing participation as part of that freedom. Rousseau defended the ideal of a self-governing citizenry on a small scale. Although both the American and French revolutions invoked republican ideas, the first reframed republicanism in ways that dovetailed with the way in which liberalism would evolve, while the second led to a reaction against the violence and tyranny associated with the Jacobin invocation of citizen virtue and participation.

Thus, in the nineteenth century, republicanism went into decline, and liberalism superseded it, defending the freedom of individuals in relation to growing social and state power, and seeking their protection through individual rights and limits on government. It thus picked up a central thread from republicanism, and carried on some of the themes and institutional provisions introduced by republicans—for example, the rule of law and institutional balance. While arguments now associated with liberalism—natural rights, consent, and constitutionally limited government— can be traced back to the seventeenth century (in John Locke), it was really only in reaction to the collectivist implications of political and philosophical utilitarianism and nationalism that a second strand of liberalism focusing on individual freedom or autonomy was clearly developed, in the thought, for example, of Benjamin Constant, Alexis de Tocqueville, and John Stuart Mill.[2]

In the twentieth century liberalism was seen as the clear alternative to a variety of collectivist authoritarian positions, and especially to socialism. When socialism became discredited with the fall of communism in Eastern Europe, liberalism appeared to emerge as the undisputed political perspective.

---

[2] Also concerned with civic virtue, these have been referred to as 'civic liberals'. Cf. Dale Miller, 'John Stuart Mill's Civic Liberalism', *History of Political Thought* 21, no. 1 (2000): pp. 88–113; Bell (n 1).

Contemporary liberalism, then, is arguably a defence of freedom, or, for neutralist liberals who rule out the state's promoting any particular idea of the good life, an attempt to treat all persons with equal respect and concern.[3] Liberalism addresses the potential conflict arising from individuals' different interests and divergent moral perspectives by creating a political authority. Because government itself may become oppressive, it must be constrained. This spells out as requiring that citizens have an equal civil status, strong legal rights, including freedom of speech and conscience, and constitutional limitations on any form of government. While some interpret freedom negatively as non-interference, and others interpret it more positively as autonomy,[4] liberals focus primarily on structures that protect individual rights, seen as pre-political, and tend to agree that, as far as the state is concerned, freedom represents more a constraint on government than a goal it should promote. Central to the liberal protection of freedom is the distinction between the public—what the state may control—and the private—what the state may not control. Citizenship is a universal, formal legal status, with certain rights and duties, which transcends the differences between individuals. While electoral representation is an important part of the institutional arrangements, active participation in self-government is not an essential part of citizenship.

While the liberal perspective is open to recognizing some common goods, this is mainly understood in terms of the aggregate of individual goods, or even as a basic precondition (as, for example, peace) for such goods. It does not prioritize shared goods or a broader common good among citizens. Nor does it emphasize the commitment or civic virtue of citizens.

But freedom is not the sole value of liberalism. The emphasis on equal freedom and respect for individual citizens has led to the development of a prominent egalitarian liberal strand for which this implies a degree of social and economic equality and accordingly of state-led redistribution. This found its canonical expression in the political theory of John Rawls, in which two basic principles were central—equal freedom and the limiting of inequalities to those which may benefit the least well-off.[5] Much liberal theory since then has been concerned with responding to, or working out, the implications of this influential position, especially with respect to the distribution of social and economic opportunities.

Despite the apparent triumph of liberal ideas, criticism of their limits, both conceptual and practical, soon emerged. Indeed the revival of republicanism from the 1990s may be seen as arising from concerns (initially communitarian

---

[3] John Rawls, *Theory of Justice* (Oxford: Oxford University Press, 1971); Ronald Dworkin, *Taking Rights Seriously* (Cambridge: Harvard University Press, 1977).

[4] Joseph Raz, *The Morality of Freedom* (Oxford: Clarendon Press, 1986); John Christman and Joel Anderson, eds., *Autonomy and Challenges to Liberalism* (Cambridge: Cambridge University Press, 2009).

[5] Rawls (n 3). For others, equality is primary (Ronald Dworkin, *Sovereign Virtue. The Theory and Practice of Equality* (Cambridge: Harvard University Press, 2000)).

in focus) about such limits, ranging from liberalism's individualist assumptions, and failure to focus on shared goods, to its limited capacity to identify certain kinds of oppression, or to motivate citizens to act in ways that would sustain liberal institutions. The more politically focused republican revival took the form first of rediscovering republicanism as an historical tradition (in the work of J. G. A. Pocock and Quentin Skinner),[6] and then of rearticulating it in a variety of expressions, for each of which freedom is realized through membership of a self-governing political community. These include a more participatory strand—from Hannah Arendt to Michael Sandel—and a more protective strand elaborated by Skinner and Philip Pettit, the leading exponent of what has come to be called 'neo-republicanism'.[7]

For contemporary neo-republicans, the starting point is the fact of interdependence that makes people vulnerable to domination. Unfreedom is identified in terms of domination: more than interference, this is systematic vulnerability to the threat of interference, or subjection to the exercise of arbitrary, or unchecked power.[8] This may loom over people even when they are not actually being interfered with, and undermines their ability to live free lives. The status of a slave, or a wife in a Victorian marriage makes them vulnerable to the exercise of arbitrary power even if, at any point in time, a kind or absent master or husband is not inclined to interfere with them; but they still need to take account of the possibility of a change of temper or conditions. They depend on the good will of the master or husband.[9]

But interdependence also offers the possibility of collective self-government, through which citizens can enjoy common goods that individuals cannot achieve alone. Freedom itself is such a good: it is not a natural property, but is realized first through legal and political institutions that establish a secure public status of legal and political equality. This protects citizens from arbitrary exercises of power, and allows them 'to look the other in the eye',[10] rather than accommodating themselves to domination; it requires that this knowledge of equal status is mutual and internalised by citizens. This constitutes freedom as non-mastery (rather than as

---

[6] J. G. A. Pocock, *The Machiavellian Moment* (Princeton: Princeton University Press, 1975); Quentin Skinner, *Foundations of Modern Political Thought*, 2 volumes (Cambridge: Cambridge University Press, 1978); Quentin Skinner, *Liberty before Liberalism* (Cambridge: Cambridge University Press, 1998).

[7] Hannah Arendt, *The Human Condition* (Chicago: Chicago University Press, 1958); Hannah Arendt, *On Revolution* (New York: Penguin, 1977); Philip Pettit, *Republicanism: A Theory of Freedom and Government* (Oxford: Oxford University Press, 1997); Michael Sandel, *Democracy's Discontent* (Cambridge: Harvard Belknap, 1998). See further Iseult Honohan, *Civic Republicanism* (Abingdon and New York: Routledge, 2002).

[8] Pettit (n 7); Frank Lovett, *A General Theory of Domination and Justice* (Oxford: Oxford University Press, 2010).

[9] Pettit (n 7), p. 69.   [10] Pettit (n 7), p. 71.

self-mastery, which Isaiah Berlin identified as positive freedom and contrasted to negative freedom or non-interference).[11]

Pettit distinguishes freedom as non-domination from both non-interference and more positive notions of freedom as autonomy, and sees this as what distinguishes republicanism from liberalism. It has been argued, however, that non-domination remains a negative conception of freedom, albeit more securely established. If so, neo-republicanism may seem not to differ that much from liberalism (as Rawls agreed).[12] Furthermore, both outline similar institutional protections and see citizenship (initially at least) as a legal status; and, although neo-republicanism emphasizes the intersubjective dimension of non-domination, it can be seen as relying on something very like the liberal notion of respect.[13] While some have aimed to reconcile the insights of both traditions in a civic liberalism or a liberal republicanism, others have argued that to the extent that republicanism is similar to liberalism it is redundant, and to the extent that it is different, it is anachronistic, populist, oppressive, or impractical.[14]

Even if non-domination remains a negative conception and neo-republicanism and liberalism share certain commonalities, the assumptions underpinning their institutional provisions, however, are different. Liberals think of individuals as inherently independent and of freedom in pre-political terms, protected by laws that constrain the exercise of power of others and the state. Furthermore, government power and law, although necessary, are constraints on freedom. For republicans, freedom is politically realized, and rights are politically constituted.[15] Laws establishing equal status constitute part of freedom, rather than a necessary infringement on it—freedom 'by the law', rather than from the law.[16] In addition, because only arbitrary exercises of power dominate, republicans are less inherently reluctant to envisage state intervention as long as this is subject to accountability procedures. The institutional requirements of non-domination are the rule of law

---

[11] Isaiah Berlin, 'Two Concepts of Liberty', in *Four Essays on Liberty* (Oxford: Oxford University Press, 1969).

[12] John Rawls, *Political Liberalism*, 2nd, paperback edition (New York: Columbia University Press, 1996), pp. 205–206.

[13] Charles Larmore, 'Liberal and Republican Conceptions of Freedom', in Daniel Weinstock and Christian Nadeau, eds., *Republicanism; History, Theory, Practice* (London: Frank Cass, 2004), pp. 96–119.

[14] Compatibility is proposed by, e.g., Charles Taylor, 'Cross-Purposes: The Liberal-Communitarian Debate', in *Philosophical Arguments* (Cambridge: Harvard University Press, 1995), pp. 181–203; Richard Dagger, *Civic Virtues: Rights, Citizenship, and Republican Liberalism* (Oxford: Oxford University Press, 1997). Rejecting any distinctive republican appeal are, e.g., Alan Patten, 'The Republican Critique of Liberalism', *British Journal of Political Science* 26, no. 1 (1996): pp. 25–44; Robert Goodin, 'Folie Républicaine', *Annual Review of Political Science* 6 (2003): pp. 55–76.

[15] Likewise, Habermas sees private and public freedom as co-original (Jürgen Habermas, *Between Facts and Norms: Contributions to a Discourse Theory of Law and Democracy* (Cambridge: MIT Press, 1996)).

[16] Pettit (n 7), p. 39.

and the accountability of political institutions to citizens by giving them a voice to contest political decisions.

Moreover, even neo-republicanism is more demanding in what equal status requires; this depends not on law alone, but on social recognition. For all republicans, the realization of freedom depends on the commitment of citizens internalizing the values of the republic, being disposed to treat others as equals rather than seeking to dominate them, and recognizing the common goods that they share as citizens. This makes central a stronger notion of the common good as collectively realized and enjoyed. Here public and private are contrasted primarily in terms of interest rather than control—what is public is in the common interest, what is private is in the individual or sectional interest. This emphasis on the character of citizens and the shared common good highlights the way in which the republican perspective entails more substantial relationships and commitments among citizens than liberals focusing on institutions generally recognize.

In addition, republicanism makes more central some kind of political activity, whether this be the opportunity for contestation for Pettit, or more substantial participation in decision-making. Indeed it has been argued that non-domination itself requires both more civic virtue and more provision for political determination relative to institutional balance than Pettit recognizes.[17]

It may further be argued that non-domination is more closely connected to autonomy than Pettit or other neo-republicans suggest. The value of non-domination lies partly in its being a precondition for the exercise of autonomy, both personal and political. If freedom is understood as an ideal to be promoted, rather than a constraint to be observed, non-domination appears to point beyond itself, if not to full mastery, towards the possibility of those who are mutually vulnerable and subject to a common authority jointly exercising some collective direction over their lives. Thus, for some republicans, as we shall see when we consider the role of political participation in citizenship in the next section, a still more participatory account may be seen as more consistent with the commitments of republicanism.

We may conclude that republicanism is not opposed to liberalism's central value of freedom, but interprets it differently, and has a different centre of gravity, in which freedom is part of a cluster of related values including civic commitment and participation in self-government. It is the conjunction of these other concerns of civic engagement with freedom that defines the distinctive character of republicanism and the continuity among its various strands. Neo-republicanism has excavated the essential underpinning of freedom as non-domination for self-government,

---

[17] John Maynor, *Republicanism in the Modern World* (Cambridge: Polity, 2003); Richard Bellamy, *Political Constitutionalism: A Republican Defense of the Constitutionality of Democracy* (Cambridge: Cambridge University Press, 2007).

but does not supersede the focus on the common good or participation in self government.[18]

Contrasting Conceptions
of Citizenship

Despite the complexities of characterizing and distinguishing liberal and republican political theories, when we compare their accounts of citizenship more specifically these differences appear in sharper perspective.

Citizenship has three distinct dimensions: legal status and rights, activity, and membership. Different conceptions of citizenship interpret, connect, and prioritize these differently. Risking oversimplifying, we may say that the liberal conception focuses more on legal status and rights, and the republican conception relatively more on activity.

For liberals, citizenship is a relatively formal legal status that establishes a significant range of rights against the state and others; the obligations of citizenship have traditionally been seen as fairly thin, amounting to obeying the laws, paying taxes, serving on juries, and other quite determinate duties that do not affect the character or identity of the individual. Some might see voting or participation as a moral, but not generally as a legal obligation. Liberalism relies heavily on institutions and laws to achieve a liberal society; although some have drawn attention to the need for certain liberal virtues or dispositions (such as tolerance and reasonableness) among citizens if liberalism is to flourish, activity over and above status, whether in terms of civic virtue or political participation, is not central.

Citizenship itself (as distinct from individual rights and constitutional limits) was not always given a central position in liberal political theory. What is often cited as the classic statement of liberal citizenship was articulated by the sociologist, T. H. Marshall, identifying its expansion from civil (from the seventeenth century) to include political (in the nineteenth century) and finally social and economic status (in the twentieth century).[19]

Subsequently, in the work of John Rawls, the idea of the free and equal citizen does play a more central role. Thus Rawls describes 'a free and equal citizen, the

---

[18] Thus, while the two strands are sometimes contrasted as 'civic humanism' and 'civic republicanism', as in Rawls (n 12), this overlooks the continuity between them.

[19] Thomas H. Marshall, *Citizenship and Social Class and Other Essays* (Cambridge: Cambridge University Press, 1950).

political person of a modern democracy, with the political rights and duties of citizenship, and standing in a political relation with other citizens', noting that these rights and duties are distinct from and more limited than the more comprehensive moral rights and duties of the moral person.[20]

For both liberals and republicans the citizen is defined in contrast to the 'subject'—a person under the command of a ruler. While also starting from legal status and structures needed to secure it, republicans place more emphasis than liberalism on the second dimension of citizenship—activity. Thus the republican citizen is defined also in contrast to the consumer, client, or free rider, or those who are indifferent to or inactive in the political community. But this status/activity account differs from 'thicker' membership accounts (where citizens—contrasted to non-members—share deep commonalities). On the republican account, as Arendt put it, citizens are 'with' others rather than being either for or against them.[21]

In the public mind, political participation may be the activity most widely associated with citizenship, distinguishing citizens from subjects. For liberals, as we have seen, participation is optional and protection may be achieved through representation. More important may be consent and constitutional protections restricting the scope of political power and even of public argument. Liberalism institutionalizes democracy through representation of diverse interests. Furthermore it may conceive of democratic decision-making as a matter of necessary compromise among interests. Although there are many variants of liberalism, it may be argued that in general it more easily accommodates a 'market' model of democracy, in which fixed individual preferences are aggregated, than a 'forum' model, in which views are articulated and developed in public.[22]

If there are political virtues in participation that citizens need to develop and practice, they are matters of rationality and impartiality rather than connection: for Rawls,

the virtues of reasonableness and fair-mindedness as shown in the adherence to the criteria and procedures of commonsense knowledge and to the methods and conclusions of science when not controversial. These values reflect an ideal of citizenship: our willingness to settle the fundamental political matters in ways that others as free and equal can acknowledge are reasonable and rational.[23]

Thus, when liberals have become engaged in the modern turn to deliberative democracy, in which deliberation between alternative viewpoints in a public space becomes more central, their accounts tend to be rational and legal or constitutionalist in their focus, or to limit both the kinds of contribution that can be made in public debate and the scope of that deliberation.

---

[20] Rawls (n 12), p. xlv.   [21] Arendt, *Human Condition* (n 7), p. 160.

[22] Jon Elster, 'The Market and the Forum', in James Bohman and William Rehg, eds., *Deliberative Democracy: Essays on Reason and Politics* (Cambridge: MIT Press, 1997), pp. 3–33.

[23] John Rawls, *Justice as Fairness: A Restatement*, edited by Erin Kelly (Cambridge: Harvard University Press, 2001), p. 92.

Contemporary republicans call for a more active citizenry and more extensive popular involvement in political activity than the liberal consensus on limited government, electoral representation of interests, and consent of the governed. Rather than either a politics of bargaining among interests or the expression of a collective will, they emphasize the deliberative interpretation of the common good.

Some republican views construe deliberative input more in terms of the ability to contest decisions and others more in terms of determining or contributing to decisions. Again, any sharp distinction between the neo-republican instrumental approach to participation and a more participatory republicanism conceals significant continuities. Both fit better with a view of democracy as a forum or public sphere in which alternative views are expressed and given consideration among diverse people. For those emphasizing more active participation in decision-making than the neo-republican strand, participation can be seen as having intrinsic as well as instrumental value, whether as a form of self-expression or participation in collective self-government,[24] rather than as part of a political nature, attributing to it ultimate value, or thinking that extensive participation, or even voting, should be compulsory.[25]

Democratic republicanism can envisage the role of active citizens as deliberating on the common good rather than imposing a collective will or realizing collective self-mastery. The republican goal of determining the common good and encouraging civic commitment gives deliberation a particular focus and importance distinct from, for example, its possible role in giving individual interests a better hearing.

Republicans and liberals differ also on the question of civic education. The largely formal liberal account, and its focus on institutions limiting state power have led liberals to place little emphasis on civic virtue or education for citizenship. Even where liberals identify need for civic virtues, whether and how they can be promoted, and whether education promoting them is legitimate, is much disputed. For some, education is hard to reconcile with autonomy; indeed, since Mill, many liberals argue that education should not be within the purview of the state, or that state education should not promote particular values. Those who think that liberal citizens need a more specific attachment to their country, however, see this as requiring education in history, common culture, or liberal democratic values.[26]

In contrast, for republicans, education is central to citizenship. Because people experience a natural tension between particular and common interests,

---

[24] Arendt (n 7); Sandel (n 7).   [25] Honohan (n 7), chapter 7.

[26] For a range of views, see Eamonn Callan, *Creating Citizens: Political Education and Liberal Democracy* (Oxford: Oxford University Press, 1997); Meira Levinson, *The Demands of Liberal Education* (Oxford: Oxford University Press, 2002); Harry Brighouse, *On Education* (London and New York: Routledge, 2006); Matthew Clayton, *Justice and Legitimacy in Upbringing* (Oxford: Oxford University Press, 2006); Will Kymlicka, 'Education for Citizenship', in *Politics in the Vernacular* (Oxford: Oxford University Press, 2001), pp. 291–316.

commitment to the common good is not guaranteed, but is a disposition that may be developed—in part at least through education. This applies to all varieties of republicanism, whether the ideal is framed in terms of a culture of non-domination or a more substantial political autonomy.[27] But this may be not so much a matter of instilling a particular doctrine, values, or identity as an awareness of interdependence, self restraint, and a capacity for deliberation.[28]

CURRENT CHALLENGES: INCLUDING DIVERSITY AND EXTENDING BEYOND THE NATION-STATE

Leaving aside radical challenges to the very concept of citizenship, it is indisputable that the frame of reference for freedom and equality, non-domination, and self-government needs to change in response to greater diversity within states, and to increasing global interdependence.

Here I consider two kinds of challenge faced specifically by liberal and republican conceptions of citizenship. How potentially inclusive of diversity are they? How extensible beyond the nation-state is their concern with freedom and equality?

While liberal and republican citizenship are framed in terms of values that appear to be inclusive, the extent to which they can accommodate diverse citizens as equals has been significantly questioned in at least three important areas: gender, culture, and religion. In brief: while not focusing primarily on drawing boundaries, liberals and republicans have been seen as enforcing boundaries, explicitly and implicitly, through the very content they attribute to citizenship.

In principle liberal citizenship, as only a 'thin' formal legal status, can potentially accommodate all: what differentiates citizens can be expressed in private, and the state does not promote any particular values or visions of the good life over others. Feminists were early critics of the liberal privatization strategy, drawing attention to the difficulty of separating public and private, that this can obscure and depoliticise certain kinds of unfreedom and inequality, and that an ideal of citizenship modelled on a rationalist, independent individual has either excluded or imposed high costs of inclusion on women and other minorities.[29] Indeed in a broad criticism encompassing both liberal and republican models of citizenship, Young maintains:

---

[27] Maynor (n 17); Sandel (n 7).   [28] Sandel (n 7); Honohan (n 7), pp. 170–179.
[29] Carole Pateman, 'Feminist Critiques of the Public/Private Dichotomy', in Stanley Benn and Gerald Gaus, eds., *Public and Private in Social Life* (New York: St Martin's Press, 1983), pp. 281–303;

The ideal of the public realm of citizenship as expressing a general will, a point of view and an interest that citizens have in common that transcends their differences, has operated in fact as a demand for homogeneity among citizens.[30]

Liberal responses have included reforming the ideal of citizenship to fulfil its promise of universality, redrawing the boundary of the private around the individual rather than the domestic sphere, loosening the private-public distinction, and acknowledging the role of emotions in the liberal individual.[31]

The republican public-private distinction, never as sharp as in liberalism, maps primarily on to common and particular interests, even if these were in practice often elided with the public and domestic spheres. So it does not have the same intrinsic liability to overlook oppression, and indeed neo-republicanism has highlighted as exemplary the domination of women within marriage that liberalism found hard to problematize.

Nonetheless, republicanism has tended to see citizenship as incompatible with dependence (and historically excluded women and others on this account).[32] It could be argued that the republican requirement for capacities and dispositions for commitment and participation suggest grounds for excluding those who are inevitably dependent.[33] Yet it may be more consistent with its concern for freedom in interdependence to acknowledge necessary dependence and the importance of securing non-domination and participation in self-government in that context. Thus non-domination has the potential to highlight unfreedom in further cases of dependence, including children and those with disabilities and mental health diagnoses, who are vulnerable to exercises of arbitrary power. Indeed, this requires understanding civic virtue and participation in less heroic or masculinist terms than in historical republicanism. Acknowledging necessary dependence entails, for example, not only counting practices of care as active citizenship, but also accepting a wide range of levels and modes of participation by those hitherto deemed incapable of inclusion.[34]

Still, feminists have been suspicious of the very idea of the common good as masking the imposition of particular dominant interests.[35] But while it has often

---

Susan Moller Okin, *Justice, Gender, and the Family* (New York: Basic Books, 1989). See also Volpp in this volume.

[30] Iris Marion Young, 'Polity and Group Difference', *Ethics* 99 (1989): pp. 250–274.

[31] Okin (n 29); Martha Nussbaum, *Political Emotions: Why Love Matters for Justice* (Cambridge: Harvard University Press, 2013).

[32] Marilyn Friedman, 'Pettit's Civic Republicanism and Male Domination', in Cécile Laborde and John Maynor, eds., *Republicanism and Political Theory* (Oxford: Blackwell, 2008); M. Victoria Costa, 'Is Neo-Republicanism Bad for Women?', *Hypatia* 28, no. 4 (2013): pp. 921–936.

[33] See Donaldson and Kymlicka in this volume.

[34] Tom O'Shea, 'Disability and Domination: Lessons from Republican Political Philosophy', *Journal of Applied Philosophy*, early view (2016) doi: 10.1111/japp.12149.

[35] Anne Phillips, 'Feminism and Republicanism; is this a Plausible Alliance?', *Journal of Political Philosophy* 9, no 2 (2000): pp. 270–293.

been used hypocritically, it is not clear this is a reason for abandoning the idea altogether. Freedom itself depends on an orientation towards the possibility of common goods realized in conjunction with others.[36] That citizens should be prepared to transcend their narrow interests is not oppressive, unless they are forced to conform to a predetermined end.

In the late twentieth century the increasing emphasis on cultural identity expanded the scope of the critique of liberal privatization; in practice this strategy meant that citizenship was marked by the dominant culture, so that members of national or immigrant minority cultures, even if in principle equal citizens, encountered obstacles to participation in social and public life.[37]

To treat members of cultural minorities equally, a more inclusive conception of multicultural liberal citizenship has been proposed by, for example, Will Kymlicka, accommodating cultural minorities through exemptions, special representation, and resources, without infringing on liberal principles of individual freedom or equality.[38] This departure from formal universal citizenship was resisted by some liberals who identified dangers to equality (between and within groups) of special treatment for groups, and argued instead for genuinely equal treatment—for example, changing the rules for all if this was warranted, rather than having rules with exemptions for minorities.[39]

On the other hand, with the increased salience of culture, others suggested that cultural diversity poses a threat to solidarity among citizens.[40] If liberal citizenship is thin—does not engage the identity or character of citizens—it overlooks the solidarity needed for support of liberal institutions, especially the redistribution associated with the welfare state. Thus some suggest that liberal citizenship should include commitment to a common public culture of liberal nationality, entailing education in that common culture, while also allowing that it may be reshaped over time.[41] This supports some thickening of the basis of liberal citizenship. But attempting to fill out formal citizenship with (even limited, public) cultural content, makes it intrinsically more difficult to integrate others. Moreover, while a shared culture may give a sense of membership of the imagined community, whether it is necessary or sufficient to motivate solidarity is contested.[42]

Republicanism, since it involves more specific commitment and activity, could initially be seen as less accommodating of cultural diversity. But unlike thicker communitarian citizenship, republican concern for the common good requires

---

[36] See Raz (n 4).   [37] See Gans in this volume.

[38] Will Kymlicka, *Multicultural Citizenship* (Oxford: Clarendon Press, 1995).

[39] Brian Barry, *Culture and Equality* (Cambridge: Cambridge University Press, 2001).

[40] Robert Putnam, 'E Pluribus Unum: Diversity and Community in the Twenty-first Century', *Scandinavian Political Studies 30*, no. 2 (2007): pp.137–174.

[41] Kymlicka (n 26); David Miller, *On Nationality* (Oxford: Oxford University Press, 1997).

[42] Cf., e.g., Tom van der Meer and Jochem Tolsma, 'Ethnic Diversity and Its Effects on Social Cohesion', *Annual Review of Sociology 40* (2014): pp. 459–478.

citizens to transcend not cultural or moral difference per se, but purely particular preferences that do not take account of interdependence. This suggests that it does not in principle exclude, and can more easily accommodate, citizens in their cultural diversity. It identifies ways in which cultural differences may entail specific needs and vulnerabilities to domination, and authorizes their voices in the political process.[43] From this perspective equality of diverse citizens may be realized by promoting broad-ranging public deliberation. The ideal here is that solidarity may be realized less through cultural commonality than intersubjective recognition and interaction; as Benhabib puts it, 'feelings of friendship and solidarity result … from … the actual confrontation in public life with those who would otherwise be strangers to us.'[44] Here too, whether and to what extent this can be borne out in practice is a matter of dispute.

Religion and its accommodation has more recently come to be the most critical issue of diversity in contemporary debates. As epitomizing comprehensive views for which compromise is problematic, religion, in the liberal view, should be tolerated in private, but excluded from public life. Even those liberals willing to accommodate cultural diversity are less willing to extend this to religion—not only ruling out any religious establishment and any state promotion of religious doctrine, but constraining citizens' political expression of religiously justified beliefs. Rawls particularly identifies as a duty of 'public civility' that citizens should not advance arguments based on religious comprehensive doctrines in discussions on constitutional essentials and questions of basic justice, or do so only if in due course they provide 'properly public reasons'.[45] With the increasing salience of new kinds of religious diversity, this approach, and whether it applies to the purely political or to all public expressions of religion, has become the focus of intense discussion.[46]

A similar approach is advanced in the strict secularism (laïcité) of official French republicanism, itself a distinctive hybrid of republican and liberal concerns, which Cécile Laborde has termed 'a tough-minded version of egalitarian, difference-blind liberalism'.[47] In the interests of freedom, equality, and fraternity, laïcité has

---

[43] Frank Lovett, 'Cultural Accommodation and Domination', Political Theory 38, no. 2 (2010): pp. 243–267; Mira Bachvarova, 'Multicultural Accommodation and the Ideal of Non-domination', Critical Review of International Social and Political Philosophy 17, no. 6 (2014): pp. 652–73, doi:10.1080/13698230.2013.826500.

[44] Seyla Benhabib, 'Judgement and the Moral Foundations of Politics in Arendt's Thought', Political Theory 16, no. 1 (1988): pp. 29–51.

[45] John Rawls, 'The Idea of Public Reason Revisited', University of Chicago Law Review 64, no. 3 (1997): pp. 765–807, p. 776.

[46] Nicholas Wolterstorff, Justice: Rights and Wrongs (Princeton: Princeton University Press, 2008); Jürgen Habermas, 'Religion in the Public Sphere', European Journal of Philosophy 14, no. 1 (2006): pp. 1–25; Robert Audi, Democratic Authority and the Separation of Church and State (Oxford: Oxford University Press, 2011); Jeremy Waldron, 'Two-Way Translation: The Ethics of Engaging with Religious Contributions in Public Deliberation', Mercer Law Review 63 (2012): pp. 845–868.

[47] Cécile Laborde, Critical Republicanism: The Hijab Controversy and Political Philosophy (Oxford: Oxford University Press, 2008), p. 40.

been interpreted as requiring a rigid neutrality, excluding all religious expressions from the public sphere, including wearing Muslim headscarves or Sikh turbans in school.[48]

The privatizing strategy can be seen as imposing differential costs on members of different religions, affecting less those that focus on belief and conscience rather than ritual and practice, or whose practices fit more easily into the distinction between public and private. Members of religious minorities who have to choose between following religious practices or participating in education may be seen as dominated by the state that imposes this conditionality. It may also be argued that if expressions of citizens' deepest convictions are restricted to the private realm, this downgrades their significance, and fails to treat them as equal citizens. If, further, political arguments based on religious reasoning are disallowed in the political realm, this reinforces any majority bias in the status quo, and remains an exercise of power in which (especially minority) religious citizens are at a disadvantage.[49]

If, in contrast to this approach, we see as the key principle of the republican approach not public neutrality, but non-domination and participation in self-government, rather than excluding religion from the public realm, this allows religious practices in public and authorizes members of religious minorities to express views based on religious perspectives in politics.[50] It also requires government to be continually open to consider and change any existing state arrangements that dominate citizens of diverse beliefs. It thus allows for even-handed accommodation of religious practices.[51] To the objection that this facilitates oppression within religious groups, it can be replied that a concern with non-domination should make the state more rather than less alert to the threat of oppression, and allows it to intervene in, and constrain, dominating practices. As John Maynor puts it: 'Individuals and groups within a republican state [committed to non-domination] can be non-liberals, but they cannot be dominators.'[52]

In this vein, Cécile Laborde's alternative 'critical republicanism' aims to formulate a theory of secularism that, like egalitarian liberalism, prioritizes egalitarian justice and solidarity over identity-based claims, and, like republicanism, recognizes the importance of civic attitudes and robust public interaction. This entails greater neutrality of political institutions than at present, but fewer constraints on the expression of religious minorities.[53]

---

[48] Though at the time of writing, the French Conseil D'Etat has just struck down mayoral bans on wearing burkinis on public beaches.

[49] Veit Bader, *Secularism or Democracy? Associational Governance of Religious Diversity* (Amsterdam: Amsterdam University Press, 2007).

[50] Honohan (n 7), pp. 250–266.

[51] On 'even-handedness' see also Joseph Carens, *Culture, Citizenship and Community* (Oxford: Oxford University Press, 2000).

[52] Maynor (n 17), p. 134.   [53] Laborde (n 47), pp. 12, 86.

More than ever before, issues concerning freedom and equality spill over the bounds of the nation-state. Globalization has undermined the capacity of political communities to protect or realize freedom. Exercises of power over individuals and less powerful states by international economic actors and more powerful states make more significant differences in security of non-domination and self-government. Can liberal and republican citizenship be extended beyond the nation-state? Furthermore, does their concern for the freedom and equality of citizens justify or proscribe limiting others' freedom to migrate or to become members?[54]

Neither theory focuses primarily on the dimension of membership, or offering criteria for its allocation. Neither is intrinsically wedded to the nation as the foundation of the state, and there are resources within both that suggest their potential extensibility. Yet both have long operated under the assumption of a bounded polity, and have only relatively recently begun to address whether and how their principles and concerns might extend beyond the nation-state.[55]

On the one hand, liberal freedom and equality applies to individuals rather than to members of a specific polity. The (in principle) universality of liberal citizenship might be thought to lend itself to cosmopolitan scope to the extent that transnational institutions of liberalism can emerge.[56] But the absence of such authoritative institutions and the reluctance of liberals to entrust power on a larger—let alone on a global—scale undermines the potential for liberal citizenship beyond the nation-state. In addition, if liberalism is seen as too thin to motivate at the national level, this problem is surely multiplied at higher levels. Egalitarian liberals focusing on distributive justice have been divided on the scope of that justice. For an increasing number of liberals, the scope of justice must be global. For others, it can apply only within a bounded society; in the context of a world of states, something like the principle of non-interference was proposed by Rawls as the appropriate relationship of liberal states with other peoples.[57]

Republicanism might be thought of initially as more firmly bounded since it relies not only on institutions, but also on commitment and the opportunity for participation among citizens. If commitment to a shared common good is thought already too demanding at national level, it may be hard to see how it could be more widely

---

[54] Whether these conceptions are extensible beyond the west is a further issue; for discussion whether republicanism may be more congenial than liberalism in the Asian context, e.g., see Jun-Hyeok Kwak and Leigh Jenco, eds., *Republicanism in North East Asia* (London: Routledge, 2014).

[55] Arguably neither theory can provide definitive criteria for allocating membership: while for liberals in the social contract tradition, voluntary consent to a political authority, and, for republicans, sustained interdependence in subjection to a coercive authority can be seen as grounds for membership, neither on their own can determine boundary issues. See Bauböck in this volume.

[56] See Tan in this volume for an argument in favour instead of a non-political cosmopolitan citizenship.

[57] Charles Beitz, *Political Theory and International Relations,* 2nd edition (Princeton: Princeton University Press, 1999); Thomas Pogge, *World Poverty and Human Rights,* 2nd edition (Cambridge: Polity Press, 2008); John Rawls, *The Law of Peoples* (Cambridge: Harvard University Press, 1999).

extensible. But while neo-republicanism has been developed initially in terms of securing non-domination for citizens within a state, domination extending across borders must surely be seen as problematic. Thus the need for structures realizing non-domination and self-government might be seen as extending the potential scope of citizenship.

It can be argued that globalization has involved an increase in the potential for domination, with increasing connectedness, asymmetry of power, and dependence across borders, affecting individuals both directly and indirectly (by making their states incapable of fulfilling their protective role).[58] If freedom requires not just non-interference, but reducing domination and a share in self-government, it may be precisely this increased potential for domination that makes a republican approach relevant. It is less clear whether this means that we should aim to secure weaker states better from domination, to create a global republic, or, as James Bohman argues, to build on the incipient world political community and multi-level democracy that existing international institutions, although partial, have created.[59]

The second global challenge is whether liberal and republican citizenship can address the issue of movement between states. Since neither liberal nor republic conceptions of citizenship are defined essentially in terms of specific membership, they do not immediately entail a communitarian right of political communities to exclude non-citizens.[60] Thus it has been argued variously that the logical conclusion of the liberal principles of freedom and equality is opening borders so that people are free to migrate wherever they wish, or giving outsiders a say in the determination of border controls.[61] With respect to migrants already admitted, liberal principles suggest a broad range of rights applying to all, and relatively easy access to full citizenship through naturalization. Against this, however, other liberals have denied that borders infringe on the freedom of outsiders, invoking the principle of free association or the need for commonality among citizens to support state powers to exclude migrants and to make citizenship for residents conditional.[62]

The focus of republicanism on a political community may seem potentially more exclusive. But a state that dominates non-citizens (within or outside the state) has

---

[58] Cécile Laborde and Miriam Ronzoni, 'What is a Free State? Republican Internationalism and Globalisation', *Political Studies* 64, no. 2 (2016): pp. 279–296, doi:10.1111/1467-9248.12190.

[59] Laborde and Ronzoni (n 58); Jose Luis Marti, 'A Global Republic to Prevent Global Domination', *DIACRÍTICA* 24, no. 2 (2010): pp. 31–72; James Bohman, *Democracy across Borders: From Dêmos to Dêmoi* (Cambridge: MIT Press, 2007).

[60] Michael Walzer, *Spheres of Justice* (Oxford: Martin Robertson, 1983).

[61] Joseph Carens, *The Ethics of Immigration* (Cambridge: Cambridge University Press, 2013); Phillip Cole, *Philosophies of Exclusion: Liberal Political Theory and Immigration* (Edinburgh: Edinburgh University Press, 2000); Arash Abizadeh, 'Democratic Theory and Border Coercion: No Right to Unilaterally Control Your Own Borders', *Political Theory* 36, no. 1 (2008): pp. 37–65.

[62] Kit Wellman, 'Immigration and Freedom of Association', *Ethics* 119, no. 1 (2008): pp. 109–141; David Miller, *Strangers in Our Midst: The Political Philosophy of Immigration* (Cambridge: Harvard University Press, 2016).

to be seen as invidious. Within a state, if non-citizen residents constitute a class vulnerable to domination, this clearly gives rise to a problem that republican theory needs to address.[63] Whether or not those outside borders are inherently dominated is a matter of more debate. Philip Pettit sees bounded states as essential to the project of minimizing domination, and argues that, as a state cannot guarantee membership of a non-dominating polity to all, border controls per se may be seen less as an exercise of arbitrary power, and more as external factors conditioning the freedom of outsiders.[64] But others argue that border controls do represent an exercise of agency, and thus constitute domination of those whose freedom of choice to move for significant reasons they reduce. Thus the logic of republican citizenship requires, if not immediate access to the benefits of citizenship, at least limits on discretionary exclusion and the possibility of contesting those controls.[65]

These are actively debated issues on which considerable disagreement within both traditions continues.

CONCLUSION: THE FUTURE OF LIBERAL AND REPUBLICAN CITIZENSHIP

While the central insights of liberalism stress the importance of respecting individuals as distinct, republicanism emphasizes the relatedness of individuals and the possibilities and problems to which that gives rise. While contemporary republicanism displays a variety and complexity of arguments and perspectives comparable to liberalism, it distinctively combines concerns for liberty and civic engagement in a self-governing political community. Less diametrically opposed to liberalism than a corrective to it, it approaches politics with a different angle of vision. Its perspective on liberty and the participation and solidarity that it entails bring into relief features that contemporary liberals have tended to overlook, or at least to prioritize differently.

Liberal and republican citizenship advance alternative perspectives on the ideals and the possibilities for realizing freedom and equality among citizens. As we

---

[63] Megan Benton, 'The Problem of Denizenship: A Non-domination Framework', *Critical Review of International Social and Political Philosophy* 17, no. 1 (2014): pp. 49–69; Sarah Fine, 'Non-Domination and the Ethics of Migration', *Critical Review of International Social and Political Philosophy* 17, no. 1 (2014): pp. 10–30.

[64] Philip Pettit, *On the People's Terms* (Cambridge: Cambridge University Press, 2012), pp. 161–162.

[65] M. Victoria Costa, 'Republican Liberty and Border Controls', *Critical Review of International Social and Political Philosophy* 19, no. 4 (2016): pp. 400–415, doi: 10.1080/13698230.2015.1066046.

have seen, both face significant challenges that put the very viability of liberal and republican citizenship in question. Here I point to three areas that particularly need further exploration

The first issue is how citizenship can be realized under current conditions of increasing social and economic inequality. How can citizens be seen as free and equal, identify with a common good, or be active citizens when those with work have no time, and those without work lack resources? While egalitarian liberals have emphasized the need for economic redistribution in terms of individual claims of justice and equal opportunity, for republicans it is as the foundation for equal citizenship that economic inequalities among citizens need to be limited. But the contemporary implications of this have so far received limited attention. While Pettit sees the need for a moderate level of redistribution on grounds internal, rather than (as for Rawls) additional, to freedom, others argue that more radical socio-economic implications follow from a concern with republican freedom.[66]

A second issue is whether there is a conception of citizenship that can contribute to addressing the collective action problems that confront us, in particular climate change, and elicit a sense of the common good and collective responsibility at a global level. Here republican citizenship may offer more possibilities, since it focuses on the importance in politics of realizing common as well as protecting individual goods, and is particularly sensitive to the threat to their realization that is posed by sectional interests. Yet there is an issue whether and how citizens, already disengaged and disempowered within nation-states, may be motivated to support such global common goods, and envisage the possibility of effective collective action.

This leads to the final issue: the motivation to participation and solidarity among citizens. How can citizenship motivate without being exclusive? While there has been much discussion of the question whether cultural commonality is a necessary and sufficient basis for solidarity, the possibilities of participation and interaction among citizens are increasingly in question. On the one hand, there is a long-standing view that citizen participation in decision-making on a large scale is impossible or undesirable. However, a wide range of experiments in participation suggest that there may be approaches other than large scale direct democracy or representation for realizing participation, and some theorists suggest that this may be a way to engage citizens in ways that elicit a deliberative approach and concern for the common good at a range of levels. Whether and how these can be elaborated in liberal

---

[66] Pettit (n 7 and n 64); cf. more radical accounts at, e.g., Stuart White, 'The Republican Critique of Capitalism', *Critical Review of International Social and Political Philosophy* 14, no. 5 (2011): pp. 561–579, doi:10.1080/13698230.2011.617119; Alex Gourevitch, *From Slavery to the Cooperative Commonwealth: Labor and Republican Liberty in the Nineteenth Century* (Cambridge: Cambridge University Press, 2014).

and republican terms and whether this possibility can be borne out in practice need further examination.

BIBLIOGRAPHY

Abizadeh, Arash, 'Democratic Theory and Border Coercion: No Right to Unilaterally Control Your Own Borders', *Political Theory* 36, no. 1 (2008): pp. 37–65.

Arendt, Hannah, *The Human Condition* (Chicago: Chicago University Press, 1958).

Arendt, Hannah, *On Revolution* (New York: Penguin, 1977).

Audi, Robert, *Democratic Authority and the Separation of Church and State* (Oxford: Oxford University Press, 2011).

Bacharova, Mira, 'Multicultural Accommodation and the Ideal of Non-domination', *Critical Review of International Social and Political Philosophy* 17, no. 6 (2014): pp. 652–673, doi:10.1080/13698230.2013.826500.

Bader, Veit, *Secularism or Democracy? Associational Governance of Religious Diversity* (Amsterdam: Amsterdam University Press, 2007).

Barry, Brian, *Culture and Equality* (Cambridge: Cambridge University Press, 2001).

Beitz, Charles, *Political Theory and International Relations*, 2nd edition (Princeton: Princeton University Press, 1999).

Bell, Duncan, 'What is Liberalism?', *Political Theory* 42, no. 6 (2014): pp. 682–715, doi: 10.1177/0090591714535103.

Bellamy, Richard, *Political Constitutionalism: A Republican Defense of the Constitutionality of Democracy* (Cambridge: Cambridge University Press, 2007).

Benhabib, Seyla, 'Judgement and the Moral Foundations of Politics in Arendt's Thought', *Political Theory* 16, no. 1 (1988): pp. 29–51.

Benton, Megan, 'The Problem of Denizenship: A Non-Domination Framework', *Critical Review of International Social and Political Philosophy* 17, no. 1 (2014): pp. 49–69.

Berlin, Isaiah, 'Two Concepts of Liberty', in *Four Essays on Liberty* (Oxford: Oxford University Press, 1969).

Bohman, James, *Democracy across Borders: From Dêmos to Dêmoi* (Cambridge: MIT Press, 2007).

Brighouse, Harry, *On Education* (London and New York: Routledge, 2006).

Callan, Eamonn, *Creating Citizens Political Education and Liberal Democracy* (Oxford: Oxford University Press, 1997).

Carens, Joseph, *Culture, Citizenship and Community* (Oxford: Oxford University Press, 2000).

Carens, Joseph, *The Ethics of Immigration* (Cambridge: Cambridge University Press, 2013).

Christman, John and Joel Anderson, eds., *Autonomy and Challenges to Liberalism* (Cambridge: Cambridge University Press, 2009).

Clayton, Matthew, *Justice and Legitimacy in Upbringing* (Oxford: Oxford University Press, 2006).

Cole, Phillip, *Philosophies of Exclusion: Liberal Political Theory and Immigration* (Edinburgh: Edinburgh University Press, 2000).

Costa, M. Victoria, 'Is Neo-Republicanism Bad for Women?' *Hypatia 28*, no. 4 (2013): pp. 921–936.

Costa, M. Victoria, 'Republican Liberty and Border Controls', *Critical Review of International Social and Political Philosophy 19*, no. 4 (2016): pp. 400–415, doi: 10.1080/13698230.2015.1066046.

Dagger, Richard, *Civic Virtues: Rights, Citizenship, and Republican Liberalism* (Oxford: Oxford University Press, 1997).

Dagger, Richard, *Sovereign Virtue. The Theory and Practice of Equality* (Cambridge: Harvard University Press, 2000).

Dworkin, Ronald, *Taking Rights Seriously* (Cambridge: Harvard University Press, 1977).

Dworkin, Ronald, *Sovereign Virtue. The Theory and Practice of Equality* (Cambridge: Harvard University Press, 2000).

Elster, John, 'The Market and the Forum', in James Bohman and William Rehg, eds., *Deliberative Democracy: Essays on Reason and Politics* (Cambridge: MIT Press, 1997): pp. 3–33.

Fine, Sarah, 'Non-Domination and the Ethics of Migration', *Critical Review of International Social and Political Philosophy 17*, no. 1 (2014): pp. 10–30.

Friedman, Marilyn, 'Pettit's Civic Republicanism and Male Domination', in Cécile Laborde and John Maynor, eds., *Republicanism and Political Theory* (Oxford: Blackwell, 2008).

Goodin, Robert, 'Folie républicaine', *Annual Review of Political Science 6* (2003): pp. 55–76.

Gourevitch, Alex, *From Slavery to the Cooperative Commonwealth: Labor and Republican Liberty in the Nineteenth Century* (Cambridge; Cambridge University Press, 2014).

Habermas, Jürgen, *Between Facts and Norms: Contributions to a Discourse Theory of Law and Democracy* (Cambridge: MIT Press, 1996).

Habermas, Jürgen, 'Religion in the Public Sphere', *European Journal of Philosophy 14*, no. 1 (2006): pp. 1–25.

Honohan, Iseult, *Civic Republicanism* (Abingdon and New York: Routledge, 2002).

Kwak, Jun-Hyeok, and Leigh Jenco, eds., *Republicanism in North East Asia* (London: Routledge, 2014).

Kymlicka, Will, *Multicultural Citizenship* (Oxford: Clarendon Press, 1995).

Kymlicka, Will, 'Education for Citizenship', in *Politics in the Vernacular* (Oxford: Oxford University Press, 2001), pp. 291–316.

Laborde, Cécile, *Critical Republicanism: The Hijab Controversy and Political Philosophy* (Oxford: Oxford University Press, 2008).

Laborde, Cécile and Miriam Ronzoni, 'What is a Free State? Republican Internationalism and Globalisation', *Political Studies 64*, no. 2 (2016): pp. 279–296, doi:10.1111/1467-9248.12190.

Larmore, Charles, 'Liberal and Republican Conceptions of Freedom', in Daniel Weinstock and Christian Nadeau, eds., *Republicanism; History, Theory, Practice* (London: Frank Cass, 2004), pp. 96–119.

Levinson, Meira, *The Demands of Liberal Education* (Oxford: Oxford University Press, 2002).

Lovett, Frank, *A General Theory of Domination and Justice* (Oxford: Oxford University Press, 2010).

Lovett, Frank, 'Cultural Accommodation and Domination', *Theory 38*, no. 2 (2010): pp. 243–267.

Marshall, Thomas H., *Citizenship and Social Class and Other Essays* (Cambridge: Cambridge University Press, 1950).

Marti, Jose Luis, 'A Global Republic to Prevent Global Domination', *DIACRÍTICA* 24, no. 2 (2010): pp. 31–72.

Maynor, John, *Republicanism in the Modern World* (Cambridge: Polity, 2003).

Miller, Dale, 'John Stuart Mill's Civic Liberalism', *History of Political Thought* 21, no. 1 (2000): pp. 88–113.

Miller, David, *On Nationality* (Oxford: Oxford University Press, 1997).

Miller, David, *Strangers in Our Midst: The Political Philosophy of Immigration* (Cambridge: Harvard University Press, 2016).

Nussbaum, Martha, *Political Emotions: Why Love Matters for Justice* (Cambridge: Harvard University Press, 2013).

Okin, Susan Moller, *Justice, Gender, and the Family* (New York: Basic Books, 1989).

O'Shea, Tom, 'Disability and Domination: Lessons from Republican Political Philosophy', *Journal of Applied Philosophy*, early view (2016), doi: 10.1111/japp.12149.

Pateman, Carole, 'Feminist Critiques of the Public/Private Dichotomy', in Stanley Benn and Gerald Gaus, eds., *Public and Private in Social Life* (New York: St Martin's Press, 1983), pp. 281–303.

Patten, Alan, 'The Republican Critique of Liberalism', *British Journal of Political Science* 26, no. 1 (1996): pp. 25–44.

Pettit, Philip, *Republicanism: A Theory of Freedom and Government* (Oxford: Oxford University Press, 1997).

Pettit, Philip, *On the People's Terms* (Cambridge: Cambridge University Press, 2012).

Phillips, Anne, 'Feminism and Republicanism; Is This a Plausible Alliance?', *Journal of Political Philosophy* 9, no. 2 (2000): pp. 270–293.

Pocock, J. G. A., *The Machiavellian Moment* (Princeton: Princeton University Press, 1975).

Pogge, Thomas, *World Poverty and Human Rights*, 2nd edition (Cambridge: Polity Press, 2008).

Putnam, Robert, 'E Pluribus Unum: Diversity and Community in the Twenty-first Century', *Scandinavian Political Studies 30* (2007): pp. 137–174.

Rawls, John, *Theory of Justice* (Oxford: Oxford University Press, 1971).

Rawls, John, *Political Liberalism*, 2nd, paperback edition (New York: Columbia University Press, 1996).

Rawls, John, 'The Idea of Public Reason Revisited', *University of Chicago Law Review 64* (1997): pp. 765–807.

Rawls, John, *The Law of Peoples* (Cambridge: Harvard University Press, 1999).

Rawls, John, *Justice as Fairness: A Restatement*, edited by Erin Kelly (Cambridge: Harvard University Press, 2001).

Raz, Joseph, *The Morality of Freedom* (Oxford: Clarendon Press, 1986).

Sandel, Michael, *Democracy's Discontent* (Cambridge: Harvard Belknap, 1998).

Skinner, Quentin, *The Foundations of Modern Political Thought*, 2 volumes (Cambridge: Cambridge University Press, 1978).

Skinner, Quentin, *Liberty before Liberalism* (Cambridge: Cambridge University Press, 1998).

Taylor, Charles, 'Cross-Purposes: The Liberal-Communitarian Debate', in *Philosophical Arguments* (Cambridge: Harvard University Press, 1995), pp. 181–203.

Van der Meer, Tom and Jochem Tolsma, 'Ethnic Diversity and Its Effects on Social Cohesion', *Annual Review of Sociology 40* (2014): pp. 459–478.

Waldron, Jeremy, 'Two-Way Translation: The Ethics of Engaging with Religious Contributions in Public Deliberation', *Mercer Law Review 63* (2012): pp. 845–868.

Walzer, Michael, *Spheres of Justice* (Oxford: Martin Robertson, 1983).

Wellman, Kit, 'Immigration and Freedom of Association', *Ethics 119*, no. 1 (2008): pp. 109–141.

White, Stuart, 'The Republican Critique of Capitalism', *Critical Review of International Social and Political Philosophy 14*, no. 5 (2011): pp. 561–579, doi:10.1080/13698230.2011.617119.

Woltersdorff, Nicholas, *Justice: Rights and Wrongs* (Princeton: Princeton University Press, 2008).

Young, Iris Marion, 'Polity and Group Difference', *Ethics 99* (1989): pp. 250–274.

CHAPTER 6

CITIZENSHIP AND NATIONHOOD

CHAIM GANS*

INTRODUCTION

THE concepts which constitute the title of this chapter refer to two distinct phenomena. Citizenship means membership of a state. Nationhood means membership of a 'nation,' which is a particular type of cultural and/or ethnic collective. A third term, 'nationality,' is equivocal, sometimes meaning

* I worked on this chapter during my 2015–16 stay at the IAS, Princeton. I am most grateful to the Institute for providing me with a wonderful intellectual environment and resources for my work. I am deeply indebted to Rainer Bauböck, Alan Patten, and Anna Stilz for their invaluable comments on earlier drafts of this article.

citizenship, sometimes nationhood. However, the two phenomena are related by much more significant factors than this semantic fact. Some factors spring from normative thinking since the eighteenth century Enlightenment and the subsequent dawn of nationalism. This thinking, in both its liberal and its anti-liberal versions, supported making states' citizenries congruent with groups enjoying a common nationhood; states that achieve this, at least in principle, are therefore called 'nation states.'[1] Other factors that produced a demographic overlap of states' citizenries and national communities reflect social and economic developments. Certain socio-historical theories maintain that capitalism, the transition from an agrarian economy to an industrial one, and the decline of religion produced the need for such congruence.[2] These factors, together with popular support for the normative arguments proposed for making citizenries coterminous with [ethno-] cultural nations, produced the ideologies that justified this overlap and the political movements that aspired to implement it, which together are commonly called 'nationalism.'[3]

In this chapter I first set out the reasons that liberals and anti-liberals have given for making citizenship and nationhood coterminous. Second, I describe the major historical and sociological explanations that were advanced for the processes that helped create this overlap, the methods that states and other political agents have adopted to realize it, and the practical and moral obstacles that these agents have always faced. Third, I discuss the positions of contemporary liberals on the issue, including the position I believe to be appropriate. The discussion concludes that the ideal of full overlap between citizenry and nationhood should be rejected both constitutionally and certainly demographically. However, it endorses arrangements allowing for a limited identification of states' citizenries with one or a few national groups.

[1] Some current uses of the terms 'nation state' and 'national' justify the non-nationalist use of the term nation state. Sometimes it is used to distinguish the modern state from pre-WW I empires, or from pre-Westphalia European city-states, or the ancient Greek polis. The term 'national' is sometimes used for a distinct level of government (national vs. provincial or local). The term 'nation-building' is often used to refer to developing central state capacities rather than cultural homogenization. In this chapter the concept of 'nation state' is used in its nationalist sense. It refers to states that aspire to realize a common nationhood for their citizenries. See also Diener in this volume (situating the notion of citizenship associated with the Westphalian nation state within the whole history of the notion of citizenship).

[2] See below.

[3] Although all ideologies arguing that citizenries should be coterminous with nationhood are nationalist, not all nationalist ideologies demand that citizenries should always be coterminous with nationhood. Ethno-cultural nationalism need not aspire to more than sub-statist forms of self-government (see Chaim Gans, *The Limits of Nationalism* (Cambridge, New York: Cambridge University Press, 2003), chapter 1).

Making Citizenship and Nationhood Coterminous: The History of the Idea

The birth of the modern nation state is commonly dated to the Peace of Westphalia (1648). However, this historical event in fact brought about the birth of European territorial states' sovereignties that were meant to replace the regime of non-territorial sovereignties intertwined on different matters and for different groups of people that dominated Europe before Westphalia.[4] The treaty of Westphalia did not aim to create states whose citizenries each formed a single nation. This ideal developed during the centuries since the treaty, reflecting a variety of considerations which assume that the role of the territorial state is greater than just providing passports to its members and/or dominating them. As we shall see, this variety of considerations has imbued the concept of the nation state with two conceptions of nationhood which differ significantly.[5]

One group of such considerations derives from the advantages of congruency between citizenship and nationhood in establishing both the legitimacy of these states and their capacity to realize certain values and goals and to perform certain necessary roles. For example, if we accept the liberal view that the agents and beneficiaries of political morality are individual human beings, then the authority that states exercise over their citizens can be justified only if they serve their freedom and well-being and respect their moral equality. Many thinkers have argued that a shared nationhood is necessary, or at least helpful, for the state's ability to exercise legitimate authority over its citizens, perform its functions, and realize the essential values just mentioned.

John Stuart Mill famously expressed this view in chapter 16 of *Considerations on Representative Government* (1861). He argued that shared nationhood is almost always necessary for representative government. 'Free institutions are next to impossible in a country made up of different nationalities. Among a people without fellow-feeling, especially if they read and speak different languages, the united public opinion, necessary to the working of representative government, cannot exist.'[6] Thus, for Mill, shared nationhood usually involves a shared language, which is a necessary means for communicating and deliberating about ideas, forming informed views, and reaching shared political understandings. Mill also argued that multinational armies can be turned into instruments for oppression

[4] For a description of this type of regime see Hedley Bull, *The Anarchical Society* (London: Macmillan, 1977), pp. 254–255.

[5] Note 1 above.

[6] John Stuart Mill, *Considerations on Representative Government* (London: Parker, Son, and Bourn, 1861), chapter 16.

if ordinary soldiers consider large parts of the citizenry as if they were foreigners. Contemporary writers such as David Miller and Yael Tamir apply similar arguments to the other roles of the state and the values it is expected to promote, especially social justice.[7]

These arguments for making citizenship coterminous with nationhood have two crucial logical characteristics. First, the arguments reflect values purporting to be universal, that is, values that all humans would subscribe to qua humans and not qua members of any national group, such as freedom, equality, well-being, security, and stability. They are therefore values that *all* states must promote on behalf of *all* their citizens, not merely those citizens who share a particular ethno-cultural nationhood. Second, the arguments assume that the state and its functions enjoy at least a normative priority (even if not always a chronological precedence) over the particular nationhood that should become coterminous with the state's citizenry. Moreover, this particular nationhood is viewed as *a means* for the state to perform the roles it must play on behalf of all its citizens.

These two characteristics generated political and social processes ostensibly designed to ensure congruency between citizenries and nationhood within states. This goal was pursued not only by establishing states for pre-existing ethno-cultural nations, but also by merging different pre-existing cultural and ethnic identities within states into single nations, usually around one of these pre-existing groups.[8] The arguments for making citizenship coterminous with nationhood permit or even require practices called 'melting pots' and 'nation-building.' The ideology endorsing the assimilation of diverse groups and individuals into one nation is called 'civic nationalism,' since the purpose of the shared nationhood is to serve humans as citizens of a state, not to use the state to serve humans as members of a pre-existing ethno-cultural nation. Nevertheless, the methods states employed to achieve such nation-building were often strongly coercive and illiberal.[9]

Civic nationalism was espoused mainly by liberal states invoking Enlightenment values. Such liberalism has also been described as 'color-blind,' since the only nationhood which may be realized at the state and constitutional levels accommodates all citizens. The more particular nationhoods of all other communities within the state are not legally recognized but are allowed expression within civil

---

[7] Yael Tamir, *Liberal Nationalism* (Princeton: Princeton University Press, 1993), especially chapter 6; David Miller, *On Nationality* (Oxford: Clarendon Press, 1995), pp. 93–99. These instrumentalist arguments can also apply to values such as security and stability that are also endorsed by non-liberal ideologies (see Gans (n 3), pp. 18–20).

[8] Anthony D. Smith, *The Ethnic Origins of Nations* (Oxford: Blackwell, 1982), part 2, especially pp. 138–140.

[9] See Gans (n 3), p. 13.

society under the freedoms of expression, association, and religion. France is the most prominent example of a state that purports to implement the ideology of civic nationalism.

It is, however, doubtful whether all current nation-building practices in France could be justified in such terms. France defends its current anti-*hijab* policies principally by reference to the particular French value of *laïcité*, which calls for the separation of church and state and therefore expresses the universal values of civic equality and religious freedom. But the practices of other liberal democracies, especially the U.S., demonstrate that these values do not imply the peculiar French practices. By stressing *laïcité*, France invokes an argument from the second group of reasons for turning the post-Westphalian sovereign states into nation states in the nationalist sense. These reasons are based not on the idea that shared nationhood can help all states promote universal values such as freedom and equality among their citizens, but on the converse idea, namely that the state can be an instrument for an ethno-cultural nation to pursue its particularist values and traditions. This ideology has been dubbed 'ethno-cultural' or 'cultural' nationalism.

All versions of this type of nationalism maintain that people have interests in adhering to their ethnic or original cultures or the groups within which they were raised, in living within them, and in their continued existence.[10] As we shall see, these assumptions can be based and interpreted in various ways which do not necessarily demand full congruency between states' citizenries and nationhood. However, the historically most influential basis of these assumptions in the period between Westphalia and the mid-twentieth century does demand full congruency. This is the world view of anti-Enlightenment nationalism, which is diametrically opposed to liberalism.

According to Isaiah Berlin and Ernest Gellner, this view is characterized by essentialism, moral collectivism, relativism, and particularism.[11] It is essentialist in regarding the division of humans into nations as quasi-natural, akin to the division of animals into different species.[12] Therefore, it is almost impossible for an individual to change national identity. It embraces moral collectivism if national groups enjoy existential and moral priority over their members just as a natural organism enjoys priority over its limbs. The good of the members must therefore derive from the good of the nation and be subordinate to it.[13] This world view endorses moral relativism if it denies the possibility of a universal moral code

---

[10] For the claim that this is the common normative denominator of all versions of nationalism dubbed by historians and sociologists 'ethno-cultural nationalism,' see Gans (n 3), chapter 1.

[11] Ernest Gellner, *Nations and Nationalism* (Oxford: Basil Blackwell, 1983), pp. 48–49; Isaiah Berlin, 'Nationalism: Past Neglect and Present Power,' in *Against the Current: Essays in the History of Idea* (New York: Viking Press, 1980), pp. 333–355.

[12] Gellner (n 11), pp. 6, 49.   [13] Berlin (n 11), pp. 341–342.

applicable to all humans as such. Rather, the substance of morality reflects the codes current within one's nation and the purposes which nature has constituted for it.[14] Finally, it is particularist since moral duties flow not from the rational acknowledgment that like cases must be treated alike, but from commitments based on natural personal relationships such as those existing within the family.[15]

The need for citizenship and nationhood to be coterminous is entailed in more than one way by the assumptions underlying the anti-Enlightenment version of ethno-cultural nationalism. If people's interests in adhering to their cultures and living within their frameworks flow from conceiving of humankind's division into nations as analogous to animals' division into species, then a state which serves the purposes of a certain nation cannot serve the purposes of members of other nations any more than a dog kennel can serve to accommodate horses. Therefore, each nation must have a state of its own which serves its particular needs and goals, and all members of this nation are exclusively eligible to become its citizens. If you are a Turk and wish to become a citizen of Germany, you must become first a member of the German nation, in the same way as, if you are a horse wishing to live in a dog's kennel, you had better first become a dog. Neither is really possible.[16] Less extreme conclusions would be entailed by the other components of the world view under consideration: if the substance of important moral principles applying to particular human beings depends on the code existing within their nations and derives from the purposes of this nation as determined by nature, and if the moral power of these principles stems from common membership in the nation, then a person cannot enjoy citizenship rights in a state without first becoming a member of the nation whose state it is. If you are a Turk and wish to become a German citizen, you must first become a member of the German nation, namely, adapt to German ways of life and accept that Germany is your house, in the same way as, if you are a member of the Doğulu family and wish to live at the Schulz's house, you had better first accept that this is their house, become one of them, and behave accordingly.[17]

---

[14] Berlin (n 11), pp. 341–342.

[15] Berlin (n 11), pp. 342–343. For this particularism and its universalist antithesis in the context of nationalism, see Miller (n 7), chapter 3; Gans (n 3), chapter 6, especially pp. 149–160.

[16] The impossibility of such conversion is suggested by Joseph de Maistre's infamous dictum: 'I have seen Frenchmen, Italians, Russians . . . ; But men I have never met...' (Joseph Marie de Maistre, *Oeuvres complètes de J. Maistre* (Lyon: Librairie Generale Catholique et Classique, 1884), p. 74). This notion of the nation has led to racist conceptions of citizenship. On the history of racist conceptions of citizenship see Fitzgerald in this volume.

[17] The difference between the two analogies illustrates the distinction between racist and assimilationist ethno-cultural nationalisms.

Making Citizenship and Nationhood Coterminous: Socio-historical Explanations and Political Practices

According to the modernist sociologists of nationalism, Ernest Gellner and Benedict Anderson, the two nationalist ideologies, civic and ethno-cultural, were encouraged by socio-historical, economic, and psychosocial forces.[18] Gellner sees nationalism as a necessary socio-historical product of the shift from the agrarian economy typical of Europe until the seventeenth century to the industrial economy that started developing during the eighteenth century to reach its peak in the twentieth century. This shift could not have occurred within small societies divided politically and detached from each other culturally and socially, as European societies were while their economies were mainly agricultural. The shift to industrial society demanded cultural and political unification of large numbers of people in large territories so that they could acquire common languages, traditions, and knowledge enabling them to produce, market, and consume standard goods in large volumes. Gellner's socio-historical explanation for nationalism is compatible with the assimilationist moves adopted by France and other countries in the name of civic nationalism, which helped states to perform their standard tasks and to realize universal human values. Other regions in Europe that lacked a unified government or high culture produced other types of nationalisms. Though Gellner identifies various types (e.g. unifying nationalism, diaspora nationalism[19]), they were all ethno-cultural nationalisms of groups conceiving of themselves as single nations demanding political unification (the Italians and the Germans) or striving to create a nation state of their own (the Irish, the Czechs, the Jews) and often embracing an anti-Enlightenment world view.

The main social and historical forces that Benedict Anderson identifies as motivating nationalism are the invention of print, the weakening of dynastic power as a source of governmental legitimacy, and the demise of religion. The invention of print enabled the creation of large communities conceiving of themselves as unified by one historical story despite the lack of face-to-face acquaintance among their members ('imagined communities'). The weakening of religion created a strong need for an alternative remedy for human distress in the face of mortality, whereas the weakening of dynastic legitimacy created a need for an alternative justification for the exercise of political power.[20] Shared nationhood provides such a source. It also provides a substitute for religion's metaphysical comfort by enabling

---

[18] Gellner (n 11); Benedict Anderson, *Imagined Communities: Reflections on the Origin and Spread of Nationalism*, revised edition (London: Verso, 1991).
[19] Gellner (n 11), pp. 97–109.   [20] Anderson (n 18), pp. 9–22.

humans to conceive of themselves as taking part in, and contributing to, something that began long before their own lives began and hopefully would persist long after their lives end.[21]

Citizenries and communities sharing nationhood became congruent in European and other states using diverse methods. In states where civic nationalism was prominent, the methods were mainly assimilationist. In France Bretons and the people of Provence were forced to give up their languages. In Britain the Welsh were, before the twentieth century, discouraged from using the Welsh language. In states where ethno-cultural nationalism was prominent those people that did not share the appropriate nationhood were excluded in various ways. However, sometimes the two types of nationalism employed the same methods. Ethno-culturalist Poland between the two world wars excluded Jews but attempted to assimilate Ukrainians; nineteenth century Britain, while assimilating the Welsh, excluded Catholics and Jews from full citizenship.

Events in Europe during and after the two world wars show that states and national groups are prone to adopt dreadful measures in order to render their citizenries congruent with the desired nationhood, especially when inspired by the collectivist and essentialist versions of ethno-cultural nationalism described above. Since World War II until recently this version of nationalism had therefore seemed fatally discredited almost throughout the West because of the crimes that were committed on its behalf.[22] The waves of immigration since World War II, which are continuing today with increased intensity, have demonstrated that realizing the ideal of citizenry–nationhood congruency is a Sisyphean task demographically speaking, and an unconscionable one morally speaking. It dooms states attempting to realize this ideal to create vast legal and social inequalities among their citizens and sometimes also systematically to violate their human rights. This holds both for ethno-cultural nationalism, which had implemented ethnic cleansings and genocides, and civic nationalism, which has enforced assimilations, obliterated identities and oppressed minority cultures.

Moreover, the technology, transportation, and communication revolutions of recent decades and the globalization of economies have made the human interests that justified the overlap between citizenship and nationhood much less demanding than previously, for three reasons. First, the conditions they created gave rise to, or increased the importance of, human interests conflicting with those supporting the ideal of citizenship–nationhood congruency, especially individual human interests

---

[21] See Tamir (n 7), chapter 1; Gans (n 3), pp. 52–55; Alan Patten, 'The Humanistic Roots of Linguistic Nationalism,' *History of Political Thought 27*, no. 2 (November 2006): pp. 221–262.

[22] Israel in recent decades is an exception. See my *A Political Theory for the Jewish People* (New York: Oxford University Press, 2016). There are many other exceptions in the post-colonial and post-communist countries alluded to in Will Kymlicka's book *Multicultural Odysseys: Navigating the New International Politics of Diversity* (Oxford: Oxford University Press, 2007). And in recent years some EU countries seem to be on the verge of reviving illiberal ethnic nationalism.

in global economic, social, and professional mobility and more varied and higher education than previously required for conducting a reasonably fulfilling human life. Second, these revolutions also enabled people to satisfy their interests in adhering to their original cultures and continuing to live (partly) within them while being geographically distant from the homelands of these cultures through creating or participating in diaspora communities where they can feel at home when abroad, remain actively involved in a distant home and visit that home frequently.[23] Third, these revolutions produced ever more diverse populations in ever more states, and therefore made a compromise more urgent among the cultural needs of the various groups of which citizenries consist, and between these needs as a whole and the cultural and moral values that citizens must share in order for their states to function.

CONTEMPORARY LIBERALISM: MAKING CITIZENSHIP AND NATIONHOOD PARTLY COTERMINOUS

The pressures to make citizenship and nationhood coterminous have thus waned significantly, at least in the West. However, they have not disappeared. This is so in terms of the meaning they have acquired either within civic or ethno-cultural nationalism. The ethno-cultural demand for congruency, which liberals largely ignored throughout most of the twentieth century, has been discussed widely since the 1980s. Many liberal thinkers, though they reject demands for full congruency between citizenship and cultural nationhood and justly dub their positions 'multicultural' or '[ethno-cultural] liberal nationalist,' support a *partial overlap* between the two. That is, they endorse *the identification of citizenship in different countries with particular cultural or ethno-cultural nations* and advocate directly or indirectly supporting *the preservation of such identities* even where not all citizens of the states in question are members of the ethno-cultural nations identified with the particular country. The congruency ideal within civic nationalism—which seems to have been its sole legitimate meaning for liberals during most of the twentieth century and which has seemed to imply that states' citizens should share a rather *culturally deep* nationhood—has ceased to be understood in this way. Liberal thinkers concerned with the cultural homogeneity required to allow states to function call for much *shallower cultural unity* than has been required and practiced during the

---

[23] See Collyer in this volume.

nineteenth and most of the twentieth centuries. One prominent version of this civic unity requirement hardly deserves the name of nationhood: it requires only a commitment to certain constitutional principles, which is called 'constitutional patriotism'. Below I discuss these two developments.

Shrinking the Overlap between Citizenship and (Ethno-)cultural Nationhood

When interpreting the interests people have in adhering to their cultures and living within their cultural frameworks, liberal thinkers surely cannot share the anti-Enlightenment assumptions that these interests arise from the roles people play as members of a group (like limbs of an organism), and that the collective good of this group, not the good of each individual, is the supreme criterion of political morality. They must assume that human individuals themselves are the basic subjects and beneficiaries of political morality and that as individuals they enjoy a normative priority over their nation. Liberals must assume that nations are not natural but rather social constructs that can be justified only in terms of individual human needs, goals, and values, even where the membership of nations requires real or imagined kinship ties.

Assuming all this, liberal writers in recent decades have proposed several foundations of the interests many people have in adhering to their ethnic or cultural nations. Some writers have focused mainly on justifying the rights of national minorities, others on justifying the right to national self-determination and self-government in general, or the possibility of liberal [ethno-cultural] nationalism. Will Kymlicka and Alan Patten are prominent examples of the first group of writers.[24] Kymlicka emphasizes the importance of culture for individual freedom, arguing that freedom requires a reasonable range of meaningful ways of life from which to choose (different occupations, different ways to develop personal relationships, etc.). Societal cultures provide such options and, since people have deep and strong psychological identity ties with their own culture, the state should enable them to realize their freedom-based interest in culture through assisting them in preserving this very culture, if they so choose.[25] It has to grant them the right to self-government, including the right to be represented in the public sphere (its language, symbols, holidays, etc.). Against this, Alan Patten argues that minorities can exercise freedom by accessing the majority's culture, but that they have a right to their own culture

---

[24] See mainly Will Kymlicka, *Multicultural Citizenship: A Liberal Theory of Minority Rights* (Oxford: Clarendon Press, 1995); Alan Patten, *Equal Recognition: The Moral Foundations of Minority Rights* (Princeton: Princeton University Press, 2014).

[25] Kymlicka (n 24), pp. 84–93.

because of its role in constituting their conceptions of the good, and that the liberal state has a duty to be neutral towards its citizens' conceptions of the good. This neutrality means avoiding granting unequal opportunities for citizens to realize their preferences. Since the state must conduct its affairs through a language and culture, it must establish at least one culture for this purpose, and usually selects the majority's culture. It thereby provides opportunities to the majority's members to pursue their conceptions of the good. Therefore, it must also provide equal opportunities to minority cultures—that is, grant them rights to self-government and to representation in the public sphere.[26]

Kymlicka and Patten focus on the rights of minorities to live within the framework of their culture, but their arguments also apply to majority cultures. In Kymlicka's case, if people have a freedom-based interest in a cultural context which needs to be realized through their own culture, this is true equally of members of majority cultures and members of minority cultures. In Patten's case, the state grants rights to members of minority cultures to live within the framework of their culture because of the formative role culture plays in constituting their conceptions of the good. However, if minority cultures play this role, majority cultures must play a similar role vis-à-vis their members' conceptions of the good.[27]

Moreover, though both Kymlicka and Patten insist that the interests people have in living within their cultures are based on the core liberal values of freedom, equal opportunity, and state neutrality, they end up invoking concerns such as people's interest in adhering to components of their identity under a non-essentialist interpretation of this notion that is compatible with liberalism. Kymlicka argues that people's freedom-based cultural interest needs to be concretized by their own culture because of their strong identity ties with it. Patten argues for minority cultural rights because of the role cultures play in constituting what he calls 'identity-related' preferences, which, he argues, enjoy a special status within peoples' conceptions of the good. It seems to me therefore that one's interest in continuing to be what one

---

[26] Patten (n 24), chapters 3–5.

[27] The rights in question are therefore rights of groups by virtue of their being cultural or ethnocultural nations, not by virtue of being minorities or majorities. For a detailed elaboration of this point as against those who argue for these rights qua minorities' rights, see Gans (n 3), chapter 3; Chaim Gans, 'On Patten's Theory of Minority Rights', *Jerusalem Review of Legal Studies 12*, no. 1 (2015): pp. 66–80, especially section 2. In a book recently published, *The Cultural Defense of Nations: A Liberal Theory of Majority Rights* (Oxford University Press, 2015), Liav Orgad invokes a similar argument against the notion of minority rights in order to argue for what he calls 'majority rights.' Whereas I find the notion of 'minority rights' just theoretically imprecise, I find the notion of 'majority rights' also morally dangerous. It might lead to unjustified hierarchical conceptions of (ethno-) cultural nationalism, wherein national majorities claim to have privileges not only vis-à-vis immigrant groups, but also vis-à-vis other homeland *national* minorities living in the same state. This in fact has happened in Israel, where some academics justify the privileges of the Jewish majority over the Arab minority, though the latter are not immigrants. See Gans (n 22), pp. 72–83.

has been so far, or in leading a life that is compatible with one's basic identity components, is the interest which forms the basis of their arguments.[28]

This interest fulfills a direct, primary, and central role in liberal arguments advanced by thinkers such as Raz and Margalit, Tamir, Miller, and others,[29] who argue for people's cultural interests not only from the perspective of minority rights, but from the perspective of [ethno-]cultural groups generally, both majorities and minorities. To the list of considerations raised by Kymlicka and Patten which imbue the cultural component in people's identities with a specifically liberal aspect—considerations such as freedom and equal opportunity—the aforementioned authors add an array of others. For example, the fact that national cultures penetrate the characters of those who are raised within them and color most of what they do explains why the prosperity or decay of such cultures greatly affects people's well-being and personal self-respect.[30] The fact that many people's endeavors derive their meaning from, or take root and exist mainly within the framework of their national cultures explains not only why people wish to live within their culture, but also why they have an interest in being able to hope that their culture will persist after their death.[31]

All these authors present themselves as liberal multiculturalists or (ethno-) cultural nationalists. They argue either for national minorities' rights only or for the rights of ethno-national groups generally. They do so by invoking either liberal core values or considerations that may be compatible with liberalism and strengthened by its core values. They all invoke these values and considerations as bases for people's interests in living within the framework of their culture, for the self-government of national groups, and for their rights to be present in, and to mold, the public spheres of the states where their members live.

Significantly, none of these liberal writers believes that the rights to self-government and representation in the public sphere entail a right to a distinct statehood. Certainly they do not entail ethno-national groups' right to grant citizenship only to their own members. In this sense, their theories are diametrically opposed to the anti-Enlightenment ethno-cultural nationalism described earlier. However, though their position doesn't require a *full congruency* between cultural nationhood and citizenry, it leads in many cases to a *partial overlap* of this type as a consequence of two facts. The first is the actual ethno-cultural diversity of states' populations, which is not a new phenomenon but is more widespread and intense today. Second,

---

[28] See also Avishai Margalit and Moshe Halbertal, 'Liberalism and the Right to Culture,' *Social Research* 61 (1994): pp. 491–510, p. 504.

[29] Joseph Raz and Avishai Margalit, 'National Self-Determination,' in Joseph Raz, ed., *Ethics in The Public Domain: Essays in the Morality of Law and Politics*, revised edition (Oxford: Clarendon Press, 1994), pp. 125–145; Tamir (n 7); Miller (n 7); Gans (n 3); Margaret Canovan, *Nationhood and Political Theory* (Cheltenham: Edward Elgar, 1996); Margaret Moore, *The Ethics of Nationalism* (Oxford, New York: Oxford University Press, 2001).

[30] Raz and Margalit (n 29).   [31] Gans (n 3), pp. 49–55.

most states don't have territorial and other sufficient resources to grant all their citizens strong cultural rights. The writers supporting these rights are forced, therefore, to provide a criterion for deciding which groups are eligible for such rights. The predominant criterion is: national or homeland groups are eligible; immigrant groups are not.[32] The latter should at most be accorded weaker cultural accommodation rights such as the rights Sikhs have in Britain and Canada not to wear safety helmets when riding motorcycles but to wear their turbans instead. Such rights allow them to individually and partly adhere to their culture. They do not enable them to fully live the major parts of their lives within it.[33]

This criterion implies support for partial congruency between citizenship and nationhood: the citizenries of a particular state, even if they are not necessarily coterminous with one nation, are still identified with one nation or a limited number of nations to which many but not all this state's citizens belong. This partial overlap creates two types of citizens: those whose nationhood is present in the public sphere of the state and is being served by its politics, and those whose cultural nations do not enjoy these privileges. Of course, immigrants are free to assimilate into the host nations, but if they choose not to do so, as such they have lesser cultural rights than citizens belonging to the host nations.

On the face of it the partial overlap of citizenship and nationhood produces two significant problems for liberals: inequality in citizenship, and insufficient social cohesion.[34] Such cohesion was described above as the main concern of civic nationalism, to which it responded by advocating full congruency of citizenship and nationhood through cultural mingling and nation-building.

As for inequality in cultural rights between homeland and immigrant groups, liberals respond to it in three different ways. Some consider it an unavoidable but morally explainable and tolerable evil; others deny that it is an evil; yet others view it as unacceptable. Authors in the first group argue that immigration is in most cases voluntary. Most immigrants intend to integrate into the culture or one of the cultures of their host state, and those who do not should be considered to have known that their new state could not allow them to live fully within the framework of their original culture. Immigrants should therefore be considered as having voluntarily surrendered their right to live within the framework of their original culture

[32] By 'homeland groups' I mean all groups that have a historical justification for considering a country to be the place where they acquired their distinctness as an [ethno-]cultural group. Such groups would of course include indigenous communities, native populations, original nations, aborigines, but also groups such as African-Americans in the U.S, Jews in Israel/Palestine, and settlers' nations in the new world countries.

[33] See Kymlicka (n 24), pp. 26–33; Gans (n 3), pp. 58–65; Chaim Gans, 'Individuals' Interest in the Preservation of Their Culture: Its Meaning, Justification and Implications,' *Journal of Law and Ethics of Human Rights 1*, no. 1 (2007): pp. 6–16, doi: 10.2202/1938-2545.1001.

[34] Maas in this volume discusses multilevel federal differentiation as another potential source of inequality of citizenship in contemporary democratic states.

in their new state. The main problem with this explanation for the lesser rights of immigrants is that it cannot apply to their descendants,[35] who sometimes wish to live in the new country within the framework of a distinct culture related to that of their ancestors.[36]

The position that denies the moral significance of unequal citizenship between immigrants and homeland groups invokes the inherent geographic and historic particularity of ethno-cultural nationhood. According to it, people's interest in living within the framework of their culture and preserving it historically is anchored in this particularity. It is characteristic of the Sikhs' interest in living within the framework of their culture and of the Poles' interest in doing the same that they are interests in doing so respectively in the Punjab and in Poland, that is, their cultural homelands.[37] Refraining from recognizing the rights of Sikh and Polish immigrants in Britain to fully live within the framework of their original cultures in Britain is therefore not an unavoidable evil resulting from the British state's lack of resources: it is hardly an evil at all and analogous to the British state's refraining from providing medicines to healthy citizens while providing them to the sick.

An additional argument is that ethno-cultural nations are social constructs that, like states, primarily exist in the global social arena, not in the domestic one. The distribution of goods necessary for their existence—territories and public spaces in which they rule themselves and reproduce themselves—should therefore be a matter for global, not intra-state, distributive justice.[38] If such global distribution is in force, then it is existentially feasible (and should also be legally feasible) for British citizens of Sikh or Polish origin to be partly involved with their original cultures as they are being lived in their homelands and to return to live there if they so wish.[39]

[35] Some writers have also questioned the soundness of attributing voluntariness to many first-generation immigrants. For references and important discussions of these issues, see Rainer Bauböck, 'Cultural Citizenship, Minority Rights, and Self-Government,' in Thomas Alexander Aleinikoff and Douglas Klusmeyer, eds., *Citizenship Today: Global Perspectives and Practices* (Washington: Carnegie Endowment for International Peace, 2001), pp. 319–348, pp. 337–341; Patten (n 24), chapter 8.

[36] We should distinguish between immigrants' descendants as such, who demand strong cultural rights, and immigrants' descendants who become a distinct homeland group. On this category see below. The justification from voluntariness for not granting immigrants strong cultural rights applies to none.

[37] The groups in question typically are historical groups with geographic particularity (see Raz and Margalit (n 29), p. 445; Gans (n 3), chapter 4).

[38] Such a globalist conception of cultural and national rights is presupposed, I think, by international law. Philippe Van Parijs also seems to allude to it in *Linguistic Justice for Europe and for the World* (Oxford, New York: Oxford University Press, 2011). I assume such a conception explicitly in my books *The Limits of Nationalism* (n 3); *A Just Zionism: On the Morality of the Jewish State* (Oxford, New York: Oxford University Press, 2008); *A Political Theory for the Jewish People* (n 22). This implies that ideally there should be a global authority that has the power to bring about, when this is possible, a distribution of territories and public spaces.

[39] This possibility is associated with the notion of transnational citizenship, which is one of the types of what Smith in this volume calls 'quasi-citizenship.' See also Rainer Bauböck, 'Stakeholder Citizenship and Transnational Political Participation: A Normative Evaluation of External Voting,' *Fordham Law Review 75*, no. 5 (2007): pp. 2393–2447.

This option would not be open to British citizens of Scottish origin unless Scotland enjoys powers to establish a specific Scottish culture.

Two types of hard cases regarding entitlements to strong nationhood rights remain also hard under this global distribution approach: one is dispersed groups such as the Roma in Europe and the Jews there prior to the establishment of Israel; the other is the descendants of immigrants who become a kind of a homeland group or quasi-national group in the country to which their ancestors migrated by developing a culture and a history that is distinct both from the groups existing in the country where they live, and from those existing in the country or countries whence their ancestors came. The latter type may or may not be territorially concentrated. The problems these two types of hard cases pose can sometimes be solved partly by the ordinary remedies provided by liberal ethno-cultural nationalism: some strong territorial rights in the case of the newly formed national groups, and strong language rights and institutional arrangements in the case of dispersed groups.

The last two justifications of the distinction between the citizenship rights of homeland groups and immigrant groups do not suffer from the weakness of the first response, which was based on the voluntary nature of immigration and therefore did not apply to immigrants' descendants.

The third liberal response to the current problem of inequality in citizenship is to treat it as an evil which is avoidable and therefore intolerable. One version of this response holds that the state should grant positive constitutional or legal rights supporting equally all its resident cultural groups without distinguishing between immigrants and non-immigrants. A second version employs the traditional liberal tools for dealing with pluralism and diversity: the privatization of identities and cultural concerns, allowing citizens to pursue them via their rights to freedom of speech, association, and religion. The liberal state should therefore refrain from granting any 'group-differentiated' rights to national and cultural groups, and should avoid creating inequality among citizens originating in different ethnic or cultural groups.

Liberals holding the first version of this response to the inequality problem, who believe that the state should grant positive supportive rights to homeland and immigrant cultures alike, may be called 'radical multiculturalists.'[40] Among liberal writers they alone seem ready to disconnect the ties between citizenship and nationhood. The standard argument against their proposal is that it is impractical since states' public life can be conducted in only a few languages, and therefore states would necessarily not be able to grant equal recognition to all the languages their citizens might use. Anna Stilz, currently the main spokesperson of this type of multiculturalism, acknowledges this practical difficulty but thinks it is not an obstacle to an equal

---

[40] The term is Miller's in *On Nationality* (n 7), pp. 120, 131–140, referring to Iris Marion Young. A more recent proponent of this view is Anna Stilz, discussed below.

distribution of cultural rights among national and immigrant groups.[41] According to her, the decision on who gets strong cultural (mainly language) rights within a state and who doesn't should be based not on the distinction between national and immigrant groups but rather on democratic majority language use in the state as a whole and in those regions of it where minority national or immigrant groups are concentrated. If a particular ethno-cultural group, either national or immigrant, doesn't have such majority, it would not enjoy these rights—but because the group fails democratically, not because it is initially less privileged.

I am not certain that this solution would solve the problem of equality even in light of the example Stilz cites, namely Iceland. Iceland grants strong language rights to its Polish immigrant minority. However, it requires all its citizens to speak Icelandic, because this is the language in which Iceland conducts its public life. Moreover, Iceland requires all its citizens to learn to speak English, because its economy depends on the EU and the world economy.

I doubt that Stilz's democratic criterion for the distribution of strong language rights explains the Icelandic case as described. If all citizens of Iceland learn to speak English, it could become the state's language of politics and economy. By accepting that it is justified nevertheless to demand that Icelandic Poles be able to speak Icelandic as well, because this is the language of Iceland's politics and economy, Stilz must either accept the privileged status of national groups vis-à-vis immigrants or reject Iceland's demand that Icelandic should be the country's language of politics and economy. Moreover, by accepting that Iceland's Poles must learn to speak both Icelandic and English, while demanding that native Icelanders learn to speak only English, Stilz fails to establish equality between these two groups. She just exchanges one inequality (granting collective language rights not to immigrants but only to national groups) with another.

Let me turn now to liberals who believe that equality in citizenship can be ensured by the traditional liberal freedoms of expression, association, and religion. Contemporary liberals who argue this generally differ from the color-blind liberals of most of the twentieth century. They discuss the interests people have in their original cultures in great detail. They don't just ignore them. Brian Barry's book *Culture and Equality* is the most salient example.[42] However, I doubt the sufficiency of his account. To the traditional liberal freedoms mentioned above as means for

---

[41] See Anna Stilz, 'Civic Nationalism and Language Policy,' *Philosophy and Public Affairs* 37, no. 3 (2009): pp. 257–292, doi: 10.1111/j.1088-4963.2009.01160.x.

[42] Brian Barry, *Culture and Equality* (Cambridge: Polity Press, 2001). There are other prominent contemporary liberal thinkers holding this position, e.g., Jeremy Waldron, 'Minority Cultures and the Cosmopolitan Alternative,' *University of Michigan Journal of Law Reform* 25 (1991–1992): pp. 751–793; Samuel Scheffler, 'Immigration and the Significance of Culture,' *Philosophy and Public Affairs* 35, no. 2 (2007): pp. 93–125, doi: 10.1111/j.1088-4963.2007.00101.x. Chandran Kukathas, *The Liberal Archipelago: A Theory of Diversity and Freedom* (Oxford: Oxford University Press, 2003) defends a more libertarian argument about equal toleration based on strong individual rights to freedom of conscience, association, and dissociation and a weak liberal state conceived as a commons that distinct communities agree to share.

accommodating citizens' cultural interests, Barry adds the requirement to attenuate the majority's cultural identity so that the burden of relinquishing components of cultural identity is imposed on the majority as well as on minorities; more import-antly, as a consequence of attenuating the majority's cultural identity (e.g., relin-quishing the dress codes that have formed part of its public culture), the advantage of being able to adhere to some components of one's cultural identity becomes open also to the members of minorities without making special exceptions on their behalf to general laws.[43] This latter proposal might satisfy people's interests in adhering to their identity, though not as fully as the other liberal approaches discussed above do. However, if we distinguish the *interest* people have *in adhering individually* and partly to their culture from their stronger interest in *living as fully as possible within the framework* of their culture, then Barry's proposals in *Culture and Equality* do not seem to even begin to address the latter—especially if, as Barry implies, people are required to relinquish their original languages.[44] Barry thus seems to underrate the significance of the effect of color-blind liberalism on the ability of citizens belonging to minority nations to continue living within the framework of their culture.[45] He seems to ignore the collective action problems this poses for them, problems that will surely prove to be insurmountable, even though national minorities have as great an interest as the majority in continuing to live within the framework of their culture.

If my reservations regarding the radical multiculturalists' and the color-blind lib-erals' proposals for accommodating ethno-cultural diversity within citizenries are sound, a distinction between the rights of citizens belonging to homeland groups and the rights of citizens belonging to immigrant groups regarding their cultural or ethnic nationhood—as opposed to their civil, political, and economic rights—seems unavoidable. My view is that the inequality this distinction creates is mor-ally insignificant or justifiable: as noted above, migrants should be allowed to fully assimilate into one of the homeland groups in their new country, or to realize their aspirations to live within their culture of origin through forming diasporas within which they can maintain their culture without establishing it within a territory, or to return to their country of origin where their culture is established. If this view or the view that homeland groups and immigrants are morally distinct because migra-tion is voluntary, is right, then a partial overlap between citizenship and ethno-cultural nationhood is acceptable.

---

[43] Barry (n 42), pp. 80–81.
[44] A common language is one of the components of Barry's required 'civic nationalism,' which should unify all citizens. This implies that members of minorities must not use their original languages when acting in the public sphere.
[45] Barry (n 42) does not pay any serious attention to the distinction between immigrant groups and national groups. He mentions the latter in passing, and seems to consider their separate existence (also linguistically) as an unavoidable necessity that should be lamented by liberals (p. 227). Barry seemed to have different views in an earlier piece: 'Self-Government Revisited,' in David Miller and Larry Siedentop, eds., *The Nature of Political Theory* (Oxford: Clarendon Press, 1983), pp. 121–154.

Shallowing the Cultural Depth of Civic Nationhood

All the liberal approaches to the cultural diversity and nationhood plurality of contemporary states' citizenries I have set out must confront the problem of social cohesion. States require a minimum of social cohesion in order to fulfill their roles and realize general political values. This problem, as we saw, was the main concern of classical civic nationalism, the one that France exemplifies, or at least used to exemplify, in its most paradigmatic form. Each of the contemporary liberal approaches discussed above acknowledges cultural diversity and nationhood plurality of citizenries as a matter of fact, but also advocates some constitutional or legal accommodation of this diversity and plurality. Can they also solve the problem of cohesion of states' citizenries?

Several writers answer this question affirmatively, and in my view rightly. They all propose to solve the cohesion problem by attenuating the cultural commonalities of citizens. Some—David Miller is a prominent example—believe that these commonalities should be only minimally reduced, approximating the French classic paradigm of civic nationhood. Yet he finds the American 'hospitable character of identity,' which Michael Walzer describes as consisting of '... the flag, the Pledge, the Fourth, the Constitution,' too thin to perform the task of forging common identities among citizenries of states.[46]

Conversely, other writers believe that civic nationhood can be attenuated to a point where it doesn't, in my view, deserve to be called nationhood at all: they believe that, to generate sufficient social cohesion for states to function, it is enough that their citizens are all committed to basic constitutional principles such as democracy, equality, and freedom. This view has been dubbed 'constitutional patriotism,' a view that became popular after Jürgen Habermas endorsed it.[47]

Between these two extremes there is a great variety of options, each with its own nuances. Two salient intermediary options are (1) the demand that citizens identify not only with the normative content of the basic constitutional principles of justice and freedom, but also 'with the particular, historically situated way in which [their country's] institutions embody values such as liberty, justice and democracy';[48] and (2) the demand for a common language.

It seems to me that all the proposals listed above are justified in the following manner: First, constitutional patriotism can serve as a sufficient (minimum)

---

[46]   Miller's reference to Walzer is in Miller (n 7), p. 136, note 29. His general discussion of the issue is in pp. 141–145.

[47]   On the concept of constitutional patriotism, the way it has developed, its possible meanings, and the demands it could involve, see Jan-Werner Müller, *Constitutional Patriotism* (Princeton: Princeton University Press, 2007).

[48]   Andrew Mason, *Community, Solidarity and Belonging* (Cambridge, New York: Cambridge University Press, 2000). See also Maurizio Viroli, *For Love of Country: An Essay on Patriotism and Nationalism* (New York: Oxford University Press, 1995).

requirement with regard to multinational components of states' citizenries. States that cannot reach at least a consensus among their national groups around some basic universal constitutional principles cannot really function peacefully in a non-authoritarian manner. They would do better to fall apart and somehow reconstitute themselves. Second, when the ethno-cultural diversity of a citizenry is a consequence not only of its multinationality but also of the presence of immigrant minorities, the members of such minorities should be required to speak the language of the national group amongst whom they live and predominantly conduct their political and economic lives. This principle follows from acknowledging the privileges of homeland groups discussed above. Third, any additional cohesion requirement of common nationhood should be considered desirable but not necessary. It should be adopted if the economic and moral price of doing so is not too high, for it would be conducive for the functioning of the state. Fourth, each state should choose a point on the spectrum of options described above—constitutional patriotism or thicker options—in light of the particular mixes and circumstances of its citizenry, the histories of its various components, their numbers, their geographies, their economies, etc. It is pointless to propose a single universal right answer. Moreover, balancing between these various complex normative and practical considerations will usually not lead to clear-cut solutions. Compromise between the groups by resorting to moral considerations which do not belong particularly to the realm of cultural and national justice would be necessary.

I discussed above the relationship between citizenship and nationhood while assuming a conception of citizenship which, following the distinctions between liberal and republican conceptions of citizenship, might be considered a legal and formal conception. This conception, which in her chapter in this volume Iseult Honohan attributes to liberalism, is opposed to the more robust republican conception. The latter refers to participation in a common good whose sharers have active concerns and interests in and therefore may not be dominated in this regard by other citizens. This republican conception of citizenship arguably creates tensions between notions of citizenship and nationhood which are not solvable by what I have described as the current liberal response to it: shrinking the overlap between ethno-cultural nationhood and citizenship, shallowing the cultural depth of civic nationhood, and discriminating against members of immigrant groups with regard to their possible interest in common goods shared by the vast majority of their fellow citizens.

I cannot here fully explore this issue. But I'm not convinced that this criticism is justified. First, the liberal solution to the tension between citizenship and nationhood does leave a common good in which all citizens, including those who belong to immigrant groups, can share: the goods underlying civic nationhood. Even if these are as culturally thin as in the case of constitutional patriotism, they are thick enough to attract the engagement of all citizens. Second, the liberal solution allows most citizens, who belong to homeland groups, to share in culturally thick common goods. Third, the liberal solution to the tension between citizenship and nation-hood leaves citizens who are members of immigrant minorities the choice between fully integrating within the homeland group or one of the homeland groups of their host country, or preserving their original nationhood as members of a national diaspora. The latter will not be full members of the homeland group or groups of their host country, but this would be their own choice, not a result of being domi-nated by other citizens. At the same time they will also be partial members of their country of origin.

Conclusion

I have described in this chapter a process whereby the idea that states' citizenries should become fully coterminous with nationhood developed from two different directions since the Peace of Westphalia until the mid-twentieth century, and the process whereby this idea has since been attenuated from both directions. Strong counter-Enlightenment and anti-liberal ethno-cultural nationalism and strong civic nationalism have learnt how to match each other, taking the forms of liberal multiculturalism or liberal ethno-cultural nationalism, on the one hand, and thin civic nationalism, or constitutional patriotism, on the other.

My description of the latter process, namely, of the ways in which strong ethno-cultural nationalism and strong civic nationalism learned how to fit each other, was accompanied by a normative argument sympathetic to this process and its current outcomes in some Western countries. It is difficult to foresee the ways in which this process will evolve. The rights and wrongs on these matters depend on historical developments that no one can fully foresee.

Bibliography

Anderson, Benedict, *Imagined Communities: Reflections on the Origin and Spread of Nationalism*, revised edition (London: Verso, 1991).

Barry, Brian, 'Self-Government Revisited,' in David Miller and Larry Siedentop, eds., *The Nature of Political Theory* (Oxford: Clarendon Press, 1983), pp. 121–154.

Barry, Brian, *Culture and Equality* (Cambridge: Polity Press, 2001).

Bauböck, Rainer, 'Cultural Citizenship, Minority Rights, and Self-Government,' in Thomas Alexander Aleinikoff and Douglas Klusmeyer, eds., *Citizenship Today: Global Perspectives and Practices* (Washington: Carnegie Endowment for International Peace, 2001), pp. 319–348.

Bauböck, Rainer, 'Stakeholder Citizenship and Transnational Political Participation: A Normative Evaluation of External Voting,' *Fordham Law Review* 75, no. 5 (2007): pp. 2393–2447.

Berlin, Isaiah 'Nationalism: Past Neglect and Present Power,' in *Against the Current: Essays in the History of Idea* (New York: Viking Press, 1980), pp. 333–355.

Bull, Hedley, *The Anarchical Society* (London: Macmillan, 1977).

Canovan, Margaret, *Nationhood and Political Theory* (Cheltenham: Edward Elgar, 1996).

de Maistre, Joseph Marie, *Oeuvres complètes de J. Maistre* (Lyon: Librairie Generale Catholique et Classique, 1884).

Gans, Chaim, *The Limits of Nationalism* (Cambridge, New York: Cambridge University Press, 2003).

Gans, Chaim, 'Individuals' Interest in the Preservation of Their Culture: Its Meaning, Justification and Implications,' *Journal of Law and Ethics of Human Rights* 1, no. 1 (2007): pp. 6–16, doi: 10.2202/1938-2545.1001.

Gans, Chaim, *A Just Zionism: On the Morality of the Jewish State* (Oxford, New York: Oxford University Press, 2008).

Gans, Chaim, 'On Patten's Theory of Minority Rights,' *Jerusalem Review of Legal Studies* 12, no. 1 (2015): pp. 66–80.

Gans, Chaim, *A Political Theory for the Jewish People* (New York: Oxford University Press, 2016).

Gellner, Ernest, *Nations and Nationalism* (Oxford: Basil Blackwell, 1983).

Kymlicka, Will, *Multicultural Citizenship: A Liberal Theory of Minority Rights* (Oxford: Clarendon Press, 1995).

Kymlicka, Will, *Multicultural Odysseys: Navigating the New International Politics of Diversity* (Oxford: Oxford University Press, 2007).

Kukathas, Chandran, *The Liberal Archipelago: A Theory of Diversity and Freedom* (Oxford: Oxford University Press, 2003).

Margalit, Avishai and Moshe Halbertal, 'Liberalism and the Right to Culture,' *Social Research* 61 (1994): pp. 491–510.

Mason, Andrew, *Community, Solidarity and Belonging* (Cambridge, New York: Cambridge University Press, 2000).

Mill, John Stuart, *Considerations on Representative Government* (London: Parker, Son, and Bourn, 1861).

Miller, David, *On Nationality* (Oxford: Clarendon Press, 1995).

Moore, Margaret, *The Ethics of Nationalism* (Oxford, New York: Oxford University Press, 2001).

Müller, Jan-Werner, *Constitutional Patriotism* (Princeton: Princeton University Press, 2007).

Orgad, Liav, *The Cultural Defense of Nations: A Liberal Theory of Majority Rights* (Oxford: Oxford University Press, 2015).

Patten, Alan, 'The Humanistic Roots of Linguistic Nationalism,' *History of Political Thought* 27, no. 2 (November 2006): pp. 221–262.

Patten, Alan, *Equal Recognition: The Moral Foundations of Minority Rights* (Princeton: Princeton University Press, 2014).

Raz, Joseph and Avishai Margalit, 'National Self-Determination,' in Joseph Raz, ed., *Ethics in The Public Domain: Essays in the Morality of Law and Politics*, revised edition (Oxford: Clarendon Press, 1994), pp. 125–145.

Scheffler, Samuel, 'Immigration and the Significance of Culture,' *Philosophy and Public Affairs* 35, no. 2 (2007): pp. 93–125, doi: 10.1111/j.1088-4963.2007.00101.x.

Smith, Anthony D., *The Ethnic Origins of Nations* (Oxford: Blackwell, 1982).

Stilz, Anna, 'Civic Nationalism and Language Policy,' *Philosophy and Public Affairs 37*, no. 3 (2009): pp. 257–292, doi: 10.1111/j.1088-4963.2009.01160.x.

Tamir, Yael, *Liberal Nationalism* (Princeton: Princeton University Press, 1993).

Van Parijs, Philippe, *Linguistic Justice for Europe and for the World* (Oxford, New York: Oxford University Press, 2011).

Viroli, Maurizio, *For Love of Country: An Essay on Patriotism and Nationalism* (New York: Oxford University Press, 1995).

Waldron, Jeremy, 'Minority Cultures and the Cosmopolitan Alternative,' *University of Michigan Journal of Law Reform 25* (1991–1992): pp. 751–793.

CHAPTER 7

....

THE HISTORY OF RACIALIZED CITIZENSHIP

....

DAVID SCOTT FITZGERALD[*]

MOMENTS OF RACIALIZED CITIZENSHIP: KEY CONCEPTS

....

How have governments over the last two and half millennia used race to decide who can be a citizen? Major cycles defy a teleological description of progress toward deracialization over the entire period. High points of racialized citizenship in ancient Athens, late medieval Iberia, the United States from the late eighteenth to mid-twentieth centuries, several countries around World War II, and apartheid

* The author thanks Rawan Arar and Areli Palomo-Contreras for their research assistance.

South Africa were followed by lulls. Since the mid-twentieth century, a strong international norm has emerged against racialized citizenship, though it is not dead in practice.[1] The following pages define race, the different moments at which citizenship can be racialized, and the broad patterns of racialization and deracialization at each of those moments. While there are no irons laws of history that define the precise conditions under which policies are racialized, these outcomes have been shaped by the formation of polities based on a strong sense of common descent,[2] colonization and decolonization,[3] and interstate relations.[4] A historical record centuries older than standard accounts of racialized citizenship reveals patterns of policy and their causes.

Racism refers to the sorting of social groups by their supposedly inherited and unchangeable physical attributes and/or phenotype, attributing differential moral and mental capacities to those physical characteristics, and then using those putative differences to legitimate the unequal distribution of resources and treatment. Race is a subset of ethnicity—the social process of making ascriptive distinctions among groups using language, history, descent, traditions, or religion. What makes race distinctive from other forms of ethnicity is the perceived inalterability of belonging to the category and/or emphasis on phenotype.

Citizenship may be ethnicized, or more narrowly racialized, at four distinct moments. Three of these moments emphasize the external dimension of citizenship—the legal nationality of an individual vis-à-vis other states. Nationality is defined through rules of birthright acquisition, naturalization, and denationalization. The fourth moment of potential racialization is the internal dimension of citizenship—the status, rights, and obligations of a group or individual within a state. Across all of these moments, racialization may consist of negative discrimination against a particular group and/or a positive preference that favors a particular group.

[1] On the role of international norms in immigration and nationality law, see Kristin Surak, 'Convergence in Foreigners' Rights and Citizenship Policies? A Look at Japan,' *International Migration Review* 42, no. 3 (2008): pp. 550–575; David Scott FitzGerald and David Cook-Martín, *Culling the Masses: The Democratic Origins of Racist Immigration Policies in the Americas* (Cambridge: Harvard University Press, 2014). See, more generally, John W. Meyer et al., 'World Society and the Nation State,' *American Journal of Sociology* 103, no. 1 (1997): pp. 144–181.

[2] Aristide R. Zolberg, 'The Formation of New States as a Refugee-Generating Process,' *The Annals of the American Academy of Political and Social Science* 467, no. 1 (1983): pp. 24–38; Rogers Brubaker, *Citizenship and Nationhood in France and Germany* (Cambridge: Harvard University Press, 1992); Michael Mann, *The Dark Side of Democracy: Explaining Ethnic Cleansing* (Cambridge: Cambridge University Press, 2005).

[3] George M. Fredrickson, *Racism: A Short History* (Princeton: Princeton University Press, 2002); Christian Joppke, *Selecting by Origin: Ethnic Migration in the Liberal State* (Cambridge: Harvard University Press, 2005).

[4] Rogers Brubaker and Jaeeun Kim, 'Transborder Membership Politics in Germany and Korea,' *European Journal of Sociology* 52, no. 1 (2011): pp. 21–75; FitzGerald and Cook-Martín (n 1).

Rules about birthright define who owns the status of citizen from the moment a baby draws its first breath. 'All states are "ethnic" in the loosest sense that birth is the usual way of becoming a member of a state.'[5] If all states are ethnic in this loose sense, far fewer are racial in the narrower sense that they only give citizenship to some racially defined group at birth while excluding others. The history of birthright citizenship in the longue durée includes cycles of racialization and deracialization. The principal theoretical dispute about what explains these configurations has revolved around the nature of *jus sanguinis*, the principle of descent, and *jus soli*, the principle of territory, in guiding birthright citizenship. According to the controversial legacies of nationhood perspective associated with Rogers Brubaker, states tend to adopt *jus sanguinis* where an understanding of nationhood is based on ethnicity or descent, while states tend to adopt *jus soli* where an understanding of nationhood is framed by the political and territorial boundaries of the state.[6]

A second potential moment for assigning nationality is through naturalization. The most obvious, but historically rare, form of racist naturalization is to restrict eligibility to foreigners who are part of a racially defined group and to deny it to all others. The United States from 1790 to 1952 and Nazi Germany practiced such policies. Contemporary cases are easier to identify when naturalization is analyzed as a whole system of policy regulating admission and membership rather than by narrowly focusing on naturalization rules alone. In most cases, admission to the territory is a precursor to naturalization. Many naturalization rules are not themselves racialized, but when considered together with immigrant admissions rules and practices, a system of racialized naturalization is revealed. There has been a sharp reduction since the late 1930s in the use of race as a criterion of selection in immigration policy. That fact does not mean that hidden racial criteria have been eliminated altogether or that they are guaranteed to vanish in the future. Positive preferences for named ethnic groups are more prevalent than negative discrimination against named groups.[7]

The third moment of potential racialization is denationalization. 'Corporate expulsions' of whole groups, as compared to forcibly moving groups within a country, first began in Western Europe during the Middle Ages.[8] Even practices as abhorrent as ethnic cleansing are not necessarily racist when groups or individuals are given the coerced option to assimilate, because assimilation suggests that a social boundary can be crossed. Racialized denationalizations accompanied expulsions and population transfers on a massive scale following the remaking of nation-states around the two world wars. Of all the moments where nationality is defined, the use of racial criteria in denationalization has become the most illegitimate.

   [5] Joppke (n 3), p. 240.   [6] Brubaker (n 2).   [7] FitzGerald and Cook-Martín (n 1).
   [8] Benjamin Z. Kedar, 'Expulsion as an Issue of World History,' *Journal of World History* 7, no. 2 (2005): pp. 165–180, p. 168.

Denaturalization for racial reasons continues in thin disguise to the present day but is relatively rare and the object of international opprobrium.

The fourth moment of potential racialization is the internal dimension of citizenship, which can be separated into legal status and substantive practice. As with the acquisition of citizenship, cycles of racialization and deracialization have marked this history, though racism has become increasingly illegitimate since the postcolonial Cold War era. The practice of citizenship continues to be racialized much more than citizenship status. Even the most homogeneous countries include ethnic, if not specifically racial divisions, and differential access to the social, political, and civil rights of citizenship reflects these divisions.

Barbarians and Infidels

In the prevailing scholarly view, racism was unknown to the ancients. For example, ancient Chinese thought barbarians could become Chinese through a process of cultural transformation, suggesting a civilizational but not strictly racial hierarchy.[9] The standard scholarly position is that racism did not emerge until the onset of long-distance European colonization of the rest of the world beginning in the late fifteenth century.[10]

However, there is extensive evidence of at least proto-racialized citizenship in antiquity. Racial citizenship arguably may have been associated with democracy. The classical Athenian notions of citizenship were proto-racial in that they were based on the notion that ecological environments created immutable physical and moral differences between groups. Greeks were superior to racialized barbarians in this scheme.[11] Eligibility for citizenship in ancient Athens required the perceived capacity to rule. Aristotle's *Politics* argued that 'natural slaves' are incapable of ruling and benefit from being governed by masters inherently endowed with a higher capacity. Most slaves in ancient Greece were barbarians, particularly in Athens, where the enslavement of Athenians was prohibited. Prominent philosophers claimed that metics, foreign denizens, also lacked the capacity for self-rule.[12] Legally, Athenian

[9] Frank Dikötter, 'Group Definition and the Idea of "Race" in Modern China (1793–1949),' *Ethnic and Racial Studies* 13, no. 3 (1990): pp. 420–432, p. 421.
[10] Lewis Hanke, *Aristotle and the American Indians* (London: Hollis and Carter, 1959); David Theo Goldberg, *Racist Culture* (Cambridge: Blackwell, 1993); Fredrickson (n 3).
[11] Benjamin H. Isaac, *The Invention of Racism in Classical Antiquity* (Princeton: Princeton University Press, 2004).
[12] J.G.A. Pocock, 'The Ideal of Citizenship Since Classical Times,' in Gershon Shafir, ed., *The Citizenship Debates* (Minneapolis: The University of Minnesota Press, 1998), pp. 31–42, p. 33.

citizenship required birth to an Athenian father, and after the passage of the Periclean law in 451 BCE, birth to both an Athenian mother and father. Marriage to foreigners was banned.[13] Thus, Athenian citizenship was based on a strong version of *jus sanguinis*—the principle of descent. Regardless of whether Athens was the first society to develop a proto-racialized understanding of citizenship, its model enjoyed extraordinary influence on the later traditions of the Enlightenment and modernity.[14]

By contrast, an expansionist Rome used a territorial version of citizenship to assimilate diverse peoples and consolidate its grip over a vast empire. Even though xenophobia against groups like the Gauls, Germans, and Persians appears to have been the norm among Roman elites, the Roman foundational myth was not based on the idea of common descent.[15] Rome lacked a proto-racial citizenship despite deep prejudice against foreigners because it was an empire based on diverse peoples unified by allegiance to Caesar rather than a democracy like Athens obsessed with self-rule by a single community.

The division of Eurasia and the Mediterranean into empires organized around the universalistic religions of Islam and Christianity also failed to create racialized citizenships.[16] Racial distinctions are based on the perceived inalterability of inherited group characteristics, which raises the critical question of whether it was possible to assimilate to a higher citizenship status via conversion. Early expulsions of Jews and Muslims from medieval Christian jurisdictions do not appear to have been racialized. Conversion was an option.[17] The ubiquity of sumptuary laws that required Muslims and Jews to wear distinctive clothing suggests that phenotypical and religious distinctions did not overlap neatly.[18] The mutability of the religious categories—indeed the encouragement of conversion—and the apparent inability to make phenotypical distinctions among Christians, Jews, and Muslims—suggests that early medieval hierarchies of membership and expulsions were based on religious bigotry rather than racism.

It was only in the wake of forced mass conversions from Judaism and Islam to Christianity that a specifically racial form of citizenship took hold in sixteenth century Iberia and in its conquests in the Americas. The *limpieza de sangre* (blood purity)

---

[13] Susan Lape, *Race and Citizen Identity in the Classical Athenian Democracy* (Cambridge, New York: Cambridge University Press, 2010), p. 33.

[14] Isaac (n 11), p. 130.   [15] Isaac (n 11).

[16] Antoine Fattal, *Le statut légal des non musulmans en Terre d'Islam* (Beyrouth: L'imprimerie Catholique, 1958); Bernard Lewis and Benjamin Braude, eds., *Christians and Jews in the Ottoman Empire* (New York: Holmes & Meier, 1982).

[17] David Nirenberg, *Communities of Violence: Persecution of Minorities in the Middle Ages* (Princeton: Princeton University Press, 1996).

[18] Marjorie Ratcliffe, 'Judíos y musulmanes en la jurisprudencia medieval española,' *Revista canadiense de estudios hispánicos* (1985): pp. 423–438; John Tolan, 'The Legal Status of the Jews and Muslims in the Christian States,' in Abdelwahab Meddeb and Benjamin Stora, eds., *A History of Jewish-Muslim Relations: From the Origins to the Present Day* (Princeton: Princeton University Press, 2013).

laws defined anyone with at least one Jewish ancestor not just as a *converso* who had made the desirable decision to become a Christian, but as a despised 'Crypto-Jew' who secretly maintained Jewish practices and tried to Judaize Christianity. Some Spanish communities explicitly banned *conversos* and their progeny from local citizenship, and *conversos* were excluded from rights enjoyed by Catholic subjects of the Spanish kings. *Moriscos*, converts from Islam to Christianity and their descendants, were expelled from Spain in 1609.[19] The legal impossibility of full membership for people of Jewish or Moorish background reveals the racialization of religious prejudice by the sixteenth century.[20] In effect, the *limpieza de sangre* laws were a strong, multi-generational form of *jus sanguinis* corresponding to a common religious community of descent.

Although the racialized treatment of Jews and Muslims suggests that overseas European colonization did not invent racism, notwithstanding the claim of many scholars,[21] colonization *did* generate many features of modern racism as European settlers sought to justify their military and economic conquests. The first permanent overseas European colonization of large populations took place in Spanish America, which engendered fundamental questions about the political and religious status of the indigenous population. During the Valladolid debate of 1550 to 1551, Bishop Bartolomé de las Casas drew on doctrines of Christian universalism to argue that the indigenous were rational beings with the right not to be enslaved. His opponent, the philosopher Juan Ginés de Sepúlveda, cited Aristotelian notions that natural slaves cannot rule and should be governed by a group inherently endowed with a higher capacity. His conclusion was that Spaniards should rule the indigenous.[22] In the wake of the debate, the *encomienda* system of forced indigenous labor was weakened, but harsh exploitation and a caste system continued to define colonial relationships. At independence, Spanish American governments abolished black slavery and the caste system even as blacks' and indigenous peoples' substantive rights of citizenship remained sharply curtailed.[23]

European colonization of nearly the entire planet was based on the logic of racial, religious, and civilizational superiority of white Christian Europeans. Native peoples and slaves, usually imported from Africa, had secondary or no citizenship in these colonial arrangements. Early European colonization of Southern Africa

---

[19] Seymour B. Liebman, *The Inquisition and the Jews in the New World* (Coral Cables: University of Miami Press, 1975); Jerome Friedman, 'Jewish Conversion, the Spanish Pure Blood Laws and Reformation: A Revisionist View of Racial and Religious Antisemitism,' *The Sixteenth Century Journal* 18, no. 1 (1987): pp. 3–30.

[20] Yosef H. Yerushalmi, *Assimilation and Racial Anti-Semitism: The Iberian and the German Models* (New York: Leo Baeck Institute, 1982).

[21] Hanke (n 10); Fredrickson (n 3).   [22] Hanke (n 10).

[23] Robert H. Jackson, *Race, Caste, and Status: Indians in Colonial Spanish America* (Albuquerque: University of New Mexico Press, 1999); Peter Wade, *Race and Ethnicity in Latin America*, 2nd edition (London: Pluto Press, 2010).

initially justified European dominance over the native populations in religious terms. Similarly, in North America, English settlements in Virginia justified slavery as the rightful condition of heathens. When native populations and slaves in Africa and the Americas converted to Christianity, however, this justification was quickly eliminated. Slaveholders turned to race to legitimate slavery and discrimination against non-whites more generally. European colonists built political communities based on racial descent rather than religion.[24]

In a parallel process in Europe, the notion of shared religious descent was shunted aside by scientific racism. The leading racial theorists in the eighteenth century turned toward a lineage-based understanding of race and typically ignored the classification of Jews or classified them as Caucasian.[25] Jews eventually gained access to the full rights of citizenship in European countries in an uneven process across the continent that unfolded from the eighteenth to early twentieth centuries during the formation of nation-states.[26]

NATION-STATES

The codification of nationality became a constitutive act in the construction of nation-states. In Brubaker's classic discussion of *jus sanguinis* and *jus soli*, the correspondence between nationality law and particular conceptions of nationhood is based on institutionalized historical idioms that shape the way political actors think and talk about nationality. An ethnic understanding of German nationhood sustained a *jus sanguinis* regime for most of modern German history, while a state-framed and territorial conception of French nationhood sustained a primarily *jus soli* regime. Brubaker recognized that there is no *automatic* connection between an ethnic conception of nationhood and *jus sanguinis*. Some versions of *jus sanguinis* are based on the idea that the accidental fact of birthplace on a territory is insufficient to create durable and legitimate bonds of citizenship, and thus *jus sanguinis* is used to ensure a substantive tie. Other versions of *jus sanguinis* are based on the idea that the nation is a 'community of descent.'[27]

[24] Pierre L. van den Berghe, *Race and Racism: A Comparative Perspective* (New York: John Wiley & Sons, 1967); George M. Fredrickson, *White Supremacy* (New York: Oxford University Press, 1981); Michael P. Banton, *Racial Theories*, 2nd edition (New York: Cambridge University Press, 1998).

[25] George L. Mosse, *Toward the Final Solution: A History of European Racism* (New York: Howard Fertig, 1978).

[26] Ibid.   [27] Brubaker (n 2), pp. 123–124.

Scholars sharply dispute the legacies of nationhood argument. Weil shows that France, renowned in the twentieth century for its *jus soli*, adopted *jus sanguinis* in 1803 to promote socialization as the basis of nationality rather than the feudalistic allegiance to a territorial sovereign expressed in *jus soli*. Prussia adopted *jus sanguinis* in 1842, not out of a sense of ethnic nationalism, but because Prussian jurists considered France to have developed the most modern legal model. This policy transfer is evidence for the importance of international norms in shaping citizenship. Prussian *jus sanguinis* also allowed for the transmission of nationality to ethnic Poles and Jews, thus providing further evidence that *jus sanguinis* was not based on ethnic descent.[28] Brubaker's crystal ball was clouded when he predicted of Germany in 1992 that 'there is no chance that the French system of *jus soli* will be adopted; the automatic transformation of immigrants into citizens remains unthinkable in Germany.'[29] French and German nationality laws converged toward a mixed *sanguinis/soli* system in the 1990s, and the intergenerational transmission of German nationality by *jus sanguinis* was limited. Tests of German linguistic competency administered to the *Aussiedler* (ethnic Germans in Eastern Europe seeking to enter Germany) also reveal a mutable conception of ethnic Germanness.[30] 'The comparative history of German and French nationality law thus does not show any equivalence, any directly causal link between *jus sanguinis*, an ethnic conception of the nation, and Germany on the one hand, or between *jus soli*, a civic or elective conception of the nation, and France on the other hand,' concludes Weil.[31] Subsequent work by Brubaker and Kim comparing German and Korean policies toward co-ethnics emphasized the contingency and geopolitical dimensions of nationality policies and downplayed the importance of distinctive 'idioms of nationhood.'[32]

The Mexican and Japanese cases show the importance of the diffusion of foreign models of nationality and that *jus sanguinis* may simply reflect ideas about family rather than race. An analysis of all references to *jus sanguinis* and related terms of descent in Mexican congressional debates from 1916 to 1997 reveals that politicians generally framed blood ties in terms of parental or familial descent rather than race. Claims of a common, primordial descent group would not make sense within a dominant national narrative that celebrates Mexico as the mixing of Spanish and native elements. Mexican policymakers often referred to European and U.S. models of *jus sanguinis* and *jus soli* as standard principles to follow.[33] In Japan, the very strong version of *jus sanguinis* and absence of *jus soli* has an apparent affinity with

---

[28] Patrick Weil, *How to be French: Nationality in the Making Since 1789* (Durham: Duke University Press, 2008).

[29] Brubaker (n 2), p. 185.

[30] Joppke (n 3), p. 241; Doris Schüpbach, 'Testing Language, Testing Ethnicity? Policies and Practices Surrounding the Ethnic German Aussiedler,' *Language Assessment Quarterly* 6, no. 1 (2009): pp. 78–82.

[31] Weil (n 28), p. 191.   [32] Brubaker and Kim (n 4), p. 67.

[33] David FitzGerald, 'Nationality and Migration in Modern Mexico,' *Journal of Ethnic and Migration Studies* 31, no. 1 (2005): pp. 171–191.

the notion of Japan as an ethnically homogeneous community.[34] Yet Kashiwazaki shows that 'ethnic nationalism in the Meiji era had little direct impact on the legislation of the 1899 nationality law.'[35] The origins of *jus sanguinis* in the 1899 law lie in the adoption of European models and the family registration system adopted from China around the sixth century. The Meiji government attributed the same legal status to minority groups subject to discrimination in practice, such as the Burakumin, Okinawans, and the Ainu, underscoring the importance of separating out racialized access to status from racialized access to substantive enjoyment of citizenship rights. Family ties and legal emulation once again shaped formal access to citizenship through *jus sanguinis*.

Decolonized states have used *jus sanguinis* to separate indigenous populations from colonizers, their descendants, and other foreigners. For example, in postcolonial Algeria, a strict *jus sanguinis* policy reserved the status of 'national by origin' to Muslims whose parents were born in Algeria.[36] The Gulf Cooperation Council states created strong versions of *jus sanguinis*. In the United Arab Emirates, full citizenship is restricted to those who can trace their lineage to an Arab settled in the territory by 1925. A secondary form of citizenship is available for those who cannot trace their lineage back to 1925 through the 'family book' that registers parentage. *Bidoon jinsiyya* (those without nationality) do not have citizenship because they are considered nomads. Practically all other foreigners are temporary migrants with very little chance of becoming citizens. The origin of these differentiated citizenship policies does not appear to be specifically racial, however. The year 1925 was chosen because it preceded the development of the oil economy that attracted so many foreigners to share in its wealth, and registration of nomads was considered too inconvenient by British administrators under the protectorate that ended in 1971.[37] It could be argued that the UAE *jus sanguinis* policies have a racial element to the extent that they privilege Arabs, but they are not plainly racist in their origins. Rather, they reflect efforts to define nationality through familial ties at the moment nation-states were created from European colonies.

Brubaker argues that unlike the multiplicity of meanings that are attached to *jus sanguinis*, *jus soli* has a more restricted affiliation with a statist, civic understanding of nationhood. From an ethnonational point of view, *jus soli* is 'rejected because it

[34] Hideki Tarumoto, 'Multiculturalism in Japan: Citizenship Policy for Immigrants,' *International Journal on Multicultural Societies 5*, no. 1 (2003): pp. 88–103, p. 89.

[35] Chikako Kashiwazaki, 'Jus Sanguinis in Japan,' *International Journal of Comparative Sociology 39*, no. 3 (1998): pp. 278–300, pp. 290–291.

[36] Zouhir Boushaba, *Etre Algérien: Hier, Aujourd'hui et Demain* (Alger: Editions Mimouni, 1992). See also Sadiq in this volume.

[37] Manal A. Jamal, 'The "Tiering" of Citizenship and Residency and the "Hierarchization" of Migrant Communities: The United Arab Emirates in Historical Context,' *International Migration Review 49*, no. 3 (2015): pp. 601–639; Jane Kinninmont, 'Citizenship in the Gulf,' in Ana Echagüe, ed., *The Gulf States and the Arab Uprisings* (Madrid: FRIDE, 2013).

grounds citizenship in territory rather than descent.[38] While it is true that there is an inherent tension between the abstract principles of *jus soli* and an ethnonational understanding of the nation, governments have found many ways to resolve this tension in ways that are blatantly racist. Of thirty-five countries in the Western Hemisphere, thirty have *jus soli*.[39] The Americas is thus a strategic site to understand the contingent relationship between race and *jus soli*.

The United States was the first country in the Americas to gain independence and define racial eligibility for citizenship. The 1789 constitution treated Native Americans as 'outside, though not necessarily independent of, the American political community.'[40] Supreme Court Chief Justice John Marshall characterized their status as 'domestic dependent nations.'[41] As early as 1861, some Native Americans were able to gain citizenship through federal treaties, but the Supreme Court ruled in 1884 that the Fourteenth Amendment did not confer citizenship on Native Americans born under tribal jurisdiction, thus weakening *jus soli*. All Native Americans born in the United States were not recognized as U.S. citizens until 1924.[42]

Black slaves were not citizens by definition. Individual states varied in whether and to what extent they considered free blacks to be citizens. The federal government did not have a consistent position until the Supreme Court's 1857 *Dred Scott v. Sandford* decision effectively stripped all blacks, including free blacks, of their federal citizenship. In practice, the ruling separated U.S. citizenship from U.S. nationality. Blacks could hold the latter but not the former.[43] Following the Union's victory in the Civil War, the 1866 Civil Rights Act and 1868 Fourteenth Amendment established a strong version of *jus soli*—citizenship for all persons born in the United States regardless of their racial categorization, with the exception of Native Americans described above.

The 1790 Uniform Rule of Naturalization had restricted eligibility to naturalize to free whites. Following the Civil War, the Naturalization Act of 1870 extended eligibility to naturalize 'to aliens of African nativity and to persons of African descent' as well as whites.[44] A contradictory series of fifty-two court cases from 1878 to 1952 gradually defined who was *not* white, even though these cases never positively defined who *was* white. From 1878 to 1909, eleven of twelve cases deciding racial prerequisites to naturalize ruled against their plaintiffs, thus declaring people

---

[38] Brubaker (n 2), pp. 123–124.

[39] Olivier Willem Vonk, *Nationality Law in the Western Hemisphere: A Study on Grounds for Acquisition and Loss of Citizenship in the Americas and the Caribbean* (The Hague: Martinus Nijhoff Publishers, 2014).

[40] Rogers M. Smith, *Civic Ideals: Conflicting Visions of Citizenship in U.S. History* (New Haven: Yale University Press, 1997), pp. 131–132.

[41] *Cherokee Nation v. State of Georgia* 30 US 1 (1831).

[42] Thomas Alexander Aleinikoff, *Semblances of Sovereignty* (Cambridge: Harvard University Press, 2002), p. 20.

[43] Smith (n 40), pp. 26, 257–258.   [44] 16 *Stat.* 254, Sec. 7.

from China, Japan, Burma, and Hawaii to be non-white.[45] The Supreme Court ruled in 1922 in *Ozawa v. United States* that Japanese were not eligible for naturalization.[46] The courts often ruled inconsistently on the whiteness of particular groups. Syrians were ruled non-white in 1913 and 1914 but white in 1909, 1910, and 1915. Between 1909 and 1923, Armenians were declared white despite their origins in Asia. Filipinos were not considered white, but they could naturalize if they immigrated to the United States and served in the U.S. military in World War I.[47] Asian Indians were ruled white in 1910, 1913, 1919, and 1920 but non-white in 1909 and 1917. The Supreme Court's 1923 ruling in *U.S. v. Bhagat Singh Thind* definitively categorized Indians as non-white.[48] These rulings demonstrate the unusually high level of judicial autonomy to define race in the U.S. case.

Geopolitical considerations shaped the racialization of U.S. law as well. The 1897 *In re Rodriguez* case upheld the right of a Mexican immigrant to naturalize based on U.S. obligations in the 1848 Guadalupe Hidalgo and 1853 Gadsden treaties with Mexico. The Nationality Act of 1940 ensured Mexican racial eligibility to naturalize, regardless of indigenous background, with a provision that extended eligibility to naturalize to 'descendants of races indigenous to the Western Hemisphere.'[49] The 1940 statute was aimed at shoring up the incipient U.S. alliance with Latin American countries as the European war threatened to reach the Americas.[50] Similarly, the U.S. alliance with China in World War II and the decolonization of Asian countries in the subsequent Cold War competition to curry favor with the Third World drove the end of U.S. racialized bans on naturalization. The 1943 Magnuson Act made 'Chinese persons or persons of Chinese descent' eligible for naturalization.[51] Racial restrictions further eased in a 1947 amendment that allowed all Asians to obtain U.S. citizenship by marriage. As soon as India and the Philippines entered the final stages of independence, their citizens became eligible for U.S. naturalization.[52] Racial restrictions on naturalization ended in 1952.[53]

The main racial trajectory in U.S. nationality law has been the decreasing salience of race with a few major exceptions.[54] The most important early exception was the wholesale stripping of blacks' ambiguous citizenship status in 1857. The second was the denationalization of several thousand Japanese Americans in the immediate aftermath of World War II. Just as Japanese were singled out for mass internment

---

[45] Ian Haney-López, *White by Law: The Legal Construction of Race* (New York: New York University Press, 1996).

[46] *Ozawa v. United States* 260 US 178 (1922).

[47] Charles Gordon, 'The Racial Barrier to American Citizenship,' *University of Pennsylvania Law Review 93*, no. 3 (1945): pp. 237–258, p. 244.

[48] *U.S. v. Bhagat Singh Thind* 261 US 204 (1923); Haney-López (n 45), pp. 67, 90–91.

[49] 54 *Stat.* 1137. Ch. III, Sec. 303.

[50] P.D. Lukens, *A Quiet Victory for Latino Rights: FDR and the Controversy Over 'Whiteness'* (Tucson: University of Arizona Press, 2012).

[51] 57 *Stat.* 600.   [52] 60 *Stat.* 416.   [53] 66 *Stat.* 163.   [54] Smith (n 40).

during the war, Japanese were singled out for denationalization while German and Italian Americans remained untouched.[55] The less obvious way that U.S. nationality was racialized was via its interaction with immigration policy. Admission to the territory is the first step toward naturalization, and the racialization of U.S. admissions policy was sustained until 1965. Restrictions on blacks in 1803, Chinese exclusion in 1882, the establishment of the Asiatic Barred Zone in 1917, and the 1921–1965 quota system that restricted entry by southern and eastern Europeans while all but banning Asians and Africans, shaped who could naturalize by limiting who could enter the United States in the first place.[56]

The U.S. case also stands out for its thorough racialization of the internal dimension of citizenship until the Civil Rights movement of the 1950s and 60s. By way of illustration, voting rights,[57] access to education,[58] the administration of criminal justice,[59] and social policy[60] have all been deeply racialized. Legal tools of racialized citizenship have included anti-miscegenation statutes,[61] residential segregation,[62] and 'alien land laws' preventing 'aliens ineligible to naturalization' from owning land.[63] The Civil Rights movement ended de facto statuses of racial hierarchy, but equal access to the substance of citizenship continues to elude African Americans in particular.

Despite being a *jus soli* country, Canadian law experimented briefly with racialized nationality law in ways that show the importance of geopolitical considerations for shaping the law. Free of British treaty obligations with China and Japan under Canada's new dominion status, a 1931 Canadian law created naturalization requirements that only applied to Chinese and Japanese applicants.[64] The discriminatory requirement for Chinese lasted until 1947. Even when Chinese were born Canadians, they could not vote in British Columbia or Saskatchewan until reforms following

---

[55] Mae M. Ngai, *Impossible Subjects: Illegal Aliens and the Making of Modern America* (Princeton: Princeton University Press, 2004).

[56] FitzGerald and Cook-Martín (n 1).

[57] E. Earl Parson and Monique McLaughlin, 'Persistence of Racial Bias in Voting: Voter ID, the New Battleground for Pretextual Race Neutrality', *Journal of Law and Society 8*, no. 2 (2007): pp. 75–104.

[58] Adrienne D. Dixson and Celia K. Rousseau, 'And We are Still Not Saved: Critical Race Theory in Education Ten Years Later', *Race Ethnicity and Education 8*, no. 1 (2005): pp. 7–27.

[59] Michelle Alexander, *The New Jim Crow: Mass Incarceration in the Age of Colorblindness*, revised edition (New York: New Press, 2010).

[60] Ian Haney-López, *Dog Whistle Politics: How Coded Racial Appeals have Reinvented Racism and Wrecked the Middle Class* (New York: Oxford University Press, 2013).

[61] Peggy Pascoe, 'Miscegenation Law, Court Cases, and Ideologies of "Race" in Twentieth-Century America', *The Journal of American History 83*, no. 1 (1996): pp. 44–69.

[62] Douglas S. Massey and Nancy A. Denton, *American Apartheid: Segregation and the Making of the Underclass* (Cambridge: Harvard University Press, 1993).

[63] Keith Aoki, 'No Right to Own?: The Early Twentieth-Century Alien Land Laws as a Prelude to Internment', *Boston College Third World Law Journal 40*, no. 1 (1998): pp. 37–72.

[64] P.C. 1378 of June 17, 1931.

World War II.[65] As in the United States, several thousand Japanese Canadians were singled out for coerced denationalization after the war.[66]

Jus soli Panama and Costa Rica were the only Latin American countries with negative racial discrimination in their nationality laws. For example, the Panamanian government suspended the citizenship of Chinese, Syrian, and Turkish migrants in 1909, and the 1941 constitution only awarded citizenship to the children of prohibited migrant races if one of the parents was a Panamanian by birth. This small exception was not extended to non-Spanish-speaking blacks. Racial discrimination continued until 1945.[67] Racial selection of citizens in the Americas was much more pervasive if one considers how nationality law works together with immigrant admissions law. Between 1803 and 1930, every one of the independent countries in the Americas passed laws explicitly seeking to restrict or exclude at least one particular ethnic group. Many of those laws were written in racial rather than national-origin categories, particularly for definitions of Asians and blacks.[68]

In sum, there is an extensive history of countries whose nationality law is primarily based on *jus soli* adopting racialized nationality policies, either in nationality law itself or, more widely, in interaction with immigration policy. The theoretical lesson is that neither *jus soli* nor *jus sanguinis* are useful predictors of whether race is a basis for assigning nationality. Interstate relations, efforts to separate colonizers from the colonized in post-independence contexts, and family registration have shaped the balance of *jus sanguinis* and *jus soli*.

RACIAL DENATURALIZATIONS

In *The Dark Side of Democracy*, Michael Mann warns that 'murderous ethnic cleansing is a hazard in the age of democracy' as the *demos* becomes entwined with the *ethnos*. People who do not fit in the ethnos are killed or expelled.[69] The construction of nation-states in a context of unstable borders favors the elimination of groups outside a racialized vision of the nation. The destruction of the multi-ethnic Austro-Hungarian, Russian, and Ottoman Empires in World War I ignited a massive 'unmixing' of people.[70] The creation of nation-states from the debris of empire

---

[65] S.B.C., 1920, c.27; S.S. 1908, c.2; *Dominion Election Act* S.C. 1948, c.46, s.6.

[66] Audrey Macklin, 'Citizenship Revocation, The Privilege to Have Rights and the Production of the Alien,' *Queen's Law Journal 40*, no. 1 (2014): pp. 1–54.

[67] Virginia Arango Durling, *La inmigración prohibida en Panamá y sus prejuicios raciales* (Panama: PUBLIPAN, 1999).

[68] FitzGerald and Cook-Martín (n 1).   [69] Mann (n 2), pp. 3–4.   [70] Brubaker (n 2).

prompted mass deportations and population exchanges, such as the 1.5 million ethnic Greeks and ethnic Turks exchanged between Greece and Turkey. These de facto
denationalizations and creations of secondary citizenship for the ethnic minorities
left behind arguably carried a racial element as they emphasized organic notions of
national communities of descent.[71]

Germany carried the racialization of citizenship the farthest of the European
states. *Mein Kampf* praised the United States for its 'modest start' in creating a
racialized national state, noting that it refused 'to allow immigration from elements
which are bad from the health point of view, and absolutely forbid naturalization in
certain defined races.'[72] After the Nazis came to power, Hitler passed a denaturalization decree based on 'ethnic national principles' to denaturalize many immigrants
who had arrived between 1918 and 1933. 'Jews from the East' were the first named
target.[73] The Nuremberg Laws and supplementary decrees passed in 1935 then
reserved the status of 'Reich citizen' (as opposed to merely 'subject of the state') to
those of 'German or related blood.' Anyone with three Jewish grandparents, regardless of the individual's religious confession, was stripped of German citizenship. All
German Jews who had left Germany were stripped of their German nationality in
1941, having already lost their citizenship in 1935. Similar decrees denaturalized Jews
in fascist Hungary, Romania, Vichy France, French Algeria, and Italy.[74]

The immediate aftermath of World War II continued the pattern at the end of
World War I, which was a massive expulsion of populations along ethnic lines.
At least eight million ethnic Germans were expelled from Eastern Europe.[75] The
destruction of the Japanese empire also led to mass denationalizations. During the
Japanese imperial period, Koreans and Taiwanese were Japanese nationals even as
they were excluded from the full rights of citizenship. The 1947 Alien Registration
Law during the U.S. occupation recategorized Korean and Chinese residents of
Japan as aliens. Five years later, Koreans and Taiwanese, whether they were living in
Korea, Taiwan, or Japan, were stripped of their Japanese nationality.[76]

Notwithstanding the spasms of ethnoracial cleansing immediately after World
War II, in the long run, the reaction against Nazism contributed strongly to the
delegitimization of racism.[77] Post-colonialism and the formation of nation-states
in Africa and Asia consolidated a nation-state system organized by rules in which
racial denaturalization is illegitimate. The template for a modern nation-state, along

---

[71] Mann (n 2), pp. 3–4.

[72] Adolf Hitler, *Mein Kampf* (New York: Houghton Mifflin, 1971) [1925], p. 182.

[73] Weil (n 28), pp. 188–189.

[74] Myres S. McDougal, Harold D. Lasswell, and Lung-chu Chen, 'Nationality and Human Rights: The
Protection of the Individual in External Arenas,' *Yale Law Journal* 83, no. 5 (1974): pp. 900–998, p. 948;
Weil (n 28), pp. 87, 128.

[75] Dariusz Stola, 'Forced Migrations in Central European History,' *International Migration Review*
26, no. 2 (1992): pp. 324–341, p. 336.

[76] Surak (n 1).   [77] Banton (n 24).

the lines described by John Meyer in his work on the international diffusion of organizational norms, excludes overtly racial citizenship.[78] None of this is to say that racial expulsions have ended, but rather, that they are typically hidden or framed in other terms because they are no longer considered politically acceptable.

South Africa stands out for creating a more racialized system and sustaining it long after World War II. Beginning in 1948, the National Party built on colonial-era discrimination to establish a system of apartheid in which every South African was legally assigned to the white, Bantu (black), Colored, or Asian categories. Sex, marriage, housing, work, internal mobility, and access to recreational spaces was strictly divided by race under the guiding principles of 'separate development' and white supremacy. Blacks held South African nationality but did not have the right to vote and in practice held extremely limited rights of citizenship. Only whites enjoyed full rights in this *Herrenvolk* democracy.[79] In the face of strong international pressure to dismantle apartheid, the South African government created a 'Bantustan' system to denationalize the majority black population while retaining access to its labor. South African officials openly described to local white audiences why the policy was needed to placate international political pressure, specifically from the UN and the International Court of Justice.[80] A 1970 law provided that every black in South Africa who was not already a 'citizen' of a Bantu homeland would become a 'citizen' of a homeland to which he or she was attached by birth, residence, or cultural affiliation.[81] In keeping with even the apartheid government's sensitivity to international norms, the law did not say that affiliation would be created on a racial basis, but rather through ties of language and culture, even though racial segregation was the obvious intent. From 1976 to 1981, South Africa granted four homelands 'independence' in an 'exercise in political fantasy' that denationalized millions of blacks by assigning their nationality to the fictive new states and stripping them of their South African nationality.[82] The Bantustan system was disbanded with the fall of apartheid.[83]

Denationalizations on racial grounds violate strong international norms, but in the twenty-first century the Dominican government has pushed against those limits. The Dominican Republic, which shares an island territory with Haiti, has a long history of discrimination against immigrants and their descendents from Haiti. Dominican national identity is built on identification with *hispanidad* in contradistinction to Haitian blackness. Since the early twenty-first century, the Dominican government has sought to restrict Haitians from acquiring Dominican nationality and even retroactively strip people of Haitian descent of their nationality, without

---

[78] See Meyer et al. (n 1).   [79] van den Berghe (n 24); Fredrickson (n 24).

[80] John Dugard, 'South Africa's Independent Homelands: An Exercise in Denationalization,' *Denver Journal of International Law and Policy 10*, no. 1 (1980): pp. 11–36, p. 14.

[81] *Bantu Homelands Citizenship Act* (1970).   [82] Dugard (n 80).

[83] Gay Seidman, 'Is South Africa Different? Sociological Comparisons and Theoretical Contributions from the Land of Apartheid,' *Annual Review of Sociology 25*, no. 1 (1999): pp. 419–440.

saying as much in the letter of the law. Migration Law 285-04 passed in 2004 stated for the first time that foreigners who did not enter legally were 'in transit.'[84] The following year, the Secretary of Labor announced a plan to 'dehaitianize' the Dominican Republic. After the government refused to issue birth certificates to two girls of Haitian descent because their parents did not have legal residency and thus were 'in transit,' the Inter-American Court of Human Rights ruled that the girls' rights to Dominican nationality had been violated.[85] A new constitution in 2010 restricted *jus soli* by specifying that it did not apply to children of those who illegally resided in Dominican territory. In 2013, the Dominican Constitutional Court ruled that children of 'irregular migrants' or foreign workers on non-immigrant visas were not Dominican nationals. The court ordered authorities to review all birth registries dating back to 1929 to determine who no longer qualified for citizenship. The decision thus retroactively stripped thousands of people of Haitian descent of their Dominican nationality.[86] The Inter-American Commission on Human Rights investigated and denounced the mass denationalization. Its report estimated that around 200,000 people of Haitian origin would be arbitrarily deprived of Dominican nationality.[87] While Dominican law does not use racial categories, and it is cast as the retroactive enforcement of qualifications around *jus soli*, the policy has received tremendous censure internationally because it is clearly motivated by an effort to reduce the black Haitian-origin population of the Dominican Republic and restrict the rights of those who stay. Denationalizations on racial grounds are now hidden by pretexts.

RACIAL OR CULTURAL PREFERENCES?

Negative racial discrimination in nationality policy has become deeply and widely illegitimate since the mid-twentieth century. Positive racial preferences are also illegitimate, but some kinds of positive preferences continue, though they are often contentious. Proponents of preferences for particular groups cast them as being legitimately about family and cultural ties while opponents decry them as racist.

[84] Nicia C. Mejia, 'Dominican Apartheid: Inside the Flawed Migration System of the Dominican Republic,' *Harvard Latino Law Review 18* (2015): pp. 201–229, p. 208.
[85] Monique A. Hannam, 'Soy Dominicano—The Status of Haitian Descendants Born in the Dominican Republic and Measures to Protect Their Right to a Nationality,' *Vanderbilt Journal of Transnational Law 47*, no. 4 (2014): pp. 1123–1166, pp. 1123, 1143.
[86] Mejia (n 84), pp. 202–203.
[87] Inter-American Commission on Human Rights, *Situation of Human Rights in the Dominican Republic* (2015), online http://www.oas.org/en/iachr/reports/pdfs/DominicanRepublic-2015.pdf.

Following decolonization in Africa and Asia, European metropolitan countries became major destinations for the formerly colonized as well as the 'return
migration' of their former colonizers. European countries created special statuses
for current or former colonial subjects amid highly dynamic and varied contexts
of sovereignty.[88] For example, the 1948 British Nationality Act established a 'UK
and Colonies (UKC)' status that expressed the apex of the imperial monarchist
notion of subjecthood regardless of color.[89] In the face of a nativist white British
reaction against non-white Commonwealth immigration, the 1968 Commonwealth
Immigrants Act restricted entry to the UK to UKC citizens who were themselves
or whose parents or grandparents had been born, adopted, registered, or naturalized in the UK.[90] The racialization of British nationality became even more trans-
parent in the 1971 Immigration Act, which divided British subjects into 'patrials'
and 'nonpatrials.' Patrials were those individuals with ties to Britain detailed above
in the 1968 Act or UKCs who had lived in the UK for at least five years. In effect,
almost all patrials were whites and non-patrials were people of color. Ten years
later, the 1981 British Nationality Act included a provision to deny patrial status to
Commonwealth citizens born after 1981, thus ensuring that patriality would end
within a generation and bring the UK into line with the growing anti-racist international norm.[91]

In France, post-war efforts to establish a racialized policy of immigration and
nationality failed or were short lived. The Ministry of Justice stopped the government's 1945 strict racial immigration quota plan that would have given 50 percent
of visas to Nordics, 30 percent to Mediterraneans, and 20 percent to Slavs. A 1945
ordinance allowed nationality of origin to be considered by officials when deciding whether to grant naturalization.[92] Between April 23, 1952 and November 23,
1953, naturalization guidelines were explicitly 'to favor to the fullest extent possible
the naturalization of foreigners originating in countries of Western Europe.' New
instructions in 1953 ended this policy, because its continuance would 'demonstrate
an unacceptable racism.'[93]

While negative racial discrimination has become illegitimate, there is greater
legitimacy for positive preferences framed in cultural terms. Sixteen countries
in Latin America retain naturalization preferences for Spaniards, ten for Latin
Americans, and three for Portuguese. The number of countries with positive ethnic
preferences in their nationality law actually increased in the twentieth century as a

---

[88] See Thomas Janoski, *The Ironies of Citizenship: Naturalization and Integration in Industrialized Countries* (Cambridge: Cambridge University Press, 2010).

[89] Randall Hansen, *Citizenship and Immigration in Postwar Britain* (New York: Oxford University Press, 2000), p. 251.

[90] Ibid., p. 179.

[91] Kathleen Paul, *Whitewashing Britain: Race and Citizenship in the Postwar Era* (Ithaca: Cornell University Press, 1997), p. 181; Joppke (n 3), p. 103.

[92] Weil (n 28), p. 145.   [93] Weil (n 28), p. 149.

result of bilateral treaties between Spain and various Latin American countries and the growth of multilateral institutions such as the Organization of Ibero-American States.[94] Spanish and Portuguese ties have revolved around preferential naturalization for nationals of former colonies even if those nationals are not of Spanish ancestry. Ties with Iberia are framed not as common familial or racial descent, but as membership in a cultural and historic community.[95]

In Israel, the foundational Law of Return of 1950 grants that 'every Jew has the right to come to this country.' The Israeli Supreme Court ruled in the *Rufeisen* case of 1962 that a Jew who had converted to Catholicism could not be considered a Jew with a right of return,[96] thereby suggesting that Jewishness is mutable and a religious rather than exclusively descent-based category. A 1970 reform further weakened the descent-based notion of Jewishness by making converts to Judaism eligible for the right of return.[97] The various conditions for moving into or out of Jewishness suggest a non-racial definition, though Israeli secularists decry making biological descent the normal path of entry and for granting Orthodox rabbis the exclusive competence to determine legitimate conversions.[98]

In practice, naturalization discrimination may continue outside the black letter of the law. Until 2003, many Swiss cantons used local referenda to decide which applicants to accept for naturalization. A study of naturalization petitions decided at the ballot box between 1970 and 2003 found that Yugoslavs and Turks were 40 percent more likely to be rejected than similar applicants from northern or Western Europe, and the applicants' language skills or level of integration had almost no effect on the decisions.[99] It is impossible to tell from the study whether differential treatment was the result of religious or racialized bias. Cultural discrimination retains greater legitimacy than biological racial discrimination.

INTERNATIONAL LEGAL CONSTRAINTS

Overt racism is in disfavor internationally, but the recurrence of populist demands to restrain the immigration of Muslims to Europe and North America and Latin Americans to the United States raises questions about what might prevent these demands from creating racialized forms of citizenship. There are slightly ambiguous international legal constraints on racial discrimination in the assignation of

---

[94] FitzGerald and Cook-Martín (n 1).   [95] Joppke (n 3).   [96] Joppke (n 3).
[97] *Law of Return* 5710-1950.   [98] Joppke (n 3), p. 181.
[99] Jens Hainmueller and Dominik Hangartner, 'Who Gets a Swiss Passport? A Natural Experiment in Immigrant Discrimination,' *American Political Science Review 107*, no. 1 (2013): pp. 159–187.

nationality and much clearer prohibitions on denationalization and discriminatory statuses for citizens on racial grounds.

The International Convention on the Elimination of All Forms of Racial Discrimination (ICERD), which entered into force in 1969 and which had 177 state parties as of 2016, condemns

any distinction, exclusion, restriction or preference based on race, colour, descent, or national or ethnic origin which has the purpose or effect of nullifying or impairing the recognition, enjoyment or exercise, on an equal footing, of human rights and fundamental freedoms in the political, economic, social, cultural or any other field of public life.

However, Article 1(2) provides that the convention does not apply to distinctions between citizens and noncitizens. According to Article 1(3), 'Nothing in this Convention may be interpreted as affecting in any way the legal provisions of States Parties concerning nationality, citizenship or naturalization, provided that such provisions do not discriminate against any particular nationality.' The U.N. Committee on the Elimination of Racial Discrimination interprets this clause to mean that illegitimate discrimination occurs only if the criteria 'are not applied pursuant to a legitimate aim, and are not proportional to the achievement of this aim.'[100] The Inter-American Court of Human Rights ruled in a 1984 advisory opinion that Costa Rica's less stringent naturalization residency requirements for Central Americans, Ibero-Americans, and Spaniards compared to other nationals were justified given their 'much closer historical, cultural and spiritual bonds with the people of Costa Rica.'[101] Thus, the ICERD does not appear to be a legal deterrent against policies that maintain at least some kinds of ethnic distinction in naturalization policy. On the other hand, denationalization on racial grounds is highly illegitimate and illegal under international law. Article 9 of the 1961 Convention on the Reduction of Statelessness, which entered into force in 1975, specifies that 'A Contracting State may not deprive any person or group of persons of their nationality on racial, ethnic, religious or political grounds.' By 2016, sixty-five states were parties to the convention.

International law does not itself prevent governments from doing as they please. The main deterrent is political. The postcolonial division of the world into sovereign states makes the external nationality dimension of citizenship policy subject to international as well as domestic scrutiny. Singling out particular groups for discrimination provokes the ire of the governments who claim to represent their targets. The organization of sovereign states into the United Nations and other fora also provides venues for shifting debates about racist laws from the national up to the international level and linking them to a wide range of issues. None of this is

---

[100] Liav Orgad, 'Illiberal Liberalism: Cultural Restrictions on Migration and Access to Citizenship in Europe,' *American Journal of Comparative Law* 58, no. 1 (2010): pp. 53–105, p. 92.

[101] Inter-American Court of Human Rights, Advisory Opinion OC- 4/84 of Jan. 19, 1984, 16.

to say that explicitly racist citizenship laws are now impossible. Rather, there are strong structural barriers that complement a global political culture in which racialized policies are stained by their association with Nazi Germany and South Africa under apartheid.[102]

CONCLUSIONS

There is no clear trajectory in the racialization of citizenship from ancient Athens to the mid-twentieth century. The proto-racialization of citizenship in Athens was followed by a much more open model in ancient Rome. Differentiated citizenship in early medieval Europe and under classical Islamic rule and the Ottoman Empire was based on religious rather than racial discrimination. The racialization of religious bigotry did not become formalized until the anti-Jewish and anti-Moorish measures developed in sixteenth century Iberia. By 1917, Jews had become politically emancipated throughout Europe, but this deracialization was cut short by the extreme racialization of citizenship under fascist regimes.

Since the mid-twentieth century, citizenship has entered a deracialization phase. Ethnic preferences do remain in nationality law. These preferences are sometimes based on ideas about common culture rather than common racial descent, such as in Iberia and Latin America. Preferences in other settings, such as the British patrial system in its twilight, are consistent with notions of common racial descent. Racialized denaturalization has become the most illegitimate of the four forms of racialized citizenship practices discussed in the chapter. Substantive racialized denaturalization, such as Dominican denaturalization of Haitians in the early twenty-first century, is disguised as enforcement of new *jus soli* qualifiers because open racial denaturalization would be considered even more illegitimate.

Much scholarship on the acquisition of nationality has debated the extent to which *jus sanguinis* expresses ethnocentrism, or even racism, while *jus soli* expresses a civic and state-framed vision of the nation. Examining the historical record across diverse contexts suggests that *jus sanguinis* is not inherently racist. While in an abstract sense, *jus soli* might sustain a civic vision of nationality, in practice, the examples of Western Hemisphere states, particularly the United States, shows that *jus soli* is fully compatible with racialized citizenship. Racialization is found most obviously in rules around naturalization, including the admissions policies that usually are the first step toward possible naturalization.

---

[102] FitzGerald and Cook-Martín (n 1).

The construction of nation-states from empires is consonant with the racialization of policies. However, the consolidation of the nation-state system mitigates
against legal racialization. Predictions are hazardous, but the institutionalization of
an anti-racist norm in a world system of nation-states where both international and
domestic actors patrol the boundaries of the law suggest that the current phase of
legal deracialization is likely to be sustained, even as agents of religious bigotry and
xenophobia test the strength of those institutions. Future research will continue to
uncover techniques and patterns of selecting citizens that appear racially neutral,
but which are racially discriminatory in practice, and the collision of logics of selection based on ascriptive and acquired social characteristics.

BIBLIOGRAPHY

Aleinikoff, Thomas Alexander, *Semblances of Sovereignty* (Cambridge: Harvard University
    Press, 2002).
Alexander, Michelle, *The New Jim Crow: Mass Incarceration in the Age of Colorblindness*,
    revised edition (New York: New Press, 2010).
Aoki, Keith, 'No Right to Own?: The Early Twentieth-Century Alien Land Laws as a Prelude
    to Internment', *Boston College Third World Law Journal 40*, no. 1 (1998): pp. 37–72.
Banton, Michael P., *Racial Theories*, 2nd edition (New York: Cambridge University
    Press, 1998).
Boushaba, Zouhir, *Etre Algérien: Hier, Aujourd'hui et Demain* (Alger: Editions
    Mimouni, 1992).
Brubaker, Rogers, *Citizenship and Nationhood in France and Germany* (Cambridge: Harvard
    University Press, 1992).
Brubaker, Rogers and Jaeeun Kim, 'Transborder Membership Politics in Germany and
    Korea', *European Journal of Sociology 52*, no. 1 (2011): pp. 21–75.
Dikötter, Frank, 'Group Definition and the Idea of "Race" in Modern China (1793–1949)',
    Ethnic and Racial Studies 13, no. 3 (1990): pp. 420–432.
Dixson, Adrienne D. and Celia K. Rousseau, 'And We are Still Not Saved: Critical Race Theory
    in Education Ten Years Later', *Race Ethnicity and Education 8*, no. 1 (2005): pp. 7–27.
Dugard, John, 'South Africa's Independent Homelands: An Exercise in Denationalization',
    Denver Journal of International Law and Policy 10, no. 1 (1980): pp. 11–36.
Durling, Virginia Arango, *La inmigración prohibida en Panamá y sus prejuicios raciales*
    (Panama: PUBLIPAN, 1999).
Fattal, Antoine, *Le statut légal des non musulmans en Terre d'Islam* (Beyrouth: L'imprimerie
    Catholique, 1958).
FitzGerald, David, 'Nationality and Migration in Modern Mexico', *Journal of Ethnic and
    Migration Studies 31*, no. 1 (2005): pp. 171–191.
FitzGerald, David Scott and David Cook-Martín, *Culling the Masses: The Democratic
    Origins of Racist Immigration Policies in the Americas* (Cambridge: Harvard University
    Press, 2014).
Fredrickson, George M., *White Supremacy* (New York: Oxford University Press, 1981).

Fredrickson, George M., *Racism: A Short History* (Princeton: Princeton University Press, 2002).

Friedman, Jerome, 'Jewish Conversion, the Spanish Pure Blood Laws and Reformation: A Revisionist View of Racial and Religious Antisemitism,' *The Sixteenth Century Journal 18*, no. 1 (1987): pp. 3–30.

Goldberg, David Theo, *Racist Culture* (Cambridge: Blackwell, 1993).

Gordon, Charles, 'The Racial Barrier to American Citizenship,' University of *Pennsylvania Law Review 93*, no. 3 (1945): pp. 237–258.

Hainmueller, Jens and Dominik Hangartner, 'Who Gets a Swiss Passport? A Natural Experiment in Immigrant Discrimination,' *American Political Science Review 107*, no. 1 (2013): pp. 159–187.

Haney-López, Ian, *White by Law: The Legal Construction of Race* (New York: New York University Press, 1996).

Haney-López, Ian, *Dog Whistle Politics: How Coded Racial Appeals have Reinvented Racism and Wrecked the Middle Class* (New York: Oxford University Press, 2013).

Hanke, Lewis, *Aristotle and the American Indians* (London: Hollis and Carter, 1959).

Hannam, Monique A., 'Soy Dominicano—The Status of Haitian Descendants Born in the Dominican Republic and Measures to Protect Their Right to a Nationality,' *Vanderbilt Journal of Transnational Law 47*, no. 4 (2014): pp. 1123–1166.

Hansen, Randall, *Citizenship and Immigration in Postwar Britain* (New York: Oxford University Press, 2000).

Hitler, Adolf, *Mein Kampf* (New York: Houghton Mifflin, 1971) [1925].

Isaac, Benjamin H., *The Invention of Racism in Classical Antiquity* (Princeton: Princeton University Press, 2004).

Jackson, Robert H., *Race, Caste, and Status: Indians in Colonial Spanish America* (Albuquerque: University of New Mexico Press, 1999).

Jamal, Manal A., 'The "Tiering" of Citizenship and Residency and the "Hierarchization" of Migrant Communities: The United Arab Emirates in Historical Context,' *International Migration Review 49*, no. 3 (2015): pp. 601–632.

Janoski, Thomas, *The Ironies of Citizenship: Naturalization and Integration in Industrialized Countries* (Cambridge: Cambridge University Press, 2010).

Joppke, Christian, *Selecting by Origin: Ethnic Migration in the Liberal State* (Cambridge: Harvard University Press, 2005).

Kashiwazaki, Chikako, 'Jus sanguinis in Japan,' *International Journal of Comparative Sociology 39*, no. 3 (1998): pp. 278–300.

Kedar, Benjamin Z., 'Expulsion as an issue of World History,' *Journal of World History 7*, no. 2 (2005): pp. 165–180.

Kinninmont, Jane, 'Citizenship in the Gulf,' in Ana Echagüe, ed., *The Gulf States and the Arab Uprisings* (Madrid: FRIDE, 2013), pp. 47–58.

Lape, Susan, *Race and Citizen Identity in the Classical Athenian Democracy* (Cambridge, New York: Cambridge University Press, 2010).

Lewis, Bernard and Benjamin Braude, eds., *Christians and Jews in the Ottoman Empire* (New York: Holmes & Meier, 1982).

Liebman, Seymour B., *The Inquisition and the Jews in the New World* (Coral Cables, FL: University of Miami Press, 1975).

Lukens, P.D., *A Quiet Victory for Latino Rights: FDR and the Controversy Over 'Whiteness'* (Tucson: University of Arizona Press, 2012).

Macklin, Audrey, 'Citizenship Revocation, The Privilege to have Rights and the Production of the Alien,' *Queen's Law Journal 40*, no. 1 (2014): pp. 1–54.

Mann, Michael, *The Dark Side of Democracy: Explaining Ethnic Cleansing* (Cambridge: Cambridge University Press, 2005).

Massey, Douglas S. and Nancy A. Denton, *American Apartheid: Segregation and the Making of the Underclass* (Cambridge: Harvard University Press, 1993).

McDougal, Myres S., Harold D. Lasswell, and Lung-chu Chen, 'Nationality and Human Rights: The Protection of the Individual in External Arenas,' *Yale Law Journal 83*, no. 5 (1974): pp. 900–998.

Mejia, Nicia C., 'Dominican Apartheid: Inside the Flawed Migration System of the Dominican Republic,' *Harvard Latino Law Review 18* (2015): pp. 201–229.

Meyer, John W., John Boli, George M. Thomas, and Francisco O. Ramirez, 'World Society and the Nation State,' *American Journal of Sociology 103*, no. 1 (1997): pp. 144–181.

Mosse, George L., *Toward the Final Solution: A History of European Racism* (New York: Howard Fertig, 1978).

Ngai, Mae M., *Impossible Subjects: Illegal Aliens and the Making of Modern America* (Princeton: Princeton University Press, 2004).

Nirenberg, David, *Communities of Violence: Persecution of Minorities in the Middle Ages* (Princeton: Princeton University Press, 1996).

Orgad, Liav, 'Illiberal Liberalism: Cultural Restrictions on Migration and Access to Citizenship in Europe,' *American Journal of Comparative Law 58*, no. 1 (2010): pp. 53–105.

Parson, E. Earl and Monique McLaughlin, 'Persistence of Racial Bias in Voting: Voter ID, the New Battleground for Pretextual Race Neutrality,' *Journal of Law and Society 8*, no. 2 (2007): pp. 75–104.

Pascoe, Peggy, 'Miscegenation Law, Court Cases, and Ideologies of "Race" in Twentieth-Century America,' *The Journal of American History 83*, no. 1 (1996): pp. 44–69.

Paul, Kathleen, *Whitewashing Britain: Race and Citizenship in the Postwar Era* (Ithaca: Cornell University Press, 1997).

Pocock, J.G.A., 'The Ideal of Citizenship Since Classical Times,' in Gershon Shafir, ed., *The Citizenship Debates* (Minneapolis: The University of Minnesota Press, 1998), pp. 31–41.

Ratcliffe, Marjorie, 'Judíos y musulmanes en la jurisprudencia medieval española,' *Revista canadiense de estudios hispánicos* (1985): pp. 423–438.

Schüpbach, Doris, 'Testing Language, Testing Ethnicity? Policies and Practices Surrounding the Ethnic German Aussiedler,' *Language Assessment Quarterly 6*, no. 1 (2009): pp. 78–82.

Seidman, Gay, 'Is South Africa Different? Sociological Comparisons and Theoretical Contributions from the Land of Apartheid,' *Annual Review of Sociology 25*, no. 1 (1999): pp. 419–440.

Smith, Rogers M., *Civic Ideals: Conflicting Visions of Citizenship in U.S. History* (New Haven: Yale University Press, 1997).

Stola, Dariusz, 'Forced Migrations in Central European History,' *International Migration Review 26*, no. 2 (1992): pp. 324–341.

Surak, Kristin, 'Convergence in Foreigners' Rights and Citizenship Policies? A Look at Japan,' *International Migration Review 42*, no. 3 (2008): pp. 550–575.

Tarumoto, Hideki, 'Multiculturalism in Japan: Citizenship Policy for Immigrants,' *International Journal on Multicultural Societies 5*, no. 1 (2003): pp. 88–103.

Tolan, John, 'The Legal Status of the Jews and Muslims in the Christian States,' in Abdelwahab Meddeb and Benjamin Stora, eds., *A History of Jewish-Muslim Relations: From the Origins to the Present Day* (Princeton: Princeton University Press, 2013), pp. 145–155.

van den Berghe, Pierre L., *Race and Racism: A Comparative Perspective* (New York: John Wiley & Sons, 1967).

Vonk, Olivier Willem, *Nationality Law in the Western Hemisphere: A Study on Grounds for Acquisition and Loss of Citizenship in the Americas and the Caribbean* (The Hague: Martinus Nijhoff Publishers, 2014).

Wade, Peter, *Race and Ethnicity in Latin America*, 2nd edition (London: Pluto Press, 2010).

Weil, Patrick, *How to be French: Nationality in the making since 1789* (Durham: Duke University Press, 2008).

Yerushalmi, Yosef H., *Assimilation and Racial Anti-Semitism: The Iberian and the German Models* (New York: Leo Baeck Institute, 1982).

Zolberg, Aristide R., 'The Formation of New States as a Refugee-Generating Process,' *The Annals of the American Academy of Political and Social Science 467* (1983): pp. 24–38.

CHAPTER 8

FEMINIST, SEXUAL, AND QUEER CITIZENSHIP

LETI VOLPP*

INTRODUCTION

CITIZENSHIP is 'Janus-faced,' simultaneously projecting the warm embrace of inclusion while excluding those who are outside the borders of belonging.[1] Janus, the Roman god of doors and gates, was portrayed as having two faces, gazing in

* Robert D. and Leslie Kay Raven Professor of Law, UC Berkeley. My profound thanks to Truc Doan and Abigail Stepnitz for wonderful research assistance, and to Irene Bloemraad, Cathryn Costello, Richard Perry, Ayelet Shachar, and participants in the Authors' Workshop for their extremely helpful comments.
   [1] Linda Bosniak, *The Citizen and the Alien: Dilemmas of Contemporary Membership* (Princeton: Princeton University Press, 2008), p. 99; Ruth Lister, *Citizenship: Feminist Perspectives* (New York: New York University Press, 1997), p. 4.

opposite directions. Citizenship is similarly split. One face of citizenship welcomes 'we the people' within the circle of membership; the other face refuses admission to those outside.

That citizenship is phrased in a language of universalism helps mask its dual nature. Iris Marion Young observed that citizenship is said to express 'a general will, a point of view and interest that citizens have in common which transcends their differences.'[2] Yet at the same time, it imposes 'a demand for homogeneity among citizens.'[3] As citizenship evolved in tandem with the Western nation-state, it incorporated a presumptively masculine and heteronormative subject. Women and sexually non-normative subjects were considered unfit candidates for full membership.

Citizenship's ambit has recently expanded, in recognizing some women and sexual minorities as full citizens, granting them the equality or autonomy they had been historically denied. But this remains an incomplete project, and citizenship may not be capable of infinite extension. As citizenship stretches to incorporate new bodies, it excludes fresh targets of unbelonging.

Feminist, sexual, and queer approaches to citizenship have foregrounded human questions of dependency, reproduction, and sexuality that had been long neglected in citizenship discourse. As explained by feminist theorists, such issues historically had been invisible to citizenship discourse because of the dichotomy between public and private, which split the human universe into gendered bodily spheres. Yet recent attention to relationships of care work, reproduction, and sexual intimacy has raised anew complicated questions about the bifurcation of the personal and the political. At the same time, other themes are emerging in the field. How do ever-intensifying market consumption and shifting categories of sexual freedom re-shape a perception of the citizen self? The self-governing, privatized, and sexually free individual arguably has become the prototypical citizen against which others are found wanting. These are racialized and illiberal others, whose purported lack of sexual freedom relegates them to the wrong side of history, and to the outside of citizenship.

Gendered Histories

A brief history shows how gender shaped specific exclusions from citizenship. Incorporating women as political subjects forces a revision of the famous trajectory

---

[2] Iris Marion Young, 'Polity and Group Difference: A Critique of the Ideal of Universalist Citizenship,' *Ethics 99*, no. 2 (1989): pp. 250–274, p. 252.
[3] Ibid.

of citizenship rights articulated by T.H. Marshall. Marshall asserted that in Western liberal democracies over the eighteenth, nineteenth, and twentieth centuries, respectively, civil rights of property and protection, political rights of participation, and finally and incompletely, social rights were secured.[4] But this narrative did not hold true for women. Into the late nineteenth century, women in countries such as Britain and the United States were not considered independent legal subjects, and thus could not control property or make contracts. At the same time, the campaign to recognize equality between men and women was an intersectional story. As one example, the first Married Women's Property Act passed in the United States, enacted in Mississippi in 1839, aimed primarily to secure the ownership rights of women slaveholders over black persons who were enslaved.[5] We see here how a step toward full citizenship for some women relied upon the denial of personhood of others.

The doctrine of coverture, shaping property relations between man and wife, also ensured that a woman's body was not her own; marital rape and domestic violence did not begin to be criminalized until the twentieth century. Both remain unrecognized as criminal acts in several nation-states today. Women lacked the right to control their own bodies through abortion or contraception, a right which continues to be challenged and so controversial that in 2016 then candidate for U.S. president Donald Trump stated that women who sought abortions should be punished. Women's access to political citizenship began to be guaranteed only at the end of the nineteenth century; the right to vote was only granted nationally in the United States in 1920 and the United Kingdom in 1928, and women were not awarded the right to vote throughout Switzerland until 1990. When suffrage activist Virginia Minor argued in 1874 that her citizenship in the American Republic mandated that she be granted voting rights, the Supreme Court ruled that her citizenship was merely a thin construction, correlating with no assurance of political rights: citizenship for women actually meant only 'membership of a nation and nothing more.'[6]

Yet women were also denied access to this 'membership of a nation,' by which the court meant the formal legal status of citizenship. Citizenship differentiates the citizen from the alien and thus refers not only to civil, political, and social rights; it also concerns membership within the community of the nation-state. Due to the doctrine of dependent citizenship, which placed the husband in the embodied position of the nation-state, married women suffered expatriation when marrying non-citizens. Until World War I, the nationality laws of virtually all countries

[4] T.H. Marshall, *Citizenship and Social Class and Other Essays* (Cambridge: Cambridge University Press, 1950).

[5] Rogers Smith, *Civic Ideals: Conflicting Views of Citizenship in U.S. History* (New Haven, London: Yale University Press, 1999), p. 233.

[6] *Minor v. Happersett*, 88 U.S. 162 (1874); Smith (n 5), p. 341.

made a married woman's nationality contingent upon that of her husband.[7] While this provided an expedited path to citizenship for immigrant women who married citizens, U.S. citizen women who married noncitizens lost their citizenship from 1907 well into the 1930s. Legislation enacted in 1922 secured independent citizenship for white women who married white noncitizen men, but explicitly divested citizenship from women who either were racially ineligible to become U.S. citizens or who married men who were similarly ineligible.[8] Women still do not have an equal right to pass their citizenship to their children in twenty-seven countries, a disability which can leave their children vulnerable to statelessness.[9] The idea that citizenship as a form of property can be thus restricted in its transfer was challenged famously in the 1992 *Unity Dow* case, which found that a law allowing only a father or an unmarried mother to pass citizenship to his or her children born in Botswana was unconstitutional on the ground of sex discrimination.[10] Which persons have been recognizable as citizens, and what attendant rights they can enjoy, has been highly gendered since the foundation of the very notion of nation-state citizenship.

Even when nationality laws are not explicitly gendered, the 'dirty work' of citizenship is carried out by immigration law's restrictions in shaping access to the political community.[11] Immigration admission has never been open to undesirable subjects. Those who are allowed entry primarily provide valuable human capital or permit family reunification; historically women were admitted only as dependents with a migration status tied to that of their male relatives.[12] In U.S. immigration law, for example, the right to family unity only belonged to the male head of the household, until 1952.[13]

What underlay these exclusions was an unquestioned public/private dichotomy, one that consigned women to the private or domestic sphere, reserving citizenship's sphere of the public domain for men. This was a division not only of the appropriate realms for gendered action but of putatively immutable characteristics (dependency, sentiment, and passivity, versus autonomy, rationality, and self-possession) thought integral to each realm.

The gendered boundary between 'public' and 'private' spheres correlated with two different kinds of claims to social resources, one based on market labor, and the other based upon family ties. (This gendered public/private dichotomy thus links to another

[7] Karen Knop, 'Relational Nationality: On Gender and Nationality in International Law,' in T. Alexander Aleinikoff and Douglas Klusmeyer, eds., *Citizenship Today: Global Perspectives and Practices* (Washington: Brookings Institution Press, 2010), pp. 89–124.

[8] Leti Volpp, 'Divesting Citizenship: On Asian American History and the Loss of Citizenship Through Marriage,' *UCLA Law Review 53*, no. 2 (2005): pp. 405–483.

[9] UNHCR, 'Background Note on Gender Equality, Nationality Laws and Statelessness 2014,' online http://www.unhcr.org/4f5886306.pdf.

[10] Knop (n 7), pp. 104–105.

[11] Catherine Dauvergne, 'Citizenship, Migration Laws and Women: Gendering Permanent Residency Statistics,' *Melbourne University Law Review 11* (2000): pp. 280–309.

[12] On states admitting immigrants for reason of human capital see Shachar in this volume.

[13] Sabrina Balgamwalla, 'Bride and Prejudice: How U.S. Immigration Law Discriminates Against Spousal Visa Holders,' *Berkeley Journal of Gender, Law & Justice 29*, no. 1 (2014): pp. 25–71.

public/private dichotomy: that between the state and the market, both arenas domi-nated by men.) In the 'male' sphere contractual relations of exchange flourished. Such relations existed between individuals who were presupposed to be free and independ-ent and in control of their objects of exchange.[14] This 'possessive individualism' cor-related with the idea of self-ownership.[15] Coverture, argue Nancy Fraser and Linda Gordon, like slavery, rationalized subjection of those who could not claim their labor power as their own, separating the universe into those who were free citizens, and those who were not.[16]

Judith Shklar famously identified the essential role played by the right to earn, along with voting, as the foundation of American citizenship, as both a matter of dignity and public respect: 'A good citizen is an earner, because independence is the indelibly necessary quality of genuine, democratic citizenship.'[17] Thus, eli-gibility for paid work outside the home was an explicit criterion for citizenship. Relegated exterior to citizenship were the degraded and enslaved, as well as the citizen's dependents, whose field of action was confined to the domestic sphere of the intimate family. In that sphere, resources were to flow through blood and sen-timent, unlinked to any public circuit of exchange. Single mothers who faced diffi-culty providing such care and who became the recipients of 'mother's pensions' in the United States, so that the state stepped in for the absent male wage, were 'pitied but not entitled.'[18] Care work was perceived to be a product of 'charity,' rather than of 'contract.'[19] Otherwise articulated, the public sphere was characterized as the realm of rights and the pursuit of self-interest, while the private was perceived as the realm of needs, bonds, and selflessness of family.[20]

REPRODUCING THE STATE

This short history elucidates why women faced obstacles to equal pay in the employ-ment context, and why care work has rarely been perceived as a performance of

[14] Nancy Fraser and Linda Gordon, 'Contract versus Charity: Why is There No Social Citizenship in the United States?,' *Socialist Review* 22 (1992): pp. 45–68, p. 52.
[15] C.B. Macpherson, *The Political Theory of Possessive Individualism: Hobbes to Locke* (Oxford: Oxford University Press, 1974).
[16] Fraser and Gordon (n 14), pp. 54–55.
[17] Judith Shklar, *American Citizenship: The Quest for Inclusion* (Cambridge: Harvard University Press, 1991), p. 92.
[18] Linda Gordon, *Pitied but Not Entitled: Single Mothers and the History of Welfare, 1890–1935* (New York: The Free Press, 1994).
[19] Fraser and Gordon (n 14), p. 59.
[20] Wendy Brown, *States of Injury* (Princeton: Princeton University Press, 1995), p. 161.

citizenship. But how, precisely, ought caregiving be understood as a practice of citizenship? And what is the relationship between citizenship and reproduction?

Some scholars argue that care work should be acknowledged as an expression of the responsibilities of social citizenship and should be accorded equal value with paid work obligations.[21] This can lead to an argument in favor of wages for housework, or for the state's responsibility for dependency care to be considered a right no less significant than civil or political rights.[22] Unpaid domestic work functions as the precondition for the illusion of unencumbered participation of male citizens in the public. Yet this domestic labor is necessary for the social reproduction of the citizenry.

Care work is overwhelmingly performed by women. This care work is both provided within families, and in the form of 'global care chains', which are staffed by women who are hired for the purpose of providing domestic labor.[23] Such women are then unable to provide the same level of care for their own families.[24] Women who work on the global care chain are often immigrants, who lack formal citizenship status in the polity where they labor to care for others. Because many have argued that women need to be fully integrated into the labor market in order to achieve equal citizenship, Linda Bosniak asks whether women who hire domestic workers enjoy citizenship at the expense of the citizenship of their household workers, and whether this can be considered a kind of transfer of citizenship. She says not, as the different forms of citizenship at issue makes them nontransferable.[25]

At the same time, we might note that the global care chain illustrates how actual citizenship is not infinitely expandable. Rather, one group claiming citizenship does so through either explicit or implicit distinction from others who cannot. Inclusion in the waged workforce enabling the full citizenship of first world women empowers them to assert their role as 'good citizens' through paid labor in what earlier had been the male sphere, thereby demonstrating their self-possession and market independence. Yet the freedom to engage in such waged work often rests upon the noncitizenship status of their domestic workers, who labor within the domestic sphere of the intimate family, but for a family that is not their own.

[21] Ruth Lister, 'Inclusive Citizenship: Realizing the Potential', in Engin F. Isin, Peter Nyers, and Bryan S. Turner, eds., *Citizenship between Past and Future* (Abingdon, Oxon: Routledge, 2008), pp. 48–60.

[22] On wages for housework see Silvia Federici, *Revolution at Point Zero: Housework, Reproduction and Feminist Struggle* (Oakland: PM Press, 2012). On the need for government subsidy for dependent care see Martha Albertson Fineman, *The Neutered Mother, the Sexual Family and Other Twentieth Century Tragedies* (Abingdon, Oxon: Routledge, 1995).

[23] Arlie Russell Hochschild, 'The Nanny Chain', *The American Prospect 11*, no. 4 (January 3, 2000): pp. 32–36.

[24] Rhacel Salazar Parreñas, *Servants of Globalization: Women, Migration and Domestic Work* (Stanford: Stanford University Press, 2001).

[25] Bosniak (n 1), p. 115.

But could care work, no matter who accomplishes it, actually be considered an exercise of citizenship, despite the fact that it takes place in the domestic sphere? Is a distinction to be recognized between a woman campaigning for men to share in care work versus a woman negotiating how to divide care work at home with her partner?[26] Perceiving a divergence between public campaigning versus private negotiating, Ruth Lister once argued that 'in the case of the former, we are acting as citizens, in the case of the latter, which is nevertheless significant for citizenship, we are not.'[27] Parsing out the difference, she suggests that 'the terrain of political citizenship action is the public sphere [yet] it cannot be divorced from what happens in the private, which shapes its contours and which can be the proper object of citizenship struggles.'[28] In other words, care work provides a resource for political citizenship but should not be considered a form of citizenship activity itself.

Other scholars have asserted, however, that the boundary between the social and political becomes less clear when one centers the experiences of women of color in building one's theory. Caregiving by women of color can teach their children to resist dominant messages about the identities of racialized ethnic groups and thus has been described as a 'political act of citizenship.'[29] One might also consider the critical role of the intimate realm in the consolidation of colonial power, as well as the importance of domestic life in shaping resistance to such power.[30] More recently, Lister has written that in certain circumstances caring can 'represent political citizenship,' and that perhaps what is most relevant is '*what* a person does and with what public consequences' rather than *where* they do it, meaning whether the care work transpires in the 'public' or 'private.'[31]

This debate begs a question: can the public and private be divorced in this way? Their continued dichotomization suggests a habit of thought which assumes that the modern state is not already enmeshed in the supposedly 'non-political' realm of the family. Can the personal be apolitical? Surely not; the modern state regulates even the most 'private' realms of the family, the body, and sexuality through forms of surveillance, self-discipline, and social welfare.[32] From a Foucauldian perspective,

---

[26] See Lister (n 1), p. 28, citing to Anne Phillips, *Democracy and Difference* (University Park: Pennsylvania State University Press, 1993).

[27] Lister (n 1), p. 30.   [28] Ibid., p. 30.

[29] Paul Kershaw, 'Caregiving for Identity is Political: Implications for Citizenship Theory,' *Citizenship Studies 14*, no. 4 (2010): pp. 395–410. See also Chia Longman, Katrien De Graeve, and Tine Brouckaert, 'Mothering as a Citizenship Practice: An Intersectional Analysis of "Carework" and "Culturework" in Non-Normative Mother-Child Identities,' *Citizenship Studies 17*, no. 3–4 (2013): pp. 385–399.

[30] Ann Stoler, ed., *Haunted By Empire: Geographies of Intimacy in North American History* (Durham: Duke University Press, 2006); Beth Piatote, *Domestic Subjects: Gender, Citizenship and Law in Native American Literature* (New Haven: Yale University Press, 2013).

[31] Lister (n 21), p. 56.

[32] Jacques Donzelot, *The Policing of Families* (Baltimore: Johns Hopkins University Press, 1977); Michel Foucault, 'Governmentality,' in Graham Burchell, Colin Gordon, and Peter Miller, eds., *The Foucault Effect* (Chicago: University of Chicago Press, 1991), pp. 87–104.

a public/private distinction that appears to exempt the personal from the disciplinary gaze is illusory: citizenship 'always lays hold of bodies, ensuring their domestication and normalization.'[33] As Engin Isin has suggested, perhaps citizenship is 'social before it is civil or political.' Because governing the social is a significant object of governing the state, activities such as reproducing, consuming, sexual habits, and one's choice of dress become objects of government, and therefore sites of contestation.[34]

Yet the prototypical citizen of liberal theory is an abstract being, and disembodied from such social activities. The question of embodiment, especially of the female body, has largely escaped citizenship theory. Men are recognized as having bodies, but it is denied that they *are* bodies.[35] Put differently, their identities are not subsumed by their bodies; rather, their bodies are controlled by their minds.[36] The male disassociation from the body casts concerns of the flesh—desire, sex, and reproduction, along with care—into the realm of the female and outside the purview of the public citizen. Making politics 'fleshly'—centering a 'shared fleshly sociality' and a focus on bodies in political theorizing—challenges this construction.[37] Attending to the body would remind us that reproductive self-determination must be understood as central to women's citizenship, although it remains a distant goal in much of the world. Power over one's own reproduction is a basic civil right to one's person.

But the relationship between citizenship and reproduction spans additional dimensions beyond autonomy over one's person. Women have been the reproducers of citizenship. They mother, both in the sense of their capacity to give birth to future citizens, and as those whose duty it is to care for and inculcate the virtues of the future citizenry. (Men only 'father' offspring—or nations, responsible only for the original moment of conception.) Women's bodies, and not men's, are located as the symbolic center and boundary marker of the nation.[38] As their bodies represent the nation's purity and honor, women are subjected to reproductive and other forms of control; their bodies become sites of conflict about national

[33] Margrit Shildrick, 'Sexual Citizenship, Governance and Disability: From Foucault to Deleuze,' in Sasha Roseneil, ed., *Beyond Citizenship? Feminism and the Transformation of Belonging* (Hampshire: Palgrave Macmillan, 2013), pp. 138–159.

[34] Engin F. Isin, 'Conclusion: the Socius of Citizenship,' in Engin F. Isin, ed., *Recasting the Social in Citizenship* (Toronto: University of Toronto Press, 2008), pp. 281–286, p. 282.

[35] Shane Phelan, *Sexual Strangers: Gays, Lesbians and Dilemmas of Citizenship* (Philadelphia: Temple University Press, 2001), p. 41.

[36] Ibid., p. 42.

[37] Chris Beasley and Carol Bacchi, 'Making Politics Fleshly: the Ethic of Social Flesh,' in Angelique Bletsas and Chris Beasley, eds., *Engaging with Carol Bacchi: Strategic Interventions and Exchanges* (Adelaide: Adelaide University Press, 2012), pp. 99–120.

[38] Anne McClintock, *Imperial Leather: Race, Gender and Sexuality in the Colonial Contest* (London and New York: Routledge, 1995), pp. 354–357.

cultural identity. Women whose reproductive capacities are valued are greeted by pro-natalist policies; women whose reproduction is not desired have suffered sterilization, forced abortion, and immigration exclusion.[39] In those jurisdictions which follow *jus soli*, or birthright citizenship through right of soil, fear is routinely expressed about undesirable women 'dropping babies' on the territory in order to anchor citizenship; this has led to calls in the United States and elsewhere to abolish the guarantee of *jus soli*.[40]

There is a procreative norm which structures social organization, in the sense of good (and not bad) citizens encouraged to have children. This is visible in Oliver Wendell Holmes' declaration of Progressive Era eugenics on behalf of the Supreme Court: 'Three generations of imbeciles are enough,' in upholding the sterilization of Carrie Buck. Echoes of such logics can be heard in recently struck down Swedish and Danish laws requiring transgendered persons to be sterilized before beginning their gender reassignment.[41] The procreative norm is also apparent in the construction of the good citizen as properly child producing.[42] Political societies project a reproductive futurism wherein the child embodies the citizen as an ideal, as the telos of the social order.[43] This vision of the child extends to the fetus as the ultimate citizen, whose claim to fetal citizenship trumps the citizenship of the pregnant woman, who 'becomes the child to the fetus, becoming more minor and less politically represented.'[44] The importance of fetal citizenship is evident in the U.S. case of Purvi Patel, who was sentenced in 2015 in the state of Indiana to twenty years for allegedly aborting her own pregnancy.[45]

Extending even further back in the chronology of fetal development, we now see what has been coined as 'embryo citizenship.' This concept shaped highly restrictive legislation concerning assisted reproduction in Italy in 2004 in the name of protecting the future interests of the 'yet to come' over the present interests of the female

[39] Jael Silliman and Ynestra King, eds., *Dangerous Intersections: Feminist Perspectives on Population, Environment, and Development* (Boston: South End Press, 1999).

[40] Priscilla Huang, 'Anchor Babies, Over-Breeders, and the Population Bomb: The Reemergence of Nativism and Population Control in Anti-Immigrant Policies,' *Harvard Law & Policy Review* 2 (2008): pp. 385–406.

[41] See *Buck v. Bell* 274 U.S. 200, 207 (1921). On the Swedish law, see Jenny Gunnarsson Payne, 'Transgendering Mother's Day: Blogging as Citizens' Media, Reproductive Rights and Intimate Citizenship,' *Citizenship Studies 17*, no. 8 (2013): pp. 928–941.

[42] Sasha Roseneil, Isabel Crowhurst, Ana Cristina Santos, and Mariya Stoilova, 'Reproduction and Citizenship/Reproducing Citizens: Editorial Introduction,' *Citizenship Studies 17*, no. 8 (2013): pp. 901–911.

[43] Lee Edelman, *No Future: Queer Theory and the Death Drive* (Durham: Duke University Press, 2004).

[44] Lauren Berlant, *The Queen of America Goes to Washington City* (Durham: Duke University Press, 1997): p. 85.

[45] Her sentence was overturned the following year ('Purvi Patel is Released after Feticide Conviction is Overturned,' *Indianapolis Star*, September 1, 2016, online http://www.indystar.com/story/news/crime/2016/09/01/purvi-patel-releases-feticide-conviction-overturned/89707582/).

citizen.[46] The law both restricted how many eggs could be fertilized during an in vitro fertilization treatment to three, and forbade embryos from being frozen or destroyed, all in the name of the rights of the 'conceived being.'

Assisted reproductive technologies both provide the possibility of delinking reproduction from the conventional family, as well as the reassertion of essentialist notions about genetic relations and racial descent.[47] Access to such technologies is shaped by the market. The global care chain staffed by women caring for the children of others is now paralleled by the global reproductive chain, staffed by women who carry the embryos of others, as surrogates. This is now a transnational market which relies upon the lesser market power of poorer countries, as wealthy families scour the globe to 'rent a womb,' paying women perhaps one tenth what a commercial surrogate would cost in the richest countries.[48] The citizenship of children produced by a global reproductive chain can raise challenging questions. As one example, for the transmission of U.S. citizenship, a child born overseas who is conceived through assisted reproductive technologies must prove that a U.S. citizen was either the sperm donor or egg donor. Failure to prove this genetic link via DNA testing can result in statelessness.[49]

How the relationship between citizenship and reproduction structures social and political orders also deserves attention. Though conventional wisdom posits kinship rules concerning race, ethnicity, and gender as 'natural' and as predating the rules that govern political societies, it is political societies that actually determine the kinship rules—relying on natality and ancestry—that are then used to reproduce these societies.[50] *Jus soli* and *jus sanguinis* (citizenship through blood descent,) which both privilege the moment of birth, are obviously bio-genetic models of producing citizens. Yet Siobhan Somerville argues, looking at the United States, that the concept of naturalization is, perhaps surprisingly, also encumbered with assumptions about a heterosexual reproductive subject, thus reinforcing the model of an organic, sexually reproduced citizenry.[51] She writes that this is metaphorically true: to naturalize is 'to introduce [a plant or animal] to a place where it is not indigenous, but in

[46] Patrick Hanafin, *Conceiving Life: Reproductive Politics and the Law in Contemporary Italy* (Aldershot: Ashgate Publishing, 1997).

[47] For an articulation and further discussion of these points, see Dumbrava in this volume.

[48] Ari Shapiro, 'Surrogate Parenting: A Worldwide Industry, Lacking Global Rules,' www.npr.org, June 11, 2015, online http://www.npr.org/sections/parallels/2015/06/11/413406325/surrogate-parenting-a-worldwide-industry-lacking-global-rules.

[49] Erika Tabke, 'Citizenship Denied to IVF Babies Born Overseas,' ivfconnections.com, March 20, 2012, online http://www.ivfconnections.com/forums/content.php/906-U-S-Citizenship-Denied-to-IVF-Babies-Born-Overseas.

[50] Jacqueline Stevens, *Reproducing the State* (Princeton: Princeton University Press, 1999).

[51] Siobhan Somerville, 'Notes toward a Queer History of Naturalization,' in Mary Dudziak and Leti Volpp, eds., *Legal Borderlands: Law and the Construction of American Borders* (Baltimore: Johns Hopkins University Press, 2006): pp. 67–83.

which it may survive and reproduce as if it were native.'[52] We can also consider this true as a matter of governmental practice. Family-sponsored immigration, whereby relatives seek family reunification and which was in the U.S. heterosexually policed until 2013, is in that country the primary avenue through which lawful permanent residence, a precondition for naturalization, is produced.[53]

Yet naturalization is also the mode of citizenship acquisition that best correlates to liberal theory's vision of the autonomous, disembodied, and self-controlled individual, who has the capacity of free choice. This figure is most clearly exemplified by the immigrant who desires to incorporate himself or herself with a new nation-state. Naturalization, rather than forms of citizenship acquisition which rely upon bodily reproduction thus seem to produce citizenry in a mode that best correlates with the self-possessed, rational actor of liberal theory, in contrast to the 'fleshly' product of reproduction.

We could make two observations here. One would be to question Peter Schuck and Rogers Smith's perplexing stand against 'citizenship without consent,' which proposes to end the guarantee of 14th Amendment birthright citizenship in the United States. They argue for changing the mode of citizenship acquisition from 'ascription' based upon the accident of birth on U.S. territory to birthright citizenship only for those whose parents are either U.S. citizens or legal permanent residents. But they do not identify naturalization as an optimal mode for citizenship transmission, even while it would seem to well align with the idea of contract or consent.[54]

The second observation would be to note the connection of naturalization with the desiring and desirable immigrant, a connection that both obscures nonconsensual bases of state formation such as conquest, colonization, and enslavement and serves to symbolize a repeated agreeing to of the social contract.[55] We thus see the importance of the naturalization ceremony, a ritualized public performance of citizenship through consent. The idea of a political community performed through consent projects a vision of the society to come produced as an ethical community, an idealized futurity particularly inherent to settler colonial regimes.[56] The ideal

---

[52] Ibid., p. 76.

[53] Siobhan Somerville, 'Queering Birthright Citizenship' (unpublished manuscript, on file with the author).

[54] Peter Schuck and Rogers Smith, *Citizenship without Consent: Illegal Aliens in the American Polity* (New Haven: Yale University Press, 1985). One could observe that being born to your parents is as accidental as it is to be born in a particular territory. For critiques of the injustices inherent in birthright citizenship see Ayelet Shachar, *The Birthright Lottery: Citizenship and Global Inequality* (Cambridge: Harvard University Press, 2009); Jacqueline Stevens, *States without Nations: Citizenship for Mortals* (New York: Columbia University Press, 2009).

[55] See Bonnie Honig, *Democracy and the Foreigner* (Princeton: Princeton University Press, 2001); Lauren Berlant (n 44).

[56] For a further discussion see Leti Volpp, 'The Indigenous as Alien,' *UC Irvine Law Review* 5 (2015): pp. 289–325.

citizen, capable of autonomy, imagined free of bodily concerns, can thus magically reproduce a state without the sedimentation of flesh or history.

SEXING CITIZENSHIP

What of sexual activity absent reproduction? Could such practice be understood as an enactment of citizenship? Citizenship can be understood as a matter of rights; citizenship can also be understood as an active practice. When the ideal citizen is imagined to act, engaged in practices of citizenship, the citizen is assumed to subordinate individual interests to those of the common good. Acts of citizenship, which constitute a participatory democracy through acts of civic virtue, might include 'voting, volunteering, organizing a book group, or attending a PTA meeting.'[57] Will Kymlicka and Wayne Norman describe the vision of civic republicans thus: 'political life is superior to the merely private pleasures ...'[58] Certainly, sexual activity, unless appropriately channeled in a procreative direction, would not be foregrounded as an act of citizenship by civic republicans or many other advocates of participatory citizenship. In fact, the concept of 'sexual citizenship' has been 'dismissed as an oxymoron.'[59]

But it is precisely the intersection between the terms sexual and citizenship that deserves scrutiny. First coined by David Evans in 1993, to refer to how the intertwining of market and state allowed sexual minorities only a partial and privatized citizenship in the realms of leisure and lifestyle, 'sexual citizenship' has taken on multiple meanings.[60] Some take the term to suggest that questions of intimacy are a necessary addition to Marshall's trio of civil, political, and social rights. This has been alternatively couched as intimate citizenship or affective citizenship. The former refers to 'private practices, moralities, identities and right claims pertaining to issues of the body, sexuality, relations, reproduction and family,' while the latter

---

[57] Sara Bosin, 'Civic Virtue,' *Learning to Give*, online http://www.learningtogive.org/resources/civic-virtue.

[58] Will Kymlicka and Wayne Norman, 'Return of the Citizen: A Survey of Recent Work on Citizenship Theory,' *Ethics 104* (1994): pp. 352–381, p. 362.

[59] Ruth Lister, 'Sexual Citizenship,' in Engin F. Isin and Bryan S. Turner, eds., *Handbook of Citizenship Studies* (London: Sage, 2002), pp. 191–208, p. 191 (describing how sexual citizenship has been dismissed by others).

[60] David Evans, *Sexual Citizenship: The Material Construction of Sexualities* (London, New York: Routledge, 1993).

'draws on the economy of feelings of belonging that tie the citizenship subject to multiple communities, including the nation-state.'[61]

Others have used the term sexual citizenship to characterize non-normative sexual subjects whose aspirations to inclusion have been thwarted, such that '[h]eterosexuality comprised a thick border of citizenship.'[62] Centering the sexually non-normative might thus require adding new claims, perhaps sexual rights, to the array of citizenship rights, or it could mean identifying sexual minorities as a group denied access to civil, political, and social rights.[63] How precisely to capture the relationship of these subjects to the state? Terms such as partial citizens, semi-citizens, second-class citizens, anticitizens, and strangers have been proffered. Each of these terms articulates a different relationship to citizenship, varying as to whether the person is positioned outside of citizenship, and if so, how.

Writing in 1998, Diane Richardson asserted that the appropriate descriptor would be partial citizenship. Her evidence: lesbians and gay men are excluded from civil rights such as formal marriages, similar legal status within the armed forces, protection from discrimination in employment or housing, and safety from harassment. The ability of gays and lesbians to exercise political power, in the form of standing for political office, is limited. And they are also denied social rights: pension, inheritance, and tax rights are all affected by the failure to officially recognize same sex relationships. In Britain homosexuality had been perceived as both undermining the heterosexual family and posing a danger of treachery and treason. Thus, not full citizens, but partial ones: 'Lesbians and gay men are entitled to certain rights of existence, but these are extremely circumscribed, being constructed largely on the condition that they remain in the private sphere and do not seek public recognition or membership in the political community.'[64]

Partial citizens could perhaps be considered a synonym for semi-citizens. Elizabeth Cohen coined the term 'semi-citizens' in order to underline that people do not hold one uniform public status; there are differentiated bundles of rights, available in different degrees and forms.[65] She positions LGBT citizens today on the 'outer bound' of semi-citizenship, as a group with stronger political rights than, say, children, undocumented immigrants, or ex-felons.

'Second-class citizens' appears ubiquitously as a term to describe nominal citizens who face systematic discrimination. It expresses the inequality between those who are already formal members of the state and suggests 'a failure to vindicate, fulfill or

[61] Longman et al. (n 29), p. 386. For more on intimate citizenship see Ken Plummer, 'The Square of Intimate Citizenship: Some Preliminary Proposals,' *Citizenship Studies* 5, no. 3 (2001): pp. 237–253.

[62] Brenda Cossman, *Sexual Citizens: The Legal and Cultural Regulation of Sex and Belonging* (Stanford: Stanford University Press, 2007), p. 7.

[63] Lister (n 59).

[64] Diane Richardson, 'Sexuality and Citizenship,' *Sociology* 32, no. 1 (1998): pp. 83–100.

[65] Elizabeth Cohen, *Semi-Citizenship in Democratic Politics* (New York: Cambridge University Press, 2009).

respect the substantive entitlements of extant citizenship.'[66] The freedom to marry campaign in the United States explicitly argued that the 1996 Defense of Marriage Act, which defined marriage for federal purposes as a marriage between one man and one woman, and which was only overturned in 2013, created a second-class citizenship. 'We are only second-class citizens' has also been a familiar rallying cry in criticizing discrimination against sexual minorities in housing, blood donation, adoption, the military, and employment. Similarly, the ACLU described the state of North Carolina's 2016 prohibition against transgendered persons from using bathrooms not assigned to their 'biological sex' as signaling second-class citizenship.

Citizenship is sometimes narrated as a story of teleological progress; those previously excluded begin to no longer be regarded as outsiders, as gradually the definition of who belongs becomes more inclusive.[67] The term 'second-class citizenship' arguably implies that, over time, groups can move from second class status to first, but this may be possible for only some groups and not others. At the same time, the idea of second-class citizenship does not capture the way in which non-heterosexuals are made visible as dangers to the community—either threatening invasion from outside, or internal degeneration from inside. Shane Phelan thus argues they are best understood to occupy the position of strangers: 'neither enemies nor friends, neither natives nor foreigners; they are near and not near, far, yet here ...'[68] and in the process abjected from 'us.'

The teleological triumphal story also ignores the extreme governmental repression of sex and gender nonconformity which coalesced in the mid-twentieth century of the United States: 'purged from the civil service and military in astounding numbers at midcentury'; barred from federal benefits; faced with FBI and Post Office surveillance; subjected to immigration and naturalization exclusions barring aliens from being admitted on the basis of 'psychopathic personality' and 'sexual deviation' from 1952 to 1990; and, finally, accused of political subversion.[69] Thus, simultaneous to the incremental enfranchisement of women and the halting efforts to dismantle Jim Crow, the post-WWII United States newly constructed the homosexual as the 'anticizen'—creating a hard line posing citizenship against perversion. Here, the anticitizen suggests an oppositional quality, namely, one whose identity threatens to undermine the nation-state, linking political subversion to perversion, a theme to which I will return.

---

[66] Audrey Macklin, 'Who is the Citizen's Other? Considering the Heft of Citizenship,' *Theoretical Inquiries in Law* 8, no. 2 (2007): pp. 333–366, p. 337.

[67] For an example, see Kenneth L. Karst, *Belonging to America: Equal Citizenship and the Constitution* (New Haven: Yale University Press, 1989).

[68] Phelan (n 35), p. 30.

[69] Margot Canaday, *The Straight State: Sexuality and Citizenship in Twentieth-Century America* (Princeton: Princeton University Press, 2009). On the immigration provisions see also Eithne Luibhéid, *Entry Denied: Controlling Sexuality at the Border* (Minneapolis: University of Minnesota Press, 2002).

Queer Liberalism, Homonormativity, Homonationalism, and Sexual Citizenship

But do gays and lesbians in countries such as the United States still experience a form of lesser citizenship, however defined, or are they now, in some contexts, in fact considered normative citizen subjects? A number of scholars have recently suggested that gay and lesbian subjects at this moment in fact occupy a privileged position and that their role as model (minority) citizens is used to discipline illiberal minorities or regions of the world. Significant here are the formulations of 'queer liberalism,' 'homonormativity,' and 'homonationalism,' all of which link contemporary normative citizenship to privatization, consumption, and self-governance, while also connecting that citizenship with racial exclusion.

Such a move correlates with a transition away from the notion that participation in the paid labor force is the essential criterion for the conception of citizenship (a conception which, as noted above, limited the means of recognizing feminist claims for equality). Writing in 1990, Nikolas Rose marked a shift in the identity and economic role of the citizen from the producer of work to the consumer: 'Through consumption we are urged to shape our lives by the use of our purchasing power … The image of the citizen as a choosing self entails a new image of the productive subject.'[70] In the neoliberal context of a declining welfare state, '"[f]reedom" and "power" are thus increasingly (even exclusively) articulated through the market.'[71] Here, the power to consume becomes the cornerstone of citizenship. The choosing self is a self-regulating self, freed of a 'nanny state,' who can 'go shopping' as a patriotic affirmation of citizenship (as President George W. Bush suggested Americans do after the terrorist attacks of September 11, 2011).

This consumer citizen no longer expects redistribution or social rights guaranteed by the state, but instead anticipates an ethos of freedom in the marketplace. This freedom now means that the citizen is urged to maximize her own utility, by participating, not in a shared political project, but in the 'sharing economy.'[72] This shift accompanies obligations transferred from the state to the individual citizen, a 'thousand points of light' whereby volunteerism can take the place of a shrunken

---

[70] Nikolas Rose, *Governing the Soul: The Shaping of the Private Self* (London, New York: Routledge, 1990): p. 103.

[71] David Bell and Jon Binnie, 'Authenticating Queer Space: Citizenship, Urbanism and Governance,' *Urban Studies 41*, no. 9 (2004): pp. 1807–1820, p. 1809.

[72] Arguably, no longer just a citizen-consumer, the responsible citizen is now also an individual entrepreneur.

state. The social welfare state is being replaced by the market citizen.[73] Active citizenship, then, means a refashioning by the citizen of the self, within a polity newly conceived as a market-state.[74] The Fab Five, the team of gay men who undertook emergency makeovers of heterosexual men on the hit television show, Queer Eye for the Straight Guy, can thus appear as iconic citizens: they inculcate discipline and self-improvement in others, while shopping.[75]

Queer theorists have noted that this transformation in citizenship appears in the ascendance of a new 'homonormativity' which redefined gay equality as access to previously heteronormative institutions of domestic privacy, the 'free' market and patriotism, shrinking the gay public sphere in the process.[76] This new politics no longer contested dominant heteronormative assumptions about marriage, monogamy, or reproduction, but upholds them. In the words of the self-described conservative gay rights activist Andrew Sullivan, in 1989: 'Legalizing gay marriage ... would foster social cohesion, emotional security, and economic prudence ... it could also help nurture children ... It would also, in the wake of AIDS, qualify as a genuine public health measure.'[77] This argument spurred Michael Warner to point out what was the 'trouble with normal': a retreat from radicalism to respectability, premised in sexual shame.[78]

The focus on access to institutions of domestic privacy coincided with what Lauren Berlant named the 'privatization of citizenship': a collapsing of the political and the personal into a world of 'public intimacy' where citizenship was produced by personal acts and no longer directed toward public life.[79] The body politic had become partitioned off into 'residential enclaves'; citizenship was 'downsized' to voluntarism and privacy. Civic ethics centered around sexual and familial practices, while political duty required no more than individual acts of consumption and accumulation.[80] Excluded from this vision of citizenship are those who make fiscal demands upon the state, as well as the sexually non-normative who do not fit neatly into domestic marriages, those who remain sexual 'outlaws', and 'citizen perverts'.[81] Precluded are those considered too dependent upon the state for support,

[73] Judy Fudge, 'After Industrial Citizenship: Market Citizenship or Citizenship at Work?', *Relations Industrielles/Industrial Relations* 60, no. 4 (2005): pp. 631–656.

[74] On the rise of the market-state, see Philip Bobbitt, *The Shield of Achilles: War, Peace, and the Course of History* (New York: Knopf, 2002).

[75] For a discussion, see Cossman (n 62).

[76] Lisa Duggan, *The Twilight of Equality? Neoliberalism, Cultural Politics, and the Attack on Democracy* (Boston: Beacon Press, 2003), pp. 50–51.

[77] Andrew Sullivan, 'Here Comes the Groom: A Conservative Case for Gay Marriage', *The New Republic*, August 27, 1989, online https://newrepublic.com/article/79054/here-comes-the-groom

[78] Michael Warner, *The Trouble with Normal: Sex, Politics, and the Ethics of Free Life* (New York: Free Press, 1999).

[79] Berlant (n 44).   [80] Ibid.

[81] On 'citizen perverts', see David Bell, 'Pleasure and Danger: The Paradoxical Spaces of Sexual Citizenship', *Political Geography* 14 (1995): pp. 139–153. On not fitting into domestic marriages, see Chiara Bertone, 'Citizenship Across Generations: Struggles Around Heteronormativities', *Citizenship Studies* 17, no. 8 (2013): pp. 985–999.

and those who are too unruly, with their deviant sexual lives and practices, to be good sexual citizens.[82]

But, importantly, also rejected are those who are thought to be too oppressed to be considered proper citizens. These include racialized immigrant communities, perceived as intolerant, uncivilized and illiberal, embodying the parts of the world from where they come. In David Eng's conception of 'queer liberalism', newly emancipated gay and lesbian U.S. citizens have been engaged in an increasingly visible and mass-mediated consumer lifestyle, foregrounded as model citizens coupled in conjugal marriage, enacting intimacy as a kind of legally protected property right. This intimacy is imagined to be colorblind, but race is now 'sublated into normative discourses of privacy, intimacy, bourgeois domesticity, marriage, family and kinship'. Simultaneously produced, then, as two sides of the same coin, are both queer liberalism and a discourse of racialized immigrant homophobia.[83] Normal, now, is white gay visibility; immigrant and nonwhite culture are cast as repressive and dysfunctional.[84] We could consider here the activity of European nationalists such as the Dutch politicians Pim Fortuyn and Geert Wilders, linking gay rights with the need to restrict Muslim immigration, or the speech of Donald Trump after the 2016 massacre of forty-nine people at a gay club in Orlando, Florida, where he vowed to protect 'gay and lesbian citizens' against 'radical Islam'. One could also look to President Trump's January 2017 executive order, barring citizens from seven majority Muslim countries from entering the United States, which stated that the United States should not admit 'those who would oppress Americans' on the basis of 'sexual orientation'.[85]

The term sexual citizenship now bears a new meaning, but with a highly negative valence. Rather than an exhortation to expand the rights of sexual minorities in the name of justice, its message is now one of a completed Euro-American project, which justifies efforts such as the war on terror or anti-immigrant policies by depicting parts of the world and particular communities as sexually backward.[86] The sexual-rights-bearing subject created through sexual citizenship, as Leticia Sabsay writes, is reconceived as an entitlement that is both universal and, ahistorically, as one that has always existed.[87] Instead of perceiving all societies as characterized

---

[82] Katherine Franke, *Wedlocked: The Perils of Marriage Equality* (New York: NYU Press, 2015).

[83] David L. Eng, *The Feeling of Kinship* (Durham: Duke University Press, 2010), p. 47.

[84] Sima Shaksari, 'After Orlando,' Middle East Research and Information Project (June 17, 2016), online http://www.merip.org/after-orlando.

[85] Leti Volpp, 'Trump's Mention of "Honor Killings" Betrays the Truth of His "Muslim Ban,"' *The Hill*, February 22, 2017, online http://thehill.com/blogs/pundits-blog/immigration/320632-trumps-mention-of-honor-killings-betray-the-truth-of-his.

[86] Leticia Sabsay, 'The Emergence of the Other Sexual Citizen: Orientalism and the Modernisation of Sexuality,' *Citizenship Studies* 16, no. 5–6 (2012): pp. 605–623. See also Francesca Romana Ammaturo, 'The "Pink Agenda": Questioning and Challenging European Homonationalist Sexual Citizenship,' *Sociology* 49, no. 6 (2015): pp. 1151–1166.

[87] Sabsay (n 86).

by sexism, homophobia, and transphobia, simply manifested in alternate forms, the world thus becomes organized along a hierarchy of gender and sexual equality development. Cultures outside the North Atlantic are figured as mired in gender oppression, homophobia, and transphobia, in contrast to modernity, tolerance, and democratic values.[88] This conceptualization of 'homonationalism,' as articulated by Jasbir Puar, illuminates how acceptance of and tolerance for gay and lesbian subjects has become a barometer by which the right to and capacity for national sovereignty is measured.[89]

As Puar has pointed out, there is a correlation made, not accidentally, between the terrorist and the perverse, indebted to Orientalist constructions of Muslim male sexuality as simultaneously excessively queer and dangerously premodern.[90] This linkage between the perverse and the Oriental dates to the conception of the Western polity as a civilized space in which free men met as individuals and made rational decisions.[91] This democratic Occident was juxtaposed with the despotic Orient, which was tribal, irrational, and dangerously immoral.[92] The Orient was conflated with the sphere of the private, and gendered as female. Characterized by weakness, as well as by vulnerability, female and Oriental bodies created, and continues to create, a justifying circumstance for Western imperial intervention.[93]

The kind of nineteenth-century civilizational hierarchy now being re-configured through homonationalism means that sexual rights can be made to function as a kind of political currency for states. This is a currency which can be expended either to deflect attention from oppressive acts in which those states engage (in what has been called 'pinkwashing') or it may be put to work to produce a moral high ground enabling those states to discipline others.[94]

Perhaps this should surprise no one. As Sabsay identifies, the problem is that the 'citizenship' of sexual citizenship remains anchored to the notion of the abstract individual and the universal subject-citizen.[95] The citizen is a self who envisions himself or herself as 'whole and free' in contradistinction to suffering women in what were once called developing countries, or whose ethno-religious origins link them to those backward regions of the world.[96] The idea of sexual freedom is

[88] Ibid.

[89] Jasbir Puar, *Terrorist Assemblages: Homonationalism in Queer Times* (Durham: Duke University Press, 2007).

[90] Ibid.

[91] Engin Isin, 'Citizenship after Orientalism,' in Engin F. Isin and Bryan S. Turner, eds., *Handbook of Citizenship Studies* (London: Sage, 2002), pp. 117–128.

[92] Tara Atluri, 'The Prerogative of the Brave: Hijras and Sexual Citizenship After Orientalism,' *Citizenship Studies* 16, no. 5–6 (2012): pp. 721–736; Edward Said, *Orientalism* (New York: Pantheon, 1978).

[93] Meyda Yeğenoğlu, *Colonial Fantasies: Towards a Feminist Reading of Orientalism* (London: Cambridge University Press, 1998).

[94] For a discussion of how this functions in the context of refugee protection, see Costello in this volume.

[95] Sabsay (n 86).

[96] See Inderpal Grewal, *Transnational America* (Durham: Duke University Press, 2005), p. 16.

bound up with the 'sovereign-free' individual of liberalism.[97] This ideal citizen is constructed as liberated through her distinction from her constitutive other, who is imagined to be living a life of utter subjection and constraint. Thus, sexual citizenship serves as the 'access gate to juridical, political and social intelligibility.'[98] Those who fail the test of sexual citizenship, those culturally bodied others, are unable to make themselves belong, even while the cultural specificity of sexual citizenship goes unmarked.[99] This is apparent in the attempt of multiple towns in France in 2016 to enact a 'burkini ban,' to take one striking example, leading to the spectacle of armed police officers ticketing women on beaches for covering too much of their bodies and thus refusing to display their bodies to the public in a manner deemed appropriate.

CONCLUSION: QUEER CITIZENSHIP?

Does it make sense to talk of any alternative to normative sexual citizenship in the form of queer citizenship? The term 'queer' was once understood as 'the name for a political movement and an extensive critique of a wide range of social normalizations and exclusions.'[100] However the term 'queer' has become increasingly unmoored from any standpoint of critique and contestation, coopted to simply serve as an alternative term for LGBTQ identity. Once, to speak of 'queering citizenship' suggested subverting citizenship's foundations, to, for example, challenge its ideology of independence and masculinity and not simply to proclaim 'citizenship for queers.'[101] It seems difficult, if not impossible, for queer citizenship to escape the pathway of sexual citizenship, that is, as also smuggling in its baggage a cultural hierarchy of the world. As one example, we could think here of how queer citizenship in the United States has been critiqued as another form of settler citizenship, so that sexual minority politics and culture is defined against the indigenous and engages in indigenous appropriation.[102]

Being included in citizenship may require engaging in a framework of normality and deviance, of legitimacy and illegitimacy, a framework that forecloses other

---

[97] Sabsay (n 86), p. 619.   [98] Ammaturo (n 88), p. 53.

[99] See Leti Volpp, 'The Culture of Citizenship,' *Theoretical Inquiries in Law* 8, no. 2 (2007): pp. 571–602.

[100] Eng (n 83), p. xi.   [101] Phelan (n 35), p. 62.

[102] Scott Lauria Morgensen, *Spaces between Us: Queer Settler Colonialism and Indigenous Decolonization* (Minneapolis: University of Minnesota Press, 2011).

ways of thinking about the sexual field.[103] Citizenship, arguably, is not available to be 'queered.' Citizenship, while representing membership, recognition, and belonging, is also a technology of governance: citizenship 'always lays hold of bodies, ensuring their domestication and normalisation.'[104]

But what of bodies even more unruly that may resist such normalization? If a trans person states, 'I'm a citizen just like you' might this actually simultaneously perform both assimilation and radical alterity?[105] In other words, can citizenship both discipline and serve as a means of resistance?[106] Of course, when those who historically have fallen outside citizenship's protections successfully claim its status, rights, and identity, this claim constitutes a foundational change to political societies. And as citizenship stretches to encompass the formerly excluded its character may shift. Yet even as it moves to embrace these new bodies, citizenship relentlessly, by its foundational logic, continues to rely upon and create new exclusions of 'those who do not or cannot fit.'[107]

What might be such new expansions and exclusions of citizenship? Future directions for research should attend to how citizenship discourse and practice shape a hierarchy of human life. I suggest here three specific areas of inquiry. An important question to examine is how ideas of citizenship relate to notions of disposability and social death. Disposability refers to the way in which individuals and entire populations are made redundant, abandoned, or expendable.[108] Social death captures the idea of alienation, of ineligibility for personhood, of rightlessness.[109] Both concepts express racialized dispossession, with which theories of feminist, sexual, and queer citizenship productively intersect. Second, animal studies has recently emerged as a significant lens through which to understand conceptions of the human, as who counts as fully human, and which lives matter. Animals function to displace questions about humans, provide a means through which to understand relations between humans, and, of course, humans are also animals.[110] What might feminist, sexual, and queer citizenship learn from

---

[103] Judith Butler, 'Is Kinship Always Already Heterosexual?', *differences: A Journal of Feminist Cultural Studies* 15, no. 1 (2001): pp. 14–44.

[104] Shildrick (n 33), p. 146.

[105] Isaac West, *Transforming Citizenships: Transgender Articulations of the Law* (New York, London: NYU Press, 2014), p. 27.

[106] Carl F. Stychin, 'Sexual Citizenship in the European Union,' *Citizenship Studies* 5, no. 3 (2001): pp. 285–291.

[107] Shildrick (n 33), p. 138.

[108] Sherene Razack, 'Gendered Disposability,' *Canadian Journal of Women and the Law* 26, no. 2 (2016): pp. 285–307.

[109] Lisa Marie Cacho, *Social Death: Racialized Rightlessness and the Criminalization of the Unprotected* (New York: NYU Press, 2012).

[110] See Irus Braverman, 'Captive: Zoometric Operations in Gaza,' *Public Culture* 29, no. 1 (2017): pp. 191–215; Mel Chen, *Animacies: Biopolitics, Racial Mattering, and Queer Affect* (Durham, London: Duke University Press, 2012).

animal studies?[111] And, finally, we live in a world that is ever violent, and in one where some believe there to be a civilizational war between the West and Islam. Building on the work on sexual citizenship, more study should focus upon how this perception relates to the conventional, and problematic, presumption that secularism is a precondition for the sexual freedom believed to be a property of the citizen.[112]

Citizenship is about borders—both territorial and metaphorical—even while it concerns belonging. The excluded function as the other against which citizenship claims are articulated and expressed, even in calls for feminist, sexual, or queer citizenship. As this chapter shows, the fact of belonging to citizenship's inside is made intelligible, through citizenship's outside.

BIBLIOGRAPHY

Ammaturo, Francesca Romana, 'The "Pink Agenda": Questioning and Challenging European Homonationalist Sexual Citizenship,' *Sociology 49*, no. 6 (2015): pp. 1151–1166.

Atluri, Tara, 'The Prerogative of the Brave: Hijras and Sexual Citizenship After Orientalism,' *Citizenship Studies 16*, no. 5–6 (2012): pp. 721–736.

Balgamwalla, Sabrina, 'Bride and Prejudice: How U.S. Immigration Law Discriminates Against Spousal Visa Holders,' *Berkeley Journal of Gender, Law & Justice 29*, no. 1 (2014): pp. 25–71.

Beasley, Chris and Carol Bacchi, 'Making Politics Fleshly: the Ethic of Social Flesh,' in Angelique Bletsas and Chris Beasley, eds., *Engaging with Carol Bacchi: Strategic Interventions and Exchanges* (Adelaide: Adelaide University Press, 2012), pp. 99–120.

Bell, David, 'Pleasure and Danger: The Paradoxical Spaces of Sexual Citizenship,' *Political Geography 14* (1995): pp. 139–153.

Bell, David and Jon Binnie, 'Authenticating Queer Space: Citizenship, Urbanism and Governance,' *Urban Studies 41*, no. 9 (2004): pp. 1807–1820.

Berlant, Lauren, *The Queen of America Goes to Washington City* (Durham: Duke University Press, 1997).

Bertone, Chiara, 'Citizenship Across Generations: Struggles Around Heteronormativities,' *Citizenship Studies 17*, no. 8 (2013): pp. 985–999.

Bobbitt, Philip, *The Shield of Achilles: War, Peace, and the Course of History* (New York: Knopf, 2002).

Bosin, Sara, 'Civic Virtue,' *Learning to Give*, online http://www.learningtogive.org/resources/civic-virtue.

Bosniak, Linda, *The Citizen and the Alien: Dilemmas of Contemporary Membership* (Princeton: Princeton University Press, 2008).

---

[111] For the argument that citizenship should be extended to domesticated animals see Donaldson and Kymlicka in this volume.

[112] For an analysis of secularism, see Saba Mahmood, *Religious Difference in a Secular Age: A Minority Report* (Princeton: Princeton University Press, 2015).

Braverman, Irus, 'Captive: Zoometric Operations in Gaza,' *Public Culture* 29, no. 1 (2017): pp. 191–215.

Brown, Wendy, *States of Injury* (Princeton: Princeton University Press, 1995).

Buck v. Bell 274 U.S. 200, 207 (1921).

Butler, Judith, 'Is Kinship Always Already Heterosexual?,' *differences: A Journal of Feminist Cultural Studies* 15, no. 1 (2001): pp. 14–44.

Cacho, Lisa Marie, *Social Death: Racialized Rightlessness and the Criminalization of the Unprotected* (New York: NYU Press, 2012).

Canaday, Margot, *The Straight State: Sexuality and Citizenship in Twentieth-Century America* (Princeton: Princeton University Press, 2009).

Chen, Mel, *Animacies: Biopolitics, Racial Mattering, and Queer Affect* (Durham, London: Duke University Press, 2012).

Cohen, Elizabeth, *Semi-Citizenship in Democratic Politics* (New York: Cambridge University Press, 2009).

Cossman, Brenda, *Sexual Citizens: The Legal and Cultural Regulation of Sex and Belonging* (Stanford: Stanford University Press, 2007).

Dauvergne, Catherine, 'Citizenship, Migration Laws and Women: Gendering Permanent Residency Statistics,' *Melbourne University Law Review* 11 (2000): pp. 280–309.

Donzelot, Jacques, *The Policing of Families* (Baltimore: Johns Hopkins University Press, 1977).

Duggan, Lisa, *The Twilight of Equality? Neoliberalism, Cultural Politics, and the Attack on Democracy* (Boston: Beacon Press, 2003).

Edelman, Lee, *No Future: Queer Theory and the Death Drive* (Durham: Duke University Press, 2004).

Eng, David L., *The Feeling of Kinship* (Durham: Duke University Press, 2010).

Evans, David, *Sexual Citizenship: The Material Construction of Sexualities* (London, New York: Routledge, 1993).

Federici, Silvia, *Revolution at Point Zero: Housework, Reproduction and Feminist Struggle* (Oakland: PM Press, 2012).

Fineman, Martha Albertson, *The Neutered Mother, the Sexual Family and Other Twentieth Century Tragedies* (Abingdon, Oxon: Routledge, 1995).

Foucault, Michel, 'Governmentality,' in Graham Burchell, Colin Gordon, and Peter Miller, eds., *The Foucault Effect* (Chicago: University of Chicago Press, 1991), pp. 87–104.

Franke, Katherine, *Wedlocked: The Perils of Marriage Equality* (New York: NYU Press, 2015).

Fraser, Nancy and Linda Gordon, 'Contract versus Charity: Why is there no Social Citizenship in the United States?,' *Socialist Review* 22 (1992): pp. 45–68.

Fudge, Judy, 'After Industrial Citizenship: Market Citizenship or Citizenship at Work?,' *Relations Industrielles/Industrial Relations* 60, no. 4 (2005): pp. 631–656.

Gordon, Linda, *Pitied but Not Entitled: Single Mothers and the History of Welfare, 1890-1935* (New York: The Free Press, 1994).

Grewal, Inderpal, *Transnational America* (Durham: Duke University Press, 2005).

Hanafin, Patrick, *Conceiving Life: Reproductive Politics and the Law in Contemporary Italy* (Aldershot: Ashgate Publishing, 1997).

Hochschild, Arlie Russell, 'The Nanny Chain,' *The American Prospect* 11, no. 4 (January 3, 2000): pp. 32–36, online http://prospect.org/article/nanny-chain.

Honig, Bonnie, *Democracy and the Foreigner* (Princeton: Princeton University Press, 2001).

Huang, Priscilla, 'Anchor Babies, Over-Breeders, and the Population Bomb: The Reemergence of Nativism and Population Control in Anti-Immigrant Policies,' *Harvard Law & Policy Review 2* (2008): pp. 385–406.

Isin, Engin F., 'Citizenship after Orientalism,' in Engin F. Isin and Bryan S. Turner, eds., *Handbook of Citizenship Studies* (London: Sage, 2002), pp. 117–128.

Isin, Engin F., 'Conclusion: the Socius of Citizenship,' in Engin F. Isin, ed., *Recasting the Social in Citizenship* (Toronto: University of Toronto Press, 2008), pp. 281–286.

Karst, Kenneth L., *Belonging to America: Equal Citizenship and the Constitution* (New Haven: Yale University Press, 1989).

Kershaw, Paul, 'Caregiving for Identity is Political: Implications for Citizenship Theory,' *Citizenship Studies 14*, no. 4 (2010): pp. 395–410.

Knop, Karen, 'Relational Nationality: On Gender and Nationality in International Law,' in T. Alexander Aleinikoff and Douglas Klusmeyer, eds., *Citizenship Today: Global Perspectives and Practices* (Washington: Brookings Institution Press, 2010), pp. 89–124.

Kymlicka, Will and Wayne Norman, 'Return of the Citizen: A Survey of Recent Work on Citizenship Theory,' *Ethics 104* (1994): pp. 352–381.

Lister, Ruth, *Citizenship: Feminist Perspectives* (New York: New York University Press, 1997).

Lister, Ruth, 'Sexual Citizenship,' in Engin F. Isin and Bryan S. Turner, eds., *Handbook of Citizenship Studies* (London: Sage, 2002), pp. 191–208.

Lister, Ruth, 'Inclusive Citizenship: Realizing the Potential,' in Engin F. Isin, Peter Nyers, and Bryan S. Turner, eds., *Citizenship between Past and Future* (Abingdon, Oxon: Routledge Press, 2008), pp. 48–60.

Longman, Chia, Katrien De Graeve, and Tine Brouckaert, 'Mothering as a Citizenship Practice: An Intersectional Analysis of "Carework" and "Culturework" in Non-Normative Mother-Child Identities,' *Citizenship Studies 17*, no. 3–4 (2013): pp. 385–399.

Luibheid, Eithne, *Entry Denied: Controlling Sexuality at the Border* (Minneapolis: University of Minnesota Press, 2002).

Macklin, Audrey, 'Who is the Citizen's Other? Considering the Heft of Citizenship,' *Theoretical Inquiries in Law 8*, no. 2 (2007): pp. 333–366.

Macpherson, C.B., *The Political Theory of Possessive Individualism: Hobbes to Locke* (Oxford: Oxford University Press, 1974).

Mahmood, Saba, *Religious Difference in a Secular Age: A Minority Report* (Princeton: Princeton University Press, 2015).

Marshall, T.H., *Citizenship and Social Class and Other Essays* (Cambridge: Cambridge University Press, 1950).

McClintock, Anne, *Imperial Leather: Race, Gender and Sexuality in the Colonial Contest* (London, New York: Routledge, 1995).

Minor v. Happersett, 88 U.S. 162 (1874).

Morgensen, Scott Lauria, *Spaces between Us: Queer Settler Colonialism and Indigenous Decolonization* (Minneapolis, University of Minnesota Press, 2011).

'Purvi Patel is Released after Feticide Conviction is Overturned,' *Indianapolis Star*, September 1, 2016, online http://www.indystar.com/story/news/crime/2016/09/01/purvi-patel-releases-feticide-conviction-overturned/89707582/.

Parreñas, Rhacel Salazar, *Servants of Globalization: Women, Migration and Domestic Work* (Stanford: Stanford University Press, 2001).

Payne, Jenny Gunnarsson, 'Transgendering Mother's Day: Blogging as Citizens' Media, Reproductive Rights and Intimate Citizenship,' *Citizenship Studies* 17, no. 8 (2013): pp. 928–941.

Phelan, Shane, *Sexual Strangers: Gays, Lesbians and Dilemmas of Citizenship* (Philadelphia: Temple University Press, 2001).

Phillips, Anne, *Democracy and Difference* (University Park: Pennsylvania State University Press, 1993).

Piatote, Beth, *Domestic Subjects: Gender, Citizenship and Law in Native American Literature* (New Haven: Yale University Press, 2013).

Plummer, Ken, 'The Square of Intimate Citizenship: Some Preliminary Proposals,' *Citizenship Studies* 5, no. 3 (2001): pp. 237–253.

Puar, Jasbir, *Terrorist Assemblages: Homonationalism in Queer Times* (Durham: Duke University Press, 2007).

Razack, Sherene, 'Gendered Disposability,' *Canadian Journal of Women and the Law* 26, no. 2 (2016): pp. 285–307.

Richardson, Diane, 'Sexuality and Citizenship,' *Sociology* 32, no. 1 (1998): pp. 83–100.

Rose, Nikolas, *Governing the Soul: The Shaping of the Private Self* (London, New York: Routledge, 1990).

Roseneil, Sasha, Isabel Crowhurst, Ana Cristina Santos, and Mariya Stoilova, 'Reproduction and Citizenship/Reproducing Citizens: Editorial Introduction,' *Citizenship Studies* 17, no. 8 (2013): pp. 901–911.

Sabsay, Leticia, 'The Emergence of the Other Sexual Citizen: Orientalism and the Modernisation of Sexuality,' *Citizenship Studies* 16, no. 5–6 (2012): pp. 605–623.

Said, Edward, *Orientalism* (New York: Pantheon, 1978).

Schuck, Peter and Rogers Smith, *Citizenship without Consent: Illegal Aliens in the American Polity* (New Haven: Yale University Press, 1985).

Seidman, Steven, 'From Identity to Queer Politics: Shifts in Normative Heterosexuality and the Meaning of Citizenship,' *Citizenship Studies* 5, no. 3 (2001): pp. 321–328.

Shachar, Ayelet, *The Birthright Lottery: Citizenship and Global Inequality* (Cambridge: Harvard University Press, 2009).

Shaksari, Sima, 'After Orlando,' *Middle East Research and Information Project* (June 17, 2016), online http://www.merip.org/after-orlando.

Shapiro, Ari, 'Surrogate Parenting: A Worldwide Industry, Lacking Global Rules,' www.npr.org, June 11, 2015, online http://www.npr.org/sections/parallels/2015/06/11/413406325/surrogate-parenting-a-worldwide-industry-lacking-global-rules.

Shildrick, Margrit, 'Sexual Citizenship, Governance and Disability: From Foucault to Deleuze,' in Sasha Roseneil, ed., *Beyond Citizenship? Feminism and the Transformation of Belonging* (Hampshire: Palgrave Macmillan, 2013), pp. 138–159.

Shklar, Judith, *American Citizenship: The Quest for Inclusion* (Cambridge: Harvard University Press, 1991).

Silliman, Jael and Ynestra King, *Dangerous Intersections: Feminist Perspectives on Population, Environment, and Development* (Boston: South End Press, 1999).

Smith, Rogers, *Civic Ideals: Conflicting Views of Citizenship in U.S. History* (New Haven, London: Yale University Press, 1999).

Somerville, Siobhan, 'Queering Birthright Citizenship' (unpublished manuscript, on file with the author).

Somerville, Siobhan, 'Notes toward a Queer History of Naturalization,' in Mary Dudziak and Leti Volpp, eds., *Legal Borderlands: Law and the Construction of American Borders* (Baltimore: Johns Hopkins University Press, 2006): pp. 67–83.

Stevens, Jacqueline, *Reproducing the State* (Princeton: Princeton University Press, 1999).

Stevens, Jacqueline, *States without Nations: Citizenship for Mortals* (New York: Columbia University Press, 2009).

Stoler, Ann, ed., *Haunted By Empire: Geographies of Intimacy in North American History* (Durham: Duke University Press, 2006).

Stychin, Carl F., 'Sexual Citizenship in the European Union,' *Citizenship Studies* 5, no. 3 (2001): pp. 285–291.

Sullivan, Andrew, 'Here Comes the Groom: A Conservative Case for Gay Marriage,' *The New Republic* August 27, 1989, online https://newrepublic.com/article/79054/here-comes-the-groom.

Tabke, Erika, 'Citizenship Denied to IVF Babies Born Overseas,' ivfconnections.com, March 20, 2012, online http://www.ivfconnections.com/forums/content.php/906-U-S-Citizenship-Denied-to-IVF-Babies-Born-Overseas.

UNHCR, 'Background Note on Gender Equality, Nationality Laws and Statelessness 2014,' online http://www.unhcr.org/4f5886306.pdf.

Volpp, Leti, 'Divesting Citizenship: On Asian American History and the Loss of Citizenship Through Marriage,' *UCLA Law Review* 53, no. 2 (2005): pp. 405–483.

Volpp, Leti, 'The Culture of Citizenship,' *Theoretical Inquiries in Law* 8, no. 2 (2007): pp. 493–601.

Volpp, Leti, 'The Indigenous as Alien,' *UC Irvine Law Review* 5 (2015): pp. 289–325.

Volpp, Leti, 'Trump's Mention of "Honor Killings" Betrays the Truth of His "Muslim Ban,"' The Hill, February 22, 2017, online http://thehill.com/blogs/pundits-blog/immigration/320632-trumps-mention-of-honor-killings-betray-the-truth-of-his.

Warner, Michael, *The Trouble with Normal: Sex, Politics, and the Ethics of Free Life* (New York: Free Press, 1999).

West, Isaac, *Transforming Citizenships: Transgender Articulations of the Law* (New York, London: NYU Press, 2014).

Yeğenoğlu, Meyda, *Colonial Fantasies: Towards a Feminist Reading of Orientalism* (London: Cambridge University Press, 1998).

Young, Iris Marion, 'Polity and Group Difference: A Critique of the Ideal of Universalist Citizenship,' *Ethics* 99, no. 2 (1989): pp. 250–274.

CHAPTER 9

....

POSTCOLONIAL
CITIZENSHIP

....

KAMAL SADIQ

INTRODUCTION

....

WHILE citizenship has a long lineage in developed Western states, we know very little about citizenship's advance in postcolonial developing states.[1] Postcolonial citizenship is the status, and the rights and obligations associated with it, of individuals and groups in independent, often multiethnic, states formerly controlled by European colonial powers.[2] It is structured by a history of colonial rule and the inherent power differentials and social control implicit in European imperial

[1] On European citizenship see T.H. Marshall and Tom Bottomore, *Citizenship and Social Class* (London: Pluto Press, 1987).
[2] Postcolonial literature commonly refers to 'West European' experiences as 'European.' Most of the British colonies were multiethnic but there are a small number that are not, because the colonies were delineated along political boundaries not attentive to the ethnic groups on the ground.

projects. Postcolonial citizenship is also associated with nationalist movements that sought to redefine political communities through self-determination and democratization. A touchstone of this chapter is decolonization after World War II, with a specific examination of post-independence citizenship among colonies of the British Empire in Asia and Africa. A postcolonial lens offers an understanding of citizenship from the viewpoint of the marginalized, a critique of European experiences, and a reexamination of liberal constructions of citizenship.

Independence from colonial powers was spread over forty years between the 1940s and the 1970s for many developing countries in Asia and Africa.[3] This process of decolonization involved the withdrawal of European powers from their colonies, the establishment of new distinct territorial boundaries, and the construction of modern nation-states and political institutions. With independence, countries such as India, Malaysia, and Sudan amongst others, began altering political, social, and economic institutions in order to redefine their political communities. During imperial rule these institutions were meant to control and regulate colonial subjects with a racially determined secondary status; at independence these same institutions required a reworking in order to serve the needs of independent citizens configured as equals by new constitutions. A reworking of the institutional purpose and form of newly established states meant redefining the legal relationship and responsibilities between multiethnic populations—as individuals and ethnic groups—and their newly appointed governments. I do not examine all the varieties of membership struggles and institutional forms that generated a range of citizenships across postcolonial countries in Asia and Africa. My goal instead is to trace dominant themes in citizenship studies, such as membership criteria, citizenship regimes, features of citizenship such as status, rights, and obligations, with the various postcolonial perspectives that inform such debates.[4] This imposes coherence on a field that is ambiguous, ill-defined, and spans the humanities and the social sciences.

This chapter will first examine the categories of imperial subjects established in European colonies, noting that the foundation of colonial rule relied on a graded, racialized, and hierarchical conception of membership to the imperial center.[5] Each of these claims to territory and empire created a racial hierarchy of colonial subjects vis-à-vis one another. Second, I examine the transition from imperial subject to postcolonial citizen at independence. This section argues that the legacies of

---

[3] The following is a brief list of developing countries and their main imperial powers (in brackets): India, Pakistan, Malaysia, Nigeria (Britain); Congo (Belgium); Indonesia (the Netherlands); Ivory Coast, Algeria, Vietnam (France); Angola, Mozambique (Portugal).

[4] For example, debates on membership criteria commonly mean institutional access to membership via birth, naturalization, descent, or territorial annexation. Influenced by European citizenship making, this assumes higher state capacity, institutionalization, legitimacy, and an ability to control and separate the boundaries of membership (citizens versus immigrants) and territory (borders).

[5] Graded, racialized, and hierarchical forms of imperial membership are based on the various official categories of imperial subjects determined by biological race, lineage, and social standing.

divide-and-rule colonialism and subsequent emergent nationalism and majoritarianism gave rise to legal tensions between *jus soli* (birthright) citizenship and *jus
sanguinis* (blood based) citizenship.[6] Citizenship law was significantly influenced
by struggles over defining a national political identity. In the third section I examine the rise of a welfare citizenship in the newly established postcolonial state. The
experiences of postcolonial states destabilize traditional European accounts of citizenship expansion from civil, political, to social rights, famously articulated by T. H.
Marshall.[7] Marshall's traditional ordering of rights is mismatched and uneven in
both postcolonial and non-Western contexts.[8] The chapter concludes by analyzing
contemporary postcolonial citizenship building through legal activism over various
silos of rights. The failures or partial successes of citizenship in postcolonial states
require us to re-examine the legacy of colonial institutions on the political, social,
and economic needs of countries that were formed at the end of Empire.

Imperial Subjects

Missing from European accounts of citizenship are the rights and experiences of
people in the colonies and their imperial centers. With some notable exceptions,
most debates on citizenship and corresponding state formation are localized to area
studies (African or Asian or Middle Eastern studies), barely interacting with discussions in Europe and the Americas.[9]

The inclusionary liberal European account of citizenship is marked by membership struggles over status, rights, and duties, how to define a political community

[6] Erin Chung's chapter in this volume shows how non-Western citizenship is mostly based on *jus
sanguinis* norms (see Chung in this volume, section titled 'Hierarchies of Citizens and Noncitizens').

[7] Marshall and Bottomore (n 1).

[8] Chung in this volume. Postcolonial states are a subset of the larger 'non-Western' developing world. States like Bhutan, China, Nepal, Japan, Thailand, among others, were not colonized by
European imperial powers.

[9] The following accounts are an exception, both due to their regional depth and their ability to
engage theoretical and empirical literatures across continents: Partha Chatterjee, *The Politics of
the Governed: Reflections on Popular Politics in Most of the World* (New York: Columbia University
Press, 2004); Niraja Jayal, *Citizenship and its Discontents* (Cambridge: Harvard University Press,
2013), Naila Kabeer, ed., *Inclusive Citizenship: Meanings and Expressions* (London: Zed Books, 2005);
Mahmood Mamdani, *When Victims Become Killers: Colonialism, Nativism, and the Genocide in
Rwanda* (Princeton: Princeton University Press, 2002); T.K. Oommen, *Citizenship, Nationality and
Ethnicity* (Cambridge: Polity Press, 1997); Kamal Sadiq, *Paper Citizens: How Illegal Immigrants Acquire
Citizenship in Developing Countries* (New York: Oxford University Press, 2009); Uday Singh Mehta,
Liberalism and Empire: A Study of Nineteenth Century Liberal Thought (Chicago, London: University
of Chicago Press, 2000).

(membership criteria) and what regime type is most appropriate. These accounts skim over the exclusionary reality of racialized citizenship that historically barred many, if not most, populations from citizenship and equal membership.[10] Postcolonial citizenship exposes how colonial powers built liberal citizenship regimes in Europe, while simultaneously engaging in exploitative racial hierarchy policies in conquered lands. Europe's liberal conceptions of citizenship reconciled racial segregation, forced and slave labor, and land confiscation, precisely because they were sutured together with broader claims of religious and racial superiority and civilizational maturity.[11] Belief in the universal rights of man did not apply to those who were deemed less human, less civilized—the colonial subjects.[12]

Classic works on citizenship, such as T. H. Marshall's account of civil, political, and social rights, ignore the suppression of the colonized and their challenges to membership in imperial states within Europe.[13] Marshall's synthesis of expanding social rights in Britain amid capitalist market relations neglects the brutal resource extraction by the Empire for an industrializing Europe.[14] Marshall's observation of expanding rights sits uncomfortably with the reality of minorities in Europe, and in former colonies alike. Nancy Fraser and Linda Gordon take on Marshall's vision of the expansion of social citizenship by highlighting,

[h]is periodization of the three stages of citizenship, for example, fits the experience of white workingmen only, a minority of the population. His conceptual distinctions between civil, political, and social citizenship tend to take for granted, rather than problematize, gender and racial hierarchies. Finally, his assumption, continued in later social-democratic thought and practice, that the chief aims of social citizenship are erosion of *class* inequality and protection from *market* forces slights other key axes of inequality and other mechanisms and arenas of domination.[15] (emphasis in original)

Europe's liberal claim becomes unstable once the conceptual lens is expanded to include a broader range of minorities and their various experiences of political, social, and economic discrimination. From the vantage point of the postcolony, Naila Kabeer critiques Marshall for his silence 'on gender and race and on the rights of those whose lands were colonized, whose way of life was disrupted and whose humanity denigrated by the imperial powers, including, of course, Britain.'[16]

---

[10] See FitzGerald in this volume.   [11] Mehta (n 9).
[12] Colonial subjects are natives who were racially deemed as inferior and thus second-class citizens while imperial subjects also included white Europeans.
[13] Naila Kabeer, 'Citizenship, Affiliation and Exclusion: Perspectives from the South,' *IDS Bulletin 37*, no. 4 (September 2006): pp. 91–101, p. 93.
[14] Marshall and Bottomore (n 1).
[15] Nancy Fraser and Linda Gordon, 'Contract vs. Charity: Why is there no Social Citizenship in the United States,' *Socialist Review 22*, no. 3 (1992): pp. 45–68, pp. 49–50.
[16] Kabeer (n 13), p. 92. See also her excellent insights in 'Introduction' in Kabeer (n 9).

Throughout the two world wars, long-term colonial subjects were not given the option of adopting the citizenship of their imperial powers in Europe. They were instead British 'subjects' not 'citizens.'[17] Even as many Sikhs, Gurkhas, Pathans, and tens of thousands of colonial locals actively served imperial armies during World War I and II, they were denied equal imperial membership based on race and identity.[18] Property ownership, good behavior, dutiful conduct, even service in the imperial military with highest honors did not lead to equal subjecthood in European empires; instead these individuals were classified as racial, ethnic, and religious inferiors, positioned outside the confines of a civilized body politic. Denied equal membership within European empires, colonial subjects were restricted to a racialized secondary status in colonies in Asia and Africa.

Who were the imperial subjects within Empire? They can be disaggregated into four categories, where often distinctions are made between the native population and the non-native colonial rulers, the legal categorization of imperial subjects was often more nuanced.[19] First, there were *land based native claims* from those with indigenous status due to spiritual and cultural claims to specific ecological environments such as distinct lands, forests, and regions. These include among others the Assamese, Nagas, Santhals in India, the Kadazandusun, Murut, and Orang Asli in Malaysia, and Dayaks in Indonesia.[20] Some natives were majorities in one region while being a minority in another—different native groups had differing claims on rights by region. This was the norm in multiethnic states of Asia and Africa.

Second, there were *lineage/ancestral based claims* by long-term natives who traced their historical residence and subjecthood to prior kingdoms and principalities, emperors and chiefs. For example, a subject of such principality or protectorate was controlled (but not directly ruled) by the British Empire. Their allegiance was to the locally powerful village head, tribe leader, or regional raja/sultan. As such this subject was considered 'protected' by virtue of a larger collective loyalty within an imperial 'protectorate.' For example, such subjects emerged under British imperial rule in the Middle East with their vast protectorate territories including among others Qatar, Bahrain, and Abu Dhabi.[21]

Third, *merchant/slave labor* based claims were made by long-term immigrants historically brought as merchant or slave labor by imperial powers from one colony to another. These communities, and subsequent traders who followed, made native

[17] For a discussion on the distinctions between political subjects and citizens please see Engin F. Isin, 'Citizenship after Orientalism: An Unfinished Project,' *Citizenship Studies 16*, no. 5 (2012): pp. 563–572.

[18] Kaveri Qureshi, 'Diasporic Citizenship and Militarization: Punjabi Soldiers in the World Wars,' *Citizenship Studies 17*, no. 3–4 (2013): pp. 400–413.

[19] See the excellent section on imperial citizenship by Jayal (n 9), pp. 29–36.

[20] R.H. Barnes, Andrew Gray, and Benedict Kingsbury, eds., *Indigenous Peoples of Asia* (Ann Arbor: Association for Asian Studies, 1995).

[21] However as Jayal points out 'political equality with other white subjects of the empire was by definition precluded' (Jayal (n 9), p. 31).

claims in their colony of settlement. For example, at Indian independence in 1947, approximately 4 million Indians were spread out in the British Commonwealth, largely descendants of slave labor brought in the nineteenth century.[22] Slave labor was brought in to work in plantations and mines, extracting mineral and agricultural resources in the colonies. Chinese and Indian laborers in British Malaysia; Chinese laborers in Dutch Indonesia; and Indian laborers in Guyana, Fiji, Uganda, Kenya, and the West Indies among others. All generated local anti-immigrant discrimination and restrictions. Immigrants who arrived closer to decolonization were often treated as outsiders, or separated for citizenship purposes by newly established postcolonial states. An example of this was the public expulsion of South Asians from Uganda in 1972, where anti-Asian sentiments persisted decades after independence.

Finally, there were imperial European subjects who were brought in for governance, law and order, in the business of extraction and trade in resources of the colonies. These individuals claimed *elite European* membership in imperial centers and their colonies. These imperial subjects were clearly recognized as non-natives with no historical claim to membership in the colonies. They were often privileged if not wealthy, and were allocated a superior European citizenship. Due to their race and ethnicity, they had a natural claim to their imperial citizenship in Europe, and could therefore opt to return to Europe as equal subjects of the imperial sovereign. In fact, inter-marriages between local native populations and European settlers led to the rise of a small, often Christian community in the colonial states such as the Anglo Indians in India, and Indo-Belanda (or Indo) in Indonesia.[23] While eligible for European citizenship based on descent and race, some remained with their families as postcolonial citizens in former colonies.

A racial citizenship separated and defined the non-European native and immigrant subjects in the colonies from the naturalized European white subjects of the empire. Race trumped any claim by rights or duties or birthplace. The white European workforce located in the colonies were at the top of this racial hierarchy—they were European after all—and were conferred equal subject status to their white European counterparts. Race separated, and firmly excluded local subjects (colored races) in the colonies from imperial European citizens. Biologically determined racial hierarchies separated imperial subjects who shared in liberal conceptions of citizenship, from those who were excluded with secondary status.

---

[22] Jayal (n 9), p. 54.
[23] In some contexts specific legal categories were used for the offspring of mixed unions. See Patricia Jerónimo and Maarten Peter Vink, 'Citizenship in a Post-Colonial Context: Comparing Portugal and the Netherlands,' *Perspectivas: Portuguese Journal of Political Science and International Relations* 6 (2011): pp. 109–129.

FROM IMPERIAL SUBJECT TO 'CITIZEN'

Anticolonial nationalism was fueled in part by imperialism's graded, racialized, and hierarchical citizenship practices, which excluded the vast majority of imperial subjects from equal membership. The transition from imperial 'subject' to 'citizen' in a newly established nation state was plagued by various group contestations. Subjecthood implied an enforceable allegiance to Empire, however becoming a citizen required formal membership with rights and duties never experienced before. How is political membership determined? What is the content of such citizenship? These were critical questions that nascent democracies in Asia and Africa faced, and this period of decolonization amid new nationalism highlights how the concept of citizenship, as status, rights, nationality, and privilege are not ideal universals (as in the European tradition), but are instead contingent, malleable, and open to redefinition.[24]

Defining the boundaries of a new nation after independence produced two types of group differentiated conflicts, 1) conflicts *within* groups; and 2) conflicts *between* groups. Ironically, the emphasis on individuals as equal and autonomous rights-bearing citizens—the norm in post-enlightenment Europe—was submerged under group or community claims in the post-colony. One appeared only as a member of a recognized ethnic, religious, caste, or tribal group. Group identity and nationality were fused together, such that they collectively determined one's citizenship. This is evident in the postcolonial separation between a Hindu India and a Muslim Pakistan in 1947, and the separation of a Chinese dominated Singapore and a Malay Malaysia in 1965. Group contestations over the content of citizenship in postcolonial states highlight citizenship as multilayered, not just an individual's status, privilege, or right granted by the nation state, but as a broader tool and control mechanism to influence political membership in a state. Viewed in this way, postcolonial citizenship is tethered to two competing concepts, citizenship as a preferential status and recognition on one hand, and citizenship as a bundle of *exercisable* social and economic rights and obligations on the other. In postcolonial citizenship the former does not necessarily lead to the latter.[25]

In the scramble to ensure national territorial integrity, otherwise stable heterogeneous communities were arbitrarily, socially, and geographically re-engineered to match the political envisioning's of modern nation states. New national borders cut across previously integrated group identities, fuelling both anticolonial nationalism and power struggles, but also newly felt religious, ethnicized, or tribal

---

[24] See Sadiq (n 9), pp. 15–22. See also Erin Aeran Chung, *Immigrant Incorporation in East Asian Democracies* (New York and Cambridge: Cambridge University Press, forthcoming).

[25] Sadiq (n 9).

group identities. Majorities became minorities, natives became immigrants. As Roy poignantly points out, postcolonial citizenship highlights how 'citizenship is deeply contested and is experienced and unfolds in specific social fields amidst hetero-geneous and often contesting political imaginaries, assumptions and practices.'[26] Engulfed in passionate nationalism and entrenched group identities, the immediate postcolonial period highlights these contradictions within citizenship.[27]

Even though contemporary citizenship regimes in former postcolonial states such as India, Malaysia, and Indonesia now apply a mixture of *jus soli* and *jus san-guinis* principles, historically a tension arose between these regimes as they are often taken to reflect ideals of constitutional equality and ethno-nationalism. Some accounts of this period propose that citizens of newly independent postcolonial states were born into *a spirit* of constitutional equality through *just soli* princi-ples.[28] This view holds that at independence, all resident subjects of former colonies emerged as constitutionally equal citizens in the struggle for national independence from imperial powers. The long struggle for independence produced solidarities that cut across varying socio-political distinctions such as class, group, and regional identities. Post-independence solidarities implied (and relied on) citizenship acqui-sition through *jus soli*, because territorial based unity to the new nation was seen as the only way to bring together different religious, ethnic, and tribal stakeholders. As new nations were made overnight, citizens were bound into new equalities.

In a second view, scholars such as Niraja Jayal instead argue that in India, for example, the tension between *jus soli* and *jus sanguinis* 'was present from the found-ing moment of the republic.'[29] The British partition of the Indian subcontinent along religious lines of Hindu majority India from Muslim majority Pakistan generated a path-dependence towards majoritarian *jus sanguinis* citizenship over *jus soli*. However, as she argues, 'in a territorially defined political community, the Indian choice of *jus soli* could not but be premised on a delinking of citizenship from nation-ality.'[30] Colonial independence and partition further reified differences in multiethnic communities and contradicted the adoption of *jus soli* principals. Thus, the new state was born with unresolved tensions between civic and ethno-nationalist aspirations.

A third perspective on the citizenship in the initial post-independence period highlights how within a few decades *after* independence, the initial euphoria of an emergent nationalism—which bonded together inter-regional, ethnic, religious, caste, tribal disparities—quickly eroded. The erosion of these solidarities underlies

---

[26] Anupama Roy, *Mapping Citizenship in India* (Delhi: Oxford University Press, 2010), p. 3.

[27] It is well known that identity-driven cleavages plagued many postcolonial states that had heteroge-neous populations, resulting in varying degrees of ethnic, religious, and tribal conflict that reverberate currently. See Timothy P. Daniels, 'African International Students in Klang Valley: Colonial Legacies, Postcolonial Racialization, and Sub-Citizenship,' *Citizenship Studies* 18, no. 8 (2014): pp. 855–870; Patricia McFadden, 'Becoming Postcolonial: African Women Changing the Meaning of Citizenship,' *Citizenship Studies* 6, no. 1 (2005): pp. 1–22; Wale Adebanwi, 'Terror, Territoriality and the Struggle for Indigeneity and Citizenship in Northern Nigeria,' *Citizenship Studies* 13, no. 4 (2009): pp. 349–363.

[28] Sadiq (n 9); Roy (n 26).   [29] Jayal (n 9), p. 52.   [30] Ibid.

the ethnicization of citizenship laws, which I will elaborate on later. The positive ideals of a postcolonial nationalism framing initial citizenship were soon eclipsed by majoritarian nationalism, ethnic conflict, competing claims to indigeneity, even genocide.[31] The brief period of a horizontal citizenship, an inclusive postcolonial stage, gave way to conflictual and hierarchical claims on citizenship. Over time, *jus soli* gave way to narrower majoritarian, blood, and kinship based *jus sanguinis* norms of citizenship. As anticolonial nationalism waned, citizenship practices transformed into religious, ethnic, or tribal majoritarianism.

Why did the initial spirit of equality, stimulated by independence movements, give way to ethnic, religious, tribal, regional-based citizenship in postcolonial Africa and Asia? Oxana Shevel's chapter in this volume highlights the ethnicization of citizenship laws in communist transition states which varied in countries with little civic nationalism, noting that territorial and residential criteria emerged as a possible default position, or as a way to safeguard territorial sovereignty.[32] In many postcolonial states, well before the transition of communist states, ethnicization of citizenship laws emerged for the following three reasons.

First, in postcolonial states many regionally concentrated ethnic, tribal, religious groups were given priority in regional claims to identity and economy. This created a de-facto internal dual membership shared between federal and regional citizenship. It separated natives of *this* homeland from natives of *that* homeland, and separated local natives from migrant settlers, thus creating duality in law.[33] Parallel to national level laws, other laws were introduced, which were applicable only to particular regions and their groups. Internal dual citizenship became the norm in states where identity groups lay claim to specific regional territories. For example, East Malaysia (states located on the island of Borneo) obtained special constitutional and legal protections, including the right to regulate internal (from West Malaysia) and international migration. Native East Malaysians hold dual allegiances, to the federal nation state of Malaysia, but equally to their protected regional states.[34] Similarly, the seven 'sister states' that comprise Northeast India, have special regional protections and exemptions from the federal union of India.[35]

Second, the adoption of *jus sanguinis* ad-hoc policy measures crept into citizenship standards due to the threat of the postcolonial migrant, immigrant, and refugee. This echoes Erin Chung's chapter in this volume, which discusses restrictive citizenship laws towards internal migrants and selective *jus sanguinis* norms to

---

[31] Mamdani (n 9).   [32] Shevel in this volume.

[33] Sanjib Baruah, 'Citizens and Denizens: Ethnicity, Homelands, and the Crisis of Displacement in Northeast India,' *Journal of Refugee Studies* 16, no. 1 (March 2003): pp. 44–66.

[34] Kamal Sadiq, 'When Being "Native" is Not Enough: Citizens as Foreigners in Malaysia,' *Asian Perspective* 33, no. 1 (2009): pp. 5–32; Kamal Sadiq, 'When States Prefer Non-Citizens over Citizens: Conflict over Illegal Immigration into Malaysia,' *International Studies Quarterly* 49, no. 1 (March 2005): pp. 101–122.

[35] Baruah (n 33).

control migration and residence within the context of contemporary non-Western citizenship.[36] According to analysis of British decolonization in South Asia, both India and Pakistan moved away from an inclusive *jus soli* spirit to a more exclusive citizenship due to 'a series of draconian executive actions' that reduced groups to minority citizens.[37] For example, a series of contingent, ad-hoc measures, were adopted in response to claims by partition refugees over property, protection, and mobility across India and Pakistan. To control the return of 'stranded' refugees, both India and Pakistan put in place a permit system. For example, restricting the return of Muslim refugees from Pakistan to India was the Influx from Pakistan (Control) Ordinance of January 1948 which was followed by a similar act by Pakistan in October 1948, its aim to foil the return of Hindu and Sikh refugees from India.[38] Introducing such ad-hoc measures to regulate the re-entry and residence of minority groups further diluted any commitments to *jus soli*.

Citizenship was qualified by such executive actions, and full formal citizenship remained outside the reach of many 'minority citizens.'[39] Religion-based nationality (Hindus in India, Muslims in Pakistan) became linked to citizenship. Similar group-based contestations emerged in other postcolonial states such as Malaysia and Indonesia in Southeast Asia, and Sudan and Nigeria in Africa among others. In this view, postcolonial citizenship arose from ad-hoc but ongoing processes of citizenship making through legislative and executive restrictions, not inclusions.

Third, other scholars point out the restrictive impact of long-term colonial law on postcolonial citizenship. For example, in a top-down account highlighting the long-term institutional impact of colonialization on the formation of individual and group identities, Mahmood Mamdani explains the rise of hierarchical identity-driven membership in postcolonial Africa.[40] He argues that ethnic, racial, or nationality-based citizenship was inevitable, because rather than unite natives under a common, equal constitution or law, imperial powers cemented and politicized customary, religious, indigenous, and traditional law, further segmenting populations.[41] Colonial rules and regulations further promoted hierarchy and heterogeneity, such that fragmented communities could not challenge the hegemony and 'indirect' or 'direct' rule of the imperial powers. This eroded any attempts at collective action or a shared citizenship. Colonial laws, rules, and regulations meant to control and manage populations inhibited democratic participation, struggles for recognition, or calls for accountability. For example, under colonial rule, separate electorates marked Hindu or Muslim majority localities in India; in Malaysia, communal separation occurred between the Chinese and

---

[36] Chung in this volume.
[37] Joya Chatterji, 'South Asian Histories of Citizenship, 1946-1970,' *The Historical Journal* 55, no. 4 (2012): pp. 1049–1071, p. 1070.
[38] Ibid., p. 1063.   [39] Ibid., p. 1049.   [40] Mamdani (n 9). See also Jayal (n 9).
[41] Mamdani (n 9).

the Malays and in Nigeria between Christian and Muslim indigenous tribes.[42] As a result, the path-dependence of imperial attempts at hegemony and rule left Africa and Asia institutionally divided by customary, religious, and traditional forms of authority.[43]

Specifically looking at customary law, Christopher Zambakari's examination of identity and citizenship in Sudan and South Sudan demonstrates how colonial customary laws for natives—a diversity of ethnic groups—restricted mobility, settlement, even employment of one native group while effectively de-nationalizing other native groups.[44] Soon 'each ethnic group needed to have its own homeland,' ethnically excluding other native groups, and importantly, excluding any migrants, displaced populations, refugees, and nomadic communities.[45] Claims to nativity and particular lands go together. For example in colonial Sudan, the Closed District Ordinances between 1920 and 1946 and the Permits to Trade Order of 1925 effectively determined who belonged to the area and who did not, restricting the movement and opportunities to trade of non-native groups.[46] Over time, those deemed non-native were stripped of their political right, right to free movement, and economic rights, among others. Post-independence political parties and movements found a fertile public space for political mobilization based on customary, religious, caste, regional, and indigenous identities.

The misfit between colonial institutions of division and rule, and postcolonial attempts at rights-bearing autonomous individuals sharing in common law and citizenship, produces a contested citizenship within the post-colony. Contemporary conflicts over the institutional accommodation of diverse identities and membership are common. Groups claim internal homelands, generating violence and displaced populations. Expulsion of groups that do not belong to a native-owned homeland become common: for example, in India, Bengali migrants in Assam, Chakmas in Bangladesh, Kacha in Sudan, Burkinabe in Ivory Coast—all are seen as native outsiders.[47] Even as de-jure citizenship exists at the federal level, a de-facto ethnicized (or nationality) based dual citizenship emerges as regions are claimed by ethnic homelands. In this view, fractured, conflict-ridden Africa and Asia inevitably produce a contested citizenship shaped by the tension between *jus soli* and *jus sanguinis*.[48]

Such analysis reifies postcolonial citizenship as an outcome of divisive colonial polices, and proposes that only a reform or removal of hierarchical colonial laws and colonial inspired executive actions will lead to a new citizenship fit for the diverse multiethnic societies of Asia and Africa. Given that Asia and Africa have some of the largest populations of internally displaced people and that statelessness

---

[42] Regarding Nigeria see Adebanwi (n 27).   [43] Mamdani (n 9).
[44] Christopher Zambakari, 'Sudan and South Sudan: Identity, Citizenship, and Democracy in Plural Societies,' *Citizenship Studies* 19, no. 1 (2015): pp. 69–82.
[45] Ibid., p. 74.   [46] Ibid., p. 72.   [47] On Northeast India see Baruah (n 33).
[48] Mamdani (n 9); Jayal (n 9).

is widespread, for a new citizenship to emerge, these societies will have to purge their citizenship laws and institutions of any discriminatory colonial principles, laws, rules, and guidelines. According to Mamdani, Africa faces a dilemma where the majority calls for democracy while the minority seeks justice.[49] Can institutional reform and adaptation reconcile the majoritarian search for a democratic nation based on majoritarian culture and power with a minority's quest for equal recognition and shared power? Can nationality, ethnicity, religion, caste, and tribe be delinked from postcolonial citizenship?[50] These are important questions for future research.

In this regard, Zambakari is emphatic that Africa has to remove the colonial customary laws that fragment land into ethnic homelands and move to a citizenship that reconciles a range of nationalities and ethnic groups.[51] Institutional reform can only begin by basing claims to citizenship on residence—a civic conception—rather then on a colonial legacy of ethnic and tribal indigeneity.[52] He argues that a beginning has been made with the New Sudan Framework, which captures inclusive norms of citizenship from post-apartheid South Africa, Tanzania, and Senegal.[53] Other scholars such as Oommen are more cautious, arguing that the 'citizenization of the underclass' is possible as long as a group's 'internality' to society is not questioned.[54] That is, equal citizenship to minorities and the underclass is only possible if they are seen as already inside the group that defines the political community. Hence, insiders such as the 'untouchables' and 'lower castes' in India, who are never viewed as external to a Hindu society just located at the bottom of it, could be accommodated through 'citizenization'—the expansion of formal and social citizenship. This may not be the case for indigenous Christians or Muslims in India, who despite their historical indigeneity are viewed outside Hindu society. In these ways, Asia and Africa are littered with multiple outsiders, entire groups considered outside a ruling majority's nationality. The growth of contemporary ethno-nationalism and the ascent of *jus sanguinis* norms in Indian, Malaysian, or Sudanese citizenship laws give us pause.

POSTCOLONIAL WELFARE CITIZENSHIP

Postcolonial citizenship as welfare—often seen as a subset of social citizenship—highlights the contestations that emerge from the expansion of rights through

---

[49] Mamdani (n 9), pp. 272–281. [50] Oommen (n 9), pp. 240–241.
[51] Zambakari (n 44) , pp. 76–77. [52] Ibid., pp. 76–78. [53] Ibid., p. 77–78.
[54] Oommen (n 9), p. 234.

state-sponsored welfare schemes. These contestations center on which communities and marginalized groups qualify and are deserving of state-sponsored welfare intervention, and the social fragmentation that emerges from such processes of inclusion.

Welfare citizenship refers to state-sponsored assistance programs that target specific minorities, and the poor, who are deserving of state assistance and preferential policies. These state programs are designed to help specific citizens become socially and economically self-sufficient. At independence, postcolonial leaders such as Nehru (in India), Sukarno (in Indonesia), and Nyerere (in Tanzania) were aware of the need to fight social and economic inequality.[55] Such leaders embraced protectionist industrialization that sought economic autonomy externally (from former imperial powers) and domestic economic self-sufficiency through welfare redistribution and rising public employment. Two parallel socio-political movements marked this period.

First, since most native residents lived in poverty, an anti-imperial nationalism united locals in a social movement for independence. Such nationalism glued together a diverse citizenry with a national ideology such as 'Pancasila' in Indonesia, 'Rukunegara' in Malaysia, 'Unity in Diversity' in India, among others. An expansive, horizontal camaraderie tied together a majority of the populations in these newly independent states who were living around the poverty line or tentatively above it in the middle class.

Second, there emerged a new political economy focused on economic development that emphasized poverty eradication, welfare policies meant to reduce inequality and limit confrontation between a newly liberated mass of working class citizens and a small group of influential elites. A class-based citizenship driven by a successful postcolonial nationalism marked this initial period of independent states. Nationalism was fused with welfare, whereby states' focus turned to delivery of resources for the masses of poor. This growth in welfare rights and services was meant to narrow the inequalities that colonialism and capitalism had generated.

The need for and expansion of social and economic welfare for the vast poor in newly independent postcolonial states is markedly different from T.H. Marshall's analysis of expanding civil, political, and social rights in England. The experiences of postcolonial states indicate that such rights were separated from the top, in which equal status (civil and political rights) had no bearing on the ability to engage in social rights at the bottom. Marshall's tripartite and sequential expansion of rights, unfolds as a spectrum in the postcolonial context. On one end of the spectrum are civil and political rights (such as equality before the law and the right to vote), in the form of equal status, which was granted by new constitutions to all eligible citizens at independence. On the other end of the spectrum, lies the ability to engage in

---

[55] See Gemma Bird, 'Beyond the Nation State: The Role of Local and Pan-National Identities in Defining Post-Colonial African Citizenship', *Citizenship Studies* 20, no. 2 (2015): pp. 260–275.

social rights (such as the right to education or basic health care). For the vast majority of newly independent and free citizens, civil and political rights were bifurcated
from social and economic rights. For example, while all Indians were constitutionally equal at independence, very few groups had the ability or resources to go to
school or receive health care.

Marshall's expansion of social rights premised that poverty, ill health, or lack of
education should not be barriers to entry for full social participation in a political
community, and that governments should intervene actively.[56] In postcolonial states
alleviating poverty was seen as an economic and political goal, tied to infrastructure
development, management of natural resources, and redistributive welfare schemes.
Preexisting social hierarchies between various ethnic, caste, and tribal communities, while on the one hand 'leveled' by constitutional decree, remained vibrant and
were culturally upheld in social practice with long-lasting effects.[57] There was no
question that the new postcolonial state needed to intervene in the expansion of
social and economic development, what was more contentious was the scope and
range of such interventions amid weak institutional resources.[58] Welfare policies to
help the poor and the marginalized were concerned with determining who was and
was not eligible; the justiciability of such rights was not prioritized. As I will discuss in the concluding section, making these rights justiciable, that is implemented
and legally exercisable, is a major goal of contemporary legal and social activists in
postcolonial states.

In order to make citizenship deliverable, the new state needed to fragment classes
of people, those targeted for interventions and those who were excluded from such
policies. Thus, administrative, spatial, and regional specifications generated a variety of circumscribed targets of welfare citizenship. However, as Kabeer points out,
newly independent states did not restructure local economies and social hierarchies anew. Instead, persisting colonial hierarchies were 'actively strengthened and
reified ... through the defining powers of a modern state apparatus and a codified
system of law.'[59]

To achieve redistributive goals of welfare, specific disadvantaged groups had to
be recognized and targeted for enhancement of rights. Hence in India, compensation addressing the historically disadvantaged or 'backward' groups became central
to the expansion of welfare, for example, in preferential policies in federal and state
employment that targeted Scheduled Castes, Scheduled tribes, or Other Backward
Castes in India. Each state scheme identified the poor, tagged them with a particular
identity card, and made them eligible for specific benefits. Many destitute individuals

---

[56] Marshall and Bottomore (n 1).

[57] For example, in contemporary Malaysia and Indonesia marriage across religions is socially discouraged; in India, religion, caste, regional and linguistic ties continue to create divisive social distinctions in society regarding marriage, education, and employment outcomes.

[58] Jayal (n 9), p. 165.   [59] Kabeer (n 9), p. 96.

who were marginalized and undocumented during colonial rule, remained outside the purview of such postcolonial schemes. Their 'blurred membership,' characterized by uneven documentary registration, social and physical exclusion, coupled with weak institutional capacity, resulted in erratic anti-poverty alleviation.[60]

In Malaysia, group-defined compensatory educational quotas for Malays were established. Malays and other 'indigenous'[61] groups such as Dayaks, Murut, and Kadazandusun were identified as rural peasants with high rates of poverty, and therefore deserving of targeted compensatory schemes as opposed to the wealthy Chinese merchant class. Such group targeted anti-poverty schemes were the mainstay of the 1971 Malaysian New Economic Policy (NEP) and its successor the 1991 National Development Policy (NDP).[62] Over time in Malaysia, ethnic quotas spread to the economy, including infrastructure construction contracts, health coverage, tourism and transport contracts, and most other social services.[63]

Economic data from Malaysia suggests that the gap between the 'indigenous,' 'bumiputera' groups (Malays, Orang Asli) and the economically dominant Chinese community has narrowed in West Malaysia. Malaysia is one of a small group of postcolonial states where economic welfare polices for targeted groups have been effective. For example, poverty rates for targeted bumiputera groups have declined from 70.5 percent in 1957/58 down to 8.3 percent in 2004.[64] While poverty has declined for other groups such as the Chinese and Indians between 1957/58 and 2004, the decline in poverty rates has been substantial for the targeted bumiputera groups.[65] Clearly, group-targeted economic programs are working in West Malaysia. However, an unintended consequence of this state-sponsored goal of equity through welfare is the further ethnicization of the economy and society by group.[66] Many Chinese and Indians resent affirmative action for Malays in West Malaysia.

Malaysia may be an exception, because in most postcolonial states, welfare coverage has been erratic, if not absent. Corruption, elite capture, and inefficient delivery of benefits have marred selectively targeted state social programs. Jayal critiques the Indian state for a 'strong rhetorical commitment' with minimal 'social policy' for welfare, resulting in the poor delivery of social and economic rights.[67] This gap between state rhetoric and policy outcome is a feature of many postcolonial states and highlights issues of state capacity, and weak legal and bureaucratic institutions, at the core of many newly independent former colonies.

[60] Sadiq (n 9), pp. 71–99.   [61] Also known as the 'bumiputera' or 'sons of the soil'.

[62] Julie Chernov Hwang and Kamal Sadiq, 'Legislating Separation and Solidarity in Plural Societies: The Chinese in Indonesia and Malaysia,' *Nationalism and Ethnic Politics 16*, no. 2 (2010): pp. 192–215, p. 207.

[63] Ibid., p. 206.

[64] Richard Leete, *Malaysia: From Kampung to Twin Towers, 50 Years of Economic and Social Development* (Selangor: Oxford Fajar, 2007) , p. 141, see Table 4.3.

[65] Ibid., p. 141, see Table 4.3.   [66] Hwang and Sadiq (n 62).   [67] Jayal (n 9), p. 164.

Targeted social protection programs are creating resentment among non-beneficiary middle classes in contemporary postcolonial states. At independence, the mantra for postcolonial citizenship was an enhancement of rights through welfare for ascriptively identified groups. However, welfare enhancement for specific groups produced exclusions for other groups—justice was eroded for them. They were deprived of such welfare enhancing policies precisely because of *who they are*. The Chinese in Malaysia, and the high caste in India, were not targeted for state welfare policies precisely because they already held a dominant position in society. By specifically targeting identities (e.g., race, nativity, ethnicity, religion, caste, tribe, gender), the goal of a common shared 'civic' citizenship is even further away. As welfare schemes sought social and economic equality by legislating affirmative action policies in the form of quotas and compensatory schemes, their success resulted in cementing exclusive identities for targeted and (non-targeted) groups alike. This is clearly evident in the Malaysian case where ethnic identities are polarized despite progress in economic equity. In India the Scheduled Caste and Other Backward Caste groups appear as exceptions to the common citizenship of others, they remain socially and economically stigmatized. Middle class Indians question why they should bear the burden, and finance, selective welfare policies for other groups. Eliminating 'quotas', 'reservations' or preferential policies for 'backward' castes or minority religions is a popular theme among sections of the resurgent middle class in contemporary India and Malaysia. These group contestations highlight the exclusionary nature of inclusive citizenship.

Another dilemma that emerges from the implementation of selective state-sponsored welfare is that diverse groups start competing against each other to be categorized as 'backward' or 'indigenous' in order to become eligible for beneficial compensatory schemes. This produces further fragmentation and conflict between groups. As Jayal points out, this raises 'the question of whether the idea of group-differentiated citizenship can accommodate the idea of a civic community?'[68] For example, the Jats in Haryana and Rajasthan (states in India) are agitating to be included among groups identified as the backward class, in order to benefit economically.[69] Despite holding a historically dominant position in society, this group demands preferential state services in the name of an equalizing claim to national citizenship.

The differential success of some groups targeted by preferential policies has generated resentment among other eligible groups who have experienced relatively lower upliftment of their economic status. For example in Malaysia, the indigenous Kadazandusun and Murut communities in Sabah (East Malaysia) struggle to realize

---

[68] Jayal (n 9), p. 270.
[69] 'Haryana Police to Appeal to Jats to End Quota Stir,' *The Indian Express*, June 9, 2016, online http://indianexpress.com/article/india/india-news-india/haryana-police-appeal-to-jats-to-end-quota-agitation-2843480/.

the full potential of compensatory policies they are eligible for, when compared to the anti-poverty successes of the bumiputeras in West Malaysia. Competition and conflict among the deserving indigenous, backward, and marginalized groups—each eligible for compensatory welfare policies—fragments the common subjects of a welfare citizenship into competing groups.

Finally, targeted state welfare polices restrict and erode the autonomy and agency of individuals in such welfare groups. These communities internalize their lower disadvantaged status through the perceived parochial policies of state assistance. Identified at the lower end in a hierarchy of groups, they remain socially stigmatized, rarely emerging as equal civic individuals independent of such a group identity. For example in India, members of the Dalit and 'untouchable' community remain culturally and politically outcast. Such stigmatization is also present in Malaysia, among the indigenous Orang Asli community. Thus, postcolonial citizenship as welfare highlights the group fragmentation inherent in the processes of targeted welfare distribution.

FUTURE DIRECTIONS

Thus far, group differentiated citizenship has emerged from the racialization of imperial subjecthood and from ethnicization of postcolonial attempts at civic citizenship and redistributive social citizenship. Contemporary civil and political mobilization has shifted focus from claiming redistributive universal welfare from government administrative institutions, to struggles for legislative justiciability over specific but wide-ranging human rights, such as for the right to food, the right to shelter, the right to health, the right to education, and the right to gender equity, amongst others. The effort of recent political mobilization in postcolonial states has been to convert implicit rights or guidelines in directive principles justiciable, that is forcing constitutional amendments and/or new legislation to make such rights tangible and exercisable by those most marginalized. In postcolonial states, legal activism for the justiciability of rights amends the bifurcation of civil and political rights on one hand, and social and economic rights on the other. Examining the impact of legal activism on the fragmentation or aggregation of rights among the poor and the marginalized is a key element for a future research agenda.

For example in India, while the right to employment and minimum wage was in the constitution and many wage employment programs were initiated (such as the 1960s Rural Manpower Programme, the 1970s Employment Guarantee Scheme in Maharashtra, among others), the right to work in rural areas only became a legal entitlement with the 2006 National Rural Employment Guarantee

Act (NREGA).[70] Rural households can now demand 100 days of employment per household per year in state-sponsored public works activities.[71] This right has become justiciable, because now unlike before, the rural unemployed can demand and enforce their right to minimal employment. Similarly, the right to education only became justiciable with the 2009 passing of The Right of Children to Free and Compulsory Education Act (or Right to Education Act). The act guarantees free and compulsory education— a minimum of eight years of elementary schooling—for all children aged six to fourteen years.[72] Through litigation and new legislation, states are being held accountable for specific rights, converting implicit rights or policy promises into individually enforceable rights. Having abandoned earlier struggles for class-based welfare and state protections, civil society actors and judicial supporters are mobilizing behind specific rights of education, shelter, and health. The viability of this mobilization is possible in postcolonial states with strong and free legal institutions and judiciary. Future scholarship will benefit from investigating if authoritarian or despotic postcolonial conditions impose limits on such rights based advocacy.

The role of civil society is a critical element in the struggle for postcolonial welfare rights. An examination of bottom-up political or civil society mobilization amid an institutionally weak postcolonial state requires one to focus on individual agency (and action) as well as collective associational responses.[73] However, Partha Chatterjee argues that a market and institutional based 'civil' society is only a partial account of postcolonial citizenship.[74] In his view, civil society, which consists of formalized associations and political party groups, does not effectively represent the interests of minorities and the masses of the urban poor. In contrast to 'civil' society he reiterates the agency and struggles of a marginalized 'political' society— consisting of minorities and the urban poor who live in slums, on footpaths, streets and work in informal markets.[75] In this view, a formal 'civil society' is distinct from an informal, but vibrant and visible 'political society.' Chatterjee's critique argues for the need to 'bring back' people into the study of citizenship, their experiences, struggles, and desire for rights. The field of citizenship studies will benefit from research that incorporates the desires and experiences of the marginalized with the institutional processes that eclipse their everyday existence. This requires innovative

[70] Santosh Mehrotra, Neha Kumra, and Ankita Gandhi, 'India's Fragmented Social Protection System: Three Rights Are in Place; Two Are Still Missing,' Working Paper 2014-18 (Geneva: United Nations Research Institute for Social Development (UNRISD), December 2014) , p. 5. The NREGA was renamed and succeeded by Mahatma Gandhi National Rural Employment Guarantee Act (MGNREGA).

[71] Ibid., pp. 1, 5.   [72] Ibid., pp. 1, 6–7.

[73] Diane Singerman, *Avenues of Participation: Family, Politics and Networks in Urban Quarters of Cairo* (Princeton: Princeton University Press, 1995); James Holston, *Insurgent Citizenship: Disjunctions of Democracy and Modernity in Brazil* (Princeton: Princeton University Press, 2008).

[74] Chatterjee (n 9) .   [75] Ibid.

archival, ethnographic and participant methods that closely interact with the poor and reveal the impact of law and institutions on their rights acquisition.

Works by scholars such as Engin Isin move the field in this direction by renewing a focus on human agency and new forms of activist citizenship.[76] Emerging scholarship makes distinctions between activist citizenship and social movements on one hand, and the politics of presence on the other. For example, just the ordinary presence and survival of the poor on the street becomes a political claim to citizenship argues Asef Bayat.[77] He observes how the contemporary urban poor in the Middle East challenge government authorities by engaging in informal activities to meet their needs incrementally—'a social non-movement.'[78] Even as formal rights are incrementally achieved through varying social, legal, or informal strategies, these rights are insufficiently protected in daily life. As Kabeer notes, without institutional force to make such rights deliverable and exercisable such rights remain 'formal, rather than real, and enjoyed with varying degrees of certainty by the population.'[79] In this view, the mismatch between 'formal rights' and 'real rights' serves to reify rather than disturb, deeply entrenched group hierarchies based on race, religion, ethnicity, caste, and gender.[80]

Future research will also benefit from investigating these gaps between formal rights and 'rights in practice' by investigating the impact of neoliberal economic development in the post-colony, where citizens are converted into individual consumers or litigants.[81] Leela Fernandez has observed the emergence of middle class 'consumer-citizens' amid an economically liberalizing India.[82] These middle class citizens engage in a 'politics of forgetting,' disregarding their fellow urban poor citizens who are marginalized by neoliberal development. Similarly, scholars such as Gautam Bhan and Asher Ghertner indicate the presence of a middle class aesthetic consciousness in India, which pits their cosmopolitan visions against the destitute poor, who are deemed as a hindrance to economic growth and thus relegated to lesser citizens with lesser rights.[83]

---

[76] Engin Isin, 'Citizenship in Flux: The Figure of the Activist Citizen,' *Subjectivity 29*, no. 1 (2009): pp. 367–388.

[77] Asef Bayat, *Life as Politics: How Ordinary People Change the Middle East* (Stanford: Stanford University Press, 2010) .

[78] Ibid.   [79] Kabeer (n 9) , p. 97.

[80] Ibid., p. 97; see also Ruth Lister, 'Inclusive Citizenship: Realizing the Potential,' *Citizenship Studies 11*, no. 1 (2007): pp. 49–61; Steven Robins, Andrea Cornwall, and Bettina von Lieres, 'Rethinking "Citizenship" in the Postcolony,' *Third World Quarterly 29*, no. 6 (2008): pp. 1069–1086.

[81] This gap between formalized citizenship and 'actual lived reality' common to postcolonial contexts may also be generalizable to non-colonized developing countries such as China, Thailand, Ethiopia, Nepal among others, thus questioning the colonial roots of such citizenship.

[82] Leela Fernandes, 'The Politics of Forgetting: Class Politics, State Power and the Restructuring of Space in India,' *Urban Studies 41*, no. 12 (2004): pp. 2415–2430.

[83] Gautam Bhan, 'The Impoverishment of Poverty: Reflections on Urban Citizenship and Inequality in Contemporary Delhi,' *Environment and Urbanization 26*, no. 2 (2014): pp. 1–14; Asher D. Ghertner, 'India's Urban Revolution: Geographies of Displacement beyond Gentrification,' *Environment and Planning A 46*, no. 7 (2014): pp. 1554–1571.

These developments raise important questions for the future regarding the overlap between postcolonial economic development and citizenship building through exclusion of the poor. Many of the poor and marginalized in Asia and Africa have neither the resources nor the time away from working to survive, to pursue individual citizenship rights, limiting their agency and participation. Popular struggles, legal and legislative mobilizations are confined to specific manageable basic rights—food, health, shelter, further narrowing the pool of interconnected, indivisible rights of the poor. An interesting avenue of future research is to ask why and how a narrow regime of rights has become acceptable as the postcolonial citizenship of the poor.[84] As many postcolonial states are experiencing a narrowing of rights among the poor and marginalized, it is important to investigate the historical roots of this impoverishment of rights and the impact of such political, social, and economic inequality on state stability.

Parallel to this, concerns with lived experience may be imagining individual agency (identity, freedom, liberty) and actors (civil society, consumer, litigant) in modern 'Western' terms. This poses a fundamental question for postcolonial citizenship theorists: are bottom-up citizenship struggles structurally 'conscripted by modernity',—a European project unfit for the diverse cultural heritage of postcolonial states? [85] On the other hand, if non-Western post-colonial citizenship continues to rely on enduring traditional categories of culture, kinship, community relations, and group identities, existing social hierarchies will only be entrenched. Can a Marshallian individual with civic, political, and social rights emerge independent of group identities that over-determine postcolonial citizenship? Understanding the gaps generated by state practices and processes of citizenship building is a critical first step. Emerging scholarship may identify these gaps as between individuals and groups, between formal rights and substantive outcomes, or between Western and postcolonial experiences of civic, political, and social rights. In this regard, postcolonial citizenship becomes a critique of the European assumptions underlying mainstream citizenship studies, and is a guidepost for future research attentive to those most marginalized.

BIBLIOGRAPHY

Adebanwi, Wale, 'Terror, Territoriality and the Struggle for Indigeneity and Citizenship in Northern Nigeria,' *Citizenship Studies* 13, no. 4 (2009): pp. 349–363.

[84] Postcolonial citizenships' attention to historical legacies of power differentials, racial hierarchy, and cultural and ethnic group identity is critical to citizenship regime formation. See Vink in this volume.

[85] Kevin Olson, *Imagined Sovereignties: The Power of the People and Other Myths of the Modern Age* (Cambridge: Cambridge University Press, 2016).

Baruah, Sanjib, 'Citizens and Denizens: Ethnicity, Homelands, and the Crisis of Displacement in Northeast India,' *Journal of Refugee Studies 16*, no. 1 (March 2003): pp. 44–66.

Barnes, R.H., Andrew Gray, and Benedict Kingsbury, eds., *Indigenous Peoples of Asia* (Ann Arbor: Association for Asian Studies, 1995).

Bayat, Asef, *Life as Politics: How Ordinary People Change the Middle East* (Stanford: Stanford University Press, 2010).

Bhan, Gautam, 'The Impoverishment of Poverty: Reflections on Urban Citizenship and Inequality in Contemporary Delhi,' *Environment and Urbanization 26*, no. 2 (2014): pp. 1–14.

Bird, Gemma, 'Beyond the Nation State: The Role of Local and Pan-National Identities Defining Post-Colonial African Citizenship,' *Citizenship Studies 20*, no. 2 (2015): pp. 260–275.

Chatterjee, Partha, *The Politics of the Governed: Reflections on Popular Politics in Most of the World* (New York: Columbia University Press, 2004).

Chatterji, Joya, 'South Asian Histories of Citizenship, 1946–1970,' *The Historical Journal 55*, no. 4 (2012): pp. 1049–1071.

Chung, Erin Aeran, *Immigrant Incorporation in East Asian Democracies* (New York and Cambridge: Cambridge University Press, forthcoming).

Daniels, Timothy P., 'African International Students in Klang Valley: Colonial Legacies, Postcolonial Racialization, and Sub-Citizenship,' *Citizenship Studies 18*, no. 8 (2014): pp. 855–870.

Fernandes, Leela, 'The Politics of Forgetting: Class Politics, State Power and the Restructuring of Space in India,' *Urban Studies 41*, no. 12 (2004): pp. 2415–2430.

Fraser, Nancy and Linda Gordon, 'Contract vs. Charity: Why is there no Social Citizenship in the United States,' *Socialist Review 22* (1992), pp. 45–68.

Ghertner, Asher D., 'India's Urban Revolution: Geographies of Displacement beyond Gentrification,' *Environment and Planning A 46*, no. 7 (2014): pp. 1554–1571.

'Haryana Police to Appeal to Jats to End Quota Stir,' *The Indian Express*, June 9, 2016, online http://indianexpress.com/article/india/india-news-india/haryana-police-appeal-to-jats-to-end-quota-agitation-2843480/.

Holston, James, *Insurgent Citizenship: Disjunctions of Democracy and Modernity in Brazil* (Princeton: Princeton University Press, 2008).

Hwang, Julie Chernov and Kamal Sadiq, 'Legislating Separation and Solidarity in Plural Societies: The Chinese in Indonesia and Malaysia,' *Nationalism and Ethnic Politics 16*, no. 2 (2010): pp. 195–215.

Isin, Engin F., 'Citizenship in Flux: The Figure of the Activist Citizen,' *Subjectivity 29*, no. 1 (2009): pp. 367–388.

Isin, Engin F., 'Citizenship after Orientalism: An Unfinished Project,' *Citizenship Studies 16*, no. 5 (2012): pp. 563–572.

Jayal, Niraja, *Citizenship and its Discontents* (Cambridge: Harvard University Press, 2013).

Jerónimo, Patricia and Maarten Peter Vink, 'Citizenship in a Post-Colonial Context: Comparing Portugal and the Netherlands,' *Perspectivas: Portuguese Journal of Political Science and International Relations 6* (2011): pp. 109–129.

Kabeer, Naila, ed., *Inclusive Citizenship: Meanings and Expressions* (London: Zed Books, 2005).

Kabeer, Naila, 'Citizenship, Affiliation and Exclusion: Perspectives from the South,' *IDS Bulletin 37*, no. 4 (September 2006): pp. 91–101.

Leete, Richard, *Malaysia: From Kampung to Twin Towers, 50 years of Economic and Social Development* (Selangor: Oxford Fajar, 2007).

Lister, Ruth, 'Inclusive Citizenship: Realizing the Potential,' *Citizenship Studies 11*, no. 1 (2007): pp. 49–61.

Mamdani, Mahmood, *When Victims Become Killers: Colonialism, Nativism, and the Genocide in Rwanda* (Princeton: Princeton University Press, 2002).

Marshall, T.H. and Tom Bottomore, *Citizenship and Social Class* (London: Pluto Press, 1987).

McFadden, Patricia, 'Becoming Postcolonial: African Women Changing the Meaning of Citizenship,' *Citizenship Studies 6*, no. 1 (2005): pp. 1–22.

Mehrotra, Santosh, Neha Kumra, and Ankita Gandhi, 'India's Fragmented Social Protection System: Three Rights Are in Place; Two Are Still Missing,' Working Paper 2014-18, (Geneva: United Nations Research Institute for Social Development (UNRISD), December 2014).

Olson, Kevin, *Imagined Sovereignties: The Power of the People and Other Myths of the Modern Age* (Cambridge: Cambridge University Press, 2016).

Oommen, T.K., *Citizenship, Nationality and Ethnicity* (Cambridge: Polity Press, 1997).

Qureshi, Kaveri, 'Diasporic Citizenship and Militarization: Punjabi Soldiers in the World Wars,' *Citizenship Studies 17*, no. 3–4 (2013): pp. 400–413.

Robins, Steven, Andrea Cornwall, and Bettina von Lieres, 'Rethinking "Citizenship" in the Postcolony,' *Third World Quarterly 29*, no. 6 (2008): pp. 1069–1086.

Roy, Anupama, *Mapping Citizenship in India* (Delhi: Oxford University Press, 2010)

Sadiq, Kamal, 'When States Prefer Non-Citizens over Citizens: Conflict over Illegal Immigration into Malaysia,' *International Studies Quarterly 49* no. 1 (March 2005): pp. 101–122.

Sadiq, Kamal, *Paper Citizens: How Illegal Immigrants Acquire Citizenship in Developing Countries* (New York: Oxford University Press, 2009).

Sadiq, Kamal, 'When Being "Native" is Not Enough: Citizens as Foreigners in Malaysia,' *Asian Perspective 33*, no. 1 (2009): pp. 5–32.

Singerman, Diane, *Avenues of Participation: Family, Politics and Networks in Urban Quarters of Cairo* (Princeton: Princeton University Press, 1995).

Singh Mehta, Uday, *Liberalism and Empire: A Study of Nineteenth Century Liberal Thought* (Chicago, London: University of Chicago Press, 2000).

Zambakari, Christopher, 'Sudan and South Sudan: Identity, Citizenship, and Democracy in Plural Societies,' *Citizenship Studies 19*, no. 1 (2015): pp. 69–82.

CHAPTER 10

ECONOMIC THEORIES OF CITIZENSHIP ASCENSION

DON J. DEVORETZ
AND NAHIKARI IRASTORZA

INTRODUCTION

THE economic analysis of the acquisition and impact of citizenship ascension in its modern form *circa* 2000 onwards is limited to a complex, heterogeneous model that includes ascending immigrants' human capital endowments. Empirical studies based on this model lead us to conclude that there is an economic premium derived when immigrants acquire citizenship in their destination countries. However naïve economic models that focus on labour market outcomes have left these premiums undetected in the past (see, e.g., the classic work by Becker in the US).[1] This purported lack of economic premiums from citizenship ascension left the economic analysis of citizenship ascension dormant until the early twenty-first century.

Even today, scholars in different countries arrive at varying conclusions on the causes and magnitude of this premium. Moreover, while the majority of these studies focus on the citizenship effects for immigrants, there are two important gaps in the literature: the effect of citizenship acquisition on others in the destination country and on residents in their origin countries.

Beyond the general question of the existence of an economic citizenship premium lies a host of more specific questions that must be addressed with a modern economic ascension model. First, how and why does the economic citizenship premium vary by gender, immigrant source country, immigrant entry class, and waiting period for citizenship ascension? The answers have important host country policy implications since addressing the influx of immigrants and time to ascension will allow the host country to maximize the derived economic benefits of citizenship ascension.

Another major question to address with an economic model of ascension is who are the economic winners or losers in the ascension process? Do host country residents economically gain or lose when a newly ascended immigrant appears? Moreover, what are the tax implications in the host country from citizenship ascension? Do new citizens pay more in taxes than they use in services, implying a net gain to existing residents? Both the average citizenship age and remaining lifetime income will influence the answer and a life cycle economic model of citizenship ascension will be needed to aid in the tax analysis. In a wider sphere, we must ask if the immigrant sending country is negatively or positively affected, economically, by citizenship ascension in the host country. Does the presence or absence of dual citizenship provisions in both the sending and host countries affect the size of the positive economic contributions for the sending countries after citizenship ascension in the host country?

Any economic model of citizenship ascension must be able to measure the impacts of existing immigrant and citizenship selection policies in a precise manner to decompose the source of the generally observed economic gain from citizenship ascension. The immigrant sending country and immigrant human capital selection criteria, along with a knowledge of the optimal waiting period for ascension, will allow the host country to absorb new citizens at no cost or maximize the benefit to the resident population depending on the host country's goal. This policy-oriented analysis of the economic impact of citizenship ascension expands on the 'club theory' model, which suggested that the admission of immigrants into the 'citizenship club' was predicated on existing club members gaining from new citizens' ascension. Without denying this general principle, the more modern economic model of citizenship ascension allows

---

[1] Gary Becker, *The Economics of Discrimination* (Chicago: University of Chicago Press, 1973).

both an analysis of the sources of any premium and provides policy instruments to increase the size of these economic benefits to existing club members.

A summary question thus emerges: what modern economic theory of citizenship ascension provides a tool to answer the questions posed above? An endogenous human capital model involving citizenship ascension is the only extant economic theory to analyse and provide answers for a variety of immigrants across source countries with different levels of human capital. Such a model recognizes that the accumulation of various forms of human capital needed for citizenship ascension and the resulting economic premium from citizenship ascension lead to a select group of citizenship candidates.

The rest of this chapter is organized as follows: first, we present earlier economic approaches to citizenship ascension based on the club goods theory and we discuss their limitations. In the next section, we further develop the human capital theory of the economic impact of citizenship ascension introduced above. We then discuss the economic costs and benefits of citizenship acquisition for immigrants, origin and destination countries, and we illustrate these ideas with empirical examples from Europe and North America. The last section presents our conclusions.

ECONOMIC THEORY OF CLUBS
AND CITIZENSHIP ASCENSION

In his book *Citizenship and Immigration*, Christian Joppke refers to Straubhaar in order to compare state membership (i.e. citizenship) to club membership.[2] One of the points of comparison concerns the economic aspect of citizenship. In a world of migration, where an increasing number of people choose their states, these states become instrumental associations with robust admission policies. According to these policies, for existing members, the benefits of accepting new members must be higher than the costs implied in this decision. He cites two 'legitimate' admission criteria: the willingness to accept the club rules and the new members' ability to pay.

These state and club membership concepts point us to the further impacts of naturalization on the state as outlined by Tiebout and Buchanan.[3] In Tiebout's attempt to build a satisfactory theory of public finance, one of the assumptions he makes is that there is an optimal community size for every public service provided by the

---

[2] Christian Joppke, *Citizenship and Immigration* (Cambridge: Polity Press, 2010).

[3] James M. Buchanan, 'An Economic Theory of Clubs', *Economica* 32, no. 125 (1965): pp. 1–14; Charles M. Tiebout, 'A Pure Theory of Local Expenditures', *Journal of Political Economy* 64, no. 5 (1956): pp. 416–424.

state to the members of such a community. This optimum, which implies that public goods are limited, is defined by the number of residents for which such services can be produced at the lowest average cost.

Likewise, according to Buchanan's economic theory of clubs, there is an optimal membership for almost any public or private activity people may engage in. The central question, according to him, is to determine the membership margin or the size of the most desirable cost and consumption sharing arrangement. As stated by Samuelson, unlike in the case of purely private goods, consumption of public goods by any one individual implies equal consumption by all others.[4] However, the utility that each member receives from the consumption of any public or private good or service depends on the number of individuals who share their benefits, i.e. the size of the club. Full equilibrium in club size will be reached when the marginal benefits and costs of having a new member for any existing member are equal.

While Tiebout and Buchanan's ideas have inspired many scholars, they have also been contested by a few. In his proposal for a new concept of citizenship, which he names 'Citizenship: Organizational and Marginal', Frey refers to Buchanan's theory of clubs in the sense that (i) non-members can be excluded and (ii) the consumption among the citizens has public good characteristics.[5] However, he argues that while Buchanan's analysis focuses on the benefits and costs of adding a member, the special relationship between the members and their club based on intrinsic motivations such as trust and loyalty is neglected.

Ruhs and Martin also address the question of the optimal community size by exploring the relationship between migrant numbers and rights.[6] In this case, however, this optimal relationship refers to migrants' rights rather than to the benefits and costs for the host community. These authors claim that there is an inverse relationship between the number and rights of migrants employed in low-skilled jobs in high-income countries. This is generated by (i) the increased labour costs associated with more employment rights for workers, from the employers' perspective and (ii) the desire of governments in destination countries to minimize the fiscal costs of low-skilled immigration, by keeping migrant numbers low or by restricting their access to welfare. These immigrants' rights, as described by Ruhs and Martin, could be extended to include their right to apply for citizenship in the host country and the host country's rules for naturalization. For example, countries could discourage low-skilled immigrant residents from applying for citizenship—and therefore, favour the highly skilled ones—by setting restrictive conditions such as a high application fee, a high language proficiency requirement, or a challenging citizenship test.

---

[4] Paul A. Samuelson, 'The Pure Theory of Public Expenditures', *Review of Economics and Statistics* 36, no. 4 (1954): pp. 387–389.

[5] Bruno Frey, 'Flexible Citizenship for a Global Society', *Politics, Philosophy & Economics* 2, no. 1 (2003): pp. 93–114.

[6] Martin Ruhs and Philip Martin, 'Numbers vs. Rights: Trade-Offs and Guest Worker Programs', *International Migration Review* 42, no. 1 (2008): pp. 249–265.

If we apply the ideas above to the study of the economic aspects of citizenship, we could state that: (i) even if all immigrant residents are allowed to apply for naturalization if they meet the conditions to do so, host countries have some mechanisms to restrict the number of successful applications from less profitable immigrant groups such as low-skilled immigrants, refugees, and family migrants; and (ii) granting citizenship will be economically sustainable and even profitable for countries and their long-term members or citizens if the benefits of such action equal or surpass the costs involved. Costs include not only the initial legal-administrative process costs associated with admitting new citizens, but also the relationship between the consumption of public goods and the total taxable income generated by immigrants after they become citizens. To establish whether this correlation is positive or negative, a comparison should be made between the new citizen's public expenditure and revenue profiles in their pre-ascension versus post-ascension periods.

The discussion about numbers and rights is also relevant to assess the economic implications, for host countries, of granting citizenship to migrants. The costs and benefits of accepting new citizens vary among destination countries depending on a number of factors including: (i) the cost of the administrative process of citizenship ascension and who pays for them; (ii) the cost of the services provided by the state to their citizens versus the permanent residents in the host country; (iii) the tax revenue collected by the state from their citizens versus their permanent residents; and (iv) the economic premium of citizenship for new citizens versus permanent residents and its tax implications for the state. However, citizenship does not only have economic implications for the countries that grant it, but also for the new citizens themselves and for their countries of origin, as we will see in the next section.

In sum, the theory of clubs as applied to the economics of citizenship provides a quasi-economic theoretical framework to address this topic but, by being too general, it lacks the precision to measure the economic impacts of citizenship ascension for a diversity of potential citizen candidates over time. Such an approach is better provided by human capital theory, which we develop in the next section.

Human Capital Theory of the Economic Impact of Citizenship Ascension

Evidence for an economic impact of citizenship ascension, finding for example higher earnings among naturalized than non-naturalized immigrants, might stem from diverse effects. It is possible that immigrants who acquire citizenship

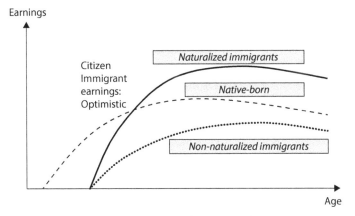

Figure 10.1 Age-Earnings Profiles Before and After Citizenship Ascension
Source: DeVoretz and Pivnenko (2006)[7]

are just different from non-citizens (e.g., in their levels of education), and that these differences drive both ascension to citizenship and earnings, without any causal relationship between citizenship status itself and economic outcomes. Alternatively, the investment required to attain citizenship (e.g., acquisition of language skills), and the subsequent security or benefits that come with citizenship might lead to productivity and earnings gains for new citizens (technically, changing the earnings slope) or help them get better jobs (producing a bump in income after naturalization).

To better appreciate the main economic factors that yield citizenship ascension premiums, we provide a stylized version of this modern economic theory's outcomes. Figure 10.1 represents an age-earnings profile for immigrant citizens and non-citizens in their chosen host country.

In this two dimensional diagram, time (age) and earnings are the primary analytical variables, with citizenship ascension and earnings affected by age for any stylized immigrant contemplating citizenship ascension. There exist several possible combinations of age-earnings profiles to deduce the size of the citizenship economic premium. In Figure 10.1 we produce three different age earnings profiles for the host country native-born (dashed line), the host country immigrant population (dotted line), and finally their naturalized counterparts (solid line). Given these three profiles it is possible to produce two measures of the citizenship economic premium. The first measure of the citizenship premium would be the anticipated higher earnings of naturalized citizens relative to resident alien earnings. It is also

[7] Don J. DeVoretz and Sergy Pivnenko, 'The Economic Determinants and Consequences of Canadian Citizenship Ascension', in Pieter Bevelander and Don J. DeVoretz, eds., *The Economic of Citizenship* (Malmo: Malmo University, 2008).

possible to measure the citizenship premium of naturalized citizens relative to the native-born.[8]

According to Figure 10.1, naturalized immigrants would earn more than both the native-born and their non-naturalized immigrant counterparts. However, empirical studies show significant variations in the effect of naturalization on immigrants' labour market outcomes among different national origins and across host countries.

Economists find that the rules governing how countries admit immigrants, and the rules governing naturalization are additional factors that affect the ultimate size of the economic premium gained from immigrants' naturalization. Too short a waiting period after immigration, for example, may inhibit the ability of a prospective citizen to gain enough human capital and labour force attachment to produce a substantial economic premium after naturalization. On the other hand, too long a waiting period may mean that candidates who have integrated into the labour market and gained valuable skills leave the country before they can become citizens.

The length of time before one can become a citizen is only one factor that shapes the economic premium from citizenship. Language requirements, for example, may help immigrants integrate into the country, but too strict a language provision might unduly restrict who attains citizenship (example.g., older candidates), diminishing any economic gains. Likewise the fact that many host countries do not allow naturalized citizens to keep dual nationalities reduces citizenship ascension rates and the aggregate economic premium.

For illustrative purposes, consider a theoretical country attempting to maximize both rates of naturalization and the economic benefit derived from them. Figure 10.2 depicts a hypothetical demand curve showing ascension rates—of the percentage of immigrants becoming citizens—and the citizenship premium—the economic bump that comes with naturalization.

With only a minimal waiting period, for example three years, the amount of immigrant accumulated country-specific human capital and the subsequent signal sent to employers is small. In this case, the short waiting period results in a small present value citizenship premium, in this hypothetical case only $50. As the ascension waiting period grows to five years the present value of the derived citizenship premium increases to a maximum of $100, as prospective citizens acquire more human capital which sends a stronger signal to employers who now pay more to these newly naturalized citizens.

Waiting periods greater than five years produce a gradual decline in the citizenship premium for two reasons. First, the payoff period shortens and thus there is less incentive to accumulate human capital while waiting to ascend to citizenship.

---

[8] Formally, these citizenship premiums are measured in terms of the differences in lifetime discounted incomes from age of citizenship ascension to retirement. In other words, $E((Y_{ct}-Y_{ct'})-(N_{ct}-Nct))/(1+t)$ where t=age of citizen or non-citizen. If this value is greater for a citizen than non-citizen it measures the discounted lifetime economic premium associated with citizenship ascension.

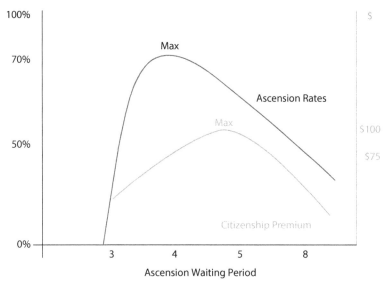

Figure 10.2 Ascension Rate and Economic Premium Trade Off
Source: Bevelander and DeVoretz (2014)[9]

Next, a longer ascension waiting period produces some outmigration as the more economically capable candidates for citizenship leave the host country to seek a citizenship premium in their home or third country.

Comparative Empirical Evidence from Europe and North America under the Human Capital Model of Citizenship Ascension

The acquisition of citizenship by immigrants has economic implications for three major parties: naturalized immigrants themselves, their countries of origin, and the host countries. These economic considerations may vary across countries of origin and destination but also depending on the human capital and socio-demographic

---

[9] Pieter Bevelander and Don J. DeVoretz, *The Economic Case for a Clear, Quick Pathway to Citizenship: Evidence from Europe and North America* (Washington: Center for American Progress, 2014).

characteristics of migrants such as their level of education or gender, and different combinations of the three parties involved.

Naturalized Migrants

In a now famous essay, Barry Chiswick claimed that there was no positive economic impact from citizenship accruing to naturalized immigrants in the US in the 1970s.[10] By the twenty-first century this conclusion was proved invalid in countries such as France, Germany, Sweden, Denmark, Norway, the US, and Canada.[11] Yet the core of the controversy remains. While most scholars agree that naturalized immigrants perform better in the labour market than non-naturalized immigrants, there is a lack of consensus over the reasons for this gap.

They also found economic performance differences across naturalized citizens by countries of origin and their associated level of development, immigrants' entry path as well as gender. Women, humanitarian migrants, and those coming from less developed countries appear to benefit most from citizenship ascension in Canada, Denmark, France, Germany, Norway, Sweden, and the US.[12]

---

[10] Barry R. Chiswick, 'The Effect of Americanization on the Earnings of Foreign-Born Men', *Journal of Political Economy 86*, no. 5 (1978): pp. 897–921.

[11] Pieter Bevelander and Don J. DeVoretz, eds., *The Economics of Citizenship* (Malmo: Malmo University, 2008); Pieter Bevelander and Ravi Pendakur, 'Citizenship, Co-Ethnic Populations, and Employment Probabilities of Immigrants in Sweden', *International Migration and Integration 13* (2012): pp. 203–222; Pieter Bevelander, Jonas Helgertz, Bernt Bratsberg, and Anna Tegunimataka, 'Who Becomes a Citizen, and What Happens Next? Naturalization in Denmark, Norway and Sweden', Delmi Report 6 (2015), online http://www.delmi.se/en/democracy#!/en/who-becomes-a-citizen-and-what-happens-next; Bernt Bratsberg, James F. Ragan, and Zaffar M. Nasir, 'The Effect of Naturalization on Wage Growth: A Panel Study of Young Male Immigrants', *Journal of Labor Economics 20*, no. 3 (2002): pp. 568–597; Denis Fougère and Mirna Safi, 'Naturalization and Employment of Immigrants in France (1968-1999)', *International Journal of Manpower 30*, no. 1-2, (2009): pp. 83–96; Christina Gathmann and Nicolas Keller, 'Returns to Citizenship? Evidence from Germany's Recent Immigration Reforms', IZA discussion paper no. 8064 (2014), online http://ftp.iza.org/dp8064.pdf; Jonas Helgertz, Pieter Bevelander, and Anna Tegunimataka, 'Naturalization and Earnings: A Denmark-Sweden Comparison', *European Journal of Population 30*, no. 3 (2014): pp. 337–359; Manuel Pastor and Justin Scoggins, 'Citizen Gain. The Economic Benefits of Naturalization for Immigrants and the Economy' (Center for the Study of Immigrant Integration, 2012), online http://dornsife.usc.edu/assets/sites/731/docs/citizen_gain_web.pdf; Ravi Pendakur and Pieter Bevelander, 'Citizenship, Enclaves and Earnings: Comparing Two Cool Countries', *Citizenship Studies 18*, no. 3–4 (2014): pp. 384–407; Heidi Shierholz, 'The Effects of Citizenship on Family Income and Poverty', EPI briefing paper no. 256 (2010), online http://www.epi.org/files/page/-/bp256/bp256.pdf; Max Steinhardt, 'Does Citizenship Matter? The Economic Impact of Naturalizations in Germany', *Labour Economics 19*, no. 6 (2012): pp. 813–823; Madeleine Sumption and Sarah Flamm, 'The Economic Value of Citizenship for Immigrants in the United States' (Washington: Migration Policy Institute, 2012), online file:///C:/Users/Matthew/Downloads/citizenship-premium.pdf.

[12] Ather H. Akbari, 'Immigrant Naturalization and its Impacts on Immigrant Labour Market Performance and Treasury', in Pieter Bevelander and Don J. DeVoretz, eds., *The Economics of*

In interpreting these findings, researchers debate whether there is a self-selection bias among naturalized immigrants or not. In other words, do immigrants who plan to acquire a new citizenship have or equip themselves with human capital and other social skills prior to citizenship ascension, which in turn allows them to enjoy the observed citizenship premium? Furthermore, do all immigrants who ascend to citizenship experience an economic premium or is this observed economic gain reserved for a select group of immigrants who arrive with premium social and human capital endowments? And, finally, do country-level immigration policies targeted to selecting immigrants influence the potential citizenship premium for their immigrants?

Bevelander and DeVoretz address these questions for five European and North American countries with different immigrant selection and citizenship-granting procedures—namely, Sweden, Norway, the Netherlands, the US, and Canada.[13] This comparative analysis leads to the conclusion that the design of a country's immigration and citizenship policies influences the degree of economic integration of its potential citizens and, as a result, also the size of the economic premium derived from citizenship.

Three specific ascension rules are cited as the main policy factors affecting the size of the citizenship premium: the length of the waiting period, language require-ments, and the absence of dual citizenship. A short waiting period may inhibit the ability of the citizenship candidate to acquire enough human capital to produce a substantial economic premium after naturalization, but the opposite can act per-versely as immigrant candidates with a large amount of human capital may leave the host country before the waiting period has expired. Language requirements may also have differing effects: greater required language facility may increase immi-grants' economic premium, whereas a more rigorous language requirement can dis-courage potential candidates to apply and encourage them to leave the host country for another country with lower or no language requirements. Finally, the literature is not conclusive on the correlation between dual citizenship policies by immigrant sending and host countries, and naturalization rates: while some studies show that the absence of dual citizenship provisions in either the host country or the immi-grant's sending country would reduce citizenship ascension rates (see, e.g., Peters et al. 2016 or Vink et al. 2013)—which would ultimately also decrease the size of the economic premium derived from naturalization—others conclude the opposite (e.g., Helgertz and Bevelander 2016).[14]

Citizenship (Malmo: Malmo University, 2008); Pendakur and Bevelander (n 11); Bevelander et al. (n 11); Fougère and Safi (n 11); Gathmann and Keller (n 11); John E. Hayfron, 'The Economics of Norwegian Citizenship', in Pieter Bevelander and Don J. DeVoretz, eds., *The Economics of Citizenship* (Malmo: Malmo University, 2008); Pastor and Scoggins (n 11); Shierholz (n 11); Sumption and Flamm (n 11).

[13] Bevelander and DeVoretz (n 11).

[14] Jonas Helgertz and Pieter Bevelander, 'The Influence of Partner Choice and Country of Origin Characteristics on the Naturalization of Immigrants in Sweden: A Longitudinal Analysis', *International Migration Review*, early view (2016), online http://dx.doi.org/10.1111/imre.12244; Floris Peters, Maarten

One of the main hypotheses posed by Bevelander and DeVoretz states that potential immigrant citizens will get higher or lower economic benefits from naturalization depending on whether they have been through a double selection process or not. The first selection occurs when immigrants select themselves and make the decision to migrate. Receiving states with policies aiming to attract immigrants with specific profiles make the second selection. These policies are more common in North American and Australia than in Europe. A third selection happens when an immigrant decides to apply for citizenship acquisition and it is granted to him or her. Doubly selected immigrants should have higher human capital endowments, which will provide immigrants with more benefits from the process of naturalization.

Based on the results obtained in the case studies and depending on the benefits derived from naturalization for migrants, the above-cited countries can be classified in three categories: high (Canada), moderate (US), and low (Norway, Netherlands, and Sweden) citizenship premium countries. The economic premium was measured in terms of earnings or employment opportunities. This classification is also illustrative of country-level differences in immigration policies and, in particular, differences in their immigrant selection criteria.

For example, DeVoretz and Pivnenko reported significantly positive earning effects derived from naturalization in Canada.[15] However, they conclude that a self-selection bias caused by a triple positive selection may have blurred their results, resulting from Canadian immigration policies, a significant presence of highly skilled immigrants, and immigrants' investments in human capital prior to naturalization.

Interesting results were reported by Akbari from the American case study: while immigrants from developing countries experienced a positive effect on earnings after naturalization, this effect was not as significant for immigrants from developed countries.[16] Later studies confirm these findings.[17]

The Netherlands, Norway, and Sweden were included in the low economic premium group of countries as reported by Bevelander and DeVoretz.[18] After controlling for human capital and sociodemographic factors, no citizenship premium was found for immigrants to these countries, with the exception of refugees to Norway.[19]

Vink, and Hans Schmeets, 'The Ecology of Immigrant Naturalisation: A Life Course Approach in the Context of Institutional Conditions', *Journal of Ethnic and Migration Studies* 42, no. 3 (2016): pp. 359–381, online http://dx.doi.org/10.1080/1369183X.2015.1103173; Maarten Peter Vink, Tijana Prokic-Breuer, and Jaap Dronkers, 'Immigrant Naturalization in the Context of Institutional Diversity: Policy Matters, but to Whom?', *International Migration* 51, no. 5 (2013): pp. 1–20, doi:10.1111/imig.12106.

[15] DeVoretz and Pivnenko (n 7).
[16] Akbari (n 12).
[17] Pastor and Scoggins (n 11); Shierholz (n 11); Sumption and Flamm (n 11).
[18] Bevelander and DeVoretz (n 11).
[19] Hayfron (n 12); Kirk Scott, 'The Economics of Citizenship: Is There a Naturalization Effect', in Pieter Bevelander and Don J. DeVoretz, eds., *The Economics of Citizenship* (Malmo: Malmo University, 2008); Pieter Bevelander and Justus Veenman, 'Naturalization and Socioeconomic Integration: The Case of the Netherlands', in Pieter Bevelander and Don J. DeVoretz, eds., *The Economics of Citizenship* (Malmo: Malmo University, 2008).

In a later study, however, Bevelander and Pendakur[20] found that citizenship acquisition has a positive impact on employment for a number of immigrant groups living in Sweden, notably, for non-EU/non-North American immigrants. Moreover, refugees—but not their family members—were reported to experience substantial gains from citizenship acquisition. These results were confirmed and extended by the same scholars in a study that compared the citizenship effect on the earnings of immigrants to Canada and Sweden.[21] Finally, in a recent study by Bevelander et al., which compared the effect of naturalization on immigrants' employment and income outcomes in Denmark, Norway, and Sweden, a positive correlation was found between naturalization and a better economic performance among people from countries generally marked by having poor labour market integration.[22] Only in a few cases, however, was this improved labour market outcome directly linked to the time of naturalization.

Studies conducted in France and Germany replicate most of these findings. Fougère and Safi (2009) found that acquiring French nationality has a significant positive relationship on naturalized immigrants' subsequent employability and that this is particularly true for groups who have a low probability of employment in the host country. Steinhardt[23] documents strong self-selection within the immigrant workforce concerning naturalization in Germany. However, he still finds a wage premium earned by naturalized German immigrants, with a larger impact for non-EU immigrants. Gathmann and Keller (2014) ask whether a more liberal access to citizenship, resulting from two major citizenship ascension reforms in Germany, improved the economic integration of immigrants.[24] Their estimates show a positive correlation between naturalization and labour market performance, with the returns of citizenship being more substantial for women and recent immigrants than for men and traditional guest workers. The authors conclude that while the liberalization of citizenship provides some benefits in the labour market, it is unlikely to result in full economic and social integration of immigrants to Germany.

In sum, these studies provide similar conclusions. Naturalized immigrants have higher human capital endowments than their counterparts and this explains their higher employment rates and income. Yet even after controlling for human capital and socio-demographic factors, there exists a separate citizenship effect for naturalized immigrants' labour market incomes in the majority of country case studies reported. This effect seems to be larger for immigrants from low-income countries, refugees and for women, and for immigrants naturalized in countries where they

---

[20] Pieter Bevelander and Ravi Pendakur, 'Citizenship, Co-Ethnic Populations, and Employment Probabilities of Immigrants in Sweden', *International Migration and Integration* 13 (2012): pp. 203–222.

[21] Pendakur and Bevelander (n 11).   [22] Bevelander et al. (n 11).

[23] Steinhardt (n 11).

[24] Between 1991 and 1999, adolescents could obtain citizenship after eight years of residency in Germany, while adults faced a fifteen-year residency requirement. Since 2000, all immigrants face an eight-year residency requirement.

are doubly selected. However, due to the possible existence of endogeneity between naturalization and greater human capital acquisition, it is difficult to establish causality. For example, Sumption and Flamm note that despite the potential economic and other benefits of citizenship, far fewer immigrants naturalize than are eligible to do so.[25] They report that immigrants are more likely to naturalize if they have high levels of education, speak English well, and have been in the US for a long time. Moreover, due to data limitations, the reported studies were unable to control for unobservable characteristics that affect both citizenship and economic progress such as inherent skills, perseverance, or personal connections. Thus, we claim that qualitative studies are needed to control for the role of current unobservable characteristics and economic outcomes of naturalized immigrants.

The studies cited above focus on the potential economic premium earned by naturalized immigrants through the improvement of their labour market performance. However, naturalized immigrants may also benefit from public services provided to citizens but not to permanent residents in certain countries.

There are also some costs related to the naturalization process itself that migrants need to take into account when making the decision to apply. In chronological order, and depending on the migrants' knowledge of the host country language and other country-specific human capital attributes and administrative matters such as the validation of foreign degrees, the first step for prospective citizens is further investment in language courses and other courses to raise their professional standards or to help them pass often rigorous host country credential exams. Second, they may have to pay application fees that range from zero euros in France to 1,005 GB pounds in the United Kingdom. Finally, whereas in some countries becoming a citizen may have tax benefits, in others, naturalization may carry negative tax implications. In the US, citizens, but not permanent residents, are taxed on their worldwide income.

Among the direct and indirect costs associated with ascending to citizenship, Bevelander and DeVoretz highlight the absence of dual citizenship provisions in the host or sending country and the potential lost productivity and income absorbed by the immigrant during the waiting period before citizenship ascension.[26] Recent research shows that migration flows are more intense among origin and destination countries that allow dual citizenship.[27] Loss of citizenship in the sending country when either or both countries deny 'dual citizenship' is a large opportunity cost for some citizenship candidates who intend to return home to either work or retire. According to these authors, the loss of home country citizenship implies limited access to their home country's labour market; a potential loss of the right to hold

[25] Sumption and Flamm (n 11).   [26] Bevelander and DeVoretz (n 11).
[27] Hannah M. Alarian and Sara Wallace Goodman, 'Dual Citizenship Allowance and Migration Flow: An Origin Story', *Comparative Political Studies*, early view (7 February 2016), doi:10.1177/0010414015626443.

land, or the requirement to pay higher land taxes; the loss of entitlement to home country public services, such as subsidized education for their children; and the loss of entitlement to participate in the political process in the source country.

Countries of Naturalization

Most existing studies examine the effects of citizenship acquisition on *immigrants'* labour market performance; we have only found two studies that address the association between naturalization and host country's economy over all, and none that link naturalization and the sending country's economy. One way to think about the effects on countries is to consider tax benefits for host countries. Naturalization countries may also benefit from immigrants' citizenship acquisition if the labour market performance improves resulting in (i) higher income taxes receipts or (ii) greater economic contributions of naturalized immigrants versus permanent residents to the host country's economy.

According to Bevelander and DeVoretz, as immigrants' salaries and lifetime earnings increase as a result of naturalization, naturalized immigrants' federal and local treasury contributions also do.[28] They add that these treasury contributions, in turn, yield benefits to non-immigrant residents in most host countries. Beyond economic benefits, host countries may also benefit from immigrants' citizenship acquisition when this increases immigrants' sense of belonging to the country of naturalization and in turn, has a positive effect on local peoples' attitude towards naturalized immigrants and therefore, increases social cohesion.

Pastor and Scoggins also asked about the economic impact on the overall host country's economy, from the hypothetical naturalization of immigrants who were eligible to do so in the US.[29] In other words, they estimate the opportunity cost of having a low level of naturalization in the US. By using the mid-point between lower-bound and upper-bound estimates of gains and by setting a goal of shrinking the number of the eligible non-naturalized by half over five years, they estimated an earnings' boost of nearly 40 billion dollars to the US economy over the next decade. They also concluded that the impact on GDP can be even larger once the secondary effects of higher incomes on spending and demand are taken into account.

The last question asked by these scholars, based on their results, is why immigrants and policy makers do not pursue this citizenship premium. They respond that low host country language proficiency, a lack of knowledge about the application process, and the relatively high application fees discourage immigrants from applying for citizenship. These ideas coincide with Sumption and Flamm's conclusions.[30] Pastor and

---

[28] Bevelander and DeVoretz (n 11).   [29] Pastor and Scoggins (n 11).
[30] Sumption and Flamm (n 11).

Scoggins also claim that the US government could help by streamlining the process and considering reductions in application fees and other indirect costs.[31]

From the receiving state's perspective, naturalization costs involve a one-time expense in processing the potential naturalized citizen for security clearance as well as administering the citizenship examination and validating other papers such as country of origin and entry date into the host country.[32] The host country's government will also have more citizens to protect and provide services for, such as in emergencies caused by natural disasters abroad. On a more symbolic level, these now naturalized outsiders may challenge the limits of the 'imagined' contours of the national political community.

Some other negative economic effects, at the country level, are more subtle and require a more detailed discussion. For example, what if immigrant ascension to citizenship results in return migration? The literature shows different behaviour for immigrants from different origin countries and human capital endowments. For example, while naturalized non-Turkish immigrants were found to be less likely to leave Germany, citizenship is not significantly correlated with the return migration of Turkish immigrants living in the same country.[33] A more general study of the outmigration of the foreign-born conducted in the US reports substantial variation in outmigration rates across national origin groups and indicates that immigrants tend to return to wealthy countries not far from the US. Furthermore, according to the same study, if the immigrant flow is positively selected—in other words, if immigrants have above-average skills—the return migrants will be the least skilled immigrants; whereas if the immigrant flow is negatively selected, the return migrants will be the most skilled.[34]

The return migration of naturalized immigrants may have significant economic implications for countries of destination, especially in the case of highly skilled immigrants with higher contributions to the treasury. Dual citizenship allows immigrants who ascend to host country citizenship to enjoy social and economic benefits in both their countries of naturalization and origin. Substantial return migration to the sending country immediately after citizenship ascension implies potentially substantial post-retirement liabilities to the host country. This outcome arises if naturalized citizens leave their host country soon after citizenship ascension then proceed to work outside the host country for their labour market years

---

[31] Pastor and Scoggins (n 11).

[32] Note that these costs may vary depending on the country of naturalization and that, more importantly, will not always be assumed by the host country (this is, e.g., the case of France) but they may also be fully or partially paid by the applicant immigrant (like in the UK, US, or Netherlands).

[33] Torben Kuhlenkasper and Max Friedrich Steinhardt, 'Who Leaves and When?–Selective Outmigration of Immigrants from Germany', HWWI research paper no. 123 (2012), online http://www.hwwi.org/uploads/tx_wilpubdb/HWWI-Research-Paper-128.pdf.

[34] George J. Borjas and Bernt Bratsberg, 'Who Leaves? The Outmigration of the Foreign-Born', *The Review of Economics and Statistics 78*, no. 1 (1996): pp. 165–176.

and are not subject to host country income taxes and then return to the host country upon retirement.

Furthermore, citizenship ascension can be motivated by and produce third country effects. For example, in either North America under the NAFTA agreement or
in the European Union, ascension to citizenship in a member country allows heretofore uni-state immigrants a legal opportunity to move from their original host
country to a third country to exploit their economic and social skills.

An economist would never view these third party effects as sub-optimal since any
migration that increases the productivity of international immigrants is a positive
outcome. Witness the multitude of recent Chinese-born Canadians working suc-
cessively in the US courtesy of now holding a Canadian passport.[35] However, the
immigrant host country may resent these induced third party movements, especially if a combination of immigrant host country citizenship acquisition yields a
passport with greater mobility provisions and if the prior accumulation of subsidized human capital in the host country facilitated their third country movement.
This third country presence of naturalized dual citizens implies the existence of an
infinite chain of naturalized progeny of a dual citizen couple living abroad. Thus
countries have limited the prospect of the progeny of dual citizens from gaining
citizenship under the principle of *jus sanguinis* leaving these progeny stateless.[36]

These above examples of potential economic loss to the host country caused by
the onward mobility of newly created dual citizens must be compared to the magnitude of economic gains derived when the recently naturalized remain economically
active in their host country. A successful host country naturalization policy would
maximize the net economic gains not only to recently naturalized immigrants but
also to resident citizens in the host country.

Countries of Origin

An understudied aspect of the economic implications of immigrants' naturalization
is the effect of host country naturalization on the immigrant sending countries' economies. Some of the benefits resulting from migrants' citizenship ascension—and the
resulting better economic situation of these naturalized citizens—for their countries
of origin could include higher remittances, investment in property or a business in the
homeland, the building of a retirement house, donations to their origin communities,
etc. However, the opposite is also possible: the act of ascending to citizenship could

---

[35] Under the NAFTA agreement naturalized Canadians (or Americans) can work in the United
States (or Canada) in sixty-seven professions without having to obtain a visa.

[36] For example Canada does not allow the progeny of naturalized Canadians born abroad to obtain
Canadian citizenship. However, progeny of Canadian-born couples born abroad are considered
Canadian citizens.

be part of a settlement process in the host country, to which the new citizens may feel more committed. As migrants' attachment from the origin to the destination country shifts, the frequency of their contacts, visits, and investments in their country of origin may also decrease over time. These two possible scenarios are not only influenced by time elapsed since migration but also by other factors such as the civil status of migrants in both countries, whether they have children and where the children live, whether the parents are still alive and where they live. Migrant sending countries such as China, which do not recognize dual citizenship, often economically penalize their third country naturalized citizens, reducing their incentive to return.[37] Other countries such as India, which also does not recognize dual citizenship, have flexible admission and residency policies for heretofore Indian citizens.[38]

From a wider view of migration, citizenship ascension, and world productivity, naturalization may, at the same time, benefit both sending and destination countries. Let's take for example the case of naturalized Gujarati immigrants to the US or Canada. The fact that India has instituted a modified form of dual citizenship recognition results in two citizenship ascension premiums. First, Gujarati immigrant entrepreneurs and engineers will ascend to US or Canadian citizenship faster and at a greater rate with the impending loss of Indian citizenship removed, which in turn lowers the cost of host country citizenship acquisition. Beyond this lower cost of host country immigrant citizenship ascension is the prospect of naturalized Indo-Canadians or Indo-Americans working and investing in India.

One of the major potential costs absorbed by sending countries—namely the loss of their citizens and, as a result, sometimes of their tax-payers—is linked to the non-recognition of dual citizenship by either sending or host countries. However, this is not a commonly found scenario because (i) most sending countries are low-income countries that do recognize dual citizenship (with the important exception of China) and (ii) naturalization countries that in theory do not accept it, in practice do not tend to prosecute their dual citizens.

SOME CONCLUSIONS

In this chapter we have reflected on the potential economic implications of citizenship acquisition using a human capital model for citizenship ascension for the three

---

[37] For example, working visas are required for working age dual citizens while the dependents of these dual citizens are charged substantial school fees.

[38] India allows a form of dual citizenship such that naturalized Indian citizens abroad can return to India to work. However, they cannot be politically active and run for office or vote in Indian elections.

major parties affected: naturalized immigrants themselves, their countries of origin, and the countries of naturalization. We have claimed that earlier approaches, such as the economic theory of clubs, lack the complexity to fully address this topic. In an attempt to do so, this chapter further develops the human capital model and the analysis of net tax transfers between three groups: immigrants, naturalized citizens, and the native-born. In addition, the human capital model has been expanded to incorporate new analytical challenges including the effects derived from the presence of dual citizenship and free trade zones. The economic costs and benefits of citizenship acquisition are then discussed from the point of view of naturalized immigrants, and their sending and host countries. Finally, these ideas have been illustrated by empirical studies conducted in North America and Europe. These studies show that the costs and benefits of naturalization vary depending on immigrants' characteristics such as human capital and gender, the standard of living of origin countries, type of migration, and immigration and naturalization policies in host countries, among which the immigrant selection policies, the provision of dual citizenship, language requirements, and the waiting time for naturalization are some of the most relevant factors.

We have stated that the vast majority of the studies on immigrants' naturalization focus on the labour market impact of citizenship ascension for the naturalized immigrant and the host labour market, and the subsequent fiscal impacts derived from naturalization. In comparison, the effect of naturalization on sending economies has received little or no attention. Below we present a research agenda based on this and other gaps and limitations we found in our literature review. We claim that more comparative and qualitative research is needed to address these questions.

How could we work around the self-selection bias to assess the real citizenship effect? Since the prospect of reaping economic benefits from naturalization entices immigrants to accumulate human capital prior to naturalization, comparative studies must be conducted to detect the 'pure' economic effect owing to citizenship ascension. One test that could be conducted across countries is to detect the differential rates of citizenship ascension and the resulting income effects for immigrants who accumulate similar amounts of capital.

Further ideas to analyse the effect of naturalization on host country's economy. There are numerous secondary economic effects that can impact the economic outcomes of host country born citizens. These economy-wide impacts on unemployment, wage rates, or income distribution of the host country born citizen can be detected *via* counterfactual experiments. For example, what would happen if all undocumented US residents gained citizenship? Would the effects differ if different groups, such as those under age thirty, or skilled workers, or the full-time employed, were granted citizenship rights? Obviously different counterfactual questions of a similar nature can be posed for other immigrant host countries.

How could we analyse the effect of naturalization on a sending country's economy? This is a difficult question to answer since few data sets exist to trace the origins and ultimate residency of host country naturalized citizens. For example, China does not recognize any naturalized Chinese born people who work or invest in China. These naturalized Chinese Canadians or Chinese Americans are recorded in China as Canadians or Americans working or living in China. Thus, small scale and specific studies must be conducted which can clearly identify the birthplace and ultimate citizenship of the return migrant. One area is promising, namely tracing the flows of naturalized citizens' human capital to their host countries. This has been done on a limited scale since the physical place of where the first and subsequent degrees are earned can identify the origin and host country of a returned naturalized citizen.

What factors condition a clear path to citizenship for individual host countries and specific groups of immigrants? Some countries have multiple paths to citizenship for different immigrant resident groups. A straightforward test would be to run controlled experiments across these multiple paths to observe possible differential rates of ascension and economic impacts owing to citizenship ascension.

Naturalization allows immigrants to not only enjoy formal rights and protections through the legal status of citizenship, but to become members of a national political community through citizenship status. It also allows naturalized migrants to have access to certain job opportunities restricted to host country citizens, freer movement between host country and third countries, accelerated rights to family unification, and so forth. On top of these rather obvious and measurable benefits of naturalization, citizenship acquisition may also be a 'natural' consequence of an immigrant's integration process and a shift in their sense of belonging from their country of origin towards their destination country. Therefore, we could state that naturalization does not always need to be a rational economic choice but it could also be an expression of more subjective identity and appreciation of legal and social institutions in the host country. Thus naturalization may still occur when there are no clear civic or economic benefits for the naturalized immigrant. However, the economic benefits derived from citizenship ascension can often be the force that entices the hesitant immigrant to become a citizen.

BIBLIOGRAPHY

Akbari, Ather H., 'Immigrant Naturalization and its Impacts on Immigrant Labour Market Performance and Treasury', in Pieter Bevelander and Don J. DeVoretz, eds., *The Economics of Citizenship* (Malmo: Malmo University, 2008).

Alarian, Hannah M. and Sara Wallace Goodman, 'Dual Citizenship Allowance and Migration Flow: An Origin Story', *Comparative Political Studies*, early view (7 February 2016), doi:10.1177/0010414015626443.

Becker, Gary, *The Economics of Discrimination* (Chicago: University of Chicago Press, 1973).

Bevelander, Pieter and Don J. DeVoretz, *The Economic Case for a Clear, Quick Pathway to Citizenship: Evidence from Europe and North America* (Washington: Center for American Progress, 2014).

Bevelander, Pieter and Don J. DeVoretz, eds., *The Economics of Citizenship* (Malmo: Malmo University, 2008).

Bevelander, Pieter and Ravi Pendakur. 'Citizenship, Co-Ethnic Populations, and Employment Probabilities of Immigrants in Sweden', *International Migration and Integration* 13 (2012): pp. 203–222.

Bevelander, Pieter and Justus Veenman, 'Naturalization and Socioeconomic Integration: the Case of the Netherlands', in Pieter Bevelander and Don J. DeVoretz, eds., *The Economics of Citizenship* (Malmo: Malmo University, 2008).

Bevelander, Pieter, Jonas Helgertz, Bernt Bratsberg, and Anna Tegunimataka, 'Who Becomes a Citizen, and What Happens Next? Naturalization in Denmark, Norway and Sweden', Delmi Report 6 (2015), online https://www.google.se/url?sa=t&rct=j&q=&esrc=s&sou rce=web&cd=2&ved=0ahUKEwituqKylcjNAhXLJSwKHaffCL4QFgghMAE&url=http %3A%2F%2Fwww.delmi.se%2Fupl%2Ffiles%2F120588.pdf&usg=AFQjCNHgk7Z9BR-FHmGB000EMqfleYo6nw&sig2=v0ACHUj7ilt_j48p70GXNA.

Borjas, George J. and Bernt Bratsberg, 'Who Leaves? The Outmigration of the Foreign-Born', *The Review of Economics and Statistics 78*, no. 1 (1996): pp. 165–176.

Bratsberg, Bernt, James F. Ragan and Zaffar M. Nasir, 'The Effect of Naturalization on Wage Growth: A Panel Study of Young Male Immigrants', *Journal of Labor Economics 20*, no. 3 (2002): pp. 568–597.

Buchanan, James M., 'An Economic Theory of Clubs', *Economica 32*, no. 125 (1965): pp. 1–14.

Chiswick, Barry R., 'The Effect of Americanization on the Earnings of Foreign-Born Men', *Journal of Political Economy 86*, no. 5 (1978): pp. 897–921.

DeVoretz, Don J. and Sergy Pivnenko, 'The Economic Determinants and Consequences of Canadian Citizenship Ascension', in Pieter Bevelander and Don J. DeVoretz, eds., *The Economics of Citizenship* (Malmo: Malmo University, 2008).

Fougère, Denis and Mirna Safi, 'Naturalization and Employment of Immigrants in France (1968–1999)', *International Journal of Manpower 30*, no. 1–2 (2009): pp. 83–96.

Frey, Bruno, 'Flexible Citizenship for a Global Society', *Politics, Philosophy & Economics 2*, no. 1 (2003): pp. 93–114.

Gathmann, Christina and Nicolas Keller, 'Returns to Citizenship? Evidence from Germany's Recent Immigration Reforms', IZA discussion paper no. 8064 (2014), online http://ftp.iza.org/dp8064.pdf.

Hayfron, John E., 'The Economics of Norwegian Citizenship', in Pieter Bevelander and Don J. DeVoretz, eds., *The Economics of Citizenship* (Malmo: Malmo University, 2008).

Helgertz, Jonas and Pieter Bevelander, 'The Influence of Partner Choice and Country of Origin Characteristics on the Naturalization of Immigrants in Sweden: A Longitudinal Analysis', *International Migration Review*, early view (2016), online http://dx.doi.org/10.1111/imre.12244

Helgertz, Jonas, Pieter Bevelander, and Anna Tegunimataka, 'Naturalization and Earnings: A Denmark-Sweden Comparison', *European Journal of Population 30*, no. 3 (2014): pp. 337–359.

Joppke, Christian, *Citizenship and Immigration* (Cambridge: Polity Press, 2010).

Kuhlenkasper, Torben and Max Friedrich Steinhardt, 'Who Leaves and When?–Selective Outmigration of Immigrants from Germany', HWWI research paper no. 123 (2012), online http://www.hwwi.org/uploads/tx_wilpubdb/HWWI-Research-Paper-128.pdf.

Pastor, Manuel and Justin Scoggins, 'Citizen Gain. The Economic Benefits of Naturalization for Immigrants and the Economy' (Center for the Study of Immigrant Integration, 2012), online http://dornsife.usc.edu/assets/sites/731/docs/citizen_gain_web.pdf.

Pendakur, Ravi and Pieter Bevelander, 'Citizenship, Enclaves and Earnings: Comparing Two Cool Countries', *Citizenship Studies 18*, no. 3–4 (2014): pp. 384–407.

Peters, Floris, Maarten Vink, and Hans Schmeets, 'The Ecology of Immigrant Naturalisation: A Life Course Approach in the Context of Institutional Conditions', *Journal of Ethnic and Migration Studies 42*, no. 3 (2016): pp. 359–381, online http://dx.doi.org/10.1080/1369183X.2015.1103173.

Ruhs, Martin and Philip Martin, 'Numbers vs. Rights: Trade-Offs and Guest Worker Programs', *The International Migration Review 42*, no. 1 (2008): pp. 249–265.

Samuelson, Paul A., 'The Pure Theory of Public Expenditures', *Review of Economics and Statistics 36*, no. 4 (1954): pp. 387–389.

Scott, Kirk, 'The Economics of Citizenship: Is There a Naturalization Effect', in Pieter Bevelander and Don J. DeVoretz, eds., *The Economics of Citizenship* (Malmo: Malmo University, 2008).

Shierholz, Heidi, 'The Effects of Citizenship on Family Income and Poverty', EPI briefing paper no. 256 (2010), online http://www.epi.org/publication/bp256/.

Steinhardt, Max, 'Does Citizenship Matter? The Economic Impact of Naturalizations in Germany', *Labour Economics 19*, no. 6 (2012): pp. 813–823.

Sumption, Madeleine and Sarah Flamm, 'The Economic Value of Citizenship for Immigrants in the United States' (Washington: Migration Policy Institute, 2012), online http://www.migrationpolicy.org/research/economic-value-citizenship.

Tiebout, Charles M., 'A Pure Theory of Local Expenditures', *Journal of Political Economy 64*, no. 5 (1956): pp. 416–424.

Vink, Maarten Peter, Tijana Prokic-Breuer, and Jaap Dronkers, 'Immigrant Naturalization in the Context of Institutional Diversity: Policy Matters, but to Whom?', *International Migration 51*, no. 5 (2013): pp. 1–20, doi:10.1111/imig.12106.

CHAPTER 11

....

COMPARING CITIZENSHIP REGIMES

....

MAARTEN VINK

DEFINING AND INVESTIGATING CITIZENSHIP REGIMES

....

CITIZENSHIP is a form of 'legalized discrimination,'[1] in the sense that polities make categorical distinctions in their laws on the basis of defined membership criteria with regard to allocation of benefits and rights. These distinctions are justified because citizenship is viewed as a constitutive element of political community: without a stable membership conception of the group of persons that is entitled to the benefits and rights of a community, political self-determination is generally held to

[1] Andreas Wimmer, *Ethnic Boundary Making: Institutions, Power, Networks* (New York: Oxford University Press, 2013), p. 74.

be impossible. Territory, an equally vital constituent element of statehood, has been divided between states as a result of warfare, international treaties, and arbitration in such a way that all permanently inhabited territories are ruled by one state and one state only. For people, the international convention is that states are sovereign in determining their own population, which entails that they can, within certain limits set by international law, exclude populations inside their territory or include others beyond their borders. As a result there is significant variation between political communities both with regard to the access to status as well as the extent to which it discriminates in terms of rights and duties.

This chapter discusses comparative research on the regulation of the acquisition and loss of citizenship status and of the implications of having this status or not, which broadly speaking can be designated as the research agenda of the comparative study of citizenship regimes. *Citizenship regimes* are understood here as institutionalized systems of formal and informal norms that define access to membership, as well as rights and duties associated with membership, within a polity. *Comparing* citizenship regimes thus implies the study of how political membership is regulated in different contexts, by states, as well as in sub-state and suprastate communities. The compelling reason for analyzing citizenship regimes across contexts is that what is normal in a particular time or place may not always have been so, or is different elsewhere.[2] Given that citizenship is so intimately linked to self-determination of communities, the regulation of political membership tends to vary significantly across time and place, while our understanding of the causes and consequences of such variation is influenced by 'self-imposed national blinders.'[3] Through comparison, when based on well-chosen case selection strategies, we can strip away such national blinders and learn not just about citizenship regimes in other contexts, but also better understand how political membership is governed within our own community.

Three further clarifications are needed, however, in terms the scope of the body of literature discussed in this chapter: citizenship regimes are defined 1) both by membership and rights; 2) by the nexus between these; and 3) by formal and informal norms.

First, as membership can be defined both by membership criteria and by the way in which membership discriminates in relevant areas of life, to understand citizenship regimes we need to look both at access to the status (and the loss of it) as well as the content of the status. In Bauböck's terminology, citizenship has both a nominal and a substantive side and to capture citizenship dynamics comprehensively,

[2] Irene Bloemraad, 'The Promise and Pitfalls of Comparative Research Design in the Study of Migration,' *Migration Studies 1*, no. 1 (2013): pp. 27–46, p. 29.

[3] David FitzGerald, 'A Comparativist Manifesto for International Migration Studies,' *Ethnic and Racial Studies 35*, no. 10 (2012): pp. 1725–1740, p. 1726.

we cannot focus solely on one of these.[4] After all, if citizenship did not provide any exclusive rights and benefits, having the status would be meaningless; conversely, if anyone can get the status, linking entitlements to citizenship would amount to little. Citizenship regimes thus include institutionalized norms both with regard to membership status as well as norms with regard to rights and duties associated with the status.

Second, it is important not only to look at both status and rights, but also at the nexus between them, as status and rights often go together, but not necessarily so. On the one hand, we can observe practices of membership without rights, such as restrictions of political rights for prisoners or for non-resident citizens. On the other hand, the extension of rights previously associated exclusively with citizenship, such as the franchise, to resident non-citizens, is seen as hollowing out or devaluing the institution of citizenship.[5] Political rights are a prime example, though by no means an exclusive one, of how the decoupling of rights and benefits from the status of citizenship invites a critical reflection on the relevance of the status itself. Comparative debate focuses both on the empirical extent of this decoupling and on the variation across government levels.[6]

Third, when analyzing citizenship regimes, especially comparatively, we need to look beyond formal norms (as defined in constitutions, laws, and jurisprudence) and also take into account how informal norms influence practice and thus the access to and meaning of citizenship. How administrations implement naturalization laws matters significantly for the extent to which immigrants are encouraged to acquire citizenship. In terms of substantive equality, formally, citizenship is a mainstreaming device. Yet in practice it may not be able to rule out discriminatory practices in the labor market. Hence it is important to recognize that formal membership rules may reflect the outcome of political contestation, yet contestation does not stop with the establishment of such rules.

In the remainder of this chapter, the focus will be on how the state of the art developed with regard to its key research questions. This discussion will follow the comparative literature on citizenship regimes, which is, broadly speaking, organized around three sets of research questions where citizenship regimes are approached, respectively, as typologies; dependent variable; and independent variable. The first question is descriptive (along which dimensions can citizenship regimes be differentiated?), the latter questions are explanatory (focusing on explaining, respectively, which factors structure variation in citizenship regimes and how citizenship

---

[4] Rainer Bauböck, *Transnational Citizenship: Membership and Rights in International Migration* (Aldershot: Edward Elgar, 1994).

[5] Peter H. Schuck, 'Membership in the Liberal Polity: The Devaluation of American Citizenship,' *Georgetown Immigration Law Journal* 3 (1989): pp. 1–18; Yasemin N. Soysal, *Limits of Citizenship: Migrants and Postnational Membership in Europe* (Chicago: University of Chicago Press, 1994).

[6] Jean-Thomas Arrighi and Rainer Bauböck, 'A Multilevel Puzzle: Migrants' Voting Rights in National and Local Elections,' *European Journal of Political Research* (forthcoming).

regimes impact on social, economic, and political outcomes). While these questions partly drive separate research agendas, they are better viewed as part of an integrated agenda where each of these questions provides necessary steps towards a comprehensive understanding of the dynamics of citizenship regimes. The concluding section reflects on such an integrated comparative research agenda and discusses theoretical and methodological challenges faced by scholars analyzing these questions.

TYPOLOGIES OF CITIZENSHIP REGIMES

Much of the comparative literature on citizenship regimes is focused on classification: what are the similarities and differences between the way in which formal and informal norms define access to membership within polities, as well as rights and duties associated with membership? In other words, along which dimensions can citizenship regimes be differentiated?

While this is in essence a descriptive exercise, the relevance of classification can hardly be exaggerated as comparative research revolves by definition around the systematic analysis of similarities and differences. Before we can answer relevant *why* and *how* questions, we first need to tackle *what* questions. Without a good sense of what variation is out there, in terms of patterns and trends, we cannot start to formulate relevant explanatory questions. The existing literature in this field attests that the deceptively straightforward 'what' question is by no means one that can be answered uncontested, especially when detecting *systematic* variation between citizenship regimes. This complexity derives from the sheer variation between regimes, both with regard to membership criteria determining access to citizenship (or 'nationality' as it is mostly termed in international law) as well as the rights attached to citizenship.

For access to citizenship, we can distinguish, on the one hand, between ascriptive membership conceptions, mostly applicable through the acquisition of citizenship at birth, and voluntary membership conceptions, which imply a degree of openness in terms of individual choice, both regarding acquisition (e.g. through ordinary naturalization) as well the loss of citizenship (e.g. through voluntary renunciation of the status). At birth, well-known distinctions exist between communities prioritizing descent from a citizen (*jus sanguinis*) or those where birth at the territory is given greater significance (*jus soli*). In practice, these principles are not mutually exclusive and most states apply a mixture of both. For example, most states in Europe prioritize descent-based transmission of citizenship but use territorial access to citizenship to prevent what is generally accepted as an undesirable phenomenon of statelessness, as in the case of newborns found on the territory of a state whose descent cannot be established (foundlings).[7] Other states prioritize territorial access to citizenship, as in the case of the United States and most states of the Americas, but simultaneously maintain rules allowing citizens residing outside the territory of the state—under varying restrictions—to transmit citizenship to their offspring.

In addition to regulations determining citizenship at birth, states also maintain a variety of rules regarding the acquisition of citizenship after birth, such as by ordinary naturalization or by facilitated naturalization for spouses of citizens or persons with cultural affinity to the political community. Moreover, not only the rules on the *acquisition* of citizenship vary between states, so do the rules on the *loss* of citizenship. For example, political attitudes towards dual citizenship have traditionally been negative and restrictive: most states had rules that implied the automatic loss of citizenship—or a discretionary power for the administration to revoke citizenship—as a consequence of the voluntary acquisition of another citizenship. Nowadays, however, such restrictive dual citizenship regulations have been abolished in the majority of states.[8]

Besides the acquisition and loss of the status of citizenship, political communities vary greatly in terms of the consequences of possessing this status. For example, franchise is traditionally tied up with citizenship, reflecting the importance of political emancipation, differentiating between those who are just subject to authoritative rules, on the one hand, and those who have a say in determining these rules.[9] From the perspective that citizenship 'is also an invitation to participate in a system of mutual governance,'[10] political rights are thus more closely linked to citizenship status than either civil or social rights. In terms of duties traditionally associated with citizenship, these are today either no longer universally imposed on all citizens (e.g. conscription) or universally imposed on residents rather than citizens (e.g. duty to obey the law, pay taxes etc.) and thus not closely linked to citizenship status.

Typological approaches aimed at capturing this variation between regimes in a systematic manner can be differentiated both by the scope of the dimensions along which regime types vary, as well as by the purposes of each approach in terms of its heuristic strengths and weaknesses. In the following, three sets of debates over citizenship regime typologies are presented, with a focus on the scope of regime typologies and their purpose.

---

[7] Maarten Peter Vink and Gerard-René de Groot, 'Citizenship Attribution across Western Europe: International Framework and Domestic Trends,' *Journal of Ethnic and Migration Studies 36*, no. 5 (2010): pp. 713–734.

[8] See Spiro in this volume.   [9] See Shaw in this volume.

[10] Irene Bloemraad, *Becoming a Citizen: Incorporating Immigrants and Refugees in the United States and Canada* (Berkeley: University of California Press, 2006), p. 1.

One-dimensional versus multi-dimensional. Given that citizenship is by definition an institution of social closure,[11] it comes as little surprise that most typological exercises in this field revolve around the relative openness/inclusiveness or closure/exclusiveness of regimes. Citizenship regimes are thus typically seen as 'closed' or 'exclusive' when the scope of provisions, for example those aimed at automatic acquisition of citizenship at birth, is relatively restricted (e.g. when only children whose father is a citizen can acquire citizenship). Or the acquisition of citizenship, for example by immigrants through ordinary naturalization, may be conditional upon meeting strict criteria, such as a long residence period, language and civic integration requirements, the renunciation of any other citizenship, or the payment of a high fee. Variation in such formal requirements, as well as the extent to which they are enforced in practice, can make a citizenship regime relatively more or less inclusive.

Whereas most existing citizenship typologies focus on the relative accessibility of the status, when considering citizenship regimes comprehensively also the rights and benefits associated with citizenship can make a regime more or less inclusive. In other words, the extent to which citizenship as a status differentiates in terms of entitlements equally affects the relative inclusiveness of the regime; even if the formal status is difficult to acquire, if rights have a universal scope and are not reserved for citizens only, this would make a citizenship regime still more 'liberal' or inclusive. Given the wide variety in ways in which citizenship can be acquired, as well as the range of civil, political, and social rights that may be either attached to the status or made available more universally, conceptualizing citizenship categorically as singularly inclusive or exclusive would make little sense; inclusiveness is clearly a matter of degree, not of kind. Hence the range of qualitative or quantitative indicators developed that aim to measure this relative inclusiveness along a number of predefined criteria for openness.

Two typological questions remain, however. First, are political dynamics of inclusion the same for status and rights? Within a one-dimensional conception of inclusiveness, status and rights can be conceived of either as complementary or as alternatives. In the first scenario, citizenship acquisition can be seen as *complementary* to the granting of social and political rights to immigrants, as a necessary step in the process of full integration in the political community. Here regimes would be expected to be equally inclusive with regard to membership and rights. In the second scenario, granting access to formal membership through naturalization may instead be seen as an *alternative* to granting social and political rights, independent of citizenship status. In this conceptualization regimes that are inclusive with regard to rights are expected to be exclusive with regard to membership. Is there a trade-off between membership, measured by access to citizenship, and access to rights?

---

[11] Rogers Brubaker, *Citizenship and Nationhood in France and Germany* (Cambridge: Harvard University Press, 1992).

Huddleston and Vink research this question on the basis of evidence in twenty-nine European regimes and find that extending membership and rights are generally used as complementary, rather than alternative, means to immigrant integration. These findings do not invalidate the 'alternative' view as a normative stance, but they do suggest that it is rarely practiced in Europe.[12] In related work, however, Ruhs finds that when membership is measured as territorial admission, thus looking at immigration control, there are trade-offs between membership and rights. This study has a broader geographical scope, focusing on global developed economies, including both democratic and authoritarian regimes. Ruhs finds that, across these states, labor immigration programs that have inclusive admission policies will be restrictive in terms of attributing rights to immigrants and, vice versa, programs that are inclusive with regard to rights tend to do so under the condition of strict admission policies. In other words, there is a 'price of rights.'[13]

The second typological question is whether it makes sense to map all variation in terms of access to status and access to rights on a single dimension of inclusiveness. Conceptually, scholars have argued that the inclusiveness of a polity's understanding of citizenship may be reflected along multiple dimensions. For example, Koopmans *et al* argue that regimes vary not just along an individual equality dimension, where citizenship status and rights are more or less accessible to immigrants, but also along a second dimension that shows how countries deal with cultural and religious diversity. On the second dimension countries range from those that are willing to recognize minority groups and adopt a pluralistic strategy by granting cultural and religious group rights to those that are reluctant to recognize such groups and do not grant any specific rights but require immigrants to assimilate to a dominant culture. This then leads to a two-by-two typology where regimes can be civic-territorial or ethnic (on the 'equality of access' dimension) and culturally monist or pluralist (on the 'cultural difference and group rights' dimension).[14] The purpose of a multi-dimensional typology is thus to cover a broader range of conceptions of inclusiveness and to allow for more fine-grained distinctions between regime types.

Comprehensive versus specific. A second line of differentiation between typologies is between those that comprehensively focus on a range of issues related to the relative inclusiveness of citizenship regimes and those that focus on specific issues only. Koopmans *et al*'s typology of citizenship rights for immigrants is an example

[12] Thomas Huddleston and Maarten Vink, 'Full Membership or Equal Rights? The Link Between Naturalisation and Integration Policies for Immigrants in 29 European States,' *Comparative Migration Studies 3*, no. 1 (2015): pp. 1–19, p. 8.

[13] Martin Ruhs, *The Price of Rights: Regulating International Labor Migration* (Princeton: Princeton University Press, 2013).

[14] Ruud Koopmans, Ines Michalowski, and Stine Waibel, 'Citizenship Rights for Immigrants: National Political Processes and Cross-National Convergence in Western Europe, 1980–2008,' *American Journal of Sociology 117*, no. 4 (2012): pp. 1202–1245.

of a comprehensive typology, in the sense that it covers indicators both for access to citizenship as well as for policies aimed at accommodating cultural and religious diversity. Another example, the Migration Integration Policy Index (MIPEX),[15] also provides a comprehensive (though one-dimensional) typology as it includes indicators measuring inclusiveness in eight broad domains of immigrant integration. The purpose of such comprehensive typologies is to capture inclusiveness on a broad range of relevant citizenship issues, yet they mostly (though not necessarily) do so at the cost of only taking into account selective target populations of citizenship regimes, in these cases immigrant populations. As a consequence, such typologies are at best partly comprehensive, in the sense that only citizenship issues relevant to the selective target population are considered.

Specific typologies are more focused in terms of the range of issues covered. For example, Howard's Citizenship Policy Index[16] and Janoski's Barriers to Naturalization Index[17] capture the restrictiveness of national citizenship regimes in terms of access to citizenship status for groups of immigrant background within, respectively, EU and OECD countries. These specific indices thus consider a narrow target population. However, other specific typologies have a broader understanding of the relevant target population. In their comparative analysis of thirty-six European citizenship laws, Vink and Bauböck argue that these laws determine the degree of inclusiveness not only towards *immigrants*, but also towards *emigrants*. For example, they find variation with regard to the automatic transmission of citizenship to second and later generations of emigrant descent. Moreover, citizenship law regulates not just the *acquisition*, but also the *loss* of citizenship. For example, in some regimes the loss of citizenship is caused by voluntarily naturalizing abroad, or even by the mere fact of residing abroad. As a consequence, typologies developed to cover all relevant variation between citizenship laws need to take into account populations of former citizen residents, their descendants, as well as broader ethno-culturally conceived kin populations, in addition to the resident population.[18] Vink and Bauböck argue that citizenship regimes can, for historical, political, or demographic reasons, prioritize one type of inclusiveness over the other, while 'expansive' regimes can also display a strong degree of inclusiveness on both dimensions and, by contrast, 'insular' regimes can restrict both types of inclusiveness. This results in four ideal-typic citizenship regimes: those that emphasize either exclusively

---

[15] Thomas Huddleston, Ozge Bilgili, Anne-Linde Joki and Zvezda Vankova, 'Migrant Integration Policy Index 2015,' edited by Migrant Policy Group (Brussels: 2015), online http://mipex.eu.

[16] Marc Morjé Howard, *The Politics of Citizenship in Europe* (Cambridge: Cambridge University Press, 2009), p. 40.

[17] Thomas Janoski, *The Ironies of Citizenship: Naturalization and Integration in Industrialized Countries* (Cambridge: Cambridge University Press, 2010).

[18] Maarten Peter Vink and Rainer Bauböck, 'Citizenship Configurations: Analysing the Multiple Purposes of Citizenship Regimes in Europe,' *Comparative European Politics* 11, no. 5 (2013): pp. 621–648.

ethnocultural or territorial selection criteria and those that combine restrictions or inclusiveness on both dimensions.[19]

Static versus dynamic. Typologies are standard elements of a comparativist's toolbox as they help in structuring our understanding of similarities and differences across political units. Yet by fitting regimes within abstract categories, typologies also come at a price, as they have the tendency to reify ideal-types, which should at best be used as heuristic device, but not be confused with constructs that have an actual correspondence with empirical reality.[20] The best, or worst for that matter, example of such misplaced reification in the comparative citizenship literature is the nationhood model distinguishing between 'ethnic' and 'civic' nations. Drawing on an older literature on types of nationalism, this distinction is frequently related to citizenship regimes where ethnic nations are associated with the prevalence of descent-based citizenship rules (*jus sanguinis*) and civic nations with territorial access to citizenship (*jus soli*). This nationhood model of citizenship regimes is often linked to Brubaker's 1992 work on *Citizenship and Nationhood in France and Germany*,[21] still a standard reference for any comparative work on citizenship regimes, despite Brubaker himself having joined authors who questioned the theoretical consistency of the dichotomy between civic and ethnocultural national citizenship models.[22]

What should be derived from Brubaker's focused comparison of two European countries with interconnected, though different political histories of state-formation is not that citizenship regimes neatly reflect ideal-typic civic or ethnic nations but rather, first of all, that understanding citizenship regimes requires a context-sensitive approach (more on historical institutionalism below). What cannot be derived from this study, and should be avoided when comparing citizenship regimes, is what Brubaker himself has later termed as 'groupism' or the 'realism of the group': 'the social ontology that leads us to talk and write about ethnic groups and nations as real entities, as communities, as substantial, enduring, internally homogenous and externally bounded collectivities.'[23] Clearly, notwithstanding the relevance of path-dependency, political reality is more complex, contested, and constructed than would be suggested by assuming the existence of pre-defined, unchanging collectivities as 'civic' and 'ethnic' nations.[24]

---

[19] Ibid.

[20] Christophe Bertossi and Jan Willem Duyvendak, 'Introduction: National Models of Immigrant Integration: The Costs for Comparative Research,' *Comparative European Politics 10*, no. 3 (2012): pp. 237–247; Christian Joppke, 'Beyond National Models: Civic Integration Policies for Immigrants in Western Europe,' *West European Politics 30*, no. 1 (2007): pp. 1–22.

[21] Brubaker (n 11).

[22] Bernard Yack, 'The Myth of the Civic Nation,' *Critical Review 10*, no. 2 (1996): pp. 193–211; Rogers Brubaker, 'Myths and Misconceptions in the Study of Nationalism,' in J. Hall, ed., *The State of the Nation* (Cambridge: Cambridge University Press, 1998), pp. 272–306.

[23] Brubaker (n 22), p. 292.

[24] Christian Joppke, *Selecting by Origin: Ethnic Migration in the Liberal State* (Cambridge: Harvard University Press, 2005), pp. 16–21.

Ideal-type models come with a second downside: they are inherently static. In the case of Brubaker's study, he arguably invited such a critique by explicitly engaging with the argument that citizenship policies had 'so far' escaped convergence.[25] Today the paradigmatic French and German citizenship regimes look much more similar, even as the extent to which this process of convergence can be generalized remains a matter of some empirical controversy.[26] Any typology must come with a strong caveat about the historical contingency of a model that aims to make sense of a contested and changing reality.

Determinants of Citizenship Regimes

Which factors structure and explain variation in citizenship regimes? The literature treating them as a dependent variable has a long tradition, most prominently within historical approaches and area studies. Scholars based in law and the social sciences, including comparative politics and international relations, have also furthered our understanding of the domestic evolution of citizenship regimes. Here I focus on three dominant sets of explanations offered in citizenship studies: historical institutionalism; comparative law and political science; and international diffusion. For analytical clarity these three approaches are discussed separately, even though within individual studies two or even all three of these approaches may be combined.

Historical institutionalism. Given that citizenship regimes are closely linked to political self-determination, accounts of why states (or other political communities, such as cities, regions, or supranational organizations) are characterized by specific types of citizenship regimes are often grounded in some path-dependent conception of state-building processes and long-term demographic trends. Brubaker's 1992 study of France and Germany[27] is an exemplary—though disputed[28]— historical contextualization of citizenship regimes. In this work the 'state-centered' nation of France is presented as a case where the political integration of all people resident

[25] Brubaker (n 11), p. 180.

[26] Patrick Weil, 'Access to Citizenship: A Comparison of Twenty-Five Nationality Laws,' in Alexander Aleinikoff and Douglas Klusmeyer, eds., *Citizenship Today: Global Perspectives and Practices* (Washington: Carnegie Endowment for International Peace, 2001), pp. 17–35; Marc Morjé Howard, 'Variation in Dual Citizenship Policies in the Countries of the EU,' *International Migration Review 39*, no. 3 (2005): pp. 697–720.

[27] Brubaker (n 11).

[28] Patrick Weil, *Qu'est-ce qu'un français? Histoire de la nationalité française depuis la Révolution* (Paris: Gallimard, 2005).

within a territory is prioritized and thus citizenship is attributed mainly via birth-place (*jus soli*). In such a case, Brubaker argues, rules for immigrant naturalization can be relatively accessible in order to achieve the inclusion of a high percentage of the resident population as formal members of the polity. By contrast, in an 'ethno-cultural' nation as pre-reunification Germany, the integration of a people across borders is prioritized and thus citizenship is attributed mainly via bloodline (*jus sanguinis*). Naturalization is difficult under such a regime for those who are not seen to belong to the ethnic nation, which means that large communities of long-term residents may not have access to citizenship. Favell's study of immigration and the idea of citizenship in France and Britain provides another classic example of 'the power of path dependency' and how responses to contemporary challenges posed by immigration are shaped by the core language and conceptual terms embedded in broader public philosophies of integration.[29]

Other notable studies within this historical institutionalism tradition serve a revisionist purpose of debunking sometimes all-too-rosy accounts of how an inclusive citizenship was established within contemporary democracies. Groundbreaking, in historical scope and theoretical depth, is Smith's account of a liberal democratic America that 'never was.' In this history of American citizenship law, Smith demonstrates how throughout most of the time from the colonial period to the Progressive era, exclusion based on race, ethnicity, and gender denied many Americans access to full citizenship.[30] FitzGerald and Cook-Martin provide an account of the relation between democracy and racism in a similar revisionist vein, but throughout the Americas. Rather than being antithetical, they argue, democratic institutions created effective channels for material and ideological interest groups to demand restriction.[31] In Europe, Hampshire's account of the racialized politics of immigration in postwar Britain, where ideas of citizenship and belonging are redefined in order to address wider concerns of demographic governance, touches on a similar theme.[32]

Comparative law and political science. Systematic comparative analyses with a broad, though usually regional, geographical focus have traditionally been the field of comparative legal scholars.[33] They are primarily focused on describing and categorizing national laws, as well as making a normative assessment in light of constitutional and international law standards. Insofar as these legal comparative

---

[29] Adrian Favell, *Philosophies of Integration: Immigration and the Idea of Citizenship in France and Britain*, 2nd edition (Basingstoke, New York: Palgrave, 2001), p. 241.

[30] Rogers Smith, *Civic Ideals: Conflicting Visions of Citizenship in US History* (New Haven: Yale University Press, 1997).

[31] David Scott FitzGerald and David Cook-Martin, *Culling the Masses* (Cambridge: Harvard University Press, 2014). See also FitzGerald in this volume.

[32] James Hampshire, *Citizenship and Belonging: Immigration and the Politics of Demographic Governance in Postwar Britain* (Basingstoke: Palgrave Macmillan, 2005).

[33] Gerard-René de Groot, *Staatsangehörigkeitsrecht im Wandel* (Köln: Heymanns, 1989).

approaches propose explanatory inferences about the origins of citizenship regimes, they point mostly towards constitutional traditions and legal transplants, such as from former metropole to colonial dominion.[34]

Building on this tradition, but making significant steps towards a social science research agenda with a global scope, Weil's comparative study of the citizenship laws of twenty-five states points at the relevance of legal traditions as a key factor explaining historical continuity of citizenship policies and especially the rules of attribution of citizenship at birth. Historically, the rule of *jus soli* derives from the feudal tradition in which persons owed allegiance to the monarch in virtue of birth in the kingdom. Seeking to discard this tradition, post-revolutionary France replaced the rule of *jus soli* with the rule of *jus sanguinis* in which legal status was transmitted from father to child like the family name. Whereas *jus soli* was preserved in the United Kingdom and exported to British colonies, *jus sanguinis* was adopted together with the Napoleonic civil law system by most continental European countries.[35]

In recent years, a number of comparative political science studies have aimed to develop more systematic explanatory accounts of variation in citizenship regimes. Howard analyses the politics of citizenship in fifteen member states of the European Union (EU) and develops an explanatory argument based on a combination of historical, demographic, and political factors. He argues that former colonial powers which democratized early were able to develop historically more liberal citizenship and immigration policies. The early exposure to diversity due to colonial experience helped these countries consolidate their national identities leading to 'more open avenues to citizenship.'[36] In a related but different vein, Janoski argues that colonialism had a liberalizing effect on citizenship only in those colonial regimes, such as the French and British cases, that developed beyond the initial stages of repression.[37]

According to Joppke the major explanatory factor for the development of national citizenship policies is the colour of the government in charge in that country, that is whether a left-wing or a right-wing political party dominates the government. Due to its 'universalist vocation,' the political left is more prone to support the political integration of immigrants and thus to push towards more liberal citizenship policies.[38] A key example here is the experience of the red-green Schröder government that took office in Germany in 1998 and as one of its first acts

---

[34] Gianluca P. Parolin, *Citizenship in the Arab World: Kin, Religion and Nation-State* (Amsterdam: Amsterdam University Press, 2009).

[35] Weil (n 26), pp. 19–21.   [36] Howard (n 16).

[37] Janoski (n 17), pp. 9–10. Cf. Ruud Koopmans and Ines Michalowski, 'Why Do States Extend Rights to Immigrants? Institutional Settings and Historical Legacies across 44 Countries Worldwide,' *Comparative Political Studies*, 50, no. 1: pp. 41–74. doi:10.1177/0010414016655533.

[38] Christian Joppke, 'Citizenship between De- and Re-Ethnicization,' *European Journal of Sociology* 44, no. 3 (2003): pp. 429–458, p. 431.

of government introduced a bill radically modernizing German citizenship law.[39] Howard, however, draws a more complex picture by arguing that, although liberalizing changes are more likely to occur when left-wing political parties are in power, the most important factor is the presence and electoral strength of right-wing anti-immigrant parties.[40] The precise relevance of colonial experience and party politics for the (changing) regulation of citizenship remains a matter of controversy and needs to be researched more systematically.

Whereas many of the explanatory accounts of citizenship regimes are focused on regulations concerning access to citizenship for immigrants, citizenship regimes also regulate access to and loss of the status for emigrants and diaspora communities. Contrasting this with a 'de-ethnicization' trend of citizenship policies for immigrants, Joppke identifies a 're-ethnicization' trend in the recent initiatives of states to maintain or re-establish formal ties with emigrants and their descendants.[41] Laws that entitle members of kin minorities to various economic, socio-cultural and symbolic benefits, as well as those granted facilitated access to citizenship, may be viewed as an indicator for an active ethnocultural agenda of the state. Shevel analyzes the citizenship policies of fifteen post-USSR states, particularly noting the preferential treatment towards co-ethnics in many of these states.[42] Ragazzi compares diaspora policies in thirty-five states worldwide, among which citizenship policies. His explanatory framework emphasizes economic and demographic factors and what he terms as 'governmentality' (fiscal pressure, financial and labor deregulation, openness to international trade).[43]

International diffusion. A third and still relatively recent body of literature looks at citizenship regimes from an international relations perspective and aims to overcome the almost inevitable methodological nationalism in a field where the dependent variable is so closely related to the core of national sovereignty. These studies recognize that even with regard to citizenship, policy makers in one country are sometimes influenced by the decisions made in other countries.

The interdependence between countries is more obvious in some regions than in others. For example, within the Council of Europe, the mostly defunct 1963 Strasbourg Convention on the Reduction of Cases of Multiple Nationality provides a clear example of a reciprocity-based framework. Today, the 1997 European Convention on Nationality[44] provides a concrete framework for intergovernmental

---

[39] Simon Green, 'Much Ado about Not-Very-Much? Assessing Ten Years of German Citizenship Reform,' *Citizenship Studies* 16, no. 2 (2012): pp. 173–188.

[40] Howard (n 16).   [41] Joppke (n 38).

[42] Oxana Shevel, 'The Politics of Citizenship Policy in New States,' *Comparative Politics* 41, no. 3 (2009): pp. 273–291.

[43] Francesco Ragazzi, 'A Comparative Analysis of Diaspora Policies,' *Political Geography* 41 (2014): pp. 74–89.

[44] Gerard-René de Groot and Olivier Willem Vonk, *International Standards on Nationality Law: Texts, Cases and Materials* (Wolf Publishers, 2016). See also Strumia in this volume.

consultations on developments in the field of citizenship law. In one of the earliest explicit studies of policy diffusion within the realm of citizenship, Checkel analyzes how the work of the Council of Europe produced a changing normative context to shared understandings of citizenship, especially with regard to the increasing acceptance of dual citizenship.[45] Similar observations about the importance of 'venues for the sharing of ideas and experiences among member states,' in light of a broader process of converging citizenship policies in Europe, are echoed by Hansen and Weil.[46]

Another sub-strand of literature, more inspired by transnationalism studies than by international relations, highlights the diffusion of diaspora engagement practices. In a recent literature review Gamlen identifies epistemic communities and policy diffusion as a key explanation of what he sees as 'the rise of diaspora institutions.'[47] For example, Delano demonstrates how Latin American countries have developed similar practices and institutions regarding consular protection and service provision for their populations in the United States as a result of formal and informal collaboration between governments.[48] In a global study, Turcu and Urbatsch find that neighbors' recent enactment of overseas voting nearly doubles the chance that a country will enfranchise its own diaspora.[49] With regard to the gradual acceptance of dual citizenship for emigrants, Escobar observes that 'regional diffusion ... was a contributing factor because the countries that established dual citizenship early served as examples and, in some instances, as providers of direct advice to the other countries.'[50] Vink *et al* test this diffusion hypothesis on the basis of a longitudinal dataset and confirm that states have a significantly higher propensity to move to a tolerant dual citizenship policy for expatriates if neighboring states have done so.[51] Conversely, states may also react unilaterally to counter policies of other states, as demonstrated by the tit-for-tat where Slovakia introduced a dual citizenship ban in 2010 following Hungary's recent expansive citizenship policy affecting its diaspora

---

[45] Jeffrey T. Checkel, 'Norms, Institutions, and National Identity in Contemporary Europe,' *International Studies Quarterly 43*, no. 1 (1999): pp. 84–114.

[46] Randall Hansen and Patrick Weil, 'Introduction: Citizenship, Immigration and Nationality: Towards a Convergence in Europe?,' in Randall Hansen and Patrick Weil, eds., *Towards a European Nationality. Citizenship, Immigration and Nationality Law in the EU* (Basingstoke: Palgrave Macmillan, 2001), pp. 1–23, p. 13.

[47] Alan Gamlen, 'Diaspora Institutions and Diaspora Governance,' *International Migration Review 48* (2014): pp. S180–S217.

[48] Alexandra Délano, 'The Diffusion of Diaspora Engagement Policies: A Latin American Agenda,' *Political Geography 41* (2014): pp. 90–100.

[49] Turcu, Anca and R. Urbatsch, 'Diffusion of Diaspora Enfranchisement Norms: A Multinational Study,' *Comparative Political Studies 48*, no. 4 (2015): pp. 407–437.

[50] Cristina Escobar, 'Extraterritorial Political Rights and Dual Citizenship in Latin America,' *Latin American Research Review 42*, no. 3 (2007): pp. 43–75, pp. 51–52.

[51] Maarten Peter Vink, Arjan H. Schakel, David Reichel, Gerard-René de Groot, and N. Chun Luk, 'The International Diffusion of Expatriate Dual Citizenship Policies' (Maastricht, 2016) (unpublished manuscript, on file with author).

in neighbouring Slovakia. In other words, the mechanisms of interdependent citizenship regimes can generate not just convergent, but also divergent or conflicting outcomes.

CONSEQUENCES OF CITIZENSHIP REGIMES

How do citizenship regimes impact other outcomes? Whereas most scholarly work has been done on citizenship regime typologies and a significant body of work exists on the determinants of regimes, there is less work on the consequences of regimes. Certain consequences are often assumed (by scholars or politicians), for example, in terms of more restrictive policies being detrimental or, by contrast, conducive to immigrant integration, but such questions are not often systematically investigated.

Citizenship acquisition rates. In this context, most scholarly attention has been devoted to the consequences of citizenship regimes for the outcome most directly related to public policies, namely the ascension to citizenship, especially among immigrants. The requirements set by law, such as scope of eligibility, years of required residence, language and integration requirements, dual citizenship acceptance, and fees determine the eligibility of persons to acquire citizenship and the conditions under which they can do so. Hence, imposing stricter requirements or, by contrast, removing or lowering existing requirements can have a direct effect on acquisition rates among target groups of these regulations. Given that requirements vary significantly between countries it is unsurprising that immigrant naturalization rates vary greatly across countries.

Research in this field, especially the North American literature, has focused traditionally on explaining variation in naturalization rates among immigrant *groups*, rather than among countries. Typically, these studies look at a range of individual characteristics, such as educational attainment, age at migration, years of residence, family situation and, relating to country of origin, economic development and political regime.[52] Insofar as these studies have investigated the relevance of the citizenship regimes, they do so mostly with a view to the legislation in countries of origin, in particular in relation to toleration of dual citizenship.[53] A notable exception is

[52] Philip Q. Yang, 'Explaining Immigrant Naturalization,' *International Migration Review* 28, no. 3 (1994): pp. 449–477; Barry Chiswick and Paul W. Miller, 'Citizenship in the United States: The Roles of Immigrant Characteristics and Country of Origin,' *Research in Labor Economics* 29 (2009): pp. 91–130.

[53] Michael Jones-Correa, 'Under Two Flags: Dual Nationality in Latin American and its Consequences for Naturalization in the United States,' *International Migration Review* 35, no. 4 (2001): pp. 997–1029; Jonas Helgertz and Pieter Bevelander, 'The Influence of Partner Choice and Country of Origin

provided by Bloemraad's comparative study of immigrant incorporation in Canada and the United States, which shows the limitations of a model that only takes into account micro-level and group characteristics. By focusing on a comparable group of Portuguese immigrants, both in Toronto and in Boston, Bloemraad investigates what drives the significantly higher naturalization rates and more visible political engagement in the Canadian context. She demonstrates that the role of government goes beyond the formal regulation of access to citizenship and that hence citizenship regimes should be conceived more broadly as the opportunity structure for mobilization, including promotion of citizenship and bureaucratic practice.[54]

In the European context, due to widely varying citizenship policies both between and within countries, scholars have traditionally paid greater attention to the effects of regimes. In a comparison of sixteen European countries, controlling for micro-level characteristics, Vink *et al* demonstrate that cross-national naturalization gaps are indeed partly explained by policies. However, they find that the positive relation between citizenship policy and naturalization rates only holds among immigrants from less developed countries; in other words, policies matter for those groups who are most interested in naturalizing.[55] Peters *et al* produce similar findings on the basis of longitudinal register data from the Netherlands, utilizing a Dutch policy shift in 2003 that significantly restricted the conditions for access to citizenship.[56] Hainmueller and Hangartner, based on an original quasi-experimental design, demonstrate that in the specific context of Switzerland where, until recently, some municipalities used referendums to decide on the citizenship applications of foreign residents, discrimination on the basis of the origin country characteristics of applicants had a significant impact on naturalization rates among immigrant groups.[57]

Immigrant integration. Koopmans, controversially, observes a trade-off between citizenship rights and a broad range of immigrant integration outcomes such as labor market participation, levels of segregation, and an overrepresentation of immigrants among those convicted for criminal behavior. Based on comparative analyses of aggregate level national data, he finds that policies that grant immigrants easy access to equal rights (e.g. through easy access to citizenship) and do not provide strong incentives for host-country language acquisition and interethnic

Characteristics on the Naturalization of Immigrants in Sweden: A Longitudinal Analysis', *International Migration Review*, early access (2016).

[54] Bloemraad (n 10).

[55] Maarten Peter Vink, Tijana Prokic-Breuer, and Jaap Dronkers, 'Immigrant Naturalization in the Context of Institutional Diversity: Policy Matters, but to Whom?', *International Migration 51*, no. 5 (2013): pp. 1–20.

[56] Floris Peters, Maarten Vink, and Hans Schmeets, 'The Ecology of Immigrant Naturalisation: A Life Course Approach in the Context of Institutional Conditions', *Journal of Ethnic and Migration Studies 42*, no. 3 (2016): pp. 359–381.

[57] Jens Hainmueller and Dominik Hangartner, 'Who Gets a Swiss passport? A Natural Experiment in Immigrant Discrimination', *American Political Science Review 107*, no. 1 (2013): pp. 159–187.

contacts have produced suboptimal outcomes when combined with a generous welfare state.[58] However, Goodman Wallace and Wright, who study the effects of civic requirements for immigration, settlement, and citizenship on socio-economic and political outcomes on the basis of micro-level data, find 'little evidence that these requirements produce tangible, long-term integration change.'[59] The substantial body of literature on the 'citizenship premium' provides further clues for the economic impact of citizenship regimes.[60] Bevelander and Devoretz, synthesizing the results of six national studies in Europe and North America, conclude that the relative accessibility of citizenship matters, but they suggest a trade-off with immigration policies: liberal citizenship regimes enhance the economic integration of their potential citizens only if there is a rigorous screening device for immigrant entry.[61] Looking at the impact of citizenship regimes on the second or even subsequent immigrant generations, one study shows a positive impact of the introduction of birthright citizenship in Germany in 1999 on educational attainment.[62] Yet comparable research is scarce.

Mobility. Looking beyond the effect of citizenship regimes on acquisition rates and immigrant integration, some scholars have explored the relation between citizenship and mobility. Alarian and Goodman argue that citizenship policies, in particular the restriction or facilitation of dual citizenship, affect bilateral migration flows. Their analyses suggest that dual-citizenship-allowing sending states experience significantly more migration than dual-citizenship-forbidding sending states. They find the highest flow between sending and receiving states allowing dual citizenship.[63] Others have looked at return migration or out-migration to another destination, which economists have argued can be viewed as part of an optimal

[58] Ruud Koopmans, 'Trade-Offs between Equality and Difference: Immigrant Integration, Multiculturalism and the Welfare State in Cross-National Perspective,' *Journal of Ethnic and Migration Studies 36*, no. 1 (2010): pp. 1–26.

[59] Sara Wallace Goodman and Matthew Wright, 'Does Mandatory Integration Matter? Effects of Civic Requirements on Immigrant Socio-Economic and Political Outcomes,' *Journal of Ethnic and Migration Studies 41*, no. 12 (2015): pp. 1885–1908.

[60] Liebig, T. and F. Von Haaren, 'Citizenship and the Socioeconomic Integration of Immigrants and Their Children,' in *Naturalisation: A Passport for the Better Integration of Immigrants?* (Paris: OECD, 2011), p. 28.

[61] Pieter Bevelander and Don J. DeVoretz, 'The Economics of Citizenship: A Synthesis,' in Pieter Bevelander and Don J. DeVoretz, eds., *The Economics of Citizenship* (Malmö University (MIM), 2008), pp. 165. Cf. DeVoretz and Irastorza, 'Economic Theories of Citizenship' and Bloemraad, 'Does Citizenship Matter?', in this volume.

[62] Judith Saurer and Christina Felfe, 'Granting Birthright Citizenship—A Door Opener for Immigrant Children's Educational Participation and Success?,' Paper presented at the 'Jahrestagung des Vereins für Socialpolitik 2014: Evidenzbasierte Wirtschaftspolitik—Session: Migration II, No. E05-V4' (2014), online https://www.econstor.eu/dspace/handle/10419/100548?locale=de.

[63] Hannah M. Alarian and Sara Wallace Goodman, 'Dual Citizenship Allowance and Migration Flow: An Origin Story,' *Comparative Political Studies*, early access (2016).

life-cycle residential location sequence.[64] While the comparative citizenship litera-ture has largely overlooked the mobility effects of naturalization, one exception is Kuhlenkasper and Steinhardt who find that out-migrants are less likely to be natu-ralized German citizens and on average have spent fewer years in Germany than their counterparts who stay in Germany. This 'negative mobility' only applies to non-Turkish immigrants.[65] Due to lack of comparable studies, it is unclear whether these findings can be generalized beyond the German context but it points to the need for scholars to assess the implications of citizenship regimes in the wider sense of transnational mobility, going beyond the often strictly internal perspective of immigrant integration.[66]

Conclusions: Towards an Integrated Comparative Research Agenda

While the comparative research agenda of citizenship regimes can be broken down into analytically distinct questions and approaches, a comprehensive understand-ing of the dynamics of citizenship regimes demands a more integrated approach. For example, literature on either the determinants or the consequences of citizen-ship regimes needs to build on a nuanced understanding of the variation between regimes and, hence, draw on the state of the art on typologies of citizenship regimes. For a good understanding of the consequences of citizenship regimes, we need to take into account also the determinants of variation between regimes. In this con-cluding section, avenues for further comparative research are suggested, building on the previous discussion and taking into account some key theoretical and meth-odological challenges.

Generalizability. Much of the literature, especially the comparatively oriented work (as also reflected in this chapter), is biased towards Western Europe and North America, or more generally towards developed democracies. Though some

---

[64] George J. Borjas and Bernt Bratsberg, 'Who Leaves? The Outmigration of the Foreign-Born,' *The Review of Economics and Statistics 78*, no. 1 (1996): pp. 165–176.

[65] Torben Kuhlenkasper and Max Friedrich Steinhardt, 'Who Leaves and When? Selective Outmigration of Immigrants from Germany,' HWWI Research Paper 128 (Hamburg Institute of International Economics, 2012), online http://www.hwwi.org/uploads/tx_wilpubdb/HWWI-Research-Paper-128.pdf.

[66] Czaika and De Haas, looking at the impact of restrictive visa policies, confirm that these restric-tions decrease circulation (Mathias Czaika and Hein de Haas, 'The Effect of Visas on Migration Processes,' *International Migration Review*, early access (2016)).

advances have been made towards opening up the geographical scope of comparative citizenship research,[67] most scholarly ventures beyond what can be considered the usual suspects largely remains limited to descriptive case studies of the legal or political context of citizenship law in various countries.[68] Much theoretical work remains to be done to generalize our understanding of citizenship regimes, first by developing comprehensive regime typologies, but subsequently and even more so by enhancing our understanding of determinants and consequences of citizenship regimes.[69] For example, while scholars debate the effect of colonialism on the former imperial power, we know much less about the impact on the citizenship laws of the former colonies.

Interdisciplinarity. What you see depends on the lenses through which you look: while citizenship studies are widely considered an interdisciplinary field, most work is still structured along disciplinary lines. Lawyers describe and categorize nationality laws; historians and area studies scholars contextualize the historical and cultural origins of such laws; political scientists analyze the relevance of changing institutional conditions for variation within and between countries; political sociologists and economists estimate the impact of regime variation on micro-level outcomes; and international relations scholars look at the relevance of international cooperation and transnational diffusion. Scholarly specialization can and does enhance work within these respective subfields, but professional constraints related to publication traditions (e.g. books versus journal articles; separate journals for these subfields), publication language (e.g. publishing in a language other than in English is broadly accepted within law, history, and area studies but will make such work less accessible to political scientists, sociologists, and international relations scholars), and organization of the field (e.g. most scholarly conferences are organized by disciplinary field) significantly hamper the prospect for a more integrated comparative agenda.

Methodological nationalism. Few comparative studies go beyond the national paradigm, which may not be surprising given that citizenship (still) relates to the core of national sovereignty. However, this implies that explanatory accounts easily fall into the trap of essentializing national 'models' of citizenship, as discussed above. Scholars who take the constructivist challenge seriously would go beyond static, ideal-type approaches and develop models that better capture the contingency of citizenship regimes.[70] Furthermore, scholars comparing citizenship regimes need to

---

[67] Vink and Bauböck (n 18), for a comparative analysis of thirty-six West and East European countries. FitzGerald and Cook-Martin (n 31), for a comparative analysis of twenty-two countries in the Western Hemisphere. For a thematic comparative analysis of the nationality laws of fifty-four African countries, see Bronwen Manby, *Citizenship Law in Africa: A Comparative Study*, 3rd edition (Open Society Foundations, 2016).

[68] T. Alexander Aleinikoff and Douglas Klusmeyer, eds., *From Migrants to Citizens: Membership in a Changing World* (Washington: Carnegie Endowment, 2000).

[69] Sadiq in this volume; Chung in this volume.   [70] Wimmer (n 1).

take transnationalism seriously and develop models that better capture the embeddedness of citizenship regimes. Citizenship regimes may be largely nationally defined but the political practice of citizenship is embedded in a multilevel (local/ regional—national—supranational) and transnational constellation of citizenship regimes.[71]

Data availability and validity. Comparative research is as good as scholars' data allow it to be; the current limited generalizability of comparative work reflects to an important degree the limitations of existing data. While significant advances have been made in recent years, especially but not exclusively in quantitative studies, we need more data covering a wider geographical range and with a larger temporal scope. This is important not only to enhance generalizability of comparative accounts, but also to test dynamic models on the relation between contextual factors (e.g. political, economic, demographic) and relevant outcomes (e.g. citizenship policies, naturalization rates, integration outcomes). While there are some notable advances, such as databases from MIPEX (the 2015 version covering thirty-eight countries including Europe, North America, Oceania, and South Korea),[72] IMPALA (aiming to cover twenty OECD countries),[73] and the Global Citizenship Observatory (GLOBALCIT, covering over 150 countries from 2017), progress has focused on an expanding geographical scope. Most datasets are cross-sectional or have data for a limited number of years. Few existing datasets achieve both a global and longitudinal scope and those that do cover only selected indicators.[74] Of course, we need not just more data, but also valid indicators and reliable measurement. In the context of measuring the relative inclusiveness of citizenship regimes, some welcome but limited methodological debate has focused on how to construct quantitative policy indices from essentially qualitative provisions in national laws.[75]

Political contestation. Finally, the research agenda of comparative citizenship studies is not just theoretically and empirically, but also politically shaped: much of the research is driven, to an important extent through external funding (such as by the European Commission, or private foundations) by specific agendas focused on issues

[71] Rainer Bauböck, 'Studying Citizenship Constellations,' *Journal of Ethnic and Migration Studies 36*, no. 5 (2010): pp. 847–859.

[72] Huddleston *et al* (n 15).

[73] Beine, Michel, Anna Boucher, Brian Burgoon, Mary Crock, Justin Gest, Michael Hiscox, Patrick McGovern, Hillel Rapoport, Joep Schaper, and Eiko Thielemann, 'Comparing Immigration Policies: An Overview from the IMPALA Database,' *International Migration Review 50*, no. 4 (2016): pp. 827–863. doi:10.1111/imre.12169.

[74] Maarten Peter Vink, Gerard-René de Groot Vink, and Ngo Chun Luk, 'MACIMIDE Global Expatriate Dual Citizenship Dataset,' Harvard Dataverse, V2, online http://dx.doi.org/10.7910/DVN/TTMZ08.

[75] Marc Helbling, 'Validating Integration and Citizenship Policy Indices,' *Comparative European Politics 11*, no. 5 (2013): pp. 555–576; Sara Wallace Goodman, 'Integration Requirements for Integration's Sake? Identifying, Categorising and Comparing Civic Integration Policies,' *Journal of Ethnic and Migration Studies 36*, no. 5 (2010): pp. 753–772; Ines Michalowski and Ricky van Oers, 'How Can We Categorise and Interpret Civic Integration Policies?,' *Journal of Ethnic and Migration Studies 38*, no. 1 (2012): pp. 163–171.

such as immigrant integration and security in Western democracy, or development, democratization, and diaspora politics in a non-Western context. As a result, research often takes place within, rather than across, such predefined policy concerns. Other political agendas, such as an international one of avoiding statelessness and refugee protection, have so far hardly inspired comparative studies on citizenship regimes.

BIBLIOGRAPHY

Alarian, Hannah M. and Sara Wallace Goodman, 'Dual Citizenship Allowance and Migration Flow: An Origin Story,' *Comparative Political Studies*, early access (2016).

Aleinikoff, T. Alexander and Douglas Klusmeyer, eds., *From Migrants to Citizens: Membership in a Changing World* (Washington: Carnegie Endowment, 2000).

Arrighi, Jean-Thomas and Rainer Bauböck, 'A Multilevel Puzzle. Migrants' Voting Rights in National and Local Elections,' *European Journal of Political Research* (forthcoming).

Bauböck, Rainer, *Transnational Citizenship: Membership and Rights in International Migration* (Aldershot: Edward Elgar, 1994).

Bauböck, Rainer, 'Studying Citizenship Constellations,' *Journal of Ethnic and Migration Studies 36*, no. 5 (2010): pp. 847–859.

Beine, Michel, Anna Boucher, Brian Burgoon, Mary Crock, Justin Gest, Michael Hiscox, Patrick McGovern, Hillel Rapoport, Joep Schaper, and Eiko Thielemann, 'Comparing Immigration Policies: An Overview from the IMPALA Database,' *International Migration Review 50*, no. 4 (2016): pp. 827–863. doi:10.1111/imre.12169.

Bertossi, Christophe and Jan Willem Duyvendak, 'Introduction: National Models of Immigrant Integration: The Costs for Comparative Research,' *Comparative European Politics 10*, no. 3 (2012): pp. 237–247.

Bevelander, Pieter and Don J. DeVoretz, 'The Economics of Citizenship: a Synthesis,' in Pieter Bevelander, and Don J. DeVoretz, eds., *The Economics of Citizenship* (Malmö University (MIM), 2008), pp. 155–168.

Bloemraad, Irene, *Becoming a Citizen: Incorporating Immigrants and Refugees in the United States and Canada* (Berkeley: University of California Press, 2006).

Bloemraad, Irene, 'The Promise and Pitfalls of Comparative Research Design in the Study of Migration,' *Migration Studies 1*, no. 1 (2013): pp. 27–46.

Borjas, George J. and Bernt Bratsberg, 'Who Leaves? The Outmigration of the Foreign-Born,' *The Review of Economics and Statistics 78*, no. 1 (1996): pp. 165–176.

Brubaker, Rogers, *Citizenship and Nationhood in France and Germany* (Cambridge: Harvard University Press, 1992).

Brubaker, Rogers, 'Myths and Misconceptions in the Study of Nationalism,' in J. Hall, ed., *The State of the Nation* (Cambridge: Cambridge University Press, 1998), pp. 27–306.

Checkel, Jeffrey T., 'Norms, Institutions, and National Identity in Contemporary Europe,' *International Studies Quarterly 43*, no. 1 (1999): pp. 84–114.

Chiswick, Barry and Paul W. Miller, 'Citizenship in the United States: The Roles of Immigrant Characteristics and Country of Origin,' *Research in Labor Economics 29*, no. 2009 (2009): pp. 91–130.

Czaika, Mathias and Hein de Haas, 'The Effect of Visas on Migration Processes,' *International Migration Review*, early access (2016).

de Groot, Gerard-René, *Staatsangehörigkeitsrecht im Wandel* (Köln: Heymanns, 1989).

de Groot, Gerard-René and Olivier Willem Vonk, *International Standards on Nationality Law: Texts, Cases and Materials* (Oisterwijk: Wolf Publishers, 2016).

Délano, Alexandra, 'The Diffusion of Diaspora Engagement Policies: A Latin American Agenda,' *Political Geography 41* (2014): pp. 90–100.

Escobar, Cristina, 'Extraterritorial Political Rights and Dual Citizenship in Latin America,' *Latin American Research Review 42*, no. 3 (2007): pp. 43–75.

Favell, Adrian, *Philosophies of Integration: Immigration and the Idea of Citizenship in France and Britain*, 2nd edition (Basingstoke, New York: Palgrave, 2001).

FitzGerald, David, 'A Comparativist Manifesto for International Migration Studies,' *Ethnic and Racial Studies 35*, no. 10 (2012): pp. 1725–1740.

FitzGerald, David Scott and David Cook-Martin, *Culling the Masses* (Cambridge: Harvard University Press, 2014).

Gamlen, Alan, 'Diaspora Institutions and Diaspora Governance,' *International Migration Review 48* (2014): pp. S180–S217.

Green, Simon, 'Much Ado about Not-Very-Much? Assessing Ten Years of German Citizenship Reform,' *Citizenship Studies 16*, no. 2 (2012): pp. 173–188.

Hainmueller, Jens and Dominik Hangartner, 'Who Gets a Swiss Passport? A Natural Experiment in Immigrant Discrimination,' *American Political Science Review 107*, no. 1 (2013): pp. 159–187.

Hampshire, James, *Citizenship and Belonging: Immigration and the Politics of Demographic Governance in Postwar Britain* (Basingstoke: Palgrave Macmillan, 2005).

Hansen, Randall and Patrick Weil, 'Introduction: Citizenship, Immigration and Nationality: Towards a Convergence in Europe?,' in Randall Hansen and Patrick Weil, eds., *Towards a European Nationality. Citizenship, Immigration and Nationality Law in the EU* (Basingstoke: Palgrave Publishers, 2001), pp. 1–23.

Helbling, Marc, 'Validating Integration and Citizenship Policy Indices,' *Comparative European Politics 11*, no. 5 (2013): pp. 555–576.

Jonas Helgertz and Pieter Bevelander, 'The Influence of Partner Choice and Country of Origin Characteristics on the Naturalization of Immigrants in Sweden: A Longitudinal Analysis,' *International Migration Review*, early access (2016).

Howard, Marc Morjé, 'Variation in Dual Citizenship Policies in the Countries of the EU.' *International Migration Review 39*, no. 3 (2005): pp. 697–720.

Howard, Marc Morjé, *The Politics of Citizenship in Europe* (Cambridge: Cambridge University Press, 2009).

Huddleston, Thomas and Maarten Vink, 'Full Membership or Equal Rights? The Link between Naturalisation and Integration Policies for Immigrants in 29 European States,' *Comparative Migration Studies 3*, no. 1 (2015): pp. 1–19.

Huddleston, Thomas, Ozge Bilgili, Anne-Linde Joki, and Zvezda Vankova, 'Migrant Integration Policy Index 2015,' edited by Migrant Policy Group (Brussels: 2015), online http://mipex.eu.

Janoski, Thomas, *The Ironies of Citizenship: Naturalization and Integration in Industrialized Countries* (Cambridge: Cambridge University Press, 2010).

Jones-Correa, Michael, 'Under Two Flags: Dual Nationality in Latin American and its Consequences for Naturalization in the United States,' *International Migration Review 35*, no. 4 (2001): pp. 997–1029.

Joppke, Christian, 'Citizenship between De- and Re-Ethnicization,' *European Journal of Sociology 44*, no. 3 (2003): pp. 429–458.

Joppke, Christian, *Selecting by Origin: Ethnic Migration in the Liberal State* (Cambridge: Harvard University Press, 2005).

Joppke, Christian, 'Beyond National Models: Civic Integration Policies for Immigrants in Western Europe,' *West European Politics 30*, no. 1 (2007): pp. 1–22.

Koopmans, Ruud, 'Trade-Offs between Equality and Difference: Immigrant Integration, Multiculturalism and the Welfare State in Cross-National Perspective,' *Journal of Ethnic and Migration Studies 36*, no. 1 (2010): pp. 1–26.

Koopmans, Ruud and Ines Michalowski, 'Why Do States Extend Rights to Immigrants? Institutional Settings and Historical Legacies across 44 Countries Worldwide,' *Comparative Political Studies*, *50*, no. 1 (2017): pp. 41–74. doi:10.1177/0010414016655533.

Koopmans, Ruud, Ines Michalowski, and Stine Waibel, 'Citizenship Rights for Immigrants: National Political Processes and Cross-National Convergence in Western Europe, 1980–2008,' *American Journal of Sociology 117*, no. 4 (2012): pp. 1202–1245.

Kuhlenkasper, Torben and Max Friedrich Steinhardt, 'Who Leaves and When? Selective Outmigration of Immigrants from Germany,' HWWI Research Paper 128 (Hamburg Institute of International Economics, 2012), online http://www.hwwi.org/uploads/tx_wil-pubdb/HWWI-Research-Paper-128.pdf.

Liebig, Thomas and Friederike Von Haaren, 'Citizenship and the Socioeconomic Integration of Immigrants and Their Children,' in *Naturalisation: A Passport for the Better Integration of Immigrants?* (Paris: OECD, 2011), pp. 23–57.

Manby, Bronwen, *Citizenship Law in Africa: A Comparative Study*, 3rd edition (Open Society Foundations, 2016).

Michalowski, Ines and Ricky van Oers, 'How Can We Categorise and Interpret Civic Integration Policies?,' *Journal of Ethnic and Migration Studies 38*, no. 1 (2012): pp. 163–171.

Parolin, Gianluca P., *Citizenship in the Arab World: Kin, Religion and Nation-State* (Amsterdam: Amsterdam University Press, 2009).

Peters, Floris, Maarten Vink, and Hans Schmeets, 'The Ecology of Immigrant Naturalisation: A Life Course Approach in the Context of Institutional Conditions,' *Journal of Ethnic and Migration Studies 42*, no. 3 (2016): pp. 359–381.

Ragazzi, Francesco, 'A Comparative Analysis of Diaspora Policies,' *Political Geography 41* (2014): pp. 74–89.

Ruhs, Martin, *The Price of Rights: Regulating International Labor Migration* (Princeton: Princeton University Press, 2013).

Saurer, Judith and Christina Felfe, 'Granting Birthright Citizenship-A Door Opener for Immigrant Children's Educational Participation and Success?,' Paper presented at the 'Jahrestagung des Vereins für Socialpolitik 2014: Evidenzbasierte Wirtschaftspolitik—Session: Migration II, No. E05-V4' (2014), online https://www.econstor.eu/dspace/han-dle/10419/100548?locale=de.

Schuck, Peter H., 'Membership in the Liberal Polity: The Devaluation of American Citizenship,' *Georgetown Immigration Law Journal 3* (1989): pp. 1–18.

Shevel, Oxana, 'The Politics of Citizenship Policy in New States,' *Comparative Politics 41*, no. 3 (2009): pp. 273–291.

Smith, Rogers, *Civic Ideals: Conflicting Visions of Citizenship in US History* (New Haven: Yale University Press, 1997).

Soysal, Yasemin N., *Limits of Citizenship: Migrants and Postnational Membership in Europe* (Chicago: University of Chicago Press, 1994).

Turcu, Anca and R. Urbatsch, 'Diffusion of Diaspora Enfranchisement Norms: A Multinational Study', *Comparative Political Studies 48*, no. 4 (2014): pp. 407–437.

Vink, Maarten Peter and Rainer Bauböck, 'Citizenship Configurations: Analysing the Multiple Purposes of Citizenship Regimes in Europe', *Comparative European Politics 11*, no. 5 (2013): pp. 621–648.

Vink, Maarten Peter and Gerard-René de Groot, 'Citizenship Attribution across Western Europe: International Framework and Domestic Trends', *Journal of Ethnic and Migration Studies 36*, no. 5 (2010): pp. 713–734.

Vink, Maarten Peter, Gerard-René de Groot, and Ngo Chun Luk, 'MACIMIDE Global Expatriate Dual Citizenship Dataset' (Cambridge: Harvard Dataverse, 2015), V2, doi: http://dx.doi.org/10.7910/DVN/TTMZo8.

Vink, Maarten Peter, Tijana Prokic-Breuer, and Jaap Dronkers, 'Immigrant Naturalization in the Context of Institutional Diversity: Policy Matters, but to Whom?', *International Migration 51*, no. 5 (2013): pp. 1–20.

Vink, Maarten Peter, Arjan H. Schakel, David Reichel, Gerard-René de Groot, and N. Chun Luk, 'The International Diffusion of Expatriate Dual Citizenship Policies' (Maastricht, 2016) (unpublished manuscript, on file with author).

Wallace Goodman, Sara, 'Integration Requirements for Integration's Sake? Identifying, Categorising and Comparing Civic Integration Policies', *Journal of Ethnic and Migration Studies 36*, no. 5 (2010): pp. 753–772.

Wallace Goodman, Sara and Matthew Wright, 'Does Mandatory Integration Matter? Effects of Civic Requirements on Immigrant Socio-Economic and Political Outcomes', *Journal of Ethnic and Migration Studies 41*, no. 12 (2015): pp. 1885–1908.

Weil, Patrick, 'Access to Citizenship: A Comparison of Twenty-Five Nationality Laws', in Alexander Aleinikoff and Douglas Klusmeyer, eds., *Citizenship Today: Global Perspectives and Practices* (Washington: Carnegie Endowment for International Peace, 2001), pp. 17–35.

Weil, Patrick, *Qu'est-ce qu'un français? Histoire de la nationalité française depuis la Révolution* (Paris: Gallimard, 2005).

Wimmer, Andreas, *Ethnic Boundary Making: Institutions, Power, Networks* (New York: Oxford University Press, 2013).

Yack, Bernard, 'The Myth of the Civic Nation', *Critical Review 10*, no. 2 (1996): pp. 193–211.

Yang, Philip Q., 'Explaining Immigrant Naturalization', *International Migration Review 28*, no. 3 (1994): pp. 449–477.

PART III

MEMBERSHIP AND RIGHTS

CHAPTER 12

CITIZENSHIP AND HUMAN RIGHTS

DAVID OWEN

INTRODUCTION

AT least since Hannah Arendt's critical remarks on the appeal to human rights and her apparent identification of citizenship as the 'right to have rights',[1] the question of the relationship of citizenship and human rights has been established as one of

---

[1] Hannah Arendt, *The Origins of Totalitarianism* (Cleveland: The World Publishing Company, 1958), p. 296. For cogent discussion of the idea of the right to have rights in relation to contemporary human rights debates, see James Ingram, 'What Is a "Right to Have Rights"? Three Images of the Politics of Human Rights', *The American Political Science Review* 102, no. 4 (November 2008): pp. 401–416, online http://www.jstor.org/stable/27644535. For a contemporary use of Arendt's work, see Ayten Gündoğu, *Rightlessness in an Age of Rights* (Oxford: Oxford University Press, 2015).

central importance to political reflection. It is a remarkable feature of the post-war world, especially since the 1970s, that, in ways that Arendt could hardly have been expected to envision, the politics of human rights has found expression in institutions and practices of international, regional, and state law as well as in governmental and non-governmental organizations whose scope ranges from the local to the global. This period has also seen significant transformations in the politics of citizenship, in part under the impact of the spreading and embedding of human rights norms. Yet the problem of statelessness to which Arendt drew attention has not been resolved and, on the sixtieth anniversary of the 1954 *Convention relating to the status of Stateless Persons*, the UNHCR 'launched a global campaign aimed at ending the devastating legal limbo of statelessness, which affects millions of people around the world.'[2] Although the numbers of *de jure* stateless persons (approx. 10 million) represent little more than 0.001 per cent of a global population that has exceeded 7 billion, the condition that they inhabit draws attention to the continuing salience of the nexus between citizenship and human rights that Arendt identified.[3]

For this reason, after a brief overview of theories of human rights, the first substantive question to be addressed in this chapter is that of the human right to citizenship as membership of a state. Addressing this question will lead us to the further issue raised by considering citizenship in the classic political sense of being an equal member of a self-governing polity and addresses the question of whether there is a human right to democracy. We turn next to the actual salience of the international human rights regime for citizenship and human rights. The chapter concludes with consideration of the relationship of human rights as cosmopolitan norms to the principle of the self-determination of peoples.

Theories of Human Rights

We can distinguish between human rights as moral-political rights (independent of their expression in positive law) and human rights as entitlements expressed in positive law as justifiable limits on the political authority of states—limits not only in terms of a state's authority to determine access to, or loss of, citizenship but also in terms of its authority to determine the distribution of rights and duties among persons within its territorial jurisdiction. A theory of human rights aims to provide

---

[2] Divers, 'UNHCR Launches 10-Year Global Campaign to End Statelessness', 4 November 2014, online UNHCR http://www.unhcr.org/545797f06.html.
[3] See Brad K. Blitz and Maureen Lynch, eds., *Statelessness and Citizenship: A Comparative Study on the Benefits of Nationality* (Cheltenham: Edward Elgar Publishing, 2011).

an account of human rights as moral-political rights, although this account may, for methodological reasons, reflectively engage legally instituted human rights regimes. Human rights specify both a range of general rights that cannot be restricted to citizens but to which all persons within the territorial jurisdiction of the state are entitled and a range of membership-specific rights due to all citizens (although states may extend these to others as civic rights).[4]

There are two major approaches to theorizing human rights. The first, which most directly descends from natural right theory,[5] conceptualizes human rights as *human* rights, that is, in terms of rights held by persons simply in virtue of their humanity, where this refers to some property or features shared by (normally functioning) human beings. Three prominent variants on the 'humanity'-based approach are the 'personhood' account,[6] the 'capabilities' account,[7] and the 'basic needs' account.[8] The first appeals to 'personhood' as an expression of the idea of dignity and identifies autonomy, freedom, and minimum provision as the necessary conditions of normative agency that comprise 'personhood' and the protection of which generates human rights. The second appeals to a (defeasible) list of basis capabilities that are taken to be integral to human flourishing. The third grounds human rights on those basic needs (generic human interests) that are held to be universal conditions of a minimally decent life.

The second main approach considers human rights as a public political doctrine or practice designed to specify conditions of membership of global political society. Here we can distinguish between accounts based on international or global public reason,[9] on discourse ethics,[10] and on discursive practices.[11]

These different approaches to the justification of human rights have implications for the range of rights identified as human rights and what count as 'primary' or

---

[4] I draw this distinction between 'general' and 'membership-specific' human rights from Joseph Carens, *The Ethics of Immigration* (Oxford: Oxford University Press, 2013), p. 97.

[5] See Peter Jones, *Rights* (Basingstoke: The MacMillan Press, 1994), especially chapters 4 and 5; James Griffin, *On Human Rights* (Oxford: Oxford University Press, 2008), pp. 9–28.

[6] Griffin (n 5).

[7] Martha C. Nussbaum, 'Capabilities and Human Rights', *Fordham Law Review* 66, no. 273 (1997): pp. 273–300, online http://ir.lawnet.fordham.edu/r/vol66/iss2/2.

[8] David Miller, *National Responsibility and Global Justice* (Oxford: Oxford University Press, 2008), pp. 163–200.

[9] John Rawls, *The Law of Peoples* (Cambridge: Harvard University Press, 1999); Joshua Cohen, *The Arc of the Moral Universe* (Cambridge: Harvard University Press, 2010).

[10] Jürgen Habermas, *Between Fact and Norm* (Cambridge: Polity Press, 1996); Jürgen Habermas, 'Constitutional Democracy: A Paradoxical Union of Contradictory Principles?' *Political Theory* 29, no. 6 (December 2001): pp. 766–781, doi: 10.1177/0090591701029006002; Seyla Benhabib, *Dignity in Adversity: Human Rights in Troubled Times* (Cambridge: Polity Press, 2011); Rainer Forst, *The Right to Justification* (New York: Columbia University Press, 2012).

[11] James Tully, *Public Philosophy in a New Key, volume 2: Imperialism and Civic Freedom* (Cambridge: Cambridge University Press, 2008); Charles R. Beitz, *The Idea of Human Rights* (Oxford: Oxford University Press, 2009).

'derivative' human rights. One way of expressing the distinction between them is to note that the first approach holds that 'primary' human rights can be conceived independently of the practice of human rights as public, international standards of global political life, whereas the second approach conceives of human rights precisely in terms of their role as such standards. We can bring this difference between the two approaches (as well as some differences within each approach) into focus by taking up the topic of a human right to national citizenship.

A Human Right
to National Citizenship

In this section, we will be concerned with moral-political justifications of the human right to national citizenship expressed in Article 15(1) of the UDHR: 'Everyone has the right to a nationality.'

As already noted, the contrasting status to that of having a nationality is the condition of being *stateless*, a point made explicit in Article 1 of the 1954 *Convention Relating to the Status of Stateless Persons*: 'the term "stateless person" means a person who is not considered as a national by any State under the operation of its law.' The background to the statelessness issue as a matter of customary and treaty-based international law is the establishment of state nationality laws in the late eighteenth and nineteenth century. The right of states to determine their own national citizenship laws is seen as integral to state sovereignty, but the fact that states adopt different laws ranging from pure *jus soli* to pure *jus sanguinis* with varied combinations in-between leads to some persons being dual citizens and others being stateless. While the primary concern in the late nineteenth century was the avoidance of dual citizenship, the 'Bancroft Treaties' established, as a matter of customary international law, the norm 'that every person should have a nationality and should have one nationality only' as this was later codified in the 1930 *Hague Convention on Certain Questions Relating to the Conflict of Nationality Laws*. However, as a consequence of both the denaturalization of citizens by Germany and other states in the years approaching the Second World War and the massive population displacements that marked its aftermath, the issue of statelessness once again assumed international political significance. It is in this context that Hannah Arendt's critique of human rights discourse and practice in which she charged that access to human rights was dependent precisely on being recognized as a citizen had its bite. But the same events may also be seen as motivating the legal expression of a human right to a national citizenship. We should note, with Arendt's caution against idealizing human rights in mind, that when in 2014 the UNHCR launched its campaign to end statelessness, there were only eighty-three signatory states to the 1954 *Convention Relating to the Status of Stateless Persons* which seeks to secure basic rights for stateless persons and even fewer, sixty-one, to the 1961 *Convention on the Reduction of Statelessness* which seeks to prevent statelessness at birth and prohibit loss of nationality resulting in statelessness. It is the case that the legally declared human right to a national citizenship has played a significant political and legal role in blocking processes of denationalization that would render persons stateless, even if it has not yet established an effective international legal norm for the general prevention of statelessness. However, it should also be noted that within the current 'Global War on Terror', the issue of statelessness has once again become significant in two ways. First, there are renewed political projects of denationalization of citizens, particularly naturalized citizens.[12] Second, large-scale refugee flows are liable to result in increases in the number of children born into statelessness.[13]

What justifications serve to ground a human right to national citizenship? From the standpoint of the 'humanity'-based approach to human rights, because this right appeals to a particular contingent state of affairs (a world politically organized in terms of states), it can only be a derivative right, rather than a primary right. We can distinguish two forms of derivation: contextual and instrumental. The former derives a secondary human right as the context-specific expression of a primary human right—thus, for example, a human right to a national citizenship as the context-specific expression of a primary human right to membership of a political community. The latter derives a secondary human right as instrumentally necessary to enjoyment of (at least some) primary human rights—thus, for example, a human right to national citizenship as an empirically necessary condition for secure access to (at least some) primary human rights. In this respect, the justification of a human right to national citizenship is dependent on *either* the existence of a primary human right to membership of a political community with membership of a state being the appropriate expression of this right in our global political context *or* the empirical claim that secure access to (at least some) primary human rights is dependent on membership of a state. The former is the case for 'personhood' and 'capability' accounts; the latter for the 'basic needs' account.

Contrastingly, on the 'political' approach to theorizing human rights, a human right to national citizenship is primary rather than derivative. Developing the 'public reason' account, Joshua Cohen proposes a justificatory minimalist account of human rights as part of an ideal of global public reason, where human rights norms 'are best thought of as norms associated with the idea of *membership or inclusion* in an organised political society'. On this view:

---

[12] See Gibney in this volume.

[13] Charlie Dunmore, 'Born in Exile, Syrian Children Face Threat of Statelessness', 4 November 2014, online UNHCR http://www.unhcr.org/54589fb16.html.

A conception of human rights ... has three elements: a statement of what the rights are; an account of the role of human rights as standards of practical reason that can be used by a range of different agents in assessing all political societies in their treatment of their members; and a view about why the rights are as they are, given that role. The idea of justificatory minimalism is that each of these elements—including the account of membership and affirmation of its importance—should be presented autonomously or independently, so that all may be affirmed by a range of ethical outlooks, for the varying reasons provided by the terms of these ethical outlooks, and then used as a basis for further argument about and elaboration of the content of human rights.[14]

Given the role of membership in political society to this 'free-standing' conception of human rights as an object of (potential) overlapping consensus, membership of a state as the predominant form of organized political society in the current global order is necessarily seen as a primary human right.

The discourse ethical account of human rights (at least in Habermas' version of this theory[15]) advances a view of the concept of human rights as exhibiting a duality in facing both morality and law; like moral norms, human rights claim universal validity, but unlike moral norms, human rights belong to (i.e., are only fully realized through) a positive legal order. Importantly this view sees an internal connection between human rights and democracy, and takes the fundamental rights of constitutional democracy as paradigmatic human rights. Given this stance, a right to membership of a state is itself a primary human right.

The third type of 'political' account, that of approaching human rights as a discursive practice, proposes that human rights are best seen as 'peculiarly, matters of international concern: they are norms worked out for one among many possible situations of human interaction found in a world order in which political authority is vested primarily in territorial states'.[16] This framing of human rights, unsurprisingly, also leads to the view that in a world order in which territorial states exercise political authority and are the primary agents for ensuring the protection of human rights, a human right to national citizenship is a primary human right.

From a normative standpoint, it appears that a human right to a national citizenship is robustly supported irrespective of the general approach to, or particular theoretical articulation of, human rights that one adopts. The robust grounds of a human right to national citizenship identify statelessness as a double threat to individuals in that it is both the denial of a human right and is pivotal for secure access to other important human rights. The moral-political requirement on the international community to eradicate statelessness is an urgent one that justifies limiting the discretionary power of states to determine their own

[14] Joshua Cohen, 'Minimalism about Human Rights: The Most We Can Hope For?', in *The Arc of the Moral Universe* (Oxford: Oxford University Press, 2010), pp. 319–348, p. 329.

[15] Habermas, *Between Fact and Norm* (n 10); Habermas, 'Constitutional Democracy' (n 10).

[16] Beitz (n 11), p. 160.

membership in two ways. First, by denying states the right to strip citizenship from a citizen if that would render them stateless and, second, by requiring states to grant citizenship to stateless persons. The human right to change one's citizenship that is expressed in Article 15(2) of the UDHR equally justifies limiting the discretionary power of states. The grounds for this latter right are closely related to the grounds of the human right not to be prevented from leaving the territory of a state. If these rights to exit from the territory or from citizenship status are denied, citizens (and residents in the territorial case) are subject to the *dominion* of the state irrespective of their own choices or circumstances. From a liberal perspective, this is an unjustifiable interference with the free choices of individuals concerning those with whom they choose to engage in civic association. From a republican point of view, it is a political form of servitude in that it leaves citizens exposed to the arbitrary power of the state by blocking renunciation of their status. In this respect, it is a normatively important feature of global political society that there are a significant number of states that do not permit voluntary renunciation of citizenship or only permit it for naturalized citizens. A related issue concerns the human right not to be 'arbitrarily deprived' of one's citizenship declared in the same Article 15(2) of the UDHR (which would be analogous to a right not to be arbitrarily banished from the territory of one's state). Both of these rights—to change one's citizenship and not to be arbitrarily deprived of it—have acquired new salience in the context of contemporary global migration.

In this section, I have discussed a human right to *national* citizenship. Considerably more controversial is the issue of whether there is a human right to *democratic* citizenship.

A HUMAN RIGHT TO DEMOCRACY?

Article 21 of the UDHR runs thus:

(1) Everyone has the right to take part in the government of his country, directly or through freely chosen representatives.
(2) Everyone has the right of equal access to public service in his country.
(3) The will of the people shall be the basis of the authority of government; this will shall be expressed in periodic and genuine elections which shall be by universal and equal suffrage and shall be held by secret vote or by equivalent free voting procedures.

We should note that only (3) strictly entails democratic rule and does so by linking popular sovereignty to a specific and minimalist model of democratic rule. But what is the justificatory basis for a human right to democracy or for expressing it in terms of a minimalist model of democracy?

Each of the approaches to, and accounts of, human rights reviewed in the preceding section supports a human right to political participation. But not all of them support a human right to democracy. In this section, I consider Cohen's argument for rejecting the claim of a human right to democracy before considering two defences.

The central claims of Cohen's argument are that (a) human rights are a part of global public reason conceived as a common terrain of debate on conditions of membership of political society that can be shared by anyone in a deeply pluralistic world and (b) democracy, as a demanding egalitarian political ideal, is not a human right because a human right to democracy would entail imposing controversial standards of justice on peoples who do not share these standards.[17] On Cohen's view, the rights required for individuals to be members of a political society entail that the laws and policies of the political society attend to the common good of the individuals over whom it rules. For Cohen a right to political membership in this sense is a condition for duties entailed by such rule to be genuine obligations rather than mere impositions. Human rights specify the conditions of political obligation in political societies and thereby set the standards by which we judge political societies. Cohen's argument is that these conditions of political obligation can be met by states characterized by arrangements of collective self-determination in which:

(1) binding collective decisions result from, and are accountable to, a political process that represents the diverse interests and opinions of those who are subject to the society's laws and regulations and expected to comply with them ... (2) rights to dissent from, and appeal, those collective decisions are assured for all; and (3) government normally provides public explanations of its decisions , and those explanations ... are founded on a conception of the common good of the whole of society.[18]

There is nothing, Cohen argues, that in principle rules out these conditions being met by an undemocratic political society characterized by what Rawls' calls a 'decent consultation hierarchy'[19] in which, for example, official positions and special privileges are reserved for adherents to the polity's official religion, although any other religions are politically represented through other routes.[20]

Yet even if we accept this as an argument in political morality, there may be good reasons to establish a human right to democracy as a legal entitlement even in contexts in which political morality does not logically entail such a right. Thus, for example, if we have good empirical grounds for thinking that only states meeting some threshold standard of democracy *reliably* meet and

---

[17] Joshua Cohen, 'Is There a Human Right to Democracy?', in *The Arc of the Moral Universe* (Oxford: Oxford University Press, 2010), pp. 340–372.

[18] Ibid., pp. 357–358.   [19] Rawls (n 9), p. 61.   [20] Cohen (n 17), p. 358.

sustain *either* these conditions of collective self-determination *or* conditions for the protection of (at least some) primary human rights, this would provide *pro tanto* reasons for such a legal entitlement[21] (although any such argument would also need to address the potential costs of establishing democracy as a human right in international law rather than as a desirable medium to long-term goal of international policy).[22] Notice that such instrumental arguments do not establish a human right to democracy conceived in terms of the demanding ideal that Cohen specifies but only to that threshold level of democracy required for the empirical claims to go through. Thus, for example, Thomas Cristiano's instrumental argument requires only what he calls 'minimally egalitarian democracy',[23] a standard that aligns closely with the minimalist conditions specified by the UDHR.[24] However, if the instrumental case for some specified level or type of democratic governance is robust, it not only serves to justify a derivative human right to democracy (in this form) from a public political approach to human rights but also to justify such a derivative right from the contrasting *humanity*-based approach. It is on this basis, for example, that James Griffin tentatively endorses an empirically based human right to democracy under contemporary political conditions.[25]

However, Cohen's argument has also been contested as an argument in political morality. Recall the hypothetical 'decent society' that meets the criteria of collective self-determination but in which official positions and special privileges are reserved for adherents to the polity's official religion. Let us imagine that the members of a non-official religion protest at their exclusion from official positions and claim a right to *equal* consideration and representation. Here it is not a question of imposing controversial standards of justice on a people who do not share these standards, but of a disagreement about justice expressed through the struggle of a minority against discriminations in political standing and access to advantage—and the place of human rights in such struggles. In this context, Forst claims that Cohen's argument illicitly supports the inference 'that these members

---

[21] See Thomas Cristiano, 'An Instrumental Argument for a Human Right to Democracy', *Philosophy & Public Affairs 39*, no. 2 (Spring 2011): pp. 142–176, doi: 10.1111/j.1088-4963.2011.01204.x.

[22] David Miller, 'Is There a Human Right to Democracy?', in R. Kreide, R. Celikates, and T. Wesche, eds., *Transformations of Democracy: Crisis, Protest and Legitimation* (Lanham: Rowman and Littlefield, 2015), pp. 177–192.

[23] Cristiano (n 21).

[24] This involves three features: '(1) Persons have formally equal votes that are effective in the aggregate in determining who is in power ... (2) Persons have equal opportunities to run for office, to determine the agenda of decision making, and to influence the processes of deliberation.... (3) Such a society also acts in accordance with the rule of law and supports an independent judiciary that acts as a check on executive power. This cluster of rights can be characterized simply as a right to participate as an equal in the collective decision making of one's political society, which I refer to as a *right to democracy*.' (Ibid., p. 146.)

[25] Griffin (n 5), p. 254.

do not have a human right to resist unequal and undemocratic forms of organizing political government'.[26] However, having a set of human rights that amount collectively to a human right to engage effectively in struggles for democracy is not equivalent to having a right *to* democracy. Rather the critical question is whether the human rights that must be in place for a 'decent society' to meet the criteria of collective self-determination amount collectively to a human right to resist 'unequal and undemocratic forms of organizing political government' or, put another way, whether the right to collective self-determination entails a human right to *democratization*. Forst's argument that the principle of collective self-government 'is a recursive principle with a built-in dynamic of justification that favours those who criticize exclusions and asymmetries'[27] is the crucial consideration here and supports the claim that a legitimate political society must provide the human rights required for its members to be able to democratize its governmental practices. This, however, need not be seen as a criticism of Cohen's argument rather than as an elaboration or extension of it.

There are a number of reasons to favour a human right to *democratization* over a human right to *democracy* but primary among these is that it respects the standing of the members of a political society as the critical agents in determining how they are governed. Consider two points to illustrate this. First, there is a significant difference between a standard that focuses on whether members of a political society are able to engage effectively in democratizing its governance structures, on the one hand, and a standard that requires (or imposes) a set of criteria specifying a minimal form of democratic rule, on the other hand. Second, and consequently, this human right is not restricted to a focus on the transition from undemocratic to (some specified form of) democratic governance but also encompasses further democratization—or what Benhabib calls 'democratic iterations'[28]—within existing structures of democratic governance. A human right to *democratization* thus acknowledges the basic right of members of a political society to codetermine the ways in which they are governed in the only way that ensures that they can conceive of themselves as authorizing this structure of rule.

In summary, the case for a human right to democracy of the kind specified in Article 21 of the UDHR hangs largely on instrumental considerations, but a more general case can be made, at least from a view of human rights as a public political doctrine or practice, for the claim that a human right to democratization is entailed by the human right to collective self-determination.

---

[26] Rainer Forst, 'The Justification of Human Rights and the Basic Right to Justification: A Reflexive Approach', *Ethics 120*, no. 4 (July 2010): pp. 711–740, p. 730.

[27] Ibid., p. 730.

[28] Seyla Benhabib, *Another Cosmopolitanism* (Oxford: Oxford University Press, 2006).

CITIZENSHIP AND THE POLITICS
OF HUMAN RIGHTS

The development of—and disagreements concerning—the theory of human rights are partially bound up with its practice, not least since its practice in the form of declarations and multilateral treaties provides a basis for reflecting on competing theories. But how effective has the spread of the international legal regime of human rights been in supporting access to human rights? Over the past sixty years, a wide range of human rights treaties have been widely adopted, but there is also considerable scepticism concerning the effectiveness of international law as a mechanism for securing access to human rights, especially in states that are not already broadly committed to human rights. Does signing up to human rights treaties actually matter for domestic politics or, more specifically, for citizenship?

When the UN General Assembly adopted the UDHR on 10 December 1948, it was as a statement of principles rather than as a binding treaty with the hope that, as Eleanor Roosevelt put it, the Declaration might become 'an international Magna Carta of all mankind'.[29] By the start of a new century characterized by a dense and complex human rights regime, international law is increasingly centred not on the law of nations, but on that of human rights.[30] Early agents focused on actualizing the rights proposed in the Declaration through binding treaties included a transnational network of individuals (many of whom worked for the UN, most obviously John Humphrey), organizations for legal activism such as the *International Commission of Jurists* (ICJ), smaller democracies and new decolonized states for whom:

The ICCPR [International Covenant of Civil and Political Rights], the ICESR [International Covenant of Economic and Social Rights] ... , and the Convention on the Elimination of Racial Discrimination (CERD) ... were among the earliest products of this effort.[31]

This initially slow progress accelerated significantly from the mid-1970s not least because of the efforts of nongovernmental organisations such as Amnesty International (founded 1961), Human Rights Internet (1976), Human Rights Watch (1978) as well as the ICJ which, in coalition with smaller democracies, significantly contributed to 'the institutionalization of legally binding accountability structures over the course of the 1980s and 1990s.'[32]

---

[29] Thomas Risse and Kathryn Sikkink, 'The Socialization of International Human Rights Norms into Domestic Practices', in T. Risse, S.C. Ropp and K. Sikkink, eds., *The Power of Human Rights: International Norms and Domestic Change* (Cambridge: Cambridge University Press, 1999), pp. 1–38, p. 1.

[30] Samuel Moyn, *The Last Utopia: Human Rights in History* (Cambridge: The Belknap Press of Harvard University Press, 2010), p. 176.

[31] Beth A. Simmons, *Mobilizing for Human Rights: International Law in Domestic Politics* (Cambridge: Cambridge University Press, 2009), p. 49.

[32] Ibid., p. 51.

Why and when do states commit or not commit themselves to binding human rights treaties? In general, states that already support the rights found in such treaties will sign up to them, although democratic states with common law legal systems are less prone to do so—or do so fully—than those with civil law legal systems.[33] Importantly though states that do not support—and may have no intention of complying with—the rights expressed in a treaty often ratify such treaties, notably in contexts in which regional peers also ratify.[34] Reluctance to be seen internationally as opposed to human rights and short-term strategic gains are important factors here but such strategic ratification raises the question of whether such commitment is—or can be—largely costless for these states?

In accounting for the effects of international law on domestic politics, Thomas Risse et al.[35] highlight the significance of advocacy networks and argue that 'the diffusion of international norms in the human rights area crucially depends on the establishment and sustainability of networks among domestic and transnational actors' which engage in consciousness raising about norms and norm-violation, legitimation and mobilization of domestic human rights actors. Sustaining human rights practices requires thus creating a transnational structure that combines external and internal pressure on domestic governments. In a more fine-grained analysis, Simmons has demonstrated the power of 'domestic mechanisms—new agendas, litigation, and especially social mobilization—in harnessing the potential of treaties to influence rights practices', where 'a treaty's greatest impact is likely to be found not in the stable extremes of democracy and autocracy, but in the mass of nations with institutions in flux, where citizens potentially have both the motive and means to succeed in demanding their rights'.[36] There are good reasons then to think that ratifying human rights treaties can be a significant factor in mobilizing citizens to engage in civic acts of rights claiming and altering the political institutions and imaginary of the state.

These empirical observations support the claim that the spread of the international legal regime of human rights has had significant consequences for access to, and the practice of, human rights. To the extent to which human rights are partly constitutive of democratic citizenship, this also matters for citizenship rights. These reflections also draw attention to the central role of the mobilization of citizens in the actualization of human rights practices in states and across states. However, they have a broader theoretical import beyond these points.

It is widely acknowledged that the classic (albeit Anglocentric) account of social citizenship offered by T.H. Marshall[37] does not align with the situation of migrants for whom civil and socio-economic rights typically precede political rights. Moreover, the enmeshment of contemporary states within the international

---

[33] Ibid., p. 109.   [34] Ibid., pp. 110–111.   [35] Risse and Sikkink (n 29).
[36] Simmons (n 31), pp. 154–155.
[37] T.H. Marshall. *Citizenship and Social Class* (Cambridge: Cambridge University Press, 1950).

legal order of human rights suggests that an account of social citizenship today will exhibit rather different features and dynamics than those theorized by Marshall. An early alternative account articulated in terms of a conception of post-nationalism in which civic membership is seen as being displaced by a human rights-based focus on persons has been widely criticized on empirical and normative grounds[38] in favour of a transnationalist approach that draws attention to how the border-crossing activities and rights claims of migrants involve the empirical and normative reconfiguring of citizenship without reducing the salience of civic membership to that of human rights.[39] The important point here is that citizenship and human rights each provide resources for the articulation and entrenchment of the other, for a mutual bootstrapping in the effective performance of rights claims. Thus, for example, human rights may not only provide non-citizens with protection from private and public forms of domination, but also with resources for contesting their exclusion from civic membership. International law cannot be expected to resolve political problems by itself but it can help provide the conditions that enable citizens and non-citizens to address their political concerns.

RECONCILING CITIZENSHIP
AND HUMAN RIGHTS

The spread of human rights practices, variably and patchily across the globe, has restructured the relationship between the rights of citizens and of residents as well as the entitlements of state citizenship itself. More generally still, the globalization of human rights has given rise to a *political imaginary* in which the relationship of persons and citizens to states is pictured in terms of rights to which, as a matter of human dignity, they are entitled. The significance of this point is not only played out in national political contexts but through international organizations and transnational advocacy networks in the propagation of a distinctive mode of politics. Consider the campaign to end statelessness within ten years launched by

---

[38] For an example, see Yasemin N. Soysal, *Limits of Citizenship: Migrants and Postnational Membership in Europe* (Chicago: University of Chicago Press, 1994). For a representative critique, see Randall Hansen, 'The Poverty of Postnationalism: Citizenship, Immigration, and the New Europe', *Theory and Society 38*, no. 1 (January 2009): pp. 1–24, doi: 10.1007/s11186-008-9074-0.

[39] For a normative account, see Rainer Bauböck, 'How Migration Transforms Citizenship: International, Multinational and Transnational Perspectives', IWE, working paper series no. 24 (February 2002), online https://eif.univie.ac.at/downloads/workingpapers/IWE-Papers/WP24.pdf.

the UNHCR in 2014. As I noted, the number of stateless persons is less than 0.001 per cent of the global population, about 10 million in a global population of more than 7 billion. It is a testimony to the grip that human rights have established on our political imagination that, despite the tiny fraction of the global population affected, the existence of stateless persons is constituted as a problem of global concern around which international organizations and transnational advocacy groups focus their work. At the same time, the very fact that such a campaign is necessary also illustrates the continuing resistance of states to the authority of human rights when this entails limiting their sovereignty (perhaps particularly in relation to issues of membership). The tension between the moral-political authority of human rights and the sovereignty of a people to engage in collective self-determination has been an integral part of the politics of human rights since the proclamation of *The Declaration of the Rights of Man and the Citizen* by the National Constituent Assembly of France on 26 August 1789 which, in its first three articles, simultaneously proclaimed the principle of universal rights of man and the principle of popular sovereignty.[40] It is worth focusing briefly on this *Declaration* before returning to contemporary politics.

The Declaration of the Rights of Man and the Citizen had been preceded and influenced by the American Declaration of Independence as well as specific Declarations of Rights adopted by colonies. However, as Bobbio comments

Although the revolution of the thirteen colonies had an immediate impact in Europe and the American myth was rapidly formed in the old continent, it was the French Revolution which for about two centuries constituted the ideal model for those who fought for their own emancipation and the liberation of the people. The principles of 1789 constituted, whether we like it or not, an obligatory reference point for the friends and foes of liberty.[41]

The signing of the 1789 *Declaration* is an *exemplary* act of political founding by an assembly that asserts this sovereign people's understanding of the universal conditions of legitimacy of the state[42] and, hence, the conditions under which it recognizes the legitimacy of other states.[43] This exemplar (as Kant and his equally enthusiastic contemporaries were quick to recognize) reshaped the space of political reasons not

---

[40] Article I—Men are born and remain free and equal in rights. Social distinctions can be founded only on the common good.

Article II—The goal of any political association is the conservation of the natural and imprescriptible rights of man. These rights are liberty, property, safety and resistance against oppression.

Article III—The principle of any sovereignty resides essentially in the Nation. No body, no individual can exert authority which does not emanate expressly from it.

[41] Norberto Bobbio, *The Age of Rights* (Cambridge: Polity Press, 1996), p. 81.

[42] It does so by advancing claims concerning general conditions of freedom for any political society as well as particular conditions of freedom intrinsic to the political form of a constitutional democratic state.

[43] This is the import of Article XVI: 'Any society in which the guarantee of rights is not assured, nor the separation of powers determined, has no Constitution.'

only within France but also, through varying kinds of uptake, within the empires and states that were spectators to this event. The Declaration represents an example of what Ferrara calls 'politics at its best': '*the prioritization of ends in the light of good reasons that can move our imagination*'.[44]

It is an important feature that the French Declaration proclaims and performs the constitution of the people as sovereign at the same moment and in the same gesture that it declares and performs the self-limitation of this sovereignty. It does so by binding the legitimacy of its authority to the constitutional acknowledgment of both, internally, the rights of persons and of citizens, and, externally, the rights of other peoples to constitute themselves as sovereign people on the same basis. But what grounds the moral-political claim to universality of the conditions of state legitimacy that this act asserts and, hence, the legitimacy of the act of self-constitution it performs? This question arose immediately with respect to the 1789 *Declaration*. For example, the *Declaration* was challenged on its claim to universality within France by women (who were denied political rights), most notably in the biting ironies of Olympe de Gouges' *Declaration of the Rights of Women and the Female Citizen* (1791), and without by the Haitian Revolution which highlighted the silence of the 1789 *Declaration* on the practice of slavery. Through a violent process of revolutionary struggle, symbolically supported by the declaration of the freedom of slaves by the French National Assembly in 1792, the establishment of the Republic of Haiti in 1804 became the major exemplar, especially for the slave societies of the Americas, of a multitude constituting itself as a sovereign people.

These criticisms raise two related issues which remain highly salient to contemporary debates concerning human rights. The first addresses the legitimacy of claims to determine the form and content of universal rights, and hence the issue of international human rights law as a potential mechanism of imperialism. The second addresses the legitimacy of the act of self-constitution. Notably in both the 1789 and 1948 Declarations, there is built into the articulation of human rights a presumption that the constitutional state is the legitimate form of organized political society through which peoples are constituted as sovereign peoples entitled to the right of collective self-determination and to legal standing as subjects of international law. While this presumption undoubted shaped many of the national liberation struggles against imperial rule in the postwar period as well as the politics of separatism in some multinational states, it also significantly disabled the struggles of indigenous peoples in settler societies such as Australia, Canada, New Zealand, and the USA as well as across Latin America. The issues are related in that it is the claim to legitimacy of the specified universal rights that grounds the claim to legitimacy of the self-constitution of the people, while, at the same time, it is peoples

---

[44] Alessandro Ferrara, *The Democratic Horizon* (Cambridge: Cambridge University Press, 2015), p. 38.

self-constituted as states that authorize, through self-binding treaties, the political authority of human rights.

However, we should not be misled by the dramatic picture of political founding offered by the American war of independence and the French revolution into conceiving of the self-constitution of the people as an event that occurs only in moments of radical political rupture. Rather, as Benhabib has noted: 'every act of self-legislation is also an act of self-constitution'.[45] The importance of this point is that it identifies a way not of resolving the tension between the universalism of human rights and the particularism of the collective self-determination of peoples (given institutional expression as state sovereignty) but of mediating this tension. Such mediation occurs, for example, when a sovereign people enables stateless persons or long-term residents to acquire citizenship or acknowledges its own plurality as 'sovereign peoples' by constructing institutions of self-rule for national minorities. In performing such acts, the sovereign people mediates between a cosmopolitan order in which all human beings are entitled to justification with respect to the coercive structure of global political order and the national order in which members of the political community are entitled to determine the rules which govern them.

This focus on mediating cosmopolitan right and national self-determination also points to a further way of specifying a necessary class of primary human rights. These are the rights that enable non-members to engage in struggles for and over their civic statuses (including access to citizenship). Such rights of inclusion for non-members are analogous to the human right to democratization that enables members to struggle for and over democracy. This point applies, albeit differently, to both resident and non-resident non-citizens. With respect to the former, who are subject to the exercise of public power in determining their civic status, what is central is their ability to exercise rights of, for example, protest and assembly in contesting the determinations of public power without fear of domination (such as, for example, the downgrading of residency rights or deportation from the state). With respect to the latter, there are two important dimensions. First, there is the ability of external affected persons to participate in the political discussions of the affecting state. This is a central justification for the distinctive border-crossing character of free speech stressed in Article 19 of the UDHR: 'Everyone has the right to freedom of opinion and expression; this right includes freedom to hold opinions without interference and to seek, receive and impart information and ideas through any media and *regardless of frontiers* (my italics).' Second, there is the ability to hold states to account for actions that breach (or undermine) the human rights of non-resident non-citizens through national, regional, international, or global institutions. We might, echoing Arendt, call this 'the right to have human rights' and while it is the case that the practice of human rights has developed in the period since

---

[45] Benhabib (n 28), p. 33.

the UN Declaration, the right to have human rights is, at best, emerging through the entrenchment of human rights in national constitutions and international law and developments such as universal jurisdiction of national courts alongside supra-national institutions, such as the European Court of Human Rights and, more dramatically, the International Criminal Court.

James Tully's reconceptualization of both citizenship and human rights as situated democratic practices provides a more radical response than Benhabib's to the tension between human rights and democratic self-rule. Tully sets up a contrast between two 'modes of citizenship':

> Whereas modern citizenship focuses on citizenship as a universalisable legal status underpinned by institutions and processes of rationalisation that enable and constrain the possibility of civil activity (an institutionalised/universal orientation), diverse citizenship focuses on the singular civic activities and diverse way that these are more or less institutionalised or blocked in different contexts (a civic activity/contextual orientation). Citizenship is not a status given by the institutions of the modern constitutional state and international law, but negotiated practices in which one becomes a citizen through participation.[46]

This contrast has significant implications for how we understand rights in citizenship contexts. On the modern view, civil rights[47] are necessary institutional preconditions of citizenship in that they comprise the entitlements, liberties, immunities, and powers that compose the condition of being *at liberty*. On the civic view, rights are neither necessary nor sufficient conditions of civic freedom. Rather, Tully argues, rights are products of civic activity and are secured by such activity.[48] But what is the value of rights on this view?

While rights are not necessary or sufficient conditions of civic freedom, they are (or can be) *enabling* conditions of civic freedom and, in particular, of the *effective* exercise of civic freedom. Rights can play a variety of roles here; reducing the costs of political participation, distributing powers to citizens, and stabilizing forms of recognition-respect. Civic citizens thus have compelling reasons to struggle—as historically they have—for those rights that are sufficient to make the exercise of civic freedom effective. This political approach to citizenship thus refigures citizenship by placing activity before status and explaining the salience of the latter in terms of the former. Human rights, on this view, are proposals that have acquired authority in and through negotiated democratic practices as enabling the 'civicization' of relations of political rule within and beyond relations between those with the status of citizenship and the state. On this view, the problem with the 'modern' view of human rights as 'universal truths' is that it risks universalizing a particular way of picturing human relations and one institutionalized form of citizenship

---

[46] Tully (n 11), p. 248.

[47] 'Civil rights' here refers to what are more usually called civil, political, socio-economic, and cultural rights. Ibid., pp. 250–256.

[48] Ibid., p. 273. See also Isin in this volume.

whose dominance itself owes much to a history of imperialism, formal and informal, with which it is intimately related.[49] By contrast, seeing human rights as the expressions of civic activity, of negotiated practices, that further enable the 'civicizing' of political rule by those subject to, or affected by, this rule, locates human rights as internal to the political struggles of a globalizing world. Tully's view reminds us of Arendt's reasons for stressing the importance of citizenship as activity and of the civic work that is integral to the constitution of the practice of human rights claims and responses to them.

Conclusion

This chapter has focused on the relationship between citizenship and human rights. In doing so, it has also drawn attention to the point that citizenship is both a status and an activity. I have argued that there is a human right to the status of citizenship and that this status is partly constituted by human rights. Human rights may also be seen as enabling conditions of citizenship as an activity: (a) an activity of political struggle within and over the constitution of citizenship as a status in terms of *who* is entitled to this status in a given state and *what* rights should be integral to this status, and (b) an activity of political struggle within and over the scope and content of human rights. It is important to note here that citizenship as an activity is not circumscribed by citizenship as a status, that is, that civic activity is not bounded by the state and human rights may be conceived as enabling conditions of transnational civic activity. When Arendt points to the status of citizenship as marking the right to have rights, her point was that, within the modern state system, the status of citizenship grounded conditions of a public realm in which the activity of citizenship could be performed. However, the spread of human rights may be seen as, incompletely and often weakly, enabling the performance of citizenship beyond the state, of enabling the formation of transnational publics in which forms of non-state transnational citizenship can be enacted.[50]

This last point draws attention to the fact that while the discourse of human rights is bound up with the development of the modern state and international state system and the form of much of this discourse is statist in character, it may enable new forms of political ordering that move beyond the dominance of the state form. It is possible to imagine a global order of human rights that makes possible a global political order without states that would, in turn, require the re-articulation of

---

[49] Tully (n 11).   [50] See also Isin in this volume.

many of our human rights. In one respect, this appears to pose more of a challenge to 'political' than 'humanity'-based accounts of human rights since the latter takes the statist form of many human rights to be derivative of the contingent political ordering of the globe, whereas the former may appear to bind human rights more closely to the modern state system. However, if we reflect on why the 'political' approach to human rights focuses on the state, it becomes clear that it too does not bear a necessarily relation to the political form of the state. For example, a political approach focused on non-domination will attend to private and public forms of domination in whatever concrete forms these take and articulate human rights that identify and protect the basic conditions of private and public autonomy. The salience of this point is not merely one tied to imagined futures however. Under contemporary conditions of globalization, the growth of the power of transnational corporations relative to states, to social groups, and to individuals may be of an order that requires the formulation of new human rights to protect such actors from forms of private domination, whether these apply to them directly or, in the case of social groups and individuals, are mediated through domination of the state. Whether or not this particular example is seen as compelling, the broader point is twofold. First, that the form and range of human rights—whether as primary in the 'political' approach or derivative in the 'humanity' approach—must be seen as open to re-articulation as the political circumstances change. Second, that part of the importance of citizenship, human rights and their relationship is securing the conditions under which this civic re-articulation can occur. This is a core agenda for future research on citizenship and human rights.

BIBLIOGRAPHY

Angeli, Oliviero, *Cosmopolitanism, Self-Determination and Territory* (Basingstoke: Palgrave, 2015).

Arendt, Hannah, *The Origins of Totalitarianism* (Cleveland: The World Publishing Company, 1958).

Bauböck, Rainer, 'How Migration Transforms Citizenship: International, Multinational and Transnational Perspectives', IWE working paper series no. 24 (February 2002), online https://eif.univie.ac.at/downloads/workingpapers/IWE-Papers/WP24.pdf.

Bauböck, Rainer, 'Morphing the Demos into the Right Shape. Normative Principles for Enfranchising Resident Aliens and Expatriate Citizens', *Democratization* 22, no. 5 (Autumn 2015): pp. 820–839, doi: 10.1080/13510347.2014.988146.

Beitz, Charles R., *The Idea of Human Rights* (Oxford: Oxford University Press, 2009).

Benhabib, Seyla, *Another Cosmopolitanism* (Oxford: Oxford University Press, 2006).

Benhabib, Seyla, *Dignity in Adversity: Human Rights in Troubled Times* (Cambridge: Polity Press, 2011).

Bobbio, Norberto, *The Age of Rights* (Cambridge: Polity Press, 1996).

Carens, Joseph, *The Ethics of Immigration* (Oxford: Oxford University Press, 2013).

Cohen, Joshua, *The Arc of the Moral Universe* (Cambridge: Harvard University Press, 2010).

Cristiano, Thomas, *The Constitution of Equality* (Oxford: Oxford University Press, 2008).

Cristiano, Thomas, 'An Instrumental Argument for a Human Right to Democracy', *Philosophy & Public Affairs 39*, no. 2 (Spring 2011): pp. 142–176, doi: 10.1111/j.1088-4963.2011.01204.x.

Dahl, Robert, *Democracy and its Critics* (New Haven: Yale University Press, 1989).

Dumbrava, Costica, *Nationality, Citizenship and Ethno-Cultural Belonging: Preferential Membership Policies in Europe* (Basingstoke: Palgrave, 2014).

Ferrara, Alessandro, *The Democratic Horizon* (Cambridge: Cambridge University Press, 2015).

Forst, Rainer, 'The Justification of Human Rights and the Basic Right to Justification: A Reflexive Approach', *Ethics 120*, no. 4 (July 2010): pp. 711–740, doi: 10.1086/653434.

Forst, Rainer, *The Right to Justification* (New York: Columbia University Press, 2012).

Griffin, James, *On Human Rights* (Oxford: Oxford University Press, 2008).

Gündoğu, Ayten, *Rightlessness in an Age of Rights* (Oxford: Oxford University Press, 2015).

Habermas, Jürgen, *Between Fact and Norm* (Cambridge: Polity Press, 1996).

Habermas, Jürgen, 'Constitutional Democracy: A Paradoxical Union of Contradictory Principles?', *Political Theory 29*, no. 6 (December 2001): pp. 766–781, doi:10.1177/0090591701029006002.

Hansen, Randall, 'The Poverty of Postnationalism: Citizenship, Immigration, and the New Europe', *Theory and Society 38*, no.1 (January 2009): pp 1–24.

Ingram, James, 'What Is a "Right to Have Rights"? Three Images of the Politics of Human Rights', *The American Political Science Review 102*, no. 4 (November 2008): pp. 401–416, online http://www.jstor.org/stable/27644535.

Jones, Peter, *Rights* (Basingstoke: The MacMillan Press, 1994).

Joppke, Christian, *Selecting by Origin: Ethnic Migration in the Liberal State* (Cambridge: Harvard University Press, 2005).

Marshall, T.H., *Citizenship and Social Class* (Cambridge: Cambridge University Press, 1950).

Miller, David, *National Responsibility and Global Justice* (Oxford: Oxford University Press, 2008).

Miller, David, 'Is There a Human Right to Democracy?', in R. Kreide, R. Celikates, and T. Wesche, eds., *Transformations of Democracy: Crisis, Protest and Legitimation* (Lanham: Rowman and Littlefield, 2015), pp. 177–192.

Moyn, Samuel, *The Last Utopia: Human Rights in History* (Cambridge: The Belknapp Press of Harvard University Press, 2010).

Nussbaum, Martha C., 'Capabilities and Human Rights', *Fordham Law Review 66*, no. 273 (1997): pp. 273–300, online http://ir.lawnet.fordham.edu/cgi/viewcontent.cgi?article=3391&context=flr.

Owen, David, 'Transnational Citizenship and the Democratic State', *Critical Review in Social and Political Philosophy 14*, no. 5 (Autumn 2011): pp. 641–663, doi:10.1080/13698230.2011.617123.

Rawls, John, *The Law of Peoples* (Cambridge: Harvard University Press, 1999).

Risse, Thomas and Kathryn Sikkink, 'The Socialization of International Human Rights Norms into Domestic Practices', in T. Risse, S.C. Ropp and K. Sikkink, eds., *The Power of Human Rights: International Norms and Domestic Change* (Cambridge: Cambridge University Press, 1999), pp. 1–38.

Simmons, Beth A., *Mobilizing for Human Rights: International Law in Domestic Politics* (Cambridge: Cambridge University Press, 2009).

Soysal, Yasemin N., *Limits of Citizenship: Migrants and Postnational Membership in Europe* (Chicago: University of Chicago Press, 1994).

Tully, James, *Public Philosophy in a New Key, volume 2: Imperialism and Civic Freedom* (Cambridge: Cambridge University Press, 2008).

CHAPTER 13

CITIZENSHIP AND CULTURAL DIVERSITY

DANIEL WEINSTOCK*

INTRODUCTION

THE aim of the present chapter it to canvas the arguments that have been put forward by political philosophers as to what an ideal of citizenship would look like in
a culturally diverse society. I will proceed as follows. In the first two sections, I will
engage in some conceptual ground-clearing aimed at transforming what might at
first glance seem to be an intractably large question, given the polysemic nature of

* An initial version of this chapter was presented at an authors' workshop at the European University
Institute in Florence. For their extensive written comments, thanks are due to Will Kymlicka, Sue
Donaldson, Rainer Bauböck, and Ayelet Shachar.

the terms involved, into a manageable one. The third section of the chapter will be devoted to diversity-based arguments that militate against a unified conception of citizenship, and the fourth will survey arguments that push in the other direction, mitigating the claims of cultural diversity in the name of a normatively acceptable shared conception of citizenship.

One clarification must be made at the outset. My survey will be largely (though not exclusively) cast within the parameters of liberal democratic theory. A tension introduced into this inquiry from the outset by this limitation is that the main virtue of political institutions for liberal-democratic theory is *justice*, or what John Rawls famously called 'the right'. According to this view, individuals should be allowed by the state to be the authors of their own lives, the role of the state being to enforce the rights that all people should be able to count on in the pursuit of an autonomously arrived at plan of life. The right is distinguished within the liberal edifice from what Rawls called 'the good'—a term by which he understood any account of the appropriate ends of human life. The state, according to liberals, should be agnostic about the human good.[1]

Accounts of citizenship have tended in the history of political philosophy to be associated with the good, rather than the right. As we shall see, they have tended to celebrate ideals of public-spiritedness, of attunement to the common good, of civic virtue. They have, in other words, been *perfectionist*, whereas liberals have tended to cleave to the ideal of *neutrality* with respect to the common good.[2] This fact imposes a challenge upon *any* theoretical quest for an ideal of citizenship that seeks to remain true the spirit of liberal-democratic theory. But the challenge is particularly acute if it turns out that liberal norms lend normative support to the centripetal logic of claims that emerge from individuals and groups on the basis of their culturally distinct properties. In other words, if we take the claims of cultural diversity as seriously as many liberal theorists claim that we ought, it might seem at first glance as if the answer to our normative question is that the ideals of citizenship ought to be rejected by liberal democratic theory. A central task for (broadly) liberal-democratic political philosophy is thus to come up with a justification for shared citizenship, and a picture of what that citizenship might look like, that does not stray from liberal ideals. It should pursue the agenda defined for political philosophers almost a generation ago by Will Kymlicka and Wayne Norman: 'if there is some conflict between respecting the legitimate claims of minorities and promoting desirable citizenship virtues and practices, what sorts of trade-offs between these values are appropriate and morally defensible?'[3]

---

[1] John Rawls, 'The Priority of the Right and Ideas of the Good,' *Philosophy and Public Affairs* 17, no. 4 (1988): pp 251–276.

[2] Jonathan Quong, *Liberalism without Perfection* (Oxford: Oxford University Press, 2013).

[3] Will Kymlicka and Wayne Norman, 'Citizenship in Culturally Diverse Societies: Issues, Contexts, Concepts,' in Will Kymlicka and Wayne Norman, eds., *Citizenship in Diverse Societies* (Oxford: Oxford University Press, 2000): pp. 1–41, p. 17.

CITIZENSHIP

Citizenship can be understood as a descriptive concept, denoting simple membership in a polity. It can also be extended to encompass the rights and obligations that, as a matter of legal fact, attach to the status of citizen in different polities. Normatively, however, it has been taken by political philosophers to refer to a wide range of properties of political agents and of their relations to each other and to their polities. Any list of ways in which the concept has been used would almost necessarily be reductive, but I don't think it is hugely inaccurate to view the uses of the term as involving the following categories:[4] first, normative conceptions of citizenship have been accompanied by normative (rather than simply factual) accounts of the bundles of rights and obligations that citizens ought to have, *qua* citizens. That is, they have emphasized not just the basic liberal bundle of rights that ought to attach to every individual agent, but also to the rights and obligations that citizens ought to have if they are to realize the values that inhere in citizenship. Thus, defenses of robust sets of political rights sometimes emphasize their connection to a vigorous practice of democratic citizenship, and some defenses of social rights similarly put weight on the impossibility of being an active citizen without the material guarantees that they afford.[5]

Second, citizenship has been associated with a set of political virtues. A virtue is a habitual disposition of character, one that inclines agents to act in certain ways spontaneously, rather than as a result of practical deliberation premised upon a general principle.[6] Virtues of citizenship have been described in various ways, that include civility, the ability to see problems from the perspective of the other, and a spontaneous orientation toward the common good, rather than one's own individual interest or that of the 'faction' to which one belongs.[7]

Third, citizenship has been thought of by political philosophers as a kind of identity. To be a citizen means viewing one's belonging to a polity as an important part of who one is. It means identifying with others on the basis of one's shared identity as

[4] Cf. Will Kymlicka and Wayne Norman, 'The Return of the Citizen: A Survey of Recent Work on Citizenship,' *Ethics* 104, no. 2 (1994): pp. 352–381. See also Daniel Weinstock, 'Citizenship and Pluralism,' in Robert L. Simon, ed., *The Blackwell Guide to Social and Political Philosophy* (Oxford: Blackwell, 2002), pp. 239–267.

[5] For the link between political rights and citizenship, see most recently Corey Brettschneider, *Democratic Rights: The Substance of Self-Government* (Princeton: Princeton University Press, 2009). For the connection between citizenship and economic rights, see Stuart White, *The Civic Minimum: On the Rights and Obligations of Economic Citizenship* (Oxford: Oxford University Press, 2003).

[6] Michael Slote, 'Virtue Ethics,' in Marcia Baron, Philip Pettit, and Michael Slote, eds., *Three Methods of Ethics* (London: Routledge, 1997), pp. 175–238.

[7] See for example Richard Dagger, *Civic Virtues: Rights, Citizenship, and Republican Liberalism* (Oxford: Oxford University Press, 1997).

a member of a polity, and also being possessed of a positive affective relation to the institutions through which citizenship in a complex modern society is mediated.[8]

Finally, citizenship denotes involvement in certain kinds of public-spirited practices, practices that are geared toward the achievement of a common good. Paradigmatic among these practices is political involvement and democratic deliberation. A citizen according to this conception is someone who actively engages with her fellow citizens in deliberation about policies that would best serve the polity as a whole, rather than one specific section thereof.[9]

Running through these diverse senses of citizenship are, I would argue, two concerns that have unified recent theories on the subject, despite their apparent disparity of focus. The first concern I would label *corrective*. Citizenship theories have in the modern literature in political philosophy sought to counter certain tendencies perceived as inherent in the dominant liberal canon. An account of rights grounded in the goods of citizenship is viewed as a useful counterweight to views of rights grounded in too individualistic and atomized a conception of the human agent. A focus on virtues of character of political agents is viewed as providing an important counterweight to the exclusively institutional focus that has according to some citizenship theorists characterized much modern political philosophy. Seen as a focus of identity, citizenship is meant to provide a locus of unity to offset the centrifugal effect that other dimensions of people's lives can have when they are viewed as central to their identities. Thus, a focus on citizenship is variously seen as a response to liberal theories that, in virtue of their recalcitrance to postulate a theory of the human good, allow, or even celebrate, particularistic identification with clan, class, religion, ethnicity, or any other exclusive attachment. Finally, a focus on citizenship as practice, and in particular as deliberative practice, is seen as an important correction for the passive rights-bearer and depoliticized citizen which is sometimes seen as an emanation of liberal theory.

A second shared concern of citizenship theorists, one that is already implicit in the thumbnail sketch that has just been provided of its corrective function, is to emphasize the unifying, universalistic logic that underpins citizenship. Normative conceptions of citizenship turn our attention to what we can share even within a diverse citizenry, rather than to what divides us. Thus, rights of citizenship implicitly denote *common* rights, rather than bundles of rights differentiated according to social position. Virtues of citizenship refer to the traits of character that we should all share to facilitate social life, as opposed to the ways of being that we possess as members of some subsection of society. Those who stress the function of citizenship as an anchor for identity implicitly or explicitly formulate it in opposition to

---

[8] Maurizio Viroli, *For Love of Country: An Essay on Patriotism and Nationalism* (Oxford: Oxford University Press, 1997).

[9] See for example Henry Richardson, *Democratic Autonomy: Public Reasoning About the Ends of Policy* (Oxford: Oxford University Press, 2004).

those other loci of identity that differentiate us, and that potentially pull us apart. Practices of citizenship, and in particular deliberative practices oriented toward the common good, are ones that we can all engage in together, irrespective of the traits that distinguish us. Some authors have noted that the universalistic logic of citizenship is self-undermining: originally meant to bind individuals to a specific, particular polity, its logic ultimately questions the moral relevance of particular polities altogether.[10] The logic of modern citizenship impels us in the direction of *global* citizenship.[11]

CULTURAL DIVERSITY

We now have a clearer (though not a simple) fix on what has been meant in recent normative literature by citizenship. What about cultural diversity? How broadly should we construe that notion? What forms of diversity does it make sense to label as 'cultural'? There can be no doubt that the term 'culture' is one of the most commonly employed, and least commonly defined, in contemporary political theory.[12] For the most part, however, the problem of cultural diversity has been largely reduced in recent political philosophy to the problem of *ethno*-cultural diversity.

Cultural diversity can in turn be understood in a variety of manners, depending on the sources of that diversity in specific countries. To schematize, political philosophers have tended to distinguish between cultural diversity that could be termed *constitutive*, in the sense that it is present at the origin of the state in question, and diversity that we could for present purposes call *contingent*, in the sense that it results from the happenstance of population movements.

Constitutive cultural diversity results from the fact that the establishment of state borders has tended to encompass more than one national group. Minority national groups can be minority nations, such as Quebec, Catalonia, Flanders, or Scotland, that are incorporated more or less whole within a larger state. Some of these manage either with the support of the state, or despite the latter's efforts at assimilation, to maintain a distinct language, civil society, and set of public institutions, while others may be in a state of greater or lesser assimilation.[13] Minority national groups

---

[10] Christian Joppke, *Citizenship and Immigration* (Cambridge: Polity, 2010), p. 115.

[11] See Daniel Weinstock, 'Prospects for Transnational Citizenship and Democracy', *Ethics and International Affairs* 15, no. 2 (2001): pp. 53–66.

[12] David Scott, 'Culture in Political Theory', *Political Theory* 31, no. 1 (2003): pp. 92–115.

[13] Karlo Basta, John McGarry, and Richard Simeon, eds., *Territorial Pluralism: Managing Difference in Multinational States* (Vancouver: University of British Columbia Press, 2015).

can also be national minorities, that is groups that have been cut off from their national group by the often arbitrary process of border-making that has resulted from post-war settlements, from colonial decisions, and the like. The presence of minority national groups on a state's territory can be a fully acknowledged fact, enshrined in various ways in constitutional documents and in foundational myths, or it can be suppressed from institutional memory, as has tended to be the case for example in states that have enacted nation-building policies aimed at producing a unified national consciousness out of what might originally have been heterogeneous cultural materials. Constitutive cultural diversity can also have come about through conquest and settler colonialism, as has been the case in countries such as Canada, Australia, New Zealand, and the United States. It can also come about through agreement and treaty, as was the case at Canada's foundation, or through processes that are neither clearly coercive nor consensual, such as the machinations of European aristocracies.[14]

Contingent cultural diversity has resulted from diverse migratory processes. It has resulted, for example, from the deliberate immigration policies put in place by countries that consider themselves 'countries of immigration,' such as Canada, the United States, and Australia, and also from the acceptance, brought about either through policy or by circumstance, of refugees fleeing conditions of war, persecution, 'natural' disaster, economic collapse, and the like. It has also resulted from the acceptance into the citizenry of migrants originally accepted only as temporary, or (as would have been the case had President Obama's immigration reform plan been accepted by the American Congress in some form or other) by the tracing of a path to citizenship of irregular migrants having set up residence and secured employment in their host country. It can result from myriad other processes as well, such as family reunification. What unites this motley category of 'culturally diverse' members of a society is that they were not present on the territory of the state at the moment of its creation.[15]

A third category that sits uncomfortably with the first two, but that has attracted a great deal of scholarly attention in recent years, is that of religious diversity. This category sits uncomfortably with the others, from a conceptual point of view, because religious diversity can emerge in an entirely ethnically homogeneous society. As Rawls has observed, significant diversity with respect to 'comprehensive conceptions of the good' can emerge easily when the basic liberal freedoms are in place, that is, when people are free to reflect upon the 'big questions' freely, and to associate with others who share the same conclusions about what the answers to

---

[14] The best account we possess of this form of cultural diversity worldwide is probably Will Kymlicka, *Multicultural Odysseys: Navigating the New International Politics of Diversity* (Oxford: Oxford University Press, 2009).

[15] For a succinct account of the way in which migration has shaped human societies through history, see Michael Fisher, *Migration: A World History* (Oxford: Oxford University Press, 2013).

those questions are.[16] But though the conceptual link between religious and ethno-cultural diversity is not a tight one, there can be no doubt that the empirical link is often very strong. Much constitutive ethno-cultural diversity has been overlaid, and made more complex, by the fact that national groups are religiously distinct. It is moreover clear that contingent cultural diversity born of diverse migratory processes is also a source of considerable religious diversity, and that much recent controversy about immigration, in Europe and in Canada, has had to do with its religious dimensions.[17]

The Claims of Diversity

These sketches of the ideals that have been associated with the notion of citizenship by political philosophers on the one hand, and on the multiform diversity of states on the other, give us an idea of the scope of the challenges that normative political philosophy faces in coming up with a (unifying) conception of citizenship.

Matters would be made simpler were the centrifugal forces set in train by the fact of cultural diversity normatively suspect. But there exists a strong quasi- consensus within contemporary political philosophy, at least within the (broadly) liberal trad-ition, that this is not the case. That is, the pressure toward differentiated citizenship is increased, rather than diminished by the weight of normative argument, at least from within a liberal axiology. In what follows I want to provide a thumbnail sketch of the arguments that have been put forward in favor of differentiated citizenship. Indeed, a survey of the literature, and of the actual practice of multiculturalism in modern liberal democracies, suggests that 'multiculturalism' can be seen as a ser-ies of implications of liberal democratic premises rather than a challenge to such premises.[18]

Let us begin with what I have in the typology just presented called 'constitutive' cultural diversity. Many minority national groups claim against the larger state the right to set up a partially independent public sphere. They claim the right to protect their languages against the assimilative pressure exercised on numerically smaller

---

[16] John Rawls, *Political Liberalism* (New York: Columbia University Press, 1993).

[17] For a series of essays that explores this connection, see Geoffrey Brahm Levey and Tariq Modood, eds., *Secularism, Religion and Multicultural Citizenship* (Cambridge: Cambridge University Press, 2008). See also Turner in this volume.

[18] For dissenting voices on this score, see Bhikhu Parekh, *Rethinking Multiculturalism*, 2nd edition (London: Palgrave Macmillan, 2006); Charles Taylor, *Multiculturalism and the Politics of Recognition* (Princeton: Princeton University Press, 1994).

languages by locally or globally dominant ones.[19] They claim the right to jurisdiction over policy domains that are seen as crucial to their ability to exercise meaningful national self-determination. And more generally they claim the legitimacy of a primary identification to their national group, rather than to the larger state within which they are encompassed.

It is arguably through the example of such constitutive minorities that the issues raised by the fact of cultural diversity entered the agenda of political philosophers in the first place. In two seminal books,[20] Will Kymlicka argued that if liberals view one of the primary responsibilities of the liberal state as being to promote the conditions in which citizens are capable of making significant life choices autonomously, then they should be concerned with the social conditions that make choice possible. Human agents do not choose in a vacuum. On Kymlicka's account, they require a stable 'societal culture' in order to make autonomous choices within a worthwhile set of options, a 'context of choice.' Now, members of majority cultural groups do not have to put any particular measures in place in order to ensure that they will have secure access to a societal culture, but members of minority national groups do, because of the assimilative force exercised by the larger culture. They must in particular be permitted to put policies in place that erect 'external protections' against this assimilative pressure.

Kymlicka's argument, though hugely influential, has also been subjected to a great deal of criticism. Most relevant to present purposes is the fact that Kymlicka's argument provides an account for the legitimacy of the claims to differentiated citizenship of only a subset of the total set of minority national groups. Briefly stated, these are the groups that have managed to maintain a robust societal culture and a set of social institutions sufficient to provide their members with adequate contexts of choice. Left out of the justificatory ambit of this argument are national groups that have not been able to sustain this level of institutional and societal completeness, in part because the cultural groups controlling the central state have been more thoroughgoing than others have been in how they have assimilated minority national groups.[21]

Other arguments have however been invoked (among others by Kymlicka himself) to supplement his central contention. In the case of indigenous peoples who have been the victims of settler colonialism, claims can quite obviously be built around an argument from historical injustice, and in some cases, from the respect of rights established by treaties and historical

---

[19] For an account of the forces that tend to corrode minority languages, see Jean Laponce, *Languages and Their Territories* (Toronto: University of Toronto Press, 1987).

[20] Will Kymlicka, *Liberalism, Community and Culture* (Oxford: Oxford University Press, 1989); Will Kymlicka, *Multicultural Citizenship* (Oxford: Oxford University Press, 1995).

[21] Daniel Weinstock, 'How Can Liberalism and Collective Rights Be Reconciled?', in Rainer Bauböck and John Rundell, eds., *Blurred Boundaries: Migration, Identity, Citizenship* (Aldershot: Ashgate, 1999), pp. 281–304.

agreements.[22] Equality is another value that has been invoked to justify differentiated citizenship for minority national groups. In a world in which the ability by national groups to control state institutions is a currency to which great value is ascribed, equality would mandate that all national groups be able to avail themselves of that currency at least to some degree.[23] To the argument according to which members of minority national groups would not be deprived of access to a societal culture were they to be linguistically and institutionally assimilated to the dominant culture within the state,[24] the objection has been raised that the idea according to which one language or culture can simply be replaced by another without loss in the lives of individuals is incompatible with the norm of equal dignity that is due to all individuals, and which is violated when individuals are told that the culture with which they identify is expendable.[25]

Thus, the right of minority national groups to exercise some degree of self-determination, with a view among other things, to protect themselves from assimilative pressures from dominant cultures, is in other words robustly underpinned by a host of values that are central to liberal democratic theory. Now, arguments that ascribe irreducible value to nations can also be adduced in order to justify differential bundles of rights for members of national minorities. The point being made here is that such arguments are not necessary for the justification of the rights of members of national minorities to exercise collective rights to self-determination. Now, a liberal justification will have as one of its implications that these collective rights ought only to be exercised in conformity with liberal-democratic values. In other words, they should not be used to violate the rights of members of the group.[26] But this can be seen as a strength, rather than as a failing, of the justification of rights to self-determination grounded in liberal values.

A similar pattern obtains in the case of the claims made by individuals for religious accommodation. Many religious individuals and groups have claimed the right to be exempted from the provisions of certain laws and administrative measures that apply to the broader society. For example, they have asked to be exempted from Sunday closing laws, from having to serve in the military, from the reach of

[22] Kymlicka, *Multicultural Citizenship* (n 20), pp. 108–120. For a highly influential account of cultural diversity placing the coexistence of settler societies and indigenous peoples to the fore, see James Tully, *Strange Multiplicity: Constitutionalism in an Age of Diversity* (Cambridge: Cambridge University Press, 1995).

[23] See Daniel Weinstock, 'Constitutionalizing Secession,' *Journal of Political Philosophy* 9, no. 2 (2001): pp. 182–203.

[24] See for example Allen Buchanan, 'Liberalism and Group Rights,' in Jules L. Coleman and Allen Buchanan, eds., *In Harm's Way: Essays in Honor of Joel Feinberg* (Cambridge: Cambridge University Press, 1994), pp. 1–15.

[25] Philippe Van Parijs, *Linguistic Justice: For Europe, and for the World* (Oxford: Oxford University Press, 2011).

[26] Kymlicka has made the distinction in this connection between 'external protections' and 'internal restrictions'. See Kymlicka, *Multicultural Citizenship* (n 20), pp. 35–44.

public school curricula, from certain dietary and clothing regimes in schools and public institutions, and so on. In so doing, they have asked that the bundles of rights that they hold as citizens differ from those of their fellow citizens.

The literature on religious accommodation has grown exponentially in recent years.[27] What's more, there is substantial disagreement among authors who have written on the topic about the *extent* of the right to religious accommodation. For example, some authors would provide religious parents with a wide berth to raise their children according to their beliefs and convictions, even when this requires exempting children from, say, educational requirements to which other children are subject, while others are more restrictive in the extent of the religious accommodation that parents can legitimately claim to raise their children according to the precepts of a faith.[28] But there is among liberal thinkers a broad consensus over two propositions. First, there exists *some* obligation on the part of the state to accommodate religious believers, and second, much of the argument about the scope of the right to accommodation can be made out without referring to religion essentially. The standard liberal rights—rights to freedom of expression, of conscience, of association, the right to equality, even freedom of movement, and the like—can be employed in order to justify a fairly broad right to accommodation. Thus, even if we were to accept arguments, such as those recently put forward by Ronald Dworkin or by Brian Leiter, to the effect that there is nothing about religion as such that warrants special protections on the part of the state, accommodation of religious convictions and practice could still be justified on liberal grounds even in the absence of an explicit constitutional guarantee to freedom of religion.[29] Indeed, even the collective dimension of religious life has been found by some writers and by some courts to be a requirement of the full realization of individual liberties.[30]

---

[27] For some prominent examples of this literature, see Jeff Spinner-Halev, *Surviving Diversity: Religion and Democratic Citizenship* (Baltimore: Johns Hopkins University Press, 2000); Charles Taylor and Jocelyn Maclure, *Secularism and Freedom of Conscience* (Cambridge: Harvard University Press, 2011); Cécile Laborde, 'Religion and the Law: The Disaggregation Approach,' *Law and Philosophy 34*, no. 6 (2015): pp. 581–600.

[28] For a latitudinarian approach, see Shelley Burtt, 'In Defense of Yoder: Parental Authority and the Public Schools,' in Joel Parker and Paul Woodruff, eds., *Nomos LIV: Loyalty* (New York: NYU Press, 2013), pp. 412–437. For a more restrictive argument, see Daniel Weinstock, 'How the Interests of Children Limit the Religious Freedom of Parents,' in Cécile Laborde and Aurélia Bardon, eds., *Religion in Liberal Political Philosophy* (Oxford: Oxford University Press, forthcoming).

[29] This argument has been made most clearly by Laborde (n 27). For the view according to which religion as such grounds no special protection, see Ronald Dworkin, *Religion without God* (Cambridge: Harvard University Press, 2013); Brian Leiter, *Why Tolerate Religion?* (Princeton: Princeton University Press, 2014).

[30] See for example Victor Muñiz-Fraticelli, *The Structure of Pluralism* (Oxford: Oxford University Press, 2014). The Canadian Supreme Court has made the recognition of the limited jurisdictional autonomy of religious institutions a condition for the realization of individual religious freedom in *Loyola High School v. Quebec (Attorney General)* 2015 SCC 12.

There are three analogies that warrant being drawn out between the liberal perspective on minority national groups and that which has characterized that perspective on the question of religious accommodation. The first is that there is no need to reach outside the range of canonical liberal values in order to justify group-differentiated rights into potentially more controversial collectivist or perfectionist notions such as 'nation' or 'religion.' The second analogy is that with respect to both exemptions and national self-determination, there is consensus that such a right exists, and disagreement over how far it extends. The third is that although they are ultimately grounded in a concern for the individual, individual rights can only be exercised if certain collective and institutional conditions are satisfied.

At first glance, there seems to be nowhere near this kind of a consensus over whether contingent cultural diversity can ground analogous claims for differentiated citizenship. On the contrary, there is a strong current of opinion that would place a significant duty of integration upon immigrants. Immigrants, it is felt by many theorists, have left their countries of origin voluntarily, and have begun a new life at the invitation of their host society. It follows for many that they have a duty to adapt to the country that has taken them in. Thus Will Kymlicka writes that 'in deciding to uproot themselves, immigrants voluntarily relinquish some of the rights that go along with their original national membership.'[31] Joe Carens writes that 'citizens of immigrant origin, especially those in the first generation, always do much more changing and adapting than other citizens, *and it is not unreasonable that they be expected to do so.*'[32] And David Miller has in his recent book emphasized the importance of integrating from a social, civic, and cultural perspective.[33] On all of these accounts, there is a moral asymmetry between the immigrant and her host society. She has decided to leave one place, and to settle in another, and that decision, according to the view being considered here, implies that she has an obligation to adapt to the mores of the place to which she has moved.

The argument from moral asymmetry can be criticized on its own terms. Indeed, in a world in which many countries actively court prospective immigrants as a matter of state policy, with a view to achieving a number of policy objectives, it is a misrepresentation of the moral facts to imply that host societies are accepting immigrants out of pure altruism.[34] Another category, that of refugees, can moreover hardly be depicted as having chosen to move into a new society.[35]

---

[31] Kymlicka, *Multicultural Citizenship* (n 20).

[32] Joseph H. Carens, *The Ethics of Immigration* (Oxford: Oxford University Press, 2013), p. 73. Emphasis added.

[33] David Miller, *Strangers in Our Midst: The Political Philosophy of Immigration* (Cambridge: Harvard University Press, 2016).

[34] Daniel Weinstock, 'Immigration and Reciprocity,' in Nils Holtug and Kasper Lippert-Rasmussen, *Nationalism and Multiculturalism in a World of Immigration* (London: Palgrave Macmillan, 2009), pp. 174–193.

[35] Matthew Gibney, *The Ethics and Politics of Asylum: Liberal Democracy and the Response to Refugees* (Cambridge: Cambridge University Press, 2006).

But the important point for present purposes is that despite the widespread view that newcomers bear a duty of integration in virtue of their status as immigrants, that view does not translate into a denial of at least some recognition of immigrant claims to differential rights. Arguably, this is in virtue of very basic liberal commitments to negative freedom.

To see this, consider three positions one might have about contingent cultural diversity. Call the first one 'multiculturalism.' It receives a clear and cogent expression in a paper by Joseph Raz, where he writes that multiculturalism 'calls on us radically to reconceive society, changing its self-image. We should learn to think of our societies as consisting not of a majority and minorities, but as constituted by a plurality of cultural groups.'[36] At the other extreme, consider a position that we might term 'assimilationism.' It would claim that immigrants are duty-bound as a condition of their being considered full-fledged citizens to divest themselves of all of the cultural traits that characterized them in their country of origin.

An intermediate position, that we might call 'integration,' claims that successful immigration requires that both the host society and immigrants adapt to each other. Immigrants must for example learn the language of the country to which they are immigrating. They must respect the laws and institutions of their host country, and learn about its history and political culture. The host society must however also acknowledge that migrants do not arrive on their shores as cultural blank slates, but rather that they bring with them cultural traits to which they are attached, which are at least at the moment of immigration deeply tied to their identities and sense of self-worth, such that it would both be wrong and in any case most likely impossible to expect full assimilation. In recognition of this fact, host societies confer what Kymlicka has called 'polyethnic rights' upon migrants. These rights, to quote Kymlicka, 'are intended to help ethnic groups and religious minorities express their cultural particularity and pride without it hampering their success in the economic and political institutions of the dominant society.'[37]

That neither multiculturalism (understood in the manner that Raz does) nor assimilationism is desirable or plausible as a goal for the successful introduction of immigrants into a host society seems to me to be a proposition largely adhered to by most of the authors who have written on the subject. There is agreement that the claims of the state against individuals' abilities to express their ethnic identities must have limits. A burden of proof is imposed upon states that would limit the freedom of immigrants to act in a manner that evinces continued attachment to their patrimonial cultures. And though that freedom can be cashed out in terms of the need on the part of immigrants for recognition or respect of their cultural traditions, it can also be justified in much the same way as religious freedom, and

[36] Joseph Raz, 'Multiculturalism: A Liberal Perspective,' *Ratio Juris* 11, no. 3 (1998): pp. 193–205, p. 197.

[37] Kymlicka, *Multicultural Citizenship* (n 20), p. 31.

the freedom of members of minority national groups to exercise some degree of meaningful self-determination, on the basis of standard liberal negative freedoms. One can justify significant freedoms on the part of minorities to live according to the precepts and practices of their cultures without needing to invoke controversial notions such as recognition.[38] As Carens puts it, 'it is reasonable for all citizens, whether of immigrant origin or not, to expect that other citizens will leave them alone and let them live as they choose to a very considerable degree.'[39] In other words, immigrants should be allowed to do a lot of the things they did in their countries of origin unless an urgent state interest justifies a legal prohibition against their being allowed to do so.

Now, a difference between immigrants on the one hand, and national minorities and religious groups on the other, is that there does not seem to be a clear path from liberal arguments to the justification of any collective or institutional dimension to their exercise of their liberal freedoms. Empirically, however, immigrants simply do not expect or request the setting up of separate institutions. Typically, they seek the wherewithal with which to participate in the broader society. The lack of any legally guaranteed collective dimension to the manifestation of immigrant cultural diversity need not be seen as posing a problem for a liberal approach to cultural diversity.

Taking a step back, the following conclusions emerge. The claims made on behalf of national minorities, of religious groups, and of immigrants to a certain amount of latitude to be able to lead their lives according to the precepts of their cultures and religions or to identify and to exercise collective self-determination with the members of their minority national groups have tended to find favor with theorists of broadly liberal bent because these claims are easily understood and justifiable in terms of basic liberal freedoms. Thus, the riotous diversity that characterizes many modern societies empirically is abetted by the norms of liberalism, which place a high burden of proof upon states wishing to limit these freedoms.

The (Unifying) Claims of Citizenship

What arguments can be marshaled by theorists wishing to oppose the centrifugal force of social diversity? Can such arguments be met by equally forceful arguments favoring a more unified conception of citizenship?

---

[38] The recent *locus classicus* of the invocation of the notion of 'recognition' as a basis for cultural rights is of course Taylor (n 18).

[39] Carens (n 32), p. 76. Cf. Joppke (n 10), p. 101.

It is possible very roughly to distinguish two families of arguments in this connection, differentiated by the degree to which those who put them forward feel bound by liberal strictures. One is perfectionist in nature. It would limit individual rights in the name of an ideal judged to be sufficiently urgent to warrant such limitation. Prominent in this category, both historically and in the more recent literature, have figured *nationalist* and *republican* arguments.

Nationalist arguments admit of at least three variants.[40] First, what might be termed moderately majoritarian nationalists argue that while national majorities cannot use their majority status to limit core liberal rights, it is nonetheless reasonable for members of an historically established cultural majority to use its majority status to protect certain aspects of the public culture from the corrosive impact of increasing cultural diversity.[41] The second might be called *intrinsic good* nationalism, and argues for the irreducible good of national identities. While there are few, if any present-day theorists willing to defend the intrinsic goodness of national identities as such, there is considerable scholarly argument to the effect that particular *languages* ought to be preserved because of their semantic irreplaceability, if necessary by constraining the linguistic choices that might otherwise be made by citizens drawn toward less vulnerable languages.[42] And though there is no perfect correspondence between language and nation, the specificity of languages as expressions of national identities has been one of the principal sources of nationalist thought.[43] (A third, instrumental variant of the nationalist argument will be considered below.)

Republican arguments emphasize the greater good of the activities that we carry out and of the identities that we bear as citizens as opposed to those that characterize us as members of ethno-cultural or religious groups.[44] They emphasize the importance of privileging the common good over the factional goods of particular groups. One variant that has attracted a great deal of scholarly attention in recent years is the secularist variant of republicanism, which emphasizes the importance of privileging one's identity as a citizen over one's religious identity, and holds that the accommodation of religious claims to differentiated rights ought to be resisted in the name of one's shared, non-religious identity.[45]

---

[40] See also Gans in this volume.

[41] This position is held by thinkers as different as Kymlicka, Miller, and Carens.

[42] Denise Réaume, 'Official-Language Rights: Intrinsic Value and the Protection of Difference,' in Will Kymlicka and Wayne Norman, eds., *Citizenship in Diverse Societies* (Oxford: Oxford University Press, 2000), pp. 245–272.

[43] Charles Taylor, *The Language Animal* (Cambridge: Harvard University Press, 2016).

[44] This corresponds with the 'civil religion' tradition identified by Ronald Beiner in the work of Machiavelli, Hobbes, and Rousseau. See Ronald Beiner, *Civil Religion* (Cambridge: Cambridge University Press, 2012).

[45] Blandine Kriegel, *Philosophie De La République* (Paris: Plon, 1998).

A second family of argument argues for the importance of shared citizenship from within the parameters of a broadly liberal political ethics.

A first prominent argument of this kind, one that can be targeted at any of the sources of diversity that have been discussed in this chapter, has invoked the interests of 'internal minorities.' The argument is that since many of the exemptions and rights that are claimed by individuals are exercised collectively, they can be used to deny 'internal minorities'—women, children, sexual minorities—their rights. According to this line of argument, when a liberal democracy allows a group—whether a national minority, a religious group, or an immigrant community—to be exempted from the norms that apply to the larger group, it is in effect allowing them to exempt themselves from liberal democracy itself, and thus to render already vulnerable internal minorities even more vulnerable than they would otherwise have been.[46] Thus, the argument continues, equal citizenship for all requires denying rights to illiberal minorities.

Theorists who have sought to justify strong shared citizenship as a counterweight to cultural diversity have also made instrumental use of nationalist arguments. They have for example argued for the importance for modern societies of solidarity among citizens in order to maintain the motivational basis for the welfare state. A society marked by solidarity, and by the willingness of the better-off to make sacrifices for the sake of the worse-off, may on this view not be compatible with a society of strangers in which a common identity is eschewed by minority groups. A sense of kinship is required in order for these sacrifices to be made, and this requires the promotion by the state of a shared identity.[47] Another argument similarly points to the importance of a sense of shared community as a condition for the healthy functioning of democratic institutions. A shared language, but beyond that as well a shared public sphere and political culture are required in order to underpin the kind of robust democratic debates and processes that are aspired to by democratic theorists who view democracy as more than just the confrontation of sectional interests.[48]

According to a fourth argument, if accommodations that would allow special rights or exemptions from citizenship duties for members of ethno-cultural or

---

[46] This is the gist of Susan Okin's argument in *Is Multiculturalism Bad for Women?* (Princeton: Princeton University Press, 1999). For a variant of the argument focussing on children, see Rob Reich, 'Minors within Minorities: A Problem for Liberal Multiculturalists,' in Avigail Eisenberg and Jeff Spinner-Halev, eds., *Minorities within Minorities: Equality, Rights and Diversity* (Cambridge: Cambridge University Press, 2005), pp. 209–226.

[47] See for example Philippe Van Parijs, 'Cultural Diversity against Economic Solidarity,' in Philippe Van Parijs, ed., *Cultural Diversity Versus Economic Solidarity* (Brussels: De Boeck, 2003), pp. 371–396.

[48] The need for a shared vernacular has been emphasized by Will Kymlicka in 'Citizenship in an Era of Globalization,' in *Politics in the Vernacular* (Oxford: Oxford University Press, 2001), pp. 317–326. See also John Stuart Mill in his *Considerations on Representative Government* (in *On Liberty and Other Essays* (Oxford: Oxford University Press, 1991)); David Miller, *On Nationality* (Oxford: Oxford University Press, 1997).

religious minorities are justified, then the question must be asked of whether the law or administrative regulation that they represent exceptions to are themselves justified, or whether to the contrary they represent undue limitations of *all* citizens' freedom. On the other hand, the argument continues, if this limitation is justified, then it is because it is in the pursuit of a good or the realization of a right that is of sufficient importance for all citizens to warrant the restriction of the right on the basis of which the claim for accommodation is made.[49]

These arguments, though appealing to different considerations, are similar in that they do not invoke controversial or perfectionist notions, to do for example with the alleged inherent goodness of a certain conception of citizenship tied to the civic republican tradition in order to justify the state in limiting the rights of members of cultural minorities. If these arguments are compelling, it follows that tradeoffs between the requirements of citizenship and those of cultural diversity must be made within the currency of a liberal axiology.

What are the prospects for the success of these arguments? The first of them is not so much an argument against accommodation of the rights of national minorities or of religious groups as it is an argument against unrestricted accommodation. Applied to religious groups it flies in the face of the fact that no liberal democracy extends unlimited religious rights to its citizens, and that the limitations that it places upon them often have to do precisely with the kinds of vulnerable internal minorities a concern for which has prompted Okin to claim that it would be better were certain groups simply to disappear. Even theorists sympathetic to a maximal extension for the religious freedoms also of fairly illiberal religious groups have argued that these rights need to be accompanied by a fairly robust set of exit rights, and of the educational conditions required in order for members of these groups to be able to exercise these rights.[50]

When applied to the claims to self-determination of national minorities, the argument is often premised upon the claim that the larger state's applications of liberal norms is neutral, and unsullied by the particularisms of the dominant culture, whereas the national group claiming some degree of self-determination within the larger state would largely eschew liberal democratic norms in order to impose its cultural preferences upon its citizenry.

As has been pointed out by theorists of otherwise quite different tempers such as Iris Marion Young and Allen Patten, the pretention to neutrality on the part of the culturally dominant group within a multinational society is often a species of self-delusion. The dominant position which groups that control the state occupy makes it possible for them to ignore the fact that their administration of the supposedly neutral state is often shot through with the symbols, values, and self-understandings

---

[49] Brian Barry, *Culture and Equality* (Oxford: Oxford University Press, 2000).

[50] See for example William Galston, *Liberal Pluralism: The Implications of Value Pluralism for Political Theory and Practice* (Cambridge: Cambridge University Press, 2002).

of the members of the dominant group, and with a blithe ignorance of the degree to which its norms end up being imposed upon minorities without the need for explicitly coercive legislation. Accommodation of the wishes formulated by members of national minorities for some degree of self-determination reflects an appreciation for the impossibility of culturally neutral administration of liberal norms and precepts.[51]

A (Unifying) Multicultural Ethos?

Instrumental arguments for a robust conception and practice of citizenship that link it to the realization of liberal values are ultimately empirical in nature. Let us assume for the sake of argument that the causal connections that these arguments hypothesize actually obtain. As some of the authors that have put them forward have acknowledged, it does not follow from the fact that it would be a good thing for members of a highly diverse polity to share a robust citizen identity, and to engage in common activities of citizenship, that the state is necessarily best placed to enforce this identity or these practices. Writing about the *desideratum* of cultural (as opposed to social and to civic) integration, David Miller writes that 'it does not even make sense to think of it as a possible *requirement*: there is no cultural equivalent to the legal acquisition of citizenship.'[52] When the state acts to enforce such an identity in too direct a manner in a context of cultural diversity, it may fail for a variety of reasons. First, identities cannot be imposed upon individuals. In order for citizens to truly identify with their fellow citizens, or with the institutions through which shared citizenship is mediated, an endorsement condition must be satisfied, one which cannot be made an object of state policy. Second, and relatedly, too direct an attempt at enforcing a shared identity, and thus at suppressing the identities and practices linked to particular identities can accelerate rather than inhibit the centrifugal tendencies inherent in cultural diversity, by giving rise to what Ayelet Shachar has called 'reactive culturalism', the tendency on the part of members of cultural minorities to exaggerate differences in the face of rejection by members of the cultural majority.[53]

---

[51] Iris Marion Young, *Justice and the Politics of Difference* (Princeton: Princeton University Press, 1990).

[52] Miller (n 33), p. 149.

[53] Ayelet Shachar, *Multicultural Jurisdiction: Cultural Differences and Women's Rights* (Cambridge: Cambridge University Press, 2001), pp. 35–36.

That liberal democratic states have themselves realized that a robust shared identity is not something that can be imposed by the state is evidenced in the citizenship tests that many of them impose on immigrants as a condition of accessing citizenship. As Christian Joppke has noted, they tend to put forward universalistic values rather than particularistic commitments that immigrants might have been obliged to take on. At the end of the day, even with respect to these citizenship tests, the best that the state can do is to require knowledge of them. Endorsement must come from within, if it is to come at all.[54]

Is this to say that states that aspire to satisfy liberal-democratic norms can do nothing to arrest the fissile tendencies that cultural diversity potentially set in motion in the body politic? I don't think that it does. For while states may be hampered both by liberal-democratic norms and by pragmatic considerations in making a shared citizenship identity a direct object of policy, perhaps it is an objective that can be pursued by indirect strategies. Shared identities are most robust, after all, when they emerge from the shared activities of citizens. If this is the case, then perhaps states act most effectively in the pursuit of a shared ideal of citizenship when they create the conditions that facilitating the pursuit by citizens of common objectives, and the achievement of shared identities 'from below.' In other work, I have argued that creating the conditions for social trust, rather than attempting to impose shared identities or values from on high, might be the best way for modern states to encourage the practices and bonds of shared citizenship. [55] Fostering trust means creating incentives for collaboration, or at the very least removing disincentives and obstacles thereto. There are myriad ways in which states can pursue this end. For example, the organization of electoral systems, of educational structures, and of many other domains in which citizens interact, can play powerful roles in either contributing to or detracting from it.[56]

In the context of highly diverse societies in which the kinds of shared national identity that nation-states attempted to create through the use of highly illiberal policies are probably no longer plausible objectives of policy, perhaps what will emerge is less a shared *identity* and something ressembling a shared *ethos*. Such an ethos could be promoted through the establishment by the state of the conditions that allow members with diverse cultural identities to interact in a manner that might make the emergence of a shared practice of citizenship, and of a mutual identification capable of offsetting what I have been referring to here as the centrifugal force of cultural diversity, and of the liberal norms that buttress

[54] Joppke (n 10).

[55] Daniel Weinstock, 'Building Trust in Divided Societies,' *Journal of Political Philosophy* 7, no. 3 (1999): pp. 287–307.

[56] For an account of the relationship between electoral systems and the prospects for citizen deliberation, see Daniel Weinstock, 'In Praise of Some Unfashionable Democratic Institutions: Political Parties, Party Discipline, and "First Past the Post",' *Journal of Parliamentary and Political Law* 9 (2015): pp. 291–306.

its claims. Jacob Levy has written for example of the kind of everyday norms of social interaction the presence of which is crucial to the viability of a highly diverse society—what he refers to as 'multicultural manners.'[57] And there has been an increase in interest among political philosophers of the social desiderata linked to the virtue of toleration. Perhaps future research on citizenship in diverse societies should take the direction of understanding the ways in which such a conception of citizenship and of its associated practices and virtues might develop, one that states aim at only indirectly, and one not as closely tied as older conceptions of citizenship have been to national identities or to perfectionist republican ideals.

Conclusion

Multicultural policies, including those that accommodate religious minorities through the granting of limited exemptions from policies applying more broadly, do not, I have argued, represent derogations from liberal-democratic norms. Rather, they are logical implications of such norms when applied in contexts of cultural diversity. Their defenders need not appeal to any controversial perfectionist claim about the irreducible value of religion, nation, or ethno-cultural belonging. A doctrine and a practice of differentiated citizenship can simply be seen as the logical extension of the exercise by members of national minorities, by immigrants, and by members of religious groups of their liberal freedoms. The exercise of these rights is of course subject to limitations. The debate within liberal democracies and within actually existing liberal democratic states has to do with the extent of these limitations, rather than with the existence of the rights themselves. In particular, states eager to counter the centrifugal force of the exercise of liberal rights by members of ethno-cultural groups will have to identify justifications for the limitations of these rights and pursue through their policy a conception and a practice of united citizenship that does not itself offend against broadly liberal-democratic norms. Whether they are able to do so, or whether they decide instead to abandon liberal-democratic constraints when these are felt to be too constraining for the pursuit of unified citizenship, will be one of the questions that will animate much political philosophy, and much political debate, in the years to come.

---

[57] Jacob T. Levy, 'Multicultural Manners,' in Michel Seymour, ed., *The Plural States of Recognition* (London: Palgrave Macmillan, 2010), pp. 61–77.

BIBLIOGRAPHY

Barry, Brian, *Culture and Equality* (Oxford: Oxford University Press, 2000).

Basta, Karlo, John McGarry, and Richard Simeon, eds., *Territorial Pluralism: Managing Difference in Multinational States* (Vancouver: University of British Columbia Press, 2015).

Beiner, Ronald, *Civil Religion* (Cambridge: Cambridge University Press, 2012).

Brettschneider, Corey, *Democratic Rights: The Substance of Self-Government* (Princeton: Princeton University Press, 2009).

Buchanan, Allen, 'Liberalism and Group Rights,' in Jules L. Coleman and Allen Buchanan, eds., *In Harm's Way: Essays in Honor of Joel Feinberg* (Cambridge: Cambridge University Press, 1994), pp. 1–15.

Burtt, Shelley, 'In Defense of Yoder: Parental Authority and the Public Schools,' in Sanford Levinson, Joel Parker, and Paul Woodruff, eds., *Nomos LIV: Loyalty* (New York: NYU Press, 2013), pp. 412–437.

Carens, Joseph H., *The Ethics of Immigration* (Oxford: Oxford University Press, 2013).

Dagger, Richard, *Civic Virtues: Rights, Citizenship, and Republican Liberalism* (Oxford: Oxford University Press, 1997).

Dworkin, Ronald, *Religion without God* (Cambridge: Harvard University Press, 2013).

Fisher, Michael, *Migration: A World History* (Oxford: Oxford University Press, 2013).

Galston, William, *Liberal Pluralism: The Implications of Value Pluralism for Political Theory and Practice* (Cambridge: Cambridge University Press, 2002).

Gibney, Matthew, *The Ethics and Politics of Asylum: Liberal Democracy and the Response to Refugees* (Cambridge: Cambridge University Press, 2006).

Joppke, Christian, *Citizenship and Immigration* (Cambridge: Polity, 2010).

Kriegel, Blandine, *Philosophie de la république* (Paris: Plon, 1998).

Kymlicka, Will, *Liberalism, Community and Culture* (Oxford: Oxford University Press, 1989).

Kymlicka, Will, *Multicultural Citizenship* (Oxford: Oxford University Press, 1995).

Kymlicka, Will, 'Citizenship in an Era of Globalization,' in *Politics in the Vernacular* (Oxford: Oxford University Press, 2001), pp. 317–326.

Kymlicka, Will, *Multicultural Odysseys: Navigating the New International Politics of Diversity* (Oxford: Oxford University Press, 2009).

Kymlicka, Will and Wayne Norman, 'The Return of the Citizen: A Survey of Recent Work on Citizenship,' *Ethics 104*, no. 2 (1994): pp. 352–381.

Kymlicka, Will and Wayne Norman, 'Citizenship in Culturally Diverse Societies: Issues, Contexts, Concepts,' in Will Kymlicka and Wayne Norman, eds., *Citizenship in Diverse Societies* (Oxford: Oxford University Press, 2000), pp. 1–41.

Laborde, Cécile, 'Religion and the Law: The Disaggregation Approach,' *Law and Philosophy 34*, no. 6 (2015): pp. 581–600.

Laponce, Jean, *Languages and Their Territories* (Toronto: University of Toronto Press, 1987).

Leiter, Brian, *Why Tolerate Religion?* (Princeton: Princeton University Press, 2014).

Levey, Geoffrey Brahm and Tariq Modood, eds., *Secularism, Religion and Multicultural Citizenship* (Cambridge: Cambridge University Press, 2008).

Levy, Jacob T., 'Multicultural Manners,' in Michel Seymour, ed., *The Plural States of Recognition* (London: Palgrave Macmillan, 2010), pp. 61–77.

Loyola High School v. Quebec (Attorney General) 2015 SCC 12.

Mill, John Stuart, *On Liberty and Other Essays* (Oxford: Oxford University Press, 1991).

Miller, David, *On Nationality* (Oxford: Oxford University Press, 1997).

Miller, David, *Strangers in Our Midst: The Political Philosophy of Immigration* (Cambridge: Harvard University Press, 2016).

Muñiz-Fraticelli, Victor, *The Structure of Pluralism* (Oxford: Oxford University Press, 2014).

Okin, Susan Moller, *Is Multiculturalism Bad for Women?* (Princeton: Princeton University Press, 1999).

Parekh, Bhikhu, *Rethinking Multiculturalism*, 2nd edition (London: Palgrave Macmillan, 2006).

Quong, Jonathan, *Liberalism without Perfection* (Oxford: Oxford University Press, 2013).

Rawls, John, 'The Priority of the Right and Ideas of the Good,' *Philosophy and Public Affairs* 17, no. 4 (1988): pp. 251–276.

Rawls, John, *Political Liberalism* (New York: Columbia University Press, 1993).

Raz, Joseph, 'Multiculturalism: A Liberal Perspective,' *Ratio Juris 11*, no. 3 (1998): pp. 193–205.

Réaume, Denise, 'Official-Language Rights: Intrinsic Value and the Protection of Difference,' in Will Kymlicka and Wayne Norman, eds., *Citizenship in Diverse Societies* (Oxford: Oxford University Press, 2000), pp. 245–272.

Reich, Rob, 'Minors within Minorities: A Problem for Liberal Multiculturalists,' in Avigail Eisenberg and Jeff Spinner-Halev, eds., *Minorities within Minorities: Equality, Rights and Diversity* (Cambridge: Cambridge University Press, 2005), pp. 209–226.

Richardson, Henry, *Democratic Autonomy: Public Reasoning About the Ends of Policy* (Oxford: Oxford University Press, 2004).

Scott, David, 'Culture in Political Theory,' *Political Theory 31*, no. 1 (2003): pp. 92–115.

Shachar, Ayelet, *Multicultural Jurisdiction: Cultural Differences and Women's Rights* (Cambridge: Cambridge University Press, 2001).

Slote, Michael, 'Virtue Ethics,' in Marcia Baron, Philip Pettit, and Michael Slote, eds., *Three Methods of Ethics* (London: Routledge, 1997), pp. 175–238.

Spinner-Halev, Jeff, *Surviving Diversity: Religion and Democratic Citizenship* (Baltimore: Johns Hopkins University Press, 2000).

Taylor, Charles, *Multiculturalism and the Politics of Recognition* (Princeton: Princeton University Press, 1994).

Taylor, Charles, *The Language Animal* (Cambridge: Harvard University Press, 2016).

Taylor, Charles and Jocelyn Maclure, *Secularism and Freedom of Conscience* (Cambridge: Harvard University Press, 2011).

Tully, James, *Strange Multiplicity: Constitutionalism in an Age of Diversity* (Cambridge: Cambridge University Press, 1995).

Van Parijs, Philippe, 'Cultural Diversity against Economic Solidarity,' in Philippe Van Parijs, ed., *Cultural Diversity Versus Economic Solidarity* (Brussels: De Boeck, 2003), pp. 371–396.

Van Parijs, Philippe, *Linguistic Justice: For Europe, and for the World* (Oxford: Oxford University Press, 2011).

Viroli, Maurizio, *For Love of Country: An Essay on Patriotism and Nationalism* (Oxford: Oxford University Press, 1997).

Weinstock, Daniel, 'Building Trust in Divided Societies,' *Journal of Political Philosophy 7*, no. 3 (1999): pp. 287–307.

Weinstock, Daniel, 'How Can Liberalism and Collective Rights Be Reconciled?,' in Rainer Bauböck and John Rundell, eds., *Blurred Boundaries: Migration, Identity, Citizenship* (Aldershot: Ashgate, 1999), pp. 281–304.

Weinstock, Daniel, 'Constitutionalizing Secession,' *Journal of Political Philosophy* 9, no. 2 (2001): pp. 182–203.

Weinstock, Daniel, 'Prospects for Transnational Citizenship and Democracy,' *Ethics and International Affairs* 15, no. 2 (2001): pp. 53–66.

Weinstock, Daniel, 'Citizenship and Pluralism,' in Robert L. Simon, ed., *The Blackwell Guide to Social and Political Philosophy* (Oxford: Blackwell, 2002), pp. 239–267.

Weinstock, Daniel, 'Immigration and Reciprocity,' in Nils Holtug and Kasper Lippert-Rasmussen, eds., *Nationalism and Multiculturalism in a World of Immigration* (London: Palgrave Macmillan, 2009), pp. 174–193.

Weinstock, Daniel, 'In Praise of Some Unfashionable Democratic Institutions: Political Parties, Party Discipline, and "First Past the Post",' *Journal of Parliamentary and Political Law* 9 (2015): pp. 291–306.

Weinstock, Daniel, 'How the Interests of Children Limit the Religious Freedom of Parents,' in Cécile Laborde and Aurélia Bardon, eds., *Religion in Liberal Political Philosophy* (Oxford: Oxford University Press, forthcoming).

White, Stuart, *The Civic Minimum: On the Rights and Obligations of Economic Citizenship* (Oxford: Oxford University Press, 2003).

Young, Iris Marion, *Justice and the Politics of Difference* (Princeton: Princeton University Press, 1990).

CHAPTER 14

CITIZENSHIP AND THE FRANCHISE

JO SHAW

INTRODUCTION

THE right to vote in elections and referendums and to stand for election is one of the most important formal legal indicators or 'hallmarks' of citizenship.[1] Elections of representatives are core elements of the democratic production and reproduction of political communities. Referendums constitute acts of direct democracy, some of which are crucial for the purposes of renewing or creating polities or for

---

[1] Piers Gardner, ed., *Citizenship: The White Paper* (London: Institute for Citizenship Studies/ BIICL, 2007).

reforming in important ways the basic constitutions of democratic polities. Modern democracies are unthinkable without universal suffrage,[2] and international law recognizes this in the form of the universal and equal suffrage guarantees in texts such as Article 21 of the Universal Declaration of Human Rights, Article 25 of the International Covenant on Civil and Political Rights, and Article 3 of Protocol 1 of the European Convention of Human Rights and Fundamental Freedoms (ECHR). The right to vote forms part of the general political freedoms allowing citizens to participate fully in the government of their countries.

Thus from a legal and political perspective, the act of voting seems obvious. It is the individual fulfilment of a right that allows for the collective self-fulfilment of a self-governing community. The challenges involved in defining the boundaries of this community and of applying these boundaries in practice are reviewed in detail elsewhere in this volume,[3] and the implications for suffrage rights are briefly discussed in the following section. We start from the supposition that the franchise[4] represents the legal articulation of political membership, although the contours of this membership are complex and contested. We then explore the history and struggles associated with extensions of and restrictions placed upon suffrage rights, which mean that both historically and also at the present time not all citizens can vote in all elections in all countries, and in some countries political membership incorporates (at least some) non-citizens as well. The particular challenges relating to immigration, emigration, and diasporas are also examined.

Finally, we turn our attention to voting in referendums and similar mechanisms of direct democracy, in particular those that have the effect of creating, renewing, or reforming polities. In such a context, the boundary problem has a particular meaning, as these political acts are specifically concerned with constructing and re-constructing (new) boundaries across territory (e.g. a new seceding state) or sometimes 'horizontally' between polities operating at different 'levels' (e.g. new sub-state or supra-state entities).

While the act of voting may seem self-evidently valuable to scholars of law and politics, given its affinity to discourses of rights and democracy, it is less obviously so for adherents of public choice theory. Scholars since Downs[5] have pointed out that, whatever the collective benefits, for the individual, considering costs and benefits,

---

[2] Daniele Caramani and Florian Grotz, 'Beyond Citizenship and Residence? Exploring the Extension of Voting Rights in the Age of Globalization', *Democratization* 22, no. 5 (2015): pp. 799–819.

[3] Bauböck in this volume.

[4] In this chapter, the words franchise and suffrage are used broadly interchangeably. 'Suffrage' is strongly associated with historical struggles and with many legal instruments which use the term 'universal suffrage'. However, 'the franchise' is a useful umbrella term for expressing the legal and political possibilities of formally accessing the mechanisms of structured political choice such as elections and referendums, and can include both the active (right to vote) and passive (right to stand or be elected) elements.

[5] Anthony Downs, *An Economic Theory of Democracy* (New York: Harper and Row, 1957).

it may not seem rational to vote. One vote will almost never sway an election. For some groups such as external voters,[6] the costs are even greater than for others, and indeed they do depress participation rates. While affording the right to vote in local elections to non-citizens might be seen as an effort to enhance inclusion, in practice other social and economic factors including language barriers and registration difficulties often continue to depress political participation rates below those of the resident citizen population. Yet voting may nonetheless assist in affording a 'we feeling' for a community that has both an individual and collective dimension to it. This can offset the costs of voting. This ideal is the premise that underlies the analysis here.

There are several steps from the franchise to the vote, many of which reduce participation in practice. These include registration and procedural requirements which may be harder for some groups to fulfil than others, and which may thus skew the outcomes of elections. Controversies in the USA surrounding voter registration, voter ID laws, and the Federal control over state measures on voting included in the Voting Rights Act until the Supreme Court case of *Shelby County v. Holder* in 2013[7] all highlight the contested terrain of voting rights practice, especially in election years such as 2016.[8] Aside from the minority (n=<30) of countries that have compulsory voting,[9] there are also social, economic, and cultural factors which affect turnout and, in some circumstances, factors affecting the way in which votes are counted[10] which in turn mediate the character of 'right to vote' when viewed from a 'street-level' rather than an 'in the books' perspective. Similar factors impact upon the right to stand for election, and these have often had the effect of reducing the numbers of women or minority ethnic or indigenous group candidates when compared to the general population. This is even before we reach the point of competing for votes, where again such candidates face obstacles to gaining political traction in the media, with political parties, and amongst the voting public.

Bearing in mind that there are many other 'citizenship acts'[11] that complete the full picture of political participation, including the utilization of political freedoms

---

[6] See Collyer in this volume.   [7] *Shelby County v. Holder* 133 S. Ct. 2612.

[8] For brief analysis see Brennan Center for Justice, 'Voting Laws Round-Up', online http://www.brennancenter.org/analysis/voting-laws-roundup-2016; Suevon Lee and Sarah Smith, 'Everything You've Ever Wanted to Know About Voter ID Laws', *Pro Publica*, 9 March 2016, online https://www.propublica.org/article/everything-youve-ever-wanted-to-know-about-voter-id-laws.

[9] IDEA, 'Compulsory Voting', online http://www.idea.int/vt/compulsory_voting.cfm. For an analysis see Sarah Birch, *Full Participation: A Comparative Study of Compulsory Voting* (Manchester: Manchester University Press, 2009).

[10] The outcome of the second round of the 2016 Austrian Presidential Election was annulled and ordered to be rerun by the Constitutional Court, on the grounds that some postal votes were mishandled. However, at the time of writing, the re-run itself was set to be postponed after further difficulties with the handling of postal votes were uncovered ('Presidential Re-Run Faces Delay as Austria Comes Unglued', *Financial Times*, 9 September 2016, online https://www.ft.com/content/e7c746f2-7695-11e6-b60a-de4532d5ea35).

[11] Engin Isin, 'Theorizing Acts of Citizenship', in Engin Isin and Greg Nielsen, eds., *Acts of Citizenship*, (London: Palgrave Macmillan, 2008).

such as speech and assembly, political party formation and engagement, and political activism and activation beyond the electoral sphere for citizens and non-citizens alike, this chapter necessarily presents only a limited snapshot of a bigger picture in its focus on the formal right to vote, to stand for election, and to participate in referendums. The premise on which this chapter proceeds is that democracy as a whole is not constituted simply by the franchise and rights to vote, but that the franchise is an important first step, deserving of detailed analysis in its own terms.

The Boundary Problem:
the Interrelationship between Citizenship Status and the Franchise

Citizenship 'creates a legal bond between individual members and a state and endows these individuals with certain rights and obligations'.[12] Stretching or diminishing the scope of citizenship has a significant impact upon a number of important dimensions of the state and political membership, and highlights the fact that citizenship, as marking out a bounded community, necessarily has a 'boundary problem'. We need to examine the political accountability of those who can set these boundaries and the process whereby boundaries are set, as well as the substantive content of 'boundary rules'. If it is the citizenry who decide who the citizenry will be in the future—and what rights and duties they will have—then the process of determining the boundary is ultimately purely internal, circular in character, and potentially lacking in legitimacy.[13] There are both practical and normative implications that arise from the setting of boundaries, in terms of deciding who can vote.

For example, what if political membership (either the formal hallmark of citizenship and/or the right to vote itself) were to be restricted only to those persons whose grandfathers were citizens or had the right to vote? Applying principles of equality, we can quickly see that such restrictions are unfair and illegitimate, as they would exclude all newcomers across at least two generations from self-government. They also distinguish between men and women in an arbitrary manner. This may be an

---

[12] Maarten Vink and Rainer Bauböck, 'Citizenship Configurations: Analysing the Multiple Purposes of Citizenship Regimes in Europe', *Comparative European Politics* 11, no. 5 (2013): pp. 621–648, p. 622.

[13] David Owen, 'Constituting the Polity, Constituting the Demos: On the Place of the All Affected Interests Principle in Democratic Theory and in Resolving the Democratic Boundary Problem', *Ethics and Global Politics* 5, no. 3 (2012): pp. 129–152.

egregious example, but it reminds us that choices are made in all polities as to where to set the boundaries of the suffrage and that these will tell us much about the character of any given democracy.

Commentators often focus on the question of the inclusion of newcomers (i.e. immigrants) as the baseline for outlining what model of citizenship a polity has adopted and for ascertaining the democratic and normative principles on which it is based. For example, the citizenship-based or 'national' approach[14] holds that immigrants should only acquire the right to vote *after* acquiring citizenship and that the acquisition of citizenship (e.g. by naturalization) should afford the polity the opportunity to test the degree of engagement of the newcomer with the society into which he or she has entered. Such an approach tends to prioritize the claims of those who acquire citizenship *at birth* over those whose claim to membership is 'merely' based on residence in the polity. Yet others have argued that residence itself should be an ascriptive mechanism for the inclusion of newcomers to ensure that their right to participate is upheld.[15]

The logic of some approaches to setting boundaries, such as the 'all affected interests' principle,[16] holds not only that all those who are within the territorial jurisdiction of the polity should be included but also, potentially, a wider range of persons (regardless of their citizenship) who could be *affected* by the extraterritorial impacts of choices made within the polity (e.g. on matters such as environmental policy which cannot be confined within territorial borders). They too should be given a voice. This is distinct from the usual approach to defending the external participation rights of *citizens*, which are premised less on the present claims of individuals who are located outside the territory as on the ongoing attachment which stems from such individuals being citizens in the formal sense. Principles such as 'all affected interests' could be criticized for being over-inclusive and also lacking coherent boundaries. A related approach involves focusing on the potential negative externalities of any given decision as the basis for according the right to vote.[17] Under that perspective, it is the impact on *rights* not *interests* that matters.

Likewise going beyond a focus primarily on incomers is Bauböck's stakeholder citizenship approach, as his model encompasses *external* citizenship and the right to vote of non-resident citizens as well as the issue of the appropriate treatment of newcomers to the polity (i.e. how long, if at all, should they wait before being able to

[14] David Miller, 'Immigrants, Nations and Citizenship', *Journal of Political Philosophy* 16, no. 4 (2008): pp. 371–390.

[15] Joseph H. Carens, *The Ethics of Immigration* (Oxford: Oxford University Press, 2013); Ruth Rubio Marín, *Immigration as a Democratic Challenge* (Cambridge: Cambridge University Press, 2000).

[16] Robert Goodin, 'Enfranchising All Affected Interests, and Its Alternatives', *Philosophy and Public Affairs* 35, no. 1 (2007): pp. 40–68.

[17] Ben Saunders, 'Defining the Demos', *Politics, Philosophy and Economics* 11, no. 3 (2014): pp. 280–301.

participate in elections).[18] Defining 'stakeholdership' thus sets justifiable boundaries for political membership. Bauböck combines 'stakeholdership' with the concept of citizenship *constellations* to highlight the importance of the interactions between sending and receiving countries in migration contexts, and to articulate the impact of citizenship ascription decisions in the context of secession and polity break-up.[19] 'Stakeholdership' can be, as his chapter in this volume demonstrates, sensitive not only to the interactions between multiple polities and their citizenries, but also between different 'nested' polities, as in the case of the EU Member States *within* the context of the European Union (and within the context, in several states, of an internal federal or quasi-federal distribution of powers). 'Rightsizing' the *demos* is therefore a task that needs to take into consideration the multi-layered character of citizenship rights and practices in multi-level constitutional contexts as well as the multiple interactions between different states in the international domain.[20]

The key point to emphasize is that there is a tension between the boundaries of the suffrage, the boundaries of the citizenry, and the literal territorial boundaries of the polity (i.e. who can gain admission). Under conditions of increasing globalization, it is clear that there is not a perfect congruence between citizenship, territory, and sovereignty, and indeed there never has been. The task then is to settle the most appropriate way of dealing with this where states are not the only relevant determinants of membership, and where states themselves have overlapping and blurred boundaries. Some states institute multiple obstacles to participation, leading to claims for more inclusion,[21] while others are more open and permeable. The EU is an interesting case. While the Member States still 'own' national citizenship (as a gateway for EU citizenship), they must give certain rights to mobile EU citizens, including rights of residence, access to the labour market and many other social goods, and the principle of non-discrimination. Yet free movement has become much more controversial in the EU in recent years, not least because of the challenges it poses to the citizenship regimes of the Member States, for example because of the rights of EU citizens to vote in the host state local elections (see below).

---

[18] Rainer Bauböck, 'Stakeholder Citizenship and Transnational Political Participation: A Normative Evaluation of External Voting', *Fordham Law Review 75*, no. 5 (2007): pp. 2393–2447.

[19] Rainer Bauböck, 'Studying Citizenship Constellations', *Journal of Ethnic and Migration Studies 36*, no. 5 (2010): pp. 847–859.

[20] Rainer Bauböck, 'Morphing the Demos into the Right Shape. Normative Principles for Enfranchising Resident Aliens and Expatriate Citizens', *Democratization 22*, no. 5 (2015): pp. 820–839; Jean-Thomas Arrighi and Rainer Bauböck, 'A Multilevel Puzzle: Migrants' Voting Rights in National and Local Elections', *European Journal of Political Research* (forthcoming 2016), doi: 10.1111/1475-6765.12176.

[21] Cristina Rodríguez, 'Noncitizen Voting and the Extraconstitutional Construction of the Polity', *International Constitutional Law Journal 8*, no. 1 (2010): pp. 30–49; Heather Lardy, 'Citizenship and the Right to Vote', *Oxford Journal of Legal Studies 17* (1997): pp. 75–100; Ludvig Beckmann, 'Citizenship and Voting Rights: Should Resident Aliens Vote?', *Citizenship Studies 10*, no. 1 (2006): pp. 153–165.

Furthermore, external citizenship is often vitally important for understanding a polity's broad approach to ascribing membership,[22] and yet internal and external inclusivity often do not go hand in hand. However, in contrast to the case of resident non-citizens whose political participation rights are still relatively sparse, the non-resident citizens seem to have gained greater traction on the body politic in terms of the argument for widening the suffrage, as shown below.

In practice, different models of membership[23] remain hard to match to actually existing political circumstances in any pure form. In his chapter, Bauböck provides examples to highlight the bewildering complexity of boundary problems in real world situations. The United Kingdom, which enjoys a complex and confusing interaction between the rules on citizenship and the right to vote, illustrates the point well. In the UK, the status of citizenship and its associated rights and duties resemble a historical bricolage more than they do a coherent constitutional design.[24] These include the right to vote and to stand in all UK elections for citizens of the countries of the Commonwealth of Nations (most but not all of which were former British colonies) and of Ireland.[25] So when this historical patchwork of voting rights came under review in a report on citizenship commissioned by then Prime Minister Gordon Brown,[26] it quickly became apparent that a decision by the UK legislature to exclude Irish citizens from the UK franchise, except where their participation is presently demanded by EU law, would have profound implications in Northern Ireland under the terms of the Good Friday Agreement. This creates a form of UK/Republic of Ireland condominium across the province, especially in relation to citizenship matters. When politicians weigh up the desirability of a neat political settlement for citizenship rights against the challenges of maintaining peace and good neighbourly relations in a place like Northern Ireland, they may understandably opt for the latter.

Similarly, in Latin America ebbing and flowing patterns of democratization and retreat from democracy, waves of immigration and emigration, and post-colonial industrialization have had an impact on a complex pattern of citizenship regimes, including the granting and withdrawal of voting rights for non-citizen residents and non-resident citizens over many years.[27] Escobar argues that while

---

[22] Bauböck (n 20).

[23] Jo Shaw and Anja Lansbergen, 'National Membership Models in a Multi-Level Europe', *International Journal of Constitutional Law 8*, no. 1 (2010): pp. 50–71.

[24] Caroline Sawyer and Helena Wray, *United Kingdom*, EUDO Citizenship Country Report on Citizenship Law (December 2014), online http://www.eudo-citizenship.eu.

[25] Lamin Khadar, *Access to Electoral Rights: United Kingdom* (EUDO Citizenship Observatory, June 2013), online http://eudo-citizenship.eu/admin/?p=file&appl=countryProfiles&f=1310-UK-FRACIT.pdf.

[26] Lord Goldsmith QC, *Citizenship: Our Common Bond*, Citizenship Review (March 2008), online http://webarchive.nationalarchives.gov.uk/+/http://www.justice.gov.uk/docs/citizenship-report-full.pdf.

[27] Cristina Escobar, 'Immigrant Enfranchisement in Latin America: From Strongmen to Universal Citizenship', *Democratization 22*, no. 5 (2015): pp. 927–950.

historically most changes could be put down to domestic factors, more recently exogenous factors including globalization, foreign relations, and regional integration have influenced countries in legislating on the scope of citizenship and voting rights.

THE 'SELECTION' OF VOTERS: LEGAL, POLITICAL, AND HISTORICAL CONSIDERATIONS

In a democracy, laws regulate who can vote in an election or a referendum, or stand for election.[28] In many instances the basic principle lies in the constitution, which is then a reference point for any challenges to the principle of universal suffrage. One interesting case where this is not so, at least not in an explicit manner, is in the USA where (restricted) access to the ballot box for certain groups has been an enduring and intensely racialized theme[29] of the country's democratic evolution. Amongst the legal and administrative mechanisms that continue to depress political participation amongst racial minorities in recent years, felon disenfranchisement has come to stand out. Nor is there an express constitutional right to vote in the UK, although it has been suggested that were Parliament to enact an egregious restriction on universal suffrage the courts could interfere with such an Act of Parliament by invoking a 'common law right'.[30]

In addition to national (and sometimes subnational) law, European and international law may also impose legal constraints on the exercise of this 'sovereign' power. As noted earlier the right to vote in democratic elections in the form of

[28] Information about the conditions for accessing electoral rights in many European and American countries is available from the EUDO Citizenship website: http://eudo-citizenship.eu/electoral-rights/conditions-for-electoral-rights-2015.

[29] Alexander Keyssar, *The Right to Vote. The Contested History of Democracy in the United States* (New York: Basic Books, 2000).

[30] *Moohan and Another v. Lord Advocate* [2014] UKSC 67 (prisoner voting and the Scottish referendum) briefly discussed by Court of Appeal in *Shindler and Maclennan v. Chancellor of the Duchy of Lancaster and Secretary of State for Foreign and Commonwealth Affairs* [2016] EWHC 957 (Admin) on the exclusion from the EU referendum franchise of UK citizens resident outside the UK for more than fifteen years. See Jo Shaw, 'Unions and Citizens: Membership Status and Political Rights in Scotland, the UK and the EU', in Carlos Closa, ed., *Secession from a Member State and Withdrawal from the European Union: Troubled Membership* (Cambridge: Cambridge University Press, forthcoming 2017).

'universal suffrage' is enshrined in a number of international instruments, and there could be said to be a consensus in international law.[31] It has been explicitly recognized by the European Court of Justice in respect of voting in European Parliament elections.[32] The European Court of Human Rights has discussed the scope of Article 3 of Protocol 1 extensively.[33] One can cite also the work of international bodies such as the Venice Commission of the Council of Europe and the UNHCR which specialize in the production of 'soft law'. They have pushed in the direction of common standards in some difficult areas, for example facilitating the political participation of refugees in the politics of the state of origin (a special case of out-of-country voting) and ensuring that they have rights to participate in the state of residence even in advance of acquisition of citizenship.[34] While the principle is well established, there is however no consensus in relation to the legitimate restrictions that may be placed upon such a right by states, in particular in relation to prisoner disenfranchisement and mental capacity and thus mixed evidence about any convergence around liberal norms amongst states.

While the most blatant gender-based or race-based examples of restrictions on the suffrage have now been removed, at least in the more stable and well developed democracies, polities can and do apply various tests of residence, age, capacity/competence, and probity in order to determine the scope of the franchise, and apply different rules for different classes of elections or votes. The history of the franchise is one of contestation and social struggles, paralleling the history of struggles by certain groups to be seen as full citizens. Persons without property or who were illiterate, women, and people of colour including indigenous peoples were routinely denied the vote during the nineteenth and well into the twentieth centuries, precisely because they were not seen as 'full' citizens denied capacity in the same way that children, for example, are still generally denied the right to vote. If these groups were not full citizens it was simply 'natural' that they should not have full civil, political, and indeed social rights. The outcomes of these struggles can be seen in legislation and sometimes in judgments of courts, as in the famous 'Persons' case in Canada in the 1920s.[35]

There is ongoing debate about the triggers of change, especially in relation to the most significant franchise extensions, namely those to working class men and

---

[31] Shai Dothan, 'Comparative Views on the Right to Vote in International Law: The Case of Prisoners' Disenfranchisement', in Anthea Roberts, Pierre Verdier, Paul Stephan, and Mila Versteeg, *Comparative International Law* (Oxford: Oxford University Press, 2016).

[32] Judgment of 6 October 2015, *Delvigne v. Commune de Lesparre Médoc and Préfet de la Gironde* C-650/13, EU:C:2015:648.

[33] Judgment of 6 October 2005, *Hirst v. the United Kingdom* (no. 2) 74025/01, CE:ECHR:2005:1006JUD007402501; Judgment of 22 May 2012, *Scoppola v. Italy* (no. 3) [GC] 126/05, CE:ECHR:2012:0522JUD000012605.

[34] Ruvi Ziegler, *Voting Rights of Refugees* (Cambridge: Cambridge University Press, 2017).

[35] *Edwards v. Canada (AG)* [1930] A.C. 124.

to women, as well as the removal of explicit racial bars. Was the vote struggled for, as class, gender, or racial politics might suggest, or conceded legislatively as part of a wider modernization process[36] in which parties competed for electoral success which a wider electorate might assist? Important national and international social movements pushed towards women's suffrage and there were dramatic changes between the end of the nineteenth century and the middle of the twentieth century.[37] But Teele argues that the granting of the vote to women in the UK was the result of a bargain between the more reformist parts of the women's movement struggling for suffrage and the nascent Labour Party, rather than social movement pressure.[38] Elsewhere, some historians of democratization have spoken of the impact of the wars and emergency situations, generating the need for armies and labour that have liberated previously disenfranchised groups, including working class men.[39] Certainly the story of women's suffrage is not simple. In Europe, for example, 'modern' states often denied women political rights they had exercised under so-called 'ancien' regimes.[40] Rubio Marín describes this as an 'inverted pathway'. For decades, women remained vulnerable to the risk of losing franchise rights they thought they had acquired in one state as a result of the almost universal practice of marital denaturalization.[41] Even today gender-based restrictions still retain some traction: for example, women were only allowed to vote for the first time in Saudi Arabia in municipal elections in December 2015.

In the USA, the story of restrictions on the right to vote is fully embedded within the broader post-slavery story of gradual black emancipation. While significant constitutional and legislative steps have been taken including the 15th Amendment and the Voting Rights Act 1965, especially at the federal level, at the state and local level *de jure* and *de facto* restrictions have proved remarkably enduring and have continued to damage the democratic fabric of the country. As was the case in many Latin American countries,[42] racially focused restrictions have often acquired the surrogate form of a literacy requirement. From the nineteenth through to the twenty-first century, many of the same concerns have coalesced about the issue of felon disenfranchisement,

---

[36] Adam Przeworski, 'Conquered or Granted? A History of Suffrage Extensions', *British Journal of Political Science 39*, no. 2 (2009): pp 291–321.

[37] Francisco Ramirez, Yasemin Soysal, and Suzanne Shanahan, 'The Changing Logic of Political Citizenship: Cross-National Acquisition of Women's Suffrage Rights, 1890–1990', *American Sociological Review 62* (October 1997): pp. 735–745.

[38] Dawn Teele, 'Ordinary Democratization: The Electoral Strategy That Won British Women the Vote', *Politics & Society 42*, no. 4 (2014): pp. 537–561.

[39] Ruth Berins Collier, *Paths toward Democracy: The Working Class and Elites in Western Europe and South America* (Cambridge: Cambridge University Press, 1999).

[40] Ruth Rubio Marín, 'The Achievement of Female Suffrage in Europe: On Women's Citizenship', *International Journal of Constitutional Law 12*, no. 1 (2014): pp. 4–34.

[41] Helen Irving, *Citizenship, Alienage and the Modern Constitutional State: A Gendered History* (Cambridge: Cambridge University Press, 2016).

[42] Tanya Hernandez, *Racial Subordination in Latin America. The Role of the State, Customary Law, and the New Civil Rights Response* (Cambridge: Cambridge University Press, 2014).

which is a standard and often permanent consequence of certain criminal convictions in the USA. This practice disproportionately impacts African Americans and it may have affected the outcomes of elections, including the 2000 US Presidential Election.[43]

Restrictions on prisoner voting are common in many other countries, albeit rarely with the same scope or effects as in the USA. In the UK, the issue of prisoner voting has become a lightning conductor for more general discontent with the impact of the UK's adherence to the ECHR, after the judgment in *Hirst (No. 2)*[44] established that the UK's current blanket ban on convicted prisoners voting infringed Article 3 of Protocol 1 and could not be saved by the principle that allows contracting states a certain level of discretion when it comes to implementing rights within a democratic society. There is an ongoing dispute between the UK's political authorities (executive and legislature) and the Court of Human Rights, with the UK Courts and the Council of Europe's political authorities standing in the middle. The UK's approach, with such a broad ban, is out of line with that across most of Europe[45] and indeed that of other states such as Australia.[46] Politically and normatively, there is no consensus about whether (all or some) prisoners should vote.[47]

Also of interest, and perhaps an example of the effective international diffusion of norms, have been the trends towards a widening of access to the franchise for persons with mental disabilities or suffering from mental illness. This has been tracked by the European Union's Fundamental Rights Agency,[48] buttressing case law of the European Court of Human Rights. Pointing out that restrictions on vulnerable social groups which have faced considerable discrimination in the past demand very weighty justifications, in *Alajos Kiss v. Hungary,* the Court overturned a blanket provision which denied voting rights to mentally disabled people under partial guardianship in Hungary.[49] New measures were introduced in Hungary after the judgment to permit case-by-case scrutiny by a judge of whether a person who is under guardianship should be disenfranchised.

Worldwide large numbers of countries continue to have blanket bans on the participation of those with mental impairments. In the USA, more than forty states disenfranchise people based on their mental status. Like so many other restrictions on the right to vote, this can have effects that are more restrictive of the voting rights of

---

[43] See Christopher Uggen and Jeff Manza, 'Democratic Contraction? Political Consequences of Felon Disenfranchisement in the United States', *American Sociological Review* 67, no. 6 (2002); pp. 777–803.

[44] *Hirst v. the United Kingdom* (n 33).   [45] Dothan (n 31).

[46] Jerome Davidson, 'Inside Outcasts: Prisoners and the Right to Vote in Australia', *Current Issues Brief*, no. 12 2003-2004, online http://apo.org.au/resource/inside-outcasts-prisoners-and-right-vote-australia.

[47] Peter Ramsay, 'Voters Should not be in Prison! The Rights of Prisoners in a Democracy', *Critical Review of International Social and Political Philosophy* 16, no. 3 (2013): pp. 421–438.

[48] Fundamental Rights Agency, *The Right to Political Participation of Persons with Mental Health Problems and Persons with Intellectual Disabilities* (Luxembourg: Publications Office of the European Union, 2013).

[49] Judgment of 20 May 2010, *Alajos Kiss v. Hungary* 38832/06, CE:ECHR:2010:0520JUD003883206.

African Americans and Native Americans, who are disproportionately affected by mental illness.[50] The same could be true in Australia,[51] when combined with the fact that Aboriginal Australians are over-represented in the prison population, prisoners are more prone to mental illness, and prisoners serving sentences of more than three years lose the right to vote. This contributes to an outcome where only 58 per cent of Indigenous Australians are registered to vote.[52]

States also continue to impose restrictions on standing for (high) office on naturalized citizens or citizens born outside the territory (most famously the US President) and on dual citizens. Here the traditional question mark over the loyalty of those apparently owing allegiance to two sovereigns raises its head, although in many other spheres states have lifted their opposition to dual citizenship. In the *Tanase* case involving parliamentary elections in Moldova,[53] the European Court of Human Rights held that a dual citizenship restriction on standing for election was intended to have political effects rather than to protect the sovereignty of the state, and was thus contrary to Article 3 of Protocol 1 of the ECHR.

RIGHT-SIZING THE ELECTORATE
IN CONTEXTS OF MIGRATION

Mobility and migration (immigration and emigration) provide important laboratories for social scientists to figure out how and why states make certain choices about voting rights, as well as for lawyers and political theorists to observe the real world traction of the models of the *demos* that they construct (see above). In other words, the issue sets up both policy and normative challenges. The main policy contexts here are diaspora engagement (i.e. citizenship, voting rights, and other policies to engage those not on the territory) and the integration of immigrants (measures to support the voting rights and practices of those who do not have citizenship or who recently acquired it). As Bauböck has argued,[54] the two questions are interconnected

[50] Rabia Belt, *Mental Disability and the Right to Vote* (PhD Dissertation, University of Michigan, 2015), online https://deepblue.lib.umich.edu/handle/2027.42/116625.

[51] For a summary of the right to vote in Australia, see Australian Human Rights Comission, 'The Right to Vote is not Enjoyed Equally by all Austalians' (February 2010), online https://www.humanrights.gov.au/our-work/rights-and-freedoms/publications/right-vote-not-enjoyed-equally-all-australians#f20a.

[52] Paul Daley, 'Only 58% of Indigenous Australians are Registered to Vote. We Should be Asking why', *The Guardian*, 30 June 2016, online https://www.theguardian.com/commentisfree/2016/jun/30/only-58-of-indigenous-australians-are-registered-to-vote-we-should-be-asking-why.

[53] Judgment of 27 April 2010, *Tanase v. Moldova* 7/08, CE:ECHR:2010:0427JUD000000708.

[54] Bauböck (n 20).

in significant ways, as are the questions of access to citizenship and access to the franchise. For example, in the USA, many Asian immigrants were effectively excluded from the franchise for many decades because they were refused access to citizenship by a combination of legislation such as the Chinese Exclusion Act of 1882 and case law which interpreted access to naturalization as being restricted to 'free white people'. In contrast, those of Asian descent born in the USA did benefit from the *jus soli* protection of the 14th Amendment.[55] The other important interconnection is between the policies and laws that grant (or deny) political participation rights and the voting behaviour and political participation of those subject to these policies. This chapter concentrates only on the first of these elements.

Some polities permit resident non-citizens to vote. More than sixty countries worldwide allow for some or all resident non-citizens to vote in some or all local or municipal elections, but fewer than ten countries allow some or all resident non-citizens to vote in national elections.[56] The best known case of so-called 'alien suffrage' is undoubtedly the European Union, which requires its Member States, since the Maastricht Treaty, to confer the right to vote in local (and European Parliament) elections on resident (i.e. mobile) non-national EU citizens. This is a unique (thus far) example of international impact upon domestic voting rights legislation and of a comprehensive reciprocal framework, with limited examples of upgrades and adjustments. The UK gives the right to vote and to stand for election to EU citizens in the elections to devolved bodies and legislatures (e.g. Scotland and Wales) under UK law. When Slovenia introduced EU voting rights prior to its accession in 2004, it included the right to vote (but not to stand for election) for third country nationals in its new legislation. Belgium and Luxembourg have benefited from limited additional derogations based on certain demographic conditions, allowing the imposition of additional residence tests on voters. In Austria and Germany, where certain cities are simultaneously also 'states' under the national federal systems, EU citizens only have the right to vote in low level civic councils with few meaningful powers.

Beyond those requirements, some EU states have instituted local electoral rights for all non-citizens (i.e. including third country nationals) with stable residence (i.e. satisfying a qualifying residence period), in most cases quite separately from the measures taken in relation to EU citizens: Belgium, Ireland, Luxembourg, Netherlands, Denmark, Sweden, Finland, Estonia, Lithuania, Hungary, Slovakia, and Slovenia.[57] In Ireland, Netherlands, and the Nordic states, these rights predate the Maastricht Treaty.

---

[55] Ian Haney Lopez, *White by Law* (New York: NYU Press, 2006).

[56] Rainer Bauböck, 'Expansive Citizenship: Voting beyond Territory and Membership', *PS: Political Science and Politics 38*, no. 4 (2005): pp. 683–687; on the EU28 see Iseult Honohan and Derek Hutcheson, 'Transnational Citizenship and Access to Electoral Rights: Defining the Demos in European States', in Johan Elkink and David M. Farrell, eds., *The Act of Voting: Identities, Institutions and Locale* (London, New York: Routledge, 2015), pp. 59–79.

[57] See Jo Shaw, *The Transformation of Citizenship in the European Union* (Cambridge: Cambridge University Press, 2007), pp. 76–82.

All bar Belgium, Luxembourg, Estonia, Hungary, and Slovenia have granted also the right to stand for election. Unsurprisingly, there is considerable overlap between this group of states and the EU Member States that have ratified or signed the 1992 Council of Europe Convention on the Political Participation of Foreigners in Local Life which commits its signatories to ensuring political freedoms for non-nationals and local electoral rights.[58] In a number of states there are also arrangements for selected groups of third country nationals to vote in local elections either on the basis of historic ties (Commonwealth and Irish citizens in the UK) or on the basis of reciprocity arrangements (often, but not always, coupled with historic ties). Reciprocity arrangements exist in Portugal (on the basis of citizenship of a Portuguese-speaking country),[59] and in Spain (originally only applicable to Norway, but extended as of 2009 towards Bolivia, Cape Verde, Chile, Colombia, Ecuador, Iceland, New Zealand, and Uruguay).[60]

Looking beyond Europe, the Commonwealth of Nations, already referred to above, is an important framework within which reciprocal electoral rights are allocated to resident non-citizens (e.g. in Caribbean countries). In Latin America, Escobar[61] has highlighted quite a strong trend towards immigrant suffrage in local elections, albeit under varied conditions and according to a variety of timescales, mapped against processes of state formation and reformation and the ebbs and flows of democratic and authoritarian government on that continent. Meanwhile, very few countries allow non-citizens to vote in national elections—the UK (Commonwealth and Irish citizens), Ireland (UK citizens) and Barbados, Uruguay and New Zealand (non-citizens satisfying certain residence requirements) being amongst that small group. In 2015 a referendum was held in Luxembourg on the question of giving electoral rights in national elections to migrants, but the proposal was rejected by 78 per cent of voters.[62]

Rodríguez argues that it is hard to discern clear patterns driving the decision to grant or to deny voting rights for third country nationals in elections, across groups of states.[63] Her comparison of the USA, New Zealand, and Ireland—states which all have a history and/or a present practice of alien suffrage—indicates that there is no fixed relationship between granting electoral rights, the national constitutional structure, or evolving perceptions of immigration. Shifts between immigration and emigration can indeed be significant, as Escobar has shown in the case

---

[58] ETS No. 144; opened for signature on 5 February 1992; entered into force on 1 May 1997.

[59] Claire Healy, *Access to Electoral Rights: Portugal* (EUDO Citizenship Observatory, June 2013), online http://eudo-citizenship.eu/admin/?p=file&appl=countryProfiles&f=138-PT-FRACIT.pdf.

[60] Ángel Rodríguez, *Access to Electoral Rights: Spain* (EUDO Citizenship Observatory, June 2013), online http://eudo-citizenship.eu/admin/?p=file&appl=countryProfiles&f=1315-Spain-FRACIT.pdf.

[61] Escobar (n 27).

[62] Michèle Finck, 'Towards an Ever Closer Union Between Residents and Citizens?', *European Constitutional Law Review 11*, no. 1 (2015): pp. 78–98.

[63] Rodríguez (n 21).

of Latin America.[64] Likewise, we can see the impact of constitutional practices. Constitutional blockages have restrained subnational entities from proceeding with more liberal policies towards third country national voters where political opinion has differed from the national-level mainstream in Germany and Austria.[65] In Ireland in the 1980s a similar constitutional blockage was removed by means of a referendum to permit UK citizens to vote in Irish national elections (but not referendums, Senate Elections, or Presidential elections). Ultimately it is hard to generalize simply on the basis of case studies, and Rodríguez concludes that 'a society's decision to adopt a particular set of alien suffrage practices reflects its own political culture'.[66]

One way of dealing with the voting rights of immigrants is simply to transfer the decision to the sphere of citizenship acquisition: immigrants may only vote after naturalization. Many states do choose that route, and consequently attention shifts to the question of how restrictive or liberal states are in relation to naturalization. Rodríguez again suggests there is no firm correlation between the decision to grant or to deny electoral rights to non-nationals and the specific approach which a polity opts for in relation to the broader issue of immigrant incorporation. In other words, it does not map directly onto what might be viewed as an overall open or restrictive policy focus. Nor is there necessarily a direct relationship between approaches to electoral rights and the possibility of citizenship acquisition, either via the time limits, conditions, and procedures attaching to naturalisation, or via the willingness of certain polities to give *jus soli* citizenship to the children of non-citizen migrants.

Political parties in some polities such as Germany and Austria have promoted non-citizen voting as part of a wider policy on migration and citizenship. Thus those on the left see giving electoral rights in advance of the acquisition of citizenship as a dimension of a pathway *towards* integration and those on the right see political participation as a reward for a specific step *of* integration, namely the voluntary acquisition of citizenship through naturalization which, in those polities given their positions on dual citizenship, requires third country nationals to give up the citizenship of birth. But steps taken by left-wing political parties have often encountered barriers erected by constitutional courts to protect the integrity of 'the people'. These can have a chilling effect on political debate on these matters, given the enhanced parliamentary majorities needed for constitutional amendments.[67]

Some political science work does move beyond case studies and examines trends on a cross-country and cross-time basis. Earnest, for example, highlights that international factors may affect the timing of changes to the right to vote for immigrants, but the content of changes at the national level are generally influenced by domestic factors.[68] In other work, Earnest has examined the relationship between

[64] Escobar (n 27).   [65] Shaw (n 57).   [66] Rodríguez (n 21), p. 49.
[67] Shaw (n 57), p. 298.
[68] David Earnest, 'Expanding the Electorate: Comparing the Noncitizen Voting Practices of 25 Democracies', *Journal of International Migration and Integration* 16, no. 1 (2015): pp. 1–25.

the extension and *reversal* of policies concerned with liberalizing citizenship as well as extending the franchise.[69] His focus here was on the interrelation between 'policy constraints' and 'national resilience'. These findings highlight the many different variables that need to be taken into account, in relation not only to the types of legal provisions that may be enacted, but also to the national and international context of changes to electoral rights. As immigration represents an increasingly 'toxic' issue in many national political debates, Justwan may well be correct to highlight that issues of 'generalized trust' across society need to be taken into consideration.[70] That has to be balanced against what others have termed the 'democratic' potential of enfranchising migrants.[71]

In contrast, surveys of external voting for emigrants and their descendants show a genuine global trend, with more than 120 countries worldwide allowing some or all external citizens to vote,[72] typically in national elections, less frequently in local or regional/state elections.[73] Collyer, in this volume, argues that external voting finds its place within a larger framework of 'transnational citizenship', with a variety of political and economic factors including party interests, development, and remittances and the ease of political information flows all contributing to the creation of more or less liberal external voting regimes. In sum, states have to balance diaspora engagement against the fear that external voters may be given too much weight in the domestic sphere and may restrict political developments that residents wish to see. For Lafleur, setting policies will include transnational negotiation processes that engage not only the citizen and the sending state, but also the host state.[74] Hutcheson and Arrighi, meanwhile, concentrate on the various hurdles that states set for external voters who exercise their rights.[75] As with non-citizen residents, their participation rates are low.

Scholarly work on emigrants and diasporas is also more heavily slanted towards single country or regional case studies, rather than being based on broader aggregate datasets, not least because of the absence of reliable data thus far. The collection

[69] David Earnest, 'The Enfranchisement of Resident Aliens: Variations and Explanations', *Democratization* 22, no. 5 (2015): pp. 861–883.

[70] Florian Justwan, 'Disenfranchised Minorities: Trust, Definitions of Citizenship, and Noncitizen Voting Rights in Developed Democracies', *International Political Science Review* 36, no. 4 (2015): pp. 373–392.

[71] Luicy Pedroza, 'The Democratic Potential of Enfranchising Resident Migrants', *International Migration* 53, no. 3 (2015): pp. 22–35.

[72] IDEA International Institute of Democracy and Electoral Assistance, *Voting from Abroad* (Stockholm: IDEA, 2007); Michael Collyer, 'A Geography of Extra-Territorial Citizenship: Explanations of External Voting', *Migration Studies* 2, no. 1 (2014): pp. 55–72.

[73] Arrighi and Bauböck (n 20).

[74] Jean-Michel Lafleur, 'The Enfranchisement of Citizens Abroad: Variations and Explanations', *Democratization* 22, no. 5 (2015): pp. 840–860.

[75] Derek Hutcheson and Jean-Thomas Arrighi, ' "Keeping Pandora's (Ballot) Box Half-Shut": A Comparative Inquiry into the Institutional Limits of External Voting in EU Member States', *Democratization* 22, no. 5 (2015): pp. 884–905.

of data on electoral rights to both emigrants and immigrants across multiple states worldwide by the EUDO Citizenship Observatory will help to offset this.

CONSTITUTING AND RENEWING THE POLITY

Referendums play a special role in the creation of polities, their renewal, and the renovation of their constitutional foundations. *A fortiori*, the question of who can vote is crucially important both normatively—in the sense of constitutional designs and polity models—and practically, not least because some states or parts of states subject to authoritarian rule may have extremely large diasporas which could outweigh the resident population. Such instances also pose particular challenges around the question of effective voter registration.

We can distinguish between a number of different cases: voting rights in self-determination plebiscites (on devolution/autonomy, on redrawing internal jurisdictional boundaries within states, on secession/independence, on EU membership, etc.) and voting rights in the first and subsequent elections in a new polity (or an emerging democracy). These topics touch upon the substance of a number of chapters in this volume including those on post-transition states (Shevel), post-colonial citizenship (Sadiq), citizenship beyond Western contexts (Chung), supranational citizenship (Strumia), and multilevel citizenship (Maas). They also interconnect with topics considered in the sections above, especially as regards the question of external voting. In what circumstances do external citizens have sufficient 'stake' in the community to be permitted to vote at such points of change? What of the case of those who are victims of forced migration, either as refugees/asylum-seekers or under some other form of internationally protected status? Should they and/or their descendants be afforded opportunities to participate when, for example, a previous authoritarian regime collapses, even if they are no longer formally recognized as citizens?

In line with that question, it is important to note that changes to voting in referendums and first/subsequent elections may eschew the 'normal' trajectory solely towards liberalization and greater inclusion. There are some examples of the franchise being narrowed down to just citizens. For example, after completing the independence process and after the crystallization of their own citizenship regimes, Canada and Australia (mostly) removed the franchise from British subjects/citizens and the USA removed the franchise from those intending to naturalize.[76] In

---

[76] Monica Varsanyi, 'The Rise and Fall (and Rise?) of Non-citizen Voting: Immigration and the Shifting Scales of Citizenship and Suffrage in the United States', *Space and Polity* 9, no. 2 (2005): pp. 113–134.

South Africa, where the post-Apartheid transitional constitutional arrangements were initially more liberal, the rules now restrict voting to citizens alone.[77] Estonia held a number of plebiscites in the process of gaining independence from the Soviet Union, with some of the earlier ones including a wider range of resident voters than were able to accede to citizenship on independence.[78] The latter cases accord with the post-conflict/transition point highlighted above. In such cases, census data (or the lack of it) can be crucial to the process of trying to document the list of voters reliably. This has been the case in Lebanon, where the last census was held in 1932, and Bosnia-Herzegovina where wars and mass population movements gave rise to huge changes between the 1991 census (as part of the Socialist Federal Republic of Yugoslavia) and the 2013 census.[79]

Even in times of 'normal' democratic political evolution, there may be intense contestation over the scope of the right to vote. We saw this in the 2014 Scottish independence referendum and the 2016 UK referendum on membership in the European Union. The interplay between the right to vote in these constitutionally significant referendums and the political choices that underpinned the Yes/No and Leave/Remain options on the voting papers is instructive.[80]

The Scottish referendum franchise was designed on the basis of the franchise for the Scottish Parliament elections, which includes EU citizens pursuant to an upgrading of their existing voting rights. The Scottish Parliament was given the task of fixing the precise modulation of the right to vote for the referendum in the Scottish Independence Referendum (Franchise) Act 2013 and it chose to include not only EU citizens but also sixteen- and seventeen-year-olds. The latter bene-fited from the argument that younger voters were those with most to gain or to lose as a result of the referendum, and that this would be a good way of catalysing the political engagement of a new generation. The franchise excluded all external voters whether resident elsewhere in the UK or outside the UK, in line with all UK local and regional elections. In comparison, the UK EU referendum franchise was based almost precisely on the current franchise for elections to the Westminster Parliament. Accordingly, this gave the right to vote not only to resident UK citi-zens, but also to Commonwealth and Irish citizens (as with every UK election) and UK citizens resident outside the UK for no more than fifteen years. However, EU citizens and the sixteen- and seventeen-year-olds were not given the vote despite

[77] Wessel Le Roux, 'Residence, Representative Democracy and the Voting Rights of Migrant Workers in Post-Apartheid South Africa and Postunification Germany (1990–2015)', *Verfassung in Recht und Übersee 48*, no. 3 (2015): pp. 284–304.

[78] Stephen Day and Jo Shaw, 'The Boundaries of Suffrage and External Conditionality: Estonia as an Applicant Member State of the EU', *European Public Law 9*, no. 2 (2003): pp. 211–236.

[79] Florian Bieber, 'The Construction of National Identity and its Challenges in Post-Yugoslav Censuses', *Social Science Quarterly 96*, no. 3 (2015): pp. 873–903.

[80] Shaw (n 30).

efforts to introduce amendments to the EU Referendum Act 2015 during its passage through Parliament. Three excluded categories of person, namely the longer term non-resident citizens, EU citizens, and the younger voters could be said to be those most acutely affected by the referendum outcome, in particular because the vote on 23 June 2016 produced a relatively narrow vote to leave (by a margin of 1.27m votes where 33.5m votes were cast). The numbers of people 'excluded' comfortably exceeded the numerical difference between the Leave voters and the Remain voters.

In many respects, these variegated solutions to the question of who should vote in two extraordinarily important referendums held in the UK within less than two years (as well as any possible future second Scottish referendum that may occur because Scotland voted by a substantial majority for the remain option[81]) reflect the mottled tapestry of citizenship and electoral rights outlined in this chapter in both the UK and many other countries. While Ziegler argued that the franchise in the Scottish referendum should have—as closely as possible—shadowed the likely future citizenry of any future independent Scotland, Bauböck's call to treat the referendum franchise as a reflection or upgrading of the actually existing regional citizenry rather than some speculative future 'national' citizenry is both normatively appealing and practically sound, given the challenge of trying to figure out and enable the registration of any other putative electorate.[82] Ziegler has also argued that the franchise in the EU referendum gives rise to the argument that the UK's general election franchise should itself be revised.[83] However, that reminds us that this franchise, like many, is the result of a set of historically contingent decisions that would be hard to change piecemeal, decisions which have significant international repercussions because of relations between the UK and Ireland over Northern Ireland noted above.

CONCLUSIONS

In this chapter, we have reviewed a range of ways in which citizenship intersects with the right to vote, allowing us to probe the contribution of citizenship as a legal

[81] Scotland voted to remain by 62 per cent to 38 per cent with no Council area recording a majority vote to leave. Northern Ireland also voted (more narrowly) to remain and Gibraltar had more than 95 per cent of its small electorate voting to remain.

[82] See Ruvi Ziegler, 'Kick off Contribution', in Ruvi Ziegler, Jo Shaw, and Rainer Bauböck, eds., *Independence Referendums: Who Should Vote and Who Should be Offered Citizenship?* EUI Working Paper no. 90 (Florence: RSCAS, 2014); Rainer Bauböck, 'Regional Citizenship and Self-Determination', in Ruvi Ziegler, Jo Shaw, and Rainer Bauböck, eds., *Independence Referendums: Who Should Vote and Who Should be Offered Citizenship?* EUI Working Paper no. 90 (Florence: RSCAS, 2014).

[83] Ruvi Ziegler, 'The "Brexit" Referendum: We Need to Talk about the (General Election) Franchise' *UK Constitutional Law Association Blog*, 7 October 2015, https://ukconstitutionallaw.org/2015/10/07/ruvi-ziegler-the-brexit-referendum-we-need-to-talk-about-the-general-election-franchise/.

status underpinning the definition of the franchise to democratic self-government as a political ideal. The struggle for universal suffrage has been a paradigmatic political struggle in the modern state, as people have striven to achieve full and equal citizenship. As a result, the right to vote now operates as an enforceable human right under national and international law, blurring the distinction between citizens' rights and human rights.[84] This is part of the ongoing transformation of citizenship as a status and as a bundle of rights.

We have also seen that these intersections raise both normative and practical questions, and that as we acquire more reliable data about the boundaries of the suffrage across place and time we will be better able to understand how these map on to other dimensions of political inclusion and exclusion. Studies of voting rights have hitherto been dominated by a case study approach and by 'Western' cases strongly influenced by postwar narratives of immigration. Work in the future will be able to draw on an increasing portfolio of evidence of democratic practices across states and other 'state-like' polities, including a small number of supranational organizations that organize elections, as well as different and perhaps increasingly fluid forms of human mobility.

Normatively, the study of electoral rights is one of the fields in which theorists can identify areas of overlap and blurring between different membership statuses. With greater mobility of populations, the global spread of elections and external voting rights, as well as the increased tolerance of dual citizenship both for those who acquire citizenship by birth and by naturalization, these complex intersections are likely to increase rather than diminish in the future.

Bibliography

Arrighi, Jean-Thomas and Rainer Bauböck, 'A Multilevel Puzzle. Migrants' Voting Rights in National and Local Elections', *European Journal of Political Research* (forthcoming 2016), doi: 10.1111/1475-6765.12176.

Bauböck, Rainer, 'Morphing the Demos into the Right Shape. Normative Principles for Enfranchising Resident Aliens and Expatriate Citizens', *Democratization* 22, no. 5 (2015): pp. 820–839, doi: 10.1080/13510347.2014.988146.

Bauböck, Rainer, 'Studying Citizenship Constellations', *Journal of Ethnic and Migration Studies 36*, no. 5 (2010): pp. 847–859, doi: 10.1080/13691831003764375.

Bauböck, Rainer, 'Stakeholder Citizenship and Transnational Political Participation: A Normative Evaluation of External Voting', *Fordham Law Review 75*, no. 5 (2007): pp. 2393–2447, online http://ir.lawnet.fordham.edu/flr/vol75/iss5/4.

Bauböck, Rainer, 'Expansive Citizenship: Voting beyond Territory and Membership', *PS: Political Science and Politics 38*, no. 4 (2005): pp. 683–687, online http://www.jstor.org/stable/30044350.

---

[84] Igor Štiks and Jo Shaw, 'Citizenship Rights: Statuses, Challenges and Struggles', *Belgrade Journal of Media and Communications 6* (2014): pp. 73–90.

Beckmann, Ludvig, 'Citizenship and Voting Rights: Should Resident Aliens Vote?', *Citizenship Studies 10*, no. 1 (2006): pp. 153–165, doi: 10.1080/13621020600633093.

Belt, Rabia, *Mental Disability and the Right to Vote* (PhD Dissertation, University of Michigan, 2015), online https://deepblue.lib.umich.edu/handle/2027.42/116625.

Bieber, Florian, 'The Construction of National Identity and its Challenges in Post-Yugoslav Censuses', *Social Science Quarterly 96*, no. 3 (2015): pp. 873–903, doi: 10.1111/ssqu.12195.

Birch, Sarah, *Full Participation: A Comparative Study of Compulsory Voting* (Manchester: Manchester University Press, 2009).

Caramani, Daniele and Florian Grotz, 'Beyond Citizenship and Residence? Exploring the Extension of Voting Rights in the Age of Globalization', *Democratization 22*, no. 5 (2015): pp. 799–819, doi: 10.1080/13510347.2014.981668.

Carens, Joseph H., *The Ethics of Immigration* (Oxford: Oxford University Press, 2013).

Collier, Ruth Berins, *Paths toward Democracy: The Working Class and Elites in Western Europe and South America* (Cambridge: Cambridge University Press, 1999).

Collyer, Michael, 'A Geography of Extra-Territorial Citizenship: Explanations of External Voting', *Migration Studies 2*, no. 1 (2014): pp. 55–72, doi: 10.1093/migration/mns008.

Davidson, Jerome, 'Inside Outcasts: Prisoners and the Right to Vote in Australia', *Current Issues Brief*, no. 12 2003–2004, online http://apo.org.au/resource/inside-outcasts- prisoners-and-right-vote-australia.

Day, Stephen and Jo Shaw, 'The Boundaries of Suffrage and External Conditionality: Estonia as an Applicant Member State of the EU', *European Public Law 9*, no. 2 (2003): pp. 211–236.

Dothan, Shai, 'Comparative Views on the Right to Vote in International Law: The Case of Prisoners' Disenfranchisement', in Anthea Roberts, Pierre Verdier, Paul Stephan, and Mila Versteeg, eds., *Comparative International Law* (Oxford: Oxford University Press, 2016).

Downs, Anthony, *An Economic Theory of Democracy* (New York: Harper and Row, 1957).

Earnest, David, 'Expanding the Electorate: Comparing the Noncitizen Voting Practices of 25 Democracies', *Journal of International Migration and Integration 16*, no. 1 (2015): pp. 1–25, doi: 10.1007/s12134-014-0334-8.

Earnest, David 'The Enfranchisement of Resident Aliens: Variations and Explanations', *Democratization 22*, no. 5 (2015): pp. 861–883, doi: 10.1080/13510347.2014.979162.

Escobar, Cristina, 'Immigrant Enfranchisement in Latin America: From Strongmen to Universal Citizenship', *Democratization 22*, no. 5 (2015): pp. 927–950, doi: 10.1080/13510347.2014.979322.

Finck, Michèle, 'Towards an Ever Closer Union Between Residents and Citizens?', *European Constitutional Law Review 11*, no. 1 (2015): pp. 78–98, doi: 10.1017/S1574019615000061.

Fundamental Rights Agency, *The Right to Political Participation of Persons with Mental Health Problems and Persons with Intellectual Disabilities* (Luxembourg: Publications Office of the European Union, 2013).

Gardner, Piers, ed., *Citizenship: The White Paper* (London: Institute for Citizenship Studies/ BIICL, 2007).

Goodin, Robert, 'Enfranchising All Affected Interests, and Its Alternatives', *Philosophy and Public Affairs 35*, no. 1 (2007): pp. 40–68, doi: 10.1111/j.1088-4963.2007.00098.x.

Healy, Claire, *Access to Electoral Rights:Portugal* (EUDO Citizenship Observatory, June 2013), online http://eudo-citizenship.eu/admin/?p=file&appl=countryProfiles&f=138-PT-FRACIT.pdf.

Hernandez, Tanya, *Racial Subordination in Latin America. The Role of the State, Customary Law, and the New Civil Rights Response* (Cambridge: Cambridge University Press, 2014).

Honohan, Iseult and Derek Hutcheson, 'Transnational Citizenship and Access to Electoral Rights: Defining the Demos in European States', in Johan Elkink and David M. Farrell, eds., *The Act of Voting: Identities, Institutions and Locale* (London, New York: Routledge, 2015), pp. 59–79.

Hutcheson, Derek and Jean-Thomas Arrighi, '"Keeping Pandora's (Ballot) Box Half-Shut": A Comparative Inquiry into the Institutional Limits of External Voting in EU Member States', *Democratization* 22, no. 5 (2015): pp. 884–905, doi: 10.1080/13510347.2014.979161.

IDEA International Institute of Democracy and Electoral Assistance, *Voting from Abroad* (Stockholm: IDEA, 2007).

Irving, Helen, *Citizenship, Alienage and the Modern Constitutional State: A Gendered History* (Cambridge: Cambridge University Press, 2016).

Isin, Engin, 'Theorizing Acts of Citizenship', in Engin Isin and Greg Nielsen, eds., *Acts of Citizenship* (London: Palgrave Macmillan, 2008).

Justwan, Florian, 'Disenfranchised Minorities: Trust, Definitions of Citizenship, and Noncitizen Voting Rights in Developed Democracies', *International Political Science Review 36*, no. 4 (2015): pp. 373–392, doi: 10.1177/0192512113513200.

Keyssar, Alexander, *The Right to Vote. The Contested History of Democracy in the United States* (New York: Basic Books, 2000).

Khadar, Lamin, *Access to Electoral Rights: United Kingdom* (EUDO Citizenship Observatory, June 2013), online http://eudo-citizenship.eu/admin/?p=file&appl=countryProfiles&f=1310-UK-FRACIT.pdf.www.eudo-citizenship.eu.

Lafleur, Jean-Michel, 'The Enfranchisement of Citizens Abroad: Variations and Explanations', *Democratization* 22, no. 5 (2015): pp. 840–860, doi: 10.1080/13510347.2014.979163.

Lardy, Heather, 'Citizenship and the Right to Vote', *Oxford Journal of Legal Studies 17* (1997): pp. 75–100.

Lee, Suevon and Sarah Smith, 'Everything You've Ever Wanted to Know About Voter ID Laws', *Pro Publica*, 9 March 2016, online https://www.propublica.org/article/everything-youve-ever-wanted-to-know-about-voter-id-laws.

Le Roux, Wessel, 'Residence, Representative Democracy and the Voting Rights of Migrant Workers in Post-Apartheid South Africa and Postunification Germany (1990-2015)', *Verfassung in Recht und Übersee 48*, no. 3 (2015): pp. 284–304, doi: 10.5771/0506-7286-2015-3-263.

Lopez, Ian Haney, *White by Law* (New York: NYU Press, 2006).

Miller, David, 'Immigrants, Nations and Citizenship', *Journal of Political Philosophy 16*, no. 4 (2008): pp. 371–390, doi: 10.1111/j.1467-9760.2007.00295.x.

Owen, David, 'Constituting the Polity, Constituting the Demos: On the Place of the All Affected Interests Principle in Democratic Theory and in Resolving the Democratic Boundary Problem', *Ethics and Global Politics 5*, no. 3 (2012): pp. 129–152, online 10.3402/egp.v5i3.18617.

Pedroza, Luicy, 'The Democratic Potential of Enfranchising Resident Migrants', *International Migration 53*, no. 3 (2015): pp. 22–35, doi: 10.1111/imig.12162.

Przeworski, Adam, 'Conquered or Granted? A History of Suffrage Extensions', *British Journal of Political Science 39*, no. 2 (2009): pp 291–321, doi: 10.1017/S0007123408000434.

Ramirez, Francisco, Yasemin Soysal, and Suzanne Shanahan, 'The Changing Logic of Political Citizenship: Cross-National Acquisition of Women's Suffrage Rights, 1890-1990', *American Sociological Review 62* (October 1997): pp. 735-745.

Ramsay, Peter, 'Voters Should Not be in Prison! The Rights of Prisoners in a Democracy', *Critical Review of International Social and Political Philosophy 16*, no. 3 (2013): pp. 421-438, doi: 10.1080/13698230.2013.795706.

Rodríguez, Ángel, *Access to Electoral Rights: Spain* (EUDO Citizenship Observatory, June 2013), online http://eudo-citizenship.eu/admin/?p=file&appl=countryProfiles&f=1315-Spain-FRACIT.pdf.

Rodríguez, Cristina, 'Noncitizen Voting and the Extraconstitutional Construction of the Polity', *International Constitutional Law Journal 8*, no. 1 (2010): pp. 30-49, doi: 10.1093/icon/mop032.

Rubio Marín, Ruth, 'The Achievement of Female Suffrage in Europe: On Women's Citizenship', *International Journal of Constitutional Law 12*, no. 1 (2014): pp. 4-34, doi: 10.1093/icon/mot067.

Rubio Marín, Ruth, *Immigration as a Democratic Challenge* (Cambridge: Cambridge University Press, 2000).

Saunders, Ben, 'Defining the Demos', *Politics, Philosophy and Economics 11*, no. 3 (2014): pp. 280-301, doi: 10.1177/1470594X11416782.

Sawyer, Caroline and Helena Wray, *United Kingdom*, EUDO Citizenship Country Report on Citizenship Law (December 2014), online http://www.eudo-citizenship.eu.

Shaw, Jo, 'Unions and Citizens: Membership Status and Political Rights in Scotland, the UK and the EU', in Carlos Closa, ed., *Secession from a Member State and Withdrawal from the European Union: Troubled Membership* (Cambridge: Cambridge University Press, forthcoming 2017).

Shaw, Jo, *The Transformation of Citizenship in the European Union* (Cambridge: Cambridge University Press, 2007).

Shaw, Jo and Anja Lansbergen, 'National Membership Models in a Multi-Level Europe', *International Journal of Constitutional Law 8*, no. 1 (2010): pp. 50-71, doi: 10.1093/icon/mop036.

Štiks, Igor and Jo Shaw, 'Citizenship Rights: Statuses, Challenges and Struggles', *Belgrade Journal of Media and Communications 6* (2014): pp. 73-90.

Teele, Dawn, 'Ordinary Democratization: The Electoral Strategy That Won British Women the Vote', *Politics & Society 42*, no. 4 (2014): pp. 537-561, doi: 10.1177/0032329214547343.

Uggen, Christopher and Jeff Manza, 'Democratic Contraction? Political Consequences of Felon Disenfranchisement in the United States', *American Sociological Review 67*, no. 6 (2002); pp. 777-803, online http://www.jstor.org/stable/3088970.

Varsanyi, Monica, 'The Rise and Fall (and Rise?) of Non-citizen Voting: Immigration and the Shifting Scales of Citizenship and Suffrage in the United States', *Space and Polity 9*, no. 2 (2005): pp. 113-134, doi: 10.1080=13562570500304956.

Vink, Maarten and Rainer Bauböck, 'Citizenship Configurations: Analysing the Multiple Purposes of Citizenship Regimes in Europe', *Comparative European Politics 11*, no. 5 (2013): pp. 621-648, doi: 10.1057/cep.2013.14.

Ziegler, Ruvi, *Voting Rights of Refugees* (Cambridge: Cambridge University Press, 2017).

Ziegler, Ruvi, 'The "Brexit" Referendum: We Need to Talk about the (General Election) Franchise', *UK Constitutional Law Association Blog*, 7 October 2015 https://

ukconstitutionallaw.org/2015/10/07/ruvi-ziegler-the-brexit-referendum-we-need-to-talk-about-the-general-election-franchise/.

Ziegler, Ruvi, Jo Shaw, and Rainer Bauböck, eds., *Independence Referendums: Who Should Vote and Who Should be Offered Citizenship?* EUI Working Paper no. 90 (Florence: RSCAS, 2014).

CHAPTER 15

STATUS NON-CITIZENS

LINDA BOSNIAK

INTRODUCTION: CITIZENSHIP'S FORMS AND NORMS

THIS chapter focuses on the condition of persons inhabiting liberal democratic political communities in which they lack the legal status of citizenship. Notwithstanding the great variations among categories and across states, it is possible to distill a profile of the rights and liabilities of status non-citizens in broad terms. This chapter offers one such profile. To frame the discussion, however, it begins by considering what status non-citizenship consists in analytically, and how this status relates to other forms and understandings of 'not being a citizen.'

The place to start in any discussion of status non-citizenship is with the international regime of bordered states. The category of status non-citizen is both product and precondition of the operation of these borders. Access to citizenship status in any given state is always to some degree restricted. Yet the state borders grounding that status are not impermeable—neither in policy terms nor in fact. Contra Rawls' famous 'closed society' thought experiment, actual states are not sealed and self-contained entities into which 'all are born' and 'no one enters from without.'[1] Instead, it is precisely because borders are neither permanently fixed nor impermeable and because the polity is therefore not a 'complete and closed system' that millions of people do, in fact, reside within the territories of national states in a variety of status situations short of citizenship, with or without those states' explicit consent. These people are, in a word, a state's status non-citizens.

At issue in this chapter is their condition and standing within liberal-democratic states. These states hold themselves out to be membership communities within which the rights of 'everyone' are to be protected and represented. Put another way, liberal states purport to adhere to norms of internal universality. Even though the scope of this universality has always been contested and the actual degree of its fulfillment incomplete, universality is the official ethos. What is more, political actors and analysts often express these universalist norms in the language of 'citizenship,' through use of such aspirational terms as 'equal citizenship,' 'democratic citizenship,' 'constitutional citizenship,' 'cultural citizenship,' and so forth.

What, then, of the condition and treatment of status non-citizens? To be among those deemed entitled to enjoy or demand equal citizenship or democratic citizenship in this universalistic sense, must a person possess the legal status of citizenship? The answer is ambiguous. At some moments and in some settings, universalist norms of citizenship are understood to extend only to those persons who possess status citizenship in the state in question. From this perspective, substantive citizenship is for status citizens only. Yet in most liberal states, this status condition for inclusion is not always observed. Instead, from liberalism's inception and ever increasingly, some inclusionary norms have been treated as territorially based and grounded, thereby extending to 'everyone' or to 'all persons within the jurisdiction,'[2] formal legal status notwithstanding. From this vantage point, the treatment of some territorially present persons as non-members or less-than-full members is unjust precisely *in light of* substantive citizenship's universalist aspirations.[3]

Even when this is the case, however, territorially present status non-citizens remain outsiders in respect to the state's constitutive border regime. Although geographically

[1] John Rawls, 'Kantian Constructivism in Moral Theory,' in John Rawls, *Collected Papers*, edited by S. Freeman (Cambridge: Harvard University Press, 1999), pp. 303–358; John Rawls, *A Theory of Justice* (Cambridge: Harvard University Press, 1971).

[2] United States Constitution, Amendment XIV.

[3] See, e.g., Linda Bosniak, *The Citizen and the Alien: Dilemmas of Contemporary Membership* (Princeton: Princeton University Press, 2006) (especially chapter 4).

present, they are defined at least to some degree as strangers, and as such, are subject to attendant legal consequences, including, most significantly, vulnerability to expulsion from the territory. State border imperatives, that is, often defeat the general individual rights non-citizens otherwise enjoy, and in practical terms, function often to trump them.

The condition of status non-citizens in liberal states, therefore, is constituted by distinct and internally complex normative orders governing edges and interior—*thresholds to* membership, and *dynamics of* membership, simultaneously. Non-citizens stand at the intersection of these regimes. Sometimes, this overlapping governance system works relatively smoothly. At other times, the relationship between the border and other internal jurisdictions becomes conflicted and confused.[4]

As we map these ambiguities, one puzzle that arises is the insistent presence of the concept of 'citizenship' in the conversation. This puzzle has at least two aspects, one analytical and one normative. First, how do we make sense of the fact that the term *citizenship* is used descriptively to reference both the constitutive edges and the internal dynamics of community membership? Second, how are we to understand the fact that the citizenship concept is widely deployed in normative terms to convey both closure/exclusivity and belonging/inclusion?

One account—the dominant one in citizenship studies and in liberal political and social theory generally—answers these questions by conceptualizing citizenship as a kind of packaged enclosure. It treats citizenship's dual facets as complementary parts of a citizenship whole. In this conception, citizenship designates membership in a political community; and membership, in turn, possesses both externally constitutive and internally substantive dimensions. Each of these dimensions embodies a distinct normative ethos: boundedness governs at the edges and inclusiveness within. On this account, citizenship is, more or less, 'hard on the outside and soft on the inside.'[5]

Familiar though this framing of citizenship is one might want to ask whether it actually satisfies analytically or empirically. Is citizenship, in fact, a single though segmented legal and political phenomenon? Or might it be more accurate to regard usages of the term as invoking analytically distinct and sometimes conflicting discourses?[6]

MANY NON-CITIZENSHIPS

Generally speaking, to understand the meaning of a concept, it is instructive to try to specify its converse—what it is not, or what we understand it not to be. Since the concept of citizenship conventionally signifies diverse modes of social

---

⁴ Ibid.   ⁵ Ibid.   ⁶ Ibid.

being and status, the '*non*-ness' of non-citizenship likewise reflects this diversity. To characterize someone as a non-citizen can mean a variety of things.

Let's begin by applying an internal gaze, one through which we survey the nature of social and political relations within the polity in which we find ourselves. From this vantage, non-citizenships or sub-citizenships may take different forms.

We might, first of all, be talking about a deficit in rights. Where we—in contemporary liberal societies—understand the citizen to be one who theoretically enjoys full equality of rights and standing in a particular polity (approximating the *citoyen* in classical political theory), the *non-citizen* is a lesser-grade member or non-member—whether subject or peon, or outlaw or slave. We might, alternatively, be addressing the question of deficits in or obstacles to democratic engagement. Where we—via a longstanding inheritance from the Greeks— regard the citizen as one who is actively engaged as a participant in the project of democratic self-rule (*politeuma*[7]), the *non-citizen* is the 'free-rider,' the passive or apathetic consumer, the oikos-confined laboring body. We might, finally, be referencing failures of mutual recognition and identification in civic terms. Where we—by way of social transformations that have come to emphasize intersubjective aspects of community[8]—understand the citizen as someone who is recognized and self-recognizes as a constituent of a particular societal community, then the *non-citizen* will be, variously, the unassimilating other(s), the felon, the deviant, the traitor, the terrorist.

Notice that despite their substantive variations, the different non-citizenships described here all plainly evoke negative associations, including deficiency, incongruity, danger, exclusion, abjectness, or suffering. Why? The answer begins with the unfailingly favorable normative valence attending citizenship in each of these modes. When 'citizenship' is a term used to characterize rights or participation or recognition, it not merely describes states of affairs but expresses their value. Its appraisive meaning is consummately positive. The *absence* of citizenship, therefore, would seem to entail the normative converse, such that to describe someone as a *non-citizen* or a *sub-citizen* is to describe them as experiencing an adverse condition.

But acknowledging this evaluative binary only deepens the question. *Why* is citizenship—as equality of rights, as democratic participation, and/or as mutual recognition—deemed so valuable that its absence or denial or incompleteness is regarded in detrimental terms? Part of the answer is that these three conceptions of citizenship are, in contemporary liberal democratic societies, decisively

---

[7] Adriel M. Trott, *Aristotle on the Nature of Community* (Cambridge: Cambridge University Press, 2014), p. 163. See also Balot in this volume.

[8] See, e.g., Charles Taylor, *Sources of the Self: The Making of the Modern Identity* (Cambridge: Harvard University Press, 1989).

associated with an ethos of internal universality.[9] Citizenship is meant to extend to 'everybody' in a society, at least in nominal or aspirational terms. This is the 'ideal of universal citizenship' to which, in many domains and in much public discourse, we have become accustomed.[10] However short of that ideal a given society falls in practice—however much actual inequality of rights, underrepresentation of persons, alienation and non-recognition of individuals or groups may characterize it at a particular moment—these notions of citizenship are discursively meant to convey a commitment to the inclusion of all persons in and of the society at issue.

Therefore, if someone in the society is treated as a *non-citizen* or *sub-citizen* in one of these modes, something has arguably gone wrong.[11] Often the claim is that the polity failed to fulfill its avowed promise of universal inclusion. The fact that some persons are treated as non-citizens or lesser citizens in some settings bespeaks a failure of the state to make good on its political and social commitments.[12] This nonfulfillment, in turn, provides the basis for political protest, critique, and resistance by those maintaining that their exclusion from citizenship, in one or all of these aspects, is an *injustice*. Such claims of injustice may take different forms: they may be claims about formal exclusion of some classes of beings from recognition as citizens (e.g., currently, nonhuman animals[13]) or, more commonly, claims about social or political conditions that result in de facto denial to some populations of meaningful or effective citizenship (e.g., voter ID and felon disenfranchisement laws in the United States; endemic structural poverty; religious attire laws).[14] Either way, the complaint is that the liberal state has fallen short of its acknowledged responsibilities to ensure citizenship's universal reach.

The state, in turn, will usually dispute the claim, but *not* by negating the salience and bindingness of the universality norm. Instead, it will profess adherence to the norm, but will either deny that the scope of citizenship's inclusionary ethos extends as far as challengers claim *or* will assert that the treatment of someone as a non-citizen or sub-citizen represents a justifiable exception to the universality

---

[9] The scope of this posited universality is hardly fixed. 'Universality for whom?' has always been subject to contestation.

[10] Iris Marion Young, 'Polity and Group Difference: A Critique of the Ideal of Universal Citizenship,' *Ethics* 99, no. 2 (January, 1989): pp. 250–274.

[11] Elizabeth Cohen has argued that citizenship in its internal mode is more accurately described as a 'gradient' than 'binary' category in that a variety of statuses 'exist between full and non-citizenship.' (Elizabeth Cohen, *Semi-Citizenship in Democratic Politics* (Cambridge: Cambridge University Press, 2009), pp. 4–5). For my purposes, I distinguish between full citizenship and everything short of this, but I recognize that in many settings gradients of citizenship matter significantly.

[12] Sometimes, the failure is attributed by certain social sectors and/or the state to particular groups in society. A recent example is claims by some that Muslim immigrants in Western states fail to sufficiently address terrorist extremism in their own communities.

[13] See Donaldson and Kymlicka in this volume.   [14] See, e.g., Volpp in this volume.

norm, as in cases of national security, terrorism, treason, or criminality.[15] The very idea of an *exception* presupposes the otherwise authoritative force of the norm from which it deviates.

In short, when speaking of citizenship in its rights, participation, and recognition modes, the attendant ethos is nominally universalist, and the treatment of persons as non-citizens generally entails a presumptive wrong—whether or not such wrong is eventually deemed justified.

But once again, these modes together constitute only part of citizenship's semantic domain. Many chapters in this volume foreground a fourth, and distinct, understanding of citizenship—one denoting a particular formal membership status in a national polity or state. Its correlative *non-citizen*, it follows, is one who lacks such status.

I will characterize in some detail in later sections the situation(s) of non-citizens produced through this understanding of citizenship. But to set the stage, I must highlight some preliminary points, beginning with the following core observation: For status-based citizenship, the normative commitment to universality does not hold. In fact, citizenship's normative underpinnings here are precisely the converse of the universalist ethos attending citizenship in its other senses. In its legal status mode, citizenship both *presupposes* exclusion of some persons by others and *produces* exclusion via legal status boundaries drawn and defended between groups of persons of different states. Possession of status citizenship in a given state is understood to be properly and justifiably restricted to the state's members, and to rightfully distinguish members from those persons designated as the state's outsiders. Exclusion here, in short, is understood to be not wrong at all, at least not in principle.

Another way of putting this is to say that the 'ideal of universal citizenship' is inapplicable in citizenship's status mode. *Not* everyone must be recognized as a status citizen by and in a given state as a matter of justice. Indeed the vast majority of persons in the world will not be citizens of that particular state, and those excluded will be prevented from joining it as citizens in all but limited circumstances. In this setting, the boundaries that divide the some from the rest are deemed constitutive of, and foundational for, the institution itself. In short, our overwhelming common-sense understanding of status citizenship is that it is a rightfully and necessarily bounded legal condition. For this reason, status non-citizenship is, in principle, a non-wrong.

But why is this the case? How do we explain the inversion here of the universalist ethos attending citizenship in its other modes?

One initial response might dispute the premise and contend that liberal thought does, indeed, contemplate a universalist ethos for status citizenship—one expressed in the aspirational precept that all persons on earth should

---

[15] See Gibney in this volume; Costello in this volume.

be ensured of possessing one.[16] This is an anti-statelessness stance that appeals to a norm of universality at the global level. But it is distinct from requiring a person to be granted citizenship status in this or that particular polity. Consequently, and, in contrast to citizenship as rights, participation, and recognition for which anything less than extension to all within the state is deemed presumptively unjust, citizenship-as-status *in that same state* is understood to be permissibly and justifiably bounded.

Furthermore, and decisively for the discussion here, status citizenship is bounded not only with respect to persons located outside the state's territory but also with respect to a great number of people present or residing within that territory. Many millions of people inhabit the territories of states of which they are not citizens.[17] To them, as well, assignment of the lesser status of non-citizen or alien is regarded as perfectly acceptable in principle, at least for some period.[18] Again, the question is: why?

THE ENCLOSURE CONCEPT

Here is the crux of the answer. In conventional liberal democratic thought, the boundaries of status citizenship are taken to be a necessary condition for the constitution and maintenance of the political community *within which* the pursuit of citizenship's otherwise aspirational universalism is to be pursued. In brief: (1) the institution of status citizenship is presumed to establish the political and social worlds or entities within which people conduct their core political lives, and (2) it is only within such bounded worlds that citizenship's nominally inclusionary aspects can even be pursued and possibly realized.

These tenets presume both a political ontology and an ethics of enclosure. On this conception, a basically exclusionary frame surrounds an interior nation-state-world

---

[16] See UN, Universal Declaration of Human Rights, 1948, Article 15: 'everyone has the right to a nationality.'

[17] The term 'inhabit' is useful here, as it may denote either 'to dwell or reside,' or 'to be present' (Merriam Webster, http://www.merriam-webster.com/dictionary/inhabit.) The denial of access to citizenship through naturalization for long-term lawfully present residents has been widely criticized, however, as violating liberal and democratic norms. See Michael Walzer, *Sphere of Justice: A Defense of Pluralism and Equality* (New York: Basic Books, 1983), chapter 3; Joseph H. Carens, *The Ethics of Immigration* (Oxford: Oxford University Press 2013).

[18] This is prevailingly true, though not always in particular cases or with respect to particular categories. Some states face criticism for failing to extend *jus soli* citizenship to children born in territory.

within which liberal democratic politics takes place.[19] This enclosure model of citizenship[20] continues to undergird the great share of contemporary legal and political theory, even today. Most often, these tenets operate subliminally, serving as the unstated theoretical baseline. Many political and social theorists—even those of progressive or critical inclination—still start by assuming the functional existence of, and practical need for, exclusionary state borders, and proceed directly to consideration of some set of political or social relations occurring within—or sometimes across—already constituted and bounded polities populated with pre-designated members.[21] This statist framing largely functions as *doxa*[22] with anterior or concurrent questions about the constitution and maintenance of the state's borders and its membership bypassed.[23]

As ever, the result is an unreflective methodological nationalism, which both distorts analytically and works to naturalize, and thereby normativize, state borders. Rawls' strategy in *Theory of Justice* of analytically bracketing borders—a strategy subsequently taken up by many strands of political and legal philosophy—produces the same naturalizing effect: where the fundamental justice conversation is posited to occur among a closed and pre-given group of status citizens—where discussion of the hows and whys of the political community's constitution and boundaries are not only ignored but analytically foreclosed—this bracketing arguably functions as a pronouncement that borders—usually actually existing borders—are indispensible for contemporary political life and for pursuit of justice therein.

Certainly, some critical and liberal theorists have criticized this methodological endogenism and have insisted that questions of immigration and territoriality

[19] For one characterization of the concept of political ontology, see Charles Tilly and Robert Goodin, 'It Depends,' in Robert E. Goodin and Charles Tilly, eds., *The Oxford Handbook of Contextual Political Analysis* (Oxford: Oxford University Press, 2006), pp. 3–32 ('ontological choices concern the sorts of social entities whose consistent existence analysts can reasonably assume' p. 10).

[20] Bosniak (n 3).

[21] For a notable recent example of ethical/ontological statism in progressive liberal thought in which the concept of 'citizenship' figures centrally, see Elizabeth Anderson, *The Imperative of Integration* (Princeton: Princeton University Press, 2010), pp. 183–184 ('The idea of integration … requires the construction of a superordinate group identity, a "we," from the perspective of which cooperative goals are framed … In a democratic society, this 'we' is most importantly a shared identity as citizens.'). Some critical theorists have highlighted both the hold and limitations of statism in political and social thought. See, e.g., Nancy Fraser, 'Reframing Justice in a Globalizing World,' *New Left Review 36* (November–December 2005): pp. 69–88.

[22] Pierre Bourdieu, *Outline of a Theory of Practice*, translated by Richard Nice (Cambridge: Cambridge University Press, 1977) [1972]; Zygmunt Bauman, *Liquid Modernity* (Cambridge: Polity Press, 2000), p. 30 (doxa is the 'unexamined frame for all further cognition.').

[23] Perhaps this disregard represents a version of what Charles Mills has called an 'epistemology of ignorance' or of erasure— in this case, ignorance or erasure as to exclusionary state borders and the way these borders frame and delimit the liberal democratic project. See Charles W. Mills, 'White Ignorance,' in Sharon Sullivan and Nancy Tuana, eds., *Race and Epistemologies of Ignorance* (Albany: SUNY Press, 2007).

cannot be purposefully 'ignored' or made to 'disappear'[24] in political theory. Yet even among those theorists who *do* attend to such questions, most go on to conclude that status citizenship and the exclusionary borders it capacitates are normatively defensible because they serve as an enabling framework for liberal democratic projects within—and are, perhaps, desirable for more affirmative reasons of identity and solidarity as well.[25]

Of course, some commentators have criticized the exclusionary effects of state borders: Ethical cosmopolitans have long contended that national borders should be subject to some of the same kinds of egalitarian and democratic critiques that have been applied to various forms of social and political exclusion within the national society.[26] More recently, various streams of No-Borders activists and academics have challenged the legitimacy of status citizenship's exclusionary boundaries, and in some cases, the justice of the institution of national citizenship altogether.[27] Compelling though these modes of critique may be, they so far remain distinctly subordinate discourses.[28] Our dominant common sense continues to regard the status of citizenship as properly rationed by states and, moreover, as legitimately employed by them as an 'instrument of social closure' in the national space (Brubaker, 1998).

And now we are in view of this chapter's main target. The fact that citizenship operates as an instrument of social closure means it functions not only as a barrier

---

[24] David Miller, *Strangers in Our Midst* (Cambridge: Harvard University Press, 2016), p. 14; Carens (n 17), p. 298, respectively.

[25] See, e.g., Christopher Heath Wellman, 'Immigration and Freedom of Association,' *Ethics 119*, no. 1 (October 2008): pp. 109–141; Miller (n 24); Michael Blake, 'Immigration, Jurisdiction and Exclusion,' *Philosophy and Public Affairs 41*, no. 2 (2013): pp. 103–130; Ryan Pevnick, *Immigration and Constraints of Justice* (Cambridge: Cambridge University Press, 2011). Joseph Carens is an ambiguous case: his early and continued articulation of a cosmopolitan, open borders project is counterposed with a feasibilist, statist frame in his recent book. For discussion of his attempted straddling of positions, see Linda Bosniak, 'Book Review: Joseph H. Carens, *The Ethics of Immigration* (Oxford: Oxford University Press, 2013),' *Ethics 125*, no. 2 (2015): pp. 571–576.

[26] Among cosmopolitan scholars of various stripes, see Chandran Kukathas, 'The Case for Open Immigration,' in Andrew I. Cohen and Christopher Heath Wellman, eds., *Contemporary Debates in Applied Ethics* (Malden, Oxford: Blackwell Publishing, 2005), pp. 207–220; Arash Abizadeh, 'Democratic Theory and Border Coercion: No Right to Unilaterally Control Your Own Borders,' *Political Theory 36, no. 1* (2008): pp. 37–65. Liberal cosmopolitan activists include promoters of the 'World Passport.' Critiques of state exclusionary policies are often brought in the name of 'universal citizenship.'

[27] Scholars include Bridget Anderson, *Us and Them? The Dangerous Politics of Immigration Controls* (Oxford: Oxford University Press, 2013); Phil Cole, 'Beyond Borders: Towards a Right to International Movement,' *The Critique*, 6 January 2016, online http://www.thecritique.com/articles/beyond-borders-towards-a-right-to-international-movement-2/. Organizations include: No One Is Illegal; Beyond Borders Networks; #NotOneMoreDeportation.

[28] David Miller maintains that most liberal political philosophers who address the immigration question challenge the legitimacy of national borders. My reading of the field is different.

vis-à- vis territorial outsiders but also as a mechanism that marginalizes persons residing *within* a democratic state as 'its' non-citizens. It is to the features and experience of this latter group—persons who inhabit a liberal democratic state of which they are not status citizens—that the chapter now turns.

WHAT IS STATUS NON-CITIZENSHIP?

Citizenship status represents formal membership in a given state. Citizenship laws are defined and regulated by each state, but are enforced in interaction with the citizenship status laws of other states. The result is a complex legal architecture of citizenship law at the global level, one which is generally recognized and defended by international law.[29] Citizenship-as-legal-status is frequently expressed in the language of nationality, with citizens of a state referred to as its nationals. At times, the interchangeability of terms is seamless because citizenship in this mode usually references membership status in the political community of the nation-state. However, citizenship status sometimes takes supra- and sub-national forms as well, extending it beyond the nationality concept in some settings.[30]

In many languages, the status citizen's antipode is the stranger, the foreign national, the alien[31] (estranjero/étranger/Ausländer/gaijin). What is conveyed by these terms is an otherness in relation to the polity and its members—an otherness produced by law which specifically denotes coming from—and perhaps properly belonging—without. The status citizen's 'other' is, in some defining respect, an outsider in relation to the community—whether or not she is geographically inside.

Importantly, though, the community's response to individual non-citizens or groups thereof present within the state is by no means always negative. The notions of 'guests,' 'visitors,' 'exchange students,' or 'permanent residents' can certainly sound favorable or innocuous, and people so designated will often find themselves welcomed by the destination state. This stands in contrast to states' responses to groups designated as 'illegal immigrants,' 'criminal aliens,' and so on.

---

[29] Peter J. Spiro, 'A New International Law of Citizenship,' *American Journal of International Law 105*, no. 4 (2011): pp. 694–746.

[30] See Bauböck in this volume; Maas in this volume.

[31] The term 'alien' is used to designate a person lacking status citizenship in the laws of the United States, the UK, and Australia, among others.

Moreover, non-citizenship is by no means a monolithic status. Persons in different non-citizenship status categories—usually, persons occupying different immigration statuses—have dramatically divergent experiences. Some non-citizens, whatever their particular legal status, intend their stay to be brief and casual, while others seek to remain, or in fact, find themselves remaining, longer term. Having limited rights and recognition in the destination state is likely to bear less significantly on those passing through than on those who have relocated more permanently or wish to do so.

Finally, substantial variations exist among non-citizenship groups regarding the extent to which the status is fixed, and in particular, regarding the conditions prevailing for promotion to citizenship status within the state. Rules governing transition by non-citizens to citizenship status via naturalization vary greatly among polities.[32] In most cases, only an extremely limited and privileged group of non-citizens has the opportunity to accede to that state's citizenship or nationality (though not all those eligible will choose to do so, for any number of reasons).[33]

Still, despite these many divergences, all status non-citizens—so long as they are non-citizens—remain foreigners or aliens within the framework of the state's citizenship laws.[34] They thereby represent, in status form, an internalized part of the national community's outside. True, legal basis of this outsiderness can vary. In a given case or class of cases, it may be grounded in geography—i.e., the individual came physically from without; s/he is not 'of the soil' or the state's territory; or it may turn on consanguinity—i.e., the individual was born in a state where territorial birthright citizenship is not recognized to parents designated as outsiders according to blood-based or descent-based rules of citizenship. Either way, though, the status foreigner is, at least in some formal respect, a being legally classified as distinct and separate from an already-constituted interior political 'we.'

That said, keep in mind that the vast majority of people designated as a state's non-citizens in this sense are not non-citizens everywhere. Today, most people are born as citizens of somewhere, sometimes of more than one place, by virtue of the transnationally overlapping rules of citizenship attribution via blood and soil (*jus sanguinis* and *jus soli*) together with post-birth citizenship attribution rules tolerating multiple citizenship. Only the stateless—estimated by the UNHCR to number approximately 10 million among the estimated 7 billion persons on earth[35]—are non-citizens everywhere. In this respect, describing a person as a status non-citizen

---

[32] See Vink in this volume.

[33] Additional bases for variation among experiences of non-citizens turn on variables shaping the experiences all persons present in the state such as race, ethnicity, gender, social class.

[34] On the other hand, some polities consider nationals of certain other states more as 'quasi-citizens' than foreigners, e.g. EU citizens residing in other Member States, Irish and Commonwealth citizens in the UK, Australian and NZ citizens in the respective other country.

[35] UNHCR, 'Ending Statelessness,' online http://www.unhcr.org/en-us/.

is, in most settings, a *relative* term; it is only in relation to a specific state's citizen-ship setting that that person is a non-citizen in the sense discussed here.

Note that the increasing pervasiveness of citizenship attribution at birth via *jus soli* rules means that a great many non-citizens now acquire non-citizenship sta-tus only after having physically crossed a border from their country of citizenship into another citizenship jurisdiction. However, some people become non-citizens without moving at all; non-citizenship occurs, that is, *in situ*. They may have been born as non-citizens in a place where they are not accorded automatic *jus soli* citi-zenship (though once again, they may well hold citizenship elsewhere, by descent). Alternatively, and significantly in some regions (e.g., the former Soviet Union), they may become non-citizens post-natally, after imposed loss of citizenship in cases when borders move following conflict, secession, or state/empire dissolution, or in cases of outright citizenship stripping. In short, though most non-citizens become such because of cross-border movement of either themselves or their parents, some become non-citizens by dint of geopolitical transformations around them.

Other chapters in this volume[36] address the complexities of status citizenship's attribution, acquisition, and loss, as well as the ensuing disjunctures between the geographic location, degree of legal protection, and citizenship status of persons produced via these intersecting regimes. Certain international trends—not only the expanding worldwide recognition of *jus soli* citizenship but also greater state toler-ation of multiple citizenships held by their members and increasing pursuit by indi-viduals of the same—might mean that, on a net global basis, there are now fewer long-term international migrants residing as non-citizens in their states of inhab-itance than in times past. Cutting in the converse direction, however, increasing cross-border mobilities of persons in various regular and irregular forms produce new categories of non-citizens in destination states. States vary greatly in their will-ingness to incorporate classes of resident (and non-resident) non-citizens into their national body of citizens, whether via naturalization or ancestral recognition. Some formerly incorporative states have become more restrictive in recent years.[37] All told, therefore, the incidence of non-citizenship status in each state must be under-stood to vary according to interacting legal, political, and demographic factors that operate at the individual state, international, and global levels simultaneously.

All of these variations notwithstanding, however, the point at present is that many persons across the globe inhabit bounded liberal political communities in which they lack the legal status of citizenship. And so we ask: What does occupying such a position entail?

Before beginning to answer, notice that consideration of this question inevit-ably brings us back into conversation with citizenship in its other senses. Because to inquire about the standing and experiences, the rights and disabilities, of

---

[36] See Gibney in this volume; Lori in this volume.
[37] See Joppke in this volume; Orgad in this volume; Vink in this volume.

status-non-citizens in a given state is, in part, to ask about their treatment under the state's norms pertaining to (what we now know is sometimes denominated) 'citizenship' in its rights, participation, and recognition senses.[38]

Of course, bringing these citizenship conversations together may appear to lead us to seemingly gratuitous inquiries about the extent to which non-citizens can be said to enjoy or lack ... citizenship. No doubt, contemplating the 'citizenship of non-citizens' may appear to be a paradoxical exercise; yet doing so is necessary in light of the prevailing 'enclosure' conception of citizenship discussed above. In this conception, the nationally bordered institutions comprising citizenship-as-status are presumed to represent the preconditional frame for pursuit of practices of liberal democratic citizenship within. Thus, we need to ask: what does the condition of status non-citizenship look like in an avowedly liberal democratic citizenship regime?

ELEMENTAL FEATURES: TERRITORIALITY AND (IN)SECURITY

To begin to identify specific characteristics of status non-citizenship, one might first want to try to designate some features—rights, capacities, duties—that exclusively attend status citizenship. After all, by definition, non-citizens will not possess them. Speaking in general terms, however, there are not so many of these. In international law, citizens have the right to territorial security in the state of their citizenship; they may not be expelled. And if they do exit, they have the right to re-enter those states. International law arguably constrains states in stripping citizenship from its holders (though in recent years, liberal states have implemented policies to forcibly expatriate their citizens on national security grounds).[39] When traveling abroad, their country of citizenship is bound to protect them in some way—though dual nationality may complicate the operation of this norm.[40]

This strikingly short list enumerates the principal attributes dividing citizens from non-citizens en masse. Non-citizens are deemed to be subject to the state's

---

[38] For non-citizens located outside of that state's borders, the ideals of 'universal citizenship' would, *ex ante*, be inapplicable since citizenship's universality is ordinarily conceived in nationally bounded terms.

[39] Audrey Macklin, 'The Return of Banishment: Do the New Denationalisation Policies Weaken Citizenship?,' online http://eudo-citizenship.eu/commentaries/citizenship-forum/1268-the-return-of-banishment-do-the-new-denationalisation-policies-weaken-citizenship.

[40] See Spiro in this volume.

exclusion power and, in most circumstances,[41] its expulsion power as well. They may be precluded from entering, whether initially or upon seeking return, and they may be removed when already present. Ordinarily, they cannot claim the diplomatic protection of a state of which they are not citizens when not within that state's territory.[42]

Of these, it is territorial access and security that is the distinction of greatest practical importance. The consequences of non-citizens' conditionality of presence are manifold and significant. Whatever other rights and protections they possess in that state, these are held contingent on the state's non-exercise of its expulsion power. Possible deportability, and the fact that the non-citizen may be excluded from re-entry after departing the territory, will have a constraining effect on mobility.

Keep in mind that in a world of bordered polities, the fact that only status citizens possess the right to enter the territory of a particular state means that the pool of persons who constitute that state's non-citizens are persons who are *not* present by right.[43] Except in those cases in which aliens are born as such in the territory or are rendered foreigners by dint of secession or conflict (in either case, call them 'autochthonous aliens'), non-citizens come to the state from without. Either such persons have been permitted to enter the territory in some capacity or they are territorially present in some unauthorized status in spite of, and contra to, border constraints. Either way, and whether born there or having arrived post-natally, all non-citizens are subject to potential removal. It is the contingency and conditionality of their territorial presence that is thus integral to—and in fact, usually constitutive of—the legal status of alienage.

On the other hand, these rules about citizenship and territoriality don't always apply in practice, nor do they always apply literally. For example, some people find themselves territorially banished from states of which they are status citizens, whether via extradition, rendition, passport revocation, or even mistaken deportation.[44] Inversely, states sometimes find themselves unable to expel some territorially-present status non-citizens, whether for geo-political reasons (e.g., the

---

[41] The principal exception to this otherwise extensive power is the norm of nonrefoulement. See Costello in this volume; Gibney in this volume.

[42] This last feature is clearest in practice, and draws a relatively sharp divide between citizen and alien. If a person who is a non-citizen in state A is outside of state A, she cannot count on State A to specifically protect her against the action of other states or non-state actors. This may matter in only limited circumstances since (i) many non-citizens in relation to state A possess citizenship in state B, and that latter state is in theory responsible for their diplomatic protection, (ii) all states are required under international law to provide basic protections to all territorially present persons, so the state of presence maintains obligations to the non-citizen, and (iii) in cases where state A's citizen possesses another nationality, state A may not regard itself as diplomatically responsible for that citizen in any case.

[43] This is the general rule but there are particular exceptions as a matter of bilateral agreement. See, e.g., Australian Government, Department of Immigration and Border Protection, 'Facesheet: New Zealanders in Australia', online https://www.border.gov.au/about/corporate/information/fact-sheets/17nz.

[44] See, e.g., Jacqueline Stevens, 'U.S. Government Unlawfully Detaining and Deporting U.S. Citizens as Aliens,' *Virginia Journal of Social Policy & The Law 18*, no. 3 (2011): pp. 606–720.

state of citizenship refuses to accept their citizen-deportees or there is no state/a failed state to send to) or due to other legal constraints (e.g., demands of nonrefoulement).

Moreover, the extent and nature of territorial conditionality varies enormously among classes of aliens. Status non-citizenship is everywhere a tiered institution: some categories have greater territorial access and greater territorial security than others. Non-citizens who are lawful permanent residents can, in principle, remain indefinitely; visitors of various kinds may stay only briefly; and the presence of others is *ex ante* and ongoingly unauthorized. Some categories of non-citizens may travel freely in and out of the state/supra-state territory, whereas others will lose their residence permission upon traveling away. Non-citizens qualifying as refugees or related categories may enjoy legal protections against state removal that others do not have.

Still, with all of these variations and qualifications, it is this conditionality-of-territorial-presence in a given citizenship state that most significantly defines what being a status non-citizen entails. Significantly, many of a state's own citizens will not be present in that state's territory at a given moment for any variety of reasons, but in ordinary circumstances, those citizens cannot be precluded by their state of nationality from being present, nor may they be forced to depart when they are there. This stands in contrast to status non-citizens, for whom both exclusion and deportation from that state are possible and routine.

POLITICAL VOICE
AND NON-CITIZENS: AMBIGUITIES

It is a commonplace in some liberal democracies, including the United States, to say that citizenship's greatest significance for its holders is that it guarantees the right to vote. Access to the franchise, according to many accounts, is the feature that most meaningfully distinguishes citizens from foreigners.[45] Empirically, in most public elections in most polities, only citizens may vote.[46] Nevertheless, voting and citizenship are hardly synonymous, nor are they mutually entailed. As much scholarly literature has now documented, voters and status citizens are only partially convergent categories.

---

[45] The right to vote is listed as the first 'benefit of citizenship' by the United States Citizenship and Immigration Services (online https://www.uscis.gov/sites/default/files/files/article/chapter2.pdf).

[46] There is, however, a significant number of European and Latin American countries where non-citizens can vote in local elections. See Shaw in this volume.

For one thing, throughout the history of liberal democratic states, many persons possessing the status of citizenship have nonetheless suffered disenfranchisement. The propertyless and women were denied the vote well into the twentieth century in some countries. In the United States and elsewhere, voting rights were routinely denied to racial minorities until the 1960s, and de facto racial exclusions continue today, whether in the form of voter identification laws or felon disenfranchisement policies.[47] Moreover, systemic structures of inequality and cultural nonrecognition effectively disenfranchise extensive populations of status citizens who are, in consequence, disinclined to vote.

Conversely, and more to the point in this chapter, lack of status citizenship has not always meant lack of democratic voice. In some elections in some democratic states, certain non-citizens (usually permanent residents) are entitled—or were at one time entitled—to cast a vote. The United States has extensive histories of non-citizen ('alien') voting,[48] and in a handful of U.S. localities today, non-citizens may vote on local matters. Within the EU system, citizens of other member states enjoy the local franchise, and twelve states extend this right to all non-citizen residents.[49] Furthermore, scholars have noted that actual political voice in some electoral systems derives far more significantly from financial investments, social capital networks, and even campaign contributions than from the franchise. Under the law of many states, non-citizens, or some categories thereof, are at no disadvantage in these arenas.[50]

Lastly, and significantly, voting and campaign contributions do not exhaust political efficacy. Political influence is delivered through grassroots action including local and national civic participation, protest, and organizing. Non-citizens (including, sometimes, undocumented non-citizens) have engaged as grassroots political actors across a range of settings, from labor disputes to local 'quality of life' battles, religious freedom manifestations, and anti-racism initiatives. In recent years, non-citizens have weighed in publicly on matters of immigration, refugee, and naturalization policy.

[47] In parts of the United States and in limited cases elsewhere, hundreds of thousands of convicted felons are formally precluded from voting in perpetuity. Given the hugely disproportionate number of convicted felons who are minority males, this exclusion functions as a racial (and gendered) bar on voting. See Ali Rickart, 'Disenfranchisement: A Comparative Look at the Right of the Prisoner to Vote' (6 February 2015), online *Ius Gentium*, https://ubaltciclfellows.wordpress.com/2015/02/06/disenfranchisement-a-comparative-look-at-the-right-of-the-prisoner-to-vote/.

[48] Jamin B. Raskin, 'Legal Aliens, Local Citizens: The Historical, Constitutional and Theoretical Meanings of Alien Suffrage,' *University of Pennsylvania Law Review 141*, no. 4 (1993): pp. 1391–1470; Ron Hayduk, *Democracy for All: Restoring Immigrant Voting in the United States* (New York: Routledge, 2006).

[49] See Bloemraad in this volume; Shaw in this volume.

[50] Bruce D. Brown, 'Alien Donors: The Participation of Non-Citizens in the U.S. Campaign Finance System,' *Yale Law and Policy Review 15*, no. 2 (1997): pp. 503–552. For an overview of states' laws on contributions to campaigns by non-nationals, including resident non-citizens, see IDEA (International Institute for Democracy and Electoral Assistance), 'Is There a Ban on Donations from Foreign Interests to Candidates?,' online http://www.idea.int/political-finance/question.cfm?id=247.

This means that citizenship-as-status and citizenship-as-democratic-participation are significantly overlapping but partially nonconvergent in both directions. Not only have many disadvantaged status citizens been denied 'citizenship rights'—in response to which various social movements have specifically called for the 'restoration of citizenship,'[51] but status non-citizens have found ways, both formal and informal, to exercise democratic voice in such a way as to permit analysts to speak coherently of the citizenship practices of non-citizens. Strange coinage, perhaps, but also useful in its paradoxical clarity.

NON-CITIZENSHIP AND THE RIGHT
TO HAVE RIGHTS

Beyond territorial insecurity and political dis- or under-enfranchisement, there is not a great deal that non-citizens, as such, have in common. As indicated already, alienage categories are highly differentiated, not merely across states, but also within them. The effect of being a status non-citizen on a person's experience turns fundamentally on the particular legal status category she occupies as well as the kind of right or liability in question. In any given state, some categories of non-citizens will be authorized to work; others will not. Some will be eligible for certain forms of social support, and some will not. Some non-citizens in some categories will be criminally liable for their presence and some will not. Some are permitted to be present for a short period, some indefinitely. Some will owe the state income taxes and some will not. Some will have the opportunity to apply for citizenship via naturalization and some will not. In this regard, it is difficult to generalize about what non-citizenship status entails *tout court*.

Still, in liberal democracies, differentiation among classes of non-citizens only goes so far. This is because liberal legalism provides a floor. At least as a matter of formal law, all non-citizens, whatever their immigration status, enjoy recognition as legal subjects by the state they inhabit (so long as they are recognized by the state as being 'inside').[52] In fact, when it comes to many of the most basic rights under law—what some states call 'fundamental rights'—territorially-present non-citizens of all categories are, at least formally, indistinguishable from citizens.

---

[51] See, e.g., Laurene Kelley, 'Public Defender Helps Reframe Memphis History,' The Shelby County Public Defender, 3 May 2016, online http://defendshelbyco.org/.

[52] States often deploy legal fictions through which they deny that certain persons who are physically inside the borders are in fact territorially present as a legal matter. This allows states to evade responsibility for affording the legal protections that would otherwise be required. Linda Bosniak, 'Being Here: Ethical Territoriality and the Rights of Immigrants,' *Theoretical Inquiries in Law* 8, no. 2 (2007): pp. 389–410.

How do we account for this leveling effect, not merely among different classes of non-citizens, but also as between non-citizens and citizens? The answer lies in a core feature of liberal constitutional states. In liberal constitutionalism, many basic rights, including the rights to sue and be sued, to make and enforce contracts, to marry and divorce, and to invoke basic government protections including due process rights in the criminal justice setting—are contingent on the facts of personhood and territorial presence rather than on any particular legal status.[53] The commitment to personhood protection is expressly embedded in the fundamental law of the individual states, as well as the European Union. Some constitutions extend basic rights to 'everyone;' others to 'any person' or 'all persons.' Some constitutions provide that 'no one' shall be subject to certain indignities or abuses. As for the territorial element, while in some cases it is only implicit, in others, it is made plain. For example, the U.S. Constitution provides that no government entity shall 'deny to any person within its jurisdiction the equal protection of the laws.'[54] Although the scope of the term 'within its jurisdiction' has a long history of contest and manipulation (one implicating the nation's colonial and military histories),[55] it is, like analogous concepts elsewhere, generally read to limit government responsibility to protection of persons who are 'present' from the state's point of view.[56]

This means that in most democratic settings, it is territorially present individuals—both citizens and non-citizens—who are the state's basic legal subjects.[57] That this should be so is striking. Among other things, it means that to characterize citizenship status as 'the right to have rights,' as Hannah Arendt did decades ago,[58] is simply not accurate today. A great many core rights extend to individuals present in the territory, independent of their status under the state's border rules.[59] Strikingly,

---

[53] Linda Bosniak, 'Persons and Citizens in Constitutional Thought,' *International Journal of Constitutional Law 8*, no. 1 (2010): pp. 9–29.

[54] Amendment 14, Sec. 1, in relevant part: 'nor shall any state deprive any person of life, liberty, or property, without due process of law; nor deny to any person within its jurisdiction the equal protection of the laws.' These 'equal protection' and 'due process' clauses have been judicially interpreted to constrain national and local government action as well as that of the states. For further discussion, see Bosniak (n 3).

[55] These are histories of territorial ambiguity that implicate a state's past and ongoing colonial and military engagements. For legal territoriality in United States law, see, e.g., Kal Raustiala, *Does the Constitution Follow the Flag?: The Evolution of Territoriality in American Law* (New York: Oxford University Press, 2010). For the French case, see Emmanuel Saada, *Empire's Children: Race, Filiation, and Citizenship in the French Colonies*, translated by Arthur Goldhammer (Chicago: University of Chicago Press, 2012).

[56] See footnote 52.

[57] Although other structural and identity variables, including race, perceived national origin, gender, and class, will affect the application and experience of these protections in practice.

[58] Hannah Arendt, *The Origins of Totalitarianism* (San Diego, New York, London: Harcourt, 1968), p. 296.

[59] Such extension has been incorporated into, and backed up by, international human rights law. Human rights law, in turn, serves in some cases to render national constitutional rights law more robust. Speaking genealogically, however, the individual rights commitments embedded in the international human rights regime were first developed in the liberal constitutionalist setting.

these are precisely the rights that liberal democratic discourse often characterizes in the language of 'citizenship.'

This is not to say, however, that non-citizens' actual experience of basic rights protection is identical to that of citizens. The reason, once again, is that the borders associated with citizenship status and immigration regulation are enforced inside the state as well as at its edges. When they are applied internally, they sometimes serve to undermine exercise of the personhood rights non-citizens formally enjoy. Such undermining can occur both directly and indirectly.

To start with the direct effect: While a territorially present non-citizen is entitled to personhood rights, these may often be trumped by the concurrent fact of their subjection to the government's immigration control authority. As one example, a non-citizen in criminal proceedings is entitled to the same full due process rights as any citizen. Yet if resulting in a conviction, these same criminal proceedings, will often thereafter trigger deportation proceedings. There, the right to remain territorially present itself now becomes the issue. And in the deportation setting, procedural protections are typically far more limited because such decisions are regarded as part of the state's legitimate border authority. Indeed, if the non-citizen is deported after criminal conviction and punishment, she arguably faces a double penalty that no criminally convicted citizen encounters.[60] And once deported, she is now outside the scope of that state's territorially grounded basic rights altogether.

The border law's undermining effect on the rights of non-citizens works indirectly as well. Some non-citizens—especially, but not only, those present on an unauthorized basis—often avoid invoking the basic rights they formally possess for fear of triggering the attention of the immigration authorities. To give an example: in most liberal democratic states, all employees, irrespective of status, are entitled to some state-managed workers compensation protection if injured on the job. But an irregularly employed non-citizen might choose to avoid claiming the benefit for fear of exposure to immigration authorities. Perhaps the employer will report her; perhaps the workers compensation office will share information with the immigration office in a system permitting information-sharing between government entities.[61]

Finally, in some moments designated as emergencies, the ordinary rules protecting territorially present persons are eclipsed. Non-citizens classified as enemies during states of exception may be subject to treatment that amounts, in Agamben's now-iconic phrase, to that of 'bare life.'[62] In those states with a strong commitment to constitutional territoriality, the state might (re)locate the individual to a space

---

[60] For general discussion of the double punishment issue, see Juliet Stumpf, 'The Process is the Punishment in Crimmigration Law,' in Katja Franco Aas, ed., *The Borders of Punishment: Migration, Citizenship and Social Exclusion* (Oxford: Oxford University Press, 2013), pp. 58–75.

[61] See generally Bosniak (n 3).

[62] See Muneer I. Ahmed, 'Resisting Guantanamo: Rights at the Brink of Dehumanization,' *Northwestern University Law Review* 103, no. 4 (2009): pp. 1683–1763.

outside the formal territory of the state—as, for example, to Guantanamo in the U.S. case, in order to claim exemption from basic rights conferral. Or, once again, the state may seek to deny territorial recognition to physically present non-citizens— treating them as still, and always, at the border.[63]

In sum, non-citizenship statuses are highly differentiated in many respects, making it difficult to generalize about the character of the non-citizen experience. Still, one can make two broad points about non-citizens as a class. First, liberal democratic states' formally recognize persons who are territorially present—including non-citizens—as liberal legal subjects. This represents a striking leveling, not only between non-citizens and citizens but among categories of status non-citizens as well. Second, because liberal democratic states claim the authority to regulate the border in the interior, the protections of territorial personhood that status non-citizens formally enjoy are often undercut in practice. It is their common subjection to the state's border authority that constitutes status non-citizens' principal structural vulnerability.

Conclusion: Non-Citizens in Liberal Democratic Citizenship Regimes

This chapter has addressed the condition of persons inhabiting liberal democratic political communities in which they lack the legal status of citizenship. It has sought to distill a profile of the status non-citizen in broad terms, notwithstanding the great variations among categories and across states. The chapter's focus, however, is equally theoretical. It is motivated by the questions: What *is* status-non-citizenship? And: How are we to understand the relationship between lack of citizenship in the status sense and other modes of non-citizenship, or non-possession of (full) citizenship?

We have seen that status non-citizenship is both product and precondition of the operation of state borders. Millions of people designated as status non-citizens under the state's border rules reside within the territory of democratic states in a variety of situations. Once inside, status non-citizens remain governed by the regime of state border control as it is internally applied and enforced. And yet, that regime shares jurisdictional space with another set of internal norms—basic liberal democratic norms which (formally) deem the treatment of persons as less-than-full-members

---

[63] In cases such as Guantanamo, the constitutional argument may shift to the question whether the individual held is, in fact, still within the state's constitutional territory such that basic protections must continue to apply (Bosniak (n 52)).

to be unjust. Significantly, these latter, ethically universalist norms are often articulated via the language of 'citizenship.'

The experiences of territorially present status non-citizens are, in consequence, produced conjointly by these overlapping but often dissonant governing logics. At times, these logics concord without great event. At others, the tensions between citizenship's borderism and its egalitarianism are fraught and unremitting.

BIBLIOGRAPHY

Abizadeh, Arash, 'Democratic Theory and Border Coercion: No Right to Unilaterally Control Your Own Borders,' *Political Theory 36*, no. 1 (2008): pp. 37–65.

Ahmed, Muneer I., 'Resisting Guantanamo: Rights at the Brink of Dehumanization,' *North western University Law Review 103*, no. 4 (2009): pp. 1683–1763.

Anderson, Bridget, *Us and Them? The Dangerous Politics of Immigration Controls* (Oxford: Oxford University Press, 2013).

Anderson, Elizabeth, *The Imperative of Integration* (Princeton: Princeton University Press, 2010).

Arendt, Hannah, *The Origins of Totalitarianism* (San Diego, New York, London: Harcourt, 1968).

Bauman, Zygmunt, *Liquid Modernity* (Cambridge: Polity Press, 2000).

Blake, Michael, 'Immigration, Jurisdiction and Exclusion,' *Philosophy and Public Affairs 41*, no. 2 (2013): pp. 103–130.

Bosniak, Linda, *The Citizen and the Alien: Dilemmas of Contemporary Membership* (Princeton: Princeton University Press, 2006).

Bosniak, Linda, 'Being Here: Ethical Territoriality and the Rights of Immigrants,' *Theoretical Inquiries in Law 8*, no. 2 (2007): pp. 389–410.

Bosniak, Linda, 'Persons and Citizens in Constitutional Thought,' *International Journal of Constitutional Law 8*, no. 1 (2010): pp. 9–29.

Bosniak, Linda, 'Book Review: Joseph H. Carens, *The Ethics of Immigration* (Oxford: Oxford University Press, 2013),' *Ethics 125*, no. 2 (2015): pp. 571–576.

Bourdieu, Pierre, *Outline of a Theory of Practice*, translated by Richard Nice (Cambridge: Cambridge University Press, 1977) [1972].

Brown, Bruce D., 'Alien Donors: The Participation of Non-Citizens in the U.S. Campaign Finance System,' *Yale Law and Policy Review 15*, no. 2 (1997): pp. 503–552.

Brubaker, Rogers, *Citizenship and Nationhood in France and Germany* (Cambridge: Harvard University Press, 1998).

Carens, Joseph H., *The Ethics of Immigration* (Oxford: Oxford University Press, 2013).

Cohen, Elizabeth, *Semi-Citizenship in Democratic Politics* (Cambridge: Cambridge University Press, 2009).

Cole, Phil, 'Beyond Borders: Towards a Right to International Movement,' *The Critique*, 6 January 2016, online http://www.thecritique.com/articles/beyond-borders-towards-a-right-to-international-movement-2/.

Fraser, Nancy, 'Reframing Justice in a Globalizing World,' *New Left Review 36* (November–December 2005): pp. 69–88.

Hayduk, Ron, *Democracy for All: Restoring Immigrant Voting in the United States* (New York: Routledge, 2006)

https://ubaltciclfellows.wordpress.com/2015/02/06/disenfranchisement-a-comparative-look-at-the-right-of-the-prisoner-to-vote/.

IDEA (International Institute for Democracy and Electoral Assistance), 'Is There a Ban on Donations from Foreign Interests to Candidates?,' online http://www.idea.int/political-finance/question.cfm?id=247.

Kelley, Laurene, 'Public Defender Helps Reframe Memphis History,' The Shelby County Public Defender, 3 May 2016, online http://defendshelbyco.org/.

Kukathas, Chandran, 'The Case for Open Immigration,' in Andrew I. Cohen and Christopher Heath Wellman, eds., *Contemporary Debates in Applied Ethics* (Malden, Oxford: Blackwell Publishing, 2005), pp. 207–220.

Macklin, Audrey, 'The Return of Banishment: Do the New Denationalisation Policies Weaken Citizenship?,' online http://eudo-citizenship.eu/commentaries/citizenship-forum/1268-the-return-of-banishment-do-the-new-denationalisation-policies-weaken-citizenship.

Miller, David, *Strangers in Our Midst* (Cambridge: Harvard University Press, 2016).

Mills, Charles W., 'White Ignorance,' in Sharon Sullivan and Nancy Tuana, eds., *Race and Epistemologies of Ignorance* (Albany: SUNY Press, 2007).

Pevnick, Ryan, *Immigration and Constraints of Justice* (Cambridge: Cambridge University Press, 2011)

Raskin, Jamin B., 'Legal Aliens, Local Citizens: The Historical, Constitutional and Theoretical Meanings of Alien Suffrage,' *University of Pennsylvania Law Review 141*, no. 4 (1993): pp. 1391–1470

Raustiala, Kal, *Does the Constitution Follow the Flag?: The Evolution of Territoriality in American Law* (New York: Oxford University Press, 2010).

Rawls, John, 'Kantian Constructivism in Moral Theory,' in John Rawls, *Collected Papers*, edited by S. Freeman (Cambridge: Harvard University Press, 1999), pp. 303–358.

Rawls, John, *A Theory of Justice* (Cambridge, Harvard University Press, 1971).

Rickart, Ali, 'Disenfranchisement: A Comparative Look at the Right of the Prisoner to Vote' (6 February 2015), online *Ius Gentium*, https://ubaltciclfellows.wordpress.com/2015/02/06/disenfranchisement-a-comparative-look-at-the-right-of-the-prisoner-to-vote/.

Saada, Emannuelle, *Empire's Children: Race, Filiation, and Citizenship in the French Colonies*, translated by Arthur Goldhammer (Chicago: University of Chicago Press, 2012).

Spiro, Peter J., 'A New International Law of Citizenship,' *American Journal of International Law 105*, no. 4 (2011): pp. 694–746.

Stevens, Jacqueline, 'U.S. Government Unlawfully Detaining and Deporting U.S. Citizens as Aliens,' *Virginia Journal of Social Policy & The Law 18*, no. 3 (2011): pp. 606–720.

Stumpf, Juliet, 'The Process is the Punishment in Crimmigration Law,' in Katja Franco Aas, ed., *The Borders of Punishment: Migration, Citizenship and Social Exclusion* (Oxford: Oxford University Press, 2013), pp. 58–75.

Taylor, Charles, *Sources of the Self: The Making of the Modern Identity* (Cambridge: Harvard University Press, 1989).

Tilly, Charles and Robert Goodin, 'It Depends,' in Robert E. Goodin and Charles Tilly, eds., *The Oxford Handbook of Contextual Political Analysis* (Oxford: Oxford University Press, 2006), pp. 3–32.

Trott, Adriel M., *Aristotle on the Nature of Community* (Cambridge: Cambridge University Press, 2014).

UNHCR, 'Ending Statelessness,' online http://www.unhcr.org/en-us/.

UN, Universal Declaration of Human Rights, 1948.

Walzer, Michael, *Sphere of Justice: A Defense of Pluralism and Equality* (New York: Basic Books, 1983).

Wellman, Christopher Heath, 'Immigration and Freedom of Association,' *Ethics* 119, no. 1 (October 2008): pp. 109–141.

Young, Iris Marion, 'Polity and Group Difference: A Critique of the Ideal of Universal Citizenship,' *Ethics* 99, no. 2 (January 1989): pp. 250–274.

CHAPTER 16

NATURALIZATION

LIAV ORGAD[*]

THE manner in which new citizens should be created is one of the most complex questions in political theory. At stake, as Ayelet Shachar observes, 'is the regulation of the most important and sensitive decision that any political community faces: how to define who belongs, or ought to belong, within its circle of members.'[1] The law of naturalization functions as one gatekeeper—it is designed to include the desirable people and exclude the undesirable ones. In so doing, naturalization provides a unique platform to reflect on three fundamental issues: [1] defining the 'We'—who 'we' are, and what kind of nation 'we' want to be; [2] setting criteria for identifying the desired 'They'—who is, in the state's view, a 'good citizen,' and the current understanding of what it means to become a citizen; and [3] finding the substance and form to which 'they' should subscribe in order to join the 'We.' Hence, to a large extent, the substance of the requirements 'we' demand of 'them' is about 'us.' Naturalization policy—the requirements that 'they' must fulfill in order

* I am indebted to Irene Bloemraad, Maarten Vink, and the participants at the Oxford Handbook of Citizenship Authors' Conference at the European University Institute for valuable comments and suggestions. Portions of this Chapter are drawn from my book, *The Cultural Defense of Nations: A Liberal Theory of Majority Rights* (Oxford: Oxford University Press, 2015).

[1] Ayelet Shachar and Rainer Bauböck, 'Should Citizenship be for Sale?,' EUI Working Paper no. 1 (Florence: RSCAS, 2014), p. 3.

to join 'us'—mirrors the qualities that 'we' value in others and reflects the essentials that define 'us' as a nation.

Liberal democracies are 'citizen makers'—they implement a variety of naturalization policies for creating citizens out of immigrants. To become German, for example, an immigrant should possess adequate knowledge of the German language, demonstrate sufficient knowledge of the German life and social order, conform to the German living conditions, and answer peculiar questions such as: 'What should parents of a 22-year-old daughter do if they do not like her boyfriend?' To become Danish, an immigrant must pass a citizenship test, meet the housing requirement by demonstrating that he or she has an independent residence of a reasonable size—at least 20 square meter per person—possess adequate knowledge of the Danish language, and hold a full-time employment for at least three out of the five years prior to the application for a permanent residence permit. Applicants should further sign a 'Declaration of Integration and Active Citizenship' in which they promise, among others, to 'make active efforts to become self-supporting … participate in the life of the community … facilitate the integration of the[ir] children,' and be aware that in Denmark parents 'are obliged to listen to their children.'[2]

To a large extent, naturalization policies look like a 'grab bag'; they include a little bit of everything. Some requirements are knowledge-based (language proficiency, civic knowledge), other are behavior-based (good moral character, full-time employment), and others are based on an attachment to the host country (family ties, ethno-cultural affinity). Very often, the goal of these policies is unknown, their format is arbitrary, their guiding ideology is controversial, their effectiveness is yet to be ascertained, and their justification is unclear. The law of naturalization has never been so central and relevant, and yet it suffers from a lack of guiding theory.

This chapter explores legal and theoretical aspects of naturalization. The first section addresses the ultimate goal of naturalization—what function does it serve?—by presenting three goals: contract, political test, and nation-building. Each goal may lead to a different process of naturalization and raise different ethical questions. The literature does not systematically discuss which goals are legitimate, and which ones are illegitimate. The second section seeks to present ways to assess the ethics of naturalization—drawing on conceptual and utilitarian grounds. Among the conceptual factors to be considered are the legitimacy of the goals of naturalization according to different conceptions of citizenship (liberalism, republicanism, cosmopolitanism, and communitarianism) and of nationhood (primordial, civic, and cultural). Among the utilitarian considerations are the efficiency of the naturalization criteria in achieving a legitimate goal. The third section moves on to examine three trends in naturalization policy in Western societies[3]—legalization,

---

[2] Declaration of Active Participation in Danish Language Learning and Integration into Danish Society, in accordance with section 9(2) of the Danish Aliens Act.

[3] The focus of the Chapter is Europe, Northern America, Australia, Israel, and Japan—the 'developed regions,' as defined by the United Nations. The Chapter does not geographically cover

devaluation, and liberalization (followed by a restrictive turn). It points out that naturalization has been internationalized in the direction of creating a right to citizenship; that citizenship is becoming a 'commodity' in the global economy market whose nature is increasingly influenced by economic factors; and that the process of liberalization in access to the status of citizenship is facing a restrictive turn—cultural considerations are becoming more central in naturalization decisions. The chapter concludes by offering new directions for the study of naturalization.

THREE FUNCTIONS OF NATURALIZATION

Naturalization is a process where a noncitizen becomes a citizen after birth. The English word 'naturalization' (or naturalisation) has its origin in the French word *naturaliser*, which means to admit an alien to citizenship. The French word *naturel* is rooted in the Latin word *natio*, which means 'birth'; naturalization, thus, means to make a person like a natural-born citizen.[4] In reality, however, naturalization policy has served various social and political functions. It is a means to control the number, pace, and nature of admission into the community and is used in order to maximize national interests—in terms of cultural identity, the economy, welfare, well-being, and justice. This section presents three functions of naturalization.

Contract

Naturalization can be viewed as a form of a contract. Membership in a community requires agreement to some rules. While existing members presumably agree to these rules by tacit consent—implied by continued residence in the host country or maintaining its citizenship, a doubtful proposition—new members are required to express explicit consent to the rules of a community. The process of naturalization intends to ensure that new members understand the community's essentials and

naturalization policies in developing regions, nor does it thematically cover access to tribal membership or sub-categories of regional membership. For the last two topics see Gover in this volume; Chung in this volume.

[4] The Chapter does not focus on mass naturalization in special moments, such as succession or the establishment of a new state, nor does it deal with facilitated modes of naturalization, such as military service. For different modes of naturalization, see Rainer Bauböck and Sara W. Goodman, 'Naturalisation,' EUDO Citizenship Policy Brief, no. 2 (2010).

explicitly consent to certain terms; it is an act of specification of obligations and expectations.

One way of demonstrating consent is through an oath of allegiance. The oath is a statement required in several countries from candidates for citizenship. In Britain, for example, there are two oaths. The traditional Oath of Allegiance requires every immigrant to 'be faithful and bear true allegiance to her Majesty Queen Elizabeth the Second, Her Heirs and Successors.' From 2004, every immigrant must also pledge loyalty to the United Kingdom: 'I will give my loyalty to the United Kingdom and respect its rights and freedoms. I will uphold its democratic values. I will observe its laws faithfully and fulfill my duties and obligations as a British citizen.' Oaths act as a form of contract between a society and newcomers; the content of the oath provides basic terms of the 'social contract' and details the most important duties and responsibilities of new citizens. An immigrant agrees to obey and uphold the law, share the democratic values of the society, act in the best interests of the state, defend the constitution, and bear true faith and allegiance to the state (Constitution, Republic, Queen, etc.), to give just a few examples from the various forms of loyalty oaths.[5] In return, the state recognizes the person as a member of the community, thereby providing her with liberties and protection. Contractual allegiance implies that allegiance is conditional; allegiance and protection are the *quid pro quo* of a mutual contract in which each is given in return for the other.

Another way of demonstrating consent is through an integration contract— a document that immigrants are often required to sign as part of the process of naturalization. In France, for example, every person should sign the 'Reception and Integration Contract' in order to receive a permanent residence permit, and another contract, 'The Charter of Rights and Duties of a French Citizen,' in order to receive citizenship.[6] The Charter is a kind of 'social contract,' specifying the terms for joining the French community. The immigrant must promise to respect French values (*Liberté, Égalité, Fraternité*) and principles (a secular, democratic, and social Republic), and be loyal to the Republic. In return, France recognizes him or her as a citizen. Reading the Charter, one gets a sense of French essentials—the fundamental values and principles that a non-French should embrace to become French.

Oaths and pacts are different forms of a contract between a noncitizen and a society, whether they are an expression of a legally binding contract—a legal promise followed by a legal sanction for breaching the terms—or merely a moral promise

---

[5] Liav Orgad, 'Liberalism, Allegiance, and Obedience: The Inappropriateness of Loyalty Oaths in a Liberal Democracy,' *Canadian Journal of Law & Jurisprudence* 27, no. 1 (2014): pp. 99–122, pp. 100–103.

[6] Décret n° 2006-1791 du 23 décembre 2006 relatif au contrat d'accueil et d'intégration et au contrôle des connaissances en français d'un étranger souhaitant durablement s'installer en France et modifiant le code de l'entrée et du séjour des étrangers et du droit d'asile (partie réglementaire); L-311-9-1 du code de l'entrée et du séjour des étrangers et du droit d'asile; Loi n° 2006-911 du 24 juillet 2006 relative à l'immigration et à l'intégration, art. 5 (Loi n° 2006-911); Décret no 2012-127 du 30 janvier 2012 approuvant la charte des droits et devoirs du citoyen français prévue à l'article 21-24 du code civil.

that serves non-legal functions, such as reminding the candidates of the seriousness of their choice and of the weighty obligation they undertake (think of wedding vows as an analogy[7]). Sometimes, these contracts reflect already existing legal duties that citizens in a political community bear, while sometimes these contracts add *new* contractual obligations to those already written in the law, thereby creating different classes of 'social contracts' because the duties taken by a naturalized citizen are broader than those applied to a natural-born citizen.

Political Test

Naturalization may function as a political test in which applicants are required to prove their worth as a prerequisite for becoming a member in the society. The process of naturalization serves as a political mechanism to test the compatibility of a candidate to the life of the community; by passing the test of naturalization, the applicant proves that he or she is a 'good citizen.' Unlike a contract, which implies two parties (even if not equal) that agree on some conditional terms, a political test is one-sided. It seeks to ensure that the migrant has made an effort to become a new member in the community by creating some obstacles that must be passed.

A well-known mechanism to put immigrants into a test is the so-called 'citizenship test.' In a way, the entire naturalization process is a test—whether one has resided in the country enough, integrated well into the society, behaved lawfully, and acquired certain skills and abilities. A citizenship test, thus, is an umbrella category. However, in the naturalization context, a citizenship test is usually a generic term to a *knowledge*-based test, examining whether the candidate has acquired the level of knowledge required in order to become a new member in the community. Citizenship tests differ greatly in their content—topical issues include history, culture, civics, geography, democracy, constitutional principles, and everyday life knowledge—and form: oral tests and writing tests are both common, but differences also exist on the format of the test and its level of difficulty.[8]

Another example of citizenship test is *character*-based. This test examines whether an immigrant possesses certain character traits. Consider the requirement of 'good moral character': this requirement tests whether an applicant has the moral character needed to become a citizen. In the United States, it had been historically

[7] Sanford Levinson, *Constitutional Faith* (Princeton: Princeton University Press, 1988), pp. 107–111.

[8] See, e.g., Christian Joppke, 'Through the European Looking Glass: Citizenship Tests in the USA, Australia, and Canada,' *Citizenship Studies 17*, no. 1 (2013): pp. 1–15; Sara W. Goodman, 'Fortifying Citizenship: Policy Strategies for Civic Integration in Western Europe,' *World Politics 64*, no. 4 (2012): pp. 659–698; Ines Michalowski, 'Required to Assimilate? The Content of Citizenship Tests in Five Countries,' *Citizenship Studies 15*, no. 6–7 (2011): pp. 749–768.

used to exclude applicants based on immoral behavior relating to lifestyle choices and sexual behavior—topics such as adultery, homosexuality, incest, prostitution, and polygamy. The requirement of good moral character was examined according to the prevalent values of the dominant majority group in the United States.[9]

Nation-Building

Naturalization can be viewed as a means of nation-building, which, alongside the ordinary means of public education, national feasts, and citizenship ceremonies,[10] serves to promote social solidarity and feeling of belonging. It intends to unify the in-group around a sense of commonness. The process of naturalization aims at cultivating a 'love of country' and attachment to its cultural identity. It often centers on national canons—real or imagined—historical events, symbols, ways of life, and patriotic rituals.

The process of nation-building is promoted by different naturalization requirements, among them are citizenship programs. The modern idea of citizenship programs was born in the United States at the beginning of the twentieth century. The U.S. Bureau of Naturalization began to develop the concept of 'Americanization' with the introduction of immigrant education programs. Immigrants were expected to become attached to American ideas and cut themselves from their old ties. New citizens had to be 'created' and 'learn to talk and think and *be* United States.'[11] The official goal was orientation: to supply immigrants with the knowledge required for examination in a naturalization court. But that was only the first step. The second step was to generate an American identity and promote the acceptance of an American way of life. The Bureau of Naturalization believed that compelling people to learn civics would shape their attitudes. Naturalization was an internal process immigrants had to undergo to develop an American consciousness and attachment to the United States. Hence, citizenship handbooks directed immigrants to love America and, importantly, to love America more than their country of origin.[12]

---

[9] Lauren Gilbert, 'Citizenship, Civic Virtue, and Immigrant Integration: The Enduring Power of Community-Based Norms,' *Yale Law and Policy Review* 27 (2009): pp. 335–397, pp. 340–361.

[10] For uses of citizenship ceremonies to promote loyalty, see Sofya Aptekar, 'Naturalization Ceremonies and the Role of Immigrants in the American Nation,' *Citizenship Studies* 16, no. 7 (2013): pp. 937–952.

[11] Theodore Roosevelt, 'True Americanism,' in *True Americanism: Four Essays* (Kessinger Publishing, 2006), pp. 27–57, pp. 51–52, 45–54.

[12] Raymond F. Crist, U.S. Department of Labor, Bureau of Naturalization, *Student's Textbook: A Standard Course of Instruction for Use in Public Schools of the United States for the Preparation of the Candidate for the Responsibilities of Citizenship* (Washington: Government Printing Office, 1918), pp. 23, 109–110 ('When I become a citizen of the United States ... I may love my native land, but I love the Government of America better ... This is not only a law of man but it is a law of God.'); Liav Orgad, 'Creating New Americans: The Essence of Americanism under the Citizenship Test,' *Houston Law Review* 47, no. 5 (2011): pp. 1227–1298, pp. 1253–1257.

The content and form of citizenship programs have been significantly changed in the last century, but the goal of nation-building remains. In 2008, upon the release of a new naturalization test, the U.S. Citizenship and Immigration Service remarked that 'We believe, through study, that the applicants will understand and attach themselves to those principles.'[13] In Europe, integration courses for immigrants have become a central mechanism to strengthen social solidarity and unity. In this regard, drafting naturalization requirements is seen as a form of nation-building. A political community, whose members are linked through a common project, is engaged in an attempt to determine the nature of the common project, the essence of the social contract, and the bond that binds the people together. Therefore, the function of naturalization as a tool for nation-building goes beyond the would-be citizens to have social implications on the citizenry.

The three functions of naturalization are always related to a specific goal that a state may seek to achieve. Take the goal of preserving a society's cultural identity. States can use a contract-based approach and ask migrants to sign a contract in which they declare having an adequate knowledge of the host society's culture and commitment to its essentials. States can further use a test-based approach to examine whether the migrants have acquired the essential knowledge and commitment. And they can use an education-based approach and require migrants to participate in integration courses in order to strengthen their cultural identity and sense of belonging. In most cases, in law and in practice, states use a blend of these functions.

ASSESSING NATURALIZATION

Every country has to decide citizenship questions: whom to admit, how many, and under which selection rules? The existing literature focuses on legitimate and illegitimate justifications to restrict immigration,[14] yet the literature on the justifications to restrict *access to citizenship* is less solid. Whatever the function of immigration

---

[13] Immigration Solutions Group, 'Frequently Asked Questions about the New Naturalization Exam' (September 27, 2007).

[14] Joseph H. Carens, 'Who Should Get In?: The Ethics of Immigration Admissions,' *Ethics & International Affairs* 17, no. 1 (2003): pp. 95–110; James L. Hudson, 'The Ethics of Immigration Restriction,' *Social Theory and Practice* 10, no. 2 (1984): pp. 201–239; David Miller, 'Immigration: The Case for Limits,' in Andrew I. Cohen and Christopher Heath Wellman, eds., *Contemporary Debates in Applied Ethics* (Malden: Blackwell Publishing, 2005), pp. 193–206; Stephen Macedo, 'When and Why Should Liberal Democracies Restrict Immigration?,' in Rogers M. Smith, ed., *Citizenship, Borders, and Human Needs* (Philadelphia: University of Pennsylvania Press, 2010), pp. 301–323.

law should be, naturalization policy raises different issues, because it governs the rights of people who are already within the territory. Many theorists take for granted that it is justified to use naturalization policy as a means for promoting patriotism and a sense of belonging, or that it is justified to use naturalization policy to put would-be citizens to test. But one may argue, for example, that nation-building should be left to public education, social institutions, and social interaction, rather than be the function of naturalization policy, or that 'the most liberal citizenship test is none,' as Joseph Carens argues.[15]

In order to assess the legitimacy of naturalization policies, clarifying their functions is not sufficient, given the contested nature of citizenship. This section discusses three ways in which naturalization policies are contested: their underlying conception of citizenship, their philosophy of nationhood, and their perceived efficiency. The first two of these challenges are essentially theoretical based on conceptual grounds, whereas the latter is an empirical challenge based on utilitarian grounds.

Conception of Citizenship

Analyzing naturalization can vary according to different theories of citizenship. Under a *cosmopolitan* theory, naturalization restrictions should be minimal because the existence of borders is seen as arbitrary. Cosmopolitan theorists are likely to object to most naturalization requirements with the possible exception of a residency requirement.[16] Under a *communitarian* theory, a state is likened to a club whose members enjoy a right of closure, meaning that they can set up a wide range of policies to restrict membership for a wide range of goals. A state is viewed as a 'community of character';[17] naturalization requirements reflect that character and new members are to accord with it. Under a *republican* theory, the virtue of citizenship is active participation in public life. The chief business of citizens is engaging in political deliberation by voting, serving on juries, participating in military service, and living a self-sufficient life. Naturalization requirements focus on active citizenship and commitment to the common good of the republic. Under a *liberal* theory, a state is neither a club whose members enjoy the right of closure, nor a global village open 'to all and sundry.' One type views liberalism as a *modus vivendi* allowing

---

[15] Joseph Carens, 'The Most Liberal Citizenship Test is None at All?,' in Rainer Bauböck and Christian Joppke, eds., *How Liberal are Citizenship Tests?*, EUI Working Paper no. 41 (Florence: RSCAS, 2010), pp. 19–20.

[16] Joseph H. Carens, 'Why Naturalization Should be Easy: A Response to Noah Pickus,' in Noah M.J. Pickus, ed., *Immigration & Citizenship in the 21st Century* (Lanham, Oxford: Rowman & Littlefield Publishers, 1998), pp. 141–146.

[17] Michael Walzer, *Spheres of Justice: A Defense of Pluralism and Equality* (New York: Basic Books, 1983), p. 62; David Miller, *On Nationality* (Oxford: Clarendon Press, 1995), pp. 22–27, 41–45, 68–70.

plural ways of life. There is no true or ideal way of life, but 'many forms of life in which humans can thrive.'[18] A second type views liberalism as an ethical project. There is a true or ideal way of life that ought to be promoted; liberalism is a moral project that holds some universal truths. Liberal theorists of the first type are likely to endorse requirements that verify whether a person is obeying the law and is committed to peaceful coexistence of the society and lawful political changes—a form of 'procedural liberalism.' Liberal theorists of the second type may go beyond it by requiring a commitment to liberal values and institutions—a form known as 'muscular liberalism.'

The legitimacy of naturalization policies may be evaluated differently under different theories of citizenship. A 'contract' may stipulate different terms according to different citizenship theories, as may the citizenship 'tests' required for naturalization. Similarly, some nation-building functions, such as the cultural preservation of the society, may be considered justified under a communitarian theory, unjustified under a cosmopolitan theory (and under some variants of a liberal theory), and context-dependent under a republican theory—if, for example, a certain way of life is an inevitable instrument of political deliberation and the public life, its use may be seen as justified. Take, for example, the U.S. requirement that a person should be attached to the principles of the U.S. Constitution: Communitarian theorists may interpret attachment to include mental attitudes and internal perceptions, while liberal theorists may focus on external respect as expressed by obeying the law and accepting the outcome of just political institutions. This classification, however, is not clear-cut. In reality, societies include a hybrid model. There may be thin and thick versions of each theory[19] and different interpretations in different contexts (for instance, one can be liberal toward refugees, and communitarian toward labor migrants).

Conception of Nationhood

Assessing naturalization policies also depends on the perceived character of the community—its implied concept of nationhood that is the political basis of citizenship. Three ideal-typical conceptions of community exist: primordial, civic, and cultural. A *primordial* community focuses on 'kinship, ethnicity and race.' Primordial characteristics are a given in the sense of being inborn; they are largely unchangeable 'by voluntary action.' One is born a member, granted membership via a relationship with a member, or achieves membership through a change of the primordial

[18] John Gray, *Two Faces of Liberalism* (New York: The New Press, 2000), p. 5.

[19] Gerald L. Neuman, 'Justifying U.S. Naturalization Policies,' *Virginia Journal of International Law* 35, no. 1 (1994): pp. 237–278. For republican and liberal citizenship, see also Honohan in this volume.

characteristics as in the case of religious conversion. There are no citizenship tests because, in principle, the test is birthright. In contrast, a *civic* community is constructed on familiarity with the community's rules of conduct, constitutional essentials, and social mores. One can learn to become a member by knowing the history and civics, participating in the political life, obeying the law, and adopting the local mores. The requirements may not be easy, but they are learnable. In between primordial and civic communities, a *cultural* community membership is open to anyone who is willing to conform to the cultural tenets of the community. Anyone can become a member 'by converting to the right faith.' The community has 'eternal values' and a 'moral zeal.' Those who do not share in the project are 'mistaken and erring; they have to be converted' by 'cultural formation.'[20]

Although no political community fits these ideal types, and concepts of nationhood are contested within states, they help understanding the conceptual starting point in assessing naturalization.[21] In *primordial* communities, one cannot become a member by just learning the language and history. In Israel, for example, unless one is a spouse of an Israeli citizen (Jewish or non-Jewish), one can become a naturalized Israeli in the regular manner only if one is born Jewish or via a close family relationship with a Jew or through religious conversion; naturalization of non-Jewish applicants, an option that officially exists, is rarely granted in reality. In *civic* communities, one can learn how to become a citizen by demonstrating knowledge of a country's civics and history, learning the language, and participating in the public life. In *cultural* communities, one can become a member by showing moral commitment to, and identification with, cultural taboos of the community; one cannot just 'learn' to be a citizen. In practice, however, most communities present a combination of the primordial, civic, and cultural naturalization types, and the question is one of weight—which type is prominent in the overall assessment? To a large extent, naturalization requirements reflect not only the character of the national community, but also help to recreate and sustain this character throughout generations.

Utilitarian Considerations

Assessing naturalization policies should be based not only on normative grounds, but also on utilitarian grounds. In this regard, the individual and societal effects of naturalization policy need further clarification. As long as the goal is to reduce the number of migrants, naturalization policy may be effective.

---

[20] Quotes are from Shmuel N. Eisenstadt and Bernhard Giesen, 'The Construction of Collective Identity,' *European Journal of Sociology 36*, no. 1 (1995): pp. 72–102, pp. 77, 82–84, 87.

[21] Rogers Brubaker, 'Myths and Misconceptions in the Study of Nationalism,' in J. Hall, ed., *The State of the Nation* (Cambridge: Cambridge University Press, 1998), pp. 272–306; Vink in this volume.

However, to the extent that it intends to promote nation-building, social science provides little evidence on how effective policies are. Take citizenship tests: it is unclear if citizenship tests, in one format or another, are an effective predictor for the applicant's adherence to certain values. It is naïve to assume that a person who can spell out what is gender equality is ipso facto integrated into the society. It is also unclear to what extent a state can assess integration merely by using a test. Similarly, there is little evidence to suggest that integration courses, in which people are asked to participate in hundreds of hours of integration lessons, or a contract-based approach, where integration is based on a contract, foster social cohesion.[22] Likewise, aside from anecdotal evidence, we do not know what transformation occurs in the hearts and minds of people taking an oath or participating in a citizenship ceremony.

The effects of naturalization policies are even more puzzling in Europe. Under EU laws, freedom of movement for EU citizens exists within Member States. In the current regime—in which there is no unified *EU* naturalization law and requirements differ among Member States—a person wishing to become European can be naturalized in a more permissive state, for instance Sweden, and then resettle in a state with a stricter migration regime, for instance Denmark. This creates a sort of 'forum shopping' where a person can choose the state with the most lenient requirements and, once a citizen, move to a different state. In this reality, the effectiveness of national naturalization policies is at least doubtful.[23]

Further research should clarify to what extent naturalization policies are effective.[24] This is essential for a legal analysis because, even if the function of the policy is legitimate, the means chosen should effectively serve the goal and there should not be other, less intrusive means to achieve this goal—the test of proportionality. To be effective, the overall benefits of certain policies (tests, oaths, contracts, etc.) should outweigh their overall costs—in terms of human rights violations, social stigmatization, and social hostility. What must be assessed is not the efficiency of the naturalization process as a whole, but the *incremental* benefit derived from the additional use of a certain policy in the entire process. The question is how effective is the policy, and for what price.

---

[22] There are some exceptions; see, recently, Sara W. Goodman and Matthew Wright, 'Does Mandatory Integration Matter? Effects of Civic Requirements on Immigrant Socio-economic and Political Outcomes,' *Journal of Ethnic and Migration Studies* 41, no. 12 (2015): pp. 1885–1908.

[23] Rainer Bauböck, 'Civic Citizenship: A New Concept for the New Europe,' in Rita Süssmuth and Werner Weidenfeld, eds., *Managing Integration: The European Union's Responsibilities towards Immigrants* (Washington: Migration Policy Institute and Bertelsmann Stiftung, 2005), pp. 122–138, pp. 127–128.

[24] For assessing empirical effects of holding the status of citizenship, see Bloemraad in this volume (finding positive effects of the status of citizenship on social integration, political participation, labor market outcome, and identification with the nation). More research is required on the efficiency and the effect of *naturalization* policy.

NATURALIZATION TRENDS

The concept of naturalization is undergoing fundamental changes—three of such changes are legal, economic, and cultural. The process of naturalization has been increasingly regulated by transnational law; economic factors have become central in regulating naturalization, mainly for high-skill immigrants; and cultural considerations have become dominant in controlling the gates, mainly for 'undesirable' immigrants.

From a Privilege to a Right?

International law does not generally regulate naturalization; it defers to state authority in setting up naturalization rules and procedures. Nationality law, as Peter Spiro notes, is 'the last bastion in the citadel of sovereignty'.[25] The decision of the International Court of Justice in the Nottebohm case (1955)[26]—according to which 'international law leaves it to each State to lay down the rules governing the grant of its own nationality', which reflected the long-established principle that 'It is for each State to determine under its own law who are its nationals'[27]—is still very much alive. Naturalization rules, unless they are completely arbitrary or discriminate against a 'particular nationality',[28] enjoy a broad spectrum of judicial immunity. With the exception of refugees and stateless persons, international law includes no common rules and procedures, nor an effective agency for monitoring naturalization policy.[29]

This state of affairs creates four problems. First, human rights law: an international legal regime should prevent some of the mistreatment of resident aliens and abuse of power in citizenship allocation.[30] Second, state interests: with the growing number of immigrants demanding citizenship, it is sometimes in the interest of states to have some guidance on how to restrict access to citizenship without being condemned for human rights violations. Third, as with other transnational issues, the

---

[25] Peter J. Spiro, 'A New International Law of Citizenship', *American Journal of International Law 105*, no. 4 (2011): pp. 694–746, p. 746.

[26] Nottebohm Case, *Liechtenstein v. Guatemala*, I.C.J. Rep. 1955 p. 23, April 6, 1955.

[27] *Convention on Certain Questions Relating to the Conflict of Nationality Laws*, art. 1, April 12, 1930, 179 L.N.T.S. 89.

[28] *International Convention on the Elimination of all Forms of Racial Discrimination* (New York, March 7, 1966, 60 U.N.T.S.), art. 1(3).

[29] Kay Hailbronner, 'Nationality in Public International Law and European Law', in Rainer Bauböck et al., eds., *Acquisition and Loss of Nationality, volume 1: Comparative Analyses: Policies and Trends in 15 European Countries* (Amsterdam: Amsterdam University Press, 2006), pp. 35–104, pp. 42–45.

[30] Owen in this volume.

movement of people requires some international cooperation. The issue is broader than naturalization because, from the perspective of states, the regulation of territorial entry pre-selects those who may later become citizens (in countries that apply the principle of *jus soli*—citizenship of a child is determined by the place of its birth—their children will be citizens). Fourth, in Europe, the lack of EU regulation leads to a reality where Member States autonomously adopt naturalization policies, which, by setting the standards for the acquisition and loss of Member State nationality, also determine the acquisition and the loss of EU citizenship.[31]

In recent years, the legal consequences of holding the status of citizenship have been changed. Significant developments occurred in Europe. On legislation, the European Union has adopted several Directives that have made national citizenship weaker. For example, the Directive on the status of third-country nationals who are long-term residents has created a status that 'should be approximated' to that of national citizens.[32] It grants long-term residents a broad set of rights—equal access to the labor market, social and cultural rights, and some political rights, such as voting in municipalities[33]—to the point that the distinction between Union citizens and long-term residents is thin.[34] In addition, the Directive on family reunification has narrowed the power of states to restrict access to citizenship of family members of EU citizens.[35] In addition, on case-law, the European Court of Justice and the European Court of Human Rights ruled that admission into citizenship is subject to EU law.

International law is far from the point of providing a legal right to citizenship, but developments in this direction have been put forward. The law of naturalization is limited today by the right to family life, equal protection, and due process of law. Human rights law imposes greater restrictions on states in governing access to citizenship.

Economic Turn

The lightening of citizenship has long been recognized.[36] Globalization has undermined national citizenship as a primary source of identity and human rights

---

[31] Strumia in this volume.

[32] Council Directive 2003/109/EC of 25 November 2003 on the Status of Third-Country Nationals Who are Long-Term Residents [2003] O.J. L. 16.

[33] Kees Groenendijk, *Local Voting Rights for Non-Nationals in Europe: What We Know and What We Need to Learn* (Washington: Migration Policy Institute, 2008).

[34] Diego A. Arcarazo, 'Civic Citizenship Reintroduced? The Long-Term Residence Directive as a Post-National Form of Membership,' *European Law Journal* 21, no. 2 (2015): pp. 200–219.

[35] Council Directive 2003/86/EC of 22 September 2003 on the Right to Family Reunification [2003] O.J. L251/12.

[36] Peter J. Spiro, 'Questioning Barriers to Naturalization,' *Georgetown Immigration Law Journal* 14 (1997): pp. 479–519; Peter J. Spiro, *Beyond Citizenship: American Identity after Globalization*

protection. With the increasing number of diaspora communities—citizens who live outside their country of citizenship and do not participate in its political life ('external citizens,' as termed by Rainer Bauböck[37])—citizenship has become a primary instrument of global mobility.

The devaluation of citizenship is also expressed itself in the conditions for citizenship. Recent years have witnessed the rise of free-market ideas in citizenship acquisition. The most radical expression is the emergence of different forms of 'citizenship-for-sale' policies in which wealthy people can 'buy' citizenship by investment. Citizenship in the West, Ayelet Shachar explains, has become 'an important recruiting tool' for attracting wealthy and talented people. Political membership is becoming a tradable asset in the global market economy, and states act as firms competing in the global race for talent; wealth candidates and other high-skilled workers are granted fast-track to citizenship and an expedited process. Western states, Shachar argues, 'are turning themselves into brokers of membership grants, all in the name of bringing home distinction and glory.'[38] Certainly, Western societies are far from a reality of 'vacancies for citizenship' according to a 'call for political membership'; and yet, economic approaches to citizenship acquisition are becoming more central.[39]

The lightening of citizenship raises interesting empirical and normative questions regarding the nexus between access to the status of citizenship and the essence of citizenship. To what extent do naturalization requirements echo a state's concept of nationhood? Is the devaluation of citizenship, as expressed in the idea of putting citizenship for sale, stronger in civic communities, compared to cultural or primordial communities? Answering these contested questions is related to the theory of citizenship—what citizenship is about—since the legitimacy of the marketization of citizenship can be seen differently under different theories. In this context, cosmopolitans and communitarians may be on the same side in objecting to the selling of citizenship, for different reasons; cosmopolitans may see it as an unjust idea that increases global inequality between the rich and the poor, while communitarians may see it as a deviation from citizenship as a sacred idea that should never be put up for sale.

(Oxford: Oxford University Press, 2008); Yasemin N. Soysal, *Limits of Citizenship: Migrants and Postnational Membership in Europe* (Chicago: University of Chicago Press, 1994).

[37] Rainer Bauböck, 'Stakeholder Citizenship and Transnational Political Participation: A Normative Evaluation of External Voting,' *Fordham Law Review 75*, no. 5 (2007): pp. 2393–2447.

[38] Ayelet Shachar, 'Picking Winners: Olympic Citizenship and the Global Race for Talent,' *Yale Law Journal 120* (2011): pp. 2088–2139, pp. 2088, 2139, 2090 (respectively). See also Shachar in this volume.

[39] There are other expressions for the lightening of citizenship, among them the acceptance of dual citizenship and the allocation of citizenship by lottery. See, respectively, Spiro in this volume; Peter Schuck, *Diversity in America: Keeping Government at a Safe Distance* (Cambridge: Harvard University Press, 2003), p. 128.

Cultural Turn

Another salient trend in Western societies is the liberalization in access to citizenship. This trend is evident by the creation of a legal option for naturalization in most countries; the decline of the principle of *jus sanguinis* as the sole criterion in determining entitlement to citizenship; the growing appeal to the principle of *jus soli* in citizenship acquisition; the shortening of the residency requirement period; the decline of group-based racial discrimination; and the increasing toleration of dual citizenship. In most Western countries, second generation immigrants are entitled nowadays to citizenship through *jus soli* principles, and noncitizens can acquire citizenship after a shorter residency period. The prevailing wisdom, as observed by Christian Joppke, holds that access to the status of citizenship is 'becoming more inclusive and universalistic.'[40]

Global migration has produced not only liberalization in access to the status of citizenship—perhaps the correct term is openness, as many of the recent trends are rooted in selfish reasons of the receiving countries, mainly economic and demographic needs (it is a mistake to automatically equate openness with liberalization)—but also a restrictive turn. This trend is evident by imposing more restrictions on access to citizenship through family reunification; increasing use of criminal law in immigration control (a phenomenon known as 'crimmigration'); growing political demands to limit birthright citizenship; and adopting cultural integration requirements.

The most visible expression of the restrictive turn is the rise of what I term elsewhere 'cultural defense policies.'[41] Generally, these are policies aimed at protecting different forms and expressions of the national culture. In Europe, this has resulted in attempts to enforce, rather than encourage, cultural assimilation—integration is mandatory and test-based. It is expressed in the extension of culture-based selection to the requirements for entry—as via pre-arrival integration. It applies to all types of immigrants, including family members, and it is more invasive than the classic requirements of familiarity with a country's civics. By and large, cultural defense policies are implemented through five measures: (a) citizenship tests; (b) integration contracts; (c) loyalty oaths; (d) attachment requirements; and (e) language requirements. Whatever we call it—a thick version of civic nationalism, a thin version of cultural nationalism, or cultural defense—culture has become increasingly dominant in keeping the gates.

Empirical research supports the proposition that there is a restrictive cultural turn in Europe. In 2002, only four out of fourteen European states had a compulsory language requirement (29 percent); in 2007, eleven out of eighteen states

---

[40] Christian Joppke, *Citizenship and Immigration* (Cambridge: Polity Press, 2010), p. 31.
[41] Liav Orgad, *The Cultural Defense of Nations: A Liberal Theory of Majority Rights* (Oxford: Oxford University Press, 2015), pp. 85–114.

had a compulsory language requirement (61 percent); in 2010, seventeen out of twenty-three European states had a compulsory language requirement (71 percent), including eight states with a language requirement to be met abroad.[42] Similarly, a citizenship test, which two decades ago was largely associated with U.S. naturalization law, has become common in Europe. In 1999, only four states had a formal test; in 2010, the number tripled to twelve.[43] Likewise, integration contracts, almost unknown a decade ago, exist nowadays in many European states, among them Austria, Denmark, France, Germany, and the Netherlands. Loyalty oaths, too, have become widespread in Western naturalization law.

One way to view the restrictive turn is as an exception to the trend of liberalization in access to citizenship. Another way sees no contradiction between the two; Christian Joppke, for one, dismisses the rising power of culture as an immigration criterion by arguing that, at the end, the 'state culture' is merely a local version of the universal concept of political liberalism.[44] In a similar direction, Sara Wallace Goodman finds that access to the status of citizenship is becoming broader in one sense (who has access?), but narrower in another sense (under which conditions?). In other words: access to citizenship becomes more liberal, but liberalism becomes more muscular by thickening the integration requirements and providing them with cultural nuances rooted in a particular culture.[45] A third way to view the restrictive turn is to connect it with low-skilled immigrants; in this view, the cultural approach to access to citizenship is mainly associated, in law or in practice, with low-skilled workers, while the economic approach to citizenship is mainly applied to high-skilled people.

The appeal to cultural criteria to filter out immigrants and monitor the naturalization process is tricky. On the one hand, international law generally allows states to select citizens by means of 'universal' criteria, such as education, wealth, skills, and family ties. On the other hand, the use of racial and ethnic criteria is considered impermissible when it discriminates against a 'particular nationality.' Culture is not explicitly included in either category and the legality of cultural selection is unclear. In 1984, the Inter-American Court of Human Rights ruled that preferences in naturalization, issued by Costa Rica for nationals of Central American countries, are compatible with the American Convention on Human Rights and presents no discrimination. The Court justified the preference for Central American nationals by noting that they have closer 'cultural and spiritual bonds with the people of

---

[42] Claire Extramiana and Piet Van Avermaet, *Language Requirements for Adult Migrants in Council of Europe Member States: Report on a Survey* (Council of Europe, 2011), pp. 8, 12.

[43] Sara W. Goodman, *Naturalisation Policies in Europe: Exploring Patterns of Inclusion and Exclusion* (Florence: RSCAS, 2010), p. 17.

[44] Joppke (n 40), p. 137.

[45] Sara W. Goodman, 'Integration Requirements for Integration's Sake? Identifying, Categorising and Comparing Civic Integration Policies,' *Journal of Ethnic and Migration Studies* 36, no. 5 (2010): pp. 753–772, p. 757.

Costa Rica ... [and] identify more readily with the traditional beliefs, values and institutions of Costa Rica, which the state has the right and duty to preserve.'[46] To the extent that this case is still a good law, it only deals with positive, rather than negative selection—exclusion based upon cultural criteria or for cultural purposes.

Recent policies reflect a retreat from the trend of liberalization in access to citizenship, but do not mark a return to policies of cultural assimilation. Perhaps paradoxically, cultural defense policies reveal how light citizenship as a source of identity becomes. Liberal states attempt to define the rules for joining the community in cultural terms, but end up with a thin version of what 'culture' is. It is too early to predict whether we are witnessing the 'swan song' of the old structure of citizenship, or its transformation.

THE FUTURE OF NATURALIZATION

Setting the rules of naturalization is one of the most important decisions that every country must make. In Europe, where the borders of citizenship are becoming blurred—'borders' in the sense of a physical line separating lands—the rules of naturalization are one of the last political means to set the boundaries of citizenship ('boundaries' in the sense of marking the cultural limits of political membership). While there are still cases in which the boundaries of citizenship are directly connected with conflicts over borders, most Western societies are debating the boundaries of citizenship. The battle is not over lands, but over the identity and 'self' that govern lands. Setting boundaries requires difficult decisions on who 'We' are, and on what type of community 'We' want to be.

With a growing number of comparative studies on access to citizenship, we know better how naturalization policies vary between countries.[47] Still, there are important open questions. Further research is required into the interrelation between the requirements for access to citizenship (who can become a citizen) and the conceptions of nationhood (what citizenship is about). Research is also needed on the

---

[46] *Proposed Amendments to the Naturalization Provisions of the Constitution of Costa Rica*, Advisory Opinion OC-4/84, Inter-Am.Ct.H.R. Series A no. 4, January 19, 1984.

[47] See, e.g., Rainer Bauböck, Sievers Wiebke, and Bernhard Perchinig, eds., *Citizenship Policies in the New Europe* (Amsterdam: Amsterdam University Press, 2006); Bauböck et al. (n 29); Patrick Weil, 'Access to Citizenship: A Comparison of Twenty-Five Nationality Laws,' in Alexander T. Aleinikoff and Douglas Klusmeyer, eds., *Citizenship Today: Global Perspective and Practices* (Washington: Carnegie Endowment for International Peace, 2001), pp. 17–35; Morjé M. Howard, *The Politics of Citizenship in Europe* (Cambridge, New York: Cambridge University Press, 2009); Sara W. Goodman, *Immigration and Membership Politics in Western Europe* (Cambridge: Cambridge University Press, 2014).

individual and societal effect of naturalization requirements. How effective are citizenship tests, loyalty oaths, and integration courses in promoting social cohesion? Is there a correlation between the length of residency requirement and the level of (cultural, economic, political) integration? As Western countries will need more immigrants in the near future, questions relating to the effect of integration courses will become more crucial. Cross-national comparative research on the various effects of naturalization requirements can lead to a more evidence-based policy.

With 250 million international migrants in 2016, the number of people who may become citizens in Western societies has been tremendously increased. Citizenship, as noted by Peter Schuck, is 'the most valuable resource that mobile foreigners can ever hope to obtain.'[48] It must be taken seriously. Among other issues, setting naturalization policy invites a discussion on what citizenship is. In particular, there should be an exploration on the legitimate goals of naturalization policy, and there must be a continuous examination of whether certain policies indeed advance the promotion of these goals. Few issues are more pivotal to our future.

Bibliography

Aptekar, Sofya, 'Naturalization Ceremonies and the Role of Immigrants in the American Nation,' *Citizenship Studies 16*, no. 7 (2013): pp. 937–952.

Arcarazo, A. Diego, 'Civic Citizenship Reintroduced? The Long-Term Residence Directive as a Post-National Form of Membership,' *European Law Journal 21*, no. 2 (2015): pp. 200–219.

Bauböck, Rainer, 'Civic Citizenship: A New Concept for the New Europe,' in Rita Süssmuth and Werner Weidenfeld, eds., *Managing Integration: The European Union's Responsibilities towards Immigrants* (Washington: Migration Policy Institute and Bertelsmann Stiftung, 2005), pp. 122–138.

Bauböck, Rainer, 'Stakeholder Citizenship and Transnational Political Participation: A Normative Evaluation of External Voting,' *Fordham Law Review 75*, no. 5 (2007): pp. 2393–2447.

Bauböck, Rainer and Sara W. Goodman, 'Naturalisation,' EUDO Citizenship Policy Brief no. 2 (2010).

Bauböck, Rainer, Wiebke Sievers, and Bernhard Perchinig, eds., *Citizenship Policies in the New Europe* (Amsterdam: Amsterdam University Press, 2007).

Bauböck, Rainer, Eva Ersboll, Kees Groenendijk, and Harald Waldrauch, eds., *Acquisition and Loss of Nationality, volume. 1: Comparative Analyses: Policies and Trends in 15 European Countries* (Amsterdam: Amsterdam University Press, 2006).

Bauböck, Rainer, Eva Ersboll, Kees Groenendijk, and Harald Waldrauch, eds., *Acquisition and Loss of Nationality, volume 2: Country Analyses* (Amsterdam: Amsterdam University Press, 2006).

---

[48] Schuck (n 39), p. 128.

Brubaker, Rogers, 'Myths and Misconceptions in the Study of Nationalism,' in J. Hall, ed., *The State of the Nation* (Cambridge: Cambridge University Press, 1998), pp. 272–306

Carens, H. Joseph, 'Why Naturalization Should be Easy: A Response to Noah Pickus,' in Noah M.J. Pickus, ed., *Immigration & Citizenship in the 21st Century* (Lanham, Oxford: Rowman & Littlefield Publishers, 1998), pp. 141–146.

Carens, H. Joseph, 'Who Should Get In?: The Ethics of Immigration Admissions,' *Ethics & International Affairs 17*, no. 1 (2003): pp. 95–110.

Carens, Joseph, 'The Most Liberal Citizenship Test is None at All?,' in Rainer Bauböck and Christian Joppke, eds., *How Liberal are Citizenship Tests?*, EUI Working Paper no. 41 (Florence: RSCAS, 2010), pp. 19–20.

Crist, F. Raymond, U.S. Department of Labor, Bureau of Naturalization, *Student's Textbook: A Standard Course of Instruction for Use in Public Schools of the United States for the Preparation of the Candidate for the Responsibilities of Citizenship* (Washington: Government Printing Office, 1918).

Eisenstadt, N. Samuel and Bernhard Giesen, 'The Construction of Collective Identity,' *European Journal of Sociology 36*, no. 1 (1995): pp. 72–102.

Extramiana, Claire and Piet van Avermaet, *Language Requirements for Adult Migrants in Council of Europe Member States: Report on a Survey* (Council of Europe, 2011).

Gilbert, Lauren, 'Citizenship, Civic Virtue, and Immigrant Integration: The Enduring Power of Community-Based Norms,' *Yale Law and Policy Review 27* (2009): pp. 335–397.

Goodman, W. Sara, 'Integration Requirements for Integration's Sake? Identifying, Categorising and Comparing Civic Integration Policies,' *Journal of Ethnic and Migration Studies 36*, no. 5 (2010): pp. 753–772.

Goodman, W. Sara, *Naturalisation Policies in Europe: Exploring Patterns of Inclusion and Exclusion* (Florence: RSCAS, 2010).

Goodman, W. Sara, 'Fortifying Citizenship: Policy Strategies for Civic Integration in Western Europe,' *World Politics 64*, no. 4 (2012): pp. 659–698.

Goodman, W. Sara, *Immigration and Membership Politics in Western Europe* (Cambridge: Cambridge University Press, 2014).

Goodman, W. Sara, and Matthew Wright, 'Does Mandatory Integration Matter? Effects of Civic Requirements on Immigrant Socio-economic and Political Outcomes,' *Journal of Ethnic and Migration Studies 41*, no. 12 (2015): pp. 1885–1908.

Gray, John, *Two Faces of Liberalism* (New York: The New Press, 2000).

Groenendijk, Kees, *Local Voting Rights for Non-Nationals in Europe: What We Know and What We Need to Learn* (Washington: Migration Policy Institute, 2008).

Hailbronner, Kay, 'Nationality in Public International Law and European Law,' in Rainer Bauböck et al., eds., *Acquisition and Loss of Nationality: Policies and Trends in 15 European Countries, volume 1, Comparative Analyses* (Amsterdam: Amsterdam University Press, 2006), pp. 35–104.

Howard, M. Morjé, *The Politics of Citizenship in Europe* (Cambridge, New York: Cambridge University Press, 2009).

Hudson, L. James, 'The Ethics of Immigration Restriction,' *Social Theory and Practice 10*, no. 2 (1984): pp. 201–239.

Joppke, Christian, *Citizenship and Immigration* (Cambridge: Polity Press, 2010).

Joppke, Christian, 'Through the European Looking Glass: Citizenship Tests in the USA, Australia, and Canada,' *Citizenship Studies 17*, no. 1 (2013): pp. 1–15.

Levinson, Sanford, *Constitutional Faith* (Princeton: Princeton University Press, 1988).

Macedo, Stephen. 'When and Why Should Liberal Democracies Restrict Immigration?,' in Rogers M. Smith, ed., *Citizenship, Borders, and Human Needs* (Philadelphia: University of Pennsylvania Press, 2010), pp. 301–323.

Michalowski, Ines, 'Required to Assimilate? The Content of Citizenship Tests in Five Countries,' *Citizenship Studies 15*, no. 6–7 (2011): pp. 749–768.

Miller, David, *On Nationality* (Oxford: Clarendon Press, 1995).

Miller, David, 'Immigration: The Case for Limits,' in Andrew I. Cohen and Christopher H. Wellman, eds., *Contemporary Debates in Applied Ethics*, (Malden: Blackwell Publishing, 2005), pp. 193–206.

Neuman L. Gerald, 'Justifying U.S. Naturalization Policies,' *Virginia Journal of International Law 35*, no. 1 (1994): pp. 237–278.

Orgad, Liav, 'Creating New Americans: The Essence of Americanism under the Citizenship Test,' *Houston Law Review 47*, no. 5 (2011): pp. 1227–1298.

Orgad, Liav, 'Liberalism, Allegiance, and Obedience: The Inappropriateness of Loyalty Oaths in a Liberal Democracy,' *Canadian Journal of Law & Jurisprudence 27*, no. 1 (2014): pp. 99–122.

Orgad, Liav, *The Cultural Defense of Nations: A Liberal Theory of Majority Rights* (Oxford: Oxford University Press, 2015).

Roosevelt, Theodore, 'True Americanism,' in *True Americanism: Four Essays* (New York: Kessinger Publishing, 2006), pp. 27–57.

Shachar, Ayelet, 'Picking Winners: Olympic Citizenship and the Global Race for Talent,' *Yale Law Journal 120* (2011): pp. 2088–2139.

Shachar, Ayelet and Rainer Bauböck, eds., 'Should Citizenship be for Sale?,' EUI Working Paper no. 1 (Florence: RSCAS, 2014).

Schuck, Peter, *Diversity in America: Keeping Government at a Safe Distance* (Cambridge: Harvard University Press, 2003).

Spiro, J. Peter, 'Questioning Barriers to Naturalization,' *Georgetown Immigration Law Journal 14* (1997): pp. 479–519.

Spiro, J. Peter, *Beyond Citizenship: American Identity after Globalization* (Oxford: Oxford University Press, 2008).

Spiro, J. Peter, 'A New International Law of Citizenship,' *American Journal of International Law 105*, no. 4 (2011): pp. 694–746.

Soysal, Yasemin N., *Limits of Citizenship: Migrants and Postnational Membership in Europe* (Chicago: University of Chicago Press, 1994).

Walzer, Michael, *Spheres of Justice: A Defense of Pluralism and Equality* (New York: Basic Books, 1983).

Weil, Patrick, 'Access to Citizenship: A Comparison of Twenty-Five Nationality Laws,' in Alexander T. Aleinikoff and Douglas Klusmeyer, eds., *Citizenship Today: Global Perspective and Practices* (Washington: Carnegie Endowment for International Peace, 2001), pp. 17–35.

CASES

Nottebohm Case, *Liechtenstein v. Guatemala*, I.C.J. Rep. 1955 p. 23, April 6, 1955.

Legislation and Directives

Council Directive 2003/109/EC of 25 November 2003 on the Status of Third-Country Nationals Who are Long-Term Residents [2003] O.J. L. 16.

Council Directive 2003/86/EC of 22 September 2003 on the Right to Family Reunification [2003] O.J. L251/12.

Décret no 2012-127 du 30 janvier 2012 approuvant la charte des droits et devoirs du citoyen français prévue à l'article 21-24 du code civil.

Décret n° 2006-1791 du 23 décembre 2006 relatif au contrat d'accueil et d'intégration et au contrôle des connaissances en français d'un étranger souhaitant durablement s'installer en France et modifiant le code de l'entrée et du séjour des étrangers et du droit d'asile (partie réglementaire).

L-311-9-1 du code de l'entrée et du séjour des étrangers et du droit d'asile.

Loi n° 2006-911 du 24 juillet 2006 relative à l'immigration et à l'intégration, art. 5 (Loi n° 2006-911).

Other

Declaration of Active Participation in Danish Language Learning and Integration into Danish Society, in accordance with section 9(2) of the Danish Aliens Act.

International Convention on the Elimination of all Forms of Racial Discrimination (New York, 7 March, 1966, 60 U.N.T.S.), art. 1(3).

Proposed Amendments to the Naturalization Provisions of the Constitution of Costa Rica, Advisory Opinion OC-4/84, Inter-Am.Ct.H.R. Series A no. 4, January 19, 1984.

Immigration Solutions Group, 'Frequently Asked Questions about the New Naturalization Exam' (27 September 2007) http://immigrationsolutions.com/blog/employers/frequently-asked-questions-about-the-new-naturalization-exam/ (on file with the author).

CHAPTER 17

DENATIONALIZATION

MATTHEW J. GIBNEY[*]

CITIZENSHIP (and nationality) in the modern state is in many ways uniquely secure as a status and thus as a ground for rights. Historically, the members of various communities, including early state forms, could and often did lose their citizenship (along with their right to reside in the state) as punishment for a range of common crimes.[1] In contemporary states, however, even individuals who commit the most heinous of domestic crimes, including murder on a large scale, are imprisoned for life or, in some jurisdictions, executed. But they are not punished by the loss of citizenship (and consequently expelled from the state). The security of citizenship

 * I am greatly indebted to my fellow contributors on the *Handbook* for helpful advice on this chapter. Peter Spiro, who served as discussant for the original paper, provided characteristically incisive observations and the comments by Irene Bloemraad, Maarten Vink, Linda Bosniak, Leti Volpp, and Noora Lori proved particularly helpful in my revision of the original piece.
 [1] Benjamin Gray, 'From Exile of Citizens to Deportation of Non-Citizens: Ancient Greece as a Mirror to Illuminate a Modern Transition', *Citizenship Studies* 15, no. 5 (2011): pp. 565–582; Matthew J. Gibney, *Deporting Citizens* (Cambridge: Cambridge University Press, forthcoming, 2018).

contrasts quite dramatically with those of non-citizenship residence statuses in many countries. Non-citizens may typically be deported for violations of immigration rules and, in many countries, face mandatory expulsion for serious violations of the criminal law.

Yet the practically inviolable nature of citizenship and nationality should not obscure the fact that states have always possessed some grounds through which to take away citizenship, including fraud, disloyalty, acquisition of another citizenship, marriage to a foreigner, and threat to public order. Indeed, in recent years, denationalization powers have gained increasing intellectual and political attention as many liberal states have created new laws or enforced old ones to strip citizenship from individuals involved with terrorism.[2]

Denationalization power has historically been seen as a simple corollary to the state's right to decide whom it shall admit to membership. Just as the state has the right to determine rules for the acquisition of citizenship, so too it can decide the rules for how citizenship can be lost. However, particularly in modern societies, denationalization is almost always a controversial state power. This is partly because the revocation of citizenship has come to be associated with totalitarian states (in particular with the Nazi and Soviet regimes). Denationalization power is in many respects state power at its zenith. By taking away an individual's citizenship, the state inflicts a kind of civic death upon one of its members, a complete exclusion from the entitlements and privileges of membership that may even result in rightlessness.[3]

Moreover, the existence of denationalization power often betrays a particular view of citizenship: one that sees the status as conditional, as a privilege the state is entitled to take away.[4] This view was captured in 2010 by the then US Secretary of State, Hilary Clinton, when she considered new proposals to strip citizenship from terrorists: 'United States citizenship is a privilege. It is not a right. People who are serving foreign powers … are clearly in violation … of the oath which they swore when they became citizens'.[5] This position runs contrary, however, to a strain of political and legal thought that sees the citizen, including the naturalized one, as sovereign.[6] In this view, suggested by the Canadian Liberal Party leader's recent claim that 'a Canadian is a Canadian is a Canadian',[7] the continued possession of citizenship should be viewed as an inviolable right.

---

[2] Gibney (n 1); Sandra Mantu, *Contingent Citizenship* (Leiden: Brill, 2015).

[3] Hannah Arendt, *The Origins of Totalitarianism* (London: Andre Deutsch, 1986), p. 296.

[4] Audrey Macklin, 'Citizenship Revocation, the Privilege to Have Rights and the Production of the Alien', *Queen's Law Journal* 40, no. 1 (2014): pp. 1–54.

[5] Quoted in 'Bill Targets Citizenship of Terrorists' Allies', *New York Times*, 6 May 2010, online http://www.nytimes.com/2010/05/07/world/07rights.html?_r=0.

[6] See, for example, Patrick Weil, *The Sovereign Citizen: Denaturalization and the Origins of the American Republic* (Philadelphia: University of Pennsylvania Press, 2012).

[7] Quoted in 'A Canadian is a Canadian', *Vice News*, 28 September 2015, online https://news.vice.com/article/a-canadian-is-a-canadian-liberal-leader-says-terrorists-should-keep-their-citizenship.

Compared to many other areas relating to citizenship, the body of scholarship dedicated to the study of denationalization is rather small. This is partly reflective of the fact that denationalization's days as a key state power have, until recently, seemed in the past because of human rights constraints on the practice since 1945. Moreover, particularly amongst liberal states, denationalization has always been a relatively rare phenomenon. Since the beginning of the twentieth century, the number of people stripped of their citizenship because they have been deemed dangerous or disloyal constitutes only a tiny fraction of those individuals who have gained citizenship through naturalization let alone birth or descent across liberal democratic states. Nonetheless, the revival of political interest in denationalization amongst Western states after 2001, particularly in response to 'home grown' terrorist threats associated with Al Qaeda and ISIS, has spawned growing academic interest in the phenomenon.

In this chapter, I will explore the fruits of this academic work. The discussion that follows is divided into two major sections. In the first section I will consider the definition, grounds, and historical development of denationalization power. In the second section, I will draw from recent work in a number of academic disciplines (including political science, law, and sociology) to show, *inter alia*, how denationalization offers insight into questions of significant moment on the ethical limits of state power, the historical development of citizenship status, and how restrictive immigration controls impact not just upon non-citizens but also state members. My discussion will conclude with a brief discussion of some outstanding issues still to be adequately reckoned with by students of denationalization.

DEFINING DENATIONALIZATION

Before proceeding further it is important to define the subject matter of our investigation. In simple terms, denationalization is the non-consensual withdrawal of nationality from an individual by his or her own state. The power transforms the individual into an alien (or at least a non-citizen) in the eyes of the law of the state concerned, thus putting an end to the special responsibilities and entitlements which result from citizenship or nationality.

Some points of clarification are immediately required. First, as this definition suggests, the act of denationalization involves the *non-consensual* withdrawal of nationality. In most states it is possible for individuals also to give up their nationality voluntarily—through a formal renunciation of citizenship—but this individual-initiated act is, in law, distinct from denationalization. This distinction may, however, be considerably less clear in practice.[8]

A second point is that the term de*nationalization* emphasizes the individual's loss of nationality; that is, the legal recognition of her as a *national* of a particular state. However, the same power is often referred to in terms of citizenship. Denationalization is thus sometimes called 'revocation of citizenship' or 'deprivation of citizenship'. Citizenship and nationality are not always perfect synonyms. They are sometimes associated with different rights and obligations (those associated with nationality establish membership in a particular state *vis-à-vis* other states, while citizenship involves the domestic relationship between individuals and the state and between fellow citizens). However, nothing crucial rests on the distinction for the discussion that follows.

Denaturalization, on the other hand, is a term that it is important to distinguish. It refers to particular category of action within denationalization power: viz., the withdrawal of citizenship from *naturalized* members (non-native born citizens of the country). Many states have (or have had) laws that allow for the denationalization only of naturalized members (such as Australia before the 1960s) or have specific provisions for this group (as is currently the case in the UK).[9]

WHY DO STATES DENATIONALIZE?

In order to understand why a state would seek to denationalize one of its citizens (or even a group of its citizens), it is helpful to distinguish between a state's *goal* in denationalizing and a state's *grounds* for denationalizing. In terms of the former, states typically denationalize because they wish to cut ties of legal and moral responsibility to a particular citizen (or group of its citizens) to enable their expulsion, deportation, or exclusion. By transforming an individual into an alien (or a non-citizen) the individual concerned may lose the right to reside in the state and become vulnerable to deportation power.[10] According to Audrey Macklin, for example, the current aim of most denationalization is to banish (suspected) terrorists. Since 9/11, she argues, 'states have turned to deportation to resolve threats to

---

[8] See, for example, Weil (n 6); Ben Herzog, *Revoking Citizenship: Expatriation in America from the Colonial Era to the War on Terror* (New York: New York University Press, 2015).

[9] Gibney (n 1).

[10] Matthew J. Gibney, 'Should Citizenship be Conditional? Denationalization and Liberal Principles', *Journal of Politics* 75, no. 3 (2013): pp. 646–658.

national security by displacing the embodied threat to the country of nationality'.[11] Historically, denationalization has sometimes served more malevolent purposes. In a striking passage, Georgio Agamben has written that during the 1940s, the Nazi regime was careful to make sure that 'Jews and gypsies were completely denationalized' before they were deported to the extermination camps.[12]

Yet the goal of denationalization has sometimes simply been to shame individuals by publicly degrading their status. The US cancelled thousands of naturalization certificates in the aftermath of a 1906 Naturalization Act because these citizenships were fraudulently acquired.[13] US authorities often made no attempt to deport the individuals involved and in many cases allowed them to reapply—this time lawfully—for US citizenship. When the UK revoked the naturalization certificates of a large number of Germans after World War I, it allowed some to stay on as non-citizen residents.[14] Under a US law of 1940, members of the military dishonourably discharged for desertion during War could be denationalized.[15] Again, this law was never intended to result in expulsion. As most members of the military only held US nationality, there would not have been anywhere to send them anyway.

Just as the goals of denationalization have been various, so too have the *grounds* justifying the practice. One can identify five major grounds for loss of citizenship frequently used by states. The first (and perhaps the most common category) has been conflicts of allegiance or loyalty. States have often denationalized to end or prevent conflicting loyalties amongst their citizens.[16] This is clearly the case with citizens denationalized because they acquire another nationality. Some states forbid dual nationality and loss of citizenship automatically results from the acquisition of another membership.[17] The principle of minimizing conflicts of loyalty also explains why some states have had rules that withdraw citizenship from (naturalized) citizens who live abroad for lengthy periods or which revoke the citizenship of women who marry a foreign national husband. In the latter case, the assumption, consistent with the dominant view of women as a simple legal appendage of their husbands, has been that they would simply take on the nationality of their spouse.[18]

[11] Audrey Macklin, 'Introduction' in Audrey Macklin and Rainer Bauböck, eds., *The Return of Banishment: Do the New Denationalisation Policies Weaken Citizenship* (Florence: EUI Working Papers, 2015), p. 1.

[12] Giorgio Agamben, 'We Refugees', *Symposium 49*, no. 2 (1995): pp. 114–119, p. 117.

[13] Weil (n 6).

[14] Matthew J. Gibney, 'A Very Transcendental Power: Denaturalisation and the Liberalisation of Citizenship in the United Kingdom', *Political Studies 61*, no. 3 (2013): pp. 637–655; Panikos Panayi, *The Enemy in Our Midst: Germans in Britain during the First World War* (Oxford: Berg, 1991).

[15] Alex Alienikoff, 'Theories of Loss of Citizenship', *Michigan Law Review 84*, no. 7 (1986): pp. 1471–1503.

[16] Anonymous, 'The Expatriation Act of 1954' *Yale Law Journal 64*, no. 8 (1954): pp. 1164–1200.

[17] Peter J. Spiro, 'A New International Law of Citizenship', *American Journal of International Law 105*, no. 4 (2011): pp. 694–746.

[18] For elaboration, see: Linda Kerber, 'The Stateless as the Citizen's Other: A View from the United States', *The American Historical Review 112*, no. 1 (2007): pp. 1–34; Helen Irving, *Citizenship, Alienage,*

A second and generally uncontroversial ground for denationalization has been fraud and misrepresentation in the original acquisition of citizenship. *All* states have rules enabling them to revoke the citizenship of the naturalized if it is proven that their citizenship was fraudulently acquired or otherwise attained through deception. Such laws have often been considered as analogous to the invalidation of other legal statuses or contracts (like patent or marriage certificates) granted under fraudulent circumstances.[19] In this case, it is typically reasoned that the citizenship or nationality never lawfully existed in the first place and thus may be cancelled *ab initio*. In many countries, including the UK, denationalization for this reason is legally permissible even if it makes the individual stateless.

A third ground has been disloyalty or lack of allegiance. Historically, most states have had legal provisions enabling them to denationalize citizens (though in some countries only *naturalized* citizens) for behaviour that demonstrates serious hostility to the key principles or government of the state in question. Examples of such behaviour have included spying for another country, trading with the enemy, joining the military forces of another (enemy country), etc.[20] In some countries, including the US, membership of certain organizations or adherence to certain ideologies, such as communism or anarchism, have been seen as incompatible with loyalty and allegiance and thus as warranting denationalization.[21]

A fourth ground is constituted by what we might term unworthiness. In the general terms, most denationalization grounds involve behaviour or actions that make an individual *unworthy* of keeping citizenship. However, some individuals have been denationalized because they possess ascriptive characteristics that make them unsuitable for citizenship. US authorities in the 1910s and 1920s denationalized some US citizens of Japanese origin who had managed to gain citizenship years earlier despite racial restrictions on their access to citizenship.[22] However, the Nazi conceptualization of the Jews as an inferior race intrinsically unfit for German citizenship in the Nuremberg laws remains the archetype of unworthiness as a denationalization ground.[23]

A final major ground is what might one term security.[24] Denationalization is sometimes justified by the risk that some individuals—with particular ideological predispositions or associations—pose to the well-being of the citizen-community.

and the Modern Constitutional State: A Gendered History (Cambridge: Cambridge University Press, 2016); Nancy F. Cott, 'Marriage and Women's Citizenship in the United States: 1880-1934', *The American Historical Review 103*, no. 5 (December 1998): pp. 1440-1474.

[19] See Walter H. Maloney, 'Involuntary Loss of American Citizenship', *St. Louis University Law Journal 4* (1956): pp. 50-77.

[20] Gibney (n 10).   [21] Weil (n 6).   [22] Ibid.

[23] Martin Dean, 'The Development and Implementation of Nazi Denaturalization and Confiscation Policy up to the Eleventh Decree to the Reich Citizenship Law', *Holocaust and Genocide Studies 16*, no. 2 (2002): pp. 217-242.

[24] Shai Lavi, 'Punishment and the Revocation of Citizenship in the United Kingdom, United States, and Israel', *New Criminal Law Review: An International and Interdisciplinary Journal 13*, no. 2 (2010): pp. 404-426, p. 409.

This is increasingly a stated rationale behind the withdrawal of citizenship from those linked to terrorist groups who might engage in domestic attacks. This rationale is sometimes difficult to separate completely from the questions of lack of allegiance, not least because the relevant acts typically must have an international dimension and not be common crimes. Nonetheless, it is the perceived threat of violent future actions by such individuals (rather than any previous actions) that often forms the primary justification for denationalization.

Historically, many different paths have thus led to denationalization. State authorities have justified the removal of citizenship on the grounds that an individual has possessed certain ascriptive characteristics (for example, being a member of a specific racial or ethnic group) or because of actions (like marriage to a foreigner, extended residence overseas, or adherence to a particular political ideology) unrelated to any direct display of disloyalty or lack of allegiance. Denationalization has resulted from acts that indicated an individual's desire for citizenship (fraudulent acquisition), as well as acts—accomplished or, sometimes merely predicted—perceived to demonstrate hostility or danger to the citizen-community or state (such as spying or terrorist activity.) If denationalization has historically been a relatively rare act of state power (at least in comparison to some other state sanctions, like imprisonment), the grounds for the power's use have been diverse and wide-ranging.

DENATIONALIZATION'S HISTORY

How has denationalization moved over historical time between these different grounds? While denationalization has evolved quite differently across regions and states, my discussion here of denationalization's historical trajectory shall for reasons of space concentrate solely on the experiences of Western states. Beginning in the early 1900s, four fairly distinct periods in denationalization's recent history are identifiable.

The first such period might be labelled the period of denationalization's emergence. This period occurs from the late nineteenth century to the end of World War I. While the punishment of banishment (which was common practice in Europe before the 1800s) is in many ways its precursor, denationalization really emerges in its modern form only with the development of formal immigration controls that clearly distinguish citizens (with the right to reside on state territory) from aliens (with no such right) through travel documentation in the nineteenth century.[25] It

---

[25] See, for example, John Torpey, *The Invention of the Passport: Surveillance, Citizenship and the State* (Cambridge: Cambridge University Press, 2000).

is in the late nineteenth century and early twentieth century that denationalization laws were first put in place by countries such as the UK, France, the US, Australia, Canada, and South Africa. These laws concentrated initially on creating a legal basis for cancelling fraudulently acquired certificates of naturalization, often because applicants had directly lied to procure citizenship or withheld from state authorities their intention to reside abroad. This singular focus on fraud tended to be quite short-lived, as focus soon shifts to laws that enable the state to denaturalize undesirable or dangerous citizens more broadly.

New laws passed in the period just before and during World War I were used to denationalize anarchists, communists, and citizens of German origin. In the UK, for example, *British Nationality and Status of Aliens Act of 1918*, resulting from anti-German hysteria during WWI, provides for denaturalization on a number of grounds, including disloyalty, trading with the enemy, and extended residence overseas.[26] Some two hundred denationalizations sprung from the provisions of the Act in the period immediately after the end of the War. In the US, similar hostilities towards Germans jostle with government concerns about anarchists and communists, and led the courts to expand fraud and expatriation provisions to make it possible to strip citizenship from individuals for disloyal actions occurring many years after the initial grant of citizenship.[27] Legislation in 1907 also allowed for the expatriation of women and naturalized citizens residents overseas for an extended period, ostensibly on grounds of preventing conflicts of nationality.[28] By the end of 1920, the US had denaturalized more than 4000 people.[29]

The second period represents the era of denationalization's apogee. This period, which ran from the early 1920s to the end of World War II in 1945, saw the rise of mass denationalization by totalitarian states. A Soviet decree in 1921 which stripped citizenship from all Soviet citizens abroad for more than five years without returning, anyone who had left Russia without permission after November 1917, and those who had fought in armies against the Soviets, left more than 1.5 million people stateless and stranded in a range of European countries.[30] Legislation in 1934, passed by the Nazi government in Germany, created wide-ranging powers to strip citizenship from so-called 'undesirables', with the use of denationalization intensifying with war in the 1940s, in part to enable the regime to appropriate the assets of Jewish emigres who had fled the country. Even democratic countries, like the US and Canada, attempted (albeit more muted versions of) similar denationalization practices, primarily as an expression of war-time hostility to their citizens of Japanese descent. The Renunciation Act of 1944 passed by the US Congress facilitated the loss of

---

[26] Panayi (n 14).   [27] Weil (n 6).   [28] Herzog (n 8).   [29] Weil (n 6), p. 197.
[30] See George Ginsburgs, 'The Soviet Union and the Problem of Refugees and Displaced Persons 1917–1956', *The American Journal of International Law 51*, no. 2 (1957): pp. 325–361.

citizenship of Japanese Americans who had—under considerable state pressure—renounced their citizenship;[31] similar measures were used in Canada to facilitate the deportation of a substantial proportion of Japanese-Canadians interned during the War.[32] However, in each case, mass denationalization was effectively foiled. In the US, this emerged through court action; in Canada, changing public attitudes to Japanese-Canadians with the end of the Pacific War, made it impossible for the government to execute its deportation plans.

The period from 1945 to 2001 saw denationalization in retreat. The Nazi experience greatly tarnished the legitimacy of stripping citizenship and the greater emphasis in the post-War world on human rights, both at domestic and (through the newly formed United Nations) at international levels, undercut the state's room to manoeuvre in denationalization.[33] Norms against discriminatory treatment based in particular on gender, race, and even mode of citizenship acquisition, and protections against statelessness impacted upon the legitimacy of the practice.[34] In the US, the Supreme Court, in several decisions, virtually outlawed involuntary expatriation, rewriting the citizen/state relationship.[35] Across a range of other countries, including Australia, Canada, and the UK, domestic legislation clawed back expansive powers, with an eye to protecting the naturalized and preventing statelessness. In Germany, the site of mass denationalization during World War II, denationalization is constitutionally limited largely to cases where citizenship is fraudulently acquired or forfeited through dual nationality.[36] Across many states, however, (including Germany by the early 2000s) dual nationality is increasingly accepted, undermining this avenue for loss of citizenship. Even where quite broad powers remain on the statutes, denationalization becomes an occasional and rare act. In the UK, for example, only one person was denationalized between 1971 and 2001.[37]

The final and current period commences with the Al Qaeda terrorist attacks of September 11, 2001 and might be described as a time of modest revival in denationalization. In the UK, September 11 and the subsequent July 7, 2005 tube and bus bombings in London has led to legislation that revamped denationalization and, in the case of the latter event, dramatically expanded the power's grounds. In the US a number of politicians have proposed legislation calling for terrorists to be stripped of citizenship on grounds of joining foreign terrorist organizations ostensibly at war with the US.[38] While these proposals have founded on the US Constitution, new legislation has emerged in Canada, Australia, the Netherlands, and Belgium (and is proposed in many other countries) to deal with Islamist extremist

---

[31] Mai Ngai, *Impossible Subjects: Illegal Aliens and the Making of Modern America* (Princeton: Princeton University Press, 2004).

[32] Ann Gomer Sunahara, *The Politics of Racism: The Uprooting of Japanese Canadians during the Second World War* (Toronto: Lorimer, 1981).

[33] Gibney (n 1).   [34] Spiro (n 17).   [35] Weil (n 6).   [36] Mantu (n 2).

[37] Gibney (n 14).   [38] Gibney (n 10).

terrorist organizations, particularly after the beginning of the war in Syria in 2011. Denationalization has become associated with the fight against various forms of jihadism.

A distinguishing feature of the current period of revival is that the focus of state justification for denationalization has shifted from 'punishing' acts of disloyalty or eliminating divided loyalties (indeed, states have become increasingly tolerant of dual nationality in recent decades) to protecting citizens against future terrorist attacks through deportation. Denationalization has become primarily a pre-emptive strike against dangerous individuals, particularly those associated with ISIS or Al Qaeda. This move towards pre-emption has however resulted in only a *modest* revival because new provisions tend to be hemmed in by liberal constraints. Reflecting international norms against the generation of statelessness, new denationalization provisions are typically applicable only to dual national citizens who may be deprived of citizenship without being made stateless, replacing the earlier focus on the naturalized. Consequently, despite a marked rise in political rhetoric about citizenship as a privilege and the flourishing of new laws, denationalization remains a rare act across Western states. Even in the UK, a country more willing to denationalize than any other Western country, the number of denationalizations in the last decade has amounted to about five to six people annually.[39]

EARLY DENATIONALIZATION SCHOLARSHIP

Despite its dramatic impact on the lives of those individuals who lose citizenship and its role as a high point of formal state power, denationalization received relatively little sustained attention from scholars before its recent revival. Most scholarship on denationalization before the 2000s was legal in focus and emanated from the US. A number of articles in US law journals between the 1920s and the 1960s mapped the evolution of the power in US law, focussing, in particular, on the legal acrobatics of US courts to show that citizens had expatriated themselves or proven that their initial oath of allegiance was invalid. In the US, these discussions were animated by the question of whether—and if so under what conditions—denationalization provisions might be considered constitutional, especially given the provisions of 14th Amendment of the Constitution which guaranteed that every individual born

---

[39] Gibney (n 1).

in the US was a citizen.[40] There was very little focus on explaining the dynamics behind denationalization's rise and fall as a matter of political focus.

While much legal scholarship tended to be domestically focussed, the use of mass denationalization by Communist Russia and Nazi Germany in the 1920s and 1930s respectively did stir the interest of International Law scholars. They were concerned with the obvious tension between the norm that states could fashion their own nationality laws—in the words of one author: 'freely to fix the conditions under which they grant and withdraw citizenship'[41]—and the baleful consequences for other states faced with large numbers of stateless people on their territory whom they were reluctant to integrate and unable to deport. As the British scholar Fischer-Williams indelicately noted in 1927, 'it is no longer possible to send undesirables abroad. Slops may be thrown out of the window of a settler's hut on a prairie; in a town such practice is inadmissible.'[42]

But it was only in response to the actions of Nazi Germany that legal scholars began to consider the question denationalization as an issue of human rights rather than simply a matter of international order. In a 1934 article, the Harvard scholar Lawrence Preuss argued that no denationalization law can 'arbitrarily disregard, from motives of pure national interest ... the natural ties by which an individual is attached to a determined society within the framework of the international community'.[43] The noted international law academic Hans Lauterpacht went even further a few years later in articulating the individual rights affected. He argued that 'the indiscriminate exercise by a State of the right of denationalizing its subjects, when coupled with a refusal to receive them when deported from a foreign country, constitutes an abuse of rights which could hardly be countenanced by an international tribunal'.[44] If these criticisms fell short of a complete critique of denationalization, they suggested international legal grounds for constraining its use.

Yet amongst scholars of politics and history the practice of denationalization, though certainly described in a range of works outlining the circumstances of mass forced migrations, received scant attention as a practice with far reaching human and political implications. A major and significant exception to this trend was Hannah Arendt's *The Origins of Totalitarianism* of 1951.[45] In many respects, political analysis on denationalization begins with this seminal work. This is because, for Arendt, the refugee—who, for her, is synonymous with the denationalized citizen embodied in the figure of stateless Jews and Russians—is 'the most symptomatic

---

[40] See, for example, Maloney (n 19); Anonymous (n 16); John P. Roche, 'The Loss of American Nationality. The Development of Statutory Expatriation', *University of Pennsylvania Law Review 99*, no. 1 (1950): pp. 25–71.

[41] Paul Abel, 'Denationalization', *Modern Law Review* (December 1942): pp. 57–68.

[42] John Fischer Williams, 'Denationalization', *British Yearbook of International Law 8* (1927): pp. 45–61, p. 57.

[43] Lawrence Preuss, 'International Law and Deprivation of Nationality', *Georgetown Law Journal 23* (1934): pp. 250–276, p. 250.

[44] Quoted in ibid., p. 250.   [45] Arendt (n 3).

group in contemporary politics'.[46] The refugee is symptomatic of the nation's capture of the state and the state's consequent inability to tolerate ethnic and racial diversity amongst its members. This intolerance reaches its fruition with mass denationalizations and the extermination of misfit ethnic groups implemented by totalitarian regimes in the 1920s and 1930s. The implications of Arendt's observation were captured some years later by Giorgio Agamben when he argued that the use of mass denationalization marks 'a decisive turning point in the life of the modern nation-state and its definitive emancipation from the naive notions of "people" and "citizen"'.[47]

Arendt does not only provide an explanation of the broader significance of denationalization on a mass scale through its connection to the rise of the exclusionary nation state. She also paints a powerful picture of the consequences of loss of citizenship for the individuals concerned. The denationalized are cast into a realm where they lack not only specific rights but also the 'right to have rights'. Loss of citizenship inflicts upon them not one calamity, but three: the loss of a home, the loss of government protection, and the loss of a place in the world that makes their 'opinions significant and actions effective'.[48] Arendt's description was, within a few years, to be picked up the US Supreme Court as part of its justification in the famous *Trop v. Dulles* decision for barring punitive denationalization.[49]

If scholarship on denationalization has been rather thin in the past, interest has grown rapidly in recent years, tracking the practical revival of the power after September 11. In the next two sections I want to turn to the fruits of this research which have ranged across law, politics, ethics, and sociology. In broad terms scholars have been concerned with two major questions: first, under what conditions—if any—is denationalization a legitimate practice? And second, what is the significance for the development of citizenship and of state power of denationalization policies and practices? The former question is normative and has been the focus on scholars in political theory, ethics, and law. The latter is explanatory and causal and has been addressed largely by scholars in political science, criminology, and sociology.

THE LEGITIMACY OF DENATIONALIZATION

Given its enormous consequences for the security and well-being of individuals, the power of states to denationalize obviously raises important questions of

---

[46] Ibid., p. 277.   [47] Agamben (n 12), p. 115.   [48] Arendt (n 3), p. 296.
[49] Weil (n 6).

legitimacy. Scholars of a normative inclination, primarily in law and ethics, have examined denationalization in relation to three major questions: do individuals have an absolute right to keep citizenship lawfully attained? Under what conditions is denationalization arbitrary and thus unacceptable? And are other states (or the international community) obliged to accept another state's denationalization decisions?

Citizenship as absolute

The question of whether there is an absolute right to retain one's citizenship has been most thoroughly explored by ethical theorists. One answer to this question has been offered by utilitarian philosopher, Peter Singer.[50] Writing in response to attempts by the British government to pass new legislation allowing denationalization for single nationals, Singer has rejected the idea that citizenship should be considered an absolute right (even when it results in statelessness). Rather, an ethical approach to denationalization should, he argues, search for the most 'desirable balance between individual rights, including the right to citizenship and the public good'.[51] At first glance, this position would seem to justify denationalization when the harms of keeping a particular individual as a citizen (for example, the potential that she might plot a mass terrorist attack) outweigh the harm to the particular individual caused by statelessness. Surely it is better to make one individual stateless than jeopardize the lives of many innocents? But, according to Singer, one needs also to consider that 'when a democratic government starts to revoke citizenship and make people stateless',[52] they provide a model for authoritarian states to strip citizenship indiscriminately (for example, to get rid of dissidents). This leads Singer to conclude that denationalization leading to statelessness can be acceptable but not 'without a judicial hearing'.[53]

Singer's consequentialist approach to ethics leads him to adopt a rather insouciant attitude towards the individual's right to citizenship. But many political theorists, informed by liberal conceptions of justice, have been more troubled. Indeed, in contrast to Singer, one issue on which they agree is that denationalization is unacceptable when it leads to statelessness.[54] This position stems from basic liberal commitments. Statelessness leaves individuals subject to state power without

---

[50] Peter Singer, 'Is Citizenship a Right?', *Project Syndicate* (6 May 2014), online https://www.project-syndicate.org/commentary/peter-singer-on-the-uk-s-proposed-legislation-to-denaturalize-britons-suspected-of-links-to-terrorism.

[51] Ibid.   [52] Ibid.   [53] Ibid.

[54] Gibney (n 10); Christian Barry and Laura Ferracioli, 'Can Withdrawing Citizenship Be Justified?', *Political Studies*, early view (5 July 2015), online http://onlinelibrary.wiley.com/doi/10.1111/1467-9248.12221/full.

citizenship's basic protections against that power, including security of residence, political rights, and potentially a host of other entitlements. Citizenship is thus appropriately conceived of as a basic right, in Henry Shue's terms, one without which it is impossible to exercise other fundamental rights.[55]

Putting to one side the statelessness issue, one might expect liberal theorists to support denationalization. After all, the idea that one should lose one's citizenship for violating society's fundamental norms seems completely consistent with the idea of society as a social contract. Many canonical liberal thinkers, like Kant and Beccaria, were supporters of the practice of banishment (which typically involved loss of citizenship) for this reason.[56] Indeed, a contemporary (if heavily moderated) version of this view has recently been articulated by Christian Joppke.[57] He suggests that it is counter-intuitive to protect the right to citizenship of individuals hell-bent on destroying the liberal societies of which they are members. Liberal states are completely justified in taking from terrorists the citizenship 'they have factually renounced and even wish to destroy.'[58]

More recent liberal theorists have shied away from such muscular contractualism. One reason, which has also been of concern to legal scholars, is that denationalization inevitably involves questionable forms of discrimination, as some citizens—notably, dual nationals—can be subjected to the practice while others cannot. Such unequal treatment is not only invidious, it also offends the idea that citizenship, as the grounding principle of state membership, simply ought to be a status which admits of no gradations. Citizenship worth its name entails equal standing amongst the members of a political community.[59]

Another ethical concern is that the state has no moral right to deprive an individual of citizenship in a country where the individual has made his or her life. Extended residence in a state over time, some political theorists argue, gives rise to a moral right to citizenship in the state concerned because uprooting a person from the place in question would be 'cruel and inhumane'.[60] If this position is right, it not only establishes a basis for saying that certain individuals should have the right to *acquire* citizenship, it also shows why it would be wrong for a state to *revoke* citizenship (and expel the individual). Denationalization would violate the principle that citizenship should correspond to an individual's connections and residence.

[55]   Henry Shue, *Basic Rights* (Princeton: Princeton University Press, 1980).

[56]   Gibney (n 10).

[57]   Christian Joppke, 'Terrorists Repudiate their own Citizenship' in *The Return of Banishment: Do the New Denationalisation Policies Weaken Citizenship* (Florence: EUI Working Papers, 2015), pp. 11–14.

[58]   Ibid., p. 13.   [59]   Macklin (n 11).

[60]   Joseph H. Carens, 'The Case for Amnesty', *Boston Review*, May/June (26 April 2012), online http://bostonreview.net/BR34.3/ndf_immigration.php. See also Joseph H. Carens, *The Ethics of Immigration* (New York: Oxford University Press, 2013); Rainer Bauböck, 'The Rights and Duties of External Citizenship', *Citizenship Studies 13*, no. 5 (2009): pp. 475–499.

Despite its evident force, the moral membership position would furnish a bar on denationalization only for some citizens. It would provide a ground for protecting those (dual national) citizens who had a genuine connection to, or residence in, the state in question.[61] Individuals who, perhaps by living overseas, lacked such connections or residence, could not, under this principle, claim protection against denationalization.[62]

A different argument for an absolute right against denationalization has emerged from judicial decision-making. In *The Sovereign Citizen* Patrick Weil illuminates the process through which legal reasoning in the US Supreme Court moved from the 1910s to the 1960s from a conditional conception of citizenship in which the sovereign (acting through the courts) could revoke citizenship for a host of reasons (including lack of allegiance), to a conception, informed by the individual as rights-holder. In this new conception, the citizen herself came to be considered, in Weil's words, 'the fount of sovereignty'.[63] The state could no more claim a sovereign right to denationalize than it could a right to dissolve its citizenry.

Evidently, there has been much debate amongst scholars on the ethics of denationalization with some seeing the practice as violating an absolute right to citizenship and others seeing it as permissible under tightly defined conditions (for example, when it is practised on dual nationals, when it follows a criminal conviction, and when an individual has not established an independent moral claim to membership). In practice, the gap between these two positions may not be that large. There may be reasons to doubt that states could be trusted to adhere to the kinds of constraints that would make denationalization ethically acceptable.[64]

Arbitrariness

Most international legal scholars accept that international law does not explicitly prohibit the practice of denationalization. They have thus been less concerned than moral theorists with the question of whether an individual has an absolute right to retain her citizenship and more concerned with exploring the specific circumstances under which denationalization is unlawful. Under international treaties like the Convention on the Reduction of Statelessness (1961) and the European Convention on Nationality (1997), denationalization is prohibited when it is 'arbitrary'.[65] This has

---

[61] Cf. Barry and Ferracioli (n 54).   [62] Gibney (n 10).   [63] Weil (n 6), p. 9.

[64] Christian Joppke, 'Terror and the Loss of Citizenship', *Citizenship Studies* 20, no. 6–7 (2016): pp. 728–748; Gibney (n 11).

[65] Jorunn Brandvoll, 'Limitations on Rendering Persons Stateless Under International Law' in Alice Edwards and Laura Van Wass, eds., *Nationality and Statelessness under International Law* (Cambridge: Cambridge University Press, 2014).

led legal scholars to ask: what features might make particular denationalization laws arbitrary and thus illegitimate?

One key issue has concerned procedural protections. In many states, including the UK and Australia, denationalization has been an administrative act, with individuals possessing far fewer procedural protections to contest decisions against them than are available to criminal defendants. A number of scholars have pointed to inadequate procedural protections including the absence of effective appeal rights and evidentiary issues related to national security information.[66]

A more fundamental, though related, issue has been whether denationalization should be considered a form of punishment, and, as such, be used only following conviction for a crime. States have powerful reasons to resist this conceptualization. Denationalization's appeal often stems from the fact that it allows authorities to rid themselves of unwanted or dangerous individuals without the bother of a criminal trial (where, for example, delicate national security information may be revealed). Regardless, many legal scholars hold the view that, given the huge impact loss of citizenship has upon an individual's fundamental rights, denationalization can only be lawful when it follows criminal conviction for serious offences against the state.[67]

The question of arbitrariness is relevant also to the grounds for denationalization. Why is it that an individual who engages in a terrorist bombing inspired by ISIS ideology that kills three people should lose his citizenship but not a mass murderer who kills his several victims for sexual gratification? It is not, as Dora Kostakopoulou notes, obvious why the former act is deemed 'prejudicial to the vital interest of the state' (or, to take the UK standard, not 'conducive to the public good') but the latter which involves 'violent criminal behaviour which shatters the lives of people' is not.[68] To be sure, there have recently been attempts to argue that terrorism is a *sui generis* criminal act, distinctive from other forms of violence, and thus justifying a distinctive kind of sanction.[69] Yet mass murder and hate crimes are also distinctive kinds of crimes and their particularity is registered in stiffer penalties (increased jail time) not, as in terrorist offences, in qualitatively different ones like denationalization.

The issue of arbitrariness has also been relevant to the question of who should be vulnerable to denationalization. As we have seen, laws that pick out naturalized

[66] Macklin (n 12); Kim Rubenstein and Niamh Lenagh-Maguire, 'More or Less Secure? Nationality Questions, Deportation and Dual Nationality' in Alice Edwards and Laura Van Waas, eds., *Nationality and Statelessness under International Law* (Cambridge: Cambridge University Press, 2014), pp. 264–291.

[67] Cf. Macklin (n 11); Lavi (n 24); Peter H. Schuck, 'Should Those Who Attack the Nation Have an Absolute Right to Remain its Citizens?' in Audrey Macklin and Rainer Bauböck, eds., *The Return of Banishment: Do the New Denationalisation Policies Weaken Citizenship* (Florence: EUI Working Papers, 2015).

[68] Dora Kostakopoulou, *The Future Governance of Citizenship* (Cambridge: Cambridge University Press, 2008), p. 137.

[69] Samuel Scheffler, 'Is Terrorism Morally Distinctive?', *Journal of Political Philosophy* 14, no. 1 (2006): pp. 1–17; Joppke (n 64).

citizens as uniquely vulnerable to loss of citizenship have been rendered unconstitutional or unlawful in many countries. But what should one make of the current trend to confine denationalization to dual nationals? Some scholars have suggested that this focus signals an anachronistic return to a period when dual nationals were distrusted because of their dual loyalty.[70] Recent laws subject dual nationals to invidious discrimination because they are subject to a penalty that cannot be imposed on other citizens.[71]

This position is contestable. Arguably, there are good reasons for treating dual nationals differently. After all, they would not suffer the same hardships as single nationals, since they would not be made stateless. Moreover, they already stand in a different position to the state in question than other citizens (undermining the equality argument) because their second citizenship provides them with an exit option should they desire to take it.[72]

These concerns about the lawfulness of denationalization reflect the way citizenship and nationality are now important foci of international law. According to Peter Spiro the direction of travel in international law in the post-war period has been towards ever growing human rights based constraints on states in the area of nationality, evinced in international norms relating to statelessness, dual nationality, and denationalization.[73] Taken together, these norms limit the lawful ability of states both to deny citizenship to certain groups of residents and to revoke citizenship once it is gained. While this sanguine conclusion may seem odd in the light of the recent denationalization turn, Spiro's analysis may help explain why new laws enabling the revocation of citizenship have, in spite of much clamour, so far been limited to relatively few states.

Responsibilities to Other States

As well as impacting upon human rights, denationalization raises questions about a state's responsibilities to other states. One interesting question to emerge from recent legal scholarship is whether other states are obliged to accept a state's denationalization decisions. Writing in the shadow of recent UK discussions of stripping citizenship from UK nationals fighting abroad in Syria, for example, Guy Goodwin-Gill has stressed that a promise to host countries that a national's state will accept the individual back at the end of her lawful stay is guaranteed in any national passport.[74] Indeed, this guarantee constitutes one of the foundational principles of international

---

[70] Rubenstein and Lenagh-Maguire (n 66).   [71] Macklin (n 11).   [72] Gibney (n 10).
[73] Spiro (n 17).
[74] Guy S. Goodwin-Gill, 'Deprivation of Citizenship Resulting in Statelessness and Its Implications in International Law', (12 March 2014), online https://www.documentcloud.org/documents/1086878-guy-s-goodwin-gill-legal-opinion-on-deprivation.html.

migration law. Consequently, even if denationalization dissolves the state/citizen relationship it may not put an end to the state of citizenship's international law duty to allow entry and residence to its (former) citizen.

From the perspective of political theory, denationalization raises questions of international justice. A state that denationalizes a member for whom it has moral responsibility (for example, one that—remembering the discussion above—is a resident with strong connections) may be committing a wrong against another state if it forces that individual on to it, even if the individual holds citizenship there.[75] The situation is analogous to the wrong committed by countries, like the US, when they deport non-citizen criminals (often in large numbers) back to ill-resourced countries, like Haiti, regardless of the fact that these individuals grew up in the US and are a product of that society.[76] But the injustice is even sharper in the case of denationalization because the people in question are often dangerous terrorists likely to pose a grave risk to the countries to which they are being sent.

Supranational memberships also pose challenges for denationalization practices. Citizens of EU member states are both national citizens and, via their national membership, citizens of the EU, and gain distinctive entitlements from each of these statuses. Is an individual's loss of citizenship in a member state enough to void her status as an EU citizen? This is one of the complicated questions that emerged in the *Rottmann* case of 2011, in which the European Court of Justice ruled that national decisions on denationalization were required to take into account EU law and specifically the requirement of proportionality. A number of scholars have seen this decision as curtailing the traditional autonomy of governments in nationality decisions. The decision, moreover, suggests the possibility of conceptualizing EU citizenship as a status independent in important respects from national citizenship.[77]

Understanding Denationalization's Significance

Denationalization's legitimacy has not been the only concern of scholars. Historians and social scientists have also used denationalization as a prism through which to explore the changing nature of citizenship and the character of state power.

---

[75] Carens, *The Ethics of Immigration* (n 60).

[76] See, for example, Daniel Kanstroom, *Aftermath: Deportation Law and the New American Diaspora* (New York: Oxford University Press, 2012).

[77] Jo Shaw, ed., *Has the European Court of Justice Challenged Member State Sovereignty in Nationality Law?* EUI Working Paper 62 (Badia Fiesolana: RSCAS, 2011).

Denationalization and the Development of Citizenship

Denationalization has provided insights into how citizenship has historically been characterized by both formal and informal inequalities. The assumptions behind and consequences of laws that have made the citizenship of some societal groups conditional has been highlighted in recent scholarship on the status of (married) women,[78] naturalized citizens,[79] and dual nationals.[80] The inferior status of specific ethnic, religious, and national groups in the citizen body has been demonstrated through examination of the experiences of citizens of German origin in Australia during World War I;[81] Japanese-Americans and Japanese–Canadians during World War II;[82] Israeli-Palestinians since the formation of the state of Israel;[83] and French Muslims facing an Islamophobic climate in contemporary France.[84] This work has shown how (seemingly impartial) denationalization laws have often served as a cover for racial and ethnic based discrimination.[85] Through these studies the gap between the official presentation of the citizenry as a community of equals and the historical reality that the citizenship embodies hierarchies of race, ethnicity, and gender has been exposed.

Scholars from the social sciences have also attempted to understand when and how denationalization power emerges in different national contexts. Recent analysis has identified a number of factors that have influenced the legal power and practical willingness of states to denationalize. Studies have pointed to the context of war,[86] (with its inevitable sharpening of the friend/foe contrast) and the roles of the judiciary (particularly in the US),[87] the bureaucracy,[88] and civil society, and public opinion in shaping legislation and enforcement.[89] Importantly, changes in the types of citizenship recognized by states have also influenced denationalization's development. The growing acceptance of dual nationality, for example, has been integral to the denationalization's current revival because the status enables states to strip citizenship from an individual without violating international norms on statelessness.[90]

The study of denationalization has unsurprisingly, then, offered distinctive insights into debates about the general trajectory of citizenship in Europe. A number

---

[78] For example, Irving (n 18); Leti Volpp, 'Divesting Citizenship: On Asian American History and the Loss of Citizenship through Marriage', *UCLA Law Review 52* (2005): pp. 405–483; Cott (n 18).

[79] Weil (n 6).

[80] Gibney (n 14); Ben Herzog, 'Dual Citizenship and the Revocation of Citizenship', *Research in Political Sociology 18* (2010): pp. 87–106.

[81] Gerhard Fischer, *Enemy Aliens: Internment and the Homefront Experience in Australia, 1914–1920* (St Lucia: University of Queensland Press, 1989).

[82] Ngai (n 31); Sunahara (n 32).

[83] See Ben Herzog, 'The Revocation of Citizenship in Israel', *Israel Studies Forum 25*, no. 1 (2010): pp. 57–72; Lavi (n 24).

[84] Marie Beauchamps, 'The Forfeiture of Nationality in France Discursive Ambiguity, Borders, and Identities', *Space and Culture 19*, no. 1 (2015): pp. 31–42.

[85] Gibney (n 14).   [86] Herzog (n 80); Gibney (n 10).   [87] Weil (n 6).   [88] Ibid.

[89] Sunahara (n 32).   [90] Gibney (n 10).

of scholars have argued that citizenship acquisition has increasingly been liberalized in Western states.[91] They have highlighted a range of changes (including the spread of *jus soli* rules and greater acceptance of dual nationality) that curtail the ability of the state to withhold citizenship from resident non-citizens, allowing citizenship to emerge as an individual *entitlement*. By contrast, scholars of denationalization have pointed to recent citizenship stripping laws and developments in immigration control, particularly since 9/11, to suggest that a logic of securitization has penetrated the realm of citizenship.[92] Denationalization evidences a clear attempt by states to affirm citizenship as a *privilege*, one conditional on a certain standard of behaviour.

The jury is still out on whether the current turn to denationalization truly undermines the broader liberalizing trends identified by scholars or simply constitutes an isolated exception to them. Yet it is clear that new denationalization laws do pose a problem for the citizenship liberalization thesis.[93]

Denationalization and the Development of State Power

Scholars have also attempted to understand the distinctiveness of denationalization, both as a historical power and in relation to other current state practices. This work has been undertaken particularly in the fields of sociology, criminology, and political science.

In some respects denationalization is, as I have suggested, a distinctly modern power, tied to the loss of a status—nationality—that first appeared in law only in the nineteenth century. Yet the practice of expelling the offending or dangerous citizen has a much longer history, as recent pejorative descriptions of denationalization as equivalent to 'exile' and 'banishment' indicate.[94] Historically informed work has traced connections between historical practices of banishment (which, before the 1900s, existed in different forms, including exile and penal transportation) and the emergence of denationalization power.[95] Denationalization might be seen, then, not as a historically novel practice, but as simply a form of punitive exile made fit for the modern international nation state system where states jealously guard their borders and nationality is fundamental.

---

[91] See, for example, Randall Hansen and Patrick Weil, eds., *Towards a European Nationality* (Basingstoke: Palgrave, 2001); Christian Joppke, *Citizenship and Immigration* (Cambridge: Polity, 2010); Spiro (n 17).

[92] James Hampshire, *The Politics of Immigration: Contradictions of the Liberal State*, (Cambridge: Polity, 2013); Macklin (n 4).

[93] Gibney (n 14).

[94] See, for example, Ben Saul, 'Plan to Strip Citizenship is Simplistic and Dangerous', *The Drum* (26 May 2015); Macklin (n 11).

[95] Gibney (n 1).

One key difference is that, at least in its most widely used forms, banishment was a formal and regular punishment, a penalty handed down as part of a criminal sentence.[96] Modern denationalization, however, is in many cases executive or administrative in nature, and states often go to great lengths to deny that it is a punishment. This contrast between the punitive and administrative mirrors modern deportation law and, consequently, another way of understanding denationalization's recent revival is as an extension of immigration (and specifically deportation) practices against non-citizens into the hallowed realm of citizenship.[97] This extension has been evident not only in the way the goal of denationalization is often expulsion. It has also been on display in the way the scant procedural protections available to citizens wishing to contest denationalization tend to mirror those of non-citizens contesting deportation.[98]

If contemporary denationalization has features in common with historical banishment, it also shares affinities with some current state practices. The criminologist Lucia Zedner, for example, has situated denationalization in the UK as merely one element in a raft of recent counter-terrorism measures designed to immobilize or contain the movement of individuals deemed harmful to the state and its citizens.[99] These measures include the confiscation of passports, control and exclusion orders (preventing individuals from entering certain zones or places or requiring them to stay in a particular zone or place), and temporary exclusion orders (which bar UK citizens overseas suspected of terrorist offences from returning to Britain for a period).[100] If one looks beyond the UK, even shadier state practices, like extraordinary rendition and the lawless off-shore internment associated with it, seem to be analogous measures.

Once one locates denationalization amongst these other state practices designed to control movement and deprive individuals of nationality entitlements, an important questions emerges: How should we conceptualize for analytic purposes what constitutes contemporary denationalization power? This question presses hard because of the existence of facilities like Guantanamo Bay in Cuba where the US has held suspected terrorists for many years without trial. When the countries of nationality of these prisoners collude in their indefinite detention have they not effectively denationalized them? Equally, what should one make of practices like the UK's Temporary Exclusion Orders that allow the state to leave a citizen in limbo overseas, barred from returning and thus unable to access the entitlements of citizenship? Should this type of—time-limited—civic death be considered a form of denationalization?

---

[96] See, for example, Gibney (n 1); Rebecca Kingston, 'The Unmaking of Citizens: Banishment and the Modern Citizenship Regime in France', *Citizenship Studies* 9, no. 1, (2005): pp. 23–40.

[97] Macklin (n 4).

[98] Daniel Kanstroom, *Deportation Nation* (Cambridge: Harvard University Press, 2007).

[99] Lucia Zedner, 'Citizenship Deprivation, Security and Human Rights', *European Journal of Migration and Law* 18 (2016): pp. 222–242.

[100] Ibid.

Conclusion

It is clear, then, that both normative and explanatory scholarship on denationalization has flourished in recent years. At the same time, it is evident from the preceding discussion that a number of key questions are still in need of address by scholars. Conceptually, it is important to rethink how the boundaries of denationalization are most appropriately conceived. In order to capture the way that modern denationalization power is developing, it may be necessary to focus more attention on *de facto* denationalization practices, like Temporary Expulsion Orders, rather than confine analysis solely to denationalization's more formal manifestations. Normatively, the most prominent question concerns the status of dual nationals, a group which constitutes a growing proportion of the citizen body of many states. Should dual citizens enjoy the same level of protection against denationalization as single nationals who would be made stateless by citizenship's withdrawal? Finally, for explanatory social science, the significance of recent moves to pass laws enabling denationalization need to be examined in depth. Is denationalization's recent revival a mere passing fad— all thunder with no lightning—made so by practical and human rights based constraints on state activity or are such laws the prelude to a new era of more contingent citizenship?

Denationalization has played a dark role in the history of citizenship. As a practice and as a power it has enabled states to throw off their obligations and responsibilities to unwanted, dangerous, or duplicitous members. At various historical moments, denationalization has reshaped nations, revealed the racial and ethnic hierarchies that lie underneath citizenship, and cast individuals into the great vulnerability and insecurity of statelessness. Moreover, denationalization is not simply a matter for citizenship's past. Every modern state claims the power to revoke the citizenship of those who gained their nationality through fraud or deception. More contentiously, the denationalization of Islamist terrorists has now become a live political issue in many countries.

To be sure, in spite of new laws across several states and heated political rhetoric about groups like Al Qaeda and ISIS, very small numbers of people have actually lost their citizenship since the early 2000s. As I have shown, the power of states to revoke citizenship has, particularly since 1945, become hemmed in by human rights norms and practical constraints. Yet denationalization, like capital punishment, remains a powerful reminder of the apex of state power. Little wonder then that scholars have seen the practice as raising profound legal, ethical, and political questions, and that, even when used infrequently, denationalization continues to be hugely controversial.

BIBLIOGRAPHY

Abel, Paul, 'Denationalization', *Modern Law Review 6* (December 1942): pp. 57–68.

'A Canadian is a Canadian', *Vice News*, 28 September 2015, online https://news.vice.com/article/a-canadian-is-a-canadian-liberal-leader-says-terrorists-should-keep-their-citizenship.

Agamben, Giorgio, *Homo Sacer* (New York: Columbia University Press, 1988).

Agamben, Giorgio, 'We Refugees', *Symposium 49*, no. 2, (1995): pp. 114–119.

Alienikoff, Alex, 'Theories of Loss of Citizenship', *Michigan Law Review 84*, no. 7 (1986): pp. 1471–1503.

Anderson, Bridget, Matthew J. Gibney, and Emanuela Paoletti, 'Citizenship, Deportation and the Boundaries of Belonging', *Citizenship Studies 15*, no. 5 (2011): pp. 547–563.

Anonymous, 'The Expatriation Act of 1954', *Yale Law Journal 64*, no. 8 (1954): pp. 1164–1200.

Arendt, Hannah, *The Origins of Totalitarianism* (London: Andre Deutsch, 1986).

Barry, Christian and Laura Ferracioli, 'Can Withdrawing Citizenship Be Justified?', *Political Studies*, early view (5 July 2015), online http://onlinelibrary.wiley.com/doi/10.1111/1467-9248.12221/full.

Bauböck, Rainer, 'The Rights and Duties of External Citizenship', *Citizenship Studies 13*, no. 5 (2009): pp. 475–499.

Bauböck, Rainer, 'Whose Bad Guys are Terrorists?' in *The Return of Banishment: Do the New Denationalisation Policies Weaken Citizenship* (Florence: EUI Working Papers, 2015): pp. 27–30.

Beauchamps, Marie, 'The Forfeiture of Nationality in France Discursive Ambiguity, Borders, and Identities', *Space and Culture 19*, no.1, (2015): pp. 31–42.

'Bill Targets Citizenship of Terrorists' Allies', *New York Times*, 6 May 2010, online http://www.nytimes.com/2010/05/07/world/07rights.html?_r=0.

Brandvoll, Jorunn, 'Limitations on Rendering Persons Stateless Under International Law' in Alice Edwards and Laura Van Wass, eds., *Nationality and Statelessness under International Law* (Cambridge: Cambridge University Press, 2014).

Carens, Joseph H., 'The Case for Amnesty', *The Boston Review*, May/June (26 April 2012), online http://bostonreview.net/BR34.3/ndf_immigration.php.

Carens, Joseph H., *The Ethics of Immigration* (New York: Oxford University Press, 2013).

Cott, Nancy F., 'Marriage and Women's Citizenship in the United States: 1880–1934', *The American Historical Review 103*, no. 5 (December 1998): pp. 1440–1474.

Dean, Martin, 'The Development and Implementation of Nazi denaturalization and Confiscation Policy up to the Eleventh Decree to the Reich citizenship Law', *Holocaust and Genocide Studies 16*, no. 2 (2002): pp. 217–242.

Fischer, Gerhard, *Enemy Aliens: Internment and the Homefront Experience in Australia, 1914–1920* (St Lucia: University of Queensland Press, 1989).

Fischer Williams, John, 'Denationalization', *British Yearbook of International Law 8* (1927): pp. 45–61.

Gibney, Matthew J., 'A Very Transcendental Power: Denaturalisation and the Liberalisation of Citizenship in the United Kingdom', *Political Studies 61*, no. 3 (2013): pp. 637–655.

Gibney, Matthew J., 'Should Citizenship be Conditional? Denationalization and Liberal Principles', *Journal of Politics 75*, no. 3 (2013): pp. 646–658.

Gibney, Matthew J., 'Beware States Piercing Holes in Citizenship' in Audrey Macklin and Rainer Bauböck, eds., *The Return of Banishment: Do the New Denationalisation Policies Weaken Citizenship* (Florence: EUI Working Papers, 2015): pp. 39–41.

Gibney, Matthew J., *Deporting Citizens* (Cambridge: Cambridge University Press, forthcoming).

Ginsburgs, George, 'The Soviet Union and the Problem of Refugees and Displaced Persons 1917-1956', *The American Journal of International Law 51*, no. 2 (1957): pp. 325–361.

Goodwin-Gill, Guy S., 'Deprivation of Citizenship Resulting in Statelessness and its Implications in International Law', 12 March 2014, online https://www.documentcloud.org/documents/1086878-guy-s-goodwin-gill-legal-opinion-on-deprivation.html.

Gray, Benjamin, 'From Exile of Citizens to Deportation of Non-Citizens: Ancient Greece as a Mirror to Illuminate a Modern Transition', *Citizenship Studies 15*, no. 5 (2011): pp. 565–582.

Hampshire, James, *The Politics of Immigration: Contradictions of the Liberal State* (Cambridge: Polity, 2013).

Hansen, Randall and Patrick Weil, eds., *Towards a European Nationality* (Basingstoke: Palgrave, 2001).

Herzog, Ben, 'Dual Citizenship and the Revocation of Citizenship', *Research in Political Sociology 18* (2010): pp. 87–106.

Herzog, Ben, 'The Revocation of Citizenship in Israel', *Israel Studies Forum 25*, no. 1 (2010): 57–72.

Herzog, Ben, *Revoking Citizenship: Expatriation in America from the Colonial Era to the War on Terror* (New York: New York University Press, 2015).

Irving, Helen, *Citizenship, Alienage, and the Modern Constitutional State: A Gendered History* (Cambridge: Cambridge University Press, 2016).

Joppke, Christian, *Citizenship and Immigration* (Cambridge: Polity, 2010).

Joppke, Christian, 'Terrorists Repudiate Their own Citizenship' in Audrey Macklin and Rainer Bauböck, eds., *The Return of Banishment: Do the New Denationalisation Policies Weaken Citizenship* (Florence: EUI Working Papers, 2015), pp. 11–14.

Joppke, Christian, 'Terror and the Loss of Citizenship', *Citizenship Studies 20*, 6–7 (2016): pp. 728–748.

Kanstroom, Daniel, *Deportation Nation* (Cambridge: Harvard University Press, 2007).

Kanstroom, Daniel, *Aftermath: Deportation Law and the New American Diaspora* (New York: Oxford University Press, 2012).

Kerber, Linda, 'The Stateless as the Citizen's Other: A View from the United States', *The American Historical Review 112*, no. 1 (2007): pp. 1–34.

Kingston, Rebecca 'The Unmaking of Citizens: Banishment and the Modern Citizenship Regime in France', *Citizenship Studies 9*, no. 1 (2005): pp. 23–40.

Kostakopoulou, Dora, *The Future Governance of Citizenship* (Cambridge: Cambridge University Press, 2008).

Lavi, Shai, 'Punishment and the Revocation of Citizenship in the United Kingdom, United States, and Israel', *New Criminal Law Review: An International and Interdisciplinary Journal 13*, no. 2 (2010): pp. 404–426.

Lavi, Shai, 'Citizenship Revocation as Punishment: On the Modern Duties of Citizens and Their Criminal Breach', *University of Toronto Law Journal 61*, no. 4 (2011): pp. 783–810.

Macklin, Audrey, 'Citizenship Revocation, the Privilege to Have Rights and the Production of the Alien', *Queen's Law Journal 40*, no. 1 (2014): pp. 1–54.

Macklin, Audrey, 'Introduction' in Audrey Macklin and Rainer Bauböck, eds., *The Return of Banishment: Do the New Denationalisation Policies Weaken Citizenship* (Florence: EUI Working Papers, 2015).

Mantu, Sandra, *Contingent Citizenship* (Leiden: Brill, 2015).

Maloney, Walter H., 'Involuntary Loss of American Citizenship', *St. Louis University Law Journal 4* (1956): pp. 50–77.

Ngai, Mai, *Impossible Subjects: Illegal Aliens and the Making of Modern America* (Princeton: Princeton University Press, 2004).

Panayi, Panikos, *The Enemy in Our Midst: Germans in Britain during the First World War* (Oxford: Berg, 1991).

Preuss, Lawrence, 'International Law and Deprivation of Nationality', *Georgetown Law Journal 23* (1934): pp. 250–276.

Roche, John P., 'The Loss of American Nationality. The Development of Statutory Expatriation', *University of Pennsylvania Law Review 99*, no. 1 (1950): pp. 25–71.

Rubenstein, Kim and Niamh Lenagh-Maguire, 'More or Less Secure? Nationality Questions, Deportation and Dual Nationality' in Alice Edwards and Laura Van Wass, eds., *Nationality and Statelessness under International Law* (Cambridge: Cambridge University Press, 2014), pp. 264–291.

Saul, Ben, 'Plan to Strip Citizenship is Simplistic and Dangerous', *The Drum* (26 May 2015).

Scheffler, Samuel, 'Is Terrorism Morally Distinctive?', *Journal of Political Philosophy 14*, no. 1 (2006): pp. 1–17.

Schuck, Peter H., 'Should Those Who Attack the Nation Have an Absolute Right to Remain its Citizens?' in Audrey Macklin and Rainer Bauböck, eds., *The Return of Banishment: Do the New Denationalisation Policies Weaken Citizenship* (Florence: EUI Working Papers, 2015), pp. 9–10.

Shaw, Jo, ed., Has the European Court of Justice Challenged Member State Sovereignty in Nationality Law? EUI Working Paper 62 (Badia Fiesolana: RSCAS, 2011).

Shue, Henry, *Basic Rights* (Princeton: Princeton University Press, 1980).

Singer, Peter, 'Is Citizenship a Right?', *Project Syndicate* (6 May 2014), online https://www.project-syndicate.org/commentary/peter-singer-on-the-uk-s-proposed-legislation-to-denaturalize-britons-suspected-of-links-to-terrorism.

Spiro, Peter J., 'A New International Law of Citizenship', *American Journal of International Law 105*, no. 4 (2011): pp. 694–746.

Sunahara, Ann Gomer, *The Politics of Racism: The Uprooting of Japanese Canadians during the Second World War* (Toronto: Lorimer, 1981).

Torpey, John, *The Invention of the Passport: Surveillance, Citizenship and the State* (Cambridge: Cambridge University Press, 2000).

Volpp, Leti, 'Divesting Citizenship: On Asian American History and the Loss of Citizenship through Marriage', *UCLA Law Review 52* (2005): pp 405–483.

Weil, Patrick, *The Sovereign Citizen: Denaturalization and the Origins of the American Republic* (Philadelphia: University of Pennsylvania Press, 2012).

Zedner, Lucia, 'Citizenship Deprivation, Security and Human Rights', *European Journal of Migration and Law 18* (2016): pp. 222–242.

PART IV

CONTEXT AND PRACTICE

CHAPTER 18

CITIZENSHIP IN IMMIGRATION STATES

CHRISTIAN JOPPKE*

CITIZENSHIP, understood in its core meaning of membership in a state, is profoundly paradoxical: inclusive to the inside but exclusive to the outside.[1] In other words, citizenship flags both equality and inequality. To the inside, citizenship allows only one status of membership; citizens are equal. The idea of citizen equality has consequently been the lodestar of most modern protest movements, to the point that even animals may be citizens.[2] To the outside, however, citizenship appears as the 'modern equivalent of feudal privilege,'[3] usually ascribed at birth and an increasingly potent source of inequality in today's globalizing world,[4] perhaps even replacing the intra-societal category of class in this respect.[5] Citizenship allows the state to

* I acknowledge helpful suggestions by Irene Bloemraad, Maarten Vink, Neil Walker, and other participants of the workshop preceding the publication of this volume.

[1] See Rogers Brubaker, *Citizenship and Nationhood in France and Germany* (Cambridge: Harvard University Press, 1992), chapter 1.
[2] See Sue Donaldson and Will Kymlicka, *Zoopolis* (New York: Oxford University Press, 2011).
[3] Joseph Carens, 'Aliens and Citizens,' *Review of Politics 49*, no. 2 (1987): pp. 251–273, p. 252.
[4] See Ayelet Shachar, *The Birthright Lottery* (Cambridge: Harvard University Press, 2009).
[5] See Yossi Harpaz, 'Compensatory Citizenship' (2016) (unpublished manuscript, on file with author).

be a relatively closed, self-reproducing community, a, 'nation-state,' which happens to be the unit of international politics.

This is a most astonishing development if one considers that the human species, moving out of Africa some 50,000 to 60,000 years ago, is an intrinsically migratory species, adaptable to a greater variety of ecological condition than most other species.[6] Still, ever since humans transited from the mobile condition of hunting and gathering to settlement-requiring agriculture about 15,000 to 10,000 years ago, civilized life, with advances in technology and culture, has been dependent on sedentariness. The norm of sedentariness was sealed by the invention of the modern state in Europe ca. 1200 A.D. Ever after, 'immigration', understood as long-term migration across state borders, became at heart an anomaly within a system of exclusive territorial states, nation-states since the nineteenth century. In such a world, our world, immigration messes up the uniformity of membership as citizenship and simultaneously activates and challenges citizenship's foundational closure function.

If citizenship is both inclusive *and* exclusive, a tool of emancipation *and* a source of inequity (the latter tied up with the exigencies of political rule), could one say that one aspect is prior to the other? In a list of nine things that citizens are, Gianfranco Poggi[7] provocatively mentions as the first and most important that citizens are 'subjects.' This would prioritize citizenship's statist, inequality-engendering aspect. Of course, historically, citizens are exactly *not* subjects. However, as Poggi insists, the state, even the liberal-democratic state, 'is essentially a system of rule, a set of arrangements and practices whereby one part of a (politically and otherwise) divided society exercises domination over the other part, whether or not the individual components of the latter are vested with attributes of citizenship.'[8] This view is supported by the fact that citizenship's earliest function had been to divide up between states the responsibility for the migrating poor, so that one state would not dump its poor on the territory of the others.[9] To the degree that classic theories of the state, like that by Hans Kelsen, dealt with citizenship at all, it was tellingly deemed 'of greater importance in the relations between the States than within a State,' [10] and citizenship was dismissed as 'a legal institution lacking import.'[11] This is because, technically speaking, 'the existence of a State is dependent upon the existence of individuals that are subject to its legal order, but not upon the existence of "citizens".'[12]

The primary function of citizenship is that of inter-state instrument of rule. Moreover, for Kelsen, citizenship was just a 'personal status' to which rights and duties are attached, so that citizenship cannot logically be a right itself. In our

---

[6] See Ian Goldin et al., *Exceptional People* (Princeton: Princeton University Press, 2011), pp. 11–28.

[7] Gianfranco Poggi, *Varieties of Political Experience* (Colchester: ECPR Press, 2014), p. 63.

[8] Ibid., p. 65.   [9] See Brubaker (n 1), pp. 64–71.

[10] Hans Kelsen, *General Theory of Law and State* (Cambridge: Harvard University Press, 1949), p. 241.

[11] Ibid.   [12] Ibid.

democratic age, however, citizenship is so closely associated with the domestic idea of equal rights that it appears as a right itself, the 'right to have rights.'[13] There is an element of truth to this notion, particularly *after* Hannah Arendt had invented it with an eye on the lot of stateless people during and after World War II. This is because individuals have taken on an increasingly protected and determinative role under international law,[14] and the 'right to a nationality,' of course, is an entry in the UN Declaration of Universal Human Rights—even though today's 'market fundamentalism' may dampen the protective powers of citizenship.[15]

Having mapped the dual meaning of 'citizenship' as simultaneously inclusive and exclusive, what are 'immigration states,' to move to the second concept to work with in this chapter? These are states that are routinely immigrant-receiving and thus in need of adjusting their citizenship laws and policies accordingly. But in what direction should this adjustment be? As I shall argue, at the functional plane, which of course doesn't answer the question of causality, in a liberal-democratic constellation the natural tilt is toward more inclusiveness. Liberal democracy requires the 'congruence' between the subjects and the objects of rule,[16] and it shuns the existence of 'second-class citizens.'[17] Indeed, as we shall see, this is the direction that citizenship laws in Western immigration states qua liberal democracies have taken.

However, the inclusive response is not the only possible response. I shall also discuss the opposite response by a second type of immigration state, the autocratic rentier states of the Gulf region. The six states of the Gulf Cooperation Council (GCC)—Bahrain, Kuwait, Oman, Qatar, Saudi Arabia, and the United Arab Emirates (UAE)—constitute the world's third-largest migrant receiving region, after North America and the European Union.[18] This fact alone invites a comparison. Some might object that the GCC states are not 'immigration states' but 'slave states,' because they categorically deny permanent settlement and citizenship to their labor migrants. This would exclude these states from the ambit of meaningful comparison.[19] To this I respond that the denial of the fact of immigration is indeed the GCC states' own self-perception. In their view, the 'internationally accepted concept of migration does not apply to them,'[20] because of the strictly enforced temporariness of migration. But then not the inclusion but exclusion of GCC states from the realm of comparison would 'do them a service.'[21]

---

[13] Hannah Arendt, *The Origins of Totalitarianism* (New York: Harcourt Brace Jovanovich, 1948).

[14] See Thomas Franck, *The Empowered Self* (New York: Oxford University Press, 2000), chapter 8.

[15] See Margaret Somers, *Genealogies of Citizenship* (New York: Cambridge University Press, 2008).

[16] See Robert Dahl, *Democracy and its Critics* (New Haven: Yale University Press, 1989), chapter 9.

[17] Michael Walzer, *Spheres of Justice* (New York: Basic Books, 1983), chapter 2.

[18] See Noora Lori, 'Temporary Workers or Permanent Migrants? The Kafala System and Contestations over Residency in the Arab Gulf States,' (Paris: IFRI, 2012), online https://www.ifri.org/sites/default/files/atoms/files/notecmcnooralori1.pdf, p. 3.

[19] Thus argued Liav Orgad at a preparatory meeting for this volume.   [20] Lori (n 18), p. 7.

[21] As Liav Orgad objected to a Gulf state–Western state comparison.

An important global comparison of labor migration regimes, by Martin Ruhs, has naturally included the GCC states. He considers them as extreme case of a 'trade-off' between states' degree of openness to migration and the amount of rights they are willing to grant to migrants: 'greater openness to admitting migrant workers will be associated with relatively fewer rights for migrants and vice versa.'[22] Normatively, Martin Ruhs' 'pragmatic approach' is a provocative broadside to the prevailing human-rights orthodoxy on labor migration, exposing a dogmatically imposed strict equality standard as in reality privileging 'existing migrants' over 'potential future migrants.'[23] Empirically, however, Ruhs downplays the *simultaneousness* of openness to migration and rights-granting in Western states.[24] He must do so because he lumps together Western and Gulf states under the same category of 'high-income state.' This flattens the distinction between liberal democracy and autocracy. Instead, the following comparison takes Gulf and Western states not as instances of the same type of state ('high-income') but as fundamentally different types of state that condition opposite responses to immigration, exclusive v. inclusive, respectively.

EXCLUSION IN GULF STATES

The Gulf States are 'rentier states' that draw their income not from taxing labor and capital but from renting the land to companies that exploit its natural resources, in this case, oil and gas.[25] The citizen population is only marginally involved in generating the rent, but it receives parts of it, also to buy their compliance—rentier states tend to be autocratic. However, it is also misleading to call them 'states' to the degree that states are defined by 'impersonality,' the differentiation of the function of rule from the person or family of the ruler.[26] Growing out of societies where the 'social structure (is) exclusively based on kin,'[27] the Gulf States are

---

[22] Martin Ruhs, *The Price of Rights* (Princeton: Princeton University Press, 2013), p. 6.

[23] Ibid., p. 9.

[24] The simultaneousness of openness and rights-granting in Western states is also the finding in a re-analysis of Ruhs' data, which factors in the variable of political regime (i.e., democracy), by Samuel D. Schmid, 'Democracy, Open Borders, and the Rights of Immigrant Workers' (2016) (manuscript, on file with author).

[25] See Neha Vora, 'From Golden Frontier to Global City,' *American Anthropologist* 113, no. 2 (2011): pp. 306–318, at p. 306. See more generally Hazem Beblawi and Giacomo Luciani, (eds.), *The Rentier State* (London: Croom Helms, 1987).

[26] See Joseph Strayer, *On the Medieval Origins of the Modern State* (Princeton: Princeton University Press, 1970), p. 6.

[27] Ginaluca Paolin, *Citizenship in the Arab World* (Amsterdam: Amsterdam University Press, 2009), p. 26.

essentially tribal, owned by the leading families. By the same token, 'citizenship' in these 'states' is a misleading term, as citizenship conveys a horizontal relationship of equal members. Membership in the tribal Gulf States is instead based on the 'idea of hierarchy and vertical allegiance.'[28] For instance, a citizen of Saudi Arabia is 'Saudi by virtue of following the House of Sa'ud'[29]—which implies that the state is equivalent to the dynastic family.

A core feature of Gulf societies is that tiny native populations face huge and growing migrant populations—in four of six GCC states noncitizens outnumber citizens, and in the UAE the local non-migrant population is just 11.5 percent of the total population.[30] The logic of citizenship law may be summarized as 'we want to protect a minority—which is us.'[31]

But who is 'us' in Gulf societies? It tends to consist of three tiers: locals with full citizenship rights, locals with passports but lesser rights, and Bidoons (unregistered former nomads). One can accede to the first and most privileged tier only with a 'family book' (*khulasat al-qaid*), which in the UAE case is given to Emirati nationals who can trace their ethnic lineage in the UAE to 1925 or before. Similar cut-off dates for first-tier citizenship exist in all Gulf States: they are chosen to precede the discovery of oil, thus establishing a natural ownership in this precious resource. The privileges that accrue from this ownership are enormous, and they make look paltry what T.H. Marshall had canonized as social citizenship rights. Kuwaitis, for instance, in addition to paying no income tax, enjoy free health care (including specialist treatment abroad), free telephone service, heavily subsidized electricity, water, gasoline, and basic food stuffs (including oil, rice, sugar, milk, lentils, and tomato paste), a free education (even university abroad, including a generous stipend), free housing, and the 'right to work' (overwhelmingly in the public sector, whose main function is the state's 'redistribut[ion] [of] the oil incomes to its citizens').[32] In fact, a better description of Gulf State social citizenship would be the 'right *not* to work,' because work is what migrants do.

The so-called *kafala* system, while 'build(ing) upon tribal narratives of hospitality,'[33] farms out the entire system of entry visas, residence and work permits to private citizens, upon whose 'sponsorship' the fate of migrants hangs. Accordingly, the sale of visas is an additional source of income for GCC citizens. To stay with the Kuwaiti case studied in detail by Longva, non-Kuwaitis are not allowed to do

[28] Anh Nga Longva, 'Citizenship in the Gulf States,' in Nils Butenschon, ed., *Citizenship and the State in the Middle East* (Syracuse: Syracuse University Press, 2000), p. 192.

[29] Ibid., p. 193.

[30] Manal Jamal, 'The "Tiering" of Citizenship and Residency and the "Hierarchization" of Migrant Communities,' *International Migration Review* 49, no. 3 (2015): pp. 601–632.

[31] J. Sater, 'Citizenship and Migration in Arab Gulf Monarchies,' *Citizenship Studies* 18, no. 3–4 (2013): pp. 292–302, online http://dx.doi.org/10.1080/13621025.2013.820394.

[32] Anh Nga Longva, *Walls Built on Sand* (Boulder: Westview Press, 1997), p. 64.

[33] Lori (n 18), p. 15.

business unless a local partner owns at least 51 percent of it—which means that most Kuwaitis own 'a business of some sort',[34] even the large majority of Kuwaitis who work in the public sector. The *kafala* system 'delegate(s) to citizens the functions that ... usually belong to state institutions'.[35] It even entails the right of sponsors to retain migrants' passports, to prevent them from absconding. 'Lack of security' and distrust is the Leitmotiv. As a Kuwaiti put it, 'Look at it as an expression of our fears and helplessness. We are few, they are many, we cannot afford to be trusting'.[36]

Immigration arrived suddenly and massively after the discovery of oil, first from neighboring Arab states (especially Palestine), and later from South and East Asia. In response, the uniform direction of citizenship reform in Gulf States has been to close off access to citizenship. Take again the case of Kuwait, whose citizenry consisted of just 0.9 million people in 2005, with almost four times as many labor migrants.[37] Its first two nationality decrees of 1948, passed ten years after the discovery of oil, were still relatively inclusive, with a mix of *jus soli* (that was unique in the region) and *jus sanguinis*. It defined 'originally Kuwaiti' (*asil*) relatively broadly, including 'members of the ruling family, those permanently residing in Kuwait since 1899, children of Kuwaiti men and children of Arab or Muslim fathers also born in Kuwait'.[38] In the Nationality Law of 1959, the descendants of those established in Kuwait since 1920 (interestingly, the year of the nation-defining Battle of Jahra, fought against a Saudi invasion) came to be included in the 'originally Kuwaiti' category. However, the 'children of Arab or Muslim fathers' were dropped, and with them the element of *jus soli* that had been originally part of Kuwaiti citizenship. Henceforth, only the sons of Kuwaiti men can claim birthright citizenship, in an exclusive system of paternal *jus sanguinis* typical of the region. Naturalization also came to be severely constrained with exceedingly low annual caps; moreover, since 1981 naturalization is only available for Muslims.

It is thus almost impossible for migrants to acquire Gulf State citizenship, and they are systematically relegated to temporary resident status. There is even a sharp (and increasingly sharpened) distinction between 'original' and 'naturalized' citizens, which is perpetuated into following generations. In Kuwait, the suffrage (a farce in a state owned and ruled by one family, the Al Sabah) was limited until 1996 to 'original' Kuwaitis, whose forefathers were residents in 1920. Thus before the 1990 invasion by Saddam Hussein's Iraq, less than 5 percent of the total population had the suffrage; among others, all women and naturalized Kuwaiti males and their sons were excluded.[39] Or consider Qatar, ruled by the Al Thani family, possessing the world's third-largest gas reserves, and where a trifle of 85,000 citizens stood against 1.35 million migrant workers in 2012. Here the 'original' v. 'naturalized'

---

[34] Longva (n 32), p. 69.   [35] Ibid., p. 100.   [36] Ibid., p. 103.
[37] Philippe Fargues, 'Immigration without Inclusion: Non-Nationals in Nation-Building in the Gulf States', *Asian and Pacific Migration Journal 20*, no. 3–4 (2011): pp. 273–292, p. 280.
[38] Quoted in Longva (n 32), pp. 47–48.   [39] Ibid., p. 49.

citizen distinction implies that naturalized citizens can't vote, can't work in the public sector in the first five years, and have only limited access to social and economic benefits. A child of a Qatari naturalized father, even if born after his naturalization, is considered merely naturalized also, and thus a second-class citizen.[40] Since a reform in 2005, the children of a Qatari woman and a foreign father, who previously were locked out from citizenship altogether, can at least naturalize—but only after twenty-five years and by princely decree, and there's a maximum number of fifty naturalizations per year.[41] A study of the United Arab Emirates disqualified a wholly discretionary and exceptional naturalization process as 'not a legal-formal determination', with 'criteria (that) are only known to them.'[42]

The Gulf States' internal 'tiering' of citizenship follows a simple economic rationale: with the past few decades' growth of the citizenry, as a result of fertility-boosting policies (to counteract the huge imbalance between the small domestic citizenry and ever growing migrant populations), there is simply less rent to distribute. This tiering is likely to get further impetus by the long-term dimming prospects for oil. A new identity card in the Emirates, introduced in 2004, contains personal and biological lifetime data, registering the all-important 'family book' (*khulasat*). While previously a passport was sufficient for proving citizenship, after the introduction of the new ID card the family book matters, even for obtaining employment.[43] This is a curious case of deploying the newest (biometric) technologies (including building a universal DNA data basis of all residents) for entrenching primordialism.

Given a growing citizen population and long-term economic contraction, and considering the accentuated differences between 'original' and 'naturalized' citizens, it does not surprise that the third layer of the local non-migrant population, the Bidoons, have suffered even more. In Kuwait, these formally stateless previous nomads, who came to be recruited into the lower ranks of the police and army, lost access to free education and health services in 1986, after a sharp drop of oil prices in the two years before, thus further shielding the privileges of formal citizenship holders.[44] Kuwait is now about to emulate the UAE's solution to their nomad problem: Facing international pressure to remedy the situation of the Bidoons, the Emirates, rather than making them UAE citizens, just bought them another citizenship, that of the Comoro Islands, though one that is without much value, not including any political rights.[45] This is convenient, because it finally allows them to

[40] Zahra R. Babar, 'Citizenship Construction in the State of Qatar,' *The Middle East Journal* 68, no. 3 (2014): pp. 403–420, online http://dx.doi.org/10.3751/68.3.14.

[41] Ibid., p. 413.

[42] Noora Lori, 'National Security and the Management of Migrant Labor,' *Asian and Pacific Migration Journal* 20, no. 3–4 (September 2011): pp. 315–337, p. 331.

[43] Jamal (n 30).   [44] Longva (n 32), p. 49.

[45] See Atossa Araxia Abrahamian, *The Cosmopolites: The Coming of the Global Citizen* (New York: Columbia Global Reports, 2015).

expel unruly nomad activists, while legalizing the situation of the quiescent rest as 'guest workers.'

In the Gulf States, where citizenship equals access to an unparalleled material bounty, the response to immigration has been to further increase citizenship's inherent exclusiveness. Citizenship, in the form of descent-based *jus sanguinis* citizenship, offered a vehicle for reproducing and sealing off a tribal society from change. Particularly in the most recent period, with the need to transit toward a post-oil future, the dominant impulse is to use exclusive citizenship to avert a perceived threat to cohesion and identity. Immigrants are increasingly perceived as competitors, and 'nationalization' and 'indigenization' policies are rampant.[46] 'Demographic imbalance' and so-called 'family social security' are now dominant concerns.[47] In response, the Emirates now require private employers to hire UAE nationals as human resource and personnel managers, secretaries, etc. In 2003, a peculiar 'Cultural Diversity Policy' was launched to make Emiratis the largest 'minority' by reducing the number of other minorities and diversifying the employee pools.[48]

The Gulf States are not alone among rich autocratic states in their preference for exclusion.[49] Singapore, transformed into one of the world's richest countries under the autocratic rule of the charismatic Lee Kuan Yew, responded to unprecedented public opposition to an intensified foreign migrant intake in the early millennium by 'differentiating' between citizens and noncitizens with respect to social benefits, subsidies, and access to public services, including schools and universities (some of them now world-leading). In effect, this meant not so much to increase citizen benefits and privileges but to withdraw benefits from resident noncitizens, who now have to pay more for their children's education, have lesser tax rebates for their families, and face restricted access to predominantly state-owned housing. Interestingly, and different from the always-exclusive Gulf States, the Singaporean 'differentiation campaign' corrected a prior liberalization of citizenship in the 1990s and early 2000s, which had targeted high-skilled immigrants.[50] In this period, Singapore had branded itself as a 'talent capital', offering easy access to permanent residence and citizenship in order to attract high-skilled workers. When the number of permanent residents consequently doubled between 2000 and 2010, this created 'pressure to make a greater distinction between the rights of citizens and permanent residents.'[51] Note, in this context, that early twenty-first century Britain also had contemplated a policy of upgrading citizenship by downgrading or even abolishing legal permanent residence, though it eventually abstained from it.[52] The fact of using citizenship to recruit high-skilled immigrants, standard practice

---

[46] Fargues (n 37), pp. 273–292.   [47] Lori (n 42), p. 320.   [48] Jamal (n 30), p. 605.

[49] For a comprehensive view of citizenship in 'non-Western' states, see Chung in this volume.

[50] Eric C. Thompson, 'Immigration Society and Modalities Citizenship in Singapore', *Citizenship Studies 18*, no. 3–4 (2013): pp. 315–331, p. 326.

[51] Ruhs (n 22), p.106.

[52] Christian Joppke, *Citizenship and Immigration* (Cambridge: Polity, 2010), p. 156.

in the global 'race for talent,'[53] shows the non-rentier nature of Singapore, which draws its riches not from a finite natural resource but from the naturally expandable work of its members. This makes for more flexible boundaries of membership, not unlike in Western states. Its autocratic face, which Singapore shares with Gulf States, is fully displayed only in its harsh treatment of low-skilled migrant workers, who are not allowed to marry citizens, or to become pregnant and give birth, and who may be expelled for alleged moral turpitude, such as 'breaking up families.'[54] While differential treatment of low- and high-skilled immigrants exists in all rich countries, liberty-restricting measures of such magnitude are difficult to fathom in Western states.

INCLUSION IN WESTERN STATES

All Western state variations of managing citizenship in a context of immigration look paltry when comparing their overall inclusive thrust with the sternly exclusive citizenship logic of the Gulf States. From a Gulf State angle, the typical distinctions that permeate the Western-focused literature lose traction, such as between the classic immigrant countries of the Americas and the immigrant-averse nation-states of Europe, or within Europe between 'civic' and 'ethnic' types of nationhood. Instead, Western immigration states' joint embrace of an inclusive, liberal model of citizenship moves into the picture. To more fully describe and account for this trend, it is helpful to distinguish between the status, rights, and identity dimensions of citizenship.[55]

On the *status* dimension,[56] particularly in Europe, the tendency has been toward mixed *jus sanguinis* and *jus soli* birthright citizenship, lowered hurdles for naturalization (in terms of lessened residence time and waived or at least facilitated assimilation requirements), and a general acceptance of multiple citizenship. In all of these respects, Europe[57] has embraced a classic immigrant-nation stance of routinely transforming immigrants into citizens.

---

[53] Ayelet Shachar, 'The Race for Talent,' *New York University Law Review 81*, no. 1 (2006), pp. 148–206.
[54] Ruhs (n 22), pp. 119–120.   [55] See Joppke (n 52).
[56] I am brief on this because of the more extended discussion of 'citizenship regimes' in Vink in this volume.
[57] More precisely: the western half of Europe, which is basically the fifteen member states of the European Union before the eastern enlargement in 2004. For a comprehensive picture, see Marc Morjé Howard, *The Politics of Citizenship in Europe* (New York: Cambridge University Press, 2009).

On the *rights* and benefit dimension, it is striking to see, through the prism of Gulf State citizenship, how small the bounty of Western citizenship is, and always has been, with the tendency to become smaller still. There is one exception: political rights, practically nil in the Gulf States, have continued to be *the* citizen privilege in the West, generally not extended to immigrants (except, in some places, at local level). For all other rights, particularly civil and social rights, it is astonishing how little better, if better at all, citizens fare above the most privileged immigrants, which are legal permanent residents.[58] The withering of the distinction is the topic of an influential monograph.[59]

But one should perhaps question the degree to which the distinction between citizen and noncitizen rights was ever marked in the West. This is, again, especially clear when comparing Western and Gulf states where the citizen-noncitizen distinction had been a watertight distinction from the start, and one that was tightened further over time. In Western states, elementary civil rights, like 'liberty, property, safety', to quote Article 2 of the French Declaration of the Rights of Man and of the Citizen (in this order!), have mostly *not* been exclusive citizen rights, instead accruing to all individuals under the jurisdiction of the state. Social rights, particularly if tied to labor market participation (like pensions, unemployment benefits, or health and accident insurance), likewise were never exclusive citizen rights. Michael Bommes has stressed, in an important work on the nexus between welfare state and immigration,[60] that the Western welfare state is based on the principle of territoriality, which in principle also makes it a motor of immigrant integration.[61] The modern welfare state, dispensing its benefits as 'right' not 'charity' (in Wilensky's classic formula)[62] interestingly differs in its noncitizen but territorial focus from traditional poor relief (*Armenfürsorge*), which—in Germany at least—had been tied to citizenship (as state membership). However, the citizenship-linked tradition of poor relief lives on in 'social aid' proper, financed through general taxes instead of social insurance, which in many European countries is contingent on citizenship, as a special solidarity that only citizens are due (and that was often instituted not before the golden era of the welfare state, in the 1960s). However, European Union law has basically eliminated the possibility for keeping social aid a national citizen privilege, as this constitutes illicit nationality discrimination.[63]

---

[58] See Bloemraad in this volume.

[59] Yasemin Soysal, *Limits of Citizenship* (Chicago: University of Chicago Press, 1994).

[60] Michael Bommes, *Migration und nationaler Wohlfahrtsstaat* (Opladen: Westdeutscher Verlag, 1999).

[61] Ibid., pp. 133–134.

[62] Harold Wilensky, *The Welfare State and Equality* (Berkeley: University of California Press, 1975), p. 1.

[63] See Maurizio Ferrera, *The Boundaries of Welfare* (Oxford: Oxford University Press, 2005), chapter 4.

There is also a distinct reluctance to tolerate graded rights *within* the citizenry of Western states, much in contrast to Gulf States' stark, and starker over time, distinction between naturalized and original citizens. The 1997 European Convention on Nationality, in its Article 5, stipulates 'the principle of non-discrimination between its nationals, whether they are nationals by birth or have acquired its nationality subsequently.' In the United States, naturalized citizens cannot become President or Vice-President, but this seems to be their only legal disadvantage. In France, a recent proposal to strip convicted terrorists of their French citizenship became controversial because it threatened to divide the French citizenry into two unequal halves—those with only one citizenship, who could not be deprived of French citizenship under international law, as it outlaws statelessness; and those with an additional (or more) citizenship(s), who are the only ones who could have been affected by the measure. In their great majority, the affected happened to be Muslims from North Africa, who predictably denounced the measure as yet another affront to France's 5-million strong Muslim population.[64]

Overall, the Western development has been for the internal equality principle of citizenship to bite holes into, if not to delegitimize altogether, its external closure function. This is simply because liberalism stipulates the equal dignity of all individuals and is ill at ease with categorizing between them on the basis of unchosen characteristics. A case in point is the notorious difficulty under European Union law to distinguish between the rights of European Union citizens and third-country nationals who might want to move from their EU country of legal residence to another member state. While separate regimes exist for both, with more advantages for EU citizens, the official notion, never fully realized but also never formally withdrawn, is that the legal status of non-EU immigrants should be 'approximated' to the status of EU citizens.[65] At the European plane, it is indeed capricious to distinguish between two types of foreigners, those who originate from other EU states, and those who do not but are settled in one of them. However, the first are still 'citizens' under EU law, while the second are not. The 'approximate' standard under the Tampere Principles thus amounts to erasing the distinction between citizens and immigrants. It should be said that the very nature of citizenship, aptly described as a formula for 'strangers' to 'become associates,'[66] works in this direction, because it lifts people out of their primordial ('tribal') connections, perhaps more visibly in

---

[64] See Christian Joppke, 'Terror and the Loss of Citizenship,' *Citizenship Studies* 20, no. 6–7 (2016): pp. 728–748, online http://dx.doi.org/10.1080/13621025.2016.1191435.

[65] This is part of the Tampere Principles, passed by the European Council in October 1999, and it was restated in Stockholm in 2009. See Diego Acosta Arcarazo, 'Civic Citizenship Reintroduced?,' *European Law Journal* 21, no. 2 (2015): pp. 200–219.

[66] Ulrich Preuss, 'Problems of a Concept of European Citizenship,' *European Law Journal* 1, no. 3 (1995): pp. 267–281, p. 275. See also Michael Oakeshott, *On Human Conduct* (Oxford: Oxford University Press, 1975) (arguing that the 'civil condition' is 'not a relationship of love or affection,' associating people who are 'strangers to one another' (p. 123)).

emergent Europe than elsewhere. It is still an astonishing development, which, if carried to the end, would be destructive of citizenship as bounded membership.

In light of facilitated access to citizenship, and considering its diminished rights implications, it is no wonder that the *identity* of citizenship, the third dimension considered here, has become broad and nondescript ('universalistic'[67]), at least from the vantage point of the state. (But not necessarily from that of ordinary people, as the current populist backlash across Europe attests.) To explicate identity, one should recall that citizenship connotes not just equal status and certain rights attached to it, but also membership in a distinct political community and loyalty obligations toward it. Hence citizenship is also identity, which is tied to the semantics of nation and nationalism.

Nationalism's drumming of distinctness had already been questioned by the classic writers of sociology, who mused about what unites and integrates a modern differentiated society. They noted that what a multitude of individuals with diverse interests and outlooks hold in common can only be thin and general, and thus in essence exchangeable. For Emile Durkheim, it was 'individualism' and the 'rights of men', which he considered a secular religion of sorts, 'our moral catechism'.[68] For Georg Simmel, 'individuality' was either invested in the individual or in the group of which she is a member. He held this to be contingent on the size of the group: small groups tend to subsume the individual, while taking on an 'individual' character themselves (Simmel's example are the Quakers who are distinctly identifiable as member of their group, but not as individuals); in large groups the relationship is the inverse, giving more space for the development of the individual, at the cost of the 'individuality' of the group.[69] This is why differentiated societies can only adopt general and exchangeable identities, if any at all. Talcott Parsons captured the same relationship in his notion that the values of differentiated societies have to become increasingly 'generalized'.[70]

These sociological insights were generated without factoring in immigration as greatly increasing the diversity of differentiated societies, and above all without considering that liberalism, the dominant ideal of Western states, severely narrows the power of the state to impose group identities on people. Accordingly, when reviewing recent identity pronunciations of Western immigration states, which are all trying to utilize 'citizenship' as a formula to unify and integrate increasingly pluralistic societies, one notices that the projected citizenship identities are all essentially similar, revolving around the tenets of liberal democracy.[71] I called the conundrum the 'paradox of universalism': while the intention must be to integrate newcomers

---

[67] As I argued in Joppke (n 52), chapter 4.

[68] Emile Durkheim, 'Individualism and the Intellectuals' (1898), in *Emile Durkheim on Morality and Society*, edited and introduced by Robert Bellah (Chicago: University of Chicago Press, 1973).

[69] Georg Simmel, *Soziologie* (Frankfurt: Suhrkamp, 1992), chapter 10.

[70] Talcott Parsons, *The System of Modern Societies* (Englewood Cliffs: Prentice Hall, 1971).

[71] See Joppke (n 52), chapter 4.

into a particular society, different here from there, the liberal state lacks the power to name and enforce this particularism. Committed to the principle of ethical neutrality, it is not for the state, but for individuals to decide what kinds of lives they want to live, so that liberal state identities, or the identity of citizenship, resemble(s) closely what philosophers have articulated as 'political liberalism' or 'constitutional patriotism.'

In a sharp rebuttal, Kristian Kriegbaum Jensen and Per Mouritsen[72] have argued that there is no 'paradox of universalism,' no liberal state incapacity to name and enforce particular identities. Even liberal (and thus in principle universalistic) conceptions of nationhood leave ample ground for particularism. Their case in point is the Nordic countries, which all espouse 'thin' civic national identities that 'convene around similar comprehensive state modernism and consensus-oriented democracies.'[73] At the same time, in Denmark the picture of nationhood conveyed to newcomers is 'deterministic,' something fixed and unchangeable that newcomers have to adjust to in a 'slow, organic socialization process.'[74] By contrast, Swedish nationhood, while being as civic and political as the Danish, is also 'voluntarist' and open-ended, so that 'integration is ultimately intended to create a "we" of the ethnic and cultural diversity.'[75] Accordingly, under the same umbrella of civic or liberal nationhood, Denmark has developed Europe's harshest variant of civic integration, with tough language and civic knowledge tests as preconditions for residence and citizenship; by contrast, Sweden has abstained from passing such requirements, making it one of the last, proud bastions of multiculturalism in Europe.

The 'paradox of universalism' is closely connected to the 'citizenship lite' hypothesis, according to which the same liberal model of inclusive citizenship with diminished rights and exchangeable identities is proliferating throughout the West.[76] An important critique of it comes from Sara Wallace Goodman.[77] Her empirical test case is the new civic integration policies for immigrants, pioneered by the Netherlands in the late 1990s and now practiced in at least ten West European countries. They require immigrants to take language and civic courses or tests as a condition for entry, residence, or citizenship, in combinations and with levels of difficulty that vary from state to state. For Goodman, the new policies signal not a 'lightening' but 'fortification' of citizenship, mostly in prolongation of national citizenship traditions, which are liberal and inclusive in some places (Britain), and less liberal and more restrictive in others (Austria or Denmark). However, Goodman's depiction

---

[72] Kristian Kriegbaum Jensen and Per Mouritsen, 'Nationalism in Liberal Register,' *British Journal of Political Science* (forthcoming).

[73] Kristian Kriegbaum Jensen, 'Scandinavian Immigrant Integration Politics' (PhD dissertation, Aarhus University, 2016) (copy on file with author), p. 50.

[74] Ibid., p. 70.   [75] Ibid., p. 73.   [76] Joppke (n 52), chapter 5.

[77] Sara Wallace Goodman, *Immigration and Membership Politics in Western Europe* (New York: Cambridge University Press, 2014).

of a new post-national 'state identity,' the content of which is 'liberal values,'[78] with an accent more on 'togetherness' than on 'sameness,'[79] is not that far away from a 'citizenship lite.' Civic integration, Goodman says, is 'nation-building in the least "national" way imaginable.'[80] There may even be space in it for a notionally discarded multiculturalism, as newcomers are not obliged 'to forego home culture or traditions.'[81] In sum, in Goodman's picture also, the citizenship of Western immigrant states shows a broadly inclusive dynamic, in sharp distinction from the exclusive thrust of Gulf State citizenship.

A similar ambivalence surrounds Liav Orgad's claim that recent Western states' attempts to upgrade and strengthen citizenship signal a 'cultural defense of nations,'[82] in which citizenship is made more exclusive by means of citizenship tests, loyalty oaths, language requirements, or integration contracts. Distinguishing between a lighter 'civic-political' defense in the United States and a more illiberal 'ethno-cultural' defense in Europe, Orgad arrives at a gloomy picture of the European scene, one geared to exclude immigrant minorities: 'The immigrants' way of life, traditions, and values are largely absent from the characterization of what is British, Dutch or French. Rather, at the heart of cultural defense policies, despite the political correct language, are the ways of life, traditions, and values of non-immigrant groups, the native-born population.'[83] The attribution of 'ethno-cultural' defense to Europe takes the wind out of his spicier claim that the true risk of civic integration is 'illiberal liberalism,' the hyping up of liberalism as a 'liberal way of life itself.'[84] What exactly is the 'ethno' element in the French *communauté*, the German *Leitkultur*, or in UK *Britishness*, to take only three of the European cases discussed by Orgad?[85] The incontrovertible truth in Orgad's scenario, however, is that in the light of shrinking native populations and recurrent mass immigration in Europe, much of it from faraway lands, the old notion that the majority can 'take care of itself' may no longer apply; the time has come to reflect on something as intrinsically perplexing as 'majority rights.'

Overall, 'fortifying citizenship' à la Goodman or 'cultural defense' à la Orgad may well be the *intention* of Western European states, for which this diagnosis has mostly been made. More precisely, it is the intention of vote-competing political parties and democratically accountable governments that have to accommodate persistent public hostility to immigration. However, the martial metaphors of 'fortification' and 'defense' are misleading. The true novelty in the immigrant states of Europe is that immigration is no longer seen as a one-shot event, to be contained by 'zero immigration' policies.[86] On the contrary, there is a growing elite consensus,

---

[78] Ibid., p. 31.   [79] Ibid., p. 17.   [80] Ibid., p. 35.   [81] Ibid., p. 32.

[82] Liav Orgad, *The Cultural Defense of Nations* (New York: Oxford University Press, 2015).

[83] Ibid., pp. 116–117.   [84] Ibid., p. 135.   [85] Ibid., chapter 3.

[86] As I had still argued in Christian Joppke, *Immigration and the Nation-State* (Oxford: Oxford University Press, 1999).

disturbed only by a populist (though alarmingly strong and growing) extreme right, that immigration in the global age cannot but be recurrent, for economic and demographic reasons. This development has been fast and dramatic. Germany, for instance, the proverbial 'we are not an immigration country' well into the mid-1990s, now has a fully modernized, inclusive citizenship law, plus Europe's most advanced regime for labor migration, especially the highly skilled.[87]

Provided that liberal democracy continues to be the dominant *spiel* in the West, the reality of permanent immigration in globalizing economies and open societies requires a citizenship that is accessible to newcomers, that does not demarcate sharply and categorically between the rights of citizens and noncitizens, and that is framed by thin and elastic identities capable of coping with cultural pluralism—the exact elements of citizenship lite. But there is no functional automatism in this. The 'liberal democracy' proviso needs to be taken seriously—*this*, rather than whatever may pass as majority culture, needs protection in the age of global migrations. The Gulf States, to a degree also Singapore (though it`s more likely to eventually embrace the liberal logic of the West), show that there is an alternative, illiberal way of dealing with citizenship in immigration states. If the notions of 'fortified citizenship' or 'cultural defense' are to be more than academic or political rhetoric, it is *there*.

For Europe, it should be pointed out that the lightening of citizenship is reinforced by European Union citizenship, fleetingly instituted in the 1992 Maastricht Treaty but mightily empowered by the European Court of Justice ever since. This is a quintessentially liberal citizenship of rights, particularly of free movement, but also access to social benefits, without even the flimsiest of duties attached, nor a 'European identity' capping it. Importantly, the very existence of EU citizenship limits member states' possibility of re-nationalizing citizenship. Any exclusion or rights deprivation of other EU citizens would violate the principle of nondiscrimination on the basis of nationality, a core principle of the European Community Treaties since their inception in 1957. The decisive Article 18, in the current treaty version, 'abolishes nationality, at least within the EU, for EU citizens.'[88] EU citizenship is at cross-purposes with member states' current renationalization efforts, as the latter try to lock in people (especially by means of the new civic integration requirements), while the point of EU citizenship is to encourage people to move and become emancipated from the confines of the national. 'The new Belgians are those who choose Belgium … residence is the new nationality,'[89] as Gareth Davies imaginatively summarizes the liberating potential of European citizenship.

---

[87] See SVR (Sachverständigenrat deutscher Stiftungen für Integration und Migration), *Unter Einwanderungsländern: Deutschland im internationalen Vergleich. Jahresgutachten 2015* (Berlin: SVR, 2015).

[88] Gareth Davis, 'Any Place I Hang My Hat,' *European Law Journal* 11, no. 1 (2005): pp. 43–56, p. 55.

[89] Ibid., p. 56.

The power of EU law reinforces the trend toward de-nationalization that, in a context of global market liberalism, is already operating at member state level from which the citizenship lite hypothesis is mostly drawn. One example of further, EU-conditioned liberalization is that six member states provide relaxed naturalization rules (in terms of shortened residence requirements) for other member state citizens. This reinforces the reduction of the differences between national citizenships. The effect of EU citizenship on national citizenship is 'the reinvention of the legal essence of nationality in terms of a merely procedural connection between the individual in possession of this status and a state.'[90] While one looks in vain for any 'duties' of citizenship at the national level already, 'liberal de-dutification' is driven even further by EU law.[91] For instance, if the Greek government refuses to issue passports to diaspora citizens who have not yet completed their mandatory army service, by virtue of EU law the latter must be granted residence permits in their state of residence (and birth, for most). 'Liberty meets nationalism and prevails,'[92] as Kochenov summarizes the EU v. member state dynamics. Of course, there is always the possibility of leaving the EU. The departure of Britain, 'Brexit', is exactly motivated by clamping down on the free movement of people and taking back 'control,' though at the likely, and for some consciously accepted, cost of impairing trade and economic growth.

Outlook

Future research needs to more systematically compare citizenship structures and dynamics across political regime types, beyond the narrowly intra-Western scope that has dominated the field, and which has got stuck in the narcissism of minor differences. The Gulf v. Western state comparison in this chapter was a crude first stab, raising more questions than providing answers. Is it really the autocratic v. liberal-democratic nature of political regimes that drives the tilt toward closure or openness? Or is it, more materially, the rentier v. work-based sources of wealth? Of course, the rentier state theory conflates both elements, but this is not necessarily so. The preceding narrative gave nods in both directions, and it would indeed be

[90] Dimitry Kochenov, 'Rounding Up the Circle,' EUI Working Paper no. 23 (Florence: RSCAS, 2010), p. 24.

[91] Dimitry Kochenov, 'EU Citizenship without Duties,' European Law Journal 20, no. 4 (2014): pp. 482–498.

[92] Ibid., p. 28.

implausible to deny either factor. But what is their exact combination? Perhaps in the Western case, ideology and regime type are the main driver (their being 'liberal-democratic'), while in the Gulf case it is more the material resource ('rentier') dimension. It is perfectly conceivable that a post-autocratic citizen cabal in the Gulf States will persist with closure, as long as the black gold flows. Alternatively, a future House of Saud, after the inevitable drying out of its oil wells, may want to offer attractive immigration-cum-citizenship packages for the high-skilled, Singapore-style. On the other end, liberal democracies once practiced crude, group-level forms of closure in terms of race, so there does not seem to be anything intrinsic in them tilting towards openness.[93]

A second desirable is to move from a monistic 'immigration state' focus to thinking about citizenship as nested in a plurality of 'constellations.'[94] We intuitively did so when examining the dynamics of de-nationalizing EU v. re-renationalizing member state citizenship. The immigration state optic, predominant ever since Brubaker launched the field in the early 1990s, has exhausted itself. Instead, from a point of view of citizenship constellations, 'individuals are simultaneously linked to several ... political entities.'[95]

Vertically, a citizenship-constellation point of view distinguishes between local, national, and—in Europe especially—supranational polities, with different logics prevailing at each level. In a stimulating exploration of 'multilevel citizenship' in the European Union, Rainer Bauböck identified 'residential' citizenship at local level, 'intergenerational' citizenship at national level, and a 'hybrid type' at European level.[96] Local membership is fluid, 'generally singular at any point in time,'[97] and in principle extendable to immigrants, because what matters here is public services that are indifferent to the nationality status of their users. Today no fewer than twelve EU states allow foreigners to vote at local level. At the national level, by contrast, *jus domicilii* has long been replaced by a less flexible birthright citizenship (*jus soli* or *sanguinis*). If juxtaposed with the more flexible local residential citizenship, birthright citizenship—sometimes attacked by liberals as feudal-era relic[98]—suddenly begins to make sense. This is because birthright citizenship, whether conferred by blood or by soil, blocks exit and provides a 'stable background'[99] for the fluidity of local citizenship. Birthright citizenship generates incentives for peoples' long-term decision-making for the benefit of future generations. From the optic of citizenship constellations, birthright citizenship is not so much an undeserved

---

[93] See FitzGerald in this volume.
[94] Rainer Bauböck, 'Studying Citizenship Constellations', *Journal of Ethnic and Migration Studies 36*, no. 5 (2010): pp. 847–859.
[95] Ibid., p. 848.
[96] Rainer Bauböck, 'The Three Levels of Citizenship in the European Union', *German Law Journal 15*, no. 5 (2014): pp. 751–763, online http://dx.doi.org/10.13128/Phe_Mi-17735.
[97] Ibid., p. 3.   [98] See Carens (n 3); Shachar (n 4).   [99] Bauböck (n 96).

perk but a requirement of democracy, which could not exist without a modicum of long-termism. At the supranational level, finally, European citizenship is 'hybrid', in official diction 'additional to' and 'not replacing' national citizenship (and in the absence of a European-level passport office, a permanent derivative of national citizenship). At the same time, the guarantee of free movement rights constitutes a bulwark to any attempted re-nationalization of member state citizenship, and in its ECJ-driven expansion it has even begun to constrain the passport- or nationality-granting and defining powers of member states.

To think about citizenship in terms of 'constellations' is also fruitful at the horizontal level, now juxtaposing not hierarchically ordered levels of government but formally equal-level sending and receiving states, whose citizenship choices often have mutually influencing effects, and with instrumentally oriented individuals in between to take advantage. Each immigrant is also an emigrant, carrying with her the citizenship of her origin state. One of the most striking recent developments has been an increasing acceptance of dual citizenship, both by immigrant-receiving *and* emigrant-sending states. In 1990, merely a quarter of the countries in Europe, North and South America, and Oceania tolerated dual citizenship; by 2010, three-quarters did. The acceptance of dual nationality has become 'the new global norm.'[100] This lends unprecedented weight to the phenomenon of 'external citizenship,'[101] that is, rights or duties that new citizens have toward the state whose citizenship they continue to hold after naturalizing or even being born elsewhere. A distinct and 'genuinely new' trend has been the global expansion of the right to vote for external citizens.[102] This generates new and unforeseen democratic legitimacy problems, making even liberal-minded scholars look at dual or multiple citizenships with critical eyes.[103] External citizenship, understood as the possibility of transmitting citizenship to one's offspring in the diaspora or reacquiring the citizenship of one's ancestors, is now routinely available in certain parts of eastern and southern Europe, creating the phenomenon of 'passport citizenship.'[104] This is an instrumentally acquired citizenship, without residence obligations, that often remains unused, a kind of insurance policy if things go wrong in one's country of residence (like geopolitically imperiled Israel). Controversially, external citizenship furthers and is furthered by instrumental dispositions on part of their holders, which raises the

[100]   Harpaz (n 5), p. 5.

[101]   Rainer Bauböck, 'The Rights and Duties of External Citizenship', *Citizenship Studies* 13, no. 5 (2009): pp. 475–499, online http://dx.doi.org/10.1080/1362102090317464.

[102]   Michael Collyer, 'A Geography of Extra-Territorial Citizenship', *Migration Studies* 2, no. 1 (2013): pp. 55–72, online 10.1093/migration/mns008.

[103]   For instance, Ana-Maria Tanasoka, *The Ethics of Multiple Citizenship* (Doctoral dissertation, University of Essex, 2015) (copy on file with author).

[104]   Yossi Harpaz, 'Rooted Cosmopolitans', *International Migration Review* 47, no. 1 (2013): pp. 166–206, doi: 10.1111/imre.12017.

normative question of what is the proper citizen attitude.[105] An orthodox 'immigration state' perspective is incapable of grasping these novel dynamics of simultaneously held sending- and receiving-state citizenships, including their normative implications.

A closely connected, third desirable for future research is to look at citizenship not from the point of view of *acquiring* it, as has been the perspective of most scholarship, this chapter included, but from the vantage point of *losing* it. Should citizenship be something that the individual can never lose, unless she consents to it? This has been the dominant view until most recently, and legal developments, particularly in the United States, have worked toward it, enshrining citizenship as the unalienable 'right to have rights.'[106] But a new kind of ruthlessly fellow-citizen targeting terrorism, especially of Islamist persuasion, and often committed by dual citizens with a migrant background, has called the unalienable right to citizenship in to question. 'How can we permit a French to kill other French because they are French?' gasped a frustrated French president after having to bury a proposal that had intended to withdraw French citizenship from convicted terrorists.[107] It may have been prudent to drop a fiercely contested proposal. But this raises the question whether there aren't any minimal loyalties that citizens owe to their fellow-citizens as a condition for holding citizenship. In fact, the difficulties of instituting what critics have denounced as 'banishment,'[108] even for deadly terrorists, show the incapacity of liberal states to enforce *any* loyalty as a requirement of citizenship. This seems to be yet another step in the seemingly unstoppable profanation and devaluation of citizenship in Western immigration states.

BIBLIOGRAPHY

Abrahamian, Atossa Araxia, *The Cosmopolites: The Coming of the Global Citizen* (New York: Columbia Global Reports, 2015).

Arcarazo, Diego Acosta, 'Civic Citizenship Reintroduced?,' *European Law Journal* 21, no. 2 (2015): pp. 200–219.

Arendt, Hannah, *The Origins of Totalitarianism* (New York: Harcourt Brace Jovanovich, 1948).

Babar, Zahra R., 'Citizenship Construction in the State of Qatar,' *The Middle East Journal* 68, no. 3 (2014): pp. 403–420.

---

[105] See Christian Joppke, 'Instrumental Citizenship', (2016) (unpublished manuscript, on file with author).

[106] See Patrick Weil, *The Sovereign Citizen* (Philadelphia: University of Pennsylvania Press, 2012).

[107] Joppke (n 64).

[108] Audrey Macklin, 'The Return of Banishment' *EUDO Observatory on Citizenship*, Florence (2014).

Bauböck, Rainer, 'The Rights and Duties of External Citizenship', *Citizenship Studies* 13, no. 5 (2009): pp. 475–499.

Bauböck, Rainer, 'Studying Citizenship Constellations', *Journal of Ethnic and Migration Studies* 36, no. 5 (2010): pp. 847–859.

Bauböck, Rainer, 'The Three Levels of Citizenship in the European Union', *German Law Journal* 15, no. 5 (2014): pp. 751–763.

Beblawi, Hazem and Giacomo Luciani (eds.), *The Rentier State* (London: Croom Helms, 1987).

Bommes, Michael, *Migration und nationaler Wohlfahrtsstaat* (Opladen: Westdeutscher Verlag, 1999).

Brubaker, Rogers, *Citizenship and Nationhood in France and Germany* (Cambridge: Harvard University Press, 1992).

Carens, Joseph, 'Aliens and Citizens', *Review of Politics* 49, no. 2 (1987): pp. 251–273.

Collyer, Michael, 'A Geography of Extra-Territorial Citizenship', *Migration Studies* 2, no. 1 (2013): pp. 55–72.

Dahl, Robert, *Democracy and its Critics* (New Haven: Yale University Press, 1989).

Davis, Gareth, 'Any Place I Hang My Hat', *European Law Journal* 11, no. 1 (2005): pp. 43–56.

Donaldson, Sue and Will Kymlicka, *Zoopolis* (New York: Oxford University Press, 2011).

Durkheim, Emile, 'Individualism and the Intellectuals' (1898), in *Emile Durkheim on Morality and Society*, edited and introduced by Robert Bellah (Chicago: University of Chicago Press, 1973).

Fargues, Philippe, 'Immigration without Inclusion: Non-Nationals in Nation-Building in the Gulf States', *Asian and Pacific Migration Journal* 20, no. 3–4 (2011): pp. 273–292, doi: 10.1177/011719681102000302.

Ferrera, Maurizio, *The Boundaries of Welfare* (Oxford: Oxford University Press, 2005).

Franck, Thomas, *The Empowered Self* (New York: Oxford University Press, 2000).

Goldin, Ian, Geoffrey Cameron, and Meera Balarajan, *Exceptional People* (Princeton: Princeton University Press, 2011).

Goodman, Sara Wallace, *Immigration and Membership Politics in Western Europe* (New York: Cambridge University Press, 2014).

Harpaz, Yossi, 'Rooted Cosmopolitans', *International Migration Review* 47, no. 1 (2013): pp. 166–206.

Harpaz, Yossi, 'Compensatory Citizenship' (2016) (unpublished manuscript, on file with author).

Howard, Marc Morjé, *The Politics of Citizenship in Europe* (New York: Cambridge University Press, 2009).

Jamal, Manal, 'The "Tiering" of Citizenship and Residency and the "Hierarchization" of Migrant Communities', *International Migration Review* 49, no. 3 (2015): pp. 601–632, doi:10.1111/imre.12132.

Joppke, Christian, *Immigration and the Nation-State* (Oxford: Oxford University Press, 1999).

Joppke, Christian, *Citizenship and Immigration* (Cambridge: Polity, 2010).

Joppke, Christian, 'Instrumental Citizenship' (2016) (unpublished manuscript).

Joppke, Christian, 'Terror and the Loss of Citizenship', *Citizenship Studies* 20, no. 6–7 (2016): pp. 728–748, online http://dx.doi.org/10.1080/13621025.2016.1191435.

Kelsen, Hans, *General Theory of Law and State* (Cambridge: Harvard University Press, 1949).

Kochenov, Dimitry, 'Rounding Up the Circle', EUI Working Paper no. 23 (Florence: RSCAS, 2010).

Kochenov, Dimitry, 'EU Citizenship without Duties,' *European Law Journal 20*, no. 4(2014): pp. 482–498, doi: 10.1111/eulj.12095.

Kriegbaum Jensen, Kristian, *Scandinavian Immigrant Integration Politics* (Ph.D. Dissertation, Aarhus University, 2016) (copy on file with author).

Kriegbaum Jensen, Kristian and Per Mouritsen, 'Nationalism in Liberal Register,' *British Journal of Political Science* (forthcoming).

Longva, Anh Nga, *Walls Built on Sand* (Boulder: Westview Press, 1997).

Longva, Anh Nga, 'Citizenship in the Gulf States,' in Nils A. Butenschon et al., eds., *Citizenship and the State in the Middle East* (Syracuse: Syracuse University Press, 2000).

Lori, Noora, 'National Security and the Management of Migrant Labor: A Case Study of the United Arab Emirates,' *Asian and Pacific Migration Journal 20*, no. 3–4 (2011): pp. 315–337, doi:10.1177/011719681102000304.

Lori, Noora, 'Temporary Workers or Permanent Migrants? The Kafala System and Contestations over Residency in the Arab Gulf States,' (Paris: IFRI, 2012) online https://www.ifri.org/sites/default/files/atoms/files/notecmcnooralori1.pdf.

Macklin, Audrey, 'The Return of Banishment,' *EUDO Observatory on Citizenship*, (Florence, 2014).

Marshall, T.H., *Citizenship and Social Class* (Cambridge: Cambridge University Press, 1950).

Oakeshott, Michael, *On Human Conduct* (Oxford: Oxford University Press, 1975).

Orgad, Liav, *The Cultural Defense of Nations* (New York: Oxford University Press, 2015).

Paolin, Gianluca, *Citizenship in the Arab World* (Amsterdam: Amsterdam University Press, 2009).

Parsons, Talcott, *The System of Modern Societies* (Englewood Cliffs: Prentice Hall, 1971).

Poggi, Gianfranco, *Varieties of Political Experience* (Colchester: ECPR Press, 2014).

Preuss, Ulrich, 'Problems of a Concept of European Citizenship,' *European Law Journal 1*, no. 3 (1995): pp. 267–281.

Ruhs, Martin, *The Price of Rights* (Princeton: Princeton University Press, 2013).

Sater, J., 'Citizenship and Migration in Arab Gulf Monarchies,' *Citizenship Studies 18*, no. 3–4 (2013): pp. 292–302.

Schmid, Samuel D., 'Democracy, Open Borders, and the Rights of Immigrant Workers' (2016) (unpublished manuscript, copy on file with author).

Shachar, Ayelet. 'The Race for Talent,' *New York University Law Review 81* (2006): pp. 148–206.

Shachar, Ayelet, *The Birthright Lottery: Citizenship and Global Inequality* (Cambridge: Harvard University Press, 2009).

Simmel, Georg, *Soziologie* (Frankfurt: Suhrkamp, 1992) [1908].

Somers, Margaret, *Genealogies of Citizenship* (New York: Cambridge University Press, 2008).

Soysal, Yasemin, *Limits of Citizenship* (Chicago: University of Chicago Press, 1994).

Strayer, Joseph, *On the Medieval Origins of the Modern State* (Princeton: Princeton University Press, 1970).

SVR (Sachverständigenrat deutscher Stiftungen für Integration und Migration), *Unter Einwanderungsländern: Deutschland im internationalen Vergleich. Jahresgutachten 2015* (Berlin: SVR, 2015).

Tanasoka, Ana-Maria, *The Ethics of Multiple Citizenship* (Doctoral dissertation, University of Essex, 2015).

Thompson, Eric C., 'Immigration, Society and Modalities of Citizenship in Singapore,' *Citizenship Studies 18*, no. 3–4 (2014): pp. 315–331.

Vora, Neha, 'From Golden Frontier to Global City,' *American Anthropologist 113*, no. 2 (2011): pp. 306–318, doi:10.1111/j.1548-1433.2011.01332.

Walzer, Michael, *Spheres of Justice* (New York: Basic Books, 1983).

Weil, Patrick, *The Sovereign Citizen* (Philadelphia: University of Pennsylvania Press, 2012).

Wilensky, Harold, *The Welfare State and Equality* (Berkeley: University of California Press, 1975).

CHAPTER 19

CITIZENSHIP AND STATE TRANSITION

OXANA SHEVEL

INTRODUCTION

THIS chapter analyzes the national citizenship regimes adopted by newly independent states—that is, states first appearing on the world political map during the era of popular sovereignty—and factors that influence the content of these regimes. The chapter examines how the goal of attaining state sovereignty, different visions of and debates over the boundaries of the national community in whose name the new state is constituted, perceived implications of citizenship rules for political and economic power of different groups, and external actors, including other states in the region and international organizations, inform the content of citizenship regimes in new states. The chapter will highlight challenges, issues, and dynamics characteristic of new transition states more broadly, though most of the empirical illustration will come from the context of the fifteen successor states of the former Soviet Union. It contends that the politics of citizenship policymaking (meaning, a set of issues that impact the formation of citizenship rules, and groups whose status is at the center of domestic debates over citizenship rules) differ in the new states in important and systematic ways from the politics of citizenship policymaking in established 'older' states. Three particularly important differences will be highlighted and analyzed in the three sub-sections of this chapter.

The first difference is the link between citizenship rules and attainment and safeguard of state sovereignty. New states that emerged during the course of the twentieth century in the wake of either decolonization or collapse of the former multinational federative states face the so-called 'stateness problem'—the challenge of transitioning to democracy in a polity 'when there are profoundly different views about the territorial boundaries of the political community's state and who has the right of citizenship in that state.'[1] The novelty of sudden statehood and the associated stateness problem create an intrinsic link between citizenship regime and state sovereignty since initial citizenship regimes in new states are created simultaneously with the process of state formation. By contrast, post-World War II citizenship reforms in established states have been taking place long after state sovereignty was established and the stateness problem solved. As the evidence from the late Soviet and early post-Soviet period makes clear, citizenship legislation is commonly viewed as an instrument to attain and defend state sovereignty, and its content is seen as something that can either strengthen or weaken sovereignty and territorial integrity—and thus the very existence—of the new state. This citizenship regime-sovereignty-territoriality nexus thus adds another layer to the analysis and characterization of citizenship rules in new states, especially during the early stages of state transition. This will be discussed in the second section.

The second important difference between new and old states relates to the question of which are the main group(s) whose status is at stake in the politics of citizenship regimes. If in longer established states citizenship debates are first and foremost about the status of relatively recent immigrants and their descendants, in the new states citizenship politics revolves around the status of the former fellow countrymen—citizens of the formerly common larger multinational state or empire. While new immigrants are also present in these states (and with time in some states new immigrants may become the main group at the center of citizenship politics, reducing the new/old state difference), initially this 'foreign' immigrant community is invariably small. Citizenship policymakers in transition states first and foremost focus on defining the constituent nation, with the key questions being if all or some of the former fellow citizens will be given right to citizenship in the new state and

---

[1] Juan Linz and Alfred Stepan, *Problems of Democratic Transition and Consolidation: Southern Europe, South America, and Post-Communist Europe* (Baltimore: Johns Hopkins University Press, 1996), p. 16.

under what conditions, and whether some of those residing outside of the borders of the new states, in particular co-ethnics of the titular group abroad, should have the right to citizenship by virtue of belonging to the 'imagined community' of the nation.[2] From this follows, as the third section will further elaborate, that 'ethnic' and 'civic' characterization may need to be applied differently to citizenship rules in new and older states. That is to say, because in new states the group at the heart of citizenship politics are former citizens of a former common state, it is the treatment of this group that should be the main comparative yardstick. This section will use the post-Soviet experience to analyze factors that lead new states to adopt more and less ethnicized citizenship regimes toward former fellow citizens, in particular toward resident ethnic minorities and co-ethnics abroad.

Finally, the third important difference between new and old states that is consequential for citizenship regimes concerns the role of international actors. The post-communist states in particular are unique in this regard because, unlike either Western states or new post-colonial states in Asia and Africa, the post-Soviet states have been legislating citizenship regimes in the shadow of international institutions. If in older states citizenship regimes were formed before international institutions with a mandate over citizenship matters were established, in the post-communist period institutions such as the UN High Commissioner for Refugees (UNHCR), the Organization for Security and Cooperation in Europe (OSCE), and the Council of Europe have worked to limit statelessness and promote non-discriminatory citizenship policies. The ability of international actors to achieve their objectives has been complicated by 'ethnic unmixing' through migration which unfolded as former multinational states began to disintegrate, prompting both voluntary and forced movement of people to their purported ethnic homelands.[3] This migration complicated the application of international legal categories, to the point when the most basic distinction between immigrants and residents was no longer clear cut. Are co-ethnics who lived in another part of a common communist state during the communist era foreign immigrants in relation to their newly formed ethnic kin state if they return there? Or do they have a legitimate claim to membership in the new states of their ethnic ancestry? Do ethnic minorities in the newly formed states belong there by virtue of their residence? Or do they belong instead to their 'ethnic homeland' state? Or potentially to both? Or perhaps all citizens of the former multiethnic communist federal state have a right to claim belonging in any of the newly formed successor states?[4] Drawing on examples from the post-Soviet region,

---

[2] The term 'imagined community' is Benedict Anderson's (Benedict Anderson, *Imagined Communities: Reflections on the Origin and Spread of Nationalism* (London: Verso, 1991)).

[3] Rogers Brubaker, 'Migration of "Ethnic Unmixing" in the New Europe', *International Migration Review 34*, no. 4 (Winter, 1998): pp. 1047–1065.

[4] Similar dilemmas presented themselves when earlier multinational empires, the Habsburg and the Ottoman, dissolved in 1918–1923. Successor states crafted rules for determining citizenship that mixed criteria of residence, co-ethnicity, and individual option rights for members of ethnic minorities to

the fourth section will discuss the conditions under with international actors were able to affect the content of citizenship regimes. The concluding section will consider whether the post-Soviet experience analyzed in this chapter is indicative of the experience of other new states in the recent period, as well as the question at what point a new state ceases to be 'new', and the politics of citizenship ceases to be distinct from the politics of citizenship in established older states.

CITIZENSHIP REGIMES AS A TOOL FOR ACHIEVING AND DEFENDING SOVEREIGNTY

When new states form as a result of political shocks such as decolonization or dissolution/collapse of former states, new states formulate initial citizenship regimes based on one of the following principles. The first is attribution of citizenship to all (legal) residents in the territory at a particular moment in time, such as declaration of independence or date of the adoption of the first citizenship law. This so-called 'zero option' was the basis for citizenship regimes in all former Soviet republics except Latvia and Estonia, which followed the second principle—a 'restoration' of citizenship to those who had been citizens of an independent predecessor state before annexation.[5] Finally, the former Yugoslav republics as well as the two successor states of the former Czechoslovakia followed a third principle—attribution of citizenship to those who had been categorized as citizens of a federal entity of a predecessor state. These rules of primary attribution are an important component of citizenship regimes in new states. The choice of a particular rule is not a monocausal phenomenon, and as the post-Soviet experience in particular shows, in new states this choice is informed by policymakers' reasoning over the issue of state sovereignty.

The experience of the former Soviet republics that began to craft citizenship regimes before independence was formally achieved is particularly instructive.

live in their kin states. In the case of the Ottoman Empire, population transfers were seen to be part of the 'solution' (Igor Štiks, *Nations and Citizens in Yugoslavia and the Post-Yugoslav States: One Hundred Years of Citizenship* (London, New York: Bloomsbury Academic, 2015)); Harris Mylonas, *The Politics of Nation-Building: Making Co-nationals, Refugees, and Minorities* (New York: Cambridge University Press, 2012).

[5] Rogers Brubaker, 'Citizenship Struggles in Soviet Successor States', *International Migration Review* 26, no. 2 (Summer, 1992): pp. 269–291.

Unlike in Yugoslavia or Czechoslovakia, there was no formalized citizenship of the constituent republics in the USSR. The concept of republican citizenship existed, but union republics did not have their own citizenship laws and republican citizenship was fully subsumed into Soviet citizenship.[6] The Lithuanian Soviet Socialist Republics (SSR) was the first to adopt a republican citizenship law already in November 1989. In Estonian and Latvian SSRs citizenship legislation also became a key issue of political importance as movement for independence gained momentum in the late perestroika years and the republican Supreme Soviets proclaimed sovereignty in 1988–1989.[7] Except for Armenia (1995), Georgia (1993), Kyrgyzstan (1993), Tajikistan (1995), Turkmenistan (1992), and Uzbekistan (1992), the remaining nine republics adopted first citizenship regulations before the USSR, and with it Soviet citizenship, formally ceased to exist in December 1991.[8] Space constraints don't allow us to analyze all states, but some examples can be given to illustrate how political elites saw citizenship regimes as such (and not just specific provisions of these regimes) as having the ability to strengthen or weaken the prospects of independent statehood. In Ukraine, for example, the idea of a republican citizenship law was first introduced in June 1990, when the Supreme Soviet of Ukrainian SSR debated draft sovereignty declaration. In these deliberations, the clause 'Ukrainian SSR has its own citizenship' became the single most contested part of the declaration. The legislators spent more time discussing it than any other clause of the declaration, including such controversial ones as Ukraine's right to its own armed forces. Stenographic records of the article-by-article debate of the declaration takes up 265 pages, 66 of which (or 25 percent) are devoted to the debate of the clause

---

[6] According to Article 1 of the 1990 Citizenship law of the USSR, 'every citizen of a union republic is simultaneously a citizen of the USSR.'

[7] Citizenship policy in Estonia and Latvia has been a subject of many studies. Comprehensive accounts of the early years in particular can be found in George Ginsburgs, 'The Citizenship of the Baltic States,' *Journal of Baltic Studies 21*, no. 1 (Spring, 1990): pp. 3–26; Andras Fehervary, 'Citizenship, Statelessness, and Human Rights: Recent Developments in the Baltic States,' *International Journal of Refuge Law 5*, no. 3 (1993): pp. 392–423; Lowell Barrington, 'To Exclude or Not to Exclude: Citizenship Policies in Newly Independent States' (PhD Dissertation, University of Michigan, 1995), online ProQuest Dissertations & Theses Global (304216259), http://search.proquest.com.ezp-prod1.hul.harvard.edu/docview/304216259?accountid=11311; Joanne Skolnick, 'Grappling With the Legacy of Soviet Rule: Citizenship and Human Rights in the Baltic States,' *University of Toronto Faculty of Law Review 54*, no. 2 (Spring, 1996): pp. 387–417; Graham Smith, 'The Ethnic Democracy Thesis and the Citizenship Question in Estonia and Latvia,' *Nationalities Papers 24*, no. 2 (1996): pp. 199–216; Lowell Barrington, 'Understanding Citizenship Policy in the Baltic States', in Alexander Aleinikoff and Douglas Klusmeyer, eds., *From Migrants to Citizens* (Washington: Carnegie Endowment for International Peace, 2000), pp. 253–301; Jeff Chinn and Lise Truex, 'The Question of Citizenship in the Baltics,' *Journal of Democracy 7*, no. 1 (January, 1996): pp. 133–147.

[8] In Estonia and Latvia the first full-fledged citizenship laws were adopted after 1991 (in 1995 and 1994, respectively), but these two states created a legislative basis for regulating citizenship already in the late Soviet period on the basis of the inter-war citizenship laws and parliamentary resolutions on these laws' implementation (for details see sources in note 7).

'The Ukrainian SSR has its own citizenship.'[9] Analysis of the debate further shows that while proponents of Ukrainian independence supported the clause exactly as a symbolic step toward an independent state, supporters of Ukraine's membership in the Soviet Union opposed the very idea of the citizenship law on the same general logic: not having a citizenship law made the phantom of a Ukrainian state fully separate from the Soviet Union less likely.[10]

The citizenship regime-state sovereignty connection can also be observed in Estonia. The Estonian evidence illuminates the rationale behind inclusion or exclusion of resident minorities. Estonia is commonly grouped with Latvia as a country that adopted a 'restored' citizenship model, extending citizenship only to those with a family link to a citizen of the inter-war independent predecessor state. This principle, while formally non-ethnic, in reality excluded most of the non-titular resident minorities from citizenship. However, Estonia differed from Latvia, and shares a commonality with more inclusive Lithuania, with a provision in the initial citizenship law that granted the right to citizenship to all those Russian speakers without connections to the inter-war state who registered as Estonian citizens before independence was achieved.[11] In the Soviet period this act of registration was purely symbolic, as such registration— a civic initiative organized by the Congress of Estonia, a non-governmental organization that took a more radical pro-independence view than the official Supreme Soviet of the Estonian SSR—had no legal consequences under then-existing legal order. But this symbolic act clearly signaled support for independent Estonian statehood on the part of those who chose to register, and this loyalty to state independence was later rewarded by the newly independent Estonian state. Just as political loyalties of the Russian speakers who migrated to the Baltic states in the Soviet period were viewed with suspicion, and this perceived lack of loyalty to the newly independent state contributed to the choice of a 'restoration' rather than 'zero option' citizenship regimes, in Estonia those who showed their support for state independence through the symbolic process of citizenship registration in the Soviet period were allowed to get citizenship in the newly independent Estonian state since they were seen as posing no danger to the sovereign statehood. A similar regulation was adopted in Lithuania. The first citizenship law of November 1989 which preceded Lithuanian state

---

[9] Author's calculation from the Supreme Soviet bulletins containing stenographic reports for the period in question.

[10] I analyze the Ukrainian case in greater detail in Oxana Shevel, 'The Politics of Citizenship Policy in New States,' *Comparative Politics 41*, no. 3 (April, 2009): pp. 273–291.

[11] Vadim Poleshchuk and Priit Jarve, 'Country Report: Estonia' (Florence: RSCAS, EUDO Citizenship Observatory, 2013); Lowell Barrington, 'Nations, States, and Citizens: An Explanation of the Citizenship Policies in Estonia and Lithuania,' *Review of Central and East European Law 21*, no. 2 1995): pp. 103–148. In the 1990s 21,101 people received Estonian citizenship this way (Estonia.eu, 'Citizenship', November 1, 2016, online http://estonia.eu/about-estonia/society/citizenship.html).

independence gave two years to those who were residents of Lithuania but not pre-1940 citizens or descendents to opt for Lithuanian citizenship. This option at the time Lithuanian independence was not yet secure was also interpreted as a manifestation of loyalty to Lithuanian statehood, and those who opted in before independence were recognized as citizens by the first post-independence citizenship law of December 1991.[12]

Another aspect of citizenship regimes in new states informed by state sovereignty concerns is policy on dual citizenship. Unlike in established nation-states where battles over dual citizenship in the post-WWII era typically concern rights of co-ethnic emigrants or ethnically 'other' immigrants, gender equality, and/or perceived economic costs and benefits of dual citizenship, in new states the politics of dual citizenship is first and foremost about sovereignty. More specifically, concerns for safeguarding state sovereignty, territorial integrity, and associated fears of possibly subversive actions by other states, in particular neighboring states, have been a key factor behind opposition to dual citizenship, while moves towards acceptance of dual citizenship that several states in the region made during the last decade were conditional and crafted in ways that continued to address sovereignty preservation concerns. Examples from Ukraine, the Baltic States, and Kyrgyzstan illustrate this logic at work.

In Ukraine the issue of dual citizenship has been one of the most if not *the* most contested citizenship regime elements since the summer of 1991, when the first citizenship law came up for debate in the legislature of Ukrainian SSR.[13] Communists and other leftists, who openly supported restoration of the Soviet Union and/or formation of a new joint state with Russia, strongly favored dual citizenship, perceiving a connection between the single/dual citizenship issue and future prospects of the Ukrainian statehood. Such linkage is evident, for example, from the 1998 electoral program of the Slavic Party that stood for a union of Russia and Ukraine in a single state. The party program reads: 'the introduction of the dual citizenship principle is the way towards one CIS citizenship.'[14] The dual citizenship provision came just two votes short of being adopted in the fall of 1991, but then and ever since opponents of dual citizenship were able to uphold the single citizenship principle. Statements by Ukrainian elites make it abundantly clear that the core of the opposition to dual citizenship stems from fears of political consequences of dual citizenship with Russia in particular for Ukrainian sovereignty and territorial integrity. Thus, in a

---

[12] Neringa Klumbyte, 'Memory, Identity, and Citizenship in Lithuania,' *Journal of Baltic Studies 41*, no. 3 (September, 2010): pp. 295–313; Egidijs Kuris, 'Country Report: Lithuania' (Florence: RSCAS, EUDO Citizenship Observatory, 2010); Vesna Popovski, *National Minorites and Citizenship Rights in Lithuania, 1988-93* (Hampshire and New York: Palgrave, 2000).

[13] For details see Shevel (n 10).

[14] Quoted after party program as printed in Kyïvs'ke naukove tovarystvo imeni Petra Mohyly and Analitychno-doslidnyts'kyi tsentr 'ANOD', eds., *Politychni partii Ukrainy* (Kyiv: Tovarystvo 'K.I.S.', 1998), p. 71.

1994 article written by two senior officials of the Ukrainian Ministry of Nationalities and Migration, the officials bluntly stated their belief that 'attempts by our northern neighbor to put a dual citizenship clause in state agreements are not only misguided but also too dangerous, with long-term consequences.'[15] In a similar vein, the Head of Citizenship Directorate of the Ukrainian Presidential Administration has argued that dual citizenship could 'undermine the government's ability to exercise sovereignty,'[16] while the former speaker of the parliament was the most blunt: 'if we have dual citizenship, we will not have the state.'[17]

The greater acceptance of dual citizenship in the 2000s is clearly discernible across the post-Soviet region, but it has not been unconditional, and states continued to guard against perceived sovereignty threats. Perhaps the most telling in this regard are laws that explicitly allow dual citizenship with some countries but not others. The latest Kyrgyz and Latvian laws are telling examples. In 2007 Kyrgyzstan explicitly recognized the possibility of dual citizenship, but this reform also explicitly forbade (Article 22 paragraph 1 of the 21 May 2007 citizenship law) dual citizenship with bordering states: China, Kazakhstan, Tajikistan, Uzbekistan, where there is a threat, even if hypothetical, that dual citizenship might lead to territorial claims and threaten state sovereignty, while no such hypothetical threat exists from dual citizenship with non-contiguous states. Latvia instituted a similar country-based approach in May 2013, when it allowed dual citizenship (both for ethnic Latvians and for immigrants) with Western states that Latvia sees as its geopolitical allies (EU and NATO members, and also Australia, New Zealand, and Brazil), but not with Russia or other former Soviet states.[18] Lithuanian legislators voted for similar rules in 2008 and again in 2010, but because of the 2006 Constitutional Court ruling against widespread dual citizenship, the president vetoed both of these laws.[19] Attempts to introduce conditional dual citizenship continue, with the current government pledging to find a way to legalize dual citizenship by the end of 2019.[20] Such a change won't be easy, however, since it requires a constitutional amendment, which in turn requires a referendum.

---

[15] Nina Sokil and Vasyl' Hubarets, 'Chym nebezpechne i komu zahrozhue podviine hromadianstvo,' *Holos Ukrainy*, 17 February 1994.

[16] Petro Chaly, 'Element derzhavnosti—instytut hromadianstva,' *Polityka i Chas* (November 21, 2001): pp. 38–46.

[17] *Chas 2000*, February 28, 2003.

[18] Peter Roudik, 'Latvia: Extension of Citizenship to Emigrants,' *Library of Congress Global Legal Monitor*, 2013, online http://www.loc.gov/lawweb/servlet/lloc_news?disp3_l205403732_text.

[19] 'President Vetoes Dual Citizenship,' *The Lithuanian Tribune*, November 18, 2010, online http://www.lithuaniatribune.com/4481/president-vetoes-dual-citizenship-20104481/.

[20] 'V planakh pravitel'stva—do 2020 uzakonit' dvoinoie grazhdanstvo,' *Delfi*, February 28, 2017, online http://ru.delfi.lt/news/live/v-planah-pravitelstva-do-2020-goda-uzakonit-dvojnoe-grazhdanstvo.d?id=73887902.

ETHNICIZATION OF CITIZENSHIP LAWS
IN NEW STATES

Much of the existing literature that analyzes citizenship regimes' exclusiveness, or ethnicization, focuses on Western states, and, reflecting the key issue at stake in societal and elite debates over citizenship rules in most Western democracies, 'focuses almost exclusively on access to citizenship for immigrants.'[21] This chapter argues however that because in new states the group at the heart of citizenship politics are former citizens of a formerly common state rather than immigrants from other states, it is the treatment of this group that ought to be the main comparative yardstick, and an ethnic/civic assessment and comparisons (cross-national or cross-temporal) ought to be applied first and foremost to rules governing access to citizenship for this group. More specifically, there are two broad categories at the heart of citizenship politics in new states: first, residents at the time of independence who held citizenship of the prior larger common state, and, second, non-residents at the time of independence who nevertheless can claim some connection to new state. The first category (of residents) comprises two distinct sub-categories—residents who belong to the titular majority of the new state, and long-term resident ethnic minorities. The second group (of non-residents with a claimed connection to the new state) also has two sub-categories: co-ethnics of the titular group, and ethnic 'other' who have a family linkage to the territory of the new state (usually through an ancestor's birth or residence on the territory).[22] Excluded from this categorization are recent immigrants from third countries, as well as residents of the former common state who have no connection to the new state (either ethnic or territorial). This is not to say that access to citizenship for the excluded groups is altogether irrelevant, but just to highlight that the politics of citizenship in new states is not centered on the status of these groups (something that may change over time, as will be discussed in the concluding section).

---

[21] Maarten Peter Vink and Rainer Bauböck, 'Citizenship Configurations: Analysing the Multiple Purposes of Citizenship Regimes in Europe,' *Comparative European Politics 11*, no. 5 (September, 2013): pp. 621–648, pp. 622–623. At the same time, more recent studies categorize and compare a broader set of citizenship indicators, including rules regulating birthright access to citizenship, facilitated access to citizenship for co-ethnics, loss of citizenship and more. See, for example, Costica Dumbrava, *Nationality, Citizenship and Ethno-Cultural Belonging: Preferential Membership Policies in Europe*, Palgrave studies in citizenship transitions (Basingstoke: Palgrave Macmillan, 2014) (distinguishing four modes of acquisition and loss (birthright citizenship, ordinary and preferential naturalization, and rules of voluntary and involuntary loss of citizenship)). See also Vink in this volume (reviewing existing typologies of citizenship regimes).

[22] The non-residents comprising the second group could be citizens of a former common state or long-term emigrants in third countries, although in domestic debates in new states it is usually the situation of citizens of the former common state that attracts the most attention.

So how do citizenship rules regulating access to citizenship to the two categories (and four sub-categories) highlighted above vary in new states, and what are the reasons behind this variation? To begin, post-Soviet citizenship regimes vary substantially on whether they contain *any* provisions privileging co-ethnics of the titular majority group or excluding resident ethnic minorities. Citizenship regimes that do not contain any such provisions can be considered non-ethnicized. Citizenship laws of seven post-Soviet states (Azerbaijan, Georgia, Moldova, Russia, Tajikistan, and Ukraine) do not contain any clauses giving preferential access to citizenship for co-ethnics, and ethnic minorities who were citizens of the USSR and were permanent residents at the time of independence were recognized as citizens in these states. Laws of eight remaining states contain provisions that give various degrees of preferential treatment to co-ethnics (Armenia, Belarus, Estonia, Latvia, Lithuania, Kyrgyzstan, Kazakhstan, Turkmenistan), and Latvia and Estonia further excluded some of the permanently resident ethnic minorities from the initial body of citizens.[23]

Inspired by Brubaker's influential study of France and Germany and his argument that historically developed conceptions of national self-understanding result in distinct citizenship models that would be more or less inclusive of the ethnic 'other,'[24] some accounts see post-communist states as having more ethnicized citizenship regimes than Western states due to the fact that they are primarily self-defined blood communities that exclude from the collective self-image of the nation 'newcomers or the children of newcomers with no blood ties or historic connections to the country.'[25] However, it is not always the case that a historically formed conception of the nation determines the content of citizenship rules in new states. Space constraints do not allow analysis of all post-Soviet cases, but a few examples pointing to the presence of different determinants of citizenship rules can be noted.

One such example is Ukraine where a citizenship regime that does not contain any provisions privileging co-ethnics of the titular majority group or excluding resident ethnic minorities, and where birth or residence on state territory are the main principles in defining the original body of citizens emerge not due to a historically formed civic-territorial understanding of the nation but essentially by default. In the fall of 1991, in the context of political battles between nationalists favoring privileges for co-ethnics of the titular group and unreformed communists opposing the idea

---

[23] This variation is documented from the author's analysis of the tests of the first set of citizenship laws of the post-Soviet states published in International Organization for Migration, *Sbornik zakonodatel'nykh aktov gosudarstv SNG i Baltii po voprosam migratsii, grazhdanstva i sviazannym s nimi aspektami* (Geneva: International Organization for Migration, 1995).

[24] Rogers Brubaker, *Citizenship and Nationhood in France and Germany* (Cambridge: Harvard University Press, 1992), p. 5.

[25] André Liebich, 'Is There (Still) an East-West Divide in the Conception of Citizenship in Europe?,' in Rainer Bauböck and André Liebich, eds., *Is There (Still) an East-West Divide in the Conception of Citizenship in Europe?* (Florence: RSCAS, 2010), pp. 1–4, p. 3.

of independent Ukrainian statehood and separate citizenship law as such, a purely territorial criteria for defining eligibility for citizenship emerged as the only acceptable compromise for all involved groups. For nationalists, having a citizenship law, even if the law did not grant preferential treatment to ethnic Ukrainians, was a key goal since the institution of citizenship by its very existence served to strengthen sovereignty, while territorial law legitimized the state and the state's claim over the territory. Communists, unable to derail the law altogether or institute dual citizenship with Russia, settled for a territorial law without any privileges for ethnic Ukrainians as the least bad option. The third politically relevant group in Ukraine, ideologically amorphous old *nomenklatura* which jumped on the bandwagon of the independence movement in the late Soviet period, saw advantages in the territorially based law for instrumental reasons. Such a law gave it a sovereign state to rule, and supporting such a law was also a useful strategy for electoral purposes as it allowed the *nomenklatura* to position itself as a desirable moderate alternative to the 'radicals' on the left and the right.[26]

Azerbaijan, Georgia, Moldova, and Tajikistan illustrate a second pathway to territorially based citizenship regimes without provisions excluding minorities or privileging co-ethnics emerging. Quite surprisingly, this pathway is through a violent conflict over territory that all these states experienced in the late Soviet or early post-Soviet period. A combination of ethnic conflict with a non-ethnic citizenship regime goes against arguments such as Joppke's that unconsolidated borders are more likely to lead to ethnicized citizenship regimes,[27] or Weil's that non-ethnic citizenship is 'impossible, even unthinkable' in states with large ethnic minorities and unconsolidated state borders.[28] In the new post-Soviet states the opposite logic seems to be at work: states that face actual or perceived challenges to their territorial integrity come to see a territorial citizenship regime without any ethnic criteria (be it to include co-ethnics abroad or to exclude domestic minorities) as a countermeasure against challenges to territorial integrity. Differently put, by defining the body of citizens through the territory of the state, which means extending citizenship to resident ethnic minorities and not extending it to ethnic kin abroad, new states legitimize sovereignty claims over desired territory. This logic was at work in states where ethnic conflict already erupted, like the four noted above, as well as in Ukraine where in the early 1990s there was no open conflict but a probability of such conflict over Crimea. In debates over citizenship the tensions in Crimea were regularly cited as a reason for a territorially based non-ethnicized citizenship regime which would solidify Ukraine's claim over the territory. This logic outlives

---

[26] For a more detailed discussion of how interests of these three political groups in Ukraine collided and aligned during the debates preceding the adoption of the initial citizenship law see Shevel (n 10).

[27] Christian Joppke, *Citizenship and Immigration* (Cambridge: Polity Press, 2010), p. 51.

[28] Patrick Weil, 'Access to Citizenship: A Comparison of Twenty-Five Nationality Laws,' in Alexander Aleinikoff and Douglas Klusmeyer, eds., *Citizenship Today: Global Perspectives and Practices* (Washington: Carnegie Endowment for International Peace, 2001), pp. 17–35, p. 33.

the immediate post-independence period, as none of these four states subsequently added ethnicized provisions to citizenship laws. It appears that as long as there is even a hypothetical threat to state sovereignty and territorial integrity (which in the content of a new state usually means an actually or potentially irredentist neighboring state, and/or a geographically concentrated resident minority that is feared to be secessionist), this threat contributes to the adoption and maintenance of territorial rather than ethnic criteria for citizenship.

Russia's experience suggests a third possible pathway to territorial and less ethnicized citizenship—the objective to exercise influence over territory larger than the existing state. Territorial criteria for initial citizenship determination Russia adopted in late 1991 reflected the perceived link between territorial principle in citizenship rules and legitimacy of claims over a territory, although here the territory in question was the former USSR and not just new Russia. The 1991 Russian citizenship law gave the right to Russian citizenship to all citizens of the USSR, and by doing so asserted Russia's 'special interest' over the entire territory of the former Soviet Union. This was not the only concern, as the Russian lawmakers also were responding to nationalizing policies in the former Soviet republics that made many ethnic Russians and Russian speakers anxious, and in many cases targeted them for discrimination. Still, debates over citizenship in the Russian republic's legislature in the fall of 1991 show that those who advocated maintaining some form of political unity of the former Soviet region under Russia's leadership saw the citizenship regime that made USSR citizenship as eligibility criteria for new Russian citizenship as a means towards this end.[29] The above examples show that, rather than being a reflection of historically formed non-ethnic and territorial understanding of the nation, territorial and non-ethnicized citizenship regimes can result from the inability of domestic actors to agree on any other principle; from the desire to hold on to territory when territorial control is threatened by secessionist conflict; or from the goal to expand territorial control—or at least institutionalize influence— beyond existing borders.

Finally, in states where citizenship legislation does contain provisions giving preferential treatment to ethno-cultural kin reasons behind the emergence of these provisions are also varied, and do not always result from a historically formed and broadly shared ethnic understanding of the nation. Particularly puzzling are ethnicized clauses in citizenship legislation of states where ethnic nationalism is

---

[29] The politics of citizenship at the time the 1991 citizenship law was adopted in Russia is discussed in detail in several studies, including George Ginsburgs, 'Citizenship and State Succession in Russia's Treaty and Domestic Repertory,' *Review of Central and East European Law 21*, no. 5 (1995): pp. 433–482; Oxana Shevel, 'The Politics of Citizenship Policy in Post-Soviet Russia,' *Post-Soviet Affairs 21*, no. 1 (January–March, 2012): pp. 111–147; Igor Zevelev, *Russia and its New Diasporas* (Washington: United States Institute of Peace, 2001); Peter Waisberg, 'Redefining Russian: Identity, Dual Citizenship, and the Politics of Post-Soviet Russian Citizenship' (MA Dissertation, Carleton University, 1995), online https://curve.carleton.ca/f5ec0c61-2fe2-46d6-84d2-1dfb64d7878d.

weak since in such states there is neither a strong ethnic nationalist party to push for ethnicized citizenship rules nor a historically formed and broadly shared ethnic understanding of the nation to underpin such rules. Belarus, Kazakhstan, and Kyrgyzstan fall in this category. Belarus is a particularly interesting example given that ethnic Belarussian nationalism is broadly recognized as being weak, both historically and in the post-independence period. Yes, Article 17 of the 1991 citizenship law grants ethnic Belarusians the right to citizenship under simplified rules (without fulfilling residency, income, or absence of other citizenship requirement). Just as in Ukraine, in Belarus the broader domestic political context at the time of the law's adoption determined this outcome. The November 1991 law was debated in the most open political climate Belarus has seen, during late perestroika, after the failed anti-Gorbachev conservative coup, and before the authoritarian regime would be consolidated under President Lukashenka a few years later. The uncertainty of the early transition period, including uncertainty about the actual strength and electoral potential of political actors and groups, helps to explain how a numerically small and politically weak Belarussian anti-communist and ethnically minded opposition was able to insert these clauses into citizenship rules by being able to credibly present itself as a political force of growing importance and to bargain its support for other pieces of legislation debated at the same time.[30]

In Russia, citizenship rules in recent years also became more ethnicized. Since April 2014, the so-called 'compatriots' are entitled to Russian citizenship under simplified rules. The definition of compatriots in the law has been purposefully ambiguous since the concept was first introduced in 1999,[31] but there is a clear ethnic tint to it as compatriots are defined as those having affinity with Russian culture and who are fluent in the Russian language.[32] The Russian case is interesting as it shows how citizenship policy can simultaneously pursue a more ethnic-oriented approach and a territorial 'imperial' one. A legal category purposefully defined ambiguously enables policies consistent with both more territorial 'imperial' interpretations (as the concept of 'compatriots' could be extended to most residents of the former Soviet

---

[30] Author's findings from an ongoing research project. More generally on the flux and profound uncertainty of the transition period, see Valerie Bunce and Maria Csanadi, 'Uncertainty in the Transition: Post-Communism in Hungary,' *East European Politics and Society 7*, no. 1 (Spring, 1993): pp. 240–275. For uncertainly induced competitiveness in Belarus in particular in the early 1990s see Lucan Way, 'Deer in Headlights: Incompetence and Weak Authoritarianism after the Cold War,' *Slavic Review 71*, no. 3 (Fall, 2012): pp. 619–646, online http://www.jstor.org/stable/10.5612/slavicreview.71.3.0619.

[31] For more on the purposes behind this ambiguity see Oxana Shevel, 'Russian Nation-Building from Yel'tsin to Medvedev: Civic, Ethnic, or Purposefully Ambiguous?,' *Europe-Asia Studies 63*, no. 2 (2011): pp. 179–202.

[32] On ethnicization of Russian nation-building policies in recent years see Helge Blakkisrud, 'Blurring the Boundary Between Civic and Ethnic: The Kremlin's New Approach to National Identity Under Putin's Third Term,' in Pål Kolstø and Helge Blakkisrud, eds., *The New Russian Nationalism: Imperialism, Ethnicity and Authoritarianism, 2000-15* (Edinburgh: Edinburgh University Press, 2016), pp. 249–274.

republics), and also policies favoring a more narrow cultural-linguistic group, as such an interpretation (including casting just ethnic Russians as compatriots) could also be consistent with the letter of the law.

All of the above examples show how the broader domestic context and the dynamics of post-communist transition in the presence of the stateness problem in a given state can explain citizenship policy outcomes, including presence and absence of more ethnicized clauses, more accurately than variables such as historically formed understandings of the nation or the strength of ethnic nationalist parties. The experience of new post-Soviet states invites further probing into causes of more and less ethnicized citizenship rules in new states, as the question remains to what extent there is a systematic set of factors behind the extent of ethnicization of citizenship regimes in new states.

INTERNATIONAL INFLUENCES
ON CITIZENSHIP RULES
IN TRANSITION STATES

As noted in the introduction, the role of international actors is an important factor that sets new transition states, especially in the former Soviet Union and in Eastern Europe, apart from established older states. In established states international influences generally are not an important cause of citizenship rules. Western states adopted initial citizenship rules decades and in some cases more than a century before the end of World War II and before international human rights, norms, and institutions rose in importance. International law acknowledges that criteria for granting citizenship are a matter of state sovereignty, and 'leaves it to each State to lay down the rules governing the grant of its own nationality.'[33] Since World War II, however, international norms are credited with contributing to the expansion of dual citizenship in particular in Western democracies, and to some degree also in the developing world.[34] International rules and norms are also credited with

---

[33] The International Court of Justice ruling in *Nottebohm (Liechtenstein vs. Guatemala)*, judgment of 6 April 1955, online http://www.icj-cij.org/docket/files/18/2674.pdf.

[34] Thomas Faist and Peter Kivisto, eds., *Dual Citizenship in Global Perspective: From Unitary to Multiple Citizenship* (New York: Palgrave Macmillan, 2007); Randall Hansen and Patrick Weil, *Dual Nationality, Social Rights, and Federal Citizenship in the US and Europe: The Reinvention of Citizenship* (New York: Berghahn Books, 2002); Tanja Brondsted Sejersen, ' "I Vow to Thee My Countries"—The Expansion of Dual Citizenship in the 21st Century,' *International Migration Review* 42, no. 3 (Fall, 2008): pp. 523–549.

contributing to reforms of citizenship regimes that brought about gender equality and reduction of statelessness.[35]

In the post-communist transition states international rules and international actors such as the EU, Council of Europe, the OSCE, and the UNHCR have been important players in citizenship politics since the early-mid 1990s. Since 1997, the Council of Europe's European Convention on Nationality has been the main international instrument setting standards of citizenship policy for member states, which includes most (nine of the fifteen) of the post-Soviet states. The EU conditionality has been recognized as a particularly important causal factor in liberalization of citizenship regimes in states wishing to join the EU,[36] most notably in Latvia and Estonia where the initial citizenship laws were the most exclusive, disenfranchising resident ethnic minorities.[37] The questions how exactly, under what conditions, and through what mechanisms international pressures impact citizenship regimes in new states is debated. This section will briefly address some important aspects of these debates, namely: whether international pressures promote more civic-territorial as opposed to ethnic citizenship rules; through what mechanisms international pressures translate into domestic policy changes; and whether and how the power of international influences varies (over time and/or across cases).

On the first question—whether international actors push for non-ethnicized citizenship rules—the evidence from transition states offers some surprises. A number of international legal instruments prohibit ethnic and racial discrimination. These instruments include the 1965 International Convention on the Elimination of All Forms of Racial Discrimination (Article 1), the 1950 European Convention for the Protection of Human Rights and Fundamental Freedoms (ECHR, Article 14), and the 1997 European Convention on Nationality (Article 5). These non-discrimination criteria do not mean, however, that international law mandates non-ethnicized and condemns ethnicized citizenship rules as a matter of course. International law prohibits only such a distinction in treatment that amounts to discrimination, while differences in treatment that have 'objective and reasonable justification' are non-discriminatory.[38] While some lawyers argue that provisions of citizenship laws that

[35] Sejersen (n 33); Maarten P. Vink and Gerard-René de Groot, 'Citizenship Attribution in Western Europe: International Framework and Domestic Trends,' *Journal of Ethnic and Migration Studies 36*, no. 5 (May, 2010): pp. 713–734.

[36] Judith Kelley, *Ethnic Politics in Europe: The Power of Norms and Incentives* (Princeton: Princeton University Press, 2004).

[37] Barrington, 'To Exclude or Not to Exclude' (n 7); Kelley (n 36); Vello Pettai, 'Estonia and Latvia: International Influences on Citizenship and Minority Integration,' in Jan Zielonka and Alex Pravda, eds., *Democratic Consolidation in Eastern Europe*, volume 2 (New York: Oxford University Press, 2001), pp. 257–280.

[38] As one international lawyer explained citing a European Court of Justice ruling, 'the difference in treatment is only discriminatory when it has no objective and reasonable justification: if it does not pursue a "legitimate aim" or if there is not a "reasonable relationship of proportionality" between the means employed and the aim thought to be realized' (Eva Ersbøll, citing the European Court of Justice ruling in the case of Abdulaziz, Cabales and Balkandali, (Series A, no. 94), in Eva Ersbøll, 'The

give preferential treatment to a particular ethnic group 'are problematic in view of Article 5(1) of the 1997 European Convention on Nationality' because they 'could be classified as positive discrimination based on ethnic origin,'[39] other legal experts argue that in the post-Soviet context provisions granting citizenship rights to co-ethnics are in fact *desirable* since their absence carried with it a risk of statelessness.[40]

Avoidance of statelessness and respect of the principle of a 'genuine and effective link' between an individual and the state when determining citizenship eligibility are key principles of the international legal instruments on citizenship.[41] The activities of international citizenship watchdogs in the post-Soviet region confirm that these organizations were primarily concerned with eliminating statelessness and ensuring that all long-term residents of the newly independent states have a right to citizenship in these states. As long as national citizenship legislation achieved these two objectives, international organizations (IOs) did *not* pressure the post-Soviet states to abandon ethnicity as a criterion for granting citizenship under simplified rules. The position the IOs took in the Baltic states is illustrative of this approach. Lithuanian citizenship legislation was the only one of the three that IOs did not criticize. However, the Lithuanian citizenship law contains an ethnic criterion and grants preferential treatment to ethnic Lithuanians.[42] Latvian and Estonian legislation similarly allowed co-ethnics to acquire citizenship under simplified rules, but used inter-war citizenship status as a criterion for determining the initial body of

Principle of Non-Discrimination in Matters Relating to National Law—A Need for Clarification,' 2nd European Conference on Nationality 'Challenges to Nation and International Law on Nationlity at the Beginning of the New Millenium' (Strasbourg, 2001), online http://www.coe.int/t/dghl/standardsetting/nationality/Conference%202%20(2001)Proceedings.pdf.

[39] Gerard-René de Groot, 'Conditions for the Acquisition of Nationality by Peration of the Law Ex Lege or by Lodging a Declaration of Option,' 2nd European Conference on Nationality, 'Challanges to Nation and International Law on Nationlty, at the Beginning of the New Millenium' (Strasbourg, 2001), pp. 65–93, pp. 83, 90, online http://www.coe.int/t/dghl/standardsetting/nationality/Conference%20 2%20(2001)Proceedings.pdf.

[40] Thus, Michele Iogna-Prat, Senior Legal Adviser of the UNHCR's Division of International Protection, reasoned that, given the fact that at the time of USSR disintegration co-ethnics of one republic lived in another republic, many such individuals were in danger of becoming stateless if they did not receive citizenship of the republic of their residence and citizenship law in their homeland republics did not grant citizenship rights to co-ethnics (Michel Iogna-Prat, *Nationality Laws in Former Soviet Republics* (Geneva: UNHCR, 1993), p. 25).

[41] For a discussion of international legal instruments pertaining to citizenship that highlight the central importance of these two principles, see Carol Batchelor, 'Statelessness and the Problem of Resolving Nationality Status,' *International Journal of Refugee Law 10*, no. 1–2 (1998): pp. 156–183; Council of Europe, *European Convention on Nationality and Explanatory Report* (Strasbourg: Council of Europe, 1997); Committee of Experts on Nationality, Council of Europe, *Statelessness in Relation to State Succession. Feasibility Study. The Necessity of an Additional Instrument to the European Convention on Nationality* (Strasbourg: Council of Europe, 2001).

[42] Article 2 paragraph 3 of the 2002 Lithuanian citizenship law uses the language 'persons of Lithuanian origin' which effectively means ethnicity since territorial origin from Lithuania and citizenship in inter-war Lithuania are treated in different paragraphs of Article 2. Similar provision was contained in Article 17 paragraph 2 of the 1991 Lithuanian citizenship law.

citizens. International actors criticized this non-ethnic principle for determining the initial body of citizens in Latvia and Estonia because it excluded from citizenship many long-term residents of Latvia and Estonia whose ancestors were not citizens of interwar Latvia and Estonia. Even though the excluded residents were for the most part ethnically non-Latvian/Estonian, the IOs objected to their exclusion first and foremost because they were long-term residents. Lithuanian citizenship law meanwhile allowed all permanent residents to become Lithuanian citizens, and *additionally* made Lithuanian ethnicity an eligibility criterion for simplified citizenship acquisition. International watchdogs likewise did not criticize citizenship laws of five other non-Baltic former Soviet republics which also contain provisions privileging co-ethnics in citizenship acquisition because the zero option principle of the law gave access to citizenship to long-term residents and thus satisfied the criterion of 'genuine and effective' link. The experience of post-Soviet transition states thus highlights that ethnicization is a matter of degree, as well as permissibility of a certain degree of ethnicization under international law.

Whether and how international actors have impacted citizenship regimes of non-EU candidate states is another question generating scholarly debate. Some studies have found that international actors can socialize citizenship policymaking elites in non-accession states into international norms on citizenship, and promote policy liberalization this way. Checkel made this argument about Ukraine, contending that IOs (in particular the Council of Europe), socialized citizenship policymaking elites in the Ukrainian Presidential Administration into learning, embracing, and promoting the Council of Europe's norms on citizenship.[43] At the same time, this author's research on citizenship regime transformation in Ukraine reached a different conclusion, finding that international actors' influence on the Ukrainian citizenship regime took the form of neither conditionality nor socialization, nor did preferences of the international actors remain unchanged while domestic actors were made to change their position.[44] Instead, in the process of interacting with each other in the mid-1990s, *both* international actors and Ukrainian political elites changed their original preferences on the question of how statelessness can be avoided. The final outcome—a set of legal changes adopted in the end of the 1990s and early 2000s that largely eliminated statelessness in Ukraine—reflected this new compromise. The outcome was thus an internationally compliant citizenship policy, but this result did not follow from either a unidirectional international pressure on the Ukrainian actors or domestic actors' acquiescence or socialization into these pressures. Mechanisms of international influences, in particular in states where the carrot of EU membership is not available, deserve further investigation.

---

[43] Jeffrey Checkel, 'Social Learning and European Identity Change,' *International Organizations 55*, no. 5 (Summer, 2001): pp. 553–588.

[44] See Shevel (n 10). See also Oxana Shevel, *Migration, Refugee Policy, and State Building in Postcommunist Europe* (New York: Cambridge University Press, 2011), chapter 4.

Another important issue concerning international influences in new states pertains to timing: does the influence of international actors increase, decrease, or remain unchanged as new states mature? In the post-Soviet states that adopted citizenship laws relatively early—in the late Soviet or the first years of the post-Soviet period—these initial citizenship regimes were adopted without much if any international involvement. It took time for international actors to familiarize themselves with the consequences of the first citizenship laws in the region and to form opinions on whether or not new states' citizenship policies are in compliance with international standards. The influence of international actors on domestic citizenship regimes may therefore proceed along an inverted U-shape of sorts: from limited or no influence on initial citizenship regimes formulated in the late Soviet and the first few years of the post-Soviet era, to most powerful influence five to ten years into transition, the time when domestic policymakers are still relative novices on citizenship issues and international law, and international agencies enjoy the role of the main, if not the only, resident expert on the subject, and when EU conditionality induces changes in domestic rules; to subsequently more limited influence of international actors as the carrot of EU accession is no longer available for states that joined the EU (and not held out to more states because of enlargement fatigue inside the EU), while in the post-Soviet states domestic elites' know-how has grown and preferences became entrenched. Recent studies show that in the post-accession period citizenship policy reforms in new member states were indeed influenced by concerns that had more to do with domestic and sometimes foreign policy considerations and bilateral relations and not fears of international sanctions.[45] So far no backsliding took place in countries such as Latvia and Estonia that were forced to liberalize citizenship regimes in order the join the EU, but at some future point domestic politics might push towards such a backsliding. If this happens, it remains to be seen if the EU and the international community more broadly have levers to prevent such developments.

Concluding Discussion

Drawing on the evidence from the post-Soviet region, this chapter sought to outline the main differences in the politics of citizenship policymaking in new versus established states. It has argued that three such differences are particularly notable

---

[45] Schulze, Jennie, 'Does Russia Matter? European Institutions, Strategic Framing, and the Case of Stateless Children in Estonia and Latvia,' *Problems of Post-Communism*, early view (October 21, 2016.

and consequential for citizenship regimes: (1) greater prominence of sovereignty concerns in new states; (2) different groups at the heart of citizenship politics (not immigrants from foreign states but former fellow citizens of an until recently common state, in particular those who become ethno-cultural minorities in their state of residence and/or an ethnic kin of another new state), which in turn has implications for analysis of ethnicization of citizenship rules; and (3) the role of international actors who have potentially more opportunities to influence citizenship regimes in new states than they have in older states, but who also face reality on the ground that may not easily map onto the categories and policy prescriptions in the international law. This concluding section will consider two further issues. First, is the post-Soviet experience analyzed in this chapter indicative of the experience of other new states in recent periods? Second, at what point does a new state cease to be 'new,' and the politics of citizenship cease to be distinct from the politics of citizenship in established older states?

Space constraints allow only a nod to the experience of new states outside the former Soviet space[46] so this section will briefly look at South Sudan, the most recent new state. Some similarities with the post-Soviet citizenship politics are present. After South Sudan became independent in 2011, it adopted a citizenship law that allocated citizenship based on one's belonging to one of the 'indigenous ethnic communities of South Sudan,' and/or habitual residency in South Sudan since 1956, the date of Sudanese independence. Sudan, for its part, amended its citizenship law and denationalized individuals who acquired ('de jure or de facto') the citizenship of South Sudan and forbade dual citizenship between the two states, while allowing dual citizenship with other states.[47] Just like in new post-Soviet states, the key group at the heart of citizenship politics in the South Sudanese and Sudanese context is not newcomer immigrants but long-term residents. Sovereignty issues are also consequential. The new state of South Sudan striving to fill its newly declared state sovereignty with all 'required elements,' including a body of citizens, claimed a group of residents of the prior common state as 'its' nation, without any expectation of consent on the part of those attributed citizenship. Sudan, for its part, pushed back against perceived encroachment on its sovereignty (although true motivations of Sudan's actions would require further investigation) and denationalized those who resided in Sudan but were 'claimed' by South Sudan, upending the lives of hundreds of thousands of people and depriving many of them of basic rights in their country of residency.[48] The prohibition of dual citizenship only with South Sudan that Sudan adopted is similar to the rules adopted by some of the

[46] But see Sadiq in this volume.

[47] Bronwen Manby, *The Right to Nationality and Secession of South Sudan: A Commentary on the Impact of the New Laws* (New York: Open Society Foundations, 2012). See also Bronwen Manby, *Citizenship Law in Africa: A Comparative Study*, 3rd edition (New York: Open Society Foundation, 2016).

[48] Human Rights Watch, 'Sudan: Don't Strip Citizenship Arbitrarily' (2012), online https://www.hrw.org/news/2012/03/02/sudan-dont-strip-citizenship-arbitrarily.

post-Soviet states discussed in this chapter—disallowing citizenship with neighboring states with which actual or potential territorial disputes impacting on state sovereignty exist, while allowing dual citizenship with states that are not seen as threatening to sovereignty.

The answer to the second question—does transition ever end?—depends on changes in the realities that make citizenship politics in new states distinct. The prominence of sovereignty concerns and the main group whose citizenship status is at the heart of domestic politics of citizenship are both factors that can change over time. In broadest terms, the longer a new state exists as a sovereign entity, the more sovereignty will become the new normal rather than something to strive for or to defend. As this happens, we can expect the politics of citizenship to gradually become decoupled from concerns over sovereignty and to center around other issues, be it the status of new immigrants, economic implications of citizenship rules, gender aspects, or others. When this happens, citizenship regimes might also become less ethnicized, following an observation made by Suny, among others, that nationalism is malleable over time, and can progress from one form to another.[49] We can thus envisage, for example, that access to citizenship for domestic minorities may become more politically acceptable the longer a new state exists, and as perceived threats to sovereignty from the domestic minority (and/or from its 'kin' state) diminishes.[50] At the same time, even if concerns over sovereignty diminish, ethnicized citizenship policies and minority exclusion may persist or develop for other reasons, so the end of transition might, but does not have to, bring less ethnicized citizenship regimes.

Another marker of a new state ceasing to be 'new' would be a change in groups whose status is at the heart of citizenship politics. The distinction between new and old states would diminish once the dust of the post-imperial migration of ethnic unmixing settles, and citizenship politics begins to center more on the status of immigrants from other states rather than on the status of former citizens of a recently defunct common state. Such refocusing of citizenship politics took place in Western states after World War II, when traditional countries of emigration became countries of immigration. This is likely to be a process rather than an abrupt change, as it has been in Western states. Once immigrants become a key group impacted by existing citizenship regimes and their situation gains prominence in domestic debates over citizenship rules, a different analytical approach to ethnicization would also become warranted, with greater attention to ethnicization (or lack thereof, as the case may be) of rules governing birthright citizenship

---

[49] Ronald Grigor Suny, 'Nationalism, Nation Making, and the Postcolonial States of Asia, Africa, and Eurasia,' in Lowell Barrington, ed., *After Independence: Making and Protecting the Nation in Postcolonial & Postcommunist States* (Ann Arbor: University of Michigan Press, 2006). pp. 279–295, pp. 284–285, 291.

[50] There is some evidence of this dynamic in Estonia, for example, as shown in Schulze (n 45).

and naturalization of immigrants and their children, as opposed to rules govern-ing status of former fellow citizens of a former common state. Attention to the temporal dimension should thus be an important element of citizenship regime studies in new states.

Bibliography

Anderson, Benedict, *Imagined Communities: Reflections on the Origin and Spread of Nationalism* (London: Verso, 1991).

Barrington, Lowell, 'Nations, States, and Citizens: An Explanation of the Citizenship Policies in Estonia and Lithuania,' *Review of Central and East European Law 21*, no. 2 (1995): pp. 103–148, doi: 10.1163/157303595X00066.

Barrington, Lowell, 'To Exclude or Not to Exclude: Citizenship Policies in Newly Independent States,' (PhD Dissertation, University of Michigan, 1995), online ProQuest Dissertations & Theses Global (304216259), http://search.proquest.com.ezp-prod1.hul.harvard.edu/docview/304216259?accountid=11311.

Barrington, Lowell, 'Understanding Citizenship Policy in the Baltic States,' in Alexander Aleinikoff and Douglas Klusmeyer, eds., *From Migrants to Citizens* (Washington: Carnegie Endowment for International Peace, 2000), pp. 253–301.

Batchelor, Carol, 'Statelessness and the Problem of Resolving Nationality Status,' *International Journal of Refugee Law 10*, no. 1–2 (1998): pp. 156–183, doi: 10.1093/ijrl/10.1-2.156.

Blakkisrud, Helge, 'Blurring the Boundary Between Civic and Ethnic: The Kremlin's New Approach to National Identity Under Putin's Third Term,' in Pål Kolstø and Helge Blakkisrud, eds., *The New Russian Nationalism: Imperialism, Ethnicity and Authoritarianism, 2000-15* (Edinburgh: Edinburgh University Press, 2016), pp. 249–274.

Brondsted Sejersen, Tanja, ' "I Vow to Thee My Countries"—The Expansion of Dual Citizenship in the 21st Century,' *International Migration Review 42*, no. 3 (Fall, 2008): pp. 523–549.

Brubaker, Rogers, *Citizenship and Nationhood in France and Germany* (Cambridge: Harvard University Press, 1992).

Brubaker, Rogers, 'Citizenship Struggles in Soviet Successor States,' *International Migration Review 26*, no. 2 (Summer, 1992): pp. 269–291.

Brubaker, Rogers, 'Migration of "Ethnic Unmixing" in the New Europe,' *International Migration Review 34*, no. 4 (Winter, 1998): pp. 1047–1065, doi: 10.2307/2547671.

Bunce, Valerie and Maria Csanadi, 'Uncertainty in the Transition: Post-Communism in Hungary,' *East European Politics and Society 7*, no. 1 (Spring, 1993): pp. 240–275.

Chaly, Petro, 'Element derzhavnosti—instytut hromadianstva,' *Polityka i Chas 1* (November 2001): pp. 38–46.

Checkel, Jeffrey, 'Social Learning and European Identity Change,' *International Organizations 55*, no. 5 (Summer, 2001): pp. 553–588.

Chinn, Jeff and Lise Truex, 'The Question of Citizenship in the Baltics,' *Journal of Democracy 7*, no. 1 (January, 1996): pp. 133–147.

Council of Europe, *European Convention on Nationality and Explanatory Report* (Strasbourg: Council of Europe, 1997).

Council of Europe, Committee of Experts on Nationality, *Statelessness in Relation to State Succession. Feasibility Study. The Necessity of an Additional Instrument to the European Convention on Nationality* (Strasbourg: Council of Europe, 2001).

de Groot, Gerard-René, 'Conditions for the Acquisition of Nationality by Peration of the Law Ex Lege or by Lodging a Declaration of Option,' 2nd European Conference on Nationality 'Challenges to Nation and International Law on Nationality at the Beginning of the New Millenium' (Strasbourg, 2001), online http://www.coe.int/t/dghl/standardsetting/nationality/Conference%202%20(2001)Proceedings.pdf.

Dumbrava, Costica, *Nationality, Citizenship and Ethno-Cultural Belonging: Preferential Membership Policies in Europe*, Palgrave studies in citizenship transitions (Basingstoke: Palgrave Macmillan, 2014).

Ersbøll, Eva, 'The Principle of Non-Discrimination in Matters Relating to National Law—A Need for Clarification,' 2nd European Conference on Nationality 'Challanges to Nation and International Law on Nationality at the Beginning of the New Millenium' (Strasbourg, 2001), online http://www.coe.int/t/dghl/standardsetting/nationality/Conference%202%20(2001)Proceedings.pdf.

Faist, Thomas and Peter Kivisto, eds., *Dual Citizenship in Global Perspective: From Unitary to Multiple Citizenship* (New York: Palgrave Macmillan, 2007).

Fehervary, Andras, 'Citizenship, Statelessness, and Human Rights: Recent Developments in the Baltic States,' *International Journal of Refuge Law* 5, no. 3 (1993): pp. 392–423, doi: 10.1093/ijrl/5.3.392.

Ginsburgs, George, 'The Citizenship of the Baltic States,' *Journal of Baltic Studies* 21, no. 1 (Spring, 1990): pp. 3–26.

Ginsburgs, George, 'Citizenship and State Succession in Russia's Treaty and Domestic Repertory,' *Review of Central and East European Law* 21, no. 5 (1995): pp. 433–482.

Hansen, Randall and Patrick Weil, *Dual Nationality, Social Rights, and Federal Citizenship in the US and Europe: The Reinvention of Citizenship* (New York: Berghahn Books, 2002).

Human Rights Watch, 'Sudan: Don't Strip Citizenship Arbitrarily' (2012), online https://www.hrw.org/news/2012/03/02/sudan-dont-strip-citizenship-arbitrarily.

International Court of Justice, *Nottebohm (Liechtenstein vs. Guatemala)*, Judgement of 6 April, online 1995. http://www.icj-cij.org/docket/files/18/2674.pdf.

International Organization for Migration, *Sbornik zakonodatel'nykh aktov gosudarstv SNG i Baltii po voprosam migratsii, grazhdanstva i sviazannym s nimi aspektami* (Geneva: International Organization for Migration, 1995).

Iogna-Prat, Michel, *Nationality Laws in Former Soviet Republics* (Geneva: UNHCR, 1993).

Joppke, Christian, *Citizenship and Immigration* (Cambridge: Polity Press, 2010).

Kelley, Judith, *Ethnic Politics in Europe: The Power of Norms and Incentives* (Princeton: Princeton University Press, 2004).

Klumbyte, Neringa, 'Memory, Identity, and Citizenship in Lithuania,' *Journal of Baltic Studies* 41, no. 3 (September, 2010): pp. 295–313. doi: 10.1080/01629778.2010.498188.

Kuris, Egidijs, 'Country Report: Lithuania' (Florence: RSCAS, EUDO Citizenship Observatory, 2010).

Kyïvs'ke naukove tovarystvo imeni Petra Mohyly and Analitychno-doslidnyts'kyi tsentr 'ANOD', eds., *Politychni partii Ukrainy* (Kyiv: Tovarystvo 'K.I.S.', 1998).

Liebich, André, 'Is There (Still) an East-West Divide in the Conception of Citizenship in Europe?,' in Rainer Bauböck and André Liebich, eds., *Is There (Still) an East-West Divide in the Conception of Citizenship in Europe?* (Florence: RSCAS, 2010), pp. 1–4.

Linz, Juan and Alfred Stepan, *Problems of Democratic Transition and Consolidation: Southern Europe, South America, and Post-Communist Europe* (Baltimore: Johns Hopkins University Press, 1996).

Manby, Bronwen, *The Right to Nationality and Secession of South Sudan: A Commentary on the Impact of the New Laws* (New York: Open Society Foundations, 2012).

Manby, Bronwen, *Citizenship Law in Africa: A Comparative Study*, 3rd edition (New York: Open Society Foundation, 2016).

Mylonas, Harris, *The Politics of Nation-Building: Making Co-nationals, Refugees, and Minorities* (New York: Cambridge University Press, 2012).

Pettai, Vello, 'Estonia and Latvia: International Influences on Citizenship and Minority Integration,' in Jan Zielonka and Alex Pravda, eds., *Democratic Consolidation in Eastern Europe*, volume 2 (New York: Oxford University Press, 2001), pp. 257–280.

Poleshchuk, Vadim and Priit Jarve, 'Country Report: Estonia' (Florence: RSCAS, EUDO Citizenship Observatory, 2013).

Popovski, Vesna, *National Minorites and Citizenship Rights in Lithuania, 1988-93* (Hampshire and New York: Palgrave, 2000).

'President Vetoes Dual Citizenship,' *The Lithuanian Tribune*, 18 November 2010, online http://www.lithuaniatribune.com/4481/president-vetoes-dual-citizenship-20104481/.

Roudik, Peter, 'Latvia: Extension of Citizenship to Emigrants,' *Library of Congress Global Legal Monitor* (2013), online http://www.loc.gov/lawweb/servlet/lloc_news?disp3_l205403732_text.

Schulze, Jennie, 'Does Russia Matter? European Institutions, Strategic Framing, and the Case of Stateless Children in Estonia and Latvia,' *Problems of Post-Communism*, early view (October 21, 2016), doi: 10.1080/10758216.2016.1239541.

Shevel, Oxana, 'The Politics of Citizenship Policy in New States,' *Comparative Politics 41*, no. 3 (April, 2009): pp. 273–291, doi: 10.5129/001041509X12911362972197.

Shevel, Oxana, *Migration, Refugee Policy, and State Building in Postcommunist Europe* (New York: Cambridge University Press, 2011).

Shevel, Oxana, 'Russian Nation-Building from Yel'tsin to Medvedev: Civic, Ethnic, or Purposefully Ambiguous?,' *Europe-Asia Studies 63*, no. 2 (2011): pp. 179–202, doi: 10.1080/09668136.2011.547693.

Shevel, Oxana, 'The Politics of Citizenship Policy in Post-Soviet Russia,' *Post-Soviet Affairs 21*, no. 1 (January–March, 2012): pp. 111–147, doi: 10.2747/1060-586X.28.1.111.

Skolnick, Joanne, 'Grappling With the Legacy of Soviet Rule: Citizenship and Human Rights in the Baltic States,' *University of Toronto Faculty of Law Review 54*, no. 2 (Spring, 1996): pp. 387–417.

Smith, Graham, 'The Ethnic Democracy Thesis and the Citizenship Question in Estonia and Latvia,' *Nationalities Papers 24*, no. 2 (1996): pp. 199–216, doi: 10.1080/00905999608408438.

Sokil, Nina, and Vasyl' Hubarets, 'Chym nebezpechne i komu zahrozhue podviine hromadianstvo,' *Holos Ukrainy*, 17 February 1994.

Štiks, Igor, *Nations and Citizens in Yugoslavia and the Post-Yugoslav States: One Hundred Years of Citizenship* (London, New York: Bloomsbury Academic, 2015).

Suny, Ronald Grigor, 'Nationalism, Nation Making, and the Postcolonial States of Asia, Africa, and Eurasia,' in Lowell Barrington, ed., *After Independence: Making and Protecting the Nation in Postcolonial & Postcommunist States* (Ann Arbor: University of Michigan Press, 2006), pp. 279–295.

Vink, Maarten P. and Gerard Rene de Groots, 'Citizenship Attribution in Western Europe: International Framework and Domestic Trends,' *Journal of Ethnic and Migration Studies* 36, no. 5 (May, 2010): pp. 713–734, doi: 10.1080/13691831003763914.

Vink, Maarten Peter and Rainer Bauböck, 'Citizenship Configurations: Analysing the Multiple Purposes of Citizenship Regimes in Europe,' *Comparative European Politics* 11, no. 5 (September, 2013): pp. 621–648, doi: 10.1057/cep.2013.14.

Waisberg, Peter, 'Redefining Russian: Identity, Dual Citizenship, and the Politics of Post-Soviet Russian Citizenship' (MA Dissertation, Carleton University, 1995), online https://curve.carleton.ca/f5ec0c61-2fe2-46d6-84d2-1dfb64d7878d.

Way, Lucan, 'Deer in Headlights: Incompetence and Weak Authoritarianism after the Cold War,' *Slavic Review* 71, no. 3 (Fall, 2012): pp. 619–646, doi: 10.5612/slavicreview.71.3.0619, online http://www.jstor.org/stable/10.5612/slavicreview.71.3.0619.

Weil, Patrick, 'Access to Citizenship: A Comparison of Twenty-Five Nationality Laws,' in Alexander Aleinikoff and Douglas Klusmeyer, eds., *Citizenship Today: Global Perspectives and Practices* (Washington: Carnegie Endowment for International Peace, 2001), pp. 17–35.

Zevelev, Igor, *Russia and its New Diasporas* (Washington: United States Institute of Peace, 2001).

CHAPTER 20

....

CITIZENSHIP
IN NON-WESTERN
CONTEXTS

....

ERIN AERAN CHUNG*

Is citizenship a fundamentally 'Western' concept, in its origin and in its essence? Is citizenship outside 'the West' necessarily derivative of Western citizenship, only capable of being represented and understood in relation to Western models of the state? How does the study of citizenship in non-Western contexts challenge, confirm, and complicate dominant understandings of citizenship?

This chapter surveys the major challenges, opportunities, and insights of scholarship on citizenship and migration in the so-called non-Western world, which, for

* The author thanks Rina Agarwala, Ryan Calder, Lingxin Hao, Noora Lori, and the editors for their insightful comments and suggestions; and Meaghan Charlton, Darcie Draudt, and Yunchen Tian for their research assistance.

the purposes of this chapter, refers to Asia, Africa, and the Middle East. The 'non-Western world' is a highly contested concept: it implies that 'the West' is a coherent entity so world-historically central that 'the rest' is best defined and essentialized as not being it. Rather than attempt to define it here, I will limit the geographical scope of this chapter to countries or regions without significant populations of European settlers, thus excluding Latin America, Eastern and Central Europe, Australia, and Israel. As I will concentrate on the most significant English-language social-science scholarship on citizenship and migration published in the last two decades, most of the examples will come from Northeast Asia, South Asia, and the Gulf States, with more limited discussion of Southeast Asia and Africa.

Building on Charles Tilly's transactional model, this chapter defines citizenship as a contested institution and cluster of practices negotiated by state and non-state actors that demarcate formal membership in a nation-state and its accompanying rights, statuses, and obligations.[1] Viewed in this way, citizenship is more than a formal set of rights and privileges granted by the state; it is also a constantly changing, interactive, and local process that is contingent on formal paperwork, informal institutions, and everyday practices. References to 'citizenship' and 'citizen' in this chapter are based on this multifaceted definition; the terms, 'nationality' and 'national,' are used to refer exclusively to legal juridical membership in a nation-state.[2]

The study of citizenship in various non-Western contexts provides a distinctive lens through which we can analyze its contradictions and contingencies. This chapter explores how technologies of citizenship create hierarchies of citizens and noncitizens that prioritize meso-level membership over individual rights, that extend beyond national boundaries, and that generate 'in-between' statuses among both native and migrant populations. The grey areas of citizenship that this chapter examines are by no means unique to non-Western contexts. On the contrary, the purpose of this chapter is to move the field of citizenship studies forward by critically reevaluating our assumptions about the concept of citizenship, its associated rights, and the lived realities of citizenship practices in different parts of the world.

---

[1] Charles Tilly, 'Citizenship, Identity and Social History,' in Charles Tilly, ed., *Citizenship, Identity and Social History* (Cambridge: Cambridge University Press, 1996); Erin Aeran Chung, 'Hierarchies of Citizenship and Non-Citizenship in East Asian Democracies,' *APSA Migration and Citizenship Section Newsletter* 2, no. 2 (Summer, 2014): pp. 48–53, online https://higherlogicdownload.s3.amazonaws.com/APSANET/e5be2e91-9721-4513-acb8-799a93991666/UploadedImages/Newsletters/Mig%20&%20Cit%20newsletter%202(2).pdf.

[2] For simplification, I refer to policies and procedures pertaining to national membership as citizenship policies, citizenship attribution, citizenship acquisition, and so forth. I also use the terms, 'naturalized citizens,' 'non-resident citizens,' and 'dual citizenship,' according to their commonly understood legal references.

THE CONTINGENCIES OF CITIZENSHIP

The dominant English-language scholarship on citizenship and immigration is based on case studies of advanced industrial democracies in North America and Europe and, thus, takes as a given that 1) citizenship policies and practices are consistent with basic liberal democratic tenets such as transparency, equality, individual rights, and universality and 2) the boundaries of citizenship are coterminous with the nation-state. The distinguishing features of citizenship in non-Western contexts upend such assumptions in three principal ways.

First, citizenship rights and obligations in non-Western contexts are generally organized and regulated at the meso level, prioritizing collective obligations toward the nation/state over individual rights. When these collectivities are codified in positive law and regulated by the state, they materially impact the allocation of goods, the provision of services, and relationships between the state, society, and economy.[3] As the next section elaborates, the formal and informal institutions grounded in kinship, ethnic, and religious networks inform citizenship attribution (and loss), the allocation of citizenship rights, and the hierarchies of citizenship, especially in the process of nation building or re-building. The household registration system, for example, was the foundation for making former nationals of the smaller Trucial States in the Gulf stateless during the process of creating a new federation in the mid-1960s to early 1970s and continues to govern citizenship attribution and rights in East Asia. In countries as diverse as Taiwan, China, India, and the United Arab Emirates (hereafter 'UAE'), the two elements of citizenship—formal membership and the rights and duties that emanate from that membership—are not necessarily embodied in a single institution. That is, one may have formal membership in a national political community but may not necessarily enjoy the full privileges of citizenship due to one's meso-level membership in a rural household, kinship system, or religious community. Meso-level institutions thus blur private-public boundaries and are the primary tools through which states render their citizen *and* noncitizen populations legible.[4]

Second, the scope of citizenship underlines its relative, or contingent, character in contrast to the idealized universality of Western citizenship.[5] Instead of a 'sharp distinction between citizen and non-citizen,' postwar immigration has contributed

---

[3] I am grateful to Noora Lori for reminding me of this point.

[4] See James C. Scott, *Seeing Like a State: How Certain Schemes to Improve the Human Condition Have Failed* (New Haven: Yale University Press, 1998).

[5] I argue elsewhere that citizenship is contingent not only in non-Western countries but throughout the world. See Erin Aeran Chung, 'The Politics of Contingent Citizenship: Korean Political Engagement in Japan and the United States,' in Sonia Ryang and John Lie, eds., *Diaspora without Homeland: Being Korean in Japan* (Berkeley: University of California Press, 2009), pp. 147–167; *Immigrant Incorporation in East Asian Democracies* (New York, Cambridge: Cambridge University Press, forthcoming).

to the development of 'a continuum of rights attached to membership of a state,' as Zig Layton-Henry noted in a seminal essay.[6] Far from the ideal of universal citizenship, this model of citizenship encompasses specific rights associated with different levels of membership among citizens and noncitizens.[7] In non-Western countries, these multiple memberships have led to the development of 'in-between' statuses that extend beyond the boundaries of the nation-state, excluding specific domestic populations based on colonial classifications, nationalist movements, kinship networks, religion, and/or spatial movement and including specific external populations based on ethnicity as I discuss further in the third and fourth sections.[8]

Finally, the rights associated with liberal democratic citizenship in the West are not necessarily guaranteed for nationals in non-Western countries, even in established democracies. Building on T. H. Marshall's seminal study of British political development, studies of immigrant rights in Europe have noted that long-term foreign residents have been extended civil and social rights, such as property rights and unemployment assistance, before political rights, such as the right to vote in local elections.[9] In non-Western countries (and a number of Western countries), the Marshallian trilogy of civil, social, and political rights has been applied unevenly to not only noncitizen but also citizen populations. In countries where the provision of social rights substituted for civil and political rights, such as Kuwait and other Middle Eastern rentier states, citizens enjoy a robust welfare system despite weak or absent democratic institutions.[10] Consolidated democracies, such as South Korea and Taiwan, guarantee citizens' civil, social, and political rights unless they run counter to national security concerns. For example, the notorious National Security Law (1948) in South Korea—which bans unauthorized contact with North Koreans, any activity that 'praises' or 'benefits' North Korea, and any involvement in organizations alleged to be pro-North Korea—was used by previous military regimes to quash any activity that could be even remotely considered pro-communist or anti-government. It continues to be a tool used by democratically elected administrations to compromise citizenship rights. The third and fourth sections explore how

---

[6] Zig Layton-Henry, ed., *The Political Rights of Migrant Workers in Western Europe* (London: Sage, 1990).

[7] See also Elizabeth F. Cohen, *Semi-Citizenship in Democratic Politics* (Cambridge, New York: Cambridge University Press, 2009); Bosniak in this volume.

[8] See Mahmood Mamdani, *Citizen and Subject: Contemporary Africa and the Legacy of Late Colonialism* (London: James Currey, 1996); Daniel Naujoks, *Migration, Citizenship, and Development: Diasporic Membership Policies and Overseas Indians in the United States* (New Delhi: Oxford University Press, 2013); Francis B. Nyamnjoh, 'From Bounded to Flexible Citizenship: Lessons from Africa,' *Citizenship Studies* 11, no. 1 (2007): pp. 73–82; Neha Vora, *Impossible Citizens: Dubai's Indian Diaspora* (Durham: Duke University Press, 2013); Lori in this volume.

[9] T. H. Marshall, *Class, Citizenship and Social Development* (Cambridge: Cambridge University Press, 1950).

[10] Anh Nga Longva, 'Nationalism in Pre-Modern Guise: The Discourse on Hadhar and Badu in Kuwait,' *International Journal of Middle East Studies* 38, no. 2 (2006): pp. 171–187.

legal inclusion or exclusion from national membership alone does not necessarily correspond with access to civil protections, social welfare benefits, or democratic institutions and representation.

In sum, citizenship in non-Western countries is characterized by the prioritization of collective regulation over individual rights, contingent membership over universal membership, and subnational and supranational hierarchies over national democratic principles.

MESO-LEVEL CITIZENSHIP

While we usually think of the undocumented as *international* migrants who enter a particular country without the proper paperwork, a significant population of undocumented individuals in non-Western countries are, in fact, native-born— usually, poor, landless, and indigenous natives who are unrecognized or unverified by the agents of the state due to the absence of official documentation.[11] In postcolonial societies, the incomplete nationalization of former colonial subjects has created pockets of unregistered native, largely rural populations who were beyond the purview of colonial authorities and remain outside of the body of documented citizens, as Kamal Sadiq's chapter in this volume explains. In Kuwait and other states in the Gulf region, the *bidūn* are effectively stateless persons denied citizenship from the moment of independence from colonial rule.[12] In Kuwait, an estimated 100,000 *bidūn* live in legal limbo.[13] Low birth registration rates in developing countries, especially among rural populations in Asia, have further contributed to the continuing growth of native-born undocumented individuals in these areas.[14] The phenomenon of *de facto* statelessness is amplified in border enclaves—such as

[11] See Kamal Sadiq, *Paper Citizens: How Illegal Immigrants Acquire Citizenship in Developing Countries* (Oxford, New York: Oxford University Press, 2009); Sadiq in this volume.

[12] This term is a truncation of *bidūn jinsīyah*, 'without nationality.'

[13] The Kuwaiti government has gone so far as to offer the government of the Comoros a large aid package in return for granting Comorian citizenship to Kuwait's *bidūn*. See Adam Taylor, 'The Controversial Plan to Give Kuwait's Stateless People Citizenship of a Tiny, Poor African Island,' *Washington Post*, May 17, 2016, online https://www.washingtonpost.com/news/worldviews/wp/2016/05/17/the-controversial-plan-to-give-kuwaits-stateless-people-citizenship-of-a-tiny-poor-african-island/. Thanks to Ryan Calder for sharing this important point. The UAE has done the same for its *bidūn* population. See Noora Lori, 'Unsettling State: Non-Citizens, State Power and Citizenship in the United Arab Emirates' (PhD dissertation, Johns Hopkins University, 2013) (pending publication December 2017, online https://jscholarship.library.jhu.edu/handle/1774.2/838).

[14] Rameez Abbas, 'Internal Migration and Citizenship in India,' *Journal of Ethnic and Migration Studies* 42, no. 1 (2016) pp. 150–168; Sadiq (n 11).

the Indian and Bangladesh enclaves in the India-Bangladesh borderlands—where transterritoriality has created unadministered, non-state spaces and nominal Indian and Bangladeshi citizens with virtually no ties to a state or nation.[15]

In much of the contemporary Arab world, nationality is informed by customary or Sharia law that defines membership in kin and religious communities. Kuwaiti and Yemeni citizenship is thus bound with Muslim identity as illustrated in the 1959 (and later 1981) Kuwaiti Naturalization Law and the 1990 Yemeni Nationality Law that bar non-Muslims from naturalization.[16] Non-Muslims are permitted to naturalize in Qatar; however, the naturalization process is highly discretionary, and naturalized citizens are not eligible for the full citizenship rights of native Qatari citizens. The determination of native Qatari status itself is highly discretionary: individuals must document their continuous settlement in Qatar from 1930 to 1961, before Qatar gained independence in 1971.[17]

The ability of the state to denaturalize citizens reminds us how the citizenship institution itself can be used to create or reinforce social hierarchies, wield political control, and create new national narratives. Citizenship may be flexible for 'cosmopolitan' individuals whose mobility transcends the boundaries of nation-states; but it is also the case for political elites who can use the citizenship institution to reshape its society.[18] Kamal Sadiq describes the linkages between ethnicity, religion, and tiered citizenship rights in Malaysia.[19] Article 160 of the Malaysian constitution defines people of Malay ethnicity as Muslims and, since the 1970s, the government's *bumiputera* ('son-of-the-soil') policies have extended affirmative-action benefits in hiring, education, lending, and government contracting specifically to Malays thusly defined. In Bahrain, which has a majority-Shia population, the Sunni royal family has naturalized Sunni Muslim migrants in order to increase the Sunni share of the population through a practice known as 'political naturalization' (*al-tajnīs al-siyāsī*).[20]

These examples moreover point to the dynamic relationship between migration and citizenship. Not only does migration shape citizenship—for example, by forcing

---

[15] Reece Jones, 'Sovereignty and Statelessness in the Border Enclaves of India and Bangladesh', *Political Geography 28*, no. 6 (2009): pp 373–381; Willem Van Schendel, 'Stateless in South Asia: The Making of the India-Bangladesh Enclaves,' *Journal of Asian Studies 61*, no. 1 (2002): pp. 115–147.

[16] Longva (n 10); Gianluca Paolo Parolin, *Citizenship in the Arab World: Kin, Religion and Nation-State* (Amsterdam: Amsterdam University Press, 2009).

[17] Zahra R. Babar, 'The Cost of Belonging: Citizenship Construction in the State of Qatar,' *The Middle East Journal 68*, no. 3 (2014): pp. 403–420.

[18] Aihwa Ong, *Flexible Citizenship: The Cultural Logics of Transnationality* (Durham: Duke University Press, 1999).

[19] Sadiq in this volume.

[20] This practice fostered resentment among Shia Bahrainis and was a contributing factor in the 2011 Arab Spring uprisings in Bahrain. See Frederic M. Wehrey, *Sectarian Politics in the Gulf: From the Iraq War to the Arab Uprisings* (New York: Columbia University Press, 2013), pp. 39–102. I am grateful to Ryan Calder for bringing these examples to my attention.

states to revise citizenship policies in response to the challenges posed by the arrival of new groups—but citizenship policies and practices may compel specific populations to migrate or *become* migrant and thus vulnerable to the encroachment of the state, businesses, and private citizens alike. The asymmetries between the small percentage of citizens and the growing population of noncitizens in the Gulf States is the product of stringent citizenship policies, foreign labor migration, *and* the deportation and denaturalization of both native and naturalized citizens.

The household registration system is also a significant institution for determining citizenship status in East Asia. As I discuss further in the next section, China's household registration system (*hukou*) is considered by some to be the single most important determinant of differential citizenship rights in China as it regulates access to education, employment, health care, housing, and geographic mobility.[21] Taiwan extends citizenship rights only to those who have established their household residence in Taiwan regardless of nationality, which means that Taiwanese nationals with household residence elsewhere do not have full citizenship in Taiwan.[22] In Japan, the household registration (*koseki*) system was the basis for denationalizing former colonial subjects shortly after the end of the Pacific War.[23] While all colonial subjects were granted Japanese nationality on the basis of their imperial subjecthood, those whose *koseki* was outside of Japan—which included all former colonial subjects, since the household registration system is based on descent—were required to carry alien registration cards from 1946 and were ineligible for voting rights beginning in 1948. These steps facilitated the formal denationalization of former colonial subjects in 1952.

HIERARCHIES OF CITIZENS
AND NONCITIZENS

The vast range of political systems and levels of development in non-Western contexts poses challenges to comparative work. This great diversity not only makes case selection challenging, but also forces us to rethink some of our assumptions about

---

[21] Xiaogang Wu and Donald J. Treiman, 'The Household Registration System and Social Stratification in China: 1955–1996,' *Demography 41*, no. 2 (2004): pp. 363–384.

[22] Shelley Rigger, 'Nationalism versus Citizenship in the Republic of China on Taiwan,' in Merle Goldman and Elizabeth J. Perry, eds., *Changing Meanings of Citizenship in Modern China* (Cambridge: Harvard University Press, 2002), pp. 353–374.

[23] See Erin Aeran Chung, *Immigration and Citizenship in Japan* (New York: Cambridge University Press, 2010).

citizenship, noncitizenship, and their associated rights. Citizenship policies in such cases may be linked to existing social hierarchies, ethnicity, residence, and/or levels of political economic development, rather than democratic principles, resulting in informal and formal hierarchies of citizenship and noncitizenship.

On one end of the spectrum are cases in which noncitizens have almost no rights. In the *kafala* system in the Arab Gulf states, foreign workers are classified as flexible laborers working for private citizens rather than as workers with state-sponsored rights. Noncitizens outnumber citizens in the UAE, Qatar, Kuwait, and Bahrain, and the majority of laborers are foreign (over 95 percent in the case of the UAE). The citizen-sponsor, rather than the state, is responsible for managing, controlling, and monitoring the foreign labor force, linking the latter's residency permit to their employment contracts.[24] Unlike guest-worker programs elsewhere, this system prohibits the permanent settlement of foreign workers but, at the same time, gives considerable discretionary power to the citizen-sponsor to repatriate (or not repatriate) workers upon the completion of their contracts, creating what Noora Lori calls 'permanently deportable' populations.[25] While guest-worker programs in Western industrial democracies have inevitably led to immigrant permanent settlement, those in the Gulf States have produced stark divisions between a largely foreign, migrant labor force and a population of citizens who are either underemployed (especially women) or employed in inefficient public-sector jobs that serve to redistribute state hydrocarbon rents to the native population.[26]

On the other end are cases in which noncitizens may have more rights in some areas than do citizens themselves. From 2003 to 2011, South Korean nationals, but not foreign nationals, were required to submit their fingerprints to their local ward offices in South Korea. South Korea had abolished the fingerprinting requirement for foreign residents in 2003 in response to international pressure and human rights concerns for foreign residents; at the same time, the continuation of the fingerprinting requirement for South Korean citizens is an institutional legacy of decades of authoritarian rule in South Korea's recent history.[27] Similarly, international

---

[24] Andrew Gardner, 'Engulfed: Indian Guest Workers, Bahraini Citizens, and the Structural Violence of the Kafala System,' in Nathalie Peutz and Nicholas De Genova, eds., *The Deportation Regime: Sovereignty, Space, and the Freedom of Movement* (Durham: Duke University Press, 2010), pp. 196–223.

[25] Lori (n 13).

[26] See Martin Baldwin-Edwards, 'Labour Immigration and Labour Markets in the GCC Countries: National Patterns and Trends,' The London School of Economics and Political Science (2011), online http://eprints.lse.ac.uk/55239/1/Baldwin-Edwards_2011.pdf; Justin Gengler and Laurent A. Lambert, 'Renegotiating the Ruling Bargain: Selling Fiscal Reform in the GCC,' *The Middle East Journal 70*, no. 2 (2016): pp. 321–329; Martin Ruhs and Philip Martin, 'Numbers Vs. Rights: Trade-Offs and Guest Worker Programs,' *International Migration Review 42*, no. 1 (2008): pp. 249–265; Adrian J. Shin, 'Tyrants and Migrants: Authoritarian Immigration Policy,' *Comparative Political Studies 50*, no. 1 (2017): pp. 14–40. I am grateful to Ryan Calder for sharing his insights and references on this point.

[27] Chung (n 5).

migrants to China or India may have greater educational and employment opportunities than native internal migrants in each country due to the former's access to formal paperwork and the latter's 'blurred membership' as unrecognized or unverified national residents.[28]

In between are hierarchies of noncitizens. The rights of temporary immigrants in any country vary according to an immigrant's legal status, country of origin, gender, or employer, among other things. While some documented migrant workers may be eligible for the same benefits given to native workers, undocumented immigrants have neither citizenship rights nor access to citizenship in most migrant-receiving societies. In contrast, select groups of immigrants and their descendants—such as co-ethnic immigrants, marriage migrants, and former colonial subjects—may hold quasi-dual citizenship rights while permanent residents, long-term residents, and some high-skilled immigrants have access to many, if not all, of the social services and benefits granted to national citizens.

The hierarchies of noncitizens within non-Western countries stem from their migration histories. With the exception of rentier economies in the Middle East, and especially the Gulf States, many non-Western countries are traditional migrant-sending societies that, until recently, had emigrant populations that well exceeded their immigrant populations. According to the United Nations Migration Report, over 40 percent of the 244 million international migrants in 2015 were born in Asia and three of the five largest overseas populations originated from Asia.[29] Although Asia hosts almost as many international migrants as does Europe—especially since intra-regional migration *within* Asia far outnumbers inter-regional migration *from* Asia—borders are, as Smart and Smart's study of Hong Kong illustrates, 'only selectively opened.'[30] Despite the continuing growth of foreign populations in each respective country, most countries in all parts of Asia—as well as in Africa and the Middle East—prohibit or discourage unskilled foreign workers' permanent settlement. Unlike North American and Western European countries with significant immigrant populations, no Asian country grants family reunification rights to unskilled migrant laborers.[31]

Labor shortages combined with relatively closed immigration policies have led to the growth of multiple visa categories that are associated with specific

[28] Sadiq (n 11).

[29] India had the largest overseas population at 16 million followed by Mexico (12 million), the Russian Federation (11 million), China (10 million), and Bangladesh (7 million). See United Nations, 'United Nations International Migration Report 2015: Highlights (ST/ESA/SER.A/375)' (New York: Department of Economic and Social Affairs of the United Nations Secretariat, 2016), online http://www.un.org/en/development/desa/population/migration/publications/migrationreport/docs/MigrationReport2015_Highlights.pdf.

[30] Alan Smart and Josephine Smart, 'Time-Space Punctuation: Hong Kong's Border Regime and Limits on Mobility,' *Pacific Affairs 81*, no. 2 (2008): pp. 175–193.

[31] Dong-Hoon Seol and John D. Skrentny, 'Why Is There So Little Migrant Settlement in East Asia?,' *International Migration Review 43*, no. 3 (2009): pp. 578–620.

citizenship rights and, for a select few, pathways to citizenship. Japan and South Korea, for example, have co-ethnic immigration policies: policies that provide special legal status to noncitizens of 'native' ethnicity who immigrate. These policies have generated a relatively ample pool of unskilled workers who are not classified as foreign labor.[32] States may privilege co-ethnics while cracking down on other migrants: the Japanese government revised the Immigration Control and Refugee Recognition Act in 1990 to impose criminal penalties on employers knowingly hiring undocumented workers and, at the same time, granted *Nikkei* (ethnic Japanese) immigrants and their descendants (up until the third generation) long-term residency visas, giving them unrestricted entrance and employment rights in Japan.[33] While their Japanese descent makes *Nikkei* immigrants the exception to Japan's otherwise closed-door immigration policies, it does not give them clear pathways to Japanese citizenship. Ethnic Japanese immigrants must undergo the same process of naturalization as all other foreigners in order to become Japanese nationals.

South Korea passed the Overseas Korean Act in 1999 that created an 'Overseas Korean' (F-4) visa category, which gave eligible co-ethnic immigrants quasi-dual-citizenship rights, including access to health insurance, pensions, property rights, unrestricted economic activity, and broad employment opportunities.[34] This act nevertheless created hierarchies among ethnic Korean immigrants to South Korea: until 2003, ethnic Koreans from China (*Chosŏnjok*), who make up the largest immigrant population of ethnic Koreans in South Korea, and the former Soviet Union (*Koryŏin*) were excluded from this status based on the provision that only those who left the Korean peninsula after the founding of the Republic of Korea in 1948 were eligible.[35]

Most non-Western countries have extended co-ethnic policies to emigrants and their descendants residing outside of their national borders. Traditional immigrant-sending countries in Asia, Africa, and the Middle East have established public agencies exclusively for their emigrant populations, such as the Overseas Chinese Affairs Office, the Commission on Filipinos Overseas, the Punjab Overseas Pakistanis Commissioner, the National Nigerian Volunteer Service, the Sierra Leone Office of

---

[32] See Erin Aeran Chung, 'Workers or Residents? Diverging Patterns of Immigrant Incorporation in Korea and Japan,' *Pacific Affairs* 83, no. 4 (December, 2010): pp. 675–696; Erin Aeran Chung, 'Japan and South Korea: Immigration Control and Immigrant Incorporation,' in James F. Hollifield, Philip L. Martin, and Pia M. Orrenius, eds., *Controlling Immigration: A Global Perspective* (Stanford: Stanford University Press, 2014), pp. 399–421.

[33] Takeyuki Tsuda, *Strangers in the Ethnic Homeland: Japanese Brazilian Return Migration in Transnational Perspective* (New York: Columbia University Press, 2003).

[34] Jung-Sun Park and Paul Y. Chang, 'Contention in the Construction of a Global Korean Community: The Case of the Overseas Korean Act,' *Journal of Korean Studies* 10 (2005): pp. 1–27; Nora Hui-Jung Kim, 'Korean Immigration Policy Changes and the Political Liberals' Dilemma,' *International Migration Review* 42, no. 3 (2008): pp. 576–596.

[35] Chung, 'Workers or Residents?' (n 32).

Diaspora Affairs, and the Presidency for Turks Abroad and Related Communities. Likewise, non-resident citizens in a wide range of countries in Asia, Africa, and the Middle East (especially since the Arab Spring in 2011), such as Japan, South Korea, Malaysia, Singapore, India, South Africa, Mali, Algeria, Egypt, Syria, and Turkey, are also eligible to vote in their home-country elections by mail or through their embassies. Dual citizenship is another tool used by some migrant-sending countries to encourage emigrant remittances and investments in their home country.[36] Over half of all countries in Africa and Southeast Asia allow or tolerate some form of dual citizenship; most Northeast and South Asian countries and Gulf States do not.[37]

In East Asia, the only immigrant group outside of co-ethnics and high-skilled professionals that have been proactively recruited by national and local governments are (female) marriage partners for the growing numbers of unmarried bachelors largely in rural areas. Facing low birth rates and aging populations, the governments of Japan, South Korea, and Taiwan have prioritized 'marriage migrants'—female immigrants marrying native male citizens—who have become one of the largest immigrant groups in these countries. Marriage to native citizens now constitutes one of the most widely recognized paths to citizenship acquisition in all three countries. Marriage migrants occupy the highest echelon in the hierarchy of noncitizens in South Korea, with the exception of high-skilled professionals (and, within that group, investors). Not only are marriage migrants among a select group eligible for simplified naturalization and dual citizenship, but they have unlimited employment rights and have access to over 180 so-called multicultural family centers created to facilitate their integration.[38] Taiwan's marriage migrants are also eligible for simplified naturalization

---

[36] See, inter alia, Thomas Faist and Peter Kivisto, eds., *Dual Citizenship in Global Perspective: From Unitary to Multiple Citizenship* (Basingstoke, New York: Palgrave Macmillan, 2007); David FitzGerald, *A Nation of Emigrants: How Mexico Manages Its Migration* (Berkeley: University of California Press, 2009); Latha Varadarajan, *The Domestic Abroad: Diasporas in International Relations* (New York: Oxford University Press, 2010); Egle Verseckaite, 'Citizenship as a Stateness Boundary Maintenance Regime: The Curious Case of Lithuanian Dual Citizenship' (PhD dissertation, Johns Hopkins University, 2015) (pending publication May 2019, online https://jscholarship.library.jhu.edu/handle/1774.2/838).

[37] Tanja Brøndsted Sejersen, '"I Vow to Thee My Countries": The Expansion of Dual Citizenship in the 21st Century,' *International Migration Review* 42, no. 3 (2008): pp. 523–549; Bronwen Manby, *Citizenship Law in Africa: A Comparative Study* (New York: Open Society Institute, 2010); Maarten Peter Vink, Gerard-René de Groot, and Ngo Chun Luk, 'MACIMIDE Global Expatriate Dual Citizenship Dataset' (2015), online http://dx.doi.org/10.7910/DVN/TTMZo8.

[38] Erin Aeran Chung and Daisy Kim, 'Citizenship and Marriage in a Globalizing World: Multicultural Families and Monocultural Nationality Laws in Korea and Japan,' *Indiana Journal of Global Legal Studies* 19, no. 1 (Winter, 2012): pp. 195–219; Daisy Kim, 'Bargaining Citizenship: Women's Organizations, the State, and Marriage Migrants in South Korea' (PhD dissertation, Johns Hopkins University, 2015) (pending publication Fall 2016, online https://jscholarship.library.jhu.edu/handle/1774.2/838); Hye-Kyung Lee, 'International Marriage and the State in South Korea: Focusing on Governmental Policy,' *Citizenship Studies* 12, no. 1 (2008): pp. 107–123.

and more employment and citizenship rights than other foreigners. At the same time, some marriage migrants are more privileged than others based on national origin. While all marriage migrants have relatively clear pathways to Taiwanese citizenship, those from mainland China cannot exercise their full citizenship rights during a post-naturalization probationary period when they have limited family reunification rights and are barred from civil service employment for ten years.[39]

Compounding noncitizen hierarchies are the multiple generations of noncitizens residing in non-Western countries. While industrial democracies in North America and Europe are grappling with the so-called second-generation immigrant incorporation question, many non-Western countries have yet to incorporate their third, fourth, or fifth-generation foreign residents. Nearly all countries in Asia and the Middle East have citizenship policies based exclusively or predominantly on *jus sanguinis*. An increasing number of non-Western countries are abolishing gender discrimination in citizenship attribution policies, thus permitting the offspring of international marriages to gain nationality either through their father or mother, and have streamlined the naturalization process for spouses of citizens; nevertheless, few have implemented facilitated naturalization procedures for native-born generations of foreign residents. Although most countries with descent-based citizenship policies do not prohibit foreign residents from acquiring nationality through naturalization, they will likely exhibit low rates of naturalization among their foreign residents across generations if dominant understandings of national citizenship and naturalization procedures reflect ethnonational conceptions of nationhood. In Japan, for example, naturalization rates have not exceeded 1 percent of the total foreign population *across* five generations of foreign residents despite the four-fold increase in annual naturalizations from the early 1990s.[40] Although Japan's official naturalization criteria are no more stringent than those of the United States, the substantial discretionary powers exercised by Justice Ministry officials during the process make naturalization procedures opaque and arbitrary. In addition to meeting official naturalization criteria and submitting tax records and extensive documentation related to their family histories, they must, in most cases, demonstrate evidence of cultural assimilation.[41]

---

[39] Sara L. Friedman, *Exceptional States: Chinese Immigrants and Taiwanese Sovereignty* (Berkeley: University of California Press, 2015).

[40] Japan Ministry of Justice, 'Heisei 26 Nenmatsu Genzaini Okeru Gaikokujintorokusha Toukeini Tsuite [Report on Current Foreign Resident Statistics at the End of 2014],' (2015), online http://www.moj.go.jp/content/001140153.pdf; SOPEMI, 'Trends in International Migration: Continuous Reporting System on Migration' (Paris: OECD, 2015).

[41] Chung (n 23).

INTERNAL MIGRATION

Although the majority of English-language scholarship on immigration focuses on flows from the Global South to the Global North, or from East to West, intra-regional and South-South migration is the dominant form of international migration in the contemporary world. The number of internal migrants, moreover, is roughly three times that of international migrants at an estimated 740 million in 2015, compared to 244 million international migrants.[42] The number of rural migrants to urban areas in China alone is almost double the total number of international migrants worldwide. In addition to China, the most internally mobile countries in the world today are South Africa, Chile, Mexico, Costa Rica, Brazil, Ecuador, Ghana, India, Indonesia, Malaysia, the Philippines, and Vietnam, according to the International Organization for Migration.[43]

Internal migrants are neither legally nor culturally foreign, but like international migrants, they often face ambiguities and differentiation with regard to their rights and privileges. Unlike domestic minority groups, internal migrants do not 'fit' into officially recognized categories and are, thus, not eligible for state-sponsored affirmative action programs, multicultural rights, or autonomous governance rights. Studies of internal migration in India demonstrate how movement—rather than nationality, race, religion, caste, or ethnicity—is tied to diminished access to voting rights, welfare benefits, health care, employment, and public services.[44] Research on rural-urban migration in China, similarly, suggests a paradoxical relationship between economic mobility and access to citizenship rights. Occupational upward mobility from farm labor to off-farm work or small businesses is accompanied by a reduction of rights to education, health insurance, residency, and voting in the urban locality in which migrants reside and work.[45] In both cases, the very documents that authenticate internal migrants' juridical citizenship in the nation-state impede their substantive citizenship in their local communities of residence.

In a seminal article, Chan and Zhang describe China's household registration, or *hukou*, system as one of the dominant tools used by the state for the purposes of social stratification and control.[46] Although the system was created in

[42] International Organization for Migration, 'World Migration Report 2015: Migrants and Cities, New Partnerships to Manage Mobility' (Geneva: International Organization for Migration, 2015), online http://publications.iom.int/system/files/wmr2015_en.pdf; United Nations (n 29).

[43] International Organization for Migration (n 42).

[44] Rameez Abbas, 'Citizen or Stranger? The Politics of Internal Migration in Mumbai and Kolkata' (PhD dissertation, Johns Hopkins University, 2011), online http://search.proquest.com/docview/880288262.

[45] Lingxin Hao and Yucheng Liang, 'The Spatial and Career Mobility of China's Urban and Rural Labor Force,' *Management and Organization Review 12*, no. 1 (2016): pp. 135–158.

[46] Kam Wing Chan and Li Zhang, 'The Hukou System and Rural-Urban Migration in China: Processes and Changes,' *The China Quarterly 160* (1999): pp. 818–855, pp. 822–823.

the early 1950s to monitor population movement, the National People's Congress promulgated the first set of *hukou* legislation in 1958 that made urban and rural household registration the basis for allocating goods, services, and eligibility for specific jobs, on the one hand, and for controlling internal movement, especially from rural to urban areas, on the other. In effect, the *hukou* system became a domestic citizenship regime, much like the Soviet *propiska* (internal passport) system, that created hierarchies of citizens within China according to a descent-based, meso-level registration system. In addition to the differential allocation of citizenship rights for urban and rural residents, rural-urban migration itself was regulated by the state, complete with migration permits, urban-entry fees, company recruitment permits, university enrollment certificates, and quotas. Those who sought to become legally sanctioned urban residents had to change both the geographical place of their *hukou* registration from rural to urban and convert their *hukou* status from agricultural to non-agricultural in a process called *nongzhuanfei*. The vast majority of internal migrants who were not eligible for *nongzhuanfei* were, in effect, informal, or undocumented, migrants who were subject to the vulnerabilities and exploitative practices that undocumented foreign migrants face throughout the world. Dorothy Solinger argues that China's rural migrants fare worse than their foreign counterparts in industrial democracies due to what she calls their 'double disadvantages.'[47] Like undocumented foreigners in countries such as Japan, Chinese migrants without urban *hukou* who nonetheless reside in urban areas are ineligible for fundamental citizenship rights such as access to education, employment, and healthcare, not to mention voting. But the latter work and reside under such conditions in an authoritarian system *as Chinese nationals* and must acquire the basic necessities of urban life at private markets, often at prices considerably higher than those available to locals, *as internal migrants.*[48]

The Xi Jinping administration abolished the *nongzhuanfei* requirement and relaxed the strict controls on spatial mobility such that residence cards are now issued to all residents in most migrant-receiving cities. While the official paperwork distinction between rural and urban residents has been phased out, the practice of differentiated citizenship remains. Since the household registration system is based on descent, there is a clear record of each household's migration history, thus demarcating urban residents who originally held a rural *hukou*.[49]

---

[47] Dorothy J. Solinger, *Contesting Citizenship in Urban China: Peasant Migrants, the State, and the Logic of the Market* (Berkeley: University of California Press, 1999); Dorothy J. Solinger, 'Citizenship Issues in China's Internal Migration: Comparisons with Germany and Japan,' *Political Science Quarterly* 114, no. 3 (1999): pp. 455–478.

[48] Solinger, 'Citizenship Issues in China's Internal Migration' (n 48), p. 469.

[49] Hao and Liang (n 45).

Such hierarchies of citizens (and noncitizens) are not exclusive to authoritarian systems, however. Power-sharing governance structures that encourage diversity and democratic countries with official multicultural policies may enable local actors to undermine the citizenship of particular minority groups or migrants from ethnically or linguistically different regions. India's constitution guarantees universal citizenship rights to its citizenry regardless of religion, race, caste, sex, or place of birth and recognizes group rights for religious, linguistic, and tribal minorities.[50] Comparing multicultural policies and programs in Asia, Kymlicka and He note that multicultural policies in India have been widely successful.[51] Not only do Indian multicultural policies accommodate minority rights but they also make special provisions to provide food, housing, education, and healthcare for the poor.[52] In contrast to China, India's constitution additionally guarantees the right to move freely within national boundaries.

But internal migrants in India, many of whom are from lower castes and tribes, face challenges of *de facto* statelessness and second-class citizenship similar to their counterparts in China due to informal practices and institutions, especially at the local level. Abbas's study of North Indian migrants to Mumbai and Kolkata focuses on the relationship between ration cards—used formally in the food rationing system—and access to citizenship status and rights.[53] Access to constitutionally guaranteed citizenship rights in India (and most parts of the world) is tied to documentation. In Mumbai and Kolkata, the ration card serves as the primary proof of identity that gives residents access to entitlements such as education, housing, healthcare, and voting rights; it is also needed for passport applications. Obtaining a ration card is often elusive for migrants—who are unfamiliar with the procedures for application, who struggle with the application due to language barriers, and/ or who encounter discrimination from presiding officials. For example, due to the anti-migration policies of the nativist Shiv Sena Party and its offshoots, ration card applications in Mumbai are available only in Marathi, which most North Indians do not speak. The barriers to entry are even higher for those who do not possess any identity documents, which is not an uncommon problem for migrant slum dwellers whose identity documents have been confiscated or destroyed by local officials. The informal practices surrounding the ration card then leads to a vicious cycle: local officials do not grant ration cards to migrants that they view as 'illegal'; without ration cards, migrants in Mumbai and Kolkata become undocumented and, thus, 'illegal.'

---

[50] Gurpreet Mahajan, 'Indian Exceptionalism or Indian Model: Negotiating Cultural Diversity and Minority Rights in a Democratic Nation-State,' in Will Kymlicka and Baogang He, eds., *Multiculturalism in Asia* (Oxford and New York: Oxford University Press, 2005), pp. 288–313.

[51] Will Kymlicka and Baogang He, eds., *Multiculturalism in Asia* (Oxford, New York: Oxford University Press, 2005). For an alternative perspective, see Rochana Bajpai, *Debating Difference: Group Rights and Liberal Democracy in India* (Oxford: Oxford University Press, 2011).

[52] Abbas (n 14), p. 159.   [53] Abbas (n 44); Abbas (n 14).

CONCLUSION

The study of migration and citizenship in any context offers opportunities to critically engage key concepts that are central to the social sciences such as power, identity, democracy, ideas, and institutions. The point of departure for theoretical development, interdisciplinary collaboration, and methodological innovation requires us to question our assumptions about what it is that we are studying, how we define and measure our variables, and, perhaps most importantly, where we mark the boundaries of our research on migration and citizenship. Rather than begin with the assumption that citizenship is universal, democratic, and inclusive, research on citizenship in non-Western contexts highlights how citizenship—as a legal status, symbol of national and/or ethnic identity, institution, and practice—is contingent.[54]

The primary challenge of studying citizenship in non-Western contexts also provides an opportunity to move the field of citizenship studies forward: we must unearth our assumptions about citizenship and its associated rights, boundaries, and practices. This process may involve re-examining the core concepts of the field, such as citizenship, nationality, citizen, immigrant, and foreigner, and disentangling them from Eurocentric frameworks. While some of these concepts need greater clarification—for example, distinguishing citizenship and nationality—others call for attention to their symbolic significance and multiple meanings—for example, 'immigrant' as foreign-born persons, 'third-country' nationals, and/or descendants of specific categories of immigrants such as second-generation French citizens of North African descent. It also requires systematic comparisons of cases that have not commonly been studied together or that may necessitate collaboration across continents and disciplines. And it will encourage research agendas that treat citizenship, migration, and racial hierarchies as mutually constitutive—not discrete—phenomena.

Explorations of the formal and informal institutions that govern the attribution, management, and loss of citizenship in Asia and the Gulf States demonstrate how states use migration and citizenship policies as control mechanisms to shape racial, ethnic, and class politics. Scholarship on African American, Asian American, and Latino politics in the United States has long examined the ways that national and local states and societies have devised mechanisms to limit the practice of citizenship among groups marginalized by racial hierarchy.[55] The research on household

---

[54] Chung (n 5).

[55] See, *inter alia*, Angelo N. Ancheta, *Race, Rights, and the Asian American Experience*, 2nd edition (New Brunswick: Rutgers University Press, 2006); Eduardo Bonilla-Silva, *Racism without Racists: Color-Blind Racism and the Persistence of Racial Inequality in the United States* (Lanham: Rowman & Littlefield Publishers, 2006); Michael Dawson, *Behind the Mule: Race and Class in African-American Politics* (Princeton: Princeton University Press, 1994); Neil T. Gotanda, 'Citizenship

registrations in East Asia and the Gulf States and ration cards in India further highlights how specific populations *come to be defined as foreign*, in policy and practice, and how citizenship policies that are based on such institutions can *make native populations migrant*. This area of research raises questions about how racial, religious, colonial, gendered, and legal classifications interact in the articulation of citizenship policies and practices. It also may be productively linked with the scholarship on subnational authoritarianism to explain intra-national and intra-regional variation.[56]

Examining internal migration in countries such as China and India further brings to relief the grey areas between internal and international migrants and citizens and noncitizens. Each group may become 'undocumented' due to its inability to produce material verification of its residency, descent, marital status, or presence in a particular territory. Foreign-born and native-born minorities may experience similar, or identical, forms of discrimination based on their common racialized identities.[57] In putatively homogeneous societies where native-born minorities may themselves be foreigners, 'immigrants' and 'racial/ethnic minorities' may be synonymous. Noncitizens in some countries may indeed have *more* citizenship rights than varieties of 'second-class' citizens. Further comparative research that analyzes both internal and international migrants in a single country or across multiple countries has the potential to contribute fresh insights into how states attempt to control migration and migrants themselves, how second-class citizenship develops over time, and the effects of migration on political institutions and economic growth.

Finally, research that grapples with the interactions between migration, citizenship, and racial politics in non-Western countries necessarily pushes us to go beyond the 'black-white' race-relations paradigm. The burgeoning comparative-historical scholarship in this area treats racial politics as a dynamic, fluid process that varies across time and space and is often coded in nonracial terms. Unlike most non-European immigrants to Western Europe and North America, many

---

Nullification: The Impossibility of Asian American Politics,' in Gordon H. Chang, ed., *Asian Americans and Politics: Perspectives, Experiences, Prospects* (Washington: Woodrow Wilson Center Press, 2001); Charles Mills, *The Racial Contract* (Ithaca: Cornell University Press, 1998); Mae M. Ngai, *Impossible Subjects: Illegal Aliens and the Making of Modern America* (Princeton: Princeton University Press, 2004); Michael Omi and Howard Winant, *Racial Formation in the United States: From the 1960s to the 1980s* (London, New York: Routledge, 1986).

[56] See, *inter alia*, Edward L. Gibson, *Boundary Control: Subnational Authoritarianism in Federal Democracies* (Cambridge: Cambridge University Press, 2012); Patrick Heller, 'Degrees of Democracy: Some Comparative Lessons from India,' *World Politics* 52, no. 4 (2000): pp. 484–519; Robert Mickey, *Paths out of Dixie: The Democratization of Authoritarian Enclaves in America's Deep South, 1944-1972* (Princeton: Princeton University Press, 2015); Richard Snyder, 'Scaling Down: The Subnational Comparative Method,' *Studies in Comparative International Development* 36, no. 1 (2001): pp. 93–110.

[57] See Reuel Reuben Rogers, *Afro-Caribbean Immigrants and the Politics of Incorporation: Ethnicity, Exception, or Exit* (New York: Cambridge University Press, 2006).

internal and international migrants within non-Western countries are physically indistinguishable from the majority population, which poses questions about the significance of culture and phenotype in immigration, citizenship, and racial politics. Examining citizenship as a tool for gaining social and political visibility among highly assimilated, phenotypically indistinguishable minority groups is especially useful for understanding the intersection of race, immigration, and citizenship in East Asia, where the concept of nationality is closely related to ethnic, racial, and national identity. If phenotypical difference is the central marker for minority status in North American and European societies, then alienage is increasingly the basis for how minorities relate to the state, mobilize themselves, and voice their collective interests in East Asia. Rather than quests for citizenship acquisition, noncitizen movements in East Asia may be viewed as *ongoing citizenship practices* that challenge dominant ideologies of ethnocultural homogeneity.[58]

In sum, the study of citizenship in non-Western contexts opens up the opportunity to interrogate conventional understandings of phenomena commonly associated with Western classifications and explore the changing character and categories of citizenship that we take for granted.[59] By expanding the boundaries of *how* and *where* we study citizenship, we can broaden our comparative lens to explore immigration politics in countries that do not acknowledge the presence of immigrants, racist discourses that circumvent direct references to race, and citizenship practices by those who are excluded from formal membership in the state.[60] The emerging areas of research on citizenship in non-Western contexts in particular challenge us to examine the grey areas of citizenship, thus helping us to better understand the gaps between policies and outcomes, the hierarchies of citizenship and noncitizenship, and the relationship between migration, citizenship, and racial politics. By questioning our area-specific assumptions, we are able to be more attentive to emergent forms of citizenship, thus generating new research agendas that can potentially travel between disciplines and move beyond isolated cases and regions.

BIBLIOGRAPHY

Abbas, Rameez, 'Citizen or Stranger? The Politics of Internal Migration in Mumbai and Kolkata' (PhD dissertation, Johns Hopkins University, 2011), online http://search.proquest.com/docview/880288262.

[58] Chung (n 23).

[59] On the study of racial politics, see Michael Hanchard and Erin Aeran Chung, 'From Race Relations to Comparative Racial Politics: A Survey of Cross-National Scholarship on Race in the Social Sciences,' *Du Bois Review* 1, no. 2 (2004): pp. 319–343.

[60] See Erin Aeran Chung, 'The Relevance Question,' *Verge: Studies in Global Asias* 3, no. 1 (Spring 2017): pp. 8–11.

Abbas, Rameez, 'Internal Migration and Citizenship in India,' *Journal of Ethnic and Migration Studies 42*, no. 1 (2016): pp. 150–168, doi: 10.1080/1369183x.2015.1100067.

Ancheta, Angelo N., *Race, Rights, and the Asian American Experience*, 2nd edition (New Brunswick: Rutgers University Press, 2006).

Babar, Zahra R., 'The Cost of Belonging: Citizenship Construction in the State of Qatar,' *The Middle East Journal 68*, no. 3 (Summer 2014): pp. 403–420.

Bajpai, Rochana, *Debating Difference: Group Rights and Liberal Democracy in India* (Oxford: Oxford University Press, 2011).

Baldwin-Edwards, Martin, 'Labour Immigration and Labour Markets in the GCC Countries: National Patterns and Trends,' The London School of Economics and Political Science (2011), online http://eprints.lse.ac.uk/55239/1/Baldwin-Edwards_2011.pdf.

Bonilla-Silva, Eduardo, *Racism without Racists: Color-Blind Racism and the Persistence of Racial Inequality in the United States* (Lanham: Rowman & Littlefield Publishers, 2006).

Chan, Kam Wing and Li Zhang, 'The Hukou System and Rural-Urban Migration in China: Processes and Changes,' *The China Quarterly 160* (1999): pp. 818–855.

Chung, Erin Aeran, 'The Politics of Contingent Citizenship: Korean Political Engagement in Japan and the United States,' in Sonia Ryang and John Lie, eds., *Diaspora without Homeland: Being Korean in Japan* (Berkeley: University of California Press, 2009), pp. 147–167.

Chung, Erin Aeran, *Immigration and Citizenship in Japan* (New York: Cambridge University Press, 2010).

Chung, Erin Aeran, 'Workers or Residents? Diverging Patterns of Immigrant Incorporation in Korea and Japan,' *Pacific Affairs 83*, no. 4 (December, 2010): pp. 675–696.

Chung, Erin Aeran, 'Hierarchies of Citizenship and Non-Citizenship in East Asian Democracies,' *APSA Migration and Citizenship Section Newsletter 2*, no. 2 (Summer, 2014): pp. 48–53, online https://higherlogicdownload.s3.amazonaws.com/APSANET/e5be2e91-9721-4513-acb8-799a93991666/UploadedImages/Newsletters/Mig%20&%20Cit%20newsletter%202(2).pdf.

Chung, Erin Aeran, 'Japan and South Korea: Immigration Control and Immigrant Incorporation,' in James F. Hollifield, Philip L. Martin, and Pia M. Orrenius, eds., *Controlling Immigration: A Global Perspective* (Stanford: Stanford University Press, 2014), pp. 399–421.

Chung, Erin Aeran, *Immigrant Incorporation in East Asian Democracies* (New York, Cambridge: Cambridge University Press, forthcoming).

Chung, Erin Aeran, 'The Relevance Question,' *Verge: Studies in Global Asias 3*, no. 1 (Spring 2017): pp. 8–11.

Chung, Erin Aeran and Daisy Kim, 'Citizenship and Marriage in a Globalizing World: Multicultural Families and Monocultural Nationality Laws in Korea and Japan,' *Indiana Journal of Global Legal Studies 19*, no. 1 (Winter, 2012): pp. 195–219.

Cohen, Elizabeth F., *Semi-Citizenship in Democratic Politics* (Cambridge, New York: Cambridge University Press, 2009).

Dawson, Michael, *Behind the Mule: Race and Class in African-American Politics* (Princeton: Princeton University Press, 1994).

Faist, Thomas and Peter Kivisto, eds., *Dual Citizenship in Global Perspective: From Unitary to Multiple Citizenship* (Basingstoke, New York: Palgrave Macmillan, 2007).

FitzGerald, David, *A Nation of Emigrants: How Mexico Manages Its Migration* (Berkeley: University of California Press, 2009).

Friedman, Sara, *Exceptional States: Chinese Immigrants and Taiwanese Sovereignty* (Berkeley: University of California Press, 2015).

Gardner, Andrew, 'Engulfed: Indian Guest Workers, Bahraini Citizens, and the Structural Violence of the Kafala System,' in Nathalie Peutz and Nicholas De Genova, eds., *The Deportation Regime: Sovereignty, Space, and the Freedom of Movement* (Durham: Duke University Press, 2010), pp. 196–223.

Gengler, Justin and Laurent A. Lambert, 'Renegotiating the Ruling Bargain: Selling Fiscal Reform in the GCC,' *The Middle East Journal 70*, no. 2 (2016): pp. 321–329, doi:10.3751/70.2.21.

Gibson, Edward L., *Boundary Control: Subnational Authoritarianism in Federal Democracies* (Cambridge: Cambridge University Press, 2012).

Gotanda, Neil T., 'Citizenship Nullification: The Impossibility of Asian American Politics,' in, Gordon H. Chang, ed., *Asian Americans and Politics: Perspectives, Experiences, Prospects* (Washington: Woodrow Wilson Center Press, 2001).

Hanchard, Michael and Erin Aeran Chung, 'From Race Relations to Comparative Racial Politics: A Survey of Cross-National Scholarship on Race in the Social Sciences,' *Du Bois Review 1*, no. 2 (2004): pp. 319–343.

Hao, Lingxin and Yucheng Liang, 'The Spatial and Career Mobility of China's Urban and Rural Labor Force,' *Management and Organization Review 12*, no. 1 (2016): pp. 135–158, doi: http://dx.doi.org/10.1017/mor.2015.35.

Heller, Patrick, 'Degrees of Democracy: Some Comparative Lessons from India,' *World Politics 52*, no. 4 (2000): pp. 484–519.

International Organization for Migration, 'World Migration Report 2015' (Geneva: International Organization for Migration, 2015).

Jones, Reece, 'Sovereignty and Statelessness in the Border Enclaves of India and Bangladesh,' *Political Geography 28*, no. 6 (2009): pp. 373–381.

Kim, Daisy, 'Bargaining Citizenship: Women's Organizations, the State, and Marriage Migrants in South Korea' (PhD dissertation, Johns Hopkins University, 2015).

Kim, Nora Hui-Jung, 'Korean Immigration Policy Changes and the Political Liberals' Dilemma,' *International Migration Review 42*, no. 3 (2008): pp. 576–596.

Kymlicka, Will and Baogang He, eds., *Multiculturalism in Asia* (Oxford, New York: Oxford University Press, 2005).

Layton-Henry, Zig, ed., *The Political Rights of Migrant Workers in Western Europe* (London: Sage, 1990).

Lee, Hye-Kyung, 'International Marriage and the State in South Korea: Focusing on Governmental Policy,' *Citizenship Studies 12*, no. 1 (2008): pp. 107–123.

Longva, Anh Nga, 'Nationalism in Pre-Modern Guise: The Discourse on Hadhar and Badu in Kuwait,' *International Journal of Middle East Studies 38*, no. 2 (2006): pp. 171–187.

Lori, Noora, 'Unsettling State: Non-Citizens, State Power and Citizenship in the United Arab Emirates' (PhD dissertation, Johns Hopkins University, 2013) (pending publication December 2017, online https://jscholarship.library.jhu.edu/handle/1774.2/838).

Mahajan, Gurpreet, 'Indian Exceptionalism or Indian Model: Negotiating Cultural Diversity and Minority Rights in a Democratic Nation-State,' in Will Kymlicka and Baogang He, eds., *Multiculturalism in Asia* (Oxford, New York: Oxford University Press, 2005), pp. 288–313.

Mamdani, Mahmood, *Citizen and Subject: Contemporary Africa and the Legacy of Late Colonialism* (London: James Currey, 1996).

Manby, Bronwen, *Citizenship Law in Africa: A Comparative Study* (New York: Open Society Institute, 2010).

Marshall, T. H., *Class, Citizenship and Social Development* (Cambridge: Cambridge University Press, 1950).

Mickey, Robert, *Paths out of Dixie: The Democratization of Authoritarian Enclaves in America's Deep South, 1944-1972* (Princeton: Princeton University Press, 2015).

Mills, Charles, *The Racial Contract* (Ithaca: Cornell University Press, 1998).

Ministry of Justice, Japan, 'Heisei 26 Nenmatsu Genzaini Okeru Gaikokujintorokusha Toukeini Tsuite [Report on Current Foreign Resident Statistics at the End of 2014]' (2015).

Naujoks, Daniel, *Migration, Citizenship, and Development: Diasporic Membership Policies and Overseas Indians in the United States* (New Delhi: Oxford University Press, 2013).

Ngai, Mae M., *Impossible Subjects: Illegal Aliens and the Making of Modern America* (Princeton: Princeton University Press, 2004).

Nyamnjoh, Francis B., 'From Bounded to Flexible Citizenship: Lessons from Africa,' *Citizenship Studies 11*, no. 1 (2007): pp. 73–82.

Omi, Michael and Howard Winant, *Racial Formation in the United States: From the 1960s to the 1980s* (London, New York: Routledge, 1986).

Ong, Aihwa, *Flexible Citizenship: The Cultural Logics of Transnationality* (Durham: Duke University Press, 1999).

Park, Jung-Sun and Paul Y. Chang, 'Contention in the Construction of a Global Korean Community: The Case of the Overseas Korean Act,' *Journal of Korean Studies 10* (2005): pp. 1–27.

Parolin, Gianluca Paolo, *Citizenship in the Arab World: Kin, Religion and Nation-State* (Amsterdam: Amsterdam University Press, 2009).

Rigger, Shelley, 'Nationalism versus Citizenship in the Republic of China on Taiwan,' in Merle Goldman and Elizabeth J. Perry, eds., *Changing Meanings of Citizenship in Modern China* (Cambridge: Harvard University Press, 2002), pp. 353–374.

Rogers, Reuel Reuben, *Afro-Caribbean Immigrants and the Politics of Incorporation: Ethnicity, Exception, or Exit* (New York: Cambridge University Press, 2006).

Ruhs, Martin and Philip Martin, 'Numbers Vs. Rights: Trade-Offs and Guest Worker Programs,' *International Migration Review 42*, no. 1 (2008): pp. 249–265, doi: 10.1111/j.1747-7379.2007.00120.x.

Sadiq, Kamal, *Paper Citizens: How Illegal Immigrants Acquire Citizenship in Developing Countries* (Oxford, New York: Oxford University Press, 2009).

Scott, James C., *Seeing Like a State: How Certain Schemes to Improve the Human Condition Have Failed* (New Haven: Yale University Press, 1998).

Sejersen, Tanja Brøndsted, ' "I Vow to Thee My Countries": The Expansion of Dual Citizenship in the 21st Century,' *International Migration Review 42*, no. 3 (2008): pp. 523–549.

Seol, Dong-Hoon and John D. Skrentny, 'Why Is There So Little Migrant Settlement in East Asia?,' *International Migration Review 43*, no. 3 (2009): pp. 578–620.

Shin, Adrian J., 'Tyrants and Migrants: Authoritarian Immigration Policy,' *Comparative Political Studies 50*, no. 1 (2017): pp. 14–40.

Smart, Alan and Josephine Smart, 'Time-Space Punctuation: Hong Kong's Border Regime and Limits on Mobility,' *Pacific Affairs 81*, no. 2 (2008): pp. 175–193.

Snyder, Richard, 'Scaling Down: The Subnational Comparative Method,' *Studies in Comparative International Development 36*, no. 1 (2001): pp. 93–110, doi: 10.1007/bf02687586.

Solinger, Dorothy J., 'Citizenship Issues in China's Internal Migration: Comparisons with Germany and Japan,' *Political Science Quarterly 114*, no. 3 (1999): pp. 455–478.

Solinger, Dorothy J., *Contesting Citizenship in Urban China: Peasant Migrants, the State, and the Logic of the Market* (Berkeley: University of California Press, 1999).

SOPEMI, 'Trends in International Migration: Continuous Reporting System on Migration' (Paris: OECD, 2015).

Taylor, Adam, 'The Controversial Plan to Give Kuwait's Stateless People Citizenship of a Tiny, Poor African Island,' *Washington Post*, May 17, 2016, online https://www.washingtonpost.com/news/worldviews/wp/2016/05/17/the-controversial-plan-to-give-kuwaits-stateless-people-citizenship-of-a-tiny-poor-african-island/.

Tilly, Charles, 'Citizenship, Identity and Social History,' in Charles Tilly, ed., *Citizenship, Identity and Social History* (Cambridge: Cambridge University Press, 1996).

Tsuda, Takeyuki, *Strangers in the Ethnic Homeland: Japanese Brazilian Return Migration in Transnational Perspective* (New York: Columbia University Press, 2003).

United Nations, 'United Nations International Migration Report 2015,' (New York: Department of Economic and Social Affairs of the United Nations Secretariat, 2016).

Van Schendel, Willem, 'Stateless in South Asia: The Making of the India-Bangladesh Enclaves,' *The Journal of Asian Studies 61*, no. 1 (2002): pp. 115–147.

Varadarajan, Latha, *The Domestic Abroad: Diasporas in International Relations* (New York: Oxford University Press, 2010).

Verseckaite, Egle, 'Citizenship as a Stateness Boundary Maintenance Regime: The Curious Case of Lithuanian Dual Citizenship' (PhD dissertation, Johns Hopkins University, 2015) (pending publication May 2019, online https://jscholarship.library.jhu.edu/handle/1774.2/838).

Vink, Maarten Peter, Gerard-René de Groot, and Ngo Chun Luk, 'MACIMIDE Global Expatriate Dual Citizenship Dataset' (2015), online http://dx.doi.org/10.7910/DVN/TTMZ08.

Vora, Neha, *Impossible Citizens: Dubai's Indian Diaspora* (Durham: Duke University Press, 2013).

Wehrey, Frederic M., *Sectarian Politics in the Gulf: From the Iraq War to the Arab Uprisings* (New York: Columbia University Press, 2013).

Wu, Xiaogang and Donald J. Treiman, 'The Household Registration System and Social Stratification in China: 1955-1996,' *Demography 41*, no. 2 (2004): pp. 363–384.

CHAPTER 21

INDIGENOUS CITIZENSHIP IN SETTLER STATES

KIRSTY GOVER*

* Many thanks to participants at the Handbook Authors' Conference (2–4 June, 2016) and to Rainer Bauböck and Irene Bloemraad for very helpful comments on earlier drafts. Thanks also to Miranda Johnson and Coel Kirkby for their good advice. This work draws on material from within Kirsty Gover, 'Gender and Racial Discrimination in the Formation of Groups: Tribal and Liberal Approaches to Membership in Settler Societies', in Kim Rubenstein, Katharine G. Young, eds., *The Public Law of Gender: From the Local to the Global*, (Cambridge: Cambridge University Press, 2016), pp. 367–390 (adapted, reproduced with permission), and from within Kirsty Gover, 'When Tribalism Meets Liberalism: Human Rights and Indigenous Boundary Problems in Canada', *University of Toronto Law Review 64*, no. 2 (2014): pp. 206–242 (adapted, reproduced with permission).

INTRODUCTION

'INDIGENOUS citizenship' encompasses a range of conceptual frameworks, denoting cultural and political membership in an indigenous community, participation in indigenous law-making, and a distinctive legal status governing the relationship between indigenous citizens and tribal or settler governments. This chapter focuses on the legal status of indigenous citizens as members of formally recognized tribal nations in the Western settler states: Canada, Australia, New Zealand, and the United States. To date, the formal constitution of historic tribal nations as legal persons with law-making powers is a practice largely confined to those states. While some tribal nations in these states have long been recognized in settler law as self-governing polities, in the past several decades many more have acquired formal status and have adopted written constitutions and laws, rendering tribal citizenship rules more legible to outsiders. This chapter examines indigenous citizenship as a contested legal status expressed in the positive law of tribal and settler nations.[1]

Contemporary expressions of indigenous citizenship reveal the legal pluralism of settler states by showing that many indigenous persons are dual nationals, and that legal indigeneity is the product of a jurisdictional relationship between settler and tribal governments. There is a growing divergence, for instance, between the long-standing category of legal indigeneity (allocated by settler governments) and the status of tribal citizenship (decided by tribal governments, within certain constraints imposed by settler law). Neither category aligns with the other, nor is either co-extensive with settler-state citizenship. Many legally indigenous persons are not members of recognized tribes, and some indigenous people, including tribal citizens, are not citizens of the state that encompasses their tribal territories. Likewise, some tribal citizens are not legally indigenous, and a growing number of people with indigenous ancestry are neither legally indigenous nor citizens of a tribal nation.

Tensions between the three status categories of tribal citizenship, national citizenship, and legal indigeneity are structured by a central difference in the way that membership is conceived in liberal and tribal democracies. Indigeneity and tribal membership are allocated primarily on the basis of biological or legal descent,[2]

---

[1] The chapter does not focus on the political and cultural meanings of indigenous citizenship as an expression of identity, nor does it engage directly the socio-legal question of whether and how written tribal laws are applied by tribal institutions.

[2] In Canada and New Zealand, but not in Australia or the United States, the adopted children of indigenous persons are legally indigenous whether or not they are biologically descended from an indigenous person.

irrespective of a descendant's birthplace or place of residence, while settler states (like most states) distribute national citizenship by using a configuration of birthplace and descent rules as mutually qualifying principles. Both *jus sanguinis* and *jus soli* birthright rules are controversial precisely because they seem to undermine the premises of liberal-democratic citizenship as a expression of consent, and because they appear to run counter to anti-discrimination norms by arbitrarily distributing membership on the basis of a person's ascriptive, immutable characteristics.[3] Unqualified *jus sanguinis* rules, however, are regarded as particularly suspect because they seem to perpetuate the racial or ethnic composition of a group by arbitrarily excluding co-residents who lack the relevant ethnic and racial origins.[4]

While liberal democratic states appear to be moving towards more civic conceptions of birthright citizenship that do not depend on ethno-cultural markers of belonging, tribal nations continue to use descent rules as the exclusive determinant of tribal birthright citizenship. Accordingly, while settler states and tribal nations both permit naturalization as a way of supplementing birthright citizenship, the crucial qualitative difference between tribal and settler citizenship is as follows; settler states supplement *jus sanguinis* rules with *jus soli* principles that accord birthright citizenship to most people born in their territory and limit the intergenerational operation of descent rules. Tribes on the other hand, do not (with rare exceptions) include birthplace criteria in their allocation of birthright citizenship. When tribal nations limit their *jus sanguinis* rules to narrow the class of eligible birthright citizens, they do so by calculating 'degrees of descent' or 'blood quantum' to exclude descendants with too few indigenous (or tribal) ancestors. *Jus sanguinis* rules used by tribes can appear in the liberal democracies to effect suspect forms of racial, ethnic, or familial discrimination. In many respects, then, legal and political disputes about tribal citizenship go directly to the core constitutive challenge faced by settler states; how to reconcile the equality-based principle of liberal democratic citizenship with the historic claims and entitlements of tribes as kinship-based polities. This chapter draws on a comparative study of the citizenship rules of 535 tribal communities in Canada, Australia, New Zealand, and the United States to argue that the absence of *jus soli* principles in tribal citizenship law is a reasonable adaptation by tribes to the exigencies of co-existence with settlers and settler governments.

[3] Ayelet Shachar, *The Birthright Lottery: Citizenship and Global Inequality* (Cambridge: Harvard University Press, 2006).

[4] See, e.g., Rainer Bauböck, 'The Rights and Duties of External Citizenship', *Citizenship Studies*, 13, no. 5 (2009): pp. 475–499, p. 484.

CITIZENSHIP AND INDIGENOUS STATE-RELATIONS: THE FIELD AND NEW DIRECTIONS

Until recently, scholarly debates about indigenous rights to self-governance and self-determination proceeded without much attention to the composition of tribal constituencies, so that the membership of the tribal 'self' remained a peripheral question. Instead, indigenous groups were more usually included as illustrative types in political theories of multiculturalism, as cultural minorities whose special collective interests, especially rights to land, should be protected by public governments in a plural society.[5] Processes of group formation have generally been absent from the wide-ranging debates in political theory about the contested status of groups in the liberal democracies. Most models have assumed the pre-constitution of minorities as identifiable communities with stable human boundaries. In such a model, an indigenous minority does not actively 'self-constitute' in the way that nation-states do (by designing and revising membership criteria), but replicates itself more or less mechanically as each new generation of members is born. This model may partly explain the tendency of some theorists to suggest that tribal laws denying citizenship to some descendants by measuring a person's 'degree' of descent are suspect and illiberal,[6] and should be abandoned in favour of more 'civic' and (arguably) non-discriminatory rules that select applicants primarily on the basis of their residency, birthplace, cultural compatibility, or other voluntaristic criteria.[7]

Indigenous claims, however, are distinct from those of other cultural minorities because they are claims to authority and property held by tribal nations before the establishment of the territorial settler state, attributes that were, or should have been, inherited by descendant communities. Measures of continuity

---

[5] Will Kymlicka, *Liberalism, Community and Culture* (Oxford: Clarendon Press, 1991); Will Kymlicka, ed., *The Rights of Minority Cultures* (Oxford, New York: Oxford University Press, 1995); Will Kymlicka, *Multicultural Citizenship: A Liberal Theory of Minority Rights* (Oxford: Clarendon Press, 1995); Jacob T. Levy, *The Multiculturalism of Fear* (Oxford: Oxford University Press, 2000); Duncan Ivison et al., eds., *Political Theory and the Rights of Indigenous Peoples* (Cambridge: Cambridge University Press, 2001).

[6] See, e.g., Duncan Ivison, 'The Logic of Aboriginal Rights', *Ethnicities* 3, no. 3 (2003): pp. 321–334, p. 334, footnote 15; Will Kymlicka, 'American Multiculturalism and the Nations Within', in Duncan Ivison et al., eds., *Political Theory and the Rights of Indigenous Peoples* (Cambridge: Cambridge University Press, 2001), p. 216–236, p. 216; Patrick Macklem, *Indigenous Difference and the Constitution of Canada* (Toronto: University of Toronto Press, 2001), p. 231.

[7] Similar anxieties are expressed in an emerging discourse in international law on 'rights to citizenship', which includes, as Peter Spiro observes, calls for the application of non-discrimination norms to citizenship rules, so placing 'racial, ethnic and gender classifications in the context of birthright citizenship ... under stress' (Peter J. Spiro, 'A New International Law of Citizenship', *American Journal of International Law* 105, no. 4 (2011): pp. 694–746, pp. 694, 717).

are therefore determinative of the form of tribal claims and contemporary state-tribal arrangements in a way that they are not in many other contexts, where a minority's contemporary cultural distinctiveness is the more central premise. Shared biological descent is a paradigmatic marker of tribal nationhood in settler law precisely because it is thought to be a more 'objective' measure of continuity and succession than contextual and mutable identity markers such as 'political integrity' or 'cultural distinctiveness'. Thus in settler constitutionalism it is historically continuous indigenous communities—tribal nations—that are increasingly recognized and embedded within the constitutional framework of the Western settler states as self-governing polities. The law and policy governing state-indigenous relationships may have, as is often the case, outpaced political theories, especially some political theories of multiculturalism. In any case, justificatory arguments drawn from theories of cultural pluralism, which are based on voluntaristic concepts of minority rights, freedom of association, and cultural or racial equality, do not quite capture the way that tribal-state relationships are managed in the Western settler states. Similarly they have not adequately accounted for the ways that indigenous citizenship is distributed and governed by settler and tribal governments.

In the past decade, however, a body of legal theoretical scholarship has emerged that addresses tribal law, nation-building, governance, and institutions as objects of study in their own right. This literature includes a growing number of works attentive to the law and jurisprudence of self-governing tribes, including membership law,[8] along with legal scholarship addressing case-studies of particular tribal membership controversies,[9] or state interventions in tribal membership governance.[10] For the time-being, however, comparative commentary on contemporary tribal membership law and attention to tribal citizenship within the field of citizenship studies remains sparse. This chapter aims to help move these conversations forward by outlining some core trends and controversies in the governance of indigenous citizenship.

---

[8] See, e.g., John Borrows, *Freedom and Indigenous Constitutionalism* (Toronto: University of Toronto Press, 2016); Matthew L. M. Fletcher, *American Indian Tribal Law* (New York: Aspen Publishers, 2011). For examples of written tribal constitutions in Canada, Australia, New Zealand, and the United States see Kirsty Gover, *Tribal Constitutionalism: States, Tribes and the Governance of Membership* (Oxford, New York: Oxford University Press, 2010); Matthew Fletcher, 'Tribal Membership and Indian Nationhood', *American Indian Law Review 37* (2012–2013): pp. 1–17; Bethany Berger, 'Race, Descent and Tribal Citizenship', *California Law Review Circuit 4* (2013): pp. 23–37.

[9] See, e.g., Greg Rubio, 'Reclaiming Indian Civil Rights: The Application of International Rights Law to Tribal Disenrollment Actions', *Oregon Review of International Law 11* (2009): pp. 1–42; Gabriel S. Galanda and Ryan D. Dreveskracht, 'Curing the Tribal Disenrollment Epidemic: In Search of a Remedy', *Arizona Law Review 57*, no. 2 (2015): pp. 383–474.

[10] See, e.g., Caroline Dick, *The Perils of Identity: Group Rights and the Politics of Intragroup Difference* (Vancouver: University of British Columbia Press, 2011).

Indigenous Citizenship: The Backdrop

The story of legal citizenship in the Western settler states typically traces the evo-lution of British subjecthood to settler-state citizenship. For indigenous peoples in those states, as for other excluded and denigrated groups, these statuses were pre-carious, because they were ascribed to and withheld from indigenous peoples at various times in the colonial enterprise. In the early stages of settlement, indigen-ous 'native' peoples of the Commonwealth colonies were British subjects by birth in accordance with Imperial law and policy, and later became citizens in accord-ance with nationality laws passed after the Second World War as these states gained formal independence from Britain. Throughout the history of colonial settlement however, indigenous peoples were denied many of the civil and political rights associated with citizenship in the liberal democratic states, including, crucially, the right to vote. Instead the franchise was used to further settler assimilative and seg-regationist policies, by variously denying indigenous peoples the right to vote in general elections, and encouraging them to sever political ties to their communi-ties in exchange for enfranchisement (an exchange that was frequently refused by members of indigenous communities). The franchise was also deployed to facilitate settler land acquisition. As responsible self-government became established in the colonies in the 1850s and 1860s, the Imperial British government insisted on the extension in the colonies of a 'liberal' and race-blind form of franchise, effected through property-based qualifications.[11] The 'property franchise' extended to some indigenous men a right to participate in colonial politics that was, at that stage, still denied to landless men and to all women.[12] Because only holders of freehold title were entitled to vote, however, the property franchise was also aligned with efforts to individualize communally held indigenous land for acquisition by freeholding settlers and to shepherd indigenous peoples away from tribal ways of life by break-ing up the tribal land base.[13]

In all three of the Commonwealth settler states, property-based voting rights for indigenous subjects were revoked in the late 1880s and 1890s, first temporarily and then in permanent exemptions (in New Zealand the property franchise was supplemented and then displaced in 1867 by four designated Maori parliamentary seats, to which Maori voters were confined until 1975).[14] In Australia, the general right of Aboriginal and Torres Strait Islanders to vote in national elections was not

[11] Julie Evans et al., *Equal Subjects, Unequal Rights: Indigenous Peoples in British Settler Colonies, 1830–1910* (Manchester, New York: Manchester University Press, 2003), p. 51; Coel Kirkby, 'Nativism and the End of the British Empire' (unpublished manuscript, on file with author), p. 15.

[12] See Shaw in this volume.   [13] Evans et al. (n 11); Kirkby (n 11), p. 16.

[14] The seats persist today in proportion to the number of Maori voters choosing to enroll on the Maori electoral roll at each five-yearly option, at the time of writing, yielding 7 seats out of a total of 120 in the single-chamber New Zealand parliament.

extended until 1962.[15] Likewise, Canadian 'status Indians' (persons deemed to be legally Indian) did not have an unconditional right to vote in federal elections until 1960. Prior to that date, the 1876 *Indian Act* ensured that status Indians could vote outside of their communities only if they had become 'enfranchised' in the terms of that Act by demonstrating a sufficient 'degree of civilisation'.[16]

The story of state-tribal citizenship in the United States has a different narrative. Since the 1830s tribes in the United States have been recognized at common law as 'domestic dependent nations'[17] exercising inherent sovereign powers,[18] including the power to determine their own membership (subject to Congress' plenary power in Indian affairs).[19] Indians who maintained relations with their tribes were not 'born in the United States and subject to the jurisdiction thereof', and so were not made citizens by the 14th Amendment to the US Constitution.[20] Birthright citizenship was not comprehensively granted to US Indians until 1924, via the federal *Indian Citizenship Act*. The extension of United States citizenship to Indians was resisted by some tribes, because of concerns that dual citizenship would result in the loss of tribal lands, the abrogation of treaties, the erosion of tribal sovereignty or the compulsory military conscription of tribal members.[21] The Act continues to be repudiated by some recognized tribes.[22]

The difficult and distinctive history of indigenous citizenship shows that indigenous peoples have long been regarded in the Western settler states as somehow 'outside' of the national body politic, or only contingently included within it. The current duality of tribal and national citizenships is one expression of this more longstanding ambivalence. It points also to what Ivison has called the enduring 'quasi-international' nature of state-indigenous relationships in the Western settler states.[23] As the next section illustrates, the divergence between the categories of national and tribal citizenship leaves open important questions about the status and rights of people who are indigenous but not tribal members, and raises further questions about the effect on indigenous peoples of the intersecting *jus soli* and *jus sanguinis* citizenship criteria used by states and tribes to define their constituencies.

---

[15] John Chesterman and Brian Galligan, *Citizens without Rights: Aborigines and Australian Citizenship* (Cambridge: Cambridge University Press, 1997), p. 15.
[16] *Indian Act* 1880 (Can.), s. 99.   [17] *Cherokee Nation v. Georgia* 30 U.S. (5 Pet.) 1 (1831).
[18] *Worcester v. Georgia*, 31 U.S. (6 Pet.) 515 (1831).
[19] *Santa Clara Pueblo v. Martinez* 436 U.S. 49 (1978).
[20] *Elk v. Wilkins* 112 U.S. 94 (1884), p 112. See discussion in Alexander Keyssar, *The Right to Vote: The Contested History of Democracy in the United States* (New York: Basic Books, 2000), p. 133.
[21] Robert B. Porter, 'The Demise of the Ongwehoweh and the Rise of the Native Americans: Redressing the Genocidal Act of Forcing American Citizenship upon Indigenous Peoples', *Harvard Black Letter Journal* 15 (1999): pp. 107–183, p. 127.
[22] Ibid.   [23] Ivison (n 6), p. 332.

THE STATE OF THE TRIBAL NATIONS: CITIZENSHIP AND INDIGENEITY IN SETTLER SOCIETIES

In the Western settler states there are now nearly 1500 officially recognized tribal nations, all exercising jurisdiction over prospective citizenship within varied limits imposed by settler law or agreed by tribal and settler governments.[24] As tribal self-government becomes more embedded in the constitutional frameworks of settler states, and tribal communities acquire more extensive powers and assets, questions about the composition of tribal communities become more pressing. In particular, the costs of non-citizenship are increased. Tribal citizenship determines a person's access to tribal land, resources, and services, rights to political and social participation in the tribal community, and increasingly, the capacity to benefit from public programs and services for indigenous peoples. Taking into account the different ways that census data are and have been collected on indigeneity and tribal affiliation, across all four countries members of formally recognized tribes comprise (at the very most) just under two-thirds of those persons who self-identify as indigenous in national censuses. Some of the most pressing governance questions faced by tribal and settler governments, then, concern the responsibilities of each to non-member indigenous peoples, and to indigenous persons who do not qualify as 'legally indigenous' in settler law.[25]

At the time of writing, the United States was home to 567 federally recognized tribes.[26] Canada had recognized 24 self-governing Aboriginal communities and 618 First Nations constituted under the Indian Act,[27] 240 of which had opted to take control of membership governance (so-called 'Section 10 First Nations', in reference to the enabling provision of the Act).[28] Australia had recognized 155 native title-holding communities represented by Registered Native Title Bodies Corporate[29] and in

---

[24] Gover (n 8).

[25] See, e.g., Sebastien Grammond, *Identity Captured by Law: Membership in Canada's Indigenous Peoples and Linguistic Minorities* (Montreal: McGill-Queen's University Press, 2009).

[26] *Federal Register 81*, no. 86 (4 May 2016) 26826-26832, online https://www.gpo.gov/fdsys/pkg/FR-2016-05-04/pdf/FR-2016-05-04.pdf. This includes 229 Alaskan Native tribes and villages, which are governed by a distinctive legal regime (*Alaska Native Claims Settlement Act* (43 U.S.C. 1601) 1971). The 2008 study of tribal documents referenced in this chapter does not include those of Alaskan Native tribes and villages.

[27] Aboriginal Affairs and Northern Development Canada, 'Self-Government and Comprehensive Claims: Completed Agreements' (2011) (unpublished document, on file with the author).

[28] *Indian Act* 1985 (Can.), s. 10(1).

[29] Australian Institute of Aboriginal and Torres Strait Islanders, 'National Registered Native Title Bodies Corporate (RNTBCs) Summary' (2 June 2016), online http://aiatsis.gov.au/sites/default/files/products/statistics_and_summaries/rntbc_summary_june_2016.pdf.

New Zealand, 99 Iwi and Hapu[30] had been recognized as beneficiaries of Treaty of Waitangi claims settlements.[31] Indigenous peoples remain vastly outnumbered in the Western settler states, constituting only a tiny minority of national populations (3 per cent in Australia,[32] 4.3 per cent in Canada,[33] 1.7 in the United States,[34] and 18 per cent in New Zealand).[35] The proportion of self-identifying indigenous persons who are also tribal members ranges between 62 per cent (Australia)[36] and 83 per cent (in New Zealand).[37]

Despite (or perhaps because of) the large degree of discretion afforded to tribal governments in the selection of members, in each state a tribe seeking recognition is obliged to prove its continuity with an identified historic group. In all four states, measures of descent play an important evidentiary role in establishing this historic connection, and in determining the original 'base' membership of a newly recognized tribe. In other words, in order to be formally recognized in contemporary processes, tribes must negotiate their original human boundaries with settler governments, and the base membership is ordinarily confined to persons who can show they are indigenous descendants of members of the predecessor group. It is the size of this constitutive population (as defined by settler governments) that determines the quantum of assets transferred in historic claims settlement (along with the estimated value of what was lost and the severity of the historic wrong).[38]

---

[30] Tribes and sub-tribes.

[31] Fifty-seven tribes are beneficiaires of the 2003 pan-tribal Treaty of Waitangi settlement of commercial fishing claims, and forty-two as beneficiaires of settled historic claims (a further seventy-two groupings in the process of negotiating historic Treaty settlements) (*Maori Fisheries Act* 2004 (N.Z.), Sch. 3; Office of Treaty Settlements, '12 Month Progress Report 1 July 2015—30 June 2016', online https://www.govt.nz/assets/Documents/OTS/Quarterly-report-to-30-June-2016.pdf.

[32] Australian Bureau of Statistics, 'National Aboriginal and Torres Strait Islander Social Survey, 2014–15', online http://www.abs.gov.au/ausstats/abs@.nsf/Lookup/by%20Subject/4714.0~2014-15~Main%20Features~Population%20context~2.

[33] Statistics Canada, 'Aboriginal Peoples Reference Guide National Household Survey, 2011', online http://www12.statcan.gc.ca/nhs-enm/2011/ref/guides/99-011-x/99-011-x2011006-eng.cfm#a6.

[34] United States Census Bureau, 'The American Indian and Alaska Native Population: 2010', p. 3, online https://www.census.gov/prod/cen2010/briefs/c2010br-10.pdf.

[35] Statistics New Zealand, '2013 Census QuickStats about Maori', p. 6, online http://www.stats.govt.nz/Census/2013-census/profile-and-summary-reports/quickstats-about-maori-english.aspx.

[36] In 2005 (the last time total tribal enrolment was estimated by the Bureau of Indian Affairs) around 31 per cent of people self-identifying as Native American in the US census were not citizens of federally recognized tribes (Bureau of Indian Affairs, 'Indian Population and Labor Force Report 2005', online http://www.bia.gov/cs/groups/public/documents/text/idc-001719.pdf). In Canada, approximately 69 per cent of self-identifying status Indians are not First Nations citizens (Statistics Canada, 'Distribution of First Nations People,2011', online http://www12.statcan.gc.ca/nhs-enm/2011/as-sa/99-011-x/2011001/tbl/tbl03-eng.cfm.

[37] Statistics New Zealand (n 35), p. 6.

[38] The Canadian federal government, for example, excludes First Nations members who are not status Indians from its First Nations populations when estimating Band funding (Allocations Indian and Northern Affairs Canada, 'Band Support Funding Program Policy' (2016), online https://www.aadnc-aandc.gc.ca/eng/1100100013828/1100100013833#chp18).

While recognized tribes are for the most part free to enrol any person they are prepared to accept as a citizen in accordance with their membership law, most continue to use descent rules to determine their prospective membership, effectively ensuring that all tribal birthright citizens are also indigenous. The lineal descent or blood quantum rules used by some tribes suggest that each prospective member must prove their degree of blood by reference to historic biological ancestors, so that the descendants do not acquire blood quantum from a non-Indian naturalized member. Further, settler states themselves continue to define indigeneity in law as a measure of descent. Thus, while *jus sanguinis* citizenship rules need not perpetuate an ethnic group (if ancestors are identified in terms other than ethnicity),[39] in the case of tribes, the correlation is much more difficult to deny, because of the way that tribes are constituted in settler law. The status categories of indigeneity and tribal citizenship therefore resonate in problematic ways with legal concepts of race and racial discrimination.

Current New Zealand and Australian legislative definitions of 'Maori' and 'Aboriginal', respectively, are measures of ancestry and race in those jurisdictions. A person either has indigenous ancestry or not and 'degrees' of ancestry are not relevant to a person's legal status as an indigenous person.[40] In North America, by contrast, measures of indigenous ancestry operate to exclude some descendants from the legally indigenous population, specifically, those persons thought by settler governments to have too few indigenous ancestors to be properly identified as indigenous in settler law. In the United States, for example, federal legislation defines 'Indian' to include 'persons of one-half or more Indian blood'.[41] Tribal membership suffices to qualify a person for most federal services and programs designed for Indians, but otherwise federal regulations usually define a qualifying Indian as a person who possesses 'one quarter or more Indian blood' (a measure that adapts the legislative 'one-half' criteria to accommodate increasing rates of exogamy).[42] Likewise in Canada, a person's parentage and the patterns of marriage among his or her predecessors have always determined their eligibility as a 'status Indian' under the *Indian Act*. Indian status is not available to persons who have only one Indian

---

[39] Costica Dumbrava, *Nationality, Citizenship and Ethno-Cultural Belonging: Preferential Membership Policies in Europe* (Basingstoke: Palgrave MacMillan, 2014), p. 27.

[40] See, e.g., the *Electoral Act* 1993 (NZ), s. 3(1) and *Indigenous Education (Targeted Assistance) Act* 2000 (Aus.), s. 4.

[41] *Indian Reorganization Act* 1934, s. 19; Paul Spruhan, 'Indian as Race/Indian as Political Status: Implementation of the Half-Blood Requirement under The Indian Reorganization Act, 1934–1945', *Rutgers Race & Law Review* 8, no. 1 (2006): pp. 27–49.

[42] These provisions provide the legislative basis for the Bureau of Indian Affairs' certification of Indian blood quanta and the issuance of Certificates of Degree of Indian Blood (CDIBs), which record a person's Indian blood quantum in increments up to 1/64 ('Certificate of Degree of Indian or Alaska Native Blood—Proposed Rule 20775', *Federal Register* 65, no. 75 (18 April 2000)). See also Paul Spruhan, 'A Legal History of Blood Quantum in Federal Indian Law to 1935', *South Dakota Law Review* 51, no. 1 (2006): pp. 1–50.

parent if that parent also has only one Indian parent. That is, after two successive generations of exogenous parenting, the descent rule terminates, and Indian status will be denied to subsequent generations.[43]

Settler states then, allocate national birthright citizenship on the basis of *jus sanguinis* rules (supplemented by *jus soli* rules), allocate legal indigeneity solely by reference to descent, and (in North America) deny indigenous status to descendants who lack the requisite number of indigenous ancestors. While contentious, these designations persist as longstanding and constitutive features of liberal democratic settler statehood. Debates about tribal citizenship rules, and specifically, about the moral justifications for the use of *jus sanguinis* rules by settler and tribal governments to define indigeneity and membership, can help shed light on the normative puzzles posed by the exclusionary birthright citizenship laws of states. The parallels between the constitutive bases of families, tribes, and states as kinship-based groups are difficult to deny. However, given their histories and the nature of their relationships with settlers and settler governments, tribes have vastly more to lose than states, if challenges to birthright rules, and *jus sanguinis* rules in particular, gain momentum in human rights and anti-discrimination law. In particular, insistence by states on the use of *jus soli* and voluntaristic criteria in tribal citizenship law to supplement or replace biological descent rules could imperil the continuity of tribal nations as self-constituting nations. This risk and the problems that arise from it are discussed in the sections that follow.

Tribal Demographies: *Jus Sanguinis* Rules and Tribal Citizenship

My 2008 survey of 535 tribal constitutions and membership codes shows that all use descent to allocate birthright citizenship. Importantly, 57 per cent of the surveyed documents empower tribal governments to 'naturalize' non-descendants at the discretion of tribal decision-makers. Usually preference is given in naturalization decisions to persons who have a kinship-based relationship to birthright citizens, so that spouses, adopted children, or collateral relatives are preferred. Some Canadian and United States tribes take into account voluntaristic criteria measuring acquired attributes in naturalization decisions, such as an aspirant member's cultural competency (for example, 'knowledge of or familiarity with the customs or language of the Band'),[44] their residence or intent to reside on tribal territory,

---

[43] *Indian Act* 1985 (Can.), s. 6(1).
[44] *Membership Code of the Serpent River Band of Ojibway* 1987, s. 17, (on file with author).

or their character, self-sufficiency, and capacity to contribute to the welfare of the tribe.[45] Overall, tribes show a strong preference for naturalized citizens who are legally indigenous (some tribes for example will naturalize spouses and adopted children only if those persons are indigenous).[46] Thus, like liberal democratic states, all tribes use *jus sanguinis* rules to allocate birthright membership, many naturalize persons who do not otherwise qualify at birth, and some prefer to naturalize persons with 'ethno-cultural ties' to citizens. As noted, the apparent absence of *jus soli* rules in tribal citizenship law is thus the core constitutive difference between nation-states and tribal nations.

So how do tribes devise and implement *jus sanguinis* citizenship rules? Descent is a relative concept and so requires the identification of an antecedent person or community from whom descent can be measured. As noted above, settler states identify a descendant's relevant ancestor by reference to that ancestor's birthplace, using *jus soli* rules to limit the number of foreign-born persons who acquire birthright citizenship by descent. Tribes on the other hand do not have recourse to birthplace to identify the persons from whom a person may derive citizenship by descent. They rely instead on a description or census of the historic group from whom they derive their official status, often recorded in documentation collected by the state. The most formal expressions in tribal law name all relevant ancestors on a written base roll (this approach is typical of United States tribes) and the least formal include very open-ended references to a named historical community or eponymous ancestor (typical of groups in New Zealand and Australia). Tribes also differ in the ways in which they measure descent. About half of Canadian and United States tribes refer to parental enrolment as the measure of descent (filiation) and thus require intergenerational continuity of citizenship. Most other tribes use lineal descent rules (linearity) to identify eligible descendants.

While tribal descent rules are not generationally or 'vertically' qualified (there is no limit to the number of generations who can acquire citizenship by descent), some tribes do impose 'horizontal' qualifications, so that not all lineal descendants in a single generation are eligible for citizenship. Many North American tribes limit the group of persons who acquire membership by descent to those with a specified proportion of Indian ancestors. This ratio is often expressed as a measure of 'blood quantum'. A majority of United States tribes, for example, require descendants to have a minimum 'blood quantum' of between one-sixteenth and three-quarters (most frequently, one-quarter). Settler state conceptions of indigeneity make no distinction between tribes as the source of indigenous ancestry or 'blood', positioning indigenous people as a racial (albeit tribally organized) population. In contrast, a large and apparently growing minority of United States tribes do not 'count'

---

[45] See, e.g., the *Membership Code of the Little Black River Band* N.d., 6(c), (on file with author).

[46] This practice is comparable to what Dumbrava terms 'preferential naturalization' (Dumbrava (n 39), chapter 3).

Indian ancestors who were members of other tribal nations, preferring to measure 'tribal blood quantum' rather than 'Indian blood quantum'.[47] These tribes have chosen to abandon measures of pan-Indian ancestry, calculated (usually) by reference to settler-state law, in favour of measures of tribal ancestry, calculated by reference to that tribe's historic rolls and genealogical records. In the United States the growing tribal preference for citizens with high 'tribal blood quantum' shows that they are moving away from the pan-Indian 'race-based' conception of Indianness used in federal Indian law in furtherance of their own genealogic conception of tribal nationhood. They are not, however, moving towards a classically liberal 'civic polity' model based on mutable criteria or *jus soli* rules. Instead they seem to be responding to the growth of the descendant population, itself a product of increased rates of exogamous marriage and parenting, by favouring applicants whose families have a history of endogamous partnering, regardless of where those applicants and their ancestors were born.

In Canada, tribal citizenship rules have a strongly pan-Indian character. The vast majority of First Nations refer to Indian ancestry rather than to tribal ancestry in their membership rules, 'counting' ancestors who were or are affiliated to any First Nation. This is an important feature of Canadian tribal membership governance. It is consistent with the strong pan-tribal sense of Indianness that has emerged from the long operation of the *Indian Act*, especially the practice of inter-Band transfers under that Act (for instance by assigning women to their husband's Band on marriage), enacting the settler-state view that while status Indians are entitled to be members of a First Nation, membership in any First Nation will suffice. Canadian First Nations themselves have not moved far from the centrality of pan-Indianness in their citizenship law. The majority of the 240 or so First Nations who have assumed control over their membership since 1985 exclude descendants who have fewer than two Indian grandparents, applying rules that are equivalent to, or more restrictive than, the *Indian Act*'s second-generation cut-off rule for status Indians.[48]

As noted, genealogical exogamy does not factor into a person's claim to legal indigeneity or tribal membership in New Zealand and Australia. The hemispheric difference is in large part referrable to the existence in North America of public records establishing a person's indigenous ancestry by reference to parentage or blood quantum, measured by tracking marriage and parenting patterns. Records of this kind were (and are) kept by the governments of the United States and Canada, but not of Australia and New Zealand.

The tribal preference for *jus sanguinis* citizenship rules may also be tied to the constraints operating on tribal territorial jurisdiction. In North America most

---

[47] Gover (n 8).

[48] Stewart Clatworthy, *Indian Registration, Membership and Population Change in First Nations Communities* (Ottawa: Ministry of Indian and Northern Affairs, 2005), p. 12 (adjusted to include those groups using blood quantum rules that are equivalent to the *Indian Act* or more).

tribes have formal jurisdiction over defined tribal territories, but as a general principle, unlike public governments, the jurisdiction ascribed to tribal governments is largely personal and status-based. Tribal jurisdiction is confined for the most part to those persons who can be said to have 'consented' to tribal authority by virtue of their membership, or have otherwise agreed to tribal jurisdiction through contract, agreement, or as a condition of residence.[49] In the United States, for example, tribal criminal jurisdiction is confined to minor crimes committed in tribal territories[50] where both the victim and perpetrator are 'Indian'.[51] Major crimes between Indians on tribal land fall under the jurisdiction of the federal government, and minor crimes involving a non-Indian victim or perpetrator fall under the jurisdiction of state governments. This 'patchwork of rules'[52] vastly complicates the task of regulating relationships between members and non-members on tribal territory.[53] Some United States tribes assert extra-territorial criminal jurisdiction over members, and several decisions have upheld this exercise of tribal jurisdiction, but the scope of the power, and the extent to which it applies in non-criminal contexts, remains uncertain.[54]

The jurisdiction of Canadian First Nations and Self-governing Aboriginal communities is limited to subject matters 'that are internal to the group, integral to its distinct Aboriginal culture, and essential to its operation as a government or institution'.[55] These include regulatory and service-provision roles on reserve lands with respect to membership, marriage, education, health, transport, natural resources, and property, while settler provincial and federal governments retain jurisdiction over national security and external relations, criminal law, banking, postal services, and shipping.[56] While tribal by-laws in these areas bind resident non-members, the agreements and legislation setting out tribal jurisdiction specify

[49] *Montana v. United States* 450 U.S. 544 (1981). Matthew L. M. Fletcher, 'Resisting Federal Courts on Tribal Jurisdiction', *University of Colorado Law Review 81*, no. 4 (2010): pp. 973–1025. See also Spruhan (n 41).

[50] Jurisdiction over major crimes lies with the federal government (*Major Crimes Act 1885*, 18 U.S.C. § 1153 (1988)). To add to confusion about the scope of tribal status jurisdiction, the meaning of 'Indian' in this statute has sometimes been interpreted by federal courts to including all members of recognized tribes.

[51] *Oliphant v. Suquamish Indian Tribe* 435 U.S. 191 (1978).

[52] Addie Rolnick, 'Tribal Criminal Jurisdiction beyond Citizenship and Blood', *American Indian Law Review 39*, no. 2 (2016): pp. 337–449, p. 340.

[53] In recognition of this difficulty Congress has recently enabled tribes to prosecute domestic violence offences perpetrated on their territories by persons who live or work on tribal territory or are in a domestic relationship with a tribal member (whether or not the offender is Indian or a tribal member) (*Violence Against Women Reauthorization Act* 2013, 25 U.S.C. § 1304(b)(4)(B) (2012)).

[54] Geoffrey D. Strommer and Stephen D. Osbourne, '"Indian Country" and the Nature and Scope of Tribal Self-Government in Alaska', *Alaska Law Review 22*, no. 1 (2005): pp. 1–34.

[55] Indian and Northern Affairs Canada, 'The Government of Canada's Approach to Implementation of the Inherent Right and the Negotiation of Aboriginal Self-Government' (2010), online http://www.aadnc-aandc.gc.ca/eng/1100100031843/1100100031844.

[56] Ibid.

that the community must provide a mechanism by which non-members can have input into decisions that 'affect their rights and interests'.[57] Likewise, in Canada the extra-territorial extension of personal jurisdiction to members living outside of the tribal territory is limited to measures to which those persons consent, and requires the agreement of the relevant provincial government.[58] Accordingly, tribal jurisdiction is largely confined to tribal members in tribal territory, so that generally speaking the personal jurisdiction of tribes (unlike that of settler governments) does not extend beyond their territorial boundaries and does not apply to non-members in those territories (or indeed to non-indigenous persons, depending on the subject matter).[59] Citizenship rules are thus the primary determinant of the scope of tribal territorial jurisdiction.

JUS SANGUINIS, RACE, DESCENT, AND INDIGENEITY: NORMATIVE CONUNDRUMS

In state allocations of birthright citizenship, whether *jus soli* or *jus sanguinis* rules are used, it is always the case that one or both of the principles is qualified.[60] States variously restrict descent-based citizenship to the first foreign-born generation, require a child or his or her parents to be residents in order for that child to be eligible for citizenship by descent, or deny birthplace citizenship to the children of persons who are not themselves permanent residents or citizens. By adjusting the inclusivity of one principle relative to another, a state can self-constitute by managing the composition of its population. In addition, most states also permit the selective naturalization of persons who do not acquire citizenship at birth. As has been shown, in contrast, while a majority of recognized tribes in the Western settler states also allow naturalization, none allocate birthright membership to non-descendants by reference to that person's birthplace.[61] Furthermore, while in North America many tribes *do* impose limits on the acquisition of *jus sanguinis* citizenship, the

---

[57] Ibid.   [58] Ibid.

[59] See, e.g., L. Scott Gould, 'The Consent Paradigm: Tribal Sovereignty at the Millennium', *Columbia Law Review 96*, no. 4 (1996): pp. 809–902.

[60] See generally Patrick Weil, 'Access to Citizenship: A Comparison of Twenty-Five Nationality Laws', in Thomas Alexander Aleinikoff and Douglas Klusmeyer, eds., *Citizenship Today: Global Perspectives and Practices* (Washington: Carnegie Endowment for International Peace, 2001), p. 17.

[61] My 2008 study shows that only a handful of US tribes assign birthright membership only to persons whose parent or parents were born on the reservation, only one refers to the birthplace of the *applicant* as a requirment of birthright citizens.

rules are not qualified by birthplace criteria. Rather, those tribes limit the number of eligible citizens by reference to additional measures of descent, often represented as degrees of ancestry or 'blood quantum'. Thus states and tribes both use descent-based rules, and both admit persons as members who did not acquire citizenship at birth, but only states allocate citizenship to persons born in the territory who are not the descendant of a citizen.

Jus soli rules have an obvious utility in countries, like the settler states, that are characterized by longstanding policies encouraging relatively high rates of immigration.[62] Unlimited *jus sanguinis* rules, applying to all descendants of all citizens (regardless of how citizenship was acquired) are used by some European states and, like tribal nations, at least eight European states do not allow anyone to acquire citizenship by *jus soli*.[63] 'Unlimited' *jus sanguinis* rules of this kind are associated in commentary with ethnic modes of citizenship because they seem intended to preserve the ethnic composition of the community over time,[64] especially where citizenship is allocated to multiple foreign-born generations and so appears not to correlate with cultural modes of belonging.[65] Some commentators worry that unlimited *jus sanguinis* rules, especially those allowing foreign-born descendants to inherit citizenship, undermine the concept of political and cultural unity that citizenship status ought to support, and draw distinctions that may be discriminatory. Bauböck et al suggest, for example, that rules of this kind can be seen to perpetuate an 'ethnic privilege derived from descent'[66] that is 'morally arbitrary'.[67]

Tribal practice however, suggests that for most tribal communities it is descent and not co-residence or birthplace that constitutes the 'genuine connection'[68] between a tribal citizen and the tribal community.[69] The fraught history of tribal relations with settlers and governments means that political and cultural continuity

[62] See discussion by Patrick Weil, 'From Conditional to Secured and Sovereign: The New Strategic Link between the Citizen and the Nations-state in a Globalized World', *International Journal of Constitutional Law* 9, no. 3–4 (2011): pp. 615–635, p. 618.

[63] Dumbrava (n 39), p. 29. Some of these states do however allow foundlings and stateless children to acquire birthright citizenship by *jus soli* principles.

[64] Ibid., p. 27. See also Joanne Mariner, 'Racism, Citizenship and National Identity, *Development*, 46, no. 3 (2003): pp. 64–70, p. 67 (noting that 'countries that strictly limit naturalization and do not recognize jus soli as a grounds for granting citizenship at birth are, in effect, limiting access to citizenship on ethnic grounds.').

[65] Christian Joppke, 'Comparative Citizenship: A Restrictive Turn in Europe?' *Law and Ethics of Human Rights* 2, no. 1 (2008): pp. 1–41, p. 29.

[66] Rainer Bauböck et al., eds., *Acquisition and Loss of Nationality: Policies and Trends in 15 European States* (Amsterdam: Amsterdam University Press, 2006), p. 30.

[67] Bauböck (n 4), p. 483.

[68] This is a phrase used by the International Court of Justice in the famous 'Nottebohm case', *Liechtenstein v. Guatemala* I.C.J. (1955), p. 23.

[69] Kirsty Gover, 'Genealogy as Continuity: Explaining the Growing Tribal Preference for Descent Rules in Membership Governance in the United States', *American Indian Law Review* 33, no. 1 (2009): pp. 243–309.

is a primary objective of tribal communities. The disruption of the tribal land-base, the very small size of reserved lands relative to traditional territories, the under-resourcing of remote and rural tribal communities, and the relocation of indigen-ous peoples away from their territories, may mean that birthplace and residence rules do not now capture what is valued by tribes as an expression of tribal con-tinuity and identity, nor what evidences a tribal citizen's 'stake' in the continuity and character of that political community. Certainly, it cannot be said that tribal descent rules are any less 'inclusive', in numerical terms, than birthplace or residence rules, given the demographies in which they operate. In a colonial setting marked by a longstanding legal distinction between indigenous and non-indigenous persons, it is reasonable for tribes to decide that continuity is best secured though shared genealogy and indigeneity, and by citizenship rules that keep the tribal community intact by allocating birthright citizenship to members of the tribal diaspora.

The *jus sanguinis* rules used by tribes, then, permit the intergenerational trans-mission of citizenship in circumstances where many people have moved or have been moved away from their ancestral territory, and preserve those connections where parents' presence in the tribal jurisdiction in question may be arbitrary (for example where reserved lands are a tiny portion of a tribe's traditional territory), in much the same way that *jus sanguinis* rules retain their importance for 'countries of emigration'.[70] In contrast to the parental-descent rules used by most states, most tribal lineal descent and blood-quantum rules measure continuity of biological descent but do not require the generation-to-generation transmission of member-ship status. Rules of this kind can serve as a way to reconstitute tribal commu-nities where there is a gap in the intergenerational inheritance of citizenship, for instance where intermediate generations became estranged from the *in situ* tribal community. Generationally unlimited *jus sanguinis* rules of this kind may assist to repair the genealogic continuity of tribal communities disrupted by policies of 'termination' (withdrawal of state recognition), forced relocations, urbanization, land individualization and confiscation, and the removal of indigenous children, all deployed by settler states in their efforts to establish control over indigenous communities and their land. Obversely, the individualization of title to land within tribal territories, and the consequent influx of settlers into those territories means that for many tribes the coherent application of a *jus soli* rule would encompass many people who are not culturally or ethnically affiliated to the tribe, and whose families have 'immigrated' into tribal territories in ways that were not fully within tribal control and are experienced by some tribal communities as the continuation

---

[70] Weil (n 62), p. 618. Weil suggests that *jus soli* principles may be unworkable where territorial boundaries are contested, or are thought to be misaligned with human boundaries, a point he illus-trates by noting that the introduction of *jus soli* rules in the Federal Republic of Germany was politic-ally possible only after reunification, because prior to that point 'millions of compatriots were living outside the borders of the [state]', and that unlimited *jus sanguinis* rules are favoured by countries with unstable territorial boundaries, giving the example of Israel.

of colonial encroachment. Given the historic dispossession and dislocation of indigenous communities, and the very large numbers of non-indigenous persons sometimes resident within tribal territories, *jus sanguinis* rules may protect the political continuity of tribes in a way that *jus soli* rules could not.

Despite these incentives and imperatives, however, the fundamental tension between liberal equality norms and descent-based citizenship criteria means that tribal nations from time to time are challenged to justify *jus sanguinis* citizenship rules in the face of claims that these rules discriminate against non-citizens on the basis of race, ethnicity, or familial status. In international law and in some domestic anti-discrimination law, descent is a cognate of 'race', alongside ethnic origin, national origin, nationality and colour, and indigeneity.[71] As critical citizenship scholars have pointed out, states and families are also kinship-based organizations, and so are arbitrarily constituted by *jus sanguinis* descent rules.[72] However, families are regarded as quintessentially private associations not governed by anti-discrimination law (just as exemptions are often granted to allow private associations and clubs to discriminate in their choice of members), while states are given very wide discretions in international law to determine their citizenship and nationality rules. The *Convention on the Elimination of all forms of Racial Discrimination*, for instance, contains an exemption for citizenship and nationality laws, allowing states to discriminate on the basis of race in these fields in ways that would otherwise be in breach of the Convention.[73] Tribes, then, are kinship-based groups occupying a precarious middle-ground between families and states. They are constituted as descent-based communities but are sometimes expected to allocate membership on grounds other than descent. Tribal nations therefore have to engage head-on with a core puzzle of democratic self-constitution: the seeming impossibility of a demos constituting itself in a way consistent with liberal principles of democratic rule, which includes the norms of equality, consent, and non-discrimination.[74]

---

[71] See, e.g., the *International Convention on the Elimination of all forms of Racial Discrimination* (1969) ('I.C.E.R.D.'), art. 1(1); U.N. Committee on the Elimination of Racial Discrimination, *General Recommendation No. 23: Indigenous Peoples* (1997); *R v. Kapp* [2008] 2 S.C.R. 483 (Canada); Cf *Morton v. Mancari* 417 U.S. 535 (1974).

[72] See especially Shachar (n 3); Jacqueline Stevens, *Reproducing the State* (Princeton: Princeton University Press, 1999); Nira Yuval-Davis, *Gender and Nation* (London: Sage Publications, 1997).

[73] See, e.g., I.C.E.R.D. (n 71), art. 1(2) and 1(3); *Convention on Certain Questions Relating to the Conflict of Nationality Laws* (League of Nations) 1930, art. 2. Cf *International Convention on the Elimination of All Forms of Discrimination against Women* (1979), art. 9(1); *European Convention on Nationality* (1997), art. 5. See generally James A. Goldston, 'Holes in the Rights Framework: Racial Discrimination, Citizenship, and the Rights of Noncitizens', *Ethics and International Affairs* 20, no. 3 (2006): pp. 321–347; Mariner (n 64).

[74] See generally Robert Goodin, 'Enfranchising All Affected Interests, and Its Alternatives', *Philosophy and Public Affairs* 35, no.1 (2007): pp. 40–68; Robert Dahl, *Democracy and Its Critics* (New Haven: Yale University Press, 1989). See also Kirsty Gover, 'When Tribalism Meets Liberalism: Human Rights and Indigenous Boundary Problems in Canada', *University of Toronto Law Review* 64, no. 2 (2014): pp. 206–242.

As long as indigeneity and descent are legally equivalent to measures of race and tribal nations are denied sovereign statehood, the vulnerability of tribes is not alleviated by subsuming membership governance within an indigenous right to self-governance or self-determination. The rights of tribal nations to self-constitute, like all collective indigenous-specific rights (including rights to self-governance) are controversial precisely because they are difficult to reconcile with the equality-based principles that animate individual human rights.[75] The question of how indigenous rights are to be reconciled with individual rights to be free from discrimination is a persistent one, and the priority of collective rights where they conflict with individual rights cannot be assumed. For example, settler-state efforts to secure indigenous collective rights, or to otherwise differentiate between indigenous and non-indigenous citizens, have been challenged as measures that racially discriminate against non-indigenous citizens or against indigenous persons who are not members of the relevant indigenous group.[76] In international law, state laws protecting indigenous rights to self-governance could be justified as measures protecting the rights of members of minorities[77] or alternatively, as the fulfilment of state obligations to take 'special measures' for the purpose of 'securing the adequate advancement' of disadvantaged racial groups.[78] However, both defences give effect to an ideal of substantive equality, so that they cannot easily be used to justify *permanent* measures for indigenous peoples. They must be discontinued when equality has been achieved so that they do not amount to 'preferential treatment' beyond what is necessary to ensure 'equal enjoyment of fundamental human rights and freedoms'.[79] These approaches supply only very awkward justifications for indigenous rights to self-governance and property, because these are rights that are to be held in perpetuity by the successors of pre-state tribal nations. For tribal communities, then, defences of this kind to date have not supported permanent distinctions designed to recognize the distinctive interests of indigenous groups as *nations*, and neither approach has yet been advanced in an international human rights forum as a way to protect the right of tribes to determine their own membership.

[75] See, e.g, Kirsty Gover, 'Equality and Non-discrimination in the United Nations Declaration on the Rights of Indigenous Peoples: Articles 2, 6 and 7(1)', in Jessie Hohmann and Marc Weller, eds., *A Commentary on the United Nations Declaration on the Rights of Indigenous Peoples* (Oxford: Oxford University Press, forthcoming 2017).

[76] See, e.g., *R v. Kapp* (n 71); *Amaltal Fishing Co Ltd v. Nelson Polytechnic* [1996] N.Z.A.R. 97 (New Zealand); *Morton v. Mancari* (n 71); *Carr v. Boree Aboriginal Corporation* [2003] F.M.C.A. 408 (Australia); *Gerhardy v. Brown* (1985) 159 C.L.R. 50 (Australia).

[77] By reference to the *International Covenant on Civil and Political Rights* (1976), art. 27; see *Lubicon Lake Band v. Canada* Comm. no. 167/1984, U.N. Doc. Supp. no. 40 (A/45/40) (H.R.C. 1991), [1].

[78] By reference to the I.C.E.R.D. (n 71), arts 1(4) and 2(2).

[79] U.N. Committee on the Elimination of Racial Discrimination, *General Recommendation No. 32: The Meaning and Scope of Special Measures in the International Convention on the Elimination of Racial Discrimination* (2009), paragraph 12. Further discussed in Kirsty Gover, 'Indigenous Membership and Human Rights: When Tribalism meets Liberalism', in Damien Short and Corrine Lennox, eds., *Handbook of Indigenous Peoples' Rights* (Abingdon, New York: Routledge, 2016), pp. 35–48.

Similarly, sovereignty, statehood, and exemptions in human rights frameworks seem not to resolve the deeper normative problem of whether racial or familial discrimination, effected by tribal or state citizenship rules, can be justified, and in what circumstances. The tendency in scholarship to date is to suggest that tribes should conform more closely to the civic model of citizenship by ceasing to make distinctions between aspirant members on the basis of their immutable and unalterable characteristics, especially race, or perhaps (implicitly in some accounts) should be able to use descent rules only as a temporary accommodation in the service of remedial justice.[80] In other words, tribal nations are at risk of being compelled to adopt subscriptive, open-ended modes of association that no nation-state has yet embraced, or to deploy residency or birthplace rules that would be extremely exclusionary given contemporary tribal and indigenous demographies.

Conclusion

For the time-being then, the question of whether tribal *jus sanguinis* rules might discriminate against non-descendants remains open. Two apparently competing principles are in play in the contemporary politics of indigenous citizenship. First, there is the principle that tribes should control their own membership as part of their inherent right to self-determination and self-governance or their right to control access to collectively held resources. The second principle is that distinctions should not be made by tribal governments between persons on the basis of their race, ethnicity, or familial status. Like the *jus sanguinis* rules used by states, tribal descent rules implicate debates about the normativity of birthright citizenship, debates that contain what FitzGerald describes as 'a great deal of ambiguity about whether the attribution of birthright citizenship by descent (*jus sanguinis*) is racial or simply familial'.[81] In settler societies, I suggest, aside from the demographic challenges faced by tribes, there is a very strong public interest in the preservation of tribal rights to differentiate on the basis of descent, because settler constitutionalism is premised on the concepts of race and descent as sources of indigenous legal status. In other words, it is the pre-colonial presence of kinship-based self-governing indigenous polities that constitutes settler states *as settler states*, and the freedom to

---

[80] See above (n 4). See also Kymlicka, *Liberalism, Community and Culture* (n 5), pp. 170, 198. On gender discrimination in tribal membership law see Will Kymlicka, *Multicultural Citizenship* (n 5), p. 165; Ayelet Shachar's response (Ayelet Shachar, *Multicultural Jurisdictions: Cultural Differences and Women's Rights* (Cambridge, New York: Cambridge University Press, 2001), pp. 18–20 and 31).

[81] See Fitzgerald in this volume.

form and maintain indigenous communities today should be protected as an essential aspect of democratic tribal and settler nationhood.

BIBLIOGRAPHY

Bauböck, Rainer, Eva Ersbøll, Kees Groenendijk, and Harald Waldrauch eds., *Acquisition and Loss of Nationality: Policies and Trends in 15 European States* (Amsterdam: Amsterdam University Press, 2006).

Bauböck, Rainer, 'The Rights and Duties of External Citizenship', *Citizenship Studies 13*, no. 5 (2009): pp. 475–499.

Berger, Bethany, 'Race, Descent and Tribal Citizenship', *California Law Review Circuit 4* (2013): pp. 23–37.

Borrows, John, *Freedom and Indigenous Constitutionalism* (Toronto: University of Toronto Press, 2016).

Chesterman, John and Brian Galligan, *Citizens without Rights: Aborigines and Australian Citizenship* (Cambridge: Cambridge University Press, 1997).

Clatworthy, Stewart, *Indian Registration, Membership and Population Change in First Nations Communities* (Ottawa: Ministry of Indian and Northern Affairs, 2005).

Dahl, Robert, *Democracy and Its Critics* (New Haven: Yale University Press, 1989).

Dick, Caroline, *The Perils of Identity: Group Rights and the Politics of Intragroup Difference* (Vancouver: University of British Columbia Press, 2011).

Dumbrava, Costica, *Nationality, Citizenship and Ethno-Cultural Belonging: Preferential Membership Policies in Europe* (Basingstoke: Palgrave Macmillan, 2014).

Evans, Julie, Patricia Grimshaw, David Phillips, and Shurlee Swain, eds., *Equal Subjects, Unequal Rights: Indigenous Peoples in British Settler Colonies, 1830–1910* (Manchester, New York: Manchester University Press, 2003).

Fletcher, Matthew L. M., 'Resisting Federal Courts on Tribal Jurisdiction', *University of Colorado Law Review 81*, no. 4 (2010): pp. 973–1025.

Fletcher, Matthew L. M., *American Indian Tribal Law* (New York: Aspen Publishers, 2011).

Fletcher, Matthew, 'Tribal Membership and Indian Nationhood', *American Indian Law Review 37* (2012–2013): pp. 1–17.

Galanda, Gabriel S. and Ryan D. Dreveskracht, 'Curing the Tribal Disenrollment Epidemic: In Search of a Remedy', *Arizona Law Review 57*, no. 2 (2015): pp. 383–474.

Goldston, James A., 'Holes in the Rights Framework: Racial Discrimination, Citizenship, and the Rights of Noncitizens', *Ethics and International Affairs 20*, no. 3 (2006): pp. 321–347.

Goodin, Robert, 'Enfranchising All Affected Interests, and Its Alternatives', *Philosophy and Public Affairs 35*, no. 1 (2007): pp. 40–68.

Gould, L. Scott, 'The Consent Paradigm: Tribal Sovereignty at the Millennium', *Columbia Law Review 96*, no. 4 (1996): pp. 809–902.

Gover, Kirsty, 'Genealogy as Continuity: Explaining the Growing Tribal Preference for Descent Rules in Membership Governance in the United States', *American Indian Law Review 33*, no. 1 (2009): pp. 243–309.

Gover, Kirsty, *Tribal Constitutionalism: States, Tribes and the Governance of Membership* (Oxford, New York: Oxford University Press, 2010).

Gover, Kirsty, 'When Tribalism Meets Liberalism: Human Rights and Indigenous Boundary Problems in Canada', *University of Toronto Law Review 64*, no. 2 (2014): pp. 206–242, online http://dx.doi.org/10.3138/utlj.0312.

Gover, Kirsty, 'Indigenous Membership and Human Rights: When Tribalism Meets Liberalism', in Damien Short and Corrine Lennox, eds., *Handbook of Indigenous Peoples' Rights* (Abingdon, New York: Routledge, 2016), pp. 35–48.

Gover, Kirsty, 'Equality and Non-Discrimination in the United Nations Declaration on the Rights of Indigenous Peoples: Articles 2, 6 and 7(1)', in Jessie Hohmann and Marc Weller, eds., *The United Nations Declaration on the Rights of Indigenous Peoples: A Commentary* (Oxford University Press, forthcoming 2017).

Grammond, Sebastien, *Identity Captured by Law: Membership in Canada's Indigenous Peoples and Linguistic Minorities* (Montreal: McGill-Queen's University Press, 2009).

Ivison, Duncan, 'The Logic of Aboriginal Rights', *Ethnicities 3*, no. 3 (2003): pp. 321–344.

Ivison, Duncan, Paul Patton, and Will Sanders, eds., *Political Theory and the Rights of Indigenous Peoples* (Cambridge: Cambridge University Press, 2001).

Joppke, Christian, 'Comparative Citizenship: A Restrictive Turn in Europe?', *Law and Ethics of Human Rights 2*, no. 1 (2008): pp. 1–41.

Keyssar, Alexander, *The Right to Vote: The Contested History of Democracy in the United States* (New York: Basic Books, 2000).

Kirkby, Coel, 'Nativism and the End of the British Empire' (unpublished manuscript, on file with author).

Kymlicka, Will, *Liberalism, Community and Culture* (Oxford: Clarendon Press, 1991).

Kymlicka, Will, ed., *The Rights of Minority Cultures* (Oxford, New York: Oxford University Press, 1995).

Kymlicka, Will, *Multicultural Citizenship: A Liberal Theory of Minority Rights* (Oxford: Clarendon Press, 1995).

Kymlicka, Will, 'American Multiculturalism and the Nations Within', in Duncan Ivison et al., eds., *Political Theory and the Rights of Indigenous Peoples* (Cambridge: Cambridge University Press, 2001), pp. 216–236.

Levy, Jacob T., *The Multiculturalism of Fear* (Oxford: Oxford University Press, 2000).

Macklem, Patrick, *Indigenous Difference and the Constitution of Canada* (Toronto: University of Toronto Press, 2001).

Mariner, Joanne, 'Racism, Citizenship and National Identity', *Development 46*, no. 3 (2003): pp. 64–70.

Porter, Robert B., 'The Demise of the Ongwehoweh and the Rise of the Native Americans: Redressing the Genocidal Act of Forcing American Citizenship upon Indigenous Peoples', *Harvard Black Letter Journal 15* (1999): pp. 107–183.

Rolnick, Addie, 'Tribal Criminal Jurisdiction beyond Citizenship and Blood', *American Indian Law Review 39*, no. 2 (2016): pp. 337–449.

Rubio, Greg, 'Reclaiming Indian Civil Rights: The Application of International Rights Law to Tribal Disenrollment Actions', *Oregon Review of International Law 11* (2009): pp. 1–42.

Shachar, Ayelet, *Multicultural Jurisdictions: Cultural Differences and Women's Rights* (Cambridge, New York: Cambridge University Press, 2001).

Shachar, Ayelet. *The Birthright Lottery: Citizenship and Global Inequality* (Cambridge: Harvard University Press, 2006).

Spiro, Peter J., 'A New International Law of Citizenship', *American Journal of International Law 105*, no. 4 (2011): pp. 694–746.

Spruhan, Paul, 'Indian as Race/Indian as Political Status: Implementation of the Half-Blood Requirement under The Indian Reorganization Act, 1934–1945', *Rutgers Race & Law Review 8*, no. 1 (2006): pp. 27–49.

Spruhan, Paul, 'A Legal History of Blood Quantum in Federal Indian Law to 1935', *South Dakota Law Review 51*, no. 1 (2006): pp. 1–50.

Stevens, Jacqueline, *Reproducing the State* (Princeton: Princeton University Press, 1999).

Strommer, Geoffrey D. and Stephen D. Osbourne, ' "Indian Country" and the Nature and Scope of Tribal Self-Government in Alaska', *Alaska Law Review 22*, no. 1 (2005): pp. 1–34.

Weil, Patrick, 'Access to Citizenship: A Comparison of Twenty-Five Nationality Laws', in Thomas Alexander Aleinikoff and Douglas Klusmeyer, eds., *Citizenship Today: Global Perspectives and Practices* (Washington: Carnegie Endowment for International Peace, 2001), pp. 17–35.

Weil, Patrick, 'From Conditional to Secured and Sovereign: The New Strategic Link between the Citizen and the Nation-state in a Globalized World', *International Journal of Constitutional Law 9*, no. 3–4 (2011): pp. 615–635.

Yuval-Davis, Nira, *Gender and Nation* (London: Sage Publications, 1997).

STATUTES

Alaska Native Claims Settlement Act (43 U.S.C. 1601) 1971.

Certain Questions Relating to the Conflict of Nationality Laws (League of Nations) 1930.

Certificate of Degree of Indian or Alaska Native Blood—Proposed Rule 20775, Federal Register, Vol. 65, No. 75 (18 April, 2000). (U.S.)

Constitution and By-laws of the Sault Ste. Marie Tribe of Chippewa Indians 1975, art. III(1)a (1975).

Electoral Act 1993 (N.Z.), s. 3(1)[KG1].

European Convention on Nationality (1997).

Federal Register, Vol. 81(86) May 4, 2016. (U.S.)

Indian Act 1880 (Can.), s. 99.

Indian Act 1985 (Can.), s. 10(1).

Indian Reorganization Act 1934, s. 19. (U.S.)

Indigenous Education (Targeted Assistance) Act 2000 (Aus.), s. 4.

International Convention on the Elimination of All Forms of Discrimination against Women (1979).

International Convention on the Elimination of all forms of Racial Discrimination (1969), art. 1(1).

International Covenant on Civil and Political Rights (1976), art. 27.

Maori Fisheries Act 2004 (N.Z.), Sch. 3.

Membership Code of the Little Black River Band N.d., 6(c).

Membership Code of the Serpent River Band of Ojibway 1987, s. 17.

U.N. Committee on the Elimination of Racial Discrimination, *General Recommendation No. 23: Indigenous Peoples* (1997).

U.N. Committee on the Elimination of Racial Discrimination, *General Recommendation No. 32: The meaning and scope of special measures in the International Convention on the Elimination of Racial Discrimination* (2009).
Violence Against Women Reauthorization Act 2013, 25 U.S.C. § 1304(b)(4)(B) (2012).

Cases

Amaltal Fishing Co Ltd v. Nelson Polytechnic [1996] N.Z.A.R. 97.
Carr v. Boree Aboriginal Corporation [2003] F.M.C.A. 408 (Australia).
Cherokee Nation v. Georgia 30 U.S. (5 Pet.) 1 (1831).
Gerhardy v. Brown (1985) 159 C.L.R. 50 (Australia).
Elk v. Wilkins 112 U.S. 94 (1884) (U.S.).
Liechtenstein v. Guatemala I.C.J. (1955).
Lubicon Lake Band v. Canada Comm. no. 167/1984, U.N. Doc. Supp. no. 40 (A/45/40) (H.R.C. 1991), [1].
Montana v. United States 450 U.S. 544 (1981).
Morton v. Mancari 417 U.S. 535 (1974).
Oliphant v. Suquamish Indian Tribe 435 U.S. 191 (1978).
R v. Kapp [2008] 2 S.C.R. 483 (Canada).
Santa Clara Pueblo v. Martinez 436 U.S. 49 (1978).
Worcester v. Georgia 31 U.S. (6 Pet.) 515 (1831).

Online Resources

Australian Bureau of Statistics, 'National Aboriginal and Torres Strait Islander Social Survey, 2014–15', online http://www.abs.gov.au/ausstats/abs@.nsf/Lookup/by%20Subject/4714.0~2014-15~Main%20Features~Population%20context~2.
Australian Institute of Aboriginal and Torres Strait Islanders, 'National Registered Native Title Bodies Corporate (RNTBCs) Summary', (2 June 2016), online http://aiatsis.gov.au/sites/default/files/products/statistics_and_summaries/rntbc_summary_june_2016.pdf.
Bureau of Indian Affairs, 'Indian Population and Labor Force Report 2005', online http://www.bia.gov/cs/groups/public/documents/text/idc-001719.pdf.
Indian and Northern Affairs Canada, 'The Government of Canada's Approach to Implementation of the Inherent Right and the Negotiation of Aboriginal Self-Government' (2010), online http://www.aadnc-aandc.gc.ca/eng/1100100031843/1100100031844.
Indian and Northern Affairs Canada, 'Band Support Funding Program Policy' (2016), online https://www.aadnc-aandc.gc.ca/eng/1100100013828/1100100013833#chp18.
Office of Treaty Settlements, '12 Month Progress Report 1 July 2015–30 June 2016', online https://www.govt.nz/assets/Documents/OTS/Quarterly-report-to-30-June-2016.pdf.

Statistics Canada, 'Aboriginal Peoples Reference Guide National Household Survey, 2011', online   http://www12.statcan.gc.ca/nhs-enm/2011/ref/guides/99-011-x/99-011-x2011006-eng.cfm#a6.

Statistics Canada, 'Distribution of First Nations People 2011', online http://www12.statcan.gc.ca/nhs-enm/2011/as-sa/99-011-x/2011001/tbl/tbl03-eng.cfm.

Statistics New Zealand, '2013 Census QuickStats about Maori', online http://www.stats.govt.nz/Census/2013-census/profile-and-summary-reports/quickstats-about-maori-english.aspx.

United States Census Bureau, 'The American Indian and Alaska Native Population: 2010', online https://www.census.gov/prod/cen2010/briefs/c2010br-10.pdf.

CHAPTER 22

SECULAR AND RELIGIOUS CITIZENSHIP

BRYAN S. TURNER

INTRODUCTION

THIS chapter examines both secular and religious patterns of civic and political membership within the institutional framework of citizenship. It will concentrate primarily on Western societies and Western notions of citizenship which may be narrowly defined here as the rights and duties of members of a political community such as a nation-state. In discussing religion. this chapter refers primarily to the Abrahamic religions (Judaism, Christianity, and Islam). Citizenship as both an institution and a theory was not indigenous to Asian societies and was introduced (if at all) late in the nineteenth century via Western influence.[1] In addition there is the complicated problem of the presence of 'religion' in Asian societies. One notorious example is Confucianism—is it a religion or a theory of the state or a state ideology? The very idea of 'world religions' has been criticized in contemporary religious studies.[2] These considerations are designed to narrow the present discussion and thereby to give the analysis greater precision.

Citizenship has obvious secular antecedents in Greek, Roman, and Enlightenment thought. For example, Aristotle in *Politics*, admitting that it is difficult to find a definition that applies to all citizens, makes no reference to religion, although he does discuss citizenship in terms of moral training.[3] Consequently citizenship is understood in the mainstream political science literature as a secular framework for the distribution of resources and corresponding obligations within a community. This chapter argues that there is typically a parallel development of religious affiliation, in which members of religious institutions, such as churches, or movements have to pay taxes, follow the commands of an authority, abide to an orthodoxy and norms of religious and ethical behaviour, and in return receive sacramental services (such as baptism and marriage ceremonies) and frequently welfare and educational services. Just as citizens in a secular state can be incarcerated for misdemeanours or expelled for serious offences, members of a religious community can also be expelled or denied ritual services.

While there are thus two distinctive spheres or forms of membership, their relationship has varied considerably over time and by national context. In the liberal politics of western societies the two spheres are assumed to be kept apart by the constitutional separation of church and state. However, the two spheres often overlap or conflict with each other. In a theocracy or under caesaro-papism, the two spheres are integrated and the monarch, as in the Church of England, is both head of state and of the Church. Other examples would include the early Mormons under Joseph Smith where Utah was both a separate state and a spatial location for a new religion. The Philippines is an interesting example where the Catholic Church virtually created a new society through baptizing the entire population.[4] However the prominent question of modern societies, given the dominance of state sovereignty and the growth of secularization, is whether religious membership enjoys some degree of autonomy or whether it is subordinated to the secular model. It is argued that in many societies religious institutions and functionaries are indeed subordinated to the state through secular law—the legislation on same-sex marriage being a prominent example. Furthermore, the

[1] Bryan S. Turner, 'Citizenship East and West: Reflections on Revolutions and Civil Society', in Gerard Delanty, ed., *Europe and Asia beyond East and West* (Abingdon: Routledge, 2006), pp. 148–160.
[2] Tomoko Masuzawa, *The Invention of World Religions: Or, How European Universalism Was Preserved in the Language of Pluralism* (Chicago: University of Chicago Press, 2005).
[3] Aristotle, *Politics* (New York: Dover Publications, 2000).
[4] Ran Hirschl, *Constitutional Theocracy* (Cambridge: Harvard University Press, 2011).

control of religious belief and practice by secular states is widespread from the United States to Singapore. This type of control can be referred to simply as 'the management of religions' by the secular state.[5]

While there is ample evidence to support the proposition that the modern state manages religious life in the interest of social and political order, there is a more profound question about whether a secular state can survive without some foundation in a religious culture or tradition. As I will explain later, the deeper issue for all secular democracies is the Böckenförde dilemma, which asks whether a secular state can function without a basis in shared values and beliefs and to what extent it could promote such a value basis without compromising its own liberal integrity. The Böckenförde dilemma states simply that a liberal democratic state cannot create the liberal values on which it depends by the usual means of 'law and order'. Yet reports from the United Kingdom and elsewhere suggest that legal protection from discrimination, laws relating to hate speech, rule of law, and protection of equality have changed the social landscape in Europe. I refer here specifically to the UK *Racial and Religious Hatred Act* 2006, the *Equality Act* of 2006, and the *Equality Act* of 2010. This legislative momentum came at first, not from a concern for religious issues but from equality legislation relating to women's rights and racial discrimination. Contemporary interest in religion and belief was a by-product of the general broadening of equality legislation. This legal protection of individual rights is clearly consistent with liberalism and does not contradict the claims of a liberal democratic state.

While one can find numerous examples where secular law appears to regulate religious practice, there are also many examples of exemptions from laws relating to equality on matters of gender, marriage and civil partnership, sexual orientation, and religion or belief itself. This finding raises the more general question as to whether legal protection of religious minorities (via exemptions) undermines a fundamental value of democracy, namely, equality of citizens.[6] It was this question—does a secular society nevertheless require some foundation in religious values?—that gave rise to the famous intervention of the secular German philosopher Jürgen Habermas, who came to acknowledge the fact that the legacy of Christianity had deeply shaped European society, and recognized that 'Religious traditions have a special power to articulate moral intuitions, especially with regard to vulnerable forms of communal life.'[7]

---

[5] Bryan S. Turner, *Religion and Modern Society: Citizenship, Secularisation and the State* (Cambridge: Cambridge University Press, 2011); Bryan S. Turner, 'The Enclave Society: Towards a Sociology of Immobility', *European Journal of Social Theory 10*, no. 2 (2007): pp. 287–304.

[6] Brian Barry, *Culture and Equality* (Cambridge: Polity Press, 2001).

[7] Jürgen Habermas, *Between Naturalism and Religion: Philosophical Essays* (Cambridge: Polity Press, 2008), p. 131.

While there has been a secular trajectory in the construction of citizenship with the rise of the sovereign nation-state, the religious and the secular often remain entangled within the same institutional framework of rights and duties. In many respects secular citizenship and religious membership are at odds precisely because they are entangled and often compete for access to and possible domination of the civic sphere. The potential conflict arises from the fact that the secular and the religious offer separate but parallel forms of membership with frequently conflicting demands regarding the rights and duties of members.

It is obvious that religion is deeply involved in modern politics, especially in the Middle East, Asia, and Africa. In the West, the churches have been forced into a defensive and reactive position with respect to abortion, contraception, and divorce. However, the debate over same-sex marriage is perhaps the most contentious issue. While the sex scandals within the Catholic Church and the 2015 Irish referendum in favour of recognizing same-sex marriage have been a major challenge to the authority of the Catholic Church, Pope Francis has sought to avoid further confrontation by treating homosexuality as a pastoral problem that does not challenge orthodox teaching. Religious problems are clearly in the public secular domain, but have the public religions survived and what of the religious citizen today?

While there are tensions between many Christian churches and the state over homosexuality and same-sex marriage, conflicts with Islam have been even more problematic. Especially after 9/11, these have raised many legal and political problems relating to dress codes and Shari'a law that indicate that the issue of Muslim integration has been a contentious issue in the public domain. While in France the principle of *laïcité* has been invoked to ban even burkinis on public beaches, the demand for accommodation of Shari'a in the West is more important from a legal and constitutional point of view. In a sovereign state, is the growth of legal pluralism involving Shari'a a challenge within the public sphere? The presence of religious laws in a sovereign state brings into sharp focus the tensions between secular and religious citizenship. In the following discussion, having examined some of the key texts in the debate about religion and the public sphere, the chapter examines the historical origins and development of secular citizenship from Greek and Roman conceptions. This sketch is followed by an analysis of religious membership with special attention to St Augustine's doctrine of the two cities. The section 'Religious Diversity and Public Reason' examines religious diversity and public reason with special consideration of the liberal theory of John Rawls, and the section 'Religious Exemptions and Equality of Membership' looks at the tensions between the notion of the equality of citizens and religious exemptions from the general requirements of equal citizenship. In conclusion, it is claimed that in modern secular societies there is a management of religion by the state and hence secular membership is dominant and religious membership is subordinate.

STATE OF THE ART

If we take two classic texts in the modern understanding of citizenship from Britain and America, we discover that religion played no part in their understanding of social rights. T.H. Marshall's *Citizenship and Social Class* has been a standard reference in the sociology of citizenship, providing an account of its development in Britain in terms of juridical, political, and social rights. Marshall had nothing to say about the role of religion in the history of citizenship rights.[8] Judith Shklar's *American Citizenship* is an equally influential view of citizenship in America. She argued that most perspectives on citizenship in political philosophy had overlooked the importance of employment and earning as the foundation of ideas about citizenship from colonial America onwards. The founding fathers feared the twin dangers of slavery and aristocracy. Slavery involved a loss of human status and dignity, while aristocracy was associated with luxury and idleness. Thus, 'We are citizens only if we "earn".'[9] Both studies presupposed the secularization of society.

The publication of José Casanova's *Public Religions in the Modern World* in 1994 was an important turning point in the contemporary debate about secularization. His commentary demonstrated that religion was not, as a result of secularization, merely a matter of private faith, but, on the contrary, played a crucial role in modern politics. Casanova brought attention to the critical role of religion in Latin American liberation theology, the Moral Majority in the United States, Solidarity in Poland, and the Iranian Revolution. His analysis was in part a reflection on the implications and consequences of Vatican II (1962–65) which had done much to modernize the Roman Catholic Church by reforming the liturgy, encouraging dialogue with other religions, accepting the validity of liberal democracy, and thereby cutting the Church's ties with authoritarianism in Latin America, and fostering the growth of Christian Democratic parties in Europe.[10] David Martin raised important criticisms of a simple linear model of secularization over a longer period, and with respect to global Pentecostalism, he showed how Pentecostal churches had empowered otherwise alienated citizens and women as second-class citizens.[11]

After 9/11 the debate about religion in the public domain became a matter of some urgency. The notion of a post-secular society in which secular citizens are obliged to take seriously the beliefs and practices of religious citizens signals a development

---

[8] Thomas H. Marshall, *Citizenship and Social Class* (Cambridge: Cambridge University Press, 1950).
[9] Judith N. Shklar, *American Citizenship: The Quest for Inclusion*, volume 3 (Cambridge: Harvard University Press, 1991), p. 67.
[10] Walter Kasper, *The Catholic Church: Nature, Reality and Mission* (London: Bloomsbury Publishing, 2015).
[11] David Martin, *The Future of Christianity* (Abingdon: Routledge, 2016 [2011]).

where the ongoing impact of religious institutions on public life is increasingly rec-ognized.[12] We might say that the effect of Vatican II was to expand religion into the secular public domain and to create the context where secular philosophers such as Habermas had to recognize the presence of the religious citizens. Alongside Habermas, Charles Taylor in his *A Secular Age* has been influential in his criticism of what we might call a naïve secularization thesis.[13]

However, after 9/11, the main focus of research has been on Islam. There is now a vast literature on the integration of Muslim communities into the West along-side extensive research on Islamophobia.[14] There has been interesting work done on minority rights in the Ottoman Empire, demonstrating that in the millet system, minority rights of religious citizens were respected.[15] This research on the Ottomans influenced Kymlicka's theory of group rights as offering one route into social and political participation by minorities.[16] A similar argument has been taken up by Saba Mahmood, noting that in Egypt state management of religion had only served to promote conflict between Copts and Muslims.[17]

In *Can Islam Be French?* John Bowen claims that Islam touches raw nerves in French culture. The entry of Islam into public culture has changed the topography of France and raised old anxieties about 'colonial repression, modern anti-Semitism, and the struggles between Catholics and Republicans'.[18] It is claimed that European hostility to Jews has been replaced by the growing fear of Muslims.[19]

While the dominant trend in research has been to argue in favour of fairly open borders, rapid naturalization of migrants, and sympathetic treatment of illegal migrants, there is also concern over the threat to sovereignty posed by migration and by the growth of legal pluralism.[20] Much of this literature defending rights on halal food, dress (the burka), and practice (customs surrounding divorce) is about

---

[12] Philip S. Gorski, David Kyuman Kim, John Torpey, and Jonathan VanAntwerpen, *The Post-Secular in Question: Religion in Contemporary Society* (New York: NYU Press, 2012).

[13] Charles Taylor, *A Secular Age* (Cambridge: Harvard University Press, 2009).

[14] Jocelyne Cesari, ed., *Muslims in the West after 9/11: Religion, Politics and Law* (London: Routledge, 2009); Jocelyne Cesari, *Why the West Fears Islam: An Exploration of Muslims in Liberal Democracies* (New York: Palgrave Macmillan, 2013).

[15] Karen Barkey, *Empire of Difference: The Ottomans in Comparative Perspective* (Cambridge: Cambridge University Press, 2008).

[16] Will Kymlicka, 'Testing the Bounds of Liberal Multiculturalism' (paper presented at the Canadian Council of Muslim Women's conference 'Muslim Women's Equality Rights in the Justice System: Gender, Religion and Pluralism', Toronto, Ontario, 2005), online: http://www.academia.edu/2397540/Testing_the_Bounds_of_Liberal_Multiculturalism_The_Sharia_Debate_in_Ontario_2005_.

[17] Saba Mahmood, *Religious Difference in a Secular Age* (Princeton: Princeton University Press, 2015).

[18] John R. Bowen, *Can Islam Be French?: Pluralism and Pragmatism in a Secularist State* (Princeton: Princeton University Press, 2011), p. 15.

[19] Paul Weller et al., *Religion or Belief, Discrimination and Equality: Britain in Global Contexts* (London: Bloomsbury Academic, 2013), p. 19.

[20] Bryan S. Turner, 'Review Essay: The Scandinavian Model of Secularities', *European Journal of Social Theory* 17, no. 4 (2014): pp. 534–543.

advocacy rather than analysis, and the basic requirements for a sociology of Islam are underdeveloped.[21]

One interesting development in religious studies and in the philosophy of religion has been to treat devotional texts as equally political texts. One sees this development most notably in recent interpretations of St Paul's letters as political reflections on the institutional problems of the early Church in managing tensions between Jewish Christians and converts from outside Judaism. We can thus read devotional literature and theological tracts as political texts or theories. A political theory of social diversity has its origins in New Testament theology. To some extent, a theology of political membership pre-dates the parallel theory of secular membership. The problem of difference arose in early Christianity, namely, the difference between Christians, Jews, and Jews who had converted to Christianity. St Paul's letters are viewed in modern scholarship as political essays relating to the problems of membership in a new 'church' that included both converted Jews and other Christians. I refer here to Jacob Taubes' *The Political Theology of Paul* and Alain Badiou's *Saint Paul: The Foundations of Universalism*.[22] The classic text, however, is Sheldon S. Wolin's *Politics and Vision* in which he interpreted Augustine's thought as privileging the 'social' over the 'political' with the consequence that 'the heavenly city was not the negation of the political society but a perfecting of it, a transmuting of its attributes to a glory that the former would never know.'[23] The resulting *socialis vita sanctorum* (the social life of saints) was the highest expression of fellowship in all creation.

The underlying issue which is alive today concerns how much of Judaism (and specifically the Old Testament) is carried over into the new dispensation. Clearly the early Christian communities were confronted by Jews who did not recognize Christ as Saviour and by Jewish converts who were unclear about the status of Jewish traditions. Thus Paul's letters are contributions to a political theory of difference that embraces universalism. Paul attempts to solve the problem by recognizing that the old laws have been superseded, that converts to Christianity are circumcised in their hearts, and that the core doctrine of faith is simply that Christ is risen. He concludes that, '[t]here is no difference between the Jew and the Greek; for the same Lord over all is rich unto all that call upon him, For whosoever shall call upon the name of the Lord shall be saved' (Romans 12–13). For Badiou, Paul is our contemporary struggling with the problems of particularity and universalism, because in fact there are Jews and Greeks existing in the same temporal and spatial reality.

[21] Bryan S. Turner, 'Sociology of Islam: The Desiderata', *Sociology of Islam* 1, no. 1–2 (2013): pp. 14–16.
[22] Jonathan Roffe, 'Book Review: Alain Badiou, *Saint Paul: The Foundation of Universalism*', *Philosophy in Review* 24 (2004): pp. 5–7; Jacob Taubes, *The Political Theology of Paul*, edited by Aleida Assmann, translated by Dana Hollander (Stanford: Stanford University Press, 2004).
[23] Sheldon S. Wolin, *Politics and Vision: Continuity and Innovation in Western Political Thought* (Princeton: Princeton University Press, 2009), p. 130.

This universalism in Paul's letters contrasted sharply with Greek political thought. While social and religious diversity is a contemporary issue—possibly *the* contemporary political issue—political theory in the ancient world was no stranger to the problem of diversity. Indeed, the origins of political theory are to be found in anxieties about social differences (gender, ethnicity, religion, and slavery) and their negative impact on political life. The security of the *polis* was threatened by social diversity: women, family, slaves, and foreigners.[24] There is therefore an interesting degree of continuity in political theory from Aristotle to the moderns.

CITIZENSHIP AS A SECULAR FORM OF POLITICAL MEMBERSHIP

In the West, citizenship was part of a cluster of notions about cities, civil society, civility, and civilization. This cluster does not translate easily into other cultures where, for example, the history of the city and civil society have taken different forms and trajectories. This argument preoccupied Max Weber in his *The City*, in which he argued that the city's relative political and economic autonomy favoured the growth of an independent bourgeoisie as the backbone of early citizenship.[25] In making these comparisons, it is easy to fall into an Orientalist approach in which there are implicit or explicit normative judgements about the superiority of the Western march towards modernity.[26] However, if we turn to the Arabic world, we find that there is no comparable term for citizenship. Two words are typically used in this context, namely, *ra'aya* (flock) indicating passive obedience or *muwatana* (homeland), derived from *watan* or nation. A much more promising approach is associated with the 'world history' approach of Marshall G.S. Hodgson who favoured the idea of 'Islamdom' as parallel to Christendom in which Muslims lived as citizens in an institutional complex that included the Shari'a, religious duties such as taxation (*Zakat*), and a civil society that included a merchant class and charitable organizations (*waqfs*).[27] Thus various secular and religious components

---

[24] Arlene W. Saxonhouse, *Fear of Diversity: The Birth of Political Science in Ancient Greek Thought* (Chicago: University of Chicago Press, 1995).

[25] Max Weber, *The City*, translated and edited by Don Martindale and Gertrud Neuwirth (Glencoe: Free Press, 1958).

[26] Bryan S. Turner, *Marx and the End of Orientalism* (New York: Routledge, 2014 [1978]).

[27] Marshall G.S. Hodgson, *The Venture of Islam*, volume 1 (Chicago: University of Chicago Press, 1974).

of what in the West we know as secular membership or citizenship were combined in Islamdom.[28]

To summarize the main argument so far, it is proposed that citizenship, starting with Aristotle and Thucydides in ancient Greece and with Cicero in Rome, assumed a secular form of political membership of free men.[29] It is secular because the normative aim of politics was to promote *eudaimonia* or the flourishing of its citizens in the context of successful statesmanship. The gods played little or no role in the flourishing of humans. The pinnacle of Greek normative thinking about secular citizenship was the famous funeral speech to the Athenians by Pericles who commanded the citizens to love the city. Religion played no significant role in this vision.

In distinguishing the 'social' from the 'political', Hannah Arendt claimed that the ancient world knew of the *polis* but relatively little of 'society' and 'free men'.[30] Political membership was to a city-state in the case of Greece and the Roman Republic. Cicero in *De natura deorum* favoured the ideas of the Stoics and Epicureans in recognizing natural law and nature as the principles to guide politics rather than the gods. However, he developed the basic ideas of Greek philosophy around the concepts of virtue, happiness, and justice, and a vocabulary of politics that embraced ideas about a commonwealth of interests, the city, and civic virtue.[31] In short, the ancient world before the rise of Christianity clearly had an understanding of religion (along with superstition, scruples, and magic) but thought of the gods as somewhat remote from human affairs. For the Greeks, they had little direct involvement in the affairs of the state.[32] The impulse behind classical political theory was a secular concern for the city and its citizens.

This secular tradition continues into modern times via the American Declaration of Independence, the Constitution, and the Bill of Rights. The Declaration of Independence refers to the 'protection of divine Providence' but it is in general terms a list of complaints against the British monarchy that justifies American independence. Substituting 'happiness' for John Locke's 'property', it famously promoted the ideas of 'life, liberty and happiness'. Similarly, in 1789, the French National Constituent Assembly, influenced by Thomas Jefferson and General Lafayette, adopted the Declaration of the Rights of Man and the Citizen. Insofar as religion entered into the political discourse on the city and the citizen, it was understood

---

[28] Armando Salvatore, *The Sociology of Islam: Knowledge, Power and Civility* (Chichester: John Wiley & Sons Ltd., 2016).

[29] See Balot in this volume; Volpp in this volume.

[30] Hannah Arendt, 'The Public and the Private Realm', in *The Portable Hannah Arendt*, edited and introduced by Peter Baehr (New York: Penguin Books, 2000), pp. 182–230.

[31] Julia Annas, *The Morality of Happiness* (New York: Oxford University Press, 1993); Marcus Tullius Cicero, *On the Commonwealth and on the Laws*, edited and translated by James E.G. Zetzel (Cambridge: Cambridge University Press, 1999).

[32] John F. Shean, 'Spiteful Zeus: The Religious Background to Axial Age Greece', *Revue internationale de philosophie 276*, no. 2 (2016): pp. 151–170.

in terms of 'civil religion'. The idea was developed by Jean-Jacques Rousseau in Chapter 8 of his *The Social Contract* of 1762 in which a civil religion was to function as the basis of social solidarity among citizens.[33] His religious view was basically one of deism, and civil religion was employed to recognize deity, an afterlife and the reward of virtue and punishment of vice as well as to reject all forms of religious intolerance. This civil religion was to be the work of lawyers rather than priests. In contemporary sociology the idea has been used extensively by Robert Bellah (1967) in a famous article on 'civil religion in America' that shaped much of the sociological debate about religion in public life in America.[34] Arguing against the narrow notion of secularization, he claimed that there is an American civil religious tradition that is separate from but connected to Christianity. This civil religion promoted the historical sense of America as the Israel of the New World. American history is one of sacrifice, commencing with the Civil War and concluding with the war in Vietnam. This public religion is periodically rejuvenated through festivals such as Thanksgiving. Adopting the language of Rousseau, Bellah concluded:

A republic will have republican customs—public participation in the exercise of power, political equality of citizens, a wide distribution of small and medium property with few very rich or very poor—customs that will lead to a public spiritedness, a willingness of the citizen to sacrifice his own interests for the common good, in a word a citizen motivated by republican virtue.[35]

RELIGIOUS CONCEPTIONS OF CITIZENSHIP

While the secularity of the idea of citizenship in the ancient world is well established, we can also conceive of religious membership as a form of religious or ecclesial citizenship. In this parallel form we can think of membership of a church in terms of the rituals, especially the sacraments such as baptism or the Eucharist that create and sustain religious communities, giving them both a theological rationalism and an emotional sense of membership. Émile Durkheim's definition of religion in *The Elementary Forms of Religious Life* (2002) as a 'unified system of belief and practice relative to the sacred, that is to say, things set apart and forbidden—beliefs and practices that unite people into a single moral community that is a church' is

---

[33] Jean-Jacques Rousseau, *The Social Contract*, translated with an Introduction by G.D.H. Cole (London: J.M. Dent and Sons, 1923).
[34] Robert N. Bellah, 'Civil Religion in America', *Daedalus* 96, no. 1 (1967): pp. 1–21.
[35] Robert N. Bellah, 'Religion and Legitimation in the American Republic', *Society* 15, no. 4 (1978): pp. 16–23, p. 18.

relevant to this analysis.[36] As with secular citizenship, there are rights, such as access to religious privileges (the sacraments), and duties (payment of church taxes or keeping the faith). In this ecclesial citizenship there are also legal traditions—canon law, the Shari'a, or the Torah. Religious citizenship can be interpreted as a parallel or alternative form of membership that is often in conflict with secular this-worldly citizenship.

Following Durkheim, there are two spheres of life—the sacred and the profane. This division of spheres was also the essence of St Augustine's political theory of two cities, which we could easily understand as a dual citizenship model. Augustine faced the problem that the Roman Empire represented the most powerful political system and the most sophisticated culture of its time. That system was diverse and typically sceptical of religious groups or cults that were overzealous and scrupulous. Was Christianity just another minority within the imperial system? Augustine attempted to solve the problem in his *De civitate Dei* in 413 CE by advocating the coexistence of an earthly (Roman) city with another celestial (Christian) city. Christians could remain loyal to Rome, while also anticipating their salvation and membership of a heavenly city. Augustine also faced the challenge that the abandonment of the Roman gods for the Christian God was an injustice to the traditional divinities which had resulted in the sacking of Rome in 410 CE. Augustine had to confront a Roman intelligentsia spread out across the Roman world that was made up of ascetic, otherworldly men, concerned, like himself, with the salvation of men's souls, yet standing aloof from the congregations of the Church, and dressed in their traditional, sober robes of their austere calling. Augustine summarized the dilemma of the Roman Christian in the notion of *Peregrinatio*, namely that the Christian is in the world but merely as a resident alien (or *peregrinus*). The resident alien is uncomfortable in the empirical world that surrounds him and he longs nostalgically for his true home. Peter Brown thus summarized *The City of God* as 'a book about being otherworldly in the world'.[37] Augustine's division between a secular and a sacred power, between secular spaces and holy ones, and between worldliness and otherworldliness has been a long-lasting political theory of the Christian churches throughout their post-Augustinian existence.

The problem with the two-cities solution is that churches typically rely on the state to crush civil strife and to supress heretics who challenge orthodox churches. Augustine was only too aware of these difficulties and for that reason is often regarded as a realist. In his struggle with the Donatists he came to abandon any opposition to religious coercion by secular powers. He also established the doctrine

---

[36] Émile Durkheim, *The Elementary Forms of the Religious Life*, translated by Joseph Ward Swain (New York: Dover Publications, 2008).

[37] Peter Robert Lamont Brown, *Augustine of Hippo: A Biography* (Berkeley: University of California Press, 2000), p. 324.

of a just war and concluded that soldiers are obliged to fight in wars that have been declared just by a lawful authority.[38]

Another way of conceiving of this relationship is exemplified by Lutheranism in Scandinavian societies where the two spheres are best described as entangled. Firstly, there is the issue that in Lutheran societies the provision of services and welfare rights involves the entwinement of religious and secular institutions (Van den Breemer, Casanova, and Wyller, 2014).[39] Secondly, in Europe, religion often appears to continue to define European identity. In Israel, there is an ongoing tension between the Zionist foundations of a secular state and the ultra-orthodox tradition. In Islam, politics and religion appear to be more closely associated from the constitution of Medina onwards and through the early Islamic empires. In the modern world, Islamic fundamentalists call for making Shari'a the basis of law for Muslims wherever they live.

Religious Diversity and Public Reason

The discussion so far has made the implicit assumption that within each nation-state there is a more or less homogeneous civil society in which there is one dominant religious tradition. This interpretation was of course the key idea behind the Treaty of Westphalia of 1648 that brought the wars of religion to a close and imposed a system where each principality would have one dominant religious tradition and where conversion would be proscribed. The Treaty provided a simple territorial solution to the problem of religious differences between Protestant and Catholic communities. The final sections of this chapter therefore examine the problems associated with growing religious diversity in Western societies as a consequence of global migration and the resulting increase in religious minorities.

Contemporary political theory and political sociology have considered various models and strategies by which different religious communities and traditions can be satisfactorily accommodated in Western liberal democratic societies with a tradition of secular citizenship. The real issue behind debates about diversity, liberalism, and multiculturalism is the specific question of the inclusion of Islam

---

[38] Paul Weithman, 'Augustine's Political Philosophy', in Eleonore Stump and Norman Kretzmann, eds., *The Cambridge Companion to Augustine* (Cambridge: Cambridge University Press, 2001), pp. 234–252, p. 247.

[39] Rosemarie Van den Breemer, José Casanova, and Trygve Wyller, *Secular and Sacred?: The Scandinavian Case of Religion in Human Rights, Law and Public Space*, volume 15 (Göttingen: Vandenhoeck & Ruprecht, 2014).

in the West that has created two controversial responses, namely, the notion of Islamofascism that flourished among Western critics after the Iranian Revolution, and Islamophobia.[40] Veiling, Shari'a, separate religious schooling, a different school curriculum, the building of mosques and minarets, halal certificates, and in Switzerland the requirement that children shake hands with the school teacher before morning classes have raised issues about the emergence of 'parallel communities' of Muslims that are not well integrated into Western democracies. It is, however, difficult to generalize about Muslim minorities, because the European experience is not uniform and there are in addition important differences between the United States and Europe. Of course, the problem of religious differences is not simply an issue about Islam but also involves ultra-Orthodox Jews, Mormons, Scientology, and Hinduism.

We have seen that the problems of social diversity in the civil sphere were regarded as a threat to sovereignty and the coherence of the Greek city-state at the very beginning of political theory. We also saw in the ancient world how the particularities of personal relationships were assumed to conflict with the processes of building solidarity in political life and in the wider sphere of civil life. In Greek political thought, the laws (*nomoi*) were the symbolic walls that protected the city and its citizens from the threat of diversity and division. Because these social ties in the civil sphere are constantly compromised by the selfish interests of actors competing in the market or by the traditional bonds of familial relationships, there is an important role for civil repair—social and political acts that are designed to rebuild confidence, solidarity, and trust.

In this section of my argument, two influential approaches to the problem of achieving difficult political objectives such as justice, equality, and tolerance in divided societies and protection of the security of citizens are considered. The work of John Rawls and Jürgen Habermas has been prominent in recent commentaries on secular and religious citizenship. At first sight this might appear to be an unusual combination of liberal and critical theory, but their concerns are similar in their quest for secure grounds of consensus in religiously divided societies. In drawing attention to their accounts of religion in their approaches to politics and civil society, I treat religion as a litmus test of theories of civil society. The reason for this strategy is that, in modern times religion and religious divisions appear to be in the vanguard of social conflict and hence an important test of any theory of social order.

Rawls's liberal solution with its unique vocabulary of 'overlapping consensus of comprehensive doctrines', 'justice as fairness', 'the original position', and 'the veil of ignorance' has been highly influential in both political and legal theory.[41]

---

[40] Norman Podhoretz, *World War IV: The Long Struggle against Islamofascism* (New York: Vintage, 2007).

[41] John Rawls, *Political Liberalism*, (New York: Columbia University Press, 1993).

He seeks to establish the basis of a liberal and lawful society with an overlapping consensus of fundamental beliefs while at the same time recognizing the difficulties in achieving that end in any society deeply divided against itself. In *The Law of Peoples*, he notes that, '[b]ecause religious, philosophical or moral unity is neither possible nor necessary for social unity, if social stability is not merely a *modus operandi*, it must be rooted in a reasonable political conception of right and justice affirmed by an overlapping consensus of comprehensive doctrines'.[42] He goes on to assert that '[t]he unity of a reasonable Society of Peoples does not require religious unity'.[43] There are, however, restrictive conditions on religious liberty, namely, that in 'a reasonably just society of well-ordered peoples, citizens do not seek to convert others to their religions'.[44] In describing such a liberal state of affairs, Rawls's theory has to rely on an important simplifying assumption, namely, that people are both rational and reasonable. Thus, if people employ 'public reason in their dealings with one another, toleration must follow'.[45] These Rawlsian assumptions became the basis for Habermas's notion of the mutual obligation on both secular and religious citizens in a post-secular society to engage in meaningful dialogue.

What is the problem to which these theories offer a solution? One response is paradoxically that the secular state needs foundations in morality and religion that a liberal state cannot coercively create. In his *State, Society and Liberty*, the German legal and political theorist Ernst-Wolfgang Böckenförde perfectly captures the dilemma for which contemporary political and social theory has sought an answer.[46] The Böckenförde dilemma states that a liberal-democratic state depends on a liberal culture that it cannot produce by the typical coercive means at its disposal, namely, law and order. More precisely, a liberal state can only survive if the civil liberties that it bestows on its own citizens acquire some moral support from civil society—both from the moral character of the individuals who make up society and from a certain homogeneity of society at large. Yet, it cannot of itself produce these internal forces of moral regulation by legal compulsion or authoritative decree without, at the same time, destroying its liberal foundations. To enforce moral and religious harmony by decree would take the state back to the confessional civil wars of the sixteenth and seventeenth centuries, from which it had departed at the time of the Treaty of Westphalia in 1648.

In January 2004, Habermas, an influential and determined defender of political modernity, engaged in an important public debate with Cardinal Ratzinger, who was later to become Pope Benedict XVI.[47] At stake was the foundational basis

---

[42] John Rawls, *The Law of Peoples; with 'The Idea of Public Reason Revisited'* (Cambridge: Harvard University Press, 1999), p. 16.

[43] Ibid., p. 8.   [44] Ibid., p. 19.   [45] Ibid., p. 19.

[46] Ernst Wolfgang Böckenförde, *State, Society, and Liberty: Studies in Political Theory and Constitutional Law* (London: Berg, 1991).

[47] Jürgen Habermas and Joseph Ratzinger, *Dialektik der Säkularisierung* (Freiburg: Herder, 2005).

of the liberal modern state and hence the debate took off from the Böckenförde dilemma. Throughout his career Habermas had been a prominent advocate of secularization, believing that religion would eventually disappear from the public domain. However, his views eventually changed in response to new developments, such as the global spread of Abrahamic religious fundamentalism. In the debate with Ratzinger, he acknowledged that religion has something important to offer in public life. Furthermore, religious citizens could participate in public discussion, provided that they accepted strict conditions (such as hermeneutical self-reflection, the awareness of the distinction between the role of religion in faith communities and in public life, the acceptance of the secular state, and the requirements of rational debate). In short, he acknowledged the role of religion within the public sphere. In fact, in a post-secular society, Christianity, and more specifically Roman Catholicism, could become a source of culture and nourishment for the moral fibre and social solidarity of democratic societies. The Böckenförde dilemma could be resolved by a democratic dialogue resulting in a workable consensus of secular and religious beliefs and values or, in terms of this chapter, between secular and religious citizenship.

In a 'post-secular society', citizens have an obligation to make their beliefs publicly accessible and to strive to understand what they have in common in terms of belief with other citizens.[48] Hypothetically Habermas recognized two apparently mutually exclusive camps in Western societies. On the one hand, there are secular rationalists, who adhere to the notion that religion is irrational and a barrier to social progress. On the other hand, there are religious fundamentalists, who believe they already possess an absolute Truth that comes ultimately from revelation and thus requires no further justification.[49] The dilemma of liberal-democratic societies is how to build a social consensus between such apparently incommensurable positions. Post-secularism demands that secular citizens cannot just assume that their beliefs are rational and valid without further argumentation; and religious citizens cannot flatly claim that their faith means that they have no need to explain or defend their beliefs. Both secular and religious citizens must strive to translate their beliefs into mutually comprehensive and intelligent statements about their values.

The problem of translation emerged from the work of Rawls, in which policies that were advanced on the basis of religion could only be accepted on the condition that they had to be corroborated in terms of properly political reasons. Religious persons can participate in public debate provided that, 'in due course', their contributions to any discussion of public issues can be rendered into a framework of intelligible secular reasons. This famous 'proviso' was said to place an onerous

---

[48] Jürgen Habermas, 'Religion in the Public Sphere', *European Journal of Philosophy* 14, no. 1 (2006): pp. 1–25.

[49] Austin Harrington, 'Habermas and the Post-Secular Society', *European Journal of Social Theory* 10, no. 4 (2007): pp. 543–560.

'cognitive burden' on religious citizens, who are likely to hold their world-views on the basis of faith rather than through reasonable reflection. In those religious traditions that hold that the divine message is ineffable, it is difficult to see how such a dialogue could begin to take place.[50] The proviso of reasonable communication presupposes the opposite, namely, that religious truths are effable. Consequently Habermas has not overcome this Rawlsian requirement, but has merely shifted the problem of translation to the sphere of formal political institutions.[51] For one thing, in his account of the public sphere, only secular reasons can enter into the legislative process, while religious ideas are confined to informal debate in terms of political advocacy. A weaker condition of accountability would not require religious citizens to translate their beliefs into a secular idiom that would in fact reject their beliefs, but simply require them to render those beliefs compatible with democratic principles of deliberation. In practice, this would mean that, if religious citizens are to be taken seriously, they must recognize the fact that they live in a society with people of other faiths and with citizens who are atheists. This weaker version does not explain why religious citizens might want to be taken seriously by people of no faith.

Clearly, there are on-going problems with attempts to defend the idea of communicative rationality in multi-faith societies when controversial issues are at stake. In recent years, religious objections to major social issues—such as abortion, euthanasia, evolutionary thought, homosexuality, and same-sex marriage—have played a critical role in political debate and the legislative process. In particular, legislation on same-sex marriage in the United States of America in 2015 has remained controversial and has produced deep divisions in the public sphere, but with a rather steady trend of more and more states recognizing same-sex marriage and the Supreme Court legalizing it throughout the US territory in its landmark decision *Obergefell v. Hodges*, 576 U.S. These unsettled disputes pose significant practical and theoretical issues to the solutions put forward by Rawls and Habermas. While philosophers grappling with the issue of religious tolerance have been concerned primarily with Islam, political and legal debates about abortion, contraception, circumcision, marriage, and divorce have also exercised Christian fundamentalists and orthodox Jews. It appears that translation cannot easily secure mutual agreement and there is no 'overlapping consensus' over a range of issues that appear to define Christian morality. Public debate appears to deepen divisions, rather than transcend them.

---

[50] Bryan S. Turner, 'T. H. Marshall, Social Rights and English National Identity', *Citizenship Studies* 13, no. 1 (2009): pp. 65–73.

[51] Cristina Lafont, 'Reason and the Public Sphere: What Are the Deliberative Obligations of Democratic Citizenship?', in Craig Calhoun, ed., *Habermas and Relgion* (Cambridge: Polity Press, 2013), pp. 230–248.

Religious Exemptions and Equality
of Citizenship

There is another challenge to liberal arguments in favour of an accommodation between religious and secular citizens. While liberals have generally welcomed cosmopolitan values that favour multiculturalism, there is a remaining issue around national sovereignty that cannot easily accept legal pluralism. Liberal tolerance of diversity in modern societies runs up against the problem of exemptions that in turn are seen to foster parallel communities and social fragmentation. It raises questions about the importance of equality over difference.[52] If the law allows for exemptions from taxation, military service, dress codes, and humane slaughtering of animals, does this erode a basic principle of equal treatment of all citizens? The presence of exemptions for religious citizens from secular laws brings into view the free rider problem. One criticism of an over-zealous accommodation of the demands of pious citizens is that they expect to enjoy the benefits of liberalism—freedom of religion, public respect, security of property and person, free elections, and so forth—while not themselves subscribing to liberal secularism or vigorously defending it.

Against this argument, religious citizens might claim that they do not in fact enjoy the benefits of a secular world that does not always give them respect or personal security. Again much of the public debate is not about religious citizens in general but about Muslims in particular. Thus, Muslims might claim reasonably that they suffer from Islamophobia in secular cultures and that they need separate schools and legal exemptions to protect their communities and their faith. How widespread is Islamophobia? Before World War II Muslims were in fact generally well integrated into European societies. In Weimar Germany they were a middle-class and socially accepted community, but this middle-class cohort of Muslims largely disappeared in the aftermath of the war.[53] It was not until 1997 that the concept of 'Islamophobia' was first defined in Britain by the Runnymede Trust (1997) to describe the nature and scope of prejudice against Muslims and to recommend that the 1976 *Race Relations Act* be amended to make discrimination on religious grounds unlawful. This amendment was rejected by the government, arguing that the *Human Rights Act* of 1998 would provide sufficient protection of minorities.[54] Perhaps unsurprisingly after 9/11, there has been a growing literature on Islamophobia, indicating widespread hostility towards and fear of Muslim communities in Western societies. There is even a view that the anti-Muslim discourse

---

[52] See Barry (n 6).

[53] Esra Özyürek, *Being German, Becoming Muslim: Race, Religion, and Conversion in the New Europe* (Princeton: Princeton University Press, 2014).

[54] Joel S. Fetzer and J. Christopher Soper, *Muslims and the State in Britain, France, and Germany* (Cambridge: Cambridge University Press, 2005), p. 32.

is rampant, in fact constituting an 'industry' and that Islamophobia is simply an illustration of a traditional Orientalist fear of Islam.[55] While Europe appears to be struggling with diversity as such, Islam is thought to be a special challenge.

Despite general public anxiety, it is important to recognize that the empirical data on the situation of Muslims in Europe present a very mixed, and often confusing, picture. Muslims make up around five million inhabitants of metropolitan France. In the Parisian suburbs (*banlieues*), Muslims from North Africa and the Middle East live in crime-ridden, depressed, and squalid housing estates. Although there is clear evidence that Muslims in Paris and Marseilles are an excluded social group, according to a survey from 2006, 74 per cent of the French population said that there was no conflict between being a devout Muslim and living in a modern society.[56] Nevertheless, evidence of the marginalization of Muslims in Europe is ample. In her broad survey of the relevant data, Jocelyne Cesari concludes that, '[a]cross the board, surveys indicate that Europeans consider Islam to be incompatible with Western values.'[57] There has been, especially in France, a divisive battle over veiling.[58] For Humayun Ansari and Farid Hafez, 'It would not be an exaggeration to say that many influential individuals and institutions in the West today have come to perceive Islam and Muslims, particularly since the end of the Cold War, as the principal threat to the survival and progress of Western civilization, a civilization founded on and formed by Christian ethos and values.'[59] As evidence they cite the Swiss minaret ban, the Danish cartoon incident, the rise of the British National Party, the leadership of the Austrian Freedom Party by Jörg Haider, and right-wing populism in Germany, such as Pegida and the *Bürgerbewegung pro Köln*. There is plentiful popular criticism of Islam, most notably in the European context, exemplified by Ayaan Hirsi Ali's *Infidel*.[60]

Perhaps the principal intellectual lesson of academic research is that understanding domestic or national conflicts cannot be undertaken without a detailed and close understanding of international affairs. The notion of a Christian Europe surrounded by barbarians does of course have a long history. *Europa* was seen as a social and political unity that was held together by emperors and popes. As Sheldon S. Wolin reminds us, such notions as *imperium christianum, regnum Europae*, or *societas christiana* were developed to distinguish the inside from the outside: 'And the same theme has recurred in twentieth-century writings concerned with the challenges of Communism, Fascism, and Asian nationalism to the common set of cultural values associated with the "West".'[61] As in mediaeval times, the domestic relation between religious and secular citizens remains defined by the liminality of the borders that circumvent European societies and their interface with Islam.

[55] Deepa Kumar, *Islamophobia and the Politics of Empire* (Chicago: Haymarket Books, 2012).
[56] Bowen (n 18), p. 3.   [57] Cesari (n 14), 2013, p. 15.
[58] Christian Joppke, *Veil: Mirror of Identity* (Cambridge: Polity Press, 2009).
[59] Humayun Ansari and Farid Hafez, *From the Far Right to the Mainstream: Islamophobia in Party Politics and the Media* (Frankfurt: Campus Verlag, 2012), p. 13.
[60] Ayaan Hirsi Ali, *Infidel* (New York: Simon and Schuster, 2008).
[61] Wolin (n 23), p. 105.

Conclusion: The Management
of Religion

In this analysis of secular and religious membership, the two spheres are concep-tually distinct but interconnected and overlapping in empirical terms. Tensions between the secular and the religious have a long history in Christianity, going back to St Paul's problems over Jews and converts to the early Church. It was, however, St Augustine who classically propounded a solution to the vexed relationship with imperial Rome by developing his two-citizenship contrast between life in the secu-lar civil society and life in the coming kingdom.

With the rise of the nation-state from the seventeenth to the late twentieth cen-tury, national citizenship as an identity was developed as the apparatus of the state (in terms of taxation, police force, a health service, and national curriculum) and was expanded in the context of international competition and conflict. Western secularization also contributed to the definition of modern citizenship. The spread of the passport as an important secular marker of membership transformed deni-zens into citizens.

The modern period is one where the global movement of people has increased social diversity and raised difficult questions about the relationship between secu-lar and religious membership. Despite liberal values and democratic constitutions, governments exercise the management of religions in creating a legal framework that regulates dress codes, interpersonal behaviour, health, and so forth. Against this trend, we have a world of exemptions by which general laws do not apply equally to all citizens. Although Islam has been increasingly regulated by Western governments, this dialectic of regulation and exemption applies to a wide range of religions and covers many issues related to sex, marriage, reproduction, divorce, and assisted death—in other words, the status of the body. The extension of govern-ment regulation over religion and the human body, especially with respect to Islam, opens up new areas of research in the social sciences.

Bibliography

Ali, Ayaan Hirsi, *Infidel* (New York: Simon & Schuster, 2008).
Annas, Julia, *The Morality of Happiness* (New York: Oxford University Press, 1993).
Ansari, Humayun, and Farid Hafez, *From the Far Right to the Mainstream: Islamophobia in Party Politics and the Media* (Frankfurt: Campus Verlag, 2012).
Arendt, Hannah, 'The Public and the Private Realm', in *The Portable Hannah Arendt*, edited and introduced by Peter Baehr (New York: Penguin Books, 2000), pp. 182–230.

Aristotle, *Politics* (New York: Dover Publications, 2000).

Barkey, Karen, *Empire of Difference: The Ottomans in Comparative Perspective* (Cambridge: Cambridge University Press, 2008).

Barry, Brian, *Culture and Equality* (Cambridge: Polity Press, 2001).

Bellah, Robert N., 'Civil Religion in America', *Daedalus 96*, no. 1 (1967): pp. 1–21.

Bellah, Robert N., 'Religion and Legitimation in the American Republic', *Society 15*, no. 4 (1978): pp. 16–23.

Böckenförde, Ernst Wolfgang, *State, Society, and Liberty: Studies in Political Theory and Constitutional Law* (London: Berg, 1991).

Bowen, John R., *Can Islam Be French?: Pluralism and Pragmatism in a Secularist State* (Princeton: Princeton University Press, 2011).

Brown, Peter Robert Lamont, *Augustine of Hippo: A Biography* (Berkeley: University of California Press, 2000).

Cesari, Jocelyne, *Muslims in the West after 9/11: Religion, Politics and Law* (London: Routledge, 2009).

Cesari, Jocelyne, *Why the West Fears Islam: An Exploration of Muslims in Liberal Democracies* (New York: Palgrave Macmillan, 2013).

Cicero, Marcus Tullius, *On the Commonwealth and on the Laws*, edited and translated by James E.G. Zetzel (Cambridge: Cambridge University Press, 1999).

Durkheim, Émile, *The Elementary Forms of the Religious Life*, translated by Joseph Ward Swain (New York: Dover Publications, 2008).

Fetzer, Joel S. and J. Christopher Soper, *Muslims and the State in Britain, France, and Germany* (Cambridge: Cambridge University Press, 2005).

Gorski, Philip S., *The Post-Secular in Question: Religion in Contemporary Society* (New York: NYU Press, 2012).

Habermas, Jürgen, 'Religion in the Public Sphere', *European Journal of Philosophy 14*, no. 1 (2006): pp. 1–25.

Habermas, Jürgen, *Between Naturalism and Religion: Philosophical Essays* (Cambridge: Polity Press, 2008).

Habermas, Jürgen and Joseph Ratzinger, *Dialektik der Säkularisierung* (Freiburg: Herder, 2005).

Harrington, Austin, 'Habermas and the Post-Secular Society', *European Journal of Social Theory 10*, no. 4 (2007): pp. 543–560.

Hirschl, Ran, *Constitutional Theocracy* (Cambridge: Harvard University Press, 2011).

Hodgson, Marshall G.S., *The Venture of Islam*, volume 1 (Chicago: University of Chicago Press, 1974).

Joppke, Christian, *Veil: Mirror of Identity* (Cambridge: Polity Press, 2009).

Kasper, Walter, *The Catholic Church: Nature, Reality and Mission* (London: Bloomsbury Publishing, 2015).

Kumar, Deepa, *Islamophobia and the Politics of Empire* (Chicago: Haymarket Books, 2012).

Kymlicka, Will, 'Testing the Bounds of Liberal Multiculturalism', paper presented at the Canadian Council of Muslim Women's conference, 'Muslim Women's Equality Rights in the Justice System: Gender, Religion and Pluralism', Toronto, Ontario, 2005, online: http://www.academia.edu/2397540/Testing_the_Bounds_of_Liberal_Multiculturalism_The_Sharia_Debate_in_Ontario_2005_.

Lafont, Cristina, 'Reason and the Public Sphere: What Are the Deliberative Obligations of Democratic Citizenship?', in Craig Calhoun, ed., *Habermas and Relgion* (Cambridge: Polity Press, 2013), pp. 230–248.

Mahmood, Saba, *Religious Difference in a Secular Age* (Princeton: Princeton University Press, 2015).

Marshall, Thomas H., *Citizenship and Social Class*, volume 11 (Cambridge: Cambridge University Press, 1950).

Martin, David, *The Future of Christianity* (Abingdon: Routledge, 2016 [2011]).

Masuzawa, Tomoko, *The Invention of World Religions: Or, How European Universalism Was Preserved in the Language of Pluralism* (Chicago: University of Chicago Press, 2005).

Özyürek, Esra, *Being German, Becoming Muslim: Race, Religion, and Conversion in the New Europe* (Princeton: Princeton University Press, 2014).

Podhoretz, Norman, *World War IV: The Long Struggle against Islamofascism* (New York: Vintage, 2007).

Rawls, John, *Political Liberalism* (New York: Columbia University Press, 1993).

Rawls, John, *The Law of Peoples; with, 'The Idea of Public Reason Revisited'* (Cambridge: Harvard University Press, 2001).

Roffe, Jonathan, 'Book Review: Alain Badiou, *Saint Paul:The Foundation of Universalism*', *Philosophy in Review 24* (2004): pp. 5–7.

Rousseau, Jean-Jacques, *The Social Contract*, translated with an Introduction by G.D.H. Cole (London: J.M. Dent and Sons, 1923).

Salvatore, Armando, *The Sociology of Islam: Knowledge, Power and Civility* (Chichester: John Wiley & Sons, 2016).

Saxonhouse, Arlene W., *Fear of Diversity: The Birth of Political Science in Ancient Greek Thought* (Chicago: University of Chicago Press, 1995).

Shean, John F., 'Spiteful Zeus: The Religious Background to Axial Age Greece', *Revue internationale de philosophie 276*, no. 2 (2016): pp. 151–170.

Shklar, Judith N., *American Citizenship: The Quest for Inclusion*, volume 3 (Cambridge: Harvard University Press, 1991).

Taubes, Jacob, *The Political Theology of Paul*, edited by Aleida Assmann, translated by Dana Hollander (Stanford, CA: Stanford University Press, 2004).

Taylor, Charles, *A Secular Age* (Cambridge: Harvard University Press, 2009).

Turner, Bryan S., 'Citizenship East and West: Reflections on Revolutions and Civil Society', in Gerard Delanty, ed., *Europe and Asia beyond East and West* (Abingdon: Routledge, 2006): pp. 148–160.

Turner, Bryan S., 'The Enclave Society: Towards a Sociology of Immobility', *European Journal of Social Theory 10*, no. 2 (2007): pp. 287–304.

Turner, Bryan S., 'T.H. Marshall, Social Rights and English National Identity', *Citizenship Studies 13*, no. 1 (2009): pp. 65–73.

Turner, Bryan S., *Religion and Modern Society: Citizenship, Secularisation and the State* (Cambridge: Cambridge University Press, 2011).

Turner, Bryan S., 'Sociology of Islam: The Desiderata', *Sociology of Islam 1*, no. 1–2 (2013): pp. 14–16.

Turner, Bryan S., *Marx and the End of Orientalism* (New York: Routledge, 2014 [1978]).

Turner, Bryan S., 'Review Essay: The Scandinavian Model of Secularities', *European Journal of Social Theory 17*, no. 4 (2014): pp. 534–543.

Van den Breemer, Rosemarie, José Casanova, and Trygve Wyller, *Secular and Sacred?: The Scandinavian Case of Religion in Human Rights, Law and Public Space*, volume 15 (Göttingen: Vandenhoeck & Ruprecht, 2014).

Weber, Max, *The City*, translated and edited by Don Martindale and Gertrud Neuwirth (Glencoe: Free Press, 1958).

Weithman, Paul, 'Augustine's Political Philosophy', in Eleonore Stump and Norman Kretzmann, eds., *The Cambridge Companion to Augustine* (Cambridge: Cambridge University Press, 2001), pp. 234–252.

Weller, Paul, Kingsley Purdam, Nazila Ghanea, and Sariya Cheruvallil-Contractor, *Religion or Belief, Discrimination and Equality: Britain in Global Contexts* (London: Bloomsbury Academic, 2013).

Wolin, Sheldon S., *Politics and Vision: Continuity and Innovation in Western Political Thought* (Princeton: Princeton University Press, 2009).

CHAPTER 23

....

PERFORMATIVE
CITIZENSHIP

....

ENGIN ISIN[*]

INTRODUCTION
....

CITIZENSHIP as a legal institution governs who may and may not *act* as a subject of rights within any given polity.[1] Being 'a subject of rights' means having

* I am happy to acknowledge this chapter as a collaborative effort. I am truly grateful to all editors, especially Maarten Vink and Rainer Bauböck, for their comments and responses to various drafts of this chapter. Maarten and Rainer have provided detailed comments and corrections. I have also immensely benefited from comments by Linda Bosniak who provided insights into this chapter that I had not seen. I am also grateful to questions and comments provided during the workshop especially by Christian Joppke, Will Kymlicka, and David Owen. Aleksandra Älund, Anne McNevin, Evelyn Ruppert, and Kim Rygiel provided insightful comments for which I am grateful. Karen Zivi provided two marvellously close readings with valuable suggestions. The chapter owes a lot to her work and her engagement with it. Jack Harrington provided a judicious and incisive copy editing. I, of course, bear responsibility for all its shortcomings.
    [1] In this chapter I will use the generic concept 'polity' to indicate any organized society with a political arrangement, including nation-states as one specific type of polity.

both the capacity and the authority to exercise rights *and* duties. Citizenship governs whether I may or may not travel to work, or study, in another country; how long I may stay there; to which country and how I pay my taxes; whether I serve as a soldier, I may drive, I may drink in public, I may vote, I receive health care or unemployment benefits, I may marry my same-sex partner, and when I may retire, and much else besides. Many such rights and duties associated with citizenship have developed especially since the eighteenth century. Today a combination of such rights and duties can be described as the regime of citizenship of any polity.[2] Yet, being a subject of these rights involves political struggle. I may or may not act to exercise my rights or claim other rights and rights for others or to refuse duties. I may ask questions about why I may not marry my partner. I may refuse to serve in the army, may refuse to vote in an election, may occupy public spaces as a protest. What citizens may or may not do involves political struggle because there will be disagreement not only about all these questions but also about who is a subject of these rights—citizens—and who does not enjoy them—non-citizens. In other words, because citizenship is *constitutive* of rights and because who can exercise and claim these rights is itself *contestable*, citizenship is practised not only by exercising these rights but also by claiming them. In this chapter I outline a perspective that broadens the conventional view of citizenship as a legal institution and expands on its performative aspects. I will argue that a performative perspective on citizenship as making rights claims across multiple social groups and polities reveals its creative and transformative possibilities. I have two main objectives. First, I want to focus our attention on the actions of actors, on how people creatively perform citizenship rather than following a script. This allows us to appreciate that how people perform citizenship plays an important role in contesting and constructing citizenship and attaching meanings to rights. Second, I hope to highlight that those engaged in the constitution of citizenship are not always citizens in the conventional sense of members of a nation-state, do not always act in the context of democratic or Euro-American polities, and may contest and constitute more than one understanding of citizenship at a time.

I shall use 'performative citizenship' in five distinct but overlapping senses, that: (a) citizenship involves political and social struggles over who may and may not act as a subject of rights; (b) these struggles feature not only citizens but also non-citizens as relational actors; (c) citizens and non-citizens include different social groups making rights claims; (d) people enact citizenship by exercising, claiming, and performing rights and duties, and; (e) when people enact citizenship they creatively transform its meanings and functions.[3] I will argue that all these senses are present when performative citizenship accomplishes its transformative

² On citizenship regimes see Vink in this volume.

³ Rutvica Andrijasevic, 'Acts of Citizenship as Methodology', in Engin F. Isin and Michael Saward, eds., *Enacting European Citizenship* (Cambridge: Cambridge University Press, 2013), pp. 47–65; Claudia

possibilities.[4] I will first expand on the five senses of performative citizenship I have just listed.[5] I will then illustrate performative citizenship in democratic and non-democratic polities. Then I will consider performative citizenship not only across social groups but also across polities. The concluding section discusses the emerging research on performative citizenship and highlights four research problems discussed in the literature.

The Senses of Performative Citizenship

The first sense in which citizenship is performative concerns the issue of struggle. Although citizenship is often considered a more or less stable membership of a state, a performative perspective considers citizenship as anything but stable. Who may and may not act as a subject of rights is determined by ongoing political and social struggles over not only the content of rights but also who are or are not entitled to them. If performative citizenship is a struggle over the subjects of rights, this struggle creates a scene in which social groups contest their similarities and differences. This argument is predicated on a sociological proposition that in any given polity there is often a social group whose *particular* characteristics dominate as seemingly *universal* characteristics.[6] If we recognize that since the eighteenth century first in Euro-America and then across the world the nation-state became

Aradau and Jef Huysmans, 'Critical Methods in International Relations: The Politics of Techniques, Devices and Acts', *European Journal of International Relations* 20, no. 3 (2014): pp. 596–619.

[4] To approach citizenship as performative acts draws inspiration from ordinary language philosophy, performance studies, and symbolic interactionism. It is beyond the scope of this chapter to discuss these sources. The word 'performative' was used by philosopher J.L. Austin in *How to Do Things with Words* (Oxford: Oxford University Press, 1962). He distinguished performative from constative utterances to emphasize how we perform acts *in* and *by* using language as opposed to describing a state of affairs. Since Austin, performativity became a particular approach in social sciences and humanities to study how people perform their subjectivity. For an overview see James Loxley, *Performativity* (London: Routledge, 2007). For performativity in performances studies see Tracy C. Davis, *The Cambridge Companion to Performance Studies* (Cambridge: Cambridge University Press, 2008). See also Andrew Parker and Eve Kosofsky Sedgwick, *Performativity and Performance* (London: Routledge, 1995). For performativity in sociology of symbolic interactionism see Erving Goffman, *Interaction Ritual: Essays on Face-to-Face Behaviour* (New York: Doubleday, 1967); *Encounters: Two Studies in the Sociology of Interaction* (Indianapolis: Bobbs-Merrill, 1961).

[5] See Bosniak in this volume.

[6] Iris Marion Young, 'Polity and Group Difference: A Critique of the Ideal of Universal Citizenship', *Ethics* 99, no. 2 (1989): pp. 250–274.

the dominant polity, we must acknowledge those who were *disqualified* as citizens. To put it conversely, the particular characteristics of a narrow social group, such as being perceived as propertied, adult, male, rational, white, Christian, heterosexual, and able-bodied became the dominant universal characteristics in the modern state. These characteristics created various other social groups as subjects without rights: the poor, young, women, irrational, black, non-Christian (Muslim, Indigenous, Jewish), ethnic minorities, queers (lesbian, gay, bisexual, transgender, questioning, intersex), and disabled people were deemed not capable of fulfilling the duties of citizenship and hence acting as citizens.

It was only in the twentieth century that the struggles of women, blacks, and queers started to significantly challenge this domination. These social struggles began unravelling the dominant characteristics of citizenship. This unravelling is still under way. We belong to an age when the dominant citizen-subject and *his* (only much later *their*) characteristics are challenged yet where the subject positions of its contestants remain as precarious and subaltern as ever. Youth, children, disabled, Muslims, the poor, blacks, women, queers—in any combination of these—make rights claims to the characteristics of citizenship so that they might cross from their precarious positions to at least more liveable positions.[7]

The second sense in which citizenship is performative concerns how social groups struggling for rights bring into play both citizens and non-citizens. The social groups I have mentioned above do not struggle to become subjects of rights from identical positions. They occupy different subject positions ranging from citizens (insiders) to strangers, outsiders, and aliens.[8] We have already suggested that citizens are those subjects whose entitlements or privileges are instituted as civil, political, and social rights. Often *strangers* are those subjects who, while accepted into citizenship, are still considered strangers in the sense that they have not yet fulfilled requirements to act as citizens. Modern examples are women (in nineteenth-century Britain) and blacks (in twentieth-century America) as both social groups that were deemed strangers of citizenship because dominant social groups considered them as lacking capacities. Yet both women and later blacks were also understood as indispensable parts of the polity that fulfilled functions for it (reproduction for women as mothers, labour for blacks as slaves first and then as workers).[9] By contrast, those social groups who are deemed *outsiders* to citizenship may find

---

[7] See Donaldson and Kymlicka in this volume (focusing on how capacity to make rights claims is denied to certain categories of subjects: small children, mentally handicapped, and domestic animals. Their argument raises a challenge for any theory that presupposes cognitive capacities for performing citizenship).

[8] See Engin F. Isin, *Being Political: Genealogies of Citizenship* (Minneapolis: University of Minnesota Press, 2002); Elizabeth F. Cohen, *Semi-Citizenship in Democratic Politics* (Cambridge: Cambridge University Press, 2009); Linda Bosniak, *The Citizen and the Alien* (Princeton: Princeton University Press, 2006).

[9] See Smith in this volume.

themselves as migrants and refugees struggling for the right to be present in a polity. The difference between strangers and outsiders is often contingent on disposability or deportability: strangers are sometimes accepted as indispensable yet corrigible (i.e., subject of/to discipline) whereas outsiders may sometimes become indispensable *yet* incorrigible (i.e., subject of/to punishment). Yet criminalization and imprisonment can also sometimes play on young black men, for example, such that they can straddle the positions of stranger and outsider. In fact, straddling between these subject positions provides the dynamics of citizenship as play rather than a static institution. Those deemed as *aliens* of a polity typically face total rejection of compatibility with or even respectability for acquiring or accessing citizenship. Categories of people such as enemy combatants or terrorists correspond to such irredeemable or rejected subjects.[10]

The subject positions of citizens, strangers, outsiders, and aliens are neither static nor impermeable. There is a huge variety of social groups that move through or across these positions. The boundaries between citizens, strangers, outsiders, and aliens are dynamic and permeable precisely because they *are* objects of social struggles. As we have already mentioned, people actually identify with or are ascribed to various social groups and constantly traverse subject positions from citizens to non-citizens. Moving across these positions or breaking down the boundaries between them involves struggles over rights.[11] Governing ourselves as political subjects means exercising rights that we may have (e.g., the right to vote) and claiming rights that we may not have (e.g., the right to same-sex marriage). It also means making claims for or against rights others do not have as members of multiple social groups. Through citizenship we sort out or negotiate these differences and settle on certain conventions by traversing these subject positions and their boundaries.

So far I have discussed performative citizenship as though each polity develops its own distinct and independent conventions of citizenship. Yet, many social groups, even those defined as nations, stretch across not only these social boundaries but also borders of polities. The ways in which people act out performative citizenship traverse not only social groups within polities but also across polities.[12] This gives rise to numerous performative contradictions in citizenship. These partly arise from the fact that, just as in relations between citizens and non-citizens, there

---

[10] About these forms of otherness in non-democratic polities, see Lori in this volume.

[11] Luin Goldring and Patricia Landolt, eds., *Producing and Negotiating Non-Citizenship: Precarious Legal Status in Canada* (Toronto: University of Toronto Press, 2013); David Weissbrodt, *The Human Rights of Non-Citizens* (Oxford: Oxford University Press, 2008).

[12] Rainer Bauböck recognizes this condition as 'citizenship constellations' where individuals simultaneously belong to several different polities (See Rainer Bauböck, 'Studying Citizenship Constellations', *Journal of Ethnic and Migration Studies* 36 (2010): pp. 847–859). Of these belongings 'external citizenship' is performed by people who live in one country but have a citizenship of another (see Rainer Bauböck, 'The Rights and Duties of External Citizenship', *Citizenship Studies* 13, no. 5 (2009): pp. 475–499).

are asymmetric power relations amongst polities. If indeed the sovereign state is the dominant polity of the modern age, it became dominant through a particular history involving Euro-American settler colonialism, colonialism, imperialism, and nationalism. Euro-American empires, such as Spanish, Portuguese, Dutch, French, British, American, and German, have left indelible marks on places they colonized through various governing strategies and technologies and imposed various citizenship arrangements on colonies. It is these arrangements that erased or displaced already existing ones between and amongst various social groups and replaced them with forms of imperial citizenship. These indelible marks of colonialism have not only inscribed names—such as the Americas, Africa, Asia, and the Middle East—but also citizenship arrangements whose legacies remain today. Euro-American empires subjected the peoples of these continents to various forms of asymmetric rule and justified this asymmetry by categorizing practices according to the presence or absence of the characteristics of the dominant social groups in imperial metropoles. So the citizen and non-citizen arrangements that obtained in each polity were disseminated across the metropole and the colony, creating both temporal and spatial arrangements of otherness. The colonial subjects were described for their fissiparous tribalism and were seen to have never understood or developed the characteristics of citizenship and its unifying powers.[13] If indeed colonial subjects were deemed to have understood citizenship, it was because it was 'borrowed' in postcolonial sovereign states. This makes studying citizenship in colonial and postcolonial states a vexed activity. Is the description 'what citizens and non-citizens perform in making rights claims' adequate to study citizenship in colonial and postcolonial states? It is important to emphasize here that approaching performative citizenship is partly inspired by this question and a direct response to it. A performative perspective on citizenship enables researchers to study various acts of making rights claims in societies and states before, during, and after colonization without making prior assumptions about the presence or absence of that which might be called citizenship.[14]

The third sense in which citizenship is performative is that it is enacted through 'making rights claims'. I have already used this phrase above to indicate both the content of struggles over rights and what people are doing when they perform citizenship.[15] It is a concept that citizenship studies inherits from social movement

---

[13] Jack Harrington, 'Orientalism, Political Subjectivity and the Birth of Citizenship between 1780 and 1830', *Citizenship Studies* 16, no. 5–6 (2012): pp. 573–586.

[14] Engin F. Isin, ed., *Citizenship after Orientalism: Transforming Political Theory* (London: Palgrave, 2015).

[15] Engin F. Isin, 'Claiming European Citizenship', in Engin F. Isin and Michael Saward, eds., *Enacting European Citizenship* (Cambridge: Cambridge University Press, 2013), pp. 19–46; Karen Zivi, *Making Rights Claims: A Practice of Democratic Citizenship* (Oxford: Oxford University Press, 2012); Horacio N. Roque Ramirez, 'Claiming Queer Cultural Citizenship: Gay Latino (Im)Migrant Acts In San Francisco', in P. Noguera, A. Hurtado, and E. Fergus, eds., *Invisible No More: Understanding the*

studies which have drawn attention to how movements for civil rights, gender struggles, environmental justice, global justice, and minority recognition have often articulated their 'claims' as rights.[16] The key lesson is that social movements use the language of rights to articulate the injustices people suffer and show that people resist the ascribing of duties to them and the denial of rights to them and others. Performative citizenship signifies both a struggle (making rights claims) and what that struggle performatively brings into being (the right to claim rights).

There is a difference between claiming to be a subject of rights and making particular rights claims. This is a crucial distinction and it is essential for understanding performative citizenship.[17] It enables researchers to study how people stage creative and transformative resistances and articulate claims against domination (e.g. oppression, repression, discrimination, inequality) and the injustices it precipitates.[18] Their focus is not only on the exercise of rights and duties as they exist but also on claiming rights and duties yet to come as a result of social struggles. As Karen Zivi writes, if we consider citizenship as making rights claims, it intrinsically enacts the right to claims rights: 'we make rights claims to criticize practices we find objectionable, to shed light on injustice, to limit the power of government, and to demand state accountability and intervention'.[19] We often focus on the content of these rights rather than on making rights claims. As Zivi writes, however, 'to approach rights and rights claiming from the perspective of performativity means, then, asking questions not simply about what a right is but also about what it is we do when we make rights claims'.[20] This distinction emphasizes that, when performing the right to claim rights, there is a putative condition of equality between citizens and non-citizens. This putative condition of equality means that citizens and non-citizens are both performing the *universal* right to claim rights but the condition of difference means that the rights that they claim are *particular*.

When making rights claims, people are effectively saying 'I, we, they have a right to' and enact performative tensions inherent in citizenship. This is the fourth sense in which citizenship is performative. Both universal and particular rights

---

Disenfranchisement of Latino Men and Boys (New York: Routledge, 2012), pp. 180–203. Karen Zivi has given the most thorough account of the concept 'making rights claims'.

[16] Charles Tilly, *Contentious Performances* (Cambridge: Cambridge University Press, 2008).

[17] The phrase 'the right to claim rights' is a variation on Hannah Arendt's well-known phrase 'the right to have rights' by which she meant the right to belong to a political community where one is judged by one's actions and ideas. See Hannah Arendt, *The Origins of Totalitarianism*, 2nd edition (New York: Harcourt Brace Jovanovich, 1973 [1951]), pp. 296–297.

[18] Or, as Judith Butler writes, 'the force of the performative is thus not inherited from prior usage, but issues forth precisely from its break with any and all prior usage. That break, that force of rupture, is the force of the performative' (See Judith Butler, *The Psychic Life of Power: Theories in Subjection* (Stanford: Stanford University Press, 1997), p. 148).

[19] Zivi (n 15), p. 3.   [20] Ibid., p. 8.

that I have mentioned above come into being and become effective through acts (e.g., declarations, proclamations, protests, demonstrations, occupations, resistance, strikes, withdrawals) and conventions (e.g., rituals, customs, practices, traditions, laws, institutions, technologies, and protocols). Often, performing acts of citizenship invokes or breaks conventions. When we make rights claims we both reference and cite these conventions and yet the performative force of our claims often exceeds or breaks them.[21] As Judith Butler puts it, performativity often involves the 'moment in which a subject—a person, a collective—asserts a right or entitlement to a liveable life when no such prior authorization exists, when no clearly enabling convention is in place'.[22] Yet, when there are clearly enabling conventions, making rights claims may still exceed those conventions. As Zivi writes, 'analyzing [citizenship] from a performative perspective means, then, appreciating the extent to which our claims both reference and reiterate social conventions, and yet have forces and effects that exceed them'.[23] There is a constitutive tension between the right to claim rights as a universal right and making claims for particular rights. When we perform acts of citizenship we play out these two tensions.[24] This is what Butler describes as a performative contradiction which arises when a person or a group is 'excluded from the universal, and yet belongs to it nevertheless, speaks from a split situation of being at once authorized and de-authorized'.[25] This is an important reason why the object of analysis in researching performative citizenship is acts and how they transform conventions.

The fifth sense in which citizenship is performative is when through struggling for their rights, the rights of others, and the rights to come, under certain conditions, people constitute themselves as citizens. Crucially, what makes citizenship performative in this sense is not only that it involves iterating or exceeding conventions about what people may and may not do but also that people often resist these conventions and transform them by applying principles such as equality, justice, liberty, emancipation, and solidarity. These principles enable or motivate people to struggle over rights by traversing the boundaries of social groups and borders of polities. By so doing citizens and non-citizens, with or without rights, assume responsibilities towards each other, across boundaries and borders, transform

---

[21] Herman Robert van Gunsteren, *A Theory of Citizenship: Organizing Plurality in Contemporary Democracies* (Boulder: Westview, 1998) (advocating a theory of citizenship as dissent rather than consent, which resonates with my view of performative citizenship). See also Holloway Sparks, 'Dissident Citizenship: Democratic Theory, Political Courage, and Activist Women', *Hypatia* 12, no. 4 (1997): pp. 74–110.

[22] Judith Butler, *Undoing Gender* (London: Routledge, 2004), p. 224.   [23] Zivi (n 15), p. 19.

[24] James Tully, *On Global Citizenship: James Tully in Dialogue* (London: Bloomsbury, 2014), pp. 44–47.

[25] Judith Butler, 'Sovereign Performatives in the Contemporary Scene of Utterance', *Critical Inquiry* 23, no. 2 (1997): pp. 350–377, p. 368.

themselves and others, the rights under which they make claims, and the rights to which they make claims.

PERFORMATIVE CITIZENSHIP IN DEMOCRATIC POLITIES

We have already seen that there are limitations on the rights of citizens in democratic polities. We can, for example, examine how these limitations generate subject positions of strangers, outsiders, and aliens with respect to specific citizenship rights. The right to vote as a right of political citizenship in some Euro-American polities already excludes various social groups such as prisoners, children, and mentally disabled.[26] We can also explore how migrants and refugees experience various limits on their rights as non-citizens.[27] We can explore how citizens are juxtaposed against aliens.[28] We can explore minorities such as Muslims in non-Muslim democratic states and how they perform their citizenship.[29] Although we can expand this list and examine how both citizens and non-citizens enact various forms of otherness as strangers, outsiders, and aliens, the broader point here is that these positions are inherent in performative citizenship in all societies. These positions are not contingent but necessary elements of citizenship. They are important reminders that citizenship is inherently a differentiating institution and that citizens and non-citizens are relational positions.[30] The obverse of these limits imposed on the rights of democracy's others is the rights that non-citizens can claim by invoking other legal orders. There has been a significant debate over the human rights of non-citizens in democratic polities. Some of these people are stateless and are able to perform some human rights.[31] Some are citizens of other polities and are able to make rights claims through international law as well as in relation to their

---

[26] Ludvig Beckman, *The Frontiers of Democracy: The Right to Vote and Its Limits* (Basingstoke: Palgrave Macmillan, 2009).

[27] David Owen, 'Citizenship and the Marginalities of Migrants', in Philip Cook and Jonathan Seglow, eds., *The Margins of Citizenship* (London: Routledge, 2014), pp. 8–25.

[28] Bosniak (n 8).

[29] Anisa Mustafa, 'Active Citizenship, Dissent and Civic Consciousness: Young Muslims Redefining Citizenship on their Own Terms', *Identities* (2015): pp. 1–16, pp. 3–4.

[30] Cohen (n 8), p. 14.

[31] Weissbrodt (n 11).

countries of origin.[32] I want to illustrate this point with two social struggles in Euro-American societies over citizenship that have had far-reaching consequences for transforming the conception of the right to claim rights and of making rights claims: the struggles of indigenous peoples and the struggles of undocumented migrants.

Indigenous peoples in democratic postcolonial polities such as Canada and Australia raise particularly vexed questions about the rights of citizens.[33] As James Tully has argued, the colonization of indigenous peoples proceeded with appropriation and usurpation of territories without consent or recognition of their resistance to colonization.[34] For these postcolonial states the status of indigenous peoples has straddled across being aliens, outsiders, strangers, and even citizens and yet they still remain as oppressed peoples. Although there is a rich and provocative history of indigenous resistance to this oppression, a more recent struggle in Canada, the Idle No More movement, is now considered to have been a turning point.[35] The movement began in November 2012 as a political response to a Canadian federal government bill that severely eroded indigenous sovereignty and environmental protections.[36] The movement continued to grow not only by using the Internet for organizing itself as a resistance movement but also through hundreds of rallies, teach-ins, and protests for articulating alternatives to neo-colonialism.[37] Arguably, the Idle No More movement staged a performative citizenship which interrogated its relationship to and status within a Canadian citizenship regime. Some would object to this statement because, it could be argued, indigenous claims are not about citizenship but about sovereign self-determination. This would appear to be appropriate if we interpreted citizenship first and foremost as membership of the nation-state. However, performative citizenship helps us to recognize different subject positions as the claiming or acting out of citizenship. Idle No More is certainly *not* about being accepted into Canadian citizenship in the sense of status. But if we understand citizenship as performative acts of the right to claim rights and making rights claims, Idle No More must be seen as not only enacting its expressive demands but also performing dissident citizenship in its most evocative and poignant form.

---

[32] Yasemin Nuhoğlu Soysal, *Limits of Citizenship: Migrants and Postnational Membership in Europe* (Chicago: University of Chicago Press, 1994).

[33] See Gover in this volume.

[34] James Tully, *Public Philosophy in a New Key: Democracy and Civic Freedom*, volume 1 (Cambridge: Cambridge University Press, 2008), p. 259.

[35] Dina Gilio-Whitaker, 'Idle No More and Fourth World Social Movements in the New Millennium', *South Atlantic Quarterly* 114, no. 4 (October 2015): pp. 866–877.

[36] Selena Couture, 'Performativity of Time, Movement and Voice in Idle No More', *Performance Research* 19, no. 6 (2014): pp. 118–120.

[37] Lesley J. Wood, 'Idle No More, Facebook and Diffusion', *Social Movement Studies* 14, no. 5 (3 September 2015): pp. 615–621.

What performative acts of Idle No More inscribe in our imaginary is that the ways in which indigenous peoples have been subjected to internal colonization should not be read as a side story of citizenship. The narrative here is not that there were indigenous peoples and that their rights were fought for within constitutional orders of colonial and then federal governments. Rather, indigenous rights and their democratic citizenship practices were subjected to strategies and technologies governments deployed to extinguish, assimilate, incorporate, and accommodate the rights of indigenous peoples to govern themselves. The claims articulated by Idle No More are not about inclusion or recognition within Canadian citizenship but about demonstrating how Canadian citizenship constitutes indigenous peoples as its strangers, outsiders, and sometimes aliens. The movement therefore not only interrogates, once again, how this oppression remains a central aspect of Canadian citizenship but, perhaps more poignantly, how the Canadian citizenship regime perpetuates this internal colonization. Whether the claims it enacted are for citizenship or not, the performative acts of Idle No More, beginning with its very naming, have moved the question of indigenous people into the centre of the politics of citizenship itself.

A similar point can also be made for another movement that has marked an important shift in citizenship politics: No One is Illegal.[38] The struggles of undocumented migrants over the last three decades have been as consequential for the politics of citizenship as the resistance of indigenous people against citizenship regimes in which they are caught.[39] What began as undocumented migrants destroying their identity documents to enable them to make rights claims as refugees, the sans-papiers (without documents) movement in countries such as Canada, France, and Spain eventually mobilized a solidarity movement between citizens and non-citizens and thus troubled the boundaries that separate them.[40] As scholars such as Iker Barbero, Anne McNevin, Mary McThomas, Peter Nyers, Kim Rygiel, and Maurice Stierl have shown, the struggles of sans-papiers have interrogated the non-citizen in Euro-American democracies and raised fundamental questions about the boundaries and borders that separate it from the citizen.[41] The key issue has been to recognize the political agency of undocumented migrants. But this requires, as McThomas writes, flipping round our 'understanding of political obligation and ask[ing] what the state owes to those who perform the role of citizen,

[38] See e.g. Iker Barbero, 'Expanding Acts of Citizenship: The Struggles of Sinpapeles Migrants', *Social & Legal Studies* 21, no. 4 (December 2012): pp. 529–547; Kathleen Coll, 'Citizenship Acts and Immigrant Voting Rights Movements in the U.S.', *Citizenship Studies* 15, no. 8 (2011): pp. 993–1009; Aoileann Ni Mhurchu, 'Unfamiliar Acts of Citizenship: Enacting Citizenship in Vernacular Music and Language From the Space of Marginalised Intergenerational Migration', *Citizenship Studies* 20, no. 2 (2016): pp. 156–172.

[39] Federico Oliveri, 'Migrants as Activist Citizens in Italy: Understanding the New Cycle of Struggles', *Citizenship Studies* 16, no. 5–6 (2012): pp. 793–806, pp. 794–795.

[40] Catherine Raissiguier, 'Troubling Borders: Sans-Papiers in France', in H. Schwenken and S. Ruß-Sattar, eds., *New Border and Citizenship Politics* (Basingstoke: Palgrave, 2014), pp. 156–170.

[41] Peter Nyers, 'No One is Illegal between City and Nation', *Studies in Social Justice* 4 (2011): pp. 127–143; Anne McNevin, 'Undocumented Citizens? Shifting Grounds of Citizenship in Los Angeles', in Peter Nyers

regardless of their documented status'.[42] By drawing our attention to the dissonance between paper citizenship and performed citizenship McThomas argues that 'instead of using a top-down approach in which we owe duties to the state because it protects us, we should use a bottom-up approach in which the performance of citizen-like duties trigger[s] the state's protections'.[43] For Butler, however, flipping between paper citizenship and performed citizenship elides the performative force of claiming rights. For her '… when undocumented workers gather in the city of Los Angeles to claim their rights of assembly and of citizenship without being citizens, without having any legal right to do so, [by] acting like citizens, they make a [performative] … claim to citizenship …'.[44] I would argue that from a performative citizenship perspective undocumented migrants are not only performing civic duties as currently understood but also resignifying these duties and transforming them.[45]

What makes both indigenous resistance struggles and sans-papiers solidarity struggles instances of performative citizenship? Both struggles involve performative citizenship in all five senses that we have identified above: (a) contest who is the subject of rights; (b) question citizens and non-citizens distinction as absolute subject positions; (c) act across these positions through making rights claims; (d) enact the right to claim rights of those who are not subjects of at least citizenship rights by performing acts to draw attention to these struggles; and (e) transform conventions by enacting provocative acts such as No One is Illegal and Idle No More.

PERFORMATIVE CITIZENSHIP IN NON-DEMOCRATIC POLITIES

We have seen that the performative acts of indigenous people and undocumented migrants disrupt the conventional narratives between citizens and non-citizens. We

and Kim Rygiel, eds., *Citizenship, Migrant Activism and the Politics of Movement* (London: Routledge, 2012), pp. 165–183; Maurice Stierl, ' "No One Is Illegal!" Resistance and the Politics of Discomfort', *Globalizations* 9, no. 3 (2012) pp. 425–438; Mary McThomas, *Performing Citizenship: Undocumented Migrants in the United States* (London: Routledge, 2016); Anne McNevin, 'Political Belonging in a Neoliberal Era: The Struggle of the Sans-Papiers', *Citizenship Studies 10* (2006): pp. 135–151.

[42] McThomas (n 41), p. 37.   [43] Ibid., p. 12.

[44] Judith Butler, *Notes toward a Performative Theory of Assembly* (Cambridge: Harvard University Press, 2015), p. 79.

[45] Kathryn R. Abrams, 'Performative Citizenship in the Civil Rights and Immigrant Rights Movements', UC Berkeley Public Law Research Paper no. 2409971, 17 September 2014, online http://ssrn.com/abstract=2409971 (arguing that performative citizenship enacted by undocumented migrants '… demonstrates that the conceptual and tactical vocabulary developed to claim the full measure of citizenship can also be deployed by those who lack even its formal guarantees' (p. 24)).

observe performative struggles over rights claims enabling outsiders or even aliens to constitute themselves as political subjects—as citizens—not in the way in which it is already understood but as a transformed conception. This perspective sheds light on the struggles of many social groups who find themselves 'outside' political arrangements or are defined as strangers, outsiders, and even aliens such as women, blacks, slaves, queers, prisoners, and others who always remain subjects outside citizenship and yet somehow constitute themselves as citizens. To put it differently, for these social groups, or more precisely for those persons belonging to or identifying with one or more of these social groups, performing Euro-American citizenship is much more precarious and subaltern than for those who belong to dominant social groups. There is an obverse narrative, to which we now want to turn, whereby people constitute themselves as citizens in polities where democracy is not the explicit arrangement, or at least if it is the arrangement, it is not guaranteeing the equality that performative citizenship requires.

This is where we turn our attention away from Euro-American polities to postcolonial or decolonizing societies. For reasons discussed earlier, the ways in which citizenship is performed in Euro-American polities is historically and presently implicated in the ways in which it is performed in postcolonial or decolonizing polities. We may argue for example, that Chinese citizens ostensibly lack certain democratic rights such as civil and political freedoms but this neither means that Chinese history is bereft of performative rights claiming nor that contemporary China is alien to such performative acts. As Dorothy Solinger and Merle Goldman have demonstrated in both urban and rural China citizens perform citizenship in various ways through local or factory assemblies, protests, and demonstrations.[46] So although we would not describe China as a democratic polity we cannot overlook the fact that its citizens perform democratic citizenship through neighbourhood assemblies and associations.[47] Similarly, Shirin Saeidi illustrates how the wives and daughters of soldiers killed during the Iran-Iraq War (1980–1988) radically intervened in the flourishing of democratic citizenship practices in the Republic of Iran that were otherwise suppressed during the war. She argues that 'as martyrs became supreme architects of a revolutionary state at war through self-sacrifice, relatives—particularly mothers, wives and daughters—were nationally bequeathed a noble citizenry status and responsibility to sculpt the state that their loved ones were dying to create'.[48] By assembling neighbourhood associations, organizing solidarity networks, reaching out to other wives and daughters, and enacting various

[46] Dorothy J. Solinger, *Contesting Citizenship in Urban China: Peasant Migrants, the State, and the Logic of the Market* (Berkeley: University of California Press, 1999); Merle Goldman, *From Comrade to Citizen: Struggle for Political Rights in China* (Cambridge: Harvard University Press, 2005).

[47] Zhonghua Guo and Sujian Guo, eds., *Theorizing Chinese Citizenship* (New York: Lexington Books, 2015).

[48] Shirin Saeidi, 'Creating the Islamic Republic of Iran: Wives and Daughters of Martyrs, and Acts of Citizenship', *Citizenship Studies* 14, no. 2 (2010): pp. 113–126, p. 115.

forms of rights claims, wives and daughters of martyrs eventually overcame the negative reactions to their subject position, mostly created by the state, and transformed it into an affirmative and activist image through acts of citizenship.[49] This has parallels with the inclusion of women in citizenship in Europe and America where often war efforts mobilized a female labour force by attributing heroic qualities to women.[50] Maya Mikdashi illustrates how deeply the Lebanese state regulates sexuality by means of regulating religion. Its eighteen officially recognized sects and fifteen personal status laws regulate marriage, divorce, inheritance, and adoption and taken together, deeply divide the rights of women and men and of adults and minors. She argues that 'the most far-reaching legal discrimination is citizenship law itself, which prohibits female citizens from transferring their legal status to spouses and children. Thus there are almost thirty articulations of structural sex-based differentiated citizenship in operation.'[51] Mikdashi, however, documents how strategic conversions from one sect to another and from one sex to another challenge the gendered constitution of Lebanese citizenship law as performative acts.[52] This is a poignant illustration of crossing borders of ascriptive social categories to make rights claims.[53]

These performative acts became even more poignant during the so-called Arab Spring of 2011 where millions of people performed citizenship by making rights claims including to constitutional change and democratic freedoms such as association and assembly rights. There were numerous performative acts across the Middle East as demonstrations of people assembled conventional and critical practices to articulate such rights claims.[54] We will discuss here only one significant episode in Morocco because it involves much less visible and ordinary acts. Morocco became a postcolonial state in 1956 after gaining its independence from France and Spain which had colonized it since 1912. Like many other postcolonial states Morocco embarked on building a national state with ownership of communications and transportation infrastructure. Ostensibly a constitutional democracy for much of this period but operating as a state dominated by a social group called *makhzen* composed of royalty, civil and security service personnel, military, and landowning groups originally groomed by French and Spanish imperial

---

[49] Ibid., pp. 123–124.

[50] Renate Bridenthal, Susan Mosher Stuard, and Merry E. Wiesner, *Becoming Visible: Women in European History*, 3rd edition (Boston: Houghton Mifflin, 1998).

[51] Maya Mikdashi, 'Queering Citizenship, Queering Middle East Studies', *International Journal of Middle East Studies 45*, no. 2 (2013): pp. 350–352, p. 351.

[52] Ibid., pp. 351–352.   [53] Ibid., p. 352.

[54] Zachary Lockman, *Contending Visions of the Middle East: The History and Politics of Orientalism* (Cambridge: Cambridge University Press, 2010); Steve Hess, 'From the Arab Spring to the Chinese Winter: The Institutional Sources of Authoritarian Vulnerability and Resilience in Egypt, Tunisia, and China', *International Political Science Review 34*, no. 3 (June 2013): pp. 254–272; Elizabeth Thompson, *Justice Interrupted: The Struggle for Constitutional Government in the Middle East* (Cambridge: Harvard University Press, 2013).

authorities, Morocco until the twenty-first century provided only a modicum of equality for its citizens.[55]

Up to the early years of the twenty-first century, the *makhzenian* state managed, at times brutally, to mitigate the potentially destabilizing effects of dissident citizenship. Since 2011 the Internet and the spreading waves of dissidence across the region empowered many social groups, especially the youth, where Morocco acquired the highest penetration of Internet users recorded anywhere in Africa.[56] As El Marzouki says, 'the old passive television spectators now have the tools to become producers of their own programmng and thus challenge elitist and statist narratives of cultural identity and citizenship'.[57] The emergence of satire as an expression of performative citizenship was spectacular. Morocco, of course, had rich traditions of story-telling, play, and drama before colonization, yet a sharp, courageous, and insightful satire through the Internet surprised everyone not least the dominant social groups in Moroccan society. The two YouTube satire programmes produced by young Moroccan activists using a dialect called *darija* brought performative democratic citizenship face to face with the *makhzen* regime.[58] The first show BM or 'black mousiba' destabilizes the *makhzen's* dour and dull representation of itself as the guardian of modern life in Morocco. The second show, *Skizofren*, specifically focuses on figures or agents of the *makhzen* by catching them in their duplicity. As El Marzouki illustrates, neither show is itself free from contradictions, inconsistencies, and essentialism, combining elements of cosmopolitanism, nationalism, Islamism, and conservatism in turns. Yet, both illustrate that with a combination of drawing on historical traditions and engaging critically with images of modern life projected upon them by dominant social groups and subversively ridiculing these images, young people in Morocco and beyond also began producing imaginaries that are neither traditional nor modern.

What these performative acts from non-democratic polities demonstrate is that when we assume that democratic citizenship can only be found in legal and political institutions, we may overlook how people perform citizenship in different contexts by assembling traditions. In contrast, by studying performative citizenship in postcolonial or decolonizing societies, not only can we unearth performative acts of making rights claims in traditions but also understand how these traditions have been transformed by the right to claims rights. Moreover, studying performative acts enables us to engage in comparative research in a different key without making prior assumptions about the absence or presence of Euro-American institutions as

[55] Lawrence Rosen, *Two Arabs, a Berber, and a Jew: Entangled Lives in Morocco* (Chicago: University of Chicago Press, 2015).
[56] Mohamed El Marzouki, 'Satire as Counter-Discourse: Dissent, Cultural Citizenship, and Youth Culture in Morocco', *International Communication Gazette 77*, no. 3 (2015): pp. 282–296, pp. 283–284.
[57] Ibid., p. 284.   [58] Ibid., pp. 286–287.

master signifiers but also without neglecting imperial and colonial histories within which comparative elements are implicated.

PERFORMATIVE CITIZENSHIP ACROSS POLITIES

As mentioned above, the right to claim rights and the making of rights claims across polities as performative acts complicate who is the subject of rights. A mention of Chinese artist Ai Weiwei, the former US intelligence agent Edward Snowden, or British artist Banksy may immediately bring these complexities into sharp focus. When, for example, Ai Weiwei lies on the beach and invokes the image of Aylan Kurdi whose body was found on that beach after attempting to cross the border with his family, is Ai Weiwei performing an act of citizenship?[59] Is it a protest for the rights that Kurdish migrants did not have? Is it a protest against the rights that European citizens have but do not perform? When Edward Snowden revealed information about mass surveillance by the US and UK governments, whose rights did he think he was protecting?[60] When Banksy paints graffiti in Gaza whose rights is he making claims for?[61] I have argued in the opening of this chapter that *because* citizenship is *constitutive* of rights and who can claim these rights is itself *contested*, citizenship is defined not just by having these rights, but also by *claiming* them. The right to claim rights and making rights claims across borders raises complex questions of performative citizenship as citizenship itself increasingly assumes a transnational character.[62]

To explore some of these questions we will briefly discuss performative acts across borders that concern the rights of refugees. The rights of refugees have been a fundamental aspect of international and human rights especially since the beginning of the twentieth century, but over the last few years increasingly, performative acts for the rights of refugees to have safe passages and settlement in Euro-American

---

[59] Monica Tan, 'Ai Weiwei Poses as Drowned Syrian Infant Refugee in "Haunting" Photo', *The Guardian*, 1 February 2016, online https://goo.gl/v5KKGN.

[60] William E. Scheuerman, 'Whistleblowing as Civil Disobedience: The Case of Edward Snowden', *Philosophy & Social Criticism 40*, no. 7 (September 2014): pp. 609–628.

[61] Raziye Akkoç, 'Banksy in Gaza: Street artist goes undercover in the Strip', *The Telegraph*, 26 February 2015, online http://goo.gl/QojKOP.

[62] Étienne Balibar, *We, the People of Europe?: Reflections on Transnational Citizenship* (Princeton: Princeton University Press, 2004); Rainer Bauböck, *Transnational Citizenship: Membership*

polities have enacted new forms of international citizenship.[63] These acts have taken many forms but perhaps the most poignant have been those that exposed borders or rather border regimes for their punitive and unjust effects on migrants and refugees. Take, for example, Boats4People. In 2012 a number of freedom of movement activists moved to the border zone between Italy and Northern Africa to draw attention to the deadly consequences of the European border regime. They formed Boats4People as an international coalition with the aim 'to end the dying along maritime borders and to defend the rights of migrants at sea'.[64] Originally intending to intervene at the border to force rescue operations, the coalition increasingly turned towards commemorative rituals bearing witness to the suffering of the migrant at sea.[65] As Maurice Stierl says 'these emotionally charged commemorative [acts] had performative effects on those participating but also on those passing by'.[66] By bringing collective grieving to European citizens, Boats4People performed a kind of European citizenship that called on people to show solidarity with migrants and refugees. But as Pierre Monforte argues these performative acts can also transform borders into zones of contention about European citizenship not only by calling into question its limits but also its force.[67] By these commemorative and disruptive acts Boats4People not only brought attention to the EU border regime but also literally re-enacted its sites where European border regime authorities would rather remain invisible such as the central areas of European cities during the Christmas shopping season.[68]

CONCLUSION

We have first signified citizenship as performative when people act as political subjects whether they are authorized or not (a). Then we resignified it by saying that citizenship is performative not only in that it enables people to act as political subjects but also as it provokes people to act across subject positions to which

---

and *Rights in International Migration* (Aldershot Brookfield: E. Elgar, 1994); Aihwa Ong, *Flexible Citizenship: The Cultural Logics of Transnationality* (Durham: Duke University Press, 1999).

[63] Engin F. Isin, 'Enacting International Citizenship', in Tugba Basaran, et al., eds., *International Political Sociology: Transversal Lines* (London: Routledge, 2017), pp. 185–204.

[64] Maurice Stierl, 'Contestations in Death: The Role of Grief in Migration Struggles', *Citizenship Studies* 20, no. 2 (2016): pp. 173–191, p. 175.

[65] Ibid., p. 176.   [66] Ibid., p. 177.

[67] Pierre Monforte, 'The Border as a Space of Contention: The Spatial Strategies of Protest against Border Controls in Europe', *Citizenship Studies* 20, no. 3–4 (2015): pp. 411–426, p. 420.

[68] Stierl (n 64), p. 177.

they are ascribed as citizens or non-citizens (b). Then we resignified it again by reiterating that it also stimulates people to act across the borders of polities for solidarity, affiliation, and association (c). Then we have stressed that performative citizenship requires performing acts through which people become citizens in exercising or claiming rights and duties (d). We finally argued that when people act as citizens they are not only actively or passively following rules but are also creatively transforming them (e). We have given examples to illustrate each sense that collectively define performative citizenship, from Idle No More (Canada), No One is Illegal (Canada, France, and Spain), BM and *Skizofren* (Morocco), and Boats4People (Europe). These illustrate how, as multiply positioned subjects (members of multiple social groups, belonging to intersecting subject positions), people find themselves in situations where a combination of various affiliations and identifications define their possibilities and potentialities and how these play out in performative citizenship. If a person is an artist, a Canadian, a woman, black, queer, and/or refugee, playing out this combination as a subject involves negotiating these positions by enacting the right to make claims and making rights claims in and by speaking against injustices, oppressions, prejudices, discriminations, and otherness.

There are two conclusions we reach from this perspective on studying citizenship. First, performative citizenship involves exercising a right: this can be a particular or universal right, but the performance itself does not affect the content and scope of the right, and it may confirm rather than contest that right. Second, performing citizenship involves claiming a right: this necessarily involves struggle, but such struggle is not necessarily transformative. Claiming a right can take various forms. There are cases where rights may be claimed towards institutions that recognize these rights and have the power to determine the content of rights (legislatures) and to settle disputes over them (courts). These types of struggle are not inherently transformative and may uphold an established system of rights. There are also cases where claimed rights are not recognized but contested and the performativity of claiming a right is that the claimant puts herself thereby forward as a subject of rights that she is not. Finally, there are also cases where the claimant herself is not recognized as having a right to claim rights (a non-citizen) and the performativity of claiming a right involves also a claim for the right to have rights.

These variations are inherent in performative citizenship and give rise to multiple tensions. We have seen that these tensions partly arise from how we have come to conventionally understand citizens and subjects as diametrically opposed actors and democratic and non-democratic polities as discrete and sovereign polities. We have called both these understandings into question and developed a critical perspective on dichotomies of subject-citizen and democratic-non-democratic. Approaching citizenship as performative acts enables us to question an enduring narrative that contrasts citizens with subjects and considers democratic and non-democratic states as discrete and enclosed regimes.[69] This narrative often considers citizens as those with rights (civil, political, and social) and subjects as those who (must) lack these rights. It considers citizens as belonging to democratic states and subjects to non-democratic states. It assumes that only citizens enjoy democratic rights (free speech, universal suffrage, the rule of law) and can perform civic duties. This conventional narrative portrays a historical progression from subjects to citizens and from non-democratic to democratic states as well downplaying the importance of acting with dissent, resistance, or even disobedience as citizens.[70]

It is this conventional narrative that becomes the object of critical interrogation from the perspective of performative citizenship that this chapter outlined. As some of the examples we have discussed illustrate, there is now a literature that uses performative citizenship or acts of citizenship as a perspective for studying citizenship. This is an emerging literature and features many studies on performative acts with a focus on specific performances or enactments of citizenship with identifiable scenes, stages, actors, and rights.[71] If indeed we see acts, as Charles Tilly illustrated, like repertoires of action that develop through time and from which actors draw when performing, we open up the possibility for comparative research to investigate how similar repertoires generate different effects when performed in different stages within or across polities.[72] An assembly, for example, to protest or dissent can have widely different consequences in squares and streets of Aleppo, Beijing, Cairo, Jerusalem, Madrid, or Seattle that requires different approaches to its enactment.

By way of closing the chapter I would like to discuss four research problems that remain contentious in the literature. The first issue concerns whether performative acts are spectacular or everyday acts. Often, examples of performative acts feature spectacular acts that appear heroic, original, and individual as the examples of Snowden and Weiwei imply. But as Catherine Neveu has argued, acts of citizenship can also involve, and perhaps even more effectively, quotidian enactments that lack the visibility of certain performative acts but nevertheless can be rather consequential.[73] Similarly, Jonathan Darling and Vicki Squire have demonstrated how

[69] Barbara Cruikshank, *The Will to Empower: Democratic Citizens and Other Subjects* (Ithaca: Cornell University Press, 1999).

[70] Pierre Boyer, Linda Cardinal, and David John Headon, *From Subjects to Citizens: A Hundred Years of Citizenship in Australia and Canada* (Ottawa: University of Ottawa Press, 2004); Alastair Davidson, *From Subject to Citizen: Australian Citizenship in the Twentieth Century* (New York: Cambridge University Press, 1997).

[71] McThomas (n 41).   [72] Tilly (n 16), pp. 41–45.

[73] Catherine Neveu, 'Of Ordinariness and Citizenship Processes', *Citizenship Studies* 19, no. 2 (2015); Catherine Neveu, 'Sites of Citizenship, Politics of Scales', in Willem Maas, ed., *Multilevel Citizenship* (Philadelphia: University of Pennsylvania Press, 2013), pp. 203–212. See also John Clarke et al., *Disputing Citizenship* (Bristol: Policy Press, 2014).

refugee politics is enacted through everyday performative acts with considerable transformative effects.[74]

The second research problem concerns whether performative acts produce ruptures when breaking conventions or incremental changes to these conventions.[75] To indicate breaks from conventions sometimes we use the term 'rupture' and this can be interpreted as a revolution, regime change, or revolt. It may well include these changes but the term rupture, following the first issue above, can also be quotidian and ordinary. The essential point is that a rupture that a performative act introduces draws people out of themselves to take notice of the taken for granted nature of a given state of affairs and turn critical attentiveness toward it.

The third problem concerns whether all performative acts are progressive or even democratic. It is clear that nationalist, racist, nativist, misogynist, and homophobic acts also exercise rights to assembly, speech, protest, and demonstrate in order to claim rights to enact a particular understanding of citizenship. As Holloway Sparks illustrates, by performatively playing into anger conservative activists have enacted a particular version of American patriotism that conceals its nativism and racism.[76] The examples that I have provided in this chapter of social groups struggling over rights are what I consider to be subaltern or oppressed or dispossessed social groups whose oppression is based on historical injustices. There is a clear orientation in performative research towards revealing subjugated social groups and their dispossession. But this does not mean that performative citizenship is inherently progressive or emancipatory. Moreover, it requires researchers making their normative decisions explicit and explain why they interpret certain acts as acts of citizenship.

The fourth problem concerns whether rights, especially the performative exercising and claiming of rights are the exclusive domain of citizenship. Amy Brandzel has expressed this problem most clearly by arguing against what she calls sweeping all dissident and resistance acts into citizenship.[77] Although she recognizes that those acts that are regarded as acts of citizenship may have transformative effects, she warns against realigning all resistant and dissident behaviours, practices, and bodies under the name of citizenship. This is an important warning for anyone approaching citizenship from a performative perspective with a view to recognizing

---

[74] Jonathan Darling, 'Asylum and the Post-Political: Domopolitics, Depoliticisation and Acts of Citizenship', *Antipode 46*, no. 1 (2014): pp. 72–91; Jonathan Darling and Vicki Squire, 'Everyday Enactments of Sanctuary: The UK City of Sanctuary Movement', in Randy K. Lippert and Sean Rehaag, eds., *Sanctuary Practices in International Perspectives: Migration, Citizenship and Social Movements* (London: Routledge, 2013), pp. 191–204.

[75] Leah Bassel and Catherine Lloyd, 'Rupture or Reproduction? "New" Citizenship in France', *French Politics 9* (2011): pp. 21–49.

[76] Holloway Sparks, 'Mama Grizzlies and Guardians of the Republic: The Democratic and Intersectional Politics of Anger in the Tea Party Movement', *New Political Science 37*, no. 1 (2014): pp. 25–47, pp. 27–28.

[77] Amy L. Brandzel, *Against Citizenship: The Violence of the Normative* (Chicago: University of Illinois Press, 2016), p. 8.

multiple, contradictory, and conflicting ways in which citizens and non-citizens challenge the meanings of citizenship and stretch its functions. This raises the question whether we can study politics without its subjects, citizens, and their relational others, strangers, outsiders, and aliens.

Bibliography

Abrams, Kathryn R., 'Performative Citizenship in the Civil Rights and Immigrant Rights Movements', UC Berkeley Public Law Research Paper no. 2409971 (17 September 2014), online http://ssrn.com/abstract=2409971.

Akkoç, Raziye, 'Banksy in Gaza: Street Artist Goes Undercover in the Strip', *The Telegraph*, 26 February 2015, online http://goo.gl/QojKOP.

Andrijasevic, Rutvica, 'Acts of Citizenship as Methodology', in Engin F. Isin and Michael Saward, eds., *Enacting European Citizenship* (Cambridge: Cambridge University Press, 2013), pp. 47–65.

Aradau, Claudia and Jef Huysmans, 'Critical Methods in International Relations: The Politics of Techniques, Devices and Acts', *European Journal of International Relations 20*, no. 3 (2014): pp. 596–619.

Arendt, Hannah, *The Origins of Totalitarianism*, 2nd edition (New York: Harcourt Brace Jovanovich, 1973 [1951]).

Austin, J.L., *How to do Things with Words* (Oxford: Oxford University Press, 1962).

Balibar, Étienne, *We, the People of Europe?: Reflections on Transnational Citizenship* (Princeton: Princeton University Press, 2004).

Barbero, Iker, 'Expanding Acts of Citizenship: The Struggles of Sinpapeles Migrants', *Social & Legal Studies 21*, no. 4 (December 2012): pp. 529–547.

Bassel, Leah and Catherine Lloyd, 'Rupture or Reproduction? "New" Citizenship in France', *French Politics 9* (2011): pp. 21–49.

Bauböck, Rainer, *Transnational Citizenship: Membership and Rights in International Migration* (Aldershot Brookfield: E. Elgar, 1994).

Bauböck, Rainer, 'The Rights and Duties of External Citizenship', *Citizenship Studies 13*, no. 5 (2009): pp. 475–499.

Bauböck, Rainer, 'Studying Citizenship Constellations', *Journal of Ethnic and Migration Studies 36* (2010): pp. 847–859.

Beckman, Ludvig, *The Frontiers of Democracy: The Right to Vote and its Limits* (Basingstoke: Palgrave Macmillan, 2009).

Bosniak, Linda, *The Citizen and the Alien* (Princeton: Princeton University Press, 2006).

Boyer, Pierre, Linda Cardinal, and David John Headon, *From Subjects to Citizens: A Hundred Years of Citizenship in Australia and Canada* (Ottawa: University of Ottawa Press, 2004).

Brandzel, Amy L., *Against Citizenship: The Violence of the Normative* (Chicago: University of Illinois Press, 2016).

Bridenthal, Renate, Susan Mosher Stuard, and Merry E. Wiesner, *Becoming Visible: Women in European History*, 3rd edition (Boston: Houghton Mifflin, 1998).

Butler, Judith, *The Psychic Life of Power: Theories in Subjection* (Stanford: Stanford University Press, 1997).

Butler, Judith, 'Sovereign Performatives in the Contemporary Scene of Utterance', *Critical Inquiry 23*, no. 2 (1997): pp. 350–377.

Butler, Judith, *Undoing Gender* (London: Routledge, 2004).

Butler, Judith, *Notes toward a Performative Theory of Assembly* (Cambridge: Harvard University Press, 2015).

Clarke, John, Kathleen M. Coll, Evelina Dagnino, and Catherine Neveu, *Disputing Citizenship* (Bristol: Policy Press, 2014).

Cohen, Elizabeth F., *Semi-Citizenship in Democratic Politics* (Cambridge: Cambridge University Press, 2009).

Coll, Kathleen, 'Citizenship Acts and Immigrant Voting Rights Movements in the U.S.', *Citizenship Studies 15*, no. 8 (2011): pp. 993–1009.

Couture, Selena, 'Performativity of Time, Movement and Voice in Idle No More', *Performance Research 19*, no. 6 (2014): pp. 118–120.

Cruikshank, Barbara, *The Will to Empower: Democratic Citizens and Other Subjects* (Ithaca: Cornell University Press, 1999).

Darling, Jonathan, 'Asylum and the Post-Political: Domopolitics, Depoliticisation and Acts of Citizenship', *Antipode 46*, no. 1 (2014): pp. 72–91.

Darling, Jonathan and Vicki Squire, 'Everyday Enactments of Sanctuary: The UK City of Sanctuary Movement', in Randy K. Lippert and Sean Rehaag, eds., *Sanctuary Practices in International Perspectives: Migration, Citizenship and Social Movements* (London: Routledge, 2013), pp. 191–204.

Davidson, Alastair, *From Subject to Citizen: Australian Citizenship in the Twentieth Century* (New York: Cambridge University Press, 1997).

Davis, Tracy C., *The Cambridge Companion to Performance Studies* (Cambridge: Cambridge University Press, 2008).

El Marzouki, Mohamed, 'Satire as Counter-Discourse: Dissent, Cultural Citizenship, and Youth Culture in Morocco', *International Communication Gazette 77*, no. 3 (2015): pp. 282–296.

Gilio-Whitaker, Dina, 'Idle No More and Fourth World Social Movements in the New Millennium', *South Atlantic Quarterly 114*, no. 4 (October 2015): pp. 866–877.

Goffman, Erving, *Encounters: Two Studies in the Sociology of Interaction* (Indianapolis: Bobbs-Merrill, 1961).

Goffman, Erving, *Interaction Ritual: Essays on Face-to-Face Behaviour* (New York: Doubleday, 1967).

Goldman, Merle, *From Comrade to Citizen: Struggle for Political Rights in China* (Cambridge: Harvard University Press, 2005).

Goldring, Luin and Patricia Landolt, eds., *Producing and Negotiating Non-Citizenship: Precarious Legal Status in Canada* (Toronto: University of Toronto Press, 2013).

Gunsteren, Herman Robert van, *A Theory of Citizenship: Organizing Plurality in Contemporary Democracies* (Boulder: Westview, 1998).

Guo, Zhonghua and Sujian Guo, eds., *Theorizing Chinese Citizenship* (New York: Lexington Books, 2015).

Harrington, Jack, 'Orientalism, Political Subjectivity and the Birth of Citizenship between 1780 and 1830', *Citizenship Studies 16*, no. 5–6 (2012): pp. 573–586.

Hess, Steve, 'From the Arab Spring to the Chinese Winter: The Institutional Sources of Authoritarian Vulnerability and Resilience in Egypt, Tunisia, and China', *International Political Science Review 34*, no. 3 (June 2013): pp. 254–272.

Isin, Engin F., *Being Political: Genealogies of Citizenship* (Minneapolis: University of Minnesota Press, 2002).

Isin, Engin F., 'Claiming European Citizenship', in Engin F. Isin and Michael Saward, eds., *Enacting European Citizenship* (Cambridge: Cambridge University Press, 2013), pp. 19–46.

Isin, Engin F., ed., *Citizenship after Orientalism: Transforming Political Theory* (London: Palgrave, 2015).

Isin, Engin F., 'Enacting International Citizenship', in Tugba Basaran, Didier Bigo, Emmanuel-Pierre Guittet, and R. B. J. Walker, eds., *International Political Sociology: Transversal Lines* (London: Routledge, 2017), pp. 185–204.

Lockman, Zachary, *Contending Visions of the Middle East: The History and Politics of Orientalism* (Cambridge: Cambridge University Press, 2010).

Loxley, James, *Performativity* (London: Routledge, 2007).

McNevin, Anne, 'Political Belonging in a Neoliberal Era: The Struggle of the Sans-Papiers', *Citizenship Studies 10* (2006): pp. 135–151.

McNevin, Anne, 'Undocumented Citizens? Shifting Grounds of Citizenship in Los Angeles', in Peter Nyers and Kim Rygiel, eds., *Citizenship, Migrant Activism and the Politics of Movement* (London: Routledge, 2012), pp. 165–183.

McThomas, Mary, *Performing Citizenship: Undocumented Migrants in the United States* (London: Routledge, 2016).

Mhurchu, Aoileann Ni, 'Unfamiliar Acts of Citizenship: Enacting Citizenship in Vernacular Music and Language From the Space of Marginalised Intergenerational Migration', *Citizenship Studies 20*, no. 2 (2016): pp. 156–172.

Mikdashi, Maya, 'Queering Citizenship, Queering Middle East Studies', *International Journal of Middle East Studies 45*, no. 2 (2013): pp. 350–352.

Monforte, Pierre, 'The Border as a Space of Contention: The Spatial Strategies of Protest against Border Controls in Europe', *Citizenship Studies 20*, no. 3–4 (2015): pp. 411–426.

Mustafa, Anisa, 'Active Citizenship, Dissent and Civic Consciousness: Young Muslims Redefining Citizenship on their Own Terms', *Identities* (2015): pp. 1–16.

Neveu, Catherine, 'Sites of Citizenship, Politics of Scales', in Willem Maas, ed., *Multilevel Citizenship* (Philadelphia: University of Pennsylvania Press, 2013), pp. 203–212.

Neveu, Catherine, 'Of Ordinariness and Citizenship Processes', *Citizenship Studies 19*, no. 2 (2015): pp. 141–154.

Nyers, Peter, 'No One is Illegal between City and Nation', *Studies in Social Justice 4* (2011): pp. 127–143.

Nyers, Peter and Kim Rygiel, eds., *Citizenship, Migrant Activism and the Politics of Movement* (London: Routledge, 2012).

Oliveri, Federice, 'Migrants as Activist Citizens in Italy: Understanding the New Cycle of Struggles', *Citizenship Studies 16*, no. 5–6 (2012): pp. 793–806.

Ong, Aihwa, *Flexible Citizenship: The Cultural Logics of Transnationality* (Durham: Duke University Press, 1999).

Owen, David, 'Citizenship and the Marginalities of Migrants', in Philip Cook and Jonathan Seglow, eds., *The Margins of Citizenship* (London: Routledge, 2014), pp. 8–25.

Parker, Andrew and Eve Kosofsky Sedgwick, *Performativity and Performance* (London: Routledge, 1995).

Raissiguier, Catherine, 'Troubling Borders: Sans-Papiers in France', in H. Schwenken and S. Ruß-Sattar, eds., *New Border and Citizenship Politics* (Basingstoke: Palgrave, 2014), pp. 156–170.

Ramirez, Horacio N. Roque, 'Claiming Queer Cultural Citizenship: Gay Latino (Im)migrant Acts in San Francisco', in P. Noguera, A. Hurtado and E. Fergus, eds., *Invisible No More: Understanding the Disenfranchisement of Latino Men and Boys* (New york: Routledge, 2012), pp. 180–203.

Rosen, Lawrence, *Two Arabs, a Berber, and a Jew: Entangled Lives in Morocco* (Chicago: University of Chicago Press, 2015).

Saeidi, Shirin, 'Creating the Islamic Republic of Iran: Wives and Daughters of Martyrs, and Acts of Citizenship', *Citizenship Studies 14*, no. 2 (2010): pp. 113–126.

Scheuerman, William E., 'Whistleblowing as Civil Disobedience: The Case of Edward Snowden', *Philosophy & Social Criticism 40*, no. 7 (September 2014): pp. 609–628.

Solinger, Dorothy J., *Contesting Citizenship in Urban China: Peasant Migrants, the State, and the Logic of the Market* (Berkeley: University of California Press, 1999).

Soysal, Yasemin Nuhoğlu, *Limits of Citizenship: Migrants and Postnational Membership in Europe* (Chicago: University of Chicago Press, 1994).

Sparks, Holloway, 'Dissident Citizenship: Democratic Theory, Political Courage, and Activist Women', *Hypatia 12*, no. 4 (1997): pp. 74–110.

Sparks, Holloway, 'Mama Grizzlies and Guardians of the Republic: The Democratic and Intersectional Politics of Anger in the Tea Party Movement', *New Political Science 37*, no. 1 (2014): pp. 25–47.

Stierl, Maurice, ' "No One Is Illegal!" Resistance and the Politics of Discomfort', *Globalizations 9*, no. 3 (2012): pp. 425–438.

Stierl, Maurice, 'Contestations in Death: The Role of Grief in Migration Struggles', *Citizenship Studies 20*, no. 2 (2016): pp. 173–191.

Tan, Monica, 'Ai Weiwei Poses as Drowned Syrian Infant Refugee in "Haunting" Photo', *The Guardian*, 1 February 2016, online https://goo.gl/v5KKGN.

Thompson, Elizabeth, *Justice Interrupted: The Struggle for Constitutional Government in the Middle East* (Cambridge: Harvard University Press, 2013).

Tilly, Charles, *Contentious Performances* (Cambridge: Cambridge University Press, 2008).

Tully, James, *Public Philosophy in a New Key: Democracy and Civic Freedom*, volume 1 (Cambridge: Cambridge University Press, 2008).

Tully, James, *On Global Citizenship: James Tully in Dialogue* (London: Bloomsbury, 2014).

Weissbrodt, David, *The Human Rights of Non-Citizens* (Oxford: Oxford University Press, 2008).

Wood, Lesley J., 'Idle No More, Facebook and Diffusion', *Social Movement Studies 14*, no. 5 (3 September 2015): pp. 615–621.

Young, Iris Marion, 'Polity and Group Difference: A Critique of the Ideal of Universal Citizenship', *Ethics 99*, no. 2 (1989): pp. 250–274.

Zivi, Karen, *Making Rights Claims: A Practice of Democratic Citizenship* (Oxford: Oxford University Press, 2012).

CHAPTER 24

DOES CITIZENSHIP MATTER?

IRENE BLOEMRAAD

DOES holding or providing citizenship matter? Normative or political claims about dignity, equality, or state sovereignty have limited purchase unless we know the answers to two empirical questions. Does holding citizenship status affect individuals' life experiences? By being more or less generous in providing citizenship to residents, do states reap benefits or face particular disadvantages?[1]

In a simple—and consequential—sense, citizenship matters. Citizenship secures a place to live and offers protection against expulsion. In the current international

---

[1] I do not explore the benefits or drawbacks of extending citizenship to expatriates. See Bauböck in this volume; Collyer in this volume.

system of sovereign states, having no citizenship renders one stateless, defined by the 1954 UN Convention on the Status of Stateless Persons as the condition of 'a person who is not considered as a national by any State under the operation of its law.' Lack of citizenship exposes the estimated 10 million stateless people world-wide to having no 'right to have rights,' that is, 'their plight is not that they are not equal before the law, but that no law exists for them.'[2] Even when challenged from above, through international law, or from below, through noncitizens' actions, documentation of nationality is usually required to travel across international borders and may be necessary to open a bank account, to access public services, health care or education, or to secure legal employment.[3]

Beyond the stark situation of those without any citizenship, the question of whether citizenship matters is less self-evident. For many, citizenship is no guarantee of basic security: today and in the past, governments enact violence on their citizens. Holding citizenship does not necessarily guarantee equal rights or benefits, as when female citizens lacked suffrage while men could vote. Conversely, in some countries, rights, responsibilities, and benefits are largely tied to residency, not citizenship, leading some observers to wonder about the devaluation, denationalization, or growing irrelevance of citizenship: 'The real prize is legal residency, not citizenship.'[4] Whether critiquing citizenship's hollow promise in ensuring security, equality, and justice, or identifying an emerging 'postnational' rights regime in which citizenship is eclipsed, there are serious arguments for citizenship's unimportance.[5]

This chapter identifies four facets of citizenship—status, rights, participation, and identity—and outlines arguments for citizenship's importance and its limits. I focus on participation and identity, taking a capacious view of participation to include political engagement, socio-economic participation, and social integration, and on experiences of citizenship for residents within a state. Remarkably, the empirical evidence for citizenship's importance is thin. This is partly because most residents are citizens of their state, so it is virtually impossible to evaluate the relative weight of citizenship net of class, gender, ethno-racial, religious, or other differences that influence life experiences. I consequently draw heavily on research comparing immigrants by citizenship status, or comparing foreigners with citizens, primarily in North America and Western Europe. I focus on whether holding citizenship

---

[2] See UNHCR, 'Ending Statelessness', online http://www.unhcr.org/pages/49c3646c15e.html; Hannah Arendt, *The Origins of Totalitarianism* (Cleveland: Meridian Books, 1962), pp. 295–296; Christian Joppke, *Citizenship and Immigration* (Malden: Polity, 2010).

[3] See Brad Blitz and Maureen Lynch, *Statelessness and Citizenship: A Comparative Study on the Benefits of Nationality* (Northampton: Edward Elgar Publishing, 2011).

[4] Peter J. Spiro, *Beyond Citizenship: American Identity after Globalization* (Oxford: Oxford University Press, 2007), p. 159; Peter Schuck, *Citizens, Strangers and In-Betweens: Essays on Immigration and Citizenship* (Boulder: Westview Press, 1998).

[5] Yasemin Soysal, *Limits of Citizenship: Migrants and Postnational Membership in Europe* (Chicago: University of Chicago Press, 1994); Damian Tambini, 'Post-National Citizenship,' *Ethnic and Racial Studies* 24, no. 2 (2001): pp. 195–217.

offers benefits compared to holding a secure long-term residency status. A growing body of evidence demonstrates that undocumented or precarious legal status stunts educational attainment, economic outcomes, and health status. But once secure residence rights are attained, does gaining citizenship generate further benefits? If it does, citizenship likely offers advantages over the variegated statuses held by non-citizens around the world.

To anticipate key conclusions, there is evidence that holding citizenship encourages political participation, improves labor market outcomes, and increases identification with a nation. But effects tend to be modest, although they appear stronger for immigrants from non-Western countries living in Western democracies, and for those who migrate at younger ages or acquire citizenship earlier. Existing research provides little direction in understanding when, where, for whom, and—critically—why citizenship matters in some cases but not others. There has been insufficient theorizing about the mechanisms linking citizenship status to life experiences. I elaborate six possible mechanisms and highlight the methodological difficulties in identifying them. Most scholarship examines citizenship consequences for individuals. An important future direction is theorizing and evaluating whether and why more or less generous citizenship policies affect families, local communities, and the countries that control the status.

DEFINING CITIZENSHIP

Citizenship is a form of membership in a political and geographic community. It can be disaggregated into legal status, rights, participation (political and other forms of societal engagement), and a sense of belonging or identity.[6] From a realist international relations perspective, citizenship is about states' control of political-legal borders, delineating territory and the people on it, and states' control over resources, which let them determine citizenship status and the rights and benefits that flow from it.[7] A liberal-democratic framework focuses on the equality and

---

[6] Linda Bosniak, *The Citizen and the Alien: Dilemmas of Contemporary Membership* (Princeton: Princeton University Press, 2006); Irene Bloemraad, Anna Korteweg, and Gökçe Yurdakul, 'Citizenship and Immigration: Multiculturalism, Assimilation, and Challenges to the Nation-State,' *Annual Review of Sociology 34*, no. 1 (2008): pp. 153–179.

[7] Citizenship status can be based on place of birth (*jus soli*) or parental origins (*jus sanguinis*), or both. Those without birthright citizenship can usually acquire it through naturalization. See Vink in this volume for a discussion of variation in countries' citizenship laws, the reasons for this, and the consequences for citizenship acquisition.

rights guarantees implicit in citizenship.[8] Citizenship has also long been understood as participation in governance. 'Participation' can be extended further to consider engagement in a state's economic system and social relations, linking citizenship studies to research on immigrant integration. Finally, citizenship delineates identities for an in-group and out-group, which can generate feelings of collective belonging. Analytically, these four dimensions can be distinguished and theorized even if, empirically, status, rights, participation, and identity can overlap or be mutually constitutive. Conceptualizing citizenship as multi-faceted obliges attention to a wide range of empirical research.

CITIZENSHIP MATTERS:
THEORIZING MECHANISMS

Despite their differences, international relations, rights, democratic political theory, integration models, or social psychological frameworks all tend to assume that citizenship carries consequences for people and societies. Existing scholarship is surprisingly silent however, as to *why* citizenship might matter and, more precisely, why it matters in some contexts, for some people, and in some places more than others. I outline six plausible mechanisms.

First, citizenship status provides, in many places, *access* to rights, benefits, or particular treatment under law and regulations. Citizenship provides access to territory and protection against deportation, and in doing so, access to particular labor markets, social systems, legal structures and the like. From 2006 through 2015, 3.5 million noncitizens were 'removed' from the United States.[9] The Migrant Integration Policy Index (MIPEX) documents variation in states' regulation of political participation, labor market access, health care, and family reunification by legal status. Citizenship will matter more where access is significantly determined by it, and more to people who benefit from particular jobs or social benefits tied to

---

[8] Thomas H. Marshall, *Citizenship and Social Class*, volume 11 (Cambridge: Cambridge University Press, 1950); Christian Joppke, 'Immigration and the Identity of Citizenship: The Paradox of Universalism,' *Citizenship Studies* 12, no. 6 (2008): pp. 533–546.

[9] U.S. Immigration and Customs, 'ICE Enforcement and Removal Operations Report, Fiscal Year 2015,' online https://www.ice.gov/sites/default/files/documents/Report/2016/fy2015removalStats.pdf, p. 11. Removals for FY 2014 and 2015 from this report; data for 2006–2013 from Table 33 of the U.S. Office of Immigration Statistics, 'Yearbook of Immigration Statistics, 2013,' online https://www.dhs.gov/publication/yearbook-immigration-statistics-2013-enforcement-actions.

citizenship. It also follows that in poor countries where governments can provide few benefits, rights, or resources to residents, citizenship may matter less.

Citizenship may also carry social value that provides *legitimacy*, beyond access to material benefits or legal rights. Others in society might feel stronger obligations to fellow citizens. For example, even if anti-discrimination guarantees protect citizens and noncitizens equally, public officials, employers, landlords and ordinary residents might take the claims of citizens more seriously due to shared social identity or for fear that citizens are more likely to complain. We might then expect stronger citizenship effects in countries with strong civic nationalism where national identity is linked to citizenship, or for people who are more likely to be stigmatized.

Combining access and legitimacy, citizenship might also facilitate *mobilization* for collective action. When people have access to the vote and social legitimacy, political parties, unions, and advocacy groups may be more likely to invite participation in elections, demonstrations, and strikes. To the extent that collective action produces policy change, this could generate different policy regimes between countries with more or less inclusive citizenship laws and, over time, differential living conditions for noncitizens across countries.

The process of acquiring and holding citizenship might produce *investment* or *socialization* that changes people's skills, motivations, actions, or viewpoints. In many countries, immigrants can naturalize following a period of residence, passing a language and/or civics test, paying a fee, and meeting other requirements.[10] Acquiring skills to pass naturalization tests could facilitate economic, civic, and political integration. Once naturalized, the new citizen may also pay more attention to politics because of democratic discourses that underscore civic responsibilities. The security of citizenship may also shift an immigrant's financial investments from the homeland to the adopted country, spurring business or home ownership, or it could lead to further education and training. Conversely, as DeVoretz and Irastorza hypothesize in this volume, immigrants from less developed countries might invest in a new citizenship to facilitate return migration or a move to a third country, as among European Union member states. In either the settlement or onward migration scenario, we would posit bigger citizenship gains for those who initially hold a more internationally devalued nationality and who acquire a more valued one.[11]

Citizenship might also act as a *signaling* mechanism vis-à-vis others. Employers or teachers may view immigrants who acquired citizenship as long-term employees or students, not just temporary residents. Irrespective of actual skills or motivation, citizens might be judged as having better language ability, more knowledge of

---

[10] Sara Goodman, *Immigration and Membership Politics in Western Europe* (Cambridge: Cambridge University Press, 2014).

[11] According to one tally, German citizens can enter 177 of 218 countries and territories without a visa, while citizens of Afghanistan can do so in only 25 countries (Elaine Yu, 'World's Best and Worst Passports Revealed,' *CNN*, March 1, 2016, online http://www.cnn.com/2016/03/01/travel/worlds-best-worst-passports).

social norms, or more motivation. We might expect the strongest signaling effects for those who face greater barriers to employment or who are more stigmatized by others.

Finally, being a citizen might provide people with a stronger sense of standing, self-empowerment, and identification with others in society. Such *social psychological effects* may increase people's sense of well-being, even if their material conditions do not change. Collectively, shared citizenship may produce societies with a greater sense of cohesion or solidarity, feelings potentially useful in supporting redistributive policy and positive social relations or, in a darker scenario, supporting foreign aggression.

In sum, and with no claim to being an exhaustive list, citizenship may matter because it provides access to opportunities, rights, and benefits; it connotes a degree of legitimacy; it leads to mobilization by other actors; it spurs personal investment or more rapid socialization in the economic, civic, or political life of the country; it serves as a signal to others of particular skills, motivations, or time horizons; and it carries social psychological effects.

CITIZENSHIP DOES NOT MATTER: A HOLLOW PROMISE, OR A POSTNATIONAL ERA

The view that citizenship matters can be challenged from two distinct perspectives that I conceptualize as the 'hollow promise' and 'postnational' critiques.

At the heart of the 'hollow promise' critique is the observation that substantive citizenship—defined as equality of rights, participation (including for some, outcomes), and belonging—varies so widely that formal citizenship becomes irrelevant. Examples abound, from past denials of the suffrage based on owning property, gender, race, religious affiliation, or indigeneity, to contemporary studies of inequality, which show much higher chances of incarceration among black men in the United States, or higher rates of mortality around the world for those with less education and income compared to those of higher social class. Such 'second-class' citizenship can be actively produced by the state or it endures due to the state's disregard or inability to intervene in socially generated inequality.

Hollow-promise critics may appreciate citizenship in theory, but find it useless in practice, or they may view it as a construct that exacerbates inequalities. In an optimistic vein, the ideal of citizenship may act as a 'promissory note,' in the words of Martin Luther King, Jr., allowing second-class citizens to mobilize for change. In a pessimistic vein, valorizing national citizenship divides the working class and undermines the ability of those in structurally vulnerable economic and political positions to enact change.[12]

Critiques about the substantive irrelevance of citizenship focus on a promise not achieved. A second critique contends that so much progress has been made in advancing human rights that nation-state citizenship has been eclipsed.[13] Depending on the author, the mechanisms behind citizenship's eclipse vary: international conventions constrain states' actions or influence the domestic judiciary; local officials adopt personhood orientations in drafting regulations or providing services; advocacy organizations leverage the normative discourse of human rights and symbolic value of international conventions as moral suasion in public campaigns. In most cases, 'postnational' arguments enumerate the multitude of rights given to residents based on universal humanity irrespective of citizenship or, in a more curtailed view, based on legal residency, economic contribution (for temporary or clandestine workers), or social contribution (e.g., based on being a parent, or length of residence). Human rights raise the 'floor' with regards to rights, participation, and treatment, such that life chances are loosely or not linked to citizenship. Similarly, in a globalized world, identities can be simultaneously more local and transnational, 'denationalized' from the nation-state.[14]

EVALUATING CITIZENSHIP'S IMPORTANCE: METHODOLOGICAL CHALLENGES

Is citizenship a hollow promise, or has it been eclipsed? This is hard to answer, empirically, partly because it is difficult to isolate the independent effect of citizenship

---

[12] The argument can be made from a Marxist or non-Marxist position. For the latter, arguing that the citizenship system limits the life chance of many and protects the generous conditions of the few, see Joseph H. Carens, *The Ethics of Immigration* (Oxford: Oxford University Press, 2013); Ayelet Shachar, *The Birthright Lottery: Citizenship and Global Inequality* (Cambridge: Harvard University Press, 2009). Arguing that citizenship has been transformed from state-based to market-based, see Natalie Deckard and Alison Heslin, 'After Postnational Citizenship: Constructing the Boundaries of Inclusion in Neoliberal Contexts,' *Sociology Compass 10*, no. 4 (2016): pp. 294–305.

[13] Soysal (n 5); Tambini (n 5).

[14] Saskia Sassen, 'The Repositioning of Citizenship: Emergent Subjects and Spaces for Politics,' *Berkeley Journal of Sociology 46* (2002): pp. 4–26. A related argument is that national citizenship in Europe is being eclipsed by EU 'citizenship,' which ensures virtually identical status, rights, and ability to participate throughout the Union. EU citizenship still requires, however, citizenship in a member state. See Maas in this volume; Strumia in this volume.

status and to establish its causal effect net of all the other factors that determine people's lives or affect societal outcomes.

First, in virtually all countries where some residents are noncitizens, they differ from citizens in patterned ways. Foreign-born migrants tend to have a different educational profile, language abilities, religion, and cultural background than citizens. If a researcher finds noncitizens earn less than citizens, she cannot easily determine whether income differences are due to citizenship, human capital, discrimination, or something else. In places where locally born minority groups lack citizenship due to redrawn borders or political exclusion, their noncitizenship is often tied to ethnic and religious differences that can affect life outcomes and feelings of belonging.

Researchers tackle these problems by comparing roughly similar groups of people who hold citizenship or not, or by studying the same people before and after they acquire citizenship. Cross-sectional multivariate statistical models compare people who are virtually identical, except for citizenship status, to see whether they have different levels of social trust, educational attainment, and so forth. In longitudinal studies, a researcher tracks the same person over time.[15] The problem, however, is that holding or acquiring citizenship is almost never independent of other unmeasured factors that might affect life chances. For example, consider a twenty-five-year-old immigrant who makes $25,000 a year. He becomes a citizen at twenty-eight, and a researcher finds that at age thirty-two, he earns $45,000 a year. Citizenship might have improved his economic situation. But so, too, might his increased work experience over seven years of employment, an improving labor market, a higher legislated minimum wage, or other contextual factors. We could compare this worker to a noncitizen with a similar profile who only makes $39,000 per year. Yet presumably the man who took the initiative to acquire citizenship—or who had the social networks or institutional support to naturalize—is different from the noncitizen. Individual initiative, social networks, or institutional environments may have fostered both citizenship and higher earnings, with no causal effect of citizenship per se.

Sometimes 'external shocks' can be used as a methodological strategy. When people suddenly become citizens for reasons outside the normal course of their lives, we can discount arguments about differences in individual ability or interest in citizenship. In 2000, a new German law gave *jus soli* citizenship to children with at least one long-term resident foreign parent. A few studies exploit the legislative change to compare outcomes among families whose children acquired birthright citizenship from those who did not.[16] Yet even with 'external shocks', if new citizens

---

[15] Most survey data are cross-sectional, thus data constraints hamper researchers' ability to do longitudinal analysis. Exceptions include North European datasets that combine over-time household register and administrative data.

[16] Ciro Avitabile, Irma Clots-Figueras, and Paolo Masella, 'The Effect of Birthright Citizenship on Parental Integration Outcomes,' *Journal of Law and Economics* 56, no. 3 (2013): pp. 777–810; Ciro

suddenly identify more with the adopted country, how much does identification stem from citizenship status, and how much from the political and social forces that lead to the legal reform?[17]

Methodologically, to pinpoint causality, researchers could use random assignment with citizenship as 'treatment'. Researchers could randomly assign some noncitizen Haitians in the Dominican Republic or noncitizen ethnic Russians in Latvia to receive citizenship while a 'control' group is denied citizenship. Comparing the two groups over time would show how much citizenship matters. In quasi-experimental work using a dataset of would-be Swiss citizens subject to a local vote to decide their naturalization, researchers compare citizens who barely garnered sufficient votes to those who just lost their naturalization bid.[18] Alternatively, citizens could be randomly assigned to a group stripped of citizenship or another group that is not, with comparisons over time.

Such an experiment is obviously fraught with ethical problems; most people would be aghast at stripping people of citizenship in pursuit of methodological purism. Such shock is revealing, however: many people assume citizenship does matter in a world system still dominated by state-based membership. I now turn to empirical evidence that supports this intuition, focusing on political and civic engagement, socio-economic outcomes, and social inclusion.

POLITICAL AND CIVIC ENGAGEMENT

We can evaluate the significance of citizenship for access—is it needed to participate in political life?—and for participation: to what degree does citizenship affect people's actual political and civic engagement? Access clearly matters in a circumscribed set of contemporary democracies. Social psychological, investment/socialization, and mobilization mechanisms also appear significant for participation.

Avitabile, Irma Clots-Figueras, and Paolo Masella, 'Citizenship, Fertility, and Parental Investments', *American Economic Journal: Applied Economics* 6, no. 4 (2014): pp. 35–65.

[17] Specialized techniques can also be used to try to deal with unobserved covariates, such as an instrumental variable approach, difference-in-difference analysis, Heckman selection, or fixed effects models.

[18] Jens Hainmueller, Dominik Hangartner, and Giuseppe Pietrantuono, 'Naturalization Fosters the Long-Term Political Integration of Immigrants', *Proceedings of the National Academy of Sciences* 112, no. 41 (2015): pp. 12651–12656; Jens Hainmueller, Dominik Hangartner, and Giuseppe Pietrantuono, 'Catalyst or Crown: Does Naturalization Promote the Long-Term Social Integration of Immigrants?' (forthcoming, 2017), *American Political Science Review*, online https://doi.org/10.1017/S0003055416000745.

Citizenship and Access to Political and Civic Engagement

In nondemocratic states, holding citizenship provides no guaranteed access to the ballot box, freedom of political expression, or freedom to assemble for collective action. The absence of an automatic link between citizenship status and political rights also characterizes the history of all current democracies, which—depending on the country—restricted participation based on gender, property ownership, religion, ethno-racial background, indigeneity, education or literacy, mental competency, criminal record, and age. Conversely, in some countries the historic primacy of gender, race, national origin, and other suffrage qualifications let noncitizens vote even when some citizens could not.[19]

The lack of political rights for some citizens—historically, or in the case of felon disenfranchisement, today—feeds into the hollow promise argument.[20] The argument is further fueled by inequalities in who actually casts ballots or stands for office. In the United States, for example, voters skew whiter, older, richer, and more educated than the eligible voting age population, and even more so than the resident population.

Still, citizenship status matters for access. Postnational arguments underscore how contemporary laws extend suffrage to noncitizen residents. In 2014, MIPEX documents that non-EU foreigners could vote in local elections in twenty-one of thirty-eight democratic countries. A smaller number of countries, fourteen of thirty-eight, allowed noncitizens to stand for local office.[21] European Union member states are required to provide EU citizens with the right to vote in local and European Parliament elections, but each country may establish its own rules for 'third country' noncitizens and for national elections. Indeed, noncitizenship remains one of the few accepted exclusions from voting, casting ballots in referenda or plebiscites, or standing for political office. Noncitizens only enjoy 'reasonable access' to national elections in one country, New Zealand. Paraguay, Uruguay, Ecuador, Chile, and Malawi do not explicitly require citizenship to vote nationally, only a period of residence.[22]

---

[19] For example, noncitizen white men who declared their intention to naturalize could vote in many U.S. states and territories in the late nineteenth and early twentieth century. See Shaw in this volume for more on the franchise.

[20] See Bauböck in this volume; Shaw in this volume for the political rights of expatriate citizens living in another country.

[21] See Migrant Integration Policy Index 2015, 'Political Participation', online http://www.mipex.eu/political-participation.

[22] Ludvig Beckman, 'Democratization and Inclusion,' in Jeffrey Haynes, ed., *Routledge Handbook of Democratization* (New York: Routledge Publishing, 2012), chapter 10, p. 168. This does not mean these countries allow noncitizen national voting in practice. Bilateral treaties and other arrangements also can establish reciprocal voting rights for nationals in each other's countries, as between Portugal and Brazil or the UK and Ireland.

Beyond voting, other political acts are often, but not universally, open to non-citizens. Immigrants are guaranteed basic political liberties similar to citizens in Australia, Canada, New Zealand, the United States, and Western Europe, but there are restrictions on joining a political party or founding a political association in all eleven Central European EU countries and Turkey.[23] Until 1981, France forbade foreign nationals from forming an association. Counter to the postnationalist argument, for countries tracked from 2007 to 2014, MIPEX reports little change in immigrants' political opportunities. Given that noncitizens can be deported, they may avoid participation in demonstrations or strikes—even if lawful—out of fear of police or government reprisal.[24]

Beyond Access: Citizenship Mechanisms and Participation

Researchers study a range of participatory engagement, from being a member of a political party or civic association, to signing a petition, boycotting a product or store, joining a demonstration, or attending a public meeting. They also probe people's social attitudes, trust in government, and opinion on policy and political questions.

A few studies find no effect of citizenship status on political and civic indicators, but overall, the limited evidence suggests that naturalized immigrants participate more than noncitizen immigrants, and that foreign-born citizens participate somewhat less or about the same as native-born citizens, with variation by country of origin and country of residence.[25] The participation of second-generation citizens of immigrant origins appears largely indistinguishable from other, similar native-born citizens, suggesting political socialization may be the dominant process at play.[26] Individual factors such as age, education, and length of residence explain variation

[23] See MIPEX and European Union Democracy Observatory on Citizenship Database, online http://eudo-citizenship.eu.

[24] Lisa Martinez, 'Yes We Can: Latino Participation in Unconventional Politics,' *Social Forces 84*, no. 1 (2005): pp. 135–155.

[25] Chistel Kesler and Neli Demireva, 'Social Cohesion and Host Country Nationality among Immigrants in Western Europe,' in *Naturalisation: A Passport for the Better Integration of Immigrants?* (Paris: OECD, 2011): pp. 209–235; Laura Morales and Marco Giugni, *Social Capital, Political Participation and Migration in Europe: Making Multicultural Democracy Work?* (London: Palgrave Macmillan, 2011); Hainmueller et al., 'Naturalization Fosters' (n 18); Aida Just and Christopher Anderson, 'Immigrants, Citizenship and Political Action in Europe,' *British Journal of Political Science 42*, no. 3 (2012): pp. 481–509.

[26] Irene Bloemraad and Matthew Wright, ' "Utter Failure" or Unity Out of Diversity? Debating and Evaluating Policies of Multiculturalism,' *International Migration Review 48*, no. s1 (2014): pp. S292–S334.

in participation, as do the adopted country's political institutions and policies; sending country characteristics may matter, too, but there is greater debate on this.[27]

If citizenship matters for political engagement, it is not just a function of formal access. Examining municipal and provincial elections in Sweden, in which non-citizens can vote, Bevelander and Pendakur find that attaining citizenship increases the probability of casting a ballot among foreign-born residents.[28] Comparing those who narrowly achieve Swiss citizenship to those who do not, Hainmueller, Hangartner, and Pietrantuono find that naturalization increases political knowledge and sense of political efficacy.[29] However, while non-electoral political engagement also increases, it is not significantly different from the participation of noncitizens. In contrast, Martinez observes an increase in the likelihood of protest with citizenship among Latinos in the United States, a conclusion echoed by Just and Andersen who find, across nineteen European democracies, that citizenship increases noninstitutionalized engagement, especially among those who migrate from nondemocratic countries.[30]

The differential effect of citizenship for migrants from more or less democratic countries is consistent with investment/socialization arguments and social psychological mechanisms. Migrants from nondemocratic countries may have fewer civic skills or political knowledge, and weaker political trust or participation norms. The naturalization process could develop civic knowledge and norms, as well as language skills, and reassure people that participation without fear is a right of citizenship. Indepth interviews with naturalized immigrants in North America offer mixed support for such arguments: some researchers document instrumental or defensive reasons for naturalization rather than participatory ones, while others find evidence of skill acquisition and feelings of greater legitimacy, as well as increased mobilization by other political actors.[31]

The Political Impact of More or Less Open Citizenship Policies

Researchers mostly ask how citizenship status affects individual political participation or, less frequently, collective action. We know less about the societal effects of having more or less expansive citizenship policies and, by implication, larger or

---

[27] Morales and Giugni (n 25); Just and Anderson (n 25).

[28] Peter Bevelander and Ravi Pendakur, 'Voting and Social Inclusion in Sweden,' *International Migration 49*, no. 4 (2011): pp. 67–92.

[29] Hainmueller et al., 'Naturalization Fosters' (n 18).

[30] Martinez (n 24); Just and Anderson (n 25).

[31] Sofya Aptekar, *The Road to Citizenship: What Naturalization Means for Immigrants and the United States* (New Brunswick: Rutgers University Press, 2015); Irene Bloemraad, *Becoming a Citizen: Incorporating Immigrants and Refugees in the United States and Canada* (Berkeley: University of California Press, 2006); Greta Gilbertson and Audrey Singer, 'The Emergence of Protective Citizenship in the USA: Naturalization among Dominican Immigrants in the Post-1996 Welfare Reform Era,' *Ethnic and Racial Studies 26*, no. 1 (2003): pp. 25–51.

smaller populations of noncitizens. Arguably, a high percentage of noncitizens in the population—7 per cent of the U.S. population in 2015—undermines the demo-cratic legitimacy of a political system claiming representation of, by and for the people. But normative arguments aside, what are the substantive consequences?

Citizenship policies and aggregate levels of noncitizenship might affect political decisions. In Western countries, immigrants tend to support parties of the left, perhaps because of alignment with economic concerns or stances on diversity. Electoral outcomes and policy decisions in countries with significant immigrant populations and extensive naturalization may shift in line with immigrants' preferences. An analysis of ten European countries from 1980 to 2008 found that one of the best predictors of immigrant rights expansion was growth in the immigrant electorate.[32] Citizenship laws may also affect the attitudes of the native-born population. Survey data in a range of Western countries indicate that the majority population expresses less political and social tolerance for minorities in countries with exclusionary citizenship policy, while *jus soli* citizenship regimes and higher levels of social spending correlate with more immigrant-inclusive definitions of the national community. The causal relationship between policy and attitudes is hard to determine, but some argue that policy can influence social identity processes and legitimacy norms.[33] If citizenship regimes generate legislative and attitudinal change, countries with more or less open policies may become more distinctive over time due to political feedback loops.

SOCIO-ECONOMIC PARTICIPATION
AND INCLUSION

Is there a citizenship 'premium' in the labor market, or a penalty for not having citizenship? Does citizenship policy matter for macroeconomic outcomes? Historically, holding citizenship did not stop egregious economic inequalities based on gender, ethno-racial background, religion, disability, and so forth. Today, numerous countries proscribe firing a pregnant employee or refusing to hire someone based on

---

[32] Ruud Koopmans, Ines Michalowski, and Stine Waibel, 'Citizenship Rights for Immigrants: National Political Processes and Cross-National Convergence in Western Europe, 1980–2008,' *American Journal of Sociology 117*, no. 4 (2012): pp. 1202–1245.

[33] Steven A. Weldon, 'The Institutional Context of Tolerance for Ethnic Minorities: A Comparative, Multilevel Analysis of Western Europe,' *American Journal of Political Science 50*, no. 2 (2006): pp. 331–349; Matthew Wright, 'Policy Regimes and Normative Conceptions of Nationalism in Mass Public Opinion,' *Comparative Political Studies 44*, no. 5 (2011): pp. 598–624.

race, yet researchers still find systematic differences in education, employment, and income by gender, race, and other ascriptive traits. For some, this is evidence of two-tiered citizenship, rendering the status irrelevant. Alternatively, in a context of global capitalism and deregulated markets, financial or human capital may drive socio-economic outcomes, not state-based citizenship.

Citizenship Premiums and Socio-economic Outcomes

Available research nevertheless suggests that citizenship carries employment and income benefits for individuals and families. Citizenship status can provide access. In 2014, full access to public sector jobs was limited to nationals (or EU nationals) in ten European countries, mostly in central and southeast Europe, but also in France and Luxembourg. Another thirteen countries had partial citizenship restrictions.[34] Access to high-paying professional fields, such as dentistry, medicine, and law, is also restricted to citizens in some countries. Restrictions may limit employment or channel noncitizens to private sector jobs with less security and fewer benefits than in the public sector.[35]

Once employed, noncitizen workers in Western states tend to have the same rights to union representation and labor protections as citizens, but noncitizens are excluded from parts of the social security system in seventeen of the thirty-eight countries surveyed by MIPEX, including Australia, New Zealand, the United States, the UK, and many central European nations.[36] Differential access to social benefits, shaped by welfare state and immigrant incorporation regimes, can produce lower standards of living and more poverty for noncitizens than citizens.[37] Access to education does not usually distinguish between citizens and permanent residents, but eligibility for scholarships or financial aid can.

Beyond access, acquiring citizenship appears to improve employment outcomes, wages, and movement to better jobs, especially for immigrants from poorer countries.[38]

---

[34] See Migrant Integration Policy Index 2015, 'Labour Marker Mobility', online http://www.mipex.eu/labour-market-mobility.

[35] Vincent Corluy, Ive Marx, and Gerlinde Verbist, 'Employment Chances and Changes of Immigrants in Belgium: The Impact of Citizenship', *International Journal of Comparative Sociology 52*, no. 4 (2011): pp. 350–368.

[36] Labor rights on the books do not necessarily translate into rights in practice, so citizenship might still mitigate exploitation even when noncitizen workers have formal rights (Kerry Preibisch and Gerardo Otero, 'Does Citizenship Status Matter in Canadian Agriculture? Workplace Health and Safety for Migrant and Immigrant Laborers', *Rural Sociology 79*, no. 2 (2014): pp. 174–199).

[37] Ann Morissens and Diane Sainsbury, 'Migrants' Social Rights, Ethnicity and Welfare Regimes', *Journal of Social Policy 34*, no. 4 (2005): pp. 637–660; Diane Sainsbury, *Welfare States and Immigrant Rights: The Politics of Inclusion and Exclusion* (Oxford: Oxford University Press, 2012).

[38] See, e.g., Corluy et al. (n 35); Denis Fougère and Mirna Safi, 'Naturalization and Employment of Immigrants in France (1968-1999)', *International Journal of Manpower 30*, no. 1–2 (2009): pp. 83–96;

The wage premium of citizenship, holding other personal attributes constant, is estimated at about 1 to 5 percent in countries such as Canada, Denmark, Germany, Norway, the Netherlands, Sweden, and the United States.[39]

Evidence for positive citizenship effects contrasts to earlier studies that found no economic benefits or even a negative correlation with economic outcomes. Chiswick, using U.S. data, argued that any observed effect is an artefact of years of residence until naturalization, years that increase human capital such as language skills and work experience.[40] In Sweden, some immigrants' labor market participation declined after naturalization in the 1990s.[41] The negative or null effect could stem from different foreign-born populations, distinct welfare and tax systems, or methodological and data problems. In a cross-sectional comparison of eight European countries, Koopmans argues that states with policies of open citizenship, multiculturalism, and generous welfare provisions turn immigrants 'into passive welfare-state clients' who live in more segregated neighborhoods and are more likely to be convicted of crimes.[42] However, most subsequent research finds weakly positive citizenship effects, depending on the gender and origins of the immigrants.[43] It is unclear whether recent work is a corrective to older studies' more limited data and methods, or if returns to citizenship have changed.[44]

Thomas Liebig and Friederike Von Haaren, 'Citizenship and the Socio-Economic Integration of Immigrants and their Children,' in *Naturalisation: A Passport for the Better Integration of Immigrants?* (Paris: OECD: 2011), pp. 23–64.

[39] Bernt Bratsberg, James Ragan Jr., and Zafar Nasir, 'The Effect of Naturalization on Wage Growth: A Panel Study of Young Male Immigrants,' *Journal of Labor Economics* 20, no. 3 (2002): pp. 568–597; Don J. DeVoretz and Sergiy Pivnenko, 'The Economic Causes and Consequences of Canadian Citizenship,' *Journal of International Migration and Integration* 6, no. 3–4 (2005): pp. 435–468; Jonas Helgertz, Pieter Bevelander, and Anna Tegunimataka, 'Naturalization and Earnings: a Denmark–Sweden Comparison,' *European Journal of Population* 30, no. 3 (2014): pp. 337–359; Liebig and Von Haaren (n 38); Garnett Picot and Feng Hou, 'Citizenship Acquisition in Canada and the United States: Determinants and Economic Benefit,' in *Naturalisation: A Passport for the Better Integration of Immigrants?* (Paris: OECD, 2011), pp. 153–182; Max Steinhardt, 'Does Citizenship Matter? The Economic Impact of Naturalizations in Germany,' *Labour Economics* 19, no. 6 (2012): pp. 813–823. See also DeVoretz and Irastorza in this volume.

[40] Barry Chiswick, 'The Effect of Americanization on the Earnings of Foreign-Born Men,' *The Journal of Political Economy* 86, no. 5 (1978): pp. 897–921.

[41] Kirk Scott, 'The Economics of Citizenship: Is There a Naturalization Effect?,' in Pieter Bevelander and Don J. DeVoretz, eds., *The Economics of Citizenship* (Malmö: Malmö University Press, 2008), pp. 105–126.

[42] Ruud Koopmans, 'Trade-Offs between Equality and Difference: Immigrant integration, Multiculturalism and the Welfare State in Cross-National Perspective,' *Journal of Ethnic and Migration Studies* 36, no. 1 (2010): pp. 1–26, p. 22.

[43] Bratsberg, Ragan, and Nasir (n 39); Scott (n 41); Pieter Bevelander and Ravi Pendakur, 'Citizenship, Co-Ethnic Populations, and Employment Probabilities of Immigrants in Sweden,' *Journal of International Migration and Integration* 13, no. 2 (2012): pp. 203–222; Helgertz, Bevelander, and Tegunimataka (n 39).

[44] For example, legislative changes in the United States, such as the 1985 U.S. Immigration Reform and Control Act that instituted employer penalties for hiring undocumented workers, may have led some employers to shun noncitizens, even those with work authorization.

Future research must better theorize and analyze the mechanisms that link citizenship to labor market outcomes. In the United States and Belgium, researchers find that new citizens gain access to more public sector, permanent, white collar, and union jobs, which helps accelerate wage growth.[45] Such gains might interact with life course such that benefits accrue more to younger workers, and with gender, although gender effects vary considerably by country, with no clear pattern.[46]

Citizenship might also bring a sense of security and permanent settlement, prompting investment in human, financial, and social capital through job and language training or investing in homeownership. Examining fourteen European countries, Corrigan (2015) argues that the conditionality of legal status at the country level influences non-EU immigrants' occupational attainment through skills investment and greater employment selectivity; immigrants hold higher status jobs in places where legal permanent residency is more secure and citizenship attainment is easier.[47] Citizenship might also mitigate discrimination by employers or lenders against those of foreign birth by signaling national membership, greater integration, or long-term residence. With improved employment, income, and legal security, naturalized citizens might buy a home or accumulate more savings in the adopted country rather than sending remittances or building houses in the country of origin. The limited research on legal status and asset accumulation is inconclusive on the effect of citizenship, at least for Latinos in the United States.[48]

All three mechanisms—access to (better) jobs, human and social capital investment, or a signal to employers—are plausible. To better adjudicate between them, researchers must consider variations in the citizenship premium. One consistent finding is that immigrants from poorer countries benefit more from citizenship than nationals of richer countries. Access mechanisms should not vary between immigrants from richer or poorer countries, but signaling effects might be stronger for migrants from non-OECD countries if employers hold discriminatory views or question their human capital, such as their educational credentials or work experience.

---

[45] Corluy, Marx, and Verbist (n 35); Bratsberg, Ragan, and Nasir (n 39).

[46] Floris Peters and Maarten Vink, 'Naturalization and the Socio-Economic Integration of Immigrants: A Life-Course Perspective', in Gary Freeman and Nikola Mirilovic, eds., *Handbook on Migration and Social Policy* (Northampton: Edward Elgar Publishing, 2016), pp. 362–376.

[47] Corrigan, Owen, 'Conditionality of Legal Status and Immigrant Occupational Attainment in Western Europe', *Policy & Politics 43*, no. 2 (2015): 181–202.

[48] Some studies find an increase in home ownership with citizenship, but no other asset boost as compared to legal permanent residency (Eileen McConnell, 'Diverging Dividends, Diverging Futures: Nativity, Citizenship Status, Legal Status, and the Non-Housing Asset Accumulation of Latinos', *Ethnicities 15*, no. 2 (2015): pp. 255–281; Eileen McConnell, 'Hurdles or Walls? Nativity, Citizenship, Legal Status and Latino Homeownership in Los Angeles', *Social Science Research 53*, (2015): pp. 19–33; Donald Bradley, Richard Green, and Brian Surette, 'The Impacts of Remittances, Residency Status and Financial Attachment on Housing Tenure for Mexican-Heritage Americans: Inferences from a New Survey', *Real Estate Economics 35*, no. 4 (2007): pp. 451–478).

Citizenship Regimes and the Socio-Economic Consequences for Societies

Much has been written about a possible 'progressive's dilemma,' namely that immigrants' ethno-racial, cultural, and religious diversity may undermine feelings of collective solidarity necessary to sustain the welfare state.[49] These debates focus on ethno-racial and religious diversity, not citizenship status; few academics have asked whether citizenship policies carry macro socio-economic consequences.[50] Citizenship policy could mitigate a progressive's dilemma if inclusive citizenship policy generates a sense of communal membership and solidarity.[51] Conversely, if large percentages of a state's residents lack citizenship, social redistribution could be eroded or, alternatively, exclusions based on citizenship could increase. A few observers note that neoliberal discourses of individual responsibility are intertwining with harder barriers to permanent residency and citizenship in some countries, potentially a new form of welfare chauvinism.[52]

Citizenship regimes could also generate socio-economic consequences through the mechanism of voting. Trying to explain why inequality has risen in tandem with welfare retrenchment in the United States—in contradiction to many voting models—McCarty, Poole, and Rosenthal argue that immigration facilitated a movement away from redistribution because noncitizens are ineligible to vote and thus 'less pressure to redistribute comes from the bottom of the income distribution.'[53] Since voting rights are among the most tightly tied to citizenship, this argument could apply beyond the United States. Sainsbury argues that parties of the left, in the United States and Europe, tend to facilitate immigrants' formal and substantive access to social benefits more than parties of the right.[54]

---

[49] Keith Banting and Will Kymlicka, *Multiculturalism and the Welfare State: Recognition and Redistribution in Contemporary Democracies* (Oxford: Oxford University Press, 2006); Will Kymlicka and Keith Banting, *The Strains of Commitment: The Political Sources of Solidarity in Diverse Societies* (Oxford: Oxford University Press, 2016).

[50] One macro-economic effect is on the fiscal system, balancing a state's costs in extending citizenship against gains (e.g., in taxes) from immigrants' naturalization. See DeVoretz and Irastorza in this volume.

[51] For Marshall (n 8), the inherent inequalities of market economies could be reconciled to democratic equality via citizenship since a progression of civil, political, and social rights brought benefits to the individual and fostered collective solidarity. Margaret Somers contends that citizenship can provide social justice by balancing the power of the state, market, and civil society (Margaret Somers, *Genealogies of Citizenship: Markets, Statelessness and the Right to Have Rights* (Cambridge: Cambridge University Press, 2008)). Available empirical research has not, however, evaluated whether societies with more inclusive citizenship policy experience greater social cohesion and social justice.

[52] Sainsbury (n 37); Soysal (n 5).

[53] Nolan McCarty, Keith Poole, and Howard Rosenthal, *Polarized America: The Dance of Political Ideology and Unequal Riches* (Cambridge: MIT Press, 2006), p. 13.

[54] Sainsbury (n 37).

Few studies examine whether the percentage of noncitizens affects redistribution or other social policies. Fox, Bloemraad, and Kesler attempt one test by examining over-time social spending across U.S. states.[55] They find, surprisingly, a positive correlation between social spending and the percentage of noncitizens in a state's voting age population (as well as the percentage of naturalized citizens and foreign-born), but a negative correlation with the percentage of racial minorities (blacks, Latinos, and Asians). Speculating on the positive effects of the immigration variables, they note that social movement activism does not require citizenship and that birthright citizenship may allow the second generation to exercise political voice for disenfranchised noncitizens. But they also underscore the need for more research to disentangle the effects of citizenship and racial minority status on social policy.

IDENTITY AND SOCIAL INTEGRATION

Citizenship is also about identity and collective membership. Does citizenship make someone identify more with the nation or fellow citizens? There is no necessary relationship: citizens can feel alienated from their country, while some undocumented U.S. residents feel American. The postnational argument claims that contemporary identities are simultaneously more local (e.g., a Parisian or New Yorker) and transnational (e.g., a diasporic identity as Gujarati), rather than tied to citizenship.

Still, nation-state identities remain significant. The 2013 International Social Survey Programme asked residents of over thirty countries how important holding citizenship was for being 'truly' American, French, Korean, Turkish, and so forth. In eleven countries with more than a handful of noncitizen respondents, only 24 percent of noncitizens felt citizenship was not very or not at all important, as did 8 percent of citizens; conversely, citizenship status was 'very' important to 62 percent of citizens and 41 percent of noncitizens.[56]

Shared belief in citizenship's importance appears greater in countries with more inclusive citizenship policies. In the United States, only 12 percent of noncitizens—and just 7 percent of citizens—said that citizenship was not very or not at all

[55] Cybelle Fox, Irene Bloemraad, and Christel Kesler, 'Immigration and Redistributive Social Policy,' in David Card and Steven Raphael, eds., *Immigration, Poverty and Socioeconomic Inequality* (New York: Russell Sage Foundation Press, 2013), pp. 381–420.

[56] The remainder found it 'fairly' important. Calculations using the 2013 International Social Survey Program Database, online http://www.gesis.org/issp/home/.

important for being 'truly' American.[57] Conversely, in countries with higher historic or current barriers to naturalization or *jus soli* citizenship, such as Germany or Switzerland, 54 percent and 44 percent of noncitizens, but just 17 percent and 19 percent of citizens, respectively, felt that citizenship was unimportant. In a study of Turkish immigrants, identification with the host country was higher in France and the Netherlands, countries with easier citizenship access at the time, than in Germany.[58] The data imply that calls to make naturalization more difficult in order to heighten the meaning of citizenship may do the opposite, devaluing citizenship as a marker of national identity, at least for the foreign-born.

Citizenship may also link to identity among the second generation. In North America, where children of immigrants have birthright citizenship, they strongly identify as 'Canadian' or 'American', in some cases more so than longstanding minorities like Francophones in Canada.[59] In the UK, second generation immigrants are only slightly less likely to think of themselves as British than white UK-born residents, and more likely than UK-born residents of Irish background.[60]

Identity effects appear stronger among immigrants from poorer and less democratic countries. In Britain, only 41 percent of 'white' immigrants of European or North American origin reported a British identity (another 5 percent report a dual identity), compared to 62 percent of foreign-born Bangladeshi (5 percent dual) and 64 percent of foreign-born black Caribbeans (6 percent dual).[61] The difference relates partly to citizenship take-up: those from poorer countries are more likely to acquire British citizenship, and citizenship has a statistically significant correlation with British identity in the immigrant generation.[62] The differential effect is also seen with other indicators of social integration. Comparing otherwise similar immigrants, receiving Swiss citizenship significantly increased foreign-born residents' plans to stay in Switzerland and the likelihood of reading Swiss newspapers, especially among more marginalized groups and when naturalization occurred early.[63] The differential effects echo those for political and economic integration,

---

[57] See also, Deborah Schildkraut, 'Defining American Identity in the Twenty-First Century: How Much "There" is There?', *Journal of Politics* 69, no. 3 (2007): pp. 597–615 (showing that most U.S. residents, regardless of immigrant background, share norms on what constitute American identity).

[58] Evelyn Ersanilli and Ruud Koopmans, 'Rewarding Integration? Citizenship Regulations and the Socio-Cultural Integration of Immigrants in the Netherlands, France and Germany', *Journal of Ethnic and Migration Studies* 36, no. 5 (2010): pp, 773–791, pp. 783–784.

[59] Bloemraad and Wright (n 26).

[60] Alan Manning and Sanchari Roy, 'Culture Clash or Culture Club? National Identity in Britain', *The Economic Journal* 120, no. 542 (2010): pp. F72–F100.

[61] Ibid.

[62] Ibid. On France, see Rahsaan Maxwell and Erik Bleich, 'What Makes Muslims Feel French?', *Social Forces* 93, no. 1 (2014): pp. 155–179 (showing that Muslims are less likely to report feeling French than others in the country, but citizenship (as well as socio-economic integration and French language fluency) mitigate the difference).

[63] Hainmueller et al., 'Catalyst or Crown' (n 18).

suggesting that non-OECD migrants might value Western citizenship more, or may benefit more from legitimacy, signaling, or mobilization dynamics if others perceive them as outsiders.

The integrative effects of citizenship might also extend to other family members, including those lacking citizenship. Much of the research on citizenship's political or economic impact takes an atomized view, focused on the person who holds or does not hold citizenship. But naturalization is often a family decision.[64] We also know that parents' illegality has detrimental effects on children in the United States, even when children hold U.S. citizenship.[65] In a parallel way, we have suggestive evidence of positive externalities from a family member's citizenship. Exploiting the exogenous shock of extending birthright citizenship in Germany to certain babies born after 2000, Avitabile and colleagues find that having a child granted German citizenship produced a significant increase in parents' probability of socializing with Germans (measured as visiting or being visited by Germans) and reading German newspapers, even though parents' status did not change, but no statistically significant difference in using the German language.[66]

The German reform also provided an opportunity to study citizenship effects on health. Children granted birthright citizenship were less likely to be obese, had fewer behavioral problems, and greater well-being, as reported by parents.[67] The authors explain these benefits by adopting economist Gary Becker's 'quality-quantity' model of fertility: families with citizen off-spring had fewer children, which supposedly let parents invest more in citizen children. Alternatively, a framework attentive to the structural determinants of health suggests that citizenship might reduce stress, encourage better outreach by health professionals, improve socio-economic conditions, and so forth. Riosmena and colleagues advance this argument to understand the protective role of U.S. citizenship in mitigating immigrant women's declining health over time.[68]

Additional research must investigate citizenship mechanisms further and establish a common evidentiary base. While Avitabile and colleagues find an increase in inter-group social relations with children's citizenship, Ersanilli and Koopmans report no difference by naturalization status for Turkish immigrants' inter-ethnic

[64] Alex Street, 'My Child Will be a Citizen: Intergenerational Motives for Naturalization,' *World Politics* 66, no. 2 (2014): pp. 264–292.

[65] Frank Bean, Susan Brown, and James Bachmeier, *Parents without Papers: The Progress and Pitfalls of Mexican American Integration* (New York: Russell Sage Foundation, 2015); Joanna Dreby, 'The Burden of Deportation on Children in Mexican Immigrant Families,' *Journal of Marriage and Family* 74, no. 4 (2012): pp. 829–845.

[66] Avitabile et al., 'The Effect of Birthright' (n 16), p. 779.

[67] Avitabile et al., 'Citizenship, Fertility' (n 16).

[68] Fernando Riosmena, Bethany Everett, Richard Rogers, and Jeff Dennis, 'Negative Acculturation and Nothing More? Cumulative Disadvantage and Mortality during the Immigrant Adaptation Process among Latinos in the United States,' *International Migration Review* 49, no. 2 (2015): pp. 443–478.

contacts.[69] Hainmueller and colleagues' Swiss data find no differences in perceptions of discrimination between those who gain citizenship and those denied, but Kesler and Demireva report that immigrants who acquire citizenship report less discrimination than those without citizenship across multiple European countries.[70] Studying whether citizenship mitigates discrimination could speak to citizenship's legitimacy and identity effects.

Conclusion

Does citizenship matter? The available evidence does not offer a resounding 'yes,' but it does suggest that for individuals, and possibly families, holding citizenship increases political and civic engagement, carries economic benefits, strengthens identification with the national community, and may improve social integration, from one's health to social relations with others. These findings undermine the contention that citizenship is a hollow promise with no substantive weight, or that it has been eclipsed by personhood rights or identity processes decoupled from the nation-state. Citizenship effects do, however, appear modest, at least for those with permanent residency, and it is unclear whether the importance of citizenship is increasing or decreasing. A decline would be in line with postnational arguments, but some economic research suggests increasing returns to citizenship. As it stands, the methodological and data challenges of isolating a citizenship effect, net of social class, minority status, age, and so forth, ensures that much research remains to be done.

Moving forward, scholars must not just ask whether citizenship matters, but for whom, in what contexts, and why. The way citizenship structures access to rights and resources—such as casting a ballot or holding a good public sector job—provides one explanation for its impact. But access mechanisms cannot easily explain differential effects between groups of people. A growing body of evidence suggests that the consequences of citizenship are more substantial for immigrants from less developed or less democratic nations who live in Western states. This may be because the security of citizenship, with its indefinite right of residence in a rich, stable country with the rule of law and democratic institutions, spurs investment in one's own or one's children's human, financial, and social capital, alters future plans, and accelerates political socialization. Alternatively, if the skills of these immigrants are devalued by the native-born majority, or they face greater social stigma and

---

[69] Ersanilli and Koopmans (n 58).   [70] Kesler and Demireva (n 25).

discrimination, then legitimacy, signaling, and mobilization dynamics may benefit them more than migrants who are culturally, economically, and politically similar to the majority. Acquiring or holding citizenship might also increase identification with the country or feelings of well-being. This may flow from the ability to become a member of the nation, or as a consequence of better treatment and greater economic and social integration.

It is possible that existing empirical research underestimates citizenship's salience for individual and social outcomes. Much of the research reviewed here employs quantitative methods. However, conceiving of citizenship as an independent variable with additive value in a statistical equation may seriously understate citizenship's constitutive and recursive influence. Viewing citizenship as participation may better capture constitutive and interactive processes, and bridge legal and political scholarship with work on integration and inequality in sociology, anthropology, economics, and geography. For example, citizenship broadens access to the political system as a legal right and participatory norm. Political participation in turn can carry consequences for economic and social inclusion, the allocation of rights and resources, and other collective decisions in a liberal democracy. Having political voice might also signal legitimacy and inclusion to others and affect outreach and mobilization by native-born citizens, thus influencing social cohesion, collective identities, and inter-personal practices of inclusion and exclusion. Future research should balance scholars' longstanding interest in rights with deeper consideration of participation.

In short, citizenship effects might be pervasive but seemingly invisible, perhaps better grasped by asking what would happen if significant proportions of a country's population suddenly were stripped of citizenship. Attention to loss of citizenship—more prevalent outside North America and Western Europe—also underscores the critical importance of extending empirical work beyond the small group of rich, liberal democracies usually investigated. Citizenship only gains saliency when individuals or the state can prove citizenship or noncitizenship. If states cannot reliably discern citizens with administrative markers—something more likely in weak, resource-poor states—it may not matter. Indeed, in some situations, noncitizenship may provide bargaining power or consular benefits.[71] However, any advantages of noncitizenship are likely enjoyed primarily by those who hold a valued citizenship in another country. Statelessness remains a dangerous condition.

When states can distinguish citizens from noncitizens, the status carries consequences. From the perspective of those kept out of a richer, more stable country due to a lack of citizenship, the prize of access is high: the United Nations estimates that migrating from a less to more developed country results, on average, in a fifteen-fold increase in income, a doubling of educational enrolment rates, and a

---

[71] See, e.g., Erin Aeran Chung, *Immigration and Citizenship in Japan* (Cambridge: Cambridge University Press, 2010) (arguing that Korean-origin noncitizens have benefited from avoiding Japan's stringent citizenship policies).

sixteen-fold reduction in child mortality.[72] Even for those noncitizens let in and provided with the most secure of legal statuses, permanent legal residency, this status probably fails to ensure substantive equality with citizens for many people. Those who worry about substantive citizenship are right to point to inequalities based on race, origins, religion, and so forth, but wrong in concluding that citizenship fails to mitigate, if only partially, those inequalities. Citizenship does not erase inequalities, but its lack probably exacerbates them.

Bibliography

Aptekar, Sofya, *The Road to Citizenship: What Naturalization Means for Immigrants and the United States* (New Brunswick: Rutgers University Press, 2015).

Arendt, Hannah, *The Origins of Totalitarianism* (Cleveland: Meridian Books, 1962).

Avitabile, Ciro, Irma Clots-Figueras, and Paolo Masella, 'The Effect of Birthright Citizenship on Parental Integration Outcomes,' *Journal of Law and Economics* 56, no. 3 (2013): pp. 777–810, doi: 10.1086/673266.

Avitabile, Ciro, Irma Clots-Figueras, and Paolo Masella, 'Citizenship, Fertility, and Parental Investments,' *American Economic Journal: Applied Economics* 6, no. 4 (2014): pp. 35–65, doi: 10.1257/app.6.4.35.

Banting, Keith and Will Kymlicka, *Multiculturalism and the Welfare State: Recognition and Redistribution in Contemporary Democracies* (Oxford: Oxford University Press, 2006).

Bean, Frank D., Susan K. Brown, and James D. Bachmeier, *Parents without Papers: The Progress and Pitfalls of Mexican American Integration* (New York: Russell Sage Foundation, 2015).

Beckman, Ludvig, 'Democratization and Inclusion,' in Jeffrey Haynes, ed., *Routledge Handbook of Democratization* (New York: Routledge Publishing, 2012), pp. 161–174.

Bevelander, Peter and Ravi Pendakur, 'Voting and Social Inclusion in Sweden,' *International Migration* 49, no. 4 (2011): pp. 67–92, doi: 10.1111/j.1468-2435.2010.00605.x.

Bevelander, Pieter and Ravi Pendakur, 'Citizenship, Co-Ethnic Populations, and Employment Probabilities of Immigrants in Sweden,' *Journal of International Migration and Integration* 13, no. 2 (2012): pp. 203–222, doi: 10.1007/s12134-011-0212-6.

Blitz, Brad and Maureen Lynch, *Statelessness and Citizenship: A Comparative Study on the Benefits of Nationality* (Northampton: Edward Elgar Publishing, 2011).

Bloemraad, Irene, *Becoming a Citizen: Incorporating Immigrants and Refugees in the United States and Canada* (Berkeley: University of California Press, 2006).

Bloemraad, Irene, Anna Korteweg, and Gökçe Yurdakul, 'Citizenship and Immigration: Multiculturalism, Assimilation, and Challenges to the Nation-State,' *Annual Review of Sociology* 34, no. 1 (2008): pp. 153–179, doi: 10.1146/annurev.soc.34.040507.134608.

---

[72] United Nations Human Development, *Overcoming Barriers: Human Mobility and Development* (New York: Palgrave MacMillan, 2009), p. 24, online http://hdr.undp.org/sites/default/files/reports/269/hdr_2009_en_complete.pdf.

Bloemraad, Irene and Matthew Wright, ' "Utter Failure" or Unity Out of Diversity? Debating and Evaluating Policies of Multiculturalism,' *International Migration Review 48*, no. s1 (2014): pp. S292–S334, doi: 10.1111/imre.12135.

Bosniak, Linda, *The Citizen and the Alien: Dilemmas of Contemporary Membership* (Princeton: Princeton University Press, 2006).

Bradley, Donald, Richard Green, and Brian Surette, 'The Impacts of Remittances, Residency Status and Financial Attachment on Housing Tenure for Mexican-Heritage Americans: Inferences from a New Survey,' *Real Estate Economics 35*, no. 4 (2007): pp. 451–478, doi: 10.1111/j.1540-6229.2007.00197.x.

Bratsberg, Bernt, James Ragan Jr, and Zafar Nasir, 'The Effect of Naturalization on Wage Growth: A Panel Study of Young Male Immigrants,' *Journal of Labor Economics 20*, no. 3 (2002): pp. 568–597, doi: 10.1086/339616.

Carens, Joseph, *The Ethics of Immigration* (Oxford: Oxford University Press, 2013).

Chiswick, Barry, 'The Effect of Americanization on the Earnings of Foreign-Born Men,' *The Journal of Political Economy 86*, no. 5 (1978): pp. 897–921, doi: 10.1086/ 260717.

Chung, Erin Aeran, *Immigration and Citizenship in Japan* (Cambridge: Cambridge University Press, 2010).

Corluy, Vincent, Ive Marx, and Gerlinde Verbist, 'Employment Chances and Changes of Immigrants in Belgium: The Impact of Citizenship,' *International Journal of Comparative Sociology 52*, no. 4 (2011): pp. 350–368, doi: 10.1177/0020715211412112.

Corrigan, Owen, 'Conditionality of Legal Status and Immigrant Occupational Attainment in Western Europe,' *Policy & Politics 43*, no. 2 (2015): 181–202.

Deckard, Natalie and Alison Heslin, 'After Postnational Citizenship: Constructing the Boundaries of Inclusion in Neoliberal Contexts,' *Sociology Compass 10*, no. 4 (2016): pp. 294–305, doi: 10.1007/s12111-015-9314-0.

DeVoretz, Don J. and Sergiy Pivnenko, 'The Economic Causes and Consequences of Canadian Citizenship,' *Journal of International Migration and Integration 6*, no. 3–4 (2005): pp. 435–468, doi: 10.1007/s12134-005-1021-6.

Dreby, Joanna, 'The Burden of Deportation on Children in Mexican Immigrant Families,' *Journal of Marriage and Family 74*, no. 4 (2012): 829–845, doi: 10.1111/j.1741-3737.2012.00989.x.

Ersanilli, Evelyn and Ruud Koopmans, 'Rewarding Integration? Citizenship Regulations and the Socio-Cultural Integration of Immigrants in the Netherlands, France and Germany,' *Journal of Ethnic and Migration Studies 36*, no. 5 (2010): pp. 773–791, doi: 10.1080/ 13691831003764318.

European Union Democracy Observatory on Citizenship Database, 2016, online http:// eudo-citizenship.eu.

Fougère, Denis and Mirna Safi, 'Naturalization and Employment of Immigrants in France (1968–1999),' *International Journal of Manpower 30*, no. 1/2 (2009): pp. 83–96, doi: 10.1108/ 01437720910948410.

Fox, Cybelle, Irene Bloemraad, and Christel Kesler, 'Immigration and Redistributive Social Policy,' in David Card and Steven Raphael, eds., *Immigration, Poverty and Socioeconomic Inequality* (New York: Russell Sage Foundation Press, 2013), pp. 381–420.

Gilbertson, Greta and Audrey Singer, 'The Emergence of Protective Citizenship in the USA: Naturalization among Dominican Immigrants in the Post-1996 Welfare Reform Era,' *Ethnic and Racial Studies 26*, no. 1 (2003): pp. 25–51, doi: 10.1080/0141987002200025261.

Goodman, Sara, *Immigration and Membership Politics in Western Europe* (Cambridge: Cambridge University Press, 2014).

Hainmueller, Jens, Dominik Hangartner, and Giuseppe Pietrantuono, 'Naturalization Fosters the Long-Term Political Integration of Immigrants,' *Proceedings of the National Academy of Sciences 112*, no. 41 (2015): pp. 12651–12656, doi: 10.1073/pnas.1418794112.

Hainmueller, Jens, Dominik Hangartner, and Giuseppe Pietrantuono, 'Catalyst or Crown: Does Naturalization Promote the Long-Term Social Integration of Immigrants?' (unpublished, 2015), online *SSRN* https://papers.ssrn.com/sol3/papers.cfm?abstract_id=2664101.

Helgertz, Jonas, Pieter Bevelander, and Anna Tegunimataka, 'Naturalization and Earnings: a Denmark–Sweden Comparison,' *European Journal of Population 30*, no. 3 (2014): pp. 337–359, doi: 10.1007/s10680-014- 9315-z.

International Social Survey Program Database, 2010, http://www.gesis.org/issp/home/.

Joppke, Christian, 'Immigration and the Identity of Citizenship: The Paradox of Universalism,' *Citizenship Studies 12*, no. 6 (2008): pp. 533–546, doi: 10.1080/13621020802450445.

Joppke, Christian, *Citizenship and Immigration* (Malden: Polity, 2010).

Just, Aida and Christopher Anderson, 'Immigrants, Citizenship and Political Action in Europe,' *British Journal of Political Science 42*, no. 3 (2012): pp. 481–509, doi: 10.1017/S0007123411000378.

Kesler, Chistel and Neli Demireva, 'Social Cohesion and Host Country Nationality among Immigrants in Western Europe,' *Naturalisation: A Passport for the Better Integration of Immigrants?* (2011), pp. 209–235, doi: 10.1787/9789264099104-11-en.

Koopmans, Ruud, 'Trade-Offs between Equality and Difference: Immigrant Integration, Multiculturalism and the Welfare State in Cross-National Perspective,' *Journal of Ethnic and Migration Studies 36*, no. 1 (2010): pp. 1–26, doi: 10.1080/13691830903250881.

Koopmans, Ruud, Ines Michalowski, and Stine Waibel, 'Citizenship Rights for Immigrants: National Political Processes and Cross-National Convergence in Western Europe, 1980–2008,' *American Journal of Sociology 117*, no. 4 (2012): pp. 1202–1245, online http://www.jstor.org/stable/10.1086/662707.

Kymlicka, Will and Keith Banting, *The Strains of Commitment: The Political Sources of Solidarity in Diverse Societies* (Oxford: Oxford University Press, 2016).

Liebig, Thomas and Friederike Von Haaren, 'Citizenship and the Socio-Economic Integration of Immigrants and their Children', in *Naturalisation: A Passport for the Better Integration of Immigrants?* (Paris: OECD, 2011): pp. 23–64, doi: 10.1787/9789264099104-en.

Manning, Alan and Sanchari Roy, 'Culture Clash or Culture Club? National Identity in Britain,' *The Economic Journal 120*, no. 542 (2010): pp. F72–F100, doi: 10.1111/j.14680297.2009.02335.x.

Marshall, Thomas H., *Citizenship and Social Class,* volume 11 (Cambridge: Cambridge University Press, 1950).

Martinez, Lisa, 'Yes We Can: Latino Participation in Unconventional Politics,' *Social Forces 84*, no. 1 (2005): pp. 135–155, doi: 10.1353/sof.2005.0113.

Maxwell, Rahsaan and Erik Bleich, 'What Makes Muslims Feel French?,' *Social Forces 93*, no. 1 (2014): pp. 155–179, doi: 10.1093/sf/sou064.

McCarty, Nolan, Keith Poole, and Howard Rosenthal, *Polarized America: The Dance of Political Ideology and Unequal Riches* (Cambridge: MIT Press, 2006).

McConnell, Eileen, 'Diverging Dividends, Diverging Futures: Nativity, Citizenship Status, Legal Status, and the Non-Housing Asset Accumulation of Latinos,' *Ethnicities 15*, no. 2 (2015): pp. 255–281, doi: 10.1177/ 1468796814557649.

McConnell, Eileen, 'Hurdles or Walls? Nativity, Citizenship, Legal Status and Latino Homeownership in Los Angeles,' *Social Science Research* 53 (2015): pp. 19–33, doi: 10.1016/j.ssresearch.2015.04.009.

Migrant Integration Policy Index, 'Labour Marker Mobility', online http://www.mipex.eu/labour-market-mobility.

Migrant Integration Policy Index, 'Political Participation', online http://www.mipex.eu/political-participation.

Morales, Laura and Marco Giugni, *Social Capital, Political Participation and Migration in Europe: Making Multicultural Democracy Work?* (London: Palgrave Macmillan, 2011), doi: 10.1057/9780230302464.

Morissens, Ann and Diane Sainsbury, 'Migrants' Social Rights, Ethnicity and Welfare Regimes,' *Journal of Social Policy* 34, no. 4 (2005): pp. 637–660, doi: 10.1017/S0047279405009190.

Peters, Floris and Maarten Vink, 'Naturalization and the Socio-Economic Integration of Immigrants: A Life-Course Perspective,' in Gary Freeman and Nikola Mirilovic, eds., *Handbook on Migration and Social Policy* (Northampton: Edward Elgar Publishing, 2016), pp. 362–376.

Picot, Garnett and Feng Hou, 'Citizenship Acquisition in Canada and the United States: Determinants and Economic Benefit,' in *Naturalisation: A Passport for the Better Integration of Immigrants?* (Paris: OECD Publishing, 2011), pp. 153–182, doi: 10.1787/9789264099104-11-en.

Preibisch, Kerry and Gerardo Otero, 'Does Citizenship Status Matter in Canadian Agriculture? Workplace Health and Safety for Migrant and Immigrant Laborers,' *Rural Sociology* 79, no. 2 (2014): pp. 174–199, doi: 10.1111/ruso.1204.

Riosmena, Fernando, Bethany Everett, Richard Rogers, and Jeff Dennis, 'Negative Acculturation and Nothing More? Cumulative Disadvantage and Mortality during the Immigrant Adaptation Process among Latinos in the United States,' *International Migration Review* 49, no. 2 (2015): pp. 443–478, doi: 10.1111/imre.12102.

Sainsbury, Diane, *Welfare States and Immigrant Rights: The Politics of Inclusion and Exclusion* (Oxford: Oxford University Press, 2012).

Sassen, Saskia, 'The Repositioning of Citizenship: Emergent Subjects and Spaces for Politics,' *Berkeley Journal of Sociology* 46 (2002): pp. 4–26, doi: 10.1353/ncr.2003.0028.

Schildkraut, Deborah, 'Defining American Identity in the Twenty-First Century: How Much "There" is There?,' *Journal of Politics* 69, no. 3 (2007): pp. 597–615, doi: 10.1111/j.1468-2508.2007.00562.x.

Schuck, Peter H., *Citizens, Strangers and In-Betweens: Essays on Immigration and Citizenship* (Boulder: Westview Press, 1998).

Scott, Kirk, 'The Economics of Citizenship: Is There a Naturalization Effect?,' in Pieter Bevelander and Don J. DeVoretz, eds., *The Economics of Citizenship* (Malmö: Malmö University Press, 2008), pp. 105–126.

Shachar, Ayelet, *The Birthright Lottery: Citizenship and Global Inequality* (Cambridge: Harvard University Press, 2009).

Somers, Margaret, *Genealogies of Citizenship: Markets, Statelessness and the Right to Have Rights* (Cambridge: Cambridge University Press, 2008).

Soysal, Yasemin, *Limits of Citizenship: Migrants and Postnational Membership in Europe* (Chicago: University of Chicago Press, 1994).

Spiro, Peter J., *Beyond Citizenship: American Identity after Globalization* (Oxford: Oxford University Press, 2007).

Steinhardt, Max, 'Does Citizenship Matter? The Economic Impact of Naturalizations in Germany,' *Labour Economics 19*, no. 6 (2012): pp. 813–823, doi: 10.1016/j.labeco.2012.09.001.

Street, Alex, 'My Child Will be a Citizen: Intergenerational Motives for Naturalization,' *World Politics 66*, no. 2 (2014): pp. 264–292, doi: 10.1017/S0043887114000033.

Tambini, Damian, 'Post-National Citizenship,' *Ethnic and Racial Studies 24*, no. 2 (2001): pp. 195–217, doi: 10.1080/01419870020023418.

United Nations High Commission for Refugees, 'Ending Statelessness,' online http://www.unhcr.org/pages/49c3646c15e.html.

United Nations Human Development, 'Overcoming Barriers: Human Mobility and Development' (New York: Palgrave MacMillan, 2009), online http://hdr.undp.org/sites/default/files/reports/269/hdr_2009_en_complete.pdf.

U.S. Immigration and Customs, 'ICE Enforcement and Removal Operations Report, Fiscal Year 2015', online https://www.ice.gov/sites/default/files/documents/Report/2016/fy2015removalStats.pdf.

U.S. Office of Immigration Statistics, 'Yearbook of Immigration Statistics, 2013,' online https://www.dhs.gov/publication/yearbook-immigration-statistics-2013-enforcement-actions.

Weldon, Steven A., 'The Institutional Context of Tolerance for Ethnic Minorities: A Comparative, Multilevel Analysis of Western Europe,' *American Journal of Political Science 50*, no. 2 (2006): pp. 331–349, doi: 10.1111/j.1540-5907.2006.00187.x.

Wright, Matthew, 'Policy Regimes and Normative Conceptions of Nationalism in Mass Public Opinion,' *Comparative Political Studies 44*, no. 5 (2011): pp. 598–624, doi: 0010414010396461.

Yu, Elaine, 'World's Best and Worst Passports Revealed,' *CNN*, March 1, 2016, online http://www.cnn.com/2016/03/01/travel/worlds-best-worst-passports.

PART V

MEMBERSHIP IN THE STATE AND BEYOND

CHAPTER 25

THE PLACE OF TERRITORY IN CITIZENSHIP

NEIL WALKER

THIS Chapter examines the ways in which and the extent to which territory becomes implicated in the definition of citizenship. More specifically, it asks how, and how far, territoriality, or the territorial principle—here understood as the proposition that control over a defined territory is a constitutive feature of political community—figures in our understanding of the claim of citizenship. The Chapter is divided into four main sections. An introductory section looks at the reasons why and the ways in which notions of territoriality loom so large, sometimes explicitly and often implicitly, in contemporary discussions of citizenship. A second section examines the treatment of territory as a key element in the classical understanding of the modern Westphalian system as a framework of mutually exclusive sovereign states and national citizenships. A third section investigates how the territorial principle is diluted in the non-exclusive or plural model of citizenship we find, paradigmatically, in the European Union. A fourth section takes matters a stage further and asks how far we might move beyond the territorial principle in accounting for or promoting the citizenship idea.

The Territorial Dimension of Citizenship in Recent Academic Literature

The territorial principle, particularly as instantiated in the territorial state, remains a key organizing category for citizenship and its study today. Territoriality may figure here as assumptive framework, as object of critique, as a point of reference and contestation for the claim to political identity, as a resilient but flexible theme within our legal and political vocabulary, and as subject to transformation or transcendence.

To begin with, much thinking simply takes the territorially grounded and bounded state for granted, as the largely unstated, and so tacitly accepted, framework for any discussion of citizenship. This shades into another significant, if superficially contrasting, strain of thinking. The latter has regard to the biases and limitations inherent in the territorial principle, and in the light of these subjects the way in which states apply the territorial principle in their treatment of citizenship to critical appraisal. In so doing, this second approach, albeit negatively, also confirms the centrality of the territorial principle to our understanding of citizenship. A third approach, again continuous with the first two, treats the territorial state and its privileged conception of citizenship as a point of reference and the site for the contestation of claims associated with a wider set of citizenship practices and a broader framework of political identity. A fourth approach examines how state citizenship according to the territorial principle remains a central regulative ideal but is being reshaped in the contemporary world, its form retained but its meaning and significance somewhat altered. A fifth and final approach, reflecting the broader purpose and anticipating the wider task of the present Chapter, questions whether and how far we can go beyond the territorial principle, or at least go beyond its instantiation in the territorial state or any similarly territorially grounded polity, in our understanding of citizenship.

Let us now briefly examine these five approaches to the territorial principle in the citizenship literature.

Territoriality as Assumptive Framework

Citizenship theory typically treats citizenship as comprising a number of different elements or dimensions of an individual's social position that together denote full membership of a particular political community with which that individual is understood to have a special association. The legal dimension refers both to the basic legal status of citizenship and to the rights and duties attached to that status. The political dimension refers to the particular type of agency possessed by a citizen as a participant in the institutions of a political community. The third dimension is social or cultural, referring to the way in which membership of a political community *qua* citizen supplies a distinct source and type of social identity.[1]

While analytically distinct, however, these elements are both conceptually inseparable and practically interwoven. The concept of citizenship implies the fusion of all three elements—legal, political, and social—in a single title that is common and distinctive to all full members of a polity or political community, and which signals their special tie to that community. In sociological terms, each of the three dimensions in the life of the citizen closely informs and conditions the others. In turn, what joins and holds these different elements together as one distinct title is the sense of their exclusive derivation from a particular polity source. In other words, the act of attribution of citizenship is always the *exclusive* prerogative of a *particular* polity—in the case of political modernity the state polity; the quality of what is attributed is a *single* and *distinctive* title; and the target of attribution are those deemed to have a *special association* with the particular polity.[2]

Tellingly, if we consider this cluster of five key features of citizenship—exclusivity and particularity of source, singularity and distinctiveness of title, special association of the target group with source—each depends on background assumptions about territory as a constitutive feature of the polity. Control over territory and its boundaries, and the settled and unassailable jurisdiction associated with such a regime of legal and political control, offers the means by which we differentiate one particular polity from another, and by which we identify each as the unique source of final authority within its domain. And this territorially coded framework of paramount legal and political authority provides the mechanism through which citizenship can be constructed as the 'one-stop' status-conferring title to full membership of a defined political community. The idea of attachment to the territory under the jurisdiction of the polity is expressed most immediately by *jus soli*, which

---

[1] See, e.g., Dominique Leydet, 'Citizenship', *Stanford Encyclopaedia of Philosophy* (Spring 2014 Edition), Edward N. Zalta, ed., http://plato.stanford.edu/entries/citizenship/.

[2] This overlaps Rogers Brubaker's list of core features of citizenship as egalitarian, sacred, national, democratic, unique, and socially consequential, though my list is concerned only with those core features implicit in the very form of citizenship as a territorially coded status. See Rogers W. Brubaker, 'Introduction', in Rogers W. Brubaker, ed., *Immigration and the Politics of Citizenship in Europe and North America* (Lanham, London: University Press of America, 1989), pp. 1–27, p. 3.

confers citizenship status based on the territory of one's birth. By contrast, *jus sanguinis* seems to loosen this attachment through typically conferring citizenship on the children of naturalized parents who were themselves born abroad as well as the children of citizens who have taken up permanent residence abroad. Nevertheless, *jus sanguinis* still attributes a status in a particular polity based on a presumptive attachment to its territory, and so to the community for whom that territory is considered its ancestral homeland. In either case, therefore, it is the link to territory that is deemed to forge the special association that qualifies all individuals as citizens of one polity or another and supplies the citizen with her primary political identity.[3]

As we shall see in the next section, under the modern state system the relationship between territory and citizenship is subject to contending forces. On the one hand, the relationship becomes consolidated under modernity. On the other, it undergoes a gradual process of attenuation. But what we have said so far is sufficient to show that the territorial principle is part of a key set of assumptions through which the idea of citizenship has become operationalized in the modern world and in terms of which we comprehend its operationalization. We observe and study citizenship within the container of the territorial state, yet in so doing we often do not observe the container itself. And this sense of the territorial principle as part of the invisible or taken for granted backdrop of inquiry is exacerbated by another of its framing effects—namely the idea of citizenship as involving a *uniform* set of attributes. The point here is that, most evidently in the state system, the territorial principle facilitates the creation of structurally identical political forms. Each territorially particular and exclusive container has the same formal citizen-generative attributes. And this is one reason—alongside the equally modern idea of moral universalism according to which certain rights and opportunities attach to everyone in light of their basic personhood,[4] which is also implicit in the idea of citizenship as a status bestowed upon everyone—why, at least at a certain level of generality, the understanding of citizenship need not concern itself with boundaries and borders. It has been rightly observed, for example, that T.H. Marshall's highly influential narrative of evolving citizenship rights,[5] while drawing key distinctions between civil, political, and social rights and paying close attention to the development of social class consciousness, makes no mention of citizenship's bounded quality.[6] Rather, the citizenship story, and its expected trajectory of development, is assumed to follow the same general lines within each of its uniform territorial capsules.

---

[3] On how *jus sanguinis* and *jus soli* offer variations on the one territorially predicated 'birthright' principle of citizenship allocation, see Ayelet Shachar, *The Birthright Lottery: Citizenship and Global Inequality* (Harvard: Harvard University Press, 2009), chapter 1.

[4] See, e.g., Charles Taylor, *Modern Social Imaginaries* (Durham: Duke University Press, 2003).

[5] Thomas H. Marshall, *Citizenship and Social Class* (Concord: Pluto Press, 1950).

[6] See Christian Joppke, 'Transformation of Citizenship: Status, Rights, Identity', *Citizenship Studies* 11 (2007): pp. 37–48, p. 38.

Territoriality as Object of Critique

If the achievement of exclusive control and settled jurisdiction over a territory is vital to the attribution of citizenship as a category of full membership of a distinctive political community, then much of the criticism of modern citizenship flows from consideration of how this framework of selective eligibility can lead to the privileging of certain groups over others, and from contemplation of the various forms of injustice, exclusion, and conflict associated with that privilege. What the study of citizenship is here concerned with are the various casualties of a conception of citizenship centred on territory. These might be the citizens and residents of neighbouring states, or of distant postcolonial states, immigrant communities, or historic sub-state groups.

In the first place, the 'close strangers'[7] of neighbouring states may become locked in relationships of rivalry and hostility with home citizens. Mutual exclusivity of jurisdiction combined with close geographical proximity, and often, too, with the existence of minorities in the territory of one state who share a national or ethnic identity with citizens of the other, can lead to conflicts and rivalries over national boundaries, the governing arrangements of border areas, and the relationship between the bordering states' respective legal regimes for ascribing citizenship or receiving citizenship claims. One vivid recent illustration of this is provided by the tension between Hungary and Slovakia over dual citizenship for the Hungarian language minority in Slovakia, where in retaliatory response to the Hungarian removal of a residence requirement for naturalization as a means to accommodate its Slovakian diaspora, the Slovakian state moved to deprive anyone who had voluntarily acquired citizenship of a foreign country of their Slovakian citizenship.[8]

In the second place, the legacy of empire, understood here as involving an extension of the territorial principle such that citizenship of the imperial state became the sole or dominant citizenship throughout the imperial territory, continues to inform and affect new forms of 'postcolonial citizenship'[9] today. These postcolonial citizenships, either the novel product of independence or transformed from their previous subaltern status, typically confront a tension between the collective self-vindication involved in the assertion of the kind of exclusive and nationally monolithic model of citizenship of whose most corrupted form they were historical victims, and a search for a form of political community which does not replicate the Western paradigm. The citizenship politics of imperial and postcolonial territories

[7] See, e.g., Nenad Miscevic, 'Close Strangers, Nationalism, Proximity, and Cosmopolitanism', *Studies in Eastern European Thought 2* (1999): pp. 109–125.

[8] See, e.g., Rainer Bauböck, ed., 'Dual citizenship for Transborder Minorities? How to respond to the Hungarian-Slovak Tit-for-Tat', EUI Working Paper no. 75 (Florence: RSCAS, 2010), online http://eudo-citizenship.eu/docs/RSCAS%202010_75.rev.pdf.

[9] See, e.g., Michael O. Sharpe, *Postcolonial Citizens and Ethnic Migration* (London: Palgrave, 2014). See also Chung in this volume; Gover in this volume.

are further complicated by the existence of settled diasporas in either location, often accompanied by complex patterns of dual citizenship, as well as by continuing migratory flows.

In the third place, immigrant communities, including those who come from former colonies, stand in a disadvantaged position as regards citizenship of territorially defined political communities. Actual and aspiring immigrants, whether motivated by cultural, economic, or political considerations, and whatever combination of 'push' and 'pull' factors influences their mobility, are always doubly vulnerable. They are dependent on legal rules and conditions of access and settlement over whose content and circumstances of application they have no or little influence. They are also dependent on their reception by a native community that has typically developed in tandem, and symbiotically, with the institution of national citizenship itself, and which tends to treat and protect citizenship as a badge of belonging.[10] Migrants, therefore, even if successful in passing the threshold tests for entrance, may be excluded from full membership, or denied any clear pathway to it. Instead, they may be treated as 'metics'—as 'second-class citizens' with basic civil rights, but with only limited political and social rights, and perhaps with only temporary, conditional, or revocable residence rights.[11]

In the fourth place, sub-state national groups may also be disadvantaged by not belonging to the privileged national group in whose image the singular prize of citizenship of the territorial state is fashioned. Indigenous peoples and regional minorities may feel prejudiced or alienated by the terms and cultural associations of national citizenship, and may consider their own political and cultural identity to be incapable of adequate recognition in a constitutional order and institutional architecture organized around a homogeneous sense of national identity and of citizenship modelled on the dominant national identity.[12]

[10] On the idea of 'national citizenship', see, e.g., Rogers Brubaker, *Nationalism Reframed: Nationhood and the National Question in the New Europe* (Cambridge: Cambridge University Press, 1997).

[11] On the modern application of the ancient Greek notion of the 'metic' see, e.g., Michael Walzer, *Spheres of Justice: A Defense of Pluralism and Equality* (New York: Basic Books, 1983), chapter 2. Sometimes 'metic' is used interchangeably with 'denizen', but the latter term, at least as developed by Hammar in his observation of post-war developments in Sweden and elsewhere, is also used in a more positive sense, conveying an idea of near-equality with citizens—including secure residence as well as social and political rights (such as the franchise in local elections) and naturalization options. Hammar was concerned that such a status may be preferred to full citizenship by permanently settled migrants. See, e.g., Tomas Hammer, *Democracy and the Nation State: Aliens, Denizens and Citizens in a World of International Migration* (London: Ashgate, 1990). See also Neil Walker, 'Denizenship and Deterritorialization in the EU', in Hans Lindahl, ed., *A Right to Inclusion and Exclusion? Normative Fault Lines of the EU's Area of Freedom, Security and Justice* (Oxford: Hart, 2009), pp. 261–272.

[12] See Gans in this volume; Weinstock in this volume; Joppke in this volume.

Territoriality as Point of Reference and Contestation for Claims of Political Identity

Beyond the claims of other 'nations' or 'peoples' in or around the territory of the host state, within citizenship literature and citizenship practice today an increasing number of other claims to political identity are characterized in citizenship terms. These alternative forms of citizenship include feminist citizenship, queer citizenship, religious citizenship, urban citizenship, and ecological citizenship.[13] Yet once again the territorial principle looms large in their exposition and analysis. For the relevant claims are often compared with—and in some measure comparable to—the dominant state-centred conception of territorial citizenship. Moreover, these claims are typically addressed to—and often against—the dominant state-centred conception.

These alternative forms of citizenship, certainly, have very different relationships to territory, and in that sense vary greatly in terms of their comparability to the state-centred territorial model. Sexual and gender-based citizenships, for example, clearly do not derive their criteria of community and group identity from territorial considerations. But urban citizenship does—if not in the exclusive or singular manner of state citizenship. For its part, religious citizenship can also refer to territory in its emphasis on sacred location or the historical homeland of adherents, while environmental citizenship invokes physical territory as part of the wider ecosystem whose protection should inform citizenship practice.

Yet what these alternative forms of citizenship do hold in common, at least in their local form,[14] is that they all make demands on the state. They either require the state to use its territorial authority to do certain things—for example, recognize gay rights, develop anti-discrimination laws, protect the environment—or to limit its territorial authority in recognition of the alternative or subsidiary claims of other groups—as regards, for instance, religious toleration, or respecting the integrated self-governing claims of cities and other localities under the sign of urban citizenship.[15] In all these cases, as is also true of the citizenship claims under the previous sub-heading, the struggle for recognition involves at one and the same time a demand made on the territorial state in recognition of its paramount authority and a critique and contestation of that paramount authority. Below, we will consider in greater depth whether and how some such contestations may come to alter the fundamental structure and territorial coding of citizenship.

---

[13] See, e.g., Volpp in this volume. See also Wayne Hudson, 'Religious Citizenship', *The Australian Journal of Politics and History 49* (2003): pp. 425–429; Rainer Bauböck, 'Reinventing Urban Citizenship', *Citizenship Studies 7*, no. 2 (2003): pp. 139–160; Andrew Dobson, *Citizenship and the Environment* (Oxford: Oxford University Press, 2003), chapter 3.

[14] For consideration of them in a global or transnational context, see below.

[15] See, e.g., Bauböck (n 13).

Territoriality as a Resilient but Flexible Theme

A significant body of work in recent years has investigated how, over the last half century, the territorial principle has become stretched and adapted in new ways while retaining its centrality to the definition of citizenship within a state-centred system.[16] In particular, an influential line of thought has examined the ways in which liberalization of access, and a movement away from the closed and closely reproductive pattern of citizenship associated with the idea of territorially bounded and mutually exclusive communities has brought about more plural membership identities. It shows how this opening has gone hand in hand with the development of minority rights at the partial expense of thicker social rights, and how the consequent softening of the traditional ethno-cultural core of national citizenship within the territorial state has, in its turn, been responded to by new projects of civic integration.[17]

Earlier we discussed the inherent vulnerability of migrants before a territorially centred conception of political community and membership, and we alluded to the development of sizable denizen communities in many immigration states. Yet we should also recognize that the combination of increasingly high levels of settled immigrants, the relative absence of frustrated nation-building aspirations in some regions of the world and the consequent reduction of security concerns about accommodating minority nationals, the international dissemination of a broader rights consciousness through the UN and other mechanisms, and the general spread of liberal-democratic norms 'that command a congruence of the subjects and objects of state authority'[18] has opened the gate to citizenship for many newcomers. On the one hand, general racial or gender-based barriers to citizenship have been dismantled. On the other hand, there is some evidence of a strengthening of the *jus soli* principle in supplementation of the classic *jus sanguinis* principle as a route to citizenship for settled immigrants, although this is an uneven trend and one that provokes counter-tendencies.[19] In a manner that neatly demonstrates the multi-layered connections between citizenship, territory, and state, therefore, the

---

[16] See, e.g., Christian Joppke, *Citizenship and Immigration* (Cambridge: Polity, 2007).

[17] See, e.g., Dora Kostakopoulou, 'The Anatomy of Civic Integration', *Modern Law Review* 73 (2010): pp. 933–958.

[18] Joppke (n 16), 50–51. See also Will Kymlicka, 'Liberal Nationalism and Cosmopolitan Justice', in Seyla Benhabib, *Another Cosmopolitanism* (edited and introduced by Robert Post) (Oxford: Oxford University Press, 2006), pp. 128–146.

[19] In Europe, we see contrasting movements of restriction of *jus soli* in the UK and, then Ireland, and very moderate expansion in Germany, Portugal and, most recently, in Greece. In Australia and New Zealand, *jus soli* also has become conditional. See further Joppke (n 16), chapter 2; Patrick Weil, 'Access to Citizenship', in Alexander Aleinikoff and Douglas Klusmeyer, eds., *Citizenship Today* (Washington: Carnegie, 2001), pp. 17–35; Iseult Honohan, 'The Theory and Politics of Ius Soli', EUDO CITIZENSHIP Working Paper (Florence: RSCAS, 2010), online http://eudo-citizenship.eu/docs/IusSoli.pdf.

deeper attachment-by-descent to a particular territory as the historical basis for citizenship in the nation state is today joined, however irregularly, by a more direct form of attachment-by-birthplace.

If relaxation of access to full citizenship, together with greater recognition of political and cultural autonomy for minority nationals and a general increase in rights of anti-discrimination in terms of ethnicity, race, and religion for newcomers and denizens more generally, signals the progressive aspect of the development of 'multicultural citizenship',[20] this is in some measure counterbalanced by a more cautious approach to the extension of social rights to new groups. To the extent that a choice is required between solidarity and diversity, the price of more accessible membership may be reduction of social provision to those not yet full members, or, more fundamentally, a general capping of the substantive welfare benefits attendant upon citizenship. [21]

More broadly, the general loosening of the bonds of citizenship of the territorially closed society occasioned by these liberalizing changes, as already indicated, has generated a further response on the part of many states intended to engineer the integration of diverse communities. The difficulty here is that however much these aims are presented in deracinated terms—as aspirations of good citizenship anywhere and everywhere, they are always implemented in a particular place with a particular cultural legacy and constellation of interests and associations. We are thus faced with the paradox of 'universalistic unity'. [22] Integrative measures, such as linguistic proficiency, sartorial conformity, and knowledge of the host national culture, may be presented and even conceived of merely as a means to provide a minimum floor of common 'societal culture',[23] yet they may be co-opted by dominant national groups or experienced by minority national groups as instead projecting an assimilationist understanding of citizenship identity.

Territoriality Transformed or Transcended

This leaves for discussion conceptions of citizenship that are neither framed by the territorial state nor forged through their encounter with the territorial state. This may involve a scalar transformation of the territoriality principle, such that it applies to entities other than the state, as in the case of the EU. Or it may involve the transcendence of the territoriality principle in conceptions of citizenship which are recast in terms which make no or only incidental reference to the control of territory as the key to political community and its membership. We will deal with these

---

[20] Will Kymlicka, *Multicultural Citizenship* (Oxford: Oxford University Press, 1995).
[21] The welfare reforms in the United States and Australia in the mid 1990s provide pertinent illustrations.
[22] Joppke (n 6), p. 44.   [23] Kymlicka (n 20), p. 103.

two topics below, but first let us look in more detail at how the territorial principle applies in the central case of modern state citizenship.

TERRITORY AND CITIZENSHIP IN THE WESTPHALIAN STATE SYSTEM

The classical theory of the modern state treats the coincidence of people, territory, and governmental authority as definitive of statehood,[24] with citizenship supplying the mark of personal membership of the polity within that coincidental structure. Additionally, as we have seen, the stylized logic of modern 'Westphalian' sovereign statehood as a self-replicating international system depends upon these citizenship-framing sets of statal attributes being distinctive and mutually exclusive. As Brubaker has argued, through its territorial coding citizenship is simultaneously 'internally inclusive' and 'externally exclusive',[25] so supplying 'an international filing system, a mechanism for allocating persons to states'.[26]

Yet we should not overstate the dependence of the Westphalian state system on the territoriality principle. In the first place, even according to its own inner logic, we can trace a gradual decentring of the significance of the territorial principle alongside the full flowering of modern citizenship. In the second place, the idea of a Westphalian state system *is* only a stylized representation, and the reality of global relations has always allowed many exceptions and anomalies. It is important to pursue both of these threads, as they provide a starting point for examining the wider challenge to—and the stretching and partial fraying of—the territorial principle of citizenship in the contemporary age.

Citizenship, of course, began before the Westphalian state, with its monopolistic control over territory and its bestowal of membership on all. Originating in the Greek republics, where it was restricted to economically self-sufficient male heads of families, citizenship remained a selective title when revived in the medieval Western city-state, limited to the free urban dweller. In pre-modern times, indeed, only in the exceptional case of imperial Rome do we find any intimation of citizenship as a status attaching to the broader population of a territory.[27]

---

[24] See, e.g., Georg Jellinek, *Allgemeine Staatslehre*, 3rd edition (Berlin: Springer, 1919).
[25] Rogers Brubaker, *Citizenship and Nationhood in France and Germany* (Cambridge: Harvard University Press, 1992), p. 46.
[26] Ibid., p. 31.   [27] See further Balot in this volume.

For its part, the Westphalian state, and state system, succeeded not only city states, but a range of medieval political systems whose authority centred on the social status of a ruler rooted in divine descent, religious charisma, dynastic tradition, feudal suzerainty, military virtue, and the like. This medley of political forms was gradually replaced by the supreme, indivisible, absolute, and exclusive power over territory we associate with modern sovereignty. The new form of rule was impersonal rather than personal, valid for each person within the territory irrespective of her social standing, individual attributes, or relations with the current ruling elite. More broadly, comprehensive and exclusive control over territory allowed for a more efficient, transaction-free demarcation of the scope and limits of rule, and the standardization of the forms of rule. And for the ruled, the requirement of loyalty towards social and political superiors was gradually replaced by an attitude of conformity to the demands of an abstract legal order.[28]

What this suggests in the round, however, is that just as citizenship did not begin with the modern territorial state, equally, the modern territorial state, newly equipped with the means and ambition of monopolistic control within its jurisdiction, did not begin by incorporating citizenship, at least not in the full sense we have come to associate with the modern conception of citizenship. Membership of the early modern polity, with its generalization and intensification of government authority, was more like 'equal subjectship'[29] (or 'subjecthood') rather than equal citizenship. The territorial principle allowed for the flattening of the system of rule, but it was a system within which a marked asymmetry between rulers and ruled prevailed.

The advent of the full modern sense of citizenship depended upon the supreme and exclusive power of sovereignty no longer deriving from territoriality as such, with control in the proprietary hands of the absolutist prince. Instead, sovereignty was relocated in the corporate unity of the multitude, and reconceived of as popular sovereignty. As legal status, as a catalogue of rights and obligations, as a form of political agency, and as a type of cultural identity, modern citizenship came to depend on this backdrop of collective self-rule. It was the product and reflection of a form of self-constitution given early articulation in the late eighteenth century constitutional settlements in France and United States, but also one that, in its voluntarist register, recalled earlier and more selective forms of collective agency in the ancient and medieval city states.

Territorial control, though no longer definitive of the polity, remained of great importance here, serving 'as a container which defines the boundaries of who belongs to the multitude and hence who qualifies as belonging to the people'.[30] Yet,

---

[28] See, e.g., Ulrich Preuss, 'Disconnecting Constitutions from Statehood: Is Global Constitutionalism a Viable Concept?', in Petra Dobner and Martin Loughlin, eds., *The Twilight of Constitutionalism?* (Oxford: Oxford University Press, 2010), pp. 23–46.

[29] Joppke (n 16), p. 9.   [30] Preuss (n 28), p. 36.

crucially, the transformation of the multitude into the people has nothing to do with territory and, indeed, sets itself against the authority of the erstwhile rulers of that territory. *In a nutshell, the new system of self-rule of the modern constitutional state relies upon the territorial principle just as it begins to detach itself from that same principle.* On the one hand, the new system continues to depend on the administrative achievement of an identifiable population subject to the authority of a territorial government—a legacy of the earlier system of absolute territorial rule. On the other hand, the new system additionally depends on a cultural sense of common peoplehood that also attaches itself to territory, but only as a cue for a reflexive process of common engagement and self-representation.[31]

If we turn, more briefly, to the ways in which the real pattern of development of citizenship in the global order has departed from the Westphalian model, even allowing for the more fluid understanding attendant upon the shift to popular sovereignty, we can see how the territorial principle is subject to further weakening or diffusion. In particular, we can indicate three sets of factors which show how and why citizenship under the Westphalian state system is not necessarily a unique status, one dependent upon the singular relationship of the individual with a particular territorially segmented polity.

In the first place, fluid patterns of mobility and allegiance and complexities of family lineage have always allowed the possibility of dual (or multiple) citizenship, or at least serial singular citizenship. The popularity and possibilities of dual citizenship have waxed and waned.[32] But the combination of increased migratory flows, the gradual abolition of patrilineal descent rules, the complexities of interaction between regimes which give priority to one or other of *jus soli* or *jus sanguinis*, and the particular contemporary difficulties of immigrant nations who seek to facilitate integration through reducing naturalization barriers while responding to pressure to 're-ethnicise' citizens by relaxing the rules regarding the retention of citizenship for expatriate communities abroad, means that the secular pattern favours more dual citizenship, and the adoption of a 'transnational membership' model of citizenship.[33]

In the second place, alongside the prior claim of the nation state, citizenship may also be nested in accordance with an infra-state federal pattern. This is continuous with the pattern of minority nationalism discussed above, with formal recognition of separate nationality,[34] or even of nominate forms of sub-state citizenship, more

---

[31] See, e.g., Jürgen Habermas, 'Citizenship and National Identity', in Bart Van Steenbergen, ed., *The Condition of Citizenship* (New York: Sage, 1994), pp. 20–35.

[32] See further Spiro in this volume.

[33] See, e.g., Rainer Bauböck, *Transnational Citizenship* (Aldershot: Edward Elgar, 1994). See further Rainer Bauböck, 'Political Boundaries in a Multilevel Democracy', in Seyla Benhabib and Ian Shapiro, eds., *Identities, Affiliations and Allegiances* (Cambridge: Cambridge University Press, 2007), pp. 85–112.

[34] As, e.g., in the Spanish case.

likely where sub-state nations are territorially concentrated and are coincidental with federal or quasi-federal systems of provincial government.[35]

And in the third place, imperial relations often involve the distribution of different citizenships not within a polity (as in the federal case) but across imperial and subaltern polities. This asymmetrical arrangement of multiple citizenships, indeed, has a strong pre-Westphalian pedigree, most obviously in the classical model of citizenship of imperial Rome, but one which expanded in the modern age of European overseas imperialism, from the eighteenth century to the mid twentieth century, and whose legacy, as we have seen, remains today in patterns of overlapping and interlocking membership between post-imperial and post-colonial communities.

Plural Territorial Citizenship in the European Union

This section examines the model of *plural* territorial citizenship we find, paradigmatically, in the EU.[36] Here we confront a de-centring of the territorial principle and a non-exclusive relationship between citizen and territory as a matter of systematic design rather than simply structural adaptation or contingent outcome. Since the introduction of the official category of EU citizenship in the Treaty of Maastricht in 1992, all citizens of member states possess (at least) two citizenships. This is so because as citizens of member states, they also automatically become citizens of the EU, which itself is a polity of closely specified territorial extent, and which, under the rubric of the Area of Freedom, Security and Justice, has (since 1997) increasingly come to define itself in territorial terms. The content of EU citizenship, tellingly, is heavily focused on the territorial dimension, stressing the right of every citizen of the Union to move and reside freely across all member states, as well as providing limited political rights (including the right to vote and stand as a candidate in both municipal and European Parliament elections, but not in national elections) for the new constituency of mobile citizens.

Unlike the exceptional possibilities of dual, nested, or imperial citizenship under the state system described above, the idea of one dominant or framing territorial citizenship no longer prevails within the new EU architecture, at least as a matter of

---

[35] We find this both in settled federations such as Switzerland, and in unsettled post-federations such as the former Yugoslavia. See, e.g., Dejan Stjepanovic, 'Dual Substate Citizenship as Institutional Innovation: The Case of Bosnia's Brcko District 21', *Nationalism and Ethnic Politics 21*, no. 4 (2015): pp. 379–400.

[36] See further Strumia in this volume.

official constitutional discourse. The EU is not a federal state, nor an empire, nor is it merely a voluntary and avoidable form of secondary attachment. Instead we have a compulsorily plural framework of territorially coded membership which, not being predicated upon the priority of a single level of allegiance and site of identification within a sovereign polity, treats its different levels of compulsory allegiance both as *de iure* complementary[37] and (with variable success) as *de facto* capable of mutual accommodation.

The situation is further complicated by patterns of mobility within and to Europe. Of the 510 million current residents of the EU, just over 10 per cent were born outside the member state where they are presently resident. Of that 10 per cent constituency, around two-thirds, roughly 35 million, do not (yet) possess citizenship in their country of residence. 20 million of these are 'third country nationals' born outside the EU, and able to take advantage of the EU's common quasi-citizenship or denizenship process for long-term residents of five years,[38] whereas the other 15 million are 'second country' nationals of other member states, and so enjoy the status and benefits of EU citizenship.[39] And, of course, the recent pattern of unusual migration into Europe promises to disturb the balance between third and second country nationals, with over one million refugees and other migrants crossing into the European Union in 2015 alone in a trend which has abated (however temporarily) only on account of the strict control and deterrence measures contained in the EU-Turkey return and resettlement agreement of March 2016.[40]

We can interpret the deep significance of EU citizenship for the accommodation of the territorial principle in a more or less radical manner. In so doing, we may usefully draw upon Will Kymlicka's distinction between 'taming' and 'transcending' liberal nationalism.[41] According to Kymlicka, recent developments in the law and politics of membership in the EU can be read in different ways, but for him the key interpretive code is a familiar and well established one; namely the liberal national and constitutionalist understanding of the citizenship project as it has developed within its traditional European continental domicile over the last sixty years. He

---

[37] The actual language of Article 9 of the Treaty of European Union is that EU citizenship 'shall be additional to and not replace national citizenship'. In the abortive Constitutional Treaty drafted by the Convention on the Future of Europe in 2003 the language of 'dual citizenship' had been proposed as an alternative. This would, of course, have blurred the important distinction between the EU's innovative model of necessary complementarity and the merely contingent and perhaps competing duality involved in the possession of multiple national citizenships. For critical discussion, see Grainne De Burca, 'Fundamental Rights and Citizenship', in Bruno de Witte, ed., *Ten Reflections on the Constitutional Treaty for Europe* (Florence: EUI, 2003), pp. 11–44.

[38] Council Directive 2003/109 EC.

[39] See Eurostat, 'Migration and Migrant Population Statistics', online http://ec.europa.eu/eurostat/statistics-explained/index.php/Migration_and_migrant_population_statistics.

[40] See European Council, 'EU-Turkey Statement, 18 March 2016', online http://www.consilium.europa.eu/en/press/press-releases/2016/03/18-eu-turkey-statement/.

[41] Kymlicka (n 18).

points to the fact that many but not all rights we typically understand as part and parcel of national citizenship—including residence rights, liberal freedoms, and some social rights and political rights, have become gradually 'unbundled'[42] from national citizenship in Europe. As we have seen, some, including limited political rights, full mobility rights, and certain attendant social welfare rights are part of the wider European citizenship available to second country nationals, whereas a more restricted set of residence, employment, and study rights are available also to 'denizens' of third country origin on the long-term residence track. Kymlicka then draws a distinction between what we might call a 'tiered membership' model and a 'proto-citizenship' or 'emergent citizenship' model for understanding the position of the non-first country national as holder of these unbundled rights. Under the first model, unbundling is the cue for vertically differentiated (i.e., more or less, unqualified or qualified) membership of the polity, while under the second 'proto-citizenship' model, which he favours over the first, unbundling is just a phase in a process which has as its endpoint and objective the 'rebundling' of these rights 'in the form of full and equal citizenship within the framework of liberal nationhood'.[43]

While the approach of Kymlicka, and others working along similar lines,[44] acknowledges the lack of formal hierarchy in the relationship between the different layers of political membership in this multi-tier architecture, it nevertheless continues to privilege the territorial unit of the state in the final analysis. Just as qualification for EU citizenship remains parasitic on citizenship of the state, the very *raison d'être* of the EU, on this view, remains to support what is valuable in the national citizenship model of 'belonging and originality'[45] while generating the requisite culture of tolerance and forms of material access which guard against nationalism's more inward-looking and illiberal reactions so notorious of the European past.

On the other 'transcending' side of Kymlicka's divide, however, we can begin to trace various alternative and less territorially defined trajectories of membership of political community. Arguably, the EU might also fit, or come to fit, one of these types. We can do so by parsing the Westphalian frame of national citizenship into its various components, and asking which element or elements of the frame is the focus of challenge. To recall, the Westphalian model of citizenship is premised on three different aspects of mutual exclusivity, namely membership itself, territorial jurisdiction, and political authority. Adapting a distinction drawn by Dora Kostakopoulou,[46] we may differentiate between 'transnational membership' and 'postnational membership' depending on whether just the first or all three of these elements of exclusivity is challenged.

---

[42] Kymlicka (n 18), p. 138.   [43] Kymlicka (n 18), p. 139.

[44] See in particular Joseph H.H. Weiler, *The Constitution of Europe* (Cambridge: Cambridge University Press, 1999), chapter 9.

[45] Ibid., p. 338.

[46] Dora Kostakopoulou, 'Thick, Thin and Thinner Patriotisms: Is This All There Is?', *Oxford Journal of Legal Studies 26* (2006): pp. 73–106, p. 83.

Transnational membership we have already discussed in the context of dual citizenship, and it seems better equipped to deal with the broader global patterns of movement between bounded communities and the resulting process of modest desegmentation that remains legible within a two-dimensional Westphalian map of the world than with the more radical interpenetration of the multi-layered three-dimensional EU model. Instead, if we look to the idea of 'postnational membership' developed by writers such as Yasemin Soysal,[47] not only is membership of political communities no longer presumptively mutually exclusive, but the very idea that rights and capacities are mere incidents of such memberships and their associated territorial jurisdictions rather than more general entitlements associated with personhood is also increasingly challenged in a way that may speak more closely to the EU experience, or at least to the ambitions of some of its supporters. This point is reinforced when we consider how other sub-state levels of (city, regional, or national) membership, territory and authority, as well as functionally specific and territorially fluid group statuses (workers, service-providers, women, racial minorities, etc.) are eroding the state-centred structures of mutual exclusivity. Indeed, in the EU context the sub-state and supra-state level, particularly in places like Scotland, Catalonia, and Flanders, together with the new emphasis on functional status, may be understood not merely as complementary forms of title, but also as mutually reinforcing challenges to the citadels of exclusive state prerogative.[48]

The fact that, even after sixty years, the European Union can still be plausibly understood as falling on either side of Kymlicka's taming/transcending divide, indicates just how innovative, and just how politically contentious the notion of moving beyond the model of a territorially exclusive nation state-based conception of citizenship remains. Today, the European Union continues to stand out as an experimental polity with an 'unresolved constitution'[49]—a prototype that invites curiosity and controversy in equal measure. On the one hand, participants in other less developed frameworks of regional integration, such as the Mercosur states in South America, countries belonging to the Gulf Cooperation Council, and those in the Caribbean Community, look to the European Union for inspiration in the design of plural territorial citizenship.[50] On the other hand, within the EU homelands

[47] Yasemin Soysal, *Limits of Citizenship* (Chicago: University of Chicago Press, 1994). See also Yasemin Soysal, 'Changing Parameters of Citizenship and Claims-Making: Organised Islam in European Public Spheres', *Theory and Society* 26 (1997): pp. 509–527.

[48] See, e.g., Stephen Tierney, 'Reframing Sovereignty: Sub-State National Societies and Contemporary Challenges to the Nation-State', *International and Comparative Law Quarterly* 54 (2005): pp. 161–183; Neil Walker, 'Federalism in 3D: The Reimagination of Political Community in the European Union', *Catolica Law Review* 1 (2017): pp. 67–90, online http://papers.ssrn.com/sol3/papers.cfm?abstract_id=2776798.

[49] Neil Walker, 'The European Union's Unresolved Constitution', in Michel Rosenfeld and Andras Sajo, eds., *The Oxford Handbook of Comparative Constitutional Law* (Oxford: Oxford University Press, 2012), pp. 1185–1208.

[50] See Francesca Strumia, 'Brexiting European Citizenship through the Voice of Others', *German Law Journal* 17 (Brexit Special Supplement) (2016): pp. 109–116, online http://static1.squarespace.com/

themselves –the 'Brexit' vote of June 2016 offers a sharp reminder—many nationals retain a unitary conception of political identity and view the expanding supranational edifice in general, and supranational citizenship and its removal of certain national prerogatives over border controls in particular, as an illegitimate encroachment on national sovereignty.[51]

Towards Non-Territorial Citizenship

Our final section moves beyond singular, contingently non-singular, and systemically plural forms of territorial citizenship to investigate the possibility of the long process of gradual detachment of political community from territory culminating in the emergence of more emphatically non-territorial forms of citizenship. This investigation, however, requires us to introduce one final distinction.

On one part of the 'non-territorial' spectrum, we can place those limited forms of political community that may retain some of the formal features of territorial citizenship introduced in the first section—namely, exclusivity and particularity of source, singularity and distinctiveness of title, and special association of the target group with 'national' or other local site, but where territory is no longer the dominant organizing principle. These would include models of non-territorial or cultural autonomy for 'tribal polities'[52] or national minorities of plurinational states (language, religious observance, education, etc.),[53] and, today, perhaps also new or evolving conceptions of diasporas such as a global Islamic *umma* or Romani claims to 'non-territorial' nation status.[54] The development of these forms, however, while significant, remains hampered or restricted by the fact that it clashes so directly with the territorial state-centred system of mutually exclusive sources of legal and

static/56330ad3e4b0733dcc0c8495/t/5776e641579fb3bc18d94197/1467409987447/21+PDF_Vol_17_Brexit+_Strumia.pdf.

[51] See further Shaw in this volume and Costello in this volume. See also, Neil Walker, 'The European Fallout', *German Law Journal* 17 (Brexit Special Supplement) (2016): pp. 125–130, online http://static1.squarespace.com/static/56330ad3e4b0733dcc0c8495/t/5776e65c579fb3bc18d942a5/1467410013198/23+PDF_Vol_17_Brexit+_Walker.pdf.

[52] See Kirsty Gover, *Tribal Constitutionalism: States, Tribes and the Governance of Membership* (Oxford: Oxford University Press, 2010). See also Gover in this volume.

[53] See, e.g., Alexander Osipov, 'Non-Territorial Autonomy during and after Communism: In the Wrong or Right Place?', *Journal on Ethnopolitics and Minority Issues in Europe* 12 (2013): pp. 7–26.

[54] See, e.g., Morag Goodwin, 'The Romani Claim to Non-territorial Nation Status; Recognition from an International Legal Perspective' (European Roma Rights Centre, 2004), online http://www.errc.org/article/the-romani-claim-to-non-territorial-nation-status-recognition-from-an-international-legal-perspective/1849.

political authority. For it is the case that these new forms both tend to claim the kind of original authority associated with state sovereignty, or at least to contest the supremacy, indivisibility, absoluteness, and exclusivity of the state's own claim and, in their conceptions of belonging, to retain significant reference to homelands that are already subject to the physical jurisdiction and rooted identity claims of states.

If we move further along the 'non-territorial' spectrum we begin to trace the implications for our understanding of citizenship of a more comprehensive detachment of political agency from territory—one that does not even invoke territory as part of its narrative of collective origins. Take 'global citizens',[55] or 'cyber citizens', or 'ecocitzens', or citizens of any other non-territorially defined, delimited, or traced entity. To pose the question starkly, to the extent that they do not imagine their public and political identities only through and against the 'local' lens of state citizenship, are these subjects actual or potential 'citizens' of anything new at all? If each of these domains of interest also has its own government system and regulatory regime (the UN and other global organizations, ICANN,[56] and the global climate change regime respectively, in the three cases just cited), is implication in that regulatory regime enough to make one a citizen thereof? If not, why not? Is it because the territorial model, even if not, or no longer, predicated upon a norm of exclusive allegiance, at least speaks to such scope and generality of governance function as requires a broad, political-status-defining form of involvement with the polity in question on the part of the citizen? Alternatively, or additionally, does the territorial model speak to a deep symbolic connection between geographical attachment and political belonging? In other words, does the idea of territorial citizenship provide and preserve a key functional or affective nexus between person and polity, or, more likely, some combination of the two? And to the extent that it does, what place, if any, is there for an emerging non-territorial range of citizenships? And to what extent might the flourishing of these new non-territorial citizenships, if such were possible, undermine—without replacing—the capacity of territorial citizenship to provide the key nexus of political community?

We can begin to address these questions if we return to the liberal nationalist-transcending side of Kymlicka's divide. If we take Soysal's 'post-national membership' as a point of departure, and explore what new types of positive political identity might contribute to her post-national personhood, we can engage a host of positions tending towards what we might, somewhat provocatively, call a 'post-membership', or, at least, a 'fluid membership' model.[57] The implication of this—to

---

[55] See, e.g., Hans Schattle, *The Practices of Global Citizenship* (Chicago: Rowman & Littlefield, 2008).

[56] The Internet Corporation for Assigned Names and Numbers.

[57] Authors I would locate here in terms of general focus, though they themselves might well not endorse the 'post-membership' label, include Kostakopoulou (n 46); Seyla Benhabib, 'Philosophical Foundations of Cosmopolitan Norms', in *Another Cosmopolitanism* (edited and introduced by Robert Post) (New York: Oxford University Press, 2006), pp. 13–44; Saskia Sassen, *Territory, Authority, Rights* (Princeton: Princeton University Press, 2006). See also Walker (n 11).

be clear—is not the redundancy of territorially located and enduringly author-ized polities. Short of a comprehensive cosmopolitan vision of world government, distinct if increasingly overlapping and plurally identified political communities will remain, and will remain situated, however fluidly, in particular spatial envir-onments. Rather, de-territorialization of citizenship in this more profound sense involves the decreasing salience of the very idea of fixed membership of a single political community. Following this thought experiment to its logical conclusion, if we consider the three factors which make up the social status (citizen, denizen, alien, etc.) that marks the relationship with political community within the modern political imaginary, namely the bundle of legal rights and obligations, the sense of political agency, and the recognition of cultural identity by self and others, under the post-membership model these are, or should be, decreasingly mediated through a robust idea of membership. The rights and obligations of *homo politicus* may become more accessible, either without a membership card or with one increas-ingly easily acquired (perhaps through brief residence or stakeholding), and also more likely to be divided and distributed across a range of organizational forms, of which the EU is only one particularly prominent (and unusually state-like in scope and ambition) example. The sense of membership may become less tied to an idea of a single or supervening political agency of the member. And finally, the signifi-cance of recognition of the member *qua* member by other members and, equally, the 'othering' recognition of the non-member *qua* non-member by members, and the associated conveyance of symbolic capital or deficit, may gradually diminish or dilute.

Overall, then, whereas in the other state-transcendent models of political mem-bership and also in the national post-territorial model considered earlier in this section—the rights associated with membership are somewhat split and diversi-fied, here the membership of any one particular community ceases to be a signifi-cant generic status-shaping code and medium of action. Many of our received ideas of strong membership, indeed, including the ordering of a binary legal distinction (member/non-member), highly specified entry and exit rules and regimes, and the symbolic self-and other-interpolation of belonging and not-belonging, may argu-ably be considered too rigid and too enveloping for a world of more diverse and fluid common commitments.

Of course, various considerations mean that, however fluid, such common com-mitments will nevertheless remain important.[58] Both continuity and security of social identity at the individual level and the need for a viable threshold of capability-of-putting-things-effectively-in-common political community at the collective level—with a premium placed on the generation and sustenance of the minimum of trust, respect, and mutual sympathy necessary for that viability—remain vital—all

---

[58] See, e.g., Margaret Canovan, *The People* (Cambridge: Polity, 2005).

the more so for social and economic groups vulnerable to non-political forms of power. In addition, the need for collective challenge to powerful cross-state interest constellations that threaten transnational or global public goods through political means also speaks to a more general political imperative to sustain a global counter-language of non-particular but highly collectivized 'co-operative citizenship'.[59]

Conclusions

This Chapter has argued that territoriality has been a key dimension of traditional conceptions of citizenship, be it as an assumed framework, as an object of normative critique, or as a reference for identity claims. The territoriality of citizenship was greatly strengthened and consolidated in the Westphalian system of sovereign states. Yet, in a longer perspective, the development of a more abstract model of political rule under the Westphalian system also paved the way for various developments in the role of the state as a sponsor and container of political community which, together with the emergence of transnational political entities such as the European Union, have had the effect of diluting the territorial relation in certain ways.

The final section has considered more radical notions of non-territorial citizenship. Where these envisage a post-membership conception of citizenship they ought to be strongly qualified. These qualifiers remind us that political community is never made out of co-presence alone, just as individuals operating in isolation can never effectively challenge it. The question of post-territorial citizenship, instead, inevitably remains one of degree. Yet it is not today a moot question, but one constantly being tested in a more globalized—and also globally segmented—political environment.[60] Within this environment, arguably, a graduated language of commitment, perhaps even one that no longer comfortably speaks in the traditionally dichotomizing language of citizenship, may over time become better able to depict the nuances of our increasingly non-exclusive and fluctuating relationship to collective belonging and practice, and to the conceptions of place that have for so long stood behind collective belonging and practice.

---

[59] See James Tully, 'The Crisis of Global Citizenship', *Radical Politics Today* (June 2009), online http://research.ncl.ac.uk/spaceofdemocracy/word%20docs%20linked%20to/Uploaded%202009/Tully/The_Crisis_of_Global_Citizenship_James_Tully.pdf.

[60] See, e.g., Gunther Teubner, *Constitutional Fragments: Societal Constitutionalism and Globalization* (Oxford: Oxford University Press, 2012).

BIBLIOGRAPHY

Bauböck, Rainer, *Transnational Citizenship* (Aldershot: Edward Elgar, 1994).

Bauböck, Rainer, 'Reinventing Urban Citizenship', *Citizenship Studies 7*, no. 2 (2003): pp. 139–160.

Bauböck, Rainer, 'Political Boundaries in a Multilevel Democracy', in *Identities, Affiliations and Allegiances* edited by Seyla Benhabib and Ian Shapiro (Cambridge: Cambridge University Press, 2007), pp. 85–112.

Bauböck, Rainer, ed., 'Dual Citizenship for Transborder Minorities? How to Respond to the Hungarian-Slovak Tit-for-Tat', EUI Working Paper no. 75 (Florence: RSCAS, 2010), online http://eudo-citizenship.eu/docs/RSCAS%202010_75.rev.pdf.

Benhabib, Seyla, 'Philosophical Foundations of Cosmopolitan Norms', in *Another Cosmopolitanism* (edited and introduced by Robert Post) (Oxford: Oxford University Press, 2006), pp. 13–44.

Brubaker, Rogers, ed., *Immigration and the Politics of Citizenship in Europe and North America* (Lanham, London: University Press of America, 1989).

Brubaker, Rogers, *Citizenship and Nationhood in France and Germany* (Cambridge: Harvard University Press, 1992).

Brubaker, Rogers, *Nationalism Reframed: Nationhood and the National Question in the New Europe* (Cambridge: Cambridge University Press, 1997).

Canovan, Margaret, *The People* (Cambridge: Polity, 2005).

De Burca, Grainne, 'Fundamental Rights and Citizenship', in Bruno de Witte, ed., *Ten Reflections on the Constitutional Treaty for Europe* (Florence: EUI, 2003), pp. 11–44.

Dobson, Andrew, *Citizenship and the Environment* (Oxford: Oxford University Press, 2003).

Goodwin, Morag, 'The Romani Claim to Non-Territorial Nation Status; Recognition from an International Legal Perspective' (European Roma Rights Centre, 2004), online http://www.errc.org/article/the-romani-claim-to-non-territorial-nation-status-recognition-from-an-international-legal-perspective/1849.

Gover, Kirsty, *Tribal Constitutionalism: States, Tribes and the Governance of Membership* (Oxford: Oxford University Press, 2010).

Habermas, Jürgen, 'Citizenship and National Identity', in Bart Van Steenbergen, ed., *The Condition of Citizenship* (New York: Sage, 1994), pp. 20–35.

Hammer, Tomas, *Democracy and the Nation State: Aliens, Denizens and Citizens in a World of International Migration* (London: Ashgate, 1990).

Honohan, Iseult, 'The Theory and Politics of Ius Soli', EUDO CITIZENSHIP Working Paper, (Florence: RSCAS, 2010), online http://eudo-citizenship.eu/docs/IusSoli.pdf.

Hudson, Wayne, 'Religious Citizenship', *The Australian Journal of Politics and History 49* (2003): pp. 425–429.

Jellinek, Georg, *Allgemeine Staatslehre*, 3rd edition (Berlin: Springer, 1919).

Joppke, Christian, *Citizenship and Immigration* (Cambridge: Polity, 2007).

Joppke, Christian, 'Transformation of Citizenship: Status, Rights, Identity', *Citizenship Studies 11* (2007): pp. 37–48.

Kostakopoulou, Dora, 'Thick, Thin and Thinner Patriotisms: Is This All There Is?', *Oxford Journal of Legal Studies 26* (2006): pp. 73–106.

Kostakopoulou, Dora, 'The Anatomy of Civic Integration', *Modern Law Review 73* (2010): pp. 933–958.

Kymlicka, Will, *Multicultural Citizenship* (Oxford: Oxford University Press, 1995).

Kymlicka, Will, 'Liberal Nationalism and Cosmopolitan Justice', in Seyla Benhabib, *Another Cosmopolitanism* (edited and introduced by Robert Post) (Oxford: Oxford University Press, 2006), pp. 128–146.

Leydet, Dominique, 'Citizenship', *Stanford Encyclopaedia of Philosophy* (Spring 2014 Edition), Edward N. Zalta, ed., http://plato.stanford.edu/entries/citizenship/.

Marshall, Thomas H., *Citizenship and Social Class* (Concord: Pluto Press, 1950).

Miscevic, Nenad, 'Close Strangers, Nationalism, Proximity, and Cosmopolitanism', *Studies in Eastern European Thought 2* (1999): pp. 109–125.

Osipov, Alexander, 'Non-Territorial Autonomy during and after Communism: In the Wrong or Right Place?', *Journal on Ethnopolitics and Minority Issues in Europe 12* (2013): pp. 7–26.

Preuss, Ulrich, 'Disconnecting Constitutions from Statehood: Is Global Constitutionalism a Viable Concept?', in Petra Dobner and Martin Loughlin, eds., *The Twilight of Constitutionalism?* (Oxford: Oxford University Press, 2010), pp. 23–46.

Sassen, Saskia, *Territory, Authority, Rights* (Princeton: Princeton University Press, 2006).

Shacher, Ayelet, *The Birthright Lottery: Citizenship and Global Inequality* (Harvard: Harvard University Press, 2009), chapter 1.

Sharpe, Michael O., *Postcolonial Citizens and Ethnic Migration* (London: Palgrave, 2014).

Schattle, Hans, *The Practices of Global Citizenship* (Chicago: Rowman & Littlefield, 2008).

Soysal, Yasemin, *Limits of Citizenship* (Chicago: University of Chicago Press, 1994).

Soysal, Yasemin, 'Changing Parameters of Citizenship and Claims-Making: Organised Islam in European Public Spheres', *Theory and Society 26* (1997): pp. 509–527.

Stjepanovic, Dejan, 'Dual Substate Citizenship as Institutional Innovation: The Case of Bosnia's Brcko District 21', *Nationalism and Ethnic Politics 21*, no. 4 (2015): pp. 379–400.

Strumia, Francesca, 'Brexiting European Citizenship through the Voice of Others', *German Law Journal 17* (Brexit Special Supplement) (2016): pp. 109–116, online http://static1.squarespace.com/static/56330ad3e4b0733dccoc8495/t/5776e641579fb3bc18d94197/1467409987447/21+PDF_Vol_17_Brexit+_Strumia.pdf.

Teubner, Gunther, *Constitutional Fragments: Societal Constitutionalism and Globalization* (Oxford: Oxford University Press, 2012).

Tierney, Stephen, 'Reframing Sovereignty: Sub-State National Societies and Contemporary Challenges to the Nation-State', *International and Comparative Law Quarterly 54* (2005): pp. 161–183.

Taylor, Charles, *Modern Social Imaginaries* (Durham: Duke University Press, 2003).

Tully, James, 'The Crisis of Global Citizenship', *Radical Politics Today* (June 2009), online http://research.ncl.ac.uk/spaceofdemocracy/word%20docs%20linked%20to/Uploaded%20 2009/Tully/The_Crisis_of_Global_Citizenship_James_Tully.pdf.

Walker, Neil, 'Denizenship and Deterritorialization in the EU', in Hans Lindahl, ed., *A Right to Inclusion and Exclusion? Normative Fault Lines of the EU's Area of Freedom, Security and Justice* (Oxford: Hart, 2009), pp. 261–272.

Walker, Neil, 'The European Union's Unresolved Constitution', in Michel Rosenfeld and Andras Sajo, eds., *The Oxford Handbook of Comparative Constitutional Law* (Oxford: Oxford University Press, 2012), pp. 1185–1208.

Walker, Neil, 'The European Fallout', *German Law Journal 17* (Brexit Special Supplement) (2016): pp. 125–130, online http://static1.squarespace.com/static/56330ad3e4b0733d-ccoc8495/t/5776e65c579fb3bc18d942a5/1467410013198/23+PDF_Vol_17_Brexit+_Walker.pdf.

Walker, Neil, 'Federalism in 3D: The Reimagination of Political Community in the European Union', *Catolica Law Review 1*, no. 1 (2017): pp. 67–90.

Walzer, Michael, *Spheres of Justice: A Defense of Pluralism and Equality* (New York: Basic Books, 1983), chapter 2.

Weil, Patrick, 'Access to Citizenship', in Alexander Aleinikoff and Douglas Klusmeyer, eds., *Citizenship Today: Global Perspective and Practices* (Washington: Carnegie Endowment for International Peace, 2001), pp. 17–35.

Weiler, Joseph H.H., *The Constitution of Europe* (Cambridge: Cambridge University Press, 1999).

CHAPTER 26

DIASPORAS AND TRANSNATIONAL CITIZENSHIP

MICHAEL COLLYER

INTRODUCTION: WHAT IS TRANSNATIONAL CITIZENSHIP?

OVER the last two decades, diasporas and the related notion of transnational communities have become the dominant paradigm in studying migration, yet this has had relatively little impact on studies of citizenship. This is mainly due to the territorial bias of contemporary approaches to citizenship, which associate citizenship primarily, if not exclusively, with belonging to a particular territory. As Bauböck noted more than two decades ago in the seminal *Transnational Citizenship*[1] the rights and obligations of citizenship change when an individual leaves the territory of citizenship, but they do not disappear altogether. In the decades since then the awareness of established forms of non-territorial or extra-territorial citizenship has grown. In addition, more and more states (and even sub-state organizations) have extended the rights and obligations of citizenship to those living permanently outside the territory of citizenship.

The term 'transnational citizenship' is employed in an incredibly wide variety of ways that go far beyond the recognition of enforceable rights in distant territories. Indeed, the most challenging and critical of recent scholarship concentrates on citizenship beyond state institutions.[2] Yet citizenship has always had a territorial referent, whether that is real or imagined, local, metropolitan, nation-state, supra-national or even global.[3] This chapter will insist on an interpretation of both diaspora and transnational citizenship involving dispersal and distance from that territorial referent, with the obvious exception of the global scale, which is covered elsewhere.[4] It will argue that the gradual expansion of membership beyond the territory must be viewed as a normative development of citizenship. Even within this characterization of dispersal and distance there is a broad array of interpretations about the meaning of citizenship. This varies from a narrow interpretation involving strictly enforceable rights, generally claimed from state institutions to a much broader interpretation of fluid social membership describing forms of social affiliation or identity. This breadth of interpretation is not unusual, in fact it is closely related to the range of uses of the term 'diaspora'. Still, some of these interpretations are covered in detail in other chapters, so it is important to clarify the scope of this chapter from the outset.

I will draw on three approaches to help clarify this conceptual field. First, in one of the earliest uses of the term 'transnational citizenship' Balibar argues that citizenship has always been linked to two distinctions: it is 'bound to the existence of the state' but also 'bound to the acknowledged exercise of an individual "capacity" to participate in political decisions'.[5] Thirty years later the first of these distinctions is relatively widely challenged, though probably still covers the vast majority of citizenship analysis, while the second still provides a useful generalization, even given the substantial broadening of the political. In later work, Balibar clarifies that his concern is with *trans*national, rather than *post*national citizenship, since

[1] Rainer Bauböck, *Transnational Citizenship: Membership and Rights in International Migration* (Aldershot: Edward Elgar, 1994).

[2] The special issue of *Global Networks* on 'Transnational Lived Citizenship' is a good example: Kirsi Paulina Kallio and Katharyne Mitchell, eds., *Global Networks: A Journal of Transnational Affairs 16*, no. 3 (2016).

[3] Walker in this volume.   [4] Tan in this volume.

[5] Etienne Balibar, 'Propositions on Citizenship', *Ethics* 98, no. 4 (1988): pp. 723–730, p. 723.

transnational 'does not imply that national identities are bound to disappear', rather 'national identities ... are increasingly relativized ... that is they must compete and take into account other kinds of identities, interests and norms which, seen from a national point of view, escape sovereignty and cross boundaries'.[6] This usefully focuses the concept of transnational citizenship, without providing an overly pro-scriptive definition. Balibar's own analysis turns to the empirical investigation of European citizenship[7] but this understanding of transnational citizenship as chal-lenging (rather than replacing) sovereignty as traditionally conceived and involving the crossing of boundaries clarifies the theoretical terrain to be explored in this chapter.

This still leaves a relatively wide area, so further conceptual focus is needed. Fox suggests a distinction between approaches that explore transnational rights in rela-tion to public authorities, and those that interpret citizenship in terms of a broader societal membership or identity position expressed in a distant or extra-territorial form.[8] The former concerns enforceable rights, in the sense that Bauböck refers to transnational citizenship, though this could relate both to emigrants, as non-resident citizens and immigrants, as non-citizen residents. This is a relatively clear, well-delimited category of analysis. Fox defines 'full transnational citizenship' in these terms as 'membership in more than one national political community'[9] but this is surely multiple citizenship. Although multiple memberships may arise from transnational citizenship, it does not necessarily follow and it is considered in a sep-arate chapter.[10] Membership cannot be limited to the relationship between an indi-vidual and a state institution, but must also be viewed in collective terms. Key civic rights such as freedom of assembly, expression, protest, organization, and religion, amongst others all have broader social implications relating to collective action, reciprocal respect, or communal solidarity.

All of these rights may be exercised transnationally. Although enjoyment of these rights requires an institutional guarantee too, they do not necessarily concern indi-viduals' relationship with public authorities. Instead, they relate to Fox's second, much broader conceptualization of transnational citizenship as societal member-ship or identity. It is here that conceptual debates are most vigorous. Mason, for example, is extremely critical of the conceptual stretching involved in labelling any involvement in transnational civil society as citizenship: 'It is only when identity is combined with something else, such as the shared enjoyment of rights, or shared participation in a cooperative scheme, that the language of citizenship gains a

---

[6] Etienne Balibar, 'Strangers as Enemies: Further Reflections on the Aporias of Transnational Citizenship', Globalization Working Papers 06/4 (Institute on Globalisation and the Human Condition, McMaster University, 2006).

[7] Considered in Strumia's chapter on supranational citizenship.

[8] Jonathan Fox, 'Unpacking "Transnational Citizenship"', *Annual Review of Political Science* 8 (2005): pp. 171–201.

[9] Ibid., p. 188.   [10] Spiro in this volume.

foothold.'[11] Many of these debates, such as Dobson's defence of 'ecological citizen-ship'[12] use a language of 'transnational citizenship' yet overlap substantially with more normative ideas of cosmopolitan citizenship, considered in another chapter.[13]

Bosniak's well cited distinction between the 'hard' external borders of member-ship and the 'soft' internal questions of the rights of membership provides a third and final clarification. She argues that '"transnational migration" creates a situation in which '"hard" threshold norms have now come to occupy the same (internal) terrain as the "soft" interior ones'.[14] When Bosniak writes of 'transnational migra-tion' she is referring only to immigration. This is a major concern of citizenship studies, with good reason, and provides a key focus for several other chapters in this book, most obviously Bauböck's on the borders and boundaries of membership. Although Bosniak clarifies this distinction between political membership and ter-ritorial presence, this is only one of two possible implications of the international movement of people.

Emigration has historically been overlooked, although it is increasingly com-mon for citizenship to be performed extraterritorially across the whole spectrum of formal political rights to informal civil society engagement. In Bosniak's effect-ive imagery this involves an investigation of what happens to the 'soft' interior norms of membership as they move beyond the 'hard' external border.[15] This focus on extra-territorial forms of citizenship, rather than the more common concern of non-citizen residents provides the theme of this chapter. This intersects with both of Fox's 'domains': formal relationships with public authorities and the broader forms of social engagement.

Throughout this chapter, I will combine this extra-territorial focus on a range of citizenship practices, derived from Fox and Bosniak with Balibar's suggestion that transnational citizenship should involve two things: border crossing and a trans-formation (rather than destruction) of traditional ideas of sovereignty from the per-spective of the nation-state. Although this applies to some elements of transnational civil society activism it doesn't incorporate everything that is labelled transnational citizenship. The exclusive extra-territorial focus would be challenged by many theorists of transnational citizenship and it does not exhaust several broader con-cerns. Yet these broader concerns overlap very significantly with mainstream citi-zenship studies, and frequently stray into the realm of multiple, cosmopolitan, or

---

[11] Andrew Mason, 'Environmental Obligations and the Limits of Transnational Citizenship', *Political Studies* 57 (2009): pp. 280–297.

[12] Andrew Dobson, 'Ecological Citizenship: A Defence', *Environmental Politics* 15, no. 3 (2006): pp. 447–451.

[13] Tan in this volume.

[14] Linda Bosniak, *The Citizen and the Alien. Dilemmas of Contemporary Membership* (Princeton: Princeton University Press, 2006), p. 4.

[15] Michael Collyer, 'Inside Out? Directly Elected "Special Representation" of Emigrants in National Legislatures and the Role of Popular Sovereignty', *Political Geography* 41 (2014): pp. 64–73.

supranational citizenships. The focus on what happens to 'acts of citizenship'[16] away from the territory of citizenship has the advantage of a clearly defined theoretical terrain of increasing empirical relevance.

The remainder of this chapter falls into four sections: the first two will consider ways of defining the very widely used and highly contested terms of diaspora and transnationalism. The third section turns to the apparent paradox of state focused transnational citizenship: as the extension of rights is becoming more common, the proportion of citizens taking advantage of those rights appears to be declining. Finally, the fourth section will examine the durability of these rights, asking if diaspora or transnational citizenship is a temporary epiphenomenon of the current state of globalization or a permanent structural change in the practice of citizenship.

DEFINING DIASPORAS: FROM ANALYSIS TO PRACTICE

The literature on diasporas is now so vast that there can be no hope of doing any justice to it here. If, in Wittgenstein's celebrated phrase, 'the meaning of a word is its use in the language' then 'diaspora' has many meanings. It is a fruitless task to try to identify a correct use of the word. This is essentially the point that Brubaker makes when he argues that diaspora cannot be used as a category of analysis, but only as a category of practice.[17] It also draws attention to the fact that the academic production of analysis of diaspora, substantial though that is, has been very quickly outpaced by more popular use of the term. If Google provides an effective measure of the frequency of use of particular words, 'diaspora' is about four times more frequent than 'transnational'—a rough indication of the more frequent use of the term 'diaspora' beyond the academy. Yet the modern origins of the term developed very much within academia and there is some value in briefly tracing this transition in this sub-section. It then turns to the nascent use of the term 'diasporic' or 'diaspora' citizenship, returning to transnational citizenship in the following sub-section.

The modern analytical use of the term 'diaspora' was originally popularized within academic writing in the 1980s leading to the founding of the journal *Diaspora* in 1991. It quickly captured the theoretical *zeitgeist* of the early 1990s, describing a social formation that existed before nation-states. This fitted well with the emerging

---

[16] Engin F. Isin and Greg M. Nielsen, eds., *Acts of Citizenship* (Chicago: University of Chicago Press, 2008). See also Isin in this volume.

[17] Rogers Brubaker, 'The "Diaspora" Diaspora', *Ethnic and Racial Studies* 28, no. 1 (2005): pp. 1–19.

transnational approach that was initially framed as a rejection of the theoretical dominance of the state. As with transnational citizenship, the relatively loose application of the term raised concerns around conceptual stretching and several approaches suggested clear criteria that should be met before any particular social group could be considered a diaspora. In the first issue of *Diaspora*, Safran provided a list of six such criteria, which was expanded to nine by Cohen a few years later.[18] These criteria highlight three common concerns that provide a clearly constrained set of ideas about the meaning of diaspora. First, diaspora was produced by population dispersal of some kind. This could arise from the physical movement of people to a variety of different locations. Alternatively, even without migration a slightly different 'near diaspora' may result from the movement of boundaries, so that individuals no longer live in the state of their birth. Second, some kind of 'enduring' relationship with the point of origin was thought necessary, since not any dispersed group could be a diaspora. Finally, the group should retain a distinctive identity in the places to which they moved, involving some form of 'boundary maintenance'.

The context of dispersal has proved relatively uncontroversial, but each of the criteria relating to the other two points have received widespread criticism. Moreover, the approach itself has been dismissed as overly formulaic, referred to as 'tickbox' social science by Clifford.[19] The necessity of a relationship with some kind of original home was seen as essentialist and criticized especially eloquently by Anthias.[20] The possibility of an eventual return to that homeland, one of Safran's initial criteria, was similarly criticized as teleological. Stuart Hall, an early advocate of the theoretical value of a diaspora focus, highlighted a preference for issues of boundary erosion, rather than maintenance as a key to the processes of hybridity which attracted him to the term in the first place.[21] Similarly, Gilroy's term 'changing same' in his work on the Black Atlantic captured an idea that something could be dynamic or hybrid, without losing clarity as a meaningful focus for analysis. This current of analysis has developed around a politically focused post-colonial approach that is concerned with issues of anti-racism and intersectionality. In a later discussion of Avtar Brah's work, Stuart Hall argues that

the idea of diaspora troubles the notion of cultural origin, of 'roots', of primordial identities and authenticity. It unpicks the claims made for the unities of culturally homogenous, racially purified national cultures and identities. It reaches naturally for the messy territory of the multicultural. It introduces the logic of translation and entanglement.[22]

---

[18] William Safran, 'Diasporas in Modern Societies: Myths of Homeland and Return', *Diaspora 1* (1991): pp. 83–99; Robin Cohen, *Global Diasporas: An Introduction* (London: Routledge, 1997).

[19] James Clifford, 'Diasporas', *Cultural Anthropology 9*, no. 3 (1994): pp. 302–338.

[20] Floya Anthias, 'Evaluation "Diaspora": Beyond Ethnicity?', *Sociology 32*, no. 3 (1998): pp. 557–580.

[21] Stuart Hall, 'Cultural Identity and Diaspora', in Jonathan Rutherford, ed., *Identity: Community, Culture, Difference* (London: Lawrence & Wishart, 1990): pp. 222–237.

[22] Stuart Hall, 'Avtar Brah's Cartographies: Moment, Method, Meaning', *Feminist Review 100* (2012): pp. 27–38.

This is the kind of theoretical position that recent critical work around transnational citizenship is trying to get at. Although it challenges a nation-state model of belonging it is not entirely irreconcilable with one, it is simply critical of a one-size-fits-all approach to citizenship. Hall finishes with a call for 'multiple belongingnesses'—not multiple citizenships, since the strength of diaspora in this frame of analysis is that it allows for a discussion of belonging irrespective of formal memberships.

The dominant understanding of diaspora in all of this literature remains that of ethno-national groups, although this is contextualized in important ways. First, there is some shift in this, to incorporate dispersed groups defined in other ways—queer diasporas is probably the most theoretically developed[23]—but these mostly intersect with diasporas that are defined in ethno-national terms. Second, work on diaspora within the cultural studies, post-colonial tradition has developed a very clear set of theoretical and political principles which totally rejects any primordial or essentialist interpretation of ethnicity and any understanding of the nation as homogeneous. It highlights the intersection of both ethnicity and national membership with a range of other differentiating characteristics such as gender, class, and sexuality and provides a sophisticated framework to respond to real world complexities. Yet the dense theoretical language and challenging premises of this approach means that it is very rarely cited in the policy discussions that now form the vast majority of references to diaspora.

Diaspora has been incorporated into a range of policy objectives by governments around the world as well as by NGOs and international organizations. The term is also increasingly widespread as a self-description by migrant organizations themselves. Yet almost without exception in these contexts the term is used to describe a group of people with a direct ethno-national link to an individual nation-state. At best this is a vastly simplified version of the post-colonial account of diaspora; at worst it actually contradicts the emphasis on the heterogeneity of forms of membership that characterizes that approach. The understanding of who forms part of the diaspora varies widely in these policy situations. At its narrowest, diaspora is simply an alternative name for all emigrant citizens. This is the case with discussion of the 'diaspora vote' in various contexts, since virtually without exception, citizenship is required to cast a vote externally. Several countries have a defined status that is broader than citizen. This is particularly common in countries which forbid citizens from acquiring a second nationality, such as India or Ethiopia. In the Indian case someone who has given up their Indian nationality to obtain another nationality and the foreign born children and grandchildren of Indian-born parents can register as 'Overseas Citizens of India' (OCI), a status which is not equivalent to citizenship, but nonetheless carries certain rights.[24]

---

[23] Anne-Marie Fortier, 'Queer Diaspora', in Diane Richardson and Steven Seidman, eds., *Handbook of Lesbian and Gay Studies* (London: Sage, 2002), pp. 183–198.

[24] Article 7 of the Indian Citizenship Act of 1955, amended in August 2005.

At its broadest usage in policy contexts membership of a diaspora is a completely undefined status implying some form of ancestral connection to the country in question. The widespread policy objective of 'building' a diaspora suggests that in addition to an ethno-national connection, membership of a diaspora also requires a deliberate choice. For it to be possible to build a diaspora at all there must be a wider group of *potential* diaspora members who can be encouraged to consciously express a sense of emotional attachment or belonging to a dispersed community. One of the challenges of using diaspora as a category of practice is that even within the same discursive frame, such as a ministerial speech or a particular policy, it is common for the term to be used both in the narrowest sense of expatriate citizens and in the broader sense of ancestral belonging almost indistinguishably.

Despite these definitional issues, it is increasingly common for diaspora relations to be institutionalized in some form.[25] This is partly explained by the recognition of the significant role that diasporas may play in economic development. Development policy interest in diasporas is driven by ever rising financial remittances and widely communicated through regular high level meetings such as the annual Global Forum on Migration and Development. Yet, although dedicated ministries, or at least departments of diaspora affairs are more common in low and middle income countries,[26] they can be found in wealthy countries too. Ireland, for example, has had a Minister for the Diaspora since July 2014 and Israel has a long standing Minster of Diaspora. These institutions may be short-lived. It is common for state relations with emigrant citizens to be initially characterized by suspicion and typically monitored through ministries of the interior. As the relationship matures and the diaspora is increasingly valued the location shifts to the Ministry of Foreign Affairs, though often a dedicated ministry is an intermediary step. These ministries or departments form what Gamlen has called the 'emigration state', responsible for both 'diaspora building' and 'diaspora integration' activities.[27] Formally recognized rights apply to those with citizenship or one of the forms of partial citizenship, such as OCI status in India. There are other forms of engagement involving cultural activities or language provision that apply equally to a more fluid notion of diaspora belonging.

The idea of a diaspora or diasporic citizenship remains a fairly marginal way of describing these policies, but it is becoming more widely used. In some cases it

[25] International Organization for Migration (IOM) and Migration Policy Institute (MPI), *Developing a Roadmap for Engaging Diasporas in Development: A Handbook for Policymakers and Practitioners in Home and Host Countries* (Geneva: IOM, 2012), online https://publications.iom.int/books/developing-road-map-engaging-diasporas-development-handbook-policymakers-and-practitioners.
[26] Ministries open and close regularly but at the time of writing the following countries all had dedicated ministerial level representation of the diaspora: Algeria, Armenia, Azerbaijan, Bangladesh, Benin, Georgia, Ireland, Israel, Mali, Morocco, Pakistan, Senegal, and Tunisia.
[27] Alan Gamlen, 'The Emigration State and the Modern Geopolitical Imagination', *Political Geography 27* (2008): pp. 840–856.

refers to claims for national citizenship from outside the territory of the state.[28] This typically requires the possibility of multiple citizenship but it is otherwise much the same as any other application for citizenship. There are three other situations discernable in this analysis where diasporas result in a more obvious challenge to traditionally understood practices of sovereignty. The term diaspora citizenship may be more meaningful to describe the specificity of these situations. First are those special categories of partial citizenship such as India's OCI status. Such partial enjoyment of citizenship rights results exclusively from a diaspora position, it could not happen within the territory. A second distinct meaning of diaspora citizenship is even more unusual. It results from a government in exile that, for largely political reasons grants citizenship to those of the same national origin. The only current example of this is exile Tibetan citizenship, conferred by the Tibetan government in exile through the Green Book, though the fact that it is not recognized by any other state means that its value is purely symbolic.[29]

The third sense in which diasporic citizenship may refer to a unique status is potentially the most widespread, though the use of the term remains rare. In a detailed analysis of Congolese migrants in Brussels, Swyngedouw and Swyngedouw highlight the significance of the urban scale in diasporic relations:

the diaspora condition calls into being new demands for political citizenship that transcend the territorial notion of the state [and] recognise the relevance of other geographical scales of political organisation ... Diasporic citizenship, therefore, demands thinking through a new notion of political urban citizenship, one that is not sutured exclusively by cultural or social citizenship rights.[30]

This is an innovative and imaginative attempt to combine the careful theoretical analysis of the post-colonial approach to diaspora with a language of citizenship. It is significant that this connection is made through a focus on the city, where superdiversity provides an alternative lens for examining these issues and a clear set of immediate practical implications of diversity that appear less abstract than at a national scale.[31] Multi-level belonging is examined in more detail elsewhere[32] but the challenge is to begin to translate this analysis to different forms of belonging. I now turn back to the central idea of transnational citizenship to examine how it

---

[28] This is the sense in which Sutherland uses the term (Claire Sutherland, 'Vietnamese Diasporic Citizenship', in Engin F. Isin and Peter Nyers, eds., *Routledge Handbook of Global Citizenship Studies* (London: Routledge, 2014), pp. 522–531).

[29] Fiona McConnell, *Rehearsing the State: The Political Practices of the Tibetan Government in Exile* (London: Wiley, 2016).

[30] Eva Swyngedouw and Erik Swyngedouw, 'The Congolese Diaspora in Brussels and Hybrid Identity Formation: Multi-Scalarity and Diasporic Citizenship', *Urban Research and Practice* 2, no. 1 (2009): pp. 68–90, pp. 87–88.

[31] Steven Vertovec, 'Super-Diversity and its Implications', *Ethnic and Racial Studies* 30, no. 6 (2007): pp. 1024–1054.

[32] See Maas in this volume.

can be informed by these very wide-ranging debates around diaspora. The tremendous breadth of theoretical and applied analysis of diaspora is a useful reflection of the range of concerns raised by diaspora analysis—from important principles of anti-racism and social justice to practical policy questions of economic development. For these reasons, it is difficult to go beyond the use of diaspora as category of practice, in Brubaker's terms. At its best diaspora analysis captures the tremendous complexity of the challenges raised by contemporary patterns of mobility and diversity. Transnational citizenship reintroduces the important question of enforceable rights, though also provides a framework to examine how they are negotiated.

Rights Across Borders: The Development of Transnational Citizenship

There is a very long history to the relationship between territorialized political authority and members of the polity living beyond that territory. Like diaspora, this relationship pre-dates the origins of the modern nation-state by several millennia. Leaving the territory of citizenship involves the loss of most rights associated with citizenship, though certain rights have always remained. At a minimum, citizens have a right of re-entry to their territory of citizenship since withdrawal of this right renders an individual stateless. Withdrawal of all citizenship rights, including right of return was also the basis for exile or banishment in ancient civilizations of the Eastern Mediterranean, a punishment with its own legal codes distinct from mass deportations.[33] Beyond that minimum position, the array of rights, and in some cases obligations, retained by citizens on leaving the territory have gradually expanded. Over the last few decades this development has been the subject of a growing array of scholarship and deserves to be considered as a genuinely normative development in citizenship.

In addition to these empirical developments in the framework of rights accorded to extra-territorial citizens the growing recognition of the non-formal content of citizenship has underlined the advantages of an extra-territorial location for other forms of engagement. Technological change has also made such distant involvement much easier. This varies from direct political opposition, such as long distance

---

[33] Raymond Westbrook, 'Personal Exile in the Ancient Near East', *Journal of the American Oriental Society* 128, no. 2 (2008): pp. 317–323.

nationalism to more supportive lobbying efforts and from involvement in transnational civil society to more local engagement akin to the urban citizenship discussed earlier. This sub-section tracks the expansion of formal rights and informal engagement enjoyed by extra-territorial citizens that now deserve to be seen as a distinct status of transnational citizenship.

The various activities offered through the institution of the consulate is an almost completely unexplored area of state engagement with extra-territorial citizens, although it has an extremely long history. The kind of services offered vary extremely widely from one state to another, though a historical thread can be traced involving the deliberate engagement between state officials and citizens of that state beyond the state's territory. This practice is well over 2,000 years old; the institution of the proxeny in ancient Greece, replicated many essential functions of the modern consulate.[34] Similar practices can be traced through shifting imperial allegiances in Europe in the centuries before the Peace of Westphalia, though consulates were not officially recognized until the 1963 Vienna Convention on Consular Relations. There is no comparative data available on the services offered through different consulates[35] but anecdotal evidence suggests that experiences of accessing consulates vary very widely. The rights they extend to non-resident citizens are usually very limited, often not going beyond support for transnational business initiatives. Nevertheless, the institution of the consulate provides a clear illustration that contemporary extra-territorial practices have a long history.

It is only relatively recently that the rights accorded to citizens who have left the country have begun to expand significantly beyond the minimalist right to return and consular support. Until the early nineteenth century, emigration for reasons other than trade was looked upon with suspicion across Western Europe. Nancy Green's analysis of the gradual process of change across five countries (Britain, France, Germany, Italy, and Hungary) charts the differential responses according to issues such as market transitions.[36] During the course of the nineteenth century the right to emigrate became accepted as an essential liberal democratic norm, now enshrined in the Universal Declaration of Human Rights.[37] Even so, emigration controls persist in some parts of the world, sometimes in the form of gender-specific bans on the emigration of women.[38] Despite these violations, Barry argues

[34] David Bederman, *International Law in Antiquity* (Cambridge: Cambridge University Press, 2007).

[35] Alan Gamlen (n 27) makes a very similar point.

[36] Nancy L. Green, 'The Politics of Exit: Reversing the Immigration Paradigm', *The Journal of Modern History 77*, no. 2 (2005): pp. 263–289.

[37] UN, *Universal Declaration of Human Rights*, 1948, Article 13(2) ('Everyone has the right to leave any country, including his own, and return to his country'); Aristide Zolberg, 'The Exit Revolution: Citizenship and Those Who Leave', in Nancy L. Green and François Weil, eds., *Citizenship and Those Who Leave: The Politics of Emigration and Expatriation* (Urbana and Chicago: University of Illinois Press, 2007), pp. 33–60.

[38] Nana Oishi, *Women in Motion: Globalization, State Policies and Labor Migration in Asia* (Stanford: University of Stanford Press, 2005).

that the development of this emigration norm is central in explaining the ongoing engagement with emigrants; 'the citizenship discourse will remain incomplete until it analyzes emigrant citizenship as a tool of nation-building and identity construction in emigration states.'[39]

The practical extension of rights to emigrant citizens has come even more recently than the relatively widespread acceptance of emigration itself. An array of rights that previously could not be enjoyed after departure from the territory are now extended to emigrants by an increasingly wide range of states. These include the access to certain investments or savings usually reserved for citizens, the right to run for office, the right to vote, and the coverage of social protection, most obviously the extra-territorial payment of pensions. These are balanced against a much more limited number of obligations which cover non-resident citizens in certain circumstances.[40] When conscription into the armed forces was more common emigrants typically had to apply for exemption or face draft dodging charges, though this is now of less general relevance. Most countries accept that they do not have the resources to pursue emigrants for tax obligations but famously, the US obliges all citizens, regardless of residence, to file an income tax declaration.[41] Other states, such as Eritrea, have established a voluntary levy, with mixed success.

Of all of these rights and obligations, the practice of voting from abroad has received by far the most attention.[42] This is partly for the symbolic significance of the democratic process for the practice of sovereignty, which has made the enfranchisement of emigrants particularly controversial. A tremendous variety of legislation governs this process which in some cases applies only to certain elections or particular categories of individuals. The approach dates from legislation passed 150 years ago by the state of Michigan allowing its soldiers to vote in state elections. It is not unusual for sub-state polities to enfranchise non-resident members, though developments at a national level are much easier to track. Almost all states now make provision for voting for state employees whose job obliges them to reside elsewhere, such as soldiers or diplomatic staff, but these rights are now widely extended to the entire emigrant population. Developments in this area have been concentrated in the last few decades. In the 1970s when countries such as Portugal or New Zealand made allowance for emigrants to vote the practice was still extremely rare. Even relatively recently respected scholars were arguing that 'only a few' countries

[39] Kim Barry, 'Home and Away: The Construction of Citizenship in an Emigration Context', *New York University Law Review 81* (2006): pp. 11–59, p. 19.

[40] Michael Collyer, ed., *Emigration Nations: Policies and Ideologies of Emigrant Engagement* (London: Palgrave, 2013).

[41] Through the US Government (2009) *Foreign Account Tax Compliance Act*, online https://www.congress.gov/111/bills/hr3933/BILLS-111hr3933ih.pdf.

[42] Jean-Michel Lafleur, *Transnational Politics and the State: The External Voting Rights of Diaspora* (London: Routledge, 2011).

had granted the franchise to non-resident citizens.[43] It is now widely recognized that the large majority of states allow emigrants to vote in most national elections.[44]

Although voting from abroad must now be considered the norm, it is still controversial in some settings. In 2006, discussions in the Ghanaian Parliament over a Bill to enfranchise emigrants provoked demonstrations in the streets by those opposed to the measure.[45] In this case opposition was rooted in the assumption that emigrants tended to favour the ruling New Patriotic Party and the bill was simply a way of boosting their vote. Objections to emigrant voting have more frequently been framed in more generalized, normative terms.[46] It is argued that emigrants lack information, lack a significant stake in the outcome of elections and therefore, most significantly, lack the incentive to vote responsibly. This is the basis for the 'long distance nationalism' thesis, that emigrants will naturally tend to more extreme political positions.[47] Defenders of emigrant voting counter that these objections are misplaced and rooted in a time when distance often did mean being cut off. Now that most daily newspapers can be read anywhere in the world and much political discussion takes place through social media, extra-territorial citizens are equally well informed. Crucially, they may also have a stake in the election, through family connections, ownership of property, or planned return.[48] Where such situations apply they undermine the notion that transnational citizenship reduces the likelihood of political responsibility. Indeed emigrants have frequently confounded voting expectations. In both France and Italy, extremely liberal regimes of voting from abroad were introduced by right wing governments (under Sarkozy and Berlusconi) in the apparent expectation that emigrants were more likely to support their positions. In both cases at subsequent elections, emigrants contributed to the general political trend in ejecting the governments that had enfranchised them.[49]

This informs the broader question of why state institutions should extend rights such as voting to emigrants in the first place. A range of explanations drawing on concerns around the impact of migration on development have argued that the gradual development of a rights-based status of transnational

[43] Ruth Rubio-Martin, 'Transnational Politics and the Normative Challenges of Expatriate Voting and Nationality Retention of Emigrants', *New York University Law Review 81* (2006): pp. 117–137, p. 127.

[44] International Institute of Democracy and Electoral Assistance (IDEA), *Voting from Abroad* (Stockholm: IDEA, 2007).

[45] AllAfrica, 'Chaos in House over 'Burger' Bill', 3 February 2006, online http://allafrica.com/stories/200602030513.html.

[46] Claudio López-Guerra, 'Should Expatriates Vote?', *The Journal of Political Philosophy 13*, no. 2 (2005): pp. 216–234; David Owen, 'Transnational Citizenship and the Democratic State', *Critical Review of International Social and Political Philosophy 14*, no. 5 (2011): pp. 641–663.

[47] Benedict Anderson, *Long Distance Nationalism: World Capitalism and the Rise of Identity Politics*, the Wertheim Lecture (Amsterdam: Centre for Asian Studies, 1992).

[48] Rainer Bauböck, 'Stakeholder Citizenship and Transnational Political Participation: A Normative Evaluation of External Voting', *Fordham Law Review 75*, no. 5 (2007): pp. 2393–2447.

[49] Collyer (n 15).

citizenship is driven primarily by the interests of state institutions. This interpretation has typically been explored through an empirical focus on low-income
countries which are dependent on migrants' remittances. In these situations,
dependency often relates closely to the package of rights that are extended to
emigrants.[50] Yet although this explanation fits a range of countries it is not sufficiently generalizable to be universally applicable. Even in those countries which
rely on emigrants for a substantial proportion of government revenue the development of a more formal status of transnational citizenship may not be exclusively motivated by these concerns.[51] In the Ghanaian example considered above,
as well as the background to the current electoral systems in Italy and France,
it may be that the perceived interests of the ruling party are more instrumental
than the financial interests of the country. Beyond this, many countries with no
structural dependence on the finances generated by emigrants also extend substantial packages of rights to emigrant citizens. This suggests that this is not a
purely interest-driven set of policy changes but a broader trend that highlights a
genuinely normative change in the ways that citizenship is perceived. The notion
that most formal rights of citizenship should end at the border has characterized the formal practice of citizenship for much of its history. Over the last few
decades, the connection between citizenship and territory has weakened. State
institutions have extended rights to non-resident citizens not because they have
something to gain but to reflect a more popular view that citizenship continues
even during absence from the territory. This has allowed a more formal status of
transnational citizenship to develop.

Although the transnational sphere has expanded significantly in recent years
due to the formal extra-territorialization of many rights it has always had a more
significant informal component. Indeed the two are closely related. In an analysis
of extra-territorial voting amongst Ecuadorians, Boccagni interviewed several
people who were not motivated to vote by any real desire to influence the result
of the election but because it made them *feel* Ecuadorian.[52] In other cases states
may provide support for emigrant groups directly through civil society, such as official organizations of emigrants, or direct cultural support or religious provision.
Emigrants themselves also frequently organize and campaign to alter conditions
in their countries of citizenship. These civil society engagements go well beyond
Fox's first category of citizenship as a relationship of enforceable rights with public

---

[50] Jose Itzigsohn. 'Immigration and the Boundaries of Citizenship', *International Migration Review*
34, no. 4 (2000): pp. 1126–1154.

[51] An attempt to investigate if a financial dependence on remittances was linked to the introduction
of voting from abroad found no significant relationship at all (see Michael Collyer and Zana Vathi,
'Patterns of Extra-Territorial Voting', Migration DRC Working Paper T22 (2007), online http://www.
migrationdrc.org/publications/working_papers/WP-T22.pdf.

[52] Paolo Boccagni, 'Making the "Fifth Region" a Real Place? Emigrant Policies and the Emigration-
Nation Nexus in Ecuador', *National Identities 16*, no. 2 (2014): pp. 117–137.

authorities. The broader social identity based elements of citizenship also have clear transnational implications. Once the analysis extends beyond the identifiable role of public authorities the difficulty is that it can be applied to virtually any cross-border activity.

The suggestion I draw from Balibar's framework that these practices should challenge traditionally conceived operations of state sovereignty also covers a wide range of activities, though it does provide some limits. It would preclude cross-border provision of services, support for international sports teams, or more global forms of activism, for example. Østergaard-Nielsen's analysis highlighted three situations in which emigrants may exert political influence on the government of their state of citizenship. First, homeland politics involving direct transnational influence, second the 'immigrant politics' of lobbying the host government to intervene in some way, and third translocal politics that does not involve either government directly but works through civil society mechanisms to influence public opinion.[53] The ancient practice of exile set out to cut people off from any influence over the polity, though all three of these orientations provide ways in which the political influence of emigrants may be amplified, rather than extinguished, by an extra-territorial location. This provides a clear challenge to sovereignty, in Balibar's terms.

These patterns of activism could also be extended to forms of engagement which are less overtly political, such as cultural displays. An extra-territorial location may allow emigrants to contest dominant narratives of what belonging to the nation means. One particularly prominent occasion that was used in this way was the 2003 Year of Algeria, in France.[54] Although most events were officially sponsored by the Algerian government, and advanced an ethnically homogeneous vision of the country, there were plenty of opportunities for the Berber or Amazight minority, who are over-represented amongst emigrants to France, to challenge this. In other situations, similar negotiations around belonging and the meaning of membership may take place more freely at different scales of membership, most obviously the city level. The absence of formal membership at the city level allows a more complex analysis and contestation of who can claim belonging and what this means. This has always been the case but is becoming more widely recognized as the extra-territorialization of formal rights of national membership becomes more common. There is perhaps a connection between these enactments of citizenship which may explain the tendency for a gradual decline in levels of engagement with transnational citizenship.

---

[53] Eva Østergaard-Nielsen, 'The Politics of Migrants' Transnational Political Practices', *International Migration Review 37*, no. 3 (2003): pp. 760–786.

[54] Michael Collyer, 'Transnational Political Participation of Algerians in France: Extra-Territorial Civil Society versus Transnational Governmentality', *Political Geography 25*, no, 7 (2006): pp. 836–849.

The Paradox of Transnational Citizenship: Growing Rights Shrinking Interest?

In some cases, the recognition of formal rights comes after a long history of campaigning by emigrants. In both Morocco and Mexico, legislation to allow emigrants to vote followed sustained lobbying from emigrant groups. In other cases, legal changes to extend further rights to emigrants do not appear to result from a clear demand. The planned introduction of emigrant voting in Ghana, in 2006 (discussed above) and the various changes in legislation to allow UK nationals to vote from abroad are both examples where legislation changes resulted more obviously from the interests of the ruling party at the time. Both emigrants and elites provide domestic pressure for change but a third source of influence is the growing international norm of extending rights to emigrants. The establishment of a norm of this kind requires a variety of mechanisms to inform and validate change. Again this is most obvious with a practice such as external voting where a degree of diffusion is evident in the development of particular models of operating the external vote. Certain characteristics of voting models are clustered. Most countries allowing emigrants to vote for their own representation are in Europe, for example where it is clear that governments study changes in neighbouring jurisdictions very closely before implementing similar policies.[55] International organizations, such as the Institute for Democracy and Electoral Assistance (IDEA) also provide important avenues for policy discussion, comparison and diffusion.

The gradual diffusion of norms of transnational citizenship[56] is accompanied by a related trend of re-examination of the place of emigrants in the national story. For centuries, emigration was widely seen as a suspicious, if not overtly hostile act to the government of the day. Green's discussions of emigration in nineteenth century Europe highlight how widespread this perspective was.[57] This continued in various forms. Sayad quotes an Algerian emigrant of the 1960s describing how emigrants left in the middle of the night to hide the shame of leaving.[58] This kind of working class emigration was often concentrated in marginal parts of the country, or involved groups of people who were considered marginal or surplus to requirements in some way. Emigration of predominantly female domestic workers from

---

[55] Collyer (n 15).

[56] Anca Turcu and Robert Urbatsch, 'Diffusion of Diaspora Enfranchisement Norms: A Multinational Study', *Comparative Political Studies* 48 (2015): pp. 407–437.

[57] Green (n 36).

[58] Abdelmalek Sayad, 'El Ghorba: le mécanisme de reproduction de l'émigration', *Actes de la recherche en sciences sociales*, no. 1–2 (1975): pp. 50–66.

Sri Lanka, of indigenous populations from the Peruvian altiplano, or Mexican agricultural workers to the US were all considered undesirable by mainstream society
when large scale migration began between the 1950s and 1970s. To the extent that
governments were concerned to maintain connections with these citizens once they
left the country, this was often managed through ministries of the interior, reflecting the sense of potential threat which they posed.

In recent years, this has begun to change. In a few extreme cases, such as Eritrea
or North Korea, emigration is still considered an act of treachery. In most cases,
however there has been transformation in the ways in which emigrants are viewed,
a deliberate incorporation of emigrant citizens, often from very humble back-
grounds as a more valorized part of the national story. In recent years the Scottish
first minister has formally recognised the role played by Scottish crofters who left
in the seventeenth century and the Sri Lanka Bureau of Foreign Employment has
begun a 'national heroes' campaign to celebrate the role played by migrant domestic
workers. I have argued elsewhere that this kind of inclusive approach, recognizing
emigrants as an essential part of the 'story of peoplehood', is a necessary part in the
normative trend towards transnational citizenship.[59] As emigrants are considered to
remain part of the nation, rather than to have rejected it, rights of citizenship will
more readily be extended to them.

The paradox of this development is that the gradual incorporation of emigrants
into the rights-based regime of citizenship has also coincided with a gradual
decline of uptake of those very rights on the part of emigrants themselves. Once
again emigrant voting provides the clearest indication of this. Electoral participation amongst emigrants is always lower than national participation rates. In some
cases this can be explained by the very challenging process that is often required of
emigrants to register to vote—the very low rates of participation from emigrants in
Mexican elections is typically explained by registration difficulties. Recent Turkish
elections provide an even clearer illustration of this trend. The vote from abroad
was introduced for the 2014 Presidential election in Turkey but emigrants had to
book an appointment at a Turkish consulate in order to cast their vote. Turnout
from overseas was less than 10 per cent, compared to 74.13 per cent within Turkey.
For the legislative elections the following year (June 2015) this restriction had been
removed, though voters still had to travel to consulates. Overseas turnout rose to
37 per cent, still substantially lower than the 83.92 per cent turnout in Turkey but a
clear indication that turnout amongst overseas electors is significantly influenced
by voting systems. Nevertheless, where data is available long term, there is a clear
decline. Portuguese emigrants were allowed to vote in 1976, when overseas turnout
was 86.8 per cent. It declined steadily to reach a low of just over 15 per cent in 2009,

[59] Michael Collyer, 'Introduction: Locating and Narrating Emigration Nations', in Michael Collyer, ed., *Emigration Nations: Policies and Ideologies of Emigrant Engagement* (London: Palgrave, 2013), pp. 1–24.

though it has recovered slightly since then. Within a complex picture of variability with different systems the available evidence suggests that interest in transnational citizenship rights declines over time.

This decline in participation in formal citizenship over time is a significant trend. It is possible that this gap is filled by other forms of engagement, such as participation in transnational civil society, the less formal 'translocal' activism, though this also requires a significant level of commitment and it seems unlikely that individuals would choose one or the other. Most likely those who make the effort to engage in transnational civil society are also likely to exercise formal rights in a transnational context. Other measures of engagement, such as financial remittances show a relatively stable increase, at least on a global level, although the data is not sufficiently widely available to distinguish between a continued supply of financial support from long established emigrants and the continued arrival of new emigrants who are more likely to retain immediate contacts back home. The most likely ongoing connection appears to be through the broadest notion of diaspora, the forms of transnational citizenship that rely on social and identity positions. Still, in these cases the challenge posed to sovereignty is weak or non-existent so this potentially amounts to the gradual fading away of transnational citizenship.

Conclusion: The Durability of Diasporas and Transnational Citizenship

The notion of transnational citizenship has developed over the last few decades from work that has examined the implications of human mobility for the practice of citizenship. This is a massive subject area that now covers so much of mainstream citizenship theory that it risks losing any specific theoretical purchase. Closely related themes are considered in a variety of other chapters. This chapter has argued that if it is to mean anything, transnational citizenship should provide a challenge to accepted practices of sovereignty, viewed from a state perspective. Balibar's formulation sought to focus discussion of sovereignty around developments that, from a state perspective, would be seen as a challenge. Nevertheless, this raises the difficulty of thinking about the state without using categories inherent in the existence of the state that was initially discussed by Bourdieu. Bourdieu argues that it is impossible to think about the state (*penser l'Etat*) without employing the state's perspective (*pensée d'Etat*). This is because thinking about the state involves 'applying categories of thought to the State which are produced and guaranteed by the State, hence [it is] to misrecognise its most profound truth'.[60]

In this chapter, I have argued that territoriality provides one of the ways out of this circular problem. Since the claiming of rights from within a state's territory reinforces rather than challenges accepted practices of sovereignty I have examined instances of the extra-territorial or diasporic exercise of the rights of citizenship. This narrower focus on extra-territoriality allows citizenship itself to be conceptualized relatively broadly. A transnational challenge can arise both through a rights-based relationship with public institutions at state level and a range of civil society engagements that reveal elements of social and cultural identity.

These two potential forms of challenge lead to further research in two distinct areas. First, the state focus can be pursued through further examination of extra-territorial practices of state institutions, particularly forms of engagement with non-resident citizens, about which relatively little systematic information is available. This is even the case for very well established areas of engagement, such as consular practice, where comparative research is almost completely absent. A detailed historical analysis of such practices is required to identify how and when changes became apparent: are these recent changes or has extra-territorial engagement been an unrecognized part of state practice for much longer than recent attention suggests? If this is a recent evolution, what other changes have provoked it? This analysis cannot be restricted to state activities but requires a simultaneous investigation of the perspectives and priorities of emigrant citizens themselves. How do their extra-territorial 'acts of citizenship' both claim and help to constitute the status of citizen in the polity they have left behind?

This understanding incorporates elements of research into diasporic citizenship. The extra-territorial focus gives rise to particular categories of partial citizenship granted by states that restrict dual nationality. It also refers to the particularly unusual but theoretically significant situation of governments in exile that recognize a quasi-citizenship membership for related diaspora. Although Tibetan exile citizenship is the only clear example of this, it relates closely to three further categories of potential membership which may or may not translate to formal citizenship. First, ethnic forms of belonging such as Pontic Greeks, German *Aussiedler*, or Latin Americans with a potential claim to Italian citizenship;[61] second, post-colonial forms of membership, such as the British Commonwealth where limited rights are recognized or more linguistic relationships, such as the Francophonie or the

---

[60] Pierre Bourdieu, *Raisons pratiques. Sur la théorie de l'action* (Paris: Seuil, 1994), p. 101.

[61] See Guido Tintori, 'The Transnational Political Practices of "Latin American Italians"', *International Migration* 49, no. 3 (2011): pp. 168–188.

lusophone PALOP states in Africa; third, state engagement with 'near diasporas' of individuals displaced by the movement of borders, such as the former USSR or the colonial drawing of borders to bisect ethnic or language groups. In all three of these situations states have a particular relationship with individuals who live beyond state territory and are not full or even partial citizens but are nonetheless distinct from non-citizens and may be able to claim certain rights. The transnationalization of partial or quasi forms of citizenship is likely to combine with multiple member-ships as a growing feature of transnational belonging. Finally 'diasporic citizenship' draws attention to more informal forms of membership that occur at a city level and provide the clearest point of engagement between citizenship theory and a post-colonial analysis of diaspora.

Understood in these terms, transnational citizenship has a long history. Recognizable historical examples of contemporary consular practices can be traced back more than 2,000 years though they have only been codified much more recently. Despite this long history, the recognition of significant rights for emigrant citizens has been a very recent development. Voting rights began to expand in the 1970s but it is only since 2000 that this has involved a substantial number, now a clear majority, of states.

Yet the final section has raised the possibility that this recent expansion of for-mal citizenship appears to coincide with a decline in interest in taking up these rights. The easiest measure of this is declining participation of emigrant voters. Such formal rights have a legally limited lifespan and for any particular cohort of emigrants the practice will decline as these limits are reached, requiring ongoing emigration for their continued practice. It is not yet clear if the current expan-sion of citizenship rights to those living permanently beyond the territory is a permanent change in the way citizenship is conducted or a temporary stage in the evolution of citizenship practices. Continued research into historical prac-tices and continued development of transnational citizenship is required to cre-ate a more complete picture of these changes. The durability of these forms of citizenship will only become clear over the course of the next decade or two. Yet from a broader understanding of citizenship involving a range of more informal connections beyond officially enforceable rights it is likely that the transnational/diasporic dimension will remain important. Such connections are not subject to the random time limits of formal rights. For growing numbers of people signifi-cant contacts and emotional connections occur across borders. The infrastruc-ture is now available to support this in ways that were not available even in the relatively recent past. For many people around the world the stuff of life is essen-tially transnational. Formal citizenship practices have evolved substantially in recent decades to take account of this but the more dynamic informal expression of shifting memberships and belongings is inevitably one step ahead.

Bibliography

AllAfrica, 'Chaos in House over 'Burger' Bill', 3 February 2006, online http://allafrica.com/stories/200602030513.html.

Anderson, Benedict, 'Long Distance Nationalism: World Capitalism and the Rise of Identity Politics', The Wertheim Lecture (Amsterdam: Centre for Asian Studies, 1992).

Anthias, Floya, 'Evaluation "Diaspora": Beyond Ethnicity?', Sociology 32, no. 3 (1998): pp. 557–580.

Balibar, Etienne, 'Propositions on Citizenship', Ethics 98, no. 4 (1988): pp. 723–730, p. 723.

Balibar, Etienne, 'Strangers as Enemies: Further Reflections on the Aporias of Transnational Citizenship', Globalization Working Papers 06/4 (Institute on Globalisation and the Human Condition, McMaster University, 2006).

Barry, Kim, 'Home and Away: The Construction of Citizenship in an Emigration Context', New York University Law Review 81 (2006): pp. 11–59.

Bauböck, Rainer, Transnational Citizenship: Membership and Rights in International Migration (Aldershot: Edward Elgar, 1994).

Bauböck, Rainer, 'Stakeholder Citizenship and Transnational Political Participation: A Normative Evaluation of External Voting', Fordham Law Review 75, no. 5 (2007): pp. 2393–2447.

Bederman, David, International Law in Antiquity (Cambridge: Cambridge University Press, 2007).

Boccagni, Paolo, 'Making the "Fifth Region" a Real Place? Emigrant Policies and the Emigration-Nation Nexus in Ecuador', National Identities 16, no. 2 (2014): pp. 117–137.

Bosniak, Linda, The Citizen and the Alien: Dilemmas of Contemporary Membership (Princeton: Princeton University Press, 2006).

Bourdieu, Pierre, Raisons pratiques. Sur la théorie de l'action (Paris: Seuil, 1994).

Brubaker, Rogers, 'The "Diaspora" Diaspora', Ethnic and Racial Studies 28, no. 1 (2005): pp. 1–19.

Clifford, James, 'Diasporas', Cultural Anthropology 9, no. 3 (1994): pp. 302–338.

Cohen, Robin, Global Diasporas: An Introduction (London: Routledge, 1997).

Collyer, Michael, 'Transnational Political Participation of Algerians in France: Extra-Territorial Civil Society versus Transnational Governmentality', Political Geography 25, no. 7 (2006): pp. 836–849.

Collyer, Michael and Zana Vathi, 'Patterns of Extra-Territorial Voting', Migration DRC Working Paper T22 (2007), online http://www.migrationdrc.org/publications/working_papers/WP-T22.pdf.

Collyer, Michael, 'Introduction: Locating and Narrating Emigration Nations', in Michael Collyer, ed., Emigration Nations: Policies and Ideologies of Emigrant Engagement (London: Palgrave, 2013), pp. 1–24.

Collyer, Michael, ed., Emigration Nations: Policies and Ideologies of Emigrant Engagement (London: Palgrave, 2013).

Collyer, Michael, 'Inside Out? Directly Elected "Special Representation" of Emigrants in National Legislatures and the Role of Popular Sovereignty', Political Geography 41 (2014): pp. 64–73.

Dobson, Andrew, 'Ecological Citizenship: A Defence', Environmental Politics 15, no. 3 (2006): pp. 447–451.

Fortier, Anne-Marie, 'Queer Diaspora', in Diane Richardson and Steven Seidman, eds., *Handbook of Lesbian and Gay Studies* (London: Sage, 2002), pp. 183–198.

Fox, Jonathan, 'Unpacking "Transnational Citizenship"', *Annual Review of Political Science* 8 (2005): pp. 171–201.

Gamlen, Alan, 'The Emigration State and the Modern Geopolitical Imagination', *Political Geography 27* (2008): pp. 840–856.

Green, Nancy L., 'The Politics of Exit: Reversing the Immigration Paradigm', *The Journal of Modern History 77*, no. 2 (2005): pp. 263–289.

Hall, Stuart, 'Cultural Identity and Diaspora', in Jonathan Rutherford, ed., *Identity: Community, Culture, Difference* (London: Lawrence & Wishart, 1990).

Hall, Stuart, 'Avtar Brah's Cartographies: Moment, Method, Meaning', *Feminist Review 100* (2012): pp. 27–38.

International Institute of Democracy and Electoral Assistance (IDEA), *Voting from Abroad* (Stockholm: IDEA, 2007).

International Organization for Migration (IOM) and Migration Policy Institute (MPI), *Developing a Roadmap for Engaging Diasporas in Development: A Handbook for Policymakers and Practitioners in Home and Host Countries* (Geneva: IOM, 2012), online https://publications.iom.int/books/developing-road-map-engaging-diasporas-development-handbook-policymakers-and-practitioners.

Engin F. Isin and Greg M. Nielsen, eds., *Acts of Citizenship* (Chicago: University of Chicago Press, 2008).

Itzigsohn, Jose, 'Immigration and the Boundaries of Citizenship', *International Migration Review 34*, no. 4 (2000): pp. 1126–1154.

Kallio, Kirsi Paulina and Katharyne Mitchell, eds., 'Transnational Lived Citizenship', *Global Networks 16*, no. 3 (2016).

Lafleur, Jean-Michel, *Transnational Politics and the State: The External Voting Rights of Diaspora* (London: Routledge, 2011).

López-Guerra, Claudio, 'Should Expatriates Vote?', *The Journal of Political Philosophy 13*, no. 2 (2005): pp. 216–234.

Mason, Andrew, 'Environmental Obligations and the Limits of Transnational Citizenship', *Political Studies 57* (2009): pp. 280–297.

McConnell, Fiona, *Rehearsing the State: The Political Practices of the Tibetan Government in Exile* (London: Wiley, 2016).

Oishi, Nana, *Women in Motion: Globalization, State Policies and Labor Migration in Asia* (Stanford: University of Stanford Press, 2005).

Østergaard-Nielsen, Eva, 'The Politics of Migrants Transnational Political Practices', *International Migration Review 37*, no. 3 (2003): pp. 760–786.

Owen, David, 'Transnational Citizenship and the Democratic State', *Critical Review of International Social and Political Philosophy 14*, no. 5 (2011): pp. 641–663.

Rubio-Martin, Ruth, 'Transnational Politics and the Normative Challenges of Expatriate Voting and Nationality Retention of Emigrants', *New York University Law Review 81* (2006): pp. 117–137.

Safran, William, 'Diasporas in Modern Societies: Myths of Homeland and Return', *Diaspora 1* (1991): pp. 83–99.

Sayad, Abdelmalek, 'El Ghorba: le mécanisme de reproduction de l'émigration', *Actes de la recherche en sciences sociales 1*, no. 2 (1975): pp. 50–66.

Sutherland, Claire, 'Vietnamese Diasporic Citizenship', in Engin F. Isin and Peter Nyers, eds., *Routledge Handbook of Global Citizenship Studies* (London: Routledge, 2014), pp. 522–531.

Swyngedouw, Eva and Erik Swyngedouw, 'The Congolese Diaspora in Brussels and Hybrid Identity Formation: Multi-Scalarity and Diasporic Citizenship', *Urban Research and Practice 2*, no. 1 (2009): pp. 68–90.

Tintori, G., 'The Transnational Political Practices of "Latin American Italians"', *International Migration 49*, no. 3 (2011): pp. 168–188.

Turcu, Anca and Robert Urbatsch, 'Diffusion of Diaspora Enfranchisement Norms: A Multinational Study', *Comparative Political Studies 48* (2015): pp. 407–437.

Vertovec, Steven, 'Super-Diversity and its Implications', *Ethnic and Racial Studies 30*, no. 6 (2007): pp. 1024–1054.

Westbrook, Raymond, 'Personal Exile in the Ancient Near East', *Journal of the American Oriental Society 128*, no. 2 (2008): pp. 317–323.

Zolberg, Aristide, 'The Exit Revolution: Citizenship and Those Who Leave', in Nancy L. Green and François Weil, eds., *Citizenship and Those Who Leave: The Politics of Emigration and Expatriation* (Urbana and Chicago: University of Illinois Press, 2007), pp. 33–60.

......

CHAPTER 27

FRAGMENTATION OF CITIZENSHIP GOVERNANCE

......

JOEL P. TRACHTMAN

INTRODUCTION

......

IN the absence of migration, the bundled conventional conception of citizenship serves reasonably well for structuring the relation between states and individuals. Under this conception, citizenship rights and duties are bundled, and available as a bundle to citizens, while only available selectively to immigrants. This chapter is concerned with how the international governance of migration affects this bundle of rights, duties, and state responsibilities, rather than with the formal legal status of citizenship or nationality. While dual citizenship is increasingly possible, migrants do not necessarily, or automatically, become citizens.

Increasing flows of people across borders for more than brief sojourns raise a challenge to this conventional concept of citizenship,[1] because they undermine the exclusive relationship between territorial states and their citizens. Migration, unless the migrant becomes a citizen and gives up her home country citizenship, necessarily destroys the integrity of this binary exclusive citizen-state relationship. As an ideal of a singular identity relation of individuals to states, 'citizenship represents cohesion in a world increasingly characterized by fragmentation.'[2] Indeed, it is not just migration that causes fragmentation. Increasingly, individuals look to multiple countries, and to subnational and supra-national governments, for the rights traditionally associated with citizenship. And international law is increasingly the mechanism for allocating these rights and responsibilities. [3] Thus, if citizenship relates to government, and government is increasingly fragmented, then citizenship must increasingly be fragmented too.

The act of migration may effectively obviate some of the rights of citizenship, for example, where the citizen effectively loses the right to vote in country H (home), and is not accorded the right to vote in country D (destination). Other examples could include negative rights like rights to a fair trial, or positive rights like social security, health care, or education.[4] To the extent that we see as inalienable some set of citizenship rights, migration may be understood as a back door means of alienation. And to the extent that H does not seek arrangements with D to reassemble a blended, yet full, set of rights, H may be understood to deny its citizens these rights.

Conversely, in a liberal society, the rights that citizenship entails are often understood as the social contractual predicate for the exercise by the state of jurisdiction over the citizen. Yet, when a citizen of H travels to D, assuming he does not become a citizen of D, D will find it appropriate to exercise jurisdiction over that person. So, while jurisdiction is readily divisible, citizenship conventionally is not.[5] While many

---

[1] See T. Alexander Aleinikoff and Douglas Klusmeyer, 'Plural Nationality: Facing the Future in a Migratory World,' in T. Alexander Aleinikoff and Douglas Klusmeyer, eds., *Citizenship Today: Global Perspectives and Practices* (Washington: Carnegie Endowment for International Peace, 2001); Yasemin Nuhoğlu Soysal, *Limits of Citizenship: Migrants and Postnational Membership in Europe* (Chicago: The University of Chicago Press, 1994).

[2] Kim Rubenstein and Daniel Adler, 'International Citizenship: The Future of Nationality in a Globalized World,' *Indiana Journal of Global Legal Studies* 7, no. 2 (Spring 2000): pp. 519–548.

[3] See Joel P. Trachtman, *The Future of International Law: Global Government* (New York: Cambridge University Press, 2013).

[4] But note that in many Western democracies, most of these negative and positive rights are not dependent upon citizenship status. See Peter J. Spiro, *Beyond Citizenship: American Identity after Globalization* (New York: Oxford University Press, 2008); Linda Bosniak, *The Citizen and the Alien: Dilemmas of Contemporary Membership* (Princeton: Princeton University Press, 2006).

[5] Multiple citizenship provides the possibility that citizenship can be congruent with jurisdiction. However, current state practice with regard to multiple citizenship accentuates this failure of divisibility insofar as states have done little to take account of citizenship rights and responsibilities their

countries now accept the possibility of dual citizenship,[6] citizenship is not routinely awarded to immigrants. Therefore, the predicate for the exercise of power may not be satisfied.

If citizenship can only be understood as an indivisible bundle of rights and obligations exclusively owed by and to the state with respect to a specified group of closely connected individuals (those considered citizens), then, unless migration immediately results in citizenship in D and loss of citizenship in H, the challenges become apparent. First, is unbundling necessary or appropriate, or should individuals maintain an exclusive bundled relationship with either H or D? Second, does unbundling destroy something essential: is the whole greater than the sum of its parts? Third, if citizenship is to be unbundled, what should be the method of dividing rights and obligations between H and D? These challenges remain even if the relevant individual is a dual citizen of H and D.

We will see that long-term migration necessitates that H and D divide up or share some of the rights owed to, and responsibilities owed by, migrants. These rights and responsibilities include those traditionally appertaining to citizenship. Political accountability, social services, social safety nets, and taxation are just some of these rights and responsibilities.

Once we accept unbundling, the question of this chapter becomes not 'who will govern citizenship?' but 'who will govern which components of the citizenship bundle?' The question of who governs migration is, in the first instance, equivalent to the question of control over inbound migration of non-citizens. So, in this sense, it is a separate question from that of who governs citizenship (although it is important to add that citizenship itself ordinarily includes the right of entry). But from a normative standpoint, immigration without some bundle of rights is unattractive both to immigrants and to others in society, and, conversely, permission to immigrate may, for political or economic reasons, be conditioned upon a reduced bundle of rights for immigrants. Therefore, governance of migration and of citizenship are linked.

When we ask the question 'who will govern migration and citizenship in the future,' we are asking about the future relationships between individuals and states. The governance of migration determines part of this relationship—entry and residence rights. But it is migration itself that challenges our understanding of citizenship, and raises the question of the allocation of the other rights and duties. Thus, while for analytical purposes it is useful initially to disaggregate the relationships between the individual and the state, these relationships are interdependent. So,

---

multiple citizens hold vis-à-vis other states. (Bilateral treaties on dual citizenship between Spain and Latin American states are an exception to this rule.)

  [6] See Peter J. Spiro, *At Home in Two Countries: The Past and Future of Dual Citizenship* (New York: NYU Press, 2016). See also the Global Dual Citizenship Database, https://macimide.maas-trichtuniversity.nl/dual-cit-database/.

the governance of citizenship will determine the governance of migration, and the desirability of migration. But, as we will see below, it is not a simple tradeoff of numbers and rights.[7]

In addition, some of the rights and duties included in citizenship are connected with one another, such that unbundling them may create distortions. For example, Ruth Mason has argued that the right to vote and the duty to pay taxes are connected insofar as individuals should experience the taxation consequences of their votes.[8] Generalizing this perspective, we may observe that the right to vote is linked to all of the rights and duties determined by a particular political community: voting influences much of the content of this bundle. Going a step further, if the bundle of rights and duties associated with citizenship is divided, then a desire for congruence between political accountability and the exercise of political power may suggest some division of the right to vote into subject matter components.

Furthermore, if dividing the components of citizenship between home and destination states destroys something essential about the relationship of citizenship—if the whole is greater than the sum of the parts—then migration will inevitably result in a reduced form of citizenship. This may be a reason to move toward a centralized form of citizenship, as the US did when forming a central federal citizenship to supervene state citizenship.[9] On the other hand, multiple citizenship may provide more than a 'full' set of citizenship rights to beneficiaries, creating inequalities between singular and multiple citizens with regard to their rights and duties.[10]

Once we can understand the dynamics of the allocation of these rights and duties, we can address which state will govern migration and citizenship and the extent to which state action will be governed by international law or organization.

In this chapter, I respond initially to the question 'who will govern migration,' without concern for the specific rights and obligations that citizens will have in their home and destination states. I first focus on entry. Next, I examine how migration affects who will govern citizenship, adding a layer of complexity, and an additional set of concerns about allocation of governing authority. In order to address who will govern citizenship, I examine the following issues:

i.   Rights to enter and remain.

---

[7] See Martin Ruhs, *The Price of Rights: Regulating International Labor Migration* (Princeton: Princeton University Press, 2013).

[8] Ruth Mason, 'Citizenship Taxation,' *Southern California Law Review 89* (January 2016): pp. 169–240.

[9] The European Court of Justice (ECJ) has made the following observation: 'Union citizenship is destined to be the fundamental status of nationals of the member states, enabling those who find themselves in the same situation to enjoy the same treatment in law irrespective of their nationality, subject to such exceptions as are expressly provided for.' (Judgment of 20 September 2001, *Grzelczyk v. Centre public d'aide sociale d'Ottignies-Louvain-La-Neuve* C-184/99, ECR II-6193, EU:C:2001:458, paragraph 31.

[10] See Spiro in this volume.

ii.   Negative rights. Many but not all negative rights granted by national constitutions are also supported by international law, and so the allocation of negative rights is not as interesting as the allocation of positive rights and duties.

iii. Positive rights, including voting, social safety nets, pensions, health, and education.

iv.   Duties, including taxes and military service.

As will be apparent, this chapter addresses only voluntary migration. Forced migration and refugee policy, although sometimes difficult to separate from voluntary migration, involve a different set of legal rules, motivations, and responses.[11]

At present, other than within the European Union and other special regional regimes, there is little restriction on states' autonomy to govern access, positive rights, and duties of non-citizens as they wish. Furthermore, there is a connection between mobility and rights, and also a relationship between mobility and duties. In the remainder of this chapter, I will review the possible reasons why and mechanisms by which states might constrain their autonomy in these areas.

Finally, it is also important to highlight the fact that one core component of citizenship, including multiple citizenship, is the right to enter and to remain in the country of citizenship. This right is sometimes denied, as Noora Lori discusses in her chapter in this volume, but it is generally granted. While I discuss below the possible tradeoff between unbundled citizenship rights and mobility, citizenship status entails at its core a right of entry and residence.

RIGHTS TO ENTER AND REMAIN: WHO WILL GOVERN MIGRATION?

Most states permit emigration, and may be required by international human rights law to do so.[12] Therefore, the main existing governmental control over migration is exercised by destination states. Controls on immigration began to be imposed in the late nineteenth century and are common today. Therefore, when we ask 'who will govern migration' in the future, we are asking how this exclusive national control over immigration may change.

---

[11] See Costello in this volume.

[12] See Article 12(2) of the International Covenant on Civil and Political Rights. See also Hurst Hannum, *The Right to Leave and to Return in International Law* (Dordrecht: Martinus Nijhoff Publishers, 1987).

There are compelling reasons to believe that the demand for migrants, and the supply of migrants, will grow to a new higher equilibrium, and that, in addition, national governments will be interested in new international legal structures to govern migration.[13] What are the changing social elements that may lead states to agree to reduce their authority in the field of immigration? First, demographic change will result in increasing demand for certain types of labor in the developed world. Second, individuals in poor countries will continue to seek better standards of living in wealthier countries. Third, there are large economic surpluses to be captured from mobility.

Demand to migrate is not exclusively dependent on demography and economic circumstances. It is also affected by conditions in departure countries, compared to conditions in destination countries. So, in addition to the critical factors of wages and productivity, war, poverty, human rights abuses, insecurity, disease, and other negative factors in the departure countries, combined with their opposites in the destination countries, increase demand for migration.

As these demand and supply factors change, there is no particular reason for the relevant law and organizations to remain static. The role of international law is to provide mechanisms by which one state may reciprocally induce another to take its interests into account in decision-making. By making commitments to increase market access for immigrants, states will necessarily give up a portion of their autonomous governance of immigration. Some parts of the governance of migration may be addressed through international treaties, but some aspects may be best addressed through the functions of an international organization.

States will find it in their interest to expand both emigration and immigration, in order to produce the very substantial welfare increases that will result. While most of the welfare increases accrue to the immigrant, it is also true that businesses, consumers, and government in the destination state can share in these increases. Businesses will be interested in sources of both skilled and unskilled labor and consumers will be interested in cheaper goods and services produced locally. Workers whose skills are complementary to those of immigrant workers will also advocate immigration. Government can gain from the opportunity to tax immigrants where the immigrants are net contributors to the national treasury. From a welfare (as opposed to political) standpoint, generally speaking, only competing workers in the destination state should oppose immigration, and the evidentiary picture is still uncertain regarding the extent to which competing workers are hurt by immigration.[14]

Home states can be hurt by emigration, especially where the emigration involves 'brain drain' (i.e., loss of high-skilled workers). Some of those left behind will have

---

[13] See Joel P. Trachtman, *The International Law of Economic Migration: Toward the Fourth Freedom* (Kalamazoo: Upjohn Institute for Employment Research, 2009).

[14] For a review of the literature, see ibid., chapter 2.

fewer opportunities. So home states will not necessarily seek liberalization of immigration in destination states unless there is a mechanism by which they benefit, such as remittances or the ability to tax their emigrants (a 'Bhagwati Tax').[15] Indeed, a Bhagwati tax might best be understood as retention by the home state of partial power to tax on the basis of nationality, and also as reflecting the home state's contributions to productivity of the migrant.

Negotiations will involve complex exchanges between states, and long-term commitments. These exchanges and commitments can be articulated in different forms, including in bilateral or informal agreements. However, international legal rules, with institutional arrangements to provide a forum for dispute settlement, negotiation, and other support, as described below, may be attractive. Furthermore, while it is possible to make these rules and institutional arrangements on a bilateral or narrow basis, there will be sufficient concerns regarding equal opportunities, as well as economies of scale in legal and institutional arrangements, to make a multilateral agreement, including a most-favored nation non-discrimination principle, attractive.

It is likely that liberalization commitments will be made, if at all, in connection with negotiations in which states make reciprocally attractive commitments. The range of reciprocally attractive commitments may be small if commitments are limited to the migration field, but there is little reason for such a limitation. As I suggested in the past, immigration liberalization commitments may be negotiated in exchange for diverse kinds of commitments, including trade or investment liberalization, or intellectual property protection.[16] Liberalization of migration has indeed been included (to different degrees) in several regional free trade agreements, including the EU, the North American Free Trade Agreement (NAFTA)[17] and a number of others. Importantly, citizenship in a member state is a predicate for free movement in these regional arrangements.

In addition, it may be appropriate for popular destination states to impose an entry fee, or a requirement for social insurance premiums,[18] in order to reduce concerns regarding social welfare program-driven movement.

When we say that international legal commitments regarding immigration, and perhaps an organization to support those commitments, may be desirable, we are suggesting that states themselves will, to some extent, give up their exclusive right to govern immigration. They will only do so pursuant to negotiations, by degrees, and with conditions and limitations, and so we can expect that the answer to 'who will govern migration in the future?' will be nuanced, with horizontally and vertically

---

[15] See, e.g., Jagdish N. Bhagwati, 'International Migration of the Highly Skilled: Economics, Ethics and Taxes,' *Third World Quarterly* 1 (1979): pp. 17–30.

[16] Trachtman (n 13).   [17] See DeVoretz and Irastorza in this volume.

[18] See Michael J. Trebilcock, 'The Law and Economics of Immigration Policy,' *American Law and Economics Review* 5 (2003): pp. 271–313.

shared control over migration. Because the utility of those commitments will depend on the rights and duties assigned to immigrants, negotiations will increasingly include issues concerning the rights and obligations of migrants.

Who Will Govern Negative Rights, Positive Rights, Duties, and Citizenship Horizontally?

Choice of law analysis—of the type applied by courts, regulators, and legislators to determine how best to allocate authority and responsibility among states in private or public law fields—will be required in order to determine how citizenship rights and obligations should be allocated horizontally between H and D[19] to decide who will govern citizenship. This choice of law analysis could be carried out unilaterally by both H and D, with possible gaps and overlaps that would come from unilateralism. This is the way dual citizenship is presently handled, and it is the way that many choice of law questions are addressed.

Alternatively, this choice of law analysis could inform the negotiation of an international agreement. In negotiating such an international agreement, negotiators would in effect be determining how to reassemble the bundle of citizenship rights in the way that satisfies their policy goals the most. An international agreement allocating rights and responsibilities would operate horizontally among states, but would share some characteristics with a constitutional arrangement for nested citizenship, such as those within the US or the EU.[20]

The concept of *jus nexi* explored in Ayelet Shachar's *The Birthright Lottery*[21] is best understood as a functionalist choice of law rule focused on the specific connections between an individual and a state. But as Shachar recognizes, citizenship, like property, can be unbundled into components.

Rainer Bauböck's concept of 'stakeholder citizenship' can also be understood as a choice of law rule that would accord citizenship to individuals 'whose circumstances

---

[19] Vicki Jackson explains that in federal systems, multiple citizenships may coexist, but require a 'conflicts' rule to determine which aspect of citizenship is applicable in a particular context (Vicki Jackson, 'Citizenship and Federalism,' in T. Alexander Aleinikoff and Douglas Klusmeyer, eds., *Citizenship Today: Global Perspectives and Practices* (Washington: Carnegie Endowment for International Peace, 2001)).

[20] Ibid.

[21] Ayelet Shachar, *The Birthright Lottery: Citizenship and Global Inequality* (Cambridge: Harvard University Press, 2009).

of life link their individual autonomy or well-being to the common good of the political community,' using two 'indicators:' (i) dependency on that community for protection of basic rights, or (ii) subjection to that community's political authorities for a significant period.[22] These indicators seem to align with positive rights and negative rights, and seem to assume a set of fundamental rights that depend on membership in the community that has the ability to withhold or grant those rights.

A disaggregated choice of law analysis would focus on the components, recognizing that the most satisfying distribution of rights and duties may involve fractured citizenship. This is true of all sorts of choice of law contexts. States have devised complex rules of contingent and shared jurisdiction, allowing them to regulate the same persons, the same assets, or the same transactions, in different ways and for different reasons. Similarly, individual property rights are often divided despite the myth of exclusive private property ownership: our use and disposition of these assets may be controlled through regulation, through the law of nuisance, or through other law of tort, in ways that fracture the property rights.

Of course, it is also true that there are economies of scale and scope in connection with the components of citizenship, and the very concept of citizenship may require some centralization of the relationship between individuals and a particular state. This can only be determined after analyzing the components, and through a process of negotiation and adaptation: synthesis following analysis.

Choice of law analysis would ordinarily focus on internalizing externalities—on ensuring that citizen rights and obligations are assigned to the state most likely to act accountably—most likely to experience the adverse or beneficial effects—in relation to those rights and obligations.[23] As Rainer Bauböck argues, 'everyone who is affected by a decision has a claim that her interests should be taken into account but not everyone has a claim to be a member of the political community on whose behalf the decision is taken.'[24] The underlying assumption, of course, is that there is something more to citizenship than a set of legally recognized claims and duties. For analytical purposes, I will reverse this assumption.

Some claims will be claims of citizens, while others are claims of non-citizens that often must be exerted through international legal processes. Indeed, international law is increasingly understood as the mechanism by which individuals from one political community may have their interests represented in the decisions of a different political community. Furthermore, if we concede that citizenship is a bundle of rights and obligations that can be unbundled, where the claim is about one of these rights or obligations, is it distinct from a claim about citizenship? And if it is

---

[22] Rainer Bauböck, 'The Rights and Duties of External Citizenship,' *Citizenship Studies* 13, no. 5 (2009): pp. 475–499.

[23] While Coase showed that internalizing externalities is not necessarily the role of law, the important question for efficiency is whether the actor incurs the consequences of her or his actions.

[24] Rainer Bauböck, 'Global Justice, Freedom of Movement, and Democratic Citizenship,' *European Journal of Sociology* 50, no. 1 (2009): pp. 1–31.

a claim about a different right or obligation than those ordinarily included in the bundle of citizenship, do we have a plausible basis by which to distinguish citizenship rights and obligations from others?

a.   Negative Rights Most liberal and democratic states accord national treatment in connection with negative rights to non-citizens under their authority, and most negative rights already bind host states in substantial ways under international human rights law. Furthermore, the central role of these rights is to protect the individual from the improper force of the state, and the force of most states is largely, although not exclusively, territorial. Thus, it would make little sense to assign negative rights obligations exclusively to H, when the migrant is resident in D. Under globalization, a kind of supplementary constitutionalization[25] would hold, as a choice of law matter, that the obligations that correlate to negative rights are owed by any state with power over any individual. Of course, this becomes more complicated where different states provide different negative rights.It is probably useful, in connection with commitments to liberalize migration, to confirm national treatment in negative rights, and to provide for better-than-national treatment where the overall level of negative rights protection would nullify or impair the liberalization commitments. For example, better-than-national treatment may be necessary to induce migration where the level of privacy or personal liberty rights is so low as to make immigration unattractive.

b.   Positive Rights and Duties With respect to positive rights, such as social welfare payments, and with respect to duties, a more complex analysis, focusing on each type of positive right, is required. In many respects, at least within major liberal democracies, positive rights are not denied to non-citizens, provided that those non-citizens have regular or long-term status. On the other hand, in less liberal states, and with respect to irregular immigrants, positive rights may be formally or functionally denied. Positive rights, in the aggregate and when combined with duties, comprise important parts of citizenship. But, rather than allocating them as an unfragmented unit, it may be useful to consider fragmenting them, much as has been done within the EU. The guiding principle here would be to ensure that individuals who contribute, or who otherwise have established relevant linkages, to a destination state, are accorded pension, health, safety net, education, and other relevant positive rights by the destination state. For example, if an individual has all her life been a permanent resident in D, with no continuing ties to H, under a *jus nexi* approach her voting, pension, civil rights, taxation, and military service should relate to D. On

²⁵ Jeffrey L. Dunoff and Joel P. Trachtman, *A Functional Approach to Global Constitutionalism, in Ruling the World: Constitutionalism, International Law, and Global Governance* (New York: Cambridge University Press, 2009).

the other hand, if an individual is a temporary resident of D, having lived all his life and expecting to return after a six-month sojourn to H, most of these relationships should be assigned to H. The tougher questions arise with respect to certain relationships that are central to a political community, such as political rights, and with respect to longer-term migration. The grant of these types of political rights to foreign persons may undermine the consensus in favor of a certain social structure. In addition, there may be circumstances in which these relationships are divided. For example, there may be good reasons to divide taxing authority between H and D.

H and D may find it useful, in order to internalize externalities and to provide appropriate incentives to migrants, to split responsibility for some positive rights. One example would be to share pension obligations pro rata in proportion to some measure of earnings in each country. Similarly, duties such as the duty to pay taxes may be shared in order to ensure appropriate incentives for the home state to provide education to potential emigrants. All of these arrangements would best be reflected in international legal commitments, largely to motivate states to take costly action where they otherwise might seek to renege. Thus, the horizontal allocation of authority over migration and citizenship should in the future be negotiated in international legal commitments addressing the issues described above.

c. Citizenship There are several ways in which formal citizenship may be addressed. First, individuals may be accorded unique bundled citizenship by H. Under this type of regime, migration will not affect citizenship, and citizenship will continue to be governed by the rules of H. Second, individuals may gain unique bundled citizenship in D. Under this regime, rules will be required to determine the transition from H to D citizenship. A third alternative would allow dual or other multiple citizenship, but dual citizenship will in any case require some unbundling: it is impractical to have dual responsibilities for military service, double taxation, dual rights to health care or pensions, etc.[26] As a practical matter, these components of citizenship would have to be divided. Fourth, H and D may by unilateral action, or by agreement, divide up the rights and responsibilities owed to and by the migrant. However, this approach of unilateralism or informal deference has important limitations. First, if migration is to be liberalized through commitments for liberalization, then it is important that destination states do not implicitly renege on or undermine the value of their commitments by burdening migrants or denying them expected rights. Second, unilateralism may result in some individuals being denied the full corpus

---

[26] See Rainer Bauböck, 'Studying Citizenship Constellations', *Journal of Ethnic and Migration Studies* 36, no. 5 (2010): pp. 847–859.

of rights and obligations of a citizen: if components deemed essential to a full citizenship status are lost through migration, then it is possible that a class of 'second-class citizens' will develop.[27] This class will grow as migration increases. Negotiations over migration may include negotiations over the full range of rights and duties otherwise included in the bundle comprising citizenship. Thus, the rise of migration, and of international law of migration, will demand a more nuanced view of citizenship. Individuals will need to be assigned rights and responsibilities in multiple states—not just the state of their initial citizenship or the state of their residency. Just as overlapping governmental problems require choices regarding applicable law in particular circumstances, overlapping and shifting relationships between individuals and states will require choices regarding applicable citizenship rights and duties. Under certain circumstances, horizontal allocation between states is not a satisfactory response to the question of allocation of authority. Rather, according to the principle of subsidiarity, under some circumstances, the desirable response will be to allocate authority to an international organization. The response to this horizontal and vertical choice of law exercise will determine who will govern citizenship and migration in the future. I address the question of vertical allocation of responsibility below.

Rights, Duties, and Numbers

One of the critical issues in connection with governing migration and citizenship is the question of whether there is a tradeoff between mobility and citizenship rights: whether mobility could be increased if migrants are willing to accept diminished citizenship rights. While this tradeoff is characterized as one between mobility and rights, another perspective would suggest that there are rights on both sides of the tradeoff: it is a tradeoff between the right to enter and other citizenship rights. I frame it this way in order to countenance the fact that individual migrants may value the liberty to sacrifice other citizenship rights for entry rights, while

---

[27] See Rainer Bauböck, *Transnational Citizenship* (Cheltenham: Edward Elgar, 1994); Michael Walzer, *Spheres of Justice: A Defense of Pluralism and Equality* (New York: Basic Books, 1983); Dora Kostakopoulou, 'Citizenship Goes Public: The Institutional Design of Anational Citizenship,' *Journal of Political Philosophy* 17, no. 3 (2009): pp. 275–306; Joseph Carens, 'Aliens and Citizens: The Case for Open Borders,' *The Review of Politics* 49, no. 2 (Spring 1987): pp. 251–273.

recognizing that an international system that induces this tradeoff may be ethically objectionable.

Indeed, as Martin Ruhs points out, the ability of states to make entry conditional on a reduced array of rights makes clear that at least some rights are divisible and alienable, and that migrants may make a voluntary decision to give up some rights for others, or even for simple market access. Ruhs raises the normative question which rights should be allowed to be alienable and which should not.[28] Most positive rights are not absolute in practice.

If we were to draw inferences from the distinction between, for example, the general international system and the EU internal system, or between the general international system and the US internal system of free movement, we would have to concede that there is no tradeoff: the EU and US internally generally provide both greater numbers of internal movers and greater rights. Furthermore, as Peter Spiro documents, for external immigrants to the US, for example, there is little tradeoff.[29] Yasemin Soysal also shows that for certain Northwest European states, 'the recent guestworker experience reflects a time when national citizenship is losing ground to a more universal model of membership anchored in deterritorialized notions of persons' rights.'[30] Perhaps in this sense we have seen anecdotally that in order to encourage people to migrate efficiently, while maintaining the kind of liberal community in which fundamental equality of individuals is respected, states have found it necessary to treat migrants either as full citizens already at the time of entry or as future citizens with immediate access to most citizenship rights.

Of course, we may contrast these examples with the seemingly contrary examples of states like Qatar or Saudi Arabia, which have increased their numbers of migrants at the same time that they have denied significant citizenship rights to migrants. Thus, in the general international system considered separately from the EU and US, there is some evidence of a tradeoff in connection with unilateral national decision-making. Work by Martin Ruhs, Daniel A. Bell, Phillip Martin, and Glen Weyl, among others, suggests that in the general international system, there may be a tradeoff between market access for migrants, on the one hand, and certain rights accorded migrants, on the other hand.

Glen Weyl points to the immigration policies of the Gulf Cooperation Council states, including Saudi Arabia, Qatar, Oman, Bahrain, the United Arab Emirates, and Kuwait.[31] While these states admit large numbers of immigrant workers, those workers are generally not admitted to citizenship and are accorded a level of rights

---

[28] Ruhs (n 7).

[29] Peter Spiro, *Beyond Citizenship: American Identity after Globalization* (New York: Oxford University Press, 2008).

[30] Soysal (n 1).

[31] E. Glen Weyl, 'The Openness-Equality Trade-Off in Global Redistribution,' *The Economic Journal* (forthcoming), online http://papers.ssrn.com/sol3/papers.cfm?abstract_id=2509305.

significantly lower than that enjoyed by citizens. Weyl explains that the admittance of these workers to the Gulf Cooperation Council (GCC) states reduces international income inequality far more effectively than OECD state aid programs. This raises two important questions: (i) is such inequality of rights politically or economically necessary to achieve this reduction of international income inequality, and (ii) is it ethically acceptable?

Martin Ruhs observes more broadly that 'in most high-income countries, the majority of migrant workers are admitted and employed under [temporary migration programs] that in one way or another restrict migrants' rights.'[32] We may understand the 11 million unauthorized immigrants in the US in the same way. This is consistent with the idea that wealthy destination countries would exercise market power in order to extract a portion of the increased welfare that immigrants achieve upon immigration to those countries.[33] They have generally not done so by charging migration fees, but instead by reducing access to formal citizenship, transfer programs, and other beneficial programs. Ruhs finds that restrictions on immigrant rights are greater in the case of low-skilled workers than in the case of high-skilled workers. While there is a plausible political economy rationale for this relationship, and while there is some evidence of correlation between market access for migrants and denial of certain largely positive rights, the evidence for causation is not strong.

In a sense, these wealthy destination states are able to exercise market power, despite their need for workers, because of competition among the workers for greater incomes. This circumstance is similar to the circumstance of un-unionized workers in a domestic setting competing for work by accepting lower wages, and lower labor rights, than they could obtain by organizing. If the potential migrants, organized through their home countries in blocs of labor exporting states, exercised countervailing bargaining power, it might be possible for them to achieve a superior blend of rights and numbers.

To the extent that the host state fears positive rights-driven migration, or to the extent that the host state simply wishes to extract from immigrants some of the welfare gains resulting from migration, consideration may be given to responding to these motivations through a more efficient, and less ethically troublesome, migration fee or special tax. This is because it may feel inhumane to provide lesser positive rights to a selected group of individuals working and living in close proximity, but also because the individual migrants may underestimate their need for these positive rights and thereby make the migration decision in a way that is harmful. For similar reasons, most societies do not allow their citizens to give up positive rights in exchange for monetary payments.

---

[32] Ruhs (n 7), p. 24.   [33] See Trachtman (n 13).

WHO SHOULD GOVERN MIGRATION
AND CITIZENSHIP VERTICALLY?

Above, I have described some of the reasons why, and the ways in which, migration and citizenship may increasingly be subjected to international law. In a sense, any international legal rule may be understood in terms of vertical integration, but we ordinarily think of an organization as the means for vertical integration. Once it is decided to regulate a subject matter under international law, an organization may be useful in order to serve as a secretariat for, to manage, to enforce, and to develop, a multilateral agreement on migration, or even a set of bilateral or regional agreements. The major roles include facilitation of negotiations, research, technical assistance, preparation of new treaty rules, preparation of new rules other than by treaty, surveillance, dispute settlement, and punishment. And of course, at least three important multilateral organizations already address migration, in at least some dimensions: the International Organization for Migration (IOM), the International Labour Organization (ILO), and the World Trade Organization (WTO).

There have been several proposals for the establishment of an international organization to address migration. One of the leading proponents has been Bimal Ghosh, who proposed a 'new international regime for the orderly movement of people' (NIROMP) in 1997.[34] This framework proposal was designed to reconcile the interests of sending and receiving states, and to develop a regime that would address all forms of migration. The 2005 report of the Global Commission on International Migration proposed the creation of a 'global migration facility' to respond to the challenges of international migration.[35] Jagdish Bhagwati proposed a 'world migration organization' in 2003.[36] None of these proposals specified the rationale, the functions, or the structure of an organization to address international migration.

Not all international law requires an organization. Much, if not most, international law lacks a secretariat, mandatory dispute settlement, and other organizational functions. While some additional international law appears useful in the field of economic migration and citizenship, it is not necessarily clear what, if any, organizational components are suitable. Nor is it clear what relationship international migration and citizenship law should have with other international law, or with existing international organizations.

---

[34] Bimal Ghosh, *Managing Migration: Time for a New International Regime?* (New York: Oxford University Press, 2000).

[35] Global Commission on International Migration, 'Migration in an Interconnected World: New Directions for Action' (2005), online http://www.queensu.ca/samp/migrationresources/reports/gcim-complete-report-2005.pdf.

[36] Jagdish N. Bhagwati, 'Borders Beyond Control,' *Foreign Affairs* 82, no. 1 (January/February 2003): pp. 98–104.

So the questions addressed in this section are, assuming that international law would be useful in the field of international economic migration and citizenship: Would an international organization be useful, compared to the alternatives? And if so, what organizational features and governance arrangements would be appropriate for an organization dealing with international economic migration?

In the Coasean theory of the firm, the reason for firms (in our case, organizations) depends on transaction cost reduction. The best way to think about this perspective is in terms of cost-benefit analysis. There are gains to be achieved from cooperation. Where the net gains from cooperation exceed the transaction costs of cooperation, we would expect to observe cooperation, although strategic barriers can impede cooperation. States would be expected to seek to maximize their net benefits from cooperation by utilizing the institutional structure, from case-by-case informal cooperation to organizationally structured formal cooperation (analogous to the continuum between the market and the firm), that maximizes the transaction benefits, net of transaction costs.

In connection with international cooperation in the context of migration and citizenship, the most important transaction costs are expended to establish mechanisms to complete incomplete contracts and to avoid strategic behavior. If an organization can reduce these costs, by, for example, supplying information, certifying information, or changing the structure of retaliation and the payoff from defection, then the organization may be justified. It is not possible to determine with any certainty whether an international organization would have greater net transaction benefits, compared to those resulting from a simple treaty. In important dimensions, the question of which would have greater net benefits depends on the structure of the cooperation problem and the structure of the proposed international organization. However, given the complexity of a likely migration and citizenship treaty, with many opportunities for uncertainty and defection, it is possible that an organization may provide certain useful services.

There are many parameters of any international agreement regarding migration and citizenship. These include, among others, certain commitments, exceptions and safeguards, calculation of sharing of migration fees (if imposed) between home and host states, coordination of health insurance, social security, and other positive rights. However, it is impossible to anticipate or address every contingency.

Complete contracts in international law, as elsewhere, are impossible. Rather, states must accept a degree of incompleteness *ex ante*. They may use a variety of methods to *ex post* complete their contracts. One method is simply to negotiate regarding new circumstances as they come up. This method may give rise to stalemates or strategic behavior. A second method is to provide for a legislative system that involves less than full unanimity, or that has other expediting characteristics. A third method is to provide for dispute settlement, with all of the varieties of dispute settlement structure that may be available. In particular, it is possible to delegate greater or lesser discretion to dispute settlement, through lesser or greater specificity of treaty text.

Thus, dispute settlement is not just a method of enforcing rules, but is also a method of completing an international contract. These are separate functions, and should be evaluated and structured separately. In the enforcement role, dispute settlement declares who is right and who is wrong, removing the subject treaty from the default international legal mechanism of auto-interpretation. This declarative role can have important informal effects, and may be sufficient to induce the desired level of compliance.

To the extent that the strategic context in which states find themselves maps into a prisoner's dilemma, or another strategic model that could be resolved efficiently by a change in the payoffs, an international organization might be useful. It would allow states to cooperate where cooperation is beneficial, and where it otherwise would not be possible. Commitments to liberalize might present a prisoner's dilemma in which the dominant strategy for any state is defection. An international legal rule that entails some kind of informal or formal punishment, or other negative consequences of defection, can change the payoffs so as to transform the game from a prisoner's dilemma to a coordination game, with a greater likelihood of compliance. Organizations can serve to engage in surveillance, communication, and adjudication, in order to implement rules that change payoffs.

Furthermore, if, as suggested above, exchanges of diverse commitments for liberalization or other consideration may be necessary in order to induce attractive destination states to liberalize, an international legal regime or organization that addresses the full range of areas of commitment may make enforcement of specific commitments more effective.

So, in determining whether an international organization would be useful, it would be important to evaluate the strategic setting, the magnitude of the payoffs, the capacity for informal enforcement, and other aspects of the migration and citizenship agreement circumstances. It is a complex determination, as the types of commitments that would be appropriate are interdependent with the types of institutional structures that would be appropriate to enforce them, including the design of the international organization.

Responsibility for international economic migration and citizenship could be assigned to an existing organization or to a new organization. I describe below the possible features of a new international organization addressing migration and citizenship. For purposes of discussion, let us call it the 'World Migration Organization' ('WMO'). By describing a WMO, I do not mean to prejudge the determination of whether the relevant responsibilities could be assigned to an existing international organization, such as the IOM, the ILO, or the WTO. I simply wish to describe what functions may be appropriate. A WMO could have a variety of features beyond substantive obligations, including perhaps the following:

- Purposes: Purposes would include the facilitation of international migration in order to better the welfare of individuals. A focus on the welfare of poor individuals might be appropriate. The purposes may be expressed in broad enough terms to include collateral matters such as social security, health care, and other matters to the extent that they would bear on economic migration.
- Membership Arrangements and Termination: Membership could be open to states willing to accept the obligations of the WMO Treaty, including obligations to liberalize immigration.
- Secretariat
  - Facilitating Negotiations: The WMO secretariat could be accorded responsibility to manage negotiations regarding liberalization commitments and other matters. Whether these negotiations would be continuous or focused in particular periods, like GATT/WTO rounds, would be determined by the member states.
  - Surveillance: The secretariat could be tasked with periodic review of member states' systems to evaluate the degree to which they could be improved in order to facilitate migration. This function could be modeled on the WTO's Trade Policy Review Mechanism.
  - Technical Assistance: Some member states will require technical assistance in support of their negotiation, as well as in support of their implementation, compliance, and dispute settlement activities. The secretariat, or an independent entity, could provide these services.
  - Research: Member states will require research to be performed about many aspects of migration, including especially the economic effects of different types of migration in different contexts. The secretariat could perform this service. One type of assistance that may be extremely useful is assistance in providing sophisticated, independent, and reliable economic analysis of the likely effects of liberalization of immigration.
  - Public Relations and Transparency: Immigrants can often be scapegoats for economic problems. If the anti-globalization backlash has been significant with respect to goods, it may become more active, and more dangerous, with respect to immigration. Therefore, it may be appropriate to develop an effective public relations function for the secretariat.
- Substantive Expertise and Experience: A WMO might contain experience in economic negotiations, including (i) analytical capabilities that could support negotiations and dispute settlement, (ii) expertise in the human side of migration, including the capacity of societies to absorb migrants, (iii) expertise in labor market conditions and dynamics, (iv) expertise in tax policy, (v) expertise in human rights, and (vi) experience in multilateral negotiations.

- Treaty-Making and Secondary Law-Making: It is possible for an organization to be mandated to promote future treaty-making in the field of liberalization of migration, and related matters. While the original GATT in 1947 did not contain a specific mandate along these lines, the GATT, and now the WTO, proceeded by 'rounds' of treaty-making. This treaty-making was able to operate in the same way that all international law treaty-making proceeds: by a rule of unanimity in which only signatories are bound. It is important to note that even under a rule of unanimity, there can be great pressure on states to join where the cost of exclusion is great. It would be highly unlikely that states would agree in the near term to allow significant migration liberalization, public policy or citizenship decisions to be made against their individual will, by majority voting. On the other hand, many related issues have been addressed through majority voting within the EU (although majority voting is rarely used for migration issues, and is not available for national citizenship issues), so we know that majority voting is not categorically impossible. After more experience of increased liberalization, and increased commitments for liberalization, states may determine that some matters could be addressed through majority voting.

- Dispute Settlement: As discussed above, dispute settlement is an alternative method of completing incomplete contracts, as new issues or new facts arise. Dispute settlement mechanisms may be understood as a type of agent of a collective principal, for purposes of completing the contract along the lines desired by the collective principal. Dispute settlement can be more or less limited, with more or less 'legislative' discretion. Dispute settlement should be evaluated in relation to legislative capacity. Under relatively strong and expeditious legislative capacity, dispute settlement may not require great authority to complete contracts.

- Scope for Complex Barter: In connection both with negotiations and with dispute settlement to implement negotiated concessions, greater breadth of coverage may ensure that the set of Pareto improving barter transactions among states will not be empty, and that states will have continuing incentives to comply with their obligations.

CONCLUSION: A FUTURE BETWEEN ATOMIZATION AND INTEGRATION

A future of greater migration will put pressure on the exclusive territorial model of citizenship. In the deepest analytical sense, bundled citizenship is incoherent, and made more so by extra-territorial effects of national decision-making—by the effects on persons in other territories—and, as salient for this chapter, by the mobility of persons that makes them experience effects of governmental decisions in other territories. For most historic periods since the emergence of the modern state system and in most regional contexts this mobility of persons was not significant enough, and the role of the state in providing positive rights was not great enough, to necessitate an international regime for assigning states responsibility for positive rights, and assigning individuals duties to states. However, with greater demand for mobility, greater cooperation to divide up the components of citizenship may be desirable.

Bibliography

Aleinikoff, T. Alexander and Douglas Klusmeyer, *From Migrants to Citizens: Membership in a Changing World* (Washington: Carnegie Endowment for International Peace, 2000).

Aleinikoff, T. Alexander and Douglas Klusmeyer, *Citizenship Policies for an Age of Migration* (Washington: Carnegie Endowment for International Peace, 2001).

Aleinikoff, T. Alexander and Douglas Klusmeyer, *Citizenship Today: Global Perspectives and Practices* (Washington: Carnegie Endowment for International Peace, 2001).

Barry, Kim, 'Home and Away: The Construction of Citizenship in an Emigration Context,' *New York University Law Review 81*, no. 1 (2006): pp. 11–59.

Bauböck Rainer, *Transnational Citizenship: Membership and Rights in International Migration* (Cheltenham: Edward Elgar, 1994).

Bauböck, Rainer, 'Global Justice, Freedom of Movement, and Democratic Citizenship,' *European Journal of Sociology 50*, no. 1 (2009): pp. 1–31.

Bauböck, Rainer, 'The Rights and Duties of External Citizenship,' *Citizenship Studies 13*, no. 5 (2009): pp. 475–499.

Bauböck, Rainer, 'Studying Citizenship Constellations,' *Journal of Ethnic and Migration Studies 36*, no. 5 (2010): pp. 847–859.

Bell, D. A., 'Justice for Migrant Workers? Foreign Domestic Workers in Hong Kong and Singapore,' in Sor-hoo Tan, ed., *Challenging Citizenship: Group Membership and Cultural Identity in a Global Age* (Aldershot, Burlington: Ashgate, 2005), pp. 41–62.

Bell, D. A. and N. Piper, 'National Citizenship and Migrant Workers in East Asia,' in Will Kymlicka and Baogang He, eds., *Multiculturalism in Asia* (Oxford: Oxford University Press, 2005).

Bhagwati, Jagdish N., 'International Migration of the Highly Skilled: Economics, Ethics and Taxes,' *Third World Quarterly 1* (1979): pp. 17–30.

Bhagwati, Jagdish, 'Borders Beyond Control,' *Foreign Affairs 82*, no. 1 (January/February 2003), pp. 98–104.

Bosniak, Linda, *The Citizen and the Alien: Dilemmas of Contemporary Membership* (Princeton: Princeton University Press, 2006).

Carens, Joseph, 'Aliens and Citizens: The Case for Open Borders,' *The Review of Politics 49*, no. 2 (Spring 1987): pp. 251–273.

Chang, Howard, 'The Immigration Paradox: Poverty, Distributive Justice, and Liberal Egalitarianism,' *DePaul Law Review* 52 (2003): pp. 759–776.

Dunoff, Jeffrey L. and Joel P. Trachtman, *A Functional Approach to Global Constitutionalism, in Ruling the World: Constitutionalism, International Law, and Global Governance* (New York: Cambridge University Press, 2009).

Ghosh, Bimal, *Managing Migration: Time for a New International Regime?* (New York: Oxford University Press, 2000).

Hammar, Tomas, *Democracy and the Nation State: Aliens, Denizens, and Citizens in a World of International Migration* (Brookfield: Gower, 1990).

Hannum, Hurst, *The Right to Leave and to Return in International Law* (Dordrecht: Martinus Nijhoff Publishers, 1987).

Jackson, Vicki, 'Citizenship and Federalism,' in T. Alexander Aleinikoff and Douglas Klusmeyer, eds., *Citizenship Today: Global Perspectives and Practices* (Washington: Carnegie Endowment for International Peace, 2001).

Jacobson, David, *Rights across Borders: Immigration and the Decline of Citizenship* (Baltimore: The Johns Hopkins University Press, 1996).

Joppke, Christian, *Citizenship and Immigration* (Cambridge: Polity Press, 2010).

Kostakopoulou, Dora, 'Citizenship Goes Public: The Institutional Design of Anational Citizenship,' *Journal of Political Philosophy* 17, no. 3 (2009): pp. 275–306.

Mason, Ruth, 'Citizenship Taxation,' *Southern California Law Review* 89 (January 2016): pp. 169–240.

Newland, Kathleen, 'The Governance of International Migration: Mechanisms, Processes and Institutions,' *Global Commission on International Migration* (September 2005), online http://iom.ch/jahia/webdav/site/myjahiasite/shared/shared/mainsite/policy_and_research/gcim/tp/TS8b.pdf.

Pécoud, Antoine and Paul de Guchteneire, 'International Migration, Border Controls and Human Rights: Assessing the Relevance of a Right to Mobility,' *Journal of Borderlands Studies* 21, no. 1 (2006): pp. 69–86.

Rubenstein, Kim, 'Globalization and Citizenship and Nationality,' in Catherine Dauvergne, ed., *Jurisprudence for an Interconnected Globe* (Farnham: Ashgate, 2003).

Rubenstein, Kim and Daniel Adler, 'International Citizenship: The Future of Nationality in a Globalized World,' *Indiana Journal of Global Legal Studies* 7, no. 2 (Spring 2000): pp. 519–548.

Ruhs, Martin, *The Price of Rights: Regulating International Labor Migration* (Princeton: Princeton University Press, 2013).

Shachar, Ayelet, *The Birthright Lottery: Citizenship and Global Inequality* (Cambridge: Harvard University Press, 2009).

Soysal, Yasemin Nuhoğlu, *Limits of Citizenship: Migrants and Postnational Membership in Europe* (Chicago: The University of Chicago Press, 1994).

Spiro, Peter J., *Beyond Citizenship: American Identity after Globalization* (New York: Oxford University Press, 2008).

Spiro, Peter J., *At Home in Two Countries: The Past and Future of Dual Citizenship* (New York: NYU Press, 2016).

Trachtman, Joel P., *The International Law of Economic Migration: Toward the Fourth Freedom* (Kalamazoo: Upjohn Institute for Employment Research, 2009).

Trachtman, Joel P., *The Future of International Law: Global Government* (New York: Cambridge University Press, 2013).

Trebilcock, Michael J., 'The Law and Economics of Immigration Policy,' *American Law and Economics Review* 5 (2003): pp. 271–313.

Walzer, Michael, *Spheres of Justice: A Defense of Pluralism and Equality* (New York: Basic Books, 1983).

Weyl, E. Glen, 'The Openness-Equality Trade-Off in Global Redistribution,' *The Economic Journal* (forthcoming), online http://papers.ssrn.com/sol3/papers.cfm?abstract_id=2509305.

CHAPTER 28

MULTIPLE CITIZENSHIP

PETER J. SPIRO

SHOULD the individual's relationship to the state be an exclusive one? As much as any other citizenship-related issues, the answer to this question has shifted dramatically in recent decades. Multiple citizenship was once considered an impossibility, an offense to nature, a moral abomination. Today it is a commonplace of globalization.

This entry first looks to explain this arc in terms of historical causation. In an early modern frame, dual nationality not only offended the ideology of sovereign-subject relations, it also posed a serious threat to stable bilateral relations. Dual nationality blurred otherwise clear lines that demarcated sovereign jurisdiction, triggering the human equivalent of turf battles. At the same time, states were unwilling to harmonize nationality practices to suppress the incidence of dual nationality. States laid conflicting claims to individuals, sparking sometimes intense diplomatic disputes. The United States was the common denominator in these episodes as it attempted to protect newly minted (and sometimes native-born) citizens from European states unwilling to release subjects from birth nationality.

Given the failure to eliminate the status, states developed alternative strategies to manage resulting conflict. States attempted to police the status under domestic law through expatriation mechanisms. Most came to terminate the nationality of those who naturalized in other countries and forced those born with multiple nationalities to choose one at the age of majority. Some states entered into bilateral arrangements to clarify nationality in the context of migration. International tribunals looked beyond formal status to determine the dominant among two or more nationalities as a matter of social attachment, in effect rendering the dual national a mono-national.

On top of these management techniques, strong social norms against the status supplied a backstop to leaky legal ones. These social norms were framed in terms of loyalty and allegiance. Though this vocabulary tended to associate the status with security concerns, in fact there were few cases in which dual nationals engaged in conduct subversive of the national security interests. In the Global South, meanwhile, dual nationality threatened fragile post-colonial national identities. Emigrants were thought to have forsaken their homelands in the way of traitors. Coupled with a brain-drain discourse, this framing policed against dual citizenship in the context of South-North migration.

As active dual nationality was more effectively suppressed, it dissipated as a source of bilateral conflict. The management strategies were reinforced by the rise of human rights. Dual citizens no longer posed a uniquely destabilizing threat to sovereign order; states could no longer treat their own as they pleased, so the fact (or not) of additional nationality was overtaken by the new regime affording individuals rights as humans and not just as nationals of other states. This mitigated a central, mostly submerged (at least to contemporary eyes), downside material risk of the status. This shift was reinforced by the general decline of interstate conflict, especially after the end of the Cold War.

This history presents a key causal explanation for acceptance of the status. Multiple citizenship once posed a major if prosaic threat to world order. It no longer does. Although social norms against the status proved sticky through the end of the twentieth century, an increasing number of states came to adopt a tolerant posture to multiple citizenship. States in the Global South saw an affirmative benefit in promoting the status as a tool to cement relations with prosperous diasporas, repackaged as an economic resource. Although holdout states remain, especially in Asia and Africa, a clear majority of states (sending and receiving) now allow the retention of original citizenship upon naturalization in another state. Few require those born with multiple citizenship to choose one among them in adulthood. This entry describes broad regional trends and thematic elements in the shift toward greater acceptance of the status, which appears unlikely to be reversed.

The cost/benefit calculation has also changed for individuals. Into the mid-twentieth century dual citizenship involved the risk of duplicative obligations, most importantly for males subject to mandatory military service. That risk was also managed through bilateral arrangements insuring exposure to conscription in only one country of nationality. Once this major cost was eliminated, individuals saw incentives to retain or acquire the status, both instrumental and affective. In many cases it has become a default option in the context of both birthright citizenship and naturalization.

Empiricists are starting to train their attention to multiple citizenship. Acceptance of dual citizenship by many states creates a diffusion effect in those that have not. This points to eventual near-universal acceptance of the status, which will be accelerated and reinforced by international norms. As multiple citizenship becomes entrenched on the ground, it continues to pose theoretical challenges. Multiple citizenship poses a particular dilemma for liberal nationalists. On the one hand, the status is both rights and autonomy expanding. On the other, it facilitates instrumental citizenship and challenges core citizenship ideologies centering the state and equality.

A Lost Story of Disrepute

The roots of the disfavor associated with dual citizenship can be precisely located in historical contingencies of statehood and sovereignty. During the nineteenth century, dual nationality[1] posed a serious material threat to international relations. Embedded notions of nationality could not account for migration and transfers of national affiliation. Sovereignty and self-determination defeated initial attempts at the kind of cooperation that would have resolved resulting conflicts and/or eradicated the status. Dual nationality was a central problem of international affairs. This dynamic, implicating serious global risks, was superseded by underspecified notions of 'loyalty' and largely unfounded security concerns. States eventually developed strategies on a uni- and bilateral basis and also worked to manage problems of dual nationality, but the resulting regimes were leaky. Strong legacy norms against active dual nationality helped to backstop incomplete legal ones.

Dual nationality emerged as a phenomenon only with the advent of significant migration among states and the end of sedentary conditions that characterized the

---

[1] Although 'nationality' and 'citizenship' are now used interchangeably, they once had distinct meanings. This entry will use 'nationality' for descriptions of historical developments prior to the mid-twentieth century, during which time 'citizenship' was a permissive matter of municipal law. Not all dual nationals would have had dual citizenship. The entry will also use 'dual nationality' or 'dual citizenship' to describe the phenomenon up to the present. The holding of more than two nationalities would have been rare; it is only recently that one can appropriately use the label 'multiple citizenship'.

feudal and early modern periods. (Nationality itself was epiphenomenal in the context of sedentariness, as territorial life trajectories avoided the need to facilitate the sorting of individuals among sovereigns.) Sedentariness was coupled with the concept of 'perpetual allegiance', notably articulated in the 1608 decision in *Calvin's* Case, under which those born to the territorial protection of a sovereign forever owed him their loyalty. The tie was indissoluble, dictated by nature not man. Migration to the newly independent United States challenged perpetual allegiance as individuals sought to transfer affiliation through naturalization to their new state of residence. European sovereigns refused to recognize the legitimacy of such transfers (in some countries, Russia for example, naturalization in another state constituted a crime). The ideology of perpetual allegiance masked the strong material incentive to retain manpower, by which military capacity and sovereign strength were then measured.[2]

The result was turf contests for men among states. Two states laid claim to every individual who naturalized in the United States. This was the first class of dual nationals. So long as these individuals remained physically located in their state of new nationality, no difficulty ensued. Outside that jurisdiction, competing claims could be actualized. On the high seas, Britain laid claim to its birth subjects who had naturalized in the United States and enlisted in the U.S. navy; these exercises in impressment were an important cause of the War of 1812. More chronic were cases involving new Americans returning to their homelands for temporary visits. Birth sovereigns would claim the individual for military service (or punish him for evading it), as if the individual had never left. The United States, meanwhile, would undertake to shield its naturalized citizens from the depredations of what it viewed as their former states.

These disputes played out in the realm of diplomatic protection, under which a state could intervene on behalf of its nationals in the face of mistreatment by another state. Diplomatic protection was an accepted but exceptional derogation from the otherwise prevailing tenet of sovereign territorial control, under which states were insulated from international law within their own jurisdiction.[3] Diplomatic protection could be reconciled with sovereignty insofar as individual nationals were considered to be an extension of the state; when one state harmed another's subject, it was harming the sovereign itself.[4] At the same time, states were unconstrained in the treatment of their own nationals. Dual nationality contradicted the two principles. Dual nationality could not be reconciled with the logic of sovereignty. Sovereign

[2] See, e.g., Aristide Zolberg, 'The Exit Revolution,' in Nancy L. Green and Francois Weil, eds., *Citizenship and Those Who Leave* (Urbana-Champaign: University of Illinois Press, 2007), pp. 33–62, p. 34.

[3] Annemarieke Vermeer-Künzli, 'Diplomatic Protection as a Source of Human Rights Law,' in Dinah Shelton, ed., *The Oxford Handbook of International Human Rights Law* (Oxford: Oxford University Press, 2013), pp. 250–274.

[4] Myres S. McDougal et al., 'Nationality and Human Rights: The Protection of the Individual in External Arenas,' *Yale Law Journal* 83 (1974): pp. 900–998, pp. 906–907.

power over a national was contested when another state claimed the same individual as its own.

The diplomatic digests from the nineteenth and early twentieth centuries are littered with episodes in which the U.S. diplomatic authorities intervened with European governments to protect naturalized U.S. citizens from military conscription and other actions premised on continuing claims of the birth sovereign.[5] The disputes comprised a constant irritation to bilateral relations between the United States and all major immigrant-sending European states. The proximate cause was the individual's status as a dual national. Dual nationals represented instability in a world lacking a robust institutional architecture to cabin conflict.

Targeting Dual Nationality, Imperfectly

Some coordination mitigated the incidence of dual nationality. European practice provoked U.S. calls for recognition of a 'right to expatriation,' implicating abandonment of perpetual allegiance and acceptance by homeland sovereigns of transfers of nationality. Terminating the nationality of those who naturalized before other sovereigns would eliminate the most important source of dual nationality and the interstate difficulties associated with the status. In the United States, the issue was not just one of high diplomacy but of mass politics behind which powerful German and Irish immigrant communities mobilized. The issue reached a flash point when a number of naturalized Irish-Americans were denied certain procedural trial rights extended to aliens in treason trials relating to the Fenian rebellion of 1867, and treated by Crown courts as British subjects. The U.S. Congress enacted legislation deeming expatriation 'a natural and inherent right of all people, indispensable to the enjoyment of the rights of life, liberty, and the pursuit of happiness,' and directed the President to employ all means short of war to secure the release of U.S. citizens, naturalized or native-born, from unjust imprisonment by any foreign government. The issue was the top agenda item in bilateral U.S.-UK relations.[6] The British relented with 1870 legislation terminating British nationality upon naturalization in another state. The United States entered into bilateral agreements with

---

[5] See especially John Bassett Moore, *A Digest of International Law*, volume 3 (Washington: Government Printing Office, 1906); Edwin M. Borchard, *The Diplomatic Protection of Citizens Abroad, Or, The Law of International Claims* (New York: Banks Law Publishing, 1915).

[6] See David Sim, *A Union Forever: The Irish Question and U.S. Foreign Policy in the Victorian Age* (Ithaca: Cornell University Press, 2013), p. 122.

other states, dubbed the Bancroft treaties after U.S. negotiator George Bancroft, providing for mutual recognition of naturalization based on five years' residency in the other state.

These piecemeal efforts reduced but did not eliminate the status. Many states retained perpetual allegiance into the twentieth century. Some conditioned expatriation on the satisfaction of military service obligations. Many children of immigrants to the United States were born with dual nationality through the interplay of *jus soli* and *jus sanguinis*. The visits of these individuals to their parents' homelands often triggered the same sort of disputes as those of the emigrant generation. France's military service requirement, for example, applied even to French nationals born abroad.[7]

Dual nationals continued to blur the lines between national communities in ways that resulted in instability. In theory, the problem could have been addressed through multilateral agreement. Some commentators proposed that states be required to adopt strict *jus soli* rules for birthright citizenship.[8] More measured proposals came out of blue ribbon groups at Harvard Law School and the League of Nations in the lead-up to the Hague Codification Conference of 1930, at which nationality was tabled for negotiation.[9] The resulting Convention on Certain Questions Relating to the Conflict of Nationality Laws addressed the problem only at the margins and was undersubscribed in any case. Its preamble recognized 'the ideal towards which the efforts of humanity should be directed is the abolition of all cases both of statelessness and double nationality.' But it also provided in its opening operative article that 'It is for each State to determine under its own law who are its nationals.' States agreed that dual citizenship was a serious problem. They were unwilling to cede discretion over nationality practice toward its suppression.

The context of imperfect legal devices to police the status helps explain the development of strong social norms against the status. In the United States, large numbers of individuals held dual nationality, either by birth or through naturalization. In the face of perpetual allegiance, the United States was powerless to eliminate the status on its own, short of refusing to extend citizenship to those still claimed by European sovereigns (an approach that would have retarded immigrant assimilation). To suppress the status, dual nationality was infused with moral opprobrium.

---

[7] Writing after his presidency, Theodore Roosevelt decried the Wilson Administration's failure to intervene on behalf of one such individual as 'dangerously close to treason' (Theodore Roosevelt, *Fear God and Take Your Own Part* (New York: George H. Doran, 1916), p. 277).

[8] See, e.g., James Brown Scott, *Observations on Nationality* (Oxford: Oxford University Press, 1931).

[9] See Research in International Law of the Harvard Law School, 'The Law of Nationality,' *American Journal of International Law* 23 (Special Supplement 1929): pp. 13–79; League of Nations Committee of Experts for the Progressive Codification of International Law, 'Nationality,' *American Journal of International Law* 20 (Special Supplement 1926): pp. 21–61. The Harvard group included Manley O. Hudson and Philip Jessup, both of whom would subsequently serve on the International Court of Justice.

Dual nationality was incomprehensible in the old loyalty framings of the connection of the ruler and the ruled. Exclusivity suited marriage analogies. As George Bancroft suggested in 1849, states would 'as soon tolerate a man with two wives as a man with two countries; as soon bear with polygamy as that state of double allegiance which common sense so repudiates that it has not even coined a word to express it.'[10] Naturalization, meanwhile, was advertised as 'a new political birth', severing forever allegiance to native land.[11] If the law could not stop one from holding dual nationality (the status itself was typically not 'illegal'), social norms helped mitigate the threat to world order. The moral element was situated in nationality tropes of 'loyalty' and 'allegiance'. These terms had little independent material significance. They were a cultural backstop to ineffective legal ordering. Claims of disloyalty worked as shaming mechanism against the practice of dual nationality.

Meanwhile, states improved strategies for suppressing the status. Most states came to require election of nationality for birthright dual nationals, forcing a choice between nationalities at majority. Some states assumed election in favor of the state of habitual residence unless an individual indicated otherwise with diplomatic authorities. Under the Bancroft treaties, those who returned to their homelands for two years were considered to revert to their nationality of origin, a standard made generally applicable in U.S. practice under the Expatriation Act of 1907.

An increasing number of states terminated nationality upon naturalization in another state. In a near-universal practice, women who married foreign men automatically lost their nationality, in most cases automatically securing the husband's nationality. This reflected patriarchal conceptions of the family and nation, but the practice was also intended to prevent dual nationality that might otherwise result for the wife and offspring.[12] In the United States, the grounds of expatriation were broadened to include almost any manifestation of active alternate nationality. Thousands lost their U.S. citizenship, for example, for merely voting in a foreign political election.[13]

Where the status itself could not be suppressed, states attempted to manage the associated pathologies. Some argued that states should be disabled as a matter of international law from exercising diplomatic protection against another state of nationality. Even though it was incorporated in the 1930 Hague Convention, this candidate norm never fully took hold. It was unacceptable to the United States,

---

[10] See Sen. Ex. Doc. 38, 36th Cong., 1st Sess. 160 (1850) (Bancroft to Lord Palmerston, Jan. 26, 1849). In 1915, Theodore Roosevelt was calling the status 'a self-evident absurdity'. The bigamy analogy has persisted among some conservative opponents of the status. See, e.g., Samuel P. Huntington, *Who Are We? The Challenges to America's National Identity* (New York: Simon & Schuster, 2004), pp. 5, 212.

[11] See Moore (n 5), p. 574.

[12] See Candice Lewis Bredbenner, *A Nationality of Her Own: Women, Marriage, and the Law of Citizenship* (Berkeley: University of California Press, 1998), p. 102.

[13] See Patrick Weil, *The Sovereign Citizen: Denaturalization and the Origins of the American Republic* (Philadelphia: University of Pennsylvania Press, 2012).

which continued to intervene on behalf of naturalized citizens against states that rejected expatriation. But other states incorporated the practice, the United Kingdom, for example, reducing the risk that dual nationals would provoke bilateral disputes.[14] International tribunals faced the question of when states could espouse claims on behalf of dual nationals against other states. Easily the most notable pronouncement of an international tribunal relating to dual nationality, the 1954 ruling of the International Court of Justice in the *Nottebohm* Case established that states could not represent individuals lacking genuine links of social attachment. Other tribunals established a rule of 'dominant and effective nationality' for espousing the claims of dual nationals. The test looked to determine which of two nationalities was the more significant in terms of social, political, civic, and family life, with place of habitual residence as a key factor.[15] This approach in effect took a person with two nationalities and (for international purposes) turned her into a person with one.

States also moved to resolve duplicative military service obligations of dual nationals. The 1930 Hague codification conference had addressed the issue in the Protocol Relating to Military Obligations in Certain Cases of Double Nationality, which provided that a dual national should in most cases be held to military service only in his country of habitual residence. More important were bilateral agreements to the same effect; by the mid-twentieth century, there was in place a dense web of such agreements, implicating many of the more common nationality pairings.[16] Some states adopted domestic laws that limited the exposure of external citizens to military service. In 1928, for example, France enacted a law under which French nationals born abroad were released from military service upon establishing compliance with the military law of the foreign country of which they were also a national. In a 1963 multilateral agreement, states under the auspices of the Council of Europe adopted an 'ordinary residence' presumption for military service obligations of dual nationals. An earlier nationality treaty among Latin American states had addressed the issue by implication. These efforts eliminated in most cases the major downside of dual nationality from the individual's perspective.[17]

---

[14] Conflicting views on the question were reflected in the experts' reports leading up to the Hague Convention. The European-dominated League of Nations report recommended adopting of the rule against being able to protect a national in another state in which the individual also had nationality where the Harvard report did not. See League of Nations Report (n 9), p. 46.

[15] See the *Mergé Case*, *Reports of International Arbitral Awards 14* (1955): pp. 236–248; Paul Weis, *Nationality and Statelessness in International Law*, 2nd edition (Dordrecht: Kluwer, 1979), pp. 169–197.

[16] Stephen H. Legomsky, 'Dual Nationality and Military Service: Strategy Number Two', in David A. Martin and Kay Hailbronner, eds., *Rights and Duties of Dual Nationals* (Leiden: Brill, 2003), pp. 79–126.

[17] For an extended treatment of the history of dual citizenship, see Peter J. Spiro, *At Home in Two Countries: The Past and Future of Dual Citizenship* (New York: NYU Press, 2016).

Loyalty Talk and Social Norms

These tools helped mitigate the costs of dual nationality. The threat to interstate relations was further minimized by the advent of human rights. Dual nationality was a problem in a world in which all rights were national rights. Dual nationals confounded the rule that sovereigns had full discretion over their nationals. Human rights constrained that discretion. Dual nationals no longer distinctively contradicted principles of sovereignty. This tectonic change in the global system supplies an important explanation for the eventual acceptance of the status.

As with all tectonic shifts, that change was slow. It was also masked in two ways. First, by the time that human rights gained hold, as an ideology if not as a practice, disputes relating to diplomatic protection had abated as a result of the mitigation strategies. Dual nationality was no longer clearly tethered to the kind of disputes that had imperiled nineteenth-century interstate relations. Second, as the actual risk of destabilization diminished, the social norms persisted. The loyalty discourse found new life in a security framing. The tag line shifted from bigamy to fifth columns. World War II and then the Cold War fertilized this understanding. Supporters of the wartime depredations against Japanese-Americans highlighted dual nationality in their justifications.[18] In the United States, various disabilities came to be attached to membership in the Communist Party—a proxy for loyalty to the Soviet Union—in a way that resembled an attack on dual nationality. The intensity of the Cold War magnified loyalty arguments generally on both sides.[19] Dual nationality presented a natural corollary target for this discourse.

The persistent social norm against dual nationality was thus consequential. In fact, dual nationals never posed any particular security threat. There were no notable cases of dual nationals committing espionage. Nor even was dual nationality a problem in the context of war between alternate states of nationality. Individuals in that situation elected one of their two nationalities, often through operation of law with enlistment in the armed forces of one state of nationality resulting automatically in the loss of nationality in the other. Thousands of Japanese, German, and Italian nationals who also had citizenship in the United States fought for the Axis powers during World War II. Almost all were automatically expatriated upon enlistment in the foreign armed force. Their (former) status as dual nationals by itself did not make them more dangerous. During the Cold War, Soviet spies would not have advertised the competing affiliation. Active dual Soviet-US citizenship would have presented something of a contradiction, not because of issues relating to diplomatic protection but because it would have seemed to present an impossible

[18] *Hirabayashi v. United States*, 320 US 81 (1943), p. 97.
[19] George Ginsburgs, *Citizenship Law of the USSR* (Leiden: Brill, 1983), p. 79.

conflict of interest. With the end of the Cold War and of major interstate military hostilities, the security objection to dual citizenship dissipated. The primary security threat today—terrorism—does not align to citizenship status.[20]

Even as duplicative obligations were mitigated, few individuals availed themselves to dual nationality. To the extent states more effectively policed dual nationality, the status was a precarious one. Undertaking active citizenship in an alternate state could put one's other citizenship at risk. That would have been an unappealing prospect, especially where it jeopardized the more important citizenship measured in terms of social attachment. After the decline of perpetual allegiance, birthright dual nationality was the more common source of dual nationals. For many, it lay dormant through adulthood. Through the middle of the twentieth century, only where individuals looked to permanently reside in the homeland of migrant ancestors would there have been cause to activate the additional nationality (in the early post-WWII decades), and then only with the knowledge that it would likely result in forfeiting the other.

The social norms against the status reinforced the incentive structure. Continuing to be inflected with moral opprobrium and divided loyalty, it was not a status to advertise. Through the mid-twentieth century, it was considered at best an oddity. The most important treatment of the subject from that period, a 1961 monograph by Nissim Bar-Yaacov, highlighted the 'psychological difficulties' and 'mental conflicts' associated with the status.[21] Hersch Lauterpacht spoke of 'inconveniences and hardships.'[22] Whether or not these observations held true as an empirical matter, there is no evidence that anyone celebrated the status.

In the post-colonial Global South, a different kind of loyalty discourse took hold. Dual nationality posed a threat to fragile national identities, especially where the second state of nationality was connected to a former imperial state or with a dominant regional power. The status was also inconsistent with anxieties about brain drain and aspirations to economic autarky. Individuals who naturalized elsewhere (mostly in developed economies) were considered something like traitors to the homeland.[23] The Global South thus perceived a distinctive harm in dual nationality, one that was not primarily rooted in the complications of diplomatic protection.

---

[20] That is, citizenship no longer defines adversaries in the way it once did. In the nineteenth-century world of declared hostilities between states, all persons of one nationality were presumed hostile to all persons of the other. Today, many adversaries are citizens of allied states or even of the state they attack. The old usage 'enemy alien' has been overtaken by 'homegrown terrorist.'

[21] Nissim Bar-Yaacov, *Dual Nationality* (London: Stevens, 1961), p. 265.

[22] Lassa Oppenheim, *International Law: A Treatise*, 6th edition, volume 1 'Peace,' edited by Hersch Lauterpacht (London: Longmans, Green & Co., 1947), p. 608.

[23] Rainer Bauböck, 'Towards a Political Theory of Migrant Transnationalism,' *International Migration Review* 37 (2003): pp. 700–723, p. 709. A prevalent Mexican understanding of U.S. naturalization included spitting and stomping on a Mexican flag as part of the naturalization ceremony (David FitzGerald, *A Nation of Emigrants: How Mexico Manages Its Migration* (Berkeley: University of California Press, 2008), p. 136).

Latin American, African, South and East Asian states adopted expatriation rules under which naturalization elsewhere terminated homeland citizenship and did not permit citizenship to descend to those born abroad. This suppressed the status for these states. It also reduced incidence of dual citizenship in developed states, especially to the extent that migration shifted from North-North to South-North. Even as some receiving states moved to tolerate the status, the incidence of dual citizenship remained low as others continued to enforce against it.

State Trends

States have more recently shifted to broad acceptance of dual citizenship, although they have not moved in lockstep. In part because of the sovereign discretion that states have enjoyed over citizenship practice, the experience of particular states has been impacted by historical, legal, cultural, and social contingencies. Some generalizations are nonetheless possible in explaining recent developments in country practices relating to multiple citizenship. Although holdouts remain, the overall trend has been nearly unidirectional.

Regional geographies and historical experiences with migration appear to have some crude correlation to dual citizenship practice. Migration source states have counted prominently among those pivoting from effectively suppressing the status to affirmatively encouraging it. For developing states, dual citizenship is now viewed as a tool for cementing relations with economically prosperous diaspora communities.[24] Dual citizenship is also seen by some source states as facilitating political mobilization in new states of residence by lowering the cost of naturalization. Such states as Mexico, the Dominican Republic, Turkey, and the Philippines have eliminated laws terminating citizenship upon naturalization in another state. This change has been shown to increase naturalization rates in a new state of residence.[25] This shift does not exclusively apply to states traditionally described as source states; today, all countries are source states. Italy's acceptance of dual citizenship in 1992

---

[24] See, e.g., Kim Barry, 'Home and Away: The Construction of Citizenship in an Emigration Context,' *New York University Law Review 81* (2006): pp. 11–59. An empirical correlation between dual citizenship and remittance levels has now been demonstrated (David Leblang, 'Harnessing the Diaspora Dual Citizenship, Migrant Return Remittances,' *Comparative Political Studies* (September 29, 2015), doi: 10.1177/0010414015606736.

[25] See Francesca Mazzolari, 'Dual Citizenship Rights: Do They Make More and Richer Citizens?,' *Demography 46* (2009): pp. 169–191. The correlation, however, may be weak. Maarten Peter Vink et al., 'Immigrant Naturalization in the Context of Institutional Diversity: Policy Matters, But to Whom?,' *International Migration 51* (2013): pp. 1–20.

is explained in part by an agenda to affirm ties to communities of Italian descent abroad. The shift toward acceptance by source states is overdetermined as a matter of policy insofar as emigrant communities have lobbied for the change; it is not only the state deciding to accept dual citizenship, but the state acceding to demands of those who want the status. This, again, is true not only of traditional source states but also developed countries with increasingly mobile populations.

The trend is not universal. South and East Asian states have lagged, even when they are migrant source states. Dual citizenship is prohibited under the Indian constitution, for example. Up against that bar, India has devised progressively more substantial status categories for ethnic Indians abroad (up to three generations removed from a citizen of India), from Non-Resident Indians, to Persons of Indian Origin, to Overseas Citizens of India (OCI). The label notwithstanding, OCI does not comprise citizenship in India. It does extend to its holders most of the rights of citizenship, including visa-free travel and settlement rights as well as economic rights equivalent to citizenship. Only political rights are excluded from the package.

Other South and East Asian states have moved toward sometimes selective acceptance. Pakistan allows dual citizenship as paired with more than a dozen, mostly OECD countries. Sri Lanka extends dual citizenship on a discretionary basis to professionals and those who hold investment accounts in Sri Lanka of about $20,000 or more. South Korea now accepts dual citizenship for those born with the status, those who are born in Korea and adopted by non-Koreans (a substantial population of whom resides in the United States), and those in mixed status marriages. The Philippines legislated full acceptance of dual citizenship in 2003 and is now among those states that actively encourage acquisition of the status.

East Asia includes two notable holdout states in the trend toward broadened acceptance of the status. Japan is among the few remaining states that both rejects dual citizenship and aggressively polices against the status (with passport renewal as a choke point). This correlates to its high level of ethnic homogeneity and outlier immigration policies. Even Japan is facing pressure from its external citizen community to recognize the status, however, and has moved through administrative practice to accept the status where it is acquired at birth. China is a more complex story. Dual citizenship is illegal in China, and by law naturalization in another state will result in the loss of important household registration status. But the bar is underenforced. The situation has been described by one observer as 'chaotic.' There have been calls for acceptance of dual citizenship for the same reason that it has been pressed in other migrant source states, as a way to facilitate economic engagement with a substantial diaspora.[26] There have also been proposals to extend an

---

[26] See, e.g., Ting Yan, 'Time to Allow Overseas Chinese Dual Nationality to Encourage Return of Talent, Delegate Proposes,' *South China Morning Post*, March 11, 2016, online http://www.scmp.com/ news/china/policies-politics/article/1923508/time-allow-overseas-chinese-duel-nationality-encourage.

intermediate status to former Chinese citizens on an Indian template. China's posture toward dual citizenship is unstable at this writing. Acceptance by China would represent an important step toward universal acceptance of the status.

Europe has trended toward acceptance of the status. As a new regional host to migrants, acceptance has been uneven. Some European states were among the first to fully accept the status, the United Kingdom (1947), France (1973), and Switzerland (1992) among them. In Germany, dual citizenship has been a flashpoint political issue since the mid-1990s. Fierce opposition has softened. Recent citizenship law reforms largely abandoned an election requirement (known as the 'option model') to allow those born in Germany with dual citizenship to retain the status into adulthood so long as the individual has resided for at least eight years in Germany. Although naturalizing citizens are not entitled to retain their citizenship of origin, favorable administrative discretion is now exercised in many cases to allow retention. Native-born Germans who naturalize elsewhere are also often allowed to retain their German citizenship. Dual citizenship is accepted outright with other EU and EFTA states.

The Netherlands presents an instructive example of putative backsliding on dual citizenship. From 1991 until 1997, naturalization applicants were not required to renounce prior citizenship. In 1997, the renunciation requirement was reintroduced. But even this retrenchment masks a high incidence of dual citizenship. A key exception allows naturalizing citizens to retain citizenship where the original state does not reasonably provide for termination of citizenship (essentially, those states that continue to adhere to perpetual allegiance). That exception allows all naturalization applicants in the Netherlands from Morocco to become dual citizens. The law includes other exceptions to the renunciation requirement, for refugees, for example. Under these exceptions, a majority of naturalization applicants retain prior citizenship. An estimated 7 percent of Dutch nationals resident in the Netherlands hold dual citizenship. Proposals to more effectively restrict dual citizenship, meanwhile, have triggered strong opposition from Dutch emigrants.[27]

States also appear to resist acceptance in the face of unstable territorial boundary conditions and substantial transborder kin groups. This explains the continued rejection of dual citizenship in some Central and East European states. Slovakia, for example, terminates the citizenship of those who acquire another nationality while remaining resident in Slovakia, a measure aimed at the country's large ethnic Hungarian population that became eligible for Hungarian citizenship under a 2010 Hungarian nationality reform. The Baltic states have feared

---

[27] Ricky van Oers et al., 'Country Report: The Netherlands' (Florence: European University Institute, EUDO Citizenship Observatory, January 2013); Willem Maas, 'The Netherlands: Consensus and Contention in a Migration State,' in James F. Hollifield et al., eds., *Controlling Immigration: A Global Perspective*, 3rd edition (Stanford: Stanford University Press, 2014), pp. 256–275, p. 268.

the 'passportization' by Russia of ethnic Russian populations as a pretext for military aggression, as was the case in Georgia and Ukraine. Latvia now allows dual citizenship of emigrants (including the restoration of citizenship to those exiled during the Soviet era) and their descendants whose other citizenship is in a state party to NATO, the EU, EFTA, and a handful of other states, but notably excluding Russia. Other former Soviet republics allow dual citizenship with Russia, Moldova, for example. Africa's reticence in accepting dual citizenship can be ascribed to the fragility of its borders and national identities. But several African states have moved in recent years to accept multiple citizenship, typically in response to demands from emigrant communities. The regional trend is clearly toward greater acceptance of the status.[28]

The overall trend has been toward broadened acceptance of multiple citizenship.[29] Causation has been overdetermined. The shift away from strong historical disfavor was enabled by the rise of human rights, which reduced the indirect but serious threat that dual nationals posed to interstate relations. Once that foundation was set, some states moved to tolerate the status. As more pairings of states accepting the status emerged, the number of dual citizens inevitably climbed. The United States, for example, grew more tolerant of dual citizenship through the second half of the twentieth century, but only as migrant source states came also to accept the status did the incidence of dual citizens among Americans increase significantly.

The increased incidence has fed pressure on states to move toward acceptance. The dynamic is one of emulation and/or diffusion. As more states accept the status, it becomes more difficult for states to defend rejectionist positions; the practice doesn't support arguments against the status. Those advocating acceptance, especially among emigrant communities, are able to leverage multiplying examples of smooth normalization of the status. There is evidence that states are more likely to move to accept the status to the extent that territorially proximate states have already done so, which supports an emulation/diffusion explanation.[30] The trajectory has also resembled a norm cascade. As a critical mass of states came to accept the status, the rate of change toward acceptance increased. A similar phenomenon is observable at the level of the individual. As more individuals maintain multiple citizenships, social norms against the status have largely dissipated. This remains variable by country (obviously where a country continues to reject the status) but in many states the status is held openly. In some states there are large, visible populations holding multiple citizenship.

---

[28] Bronwen Manby, *Citizenship Law in Africa: A Comparative Study*, 2nd edition (New York: Open Society Foundations, 2012).
[29] See the Global Citizenship Database, Maastricht Centre for Citizenship, Migration and Development, online https://macimide.maastrichtuniversity.nl/dual-cit-database/.
[30] Vink in this volume.

WANTING DUAL CITIZENSHIP

Parallel with changes in state policies, individual understandings of dual citizenship began to shift toward the close of the twentieth century. As states retreated from efforts to suppress the status and alleviated duplicative obligations in many contexts, the sentimental and instrumental benefits of dual citizenship came to outweigh the costs in an increasing number of pairings. In many cases, there is little cost to acquiring and no cost to retaining an additional citizenship. That translates into the possible retention or acquisition of dual citizenship even where benefits are minimal.

The benefits of dual citizenship are contingent. In some cases, it has an expressive value to its holders. Citizenship remains an important element in individual identity composites. This is clear in the context of children born to parents of mixed nationality, for instance. In a typical case, the national identities of both parents will be important to the child's identity composite. Under the historical approach, children of mixed status marriages were forced to pick one or the other, a requirement that typically resulted in the father's nationality being chosen over the mother's.[31] Dual citizenship validates both identities. Similar identity interests play out in the context of naturalization. Migrants will often identify with both the homeland and the new state of residence. The former regime in which most states terminated the nationality of those who naturalized elsewhere suppressed full expression of both identities. Dual citizenship allows them to be actualized. The new landscape reverses the problem of 'psychological difficulties.' Today it is the preclusion of multiple citizenship that is more likely to create mental conflicts by artificially forcing membership choices.

Multiple citizenship also implicates material benefits, including political rights. Individuals increasingly have self-governance interests in multiple polities.[32] This is increasingly the case in migrant communities, whose members may have self-governance interests in both their homelands and their new states of residence. Requiring termination of citizenship of origin imposes a price on the exercise of full political rights in one state or the other where dual citizenship enables political voice in both. From the migrant perspective, dual citizenship can also enhance economic rights. Some states restrict property and business ownership by non-citizens. With dual citizenship, migrants can freely pursue economic opportunity in states of original and adopted citizenship, a benefit to growing numbers of circular migrants.

---

[31] Karen Knop, 'Relational Nationality: On Gender and Nationality in International Law,' in T. Alexander Aleinikoff and Douglas Klusmeyer, eds., *Citizenship Today: Global Perspectives and Practices* (Washington: Carnegie Endowment for International Peace, 2001), pp. 89–126, p. 112.

[32] Rainer Bauböck, 'Stakeholder Citizenship and Transnational Political Participation. A Normative Evaluation of External Voting,' *Fordham Law Review 75* (2007): pp. 2393–2447, p. 2428.

Multiple citizenship can improve life opportunities by enabling migration. Increasing numbers of individuals are exploiting citizenship eligibility on an ancestral basis for the purpose of securing migration rights. Acceptance of dual citizenship is a necessary condition to activating such citizenship claims. The greater the asymmetries among citizenships, the greater the incentive to retain or acquire multiple citizenship for migration purposes. Where an individual holds a non-premium passport in terms of travel and settlement rights, there will be a higher value placed on the acquisition or retention of a premium passport. Empirical analysis has demonstrated this intuitive proposition. For example, eligible individuals in Latin American states are more likely than their U.S. citizen counterparts to acquire Spanish and Italian citizenship by descent.[33] This reflects the relative disparity of the Latin American citizenships relative to EU citizenship. Especially as Latin American economies were in crisis and EU economies remained robust (2000–08), large numbers of dual Argentine-Italian and Argentine-Spanish citizens availed themselves to settlement rights in the EU.[34] Citizens in developing or transitional states may also claim citizenship as a hedge against political instability. The incentives for U.S. citizens to acquire EU citizenship are less compelling, and many who are eligible for an additional citizenship will not bother to acquire it. Nonetheless, many have done so, on the basis of Irish, Italian, Greek, Polish, and other European heritage. During the 2016 presidential campaign there was not unserious chatter in the United States about exploiting alternative citizenships to escape a Trump Administration. The 2016 Brexit vote triggered a jump in applications by U.K. citizens for Irish citizenship (an estimated six million are eligible by virtue of a grandparent's birth anywhere on the island of Ireland), to insure continued benefits of EU citizenship.

The shift in domestic legal regimes has resulted in increased incidence of the status not always as a result of individual agency but rather through the operation of intersecting legal regimes. In many cases dual citizenship has become a default position. It does not need to be claimed as such. Those who are born with it simply retain it into adulthood. Those who naturalize in another country will now typically retain their citizenship of origin without any further action. For example, almost all of the more than one million Mexican citizens who have acquired citizenship in the United States since 1998 became dual citizens upon naturalization.

There remain a small number of contexts in which dual citizenship remains a burden. One involves states which continue to adhere to perpetual allegiance, rejecting the individual's capacity to expatriate. Iran, for example, does not allow native-born nationals to shed Iranian nationality even after naturalization elsewhere, and

---

[33] Yossi Harpaz, 'Ancestry into Opportunity: How Global Inequality Drives Demand for Long-Distance European Union Citizenship', *Journal of Ethnic and Migration Studies 41* (2015): pp. 2081–2104.
[34] David Cook-Martín, *The Scramble for Citizens: Dual Nationality and State Competition for Immigrants* (Stanford: Stanford University Press, 2013).

ascribes nationality on a *jus sanguinis* basis to the first generation born abroad with no opt-out possibilities. These involuntary Iranian dual nationals can face legal disabilities as a result of sanctions; for instance, the United States recently made dual EU-Iranian nationals ineligible for the visa waivers that they would otherwise enjoy as EU citizens. There may be complications, too, for dual citizens who travel to Iran, which refuses to recognize any additional nationality an individual may hold. The result is disputes akin to those that dogged U.S.-European relations during the nineteenth century. But this is not so much a downside of dual citizenship as it is a downside of perpetual allegiance, itself an archaic and rights-infringing practice.

Dual citizenship may also present an individual risk in the counter-terror context. A small handful of countries (Australia and Denmark among them) allow dual but not mono-nationals to have their citizenship stripped on terror-related grounds. But this will affect a tiny number of individuals (to date, measured only in the low hundreds) relative to the many millions who maintain the status to their advantage. In other countries, proposals to the same effect have been reversed (Canada) or rejected (France) precisely because they would discriminate against dual citizens.[35]

Increased acceptance of the status is unlikely to be reversed. As a political matter, validation of the status creates political constituencies who will resist dispossession. This may explain why Mexico's acceptance of dual citizenship in 1998 did not trigger meaningful attempts to suppress dual citizenship in the United States. There were powerful ethnic constituencies already invested in dual citizenship (Italian, Irish, and Jewish among them). The same dynamic is likely in countries with powerful emigrant constituencies. Once they have won the status it will be difficult to take it away, especially in the absence of a clear policy justification.

Finally, the emergence of rights-inflected norms protective of the status are likely to help reinforce existing developments and further incentivize recognition of the status. For example, the 1997 European Convention on nationality requires parties to allow those born with dual nationality to retain it into adulthood, implicitly recognizing an identitarian element to the status. The convention also bars states from requiring termination of prior nationality as a condition to naturalization where termination is not possible or cannot reasonably be required. Non-discrimination arguments have been levelled against countries that continue to bar dual citizens from holding elective office while otherwise permitting the status.[36] A different strain of non-discrimination discourse is being leveled at regimes that accept dual citizenship in some cases but not in others. Germany, for example, has been criticized for allowing unrestricted dual citizenship with European states but

---

[35] See also Matthew J. Gibney, 'Should Citizenship Be Conditional? The Ethics of Denationalization,' *Journal of Politics* 75 (2013): pp. 646–658; Peter J. Spiro, 'Expatriating Terrorists,' *Fordham Law Review* 82 (2014): pp. 2169–2187.

[36] Peter J. Spiro, 'A New International Law of Citizenship', *American Journal of International Law* 105 (2011): pp. 694–746, pp. 736–737.

not others.[37] Partial acceptance may not be sustainable as an equilibrium position; once a state accepts multiple citizenship in some cases, it may ultimately be forced to accept it in all cases. These pressures recognize interests that individuals may have in the status distinct from state interests. Further evolution of these norms could establish universal or near-universal acceptance of multiple citizenship.

Multiple Citizenship in Theory

While multiple citizenship appears to be gaining hold on the ground, theorists have not closely engaged the normative aspects of the status. Some have denounced the status on communitarian grounds, echoing conventional loyalty discourses. Those with republican tendencies consider whether multiple citizenship is consistent with responsible political participation in each state of nationality, concerns that are now being satisfied through empirical work.[38] The challenge is most difficult for liberal theorists. On the one hand, multiple citizenship is rights and autonomy enhancing. On the other, it poses an insidious threat to equality.

Some have suggested that multiple citizenship undermines political equality by giving dual citizens greater political rights than their mono-national counterparts, including double voting rights.[39] But multiple citizenship does not afford its holders greater political status within any one national polity.[40] Nor does multiple citizenship create meaningful political inequalities at the global level. The world is not organized as a polity. International organizations are premised on the equality of states, not individuals, which creates gross disparities in representation. In any case, individual voice at the global level is too attenuated for the extra vote by itself to threaten political equality.[41] The solution proposed to eliminate putative political

[37] Christian Joppke, *Citizenship and Immigration* (London: Wiley, 2013).

[38] Irene Bloemraad, 'Who Claims Dual Citizenship? The Limits of Postnationalism, the Possibilities of Transnationalism, and the Persistence of Traditional Citizenship,' *International Migration Review* 38 (2004): pp. 389–426; Andrea Schlenker, 'Divided Loyalty? Identification and Political Participation of Dual Citizens in Switzerland,' *European Political Science Review* 8, no. 4 (2016): pp. 517–546, doi: 10.1017/S1755773915000168.

[39] Robert E. Goodin and Ana Tanasoca, 'Double Voting,' *Australasian Journal of Philosophy* 92 (2014): pp. 743–758; David A. Martin, 'New Rules on Dual Nationality for a Democratizing Globe: Between Rejection and Embrace,' *Georgetown Immigration Law Journal* 14 (1999): pp. 1–34.

[40] Bauböck (n 32), p. 2428.

[41] This also answers the problem of double voting in so-called spillover contexts, those in which an individual is a citizen of two states engaged in bilateral decision-making. If the United States and Canada are negotiating a treaty, e.g., a dual U.S.-Canadian citizen would have two votes to support or oppose the action. But voting by itself is unlikely to translate into significant political power. Other

inequalities created by multiple citizenship—restricting multiple citizens to vote in one state of nationality only—would create a more substantial equality issue by depriving citizens of political equality within the polities in which voting rights are cancelled.

More serious are sociological inequalities enabled by multiple citizenship. Citizenship is an important determinant of life opportunities. The degree of socio-logical inequality associated with multiple citizenship will be contingent and rela-tive. A dual Turkish-German citizen will not be appreciably privileged relative to her native-born mono-national German compatriot, probably the contrary. But an Argentine citizen also holding Italian or Spanish citizenship will have signifi-cantly enhanced life opportunities relative to his mono-national Argentine neigh-bor. Citizens of less developed states whose citizenship does not afford travel and settlement rights in developed ones will be advantaged if they are able to secure an additional citizenship that does. To the extent that eligibility for the additional citizenship enables instrumental citizenship claims, it will look like arbitrary priv-ilege.[42] The problem will be compounded where there is a large population that has the additional premium citizenship. As Shachar notes, 'with the marked increase in dual nationality ... some will be in possession of more diversified bundles or shares in several membership "corporations," whereas others will own merely a single citi-zenship parcel ... , further deepening concerns about stratification and unequal opportunity.'[43] Citizenship has historically been a badge of equality. Under these conditions, it may become the opposite.

This difficulty explains the ambivalence with which some liberal theorists approach dual citizenship.[44] But any attempt to shelter democratic citizenship from the corrosive effects of multiple citizenship will be either unworkable or will create more serious equality concerns than the ones they would solve. Applying a genu-ine links requirement on the acquisition of additional citizenships will be satisfied in almost all cases; in the wake of globalization, such links are easily established. More robust exogenous constraints on the extension of citizenship (such as limita-tions on citizenship by descent) will have the effect of excluding some authentic members of the community. In other words, imposing limitations on the allocation of citizenship will also translate into inequality. These inequalities will be status

channels, such as political campaign donations, present more influential entry points. In many states, contributions can be made by non-citizen residents, so this is not a citizenship-contingent issue.

[42] Iseult Honohan, 'Limiting the Transmission of Family Advantage: Ius Sanguinis with an Expiration Date,' in Costica Dumbrava and Rainer Bauböck, eds., *Bloodlines and Belonging: Time to Abandon 'Ius Sanguinis'?*, EUI Working Paper no. 80 (Florence: RSCAS, 2015), pp. 32–34, online http://cadmus.eui.eu//handle/1814/37578.

[43] Ayelet Shachar, *The Birthright Lottery: Citizenship and Global Inequality* (Cambridge: Harvard University Press, 2009), pp. 130–131.

[44] E.g., Noah Pickus, *True Faith and Allegiance: Immigration and American Civic Nationalism* (Princeton: Princeton University Press, 2005), p. 181.

inequalities—inequalities before law—not sociological ones. Barring multiple citizenship will deprive individuals of political and expressive rights in communities of which they are members.

Multiple citizenship also enables instrumental allocations of and claims to citizenship. Without acceptance of multiple citizenship, there would be no Olympic citizenship, no tenuous ancestral citizenship, no investor citizenship.[45] Rules against dual citizenship are unlikely to police against these inauthentic attributions. Even if they could, no agent is available to impose the constraint. So long as it is volitional on the part of the individual and does not interfere with the sovereignty of other states, states are free to extend citizenship according to their own criteria, regardless of whether it results in multiple citizenship.

Multiple citizenship is now sufficiently pervasive to be characterized as a feature of globalization. Its incidence will increase with increased migration. It will also increase on a next-generation basis. Current holders of multiple citizenship will in most cases pass the status on to their children, sometimes with the addition of a different nationality of the other parent. In the next generation, persons born with three or more citizenships will increase through natural reproduction. Social scientists could usefully work to quantify its incidence and the societal consequences of its increase. Acceptance of multiple citizenship, meanwhile, is enabling the rise of 'citizenship planners', who will advise global elites on appropriate citizenship portfolios. This activity will inevitably cast new meanings on citizenship as an institution, presenting additional opportunities for future research in political theory and other fields.

Bibliography

Barry, Kim, 'Home and Away: The Construction of Citizenship in an Emigration Context,' *New York University Law Review 81* (2006): pp. 11–59.

Bar-Yaacov, Nissim, *Dual Nationality* (London: Stevens, 1961).

Bauböck, Rainer, 'Towards a Political Theory of Migrant Transnationalism,' *International Migration Review 37* (2003): pp. 700–723.

Bauböck, Rainer, 'Stakeholder Citizenship and Transnational Political Participation. A Normative Evaluation of External Voting,' *Fordham Law Review 75* (2007): pp. 2393–2447.

Blatter, Joachim, 'Dual Citizenship and Theories of Democracy,' *Citizenship Studies 15* (2011): pp. 769–798.

Bloemraad, Irene, 'Who Claims Dual Citizenship? The Limits of Postnationalism, the Possibilities of Transnationalism, and the Persistence of Traditional Citizenship,' *International Migration Review 38* (2004): pp. 389–426.

---

[45] See Shachar in this volume.

Bloemraad, Irene, *Becoming a Citizen: Incorporating Immigrants and Refugees in the United States and Canada* (Berkeley: University of California Press, 2006).

Boll, Alfred Michael, *Multiple Nationality and International Law* (Leiden: Martinus Nijhoff, 2006).

Borchard, Edwin M., *The Diplomatic Protection of Citizens Abroad, Or, The Law of International Claims* (New York: Banks Law Publishing, 1915).

Bredbenner, Candice Lewis, *A Nationality of Her Own: Women, Marriage, and the Law of Citizenship* (Berkeley: University of California Press, 1998).

Cook-Martín, David, *The Scramble for Citizens: Dual Nationality and State Competition for Immigrants* (Stanford: Stanford University Press, 2013).

Faist, Thomas and Peter Kivisto, eds., *Dual Citizenship in Global Perspective: From Unitary to Multiple Citizenship* (New York: Palgrave Macmillan, 2007).

FitzGerald, David, *A Nation of Emigrants: How Mexico Manages Its Migration* (Berkeley: University of California Press, 2008).

Gibney, Matthew J., 'Should Citizenship Be Conditional? The Ethics of Denationalization,' *Journal of Politics* 75 (2013): pp. 646–658.

Ginsburgs, George, *Citizenship Law of the USSR* (Leiden: Brill, 1983).

Goodin Robert E. and Ana Tanasoca, 'Double Voting,' *Australasian Journal of Philosophy* 92 (2014): pp. 743–758.

Harpaz, Yossi, 'Ancestry into Opportunity: How Global Inequality Drives Demand for Long-Distance European Union Citizenship,' *Journal of Ethnic and Migration Studies* 41 (2015): pp. 2081–2104.

Honohan, Iseult, 'Limiting the Transmission of Family Advantage: Ius Sanguinis with an Expiration Date,' in Costica Dumbrava and Rainer Bauböck, eds., *Bloodlines and Belonging: Time to Abandon 'Ius Sanguinis'?*, EUI Working Paper no. 80 (Florence: RSCAS, 2015), pp. 32–34, online http://cadmus.eui.eu//handle/1814/37578.

Huntington, Samuel P., *Who Are We? The Challenges to America's National Identity* (New York: Simon & Schuster, 2004).

Joppke, Christian, *Citizenship and Immigration* (London: Wiley, 2013).

Knop, Karen, 'Relational Nationality: On Gender and Nationality in International Law,' in T. Alexander Aleinikoff and Douglas Klusmeyer, eds., *Citizenship Today: Global Perspectives and Practices* (Washington: Carnegie Endowment for International Peace, 2001), pp. 89–126.

League of Nations Committee of Experts for the Progressive Codification of International Law, 'Nationality,' *American Journal of International Law* 20 (Special Supplement 1926): pp. 21–61.

Leblang, David, 'Harnessing the Diaspora Dual Citizenship, Migrant Return Remittances,' *Comparative Political Studies* (September 29, 2015), doi: 10.1177/0010414015606736.

Legomsky, Stephen H., 'Dual Nationality and Military Service: Strategy Number Two,' in David A. Martin and Kay Hailbronner, eds., *Rights and Duties of Dual Nationals* (Leiden: Brill, 2003), pp. 79–126.

Maas, Willem, 'The Netherlands: Consensus and Contention in a Migration State,' in James F. Hollifield et al., eds., *Controlling Immigration: A Global Perspective*, 3rd edition (Stanford: Stanford University Press, 2014), pp. 256–275.

Manby, Bronwen, *Citizenship Law in Africa: A Comparative Study*, 2nd edition (New York: Open Society Foundations, 2012).

Martin, David A., 'New Rules on Dual Nationality for a Democratizing Globe: Between Rejection and Embrace,' *Georgetown Immigration Law Journal* 14 (1999): pp. 1–34.

Martin, David A. and Kay Hailbronner, eds., *Rights and Duties of Dual Nationals: Evolution and Prospects* (The Hague: Kluwer Law International, 2003).

Mazzolari, Francesca, 'Dual Citizenship Rights: Do They Make More and Richer Citizens?,' *Demography 46* (2009): pp. 169–191.

McDougal, Myres S., Harold D. Lasswell, and Lung-chu Chen, 'Nationality and Human Rights: The Protection of the Individual in External Arenas,' *Yale Law Journal 83* (1974): pp. 900–998.

Moore, John Bassett, *A Digest of International Law*, volume 3 (Washington: Government Printing Office, 1906).

Oppenheim, Lassa, *International Law: A Treatise*, 6th edition, volume 1 'Peace,' edited by Hersch Lauterpacht (London: Longmans, Green & Co., 1947).

Pickus, Noah, *True Faith and Allegiance: Immigration and American Civic Nationalism* (Princeton: Princeton University Press, 2005).

Research in International Law of the Harvard Law School, 'The Law of Nationality,' *American Journal of International Law 23* (Special Supplement 1929): pp. 13–79.

Roosevelt, Theodore, *Fear God and Take Your Own Part* (New York: George H. Doran, 1916).

Schlenker, Andrea, 'Divided Loyalty? Identification and Political Participation of Dual Citizens in Switzerland,' *European Political Science Review 8*, no. 4 (2016): pp. 517–546, doi: 10.1017/S1755773915000168.

Scott, James Brown, *Observations on Nationality* (Oxford: Oxford University Press, 1931).

Sejersen, Tanja Brøndsted, '"I Vow to Thee My Countries"—The Expansion of Dual Citizenship in the 21st Century,' *International Migration Review 42* (2008): pp. 523–549.

Shachar, Ayelet, *The Birthright Lottery: Citizenship and Global Inequality* (Cambridge: Harvard University Press, 2009).

Sim, David, *A Union Forever: The Irish Question and U.S. Foreign Policy in the Victorian Age* (Ithaca: Cornell University Press, 2013).

Spiro, Peter J., 'A New International Law of Citizenship,' *American Journal of International Law 105* (2011): pp. 694–746.

Spiro, Peter J., 'Expatriating Terrorists,' *Fordham Law Review 82* (2014): pp. 2169–2187.

Spiro, Peter J., *At Home in Two Countries: The Past and Future of Dual Citizenship* (New York: NYU Press, 2016).

van Oers, Ricky, Betty de Hart, and Kees Groenendijk, 'Country Report: The Netherlands' (Florence: European University Institute, EUDO Citizenship Observatory, January 2013).

Vermeer-Künzli, Annemarieke, 'Diplomatic Protection as a Source of Human Rights Law,' in Dinah Shelton, ed., *The Oxford Handbook of International Human Rights Law* (Oxford: Oxford University Press, 2013), pp. 250–274.

Vink, Maarten Peter, Tijana Prokic-Breuer, and Jaap Dronkers, 'Immigrant Naturalization in the Context of Institutional Diversity: Policy Matters, But to Whom?,' *International Migration 51* (2013): pp. 1–20.

Vonk, Olivier, *Dual Nationality in the European Union: A Study on Changing Norms in Public and Private International Law and in the Municipal Laws of Four EU Member States* (Leiden: Martinus Nijhoff, 2012).

Weil, Patrick, *The Sovereign Citizen: Denaturalization and the Origins of the American Republic* (Philadelphia: University of Pennsylvania Press, 2012).

Weil, Patrick and Randall Hansen, eds., *Dual Nationality, Social Rights and Federal Citizenship in the U.S. and Europe: The Reinvention of Citizenship* (Oxford: Berghahn Books, 2002).

Weis, Paul, *Nationality and Statelessness in International Law*, 2nd edition (Dordrecht: Kluwer, 1979).

Yan, Ting, 'Time to Allow Overseas Chinese Dual Nationality to Encourage Return of Talent, Delegate Proposes,' *South China Morning Post*, March 11, 2016, online http://www.scmp.com/news/china/policies-politics/article/1923508/time-allow-overseas-chinese-duel-nationality-encourage.

Zolberg, Aristide, 'The Exit Revolution,' in Nancy L. Green and Francois Weil, eds., *Citizenship and Those Who Leave* (Urbana-Champaign: University of Illinois Press, 2007), pp. 33–62.

CHAPTER 29

MULTILEVEL CITIZENSHIP

WILLEM MAAS

INTRODUCTION

CITIZENSHIP is today usually conceived as a unitary and exclusive relationship between an individual and a sovereign state, represented by agents of that state's government; thus one can be a citizen of Canada or Brazil, but not of a company or a religious or private organization.[1] Nor is 'citizenship' often used to describe an individual's relationship with a city, region, or sub- or suprastate entity. This reflects the assertion by states of a monopoly on determining the status of individuals under international law, represented in concrete form through the issuing of passports and

[1] Willem Maas, 'Citizenship', in *The Encyclopedia of Political Science* (Washington: CQ Press, 2011), pp. 226–230.

their recognition by other states.[2] The universalizing logic of state sovereignty was recognized with the Peace of Westphalia and, certainly from the French Revolution onwards, the doctrine of nationalism undergirded state efforts to create and reinforce a homogeneous national citizenry premised on the ideal of equality between citizens—though the category 'citizen' for a long time excluded all women and most men. The dominant view of the growth of citizenship accompanying the rise of sovereign states since Westphalia sanitizes a complex history and ignores important developments both 'above' and 'below' the state. For example, the rise of European Union citizenship inspires other regional integration efforts to develop common rights as a form of supranational 'citizenship' while many states, particularly federal ones, face growing demands for special regional or group-based statuses.[3] Similarly, cities sometimes reassert what citizenship meant until current forms of statehood crowded out alternatives: a member of a city entitled to the privileges and rights of that city.[4] If only sovereign states can confer citizenship, then cities, provinces, nations (to the extent they do not coincide with a state), or supranational entities like the European Union cannot do so.[5] But this view of citizenship obscures historical and emerging forms of multilevel citizenship that span the world. This chapter argues that multilevel and federal citizenship are more prevalent than unitary citizenship, explores how multilevel citizenship operates in federal states, then discusses emerging supranational and municipal citizenships before concluding with future directions.

CONCEPTUALIZING MULTILEVEL CITIZENSHIP

The most common form of multilevel citizenship is federal citizenship, but federalism is a subset of the general phenomenon of divided and overlapping sovereignties.

---

[2] In this vein the *1930 Hague Convention* declares that 'it is in the general interest of the international community to secure that all its members should recognise that every person should have a nationality and should have one nationality only', specifying that it 'is for each State to determine under its own law who are its nationals' (*Convention on Certain Questions Relating to the Conflict of Nationality Laws*, the Hague, 12 April 1930, preamble and Article 1).

[3] Willem Maas, 'Varieties of Multilevel Citizenship', in Willem Maas, ed., *Multilevel Citizenship* (Philadelphia: University of Pennsylvania Press, 2013), pp. 1–21; Diego Acosta Arcarazo and Andrew Geddes, 'Transnational Diffusion or Different Models? Regional Approaches to Migration Governance in the European Union and Mercosur', *European Journal of Migration and Law* 16, no. 1 (2014): pp. 19–44; Willem Maas, 'Trade, Regional Integration, and Free Movement of People', in Joaquín Roy, ed., *A New Atlantic Community: The European Union, the US and Latin America* (Miami: European Union Center of Excellence/Jean Monnet Chair, University of Miami, 2015), pp. 111–121.

[4] The word 'citizenship' comes from the French cité and the Latin cīvitās, the community of citizens cited in Maas, 'Varieties of Multilevel Citizenship' (n 3), p. 1.

[5] Ibid., p. 1.

We can think of multilevel citizenship as premised on the coexistence of distinct polities on the same territory. In this way multilevel citizenship differs from simple administrative decentralization, which creates different territorial units without a corresponding differentiation of citizenship. Administrative decentralization of public services does not usually create a corresponding sense of peoplehood, even if such decentralization results in differences in welfare provision (such as differences in educational facilities, health care, or emergency services). But a substate unit with its own legislature, or a city with an elected mayor and council, could foster local loyalties. So could supranational entities such as the European Union, where we can speak of a shared citizenship even absent a sense of common peoplehood as strong as that of many nation-states.[6] Regions play an increasing role in the public policy process, even in traditionally unitary states such as France, and the growth of multilevel governance places in question the nation-state as the citizen's primary reference point.[7]

In terms of governance beyond the state, multilevel citizenship can be distinguished from regional human rights regimes, such as the Council of Europe, or international governance or trade regimes, such as NAFTA or the WTO. Such regimes lack both a polity or sense of peoplehood and a means of involving individual citizens in decision-making, which are the necessary and sufficient conditions for multilevel citizenship.[8] Citizen involvement can either be direct, such as through referendum or local citizen assemblies, or indirect through representatives

[6] Seyla Benhabib, *The Rights of Others: Aliens, Residents, and Citizens* (Cambridge: Cambridge University Press, 2004), especially chapter 4; Rogers M. Smith, *Political Peoplehood: The Roles of Values, Interests, and Identities* (Chicago: University of Chicago Press, 2015). The idea that a common European sense of peoplehood is marginal may need reconsideration: in a recent Eurobarometer survey, 51 per cent of respondents define themselves as 'nationality and European', while 6 per cent define themselves as 'European and nationality' (placing more emphasis on their European citizenship) and 2 per cent define themselves as 'European only'—only 39 per cent of respondents define themselves as 'nationality only', a proportion that is declining: 53 per cent of respondents born before 1946 define themselves as 'nationality only', but only 33 per cent of those born after 1980. Standard Eurobarometer 85 (spring 2016), European Citizenship.

[7] Romain Pasquier, 'Regional Citizenship and Scales of Governance in France', in Daniel Wincott, Charlie Jeffery, and Ailsa Henderson, eds., *Citizenship after the Nation State: Regionalism, Nationalism and Public Attitudes in Europe* (Basingstoke: Palgrave Macmillan, 2014). As one recent research project comparing eighty-one countries concludes, traditionally unitary countries may, like federal ones, have multiple levels of governance, directly elected regional assemblies, and regional governments that collect taxes, issue debt, and have extensive policy responsibilities with a high degree of autonomy from the central government (Liesbet Hooghe and Gary Marks, *Community, Scale, and Regional Governance* (Oxford: Oxford University Press, 2016), p. 153).

[8] For an argument that corporations are becoming 'citizens' in an emerging international economic regime, a growing body of trade-related entitlements in which businesses both claim rights and participate in building institutions of economic governance, see Turkuler Isiksel, 'Citizens of a New Agora: Postnational Citizenship and International Economic Institutions', in Willem Maas, ed., *Multilevel Citizenship* (Philadelphia: University of Pennsylvania Press, 2013), pp. 184–202. Here I limit consideration to natural persons—though see Donaldson and Kymlicka in this volume for another extension of citizenship beyond humans.

elected by citizens, such as members of a local, regional, or national legislature, or supranational parliament. In this conceptualization, multilevel citizenship must be democratic—that is, forms of governance in which those being governed do not also play some role in governing are better understood as subjecthood rather than citizenship.

Citizenship-based equality applies only among those who share the same citizenship status. All EU citizens are equal with regard to the rights of EU citizenship, but not necessarily with regard to rights that are within the domain of national citizenship—despite the EU rules against nationality-based discrimination. Similarly, equality of national citizenship may nevertheless permit inequality of rights in substate polities. Multilevel citizenship therefore entails a space for legitimate inequality of some citizenship rights. However, inequality can come to conflict with a general ideal of equal citizenship in at least two situations: through free internal movement with extensive mobility, or through strong asymmetry in the relation of constituent polities to the overarching state. The resulting inequalities in the multilevel bundles of rights that citizens enjoy in different parts of the polity may be regarded either as an unavoidable price of federation, or as a positive aspect allowing for federal experimentation.[9] But such inequalities become unavoidably more conflictual with higher levels of constitutionalized asymmetry and internal mobility.

With the exception of the mid-twentieth century—when alternative levels had largely been subsumed or were not considered relevant for citizenship—multilevel citizenship is the historical norm rather than an exception to unitary state citizenship. The origins of unitary state citizenship can be traced back to Westphalia, but in fact local citizenships dominated in most countries until relatively recently. In the United States, common citizenship supplanted earlier forms of plural rather than singular citizenship only after the Civil War and the Fourteenth Amendment (1868), and state-level entitlements remain important today. German and Italian citizenship simply did not exist before the unifications of Germany and Italy in 1871. Meanwhile, in Latin America, independence and state-building processes occupied most of the nineteenth century and it would be anachronistic to speak of homogeneous citizenships. The Austro-Hungarian, Ottoman, and Russian empires all featured forms of local status and rights that differed depending on territorial location or social membership. European colonial empires were characterized by forms of subjecthood in the colonies that were generally inferior to those in the metropole. Only since World War I and supported by the principle of national self-determination did unitary nation-states spread around the world; most of the world's states are less than one hundred years old and many are considerably newer.

---

[9] As argued by James Madison in Federalist 10 (in *The Federalist: A Collection of Essays, Written in Favour of the New Constitution, as Agreed upon by the Federal Convention, September 17, 1787*, 2 volumes (New York: J. and A. McLean, 1788)).

Furthermore, three of the world's most populous democracies (India, the United States, and Brazil) are formal federations, while virtually all other states also contain deviations from the ideal of equal citizenship.

One example of such deviations are barriers to freedom of movement or residence, which can impede equal citizenship even in nominally unitary states. China's *hukou* household registration system, for example, was designed explicitly to hinder internal migration and is only now slowly being reformed by allowing rural residents to purchase 'temporary urban residency permits'.[10] The relaxation of internal barriers is far from complete, however, as many provinces or municipalities provide residence permits only for migrants from the specific jurisdiction, thereby excluding millions of potential and actual migrants of equal access to public resources—meaning that the world's largest group of 'unauthorized migrants' are citizens of China moving between jurisdictions within China.[11] A related example of such 'internal passports' that prohibit or inhibit internal migration is the *propiska* system that severely restricted free movement in the former Soviet Union. It was cancelled in 1993, coupled with a constitutional guarantee that everyone lawfully on the Russian territory enjoys freedom of movement and residence.[12] Yet barriers to internal free movement continue to exist, most notably in the forty-three cities known as Closed Administrative Territorial Formations, home to well over one million people.[13] Meanwhile, a study of disparate approaches to migration by four Russian regions reveals that regional authorities have an unusual level of power over migration, creating a patchwork of citizenship and migration policies and devaluing national citizenship.[14]

The patchwork of citizenships that operate in most countries is based on jurisdictional borders between different territorial units. But jurisdiction may instead follow personal rather than territorial lines, with authority based on personal characteristics or social divisions rather than physical borders. This type of organizing

---

[10]   Ling Wu, 'Decentralization and Hukou Reforms in China', *Policy and Society* 32, no. 1 (2013): pp. 33–42 (arguing that recent decentralization policies in China do make local governments more powerful and responsible for providing social welfare to their local citizens but have also undermined the incentives for local governments to provide welfare to migrant workers. Thus decentralization has hindered integrating the large number of migrant workers into local cities and promoting equity within national social welfare delivery).

[11]   Willem Maas, 'Free Movement and Discrimination: Evidence from Europe, the United States, and Canada', *European Journal of Migration and Law* 15, no. 1 (2013): pp. 91–110, pp. 93–94.

[12]   *Law on the Right of Russian Citizens to Freedom of Movement, the Choice of a Place of Stay and Residence within the Russian Federation* (1993, amended 2004). The constitutional guarantee is article 27.1, cited in Maas (n 11), p. 94.

[13]   Roemer Lemaître, 'How Closed Cities Violate the Freedom of Movement and other International Human Rights Obligations of the Russian Federation', Leuven Institute for International Law Working Paper 77 (June 2005), online http://www.law.kuleuven.be/iir/nl/onderzoek/wp/WP77e.pdf (cited in Maas (n 11), p. 94).

[14]   Matthew A. Light, *Fragile Migration Rights: Freedom of Movement in Post-Soviet Russia* (New York: Routledge, 2016).

logic predates the idea of equal citizenship and prevailed in the Middle Ages—where society was divided into different estates, each with different laws and membership rules—as well as the millet system in the Ottoman empire, in which members of different religious communities were governed under their own laws with their own courts and own taxes.[15] Such an alternative logic is reflected in the idea of non-territorial citizenships,[16] an idea which has lost prominence with the rise of nation-states as the basis for political authority and the strengthening of the normative ideal of equal citizenship. As 'the idea of the nation-state achieved its hegemony as a territorial, all-purpose political organization, it affected aspects of citizens' identity. Out of the myriad ways in which each person can be characterized, one's territorial location in a nation has come to assume overwhelming importance.'[17]

A territorial logic usually undergirds the notion of levels of citizenship—from local to regional to national to supranational[18]—although non-territorial citizenship is another possible response to pluralism and could also be considered under multi-level citizenship. No non-territorial group has ever achieved sovereignty—exclusive control over territory is considered a requirement for sovereignty, though Walker (in this volume) documents the partial unravelling of that requirement—but some models of differentiated citizenship distinguish between territorial state citizenship and non-territorial national or cultural citizenship.[19] Such non-territorial citizenships persist in some states through contemporary versions of the millet system in which personal status depends on one's registration within a religious community: in Israel, even staunch atheists are registered as Jewish, or else as Muslim or member of an officially recognized Christian sect, if they 'belong' to that religion. And in Egypt the operation of family law similarly depends on society's compartmentalization into Muslim, Christian, or Jewish communities—which can give rise to complex jurisdictional questions whenever events involve individuals subject to different laws.[20] Categorization by authorities, particularly the registration of

---

[15] Maas, 'Varieties of Multilevel Citizenship' (n 3), pp. 9–10.

[16] Non-territorial citizenship must be distinguished from extraterritorial citizenship enjoyed by individuals residing outside a territory in relation to the authorities governing that territory. While the former conception has largely faded away, the latter has gained in strength in the context of international migration since World War II. See Collyer in this volume.

[17] David J. Elkins, *Beyond Sovereignty: Territory and Political Economy in the Twenty-First Century* (Toronto: University of Toronto Press, 1995), p. 29.

[18] Rainer Bauböck, 'The Three Levels of Citizenship within the European Union', *German Law Journal 15*, no. 5 (2014): pp. 751–763.

[19] This was true of Otto Bauer's and Karl Renner's models. See Rainer Bauböck, 'Political Autonomy or Cultural Minority Rights? A Conceptual Critique of Renner's Model', in Ephraim Nimni, ed., *National Cultural Autonomy and Its Contemporary Critics* (New York: Routledge, 2005), pp. 97–110.

[20] Will Hanley, 'When Did Egyptians Stop Being Ottomans? An Imperial Citizenship Case Study', in Willem Maas, ed., *Multilevel Citizenship* (Philadelphia: University of Pennsylvania Press, 2013), pp. 89–109.

minority and indigenous groups, determines the demographic presentation of the population.[21]

Special non-territorial citizenship statuses may also be appropriate for indigenous or Aboriginal peoples, 'nations' often dispersed territorially or too small for statehood. For example, Canada's 1966 Hawthorn Report concluded that 'in addition to the normal rights and duties of citizenship, Indians possess certain additional rights as charter members of the Canadian community'. This leads to an asymmetrical citizenship in which Aboriginal (or First Nations) individuals are 'a bit more equal than other Canadians', what Alan Cairns (echoing the Report) terms 'Citizens plus'.[22] The idea that some individuals can be 'a bit more equal' than others, becoming 'Citizens plus' with additional rights, can seem jarring to views of citizenship as premised on equal status. But historically it was not unusual to have 'multiple categories and forms of citizenship within the jurisdiction of the same state, such as the "active" and "passive" citizens the French revolutionary regime distinguished until 1792 or the intricate hierarchy of citizenships the Venetian state established during its years of imperial glory'.[23] Although not based on territorial jurisdictions and thus not fitting neatly into a traditional federal framework, such examples demonstrate how differentiated citizenship can operate in situations of divided and overlapping sovereignties.[24] Relaxing the assumption of exclusive, universal, and equal citizenship recovers older forms in which citizenship emphasized duties rather than rights, and taxation or exemption from taxation determined membership.[25]

The insight that citizenship is premised on jurisdiction, and that territory is often simply a convenient determinant of jurisdiction, rather than its sole possible source (as shown by the example of non-territorial jurisdiction) is gaining recognition in studies of federalism. Although federalism is often analyzed in terms of shared power over territory, it more accurately represents 'a division of authority over people. Unions of states which are federal are precisely more than just that: they are also unions of people.'[26] Such a political system is not only a union of states,

[21] Shourideh Molavi, 'The Israeli Logic of Exclusion' (PhD dissertation, York University, expected 2017) (on file with author).
[22] Philip Resnick and Gerald P. Kernerman, eds., *Insiders and Outsiders: Alan Cairns and the Reshaping of Canadian Citizenship* (Vancouver: UBC Press, 2005); Alan Cairns, *Citizenship, Diversity, and Pluralism: Canadian and Comparative Perspectives* (Montreal: McGill-Queen's University Press, 1999); Alan Cairns, *Citizens Plus: Aboriginal Peoples and the Canadian State* (Vancouver: University of British Columbia Press, 2000).
[23] Charles Tilly, 'Citizenship, Identity and Social History', *International Review of Social History 40*, no. 3 (1995): pp. 1–17, p. 8.
[24] Elizabeth Dale, 'The *Su Bao* Case and the Layers of Everyday Citizenship in China, 1894–1904', in Willem Maas, ed., *Multilevel Citizenship* (Philadelphia: University of Pennsylvania Press, 2013), pp. 110–126.
[25] Hanley (n 20).
[26] Gary T. Miller, 'Citizenship and European Union: A Federalist Approach', in C. Lloyd Brown-John, ed., *Federal-Type Solutions and European Integration* (Lanham: University Press of America, 1995), pp. 461–499, p. 471.

in which citizens 'remain unaffected and divided into discrete units', but indeed unites people across state borders through common institutions operating directly upon the citizens without intermediation; citizens thus have 'two sets of meaningful relationships with two centres of authority or levels of government—in effect, two citizenships'.[27] This means that any federal system contains a kind of dual citizenship, which in Europe flows from the member-states both 'upward' to the EU and 'downward' to regions and cities.[28] Multilevel citizenship in Europe is thus no longer dual, but multiple: local, regional, state, and supranational.

LITERATURES RELEVANT
FOR MULTILEVEL CITIZENSHIP

The literature on equality is relevant for multilevel citizenship, because within any state in which subjurisdictions provide social welfare, some citizens are more equal than others.[29] States attempt to minimize variation and guarantee equal citizenship through portability of welfare entitlements, prohibition of exclusionist residence requirements, mutual recognition of credentials, and other measures that facilitate mobility within the state.[30] Within the supranational European Union, the European Commission adopts similar strategies, working to remove barriers to free movement by making borders lose their significance, in an attempt to foster common EU citizenship.[31]

Variation tends to be most pronounced in states where subjurisdictions have greater authority, notably federal states. Thus the literature on federal citizenship is also relevant for general considerations of multilevel citizenship. Since the 1990s, scholars distinguish mononational from plurinational federal states, asking whether federalism allows for accommodation of plurinationalism and thus helps to preserve territorial cohesion or deepens territorial divisions and facilitates state breakup.[32] Political systems riven by territorial and linguistic divisions can

---

[27] Ibid., p. 470.

[28] Christophe Schönberger, 'European Citizenship as Federal Citizenship: Some Citizenship Lessons of Comparative Federalism', *European Review of Public Law 19*, no. 1 (2007): pp. 61–82.

[29] Willem Maas, 'Equality and the Free Movement of People: Citizenship and Internal Migration', in Willem Maas, ed., *Democratic Citizenship and the Free Movement of People* (Leiden: Martinus Nijhoff, 2013), pp. 9–30.

[30] Ibid.

[31] Willem Maas, 'The Genesis of European Rights', *Journal of Common Market Studies 43*, no. 5 (2005): pp. 1009–1025; Willem Maas, *Creating European Citizens* (Lanham: Rowman & Littlefield, 2007).

[32] Michael Keating, *Plurinational Democracy: Stateless Nations in a Post-Sovereignty Era* (Oxford: Oxford University Press, 2001); Michael Keating, 'Social Citizenship, Solidarity and

nevertheless remain stable political communities.[33] Other literature examines ways in which states work to accommodate distinct ethnic and cultural groups while maintaining national political unity, a project that can fit within traditional federalism or plurinationalism, which has been mostly understood as specific form of (or condition for) federalism.[34]

Plurinationalism refers to the existence of two or more distinct national groups within a political community, whether a state or a supranational polity like the European Union. A large and growing body of literature considers cases of plurinationalism in Western political systems such as Canada, the United Kingdom, Spain, Belgium, Switzerland, and the European Union, all of which are federal in nature, but plurinationalism has also been recognized elsewhere in unitary states, particularly in Latin America.[35] For example, in 2008 Ecuador changed its constitution, with president Rafael Correa arguing that '"Plurinationalism" means admitting that several different nationalities coexist within the larger Ecuadorean state', and that recognizing the different peoples, cultures and worldviews within the country should impact all public policies, such as education, health, and housing.[36] Bolivia went a step further and in 2009 changed its name to the Plurinational State of Bolivia, which fits with a general rise in Indigenous political activism.[37]

Outside Latin America and New Zealand, where the special status of indigenous groups shapes the kind of unique citizenship statuses available, plurinationalism can be seen both as a driver and a possible consequence of asymmetric multilevel citizenship. There is also a growing literature on territorial governance and rescaling,

Welfare in Regionalized and Plurinational States', *Citizenship Studies* 13, no. 5 (2009): pp. 501–513; Ferran Requejo Coll and Miquel Caminal i Badia, eds., *Federalism, Plurinationality and Democratic Constitutionalism: Theory and Cases* (New York: Routledge, 2012); Will Kymlicka, *Politics in the Vernacular: Nationalism, Multiculturalism, and Citizenship* (New York: Oxford University Press, 2001); Alain-G. Gagnon and James Tully, *Multinational Democracies* (Cambridge: Cambridge University Press, 2001); Jaime Lluch, *Visions of Sovereignty: Nationalism and Accommodation in Multinational Democracies* (Philadelphia: University of Pennsylvania Press, 2014).

[33] Joseph Lacey, 'Centripetal Democracy: Democratic Legitimacy and Regional Integration in Belgium, Switzerland and the EU' (PhD dissertation, European University Institute, 2015) (on file with author).

[34] Alfred Stepan, Juan J. Linz, and Yogendra Yadav, *Crafting State-Nations: India and Other Multinational Democracies* (Baltimore: Johns Hopkins University Press, 2010).

[35] Marc Becker, 'Building a Plurinational Ecuador: Complications and Contradictions', *Socialism and Democracy* 26, no. 3 (2012): pp. 72–92; Jason Tockman and John Cameron, 'Indigenous Autonomy and the Contradictions of Plurinationalism in Bolivia', *Latin American Politics and Society* 56, no. 3 (2014): pp. 46–69.

[36] Kintto Lucas, 'Ecuador: New Constitution Addresses Demand for "Plurinational" State', *Inter Press Service*, 5 May 2008, online http://www.ipsnews.net/2008/05/ecuador-new-constitution-addresses-demand-for-lsquoplurinationalrsquo-state/.

[37] Deborah J. Yashar, *Contesting Citizenship in Latin America: The Rise of Indigenous Movements and the Postliberal Challenge* (Cambridge: Cambridge University Press, 2005); Sheryl Lightfoot, 'The International Indigenous Rights Discourse and Its Demands for Multilevel Citizenship', in Willem Maas, ed., *Multilevel Citizenship* (Philadelphia: University of Pennsylvania Press, 2013), pp. 127–146.

which is relevant for multilevel citizenship because it investigates alternative sources of political authority to the state.[38] Finally, there is a more recent literature on comparative supranational regionalism,[39] and emerging forms of supranational rights regimes that invoke the language of citizenship (discussed below).

FEDERAL CITIZENSHIP

Virtually every state in the world has internal jurisdictional boundaries, but these are most important in federal states, in which the substate jurisdictions usually have significant authority in a range of fields important to individual citizens.[40] This means that federal citizenship is the most common form of multilevel citizenship today, even though the concept of citizenship is often not employed in analyses of substate policies and programs that affect citizens in differential ways.[41] The most common distinction within the literature on federal systems is between federations and confederations. However, in spite of the wide variety of ways in which today's states came into existence and developed there is probably no true confederation in the world today. The distinction between the federal and the confederal model of political organization is identified by Proudhon: In a federal state 'each citizen is subject to a dual jurisdiction—of "Centre" and of "Province"—whereas the central organs of a confederal arrangement do not have direct jurisdiction over the citizens of constituent states'.[42] Since Switzerland has become increasingly centralized, while states such as Belgium and Canada remain insufficiently decentralized to be considered confederations—because their central authorities do have direct jurisdiction over the citizens of the constituent jurisdictions—there is no example of confederal citizenship today, with the possible exception of Bosnia and Herzegovina, whose

---

[38] Michael Keating, *Rescaling the European State: The Making of Territory and the Rise of the Meso* (Oxford: Oxford University Press, 2013).

[39] Thomas Risse and Tanja A. Börzel, *The Oxford Handbook of Comparative Regionalism* (Oxford: Oxford University Press, 2016); Carlos Closa and Daniela Vintilla, 'Supranational Citizenship: Rights in Regional Integration Organizations', paper presented at European University Institute, 14 May 2015 (on file with author).

[40] Maas (n 29).

[41] In this light, see Lorenzo Piccoli, 'Regional Spheres of Citizenship? The Territorial Politics of Rights in Italy, Spain, and Switzerland', PhD dissertation, European University Institute, forthcoming, who demonstrates significant variation within Italy, usually considered a unitary state. This fits the observation that, in a democracy, when authority is conveyed to regional institutions, citizens should have some say. Hooghe and Marks (n 7), p. 161.

[42] P. J. Proudhon, *The Principle of Federation*, translated by Richard Vernon (Toronto: University of Toronto Press, 1979), p. xxiii.

'complex citizenship regime, created in response to stability challenges and freezing existing patterns of political interaction, weakens central state institutions and fails to protect basic human and political rights'.[43] By contrast, federal citizenship is quite common.

In the United States, the relationship between federal and state citizenship has long animated legal discussion. The US Articles of Confederation (1776) had established a severely underdeveloped central government, without a mechanism for enforcing its laws or collecting taxes, and dependent on voluntary compliance by the states. The US Constitution (1787, entry into force 1789) created a system of shared sovereignty between the federal government and the states, with the central government's powers limited to those enumerated in the Constitution and the states remaining sovereign in all other areas. Over time, the authority of the central government grew primarily through expansive interpretations of the interstate commerce clause and the Fourteenth Amendment (1868), which provides that 'All persons born or naturalized in the United States, and subject to the jurisdiction thereof, are citizens of the United States and of the state wherein they reside.' This was a direct rebuke of the *Dred Scott* decision (1857) which had helped spark the US Civil War by ruling that African Americans were not citizens of the United States, even if they were citizens at state level.[44] After the Civil War, the Fourteenth Amendment guaranteed individual rights in all states—particularly those states in which slavery had just been abolished; it 'was designed to make national citizenship paramount to state citizenship, to confer national citizenship upon the newly freed slaves, and to secure for the former slaves the equal enjoyment of certain civil rights'.[45]

But the move to equal citizenship encountered resistance. Responding to the Fourteenth Amendment, the *Slaughter-House Cases* (1873) established that 'there is a citizenship of the United States, and a citizenship of a State, which are distinct from each other, and which depend upon different characteristics or circumstances in the individual.'[46] This, along with the *Civil Rights Cases* (1883), limited the Amendment's impact, and as the federal government abdicated its responsibility to protect rights in the latter part of the nineteenth century, power reverted to the states.[47] As a result,

---

[43] Eldar Sarajlic, 'Multilevel Citizenship and the Contested Statehood of Bosnia and Herzegovina', in Willem Maas, ed., *Multilevel Citizenship* (Philadelphia: University of Pennsylvania Press, 2013), pp. 168–183, p. 182. The Dayton peace agreement created two constituent entities, the Republic of Srpska for Serbs and the Federation of Bosnia and Herzegovina for Bosniaks and Croats, with the federal government determined by ethnic proportionality, meaning that equal citizenship is impossible in practice.

[44] *Dred Scott v. Sandford*, 60 US 393 (1857).

[45] Earl Warren, 'Fourteenth Amendment: Retrospect and Prospect', in Bernard Schwartz, ed., *The Fourteenth Amendment* (New York: New York University Press, 1970), pp. 212–233, p. 216.

[46] 83 U.S. 36 (1873), paragraph 74.

[47] Bernard Schwartz, 'The Amendment in Operation: A Historical Overview', in Bernard Schwartz, ed., *The Fourteenth Amendment* (New York: New York University Press, 1970), pp. 29–38; Warren

individual states effectively 'retained the power to define most aspects of citizenship without interference from the national government', with racial policy, in particular, continuing to be determined by the states rather than the federal government.[48] With the New Deal, most social and labour policies except for veterans' pensions continued to be enacted and implemented at the state or local level, and eligibility was conditional on gender, race, and other norms, resulting in a 'semi-feudal' rather than rights-oriented welfare state, in which federalism permitted local differences to thrive.[49] Unemployment Insurance (UI, mostly used by men) short-circuited layers of federalism while Aid to Families with Dependent Children (AFDC, mostly used by women) granted a high degree of discretionary power to state and local officials, with eligibility determined by procedures that differed from jurisdiction to jurisdiction. Even UI eligibility differed from state to state; in 1971, for example, twenty-three states still disqualified women from collecting UI if they left work for reasons of pregnancy, childbirth, or other familial responsibilities. Over time, UI and AFDC 'evolved in a manner that separated non-elderly men and women as if they were citizens of distinct sovereignties, national versus state, wherein they experienced very different forms of governance'.[50] Although these programmes were centralized by the mid-1970s, the Personal Responsibility and Work Opportunity Reconciliation Act (1996) once again returned great authority to the states,[51] resulting in a return to divided citizenship. Federalism often continues to perpetuate illiberal and undemocratic racial, ethnic, and gender hierarchies.[52]

That the coexistence of two levels of citizenship can result in competition between the two levels need not be viewed negatively. Thus US Supreme Court Justice William J. Brennan issued in 1977 what he termed 'a clear call to state courts to step into the breach' left by what he felt was the Supreme Court's lacklustre and diminished rights protection; judicial federalism would thus provide a 'double source of protection for the rights of our citizens'.[53] He argued that 'state courts no less than federal are and ought to be the guardians of our liberties', and that 'state courts cannot rest when they have afforded their citizens the full protections of the

(n 45); Raoul Berger, *The Fourteenth Amendment and the Bill of Rights* (Norman: University of Oklahoma Press, 1989).

[48] Suzanne Mettler, 'Social Citizens of Separate Sovereignties: Governance in the New Deal Welfare State', in Sidney M. Milkis and Jerome M. Mileur, eds., *The New Deal and the Triumph of Liberalism* (Amherst: University of Massachusetts Press, 2002), pp. 231–271, p. 231.

[49] Ibid., pp. 233–237.

[50] Suzanne Mettler, 'Dividing Social Citizenship by Gender: The Implementation of Unemployment Insurance and Aid to Dependent Children, 1935-1950', *Studies in American Political Development* 12 (1998): pp. 303–342, p. 340.

[51] Ibid.

[52] Rogers M. Smith, *Civic Ideals: Conflicting Visions of Citizenship in U.S. History* (New Haven: Yale University Press, 1997).

[53] William J. Brennan Jr., 'State Constitutions and the Protection of Individual Rights', *Harvard Law Review 90*, no. 3 (1977): pp. 489–504, p. 503.

federal Constitution. State constitutions, too, are a font of individual liberties, their protections often extending beyond those required by the Supreme Court's interpretation of federal law'.[54] The aim was to reinvigorate a federalism animated by the fundamental promises of the Fourteenth Amendment—'that the citizens of all our states are also and no less citizens of our United States'.[55] Recent legal scholarship is returning to the idea of US citizenship as possessing a dual nature: the US founders arguably 'envisioned Americans with dual loyalties to their states and to the nation', with these dual loyalties serving as essential element of the system of checks and balances.[56]

The constituent units in a federation tend to operate slightly differently from the regional administrative units in a unitary state, where regional governments more likely conform to a single model, that of an administrative arm of the central government. Civil servants are interchangeable and local political identities weak or non-existent. Furthermore, unitary states are characterized by the absence or relative paucity of legal distinctions in the rights and responsibilities of citizens, reflecting a continuum from centralized unitary states to decentralized federations; in a unitary state, the relationships between the central government and those of the regional administrative units tend to exhibit lower levels of competition and differentiation than in federations. The citizens of a 'federation have a dual relationship, as citizens of both the federation and a member State. Within their respective areas of competence, both the federation and the member States create rights and obligations for such individuals'.[57] A comparative study of federations found that all forbid unreasonable discrimination between citizens of the constituent states, guarantee freedom of movement and residence throughout the federation, and do not allow individuals to possess state citizenship without also possessing federal citizenship.[58]

A subset of federal citizenship is that of federacies, which consists of a special relationship between a dominant unit and one or more smaller or distant units.[59] Examples include the Åland islands for Finland, the Faeroe islands and Greenland for Denmark, the Netherlands Antilles for the Netherlands, or Puerto Rico for the United States. Federacies often result from colonial legacies or special forms of plurinationalism where minorities are concentrated in offshore territories, and are

---

[54] Ibid., p. 491.

[55] Ibid., p. 490.

[56] Ernest A. Young, 'The Volk of New Jersey? State Identity, Distinctiveness, and Political Culture in the American Federal System', Duke Law Working Paper (2015), p. 7, online http://scholarship.law. duke.edu/faculty_scholarship/3431/. Young refers here to Alexander Hamilton in Federalist 28 (in *The Federalist: A Collection of Essays, Written in Favour of the New Constitution, as Agreed upon by the Federal Convention, September 17, 1787*, 2 volumes (New York: J. and A. McLean, 1788).

[57] William J. Schrenk, 'Citizenship and Immigration', in Robert R. Bowie and Carl J. Friedrich, eds., *Studies in Federalism* (Boston: Little, Brown, 1954), pp. 635–675, p. 635.

[58] Ibid., p. 644.

[59] The old term 'federacy' was reintroduced with this specific meaning by Daniel J. Elazar, *Exploring Federalism* (Tuscaloosa: University of Alabama Press, 1987).

by definition asymmetric whereas plurinational federations may be symmetric as a matter of constitutional principle. Citizens who are residents of the 'lesser partner' in the federacy typically enjoy a special status or certain unique rights with respect to 'normal' citizens of the state in question. This is at least partially the case because residents of the lesser partner in federacies are often geographically and politically removed from the centre of decision-making, and they may or may not possess the same participation rights as 'normal' citizens. Similarly, citizens of the dominant unit may not enjoy full citizenship rights within the federacy. This is the case on the Åland islands, where Finnish nationals who do not enjoy regional citizenship of those islands are subject to special conditions relating to the period of residence in order to be able to exercise their right to vote and to stand as candidates in municipal elections, for example. The United States has an analogous relationship with Puerto Rico, Samoa, and other dependencies. Federacies certainly deviate from the idea of equal citizenship more profoundly than other federal arrangements in which citizenships are horizontally differentiated and unequal but bound together by a single and equal federal citizenship. In federacies, by contrast, horizontal inequality is compounded by vertical inequality of citizenship across levels: not all citizens of the larger polity enjoy the same rights in relation to central state authorities.

SUPRANATIONAL CITIZENSHIP

If the levels in multilevel citizenship are usually territorial and federal citizenship represents the most common form of multilevel citizenship within states, then supranational citizenship can be viewed as a form of multilevel citizenship beyond the state, in which nation-states occupy the 'lower' level, with a common citizenship superimposed on the member states. Various forms of supranational citizenship are growing today, most notably citizenship of the European Union and the free movement and other rights attached to that status.[60] Conceived more broadly, however, the concept of supranational citizenship could include any form of supranational rights (such as the human rights that member states of the Council of Europe pledge to uphold) or regional organizations that provide special entitlements (such as preferential work visas for citizens of the United States, Canada, and Mexico within NAFTA, or similar arrangements within other regional trade organizations). Aside from the EU and the few forms of supranational citizenship discussed below,

---

[60] See Strumia in this volume.

however, such rights tend to be reciprocity-based arrangements rather than aspiring to a common citizenship.

A supranational citizenship of the European Union was discussed even before the first treaties, and supranational European rights were enshrined as early as the 1951 and 1957 treaties of Paris and Rome.[61] After years of efforts by integration-minded actors, the formal status of EU citizenship entered the treaties at Maastricht (1992), and its existence has subsequently provided a constitutional conundrum for European legal and political actors.[62] European Court of Justice judgments since 2001 have affirmed that EU citizenship is 'destined to be the fundamental status of nationals of the Member States', while the European Parliament casts it as 'a dynamic institution, a key to the process of European integration, and expected gradually to supplement and extend' national citizenship.[63] Yet member states insist that 'Citizenship of the Union shall be additional to national citizenship and shall not replace it', in the language of the Lisbon Treaty.

Supranational citizenship regimes require a level of coordination that goes well beyond that of simple trade agreements. In the EU, despite member state hesitation, functional needs driven by free movement of individuals are coupled with the growing realization that EU citizenship creates a new political sphere that is 'above' that of the member states and whose subjects, EU citizens, have rights and a status that transcends member state citizenship.[64] Desiring to increasing the role of EU institutions in citizenship questions, the European Parliament resolved in 1991 that the European 'Union may establish certain uniform conditions governing the acquisition or loss of the citizenship of the Member States', but this resolution did not make it into the Maastricht Treaty.[65] Despite the rejection of a greater EU role in determining citizenship status and the subsequent Amsterdam and Lisbon Treaties, however, coordination is necessary, as shown in the fields of electoral rights, diplomatic and consular protection, naturalization, and citizenship deprivation.[66] Although welfare provisions and social systems in Europe remain primarily national and jurisprudence safeguards the ability of member states to exclude individuals despite shared EU citizenship, political statements and legal judgments emphasize that 'the competence of Member States to enact laws concerning national citizenship has to be exercised in accordance with the Treaties' and that even member state

[61] Maas, 'The Genesis of European Rights' (n 31).

[62] Willem Maas, 'European Union Citizenship in Retrospect and Prospect', in Engin Isin and Peter Nyers, eds., *Routledge Handbook of Global Citizenship Studies* (London: Routledge, 2014), pp. 409–417; Willem Maas, 'The Origins, Evolution, and Political Objectives of EU Citizenship', *German Law Journal* 15, no. 5 (2014): pp. 797–819.

[63] Discussed in Maas, *Creating European Citizens* (n 31).

[64] Willem Maas, 'European Governance of Citizenship and Nationality', *Journal of Contemporary European Research* 12, no. 1 (2016): pp. 532–551, p. 544.

[65] European Parliament 'Resolution on Union Citizenship', 14 June 1991, discussed in ibid., p. 538.

[66] Maas (n 64).

naturalization and citizenship deprivation policies are 'amenable to judicial review carried out in the light of EU law'.[67] Member state autonomy can thus be limited by the general principles of EU law even in areas of putatively exclusive member state competence, such as decisions regarding the acquisition and loss of member state (and hence EU) citizenship.[68]

Despite its limitations, no other supranational rights regime is as advanced as that of EU citizenship. In North America, for example, the egregious misregulation of Mexican migration to the United States shows the limits of the North American Free Trade Agreement (NAFTA) free movement provisions; similarly, between 2009 and 2016, Canada required citizens of Mexico to obtain a visa not only to study or work but also simply to travel. The lack of extensive free movement provisions hampers even NAFTA's limited goals. Comparative research demonstrates that successful and stable regional integration efforts must include free movement rights for people as a priority—Karl Deutsch observed that '[f]ull-scale mobility of persons has followed every successful amalgamated security-community in modern times immediately upon its establishment' and that 'the importance of the mobility of persons suggests that in this field of politics persons may be more important than either goods or money'[69]—signalling that NAFTA may be doomed to remain forever a trade agreement rather than a truly integrated supranational community, which may correspond with the intentions of the member governments. To date, the European Union remains the only case of regional integration where free movement rights are relatively entrenched, and even EU free movement rights face opposition, as illustrated by the importance of free movement in the campaign for Brexit.

By contrast with NAFTA, emerging free movement efforts in Latin America show more promise; outside Europe, the most advanced efforts at establishing common supranational rights are occurring in Latin America. For example, the Caribbean Community treaty provides that 'Member States commit themselves to the goal of the free movement of their nationals within the Community', obviating the need for work or residence permits, and providing a common-format passport.[70] Meanwhile, the Andean Community includes an Andean Labor Migration Instrument which provides for the relative free movement of workers between member states, as well as banning discrimination based on nationality for workers from other Community member states, thus resembling the early free movement provisions of the European

---

[67] Ibid., p. 533. First quotation by the representative of the European Council at a European Parliament debate discussed in ibid., pp. 540–541; second quotation from Judgment of 2 March 2010, *Rottmann* C-135/08 EU:C:2010:104, paragraph 48, discussed in ibid., pp. 541–542.

[68] Ibid., p. 542.

[69] Karl Wolfgang Deutsch, *Political Community and the North Atlantic Area: International Organization in the Light of Historical Experience* (Princeton: Princeton University Press, 1957), pp. 53, 54.

[70] *Revised Treaty of Chaguaramas Establishing the Caribbean Community including the CARICOM Single Market and Economy*, 2001, article 45.

Community.[71] Mercosur has a Residence Agreement with similar provisions, and a Citizenship Statute, signed in 2010, which provides an action plan for full implementation of common citizenship on the thirtieth anniversary of the signing of the Treaty of Asunción (in 2021) and has three main objectives: free movement of people within the region; equal civil, social, cultural, and economic rights and freedoms for citizens of member states; and equal conditions of access to work, health, and education.[72] Meanwhile Unasur, which covers almost the entire continent of South America,[73] aims at 'the consolidation of a South American identity through the progressive recognition of the rights of nationals of a Member State resident in any of the other Member States, in order to achieve a South American citizenship'; Unasur citizenship includes creating a 'single passport' and common educational rules to give South Americans the right to live, work, and study in any Unasur country.[74] These efforts appear more rhetorical than real for the moment, but they do indicate the growth in Latin America of incipient forms of supranational citizenship.

Efforts to create forms of supranational citizenship encounter an international system which remains very much in flux. There was a flurry of declarations of independence during the last century, and many citizenships are quite new. At the same time, the tension between a theoretical world divided neatly into separate territorial containers, one for each people or nation, and a real world in which individuals and collectivities do not fit neatly into these separate containers (for example indigenous peoples, Roma, and other 'unusual' groups), means a simplistic logic is misleading.[75]

MUNICIPAL CITIZENSHIP?

As argued by Bauböck in this volume, the local is one level in multilevel citizenship that is ubiquitous in democratic states. Yet local citizenship is nowhere today

[71] Maas, 'Trade, Regional Integration, and Free Movement of People' (n 3), p. 114.

[72] Ibid., p. 115.

[73] The Union of South American Nations, usually known by its Spanish acronym Unasur (Unión de Naciones Suramericanas; Portuguese: União de Nações Sul-Americanas; Dutch: Unie van Zuid-Amerikaanse Naties), includes every country on the South American continent except for French Guiana, which is an overseas territory of France.

[74] Maas, 'Trade, Regional Integration, and Free Movement of People' (n 3), p. 116. At Unasur's December 2014 summit, Unasur general secretary Ernesto Samper emphasized that 'We have approved the concept of South American citizenship. This should be the greatest register of what has happened' (cited in ibid).

[75] Lightfoot (n 37); Jacqueline Gehring, 'Free Movement for Some: The Treatment of the Roma after the European Union's Eastern Expansion', in Willem Maas, ed., Democratic Citizenship and the Free Movement of People (Leiden: Martinus Nijhoff, 2013), pp. 143–174.

constitutive for citizenship in the larger polity and can thus be determined by different criteria: residence for local and birthright for state citizenship. By contrast, where regional polities are constitutive for the larger polity, their citizenships must be linked across levels through upwards derivation, as in the European Union and to some extent in Switzerland, or downwards derivation, as in all other contemporary federal states.

In light of policy stalemate at the federal level, many cities in the United States have been experimenting with forms of local incorporation such as municipal identity cards.[76] The proliferation of incorporation strategies at the state level creates 'a de facto regime of state citizenship, one that operates in parallel to national citizenship and, in some important ways, exceeds the standards of national citizenship' in the areas of health care, education, and access to employment opportunities.[77] Many scholars may not view sanctuary city movements for irregular migrants, municipal identity documents, and related efforts as truly creating a new level of citizenship but, as such examples demonstrate, local authorities undeniably articulate local citizenship as in conflict with regional or national citizenship by claiming powers normally reserved for 'higher' authorities.[78] By contrast, municipal citizenship is crucial in some contexts, such as that of Switzerland, where decisions about naturalization are taken at the local level.[79] Such a decentralized system ensures that regulations and laws account for regional or local specificities, as local political actors and administrative officials are close to those seeking naturalization. Yet this means differential treatment, and one might wonder about the relevant level at which foreigners become citizens: the local community, the substate region, or the nation-state.[80]

Regardless of normative concerns, cities have a long history as the primary locus of allegiance and integration into the polity. Some social scientists argue that cities are returning to their roots as the site of true governance, with mayors as key democratic leaders, and at the same time there are growing efforts at transnational cooperation by mayors of various world cities.[81] Others emphasize that cities should

---

[76] Els De Graauw, *Making Immigrant Rights Real: Nonprofits and the Politics of Integration in San Francisco* (Ithaca: Cornell University Press, 2016).

[77] Karthick Ramakrishnan and Allan Colbern, 'The California Package: Immigrant Integration and the Evolving Nature of State Citizenship', *Policy Matters* 6, no. 3 (2015): pp. 1–19, pp. 10–11.

[78] See Monica Varsanyi and Doris Marie Provine, 'Comparing Immigration Policy and Enforcement in Two Neighboring States', paper presented at the 2015 American Political Science Association Annual Conference (on file with author). For example, San Francisco recently updated its 'Due Process for All' ordinance, restricting cooperation with federal immigration law.

[79] Marc Helbling, 'Local Citizenship Politics in Switzerland: Between National Justice and Municipal Particularities', in Willem Maas, ed., *Multilevel Citizenship* (Philadelphia: University of Pennsylvania Press, 2013), pp. 149–167.

[80] Ibid., p. 165.

[81] Benjamin R. Barber, *If Mayors Ruled the World: Dysfunctional Nations, Rising Cities* (New Haven: Yale University Press, 2013).

indeed enjoy greater constitutional standing than they do, particularly because cities inspire loyalty in ways analogous to those found in processes of nation-building.[82]

FUTURE DIRECTIONS FOR MULTILEVEL AND FEDERAL CITIZENSHIP

Since federal or other forms of multilevel citizenship are the most common form of citizenship today, the relative lack of attention paid to deviations from the 'norm' is surprising. This can be expected to change in the future. Recent feminist research examines whether multilevel citizenship 'strengthens women's opportunities to experience dual citizenship or divides their energies and efforts', while other research emphasizes how women's entitlement to 'national' citizenship rights such as gender equality can compete with group rights at other levels of government.[83] Some globalization theorists, meanwhile, advocate developing political authority and administrative capacity at regional and global levels, seeing those levels as necessary supplements to the political institutions at the level of the state. Both approaches question the assumption that a homogeneous national citizenship is necessarily the best way of organizing political life, thereby interrogating the view of contemporary citizenship as a uniform political and legal status that can be bestowed only by sovereign states and must be based on political equality between citizens. The overwhelming focus of analysis on political rights, especially democratic and electoral politics, corresponds to the major concerns of citizenship theory, but deadens analysis of legal, social, civil, and other forms of citizenship.[84] A future direction of citizenship research would be to acknowledge the empirical reality of multilevel and federal citizenship and explore its implications for citizenship theory.

A key element of such work should be explorations of difference rather than equality, both in terms of policies and in terms of political identity. Discrimination

---

[82] Daniel Weinstock, 'Cities and Federalism', in James E. Fleming and Jacob T. Levy, eds., *Federalism and Subsidiarity* (New York: New York University Press, 2014), pp. 259–290; Loren King, 'Cities, Subsidiarity, and Federalism', in James E. Fleming and Jacob T. Levy, eds., *Federalism and Subsidiarity* (New York: New York University Press, 2014), pp. 290–331.

[83] Louise A. Chappell, 'Feminist Engagement with Federal Institutions: Opportunities and Constraints for Women's Multilevel Citizenship', in David H. Laycock, ed., *Representation and Democratic Theory* (Vancouver: UBC Press, 2004), pp. 65–89; Melissa Haussman, Marian Sawer, and Jill Vickers, eds., *Federalism, Feminism and Multilevel Governance* (Burlington: Ashgate, 2010). This sentence and the next two draw on Maas, 'Varieties of Multilevel Citizenship' (n 3), p. 5.

[84] Hanley (n 20), p. 163.

between 'citizens' of different constituent political communities tends to be frowned upon by the central government, but rights vary across the constituent units in most federations, raising important normative challenges of distinguishing acceptable from unacceptable rights diversity.[85] For example, US states differ or have differed on the legality of marijuana or other drugs, drinking age, age of consent for sexual activity, homosexual sex and marriage, obscenity, the death penalty and lesser penalties, age to obtain a driver's licence, voting age, access to abortion or doctor-assisted dying, and of course slavery until the Fourteenth Amendment (discussed above), followed by state-sanctioned racial segregation, which ended only with federal military intervention and passage of the 1964 Civil Rights Act. Furthermore, 'citizens' of one unit in a federation may be treated differently from those of other units not only internally but also internationally; for example, certain public scholarships in France are available to applicants from Québec but not those from of other Canadian provinces, despite shared Canadian citizenship. The ideal of the equality of all citizens counteracts such rights diversity, and an important way in which central authorities attempt to foster equality is through promoting a common identity or at least a common political culture.[86] One expression of this idea is the notion that 'democratic citizenship need not be rooted in the national identity of a people [... but] does require that every citizen be socialised into a common political culture'.[87] Identity—even a territorial and political identity—need not be exclusive or primary (one can simultaneously be a Torontonian, Ontarian, Canadian, and possibly even North American; or identify simultaneously with Munich, Bavaria, Germany, and the European Union); in a world where borders matter less than they used to, multiple political identities should be more common.

Citizenship-as-equality has become the dominant representation of what citizenship means today. Yet this dominant narrative ignores most of the differentiated forms of citizenship held by the vast majority of the world's population, particularly multilevel and federal citizenship. Nation-states assert a monopoly on the authority to bestow citizenship, but virtually all contemporary nation-states—and it must be remembered that most nation-states are quite recent creations—are characterized by often wide variation in the levels of rights and protections that they offer their citizens. Except perhaps for the mid-twentieth century, multilevel citizenship is the historical norm rather than an aberration. This can be seen in policies regarding freedom of movement within state territory, which is often restricted or subject to incentives or disincentives. It is also evident in differentiated social programmes,

[85] John Kincaid, 'Federalism and Rights: The Case of the United States, with Comparative Perspectives', in Gordon DiGiacomo, ed., *Human Rights* (Toronto: University of Toronto Press, 2016), pp. 83–113.

[86] Maas, *Creating European Citizens* (n 31).

[87] Jürgen Habermas, 'Citizenship and National Identity', in *Between Facts and Norms*, translated by William Rehg (Cambridge: MIT Press, 1996), p. 500.

or simply in differential application of common policies: despite the ideal of equal citizenship, where one lives or works often matters more than common citizenship status—to say nothing of the varied statuses Rogers Smith (in this volume) terms 'quasi-citizens'. Federal states are most explicitly identified with a kind of dual citizenship, simultaneously of the substate jurisdiction and of the centre, while at the same time there is a growth of both supranational and local citizenship regimes. Continuing political contestation surrounding the project of making equal citizens out of many different individuals means that multilevel and federal citizenship requires more attention.[88] Particular attention should be paid to comparative research on different multilevel polities and different kinds of multilevel citizenship.

BIBLIOGRAPHY

Acosta Arcarazo, Diego and Andrew Geddes, 'Transnational Diffusion or Different Models? Regional Approaches to Migration Governance in the European Union and Mercosur', *European Journal of Migration and Law 16*, no. 1 (2014): pp. 19–44.

Barber, Benjamin R., *If Mayors Ruled the World: Dysfunctional Nations, Rising Cities* (New Haven: Yale University Press, 2013).

Bauböck, Rainer, 'Political Autonomy or Cultural Minority Rights? A Conceptual Critique of Renner's Model', in Ephraim Nimni, ed., *National Cultural Autonomy and Its Contemporary Critics* (New York: Routledge, 2005), pp. 97–110.

Bauböck, Rainer, 'The Three Levels of Citizenship within the European Union', *German Law Journal 15*, no. 5 (2014): pp. 751–763.

Becker, Marc, 'Building a Plurinational Ecuador: Complications and Contradictions', *Socialism and Democracy 26*, no. 3 (2012): pp. 72–92.

Benhabib, Seyla, *The Rights of Others: Aliens, Residents, and Citizens* (Cambridge: Cambridge University Press, 2004).

Berger, Raoul, *The Fourteenth Amendment and the Bill of Rights* (Norman: University of Oklahoma Press, 1989).

Brennan, William J. Jr., 'State Constitutions and the Protection of Individual Rights', *Harvard Law Review 90*, no. 3 (1977): pp. 489–504.

Cairns, Alan, *Citizenship, Diversity, and Pluralism: Canadian and Comparative Perspectives* (Montreal: McGill-Queen's University Press, 1999).

Cairns, Alan, *Citizens Plus: Aboriginal Peoples and the Canadian State* (Vancouver: University of British Columbia Press, 2000).

Chappell, Louise A., 'Feminist Engagement with Federal Institutions: Opportunities and Constraints for Women's Multilevel Citizenship', in David H. Laycock, ed., *Representation and Democratic Theory* (Vancouver: UBC Press, 2004), pp. 65–89.

---

[88] Maas (n 29).

Closa, Carlos and Daniela Vintilla, 'Supranational Citizenship: Rights in Regional Integration Organizations', paper presented at European University Institute, 14 May 2015 (on file with author).

Dale, Elizabeth, 'The *Su Bao* Case and the Layers of Everyday Citizenship in China, 1894–1904', in *Multilevel Citizenship*, edited by Willem Maas (Philadelphia: University of Pennsylvania Press, 2013), pp. 110–126.

De Graauw, Els., *Making Immigrant Rights Real: Nonprofits and the Politics of Integration in San Francisco* (Ithaca: Cornell University Press, 2016).

Deutsch, Karl Wolfgang, *Political Community and the North Atlantic Area: International Organization in the Light of Historical Experience* (Princeton: Princeton University Press, 1957).

Elazar, Daniel J., *Exploring Federalism* (Tuscaloosa: University of Alabama Press, 1987).

Elkins, David J., *Beyond Sovereignty: Territory and Political Economy in the Twenty-First Century* (Toronto: University of Toronto Press, 1995).

Gagnon, Alain-G. and James Tully, *Multinational Democracies* (Cambridge: Cambridge University Press, 2001).

Gehring, Jacqueline, 'Free Movement for Some: The Treatment of the Roma after the European Union's Eastern Expansion', in Willem Maas, ed., *Democratic Citizenship and the Free Movement of People* (Leiden: Martinus Nijhoff, 2013), pp. 143–174.

Habermas, Jürgen, *Between Facts and Norms*, translated by William Rehg (Cambridge: MIT Press, 1996).

Hanley, Will, 'When Did Egyptians Stop Being Ottomans? An Imperial Citizenship Case Study', in Willem Maas, ed., *Multilevel Citizenship* (Philadelphia: University of Pennsylvania Press, 2013), pp. 89–109.

Haussman, Melissa, Marian Sawer, and Jill Vickers, eds., *Federalism, Feminism and Multilevel Governance* (Burlington: Ashgate, 2010).

Helbling, Marc, 'Local Citizenship Politics in Switzerland: Between National Justice and Municipal Particularities', in Willem Maas, ed., *Multilevel Citizenship* (Philadelphia: University of Pennsylvania Press, 2013), pp. 149–167.

Hooghe, Liesbet and Gary Marks, *Community, Scale, and Regional Governance* (Oxford: Oxford University Press, 2016).

Isiksel, Turkuler, 'Citizens of a New Agora: Postnational Citizenship and International Economic Institutions', in Willem Maas, ed., *Multilevel Citizenship* (Philadelphia: University of Pennsylvania Press, 2013), pp. 184–202.

Keating, Michael, *Plurinational Democracy: Stateless Nations in a Post-Sovereignty Era* (Oxford: Oxford University Press, 2001).

Keating, Michael, 'Social Citizenship, Solidarity and Welfare in Regionalized and Plurinational States', *Citizenship Studies* 13, no. 5 (2009): pp. 501–513.

Keating, Michael, *Rescaling the European State: The Making of Territory and the Rise of the Meso* (Oxford: Oxford University Press, 2013).

Kincaid, John, 'Federalism and Rights: The Case of the United States, with Comparative Perspectives', in Gordon DiGiacomo, ed., *Human Rights* (Toronto: University of Toronto Press, 2016), pp. 83–113.

King, Loren, 'Cities, Subsidiarity, and Federalism', in James E. Fleming and Jacob T. Levy, eds., *Federalism and Subsidiarity* (New York: New York University Press, 2014), pp. 290–331.

Kymlicka, Will, *Politics in the Vernacular: Nationalism, Multiculturalism, and Citizenship* (New York: Oxford University Press, 2001).

Lacey, Joseph, 'Centripetal Democracy: Democratic Legitimacy and Regional Integration in Belgium, Switzerland and the EU' (PhD Dissertation, European University Institute, 2015) (on file with author).

Light, Matthew A., *Fragile Migration Rights: Freedom of Movement in Post-Soviet Russia* (New York: Routledge, 2016).

Lightfoot, Sheryl, 'The International Indigenous Rights Discourse and Its Demands for Multilevel Citizenship', in Willem Maas, ed., *Multilevel Citizenship* (Philadelphia: University of Pennsylvania Press, 2013), pp. 127–146.

Lluch, Jaime, *Visions of Sovereignty: Nationalism and Accommodation in Multinational Democracies* (Philadelphia: University of Pennsylvania Press, 2014).

Lucas, Kintto, 'Ecuador: New Constitution Addresses Demand for "Plurinational" State', *Inter Press Service*, 5 May 2008, online http://www.ipsnews.net/2008/05/ecuador-new-constitution-addresses-demand-for-lsquoplurinationalrsquo-state/.

Maas, Willem, 'The Genesis of European Rights', *Journal of Common Market Studies* 43, no. 5 (2005): pp. 1009–1025.

Maas, Willem, *Creating European Citizens* (Lanham: Rowman & Littlefield, 2007).

Maas, Willem, 'Citizenship', in *The Encyclopedia of Political Science* (Washington: CQ Press, 2011), pp. 226–230.

Maas, Willem, 'Free Movement and Discrimination: Evidence from Europe, the United States, and Canada', *European Journal of Migration and Law* 15, no. 1 (2013): pp. 91–110.

Maas, Willem, 'Equality and the Free Movement of People: Citizenship and Internal Migration', in Willem Maas, ed., *Democratic Citizenship and the Free Movement of People* (Leiden: Martinus Nijhoff, 2013), pp. 9–30.

Maas, Willem, 'Varieties of Multilevel Citizenship', in Willem Maas, ed., *Multilevel Citizenship* (Philadelphia: University of Pennsylvania Press, 2013), pp. 1–21.

Maas, Willem, 'European Union Citizenship in Retrospect and Prospect', in Engin Isin and Peter Nyers, eds., *Routledge Handbook of Global Citizenship Studies* (London: Routledge, 2014), pp. 409–417.

Maas, Willem, 'The Origins, Evolution, and Political Objectives of EU Citizenship', *German Law Journal* 15, no. 5 (2014): pp. 797–819.

Maas, Willem, 'Trade, Regional Integration, and Free Movement of People', in Joaquín Roy, ed., *A New Atlantic Community: The European Union, the US and Latin America* (Miami: European Union Center of Excellence/Jean Monnet Chair, University of Miami, 2015), pp. 111–121.

Maas, Willem, 'European Governance of Citizenship and Nationality', *Journal of Contemporary European Research* 12, no. 1 (2016): pp. 532–551.

Mettler, Suzanne, 'Dividing Social Citizenship by Gender: The Implementation of Unemployment Insurance and Aid to Dependent Children, 1935–1950', *Studies in American Political Development* 12 (1998): pp. 303–342.

Mettler, Suzanne, 'Social Citizens of Separate Sovereignties: Governance in the New Deal Welfare State', in Sidney M. Milkis and Jerome M. Mileur, eds., *The New Deal and the Triumph of Liberalism* (Amherst: University of Massachusetts Press, 2002), pp. 231–271.

Miller, Gary T., 'Citizenship and European Union: A Federalist Approach', in C. Lloyd Brown-John, ed., *Federal-Type Solutions and European Integration*, edited by C. Lloyd Brown-John (Lanham: University Press of America, 1995), pp. 461–499.

Molavi, Shourideh, 'The Israeli Logic of Exclusion' (PhD dissertation, York University, expected 2017) (on file with author).

Pasquier, Romain, 'Regional Citizenship and Scales of Governance in France', in Daniel Wincott, Charlie Jeffery, and Ailsa Henderson, eds., *Citizenship after the Nation State: Regionalism, Nationalism and Public Attitudes in Europe* (Basingstoke: Palgrave Macmillan, 2014).

Piccoli, Lorenzo, 'Regional Spheres of Citizenship? The Territorial Politics of Rights in Italy, Spain, and Switzerland', PhD dissertation, European University Institute, forthcoming.

Proudhon, P. J., *The Principle of Federation*, translated by Richard Vernon (Toronto: University of Toronto Press, 1979).

Ramakrishnan, Karthick and Allan Colbern, 'The California Package: Immigrant Integration and the Evolving Nature of State Citizenship', *Policy Matters* 6, no. 3 (2015): pp. 1–19.

Requejo Coll, Ferran and Miquel Caminal i Badia, eds., *Federalism, Plurinationality and Democratic Constitutionalism: Theory and Cases* (New York: Routledge, 2012).

Resnick, Philip and Gerald P Kernerman, eds., *Insiders and Outsiders: Alan Cairns and the Reshaping of Canadian Citizenship* (Vancouver: UBC Press, 2005).

Risse, Thomas and Tanja A. Börzel, *The Oxford Handbook of Comparative Regionalism* (Oxford: Oxford University Press, 2016).

Sarajlic, Eldar, 'Multilevel Citizenship and the Contested Statehood of Bosnia and Herzegovina', in Willem Maas, ed., *Multilevel Citizenship* (Philadelphia: University of Pennsylvania Press, 2013), pp. 168–183.

Schönberger, Christophe, 'European Citizenship as Federal Citizenship: Some Citizenship Lessons of Comparative Federalism', *European Review of Public Law* 19, no. 1 (2007): pp. 61–82.

Schrenk, William J., 'Citizenship and Immigration', in Robert R. Bowie and Carl J. Friedrich, eds., *Studies in Federalism* (Boston: Little, Brown, 1954), pp. 635–675.

Schwartz, Bernard, 'The Amendment in Operation: A Historical Overview', in Bernard Schwartz, ed., *The Fourteenth Amendment* (New York: New York University Press, 1970), pp. 29–38.

Smith, Rogers M., *Civic Ideals: Conflicting Visions of Citizenship in U.S. History* (New Haven: Yale University Press, 1997).

Smith, Rogers M., *Political Peoplehood: The Roles of Values, Interests, and Identities* (Chicago: University of Chicago Press, 2015).

Stepan, Alfred, Juan J. Linz, and Yogendra Yadav, *Crafting State-Nations: India and Other Multinational Democracies* (Baltimore: Johns Hopkins University Press, 2010).

Tilly, Charles, 'Citizenship, Identity and Social History', *International Review of Social History* 40, no. 3 (1995): pp. 1–17.

Tockman, Jason and John Cameron, 'Indigenous Autonomy and the Contradictions of Plurinationalism in Bolivia', *Latin American Politics and Society* 56, no. 3 (2014): pp. 46–69.

Varsanyi, Monica and Doris Marie Provine, 'Comparing Immigration Policy and Enforcement in Two Neighboring States', paper presented at the 2015 American Political Science Association Annual Conference (on file with author).

Warren, Earl, 'Fourteenth Amendment: Retrospect and Prospect', in Bernard Schwartz, ed., *The Fourteenth Amendment* (New York: New York University Press, 1970), pp. 212–233.

Weinstock, Daniel, 'Cities and Federalism', in James E. Fleming and Jacob T. Levy, ed., *Federalism and Subsidiarity* (New York: New York University Press, 2014), pp. 259–290.

Wu, Ling, 'Decentralization and Hukou Reforms in China', *Policy and Society* 32, no. 1 (2013): pp. 33–42.

Yashar, Deborah J., *Contesting Citizenship in Latin America: The Rise of Indigenous Movements and the Postliberal Challenge* (Cambridge: Cambridge University Press, 2005).

Young, Ernest A., 'The Volk of New Jersey? State Identity, Distinctiveness, and Political Culture in the American Federal System', Duke Law Working Paper, 2015, online http://scholarship.law.duke.edu/faculty_scholarship/3431/.

CHAPTER 30

SUPRANATIONAL CITIZENSHIP

FRANCESCA STRUMIA[*]

INTRODUCTION

SUPRANATIONAL citizenship, as a concept, sits somewhat uncomfortably between the regional experience of European citizenship and discourses on global or cosmopolitan citizenship. To the former, supranational citizenship is semantically married, as the notions of European and supranational citizenship are often used interchangeably in relevant interdisciplinary literature. To the latter, if conceived as a genus, supranational citizenship belongs as a sub-part. However neither option offers a satisfactory account of supranational citizenship: European citizenship is too narrow to exhaust the concept, and global or cosmopolitan citizenship is too broad to embrace it firmly.

* I am indebted to Sam Hall for his invaluable research assistance for this chapter.

Hence the contours of the notion remain rather fuzzy. The objective of this chapter is to dispel this fuzziness. The first section traces a conceptual definition of supranational citizenship, distinguishing it from other forms of citizenship beyond the state. The second section reinforces this conceptual definition by distilling further elements from the experience of European citizenship. The third and fourth sections rely on this reinforced definition to, respectively, examine other concrete examples and consider the theoretical prospects of supranational citizenship.

Defining Supranational Citizenship

Literally, 'supranational' means 'extending beyond or free of the political limitations inhering in the nation state.'[1] Supranational citizenship thus points to a notion of citizenship beyond the state. In this respect, it shares the premises of accounts of global or cosmopolitan citizenship. The latter label is used in the context of a variety of intellectual projects on citizenship beyond the state, some adopting a moral viewpoint, others grounded in democratic theory, others still focusing on institutional dimensions.[2] With these projects, supranational citizenship partakes in the endeavor to re-conceptualize citizenship in a non-hegemonic sphere overcoming state boundaries.[3]

However, in contrast with accounts of cosmopolitan citizenship, the non-hegemonic sphere to which supranational citizenship points is not a world-wide one. It rather coincides with a supranational entity organized around a collective purpose and having set boundaries. From this perspective, supranational citizenship fits with regional citizenship better than with global citizenship.[4] As its very name suggests, it posits an enduring albeit reconfigured relation with nationality.

Indeed supranational citizenship stands in both continuity and contrast with other notions of membership conceived to challenge the conflation of citizenship

---

[1] Webster's Third New International Dictionary of the English Language (Springfield: Merriam-Webster, 2002).

[2] See Tan in this volume. See also Richard Falk, 'The Making of Global Citizenship,' in Bart van Steenbergen, ed., The Condition of Citizenship (London: Sage, 1994), pp. 127–140; Daniele Archibugi, The Global Commonwealth of Citizens: Towards Cosmopolitan Democracy (Princeton, Woodstock: Princeton University Press, 2008), pp. 114–119.

[3] On the idea of transnational non-domination see Kalypso Nicolaïdis, 'European Democracy and Its Crisis,' Journal of Common Market Studies 51 (2013): pp. 351–369, pp. 358–359.

[4] See Richard Falk, 'An Emergent Matrix of Citizenship: Complex, Uneven and Fluid,' in Nigel Dower and John Williams, eds., Global Citizenship: A Critical Reader (Edinburgh: Edinburgh University Press, 2002), pp. 15–29, pp. 23–25.

and nationality. An intrinsic association of citizenship and nationality is often taken for granted in discourses surrounding modern citizenship. However the demands of liberal democracy, globalization, and the human rights movement have problematized this association, prompting alternative visions.[5]

Some of these visions rely on a transformative understanding of the relationship between citizenship and nationality. Post-national citizenship, for instance, grounds the rights of membership not in nationality but in universal personhood. It distinguishes the perspective of rights fruition, where universal aspirations defeat narrow conceptions of national citizenship; and the perspective of rights dispensing, where sovereign and democratic closure lead back to the nation state as the main point of reference.[6] Other accounts instead propose a pluralist understanding of the relation between citizenship and nationality, emphasizing how the conjugation of citizenship and nationality no longer exhausts the spectrum of membership. From one perspective, pluralism in citizenship finds expression in instances of multiple citizenship, implicating the simultaneous possession of several nationalities.[7] From a different pluralist perspective, transnational citizenship emphasizes how national citizenship has become just one of several nested and overlapping circles of membership, many of which transcend national boundaries.[8] Equality of citizenship can only be preserved, from this perspective, by recognizing that nation states owe obligations also to non-members.[9]

Supranational citizenship points to yet another relation between citizenship and nationality in comparison to the above models. It denotes a status that stems from nationality, yet re-articulates citizenship beyond its boundaries. This re-articulation relies on a rule of mutual recognition: each member state in a supranational community recognizes national citizens of other member states to some extent as its own. Political and residence rights granted to supranational citizens in national communities beyond their own give concrete expression to this rule of recognition. While it has elements in common with both post-national and transnational accounts, supranational citizenship hence remains distinct from both: from the former, because it places national citizenship at the centre of gravity of belonging;

---

[5] For an articulation of relevant arguments, see Yasemin Nuhoglu Soysal, *The Limits of Citizenship* (Chicago, London: University of Chicago Press, 1994); Seyla Benhabib, *The Rights of Others: Aliens, Residents and Citizens* (Cambridge: Cambridge University Press, 2004); Rainer Bauböck, *Transnational Citizenship: Membership and Rights in International Migration* (Cheltenham: Edward Elgar, 1994).

[6] Benhabib (n 5), p. 178; Soysal (n 5).

[7] See Peter Spiro, 'The Citizenship Dilemma,' *Stanford Law Review* 51 (1998–1999): pp. 597–639, pp. 617–630. See also Spiro in this volume.

[8] See Bauböck (n 5), chapter 1. From an EU citizenship perspective, see Rainer Bauböck, 'The Three Levels of Citizenship within the European Union,' *German Law Journal* 15, no. 5 (2014): pp. 751–763; Rainer Bauböck, 'Why European Citizenship? Normative Approaches to Supranational Union,' *Theoretical Inquiries in Law* 8, no. 2 (2007): pp. 454–488, p. 455.

[9] See Bauböck (n 5), chapter 12. Also see Dora Kostakopoulou, *The Future Governance of Citizenship* (Cambridge, New York: Cambridge University Press, 2008), pp. 100–122.

from the latter because it situates nested circles of national membership within a broader, but clearly bounded supranational sphere.

Comparing and distinguishing supranational citizenship from notions of citizenship beyond the state and beyond nationality yields a concept with three key prongs: projection of citizenship beyond the state in the context of a non-hegemonic project; articulation of this beyond-state citizenship within the boundaries of a supranational entity pursuing a collective purpose; and reconfiguration of citizenship beyond nationality through a dynamic of mutual recognition of national citizenships. This conceptual sketch provides a starting point to consider concretely what forms of citizenship may count as supranational.

First, forms of multilevel citizenship that do not reconfigure citizenship beyond nationality, such as federal citizenship, fail the test of supranational citizenship.[10] The same applies to hegemonic extensions of citizenship beyond nationality. For instance, this is the case with colonial citizenships in the fashion of the status of 'British subject,' recognized since 1914 to all persons born in the British Empire, and grounding their common membership in allegiance to the crown;[11] or the status of nonmetropolitan citizenship that Italy extended to the natives of its colonies in northern and eastern Africa.[12]

Post-colonial citizenships in the frame of post-imperial arrangements that have lost their hegemonic character may however fit the concept of supranational citizenship. Commonwealth citizenship, which represents the supranational evolution of the status of 'British subject,' offers a prime example. The 'British subject' status had become inadequate, after the Second World War, to express the conundrums of rights and forms of belonging resulting from nationalist ferment in the British dominions and colonies, and of the first stages of decolonization.[13] These transformations called for configuration of a dual status, combining nationality of a colony or newly independent dominion, and Commonwealth citizenship. Such dual status, in the form of a supranational Commonwealth citizenship, was introduced, following a conference of the Commonwealth countries in 1947, with the British Nationality Act 1948.[14] The Act extended recognition as 'British subject' or 'Commonwealth

---

[10] See Maas in this volume.

[11] J.E.S Fawcett, 'British Nationality and the Commonwealth,' *The Round Table* 63, no. 250 (1973): pp. 259–269, pp. 260–261; Jatinder Mann, 'The Evolution of Commonwealth Citizenship, 1945–48 in Canada, Britain and Australia,' *Commonwealth and Comparative Politics* 50, no. 3 (2012): pp. 293–313, p. 294.

[12] See Sabina Donati, *A Political History of National Citizenship and Identity in Italy, 1861–1950* (Stanford: Stanford University Press, 2013), pp. 120–125, 128–130.

[13] See E.F.W. Gey Van Pittius, 'Dominion Nationality,' *Journal of Comparative Legislation and International Law* 13 (1931): pp. 199–202; Randall Hansen, *Citizenship and Immigration in Postwar Britain* (Oxford: Oxford University Press, 2000), pp. 42–43.

[14] *British Nationality Act 1948*. See Andrew Mycock, 'British Citizenship and the Legacy of Empire,' *Parliamentary Affairs* 63, no. 2 (2010): pp. 339–355, p. 343; Robert R. Wilson and Robert E. Clute, 'Commonwealth Citizenship and Common Status,' *American Journal of International Law* 57, no. 3 (1963): pp. 566–587, pp. 567–568; Fawcett (n 11), pp. 261–262.

Citizen,' two expressions with the same meaning, to any citizen of the UK or its colonies, as well as to citizens of the Commonwealth countries.[15] A White Paper accompanying the Act encouraged all Commonwealth countries to incorporate in their own legislation, along with a definition of their own citizens, a recognition clause whereby they would recognize citizens of other Commonwealth countries as British subjects.[16] A post-colonial supranational citizenship, centered precisely on recognition of different Commonwealth nationalities, had found its birth. In the frame of the supranational entity that survived dissolution of the British empire, this citizenship served the goal of preserving the collective identity of its English speaking holders as British people.

In terms of content, Commonwealth citizenship varied among the different Commonwealth countries.[17] In Britain, at its fullest, it entailed rights of entry and abode as well as political rights for its holders. However it lasted in this full form only a few decades. Immigration restrictions for Commonwealth citizens were introduced from 1962 and the 1981 British Nationality Act, in response to the urge to rebound British identity, redefined British citizenship and deprived the holders of Commonwealth citizenship of the right of abode in the UK.[18] Commonwealth citizenship survives today as a thin supranational status, embodying just a handful of mostly symbolic rights.[19]

Thicker contemporary examples of supranational citizenship can be found in forms of interstate citizenship in the context of regional trade arrangements. Thoughts immediately go to European citizenship. While not an isolated case, the European Union's model of supranational citizenship deserves special attention in this context and is a compulsory next step for any attempt to further spell out the concept under discussion. This is not only because European citizenship is arguably the most developed concrete form of supranational citizenship in the frame of a regional association. But also because in relevant interdisciplinary literature it is considered almost as the alter ego of supranational citizenship. The only two English language monographic works on supranational citizenship are centered on

[15] *British Nationality Act 1948*, section 1(1) and 1(2). The term 'commonwealth citizen' was introduced at the request of the Government of India to avoid misunderstandings. See Cabinet Conclusions, meeting of 6 May 1948, CAB 128/12, online http://discovery.nationalarchives.gov.uk/details/r/D7663145.

[16] Wilson and Clute (n 14), pp. 567–568; Hansen (n 13), pp. 41–50.

[17] Wilson and Clute (n 14), pp. 573–581.

[18] *British Nationality Act 1981*. Also see Mycock (n 14), pp. 342–343; Christian Joppke, 'How Immigration is Changing Citizenship: A Comparative View,' *Ethnic and Racial Studies* 22, no. 4 (1999): pp. 629–652, p. 641. Robert Moore, 'The Debris of Empire: The 1981 Nationality Act and the Oceanic Dependent Territories,' *Immigrants & Minorities* 19, no. 1 (2000): pp. 1–24, pp. 1–4; Rieko Karatani, *Defining British Citizenship: Empire, Commonwealth and Modern Britain* (London: Frank Cass, 2003), pp. 145–165.

[19] Tendayi Bloom, 'Contradictions in Formal Commonwealth Citizenship Rights in Commonwealth Countries,' *The Round Table 100*, no. 417 (2011): pp. 639–654, pp. 640–642.

European citizenship.[20] Interdisciplinary literature on global and cosmopolitan citizenship treats European citizenship as the first and foremost example of relevant models.[21] And reference books on citizenship often include an entry on European citizenship rather than more generally on supranational.[22]

European Citizenship

European citizenship was formally introduced by the 1992 Treaty of Maastricht, with which political union found its place among the objectives of European integration. It is an additional legal status that follows automatically from nationality of one of the Member States of the European Union.[23] It entails a short list of rights, the most important of which is the right to move and reside in any Member State.[24] At first sight, European citizenship appears to fit all three prongs of the above-proposed definition of supranational citizenship. It comes in the context of a non-hegemonic project of supranational union, pursuing shared economic and political goals. It represents the means to achieve one of these goals, namely fostering people's ownership of the integration project through the recognition of 'special rights' to Community citizens.[25] These 'special rights', in the model of supranational citizenship that eventually made its way into the Treaties, are based on reciprocal recognition, among the Member States, of the status of their respective nationals.

In its Treaty version, European citizenship is a rather skinny status. However the combination of expectant analyses in a vast interdisciplinary literature,[26] and of purpose-oriented interpretations of the Court of Justice of the EU, have given it

---

[20] Lynn Dobson, *Supranational Citizenship* (Manchester, New York: Manchester University Press, 2006); Francesca Strumia, *Supranational Citizenship and the Challenge of Diversity: Immigrants, Citizens and Member States in the EU* (Leiden, Boston: Martinus Nijhoff, 2013).

[21] See, e.g., Keith Faulks, *Citizenship* (London: Routledge, 2000), p. 158; Luis Cabrera, *The Practice of Global Citizenship* (Cambridge: Cambridge University Press, 2010), p. 181; Archibugi (n 2), p. 117.

[22] See, e.g., Engin Isin and Peter Nyers, eds., *Handbook of Global Citizenship Studies* (Abingdon: Routledge, 2014).

[23] Consolidated Version of the Treaty on the Functioning of the European Union, OJ C 326, 26 October 2012, pp. 47–390 (TFEU), article 20.

[24] Ibid., articles 21–24.

[25] See Pietro Adonnino, 'A People's Europe: Reports from the Ad Hoc Committee,' *Bullettin of the European Communities 7* (1985), online http://aei.pitt.edu/992/.

[26] For a small sample, see Dora Kostakopoulou, 'European Union Citizenship: Writing the Future,' *European Law Journal 13*, no. 5 (2007): pp. 623–646; Elizabeth Meehan, *Citizenship and the European Community* (London: Sage, 1993); J.H.H Weiler, 'To Be a European Citizen: Eros and Civilization,' *Journal of European Public Policy* (1997): pp. 495–519; Massimo La Torre, ed., *European Citizenship: An Institutional Challenge* (The Hague: Kluwer Law International, 1998).

body and weight. The Court, in particular, has relentlessly repeated in its jurisprudence that 'Union citizenship is destined to be the fundamental status of nationals of the Member States,'[27] and it has resorted to European citizenship to stretch, and gradually vest in constitutional garb, pre-existing free movement rights for economic actors.[28]

To achieve the latter result, the Court has aggressively deployed, in its 'classical' citizenship case law, the principle of non-discrimination on the basis of nationality: it has found that European citizens residing in a Member State other than the one of nationality are entitled to equal treatment with nationals for purposes of a number of entitlements and benefits, including social assistance.[29] Until a recent change of trend,[30] the Court has extended the reach of European supranational citizenship to embrace not economically active intra-EU migrants in the name of 'a minimum degree of financial solidarity' expected among the Member States and their citizens.[31] With the excuse to further protect the effectiveness of European citizens' free movement, the Court has recognized rights of residence and work for non-EU national family members of migrant European citizens, even beyond those secured through secondary European legislation.[32] In the same vein, the Court has pushed beyond the non-discrimination paradigm to sanction also restrictions to the right to free movement imposed in a Member State of origin.[33]

Ultimately, judicial endeavors have molded a supranational citizenship relying on a sophisticated web of rights and duties of recognition. This becomes evident when looking at European citizenship from the perspective of its subjects: the Member States, the citizens themselves, and the third country nationals (TCNs), that is nationals of a country not belonging to the EU, who are European denizens, but potentially aspirant citizens.[34]

---

[27] See, e.g., Judgment of 20 September 2001, *Grzelczyk*, C-184/99, EU:C:2001:458, paragraph 31. See also Daniel Thym, 'Towards Real Citizenship? The Judicial Construction of Union Citizenship and Its Limits,' in Maurice Adams, Henry De Waele, Johan Meeusen, and Gert Straetmans, eds., *Judging Europe's Judges: The Legitimacy of the Case Law of the European Court of Justice* (Oxford, Portland: Hart, 2013), pp. 155–174.

[28] Francesca Strumia, 'Citizenship and Free Movement: European and American Features of a Judicial Formula for Increased Comity,' *Columbia Journal of European Law* 12, no. 3 (2005): pp. 713–749. See also Willem Maas, 'The Origin, Evolution and Political Objectives of EU Citizenship,' *German Law Journal* 15 (2014): pp. 797–819, pp. 807–808, 814; Francesco De Cecco, 'Fundamental Freedoms, Fundamental Rights and the Scope of Free Movement Law,' *German Law Journal* 15, no. 3 (2014): pp. 383–406, pp. 395–397.

[29] E.g. Judgment of 7 September 2004, *Trojani*, C-456/02, EU:C:2004:488.

[30] Judgment of 11 November 2014, *Dano*, C-333/13, EU:C:2014:2358; Judgment of 14 June 2016, *Commission v UK*, C-318/14, EU:C:2016:436.

[31] *Grzelczyk* (n 27).

[32] E.g. Judgment of 19 October 2004, *Zhu and Chen*, C-200/02, EU:C:2004:639; Judgment of 12 March 2014, *O. and B.*, C-456/12, EU:C:2014:135.

[33] E.g. Judgment of 22 May 2008, *Nerkowska*, C-499/06, EU:C:2008:300.

[34] The perspective of the subjects is developed further in Strumia (n 20), pp. 258–273.

For the Member States, European citizenship grounds duties of recognition both in respect of nationals of other Member States and in respect of TCNs. The Member States have indeed an obligation to recognize the status and rights of nationals of other Member States, guaranteeing rights to any such nationals residing in their territory as well as to their TCN family members. As a result, European citizenship affects the power of each Member State to draw the boundary between insiders and outsiders, citizens and denizens.[35] Not only because it extends the obligations of each Member State as 'provider' of citizenship entitlements towards outsiders to national citizenship, but also because it limits Member States' discretion in exercising their powers to grant and withdraw their nationality.[36]

For the citizens, who are European citizens by virtue of their nationality, European citizenship brings about three classes of rights to recognition.[37] First, the right to be recognized as part insiders in the Member State of residence; this right underpins the principle of non-discrimination on the basis of nationality that informs European rules on free movement of persons. Second, the right to keep being recognized as insiders in the Member State of nationality, even while residing as European citizens in other Member States. As European citizenship does not diminish national citizenship, certain entitlements granted by the Member State of nationality to its nationals, such as for instance war victims' benefits and study finance, are 'exportable' to the Member State of residence.[38] And finally the right to have one's condition of simultaneous belonging to more than one Member State, such as the one of nationality and the one of residence, recognized and respected. For instance, a European citizen national of Spain but growing up in Belgium has an entitlement to have his last name recorded in Belgian documents according to traditional Spanish rules on name composition.[39] This can be seen as recognition of the fact that national identity, that names in part express, does not get diluted through the exercise of the transnational rights of European supranational citizenship.

In addition to these variously shaped rights to recognition, with European citizenship also comes a duty of recognition. Citizens of each Member State have an implied obligation to recognize citizens of any other Member State as part members

---

[35] See Francesca Strumia, 'European Citizenship and EU Immigration: A Demoi-cratic Bridge between the Third Country Nationals' Right to Belong and the Member States' Power to Exclude?', *European Law Journal* 22, no. 4 (2016): pp. 417–447.

[36] See Judgment of 7 July 1992, *Micheletti*, C-369/90, EU:C:1992:295; Judgment of 2 March 2010, *Rottmann*, C-135/08, EU:C:2010:104.

[37] Francesca Strumia, 'Looking for Substance at the Boundaries: European Citizenship and Mutual Recognition of Belonging', *Yearbook of European Law 32* (2013): pp. 432–459, pp. 443–448.

[38] See, e.g., *Nerkowska* (n 33); Judgment of 18 July 2013, *Prinz and Seeberger*, C-523/11 and C-585/11, EU:C:2013:524. See also Strumia (n 37), p. 448.

[39] See, e.g., Judgment of 2 October 2003, *Garcia Avello*, C-148/02, EU:C:2003:539. See also Francesca Strumia, 'Individual Rights, Interstate Equality, State Autonomy: European Horizontal Citizenship and its (Lonely) Playground in Trans-Atlantic Perspective', in Dimitry Kochenov, ed., *Citizenship and Federalism in Europe: The Role of Rights* (Cambridge University Press, forthcoming 2017).

of their national community. They have to recognize, for instance, the entitlement of other European citizens to raise claims against the welfare system into which national citizens are potentially longer term contributors. This obligation to contribute also for outsiders is the counterpart to the right of every European citizen to move to a different Member State and claim certain rights as an insider.

Turning to the TCNs, as national citizenship represents the gateway to European citizenship, it may appear that European citizenship is of little relevance for their inclusion claims. However European citizenship affects the condition of TCNs both directly and indirectly. Directly, because it brings about a discrete set of rights for TCNs who are family members of European citizens.[40] And indirectly, because as suggested above, it grounds Member States' obligations toward outsiders. In respect of TCNs, these obligations translate into a duty, a soft one for the time being, to take into account the measure of belonging that a TCN has already accrued in other EU Member States.[41] A similar duty, albeit not directly linked to European citizenship, finds concrete expression in some of the instruments adopted as part of the EU common immigration policy.[42] It also descends as a side effect from each Member State's duty to internalize, to some extent, the interests of any other Member States in discharging its functions. This duty begins to change the texture of the boundary between inclusion and exclusion that national citizenship continues to mark. Whilst not shifting this boundary, European citizenship makes it partly permeable.[43]

This web of rights and duties of recognition spells out more fully the norm of recognition that was already evident in post-colonial citizenship. It also reflects a broader notion of mutual recognition echoing into the citizenship domain from other areas of European integration. This broader notion of mutual recognition offers theoretical depth to supranational citizenship.

Mutual recognition fulfills several tasks in the context of European integration. It is a regulatory principle governing the movement of goods in the internal market and the recognition of professional qualifications for purposes of free movement of persons. It is also a model of governance informing cooperation in judicial and criminal matters.[44] And it is a political principle and normative aspiration, offering one explanation for the process of European integration, as well as a horizon for its continuation.[45] In the words of Kalypso Nicolaidis:

---

[40] Directive 2004/38, articles 7, 12, 13. See also *O. and B* (n 32).   [41] Strumia (n 35).

[42] For instance, long-term resident TCNs who have already complied with integration requirements in a first Member State cannot be subjected to integration requirements in a second Member State (Directive 2003/109, article 15(3)).

[43] For the articulation of this argument, see Strumia (n 35).

[44] For an overview, see Francesca Kostoris Padoa Schioppa, ed., *The Principle of Mutual Recognition in the European Integration Process* (Basingstoke: Palgrave Macmillan, 2005); Christian Janssens, *The Principle of Mutual Recognition in EU Law* (Oxford: Oxford university Press, 2013).

[45] See Kalypso Nicolaïdis, 'Trusting the Poles? Constructing Europe through Mutual Recognition,' *Journal of European Public Policy 14* (2007): pp. 682–698, p. 684.

As a 'demoicracy', the European Union requires its many peoples not only to open up to one another but to recognize mutually their respective polities and all that constitutes them: their respective pasts, their social pacts, their political systems, their cultural traditions, their democratic practices. It is a very demanding notion of mutual recognition.[46]

This demanding notion ultimately relies on building and managing trust among the Member States and their polities.[47] This dynamic of reciprocal trust and recognition yields a novel norm of belonging, supporting supranational citizenship. A set of polities that open up to one another and recognize one another's social contracts, trust one another's political principles, and respect one another's traditions and memories, are capable of recognizing one another's citizens as shared members. After all, those citizens are bound to respect rules, and are committed to political projects and social pacts that all participating polities recognize and respect. Hence the bond between state and individual that justifies citizenship becomes transferable across the participating states, and belonging in the participating polities becomes to some extent interchangeable. Supranational citizenship is born from this idea of interchangeable belonging: it is premised in a related right, not just to have rights, but to have rights, and ultimately belong, across national borders.[48] In this sense it problematizes the boundaries of the national citizenships to which it adds without replacing them.

A first implication is that the glue of supranational belonging is not a strong shared identity or ethno-cultural affinity. It is rather a measure of reciprocal trust, coupled with the acknowledgment of shared goals and with regular transnational interactions. Ideas of a thin civic identity grounded in recognition are well represented in European citizenship literature.[49]

From a further perspective, a right to belong across borders grounded in mutual trust requires mutual responsibility on the part of the Member States for citizens of other Member States, and on the part of the citizens for the welfare of the migrant members of their own polities. This mutual responsibility lays the ground for the web of rights and duties of recognition examined above.

This norm of belonging based on mutual recognition has reached only partial realization in the EU, of course. It provides a rationale for the architecture of supranational citizenship advanced, mostly, by the European Court of Justice. However it does not resonate in political sentiment and in societal perceptions, as evidenced by arguments about lack of solidarity and mutual trust displayed in the context of the EU referendum in the UK in June 2016. Such resonance would perhaps require

---

[46] Kalypso Nicolaïdis, 'The Idea of European Demoicracy', in Julie Dickinson and Pavlos Eleftheriadis, eds., *Philosophical Foundations of European Union Law* (Oxford: Oxford University Press, 2012), pp. 247–274, p. 248. Also see Nicolaïdis (n 45), p. 682; Pavlos Eleftheriadis, 'The Content of European Citizenship', *German Law Journal* 15, no. 5 (2014): pp. 777–796, pp. 795–796.

[47] Nicolaïdis (n 45), p. 686.   [48] Strumia (n 35).

[49] See, e.g., Dobson (n 20), pp. 137–150; Paul Magnette, 'How Can One Be European? Reflections on the Pillars of European Civic Identity', *European Law Journal* 13, no. 5 (2007): pp. 664–679.

internalization of some of the cosmopolitan ideas inspiring the global citizenship accounts with which European citizenship flirts.[50] Relatedly, this account of supranational citizenship relying on mutual recognition lends itself to two critiques.

A first critique is that it offers a too rosy account of European supranational citizenship. Part of the literature indeed emphasizes that European citizenship dilutes citizenship, failing to rearticulate several of its traditional components beyond national boundaries. From a first perspective, with European citizenship comes a loss in solidarity. European citizenship is ultimately a market citizenship that promotes a dis-embedded understanding of economic freedoms.[51] Protection of these freedoms comes at a cost for the role of the Member States as welfare providers; as it is conceived, supranational citizenship threatens the very ability of the Member States to discharge their social functions, thereby undermining the foundations of modern social citizenship.[52] In a second sense, supranational citizenship impoverishes the participation content of citizenship. Not only because the political rights attached to European citizenship are limited, but also because there is hardly a supranational public sphere in Europe; European citizens do not voice their political self through their supranational status, and despite the tools for political participation at their disposal, the agenda of the EU remains quite impermeable to the citizenry's input.[53] Further, European supranational citizenship entails a downgrade in collective identity. It appeals to atomized individuals and 'accidental cosmopolitans,'[54] whose whims it serves and whose autonomy it enhances.[55] However it does away with the collective bonds and the legacy of groupness that national citizenship stands for.[56] There is also the problem that analyses of European supranational citizenship over-rely on the meaning of the same for a tiny minority of transnational migrants. A vast majority of static European citizens finds little or no protection in European citizenship.[57] Despite the CJEU's interpretation efforts, and

---

[50] See Andrew Linklater, 'Cosmopolitan Citizenship,' *Citizenship Studies* 2, no. 1 (1998): pp. 23–41, p. 32.

[51] See, e.g., Agustín José Menéndez, 'Which Citizenship? Whose Europe? The Many Paradoxes of European Citizenship,' *German Law Journal* 15 (2014): pp. 907–934, pp. 922–928. See also Michelle Everson, 'A Citizenship in Movement,' *German Law Journal* 15 (2014): pp. 965–984.

[52] Menéndez (n 51), pp. 923–927, 931–932. Also see Alexander Somek, 'Europe: Political Not Cosmopolitan,' *European Law Journal* 20 (2014): pp. 142–163, pp. 155–156.

[53] See Jo Shaw, 'Citizenship: Contrasting Dynamics at the Interface of Integration and Constitutionalism,' in Paul Craig and Gráinne De Burca, eds., *The Evolution of EU Law* (Oxford: Oxford University Press, 2011), pp. 575–609, pp. 646–647; Joseph H. Weiler, 'In the Face of Crisis: Input Legitimacy, Output Legitimacy and the Political Messianism of European Integration,' *Journal of European Integration 34*, no. 7 (2012): pp. 825–841, p. 829; Menéndez (n 51), p. 931; Somek (n 52), p. 143.

[54] Somek (n 52), p. 145.

[55] Joseph H. Weiler, 'Van Gend en Loos: The Individual as Subject and Object and the Dilemma of European Legitimacy,' *International Journal of Constitutional Law* 12, no. 1 (2014): pp. 94–103 (European integration 'places the individual in the center and turns it into a self-centered individual).

[56] See Menéndez (n 51), pp. 909–910; Andreas Follesdahl, 'A Common European Identity for European Citizenship?,' *German Law Journal* 15 (2014): pp. 765–775, p. 766.

[57] See Menéndez (n 51), p. 917.

with the exception of the *Ruiz Zambrano* doctrine on interference with the substance of European citizenship even in internal situations,[58] European citizenship is only activated in the presence of a cross-border link. That is when a European citizen works, resides, or at least travels regularly to provide or receive services in a Member State other than the one of nationality. As a result static European citizens may incur 'reverse discrimination': as their rights are only protected under national law, and not under EU law, they may find themselves treated less favorably, in their own Member State, than a migrant European citizen.[59]

These different critiques of European supranational citizenship are shortsighted in one respect: they treat the relation between national and supranational citizenship as a zero sum game. Whatever is secured for supranational citizenship is lost to national one, and vice versa. A similar approach disregards the transformative potential of supranational citizenship. It fails to consider how supranational citizenship, in reshuffling rights, status, identity, and participation, re-engages national citizenship at a different level, so that national and supranational are better conceived on a continuum rather than in the alternative. Far from diluting or emptying national citizenships, supranational citizenship actually enhances it.[60] It stretches national citizenship's reach extra-territorially and complements it with a set of transnational rights that let it tap into the domain of other national citizenships. National citizenship emerges enriched from this process. This is true not only of the national citizenship of intra-EU migrants who concretely benefit from fruition of rights on a transnational basis. Also settled national citizens see their status strengthened by supranational citizenship, which gives them a stake in the community of any other Member State.

A further critique is that an account based on mutual recognition, with its reliance on national citizenship and focus on the horizontal capacity of European citizenship, disregards the vertical link between the supranational entity and the people, thereby discounting the *supra*national element of European citizenship. Yet the vertical link is crucial to supranational citizenship intended in this sense from at least three perspectives. First it is the Union's commitment to the people, who are both the ultimate principals and addressees of the supranational project, that provides impetus and legitimacy for the design of a supranational citizenship,

---

[58] Judgment of 8 March 2011, *Ruiz Zambrano*, C-34/09, EU:C:2011:124; Niamh Nic Shuibne, 'The Resilience of EU Market Citizenship,' *Common Market Law Review* 47 (2010): pp. 1597–1628, p. 1611; Koen Lenaerts, 'Civis Europeus Sum: From the Cross-Border Link to the Status of Citizen of the Union,' in Pascal Cardonnel, Allan Rosas, and Nils Wahl, eds., *Constitutionalising the EU Judicial System—Essays in Honour of Pernilla Lindh* (Oxford: Hart Publishing, 2012), pp. 213–232, pp. 213–215.

[59] See Judgment of 5 June 1997, *Uecker and Jacquet*, Joined C-64 and C-65/96, EU:C:1997:285. See also Niamh Nic Shuibne, 'Free Movement of Persons and the Wholly Internal Rule: Time to Move On?,' *Common Market Law Review* 39 (2002): pp. 731–771; Alina Tryfonidou, 'Reverse Discrimination in Purely Internal Situations: An Incongruity in a Citizens' Europe,' *Legal Issues of Economic Integration* 35, no. 1 (2008): pp. 43–67.

[60] But see Gareth Davies, '"Any Place I Hang my Hat?", or: Residence is the New Nationality,' *European Law Journal* 11 (2005): pp. 43–56.

albeit one concretely based in the recognition and trans-nationalization of national ones. Second, supranational citizenship does not rely on horizontal mechanisms only. The vertical link of belonging in a supranational entity enables the enforcement of recognition and provides a check on the operation of the Member States in this sense. Finally, the mutuality of interests and discourses that descends from the trans-nationalization of national citizenships is conducive to creating an enlarged public sphere. In this enlarged sphere, the supranational citizens may ultimately glean their second, 'vertical,' political capacity.

The experience of European citizenship ultimately corroborates the supranational citizenship definition proposed in the first section, helping to distinguish a functional and an aspirational role for that definition's prongs. From a functional point of view, free movement rights are a primary expression of the rule of recognition underpinning supranational citizenship. However, per se, they are not sufficient to ground supranational citizenship. For the latter to ensue, they have to be part of a strategy to reconfigure national citizenships in the context of a broader discourse of common citizenship. From an aspirational perspective, reconfiguration of national citizenships through mutual recognition must be prompted by bonds of trust and mutual responsibility developed in the context of a common supranational project. Such project must entail shared political goals or recuperate common identity elements, and it must inspire a reconceptualization of notions of belonging.

In the European context, this reinforced definition allows distinguishing supranational European citizenship from lesser forms of transnational rights such as those enjoyed by nationals of countries in the European Economic Area.[61] Beyond Europe, it provides an analytical tool to consider both other instances and the prospects of supranational citizenship.

OTHER INSTANCES
OF SUPRANATIONAL CITIZENSHIP

Aside from the most advanced instance of supranational citizenship represented by EU citizenship, free movement regimes in other regional associations and trade agreements offer a promising terrain. However, not all transnational arrangements involving free movement amount to supranational citizenship. Adopting a reinforced definition along the lines distilled from European citizenship, contemporary

---

[61] The European Economic Area is an enlarged single market including the EU Member States and Norway, Iceland, and Liechtenstein.

regional agreements can be divided into three groups in terms of supranational citizenship capability. A first, low-capability group includes the North American Free Trade Agreement (NAFTA) and the Association of Southeast Asian Nations (ASEAN). A second intermediate group includes the Economic Community of West African States (ECOWAS) and the Andean Community. A third, more advanced group, includes the Gulf Cooperation Council, the Caribbean Community (CARICOM) and the Common Market of the South (MERCOSUR). As with the European Union, in all these agreements, with the exception of CARICOM, it is national citizenship, more or less narrowly defined, that provides the gateway to supranational rights of movement and, where relevant, to a burgeoning status of supranational citizenship.

Agreements in the first group provide for sectoral and limited free movement rights. NAFTA, joining Canada, the United States, and Mexico, allows for the temporary movement among participating countries of four classes of business travelers.[62] These limited movement rights do not fit however within a broader discourse of citizenship. Similarly limited and unrelated to ideas of common citizenship are rights extended in the context of ASEAN. Established in 1967 as a regional cooperation project among ten nations in Southeast Asia, ASEAN evolved into a free trade area in 1992 and into an economic community in 2015.[63] Milestones to be reached by 2025 include strengthening rights to free movement for natural persons, through the extension of agreements on mutual recognition of professional qualifications and the recognition of rights to temporary movement for business travelers.[64] Recognition is thus restricted to limited classes of travelers and fits within the frame of a rigorously economic project, not eliciting political or identity aspirations to reconfigure national citizenships into a common transnational status.

Reconfiguration of national citizenships through mutual recognition goes a step further into the second, intermediate, group of regional agreements. ECOWAS, established among fifteen African States with the 1975 Treaty of Lagos, includes free movement of persons as one of its general objectives.[65] The right to free movement is specifically codified in the Treaty of Lagos as a right of the 'common citizens of the Community',[66] and it has been realized in three phases, abolition of visas, right to residence, and right to establishment, detailed in a 1979 Protocol on free

[62] See NAFTA agreement, chapter 16, article 1603 and annex. For an overview, see Alejandro Canales, 'International Migration and Labour Flexibility in the Context of NAFTA,' *International Social Science Journal* 52, no. 3 (2000): pp. 409–419.

[63] For an overview, see Lay Hong Tan, 'Will ASEAN Economic Integration Progress beyond a Free Trade Area?,' *International & Comparative Law Quarterly* 53, no. 4 (2004): pp. 935–967.

[64] See ASEAN Secretariat, 'ASEAN Economic Community Blueprint 2025' (November 2015), online http://www.asean.org/storage/2016/03/AECBP_2025r_FINAL.pdf, section A5, p. 10.

[65] Economic Community of West African States, Revised Treaty, 1993, online http://www.ecowas.int/wp-content/uploads/2015/01/Revised-treaty.pdf, article 3.2(d)iii. The Treaty, originally signed in 1975, was revised in 1993.

[66] Ibid., article 59.

movement.[67] Various weaknesses plague ECOWAS's burgeoning supranational citizenship however, beginning from the very definition of ECOWAS community citizenship, spelt out in a 1982 Protocol to the Treaty of Lagos. The Protocol distinguishes between nationals of an ECOWAS country by birth, and naturalized nationals, who only become ECOWAS community citizens after having resided for fifteen years in an ECOWAS country. In addition, possession of a second non-ECOWAS nationality makes the holder ineligible for community citizenship.[68] This restrictive definition of common citizenship signals weak recognition among the participating Member States. Weak recognition is confirmed by the provision of the Protocol on free movement that reserves to the Member States the right to deny entry to any ECOWAS citizen who is 'inadmissible according to their immigration laws,' without any further guarantee or specification.[69] In addition, problems of road insecurity as well as illegal barriers hamper the concrete enjoyment of free movement rights.[70] In terms of concrete guarantees toward a form of supranational citizenship based on free movement, the Andean Community between Peru, Bolivia, Colombia, and Ecuador seems to have reached a more promising level than ECOWAS. Established in 1969 with an agreement signed in Cartagena, the community evolved into a common market in the 1990s.[71] As part of the common market project, the 2003 'Instrumento Andino de Migración Laboral' extends a general right to free movement for employment purposes to nationals of the Member States.[72] The right is coupled with a guarantee of equal treatment and supported by provisions on access to social security.[73] If the frame of transnational rights appears thus more convincing than in the context of ECOWAS, on the conceptual side Andean free movement struggles at this stage to configure a true supranational citizenship. Recognition of national citizenships is limited to free movement for employment purposes, and the Instrumento de Migracion Laboral makes clear that free movement is an instrument for the 'human development of the Member States':[74] an economic goal, rather than a subtler attempt to reconfigure the boundaries of belonging in the participating national communities.

---

[67] Protocol A/P 1/5/79 Relating to Free Movement of Persons, Residence and Establishment, ECOWAS OJ 1979/1, online http://www.unhcr.org/49e47c9238.pdf.

[68] Protocol A/P.3/5/82 Relating to the Definition of Community Citizen, 1982, online http://documentation.ecowas.int/download/en/legal_documents/protocols/Protocol%20Relating%20to%20the%20Definition%20of%20Community%20Citizen.pdf.

[69] Protocol A/P 1/5/79 (n 67).

[70] See Malebakeng Forere, 'Is Discussion of the "United States of Africa" Premature? Analysis of ECOWAS and SADC Integration Efforts,' Journal of African Law (2012): pp. 29–54, p. 45.

[71] For an overview, see Karen J. Alter and Laurence R. Helfer, 'Nature or Nurture? Judicial Lawmaking in the European Court of Justice and the Andean Tribunal of Justice,' International Organization 64, no. 4 (2010): pp. 563–592.

[72] Consejo Andino de Ministros de Relaciones Exteriores de la Comunidad Andina, Decision 545 of 2003, Instrumento Andino de Migración Laboral, online http://www.comunidadandina.org/Seccion.aspx?id=84&tipo=TE&title=migracion.

[73] Ibid., articles 10, 13.

[74] Ibid., preamble.

More explicitly subversive of those boundaries are regional projects in the third group. The Economic Agreement of the Gulf Cooperation Council,[75] for instance, extends to citizens of participating countries a broad guarantee of equal treatment in all Member States.[76] Equal treatment is not limited to movement, residence, and work, but encompasses access to all professions and economic activities, real estate ownership, tax treatment, education, health and social services.[77] The preamble to the Economic Agreement sets this promise of equal treatment in the frame of a clear citizenship project, clarifying that relevant rights respond to the citizens' aspirations for a 'Gulf citizenship.'[78] In the case of CARICOM, a grouping of twenty Caribbean countries originally established with the 1973 Treaty of Charaguamas, free movement achievements and citizenship aspirations have followed an incremental path. The Treaty of Charaguamas set free movement of persons as a programmatic object-ive, and codified, as a first concrete step towards this objective, free movement rights for certain groups of skilled citizens.[79] A 2007 decision of the Conference of the Heads of Government developed the Treaty free movement objective further in the direction of common citizenship, by recognizing to all citizens of a community country the right to stay for six months in another community country. This was meant as a means to foster the citizens' sense that 'they belong to, and can move in the Caribbean Community.'[80] The Caribbean Court of Justice, interpreting the decision, saw a fundamental transformation in the nature of the Caribbean free movement project: from a project addressed to the restricted group of those seeking economic enhancement, to a project for the citizens of the Community in general.[81] A peculiarity is in that the status that qualifies for mutual recognition, in the con-text of this burgeoning Caribbean supranational citizenship, is not nationality of one of the participating countries as in the European Union, but the broader con-dition of 'belonger': that is, a person who, on the basis of a close connection to one of the Caribbean countries, has a right to enter and reside there even without being

---

[75] Cooperation Council for the Arab States of the Gulf, established in 1981 and including the United Arab Emirates, Bahrain, Saudi Arabia, Oman, Qatar, and Kuwait.

[76] Cooperation Council for the Arab States of the Gulf, Secretariat General, Economic Agreement, 31 December 2001, online http://www.wipo.int/wipolex/en/other_treaties/text.jsp?file_id=227910, article 3.

[77] Ibid., article 3.   [78] Ibid., preamble.

[79] Caribbean Community Secretariat, Revised Treaty of Chaguaramas Establishing the Caribbean Community Including the Caricom Single Market and Economy, 2001, online http://idatd.cepal.org/Normativas/CARICOM/Ingles/Revised_Treaty_of_Chaguaramas.pdf, articles 45–46.

[80] Decision of the Conference of Heads of Government at their Twenty Eighth Meeting, July 1–4, 2007, online http://archive.caricom.org/jsp/communications/communiques/28hgc_2007_com-munique.jsp. The quoted sentence comes from the draft report of the Conference, as quoted by the Caribbean Court of Justice. Caribbean Court of Justice, *Shanique Myrie v Barbados*, [2013] CCJ 3(OJ), paragraph 43. Also see David S. Berry, *Caribbean Integration Law* (Oxford: Oxford University Press, 2014), pp. 258–259.

[81] Caribbean Court of Justice, *Shanique Myrie v Barbados*, (n 80), paragraph 62. See also Berry (n 80), p. 253.

a citizen.[82] Finally, in the context of MERCOSUR, established with the 1991 Treaty of Asunción between Brazil, Argentina, Uruguay, and Paraguay (with the later addition of Venezuela), supranational citizenship has gone beyond aspirations. It has become a precise project, aimed to reconfigure national citizenships on the backdrop of concrete achievements and a clear roadmap. The MERCOSUR citizenship project builds on a number of instruments gradually implementing rights to free movement for the citizens of MERCOSUR countries, and remedying the silence in this respect of the original Treaty of Asunción.[83] A 2010 action plan details the steps to deepen the social and civic dimension of MERCOSUR integration through the achievement of a statute of common citizenship by 2021. The action plan focuses on the implementation of a regional system of free movement as well as on the equalization of the condition of nationals of the MERCOSUR Member States in respect to civic, social, cultural, and economic rights, access to work, education, and social services.[84]

Applying the three-pronged definition of supranational citizenship developed in the first section, and reinforced in the second section, it appears that the three considered groups are at different stages in the realization of supranational citizenship. Projects in the first group do not go as far as conceiving a form of belonging across national borders, and hence fail the third prong of the definition of supranational citizenship proposed in the first section. Projects in the second and third group meet all the three prongs of that definition: they are non-hegemonic, articulated within a supranational entity with a collective purpose, and they do, albeit to different extents, reconfigure national citizenships through a system of mutual recognition. However they differ in the extent to which the free movement systems they entail express the aspiration as well as fulfill the function of supranational citizenship. Projects in the second group portray weaknesses on the functional or aspirational side. In the case of ECOWAS, despite an aspiration to common citizenship, limitations and implementation shortfalls functionally betray a fulsome supranational citizenship; in the Andean Community, free movement rights remain functional to economic cooperation and citizenship aspirations are underdeveloped. Projects in the third group are the most advanced along the path of supranational citizenship. While at different stages of realization, these projects effectively couple the aspiration and discourse of common citizenship with concrete sets of rights tailored to its realization.

---

[82] Treaty of Chaguaramas (n 79), article 32(5(a)(ii); Berry (n 80), p. 250.

[83] Diego Acosta Arcarazo, 'Toward a South American Citizenship?,' *Journal of International Affairs* 68, no. 2 (2015): pp. 213–221, pp. 216–218; M. Belén Olmos Giupponi, 'Citizenship, Migration and Regional Integration: Re-Shaping Citizenship Conceptions in the Southern Cone,' *European Journal of Legal Studies* 4, no. 2 (2011): pp. 104–136, pp. 126–131.

[84] Decision of the Council of MERCOSUR, 'Estatuto de la Ciudadanìa del Mercosur. Plan de Acciòn,' n. 64/10, December 2010, article 2, online http://www.cartillaciudadania.mercosur.int/uploads/DEC_064-2010_ES_Estatuto%20de%20Cidadania.pdf.

THE PROSPECTS
OF SUPRANATIONAL CITIZENSHIP

Regardless of realization stages, most of the supranational citizenship projects considered so far share in that they challenge the nation state's role as referent and provider of citizenship. Through the rules on mutual recognition that they promote, these projects compel states to cater to both present strangers and distant nationals, thereby problematizing the monopolies of both territory and nationality that had long enabled states to discharge their functions.

This challenge to the role of the state enlarges the perspective from the concrete instances to the theoretical prospects of supranational citizenship. The concept, in this respect, faces both a hurdle and an opportunity. It faces a hurdle because the second decade of the twenty-first century has seen momentum for political narratives pushing for rebounding, rather than opening, the nation state.[85] It faces an opportunity precisely because these political sensitivities bring the perspective of the citizens at the forefront of agendas on international trade, globalization, and democracy. Supranational citizenship has an ideal conceptual toolset to deploy in redefining the place for citizenship in the context of relevant agendas. With this in mind, some research questions emerge as central in charting the future of supranational citizenship; these focus on the types of social contracts between citizens and states, as well as on the types of transnational compacts among states that support authentic supranationalization of citizenship.

With regard to social contracts between citizens and states, the problem is understanding what kinds of citizenship bonds and duties are capable of supranationalization. The notion of supranational citizenship based on mutual recognition elaborated so far entails a suggestion: the task is reinterpreting the bonds at the basis of national citizenship, in light of their becoming, in a supranational perspective, fungible and transferable. What types of bonds to a community of origin, in other words, are capable of being preserved at a distance, lived through as external citizens, or transferred in part to a host community? Supranational citizenship, which encourages its holders to wear their national citizenships with a certain casualness, has to rely, it seems, upon bonds of this latter type.

And what duties are owed then by the casual citizens that supranationalization of national citizenship yields? Dimitry Kochenov, in reference to the European context, has argued that citizenship does not entail duties, feeding, in the disconcerted eyes of some interlocutors, the de-dutification trend that accompanies the

---

[85] Witness to these is the result of the UK EU Referendum in June 2016.

cosmopolitan evolution of citizenship.[86] Even Kochenov however recognizes that the rights of citizenship mirror into some societal obligations.[87] Other scholars rather articulate these as proper 'duties' or 'obligations of justice,' aimed at enabling the state to discharge its functions and eventually at supporting a just scheme of rights.[88] With regard to these obligations, a supranational citizenship based on mutual recognition focuses the attention on the balance between duties owed to a home state (of nationality) and duties owed to a host state. The fact that supranational citizenship gravitates on national citizenship suggests that obligations of citizenship remain addressed to the home state. Each state participating in a supranational union extends rights to nationals of other participating Member States as it recognizes their belonging and contributing to a comparable system of organized justice.[89] How far, however, do obligations owed to a home state justify rights in a host state? And what obligations do recognized citizens immediately owe in a host state?

These questions implicate the complex notion of transnational solidarity. Transnational solidarity demands not only obligations among citizens, and between state and citizen, but also presupposes duties among states.[90] This drives in turn the question of the types of supranational compact among nation states justifying this bounded enhancement and reconfiguration of national citizenship, as well as the peculiar state obligations that it calls for. The question is old, at least in the context of Europe,[91] but the perspective, from citizenship, and from recognition, is new.

The mutual recognition lens suggests that, together with a perceived commitment to a minimum shared idea of common good,[92] a notion of trust must be central to the supranational compact. The nation states' recognition of each other's interests, policies, laws and, ultimately, citizenries requires a measure of reciprocal trust in one another's constitutional values, institutions, and processes.[93] While trust does not demand sameness, it does demand a measure of resonance in the participating

---

[86] Dimitry Kochenov, 'EU Citizenship without Duties,' *European Law Journal* 20, no. 4 (2014): pp. 482–498; Richard Bellamy, 'A Duty-Free Europe? What's Wrong with Kochenov's Account of EU Citizenship Rights,' *European Law Journal* 21, no. 4 (2015): pp. 558–565.

[87] Kochenov (n 86), p. 493.

[88] Bellamy (n 86), p. 561; Andrea Sangiovanni, 'Solidarity in the European Union,' *Oxford Journal of Legal Studies* 33, no. 2 (2013): pp. 213–241, p. 222; Floris De Witte, *Justice in the EU: The Emergence of Transnational Solidarity* (Oxford: Oxford University Press, 2015), pp. 2–3.

[89] For an argument along these lines see Daniel Thym, 'The Elusive Limits of Solidarity: Residence Rights of and Social Benefits for Economically Inactive Union Citizens,' *Common Market Law Review* 52 (2015): pp. 17–50; Sangiovanni (n 88), pp. 232–241.

[90] Sangiovanni (n 88), p. 217.

[91] See, e.g., from different perspectives, Weiler (n 53); Jürgen Habermas, 'The Crisis of the European Union in the Light of a Constitutionalization of International Law,' *European Journal of International Law* 23, no. 2 (2012): pp. 335–348; Gareth Davies, 'Democracy and Legitimacy in the Shadow of Purposive Competence,' *European Law Journal* 21, no. 1 (2015): pp. 2–22.

[92] For a disenchanted suggestion, see Somek (n 52), p. 161.

[93] On trust, see Nicolaïdis (n 45), p. 683.

states' conceptions of justice, commitment to their realization, and concrete ability to realize these.

The challenge for supranational citizenship projects, in this sense, is exploring institutional mechanisms and conceptual tools that may level the opportunities available to national citizens throughout a supranational entity, so that their becoming interchangeable does not raise asymmetries and related resistances;[94] whilst preserving the diverse identities, languages, heritages that characterize national citizenship, as it is from the latter that supranational citizenship ultimately derives its substance and legitimacy. The agenda is a complex one that requires hard thoughts on the transnational capability of citizenship in several spheres, social inclusion, political participation, labor market participation, governance mechanisms. It also requires considering the proper balance between the judicial advancement of supranational citizenship rights and the appropriation of supranational citizenship status in political and public opinion narratives: supranational citizenship requires trust and recognition not only among states but also among citizens.

In this latter sense, the concept navigates at present, at least in Europe, in troubled waters. Yet it remains rife with useful clues for an age of heightened instability in both transnational interactions and democratic iterations. Through its focus on mutual recognition, supranational citizenship indeed embodies a normative commitment to both preservation of national interests and bonds, and internalization of the interests of others and of an enlarged, transnational, conception of common good. For these reasons, it also offers important, and sorely needed, discerning tools to distinguish the worthwhile role of nationhood from the illusory promises of exalted nationalism.

BIBLIOGRAPHY

'British Nationality: Summary', online https://www.gov.uk/government/uploads/system/uploads/attachment_data/file/267913/britnatsummary.pdf.

Acosta Arcarazo, Diego, 'Toward a South American Citizenship?', *Journal of International Affairs* 68, no. 2 (2015): pp. 213–221.

Adonnino, Pietro, 'A People's Europe: Reports from the Ad Hoc Committee', *Bullettin of the European Communities* 7 (1985), online http://aei.pitt.edu/992/.

Alter, Karen J. and Laurence R. Helfer, 'Nature or Nurture? Judicial Lawmaking in the European Court of Justice and the Andean Tribunal of Justice', *International Organization* 64, no. 4 (2010): pp. 563–592.

---

[94] On cohesion policy as a possible starting point in the EU's frame, see Francesca Strumia, 'Remedying the Inequalities of Economic Citizenship in Europe: Cohesion Policy and the Negative Right to Move', *European Law Journal* 17, no. 6 (2011): pp. 725–743.

Amtenbrink, Fabian, 'Europe in Times of Economic Crisis: Bringing Europe's Citizens Closer to One Another?', in Michael Dougan, Niamh Nic Shuibne, Eleanor Spaventa, eds., *Empowerment and Disempowerment of the European Citizen* (Oxford, Portland: Hart, 2012), pp. 171–188.

Archibugi, Daniele, *The Global Commonwealth of Citizens: Towards Cosmopolitan Democracy* (Princeton, Woodstock: Princeton University Press, 2008).

Baldi, Gregory and Sara Wallace Goodman, 'Migrants into Members: Social Rights, Civic Requirements, and Citizenship in Western Europe', *West European Politics 38*, no. 6 (2015): pp. 1152–1173.

Bauböck, Rainer, *Transnational Citizenship: Membership and Rights in International Migration* (Cheltenham: Edward Elgar, 1994).

Bauböck, Rainer, 'Why European Citizenship? Normative Approaches to Supranational Union', *Theoretical Inquiries in Law 8*, no. 2 (2007): pp. 454–488.

Bauböck, Rainer, 'The Three Levels of Citizenship within the European Union', *German Law Journal 15*, no. 5 (2014): pp. 751–763.

Bellamy, Richard, 'A Duty-Free Europe? What's Wrong with Kochenov's Account of EU Citizenship Rights', *European Law Journal 21*, no. 4 (2015): pp. 558–565.

Benhabib, Seyla, *The Rights of Others: Aliens, Residents and Citizens* (Cambridge: Cambridge University Press, 2004).

Berry, David S., *Caribbean Integration Law* (Oxford: Oxford University Press, 2014).

Bloom, Tendayi, 'Contradictions in Formal Commonwealth Citizenship Rights in Commonwealth Countries', *The Round Table 100*, no. 417 (2011): pp. 639–654.

Bosniak, Linda, 'Citizenship Denationalized', *Indiana Journal of Global Legal Studies 7* (2000): pp. 447–510.

Cabrera, Luis, *The Practice of Global Citizenship* (Cambridge: Cambridge University Press, 2010).

Canales, Alejandro, 'International Migration and Labour Flexibility in the Context of NAFTA', *International Social Science Journal 52*, no. 3 (2000): pp. 409–419.

Ceriani Cernadas, Pablo, 'Migration, Citizenship and Free Movement in South America: A rights-Based Analysis of Regional Initiatives' (United Nations Research Institute for Social Development (UNRISD), 2013), online http://www.unrisd.org/80256B3C005BCCF 9%2F(httpAuxPages)%2F174C45EB44BF92D1C1257D6C0029E0CB%2F$file%2FCeriani_ Migration,%20Citizenship%20and%20Free%20Movement%20in%20South%20America.pdf.

Davies, Gareth, ' "Any Place I Hang my Hat?", or: Residence is the New Nationality', *European Law Journal 11* (2005): pp. 43–56.

Davies, Gareth, 'Democracy and Legitimacy in the Shadow of Purposive Competence', *European Law Journal 21*, no. 1 (2015): pp. 2–22.

De Cecco, Francesco, 'Fundamental Freedoms, Fundamental Rights and the Scope of Free Movement Law', *German Law Journal 15*, no. 3 (2014): pp. 383–406.

De Witte, Floris, *Justice in the EU: The Emergence of Transnational Solidarity* (Oxford: Oxford University Press, 2015).

Dobson, Lynn, *Supranational Citizenship* (Manchester, New York: Manchester University Press, 2006).

Donati, Sabina, *A Political History of National Citizenship and Identity in Italy, 1861-1950* (Stanford: Stanford University Press, 2013).

Eleftheriadis, Pavlos, 'The Content of European Citizenship', *German Law Journal 15*, no. 5 (2014): pp. 777–796.

Everson, Michelle, 'A Citizenship in Movement,' *German Law Journal* 15 (2014): pp. 965–984.

Falk, Richard, 'The Making of Global Citizenship,' in Bart van Steenbergen, ed., *The Condition of Citizenship* (London: Sage, 1994), pp. 127–140.

Falk, Richard, 'An Emergent Matrix of Citizenship: Complex, Uneven and Fluid,' in Nigel Dower and John Williams, eds., *Global Citizenship: A Critical Reader* (Edinburgh: Edinburgh University Press, 2002), pp. 15–29.

Faulks, Keith, *Citizenship* (London: Routledge, 2000).

Fawcett, J.E.S., 'British Nationality and the Commonwealth,' *The Round Table* 63, no. 250 (1973): pp. 259–269.

Ferrera, Maurizio, *The Boundaries of Welfare, European Integration and the New Spatial Politics of Social Protection* (Oxford: Oxford University Press, 2005).

Follesdahl, Andreas, 'A Common European Identity for European Citizenship?,' *German Law Journal* 15 (2014): pp. 765–775.

Forere, Malebakeng, 'Is Discussion of the "United States of Africa" Premature? Analysis of ECOWAS and SADC Integration Efforts,' *Journal of African Law* (2012): pp. 29–54.

Gey Van Pittius, E.F.W., 'Dominion Nationality,' *Journal of Comparative Legislation and International Law* 13 (1931): pp. 199–202.

Giubboni, Stefano, 'Free Movement of Persons and European Solidarity,' *European Law Journal* 13 (2007): pp. 360–379.

Grugel, Jean, 'Citizenship and Governance in Mercosur: Arguments for a Social Agenda,' *Third World Quarterly* 26, no. 7 (2005): pp. 1061–1076.

Habermas, Jürgen, 'The Crisis of the European Union in the Light of a Constitutionalization of International Law,' *European Journal of International Law* 23, no. 2 (2012): pp. 335–348.

Hansen, Randall, *Citizenship and Immigration in Postwar Britain* (Oxford: Oxford University Press, 2000).

Isin, Engin and Peter Nyers, *Handbook of Global Citizenship Studies* (Abingdon: Routledge, 2014).

Jacobs, Francis J., 'Citizenship of the European Union: a Legal Analysis,' *European Law Journal* 13 (2007): pp. 591–610.

Janssens, Christine, *The Principle of Mutual Recognition in EU Law* (Oxford: Oxford University Press, 2013).

Joppke, Christian, 'How Immigration is Changing citizenship: A Comparative View,' *Ethnic and Racial Studies* 22, no. 4 (1999): pp. 629–652.

Joppke, Christian, 'The Inevitable Lightening of Citizenship,' *European Journal of Sociology* 51 (2010): pp. 9–32.

Karatani, Rieko, *Defining British Citizenship: Empire, Commonwealth and Modern Britain* (London: Frank Cass, 2003).

Kochenov, Dimitry, 'Free Movement and Participation in the Parliamentary Elections in the Member State of Nationality: An Ignored Link?,' *Maastricht Journal of European and Comparative Law* 16 (2009): pp. 197–223.

Kochenov, Dimitry, 'Ius Tractum of Many Faces: European Citizenship and the Difficult Relationship between Status and Rights,' *Columbia Journal of European Law* 15 (2009): pp. 169–237.

Kochenov, Dimitry, 'The Citizenship Paradigm,' *Cambridge Yearbook of European Legal Studies* 15 (2012–1013): pp. 197–225.

Kochenov, Dimitry, 'EU Citizenship without Duties,' *European Law Journal* 20, no. 4 (2014): pp. 482–498.

Kostakopolou, Dora, 'European Union Citizenship: Writing the Future,' *European Law Journal* 13, no. 5 (2007): pp. 623–646.

Kostakopoulou, Dora, *The Future Governance of Citizenship* (Cambridge, New York: Cambridge University Press, 2008).

Kostakopoulou, Dora, 'The Anatomy of Civic Integration,' *Modern Law Review* 73 (2010): pp. 933–958.

Kostoris Padoa Schioppa, Francesca, ed., *The Principle of Mutual Recognition in the European Integration Process* (Basingstoke: Palgrave Macmillan, 2005).

La Torre, Massimo, ed., *European Citizenship: An Institutional Challenge* (The Hague: Kluwer Law International, 1998).

Lenaerts, Koen, 'Civis Europeus Sum: From the Cross-Border Link to the Status of Citizen of the Union,' in Pascal Cardonnel, Allan Rosas, and Nils Wahl, eds., *Constitutionalising the EU Judicial System—Essays in Honour of Pernilla Lindh* (Oxford: Hart Publishing, 2012), pp. 213–232.

Linklater, Andrew, 'Cosmopolitan Citizenship,' *Citizenship Studies* 2, no. 1 (1998): pp. 23–41.

Maas, Willem, 'The Origin, Evolution and Political Objectives of EU Citizenship,' *German Law Journal* 15 (2014): pp. 797–819.

Magnette, Paul, 'How Can One Be European? Reflections on the Pillars of European Civic Identity,' *European Law Journal* 13, no. 5 (2007): pp. 664–679.

Mann, Jatinder, 'The Evolution of Commonwealth Citizenship, 1945–48 in Canada, Britain and Australia,' *Commonwealth and Comparative Politics* 50, no. 3 (2012): pp. 293–313.

Margheritis, Ana, 'Piecemeal Regional Integration in the Post-Neoliberal Era: Negotiating Migration Policies within Mercosur,' *Review of International Political Economy* 20, no. 3 (2013): pp. 541–575.

Meehan, Elizabeth, *Citizenship and the European Community* (London: Sage, 1993).

Menéndez, Agustín José, 'Which Citizenship? Whose Europe? The Many Paradoxes of European Citizenship,' *German Law Journal* 15 (2014): pp. 907–934.

Mindus, Patricia, *Cittadini e No: Forme e Funzioni dell'Inclusione e dell'Esclusione* (Firenze: Firenze University Press, 2014).

Moore, Robert, 'The Debris of Empire: The 1981 Nationality Act and the Oceanic Dependent Territories,' *Immigrants & Minorities* 19, no. 1 (2000): pp. 1–24.

Mycock, Andrew, 'British Citizenship and the Legacy of Empire,' *Parliamentary Affairs* 63, no. 2 (2010): pp. 339–355.

Newbigin, Eleanor, 'Personal Law and Citizenship in India's Transition to Independence,' *Modern Asian Studies* 45, no. 1 (2011): pp. 7–32.

Nic Shuibne, Niamh, 'Free Movement of Persons and the Wholly Internal Rule: Time to Move On?,' *Common Market Law Review* 39 (2002): pp. 731–771.

Nic Shuibne, Niamh, 'The Resilience of EU Market Citizenship,' *Common Market Law Review* 47 (2010): pp. 1597–1628.

Nicolaïdis, Kalypso, 'Trusting the Poles? Constructing Europe through Mutual Recognition,' *Journal of European Public Policy* 14 (2007): pp. 682–698.

Nicolaïdis, Kalypso, 'The Idea of European Demoicracy,' in Julie Dickinson and Pavlos Eleftheriadis, eds., *Philosophical Foundations of European Union Law* (Oxford: Oxford University Press, 2012), pp. 247–274.

Nicolaïdis, Kalypso, 'European Democracy and Its Crisis,' *Journal of Common Market Studies* 51 (2013): pp. 351–369.

Nwauche, E.S., 'Enforcing ECOWAS Law in West African National Courts,' *Journal of African Law* (2011): pp. 181–202.

Olmos Giupponi, M. Belén, 'Citizenship, Migration and Regional Integration: Re-Shaping Citizenship Conceptions in the Southern Cone,' *European Journal of Legal Studies 4*, no. 2 (2011): pp. 104–136.

Orgad, Liav, 'Illiberal Liberalism: Cultural Restrictions on Migration and Access to Citizenship in Europe,' *American Journal of Comparative Law 58* (2010): pp. 53–106.

Preuss, Ulrich K., 'Problems of a Concept of European Citizenship,' *European Law Journal 1*, no. 3 (1995): pp. 267–281.

Sangiovanni, Andrea, 'Solidarity in the European Union,' *Oxford Journal of Legal Studies 33*, no. 2 (2013): pp. 213–241.

Shaw, Jo, 'Citizenship: Contrasting Dynamics at the Interface of Integration and Constitutionalism,' in Paul Craig and Gráinne De Burca, eds., *The Evolution of EU Law* (Oxford: Oxford University Press, 2011), pp. 575–609.

Somek, Alexander, 'Europe: Political Not Cosmopolitan,' *European Law Journal 20* (2014): pp. 142–163.

Soysal, Yasemin Nuhoglu, *The Limits of Citizenship* (Chicago, London: University of Chicago Press, 1994).

Spiro, Peter, 'The Citizenship Dilemma,' *Stanford Law Review 51* (1998–1999): pp. 597–639.

Spiro, Peter, 'Embracing Dual Nationality,' in Randall Hansen and Patrick Weil, eds., *Dual Nationality, Social Rights and Federal Citizenship in the US and Europe: The Reinvention of Citizenship* (New York, Oxford: Berghahn Books, 2002), pp. 19–32.

Strumia, Francesca, 'Citizenship and Free Movement: European and American Features of a Judicial Formula for Increased Comity,' *Columbia Journal of European Law 12*, no. 3 (2005): pp. 713–749.

Strumia, Francesca, 'Remedying the Inequalities of Economic Citizenship in Europe: Cohesion Policy and the Negative Right to Move,' *European Law Journal 17*, no. 6 (2011): pp. 725–743.

Strumia, Francesca, 'Looking for Substance at the Boundaries: European Citizenship and Mutual Recognition of Belonging,' *Yearbook of European Law 32* (2013): pp. 432–459.

Strumia, Francesca, *Supranational Citizenship and the Challenge of Diversity: Immigrants, Citizens and Member States in the EU* (Leiden, Boston: Martinus Nijhoff, 2013).

Strumia, Francesca, 'EU Citizenship and EU Immigration: A Democratic Bridge between the Third Country Nationals' Right to Belong and the Member States' Power to Exclude?,' *European Law Journal 22*, no. 4 (2016): pp. 417–447.

Strumia, Francesca, 'Individual Rights, Interstate Equality, State Autonomy: European Horizontal Citizenship and its (Lonely) Playground in Trans-Atlantic Perspective,' in Dimitry Kochenov, ed., *Citizenship and Federalism in Europe: The Role of Rights* (Cambridge: Cambridge University Press, 2017).

Tan, Lay Hong, 'Will ASEAN Economic Integration Progress beyond a Free Trade Area?,' *International & Comparative Law Quarterly 53*, no. 4 (2004): pp. 935–967.

Thym, Daniel, 'Towards Real Citizenship? The Judicial Construction of Union Citizenship and Its Limits,' in Maurice Adams, Henry De Waele, Johan Meeusen and Gert Straetmans, eds., *Judging Europe's Judges: The Legitimacy of the Case Law of the European Court of Justice* (Oxford, Portland: Hart, 2013), pp. 155–174.

Thym, Daniel, 'The Elusive Limits of Solidarity: Residence Rights of and Social Benefits for Economically Inactive Union Citizens,' *Common Market Law Review 52* (2015): pp. 17–50.

Tryfonidou, Alina, 'Reverse Discrimination in Purely Internal Situations: An Incongruity in a Citizens' Europe,' *Legal Issues of Economic Integration 35*, no. 1 (2008): pp. 43–67.

Von Bogdandy, Armin, Matthias Kottmann, Carlino Antpöhler, Johanna Dickschen, Simon Hentrei, and Maja Smrkolj, 'Reverse Solange: Protecting the Essence of Fundamental Rights against EU Member States,' *Common Market Law Review 49*, no. 2 (2012): pp. 489–519.

Webster's Third New International Dictionary of the English Language (Springfield: Merriam-Webster, 2002).

Weiler, Joseph H., 'In the Face of Crisis: Input Legitimacy, Output Legitimacy and the Political Messianism of European Integration,' *Journal of European Integration 34*, no. 7 (2012): pp. 825–841.

Weiler, Joseph H., 'To Be a European Citizen: Eros and Civilization,' *Journal of European Public Policy* (1997): pp. 495–519.

Weiler, Joseph H., 'Van Gend en Loos: The Individual as Subject and Object and the Dilemma of European Legitimacy,' *International Journal of Constitutional Law 12*, no. 1 (2014): pp. 94–103.

Wilson, Robert R. and Robert E. Clute, 'Commonwealth Citizenship and Common Status,' *American Journal of International Law 57*, no. 3 (1963): pp. 566–587.

....

CHAPTER 31

COSMOPOLITAN CITIZENSHIP

....

KOK-CHOR TAN*

THE term 'cosmopolitan citizen' calls to mind a broad-minded and morally progressive individual capable of transcending her parochial ties and personal interests to include humanity as a whole within her moral horizon. It is thus a rather fashionable idea in some circles of public discourse. But cosmopolitan citizenship is in fact a rather controversial concept within political philosophy and theory. To complicate matters, it is often invoked by different theorists to mean different things. My primary goal in this chapter, which is largely a survey of contemporary approaches, is to identify and clarify some of the main conceptions of cosmopolitan citizenship in the literature, and some of the philosophical and normative difficulties that they

* Many thanks to Ayelet Shachar and Rainer Bauböck for their valuable comments and suggestions. I should acknowledge that sections of this chapter draw on a previously published work, Kok-Chor Tan, 'Global Democracy: International, Not Cosmopolitan,' in Deen Chatterjee, ed., *Democracy in a Global World* (New York: Lanham, Rowman and Littlefield, 2005), pp. 161–186.

face. But I attempt, in the last part of the chapter, a defense of cosmopolitan citizenship understood as a normative ideal.

The central difficulty with the idea of cosmopolitan citizenship in fact engages the very idea of citizenship itself. Standardly, citizenship is understood as an inherently bounded concept, tied to membership in a political society. Is cosmopolitan citizenship then necessarily committed to the notion of a world state? Or can one speak sensibly of being a cosmopolitan citizen in the absence of a global political society, as an ideal independent of political membership? In part then, the discussion surrounding cosmopolitan citizenship engages the fundamental question of the possibility of reconceptualizing and recasting the ideal of citizenship.[1]

VARIETIES OF COSMOPOLITAN CITIZENSHIP

To begin, let me identify and distinguish the main conceptions of cosmopolitan citizenship that one might infer from popular and academic discourse. The first, most immediate, conception treats cosmopolitan citizenship literally as citizenship under a *world state*. Citizenship is here understood in the traditional sense as a *legal-political category* tied to political membership. In this case, instead of the nation-state, one's political membership and allegiance is extended to a world government. Defenders of cosmopolitan citizenship in this sense are thus in the main proposing and defending the creation of a world state. While this is a straightforward interpretation of cosmopolitan citizenship, it is in fact not the version most frequently proposed in the academic literature. But it has its share of stalwart defenders such as Robert Goodin, Kai Nielsen, and Andrew Wendt.[2]

Another conception of cosmopolitan citizenship understands citizenship not in terms of political membership but in terms of the function and related capacities of individuals in democratic decision-making. What the cosmopolitan citizen is, on this conception, is not a citizen of the world in the legal-political sense, but an

[1] See Bauböck in this volume, for a discussion on citizenship as political membership. See Walker in this volume, for a discussion on the territorial parameters of citizenship.

[2] Robert E. Goodin, 'World Government is Here!', in Sigal Ben-Porath and Rogers Smith, eds., *Varieties of Sovereignty and Citizenship* (Philadelphia: University of Pennsylvania Press, 2013), pp. 149–165; Kai Nielsen, 'World Government, Security, and Global Justice', in Steven Luper-Foy, ed., *Problems of International Justice* (Boulder: Westview Press, 1988), pp. 263–282; Andrew Wendt, 'Why a World State is Inevitable', *European Journal of International Relations* 9, no. 4 (2003): pp. 491–542.

individual with the entitlement and responsibility to participate in global decision-making through new transnational institutions, empowered international organizations. There is no presumption on this view of a world state. In contrast to the legal-political conception of citizenship noted above, we may call this functional conception the *democratic conception*. The main advocates of cosmopolitan democracy, such as David Held and Daniele Archibugi, have this conception of cosmopolitan citizenship in mind.[3]

Finally, cosmopolitan citizenship has been used in a normative sense. Here citizenship is used aspirationally to denote a moral perspective or point of view an individual should adopt when considering her moral obligations and duties of justice to others. It is an ideal of how the morally engaged person should view the world, that beneath our local and parochial ties like state citizenship and nationality, our obligations of justice to all persons in the world are fundamentally the same. There is no commitment on this account to a world state as such. This *normative conception* of cosmopolitan citizenship is found in the works of Martha Nussbaum and Andrew Linklater.[4]

These three conceptions of cosmopolitan citizenship can be distinguished as follows: the first associates cosmopolitan citizenship with a global *government*, the second with global democratic *governance*, and the third (primarily) with cosmopolitan *justice*. The main difficulty with the legal-political conception has to do with the practical and normative challenges surrounding the notion of a world state. The democratic conception avoids this problem, but, as we will see, it faces other difficulties having to do with the locus of democratic decision-making. The normative conception, as a moral aspiration, avoids the problem of the site of democracy, but faces challenges of its own concerning its potentially distorting (even if aspirational) use of the term 'citizenship.'

In this chapter, I will limit my discussion mostly to the democratic conception (since this is where the cosmopolitan citizen most frequently makes her entrance in the philosophical literature). I will conclude with some reflections on the plausibility and appeal of normative conception as an alternative.

---

[3] David Held, *Cosmopolitanism: Ideals and Realities* (Cambridge: Polity Press, 2010); David Held, 'The Changing Contours of Political Community,' in Barry Holden, ed., *Global Democracy: Key Debates* (London: Routledge, 2000), pp. 17–31; David Held, *Democracy and the Global Order* (Cambridge: Polity Press, 1995); Daniele Archibugi et al., 'The United Nations as an Agency of Global Democracy,' in Barry Holden, ed., *Global Democracy: Key Debates* (London: Routledge, 2000), pp. 125–142; Archibugi, Daniele et al., eds., *Re-Imaging Political Community* (Cambridge: Polity Press, 1998).

[4] Martha C. Nussbaum, *Cultivating Humanity* (Cambridge: Harvard University Press, 1997); Martha C. Nussbaum, *For Love of Country?*, edited by Joshua Cohen (Boston: Beacon Press, 1996); Andrew Linklater, 'Cosmopolitan Citizenship,' *Citizenship Studies* 2, no. 1 (1998): pp. 23–41.

Cosmopolitan Democracy
and Cosmopolitan Citizenship

Cosmopolitan democracy is proposed as a response to the problem of global demo-cratic deficit. The state-centric account of democracy, cosmopolitan democrats point out, is outmoded in an era of increasing globalization in which state borders and membership are becoming less and less central with respect to where deci-sions are made and how and where they impact people. For instance, domestic eco-nomic and social decisions and policies have global reach and effect. Environmental regulations, or the lack thereof, affect not just the country where these regulations are made, but also neighboring countries if not the rest of the world. Even when decisions with profound impact on persons are made by international institutions such as the World Bank, or the International Monetary Fund, there is an absence of democratic input by those individuals who will be most affected. As David Held, puts it, 'the idea of a democratic order can no longer be simply defended as an idea suitable to a particular closed political community or state.'[5]

Thus, Held and others like Daniel Archibugi propose, as an alternative to the traditional state-centric view of democracy, the ideal of cosmopolitan democracy. As the primary arena of human social, political, and economic endeavors is less and less limited to the confines of the domestic state, so less and less should the primary arena of democratic engagement be similarly confined. The idea that democracy is essentially a state-based practice and concept has to be replaced by an unbounded conception of democracy in order to face the new realities and challenges of a glo-balized world order.

Cosmopolitan democracy thus treats democracy as a transnational ideal in which individuals, conceived as global participants, engaged in deliberative democratic decision-making with each other on the global stage. Individuals are not merely democratic agents within their own countries, but are democratic agents in the world at large. They are to be empowered to have a voice in global decision-making through their participation at various transnational associations and institutions. Some cosmopolitan democrats propose, for instance, the creation of a world par-liament consisting of representatives *directly* elected by individuals to complement existing international bodies such as the General Assembly of the United Nations that consists of representatives of nation-states.[6] In other words, individuals will

[5] Held, 'The Changing Contours of Political Community' (n 3); Held, *Cosmopolitanism: Ideals and Realities* (n 4). See also Saskia Sassen, *Globalization and Its Discontents* (New York: New Press, 1998). Costello, in this volume, points to the international refugee crisis as another stress point for standard (state-centric) conceptions of citizenship.

[6] Archibugi et al., 'The United Nations as an Agency of Global Democracy' (n 3).

assume certain democratic citizenship functions at the global level that are traditionally state-confined, such as electing representatives to world governing bodies. Held thus writes that '[d]emocracy for the new millennium must involve *cosmopolitan citizens* able to gain access to, and mediate between, and render accountable, the social, economic and political processes and flows which cut across and transform their traditional community boundaries.'[7]

The introduction of cosmopolitan citizenship animates a potential misunderstanding that many cosmopolitan democrats should want to dispel. Cosmopolitan democracy coupled with cosmopolitan citizenship calls to mind a democratic *cosmos polis*, a democratic world political order in which individuals are citizens in the ordinary legal political sense. That is, individuals are seen as political subjects of a world sovereign that has the capacity and right to make and enforce laws that are binding on all individuals in the world qua subjects. Indeed, cosmopolitanism itself is commonly associated with the idea of a world state, and this association is one reason why some commentators reject the cosmopolitan ideal.[8]

The idea of a world state is a controversial one, for both practical and normative reasons.[9] Immanuel Kant, his cosmopolitan credentials notwithstanding, is skeptical of a world state.[10] He famously argues in his 1775 essay, 'Perpetual Peace,' that a literal world state will be hard to achieve, and even if achievable hard to maintain given the vast expanse of the globe and the challenges of human diversity.[11] Moreover, if contrary to expectations such a state is realized, it is realizable and sustainable only through some kind of global tyranny.

We must not ignore the fact that world statism has some powerful defenders in the literature, as noted above. But this is an outlier position among cosmopolitan democrats. Few actually defend a literal world state and a world citizenship conceived as citizenship in the ordinary legal-political sense in terms of a common political relationship. Most of them, like Held and Archibugi, refrain from affirming an actual world state. To the contrary, they quite explicitly state that their understanding of cosmopolitan democracy does not entail a world state as we ordinarily understand the 'state.' For Held, what cosmopolitan democracy requires primarily are trans-*national* institutions and organizations that transcend and cut across the

---

[7] Held, 'The Changing Contours of Political Community' (n 4), p. 30. Emphasis added.

[8] See example.g. the criticism in Danilo Zolo, *Cosmopolis: Prospects for World Government* (Cambridge: Polity Press, 1997); Danilo Zolo, 'The Lords of Peace: From the Holy Alliance to the New International Criminal Tribunal,' in Barry Holden, ed., *Global Democracy: Key Debates* (London: Routledge, 2000), pp. 73–86.

[9] For a survey on the pros and cons of world government, see Catherine Lu, 'World Government,' *The Stanford Encyclopedia of Philosophy* (Winter 2015 Edition), Edward N. Zalt, ed., http://plato.stanford.edu/archives/win2015/entries/world-government/.

[10] See Pauline Kleingeld, 'Kant's Moral and Political Cosmopolitanism,' *Philosophy Compass* 11, no. 1 (2016): pp. 14–23 for a survey of Kant's cosmopolitanism.

[11] Immanuel Kant, 'Perpetual Peace,' in *Kant's Political Writings*, edited and translated by Hans Reiss (Cambridge: Cambridge University Press, 1991) [1775], pp. 93–130.

boundaries of states. To put it simply, Held's cosmopolitan democracy is a call for more democratic world *governance*, not world government. Its attendant notion of cosmopolitan citizenship, then, is not citizenship in the standard legal-political sense, connoting membership in a political association and lawful subjection to its coercive powers. What the cosmopolitan citizen is, under this conception, is a *democratic* ideal. The cosmopolitan citizen is a participant in global democratic governance and who stands in relation to other individuals in the world as democratic partners but not necessarily as fellow subjects of a common political authority. What makes the cosmopolitan democratic citizen a *citizen* is her role and function as a democratic participant in global decision-making. We might say then, for a contrast with the legal-political conception of citizenship, that 'citizenship' here is defined in terms of an agent's democratic 'function' and not political membership.

The democratic conception of cosmopolitan citizenship takes it that meaningful democratic participation is possible and realizable outside the context of a political state as ordinarily conceived. Indeed, it is the motivation behind cosmopolitan democracy that meaningful individual democratic participation is not just possible but necessary beyond the confines of the domestic state. We can and ought to reconceive the traditional (state-centric) locus of democratic participation.

Yet this democratic ideal of cosmopolitan citizenship is less straightforward than might seem on first glance. According to some critics, the democratic relationship it depends on is not something to be taken for granted at the global level. Let us turn to one prominent line of objection against the democratic conception that I will call, for convenience, the liberal nationalist challenge.

THE LIBERAL NATIONALIST CHALLENGE

Deliberative democracy is 'a conception of democratic politics in which decisions and policies are justified in a process of discussion among free and equal citizens or their accountable representatives.'[12] Fundamentally, this means that a democratically arrived at public policy is one which all individuals who are affected could reasonably consent to. According to the liberal nationalist thesis, this ideal of democracy requires, foremost, that individuals share a common language, a vernacular, with which to effectively debate and to collectively decide on matters that affect them. Moreover, democratic politics presuppose a sufficient level of trust and mutual

---

[12] Amy Gutmann and Dennis Thompson, 'Why Deliberative Democracy is Different,' *Social Philosophy and Policy* 17 (2000): pp. 161–180, p. 161.

respect among citizens so as to motivate them to honor democratic decisions that are not in their favor, on the understanding that should decisions be in their favor next time, these would likewise be respected. Most democrats agree that democratic politics is possible only if citizens adequately trust and respect each other; but liberal nationalists make the additional claim that a shared national identity is the source of this solidarity, the 'fellow-feeling', necessary for generating and sustaining this mutual respect and trust among persons who are practically strangers to each other, as citizens generally are. I will elaborate on some of these points.

Before proceeding, it is worth reminding ourselves of the distinction between *liberal* nationalism and nationalism as such. Liberal nationalism takes liberalism as the starting point, and limits nationalist pursuits against liberal democratic values and principles. As Yael Tamir puts it, a liberal nationalist entity 'will endorse liberal principles of distribution inwards and outwards; its political system will reflect a particular national culture, but its citizens will be free to practice different cultures and follow a variety of life plans and conceptions of the good.'[13] Indeed, as we will see, one reason why nationalism matters (for the liberal nationalist) is that shared nationality provides the precondition for liberal democratic values and commitments. The liberal nationalist challenge does not oppose the global ends that cosmopolitan democrats aspire to. What it claims is that the (liberal) nation is the necessary setting from which to articulate and realize these ends and from which to best address the global democratic deficit problem. Henceforth, unless qualified or suggested otherwise by the context, nationalism implies *liberal* nationalism.[14]

Will Kymlicka writes that 'democratic politics is politics in the vernacular', meaning by this that democratic deliberation is possible only among individuals who share a common language.[15] One reason for this is that people ordinarily feel 'comfortable debating political issues in their own tongue.'[16] As a general rule, only a minority elite can acquire equal fluency in more than one language. Most individuals are most at home talking politics in their own tongue even if they have competency in a second language. So to require people to deliberate in a language foreign to them risks a form of political elitism to the exclusion of the majority of a society. This, of course, runs against the democratic ideal. Kymlicka thus concludes that 'the more political debate is conducted in the vernacular, the more participatory it will be.'[17]

---

[13] Yael Tamir, *Liberal Nationalism* (Princeton: Princeton University Press, 1993), p. 163.

[14] I am indebted to Rainer Bauböck for reminding me that the nationalist challenge I am discussing is a challenge from within *liberal* nationalism. He also rightly suggests that the term 'democratic nationalism' would be more exact for my purpose since my discussion will emphasize democratic rather than liberal ends and values. But for the expediency of avoiding conceptual clarifications that are inevitable when new terms are introduced, I will stick to the standard label, 'liberal nationalism', since it reasonably suffices for the present purpose.

[15] Will Kymlicka, *Politics in the Vernacular* (Oxford: Oxford University Press, 2001), p. 213.

[16] Ibid.   [17] Ibid., p. 214.

In addition to the common language that shared nationality provides, another crucial role nationality plays in servicing democratic politics is that it provides a sense of solidarity and unity that is necessary for generating the requisite level of mutual respect and trust among individuals. Democracy requires individuals to respect the reasonable views of their fellow citizens even if they are in disagreement with each other, and to only forward arguments and views that each can 'reasonably be expected reasonably to endorse.'[18]

Fellow nationals are, of course, not intimate with each other as, say, friends or kin are. But fellow feelings, nationalists argue, need not be restricted only to people who are closely related to one another. Conationals see themselves to be part of a collective and common past and with a shared future, and even if they are not actually acquainted with each other, 'in the minds of each lives the image of their communion.'[19] It is for this reason that Benedict Anderson famously refers to the nation as 'an imagined community,' meaning by this not that the nation is a fictitious association that is unworthy of people's allegiances, but that it is a significant allegiance-generating association that is premised on a people's image or collective consciousness of its historic and communal distinctness.

In sum, as David Miller has long pointed out, democratic politics 'are likely to function most effectively when they embrace just a single national community.'[20] This is because the virtues of mutual trust and respect, moderation and self-restraint, and the idea of public reason are crucial for a functioning democratic political community; and common nationality provides the 'cement' for engendering and nurturing these virtues.[21] In sum, 'national political forums with a single common language form the primary locus of democratic participation in the modern world, and are more genuinely participatory than political forums at higher levels that cut across language-lines.'[22] Shared nationality provides the cultural linguistic basis for democratic deliberation and the source of democratic trust and respect among citizens.

The nationalist thesis makes the strong positive claim about the necessity of shared nationality for democratic relations and deliberation. But this positive claim rests on a weaker negative claim that the bonds of solidarity and mutual understanding necessary for democratic relationships are absent at the global level. The truth of the weaker negative thesis suffices to put the democratic conception of cosmopolitan citizenship under pressure.

---

[18] John Rawls, 'The Idea of Public Reason Revisited,' in *The Law of Peoples* (Cambridge: Harvard University Press, 1999), pp. 129–180, p. 140.

[19] Benedict Anderson, *Imagined Communities* (London: Verso, 1993), p. 6.

[20] David Miller, *On Nationality* (Oxford: Oxford University Press, 1995), p. 90; also Miller, 'Bounded Citizenship,' in Kimberly Hutchings and R. Dannreuther, eds., *Cosmopolitan Citizenship* (New York: St. Martin's Press, 1999), pp. 60–82, p. 60–61.

[21] See Margaret Canovan, *Nationhood and Political Theory* (Cheltenham: Edward Elgar, 1996).

[22] Kymlicka (n 15), p. 227.

As mentioned, nationalist theorists point out that nationhood provides the solidarity and common language necessary for democratic politics. Yet, as some have countered, 'the cosmopolitan governance proposed by Held is for the most part silent on' this crucial point.[23] What would serve as the basis of solidarity and common understanding at the global level among people of diverse nationalities? If individuals are to be directly represented at global decision making irrespective of nationality, it is not clear whether the linguistic diversity can be overcome, and whether the diversity in worldviews and affinities can properly support a democratic deliberative order that is based on mutual trust and respect across national lines. If we actually do establish, say, a directly elected world parliament, how likely would it be for, say, a Canadian to seriously consider voting for, and to do so in an informed manner, an Indonesian candidate given the linguistic and cultural barriers?

For example, as some commentators have pointed out, the European experience has shown this to be quite unlikely. In spite of the success of the European Union (EU) in formally bringing together democratic nations under a single political organization, the creation of a unified European demos remains elusive. The diversity of and challenges of national identification remain as obstacles to the formation of transnational European democratic solidarity in spite of economic and monetary integration at the level of Europe. As some commentators have suggested, most Europeans tend to see themselves as members of particular nations, rather than as members of a European polity.[24]

Extending direct democratic participation beyond national boundaries may also undermine democratic accountability. As Dennis Thompson observes, 'when we look at the experience of extending governmental authority beyond national boundaries, we cannot be encouraged by what we see. As the EU has gained more power and become more effective, it has also drawn more criticism for its lack of democratic accountability.'[25] The more we increase the number of decision-making authorities that are directly accountable to individuals, as the cosmopolitan idea calls for, the more difficult it will be to actually hold these authorities accountable. 'By its very nature, such a network [of regional and international agencies and authorities] does not give those citizens outside particular agencies or assemblies any significant control, and does not provide any way for citizens within them to deal with the effects of the uncoordinated decisions of other agencies and assemblies.'[26] The more we multiply democratic authorities, the

---

[23] Ibid., p. 239.
[24] Richard Bellamy and R. J. Barry Jones, 'Globalization and Democracy: An Afterword,' in Barry Holden, ed., *Global Democracy: Key Debates* (London: Routledge, 2000), pp. 202–216, p. 211.
[25] Dennis Thompson, 'Democratic Theory and Global Society,' *Journal of Political Philosophy* 7, no. 2 (1999): pp. 111–125, p. 115.
[26] Ibid., pp. 115–116.

more we undermine the democratic ideals of effective control and accountability. Thompson, in other writings, has aptly labeled this 'the problem of many hands.'[27] To be sure, the problem of many hands is not uniquely a problem for cosmopolitan democracy, for it confounds domestic democrats as well to the extend that there are multiple democratically accountable decision-making entities within a society. But it is a problem that is compounded when we extend deliberative democracy globally.

There is also the problem of fostering and securing a global civil society that can underpin a functioning democracy of individuals in the global arena. Democrats take as one important precondition for a flourishing democracy the presence of a flourishing civil society. Yet it is not clear how a global civil society could be engendered. Richard Falk holds out hope, cautiously, that a global civil society may emerge as a result of globalization, in that 'as the global village becomes more an experienced, daily reality,' individuals can come to see themselves as members of a shared community of fate.[28] This optimism presupposes that the sense of solidarity and common sympathies and fellow-feelings that are the preconditions of civil society can be engendered globally because of people's common experiences and realities as a result of increased globalization. Yet shared experience and reality alone may not be sufficient. A prior sense of identity may be necessary before individuals can come to appreciate and perceive certain experiences and realities as *shared*. Why, for example, would Americans attempt to understand the effects of globalization on Chinese citizens and to share in their worldview? The felt impact of free trade and economic liberalization for Americans and the Chinese workers are quite different; unless there is first a prior sense of affinity and mutual feeling between the two peoples, experiences need not be seen as shared and held in common.

One might propose that shared values and causes could provide the glue to bind individuals from different nations together, thus creating the global civil society needed to ground cosmopolitan democracy. Held, in earlier writings, points to the 'new voices' motivated by shared principles in events such as the Rio Conference and the Beijing Conference on Women's Rights as hopeful signs of strengthening global ties and the founding of a global civil society. For more recent examples, one could look to The United Nations Climate Change Conference held in Paris in 2015 as a sign of the beginnings of a true global civil society based on shared interests and challenges. Held acknowledges that these attempts to create 'new forms of public life and new ways of debating regional and global issues' are still very nascent, and so it is too early to say whether these attempts to foster a global civil society will eventually succeed. Nonetheless, he thinks that 'they point in the direction' of such

---

[27] Dennis Thompson, *Political Ethics and Public Office* (Cambridge: Harvard University Press, 1986).

[28] Richard Falk, 'Global Civil Society and the Democratic Prospect,' in Barry Holden, ed., *Global Democracy: Key Debates* (London: Routledge, 2000), pp. 162–178, p. 176.

possibilities.[29] But in reply to Held, nationalists would urge that we should not be too hasty to conflate transnational activism motivated by shared goals and interests with transnational democratic deliberation. The former kind of coalition is unraveled once goals and interests diverge; democratic associations, on the other hand, ought to be able to withstand such value disagreements. Indeed, democratic associations presuppose divergent goals among its members, and hence the need for democratic deliberation to fairly and reasonably adjudicate divergent claims. The ties that bind a democratic order together cannot be secured by shared interests or principles for these are not robust and permanent enough to generate the kinds of shared sympathies, and mutual respect and trust, necessary for actual deliberative democracy.[30]

As an aside, it is important to note that the nationalist thesis does not deny that there is a global democratic deficit that needs fixing. They do not oppose the idea of greater global democracy as such. What they are skeptical of is that global democracy can be achieved through the direct democratic participation of individuals dislocated from local and national communities. Instead of supplanting and diluting national and local democratic relations, nationalists would call for the strengthening of the traditional sites of democracy at the local and national levels, and better international democratic institutions wherein representatives of democracies can engage in democratic decision-making with other national representatives. In short, global democracy is to be achieved by improving democratic relations between individuals at the national level and improving democratic relations between national communities at the global level. Global democracy will take the form then literally of an inter*national* democracy instead of a cosmopolitan democracy. More can be said about global democracy through international democracy instead of inter*personal* democracy); but the key point for our purpose is that this approach dispenses with the ideal of the democratic cosmopolitan citizen.

The negative claim of the nationalist thesis can be challenged of course. For just one example, Carol Gould has argued for the possibility of transnational democratic solidarity through increasing global level participation by individuals through different interactive international organizations, networks, and governmental agencies.[31] This is a live debate, so I should not give the impression that the nationalist thesis cannot be refuted. But as things are, it presents a serious challenge.

---

[29] Held, 'The Changing Contours of Political Community' (n 3), p. 29.
[30] Kymlicka (n 15), p. 325.
[31] Carol Gould, *Interactive Democracy: The Social Roots of Global Justice* (Cambridge: Cambridge University Press, 2014). See also Daniel Weinstock, 'Prospects for Transnational Citizenship and Democracy,' *Ethics and International Affairs* 15, no. 2 (2001): pp. 53–66.

Cosmopolitan Justice
and Cosmopolitan Citizenship

Besides the legal-political and democratic conceptions, cosmopolitan citizenship has also been proposed as a normative ideal. On the normative conception, cosmopolitan citizenship is a metaphor for the moral perspective or point of view that the globally engaged individual ought to adopt.

The normative conception of cosmopolitan citizenship is thus an expression of a moral outlook or aspiration. It illustrates the ideal that we are to regard all persons in the world with equal consideration and respect. The normative conception need not be silent about institutions. To the contrary, as an entailment of its moral outlook, it can require that any global arrangements we establish and support must be justifiable to all affected. And it can certainly require the establishment of new global institutional forms if equal respect for all cannot otherwise be achieved. But, unlike the legal political conception, the normative conception is not tied to the notion of a world state. And to the extent that there are independent reasons for moral skepticism against a world state, the normative conception of cosmopolitanism, even though it can make institutional demands, will eschew the creation of a world state. The normative conception is primarily a statement of our moral obligations and only derivatively a statement about global institutions.[32] It carries no necessary legal-political connotations.

This is how some of the prominent calls for cosmopolitan citizenship are to be understood. Indeed, one of the earliest known utterances of cosmopolitan citizenship is intended in exactly this metaphorical sense. When Diogenes of Sinope offered that he was 'a citizen of the world' (*kosmopolitēs*) in response to the question as to his origin, his point was that his moral allegiances and responsibilities were not confined to the state of Sinope but owed to humanity as a whole. He meant by 'citizen of the world' a moral perspective, a way of morally engaging with and relating to the world, an engagement that is broad-minded and not parochial. In our own time, when Martha Nussbaum invokes the idea of world citizenship, she is not calling for the establishment of a world state. Her purpose is to 'make all human beings part of our community of dialogue and concern,' and to motivate us to 'base our political deliberations on interlocking commonality, and [to] give the circle that defines our humanity special attention and respect.'[33] The invocation of cosmopolitan citizenship is meant to incite an expansion of our moral horizon and not a call to arms to bring about a world government.

---

[32] See Gillian Brock, 'Contemporary Cosmopolitanism,' *Philosophy Compass* 8, no. 8 (2013): pp. 689–698, for a critical survey of cosmopolitanism and justice.

[33] Nussbaum, *For Love of Country?* (n 4), p. 9.

The normative conception differs from the democratic conception as well. It does not conceive cosmopolitan citizenship in terms of individuals' capacity and responsibility to participate in actual global democratic politics. The cosmopolitan citizen, as understood here, is a conception of the individual for the purpose of cosmopolitan justice not for cosmopolitan democracy. It identifies a point of view to adopt for the purpose of assessing the rightness or wrongness of our current global conditions and of what we owe to each other in the world at large. The cosmopolitan citizen, in this context, is a person who is able to look past her local ties and interests, and to regard the whole humanity as her moral community. This is distinct from the cosmopolitan democratic conception of the individual as a person who is empowered and capable of actually participating in democratic global governance.

The above might seem rather puzzling. After all, some approaches to justice seem to involve deliberation, as in social contract theories of justice. That is, the social contract method involves deliberation, so it seems, among persons for the purpose of identifying and agreeing on principles of justice for their common social order.[34] So, at the very least, with respect to social contract theories, shouldn't the difficulties attending global democratic *deliberation* affect as well global *deliberations* about justice? Thus, it is important to clarify that these are two very different forms of deliberation.

First, unlike deliberations about justice which operate at the abstract level of determining general principles for the purpose of regulating the basic institutions of society, the ideal of deliberative democracy operates at what Gutmann and Thompson have called 'the middle range of abstraction, between foundational principles and institutional rules.'[35] To put this point across in Rawlsian terms, deliberative democracy is concerned with the legislative stage of justice, whereas deliberations about justice concern the basic principles that would regulate the social setting within which such legislative deliberations take place. As Samuel Freeman neatly puts it, deliberative democracy is a normative 'model of deliberation that legislative and other decision-making bodies are to emulate ... As a model of decision making, it is to be distinguished from the theoretical construct of hypothetical agreement that typifies contractarian theory [of justice].'[36] The ideal conditions for democratic deliberation and deliberation about justice are quite different then, as are their aims. To put it differently, deliberation about justice aims to provide principles to regulate institutions, deliberative democracy aims to clarify the laws and rules of institutions.

[34] See John Rawls, *A Theory of Justice* (Cambridge: Harvard University Press, 1971). Another prominent example of the social contract approach to justice is David Gauthier, *Morals by Agreement* (Oxford: Oxford University Press, 1986).

[35] Amy Gutmann and Dennis Thompson, *Democracy and Disagreement* (Cambridge: Harvard University Press, 1996), p. 5.

[36] Samuel Freeman, 'Deliberative Democracy: A Sympathetic Comment,' *Philosophy and Public Affairs* 29, no. 4 (2000): pp. 371–418, p. 379.

This takes us to the second, and most basic, difference between the two kinds of deliberation. Democratic deliberation about legislation and institutional specifics is *actual* deliberation that takes place in real life and subject to real world limiting conditions, whereas deliberation about justice is hypothetical and idealized.[37] John Rawls's 'original position' is one famous hypothetical device of representation that which any person, 'here and now', may utilize in deciding what justice demands.[38] The original position construction presents a deliberative model that is not limited by considerations of language, national affinity and so on because it operates at a level of abstraction that is independent of such real limitations. 'Hypothetical agreements (such as the original position …) contain conditions that are not realizable in the world,' as Freeman writes,[39] but being hypothetical, these conditions need not be bound by real constraints. That is, the conditions for deliberative democracy, such as shared language, mutual feelings etc., do not apply to the construction of hypothetical agreements about justice. These are different kinds of deliberation for which different idealized conditions are required, and in the case of deliberations about justice, differences in nationality may be put to one side. Indeed, on the cosmopolitan approach to justice, they must be put to one side.

The above remarks are largely familiar, and hopefully uncontroversial enough. I draw them to our attention to clarify how democratic deliberation differs from deliberation about justice, and, more to the point, why the nationalist thesis does not trouble the normative conception of cosmopolitan citizenship. Any individual here and now may try to work out what cosmopolitan justice requires, since no actual deliberation is required. So the linguistic and cultural solidarity problems do not even arise. Just as it is possible for a single citizen to conceive behind the veil of ignorance principles of justice for her entire society, so it is possible, by extension, for a single person to conceive of principles for the world. Deliberations about justice are hypothetical deliberations rather than actual, and so unlike the actual deliberation of democracy, are not confounded by the real problems and limitations of language and solidarity identified by the nationalist thesis.

I have not given any arguments why principles of justice ought to be conceived on cosmopolitan terms. My main point is that the nationalist thesis does not threaten the normative conception of cosmopolitan citizenship. But this is not to say that the normative conception does not face its own challengers. Some commentators feel that this metaphorical, normative, use of 'citizenship' is more trouble than it is worth. Stephen Neff, for instance, thought that it is in the end unfortunate that

[37] Ibid., p. 380. See also Gutmann and Thompson (n 35).

[38] Rawls (n 34). Rawls's original position procedure, to recall, conceives of parties to the deliberation about justice as free and equal. This condition of equality and freedom is ensured by means of the 'veil of ignorance,' behind which parties to the deliberation are to imagine that they do not know contingent and specific facts about themselves, such as their social class, the talents they have, their own conception of the good and so on.

[39] Freeman (n 36), p. 379.

cosmopolitans speak freely of world citizenship given the distractions and confusion this poses, when they mean rather generally the attractive idea of a shared humanity.[40] Indeed, the normative goals of cosmopolitanism, that of global justice, protecting human rights, and a more democratic global arena 'can be brought about in ways,' argues Neff, 'which do not require a distinct concept of cosmopolitan citizenship.'[41] As David Miller has pointed out, citizenship, properly understood, is a 'bounded' concept that expresses a membership in a distinct polity that comes with certain obligations in addition to rights.[42] To speak of cosmopolitan citizenship in the absence of a world state and a common political relationship between individuals in the world at large is a hazardous overextension of the concept of citizenship.

But why is a metaphorical use of citizenship unacceptable? Why is this a problematic overextension of the concept of citizenship? We do, for example, use the concept of university citizenship and say of our more selfless and institutionally responsive colleagues that they are good university citizens. Clearly we aren't imputing here some pretended political relationship among university colleagues. The term 'good university citizen' uses 'citizen' metaphorically, to describe a colleague who is devoted and committed to her larger academic institution beyond her own personal projects. Not only is its use not misleading; it is actually illuminating.

It might be pointed out that unlike individuals in the world, members of a university are members of an institution capable of governance. Thus it can make sense to speak of a university citizen but not of a global citizen since the latter lacks common associational and institutional ties. But my reference to the idea of the university citizen is meant to draw attention to the fact that there are (seemingly useful) uses of 'citizenship' that are disengaged from political membership. The university is an institution and an association that is governed by rules and practices. But it is not a political association in that it is largely voluntary and lacks coercive power in the sense we attribute to the state. My claim is that the idea of university citizenship is (just) one instance in which the notion of citizenship can be deployed in a productive and non-deceptive way. The appeal of this usage (and similar others) is that it points to a desired moral attitude or perspective that one could adopt.

David Miller has raised additional worries about the value of cosmopolitan citizenship even in its moral, metaphorical sense. He argues that citizenship carries with it the ideals of reciprocity and accountability. When one acts as a citizen, one expects that one's actions 'are being reciprocated by many others.' Also, a citizen expects to be held accountable to others, and they to her 'for the arguments she

---

[40] Stephen C. Neff, 'International Law and the Critique of Cosmopolitan Citizenship,' in Kimberly Hutchings and R. Dannreuther, eds., *Cosmopolitan Citizenship* (New York: St. Martin's Press, 1999), pp. 105–119, p. 118.

[41] Ibid., p. 119.   [42] Miller, 'Bounded Citizenship' (n 20).

makes and the actions she takes.'[43] These ideals are (perhaps) present in the ideal of the university citizen. The good university citizen is quick to reciprocate her colleagues, and also holds herself accountable to them. So perhaps Miller has no quarrel with using 'citizen' in this context.

But *global* citizenship would be another thing for Miller. It lacks both this reciprocity and accountability according to him. The institutional mechanisms for ensuring reciprocity and accountability are lacking at the global level, he believes. Accordingly, he writes, 'The danger is that when a concept is extended to apply in a new setting, it continues to embody assumptions that held in the original setting but cannot hold in the new one. Users of the extended concept are thereby misled, or perhaps self-deceived.'[44]

It seems reasonable to say that among the *sine qua non* of the concept 'citizenship' are the ideals of reciprocity and accountability. And it is a fair point that a usage of a concept, even if explicitly as a metaphor, that does not include its distinguishing features or ideals (the properties that make the concept the concept that it is) can be misleading and self-deceiving. At best, it is a very sloppy and distracting metaphor that has no place in serious academic discussions. At worst, we risk giving the wrong impression that we are committed to more than we really intend.

But are the ideals of reciprocity and accountability really abandoned when we use cosmopolitan citizenship non-literally, as in the normative conception? It does not seem so. To the contrary, these ideals are built into the normative conception itself. The normative conception, to recall, is an expression of the point of view that we are to acquire when we are thinking about the requirements of global justice and our moral obligations to all persons in the world. It is a feature of any theorizing about justice or moral responsibilities (whether this involves hypothetical deliberation or not) that, whatever principles we contemplate, these are principles that can be mutually affirmed by all who would be affected. Thus, reciprocity is simply a precondition of any theorizing about justice. And whatever arguments we could muster in support of these principles, they must be arguments that can survive the test of reason and potential counter-arguments. That is, when philosophizing about justice, accountability to others for the arguments we make is an integral part of the exercise.

Miller is right that 'it is wrong to think of global citizenship as though it were an alternative to local or national citizenship.'[45] As he puts it neatly, the ideal we need to strive for is 'not the global citizen, but the globally concerned citizen.'[46] This vividly states the opposition to the democratic reading of cosmopolitan citizenship. But as a normative ideal, cosmopolitan citizenship is not meant to change or displace the

---

[43] David Miller, 'The Idea of Global Citizenship,' in Sigal Ben-Porath and Rogers Smith, eds., *Varieties of Sovereignty and Citizenship* (Philadelphia: University of Pennsylvania Press, 2013), pp. 227–243, p. 242.
[44] Ibid.   [45] Ibid., p. 241.   [46] Ibid., p. 242.

'central arenas' where citizenship is actually practiced, pace Miller.[47] It is an expression of the moral perspective or point of view we ought to adopt if we are to be a *globally concerned citizen*.

My claim here is not that the rhetoric of cosmopolitan citizenship is necessary to the cause of global justice; other images are available. But it can assist that cause. In particular, it helps motivate the cosmopolitan approach to global justice which understands global justice to be primarily about how individuals stand in relation to each other in the world at large. Now, one will have no use for the cosmopolitan citizen (even as a normative conception) if one has no time for the cosmopolitan approach to global justice. For instance, one might instead prefer non-cosmopolitan alternatives to international justice as developed by Miller himself and Rawls.[48] Whether global justice should take a cosmopolitan or non-cosmopolitan form is an important debate that we unfortunately cannot get into here. But the reason for rejecting cosmopolitan justice cannot be that cosmopolitan citizenship as a normative ideal is an empty or incoherent concept. It will involve a more substantive disagreement with the idea of cosmopolitan justice.

Conclusion

Cosmopolitan citizenship has different associations and meanings. It is sometimes interpreted as a common global political relationship under a world state. That is, it is seen as a global form of citizenship in the ordinary legal-political sense. Few theorists in fact defend cosmopolitan citizenship in this sense. A more common conception of cosmopolitan citizenship understands 'citizenship' functionally in terms of individuals' capacity and responsibility to participate in global democratic governance. But this democratic conception of cosmopolitan citizenship faces the criticism that the bonds of democratic solidarity between individuals are hard to forge at the global level. Finally, another common conception of cosmopolitan citizenship is a normative one. Cosmopolitan citizenship is meant as a metaphor to capture the moral perspective that individuals are to adopt when determining their moral responsibilities and duties of justice to the world at large. There is the substantive question whether global justice should be conceived on cosmopolitan terms. But if global justice should indeed be cosmopolitan in form, then, as I tried

---

[47]   Ibid., p. 241.
[48]   David Miller, *National Responsibility and Global Justice* (Oxford: Oxford University Press, 2007); John Rawls, *The Law of Peoples* (Cambridge: Harvard University Press, 1999).

to suggest, the idea of cosmopolitan citizenship understood as a normative ideal, is a helpful pointer to the moral standpoint we should strive to adopt.

To close, let me note some underlying and further questions of this discussion. Our framing question is whether the idea of cosmopolitan citizenship entails a radical re-conceptualization of the concept and ideal of citizenship. Is citizenship an inherently bounded concept, or can it be disengaged from its traditional (e.g. state-centric) moorings without losing its normative significance and meaning? Essentially, the introduction of cosmopolitan citizenship in philosophical debates must instigate a re-examination of what citizenship is and why it is of value. Also, the premise of the nationalist challenge, that shared nationality or membership in a societal culture is a prerequisite for democratic relations and deliberations, needs to be further scrutinized. Have the nationalists exaggerated the significance of shared nationality in this regard? What is the key relationship between nationality and citizenship? Finally, I had mainly put to one side the issue of world government and the legal-political conception of cosmopolitan citizenship that this would entail. But what are the prospects for world government? Could it be both morally attractive and a historical possibility? As mentioned, not many philosophers endorse the ideas of a world state and world citizenship in the legal-political sense. But there is room for debate.

BIBLIOGRAPHY

Anderson, Benedict, *Imagined Communities* (London: Verso, 1993).

Archibugi, Daniele, Sveva Balduini, and Marco Donati, 'The United Nations as an Agency of Global Democracy,' in Barry Holden, ed., *Global Democracy: Key Debates* (London: Routledge, 2000), pp. 125–142.

Archibugi, Daniele, David Held, and Martin Köhler, eds., *Re-Imaging Political Community* (Cambridge: Polity Press, 1998).

Beitz, Charles R., *Political Theory and International Relations*, 2nd edition (Princeton: Princeton University Press, 1999) [1979].

Bellamy, Richard and R. J. Barry Jones, 'Globalization and Democracy: An Afterword,' in Barry Holden, ed., *Global Democracy: Key Debates* (London: Routledge, 2000), pp. 202–216.

Ben-Porath, Sigal and Rogers Smith, eds., *Varieties of Sovereignty and Citizenship* (Philadelphia: University of Pennsylvania Press, 2013).

Brock, Gillian, 'Contemporary Cosmopolitanism,' *Philosophy Compass 8*, no. 8 (2013): pp. 689–698.

Canovan, Margaret, *Nationhood and Political Theory* (Cheltenham: Edward Elgar, 1996).

Cunningham, Frank, *The Real World of Democracy Revisited* (Atlantic Highlands: Humanities Press, 1994).

Dryzek, John, 'Transnational Democracy,' *Journal of Political Philosophy 7* (1999): pp. 30–51.

Falk, Richard, 'Global Civil Society and the Democratic Prospect,' in Barry Holden, ed., *Global Democracy: Key Debates* (London: Routledge, 2000), pp. 162–178.

Freeman, Samuel, 'Deliberative Democracy: A Sympathetic Comment,' *Philosophy and Public Affairs 29*, no. 4 (2000): pp. 371–418.

Gauthier, David, *Morals by Agreement* (Oxford: Oxford University Press, 1986).

Goodin, Robert E., 'World Government is Here!,' in Sigal Ben-Porath and Rogers Smith, eds., *Varieties of Sovereignty and Citizenship* (Philadelphia: University of Pennsylvania Press, 2013), pp. 149–165.

Gould, Carol, *Interactive Democracy: The Social Roots of Global Justice* (Cambridge: Cambridge University Press, 2014).

Gutmann, Amy and Dennis Thompson, 'Why Deliberative Democracy is Different,' *Social Philosophy and Policy 17* (2000): pp. 161–180.

Gutmann, Amy and Dennis Thompson, *Democracy and Disagreement* (Cambridge: Harvard University Press, 1996).

Held, David, *Cosmopolitanism: Ideals and Realities* (Cambridge: Polity Press, 2010).

Held, David, 'The Changing Contours of Political Community,' in Barry Holden, ed., *Global Democracy: Key Debates* (London: Routledge, 2000), pp. 17–31.

Held, David, *Democracy and the Global Order* (Cambridge: Polity Press, (1995).

Holden, Barry, ed., *Global Democracy: Key Debates* (London: Routledge, 2000).

Hutchings, Kimberly and R. Dannreuther, eds., *Cosmopolitan Citizenship* (New York: St. Martin's Press, 1999).

Kant, Immanuel, 'Perpetual Peace,' in *Kant's Political Writings*, edited and translated by Hans Reiss (Cambridge: Cambridge University Press, 1991) [1775], pp. 93–130.

Kleingeld, Pauline, 'Kant's Moral and Political Cosmopolitanism,' *Philosophy Compass 11*, no. 1 (2016): pp. 14–23.

Kymlicka, Will, *Politics in the Vernacular* (Oxford: Oxford University Press, 2001).

Kymlicka, Will, *Multicultural Citizenship* (Oxford: Oxford University Press, 1995).

Linklater, Andrew, 'Cosmopolitan Citizenship,' *Citizenship Studies 2*, no. 1 (1998): pp. 23–41.

Lu, Catherine, 'World Government,' *The Stanford Encyclopedia of Philosophy* (Winter 2015 Edition), Edward N. Zalt, ed., http://plato.stanford.edu/archives/win2015/entries/world-government/.

Miller, David, 'The Idea of Global Citizenship,' in Sigal Ben-Porath and Rogers Smith, eds., *Varieties of Sovereignty and Citizenship* (Philadelphia: University of Pennsylvania Press, 2013), pp. 227–243.

Miller, David, *National Responsibility and Global Justice* (Oxford: Oxford University Press, 2007).

Miller, David, 'Bounded Citizenship,' in Kimberly Hutchings and R. Dannreuther, eds., *Cosmopolitan Citizenship* (New York: St. Martin's Press, 1999), pp. 60–82.

Miller, David, *On Nationality* (Oxford: Oxford University Press, 1995).

Neff, Stephen C., 'International Law and the Critique of Cosmopolitan Citizenship,' in Kimberly Hutchings and R. Dannreuther, eds., *Cosmopolitan Citizenship* (New York: St. Martin's Press, 1999), pp. 105–119.

Nielsen, Kai, 'World Government, Security, and Global Justice,' in Steven Luper-Foy, ed., *Problems of International Justice* (Boulder: Westview Press, 1988), pp. 263–282.

Nussbaum, Martha C., *Cultivating Humanity* (Cambridge: Harvard University Press, 1997).

Nussbaum, Martha C., *For Love of Country?* edited by Joshua Cohen (Boston: Beacon Press, 1996).

Rawls, John, *The Law of Peoples* (Cambridge: Harvard University Press, 1999).

Rawls, John, *Political Liberalism* (New York: Columbia University Press, 1993).

Rawls, John, *A Theory of Justice* (Cambridge: Harvard University Press, (1971).

Sassen, Saskia, *Globalization and Its Discontents* (New York: New Press, 1998).

Tan, Kok-Chor, 'Global Democracy: International, Not Cosmopolitan,' in Deen Chatterjee, ed., *Democracy in a Global World* (New York: Lanham, Rowman and Littlefield, 2005), pp. 161–186.

Tamir, Yael, *Liberal Nationalism* (Princeton: Princeton University Press, 1993).

Thompson, Dennis, 'Democratic Theory and Global Society,' *Journal of Political Philosophy* 7, no. 2 (1999): pp. 111–125.

Thompson, Dennis, *Political Ethics and Public Office* (Cambridge: Harvard University Press, 1986).

Weinstock, Daniel, 'Prospects for Transnational Citizenship and Democracy,' *Ethics and International Affairs* 15, no. 2 (2001): pp. 53–66.

Wendt, Andrew, 'Why a World State is Inevitable,' *European Journal of International Relations* 9, no. 4 (2003): pp. 491–542.

Zolo, Danilo, 'The Lords of Peace: From the Holy Alliance to the New International Criminal Tribunal,' in Barry Holden, ed., *Global Democracy: Key Debates* (London: Routledge, 2000), pp. 73–86.

Zolo, Danilo, *Cosmopolis: Prospects for World Government* (Cambridge: Polity Press, 1997).

PART VI

TOMORROW'S CHALLENGES

CHAPTER 32

ON REFUGEEHOOD AND CITIZENSHIP

CATHRYN COSTELLO[*]

INTRODUCTION

TWELVE athletes competed for Team Refugees in the Rio Olympics and Paralympics. Their presence suggests that refugeehood is an ersatz nationality, yet the team members were still listed as nationals of their home countries—Democratic Republic of the Congo (DRC), Ethiopia, Iran, Syria, and South Sudan, and also with the affiliations of the National Olympic Committees of their states of refuge. A cursory glance at

* Andrew W. Mellon Associate Professor in International Human Rights and Refugee Law, Refugee Studies Centre and Faculty of Law, University of Oxford. The author thanks Ms Emma Dunlop for her excellent research and editorial assistance, and Linda Bosniak, Eric Fripp, Matthew Gibney, James Milner, David Owen, Ayelet Shachar, Jo Shaw, Leti Volpp, and Ruvi Ziegler, for most helpful suggestions. All errors remain, of course, the author's own.

their profiles reveals the diverse predicament of refugees. Half the team live in the Global South in camps, with apparently little prospect of acquiring the citizenship of their host country, Kenya. It appears that those who have been recognized as refugees in Europe have had to use irregular means to get there. The prelude to recognition as a refugee in Europe, with a possible path to citizenship, is a dangerous journey, the cost of which is prohibitive for most refugees. I will return to their stories at the conclusion of this piece, but for now suffice to note that in spite of their common refugeehood, their rights and prospects for political inclusion vary greatly.

The purpose of this chapter is to clarify the relationship between citizenship and refugeehood.[1] In particular, the chapter explores the extent to which loss of meaningful citizenship defines the predicament of the refugee. It then examines the *status* of refugee, and how refugeehood comes to an end, in particular the role of citizenship (new or restored) in ending refugeehood. Traditionally, UNHCR employs three 'solutions' to the problems of refugees: repatriation, resettlement, or local integration. At times, various solutions have been favoured—for instance, the 1990s have been cast as the 'decade of repatriation,'[2] and since then refugees tend to be regarded as liable to being returned to their home countries when circumstances change durably. This means that refuge or asylum is generally now regarded as temporary, although that imagined temporariness may continue for prolonged periods.

The structure of this chapter is as follows. The second section distinguishes between refugees, stateless persons, and internally displaced persons (IDPs). The third section examines refugee definitions, in law and political theory, in particular how they relate to citizenship. It also considers procedures for recognizing refugees, in particular the centrality of nationality to these processes. The fourth section turns to the rights to which refugees are entitled, contrasting *non-refoulement* and refugee status, and the way the refugee regime parses out responsibility for refugees both temporally and territorially. The fifth considers so-called 'durable solutions' for refugees. Citizenship is formally viewed as bringing refugeehood to an end, whether that emerges as return to the home country or naturalization in a new state. However, in practice, both return and a new citizenship for many refugees remain out of reach, and the status of refugee often becomes an intergenerational carrier of civic and social exclusion. The fourth and fifth sections reveal the realities of refugee

---

[1] A note on terminology: Nationality is a generic term in international law, referring to how individuals are linked to particular states. Nationality is the mere 'filing system' (Rogers Brubaker, *Citizenship and Nationhood in France and Germany* (Cambridge, London: Harvard University Press, 1992), p. 32). In this chapter, I use 'nationality' when the international legal concept is at issue, and 'citizenship' when drawing on normative political accounts of membership and status, or where the context otherwise so demands.

[2] Statement by Mrs. Sadako Ogata, United Nations High Commissioner for Refugees, at the International Management Symposium, St. Gallen, Switzerland, 25 May 1992, online http://www.unhcr.org/admin/hcspeeches/3ae68faec/statement-mrs-sadako-ogata-united-nations-high-commissioner-refugees-international.html.

containment, in contrast to the vision of shared responsibility that underpins the 1951 Convention on the Status of Refugees ('Refugee Convention')[3] and the refugee regime. By containment, I mean, drawing on the seminal scholarship on this theme,[4] efforts to keep would-be refugees in their countries or regions of origin. The final section concludes with some reflections on the road not taken, genuinely global citizenship for refugees, whether Olympians or not.

REFUGEES DISTINGUISHED

Historically, mass displacement and population transfers took place in the context of the disintegration of empires and state formation. Nowadays, in contrast, most who flee stay within the boundaries of their own state. Of the 65.3 million displaced people in the world, 40.8 million are 'internally displaced' within their own countries, and 21.3 million are refugees.[5] Following the general pattern, the Syrian conflict has displaced about 7.6 million people internally, and created about 4.8 million refugees.[6]

Of the world's refugee population, many are born into refugeehood. Over 5 million of the world's refugees are Palestinian, most of whom are descendants of the c. 750,000 Palestinians displaced in 1948 and 1967, meaning that their plight remains the world's largest protracted refugee situation. While most Palestinian refugees are subject to a particular international regime,[7] protracted refugee situations are not unique to them. UNHCR defines protracted refugee situations as those where refugees spend long periods (over five years) in exile without either local integration or repatriation prospects.[8] Often, the period is exile is much longer, so refugeehood

---

[3] *Convention Relating to the Status of Refugees* (adopted 28 July 1951, entered into force 22 April 1954) 189 UNTS 150, article 1E ('CSR51').

[4] Andrew Shacknove, 'From Asylum to Containment', *International Journal of Refugee Law* 5, no. 4 (1993): pp. 516–533; B. S. Chimni, 'The Geopolitics of Refugee Studies: A View from the South', *Journal of Refugee Studies* 11, no. 4 (1998): pp. 350–374.

[5] UN High Commissioner for Refugees (UNHCR), *Global Trends: Forced Displacement in 2015* (20 June 2016), p. 2, online http://www.refworld.org/docid/57678f3d4.html.

[6] See *3RP Mid-Year Report* (June 2016), p. 9, online http://data.unhcr.org/syrianrefugees/regional. php; IDMC, Annual Report 2015, p. 8, online http://www.internal-displacement.org/assets/publications/2016/201607-annual-report-2015-en.pdf.

[7] Susan Akram, 'UNRWA and Forced Migration', in Elena Fiddian-Qasmiyeh, Gil Loescher, Katy Long, and Nando Sigona, eds., *The Oxford Handbook of Refugee and Forced Migration Studies* (Oxford: Oxford University Press, 2014), pp. 227–240.

[8] UNHCR Executive Committee of the High Commissioner's Programme (Excom), 'Conclusion on Protracted Refugee Situations', no. 109 (LXI) (2009), online http://www.unhcr.org/excom/exconc/

becomes intergenerational. The resultant communities, often both legally and socially isolated, often depend heavily or entirely on international aid. Under these circumstances, UNHCR and other actors seem to act as a 'surrogate state', on one view perpetuating these protracted refugee situations through their assistance.[9]

To give some sense of the scale of the global refugee population, it is also useful to note that the world's refugee population is dwarfed by the global migrant stock, which is estimated at 244 million.[10] So, international migrants far outnumber refugees. It should be recalled too that the vast majority of the world's population lives in their state of origin (about 97 per cent).[11] Or to put it differently, with a global population of 7.4 billion, refugees make up merely 0.0027 per cent thereof.

In contrasting refugees and migrants, a striking global distributive anomaly becomes apparent: concentrations of international migrants are highest in Europe, North America, and Oceania.[12] In contrast, refugees are contained in the Global South: developing countries host over 86 per cent of the world's refugees, compared to 70 per cent twenty years ago.[13] So refugees buck the global migratory trends and patterns. This seems to reflect the geopolitics of refugee containment that emerged at the end of the Cold War, and remains a defining feature of the global refugee regime.

Refugees and Stateless Persons Distinguished

In conceptual terms, many accounts define refugees as those who have lost the protection of their state. Most notably, Arendt's writing on refugees assumes their statelessness. Arendt could plausibly assert, writing of European refugees, that 'the core of statelessness ... is identical with the refugee question'.[14] In the

---

4b332bca9/conclusion-protracted-refugee-situations.html. See generally James Milner, 'Protracted Refugee Situations', in Fiddian-Qasmiyeh et al. (n 7), pp. 151–162.

[9] Amy Slaughter and Jeff Crisp, 'A Surrogate State? The Role of UNHCR in Protracted Refugee Situations', in Gil Loescher, James Milner, Edward Newman, and Gary G. Troeller, eds., *Protracted Refugee Situations: Political, Human Rights and Security Implications* (Tokyo: United Nations University Press, 2008), pp. 123–140, p. 128.

[10] UN dataset, 'Trends in International Migrant Stock: The 2015 Revision', online http://www.un.org/en/development/desa/population/migration/data/estimates2/estimates15.shtml.

[11] Mathias Czaika and Hein de Haas, 'The Globalization of Migration: Has the World Become More Migratory?', *International Migration Review* 48, no. 2 (Summer 2014): pp. 283–323; Ayelet Shachar, *The Birthright Lottery: Citizenship and Global Inequality* (Cambridge, London: Harvard University Press, 2009).

[12] Czaika and de Haas (n 11).   [13] UNHCR (n 5), p. 18.

[14] Hannah Arendt, *The Origins of Totalitarianism* (New York: Harcourt Brace & Co., 1978), p. 277. Cf. Audrey Macklin, 'Who Is the Citizen's Other? Considering the Heft of Citizenship', *Theoretical Inquiries in Law* 8, no. 2 (2007): pp. 333–366; Megan Bradley, *Refugee Repatriation: Justice, Responsibility and Redress* (Cambridge: Cambridge University Press, 2013).

era of which she wrote, refugees often had been denationalized as a prelude to their expulsion. Nowadays, although legal denationalization is on the rise, it does not typically define the predicament of the refugee.[15] Empirically, too, conceiving of refugees as if they had been denationalized obscures the fact that many refugees wish to return, and seek to renegotiate their relationships with their countries of origin.[16] Furthermore, defining refugees by their lack of effective nationality fits poorly in contexts of the failed and fragile states from which many refugees flee.[17]

Legally, too, the regimes for statelessness and refugees are now separate.[18] International law defines statelessness in *de jure* terms, as those who lack nationality of any state. In this way, the *de facto* effectively stateless character of many refugee populations is not enough to bring them within the formal legal regime on statelessness. Of course, stateless populations may be at risk of persecution, and if they flee, warrant recognition as refugees. In particular, the arbitrary deprivation of nationality is often a human rights violation warranting recognition as persecution on a discriminatory ground.[19] In addition, refugeehood may generate statelessness, such as when refugee children are unable to claim any nationality. The realities of flight and exile may combine with gender discriminatory nationality laws in particular, leading to children born stateless.[20] But in general, statelessness and refugeehood are now distinct.

<hr/>

[15] For exceptions, see Michael Hutt, *Unbecoming Citizens: Culture, Nationhood and the Flight of Refugees from Bhutan* (New Delhi: Oxford University Press, 2003) (on Bhutan's denationalization expulsion of ethnic Nepalese citizens (Lhotshampas)); John R. Campbell, 'The Enduring Problem of Statelessness in the Horn of Africa: How Nation-States and Western Courts (Re)Define Nationality', *International Journal of Refugee Law* 23, no. 4 (2011): pp. 656–679 (on the impact of Ethiopia's denationalization of ethic Eritreans).

[16] Megan Bradley, 'Rethinking Refugeehood: Statelessness, Repatriation, and Refugee Agency', *Review of International Studies* 40, no. 1 (2014): pp. 101–123.

[17] See Macklin (n 14).

[18] *Convention Relating to the Status of Stateless Persons* (adopted 28 September 1954, entered into force 6 June 1960) 360 UNTS 117; *Convention on the Reduction of Statelessness* (adopted 30 August 1961, entered into force 13 December 1975) 989 UNTS 175.

[19] See, for example, Hélène Lambert, 'Refugee Status, Arbitrary Deprivation of Nationality, and Statelessness within the Context of Article 1A(2) of the 1951 Convention and its 1967 Protocol Relating to the Status of Refugees', UNHCR Legal and Protection Policy Research Series, PPLA/2014/01 (Geneva: UNHCR, 2014).

[20] On gender discriminatory nationality laws, see Volpp in this volume. Syria is one of twenty-seven states that maintain nationality laws that discriminate against women. Children born to Syrian women refugees, in particular when they are heads of households, are at particular risk of statelessness (Institute on Statelessness and Inclusion and The Global Campaign for Equal Nationality Rights, *Submission to the Human Rights Council at the 26th Session of the Universal Periodic Review: Syrian Arab Republic* (24 March 2016), online http://www.institutesi.org/SyriaUPR2016.pdf).

Refugees and Internally Displaced Persons Distinguished

The basic distinction between a refugee and IDP is that the latter does not flee across an internationally recognized state border, whereas a refugee is 'outside the country of his nationality'.[21] The international regime on IDPs that emerged through soft law in the 1990s recognizes the primary responsibility of the territorial state—to avoid arbitrary displacement, protect rights during displacement, and bring displacement to an end.[22] The IDP regime is a synthesis of human rights and international humanitarian law, so it turns not on nationality, but humanity. It applies to anyone who has been forced to leave her home or place of habitual residence. Protection for IDPs may mean there is less cause to flee internationally, which may in some circumstances be a good thing. However, some aspects of IDP protection smack of containment, and may undermine the right to flee and refugee protection.[23]

REFUGEES DEFINED AND RECOGNIZED

Refugee Definitions

The preceding account demonstrates that refugees are distinct from IDPs and stateless persons. In legal terms, as will be seen, there are many refugee definitions, but the principal global one under the Refugee Convention is someone who

owing to well-founded fear of being persecuted for reasons of race, religion, nationality, membership of a particular social group or political opinion, is outside the country of his nationality and is unable or, owing to such fear, is unwilling to avail himself of the protection of that country; or who, not having a nationality and being outside the country of his former habitual residence as a result of such events, is unable or, owing to such fear, is unwilling to return to it.[24]

The 'national order of things' defines the concept of refugee.[25] If a person flees her country of residence, even if she has never lived in her country of nationality, her

---

[21] CSR51 (n 3), article 1A(2).

[22] See *Guiding Principles on Internal Displacement*, E/CN.4/1998/53/Add.2, 11 February 1998, Principle 6, online http://www.un-documents.net/gpid.htm.

[23] Bríd Ní Ghráinne, 'UNHCR's Involvement with IDPs—"Protection of that Country" for the Purposes of Precluding Refugee Status?', *International Journal of Refugee Law* 26, no. 4 (2014): pp. 536–554.

[24] CSR51 (n 3), article 1A(2).

[25] Liisa H. Malkki, 'Refugees and Exile: From "Refugee Studies" to the National Order of Things', *Annual Review of Anthropology* 24 (1995): pp. 495–523.

refugee assessment still turns on assessing her fear of persecution vis-à-vis her country of nationality.[26] To illustrate further, if a person who flees is a dual (or multiple) national,[27] the lack of effective state protection is to be assessed in light of the protection of all countries of effective nationality. Two examples of this phenomenon concern those fleeing North Korea, and their putative right to South Korean nationality,[28] and Jewish refugees from the former Soviet Union, and their right to claim Israeli nationality under Israel's Law of Return.[29] Similarly, once someone enjoys 'the rights and obligations which are attached to the possession of the nationality of that country' one is not a refugee.[30] The logic is that a secure right to nationality somewhere, indeed anywhere, obviates the need for refugee protection. As the Supreme Court of Canada has put it, '[i]nternational refugee law was formulated to serve as a back-up to the protection one expects from the state of which an individual is a national.'[31]

The basic notion is that the individual is unable or, owing to the well-founded fear of persecution, unwilling to avail herself of the 'protection' of her state. 'Protection' in this context, however, is ambiguous. Originally, the failure of protection inherent in the international community's approach to refugees was an absence of diplomatic protection.[32] But over time, it came to set a higher standard for refugees, taking a restrictive turn in the form of the 'internal protection alternative', a legal gloss that requires would-be refugees to demonstrate that they had nowhere safe to flee within their own state. This doctrine has scant textual foundation in the Refugee Convention, but has been used and sometimes misused by some governments to deny recognition to refugees.[33]

The Refugee Convention leaves undefined the central concept of 'persecution'. Read in light of the rest of the Convention and the need for nexus to political status,

---

[26] See generally Eric Fripp, *Nationality and Statelessness in the International Law of Refugee Status* (Oxford, Portland: Hart Publishing, 2016).

[27] On dual nationality generally, see Spiro in this volume.

[28] See, for example, Andrew Wolman, 'North Korean Asylum Seekers and Dual Nationality', *International Journal of Refugee Law* 24, no. 4 (2012): pp. 793–814. The practice varies, but some states do take into account that those who flee North Korea may claim South Korean nationality quasi-automatically.

[29] Audrey Macklin, 'Sticky Citizenship', in Rhoda E. Howard-Hassmann and Margaret Walton-Roberts, eds., *The Human Right to Citizenship: A Slippery Concept* (Philadelphia: University of Pennsylvania Press: 2015), pp. 223–239.

[30] CSR51 (n 3), article 1E. See UNHCR, *UNHCR Note on the Interpretation of Article 1E of the 1951 Convention relating to the Status of Refugees* (March 2009), online http://www.refworld.org/pdfid/49c3a3d12.pdf. This provision was drafted with returning ethnic Germans in mind, who were constitutionally entitled to German nationality under the German Constitution. It was also applied to refugees of Turkish origin from Bulgaria who, on entering Turkey, were quickly recognized as Turkish nationals.

[31] *Ward v. Canada* [1993] 2 SCR 689, paragraph 25.

[32] Antonio Fortin, 'The Meaning of "Protection" in the Refugee Definition', *International Journal of Refugee Law* 12, no. 4 (2000): pp. 548–576.

[33] UNHCR, *Guidelines on International Protection No. 4: 'Internal Flight or Relocation Alternative' Within the Context of Article 1A(2) of the 1951 Convention and/or 1967 Protocol Relating to the Status of Refugees* (23 July 2003), HCR/GIP/03/04, online http://www.refworld.org/docid/3f2791a44.html.

the Convention definition suggests an understanding of persecution as a serious wrongful act based on political opinion or identity. Both state acts and omissions may count as persecution. It has now also been accepted that non-state actors may commit persecution, provided there is a state failure of protection. Most authorities now look to international human rights law to elucidate the concept of persecution in the Refugee Convention.[34] The requirement to demonstrate a nexus between persecution and Convention grounds excludes those fleeing truly indiscriminate rights violations from Convention refugee status. For many this is ethically troubling, but Hathaway defends the Convention definition, on the assumption that if protection is to be rationed, the Convention grounds track 'fundamental social marginalization'. This claim is premised on the flexibility of the notion of 'particular social group'.[35]

It is often erroneously asserted that conflict refugees are not Convention refugees. However sometimes, those fleeing conflict *are* Convention refugees, as they do have a well-founded fear of persecution linked to one of the Convention grounds. To illustrate, many are fleeing Syria due to 'a direct or indirect, real or perceived association with one of the parties to the conflict', meaning that a nexus to political opinion may be established.[36] In addition, there are other sources of protection, beyond the Refugee Convention. Many regions supplement the Convention definition, either by expanding the concept of the refugee (as has been done in Latin America[37] and Africa[38]), or by adding additional statuses such as subsidiary protection in EU law.[39] The expanded refugee definitions in Africa and Latin America include those fleeing some forms of generalized violence, so remove the link with political status and persecution. Subsidiary protection builds on the forms of 'complementary protection' which international human rights law develops to protect against return to face serious human rights violations.[40]

The evolution of the refugee definition has involved a participatory process of claims making. To illustrate, gender guidelines and strategic litigation have been

[34] This move is associated with Hathaway, but has been widely endorsed, including in EU law.
[35] James C. Hathaway, 'Is Refugee Status Really Elitist? An Answer to the Ethical Challenge', in Jean-Yves Carlier and Dirk Vanheule, eds., *Europe and Refugees: A Challenge? L'Europe et les réfugiés: un défi?* (The Hague, London, Boston: Kluwer Law International, 1997), pp. 79–88.
[36] UNHCR, 'International Protection Considerations with Regard to People Fleeing the Syrian Arab Republic, Update III' (October 2014), online http://www.refworld.org/pdfid/544e446d4.pdf.
[37] *Cartagena Declaration on Refugees*, adopted by the Colloquium on the International Protection of Refugees in Central America, Mexico and Panama, 22 November 1984, conclusion 3.
[38] *OAU Convention Governing the Specific Aspects of Refugee Problems in Africa* (adopted 10 September 1969, entered into force 20 June 1974) 1001 UNTS 45, article I(2).
[39] Directive 2011/95/EU of the European Parliament and of the Council of 13 December 2011 on standards for the qualification of third-country nationals or stateless persons as beneficiaries of international protection, for a uniform status for refugees or for persons eligible for subsidiary protection, and for the content of the protection granted (recast) [2011] OJ L337/9, article 15.
[40] Jane McAdam, *Complementary Protection in International Refugee Law* (Oxford: Oxford University Press, 2007).

employed over the past two decades to challenge the androcentric character of the Convention definition.[41] Similarly, persecution related to sexual orientation and identity has been included as a basis for refugee recognition.[42] While both moves have demonstrated the Convention's capacity to adapt to newly recognized forms of human rights violations, these apparently progressive interpretative moves often simultaneously depends on a process of 'othering'. Recognition is often premised on showing particularly exoticized or orientalized human rights violations.[43]

The legal definition of the refugee excludes the undeserving, for instance war criminals and those who have perpetrated genocide, and more ambiguously those who have committed 'serious non-political crimes' and 'acts contrary to the purposes and principles of the United Nations'.[44] Exclusion practices have been subject to scholarly attention and critique of late, as states increasingly exclude people from refugee status, particularly in cases ostensibly linked to terrorism,[45] or the expansion of international criminal law.[46] However, no one may be returned to face torture, inhuman or degrading treatment, as this prohibition is absolute in international human rights law.[47] This is one of the ways in which refugee status determination (RSD) may lead to ambiguous outcomes, with some people deemed non-removable, but potentially denied a formal legal status.

In law, persecution is more about serious human rights violations than a deficit of citizenship per se. But, refugee protection is a back-up, available only if state protection is deemed to fail. In this way, while citizenship is not central to the concept of 'persecution', the entire refugee regime is premised on the normality of a

[41] Audrey Macklin, 'Refugee Women and the Imperative of Categories', *Human Rights Quarterly* 17, no. 2 (1995): pp. 213–277; Alice Edwards, 'Transitioning Gender: Feminist Engagement with International Refugee Law and Policy 1950–2010', *Refugee Survey Quarterly* 29, no. 2 (2010): pp. 21–45; Michelle Foster, 'Why We are Not There Yet: The Particular Challenge of "Particular Social Group" ', in Efrat Arbel, Catherine Dauvergne, and Jenni Millbank, eds., *Gender in Refugee Law: From the Margins to the Centre* (Abingdon: Routledge, 2014), pp. 17–45.

[42] See Thomas Spijkerboer, ed., *Fleeing Homophobia: Sexual Orientation, Gender Identity and Asylum* (Abingdon: Routledge, 2013).

[43] Thomas Spijkerboer, 'European Sexual Nationalism: Refugee Law After the Gender & Sexuality Critiques', Paper presented at the Nordic Asylum Seminar, University of Uppsala, 8 May 2015, online http://thomasspijkerboer.eu/wp-content/uploads/2015/05/Uppsala-201505081.pdf.

[44] CSR51 (n 3), article 1F.

[45] See, for example, Elspeth Guild and Madeline Garlick, 'Refugee Protection, Counter-Terrorism and Exclusion in the European Union', *Refugee Survey Quarterly* 29, no. 4 (2010): pp. 63–82.

[46] See, for example, Asha Kaushal and Catherine Dauvergne, 'The Growing Culture of Exclusion: Trends in Canadian Refugee Exclusions', *International Journal of Refugee Law* 23, no. 1 (2011): pp. 54–92.

[47] See *Convention against Torture and Other Cruel, Inhuman or Degrading Treatment or Punishment* (adopted 10 December 1984, entered into force 26 June 1987) 1465 UNTS 85, article 3; *International Covenant on Civil and Political Rights* (adopted 16 December 1966, entered into force 23 March 1976) 999 UNTS 171, article 6; *European Convention for the Protection of Human Rights and Fundamental Freedoms* (adopted 4 November 1950, entered into force 3 September 1953) 213 UNTS 221, ETS no. 5, article 3.

link between individuals and states, with refugeehood defined in contrast as exceptional. However, in the political theoretical accounts, citizenship-based and human rights accounts may be contrasted. While the contrast drawn here for the purposes of exposition may be somewhat strained, it highlights that different conceptions of citizenship generate different normative accounts of the refugee.

Some take a citizenship-loss view of refugeehood, and use it to ground a right to asylum as new membership. Price argues that refugees are those 'targeted for harm in a manner that repudiates their claim to political membership'.[48] His account also entails a conception of asylum with a strong condemnatory dimension, and in turn a view that states that are simply unable (rather than unwilling) to protect their citizens 'ought to be assisted, not condemned'.[49] This account supports a narrow construction of 'refugee'. Cherem too defends the strictures of the Refugee Convention definition, in particular in order to distinguish between those who may be assisted in their own states, and those for whom assistance may not be rendered via their own governments.[50]

These citizenship-based accounts of refugeehood contrast with the many critiques of the refugee definition as under-inclusive.[51] Gibney, for example, argues that the concept of refugee should encompass those 'who require a new state of residence, either temporarily or permanently, because if forced to return or stay at home they would, as a result of either the inadequacy or brutality of their state, be persecuted or seriously jeopardize their physical security or vital subsistence needs'.[52] Notably, theorists with different views on the ethics of immigration often share the view that the refugee definition is too narrow. For instance, David Miller, a liberal nationalist defender of discretionary immigration control, notes that 'there is clearly a good case for broadening the definition to include people who are being deprived of rights to subsistence, basic healthcare, etc'.[53] These ethical critiques are compelling, and all the more troubling given that, as will be seen, the refugee regime fails to protect even the narrowly defined category of refugee in its purview.

---

[48] Matthew E. Price, *Rethinking Asylum: History, Purpose, and Limits* (Cambridge: Cambridge University Press, 2009), p. 70.

[49] Ibid., p. 159.

[50] Max Cherem, 'Refugee Rights: Against Expanding the Definition of a "Refugee" and Unilateral Protection Elsewhere', *The Journal of Political Philosophy 24*, no. 2 (2016): pp. 183–205.

[51] Andrew Shacknove, 'Who is a Refugee?', *Ethics 95*, no. 2 (1985): pp. 274–284; Matthew Gibney, *The Ethics and Politics of Asylum: Liberal Democracy and the Response to Refugees* (Cambridge: Cambridge University Press, 2004); Alexander Betts, *Survival Migration: Failed Governance and the Crisis of Displacement* (Ithaca: Cornell University Press, 2013).

[52] Gibney (n 51).

[53] David Miller, *National Responsibility and Global Justice* (Oxford: Oxford University Press, 2007).

Recognizing and Rejecting Refugees

In international law and practice refugee status is declaratory, so refugees are refugees 'as soon as' they meet the definition.[54] However, in reality, the processes of RSD are just as important to understanding the scope of protection as the formal definitions on paper. Many refugees are recognized as such on a group basis, particularly in Africa, where the OAU definition is often combined with group determination, at least on a *prima facie* basis. In the Middle East and Asia, where many of the major host countries are not parties to the Refugee Convention, UNHCR registration may bring with it some form of refugee protection, albeit one which is very much at the discretion of the host state.

In the Global North, RSD is often a highly formalized quasi-judicial process. Nationality is often decisive in RSD, as claimants tend to be siphoned into different procedures depending on their nationality. Governments, in particular in Europe and then emulated across the Global North, introduced procedures to limit the perceived 'abuse' of asylum processes by non-refugees. European states pioneered 'Safe Country of Origin' processes and attendant acceleration of procedures to allow for swift rejection of obviously weak claims.[55]

Proving and enacting citizenship becomes a key part of RSD. The purpose is to determine not only if the refugee is who she claims, but also to ensure that she will at some point be returnable back to her state of nationality. As Bradley puts it, '[e]ven when refugees come from countries such as Somalia that have at previous times lacked the institutions to produce legitimate passports, those responsible for [RSD] dutifully copy and file the passports refugees purchased from market vendors, reflecting the regime's ideological commitment to the notion that refugees remain linked to a state to which they will one day, ideally, return.'[56] Techniques, often of dubious probity, such as language analysis[57] and genetic testing[58] are employed to assess origins.

Although there is a shared global definition of a refugee, recognition in the Global North depends on meeting evidential and procedural thresholds that are set increasingly highly. In contrast, in the Global South, many of the main refugee-hosting states

[54] UNHCR, *Handbook and Guidelines on Procedures and Criteria for Determining Refugee Status under the 1951 Convention and the 1967 Protocol relating to the Status of Refugees* (Reissued December 2011), p. 9, online http://www.unhcr.org/3d58e13b4.pdf.

[55] See Cathryn Costello, 'Safe Country? Says Who?', *International Journal of Refugee Law 28*, no. 4 (2016): pp. 601–622.

[56] Bradley (n 16), p. 111.

[57] John Campbell, 'Language Analysis in the United Kingdom's Refugee Status Determination System: Seeing through Policy Claims about "Expert Knowledge"', *Ethnic and Racial Studies 36*, no. 4 (2013): pp. 670–690.

[58] See, for example, Richard Tutton, Christine Hauskeller, and Steven Sturdy, 'Importing Forensic Biomedicine into Asylum Adjudication: Genetic Ancestry and Isotope Testing in the United Kingdom',

have not ratified the Refugee Convention.[59] Oftentimes, in these contexts, UNHCR determines refugee status, but that status often brings few rights.

Non-Refoulement and Refugee Status

Non-Refoulement and Refugee Containment

When these processes are concluded, their outcomes are varied. In the Global North, some will be recognized as Convention refugees, others may be offered a lesser status, or rejected. The status granted to Convention refugees tends nowadays to be temporary. The citizenship-loss account of the refugee posits that she needs membership in a new state, and conceives of asylum as such. However, this no longer fits the practice. Nor does it fit the approach under the refugee regime, under which refugee protection and 'solutions' (eg local integration, resettlement, or voluntary repatriation) are temporally and territorially parsed out. This section illustrates the workings of the regime and its manifest shortcomings.

The first point to note is the primary basis for the distribution of responsibility for refugees is territorial. *Non-refoulement* is required by many treaties, as well as being a norm of customary international law and arguably 'ripe for recognition' as a norm of *jus cogens*.[60] *Non-refoulement* is not just for refugees—it precludes return of anyone to a country where there is a real risk of an irreparable or serious human rights violation. But to be protected against *refoulement,* refugees must generally reach the territory of a safe state. The *non-refoulement* norm applies at the border, in the territory, or sometimes when states act extraterritorially in their border control practices.[61] But in general states, particularly those in the Global North, are able to insulate themselves from refugees through the containment policies that stop refugees arriving on their shores.

A panoply of access restrictions has developed since the late 1980s and 1990s, rendering flight in search of refuge more difficult. Those who flee face layers of restrictions. Scholarship on access to asylum clarifies the workings of

in Benjamin N. Lawrance and Galya Ruffer, eds., *Adjudicating Refugee and Asylum Status: The Role of Witness, Expertise, and Testimony* (New York: Cambridge University Press, 2015), pp. 202–220.

[59] See details of ratifications online: https://treaties.un.org/doc/Publication/MTDSG/Volume%20I/Chapter%20V/V-2.en.pdf.

[60] Cathryn Costello and Michelle Foster, 'Non-Refoulement as Custom and Jus Cogens? Putting the Prohibition to the Test', *Netherlands Yearbook of International Law 46* (2015): pp. 273–327.

[61] Judgment of 23 February 2012, *Hirsi Jamaa and Others v. Italy* 27765/09, CE:ECHR:2012:0223 JUD002776509.

containment.[62] Visa regimes reflect and exacerbate the global inequality of citizenships. Those who seek to leave war torn or tyrannical countries usually have few visa-free travel options. To start with, to obtain a visa one must have a valid passport in the first place. To get one is nigh on impossible for citizens of some countries, and for the stateless. States, particularly in the Global North, often impose visa requirements as soon as citizens from a particular state start to claim asylum. Visas are usually for short-term stay. Posing a risk of claiming asylum means that a visa will in likelihood be refused. The real sting comes as without a visa, regular travel is impeded due to carriers' sanctions, which privatize border control, and mean that those in search of refuge must generally use irregular means of travel and often employ smugglers. The Refugee Convention protects refugees from penalization for illegal entry under some circumstances,[63] but the range of access barriers that refugees now face mean most refugees simply cannot afford the expensive dangerous journeys to seek protection in the Global North.

These access barriers are the scaffolding of the containment of refugees in the Global South. While countries neighbouring conflict and oppression often face condemnation if they close borders in the face of those fleeing directly, countries at a distance may prevent refugees from reaching their shores. Containment has been written into the global regime, such that refugees are framed as if they were *obliged* to stay in their regions of origin, and that the ethical obligations of the international community are exhausted by the provision of aid and assistance. To this end, the 'safe third country' (STC) notion is now widely employed to permit states to return refugees and asylum seekers to countries where they could have sought protection. Its origins lie in European state practice, but it is now written into the refugee policies of many states and regions.[64]

Containment policies are liable to fail, and sometimes spectacularly. When land borders are sealed, and regular means of cheap and safe travel legally blocked, refugees may still be driven to flee. This creates the demand for the services of smugglers, and dangerous journeys by sea. In 2015, almost one million people made such journeys to Europe, with an estimated over 3,770 deaths at sea.[65]

Being protected against *refoulement* often generates precarity, as it does not bring with it a particular status for the non-removable person. *Non-refoulement* provides access to a place, but not a route to security of residence, let alone citizenship. While *non-refoulement* is a minimum requirement for refugee protection, the central

---

[62] Thomas Gammeltoft-Hansen, *Access to Asylum: International Refugee Law and the Globalisation of Migration Control* (New York: Cambridge University Press, 2011).

[63] CSR51 (n 3), article 31.

[64] Cathryn Costello, 'The Asylum Procedures Directive and the Proliferation of Safe Country Practices: Deterrence, Deflection and the Dismantling of International Protection', *European Journal of Migration Law* 7 (2005): pp. 35–69.

[65] IOM, Missing Migrants Project, online http://missingmigrants.iom.int/over-3770-migrants-have-died-trying-cross-mediterranean-europe-2015.

concern of the Refugee Convention, as its full title indicates, is to afford refugees a particular status. But beyond *non-refoulement*, the rights in the Convention depend on being granted legal permission to enter and stay. If states are not willing to grant such permission, the Convention requires that they *enable* refugees to find protection elsewhere,[66] in contrast to the discourse surrounding refugee containment. This rule is important and often ignored. The Convention assumes that those who have fled may not find effective protection in their first place of stay, and may move onwards. Thus, the Convention parses out refugee protection both spatially and temporally. Moreover, the Convention disaggregates protection and solutions, in contrast to the citizenship-based accounts of the refugee. A new nationality, or re-availing of one's original nationality, brings refugeehood to an end, as the next section explores.

DURABLE SOLUTIONS FOR REFUGEES

Once refugees find a place of refuge, the refugee regime envisages that protection should be followed by a 'solution'—an end to the period as a refugee, either by naturalizing (in a country of first protection or in a country of resettlement) or by being repatriated if the conditions that induced flight change durably.

Cessation and Repatriation

The Refugee Convention envisages the following 'cessation' scenarios: (1) voluntary re-availment of the protection of the country of nationality; or (2) voluntarily re-acquisition of previous nationality having lost it; or (3) acquisition of a new nationality, and enjoyment of the protection of the country of new nationality; or (4) voluntary re-establishment in the country which was left owing to fear of persecution.[67] These acts all turn on the acts of the refugee to bring her refugeehood to an end. In practice, they envisage the refugee as an exile, and refugees who return home for considerable periods risk losing their refugee status.

---

[66] Article 31(2) of the CSR51 (n 3) provides: 'The Contracting States shall not apply to the movements of such refugees restrictions other than those which are necessary and such restrictions shall only be applied until their status in the country is regularized or they obtain admission into another country. The Contracting States shall allow such refugees *a reasonable period and all the necessary facilities to obtain admission into another country*' (emphasis added).

[67] CSR51 (n 3), article 1C.

In addition, the Convention also recognizes that refugees cease to be refugees when they can no longer refuse to avail of the protection of the country of their nationality, because 'the circumstances in connection with which he has been recognized as a refugee have ceased to exist'.[68] The Refugee Convention suggests that if refugees truly have no protection needs any longer, they may be deported like other non-citizens. However, the Statute establishing the Office of the UNHCR, requires the High Commissioner to assist states in facilitating voluntary repatriation and several Executive Committee (ExCom) conclusions emphasize the necessarily voluntary character of repatriation.[69] The OAU Convention contains a detailed provision on ensuring the voluntary character of repatriation.[70] In practice, much repatriation has taken place under dubious conditions, when refugees have contested the safety of return.

The Refugee Convention has a proviso on cessation, noting that some refugees may have 'compelling reasons arising out of previous persecution for refusing to avail [themselves] of the protection of the country of nationality'. Shklar's reflections on Holocaust survivors are apposite to understanding this proviso. In her account, such refugees 'have been expelled beyond all hope of return ... After such an expulsion, there is no point in trying to reclaim one's rights' as they had been doubly betrayed, by both the state and their fellow members of German society.[71] For such refugees, return was unthinkable. For other refugees, return was impossible. For instance, for many who fled from behind the Iron Curtain to the West, no significant change of circumstances was viewed as likely, so asylum in this era generally became a route to permanent residence and citizenship.

In the 1990s, the so-called 'decade of repatriation', the opposite assumption took hold—that refugees fled transitory phenomena, and that most not only could, but *should* return, once circumstances changed. Bradley's exemplary study of the requirements of justice in repatriation shows that refugees can and do forge new relationships with the states that caused them to flee.[72] She studies not only return, but also issues of restitution and reparation. Importantly, in her account, refugees actively negotiate the terms of their return in order to re-establish their membership. Long's study too demonstrates that repatriation is a fundamentally political process, but she stresses that refugees can rejoin their original political communities

---

[68] Ibid., article 1C(5).

[69] See UNGA Resolution 428(V) 'Statute of the Office of the United Nations High Commissioner for Refugees' (14 December 1950), paragraph 1, online http://www.unhcr.org/3b66c39e1.pdf; UNHCR Excom, 'Voluntary Repatriation', no. 18 (XXXI), 1980, online http://www.unhcr.org/excom/exconc/3ae68c6e8/voluntary-repatriation.html; UNHCR Excom, 'Voluntary Repatriation', no. 40 (XXXVI), 1985, online http://www.unhcr.org/excom/exconc/3ae68c9518/voluntary-repatriation.html.

[70] *OAU Convention* (n 38), article 5.

[71] Judith N. Shklar, 'Obligation, Loyalty, Exile', *Political Theory* 21, no. 2 (1993): pp. 181–197, p. 193, cited by Bradley (n 16), p. 115.

[72] Bradley (n 14).

without physically returning.[73] Her transnational vision treats repatriation as compatible with continued mobility. These studies of repatriation demonstrate the varieties of ways in which refugees may seek to restore their bonds with their home states and fellow citizens.

Refugee Naturalization and Political Inclusion

The refugee regime nowadays tends to envisage refugee protection as temporary, although often it is impossible for refugees to return home. Legally, a refugee will cease to be a refugee when she becomes a citizen of her new country of residence. However, under international law, there is no obligation on states of refuge to naturalize refugees. Under the Refugee Convention, states are required 'as far as possible' to 'facilitate the assimilation and naturalisation of refugees. They shall in particular make every effort to expedite naturalisation proceedings and to reduce as far as possible the charges and costs of such proceedings'.[74] Refugees are in a distinctive position as they are politically excluded from their home states. On this basis, their claims for political inclusion in a new polity are even stronger than for other settled migrants. As Ziegler demonstrates, even if not naturalized, they have a particularly strong claim to political inclusion in the form of being granted voting rights.[75]

In 'durable solutions' parlance, 'local integration' of refugees is one of the three solutions. The UNHCR defines local integration as including legal, economic, and social elements, often downplaying naturalization. This reflects a deference to state sovereignty over matters of citizenship. When states came together under the auspices of the UNHCR's Executive Committee to agree a conclusion on local integration, the opening affirms that voluntary repatriation is the preferred solution, and that 'local integration is a sovereign decision and an option to be exercised by States guided by their treaty obligations and human rights principles'.[76] Downplaying naturalization and political rights reflects their lack of availability for most refugees, particularly in the main host countries of the Global South, and that *de facto* integration through economic activity is understood to be more urgent, particularly as humanitarian aid to refugee populations dwindles over time.

---

[73] Katy Long, *The Point of No Return: Refugees, Rights, and Repatriation* (Oxford: Oxford University Press, 2013).

[74] CSR51 (n 3), article 34.

[75] Ruvi Ziegler, *Voting Rights of Refugees* (Cambridge University Press, forthcoming).

[76] UNHCR Excom, 'Conclusion on Local Integration', no. 104 (LVI), 2005, online http://www.unhcr.org/excom/exconc/4357a91b2/conclusion-local-integration.html.

Manby's study of African citizenship laws notes the diversity of approaches for refugee naturalization.[77] Tanzania has been praised for offering citizenship to its long-term refugee populations, but in practice, that offer has not been implemented.[78] In host countries in the Middle East, not only is naturalization generally off the cards, but as mentioned, refugee children often become stateless. An exception may be in Turkey, where the naturalization of Syrian refugees has been suggested, in spite of their formally temporary status.[79]

The practice of Northern states regarding refugee naturalization vary, but many states offer refugees naturalization on *better* conditions than ordinary migrants, in particular by applying shorter time periods for naturalization, or waiving fees or documentation requirements.[80] Some states require those naturalizing to renounce their existing nationality, but refugees are often exempt from this requirement.[81] However, these advantages are often limited to Convention refugees, not those with other protection statuses. Moreover, given that asylum systems in the Global North tend to also create populations of non-removable non-refugees, this apparently clear path to naturalization is one from which many who seek refuge are excluded.

With some notable exceptions,[82] empirical studies and indices of integration tend to treat refugees and other migrants through the same lens. Some naturalization studies indicate that those from unstable countries of origin are more likely to naturalize, presumably in order to gain security of residence.[83] A further phenomenon in need of empirical investigation is naturalization not as integration, but rather as an exit strategy. Those who seek protection in EU countries often find themselves obliged to claim asylum in states where they do not wish to be. Even if recognized as refugees, that status is not recognized across the EU for five years, and then only once conditions are met. In this context, for many, naturalization is a route to move to their preferred country of destination, in particular given EU free movement rights.

---

[77] Bronwen Manby, *Citizenship Law in Africa: A Comparative Study*, 2nd edition (New York: Open Society Foundations, October 2010), pp. 91–94.

[78] James Milner, 'Can Global Refugee Policy Leverage Durable Solutions? Lessons from Tanzania's Naturalization of Burundian Refugees', *Journal of Refugee Studies* 27, no. 4 (2014): pp. 553–573.

[79] Ishaan Tharoor, 'Turkey's Bold New Plan for Syrian Refugees: Make Them Citizens', *The Washington Post*, 9 July 2016, online https://www.washingtonpost.com/news/worldviews/wp/2016/07/09/turkeys-bold-new-plan-for-syrian-refugees-make-them-citizens/.

[80] Sarah Wallace Goodman, 'Naturalisation Policies in Europe: Exploring Patterns of Inclusion and Exclusion' (Florence: EUDO Citizenship Observatory, November 2010), p. 33, online http://eudo-citizenship.eu/docs/7-Naturalisation%20Policies%20in%20Europe.pdf.

[81] See Spiro in this volume on the Netherlands.

[82] Irene Bloemraad, *Becoming a Citizen: Incorporating Immigrants and Refugees in the United States and Canada* (Berkeley and Los Angeles: University of California Press, 2006).

[83] Madeline Sumption and Sarah Flamm, *The Economic Value of Citizenship for Immigrants in the United States* (Migration Policy Institute, September 2012), online http://www.migrationpolicy.org/research/economic-value-citizenship; Floris Peters, Maarten Vink, and Hans Schmeets, 'The Ecology of Immigrant Naturalisation: A Life Course Approach in the Context of Institutional Conditions', *Journal of Ethnic and Migration Studies* 42, no. 3 (2016): pp. 359–381.

Resettlement as a Solution?

The hallmark of protracted refugee situations is that local integration, in particular naturalization, is politically blocked. In addition, rights restrictions usually mean that legal exclusion is combined with social and economic exclusion. In these circumstances, it would seem that refugees should simply move on, in search of the rights to which they are entitled. However, as we have seen, containment policies make this legally and physically difficult. In terms of formal 'solutions', in very limited cases at present, UNHCR organizes to 'resettle' refugees to third countries. UNHCR currently states that 'of the 14.4 million [ie the 20 million refugees minus the Palestinians] refugees of concern to UNHCR around the world, less than one per cent is submitted for resettlement'. The main countries of resettlement are the US, followed by Australia, Canada, and the Nordic countries. In 2015, by nationality, the main beneficiaries of UNHCR-facilitated resettlement programmes are refugees from Syria (53,305), DRC (20,527), Iraq (11,161), and Somalia (10,193).[84] The 1 per cent of refugees who are offered resettlement tend to get safe passage, secure legal status from the outset, and integration support. Resettlement offers them a new life, usually with a clear path to citizenship in time. And for host states, in particular those at a geographical distance from regions of origin, resettlement is an important way for them to offer tangible support to refugees and overburdened countries of first refuge.

However, there are unanswered questions about the ethics of resettlement. The UNHCR resettlement criteria focus on vulnerability,[85] a notoriously slippery concept. Some states seem to use additional criteria such as religion or ethnicity to select amongst refugees, which would be legally prohibited for a country of first asylum to employ.[86] Resettlement also plays a role in refugee containment, both by encouraging refugees to tolerate conditions that would otherwise be intolerable (on a dim hope of resettlement), and by de-legitimating other modes of seeking protection. This undermines the obligations under the Refugee Convention, in particular non-penalization for illegal entry (Article 31) and *non-refoulement*.[87] For example, in Australia, spontaneous asylum has been delegitimized, and refugee resettlement is portrayed as the only acceptable route to protection. A similar trope underlies the EU-Turkey deal, with a twist—resettlement places are offered to the extent that Turkey accepts back those who travelled irregularly to the Greek islands.[88] Refugees are expected to wait patiently in an imaginary resettlement queue and endure the

[84] UNHCR, *UNHCR Projected Global Resettlement Needs,* 22nd Annual Tripartite Consultations on Resettlement, Geneva: 13–15 June 2016, p. 55, online http://www.unhcr.org/575836267.pdf.

[85] See UNHCR, *UNHCR Resettlement Handbook* (2011), online http://www.unhcr.org/46f7c0ee2.pdf.

[86] CSR51 (n 3), article 3.

[87] Maria O'Sullivan, 'The Ethics of Resettlement: Australia and the Asia-Pacific Region', *The International Journal of Human Rights 20,* no. 2 (2016): pp. 241–263.

[88] EU-Turkey Statement, 18 March 2016, Press Release 144/16, online http://www.consilium.europa.eu/en/press/press-releases/2016/03/18-eu-turkey-statement/.

entirely discretionary assessment that underpins resettlement. Resettlement often obscures other more straightforward ways to offer legal routes to claim asylum, such as specific visas to enable legal travel to claim asylum. Indeed, discourse around resettlement suggests it provides states with a way to re-inscribe refugees in the practices of discretionary admission that characterize other forms of migration control.

Yet, at some historical junctures, resettlement has provided access to protection and solutions for millions. When Hungarians fled the Soviet invasion in 1956, within months all but 410 of the 180,000 who fled to Austria were resettled to thirty-six other states.[89] The Indochinese Comprehensive Plan of Action is another oft-cited example of cooperation to offer refugee protection, involving the resettlement of hundreds of thousands of refugees from states which were only willing to offer temporary protection.[90] Some urge that increasing resettlement is key to generating political support for refugee protection, as it means refugees cease to be associated with illegal immigration, and arrive with their status already determined.[91] 2016 saw various attempts to increase global resettlement commitments, but the results thus far have been underwhelming.

CONCLUSIONS

The hallmark of the global refugee regime since the end of the Cold War has become containment rather than cooperation to offer protection. In the absence of cooperation to provide protection, containment undermines the rights of refugees. The ideal of refugee protection as reinsertion within the protective ambit of a new state, with a clear path to either a new citizenship or voluntary safe repatriation and reintegration at home, is belied by the reality of protracted limbo, subject to constraints on movement and work rights, and provision of meagre humanitarian assistance.

A glance at the profiles of the 2016 Olympic 'Team Refugees' reveals the human face of containment. Five are South Sudanese refugees living in Kakuma camp in Kenya. Two are Congolese refugees, who claimed asylum whilst in Brazil for

---

[89] Marjoleine Zieck, 'The 1956 Hungarian Refugee Emergency, an Early and Instructive Case of Resettlement', *Amsterdam Law Forum* 5, no. 2 (2013): pp. 45–63.

[90] W. Courtland Robinson, *Terms of Refuge: The Indochinese Exodus and the International Response* (London, New York: Zed Books, 1998).

[91] Luara Ferracioli, 'The Appeal and Danger of a New Refugee Convention', *Social Theory and Practice* 40, no. 1 (2014): pp. 123–144.

the Judo world championships in 2013. Their elite athletic privilege gave them a freedom to travel their co-nationals would generally lack. Three are refugees in Europe—two Syrians (one in Germany; the other in Belgium) both of whom made dangerous boat journeys from Turkey to Greece. The youngest member of the team, Yusra Mardini (18), swam for three hours to propel a boatful of her fellow refugees to safety when its engine failed.[92] Rami Anis (25) fled Aleppo to Turkey, but it seems he gave up on life in Turkey as he was not able to work or study there. The final member is an Ethiopian refugee living in Luxembourg. In addition, two refugee athletes competed in the Rio Paralympic Games, Ibramhim Ali Hussein from Syria and Shahrad Nasajpur from Iran.[93]

Team Refugees are competing under the international Olympic flag. But in reality, their refugeehood depends on recognition by their state of residence. There is no 'country of UNHCR' to which refugees can turn for protection. Nor may refugees assert a global citizenship.

In his account of the development of the Refugee Convention, Gatrell recounts the exchange between the International Refugee Organisation (the IRO), and leading intellectuals of the day including Bernard Shaw, Albert Einstein, and Bertrand Russell.[94] They suggested to the IRO that refugees should be regarded as 'harbingers of "world citizenship"'.[95] They argued that refugees already 'by sheer force of events ... have acquired the feeling of belonging to a community larger than one nation [sic]. History made them citizens of the world'. Crucially, too, they urged that '*they should be treated as such*'.[96] 'As such' connoted that refugees not be required to apply for new nationalities, but rather 'let the ideal of world citizenship subsist not solely in theories and programs, but also in courageous experimenting and in a genuine respect for the human person'.[97] The IRO rejected this notion: 'Here are people to whom you say, be proud of your statelessness'. Much better, its officials countered, for them to be rid of that status and find a new state. Paul Weis, the IRO's chief legal adviser, argued that 'it is through his connection with a particular state by the ties of nationality that the individual finds his place in international law'.[98]

Formally, refugees are privileged aliens, in that they may stake claims against other states, above and beyond other non-citizens. However, the geopolitics of

---

[92] Heather Saul, 'Yusra Mardini: Olympic Syrian Refugee Who Swam for Three Hours in Sea to Push Sinking Boat Carrying 20 to Safety', *The Independent*, 6 August 2016, online http://www.independent.co.uk/news/people/yusra-mardini-rio-2016-olympics-womens-swimming-the-syrian-refugee-competing-in-the-olympics-who-a7173546.html.

[93] Rio 2016, 'IPC Announces Two Refugee Athletes who Will Compete at Rio 2016 Paralympic Games', online https://www.rio2016.com/en/paralympics/news/ipc-refugee-athletes-independent-team-rio-2016-paralympic-games-Ibrahim-Al-Hussein-Shahrad-Nasajpour.

[94] Peter Gatrell, *The Making of the Modern Refugee* (Oxford: Oxford University Press, 2013), p. 108, citing G. Daniel Cohen, *In War's Wake: Europe's Displaced Persons in the Postwar Order* (New York: Oxford University Press, 2012), pp. 89–90.

[95] Gatrell (n 93), p. 108.   [96] Ibid. (emphasis added).   [97] Ibid.   [98] Ibid.

refugee containment, and the global inequality of citizenship and power that under-pins it, often render refugee privilege illusory. Containment policies deny refugees' agency, and place them at risk of further human rights violations, beyond those that caused them to flee in the first place. These violations include protracted encamp-ment and denial of work and citizenship rights in exile, and dangerous illicit jour-neys where they risk further harm if they flee in search of better protection. This chapter reveals a refugee regime that often leaves refugees struggling to access the protections they are due.

Bibliography

Akram, Susan, 'UNRWA and Forced Migration', in Elena Fiddian-Qasmiyeh, Gil Loescher, Katy Long, and Nando Sigona, eds., *The Oxford Handbook of Refugee and Forced Migration Studies* (Oxford: Oxford University Press, 2014), pp. 227–240.

Arendt, Hannah, *The Origins of Totalitarianism* (New York: Harcourt Brace & Co., 1978).

Betts, Alexander, *Survival Migration: Failed Governance and the Crisis of Displacement* (Ithaca: Cornell University Press, 2013).

Bloemraad, Irene, *Becoming a Citizen: Incorporating Immigrants and Refugees in the United States and Canada* (Berkeley, Los Angeles: University of California Press, 2006).

Bradley, Megan, *Refugee Repatriation: Justice, Responsibility and Redress* (Cambridge: Cambridge University Press, 2013).

Bradley, Megan, 'Rethinking Refugeehood: Statelessness, Repatriation, and Refugee Agency', *Review of International Studies 40*, no. 1 (2014): pp. 101–123.

Brubaker, Rogers, *Citizenship and Nationhood in France and Germany* (Cambridge, London: Harvard University Press, 1992).

Campbell, John R., 'The Enduring Problem of Statelessness in the Horn of Africa: How Nation-States and Western Courts (Re)Define Nationality', *International Journal of Refugee Law 23*, no. 4 (2011): pp. 656–679.

Campbell, John, 'Language Analysis in the United Kingdom's Refugee Status Determination System: Seeing through Policy Claims about "Expert Knowledge"', *Ethnic and Racial Studies 36*, no. 4 (2013): pp. 670–690.

Cherem, Max, 'Refugee Rights: Against Expanding the Definition of a "Refugee" and Unilateral Protection Elsewhere', *The Journal of Political Philosophy 24*, no. 2 (2016): pp. 183–205.

Chimni, B. S., 'The Geopolitics of Refugee Studies: A View from the South', *Journal of Refugee Studies 11*, no. 4 (1998): pp. 350–374.

Cohen, G. Daniel, *In War's Wake: Europe's Displaced Persons in the Postwar Order* (New York: Oxford University Press, 2012).

Costello, Cathryn, 'The Asylum Procedures Directive and the Proliferation of Safe Country Practices: Deterrence, Deflection and the Dismantling of International Protection', *European Journal of Migration Law 7* (2005): pp. 35–69.

Costello, Cathryn, 'Safe Country? Says Who?', *International Journal of Refugee Law 28*, no. 4 (2016): pp. 601–622.

Costello, Cathryn and Michelle Foster, 'Non-Refoulement as Custom and Jus Cogens? Putting the Prohibition to the Test', *Netherlands Yearbook of International Law 46* (2015): pp. 273–327.

Courtland Robinson, W., *Terms of Refuge: The Indochinese Exodus and the International Response* (London, New York: Zed Books, 1998).

Czaika, Mathias and Hein de Haas, 'The Globalization of Migration: Has the World Become More Migratory?', *International Migration Review 48*, no. 2 (Summer 2014): pp. 283–323.

Edwards, Alice, 'Transitioning Gender: Feminist Engagement with International Refugee Law and Policy 1950–2010', *Refugee Survey Quarterly 29*, no. 2 (2010): pp. 21–45.

Ferracioli, Luara, 'The Appeal and Danger of a New Refugee Convention', *Social Theory and Practice 40*, no. 1 (2014): pp. 123–144.

Fortin, Antonio, 'The Meaning of "Protection" in the Refugee Definition', *International Journal of Refugee Law 12*, no. 4 (2000): pp. 548–576.

Foster, Michelle, 'Why We are Not There Yet: The Particular Challenge of "Particular Social Group"', in Efrat Arbel, Catherine Dauvergne, and Jenni Millbank, eds., *Gender in Refugee Law: From the Margins to the Centre* (Abingdon: Routledge, 2014), pp. 17–45.

Fripp, Eric, *Nationality and Statelessness in the International Law of Refugee Status* (Oxford, Portland: Hart Publishing, 2016).

Gammeltoft-Hansen, Thomas, *Access to Asylum: International Refugee Law and the Globalisation of Migration Control* (New York: Cambridge University Press, 2011).

Gatrell, Peter, *The Making of the Modern Refugee* (Oxford: Oxford University Press, 2013).

Gibney, Matthew J., *The Ethics and Politics of Asylum: Liberal Democracy and the Response to Refugees* (Cambridge: Cambridge University Press, 2004).

Goodman, Sarah Wallace, 'Naturalisation Policies in Europe: Exploring Patterns of Inclusion and Exclusion' (Florence: EUDO Citizenship Observatory, November 2010), online http://eudo-citizenship.eu/docs/7-Naturalisation%20Policies%20in%20Europe.pdf.

Guild, Elspeth and Madeline Garlick, 'Refugee Protection, Counter-Terrorism and Exclusion in the European Union', *Refugee Survey Quarterly 29*, no. 4 (2010): pp. 63–82.

Hathaway, James C., 'Is Refugee Status Really Elitist? An Answer to the Ethical Challenge', in Jean-Yves Carlier and Dirk Vanheule, eds., *Europe and Refugees: A Challenge? L'Europe et les réfugiés: un défi?* (The Hague, London, Boston: Kluwer Law International, 1997), pp. 79–88.

Hutt, Michael, *Unbecoming Citizens: Culture, Nationhood and the Flight of Refugees from Bhutan* (New Delhi: Oxford University Press, 2003).

Kaushal, Asha and Catherine Dauvergne, 'The Growing Culture of Exclusion: Trends in Canadian Refugee Exclusions', *International Journal of Refugee Law 23*, no. 1 (2011): pp. 54–92.

Lambert, Hélène, 'Refugee Status, Arbitrary Deprivation of Nationality, and Statelessness within the Context of Article 1A(2) of the 1951 Convention and its 1967 Protocol Relating to the Status of Refugees', UNHCR Legal and Protection Policy Research Series, PPLA/2014/01 (Geneva: UNHCR, 2014).

Long, Katy, *The Point of No Return: Refugees, Rights, and Repatriation* (Oxford: Oxford University Press, 2013).

Macklin, Audrey, 'Refugee Women and the Imperative of Categories', *Human Rights Quarterly 17*, no. 2 (1995): pp. 213–277.

Macklin, Audrey, 'Who Is the Citizen's Other? Considering the Heft of Citizenship', *Theoretical Inquiries in Law 8*, no. 2 (2007): pp. 333–366.

Macklin, Audrey, 'Sticky Citizenship', in Rhoda E. Howard-Hassmann and Margaret Walton-Roberts, eds., *The Human Right to Citizenship: A Slippery Concept* (Philadelphia: University of Pennsylvania Press, 2015), pp. 223–239.

Malkki, Liisa H., 'Refugees and Exile: From "Refugee Studies" to the National Order of Things', *Annual Review of Anthropology 24* (1995): pp. 495–523.

Manby, Bronwen, *Citizenship Law in Africa: A Comparative Study*, 2nd edition (New York: Open Society Foundations, October 2010).

McAdam, Jane, *Complementary Protection in International Refugee Law* (Oxford: Oxford University Press, 2007).

Miller, David, *National Responsibility and Global Justice* (Oxford: Oxford University Press, 2007).

Milner, James, 'Protracted Refugee Situations', in Elena Fiddian-Qasmiyeh, Gil Loescher, Katy Long, and Nando Sigona, eds., *The Oxford Handbook of Refugee and Forced Migration Studies* (Oxford: Oxford University Press, 2014), pp. 151–162.

Milner, James, 'Can Global Refugee Policy Leverage Durable Solutions? Lessons from Tanzania's Naturalization of Burundian Refugees', *Journal of Refugee Studies 27*, no. 4 (2014): pp. 553–573.

Ní Ghráinne, Bríd, 'UNHCR's Involvement with IDPs—"Protection of that Country" for the Purposes of Precluding Refugee Status?', *International Journal of Refugee Law 26*, no. 4 (2014): pp. 536–554.

O'Sullivan, Maria, 'The Ethics of Resettlement: Australia and the Asia-Pacific Region', *The International Journal of Human Rights 20*, no. 2 (2016): pp. 241–263.

Peters, Floris, Maarten Vink, and Hans Schmeets, 'The Ecology of Immigrant Naturalisation: A Life Course Approach in the Context of Institutional Conditions', *Journal of Ethnic and Migration Studies 42*, no. 3 (2016): pp. 359–381.

Price, Matthew E., *Rethinking Asylum: History, Purpose, and Limits* (Cambridge: Cambridge University Press, 2009).

Saul, Heather, 'Yusra Mardini: Olympic Syrian Refugee Who Swam for Three Hours in Sea to Push Sinking Boat Carrying 20 to Safety', *The Independent*, 6 August 2016, online http://www.independent.co.uk/news/people/yusra-mardini-rio-2016-olympics-womens-swimming-the-syrian-refugee-competing-in-the-olympics-who-a7173546.html.

Shachar, Ayelet, *The Birthright Lottery: Citizenship and Global Inequality* (Cambridge, London: Harvard University Press, 2009).

Shacknove, Andrew, 'Who is a Refugee?', *Ethics 95*, no. 2 (1985): pp. 274–284.

Shacknove, Andrew, 'From Asylum to Containment', *International Journal of Refugee Law 5*, no. 4 (1993): pp. 516–533.

Shklar, Judith N., 'Obligation, Loyalty, Exile', *Political Theory 21*, no. 2 (1993): pp. 181–197.

Slaughter, Amy and Jeff Crisp, 'A Surrogate State? The Role of UNHCR in Protracted Refugee Situations', in Gil Loescher, James Milner, Edward Newman, and Gary G. Troeller, eds., *Protracted Refugee Situations: Political, Human Rights and Security Implications* (Tokyo: United Nations University Press, 2008), pp. 123–140.

Spijkerboer, Thomas, ed., *Fleeing Homophobia: Sexual Orientation, Gender Identity and Asylum* (Abingdon: Routledge, 2013).

Spijkerboer, Thomas, 'European Sexual Nationalism: Refugee Law After the Gender & Sexuality Critiques', Paper presented at the Nordic Asylum Seminar, University of Uppsala, 8 May 2015, online http://thomasspijkerboer.eu/wp-content/uploads/2015/05/Uppsala-201505081.pdf.

Sumption, Madeline and Sarah Flamm, *The Economic Value of Citizenship for Immigrants in the United States* (Migration Policy Institute, September 2012), online http://www.migrationpolicy.org/research/economic-value-citizenship.

Tharoor, Ishaan, 'Turkey's Bold New Plan for Syrian Refugees: Make Them Citizens', *The Washington Post*, 9 July 2016, online https://www.washingtonpost.com/news/worldviews/wp/2016/07/09/turkeys-bold-new-plan-for-syrian-refugees-make-them-citizens/.

Tutton, Richard, Christine Hauskeller, and Steven Sturdy, 'Importing Forensic Biomedicine into Asylum Adjudication: Genetic Ancestry and Isotope Testing in the United Kingdom', in Benjamin N. Lawrance and Galya Ruffer, eds., *Adjudicating Refugee and Asylum Status: The Role of Witness, Expertise, and Testimony*, (New York: Cambridge University Press, 2015), pp. 202–220.

Wolman, Andrew, 'North Korean Asylum Seekers and Dual Nationality', *International Journal of Refugee Law 24*, no. 4 (2012): pp. 793–814.

Zieck, Marjoleine, 'The 1956 Hungarian Refugee Emergency, an Early and Instructive Case of Resettlement', *Amsterdam Law Forum 5*, no. 2 (2013): pp. 45–63.

Ziegler, Ruvi, *Voting Rights of Refugees* (Cambridge University Press, forthcoming).

ADDITIONAL REFERENCES

3RP Mid-Year Report (June 2016), online http://data.unhcr.org/syrianrefugees/regional.php.

EU-Turkey Statement, 18 March 2016, Press Release 144/16, online http://www.consilium.europa.eu/en/press/press-releases/2016/03/18-eu-turkey-statement/.

IDMC, *Annual Report 2015*, online http://www.internal-displacement.org/assets/publications/2016/201607-annual-report-2015-en.pdf.

IOM, Missing Migrants Project, online http://missingmigrants.iom.int/over-3770-migrants-have-died-trying-cross-mediterranean-europe-2015.

Institute on Statelessness and Inclusion and The Global Campaign for Equal Nationality Rights, *Submission to the Human Rights Council at the 26th Session of the Universal Periodic Review: Syrian Arab Republic* (24 March 2016), online http://www.institutesi.org/SyriaUPR2016.pdf.

Statement by Mrs. Sadako Ogata, United Nations High Commissioner for Refugees, at the International Management Symposium, St. Gallen, Switzerland (25 May 1992), online http://www.unhcr.org/admin/hcspeeches/3ae68faec/statement-mrs-sadako-ogata-united-nations-high-commissioner-refugees-international.html.

UN dataset, Trends in International Migrant Stock: The 2015 Revision, online http://www.un.org/en/development/desa/population/migration/data/estimates2/estimates15.shtml.

UNGA Resolution 428(V) 'Statute of the Office of the United Nations High Commissioner for Refugees' (14 December 1950).

UNHCR, *Global Trends: Forced Displacement in 2015* (20 June 2016), online http://www.refworld.org/docid/57678f3d4.html.

UNHCR, *Guidelines on International Protection No. 4: 'Internal Flight or Relocation Alternative' Within the Context of Article 1A(2) of the 1951 Convention and/or 1967 Protocol Relating to the Status of Refugees* (23 July 2003), HCR/GIP/03/04, online http://www.ref-world.org/docid/3f2791a44.html.

UNHCR, *Handbook and Guidelines on Procedures and Criteria for Determining Refugee Status under the 1951 Convention and the 1967 Protocol relating to the Status of Refugees* (Reissued December 2011), online http://www.unhcr.org/publications/legal/3d58e13b4/handbook-procedures-criteria-determining-refugee-status-under-1951-convention.html.

UNHCR, 'International Protection Considerations with regard to people fleeing the Syrian Arab Republic, Update III' (October 2014), online http://www.refworld.org/pdfid/544e446d4.pdf.

UNHCR, *UNHCR Note on the Interpretation of Article 1E of the 1951 Convention relating to the Status of Refugees* (March 2009), online http://www.refworld.org/docid/49c3a3d12.html.

UNHCR, *UNHCR Projected Global Resettlement Needs*, 22nd Annual Tripartite Consultations on Resettlement, Geneva: 13–15 June 2016, online http://www.unhcr.org/protection/resettlement/575836267/unhcr-projected-global-resettlement-needs-2017.html.

UNHCR, UNHCR Resettlement Handbook (2011), online http://www.unhcr.org/46f7c0ee2.pdf.

UNHCR Excom, 'Conclusion on Protracted Refugee Situations', no. 109 (LXI), 2009.

UNHCR Excom, 'Conclusion on Local Integration', no. 104 (LVI), 2005.

UNHCR Excom, 'Voluntary Repatriation', no. 18 (XXXI), 1980.

UNHCR Excom, 'Voluntary Repatriation', no. 40 (XXXVI), 1985.

CONVENTIONS

Convention relating to the Status of Refugees (adopted 28 July 1951, entered into force 22 April 1954) 189 UNTS 150.

Convention relating to the Status of Stateless Persons (adopted 28 September 1954, entered into force 6 June 1960) 360 UNTS 117.

Convention on the Reduction of Statelessness (adopted 30 August 1961, entered into force 13 December 1975) 989 UNTS 175.

Convention against Torture and Other Cruel, Inhuman or Degrading Treatment or Punishment (adopted 10 December 1984, entered into force 26 June 1987).

European Convention for the Protection of Human Rights and Fundamental Freedoms (adopted 4 November 1950, entered into force 3 September 1953) 213 UNTS 221, ETS no. 5.

International Covenant on Civil and Political Rights (adopted 16 December 1966, entered into force 23 March 1976) 999 UNTS 171.

OAU Convention Governing the Specific Aspects of Refugee Problems in Africa (adopted 10 September 1969, entered into force 20 June 1974) 1001 UNTS 45, art. I(2).

OTHER INSTRUMENTS

Cartagena Declaration on Refugees, adopted by the Colloquium on the International Protection of Refugees in Central America, Mexico and Panama, 22 November 1984.

Guiding Principles on Internal Displacement, E/CN.4/1998/53/Add.2, 11 February 1998.

Directive 2011/95/EU of the European Parliament and of the Council of 13 December 2011 on standards for the qualification of third-country nationals or stateless persons as beneficiaries of international protection, for a uniform status for refugees or for persons eligible for subsidiary protection, and for the content of the protection granted (recast) [2011] OJ L337/9.

CASES

Judgment of 23 February 2012, *Hirsi Jamaa and Others v. Italy* 27765/09, CE:ECHR:2012:0223JUD002776509.

Ward v. Canada [1993] 2 S.C.R. 689.

CHAPTER 33

....

STATELESSNESS, 'IN-BETWEEN' STATUSES, AND PRECARIOUS CITIZENSHIP

....

NOORA A. LORI

As states have monopolized the authority over legitimate interstate movement by building identity management infrastructures, they have created a margin of people who lack access to *permanent* and *secure* citizenship rights. The denial of identity documents significantly impacts livelihood outcomes, because identity management infrastructures increasingly link travel documents to employment, education, healthcare, and other public services. I use the concept of *precarious citizenship* to refer to people who are unable to gain access to secure citizenship rights and instead inhabit ad hoc and temporary legal statuses for protracted periods. Precarious citizenship is primarily experienced by two groups: (1) migrants and (2) internal 'others' who are not recognized by the states in which they reside. Why do these groups persist with precarious legal statuses for protracted periods? I argue that states increasingly adopt ad hoc and temporary statuses because they represent a strategic government response to avoid resolving larger dilemmas about citizenship, especially questions about the incorporation of minorities, refugees, or labor.

This chapter brings together recent scholarship on a wide range of groups who are unable to gain access to citizenship as a legal status; individuals in these groups are stateless or inhabit a liminal position 'in between' legal statuses. For these individuals, exclusion from the national body politic occurs not just through crisis-driven forced expulsion, but also through the gradual institutional forces of state-building, standardization, and centralization. Drawing from across world-regions and regime-types, this chapter shows that by holding people in a pending status for so long, states are creating the very ambiguity in legal status that challenges their ability to have a synoptic vision of the population and to place everyone into a discrete category. This creates the paradox of precarious citizenship as a direct result of boundary enforcement: although the drive to strengthen boundary enforcement can be motivated by a desire to eliminate undocumented or uncertain legal statuses, it often achieves the opposite, reifying uncertainty in the legal status of migrant and minority populations. This uncertainty has gradually crystalized as a constitutive ambiguity in the legal status of an increasing number of people across the globe. It is—as James Scott has so eloquently shown—the business of states to make people legible.[1] But as I illustrate below, since states continually postpone the incorporation of some groups, their legibility-producing actions also create and institutionalize ambiguity. States make populations legible—and *illegible*—often to achieve similar ends.

This chapter first provides a definition of precarious citizenship and then parses precarious citizenship into sub-types based on the documentary profiles of the individuals in each group—that is, what documents they have and how those documents align (or misalign) with the state's authorization of secure and permanent residency. This documentary lens is necessary because citizenship status must be proven through evidence. People who do not hold the right documents can be expelled from the territory even if they meet the legal conditions of citizenship in practice.[2] Secure access to citizenship means having all of the necessary identity

---

[1] James C. Scott, *Seeing Like a State: How Certain Schemes to Improve the Human Condition Have Failed* (New Haven: Yale University Press, 1999).

[2] On the deportation of U.S. citizens, see Jacqueline Stevens, 'U.S. Government Unlawfully Detaining and Deporting U.S. Citizens as Aliens,' *Virginia Journal of Social Policy and the Law* 18, no. 3 (July 2011): 606–720.

documents to be able to benefit from citizenship rights domestically and to travel internationally. The four sub-types examined below include: 1) individuals who cannot gain national identity documents and become stateless; 2) individuals who may have one state's identity documents but who lack legal status in the state of their residence and thus become 'illegal'; and a spectrum of groups with temporary statuses that are neither stateless nor fully unauthorized. Rather than being denied the authority to live in a state, these groups have temporary and circumscribed residency authorization. Such groups include 3) individuals with temporary humanitarian protected statuses, and 4) temporary guest workers.

Precarious Citizenship

I employ the overarching concept of *precarious citizenship* to refer to the structured uncertainty of being unable to secure permanent access to citizenship rights.[3] The concept of precariousness has gained prominence in recent years, but the term dates back to at least the 1600s, and its early usages refer to a sense of insecurity related to bodily harm or the means of one's subsistence.[4] The term is now most commonly used to denote economic insecurity. Precariousness is used to describe the erosion of social protections and labor rights, including drops in average job tenure, increases in long-term unemployment, outsourced and temporary work, unsafe work, and the reduction of pensions and insurance.[5] Somers connects this form of precariousness to the concept of citizenship by arguing that marketization and neoliberal reforms have led a growing number of people who are formally citizens to be stripped of the social protections associated with citizenship, rendering them socially excluded and 'internally stateless.'[6] While Somers focuses on the *content* of citizenship (rights), I use the concept of precariousness to focus exclusively on the challenges people face when trying to gain formal *access* to citizenship (status).[7]

---

[3] The chapter uses 'precariousness' and 'precarity' as synonyms for precarious legal citizenship status.

[4] 'Precariousness,' *Oxford English Dictionary*, 3rd edition (New York: Oxford University Press, 2007).

[5] Louise Waite, 'A Place and Space for a Critical Geography of Precarity?,' *Geography Compass 3*, no. 1 (2009): pp. 412–433; Guy Standing, *The Precariat: The New Dangerous Class* (London: Bloomsbury Academic, 2011).

[6] Margaret Somers, *Genealogies of Citizenship: Markets, Statelessness, and the Right to Have Rights* (Cambridge, New York: Cambridge University Press, 2008).

[7] In Joppke's citizenship triad, citizenship is comprised of three dimensions: status, rights, and identity (Christian Joppke, 'Transformation of Citizenship: Status, Rights, Identity,' *Citizenship Studies 11*, no. 1 (2007): pp. 27–48).

Citizenship status is critical because 'precarious legal status … goes hand-in-hand with precarious employment and livelihood.'[8] In other words, uncertain legal statuses compound the effects of economic exigencies by rendering certain populations more likely to experience insecurity and uncertainty. The lived experience of having a precarious legal status can impact almost every aspect of an individual's life and can lead to, among other costs: psychological trauma; increased illness and loss of access to medical services; the inability to obtain gainful employment; the loss of secure, stable, and affordable housing; the loss of educational opportunities; the increased incidence of domestic violence; and significantly higher risks of being trafficked (as forced labor, and especially for women and children, in the sex industry). Because of the systematic impact of citizenship status on economic uncertainty, Paret and Gleeson argue that migration provides the best lens through which to understand economic inequality and how it is maintained in the global capitalist system. This focus on migration also emerges in the definition of precarious legal status recently promulgated by the Upper Tribunal of the United Kingdom in its interpretation of section 117B of the 2002 Nationality, Immigration and Asylum Act.[9] The Tribunal's definition of 'precarious' encompasses any legal status that is temporary and revocable, even when such status is valid and lawfully obtained. Unlike Paret and Gleeson and the UK courts, who link precariousness to migrant deportability in general, this chapter focuses on precarious citizenship as an outcome of both migration and state building.

BOUNDARY ENFORCEMENT AND THE PROLIFERATION OF 'IN-BETWEEN' AND STATELESS POPULATIONS

What accounts for the proliferation of precarious citizenship statuses? This section provides an overview of why and how precarious citizenship is experienced by two groups of people: 1) migrants (including both migration 'forced' by political conflict or natural disaster, and the arguably 'chosen' path of clandestine economic migration); and 2) internal 'others' who are not recognized by the states in which they

---

[8] Marcel Paret and Shannon Gleeson, 'Precarity and Agency through a Migration Lens,' *Citizenship Studies* 20, no. 3–4 (2016): pp. 277–294, p. 281.

[9] *AM (S 117B) Malawi* [2015] UKUT 260 IAC, paragraph 4 of the headnote ('A person's immigration status is "precarious" if their continued presence in the UK will be dependent upon their obtaining a further grant of leave').

reside. The literature identifies a range of variables that condition the experience of precarious citizenship—the structural, institutional, and individual factors that make insecure citizenship status (and the intensity of the risks associated with it) more or less likely (Table 33.1).

The most common route to precarious citizenship is 'unauthorized' movement or residency; that is, entering a state without the proper government authorization or overstaying the duration of one's authorization. Despite the risks associated with unauthorized entry and residency, millions of people migrate without authorization—often because they are forced to. While the speed and reach of human mobility have certainly increased over the past two centuries, this mobility is hardly 'new'; what *is* relatively new is the criminalization of movement. By the

Table 33.1 Precarious Citizenship Causes and Conditioning Variables

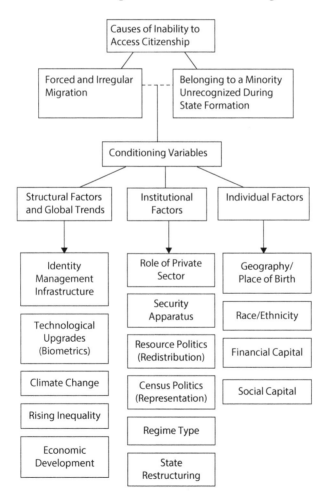

end of the nineteenth and into the twentieth centuries, modern states monopolized the authority over legitimate movement into and out of their territories, aiming to settle mobile populations.[10] Whether driven by climate change, political conflict, or economic pressures, unauthorized migration—or more accurately state responses *to* unauthorized migration—challenges the ideal of a globally inclusive citizenship system. When displaced populations are unable to access durable solutions (repatriation, local integration, or third country resettlement) they may face criminalization, becoming 'illegal' immigrants or stateless persons. Instead of being formally incorporated, these populations persist—sometimes over generations—with precarious citizenship statuses. The outcome is a vicious cycle: displacement creates illegality and in some cases statelessness, and those who experience protracted periods of precarity as illegal aliens or stateless persons are often forced to migrate for survival, creating even more displaced populations.[11]

People can also be excluded from permanent and secure access to citizenship in the absence of migration if they are unrecognized by the states in which they reside. Since the globe's heterogeneous populations do not neatly align with the current configuration of sovereign states, most (if not all) states encompass populations that do not fit into the dominant national narrative or 'imagined community.' States have three options when responding to their internal 'others': incorporate, expel, or ignore. While more scholarly attention has been paid to how and why states choose to incorporate or expel minority populations, for much of the twentieth century, states have also been able to ignore their 'others,' thereby creating pockets of populations invisible in the state's legal self-image. Unlike the physically displaced, these populations disappear from their place of residence *de jure*, without crossing a border or leaving their place of birth. Examples include the Rohingya in Myanmar/ Burma, Kenyan Nubians, or Dominicans of Haitian descent.

When states fortify their boundaries—by adopting biometric ID cards, diffusing internal identity checks, and strengthening border control—these populations become the object of intensive regularization. Identity regularization is a multifaceted process that for some can mean the issuance of an identity document, but for others can mean the loss of residence, bank accounts and assets, and expulsion, or factual, as well as legal, erasure from the state.[12] The global rise in boundary

---

[10]   Scott (n 1); Charles Tilly, 'The Geography of European State-Making and Capitalism Since 1500,' in Eugene Genovese and Leonard Hochberg, eds., *Geographic Perspectives in History* (Oxford: Blackwell 1989), pp. 159–181; John C. Torpey, *The Invention of the Passport: Surveillance, Citizenship and the State* (Cambridge: Cambridge University Press, 2000), p. 6.

[11]   On the cyclical relationship between statelessness and forced migration, see Lucy Hovil and Zachary A. Lomo, 'Forced Displacement and the Crisis of Citizenship in Africa's Great Lakes Region: Rethinking Refugee Protection and Durable Solutions,' *Refuge: Canada's Journal on Refugees* *31*, no. 2 (December 2, 2015): pp. 45–46.

[12]   See Dumbrava in this volume.

enforcement is itself part of the process that is exposing a growing number of people to the risks of precarious citizenship.

To a great extent, structural pressures beyond the control of individuals account for the proliferation of statelessness and in-between statuses. Imperial breakdown, state formation, and restructuring can lead certain populations to be excluded from new political arrangements, thus generating precarious legal statuses and statelessness through the very processes of state building.[13] The expansion of the global labor force, rising levels of income inequality, and climate change are all examples of structural factors that stimulate migration and with it, precariousness. People are forced to move for a wide range of reasons, but the international legal framework on forced displacement only legitimates a small proportion of them through its focus on persecution. Under the *1951 Convention relating to the Status of Refugees*, a refugee is a person who has been targeted on account of his/her race, religion, nationality, membership in a particular social group, or political opinion. To meet this definition, an individual must be able to show that they were individually targeted for persecution because of their identity. The emphasis on individual persecution not only excludes many push factors of forced migration, such as generalized violence, it also requires a high burden of proof that can be difficult to meet, especially when people flee without identity documents. In response to the political and procedural challenges of asylum, states have developed a range of ad hoc legal statuses to fill the gap between the 1951 Convention's refugee and the reality of contemporary forced migration.

Global trends in international security, biometric technology adoption, and deportations have heightened state efforts to enforce citizen/non-citizen distinctions, increasing the risks of precarious citizenship. As non-state actors eclipse interstate conflict as a major threat to international security, governments—particularly in the developing world—are facing mounting pressures to document their populations accurately and strengthen the infrastructure of their identity management systems. Development institutions like the World Bank promote the adoption of electronic identity management systems and the first decade of the twenty-first century witnessed a proliferation of new population identification technologies—by 2010 there were 160 cases where biometric identification was adopted in developing countries for economic, political, or social purposes.[14]

This ubiquitous adoption of biometric identification coincides with mass displacement of record-breaking levels. The heightened security imperative to accurately

---

[13] Aristide Zolberg, 'The Formation of New States as a Refugee-Generating Process,' *The Annals of the American Academy of Political and Social Science 467*, no. 1 (May 1, 1983): pp. 24–38; Oxana Shevel, *Migration, Refugee Policy, and State Building in Postcommunist Europe* (New York: Cambridge University Press, 2011); Jo Shaw and Igor Stiks, eds., *Citizenship After Yugoslavia* (New York: Routledge, 2013).

[14] See Alan Gelb and Julia Clark, 'Identification for Development: The Biometrics Revolution,' (Washington: Center for Global Development, 2013), online http://www.cgdev.org/publication/identification-development-biometrics-revolution-working-paper-315.

categorize people thus comes at a time when more and more people do not neatly fit into pre-existing national categories. With the new global security trends in identity management and the increasing dependence on digital governance, these irregular cases are brought to the fore and we are witnessing a proliferation of statelessness globally. The heighted securitization of travel and domestic ID checks, particularly after the turn of the twenty-first century, has meant that deportations are reaching record highs in almost every world region.[15]

The challenges of unauthorized travel and residence can be relatively manageable or unsustainably precarious, depending not only on individual resources but also on the strength of the host state's identity infrastructure and its incentives for enforcing legal status. Indeed, the very concept of 'unauthorized' only makes sense vis-à-vis a political authority that has the capacity to check identity documents domestically as well as at national borders. The strength of an identity management infrastructure depends not only on a state's level of economic development but also on the strength of its security apparatus and the role of public institutions in domestic migration control. Policing and monitoring can occur not only at borders but also at schools, hospitals, and housing developments.

When the infrastructure of documentary citizenship is weak, as it is in many developing states, 'unauthorized' individuals can gain access to local identity documents that become a conduit to the benefits of citizenship despite not having an official national identity in the country.[16] The weakness of domestic institutions can enable unauthorized residents to slowly gain entry into the society as they acquire local identity documents, vote in local elections, access public services, and build their families—all without official authorization, for protracted periods. As long as accessing public services or earning a livelihood at the local level are decoupled from legal status, individuals can persist with irregular citizenship statuses. However, when the state's infrastructure for enforcing legal status is entrenched, long-term residents can face exclusionary pressures.

Though larger global pressures drive migration, people fall into precarious statuses because of state policies—not depoliticized economic forces. Ad hoc and temporary statuses are proliferating because they provide political elites with a means of avoiding larger dilemmas about the boundaries of the nation. These dilemmas emerge when there is a contestation over the incorporation of ethnic minorities, refugees, or labor. In such cases, states often find it more politically expedient to postpone the larger questions about belonging and address the more immediate

[15] See, e.g., Daniel Kanstroom, *Deportation Nation: Outsiders in American History* (Cambridge: Harvard University Press, 2007); Nicholas De Genova and Nathalie Peutz, eds., *The Deportation Regime: Sovereignty, Space, and the Freedom of Movement* (Durham: Duke University Press Books, 2010); Bridget Anderson, Matthew J. Gibney, and Emanuela Paoletti, 'Citizenship, Deportation and the Boundaries of Belonging,' *Citizenship Studies* 15, no. 5 (2011): pp. 547–563.

[16] Kamal Sadiq, *Paper Citizens: How Illegal Immigrants Acquire Citizenship in Developing Countries* (New York: Oxford University Press, 2008).

issues of population management. For example, Shevel shows how an intentionally ambiguous nationality law proved to be politically expedient in post-Soviet Russia, 'the fuzzy definition of compatriots in the law allows Russia to pursue a variety of objectives and to target a variety of groups without solving the contradictions of existing nation-building discourses.'[17] Ambiguous, conditional and temporary legal statuses allow authorities to address subnational populations in a contradictory and flexible manner.

Liminal population categories emerge for a range of politically expedient reasons. Competing state actors can choose to strategically allow 'illegal' immigrants to vote, particularly when there are electoral gains at stake.[18] This fluidity in how to count people (or votes) is not limited to developing countries; the US census counts unauthorized migrants, and the resulting state population size determines each state's number of seats at the House of Representatives and federal funds distribution.[19] The extensive literature on census politics shows that political interests play a role in whether and how states count people; competing state actors may have different incentives for excluding (or ignoring) minority populations. The scholarship demonstrates that decisions to assimilate, culturally accommodate, or expel minorities are shaped by the strategic calculations of policy-makers, including their long-standing ideas about nationhood and political culture,[20] need for labor or military conscription,[21] and national security calculations and perceptions of threat.[22] The decision to exclude or incorporate particular groups can also be driven by foreign relations. The recognition of political refugees is an act of recognizing injustice in the actions of foreign states; recognized refugees thus often come from 'enemy' states—as exemplified by Cuban migrants in the US—while individuals in a very similar (or arguably worse) situation may be labeled as 'economic migrants' simply because they are fleeing foreign allies.

Finally, while many studies on the causes of precarious citizenship tend to emphasize macro and meso level conditioning variables, the ethnographic research on those who experience precarity demonstrates that individual and group

[17] Oxana Shevel, 'Russian Nation-Building from Yel'tsin to Medvedev: Ethnic, Civic or Purposefully Ambiguous?', *Europe-Asia Studies* 63, no. 2 (2011): pp. 179–202.

[18] Kamal Sadiq, 'When States Prefer Non-Citizens Over Citizens: Conflict Over Illegal Immigration into Malaysia', *International Studies Quarterly* 49, no. 1 (2005): pp. 101–122, doi: 10.1111/j.0020-8833.2005.00336.x.

[19] United States Census Bureau, 'Congressional Apportionment: FAQ', online http://www.census.gov/population/apportionment/about/faq.html#Q16.

[20] Rogers Brubaker, *Citizenship and Nationhood in France and Germany* (Cambridge: Harvard University Press, 1992).

[21] Patrick Weil, 'Access to Citizenship: A Comparison of Twenty-Five Nationality Laws', in Alexander Aleinikoff and Douglas B. Klusmeyer, eds., *Citizenship Today: Global Perspectives and Practices* (Washington: Carnegie Endowment for International Peace, 2001), pp. 17–36.

[22] Harris Mylonas, *The Politics of Nation-Building: Making Co-Nationals, Refugees, and Minorities* (New York: Cambridge University Press, 2013); Myron Weiner, 'Security, Stability, and International Migration', *International Security* 17, no. 3 (Winter 1992): pp. 91–126.

characteristics (like wealth, social capital, class, geography of birth, and race) also shape the likelihood someone will experience precarious citizenship. Financial and social capital are key factors for mitigating the extent to which uncertain citizenship status will lead to economic and bodily insecurity. Wealth generates greater avenues for travel and access to safer routes, and strong social networks can facilitate migration and expand housing and livelihood options. Capital allows individuals to use informal networks or the private sector to gain access to services (like healthcare or education) that they cannot gain from the state. Financial capital even plays a role in determining legal status. Wealth differentials create wide variation in the livelihood outcomes of migrants fleeing the same conflict, even when they end up in the same host state. For example, in Jordan, economic resources shape whether a Syrian registers as a refugee with the UNHCR or lives as a 'visitor;' those with means have been able to reside in hotels throughout the conflict and are thus counted as 'Arab guests.'[23] At higher income levels, individuals may even be able to purchase legal status through citizenship-by-investment schemes.[24] Advanced degrees or valuable skills also open avenues for mobility.

Racial, ethnic, and religious hierarchies may generate precarious legal status, but also allow some to escape precarity. For example, when minorities are unable to access hospitals or register births, their members can become stateless or fall into a liminal status.[25] Conversely, minority status can be leveraged for asylum if an individual is able to prove persecution on the basis of one's identity. Geography of birth and parental citizenship also shape the likelihood that someone will experience precarious citizenship due to the fact that the global visa regime hierarchizes mobility. For example, though both Eritrean and UK passport holders may be motivated to travel abroad to seek job opportunities during an economic crisis, an Eritrean citizen needs a visa to travel almost anywhere and is far more likely to become 'illegal' than a UK citizen who is granted authorized access to 147 countries and can securely explore alternative job markets.[26]

Precarious citizenship is produced as an intended and unintended consequence of boundary enforcement processes. In the next sections, I examine four groups of people who can be described as having precarious citizenship; for each, I show how state building and regularization processes have worked to formalize, rather than

[23] Oroub El-Abed, 'The Discourse of Guesthood: Forced Migrants in Jordan,' in Anita Fabos and Riina Isotalo, eds., *Managing Muslim Mobilities* (Basingstoke: Palgrave Macmillan, 2014): pp. 81–100.

[24] See Shachar in this volume.

[25] Sardelic explains that difficulties in registering births (and therefore inability to prove residency) were a key barrier for Romani minorities to gain access to citizenship in the former Yugoslavia (Julija Sardelic, 'Romani Minorities and Uneven Citizenship Access in the Post-Yugoslav Space,' *Ethnopolitics* 14, no. 2 (2015): pp. 159–179).

[26] Arton Capital calculates global rankings of passports based on the number of countries that allow document-holders visa-free access (Arton Capital, Passport Index: World's Passports in One Place), online http://www.passportindex.org/index.php.

alleviate or eradicate, the precarious legal statuses of these groups. The risks associated with precarious access to citizenship apply to all documentary profiles discussed in this chapter (stateless populations, unauthorized residents, or temporarily authorized residents), but there is variation across these statuses as some are more precarious than others. Individuals with temporary and circumscribed authorization experience precarity when they fall out of status and cannot gain access to permanent residency and citizenship for protracted periods. Stateless populations, on the other hand, find themselves in a permanent state of precarity—they have no authorization to either reside in their current location or travel. 'Illegal' immigrants experience precarity only when they travel without authorization or overstay their visas, but the likelihood of being forced into this status is unevenly concentrated cross-nationally due to the hierarchies of the global visa regime. All of these groups experience precarious citizenship as an indeterminate waiting for citizenship that creates a generalized state of insecurity.

No National Identity Documents: Stateless Populations

Those who are most at risk of precarious citizenship are the individuals denied national identity documents in their country of birth. This document may be a passport, or a different ID as states often use passports for international identification purposes and have separate systems for domestic identification. Stateless populations are often not entirely 'undocumented'—they can carry local documents (birth certificates, local IDs, or ration cards) but are considered stateless if those documents are not recognized by the state as establishing citizenship. Statelessness is caused both by exogenous shocks like conflicts and imperial breakdowns, as well as much slower boundary enforcement processes like state building and identity regularization.

It is not surprising that much of the early scholarship on statelessness focused on its association with the refugee cycle, interstate conflict, and state formation.[27] Zolberg develops 'political persecution' as an analytic category and argues that mass displacement 'arises most prominently as a by-product of the secular transformation of empires into nation-states.'[28] By being denied access to national identity

---

[27] Zolberg (n 13); Craig J. Jenkins and Susan Schmeidl, 'Flight from Violence: The Origins and Implications of the World Refugee Crisis,' *Sociological Focus* 28, no. 1 (1995): pp. 63–82, doi: 10.1080/00380237.1995.10571039.

[28] Zolberg (n 13), p. 24.

documents, stateless persons are deprived of the 'right to have rights.'[29] Arendt, who coined this phrase, was particularly interested in how stripping people of citizenship rights served as a prelude to persecution—paving the path to genocide. In the aftermath of World War II an international human rights framework emerged to protect people targeted for persecution because of their identity. Conflict, persecution, and forced displacement often result in statelessness, particularly when refugees are not integrated and cannot obtain identity documents in either their host country, or in their state of origin. The current challenges that displaced Syrians face in registering their children born in Lebanon, Jordan, Egypt, Turkey, and Iraq provide a case in point.[30]

Statelessness also occurs in the absence of state formation, conflict, or displacement. Perhaps counter-intuitively, the stateless are not free-floating individuals, 'the primary injustice of the stateless experience ... is not that they cannot find a state to grant them citizenship but that the state which should grant them citizenship will, for various reasons, not do so.'[31] A key reason for the emergence of statelessness in the absence of displacement is the variation among citizenship regimes. Failures to show parentage or place of birth and conflicting state citizenship laws can put people in the position of being unrecognized by any state. In the Middle East, a key path to statelessness is the predominance of patrilineal citizenship. By making it so that only fathers can confer nationality to their children, patrilineal citizenship regimes often create statelessness, for instance in cases where the father is a refugee, from an unrecognized minority, or absent.

More recent scholarship on statelessness has focused on how state-building and political restructuring can effectively strip minorities of nationality rights— expanding research to include situations of *de facto* statelessness.[32] *De jure* statelessness is explicitly treated in the 1954 Convention relating to the Status of Stateless people and the 1961 Convention on the Reduction of Statelessness.[33] By contrast,

---

[29] Hannah Arendt, *The Origins of Totalitarianism* (New York: Harcourt Brace Jovanovich, 1976), p. 296.

[30] UNHCR, 'Born in Exile,' online http://unhcr.org/FutureOfSyria/born-in-exile.html.

[31] Matthew Gibney, 'Statelessness and the Right to Citizenship,' *Forced Migration Review* 32 (April 2009): pp. 50–51, p. 50, online http://www.fmreview.org/FMRpdfs/FMR32/50-51.pdf.

[32] See Shevel (n 13); Roshan De Silva Wijeyeratne, 'Citizenship Law, Nationalism and the Theft of Enjoyment: A Post-Colonial Narrative,' *Law Text Culture* 4, (1998): pp. 37–67; Rebecca Wolozin, 'Citizenship Issues and Issuing Citizenship: A Case Study of Sri Lanka's Citizenship Laws in a Global Context,' *Asian-Pacific Law & Policy Journal* 16, no. 1 (2014): pp. 1–28; Joy K. Park, John E. Tanagho, and Mary E. Weicher, 'A Global Crisis Writ Large: The Effects of Being "Stateless in Thailand" on Hill-Tribe Children,' *San Diego International Law Journal* 10, no. 2 (2009): pp. 495–554; Joseph Harris, 'Uneven Inclusion: Consequences of Universal Healthcare in Thailand,' *Citizenship Studies* 17, no. 1 (2013): pp. 111–127, doi: 10.1080/13621025.2013.764220.

[33] Later documents include the International Law Commission's Draft Articles on Nationality of Natural Persons in Relation to the Succession of States (International Law Commission, *Report of the Commission to the General Assembly on the Work of Its Fifty-First Session*, A/CN.4/SER.A/1999/Add.l (Part 2): pp. 19–39, online http://www.refworld.org/pdfid/4512b6dd4.pdf.

de facto statelessness is a term developed by the literature to refer to individuals who were (at least at some point) formally documented by a state but continue to be systematically excluded from state protection and assistance. *De facto* statelessness lacks an international legal framework because states frame these exclusions as part of the sovereign prerogative to define the national body. *De facto* statelessness is often not produced by forced migration, but rather through the institutionalization of new nationality laws or the revocation of residency rights. For example, the cases of Slovenia, Kosovo, and other states of former Yugoslavia, demonstrate how political restructuring creates liminal and stateless populations.[34] Stiks illustrates how some groups of former Yugoslav citizens became post-Yugoslav aliens who had to go through a process of naturalization.[35] In Slovenia, the young state's attempts to establish itself in opposition to Yugoslavia led to a campaign of national homogenization that created thousands of stateless persons. In the process of this campaign, 'more than 18,000 former Yugoslav citizens were deleted from the Slovenian State register in 1992 and subsequently became known as "erased persons." '[36] These individuals were then deemed to be 'illegal aliens' and had their residency revoked.

De facto stateless persons are not always actively targeted by the state for denaturalization; individuals can also become effectively stateless over time as they experience delays or refusals when attempting to renew identity documents. This becomes especially important when the infrastructure of the state develops to integrate identity checks into the provision of public services, so that individuals who could previously access education, healthcare, or public housing are no longer able to do so. While statelessness through displacement may occur rapidly, *de facto* statelessness through state-building is more incremental. The two forms are not mutually exclusive. For example, a small community of Asian Ugandans became stateless twice in their lives—once rapidly, when Idi Amin expelled them from Uganda in 1972, and then again gradually over a period of forty years of residency in the United Arab Emirates, as their identity documents were no longer recognized and their passports were no longer renewed.[37] Their case illustrates that experiencing crisis-driven statelessness in one context does not immunize one from experiencing *de*

---

[34] Shaw and Stiks (n 13); Gezim Krasniqi and Dejan Stjepanovic, 'Uneven Citizenship: Minorities and Migrants in the Post-Yugoslav Space,' *Ethnopolitics 14*, no. 2 (2015): pp. 113–120; Brad Blitz, 'Statelessness and the Social (De)Construction of Citizenship: Political Restructuring and Ethnic Discrimination in Slovenia,' *Journal of Human Rights 5*, no. 4 (2006): pp. 453–479.

[35] Igor Stiks, 'A Laboratory of Citizenship: Shifting Conceptions of Citizenship in Yugoslavia and its Successor States,' CITSEE Working Paper 2010/2 (Edinburgh: University of Edinburgh, 2010), online http://www.citsee.ed.ac.uk/__data/assets/pdf_file/0009/108828/179_alaboratoryofcitizenshipshifting-conceptionsof citizenshipinyugoslaviaanditssucces.pdf.

[36] Blitz (n 34), p. 2.

[37] Members of this community were issued Union of Comoros passports in 2008 (Noora Lori, 'Unsettling State: Non-Citizens, State Power, and Citizenship in the United Arab Emirates' (PhD Dissertation, Johns Hopkins University, 2013) (unpublished, on file with author), pp. 151–198; Noora Lori, *Offshore Citizens: Permanent 'Temporary' Status* (unpublished manuscript, on file with author)).

facto statelessness in another; those who are in the 'margins' do not cleanly fit into any state and their precarity is often compounded over time, across multiple legal contexts and over generations.

Where the concept of statelessness is not recognized, the *de facto* stateless can easily become 'illegal immigrants.' The colloquial reference to 'illegal immigrants' presumes the bearer of the label to be a newcomer or foreigner, but locally born minorities can also fall into a state of illegality.[38] In that sense, the boundaries between the stateless and those deemed to be 'illegal' are fluid, much like the boundaries between all of these categories. That is the defining characteristic of precarity; one's citizenship status is not secure, it fluctuates.

No Authorization: 'Illegal' Immigration

Individuals become 'illegal' under the law of a state when they enter into or reside in a country without the proper authorization in the form of a valid passport and visa. Unauthorized migrants inhabit a precarious position when they are unable to draw upon any state's protections. They can face challenges procuring local IDs or national identity documents, registering births, and accessing social security benefits. Illegality only makes sense in reference to a state authority; people become 'illegal' through an active process when the state criminalizes their presence in the territory. Studies have demonstrated how unauthorized immigrants can achieve various forms of social and civic integration despite being formally excluded. Irregular migrants are often integrated at the local level—in schools, churches, community groups, art collectives, and political associations.[39] Moreover, instead of juxtaposing formal exclusion on the one hand, to informal incorporation on

[38] As a case in point, the *bidoon* in Kuwait are referred to by the government as 'illegal residents.' See, e.g., Human Rights Watch, 'Concerns and Recommendations on Kuwait Submitted to the UN Human Rights Committee in advance of its Pre- Sessional Review' (August 7, 2015): p. 3, online http://tbinternet.ohchr.org/Treaties/CCPR/Shared%20Documents/KWT/INT_CCPR_ICO_KWT_21314_E.pdf.
[39] Leo Chavez, 'Outside the Imagined Community: Undocumented Settlers and Experiences of Incorporation,' *American Ethnologist 18*, no. 2 (1991): pp. 257–278; James Holston, *Cities and Citizenship* (Durham: Duke University Press, 1994); Susan B. Coutin, *Legalizing Moves: Salvadoran Immigrants' Struggle for U.S. Residency* (Ann Arbor: University of Michigan Press, 2000); Joanne Van der Leun, *Looking for Loopholes: Processes of Incorporation of Illegal Immigrants in the Netherlands* (Amsterdam: Amsterdam University Press, 2003); Godfried Engbersen, Marion Van San, and Arjen Leerkes, 'A Room with a View: Irregular Migrants in the Legal Capital of the World,' *Ethnography 7*, no. 2 (2006): pp. 209–242.

the other, the dynamic of exclusion and incorporation 'does not always pit formal law against informal practices or social resistance, but is often located within law itself'.[40] Irregular migrants can be integrated into different parts of a state's formal institutions despite being otherwise 'illegal'.[41]

The term 'illegal' is highly problematic when used to refer to people instead of actions, as the Associate Press noted when it excluded 'illegal immigrant' from its vocabulary in 2013. Scholarship has moved away from the 'illegal immigrant' as a reified category to pay attention to an analysis of 'illegality' as a juridical status and socio-political condition.[42] Andersson examines the whole illegality 'industry', including those who partake in policing and patrolling (border guards), caring and rescuing (aid workers), and observing and knowing (media and academia).[43] This attention to the actors and processes that create conditions of illegality is key for showing that 'becoming illegal' requires an active process of targeting on behalf of state authorities (often with the complicity and assistance of the private sector, NGOs, and inter-governmental bodies like the International Organization for Migration). In her work on the experiences of West African and Filipino migrants in Tel Aviv, Willen shows how a massive regularization campaign of arrest and deportation transformed these migrants from benign 'others' into wanted 'criminals'.[44] While domestic security concerns often motivate such campaigns, foreign relations

[40] Sébastien Chauvin and Blanca Garcés-Mascareñas, 'Beyond Informal Citizenship: The New Moral Economy of Migrant Illegality,' *International Political Sociology* 6 (2012): pp. 241–259, p. 243. Earlier work that challenges the dichotomy between exclusion and membership models of undocumented immigrants includes: Linda Bosniak, 'Exclusion and Membership: The Dual Identity of the Undocumented Worker under U.S. Law,' *Wisconsin Law Review* 6 (1988): pp. 955–1042; Linda Bosniak, *The Citizen and the Alien: Dilemmas of Contemporary Membership* (Princeton: Princeton University Press, 2006).

[41] Coutin (n 39); Cecilia Menjavar, 'Liminal Legality: Salvadoran and Guatemalan Immigrants' Lives in the United States,' *American Journal of Sociology* 111, no. 4 (January 2006): pp. 999–1037; Monica Varsanyi, 'Interrogating "Urban Citizenship" vis-a-vis Undocumented Migration,' *Citizenship Studies* 10, no. 2 (2006): pp. 229–249; Paul G. Lewis and S. Karthick Ramakrishnan, 'Police Practices in Immigrant-Destination Cities: Political Control or Bureaucratic Professionalism?,' *Urban Affairs Review* 42, no. 6 (2007): pp. 874–900; Barbara Laubenthal, 'The Negotiation of Irregular Migrants' Right to Education in Germany: A Challenge to the Nation-State,' *Ethnic and Racial Studies* 34, no. 8 (2011): pp. 1357–1373.

[42] Coutin (n 39); Josiah M. Heyman, 'Class and Classification at the US-Mexico Border,' *Human Organization* 60, no. 2 (2001): pp. 128–140; Mae Ngai, *Impossible Subjects: Illegal Aliens and the Making of Modern America* (Princeton: Princeton University Press, 2004); Liliana Suárez-Navaz, *Rebordering the Mediterranean: Boundaries and Citizenship in Southern Europe* (New York: Berghahn Books, 2004); Sarah Willen, 'Exploring "Illegal" and "Irregular" Migrants' Lived Experiences of Law and State Power,' *International Migration* 45, no. 3 (2007): pp. 2–7, doi: 10.1111/j.1468-2435.2007.00408.x.

[43] Ruben Andersson, *Illegality, Inc.: Clandestine Migration and the Business of Bordering Europe* (Oakland: University of California Press, 2014).

[44] Sarah Willen, 'Citizens, "Real" Others, and "Other" Others: The Biopolitics of Otherness and the Deportation of Unauthorized Migrant Workers from Tel Aviv, Israel,' in Nicholas De Genova and Nathalie Peutz, eds., *The Deportation Regime: Sovereignty, Space, and the Freedom of Movement* (Durham: Duke University Press Books, 2010), pp. 262–294.

and external pressures can also lead states to regularize migrant populations and target 'unlawful' residents. For example, Spain's entry into the European Union enabled the Spanish nationality inhabitants of Ceuta and Melilla to become full citizens of the EU while thousands of their ethnic Moroccan counterparts who had been living in those enclaves for decades became 'illegals' subject to deportation.[45]

While irregular migrants are often treated like criminals in these regularization drives, unlawful presence does not always take on the form of criminalization. This legal distinction is important for shaping how migrants are able to respond to such deportation campaigns. In the in US, for example, unlawful presence (whether via unauthorized entry or visa violation) has been treated as an administrative violation. The fact that unauthorized migration is not formally criminalized has led US courts to conclude that deportation is not tantamount to punishment in the criminal context; this has thereby insulated the government from being constitutionally required to offer due process protections (e.g., appointment of counsel) in deportation proceedings.[46]

One of the paradigmatic experiences of precarious citizenship is the lack of certainty; those who are deemed to be 'illegal' face the danger of arrest on a daily basis once they have been targeted by the state. The next two categories of those with precarious access to citizenship also experience daily uncertainties, but they often oscillate from being authorized to being 'illegal.' This is due to the fact that they have circumscribed and temporary authorization to reside in the state, and yet tend to inhabit these temporary statuses for protracted periods.

Temporary and Circumscribed Humanitarian Authorization: Ad Hoc Protected Statuses

The precarious status holders covered in this section are neither stateless nor 'illegal'; they have temporary and circumscribed authorization to reside in the host country for humanitarian purposes. States have developed a plethora of temporary and ad hoc statuses to accommodate the large gap between those who are displaced, and those who meet the stringent criteria required for refugee resettlement. These ad hoc statuses highlight the long-standing tension between a state's right

---

[45] Iker Barbero, 'Orientalising Citizenship: The Legitimation of Immigration Regimes in the European Union,' *Citizenship Studies 16*, no. 5–6 (August 1, 2012): pp. 751–768, doi: 10.1080/13621025.2012.698504.

[46] Thanks to Linda Bosniak for her helpful decipherment of the U.S. legal system.

to control the makeup of its population, and the customary international norm of *'non-refoulement'* (the prohibition against expelling aliens who risk persecution if forced to return to their place of origin).

States have developed temporary statuses in response to the fact that most displaced people find themselves in 'refugee-like' situations but are not eligible for refugee status as defined under international law. Examples of temporary statuses include exceptions made for rejected asylum seekers or reprieve from deportation because of unstable conditions in one's country of origin. At times these temporary statuses emerge informally, in the ad hoc practices of deferring deportation and exempting passports that cannot be renewed because of conflicts. In other cases, these practices are codified, such as Temporary Protected Status (TPS) in the US, which Congress passed in 1990.[47] Temporary protection is also offered in Germany and Turkey, and, at least on paper, could be triggered in the European Union.

While ad hoc and temporary humanitarian protections emerge out of humanitarian concerns, they often have the unintended consequence of placing individuals in a position of structural ambiguity for a protracted period. The research demonstrates how people with temporary protection often oscillate from being authorized to becoming 'illegal'—both in cases of formally codified and informal protected statuses. For example, in cases of informal temporary protection, individuals are often forced between living as a 'refugee' inside a refugee camp (protected from arrest and deportation but without the freedom to work or move) or as an 'illegal' immigrant outside the camps (able to move and work in the informal sector but vulnerable to exploitation as well as arrest and deportation).[48] At times forced migrants can also gain the right to legally reside as temporary workers in the host state. Frelick explains that refugees can work legally in Thailand if they choose *not* to claim refugee status and instead present themselves as migrant workers to the Thai Ministry of Labor. This can lead to the acquisition of a temporary work visa and permit (valid for two years) that can be renewed once.[49] Refugees cannot return home so claiming asylum can lead to a rejected application and deportation, but being strategically silent can allow the forced migrant to gain temporary reprieve from deportation.

The scholarship demonstrates that individuals can also face this structural uncertainty even in contexts where temporary protection is formally recognized. For example, in her research on Central American migrants under TPS in the US, Menjivar argues that they are neither documented nor undocumented but rather fall into a gray area in between legal statuses.[50] TPS is *not* asylum because it is

---

[47] Bill Frelick and Barbara Kohnen, 'Filling the Gap,' *Journal of Refugee Studies* 8, no. 4 (1995): pp. 339–363.

[48] Bill Frelick, 'Unlocking Protracted Refugee Situations: Lessons from Four Asian Cases,' in Tom Syring, ed., *Still Waiting for Tomorrow: The Law and Politics of Unresolved Refugee Crises* (Newcastle upon Tyne: Cambridge Scholars Publishing, 2014), pp. 169–193, p. 182.

[49] Ibid., p. 182.   [50] Menjivar (n 41), p. 1000.

explicitly designed not to be an avenue for permanent residency.[51] Rather, it is a stopgap measure to protect designated nationalities from being deported during times of armed conflict, natural disasters, or 'temporary and extraordinary' conditions. While asylum is individually determined, TPS is granted to all nationals of a designated country, as a 'blanket' form of relief for people who face reasonable threats but are not individually persecuted. Though TPS was set up as a temporary measure, TPS designations have become increasingly protracted since it was established. Because TPS is not meant as a path to permanent settlement, each extension of TPS works to lock beneficiaries in 'a "legal limbo," rendering them unable to fully integrate into life in the United States.'[52] Menjivar argues that a state of 'liminal legality shapes different spheres of life' for these migrants, not just constraining livelihood outcomes but also shaping social networks and family, the place of religious institutions, and artistic expression.[53] They are neither 'legal' nor 'illegal' because they are neither fully recognized as economic migrants nor political refugees; at times they are treated as refugees and granted temporary relief from deportation, and at other times their permits are not renewed and they fall into being 'illegal' migrants again.

Temporary and Circumscribed Employment Authorization: 'Guest' Workers

Another form of temporary and circumscribed authorization that may lead to precarious citizenship exists in the sphere of transnational labor mobility. Work visa categories are designed with the host state's labor market needs in mind, rather than the needs of the migrant. Low-skilled temporary visa workers are more vulnerable to exploitation of their labor, and rarely have recourse to legal mechanisms for adjusting their status to permanent residency. In such situations, and where

---

[51] The law explicitly prevents TPS holders from adjusting to lawful permanent residence (LPR) status (*Immigration & Naturalization Act*, § 244(h)). Individuals who are on TPS may qualify for asylum—but by law one may apply for asylum only within the individual's first year in the U.S. Because asylum processing is lengthy and cumbersome, immigration judges and applicants alike often opt for TPS despite its limitations.

[52] Claire Bergeron, 'Temporary Protected Status after 25 Years: Addressing the Challenge of Long-Term "Temporary" Residents and Strengthening a Centerpiece of US Humanitarian Protection,' *Journal on Migration and Human Security* 2, no. 1 (2014): pp. 22–43, p. 22.

[53] Menjivar (n 41), p. 1000.

migrants have spent the bulk of their lives outside of the state of their citizenship, formal citizenship may lose its function as guarantee of political and legal belonging or source of protection against rights violations.

Guest worker programs are designed to increase the supply of labor without increasing the number of permanent residents. This design rarely maintains coherence in reality because migration that begins as temporary quickly takes on a more permanent quality as governments struggle to control settlement once workers have entered the country.[54] As one migration scholar put it, 'there is nothing more permanent than temporary foreign workers.'[55] Guest worker programs become permanent because of the dependence on those workers created by the private sector. The demand for workers grows and adapts to the promise of an almost unlimited cheap foreign labor supply.

In the cases of the US-Mexico Bracero programs and the German and other European guest worker schemes of the 1960s and 1970s, the employers' 'need' for guest workers lasted longer and proved to be larger than originally expected. This dynamic operates in the states of the Gulf Cooperation Council across all economic sectors.[56] Dependence occurs because employers in the receiving country come to rely on foreign workers, and those workers in turn form attachments to the receiving country, as do their families who now depend on the remittances sent home. The private sector also plays a key role in enforcing visa status. In the *kafala* guest worker system in the Gulf, the costs of migrants' violation of visa status are externalized to the private sector. Under this system, each migrant is linked to an individual citizen or company sponsor who is financially liable for the migrant.

When it comes to the vulnerability of those with temporary work authorization, regime-type differences are important because the presence of liberal democratic institutions, particularly courts and civil rights organizations, can allow individuals with insecure status to leverage different resources within the state to gain legal status. This is exemplified in the way 'temporary' workers in Europe were able to gain permanent residency and citizenship rights, while such formal inclusion is foreclosed for long-term 'temporary' workers in the Gulf. In the case of post-war migration to Western Europe, migrants were able to move from temporary work authorization to more permanent residency statuses and gain political rights at the local level.[57] These reforms occurred despite what were often heated and racialized

---

[54] For a discussion of the permanence of temporary statuses, see Elizabeth F. Cohen, *Semi-Citizenship in Democratic Politics* (Cambridge: Cambridge University Press, 2009), pp. 9–10.

[55] Phillip Martin, 'There is Nothing More Permanent Than Temporary Foreign Workers,' *Center for Immigration Studies Backgrounder* (April 2001), p. 1, online http://cis.org/TemporaryWorkers-Overstays.

[56] The states of the Gulf Cooperation Council (Bahrain, Kuwait, Oman, Qatar, Saudi Arabia, and the United Arab Emirates) are overwhelmingly dependent upon guest workers. Non-citizens make up 60 percent of the region's aggregate labor force and over 90 percent in the UAE and Qatar.

[57] Tomas Hammar, *Democracy and the Nation State: Aliens, Denizens, and Citizens in a World of International Migration* (Aldershot, Brookfield: Avery/Gower Pub. Co., 1990).

political battles about the growing number of foreigners, especially post-colonial minorities, in places like the United Kingdom, Germany, and France.[58]

In contrast, the lack of checks and balances in authoritarian states allows them to seal off naturalization policies from scrutiny as a realm of national security and to more freely employ denationalization as means of dealing with dissidence. The large oil producers in the Gulf all have citizenship policies that entitle citizens to redistributed wealth but make it nearly impossible for 'guest' workers to obtain citizenship. Foreign residents are treated as 'temporary' workers regardless of the duration of their residency. Instead of becoming legal permanent residents after long periods of residing in a state, migrants in the Gulf become permanently deportable—their authorization for remaining in the country is always conditional and circumscribed.[59]

Concluding Remarks

The notion of precarious citizenship offers one approach to systematizing the experiences of the growing number of people across the globe who cannot gain access to secure and permanent citizenship status for a wide range of reasons. This chapter presents an overview of the factors that increase or decrease the likelihood that someone will experience precarious citizenship. It identifies four forms of precarious citizenship, arguing that in each case, precarious citizenship is produced as an intended and unintended consequence of boundary enforcement processes. Ambiguous and temporary statuses are growing because they represent a strategic government response to avoid resolving dilemmas about citizenship (especially questions about the incorporation of minorities, refugees, or labor) by postponing those decisions, perhaps indefinitely. Moreover, the very processes of boundary enforcement (biometric ID management, ID regularization, and deportation drives) have pulled more and more people into the documentary power of the state system without providing them a secure place within it. In its structuring of everyday life, precarious citizenship is experienced as a protracted waiting—waiting

---

[58] See, e.g., Kathleen Paul, *Whitewashing Britain: Race and Citizenship in the Postwar Era* (Ithaca: Cornell University Press, 1997); Miriam Feldblum, *Reconstructing Citizenship: The Politics of Nationality Reform and Immigration in Contemporary France* (Albany: SUNY Press, 1997).

[59] For overview of the formal and informal institutions that regulate the *kafala* in the Gulf see Noora Lori, '"Temporary Migrants" or Permanent Residents? The Kafala System and Contestations over Residency in the Arab Gulf States,' *Center for Migrations and Citizenship, Institut Français des Relations Internationales* (November 2012), online http://www.ifri.org/sites/default/files/atoms/files/notecmcnooralori1.pdf.

for documents, waiting for resettlement, or waiting for authorization to be able to access the tools of a secure life, especially legal employment and travel.

These cases of precarity demonstrate that documents are a key variable in determining livelihood outcomes. While identity documents have no value in themselves, they impact every aspect of a person's life trajectory based on whether or not they are recognized by the state. Identity documents can thus range from being the most effective conduit for enabling access to state services, employment, and travel or the largest barrier to taking part in such quotidian activities. This chapter illustrates how boundary enforcement processes have worked to formalize, rather than alleviate or eradicate, precarious citizenship. At a time when immigration is highly politicized everywhere, it is critical to pay attention to the externalities that are emerging with the global drive to secure boundaries and 'imagined' national citizenries.

BIBLIOGRAPHY

Akram, Susan and Tom Syring, eds., *Still Waiting for Tomorrow: The Law and Politics of Unresolved Refugee Crises* (Newcastle upon Tyne: Cambridge Scholars Publishing, 2014).

Anderson, Bridget, Matthew J. Gibney, and Emanuela Paoletti, 'Citizenship, Deportation and the Boundaries of belonging,' *Citizenship Studies 15*, no. 5 (2011): pp. 547–563.

Andersson, Ruben, *Illegality, Inc.: Clandestine Migration and the Business of Bordering Europe* (Oakland: University of California Press, 2014).

Arendt, Hannah, *The Origins of Totalitarianism* (New York: Harcourt Brace Jovanovich, 1976).

Barbero, Iker, 'Orientalising Citizenship: The Legitimation of Immigration Regimes in the European Union,' *Citizenship Studies 16*, no. 5–6 (August, 2012): pp. 751–768.

Bergeron, Claire, 'Temporary Protected Status after 25 Years: Addressing the Challenge of Long-Term "Temporary" Residents and Strengthening a Centerpiece of US Humanitarian Protection,' *Journal on Migration and Human Security 2*, no. 1 (2014): pp. 22–43.

Blitz, Brad, 'Statelessness and the Social (De)Construction of Citizenship: Political Restructuring and Ethnic Discrimination in Slovenia,' *Journal of Human Rights 5*, no. 4 (2006): pp. 453–479.

Bosniak, Linda, 'Exclusion and Membership: The Dual Identity of the Undocumented Worker under U.S. Law,' *Wisconsin Law Review 6* (1988): pp. 955–1042.

Bosniak, Linda, *The Citizen and the Alien: Dilemmas of Contemporary Membership* (Princeton: Princeton University Press, 2006).

Brubaker, Rogers, *Citizenship and Nationhood in France and Germany* (Cambridge: Harvard University Press, 1992).

Chauvin, Sébastien and Blanca Garcés-Mascareñas, 'Beyond Informal Citizenship: The New Moral Economy of Migrant Illegality,' *International Political Sociology 6* (2012): pp. 241–259.

Chavez, Leo, 'Outside the Imagined Community: Undocumented Settlers and Experiences of Incorporation,' *American Ethnologist 18*, no. 2 (1991): pp. 257–278.

Cohen, Elizabeth F., *Semi-Citizenship in Democratic Politics* (Cambridge: Cambridge University Press, 2009).

Coutin, Susan B., *Legalizing Moves: Salvadoran Immigrants' Struggle for U.S. Residency* (Ann Arbor: University of Michigan Press, 2000).

De Genova, Nicholas and Nathalie Peutz, eds., *The Deportation Regime: Sovereignty, Space, and the Freedom of Movement* (Durham: Duke University Press Books, 2010).

El-Abed, Oroub, 'The Discourse of Guesthood: Forced Migrants in Jordan,' in Anita Fabos and Riina Isotalo, eds., *Managing Muslim Mobilities* (Basingstoke: Palgrave Macmillan, 2014), pp. 81–100.

Engbersen, Godfried, Marion Van San, and Arjen Leerkes, 'A Room with a View: Irregular Migrants in the Legal Capital of the World,' *Ethnography 7*, no. 2 (2006): pp. 209–242.

Feldblum, Miriam, *Reconstructing Citizenship: The Politics of Nationality Reform and Immigration in Contemporary France* (Albany: SUNY Press, 1997).

Frelick, Bill, 'Unlocking Protracted Refugee Situations: Lessons from Four Asian Cases,' in Susan Akram and Tom Syring, eds., *Still Waiting for Tomorrow: The Law and Politics of Unresolved Refugee Crises* (Newcastle upon Tyne: Cambridge Scholars Publishing, 2014), pp. 169–193.

Frelick, Bill and Barbara Kohnen, 'Filling the Gap,' *Journal of Refugee Studies 8*, no. 4 (1995): pp. 339–363.

Gelb, Alan and Julia Clark, 'Identification for Development: The Biometrics Revolution,' (Washington: Center for Global Development, 2013), online http://www.cgdev.org/publication/identification-development-biometrics-revolution-working-paper-315.

Gibney, Matthew, 'Statelessness and the Right to Citizenship,' *Forced Migration Review* 32 (April 2009): pp. 50–51, online http://www.fmreview.org/FMRpdfs/FMR32/50-51.pdf.

Hammar, Tomas, *Democracy and the Nation State: Aliens, Denizens, and Citizens in a World of International Migration* (Aldershot, Brookfield: Avery/Gower Pub. Co., 1990).

Harris, Joseph, 'Uneven Inclusion: Consequences of Universal Healthcare in Thailand,' *Citizenship Studies 17*, no. 1 (2013): pp. 111–127, doi: 10.1080/13621025.2013.764220.

Heyman, Josiah M., 'Class and Classification at the US-Mexico Border,' *Human Organization* 60, no. 2 (2001): pp. 128–140.

Holston, James, *Cities and Citizenship* (Durham: Duke University Press, 1994).

Hovil, Lucy and Zachary A. Lomo, 'Forced Displacement and the Crisis of Citizenship in Africa's Great Lakes Region: Rethinking Refugee Protection and Durable Solutions,' *Refuge: Canada's Journal on Refugees 31*, no. 2 (December 2, 2015), online: http://refuge.journals.yorku.ca/index.php/refuge/article/view/40308.

Human Rights Watch, 'Concerns and Recommendations on Kuwait Submitted to the UN Human Rights Committee in advance of its Pre-Sessional Review,' (August 7, 2015), online http://tbinternet.ohchr.org/Treaties/CCPR/Shared%20Documents/KWT/INT_CCPR_ICO_KWT_21314_E.pdf.

International Law Commission, *Report of the Commission to the General Assembly on the Work of Its Fifty-First Session*, A/CN.4/SER.A/1999/Add.l (Part 2).

Jenkins, Craig J. and Susan Schmeidl, 'Flight from Violence: The Origins and Implications of the World Refugee Crisis,' *Sociological Focus 28*, no. 1 (1995): pp. 63–82, doi: 10.1080/00380237.1995.10571039.

Joppke, Christian, 'Transformation of Citizenship: Status, Rights, Identity,' *Citizenship Studies 11*, no. 1 (2007): pp. 27–48.

Kanstroom, Daniel, *Deportation Nation: Outsiders in American History* (Cambridge: Harvard University Press, 2007).

Krasniqi, Gezim and Dejan Stjepanovic, 'Uneven Citizenship: Minorities and Migrants in the Post-Yugoslav Space,' *Ethnopolitics 14*, no. 2 (2015): pp. 113–120.

Laubenthal, Barbara, 'The Negotiation of Irregular Migrants' Right to Education in Germany: A Challenge to the Nation-State,' *Ethnic and Racial Studies 34*, no. 8 (2011): pp. 1357–1373.

Lewis, Paul G. and S. Karthick Ramakrishnan, 'Police Practices in Immigrant-Destination Cities: Political Control or Bureaucratic Professionalism?,' *Urban Affairs Review 42*, no. 6 (2007): pp. 874–900.

Lori, Noora, '"Temporary Migrants" or Permanent Residents? The Kafala System and Contestations over Residency in the Arab Gulf States,' *Center for Migrations and Citizenship, Institut Français des Relations Internationales* (November 2012), online http://www.ifri.org/sites/default/files/atoms/files/notecmcnooralori1.pdf.

Lori, Noora, 'Unsettling State: Non-Citizens, State Power, and Citizenship in the United Arab Emirates' (PhD Dissertation, Johns Hopkins University, 2013) (unpublished, on file with author).

Martin, Philip, 'There is Nothing More Permanent than Temporary Foreign Workers,' *Center for Immigration Studies Backgrounder* (April 2001), online http://cis.org/TemporaryWorkers-Overstays.

Menjavar, Cecilia, 'Liminal Legality: Salvadoran and Guatemalan Immigrants' Lives in the United States,' *American Journal of Sociology 111*, no. 4 (January 2006): pp. 999–1037.

Mylonas, Harris, *The Politics of Nation-Building: Making Co-Nationals, Refugees, and Minorities* (New York: Cambridge University Press, 2013).

Ngai, Mae, *Impossible Subjects: Illegal Aliens and the Making of Modern America* (Princeton: Princeton University Press, 2004).

Paret, Marcel and Shannon Gleeson, 'Precarity and Agency Through a Migration Lens,' *Citizenship Studies 20*, no. 3–4 (2016): pp. 277–294.

Park, Joy K., John E. Tanagho, and Mary E. Weicher, 'A Global Crisis Writ Large: The Effects of Being "Stateless in Thailand" on Hill-Tribe Children,' *San Diego International Law Journal 10*, no. 2 (2009): pp. 495–554.

Paul, Kathleen, *Whitewashing Britain: Race and Citizenship in the Postwar Era* (Ithaca: Cornell University Press, 1997).

Sadiq, Kamal, 'When States Prefer Non-Citizens over Citizens: Conflict over Illegal Immigration into Malaysia,' *International Studies Quarterly 49*, no. 1 (2005): pp. 101–122, doi: 10.1111/j.0020-8833.2005.00336.x.

Sadiq, Kamal, *Paper Citizens: How Illegal Immigrants Acquire Citizenship in Developing Countries* (New York: Oxford University Press, 2008).

Sardelic, Julija, 'Romani Minorities and Uneven Citizenship Access in the Post-Yugoslav Space,' *Ethnopolitics 14*, no. 2 (2015): pp. 159–179.

Scott, James C., *Seeing Like a State: How Certain Schemes to Improve the Human Condition Have Failed* (New Haven: Yale University Press, 1999).

Shaw, Jo and Igor Stiks, eds., *Citizenship after Yugoslavia* (New York: Routledge, 2013).

Shevel, Oxana, *Migration, Refugee Policy, and State Building in Postcommunist Europe* (New York: Cambridge University Press, 2011).

Shevel, Oxana, 'Russian Nation-Building from Yel'tsin to Medvedev: Ethnic, Civic or Purposefully Ambiguous?,' *Europe-Asia Studies 63*, no. 2 (2011): pp. 179–202.

Somers, Margaret, *Genealogies of Citizenship: Markets, Statelessness, and the Right to Have Rights* (Cambridge, New York: Cambridge University Press, 2008).

Standing, Guy, *The Precariat: The New Dangerous Class* (London: Bloomsbury Academic, 2011).

Stevens, Jacqueline, 'U.S. Government Unlawfully Detaining and Deporting U.S. Citizens as Aliens,' *Virginia Journal of Social Policy and the Law 18*, no. 3 (July 2011): pp. 606–720, online http://papers.ssrn.com/sol3/papers.cfm?abstract_id=1931703.

Stiks, Igor, 'A Laboratory of Citizenship: Shifting Conceptions of Citizenship in Yugoslavia and its Successor States,' *CITSEE Working Paper 2010/2* (Edinburgh: University of Edinburgh, 2010), online http://www.citsee.ed.ac.uk/__data/assets/pdf_file/0009/108828/179_alaboratoryofcitizenshipshiftingconceptionsof citizenshipinyugoslaviaanditssucces.pdf.

Suárez-Navaz, Liliana, *Rebordering the Mediterranean: Boundaries and Citizenship in Southern Europe* (New York: Berghahn Books, 2004).

Tilly, Charles, 'The Geography of European Statemaking and Capitalism since 1500,' in Eugene Genovese and Leonard Hochberg, eds., *Geographic Perspectives in History* (Oxford: Blackwell, 1989), pp. 159–181.

Torpey, John C., *The Invention of the Passport: Surveillance, Citizenship and the State* (Cambridge, New York: Cambridge University Press, 2000).

United States Census Bureau, 'Congressional Apportionment: FAQ,' online http://www.census.gov/population/apportionment/about/faq.html#Q16.

van der Leun, Joanne, *Looking for Loopholes: Processes of Incorporation of Illegal Immigrants in the Netherlands* (Amsterdam: Amsterdam University Press, 2003).

Varsanyi, Monica, 'Interrogating "Urban Citizenship" vis-a-vis Undocumented Migration,' *Citizenship Studies 10*, no. 2 (2006): pp. 229–249.

Waite, Louise, 'A Place and Space for a Critical Geography of Precarity?,' *Geography Compass 3*, no. 1 (2009): pp. 412–433.

Weil, Patrick, 'Access to Citizenship: A Comparison of Twenty-Five Nationality Laws,' in Alexander Aleinikoff and Douglas B. Klusmeyer, eds., *Citizenship Today: Global Perspectives and Practices* (Washington: Carnegie Endowment for International Peace, 2001), pp. 17–36.

Weiner, Myron, 'Security, Stability, and International Migration,' *International Security 17*, no. 3 (Winter 1992): pp. 91–126.

Wijeyeratne, Roshan De Silva, 'Citizenship Law, Nationalism and the Theft of Enjoyment: A Post-Colonial Narrative,' *Law Text Culture 4* (1998): pp. 37–67.

Willen, Sarah, 'Exploring "Illegal" and "Irregular" Migrants' Lived Experiences of Law and State Power,' *International Migration 45*, no. 3 (2007): pp. 2–7, doi: 10.1111/j.1468-2435.2007.00408.x.

Willen, Sarah, 'Citizens, "Real" Others, and "Other" Others: The Biopolitics of Otherness and the Deportation of Unauthorized Migrant Workers from Tel Aviv, Israel,' in Nicholas De Genova and Nathalie Peutz, eds., *The Deportation Regime: Sovereignty, Space, and the Freedom of Movement* (Durham: Duke University Press Books, 2010), pp. 262–294.

Wolozin, Rebecca, 'Citizenship Issues and Issuing Citizenship: A Case Study of Sri Lanka's Citizenship Laws in a Global Context,' *Asian-Pacific Law & Policy Journal 16*, no. 1 (2014): pp. 1–28.

Zolberg, Aristide, 'The Formation of New States as a Refugee-Generating Process,' *The Annals of the American Academy of Political and Social Science 467*, no. 1 (May 1, 1983): pp. 24–38.

CHAPTER 34

CITIZENSHIP AND TECHNOLOGY

COSTICA DUMBRAVA

INTRODUCTION

TECHNOLOGICAL developments have complex, ambiguous, and sometimes contradictory effects of on the institutions, norms, and practices of citizenship. From the ages of the discovery of fire and the invention of the wheel to today's Internet and the Human Genome Project, technologies have incessantly shaped peoples' lives and nourished their hopes and fears. The development of information and communication technologies (ICT) and advances in biotechnologies, such as assisted reproduction technologies (ART)[1] and genetics, in the second half of the twentieth century have imbued public imagination with both utopian visions of technological self-enhancement and social progress as well as with dystopian scenarios of

---

[1] ART refers to technologies used to induce pregnancy through procedures such as in vitro fertilization, artificial insemination, and surrogacy.

self-destruction and totalitarian control. With regard to citizenship and politics, technologies promise to revitalize participation, increase political accountability, and reimagine membership and solidarity. While the jury is still out on the political benefits of recent technologies, there are important concerns about persistent inequalities, increased social control, and exacerbating exclusion and discrimination.

This chapter investigates the relationship between technology and citizenship by exploring the tensions between inclusion and emancipation, on the one hand, and exclusion and control, on the other hand. It discusses inclusionary and exclusionary aspects of developments in the areas of digital and biotechnologies in respect to access to legal status, political participation, and identity. It also examines the emancipatory potential of technologies at the level of citizenship practices and issues related to social and political control, which are triggered by increased and pervasive surveillance.

As both citizenship and technology cover vast conceptual and empirical grounds, this discussion remains inevitably limited and selective. The various social implications of technologies can be studied from a number of disciplinary perspectives. Sociologists and economists look at the implications of technologies on social structures and socio-economic inequalities (digital divide, technological unemployment, demographic impact); lawyers and legal scholars deal with challenges related to the regulation of technologies and citizenship status (data protection, regulation of artificial intelligence, statelessness as a consequence of ART); political scientists analyse the role of technologies on political competition and participation (political mobilization, electronic voting); anthropologists and social psychologists study the effects of technologies on social norms and identities (kinship, solidarity, perceptions of self), etc. While many of these aspects and perspectives can be linked to citizenship, in this chapter I work with a more restricted concept of citizenship, which focuses primarily on political aspects of membership such as legal status, political rights, and national identity.[2] How does technology shape citizenship's inner tension between inclusion and emancipation,[3] on the one hand, and exclusion and social closure,[4] on the other hand? Is technology conducive to more formal inclusion, better political participation, and more inclusive identities? Does technology reinforce exclusion, social control, and parochial nationalism? By looking into key aspects of the relationship between citizenship and technology, the chapter aims to raise a number of questions that are more broadly relevant across the sub-field of citizenship studies. The second section discusses implications of digital technologies on political participation, social surveillance, and state borders.

---

[2] Joseph H. Carens, *Culture, Citizenship and Community: A Contextual Exploration of Justice as Evenhandedness* (Oxford: Oxford University Press, 2000); Bauböck in this volume.

[3] Thomas H. Marshall, *Class, Citizenship and Social Development: Essays* (New York: Doubleday, 1965).

[4] Rogers W. Brubaker, *Citizenship and Nationhood in France and Germany* (Cambridge: Harvard University Press, 1992), p. 21.

The third section examines the impact of ART and genetic technologies on formal membership, immigration control, and national identity. A final section reflects on the main points discussed in the chapter and puts forward several ideas for future research in the area of citizenship and technology.

DIGITAL CITIZENSHIP

There are various ways in which digital technologies are expected to affect citizenship and political participation. On the one hand, digital technologies may increase participation, efficiency, safety, and comfort; on the other hand, they may exacerbate social inequalities, intensify social control, and discriminate between insiders and outsiders. Isin and Ruppert identify three key dimensions of 'digital citizenship': the political impact of citizens' access to Internet; the use of digital technologies by the government in order to inform and engage citizens; and the political mobilization of citizens through digital means.[5] This section discusses the opportunities for political participation offered by new digital technologies, as well as problems related to widespread surveillance within society and at the borders. Does technology enhance political participation? Is surveillance compatible with citizens' rights? Does technology reinforce social control and exclusion?

After initial enthusiasm in the early 1990s about the democratizing effect of the Internet, it soon became apparent that a new 'digital divide' was in the making, namely a divide between those who had access and benefited from Internet and those who did not.[6] At a closer look, this gap comprises of at least three divides. The first divide refers to access to information technologies. High Internet penetration rates in Western countries have diminished (but not eliminated) the gap in access to information. The second divide is about unequal levels of knowledge and skills that separate the interacting and the interacted[7] in the electronic sphere. Having access to information means little in the absence of comprehension skills. For example, it is estimated that 'the average government Web site ... requires an eleventh-grade level of reading comprehension, even though about half of the U.S. population

---

[5] Engin Isin and Evelyn Ruppert, *Being Digital Citizens* (London: Rowman & Littlefield International, 2015).

[6] James McConnaughey, Timothy Sloan, and Cynthia Ann Nila, *Falling through the Net: A Survey of the 'Have Nots' in Rural and Urban America* (Washington: National Telecommunications and Information Administration, 1995).

[7] Manuel Castells, *The Rise of the Network Society: The Information Age: Economy, Society, and Culture*, volume 1 (Oxford: Blackwell Oxford, 1996).

reads at an eighth-grade level or lower.[8] A third divide is a global one and parts the developed countries from the developing world. While the Internet is gradually reaching most parts of the world, sometimes by means of ingenious technological solutions such as Google's solar-powered balloons, there are still significant differences between developed and developing countries in terms of number of users and the quality of service (bandwidth).

It is argued that digital technologies enable citizens to gain access to public information and to participate in formal and informal political processes and arenas.[9] Many national and local governments have launched e-government initiatives in order to provide easy access to public information and services (e.g. access to public documents, use of electronic ID, filling taxes online). These tools are seen as modern solutions to increase administrative efficiency and enhance political accountability. Technology has also made it possible for citizens, journalists, or specialized organizations to gain access to and publicize classified government information.[10] Such unauthorized (illegal) ways of information sharing may be driven by the desire to enhance transparency and government accountability but they do so at the price of undercutting the work and credibility of law enforcement agencies.

Apart from access to information, digital technologies also allow citizens to engage politically via formal channels, such as electronic voting and public consultations, or informal channels, such as online forums and campaigns. With political participation and civic engagement continuously decreasing in most democracies, information technologies have been seen as having a potentially invigorating role. The evidence about the role of technologies in boosting political participation is, however, mixed. While some found that, in the US context, the Internet promotes voting, transfer of political knowledge, and deliberation,[11] others argued that the Internet weakens social connections, reduces social trust, and discourages civic engagement.[12] Evidence from Estonia—a country that champions e-citizenship— shows that political participation remains limited even when backed by a complex e-government infrastructure (e.g. digital ID cards for all citizens). While the percentage of electronic votes increased significantly since the introduction of electronic voting in 2015 (when under 2 per cent of the votes were cast electronically), it only amounted to about one third of the votes in the 2015 parliamentary elections.[13]

---

[8] Karen Mossberger, Caroline J. Tolbert, and Ramona S. McNeal, *Digital Citizenship: The Internet, Society, and Participation* (Cambridge: MIT Press, 2007), p. 14.

[9] Pippa Norris, *Digital Divide: Civic Engagement, Information Poverty, and the Internet Worldwide* (Cambridge: Cambridge University Press, 2001).

[10] In 2010 Wikileaks released about 400,000 leaked documents under the tag 'Iraq War Logs'.

[11] Norris (n 9).

[12] Robert Putnam, *Bowling Alone, the Collapse and Revival of Civic America* (New York: Simon and Schuster, 2000).

[13] Sandra Särav and Tanel Kerikmäe, 'E-Residency: A Cyberdream Embodied in a Digital Identity Card?', in Tanel Kerikmäe and Addi Rull, eds., *The Future of Law and eTechnologies* (Cham, New York: Springer, 2016): pp. 57–79, p. 58.

Estonia also introduced an e-residency card allowing interested foreigners to use the Estonian public electronic infrastructure without taking residence in the country. While the policy explicitly delinked e-residency from formal citizenship, the government justified the scheme by appealing to a normatively strong language commonly associated with citizenship, for example 'link with the country' and 'contribution'.[14] The Estonian e-residency makes for an over-inclusive form of transactional and non-territorial membership, which is at odds with conventional views on citizenship as participatory and territorial political membership.[15]

If in established democratic states digital technologies have at least the potential to enhance political participation, in less democratic states, these technologies can enable civic and political mobilization against political power. As Reagan quipped in June 1989, 'the Goliath of totalitarianism will be brought down by the David of the microchip'.[16] The widespread use of Internet and social media are believed to have played key roles in recent protests and revolutionary movements from the Arab spring to Moldova's twitter revolution. Virtual spaces provide activists and citizens with alternative means of communication and engagement that escape traditional forms of censorship and control. However, repressive governments have been quick to adopt new technologies in order to clamp down on freedom of expression and launch indoctrination campaigns. When not blocking the Internet altogether, governments have acquired sophisticated spyware technology to monitor citizens' online activities. The more diffuse nature of the Internet makes it a less malleable ideological tool for governments than the radio and television. Yet, the governmental control of access to Internet and technologically enhanced forms of censorship undermine significantly the capacity of digital technologies to mobilize citizens and challenge political power.

For from being only a characteristic of non-democratic countries, the spread of surveillance has become a fundamental feature of contemporary societies. While surveillance has been an element of modern societies ever since the eighteenth century,[17] it is only recently that it became a fundamental feature of everyday life.[18] The widespread use of Closed Circuit Television (CCTV) cameras is a harbinger of a contemporary regime of ubiquitous and undiscerning surveillance. For example, it is estimated that in London a person is caught by CCTV cameras up to 300 times a

---

[14] Lehte Roots and Costica Dumbrava, 'E-Citizenship Opportunities in the Changing Technological Environment', in Tanel Kerikmaë and Addi Rull, eds., *The Future of Law and eTechnologies* (Cham, New York: Springer, 2016): pp. 45–56.

[15] Bauböck in this volume; Shachar in this volume; Spiroin this volume; Walker in this volume.

[16] 'Caught in the Net', *The Economist*, 23 January 2003, online http://www.economist.com/node/1534249.

[17] Kerstin Gooas, Michael Friedewald, William Webster, and Charles Leleux, 'The Co-Evolution of Surveillance Technology and Surveillance Practices', in D. Wright and R. Kreissl, eds., *Surveillance in Europe* (Abingdon: Routledge, 2015): pp. 51–100.

[18] David Lyon, 'Everyday Surveillance: Personal Data and Social Classifications', *Information, Communication & Society* 5, no. 2 (2002): pp. 242–257.

day on average.[19] The enhanced computing capacity has facilitated the replacement of the 'dossier society',[20] characterized by filling cabinets and limited analytical capacity, with the 'surveillance society',[21] which is defined by the networked database and powerful data mining capabilities. The 'new surveillance'[22] is to a great extent 'dataveillance'[23] because it relies heavily on sophisticated technologies of data collecting, sharing, and processing.[24]

The ubiquitous character of surveillance distinguishes today's 'networked society'[25] from the earlier model of 'disciplinary society',[26] where different governance techniques were employed in particular social institutions and sites (school, factory, prison) in order to discipline and construct 'docile' citizens. In contrast, the new 'societies of control'[27] are based on a 'dispersal of discipline'[28] and a generalization of social control. Whereas Foucault's Panopticon enclosed and disciplined 'abnormal' or deviant citizens, contemporary 'ban-opticon' regimes encircle 'normal' citizens and exclude the 'abnormal'.[29] Conventional moralizing accounts, such as Orwell's Big Brother metaphor, fail to capture the regime of contemporary surveillance because they focus on a clearly distinguishable, centralized and evil power that seeks to oppress individuals. Or, much of contemporary surveillance is not repressive but constitutive, meaning that it is 'the outcome of the complex ways in which we structure our political and economic relationship in societies that value mobility, speed, security and consumer freedom'.[30]

There are obvious advantages with using new surveillance technologies, as they permit 'new levels of efficiency, productivity, convenience, and comfort that many

---

[19] David Wright, Michael Friedewald, Serge Gutwirth, Marc Langheinrich, Emilio Mordini, Rocco Bellanova, Paul De Hert, Kush Wadhwa, and Didier Bigo, 'Sorting Out Smart Surveillance', *Computer Law & Security Review* 26, no. 4 (2010): pp. 343–354, p. 344.

[20] Greg Marquis, 'Private Security and Surveillance: from the "Dossier Society" to Database Networks', in David Lyon, ed., *Surveillance as Social Sorting: Privacy, Risk and Digital Discrimination* (New York, London: Routledge, 2003), pp. 226–248.

[21] David Lyon, *Surveillance Society: Monitoring Everyday Life* (Buckingham: Open University Press, 2001).

[22] Gary T. Marx, 'Ethics for the New Surveillance', *The Information Society* 14, no. 3 (1998): pp. 171–185.

[23] Roger Clarke, 'Information Technology and Dataveillance', *Communications of the ACM* 31, no. 5 (1988): pp. 498–512.

[24] These data technologies include image recognition, advanced biometrics (iris scan, DNA tests), geotracking, radio tagging, and neuroimaging.

[25] Castells (n 7).

[26] Michel Foucault, *Discipline and Punish: the Birth of the Prison* (New York: Random House, 1975).

[27] Gilles Deleuze, 'Postscript on the Societies of Control', *October 59* (Winter 1992): pp. 3–7.

[28] Clive Norris, 'From Personal to Digital: CCTV, the Panopticon, and the Technological Mediation of Suspicion and Social Control', in David Lyon, ed., *Surveillance as Social Sorting: Privacy, Risk and Digital Discrimination* (London, New York: Routledge, 2003), pp. 249–281.

[29] Didier Bigo, 'Globalized (in) Security: The Field and the Ban-Opticon', in *Illiberal Practices of Liberal Regimes: The (In) Security Games* (Paris: L'Harmattan, 2006), pp. 5–49.

[30] Lyon (n 18), p. 2.

in the technologically advanced societies take for granted'.[31] Digital surveillance allows for better law enforcement, more effective protection against crime, terrorism, fraud, etc. However, these technologies have negative consequences for individual freedom and social inclusion. Increased surveillance shrinks the space of individual freedom and renders individuals more vulnerable to interference and control. This is particularly visible in the widespread phenomenon of 'surveillance creep',[32] in which personal data are collected, transferred, and used for purposes different than those initially envisaged. For example, administrative data, medical records, banking transactions, and even shopping patterns are increasingly used for law enforcement and security purposes. In 2006 the UK introduced a national ID card to serve as an instrument for fighting fraud, combating terrorism, and controlling immigration. The card was eventually abandoned after criticism of 'being too expensive and an infringement of civil liberties'.[33] It is telling that initial efforts to develop biometric technologies were driven by eugenic objectives of identifying criminal types and races.[34] DNA data are used nowadays for an increasing number of purposes, including identification,[35] establishing family relationship, and immigration control.[36] For example, Kuwait announced recently that it would require DNA samples from all its citizens, as well as visitors and expatriates, in order to 'facilitate in solving crime and terrorism cases'.[37] As shown in the next section, DNA testing is routinely used in the context of migration policies in order to ascertain claims of preferential admission on grounds of family reunification.

Apart from limiting individual freedom, surveillance technologies can also reinforce 'social sorting'[38] when prejudices and social stereotypes are built into practices and techniques of surveillance. As a consequence, certain individuals and groups are singled out and excluded on the basis of institutionalized, technology-enabled prejudice. For example, research has shown that CCTV operators tend to focus on certain categories of people, such as the young, male, and ethnic minorities.[39] These

---

[31] Lyon (n 21), p. 18.

[32] Dorothy Nelkin and Lori Andrews, 'DNA Identification and Surveillance Creep', *Sociology of Health & Illness 21*, no. 5 (1999): pp. 689–706.

[33] 'Identity Cards Scheme will be Axed "Within 100 Days"', *BBC*, 27 May 2010, online http://news.bbc.co.uk/2/hi/8707355.stm.

[34] Mark Maguire, 'The Birth of Biometric Security', *Anthropology Today 25*, no. 2 (2009): pp. 9–14.

[35] Nelkin and Andrews (n 32).

[36] Janice D. Villiers, 'Brave New World: The Use and Potential Misuse of DNA Technology in Immigration Law', *Boston College Third World Law Journal World 30*, no. 2 (2010): pp. 239–271.

[37] Seung Lee, 'Kuwait Becomes First Country to Collect DNA Samples from all Citizens and Visitors: Report', *Newsweek*, 19 April 2016, online http://europe.newsweek.com/kuwait-becomes-first-country-world-collect-dna-samples-all-citizens-and-449830?rm=eu.

[38] David Lyon, *Surveillance as Social Sorting: Privacy, Risk, and Digital Discrimination* (New York, London: Routledge, 2003).

[39] Clive Norris and Gary Armstrong, *The Maximum Surveillance Society: The Rise of CCTV* (Oxford: Berg Publishers, 1999).

practices and algorithms generate biased categories of risk, which serve to justify the exclusion of individuals or groups from particular services or spaces.[40]

Mobility is one particular aspect of contemporary society that has both benefited of and suffered from technological development. The expansion of ICT and of cheap travel opportunities in the second half of the previous century has facilitated the unprecedented flow of people within and across international borders. Immigration has led to a partial delinking of citizenship status from territory by creating significant numbers of non-citizen residents, as well extra-territorial citizens. This phenomenon was accompanied by a partial dissociation of citizenship rights from formal status, as long-term immigrants in Western countries have come to enjoy a number of (post-national) rights[41] that were previously associated exclusively with citizenship. Apart from facilitating the physical movement of people across borders, ICT also made possible the creation of virtual transnational communities by enabling migrants to maintain connections with family and friends and to engage more broadly with their countries of origin. ICT also played an important role in various diaspora engagement strategies adopted by a growing number of states in order to keep contact with emigrants (e.g. official websites, on-line campaigns, electronic voting from abroad).

Mobility has become increasingly securitized as a consequence of a series of terrorist attacks in Europe and the US. Together with measures aiming at 'hardening' the borders in order to keep out uninvited immigrants—for example through increased capacity and the erection of physical walls—states have also moved towards 'smartening' the borders by resorting to information and surveillance technologies. A growing literature on borders focuses on how the technologization of borders and mobility has lead to a gradual 'debordering' of borders,[42] in the sense that borders have extended beyond their geopolitical locations and sprawled over 'a multiplicity of sites for the surveillance of movement'.[43] The new 'iborders'[44] are digital, automated, networked, and de-territorialized systems used to sort out good from bad mobility and to distinguish between wanted and unwanted people.

The capacity to identify and classify people is instrumental to the modern state, which has become concerned primarily with governing populations.[45] Authorities

---

[40] Mireille Hildebrandt and Serge Gutwirth, *Profiling the European Citizen* (Dordrecht: Springer, 2008).

[41] Yasemine N. Soysal, *Limits of Citizenship. Migrants and Postnational Membership in Europe* (Chicago: University of Chicago Press, 1994).

[42] Mathias Albert and Lothar Brock, 'Debordering the World of States: New Spaces in International Relations', *New Political Science 18*, no. 1 (1996): pp. 69–106, doi: 10.1080/07393149608429765.

[43] Louise Amoore, Stephen Marmura, and Mark B. Salter, 'Smart Borders and Mobilities: Spaces, Zones, Enclosures', *Surveillance & Society 5*, no. 2 (2002): pp. 96–101, p. 99; Ayelet Shachar, 'The Shifting Border of Immigration Control', *Stanford Journal of Civil Rights & Civil Liberties 3*, no. 2 (2007): pp. 165–193.

[44] Holger Pötzsch, 'The Emergence of iBorder: Bordering Bodies, Networks, and Machines', *Environment and Planning D: Society and Space 33*, no. 1 (2015): pp. 101–118, doi: 10.1068/d14050p.

[45] Michel Foucault, *Security, Territory, Population: Lectures at the Collège de France 1977-1978*, volume 4 (Basingstoke: Palgrave Macmillan, 2009).

need to be able to identify the person in order to determine whether he or she belongs to the state. The development of modern identification technologies, such as the passport, served to ensure that the state maintained the monopoly over 'legitimate means of movement'.[46] As technologies of identification became more complex and accurate, they expanded gradually from cataloguing static characteristics (physiognomy) to capturing behavioural patterns (mobility) and from reading superficial biometrics (fingerprints) to recording deeply rooted biological codes (DNA).

In the immigration context, the governance of mobility relies heavily on a digital infrastructure built through 'the collection, processing, storage and sharing of digital personal data for risk profiling'.[47] Digital data are amassed and analysed using data-matching and data-mining algorithms in order to construct digital personae or personal profiles for the purpose of identity checking and risk assessment. For example, smart IDs have been adopted in order to store and link personal data and to allow distinguishing between insiders and outsiders.[48] The collection and sharing of travellers' data is a widespread technique of border control and digital surveillance. The ongoing debate in the EU about the sharing of Passenger Name Records (PNR), i.e. personal data of flight passengers entering or leaving the EU, is indicative of the legal and political difficulties generated by digitalization of borders. For example, in 2006 the European Court of Justice annulled a time-limited agreement between the EU and the US for the provision of PNR. While the terrorist attacks in Paris and Brussels in 2015 and 2016 have given new impetus to reinforce PNR, disagreements persist about how to reconcile security imperatives with concerns about data protection and preventing abuse (what data, to whom, for what purposes).[49]

Smart technological solutions often rely on a selection of conventional, not-so-smart data (e.g. administrative records) and on human input that is susceptible to bias. Algorithms and risk profiles can be affected by 'discrimination by design',[50] in which particular groups of people, such as persons of certain national, ethnic, or racial origin, become the prominent targets of surveillance and control. This leads to a border regime in which the mobility of some is achieved with the price of the 'immobility and exclusion for others'.[51] Together with becoming more digital, borders are also being increasingly externalized and automatized. Immigration control

[46] John C. Torpey, *The Invention of the Passport: Surveillance, Citizenship, and the State* (Cambridge: Cambridge University Press, 2000).

[47] Quirine Eikjman, 'Digital Security Governance and Accountability in Europe: Ethical Dilemmas in Terrorism Risk Management', *Journal of Politics and Law* 6, no. 4 (2013): pp. 35–45, p. 35, doi: 10.5539/jpl.v6n4p35.

[48] David Lyon, 'The Border is Everywhere: ID Cards, Surveillance and the Other', in Elia Zureik and Mark Salter, eds., *Global Surveillance and Policing: Borders, Security, Identity* (Cullompton, Portland: Willan, 2005), pp. 66–82.

[49] Eikjman (n 47).

[50] Keith Guzik, 'Discrimination by Design: Predictive Data Mining as Security Practice in the United States' "War on Terrorism"', *Surveillance & Society* 7, no. 1 (2009): pp. 3–20.

[51] Maguire (n 34), p. 14.

in Europe and the West has been gradually externalized by means of visas, extra-territorial immigration checks, and asylum processing.[52]

Apart from increased efficiency and analytical capacity, the resort to computing and automation in the context of immigration and border control is triggered by attempts to avoid thorny political and moral issues. For example, an EU official recently justified the proposal to use computers for determining the distribution of refugees across EU countries by arguing that the issue was 'too complex and required too many lengthy debates with national governments'.[53] The increased automation of decision-making in the immigration context tends to remove possibilities for political contestation and to silence more fundamental moral questions about the fairness of borders and admission.

BIOLOGICAL CITIZENSHIP

The concept of biological citizenship was developed in relation to the emergence of new forms of subjectivities and collective action among patient groups and people sharing particular medical conditions or biological traits.[54] This 'new kind of citizenship ... in the age of biomedicine, biotechnology and genomics'[55] was seen as an emancipatory development that challenges bio-nationalist, eugenicist predispositions build into the model of national citizenship. Biological citizenship is also linked to a growing trend towards the democratization of biomedicine, as in the emergence of personalized medicine, such as self-tracking biomedical applications. Notwithstanding their emancipatory and democratizing effects, biotechnologies provide new tools and modes of 'surveillance, exclusion, and denial of citizenship rights on a "biological" basis.'[56] In this section I discuss the impact of key developments in the areas of ART and genetic technologies on citizenship, immigration, and national identity. In what ways do ART affect the institutions and norms of

---

[52] Ruben Zaiotti, ed., *Externalizing Migration Management: Europe, North America and the Spread of 'Remote Control Practices'* (New York: Routledge, 2016); Bernard Ryan and Valsamis Mitsilegas, eds., *Extraterritorial Immigration Control: Legal Challenges* (Boston, Leiden: Martinus Nijhoff, 2010).

[53] Nikolaj Nielsen, 'Computer to Make EU Asylum Decisions', *Euobserver*, 4 May 2017, online https://euobserver.com/migration/133341.

[54] Adriana Petryna, *Life Exposed: Biological Citizens After Chernobyl* (Princeton: Princeton University Press, 2002).

[55] Nikolas Rose and Carlos Novas, 'Biological Citizenship', in A. Ong and S. J. Collier, eds., *Global Assemblages: Technology, Politics, and Ethics as Anthropological Problems* (Oxford: John Wiley & Sons, 2008): pp. 439–463, p. 439.

[56] Ilpo Helén, 'Biological Citizenship across the Borders: Politics of DNA Profiling for Family Reunification', *Distinktion: Scandinavian Journal of Social Theory* 15, no. 3 (2014): pp. 343–360, p. 344.

citizenship? What problems arise from using DNA testing for the purpose of immigration control? How does the increased geneticization of social life shape narratives about national identity?

The rapid and global spread of ART generates problems related to children's access to citizenship and raises questions about normative models of (birthright) citizenship. A multi-million global market for ART—involving 'the movements of assisted reproduction professionals, egg and sperm donors and surrogates'[57]—has developed partly as a consequence of uneven regulation of ART among countries. Many children born through cross-border surrogacy are under the risk of becoming parentless and stateless.[58] This is because people seeking assisted reproduction care abroad, often in order to avoid legal restrictions in their own countries, face difficulties in securing the recognition of paternity and citizenship for their children. The problem of statelessness arises when a child born to a surrogate mother cannot acquire the citizenship of the intended parents, such as in cases when the law follows strictly the principle *mater semper certa est*, according to which the woman who gives birth is always the mother. If the country where surrogacy arrangements take place does not grant *jus soli* citizenship (in virtue of birth in the territory) and does not recognize the surrogate mother as the legal mother, as it enforces surrogacy contracts that recognize only the intended mother as the legal mother, the resulting child falls in between citizenship regimes and becomes stateless.[59]

Beyond the issue of inadequate regulation and coordination of ART policies, citizenship debates in the context of ART are also a result of diverse and conflicting politics of reproduction. All human societies seek to ensure continuity over generations through establishing norms on the physical and normative reproduction of membership. In modern times citizenship regulations play a key role in ensuring the intergenerational continuity of the national community. They do so by relying heavily on birthright entitlements; most children nowadays acquire citizenship through descent from citizens (*jus sanguinis*) or due to birth in the territory (*jus soli*).[60] The recent development of ART challenges these two mechanisms of birthright citizenship because it (partly) alienates individual reproduction from the conventional models of heterosexual family and territorial citizenship.

---

[57] Zeynep B. Gürtin and Marcia C. Inhorn, 'Introduction: Travelling for Conception and the Global Assisted Reproduction Market', *Reproductive Biomedicine Online* 23, no. 5 (2011): pp. 535–537, p. 535, doi: 10.1016/j.rbmo.2011.08.001.

[58] E.g., 'Australian Couple Abandon Surrogate Down's Syndrome Baby', *BBC News*, 2 August 2014, online http://www.bbc.com/news/world-asia-28617912.

[59] Costica Dumbrava and Rainer Bauböck, eds., 'Bloodlines and Belonging: Time to Abandon Ius Sanguinis?', EUI Working Paper no. 80 (Florence: RSCAS, 2015), online http://cadmus.eui.eu/bitstream/handle/1814/37578/RSCAS_2015_80.pdf;sequence=1.

[60] Ayelet Shachar, *The Birthright Lottery: Citizenship and Global Inequality* (Cambridge: Harvard University Press, 2009); Maarten P. Vink and Gerard-René de Groot, 'Birthright Citizenship: Trends and Regulations in Europe', EUDO Citizenship Comparative Report (Florence: European University Institute, 2010), online http://eudo-citizenship.eu/docs/birthright_comparativepaper.pdf.

While ART open new avenues for forging and imagining social relations, they also contribute to the reassertion of conventional and essentialist ideas about gender relations, genetic relatedness, and ethnic descent. By delinking reproduction from the conventional family, ART challenge the traditional societal model based on 'the heterosexual, co-resident nuclear family unit'.[61] However, ART also reinforce traditional biological conceptions of the family since 'the very existence of IVF pays testament to people's desire to have their "own" children'.[62] Legal procedures for the recognition of family relationship and citizenship for children born through ART often explicitly require proof of biological relationship (DNA tests). For example, children born through ART abroad can acquire Canadian derivative citizenship only if they are genetically related to Canadian parents.[63]

Contemporary legal and political controversies about ART should be viewed in the light of current family and fertility 'crises' in the West generated by high levels of divorce, separation, cohabitation, and persistent low fertility rates.[64] Feminist research has shown how gendered ideologies about the nation shape discourses and policies on family, reproduction, and citizenship.[65] In the past states have used various positive and negative reproduction policies in order to promote 'stratified reproduction',[66] i.e. to encourage the reproduction of certain groups of the population while discouraging others (e.g. immigrants, ethnic, racial, or sexual minorities). The selective access to ART and to the recognition of legal parenthood in the context of ART raises concerns about (assisted) stratified reproduction. Countries such as France and Germany restrict access to ART to heterosexual couples only. As a recent case in the UK shows, even when access to ART is not restricted to heterosexual couples, single parents still cannot apply for parental orders in order to establish parental relationship with 'their' surrogate-born children.[67] In certain cases the

[61] Beatrice Halsaa, Sasha Roseneil, and Sevil Sümer, *FEMCIT—Gendered Citizenship in Multicultural Europe: The Impact of Contemporary Women's Movements—Final Report* (University of Oslo, Birkbeck University and University of Bergen, 2011), p. 56, online http://wpms.computing.uni.no/femcit/wp-content/uploads/sites/16/2015/11/WP7_WorkingpaperNo5.pdf.

[62] Tabitha Freeman and Martin Richards, 'DNA Testing and Kinship: Paternity, Genealogy and the Search for the "Truth" of Our Genetic Origins', in Fatemeh Ebtehaj, Bridget Lindley, and Martin Richards, eds., *Kinship Matters* (Oxford: Hart, 2006), pp. 67–95, p. 82.

[63] Lois Harder, 'Does Sperm Have a Flag? On Biological Relationship and National Membership', *Canadian Journal of Law and Society 30*, no. 1 (2015): pp. 109–125.

[64] Jay Winter and Michael Teitelbaum, *The Global Spread of Fertility Decline: Population, Fear, and Uncertainty* (New Haven, London: Yale University Press, 2013).

[65] Nira Yuval-Davis, *Gender and Nation* (Cambridge: Cambridge University Press, 1997); Sasha Roseneil, Isabel Crowhurst, Ana Cristina Santos, and Mariya Stoilova, 'Reproduction and Citizenship/Reproducing Citizens: Editorial Introduction', *Citizenship Studies 17*, no. 8 (2013): pp. 901–911; Volpp in this volume.

[66] Faye Ginsburg and Rayna Rapp, *Conceiving the New World Order: The Global Politics of Reproduction* (Berkeley: University of California Press, 1995).

[67] Antony Blackburn-Starza, 'Single Father Wins Surrogacy Human Rights Ruling', *Bionews 852*, 23 May 2016, online http://www.bionews.org.uk/page_651129.asp.

rules of legal parenthood apply differently to men and women. For example, in Norway a man can claim legal parenthood and transfer citizenship to a surrogate-born child if the two are not genetically related, but this possibility is not available to women who, although genetically related to the child, have not given birth to the child.[68] Differentiated access to reproduction also occurs when states leave ART to the markets. As long as ART procedures remain costly and not covered by basic insurance packages, the beneficiaries are most likely to be the middle to upper classes, despite the fact that infertility affects more drastically persons belonging to less well-off minorities.[69]

The development of ART provides an additional layer to the nexus between reproduction and national identity. Interestingly, nationalist responses to ART can go in diametrically opposed directions. For example, in predominantly Catholic countries such as Ireland and Poland, ART are predominantly seen as a threat for the nation. In Poland, the Catholic Church staunchly opposes in vitro fertility (IVF) procedures, which it regards as a form of 'sophisticated abortion'.[70] At the other extreme, ART can be regarded as opportunities for demographic and ethno-national revival. In Romania and Bulgaria the governments defended public IVF programmes putting forward claims about the significant contribution of ART to the demographic revival of the countries.[71] In the Bulgarian context, the debate included explicit eugenic arguments as it was suggested to use ART in order to 'counteract the outnumbering of Bulgarians by the minorities' and to 'give Bulgaria back to the Bulgarians'.[72] The development of such version of in vitro nationalism is indicative of a resilient and versatile nationalist ideology in the context of disruptive socio-demographic and technological changes.

The genetic revolution triggered by the discovery of deoxyribonucleic acid (DNA) and bolstered by the recent mapping of all human genes (the Human Genome Project) has raised hopes about treating diseases, improving life, and even defeating death. However, the rapid development of genetic technologies also prompted concerns about the 'geneticization' of social life,[73] as human behaviour and social

[68] Kristine S. Knaplund, 'Baby Without a Country: Determining Citizenship for Assisted Reproduction Children Born Overseas', *Denver University Law Review 91*, no. 2 (2013): pp. 335–367.

[69] Marcia C. Inhorn, Rosario Ceballo, and Robert Nachtigall, 'Marginalized, Invisible, and Unwanted: American Minority Struggles with Infertility and Assisted Conception', in Lorraine Culley, Nicky Hudson, and Floor van Rooij, eds., *Marginalized Reproduction: Ethnicity, Infertility and Reproductive Technologies* (London, Sterling: Earthscan, 2009), pp. 181–197.

[70] Elżbieta Korolczuk, *IVF as a Threat to the Nation: The Debate on Assisted Reproduction in Contemporary Poland* (Berlin: Heinrich Boell Foundation Dossier on Overcoming Gender Backlash, 2013), p. 10.

[71] Costica Dumbrava, 'Reproducing the Nation: Reproduction, Citizenship and Ethno-Demographic Survival in Post-Communist Romania', *Journal of Ethnic and Migration Studies*, early view (2016), doi: 10.1080/1369183X.2016.1221335.

[72] Ina Dimitrova, *Populism and Pronatalism: The Assisted 'Rebirth' of the (Bulgarian) People* (2013) (unpublished manuscript, on file with author).

[73] Abby Lippman, 'Prenatal Genetic Testing and Screening: Constructing Needs and Reinforcing Inequities', *American Journal of Law & Medicine 17*, no. 1–2 (1991): pp. 15–50; Kaja Finkler, *Experiencing*

interactions are increasingly viewed through the lens of genetics. The worry is that population genomics studies will contribute to legitimizing and 'naturalizing' inequality and to the designation of new vulnerable groups based on arbitrary patterns and statistical correlations.[74]

While genetic technologies may allow for new ways of imagining identities and social relations (e.g. rediscovering and reinterpreting one's origin), they also tend to reiterate essentialist views about genetic relatedness, race, and nation. The commercial success of personal DNA testing kits indicates a renewed interest in linking personal identity with genetic 'truths'. The use of these tests has expanded across different areas to include paternity checks, immigration control, and ancestry search. While promising to provide accurate measures of biological relatedness, these instruments acquire a truth revealing function that may collide with established legal and cultural norms about social relatedness (e.g. family, paternity, race, and ethnicity).

States have begun to use DNA tests to check family relationships for the purpose of immigration control. With family reunification becoming the primary legal channel of immigration in the West, efforts to restrict immigration have focused on combating fraud and detecting 'fake' family ties (including marriages of convenience). Parental DNA testing in the immigration context has become a standard procedure in many countries.[75] Although these measures have been justified within a human rights frame, for example providing claimants with reliable proofs, combating child trafficking, they are often driven by and reinforce a 'rationale of suspicion'.[76]

There are a number of problems with using DNA tests for immigration purposes. DNA tests tend to reinforce a narrow biological concept of the family, which is often at odds with family norms prevalent in the immigrant's country of origin and even in the country of immigration. Social ties, as opposed to biological ones, form the basis of family institutions in many cultures.[77] Moreover, while many countries of immigration recognize family relationships regardless of the genetic connection between parents and children, testing such connection in the context of immigration establishes a double standard applied to native citizens and immigrants.[78] There

---

the New Genetics: Kinship and Family on the Medical Frontier (Philadelphia: University of Pennsylvania Press, 2000).

[74] Herman T. Tavani, 'Genomic Research and Data-Mining Technology: Implications for Personal Privacy and Informed Consent', Ethics and Information Technology 6, no. 1 (2004): pp. 15–28.

[75] Torsten Heinemann and Thomas Lemke, 'Suspect Families: DNA Kinship Testing in German Immigration Policy', Sociology 47, no. 4 (2013): pp. 810–826.

[76] Villiers (n 36).   [77] Helén (n 56).

[78] Tera Rica Murdock, 'Whose Child is This: Genetic Analysis and Family Reunification Immigration in France', Vanderbilt Journal of Transnational Law 41 (2008): pp. 1503–1534.

are also concerns that current DNA testing procedures violate the applicants' informational privacy and self-determination.[79]

By putting emphasis on genetic and biological ties DNA tests lead to a 'geneticization of the family'.[80] It is true that certain genetic applications, such as personal DNA-based ancestry tests,[81] may provide resources for enriching and diversifying personal identities.[82] DNA.ancestry.com, for example, invites potential clients to 'uncover [their] ethnic mix, discover distant relatives, and find new details about [their] unique family history'. However, such identity-making exercises often reinforce ethno-racial classifications and stereotypes that are built into these applications.

At the collective level, genetic science becomes instrumental for (re) constructing the nation as an 'imagined genetic community'.[83] Weaving genetic evidence into narratives of group distinctiveness contributes to a biologization and essentialization of national, ethnic, and racial identities.[84] References to genetic 'truths' lend support to claims of ethnic or racial distinctiveness, similarity or continuity. This leads to a return of racial and biological determinism, which is embodied in the belief that 'race is anchored in a person's genes and, thus, racial inequality is largely the result of biological predispositions'.[85] In Mexico the state invested considerable efforts and resources in order to identify the 'indigenous DNA', which could be moulded into the official narratives of Mexican national identity.[86] Israel has attempted to use genetic tests to determine the 'Jewishness' of certain groups of people claiming Jewish heritage.[87] In the UK the media warned against a 'Viking Baby Invasion' caused by the widespread use of sperm from Danish donors in British ART procedures.[88] While 'blood' has long been a marker and symbol of nation belonging (e.g.

[79] Martin G. Weiss, 'Strange DNA: The Rise of DNA Analysis for Family Reunification and its Ethical Implications', *Life Sciences Society and Policy 7*, no. 1 (2011): pp. 1–19, doi: 10.1186/1746-5354-7-1-1.

[80] Heinemann and Lemke (n 75), p. 811.

[81] One can order online lunch-box sized DNA laboratories, e.g. https://www.bento.bio.

[82] Catherine Nash, 'Genetic Kinship', *Cultural Studies 18*, no. 1 (2004): pp. 1–33.

[83] Bob Simpson, 'Imagined Genetic Communities: Ethnicity and Essentialism in the Twenty-First Century', *Anthropology Today 16*, no. 3 (2000): pp. 3–6, doi: 10.1111/1467-8322.00023.

[84] David Skinner, 'Racialized Futures Biologism and the Changing Politics of Identity', *Social Studies of Science 36*, no. 3 (2006): pp. 459–488, p. 462.

[85] Carson W. Byrd and Matthew W. Hughey, 'Biological Determinism and Racial Essentialism: The Ideological Double Helix of Racial Inequality', *The Annals of the American Academy of Political and Social Science 661*, no. 1 (2015): pp. 8–22, p. 10, doi: 10.1177/0002716215591476.

[86] Ernesto Schwartz-Marín and Irma Silva-Zolezzi, ' "The Map of the Mexican's Genome": Overlapping National Identity, and Population Genomics', *Identity in the Information Society 3*, no. 3 (2010): pp. 489–514.

[87] Ian V. McGonigle and Lauren W. Herman, 'Genetic Citizenship: DNA Testing and the Israeli Law of Return', *Journal of Law and the Biosciences*, early view (2015), doi: 10.1093/jlb/lsv027.

[88] An article in the newsletter *Glasgow Herald* suggested that the origins of the sperm didn't matter as long as it came from a nation that could play football (Simpson (n 83), p. 4).

jus sanguinis), the wide appeal of the gene may soon replace the blood as the true repository of identity.[89]

These new 'ideologies of genetic inheritance'[90] are, nevertheless, contested and flexible. Genetic evidence can be 'mobilised or ignored depending on the particular political and social objectives'.[91] For example, despite evidence that Lemba Bantu tribesmen from Southern Africa overwhelmingly shared the Cohen haplotype, which is believed to link back to the first Jewish priest, Israeli authorities have been reluctant to acknowledge the Jewishness of the tribe.[92] Moreover, genetic evidence can also be used in order 'to repair and recast the past'[93] by supporting claims for redress, conciliation, and solidarity. Forensic DNA technology has been used by international criminal tribunals and in transitional justice processes in order to identify bodies and missing persons. For example, DNA technology was employed in order to identify children who were kidnapped by the military during the Argentinian dictatorship, thus enabling 'to reconstruct and reconnect multiple levels of social life: the individual, the familial, and the national'.[94] Apart from reinforcing surveillance, biological determinism, and visceral nationalism, biotechnologies can also serve to attest and vindicate personal identities and to support projects of collective reconciliation.

Conclusion

The development of digital and biotechnologies has the potential to reshape the institutions and norms of citizenship as political membership. Digital technologies offer new opportunities for individual and collective public engagement, political participation, and mobilization. However, they also provide governments and other actors with effective tools for tracking, policing, and excluding people. While a growing literature on surveillance has dealt with key citizenship issues, such as individual exclusion and social control, citizenship scholars have been slow to investigate

---

[89] Simpson (n 83).   [90] Finkler (n 73).

[91] Barbara Prainsack, Yael Hashiloni-Dole, and Margaret Lock, 'Religion and Nationhood: Collective Identities and the New Genetics', in Paul Atkinson and Peter Glasner, eds., *The Handbook of Genetics and Society: Mapping the New Genomic Era* (New York: Routledge, 2009), pp. 404–421, p. 412.

[92] Ibid.

[93] Keith Wailoo, Alondra Nelson, and Catherine Lee, 'Intruduction: Genetic Claims and the Unsettled Past', in Keith Wailoo, Alondra Nelson, and Catherine Lee, eds., *Genetics and the Unsettled Past: The Collision of DNA, Race, and History* (New Jersey: Rutgers University Press, 2012), p. 8.

[94] Adams L. Smith, 'Identifying Democracy Citizenship, DNA, and Identity in Postdictatorship Argentina', *Science, Technology & Human Values* (2016): pp. 1–16, p.4, doi: 0162243916658708.

the implication of increased digitalization of social and political life on citizenship. While widespread surveillance has a negative impact on individual freedom and social inclusion, it also triggers various forms of everyday resistance.[95] From the perspective of citizenship as practice, digital technologies offer new opportunities for 'acts of citizenship', as they enable individuals to advance various 'digital rights claims'.[96] Thus the tensions between citizenship and technology are not inherent but rather derived from the circumstances in which technologies are adopted, the ways in which they are used, and the ongoing political struggles over citizenship. Further research will need to do more in order to make sense of the various aspects of digital citizenship that include both citizen resistance to oppressive surveillance and the appropriation of technologies for the purpose of political action.

The success of assisted reproduction technologies and genetics has stretched the boundaries of human possibilities and rekindled ideas about scientific progress and the continuous improvement of the human condition. However, with the spectre of eugenics still looming in the background, biotechnological advancements have been easily hijacked to serve exclusionary institutions and ideologies. Conflicting politics of national reproduction leading to different approaches to ART have generated problems with regard to access to citizenship. Ideologies of ethnic, racial, and national distinctiveness have benefited from the new language of genetics by moving the boundaries of group identity further into the body. This geneticization of national identity challenges the thesis of the gradual de-ethnicization of citizenship in the West.[97] More needs to be said about the transformation of citizenship and national identity in the genetic era. The widespread use of DNA testing in the context of immigration and citizenship seems to suggest a concern with preserving the genetic boundaries of the nation. However, as in the case of digital technologies, biotechnological devices and vocabularies also serve to create and recover personal identities and to build inclusive societies.

From citizenship's perspective technology is both a blessing and a curse. The increasing complexity of contemporary societies makes technological innovations both inevitable and unpredictable. Uncertainties about our technological future only aggravate worries about the future of citizenship in a global yet local, mobile yet static, virtual yet material world. While technological solutions can provide the necessary infrastructure for reorganizing citizenship and membership, they cannot answer to normative question about what kind of boundaries of political membership are suitable for increasingly complex and mobile contemporary societies.

[95] Gary T. Marx, 'A Tack in the Shoe: Neutralizing and Resisting the New Surveillance', *Journal of Social Issues* 59, no. 2 (2003): pp. 369–390.
[96] Isin and Ruppert (n 5).
[97] Christian Joppke, *Selecting by Origin: Ethnic Migration in the Liberal State* (Cambridge: Harvard University Press, 2005).

BIBLIOGRAPHY

Albert, Mathias and Lothar Brock, 'Debordering the World of States: New Spaces in International Relations', *New Political Science 18*, no. 1 (1996): pp. 69–106, doi: 10.1080/07393149608429765.

Amoore, Louise, Stephen Marmura, and Mark B. Salter, 'Smart Borders and Mobilities: Spaces, Zones, Enclosures', *Surveillance & Society 5*, no. 2 (2002): pp. 96–101.

Bigo, Didier, 'Globalized (in) Security: The Field and the Ban-Opticon', in Didier Bigo and Anastassi Tsoukala, eds., *Illiberal Practices of Liberal Regimes: The (In) Security Games* (Paris: L'Harmattan, 2006), pp. 5–49.

Blackburn-Starza, Antony, 'Single Father Wins Surrogacy Human Rights Ruling', *Bionews 852*, 23 May 2016, online http://www.bionews.org.uk/page_651129.asp.

Brubaker, Rogers W., *Citizenship and Nationhood in France and Germany* (Cambridge: Harvard University Press, 1992).

Byrd, Carson W. and Matthew W. Hughey, 'Biological Determinism and Racial Essentialism: The Ideological Double Helix of Racial Inequality', *The Annals of the American Academy of Political and Social Science 661*, no. 1 (2015): pp. 8–22, doi: 10.1177/0002716215591476.

Carens, Joseph H., *Culture, Citizenship and Community: A Contextual Exploration of Justice as Evenhandedness* (Oxford: Oxford University Press, 2000).

Castells, Manuel, *The Rise of the Network Society: The Information Age: Economy, Society, and Culture*, volume 1 (Oxford: Blackwell Oxford, 1996).

Clarke, Roger, 'Information Technology and Dataveillance', *Communications of the ACM 31*, no. 5 (1988): pp. 498–512.

Deleuze, Gilles, 'Postscript on the Societies of Control', *October 59* (Winter 1992): pp. 3–7.

Dimitrova, Ina, *Populism and Pronatalism: The Assisted 'Rebirth' of the (Bulgarian) People* (2013) (unpublished manuscript, on file with author).

Dumbrava, Costica, 'Reproducing the Nation: Reproduction, Citizenship and Ethno-Demographic Survival in Post-Communist Romania', *Journal of Ethnic and Migration Studies*, early view (2016), doi: 10.1080/1369183X.2016.1221335.

Dumbrava, Costica and Rainer Bauböck, eds., 'Bloodlines and Belonging: Time to Abandon Ius Sanguinis?', EUI Working Paper no. 80 (Florence: RSCAS, 2015), online http://cadmus.eui.eu/bitstream/handle/1814/37578/RSCAS_2015_80.pdf;sequence=1.

Eikjman, Quirine, 'Digital Security Governance and Accountability in Europe: Ethical Dilemmas in Terrorism Risk Management', *Journal of Politics and Law 6*, no. 4 (2013): pp. 35–45, doi: 10.5539/jpl.v6n4p35.

Finkler, Kaja, *Experiencing the New Genetics: Kinship and Family on the Medical Frontier* (Philadelphia: University of Pennsylvania Press, 2000).

Foucault, Michel, *Discipline and Punish: the Birth of the Prison* (New York: Random House, 1975).

Foucault, Michel, *Security, Territory, Population: Lectures at the Collège de France 1977-1978*, volume 4 (Basingstoke: Palgrave Macmillan, 2009).

Freeman, Tabitha and Martin Richards, 'DNA Testing and Kinship: Paternity, Genealogy and the Search for the "Truth" of Our Genetic Origins', in Fatemeh Ebtehaj, Bridget Lindley, and Martin Richards, eds., *Kinship Matters* (Oxford: Hart, 2006), pp. 67–95.

Ginsburg, Faye and Rayna Rapp, *Conceiving the New World Order: The Global Politics of Reproduction* (Berkeley: University of California Press, 1995).

Gooas, Kerstin, Michael Friedewald, William Webster, and Charles Leleux, 'The Co-Evolution of Surveillance Technology and Surveillance Practices', in D. Wright and R. Kreissl, eds., *Surveillance in Europe* (Abingdon: Routledge, 2015), pp. 51–100.

Gürtin, Zeynep B. and Marcia C. Inhorn, 'Introduction: Travelling for Conception and the Global Assisted Reproduction Market', *Reproductive Biomedicine Online* 23, no. 5 (2011): pp. 535–537, doi: 10.1016/j.rbmo.2011.08.001.

Guzik, Keith, 'Discrimination by Design: Predictive Data Mining as Security Practice in the United States' "War on Terrorism"', *Surveillance & Society* 7, no. 1 (2009): pp. 3–20.

Halsaa, Beatrice, Sasha Roseneil, and Sevil Sümer, *FEMCIT—Gendered Citizenship in Multicultural Europe: The Impact of Contemporary Women's Movements—Final Report* (University of Oslo, Birkbeck University and University of Bergen, 2011), online http://wpms.computing.uni.no/femcit/wp-content/uploads/sites/16/2015/11/WP7_WorkingpaperNo5.pdf.

Harder, Lois, 'Does Sperm Have a Flag? On Biological Relationship and National Membership', *Canadian Journal of Law and Society* 30, no. 1 (2015): pp. 109–125.

Heinemann, Torsten and Thomas Lemke, 'Suspect Families: DNA Kinship Testing in German Immigration Policy', *Sociology* 47, no. 4 (2013): pp. 810–826.

Helén, Ilpo, 'Biological Citizenship across the Borders: Politics of DNA Profiling for Family Reunification', *Distinktion: Scandinavian Journal of Social Theory* 15, no. 3 (2014): pp. 343–360.

Hildebrandt, Mireille and Serge Gutwirth, *Profiling the European Citizen* (Dordrecht: Springer, 2008).

Inhorn, Marcia C., Rosario Ceballo, and Robert Nachtigall, 'Marginalized, Invisible, and Unwanted: American Minority Struggles with Infertility and Assisted Conception', in Lorraine Culley, Nicky Hudson, and Floor van Rooij, eds., *Marginalized Reproduction: Ethnicity, Infertility and Reproductive Technologies* (London, Sterling: Earthscan, 2009), pp. 181–197.

Isin, Engin and Evelyn Ruppert, *Being Digital Citizens* (London: Rowman & Littlefield International, 2015).

Joppke, Christian, *Selecting by Origin: Ethnic Migration in the Liberal State* (Cambridge: Harvard University Press, 2005).

Knaplund, Kristine S., 'Baby Without a Country: Determining Citizenship for Assisted Reproduction Children Born Overseas', *Denver University Law Review* 91, no. 2 (2013): pp. 335–367.

Korolczuk, Elżbieta, *IVF as a Threat to the Nation: The Debate on Assisted Reproduction in Contemporary Poland* (Berlin: Heinrich Boell Foundation Dossier on Overcoming Gender Backlash, 2013).

Lee, Seung, 'Kuwait Becomes First Country to Collect DNA Samples from all Citizens and Visitors: Report', *Newsweek*, 19 April 2016, online http://europe.newsweek.com/kuwait-becomes-first-country-world-collect-dna-samples-all-citizens-and-449830?rm=eu.

Lippman, Abby, 'Prenatal Genetic Testing and Screening: Constructing Needs and Reinforcing Inequities', *American Journal of Law & Medicine* 17, no. 1–2 (1991): pp. 15–50.

Lyon, David, *Surveillance Society: Monitoring Everyday Life* (Buckingham: Open University Press, 2001).

Lyon, David, 'Everyday Surveillance: Personal Data and Social Classifications', *Information, Communication & Society 5*, no. 2 (2002): pp. 242–257.

Lyon, David, 'Surveillance as Social Sorting: Computer Codes and Mobile Bodies', in David Lyon, ed., *Surveillance as Social Sorting: Privacy, Risk, and Digital Discrimination* (New York, London: Routledge, 2003), pp. 13–30.

Lyon, David, *Surveillance as Social Sorting: Privacy, Risk, and Digital Discrimination* (New York, London: Routledge, 2003).

Lyon, David, 'The Border is Everywhere: ID Cards, Surveillance and the Other', in Elia Zureik and Mark Salter, eds., *Global Surveillance and Policing: Borders, Security, Identity* (Cullompton, Portland: Willan, 2005), pp. 66–82.

Marshall, Thomas H., *Class, Citizenship and Social Development: Essays* (New York: Doubleday, 1965).

Maguire, Mark, 'The Birth of Biometric Security', *Anthropology Today 25*, no. 2 (2009): pp. 9–14.

Marquis, Greg, 'Private Security and Surveillance: From the "Dossier Society" to Database Networks', in David Lyon, ed., *Surveillance as Social Sorting: Privacy, Risk and Digital Discrimination* (New York, London: Routledge, 2003), pp. 226–248.

Marx, Gary T., 'Ethics for the New Surveillance', *The Information Society 14*, no. 3 (1998): pp. 171–185.

Marx, Gary T., 'A Tack in the Shoe: Neutralizing and Resisting the New Surveillance', *Journal of Social Issues 59*, no. 2 (2003): pp. 369–390.

McConnaughey, James, Timothy Sloan, and Cynthia Ann Nila, *Falling through the Net: A Survey of the 'Have Nots' in Rural and Urban America* (Washington: National Telecommunications and Information Administration, 1995).

McGonigle, Ian V. and Lauren W. Herman, 'Genetic Citizenship: DNA Testing and the Israeli Law of Return', *Journal of Law and the Biosciences*, early view (2015), doi: 10.1093/jlb/lsv027.

Mossberger, Karen, Caroline J. Tolbert, and Ramona S. McNeal, *Digital Citizenship: The Internet, Society, and Participation* (Cambridge: MIT Press, 2007).

Murdock, Tera Rica, 'Whose Child is This: Genetic Analysis and Family Reunification Immigration in France', *Vanderbilt Journal of Transnational Law 41* (2008): pp. 1503–1534.

Nash, Catherine, 'Genetic Kinship', *Cultural Studies 18*, no. 1 (2004): pp. 1–33.

Nelkin, Dorothy and Lori Andrews, 'DNA Identification and Surveillance Creep', *Sociology of Health & Illness 21*, no. 5 (1999): pp. 689–706.

Nielsen, Nikolaj, 'Computer to Make EU Asylum Decisions', *Euobserver*, 4 May 2017, online https://euobserver.com/migration/133341.

Norris, Clive, 'From Personal to Digital: CCTV, the Panopticon, and the Technological Mediation of Suspicion and Social Control', in David Lyon, ed., *Surveillance as Social Sorting: Privacy, Risk and Digital Discrimination* (London, New York: Routledge): pp. 249–281.

Norris, Clive and Gary Armstrong, *The Maximum Surveillance Society: The Rise of CCTV* (Oxford: Berg Publishers, 1999).

Norris, Pippa, *Digital Divide: Civic Engagement, Information Poverty, and the Internet Worldwide* (Cambridge: Cambridge University Press, 2001).

Petryna, Adriana, *Life Exposed: Biological Citizens after Chernobyl* (Princeton: Princeton University Press, 2002).

Pötzsch, Holger, 'The Emergence of iBorder: Bordering Bodies, Networks, and Machines', *Environment and Planning D: Society and Space 33*, no. 1 (2015): pp. 101–118, doi: 10.1068/d14050p.

Prainsack, Barbara, Yael Hashiloni-Dole, and Margaret Lock, 'Religion and Nationhood: Collective Identities and the New Genetics', in Paul Atkinson and Peter Glasner, eds., *The Handbook of Genetics and Society: Mapping the New Genomic Era* (New York: Routledge, 2009), pp. 404–421.

Putnam, Robert, *Bowling Alone: The Collapse and Revival of Civic America* (New York: Simon and Schuster, 2000).

Roots, Lehte and Costica Dumbrava, 'E-Citizenship Opportunities in the Changing Technological Environment', in Tanel Kerikmaë and Addi Rull, eds., *The Future of Law and eTechnologies* (Cham, New York: Springer, 2016), pp. 45–56.

Rose, Nikolas and Carlos Novas, 'Biological Citizenship', in A. Ong and S. J. Collier, eds., *Global Assemblages: Technology, Politics, and Ethics as Anthropological Problems* (Oxford: John Wiley & Sons, 2008), pp. 439–463.

Roseneil, Sasha, Isabel Crowhurst, Ana Cristina Santos, and Mariya Stoilova, 'Reproduction and Citizenship/Reproducing Citizens: Editorial Introduction', *Citizenship Studies 17*, no. 8 (2013): pp. 901–911.

Ryan, Bernard and Valsamis Mitsilegas, eds., *Extraterritorial Immigration Control: Legal Challenges* (Boston, Leiden: Martinus Nijhoff, 2010).

Särav, Sandra and Tanel Kerikmaë, 'E-Residency: A Cyberdream Embodied in a Digital Identity Card?', in Tanel Kerikmaë and Addi Rull, eds., *The Future of Law and eTechnologies* (Cham, New York: Springer, 2016), pp. 57–79.

Schwartz-Marín, Ernesto and Irma Silva-Zolezzi, ' "The Map of the Mexican's Genome": Overlapping National Identity, and Population Genomics', *Identity in the Information Society 3*, no. 3 (2010): pp. 489–514.

Shachar, Ayelet, 'The Shifting Border of Immigration Control', *Stanford Journal of Civil Rights & Civil Liberties 3*, no. 2 (2007): pp. 165–193.

Shachar, Ayelet, *The Birthright Lottery: Citizenship and Global Inequality* (Cambridge: Harvard University Press, 2009).

Simpson, Bob, 'Imagined Genetic Communities: Ethnicity and Essentialism in the Twenty-First Century', *Anthropology Today 16*, no. 3 (2000): pp. 3–6, doi: 10.1111/1467-8322.00023.

Skinner, David, 'Racialized Futures Biologism and the Changing Politics of Identity', *Social Studies of Science 36*, no. 3 (2006): pp. 459–488.

Smith, Adams L., 'Identifying Democracy Citizenship, DNA, and Identity in Postdictatorship Argentina', *Science, Technology & Human Values 41*, no. 6 (2016): pp. 1–16, doi: 0162243916658708.

Soysal, Yasemine N., *Limits of Citizenship: Migrants and Postnational Membership in Europe* (Chicago: University of Chicago Press, 1994).

Tavani, Herman T., 'Genomic Research and Data-Mining Technology: Implications for Personal Privacy and Informed Consent', *Ethics and Information Technology 6*, no. 1 (2004): pp. 15–28.

Torpey, John C., *The Invention of the Passport: Surveillance, Citizenship, and the State* (Cambridge: Cambridge University Press, 2000).

Villiers, Janice D., 'Brave New World: The Use and Potential Misuse of DNA Technology in Immigration Law', *Boston College Third World Law Journal 30*, no. 2 (2010): pp. 239–271.

Vink, Maarten P. and Gerard-René de Groot, 'Birthright Citizenship: Trends and Regulations in Europe', EUDO Citizenship comparative report (Florence: European University Institute, 2010), online http://eudo-citizenship.eu/docs/birthright_comparativepaper.pdf.

Wailoo, Keith, Alondra Nelson, and Catherine Lee, 'Intruduction: Genetic Claims and the Unsettled Past', in Keith Wailoo, Alondra Nelson, and Catherine Lee, eds., *Genetics and the Unsettled Past: The Collision of DNA, Race, and History* (New Jersey: Rutgers University Press, 2012).

Weiss, Martin G., 'Strange DNA: The Rise of DNA Analysis for Family Reunification and Its Ethical Implications', *Life Sciences Society and Policy 7*, no. 1 (2011): pp. 1–19, doi: 10.1186/1746-5354-7-1-1.

Winter, Jay and Michael Teitelbaum, *The Global Spread of Fertility Decline: Population, Fear, and Uncertainty* (New Haven, London: Yale University Press, 2013).

Wright, David, Michael Friedewald, Serge Gutwirth, Marc Langheinrich, Emilio Mordini, Rocco Bellanova, Paul De Hert, Kush Wadhwa, and Didier Bigo, 'Sorting Out Smart Surveillance', *Computer Law & Security Review 26*, no. 4 (2010): pp. 343–354.

Yuval-Davis, Nira, *Gender and Nation* (Cambridge: Cambridge University Press, 1997).

Zaiotti, Ruben, ed., *Externalizing Migration Management: Europe, North America and the Spread of 'Remote Control Practices* (New York: Routledge, 2016).

....

CHAPTER 35

CITIZENSHIP FOR SALE?

....

AYELET SHACHAR*

Government is instituted for the common good; for the protection, safety, prosperity and happiness of the people; and not for the profit, honor, or private interest of any one man, family, or class of men.

The Constitution of the Commonwealth
of Massachusetts, Article VII

IN a world of severe inequality like our own, millions risk their lives crossing borders without authorization in search of better life prospects, often learning all too quickly that they are unwanted and unwelcome in their 'host' countries. At the same time, a growing number of countries now offer tailor-made, exclusive, and

* Earlier drafts were presented at the EUI, Max Planck, and Princeton's LAPA programme. I'm grateful to Leti Volpp, Sara Fine, and Stephen Macedo, my commentators in these respective events. Thanks are also due to Rainer Bauböck, Irene Bloemraad, Sue Donaldson, Daniel Halberstam, Turku Isiksel, Will Kymlicka, Matthew Milne, David Owen, Steven Ratner, Jen Rubio, Maarten Vink, Marinka Yossiffon, and especially Ran Hirschl, for their insightful comments and suggestions. All errors are mine.

expedited pathways for the world's super-rich to acquire citizenship 'quickly and simply, without any disruption to your life,' as a leading firm involved in the trade has succinctly put it.[1] Citizenship-for-sale programmes—the topic of this chapter—are booming in recent years, creating a fast-track for the rich to legally obtain citizenship in a new country in exchange for a substantial investment or 'donation'.[2]

A new global stratification is in the making. Across the globe, countries are promoting strategic or expedited passport grants to 'high value' migrants, offering them faster and smoother gateways to membership. In the context of a global race for talent, a growing number of governments now seek to lure and attract individuals with abundant human capital or exceptional achievements in the arts, sciences, sports and the like, with the expectation of receiving a return: bolstering their national interest or international stature.[3] Governments are willing to go as far as to turn their exclusive control over the allocation of membership goods—entry visas, residence permits, and ultimately, citizenship itself, into recruitment tools. Call this the *talent-for-citizenship* exchange.[4] These developments highlight the growing influence of the economic language of human capital accretion on the design of migration and membership priorities. Simultaneously, and even more contentiously, when it comes to attracting the world's rich and affluent—a particular subset of 'wanted and welcomed' potential entrants—policymakers increasingly rely on the size of one's wallet or bank account as a basis for swift admission, settlement, and naturalization. These new programmes allow the few—those with hefty deposits of mobile capital—an easy pass through the otherwise increasingly bolted gates of entry that make admission ever more tightly controlled for the nonwealthy many, if they are willing to dish out millions of dollars to literally purchase 'golden visas' or 'golden passports'. Witness the début of *citizenship for sale*.

From Australia's Pacific hub to America's skyscrapers, from the islands of the Caribbean to continental Europe, more than a quarter of the world's countries offer specialized entry, settlement, and passport acquisition programmes to high-net-worth individuals (HNWI, defined as those with personal *mobile* capital in excess of US\$1 million; ultra-high-net-worth individuals, or UHNWI, are those with over \$30 million of investable assets). The wealth of the total

[1] Henley and Partners, 'Citizenship-by-Investment', online https://www.henleyglobal.com/citizenship-by-investment/.
[2] Madeleine Sumption and Kate Hooper, *Selling Visas and Citizenship: Policy Questions from the Global Boom in Investor Immigration* (Washington: Migration Policy Institute, 2014).
[3] Ayelet Shachar, 'The Race for Talent: Highly Skilled Migrants and Competitive Immigration Regimes', *NYU Law Review 81* (2006): pp. 148–206; Ayelet Shachar and Ran Hirschl, 'On Citizenship, States, and Markets', *Journal of Political Philosophy 22* (2014): pp. 231–257. See also Triadafilos Triadafilopoulos, ed., *Wanted and Welcome? Policies for Highly Skilled Immigrants in Comparative Perspective* (New York: Springer, 2013).
[4] Shachar (n 3). For further discussion, see Ayelet Shachar, *Olympic Citizenship: Migration and the Global Race for Talent* (Oxford: Oxford University Press, forthcoming 2018).

population of high- and ultra-high-net-worth individuals worldwide is 'just over $56 trillion—triple the GDP of the United States, and greater than the sum of the world's fifteen largest national economies'.[5] This is the global 1 percent, the target audience of the gold-plated tracks to citizenship I explore in the following pages.[6]

These programmes create a direct link between money transfers—in large quantities—and expedited bestowal of citizenship. In certain cases, millionaire migrants need not even set foot in the new home country.[7] The capital investments involved are significant, ranging from $1 million in the United States ($500,000 for specially designated areas) for a coveted green card, to a minimum of £2 million in the United Kingdom for a leave of remain (the greater the investment, the shorter the wait time), to €500,000 in Portugal for a golden residence permit, to 'bargain' passports in the island nations of the Caribbean and the Pacific where the price tag for citizenship hovers around the $250,000 mark.

The spread of these new programmes is one of the most significant developments in citizenship practice in the past few decades, yet it has received only scant attention in the literature. My discussion in this chapter begins to fill the lacuna. The proliferation of citizenship-for-sale programmes tests our deepest intuitions about the meaning and attributes of the relationship between the individual and the political community to which she belongs.[8] While the specific details of different countries' programmes vary, they all rely on a shared premise: these schemes allow the über-rich, even those with only tenuous ties to the passport-issuing country, the opportunity to acquire citizenship based on nothing more than the heft of their wallets, bypassing standard residence, linguistic proficiency, and related requirements that states otherwise jealously enforce.[9] Such stratification and marketization processes recast membership in the community—for many the ultimate *non*market good—as a purchasable commodity.

---

[5] Brooke Harrington, *Capital without Borders: Wealth Managers and the One Percent* (Cambridge, MA: Harvard University Press, 2016), p. 201. See also Cap-Gemini, *World Wealth Report* (Paris: Cap-Gemini, 2015).

[6] The programmes differ in terms of the required monetary investment for the transaction, and the speed through which applicants reach the naturalization stage. The capital transfer may take the form of non-refundable cash payments to the government, or a fixed-term investment in bonds, real estate, or other private-sector assesses. In some cases, the funds are returned to the applicant-investor after a fixed number of years (in effect operating as an interest-gaining loan), while in others, the funds remain with the citizenship-offering state.

[7] The term millionaire migrant is drawn from David Ley, *Millionaire Migrants: Trans-Pacific Life Lines* (Malden: Wiley-Blackwell, 2010).

[8] It also raises significant questions about the scope of state obligations under international law vis-à-vis these passport holders, who lack affiliation with the membership-granting society but have officially purchased its citizenship, a topic that goes beyond the scope of analysis in this chapter.

[9] Some countries initially offer expedited admission, some permit direct access to permanent residence, whereas others turn expeditiously to issue citizenship certificates and passports.

This is a revealing conundrum. Well-off states tighten and impede passage through their cumulative gates to most categories of would-be migrants.[10] However, at the same time, countries are *facilitating* fast-tracked entry to the world's moneyed elite who desire to 'diversify' their passport portfolios. Laws and regulations governing such preferential access offer us a rare window through which to consider which qualities policymakers appear to value in their prospective 'high value' citizens and seek to incorporate into their political communities.[11] While important lessons can be learned by examining the restrictions to or denial of access to citizenship, equally revealing insights can be unearthed by focusing on *who* is given the red-carpet treatment and, especially, on *what* basis.

When a stack of cash becomes the surrogate for membership, the basic connection between the individual and the political community is unfastened, leading to a situation whereby the millionaire-turned-citizen is not required to establish any kind of tangible connection to the new home country, other than a wire transfer. These new developments challenge familiar concepts of citizenship, such as those focusing on 'identity and belonging', as well as post-Westphalian arguments that have dismissed borders and membership boundaries as relics of a bygone era that has outlived its usefulness. These entrenched perspectives can neither explain the developments recounted here, nor can they fully capture the unique mixture of state and market influences that undergirds their surge. Neither can provide answers to the puzzling transformation explored in this chapter: the re-conception of citizenship from 'sacred' bond to marketable 'commodity'.

Nothing in the conventional accounts of citizenship as a unique and reciprocal political relation, nor predictions of its demise, can explain the proliferation of these more instrumental, flexible, and market-oriented interpretations of citizenship.[12] Yet it is clear that developments in the world of law and policy now reflect such transformation, as governments not only permit but actively facilitate such transactions. Familiar considerations of (under)supply of and (over)demand for entry visas, growing competition for the rich and mobile, and the entry of new players into the fray do not adequately explain the depth of the current phenomenon; deeper processes are at work, meriting keen consideration, namely: the perpetual

---

[10] The reference to cumulative gates (admission, settlement, and naturalization) draws on the classic account offered by Tomas Hammar, *Democracy and the Nation State: Aliens, Denizens and Citizens in a World of International Migration* (Aldershot: Ashgate, 1990), pp. 16–18.

[11] This new trend brings to the fore core questions about the future of citizenship, highlighting the risks and opportunities that attach to states taking on the role of 'brokers' of paid-for citizenship grants that exacerbate inequality in global mobility and membership regimes while depleting citizenship from within.

[12] For illuminating ethnographic and geographical accounts of the flexible use of citizenship by transnational individuals and families, see Aihwa Ong, *Flexible Citizenship: The Cultural Logic of Transnationality* (Durham: Duke University Press, 1999); Ley (n 7). The focus of this chapter is, by contrast, on state policies that create avenues for the rich and wealthy to purchase citizenship, rather than the strategies employed by those taking advantage of these opportunities.

testing, blurring, and erosion of the state-market boundary regulating access to membership.

By drawing attention to these cash-for-passport practices, I wish to look more closely at some legal and normative problems and puzzles, while exploring the role of state action in facilitating these dramatic changes.[13] I refer to this new trend as the *marketization of citizenship* to highlight a dual transformation—commodifying citizenship and hollowing out the 'status, rights and identity' components of membership.[14] Marketization is never merely an economic process; it is also deeply political as it reshapes and 're-engineers' the boundaries of and interactions among states and markets, voice and power, the inviolable and the mercantile.[15]

In what follows, I trace the surge that has taken place in cash-for-passport programmes, providing illustrative examples. Next, I turn to explore the main legal strategies adopted by a growing number of countries putting their visas and passports up 'for sale', selectively opening the gates of admission to those with massive billfolds while restricting access to most other categories of would-be entrants. Moving from the positive to the normative, I then elaborate the main arguments in favour of, as well as against, citizenship-for-sale. Finally, I conceive potential responses to curb these developments, although in fact the proverbial train has already left the station.

Treating citizenship as a marketable commodity represents a new frontier as well as a new challenge. My discussion stems from the belief that citizenship worthy of its name is centred on equality and promotion of the 'common good' (however difficult it remains to define), not the 'profit, honor, or private interest of any one man, family, or class of men'. [16] Legal access to membership, not to mention the actual experience of citizenship, have never been fully immune to the influence of social class or property ownership.[17] However, turning the

---

[13] States are not alone in charting this new terrain. Intermediaries, both local and transnational, such as specialized law firms, wealth mangers and other for-profit third parties, have also exerted influence in shaping and transplanting such programmes from one country, or region, to another. See Shachar (n 3).

[14] These multiple facets of citizenship are captured well by Christian Joppke, 'Transformation of Citizenship: Status, Rights, Identity', *Citizenship Studies* 11 (2007): pp. 37–48. For related categorization, see Bloemraad et al., 'Citizenship and Immigration: Multiculturalism, Assimilation, and Challenges to the Nation-State', *Annual Review of Sociology 34* (2008): pp. 153–179.

[15] For a concise overview, see Marina Vujnovic, 'Marketization', in George Ritzer, ed., *Wiley-Blackwell Encyclopedia of Globalization* (Malden: Wiley-Blackwell, 2012), published online, DOI: 10.1002/9780470670590.wbeog368. David Harvey, *A Brief History of Neoliberalism* (Oxford: Oxford University Press, 2005), p. 160.

[16] These words are drawn from the Constitution of the Commonwealth of Massachusetts, Article VII. For different articulations of the value of equality in citizenship, see Bauböck in this volume; Donaldson and Kymlicka in this volume; Honohan in this volume; Joppke in this volume; Gibney in this volume; Volpp in this volume.

[17] Marketization processes remind us of the long durée of history whereby the vast majority of the population was denied access to equal membership through mechanisms such as property ownership (over slaves, land, or household members) and the like.

transfer of capital, *simpliciter*, into the admissibility criterion challenges the equality principle itself—not just its imperfect implementation. Thus, of the various and multifaceted recent transformations to membership explored in this Handbook, imposing market valuation on citizenship acquisition and extending it to admission into the body politic, may prove the most corrosive over time, steadily eroding out the relational and political realm of membership definition.

Citizenship for Sale:
A Thumbnail History

'There are some things that money can't buy.' Is citizenship among them? Only a few years ago, raising such a question would have seemed out of place if not oxymoronic: placing the utmost *political* relation in our lexicon—citizenship—for *sale*? This, however, is taking place and it is a practice that requires closer scrutiny.

The term marketization has various meanings, but will be used here primarily to refer to processes through which modes of monetized transacting come to displace non-market activities and relations, opening up new 'domains hitherto regarded off-limits'. In the context of citizenship, marketization both tests and strains aspirational notions of citizenship as reflecting the horizon of equality and participation, regardless of which theories of state and society—liberal, civic republican, or democratic—inform them.[18] Instead, the size of the applicant's wallet is the core, if not sole, criterion determining whether gates of admission will open.

A quick step back in time allows us to examine some precursors of today's cash-for-passport programmes. Not long ago, the market catering to wealthy purchasers, seeking 'passports of convenience', was primarily associated with unscrupulous offshore tax havens in micro-states in the Pacific and the Caribbean. Many such programmes, which began to emerge in the 1980s, were discredited, associated with fraud, corruption, and money laundering.[19] Lenient due-diligence and background review procedures made these programmes vulnerable to abuse; applicants did not need to inhabit, or even visit, the passport-issuing country. These cash-for-passport programmes offered significant tax advantages and facilitated visa-free travel;

---

[18] Margaret R. Somers, *Genealogies of Citizenship: Markets, Statelessness, and the Right to Have Rights* (Cambridge: Cambridge University Press, 2008). See Bloemraad in this volume.

[19] Anthony van Fossen, 'Citizenship for Sale: Passports of Convenience from Pacific Island Tax Havens', *Commonwealth & Comparative Politics 45* (2007): pp. 138–163.

passport holders could also elude stricter financial record-keeping and reporting requirements in their home countries.

An important step in the process of policy legitimization occurred when the world's major immigrant-receiving countries, including Canada and the United States, adopted legislation that granted direct or conditional permanent residence (or 'green card') status following an applicant's investment in government bonds (Canada) or private businesses (the United States), waiving standard admission requirements.[20]

These programmes have proliferated since the early 2000s. Surprisingly, it is in Europe—the progenitor of modern statehood and the contemporary inventor and facilitator of the world's most comprehensive model of supranational citizenship— that a new generation of pecuniary-centered transactions has emerged. The most recent data reveal that about 'half of the member states have designated immigrant-investor routes'.[21] Of these countries, some offer investment-based entry visas, many of which allow for later application for permanent residence, while others offer easier access or direct access to permanent residence status.[22] Yet others have gone further, offering express access to citizenship for direct cash transfers.

Consider, for example, Malta's amendment of its Citizenship Act in 2013, establishing a new individual investor category for facilitating a Maltese passport; this category was open to high-net-worth individuals with few requirements beyond the ability to pay.[23] Malta, the smallest member state of the European Union, initially offered speedy naturalization in return for a non-recoverable 'donation' of €650,000; this sum was later increased to €1.15 million, opening a gilded backdoor to European citizenship.[24] The Maltese programme's main attraction for investors was the government's original plan to abolish *both* the residency requirements *and* the waiting periods for citizenship—Maltese and European. Such a transaction is something that none of the other EU countries, including those now offering expedited golden visa and residency permits were willing to do—namely, to completely forego requirements ensuring that applicants have 'real and effective' ties to

---

[20] Australia, New Zealand, and the United Kingdom also offer their variants of preferred admission for investment migrants.

[21] Sumption and Hooper (n 2), p. 2.

[22] Spain and Portugal are prime examples of the surge in such golden visas and residence permits. For further discussion, see Jelena Džankic, 'Investment-Based Citizenship and Residence Programmes in the EU', EUI Working Paper no. 08 (Florence: RSCAS, 2015).

[23] Applicants also had to establish that they had no criminal record and were subject to a due diligence review.

[24] European citizenship is derivative: a person who holds the nationality of an EU country automatically gains EU citizenship. See Consolidated Version of the Treaty on the Functioning of the European Union, Article 20(1). C 326/47 Official Journal of the European Union, 26 October 2012. For further discussion, see Strumia in this volume.

the political community they join.[25] Malta's programme initially waived residency *altogether*, just as it removed any other prerequisite that there be a 'genuine link'. So much for the International Court of Justice conclusion, in the influential *Nottebohm Case*, that real and effective ties between the individual and the state must underpin the conferral of citizenship.[26] This is a textbook example of what theorists, lawyers, and political economists have referred to as 'blocked exchanges' or 'prohibited transactions' that allow advantages in one social sphere or arena (the economic) to unfairly influence another (the political).[27]

Following a storm of criticism, culminating in a special session held in the European Parliament during which the Vice President of the European Commission declared that 'citizenship is not for sale!', Malta eventually revised its policy by including a nominal one-year residency requirement for investors.[28] It did not, however, back down from its bolder scheme: placing a price tag on Maltese (and European) citizenship. Other countries in Europe have since taken cues from the Maltese programme in recasting their own programmes of membership by investment.[29]

These examples provide concrete illustrations of the broader trend toward the marketization of citizenship. The transaction is based on turning capital investment into the *core* criterion for admission, settlement, and naturalization. These developments prompt a set of novel questions of fairness, justice, and democratic accountability. For example, in the context of supranational citizenship regimes (such as the European Union membership model), *to whom*, beyond its own citizenry, must a transacting government justify its decisions? Need a country justify itself to other member states, or the Union-wide institutions such as the European Commission, and if so, with what implications? What about justification to would-be entrants who may have a shot at admission through standard migration streams (family, employment, and humanitarian), but may be priced out, or pushed to the back of the line? Should the opinions of sedentary populations of emigrants' countries of origin and destination also be heard? Or, if an expansive all-affected-interests principle is applied, perhaps *anyone* who may be unfairly and arbitrarily impacted should have a say.[30] Furthermore, non-millionaire migrants already settled in passport-selling

---

[25] The 'real and effective' standard is applied in many jurisdictions, affirming a notion of citizenship as social membership; it is most famously drawn from the *Nottebohm Case*. See *Nottebohm Case* (*Liechtenstein v. Guatemala*) [1955] I.C.J. 1. This decision focused on the claims for diplomatic protection and recognition of citizenship by other members of the international community.

[26] *Nottebohm*, p. 22.

[27] Michael Walzer, *Spheres of Justice: A Defense of Pluralism and Equality* (New York: Basic Books, 1983), pp. 95–103; Cass R. Sunstein, 'Incommensurability and Valuation in Law', *Michigan Law Review* 92, no. 4 (1994): pp. 779–861, pp. 849–850.

[28] This requirement can be fulfilled by renting out an apartment for twelve months, not necessarily residing in it.

[29] Džankić (n 22).

[30] Robert Goodin, 'Enfranchising All Affected Interests, and Its Alternatives', *Philosophy and Public Affairs* 35 (2007): pp. 40–68.

countries might have an opinion about their own ineligibility for naturalization schemes that bypass knowledge or familiarity with the country's political structures, main civic institutions, history or language, especially since these requirements become increasingly stringent. If civic and cultural integration are necessary preconditions for full membership (as restrictive citizenship tests increasingly indicate), it seems unfair and incoherent to apply the mechanisms for determining integration to some and not to others.

To begin to address these questions, the following section investigates several core puzzles associated with citizenship-for-sale transactions. Before articulating arguments *against* the proliferation of these programmes, however, I briefly examine the case in their *favour*, putting forward three major arguments in their defence: taming nationality, endorsing a 'commodify everything' approach, and increasing government revenue. These claims are frequently intertwined, but for analytical purposes, I consider each rationale in turn.

Arguments in Favour
of Selling Citizenship

The first theme is that *anything* that removes or at least reduces the air of chauvinism, historically associated with certain conceptions of membership in the state, is a welcome advance.[31] This position is implied in the work of economists who view the market as the best locale for promoting individual choice and allocative efficiency without centralized control or overarching paternalistic oversight.[32] The presumption is that turning citizenship into a commodity would offer a better sorting mechanism to help identify, through market transaction, which agents value citizenship most—by paying more for it. This analysis holds that for voluntary trades on the market to gravitate towards optimal results, access to membership must be recast and removed from the regulatory authority of the state. Entry visas, residency permits, and naturalization certificates must instead be freely sold and traded on the market, just like any other scarce and valuable good. In this account, trading in citizenship ensures that a correct pricing mechanism will emerge, through repeated transactions between 'purchasers' and 'sellers' on carefully regulated platforms.

---

[31] On the relationship between citizenship and nationhood, see Gans in this volume.
[32] There is very little literature that focuses on the idea of a market for citizenship, but these positions can be extrapolated from general pro-market liberalization arguments.

Note that no attention is paid here to background conditions of inequality that may well prohibit the vast majority of the world's population (including the less well-off segments of prosperous nations) from 'expressing'—through monetary investments that are far beyond their reach—the value that they attach to such membership goods. Nor is it clear how pure market transactions, recommended here as *the* admission ticket to citizenship, can ever fully capture and sustain the *non*monetary and intangible dimensions of human relations, social interactions, and political commitments that are encapsulated in citizenship, making it valuable in the first place.

Taking the transactional logic one step further, an open market or auction model for citizenship should, at least in theory, allow private individuals, not just states, to engage in the trade.[33] However, under current law everywhere, it is a serious offence to engage in such activity. In practice, states have *not* surrendered their monopoly over controlling access to membership—and its associated goods—and are unlikely to do so any time soon. Instead, we witness a more complex pattern emerge: governments continue to define and control the criteria for access, although the *content* they may give such criteria is more market-oriented.

Indeed, perhaps the most surprising aspect of the legal transformation of citizenship in the direction of marketization is in the willingness of governments—our political representatives and public trustees—to turn the most sacrosanct resource under their control into a tradable 'commodity'. Here, the marketization of citizenship presents a puzzle, as it defies any simple and unidirectional logic of the retreat or withdrawal of the state through deregulation or privatization. Instead, it is precisely the special character of the market in citizenship that makes it fascinating to track, explore, and explain, both empirically and normatively. For governments have created a platform for transacting citizenship that is distinctively, paradoxically, *statist*: it is created by governments and primarily implemented and monitored by them. State actors—or their authorized delegates—control core aspects of the transaction, such as the prerequisites for the sale, the review process, the conditions for and the timing of approval, and the number of available spots.[34]

Revisiting the debate about whether globalization leads to the demise of states' ability to control borders and boundaries, the trend explored here suggests that although a growing number of countries designate privileged entry routes for the wealthy as part of their 'managed' migration policies, states have *not* abandoned

---

[33] Those who view citizenship as a club good predict that it is unlikely that governments will cede control over defining and controlling membership, for a core characteristic of a club good is the ability to define the entry criteria and its price. For a critical account, see DeVoretz and Irastorza in this volume.

[34] What governments have acquiesced to, and in certain cases, encouraged, is the role played by third-party for-profit actors—including global law firms, tax planners, private-client advisors, and wealth managers—as intermediaries between those searching to buy a second or third citizenship and passport-selling countries.

their monopoly over defining who may gain access to membership, and according to what criteria. The high price of citizenship—literally, millions in investment dollars—exists precisely because of tight control over membership.[35]

The invention and implementation of citizenship-for-sale programmes is living proof of the persistent power and discretion still exercised by states in today's globalized world as they seek to regulate membership and mobility, in the process 'constitut[ing] the[ir] very "stateness".'[36] But it also shows the intrusion of market logic into the sovereign act of defining 'who belongs'. This blurred matrix yet again reveals the collapse of old borderlines between states and markets, law and transaction, principle and interest, creating new hybrids and shifting alignments under an emerging market-for-citizenship model.[37]

To recapitulate the first line of argument in favour of selling citizenship: if a connection is drawn between marketization and the tamping of nationalism, reimagining citizenship in the image of a purchasable commodity is perceived as a liberating process. It removes the shackles of tradition, culture, and patria, moving citizenship forward to a new and more competitive age of high-speed transactional global contracting, where a price mechanism is an interface for circumventing cumbersome criteria and bureaucratic review processes, stages of entry that are seen as both obsolete and passé. A critic of this line of argument might point out, however, that in many countries citizenship is progressively disassociated from thick conceptions of nationhood and that civic conceptions of membership have emerged globally without reliance on commodified market mechanisms. Primary examples of such patterns of change are found in the growing acceptance of dual nationality or the rise of supranational and multilevel citizenship, among other new types of conceptualization.[38]

A second, closely related argument, speaks more directly to the value of commodification. Perhaps the best defence of this position is found in the work of Gary Becker, endorsing what he has labelled the 'economic approach to human behavior'.[39] This approach rests on tripartite assumptions of maximizing behaviour,

---

[35] I thank Irene Bloemraad for this formulation. Proponents of open borders or more liberal mobility regimes would see governments acting here as rent-seeking monopolists; political economists may counter by arguing that the value of citizenship as a club good relies on its excludability.

[36] John Torpey, 'Coming and Going: On the State Monoplization of the Legitimate "Means of Movement"', *Sociological Theory* 16 (1998): 235–259, at p. 240.

[37] Shachar and Hirschl (n 3). In small-market economies, such as the tiny island nations involved in the citizenship trade, transnational for-profit brokers can wield significant negotiation power vis-à-vis local governments, promising to promote their product worldwide in exchange for commissions for citizenship sold through the promoted investment route. This raises, yet again, further concerns about the intertwining of market forces and state actors, democratic legitimacy concerns, as well as questions of transparency and accountability.

[38] See Spiro in this volume; Strumia in this volume; Colleyer in this volume; Maas in this volume.

[39] Gary S. Becker, *The Economic Approach to Human Behavior* (Chicago: University of Chicago Press, 1976).

market equilibrium, and stable preferences. Taken together, argues Becker, these three assumptions can explain '*all* human behavior' and should apply *regardless* of what goods are at stake.[40] As such, the economic approach knows no borders or boundaries. Accordingly, nothing prohibits selling United States entry permits, a proposal that Becker made public in the op-ed pages of *The Wall Street Journal* the day after he won the Nobel Prize in Economic Sciences.[41] Though this Beckerian line of argument will be critiqued further on, here it is important to grasp the prominence of his work in providing intellectual ammunition to various players—not just government policymakers but also third-party intermediaries, such as global law firms facilitating the transaction, tax planners, private-client advisors, and wealth managers—who have a stake in further expanding the reach of citizenship-for-sale programmes.

As studies by Vivian Zelizer and other economic sociologists have shown, the creation of an environment receptive to the commodification of institutions and aspects of life previously held 'sacred' and, as such, not suitable for trade, is not simply the result of rapid globalization or the rationalization and disenchantment of modern life (as Max Weber famously put it). Rather, it also requires a cultural, ideological, and conceptual reorientation that transforms the way we value certain relations and the legal structures that govern them.[42] Similarly, Wendy Brown employs a political theory lens to argue that the immense power of today's neoliberal governing rationality lies precisely in its ability to transform and construct 'society, institutions, subjects and the very idea of democracy in market terms'.[43] The economic approach to human behaviour as advanced by Becker and his intellectual cadre contributes to just such a reorientation, by imposing market rationality on *all* spheres of life and domains of society.[44] The novelty, in the case of monetized citizenship, is that such changes dramatically reorient long-standing liberal, civic-republican, and democratic theories of how we govern our collective life and define 'who belongs'. In this sense, it usurps the values underlying alternative conceptions of social ordering. These tendencies become particularly evident in the case of cash-for-passport programmes, which require us to reprogram deeply held cultural beliefs about the institution and ideal of membership in a political community, even while engaging in the constitutive act of *demos*-definition.

---

[40] Ibid., pp. 5, 8 (emphasis added).

[41] Gary S. Becker, 'An Open Door for Immigrants—The Auction', *The Wall Street Journal*, 14 October 1992, p. A1.

[42] Viviana A. Zelizer, *Morals and Markets: The Development of Life Insurance in the United States* (New York: Columbia University Press, 1979). On the 'sacred' aspect of citizenship, see William Rogers Brubaker, 'Immigration, Citizenship and the Nation-State in France and Germany: A Comparative Historical Analysis', *International Sociology* 5 (1990): pp. 379–407.

[43] Wendy Brown, *Undoing the Demos: Neoliberalism's Stealth Revolution* (Cambridge: MIT Press, 2015).

[44] For an early and still influential critical account, Margaret J. Radin, 'Market-Inalienability', *Harvard Law Review* 100 (1987): pp. 1849–1937.

The third defence of citizenship-for-sale programmes focuses on tangible economic benefit; this is the most common rationale offered by governments.[45] At first glance, it seems unquestionable that those states that are willing to put citizenship up for sale —despite public discomfort with the idea of rewarding cash payments with citizenship—reap significant economic benefit from the transaction.[46] As the Chairman of the UK Migration Advisory Committee (an independent non-government think tank, focusing on the economic benefits of migration) put it, there is an assertion, 'strongly [held] by law firms, accountants and consultancies that help organize the affairs of such investors', that selling citizenship is 'self-evidently beneficial'.[47]

Counter-intuitively, however, even the purported economic benefit of such programmes is *not* as obvious as it may appear. Recent studies have shown that 'policy-makers have often found the results disappointing'.[48] Data and analysis has emerged from traditional investor programs such as those in the United States, Canada, Australia, New Zealand, and the United Kingdom, countries that have tried to create some temporal distance between granting membership and monetary transactions. Even in these cases, where residence is required prior to the acquisition of citizenship, comprehensive expert consultation and comparative evidence reveal that we should be highly sceptical of the economic rewards argument.[49]

Two core examples are illustrative. First, in the United States, recent studies have concluded that the government 'cannot demonstrate that the program is improving the U.S. economy and creating jobs for U.S. citizens'.[50] In the same vein, a comprehensive government review of Canada's investor-visa programme, which had been in operation for years until it was abolished in 2014, was characterized by high regulatory costs and proved economically *in*efficient. The Canadian government disclosed that there is 'little evidence that immigrant investors … are maintaining ties to Canada or making a positive economic contribution to the country'. The longitudinal data reveal that 'immigrant investors report employment and investment income below Canadian averages and pay significantly lower taxes over a lifetime'.[51] The expectation that a hypermobile global elite will make hefty deposits in the places

[45] Sumption and Hooper (n 2).
[46] Shaheen Borna and James M. Stearns, 'The Ethics and Efficacy of Selling National Citizenship', *Journal of Business Ethics 37* (2002): pp. 193–207.
[47] Migration Advisory Committee, *The Economic Impact of the Tier 1 (Investor) Route* (London: Migration Advisory Committee, 2013), p. 1.
[48] Sumption and Hooper (n 2), p. 1.   [49] Migration Advisory Committee (n 47), pp. 1–2.
[50] Department of Homeland Security, Office of Inspector General, *United States Citizenship and Immigration Services' Employment-Based Fifth Preference (EB-5) Regional Centre Program* (Washington: OIG-14-19, 2013), p. 1, online http://www.oig.dhs.gov/assets/Mgmt/2014/OIG_14-19_Dec13.pdf.
[51] Government of Canada, Department of Finance, *The Road to Balance: Creating Jobs and Opportunities* (F1-23/3-2014E2, 2014), p. 81, online http://www.budget.gc.ca/2014/docs/plan/pdf/budget2014-eng.pdf.

where they purchase their passports requires '*evidence* rather than assertion' as the UK Migration Advisory Committee powerfully stated.[52] As the Canadian experience demonstrates, once a passport is gained, the passport-purchaser is not 'home' to pay taxes or report employment and investment income overtime.[53] Those on the market for a new passport, or maybe several, clearly gain greater mobility and other potential advantages from the transaction, otherwise they would not engage in it. But the overall economic benefit to the society that ramps up efforts to persuade high-net-worth individuals to take its passport offering is far less clear. The non-monetary cost of shifting the balance of power between states and markets is, alas, real and lasting.

Still, a proponent might argue that short-term increases in budgetary revenue justify such schemes, especially for smaller economies. Here, it is important to examine how precisely the inflows from the sale of citizenship are recorded, managed, held, and used.[54] Political economists would be quick to point out that such monies provide significant flexibility for discretional use by elected officials, partly helping explain why governments are willing to embark on the process of marketization. Another common arrangement is to create a public fund that holds the investment in trust. Evidence from St. Kitts and Nevis, whose government boasts a citizenship-for-sale programme that is the 'oldest of its kind in the world' (launched in 1984, revamped and reformed in 2007, and yet again in 2011 and 2016) reveals that following the programme's restructuring and extensive marketization by a global law firm specializing in 'residence and citizenship planning', it has indeed increased state revenue and is also credited with helping drive several luxury real estate development projects. Political pundits have argued, however, that this sudden boom is unsustainable and that the value and reputation of the country's now-commodified citizenship may diminish quickly with steeper competition or irregularities in the issuance process. It was further revealed that the country's public fund established to manage the proceeds has pumped millions of dollars into the hands of private developers and real estate moguls, whereas ordinary citizens saw little of these returns. This has led to public criticism of the programme.

From the perspective of democratic accountability to the home population, there are recurrent complaints about the lack of transparency of government-created funds into which the non-recoverable fees or donations are directed; as such, there is no guarantee that such monies will be used wisely or 'trickle down' to benefit

---

[52] Migration Advisory Committee (n 47), pp. 1–2.

[53] Harrington develops a related line of argument in relation to attracting the fortunes of foreign investors by facilitating capital mobility and offering them attractive destinations in which to shelter their wealth. See Harrington (n 5), pp. 239–243.

[54] The proceeds may be classified, for example, as non-tax revenue or as capital grants.

members of the recipient society, who remain liable to the non-fungible risks of a discredited passport or loss of reputation if a citizenship-for-sale programme runs into disrepute.

When considering the economic benefits of citizenship-for-sale, then, we must look closely not only at aggregate accounts of the monetary proceeds, but also *who* (or what set of actors, local or transnational) gain from cash-for-passport programmes. The 'lucrative' business of citizenship-for-sale, as it is often referred to, may be lucrative to intermediaries who transact in citizenship or gain from it, or, in extreme cases, government officials who become involved in corrupt behaviour, as was the case in the administration of the golden visa scheme in Portugal. It remains less clear, however, what the average citizen of a passport-selling country may gain.

Selling countries typically offer partial or full tax wavier for those who purchase membership. No similar 'discount' is offered to ordinary citizens who are expected to pay taxes, engage in civic duties such as jury service, and otherwise partake in the social and political life of the community. Those who acquire membership through a paid transaction have no share of the burdens of such non-fungible contributions. Yet it is ordinary citizens who also bear the non-monetary costs of abuse of purchased passports, for example, if they were used in the course of proscribed financial transactions or similarly prohibited acts. This has been a long-standing concern with earlier variants of such programmes, especially in micro-states, but it remains a pressing matter. In 2014, the United States Treasury published a warning that St. Kitts and Nevis had issued passports, without basic identifying details such as the passport holder's place of birth, to 'illicit actors [who were] abusing the program ... in order to mask their identity and geographic background'.[55] Canada soon thereafter revoked St. Kitts and Nevis citizens' visa-free travel, due to security and due diligence concerns about the country's cash-for-passport programme. This is a non-monetary sanction and suspicion that Kittitians and Nevisians who have no other passport (nor the luxury of switching allegiance with the speed of a wire transfer) must now bear.

When sapped of its neoliberal rationale and held up to scrutiny, the marketization of citizenship may be found to benefit significantly a close-knit subset of local and transnational actors, while imposing substantial risk on the whole population and contributing to new and powerful forms of stratification both within states and across borders.

---

[55] U.S. Department of Treasury, Financial Crimes Enforcement Network, FIN-2014-A004, *Advisory: Abuse of Citizenship-by-Investment Program Sponsored by the Federation of St. Kitts and Nevis* (20 May 2014), p.1, online: https://www.fincen.gov/resources/advisories/fincen-advisory-fin-2014-a004.

Arguments Against
Cash-for-Passport Transactions

It is time now to move to a normative exploration of the arguments against sell-ing membership in a political community. Three such lines of critique will be advanced: exacerbating inequality, the intrusion of the market, and the character of citizenship.[56] As I develop these strands of argument, I will move beyond the immediate focus on the distributive dimension in order to speak more directly to the political relational aspect of citizenship. These are not exhaustive of the hazards associated with monetizing citizenship; rather, they provide a foray into the topic, inviting further study.

The first argument is that of *exacerbating inequality*, in its various dimensions. High levels of wealth inequality exist in our world, enabling some individuals to think nothing of paying millions for a passport, while others can barely find the means to subsist. It is clear that citizenship-for-sale programmes would only exacerbate, rather than alleviate, the impact of preexisting economic inequality on the oppor-tunity to gain access to membership in desired destinations.[57] Giving preference to those who can pay hefty sums of cash-for-passport transactions adds yet another barrier to mobility for the majority of the world's non-affluent population.[58] In this way, these programmes contribute to perpetuating and deepening patterns of glo-bal inequality in contemporary mobility regimes and citizenship allocation. So, part of what is troubling about these citizenship-for-sale programmes is that they both reflect and exacerbate existing inequalities and, by extension (many might add), injustices.[59] Call this the global-inequality moral hazard of citizenship-for-sale.

There is now a flourishing discussion in political philosophy articulating the moral limits of markets, raising important concerns about queue jumping, the slip-pery slope, fairness and inequality, and the hollowing out of non-market values and motivations.[60] These accounts bypass, however, the core issue that concerns us

---

[56] These arguments partly intertwine and overlap, but for purposes of analytical clarity, I explore them separately.

[57] Such policies fit under the definition of discretionary migration. See Michael Blake, 'Discretionary Immigration', *Philosophical Topics 30* (2002): pp. 273–289. States are permitted but not bound to adopt them. This is contrast with non-discretionary policies whereby states hold domestic and international obligations towards refugees, asylum seekers, and other vulnerable populations.

[58] Additional barriers compound this inequality in mobility. See Eric Neumayer, 'Unequal Access to Foreign Spaces: How States Use Visa Restrictions to Regulate Mobility in a Globalized World', *Transactions of the Institute of British Georgraphers 31* (2006): pp. 72–84. See also Shachar and Hirschl (n 3).

[59] I thank Sarah Fine for helpful discussions elaborating this point.

[60] Major contributors to this debate include Elizabeth Anderson, Wendy Brown, Steven Lukas, Anne Phillips, Margaret Radin, Michael Sandel, and Debra Satz, among others.

here: the *legal* definition of access to citizenship—the definition of who belongs, or ought to belong—and how it, too, is being recast on the basis of pecuniary considerations and market-based valuations. Most commentators would be hard-pressed, I believe, to contest this global-inequality moral hazard of citizenship-for-sale.

The marketization of citizenship not only facilitates the intrusion of pecuniary considerations into the *demos*-sculpting sphere, it also reshapes the logic of citizenship from a membership bond that may in fact act as a *shield* against inequalities.[61] In the marketization of citizenship, then, concerns about inequality of access, from a global perspective, join forces with the stratification of citizenship in the domestic sphere. Placing a price tag on citizenship signifies a transformation of the criteria of membership from a political to an economic metric, contributing to broader processes of commodification that erode the promise of equality among existing members of the political community. In this, it intervenes in complex ways in debates about the rise and fall of citizenship solidarity within states, just as it illuminates processes that mar inequalities in access to membership globally.[62]

The second strand of critique highlights the *intrusion of the market*, and its imperialistic norms and rationale, into the sphere of the political, hitting at the heart of the sovereign act of delineating the contours of the *demos*. As much as Becker may claim the contrary, these programmes are objectionable not only because they are novel and counterintuitive, but also for deeper, more profound reasons. Citizenship as we know it (at least since Aristotle) is comprised of *political* relations; as such, it is expected to both reflect and generate notions of participation, co-governance, risk-sharing, and some measure of solidarity among those constituting the body politic.[63] It is difficult to imagine how these democratic and reciprocal commitments can be preserved under circumstances in which insiders and outsiders are distinguished merely by their ability to pay a certain price. The objection here is to the notion that *everything*, including political membership, is 'commensurable' and reducible to a dollar value. This sends a loud message that reverberates through the fields of law and social ethics about whom the contemporary market-friendly state prioritizes in the admission line and whom it most covets as future citizens. This expressive conduct and the new grammar of market-infused valuation threatens to rewrite basic

---

[61] This position is associated with the Marshallian tradition, or the ideal of social citizenship.

[62] On the erosion of social citizenship, see Somers (n 16). I do not address here the interests of those who stay in the country of origin, although questions of justice may arise there as well if the millionaire migrant is using the new citizenship to avert public disclosure rules or tax obligations in the home country.

[63] This is of course an idealized vision of citizenship. As Derek Heather observes, the 'status of citizen was in origin and indeed for by far the greatest portion of its history essentially the mark of an elite'. See Derek Heather, *A Brief History of Citizenship* (New York: NYU Press, 2004), p. 143. More inclusive, democratic, and national conceptions of citizenship emerge in the seventeenth century and came to the fore in the late eighteenth century's age of revolution, but left intact many exclusionary grounds. See FitzGerald in this volume; Volpp in this volume; Sadiq in this volume.

expectations about relationship we have with fellow members of our political community once transactional views of citizenship become entrenched.

In today's era of 'market triumphalism' or 'market fundamentalism', as Michael Sandel and Joseph Stiglitz have respectively observed, the economic logic of 'buying and selling no longer applies to material goods alone'.[64] Alas, by imposing market rationality on citizenship and extending it to perhaps the most sensitive and charged aspect of sovereignty—defining whom to admit and include in the body politic—the state is dangerously entering a high-stakes game, which may ultimately undercut its own turf and legitimacy. The invisible hand may prove more efficient at developing mechanisms for trading or auctioning citizenship than those conceived by government lawyers and bureaucrats.[65] On a full marketization scenario, the state may eventually price itself out of the business of regulating membership. It is unlikely that this scenario will materialize any time soon given the keen interest governments hold in controlling and allocating membership goods, but the conceptual shift in the perception of citizenship has already begun. It is the basis for programmes upon which the red carpet is rolled out for those buying their way into the political community. At the same time, there is deep discomfort with the implications of a *market* for citizenship. Perhaps as a result of this ambivalence, we hardly, if ever, find these cash-for-passport programmes mentioned in official study-guides for citizenship tests, which occupy a symbolic standing as 'mission statements' of their admitting societies and reflect a carefully constructed vision of the process of *becoming* members.[66]

Another set of concerns relates to the disintegrating and 'hollowing out' impact of such transactions on citizenship as membership.[67] The core observation here is that such marketization processes facilitate a legal rewriting of the basic logic of emancipatory conceptions of citizenship, giving reign instead to the imperialistic idea that 'trades' and 'transactions' can cover the full terrain of human value and meaning. This reflects a worldview according to which economics trump politics, and membership in the political community—a manifold social and relational web of connections—is reduced into mere purchase-and-sale agreement.

[64] Michael J. Sandel, *What Money Can't Buy: The Moral Limits of Markets* (New York: Farrar, Straus and Giroux, 2012), p. 6; Joseph Stiglitz, 'Moving Beyond Market Fundamentalism to a More Balanced Economy', *Annals of Public and Cooperative Economics 80* (2009): pp. 345–360.

[65] A parallel, clandestine market for smuggling people without authorization is 'a highly profitable business', as the United Nations Office on Drug and Crime recently put it. Migrant smuggling is among the most lucrative illicit trades in the world, often cited together with drugs and weapons. See United Nations Office on Drug and Crime, 'Migrant Smuggling', online https://www.unodc.org/unodc/en/human-trafficking/smuggling-of-migrants.html.

[66] Orgad in this volume; Joppke in this volume; Vink in this volume. Most observers would be at odds if asked to explain how our governments can claim coherence of these apparently conflicting messages.

[67] Bauböck in this volume.

As we saw earlier, transferred funds alone—completely detached from civic or any related requirements—serve as a 'collateral' for the issuance of a new passport. Yet a wire transfer cannot ensure that the newly minted passport will transform the citizen into a member in any recognizable way. If no ties to the new community are established, then the 'value' of citizenship for the purchaser is indeed self-serving and instrumental: it is good to keep when on the rise, better to dispose of when on the decline.[68] If pure maximization of interest undergirds the transaction, it is reasonable to assume that in times of crisis individuals who have simply bought their citizenship, but never had to establish the *relationship* of membership, will dispense themselves of their investment, or seek to recoup it as quickly as possible. Accordingly, when citizenship is no longer profitable to them, investors could simply defect, especially if certain responsibilities of citizenship are suddenly attached to them, such as paying taxes, or, at times of crisis, serving in the military.[69] The passport-buying citizens might then swiftly rescind their citizenship irrespective of what the consequences are (financial, political, and so on) for the country in which they had purchased membership. This is not a particularly solid foundation upon which to build or sustain a political community.

As such, a transactional variant of citizenship may erode the reciprocity and goodwill of those members who contribute to the civic fibre of their societies and habitually reside in them, through good times and bad. Globetrotting well-heeled millionaire migrants who have paid for a passport but never taken on corresponding membership responsibilities, in essence, free-ride on the governance reputation, standards, and civic commitments of the actual members habituating the society whose (purchased) membership goods the buyer seeks to enjoy without helping either to generate or to sustain it. While enjoying tax-exempt 'membership' and visa-free travel, their indiscretion may lead to stricter scrutiny for *all* persons travelling on that country's passport—another non-pecuniary risk of citizenship-for-sale programmes on existing members.

The third theme builds closely on the first and second and speaks to the *character of citizenship*. Cash-for-membership programmes detach the notion of citizenship from any kind of connection—be it residence, attachment, commitment—to the political community. This creates a dissonance between the familiar idea of citizenship as a valuable bond or *relationship* with a polity and its members and a moneyed elite that can nonchalantly 'parachute' into membership.[70]

---

[68] These programmes produce 'paper' citizens: formal status holders who display no societal measures of membership (participation, commitment, rights and duties, and so on). My usage of the term differs here from Kamal Sadiq, who creatively shows how documentary evidence generates visibility in the eyes of the state for the status-less. See Kamal Sadiq, *Paper Citizens: How Illegal Immigrants Acquire Citizenship in Developing Countries* (Oxford: Oxford University Press, 2008).

[69] A similar observation is made by Ana Tanasoca, 'Citizenship for Sale: Neomedieval, Not Just Neoliberal?', *European Journal of Sociology* 57 (2016): pp. 169–195, p. 179.

[70] There is a growing body of literature on citizenship as based on social membership, place-related obligations, performative acts, or equitable grounds. See, for example, Isin in this volume; Joseph H.

While citizenship has been variously defined and has undergone many trans-formations, Rogers Smith observes that the 'oldest, most basic, and most prevalent meaning [of citizenship] is a certain sort of membership in a political community'.[71] Although we know from the historical record that access to equal membership has never been open to all, this emancipatory and aspirational promise has gained tre-mendous staying power ever since the age of revolutions.[72] And while the scale and scope of the membership community has ranged from city-state to empire, citi-zenship has always been associated with *political* relations.[73] If we take as a baseline the view that 'the principal end of political society [i]s the good of its members',[74] whether understood as securing liberty, protecting public order, providing the con-ditions for a system of cooperation and shared participation, or promoting equal respect and non-domination—whatever guiding principles we adopt to organize our collective life, 'citizenship entails more than just buying a good or a service'.[75] It binds members of a community together in a distinctive political and social relation with deep regulatory significance.[76] It is the unique and reciprocal bond between the individual and the state (or other levels of government in multi-level concep-tions of membership) that distinguishes citizenship from traditional master-slave, emperor-subject, producer-consumer, or supply-demand relations of private provi-sion. The recent experience of transition democracies offers a fresh reminder that 'behavior based on civic virtue is required, and that markets cannot substitute for everything'.[77] Our government officials appear to ignore such warnings with impun-ity when they adopt a calculus of profitably. Even if enlarging their coffers may, as a matter of real-life experience, explain *why* some governments create these pro-grammes (again, with the caveat that 'healthy skepticism concerning the benefits normally asserted' is required[78]), as a normative matter, this does not constitute an

Carens, *The Ethics of Immigration* (Oxford: Oxford University Press, 2013); Ayelet Shachar, 'Earned Citizenship: Property Lessons for Immigration Reform', *Yale Journal of Law & the Humanities* 23 (2011): pp. 110–158; Bauböck in this volume; Bosniak in this volume.

[71] Rogers Smith, 'Citizenship: Political', in Neil J. Smelser and Paul B. Baltes, eds., *International Encyclopedia of the Social & Behavioral Studies* (Oxford: Elsevier, 2001), pp. 1857–1860, at p. 1857; Bauböck in this volume.

[72] Unlike classical times, today, gender, race or possessing arms no longer formally define access to (or rather exclusion from) the boundaries of membership, although their lasting impacts are hard to shake off. On the ongoing struggle for expanding the boundaries of membership, see Bosniak in this volume; Donaldson and Kymlicka in this volume; FitzGerald in this volume; Isin in this volume; Volpp in this volume.

[73] On the changing scales of citizenship, see Diener in this volume.

[74] Christopher W. Morris, 'The State', in George Kolsko, ed., *Oxford Handbook of the History of Political Philosophy* (Oxford: Oxford University Press, 2012), pp. 544–560, pp. 544, 557.

[75] Bruno S. Frey, 'Flexible Citizenship for a Global Society', *Politics, Philosophy and Economics* 2 (2003): pp. 93–114, p. 106.

[76] Opinions may reasonably differ on how precisely to define or express such bonds.

[77] Frey (n 75), p. 106.   [78] Migration Advisory Committee (n 47), p. 2.

adequate justification, since this kind of exchange threatens to 'corrupt' and recast the good being sold.[79]

What changes when citizenship is put on sale is not just the price of membership, but its substantive content as well. If political relations, valued in part because they are *not* for sale, become tradable and marketable, the ramifications may prove far-reaching, affecting not only those directly engaged in the transaction, but also broader societal perceptions of how we value these relations.[80] Laws do not simply define categories and guide action; they also constitute that which they purport to describe.[81] Likewise, markets do not just allocate goods; they also 'express and promote certain attitudes toward the goods being exchanged'.[82] Making the ability to pay a condition of citizenship may well erode the civic bonds and practices that allow a society to not merely survive but also thrive.

As citizenship-for-sale programmes play an increasingly important role in countries' selective migration policies and priorities, they may also gradually reshape the greater class of those who are likely to enjoy political membership by distorting democratic mechanisms and prioritizing market choices instead. Were citizenship allocation to become reliant on a price mechanism alone, to the exclusion of other important considerations, not only would the vast majority of the world's population be prevented from ever gaining a chance to access citizenship in well-off polities, but, taken to its logical conclusion (as *reductio*), it might also, over time lead to a dystopian world in which *anyone* included in the pool of members might have to pay to retain their membership status or risk being priced out.

Government programmes that authorize a market in purchasing and selling citizenship, turning its acquisition into a bare-bones monetized transaction, run the risk of diminishing the good itself and the norms that govern its underlying justification and purpose.[83] They may also end up reshaping the class of recipients and ultimately denying membership to those who cannot afford it. Turning citizenship into a paid transaction may contribute to crowding out public-minded motivations that currently provide the 'social glue' binding our institutions and communities.[84]

---

[79] The language of corruption, in the moral sense, is drawn from Sandel (n 64).

[80] For a relational critique of markets, see Debra Satz, *Why Some Things Should Not Be for Sale: The Moral Limits of Markets* (Oxford: Oxford University Press, 2010).

[81] On the expressive function of law, see Cass Sunstein, 'On the Expressive Function of Law', *University of Pennsylvania Law Review 144* (1996): pp. 2021–2053; on 'performative' law, see J. L. Austin, *How to Do Things with Words*, 2nd edition (Cambridge: Harvard University Press, 1975).

[82] Sandel (n 64), p. 9.   [83] Ibid., pp. 110–113.

[84] The erosion of civic commitment has been traced in other areas of public life, whereby a previously non-commodified activity becomes monetized. Perhaps best known is Titmuss' study of blood donation, which concludes with the following observation: 'From our study of the private market in blood in the United States, we have concluded that the commercialization of blood and donor relationships represses the expression of altruism, erodes the sense of community.' See Richard M. Titmuss, *The Gift Relationship: From Human Blood to Social Policy* (New York: New Press, 1970), p. 245.

For-sale programmes thus offer the legal 'shell' of citizenship, but empty it of membership content.

No equality-centred or *nexi*-based conception of membership would accept this recasting without perceiving the significant erosion it causes to the unique bond of citizenship.[85] As an early critic of the monetize-everything approach has memorably observed, 'price and value will sometimes coincide. But often enough money fails to represent value; the translations are made, but as with good poetry, something is lost in the process.'[86] Although we have almost become oblivious to the manifold ways in which the language of the market now invades every corner of our lives, the realm of citizenship is—and on these accounts, ought to remain—distinct. The public domain of rights and relations that makes up our political communities and enshrines the expression, symbolic or actual, of our legal standing as equal members—the bedrock principle underlying citizenship—cannot, without undermining itself, substitute membership for money.

Concluding Remarks and Future Directions for Research

New laws and regulations generated in the era of market citizenship allow wealth to become a golden passport. I have argued that reliance on the depth of one's pockets as a basis for granting access to membership tests our deepest intuitions about the relationship between the individual and the political community to which she belongs. As such, it offers a rare window through which to explore underlying tensions and questions about the future of citizenship. Unless confronted head-on, the prospering transactional approach may irrevocably and irreversibly rewrite citizenship as we know it, crowding out its association with political *demos*, paradoxically replacing it with government-sponsored market-oriented rationality and valuation in determining whom, among those not born as citizens, to lawfully admit as 'worthy' new members.

---

[85] I have elsewhere elaborated the *jus nexi* principle, accounting for the kinds of links and ties to a political community that may serve as an equitable basis for accessing membership when no other lawful ground for membership acquisition is present. See Shachar (n 70). Related ideas refer to notions of a stakeholder society, or to the importance of social membership in determining access to citizenship. See Rainer Bauböck, 'Expansive Citizenship—Voting beyond Territory and Membership', *Political Science and Politics 38* (2005): pp. 683–687; Carens (n 70).

[86] Walzer (n 27), p. 97.

Governments today are willing to adjust and reinterpret sovereignty and citizenship in profoundly flexible ways, making mobility more readily available in attracting 'high-net-worth' migrants, especially the rich and affluent, while imposing tighter restriction on other categories of would-be entrants. Our affiliation to a given state and society (even if defined primarily in legalistic rather than participatory terms), resists the idea that such membership relies on profit-maximizing considerations. Collapsing the logic of states into markets, by diluting their competing values and commitments and making personal wealth a precondition of political membership, threatens to eviscerate citizenship from within. It poisons the political ideal of a common enterprise committed to promoting equality, rights, and collective decision-making through processes of deliberation and participation. It places profit, self-interest, and personal gain, values we typically associate with the market, in a sphere to which they do not belong: membership in the polity. Accordingly, even in a world untainted by the injustice of disparities of power and influence, the principled argument would still hold that 'there are some things that money can't buy'.

No one is claiming that the prevailing principles for allocating access to citizenship—primarily according to morally arbitrary circumstances of where or to whom we are born (the *jus soli* and *jus sanguinis* principles, respectively), which affect the vast majority of the world's population through the birthright lottery, and in turn, are correlated to vastly unequal life chances—are free from profound quandaries and injustices. I have devoted a whole book to arguing just that and to critically reflecting on the inadequacy of existing conditions and the urgent need to challenge and amend entrenched models of fixed, entail-like, birthright citizenship regimes.[87] Yet it would be deeply misguided to conclude that the best way to overcome our current predicament is to give primacy instead the vicissitudes of market forces and the 'invisible hand'.

While it is impossible to read the tea leaves of the future of citizenship, several lessons can be drawn. First, there is nothing inevitable about the rise of a more transactional approach to citizenship. Global competitive pressures and neoliberal rationality surely push in the direction of greater marketization, but there are counter forces that may reverse or halt this trend. We might call this the 'de-marketization' response. Such a scenario may emerge if the marketization policy becomes too costly for policymakers to support, especially if it leads to political resistance and resentment, domestic or international. Such a scenario is not merely speculative; we have already seen it unfold in practice. Two recent examples highlight this. In 2015, Hong Kong closed down its highly successful investor migrant programme, following a growing tide of criticism that, among other concerns, this priced out the local population from necessary essentials, such as housing, a perennial issue in densely populated Hong Kong. In 2014, following a comprehensive longitudinal review,

---

[87] Ayelet Shachar, *The Birthright Lottery: Citizenship and Global Inequality* (Cambridge, MA: Harvard University Press, 2009).

the Canadian government terminated the country's investment route after concluding that the programme, which was popular with the world's ultra-rich (more than 40,000 applications were backlogged when the programme closed down), had failed to fulfil the stated goals of economic growth and increased foreign investment that had provided the official justification for its adoption in the first place.

Another set of constrains may emerge at the international level. No state is an island. Even in a world system guided by the principle of respect for the sovereign prerogative of each political community to define its own citizenship laws and naturalization rules, other countries, acting alone or in concert, may impact and change the calculus of a government adopting cash-for-passport policies. Concerns about programme integrity, for example, may cause other countries to restrict visa-free travel privileges for the citizens of passport-selling countries. If we follow the logic of the transactional view of citizenship, the value of a passport is in no small part reliant on its recognition by third parties *outside* the issuing country; without such recognition the value plummets.[88]

In the context of regional unions or multinational organizations, the 'unscrupulous' conduct of citizenship-selling states may potentially be tamed by credible threats of removal from the club or curtailed membership. When supranational citizenship is engaged, as in the case in the EU, it is not implausible to imagine future claims of breach of solidarity (or lack of sincere cooperation) and abuse of right against member states that blatantly commodify citizenship.[89] As lawyers would put it, such action is not neutral with regard to other member states or the Union. As such, these parties would arguably be justified to take action to tame such rampant commodification, or at least qualify the terms of the proposed 'bill of sale'.

At least in principle, under current international law, country X may refuse to recognize beneficiaries of form-over-substance citizenship issued by country Y (a passport 'selling' country) under certain circumstances due to lack of a genuine connection. One of history's little ironies is that *Nottebohm*, the main precedential case in this field, was decided by the International Court of Justice following an early exemplar of citizenship for sale: Mr. Nottebohm bought his Lichtensteinian citizenship through a 'donation' of 37,500 Swiss Francs and a commitment to play 1,000 Swiss Francs annually in taxes. This purchased membership was not backed up by any real or effective links to the citizenship-selling country. The International Court of Justice ruled that although each state is sovereign to determine its own citizenship and criteria for its acquisition under domestic law, on the international plane, a meaningful connection between the individual and the state must be established.[90]

---

[88] If the purchase of a new passport is designed primarily to allow the new 'citizen' greater mobility, e.g., by virtue of benefiting from a given country's visa-waiver programmes, then the risk of loss of value is further aggravated.

[89] *Rotmann* may serve a potential legal precedent in European context. Judgment of 2 March 2010, *Janko Rotmann v. Freistaat of Bayren* C-135/08, E.C.R. I-01449, EU:C:2010:104.

[90] This ruling referred specifically to questions of diplomatic protection.

In another recent twist, international human rights bodies, such as the United Nations Human Rights Committees, may take a stance against government-*imposed* purchase of citizenship in a third country. Such a scenario may occur when officials in a given country, call it Wealthiana, go on a shopping spree to 'relocate' to another country the membership claims of unwanted ethnic minority populations, potentially against their will and without their knowledge. The idea that one country will buy citizenship from another country to *dis*enfranchise some of its long-term residents and avoid granting them citizenship may sound more fitting for a dystopian novel than for twenty-first-century citizenship law, but precisely such a narrative emerged when Kuwait purchased Comoros citizenship for its *bidoon* population. The UN Human Rights Committee commented on the practice in its 2016 report on Kuwait, holding explicitly that the country should 'set aside plans to offer "Bidoon" the "economic citizenship" of another country'.

These comments speak loudly to the deeper concern at issue: once citizenship is merely determined by the transfer of cash and detached from any membership reference, nothing stands in the way of governments that may wish to disenfranchise 'unwanted' resident populations through the compulsory purchase of citizenship-in-another-country. This is the dark side of commodification, informed, paradoxically, by the very same logic of marketization that permits volitional citizenship-for-sale transactions between willing government and eager clients.

Even if these taming measures were in place (which is a far cry from today's reality), it is quite possible that wallet-size-based access priorities will emerge as increasingly prevalent at the expense of other, more humanistic, pluralistic, and non-pecuniary interpretations. This will make entry, settlement, and naturalization reliant upon credit lines rather than civic ties. Echoing larger processes of stratification, the surge in privileged access to membership-for-the-rich risks aggravating inequality, accentuating already deeply stratified global mobility and migration patterns, and further contributing, as we have seen, to the 'hollowing out' of citizenship from within. The mismatched confluence of market values and membership privileges counters the notion that the state belongs to the people—not to a wealth oligarchy. It unravels the basic political legitimacy upon which popular sovereignty is founded, the same legitimacy that makes citizenship attractive as a *non*market good.

As critics of commodification have been at pains to clarify in other contexts, it is not that €1 million is too high or too low a price, but that placing citizenship 'for sale', no matter what the asking price, corrodes non-market relations, unraveling the ties that bind and altering our view of what it means to belong to a political community. Just as we should be critical of granting citizenship according to nothing but the fortuitous and arbitrary circumstances of birth, we must resist, with even greater force, the notion that money can buy 'love of country'—or secure membership in it.

BIBLIOGRAPHY

Austin, J. L., *How to Do Things with Words*, 2nd edition (Cambridge: Harvard University Press, 1975).

Bauböck, Rainer, 'Expansive Citizenship—Voting beyond Territory and Membership', *Political Science and Politics 38* (2005): pp. 683–687.

Becker, Gary S., *The Economic Approach to Human Behavior* (Chicago: University of Chicago Press, 1976).

Becker, Gary S. 'An Open Door for Immigrants—The Auction', *The Wall Street Journal*, 14 October 1992, A1.

Blake, Michael, 'Discretionary Immigration', *Philosophical Topics 30* (2002): pp. 273–289.

Bloemraad, Irene, Anna Korteweg, and Gökçe Yurdakul, 'Citizenship and Immigration: Multiculturalism, Assimilation, and Challenges to the Nation-State', *Annual Review of Sociology 34* (2008): pp. 153–179, doi: 10.1146/annurev.soc.34.040507.134608.

Borna, Shaheen and James M. Stearns, 'The Ethics and Efficacy of Selling National Citizenship', *Journal of Business Ethics 37* (2002): pp. 193–207.

Brown, Wendy, *Undoing the Demos: Neoliberalism's Stealth Revolution* (Cambridge: MIT Press, 2015).

Brubaker, William Rogers, 'Immigration, Citizenship and the Nation-State in France and Germany: A Comparative Historical Analysis', *International Sociology 5* (1990): pp. 379–407.

Cap-Gemini, *World Wealth Report* (Paris: Cap-Gemini, 2015).

Carens, Joseph H., *The Ethics of Immigration* (Oxford: Oxford University Press, 2013).

Department of Homeland Security, Office of Inspector General, *United States Citizenship and Immigration Services' Employment-Based Fifth Preference (EB-5) Regional Centre Program* (Washington: OIG-14-19, 2013), online http://www.oig.dhs.gov/assets/Mgmt/2014/OIG_14-19_Dec13.pdf.

Džankic, Jelena, 'Investment-based Citizenship and Residence Programmes in the EU', EUI Working Paper no. 08 (Florence: RSCAS, 2015).

van Fossen, Anthony, 'Citizenship for Sale: Passports of Convenience from Pacific Island Tax Havens', *Commonwealth & Comparative Politics 45* (2007): pp. 138–163.

Frey, Bruno S., 'Flexible Citizenship for a Global Society', *Politics, Philosophy and Economics 2* (2003): pp. 93–114.

Goodin, Robert, 'Enfranchising All Affected Interests, and Its Alternatives', *Philosophy and Public Affairs 35* (2007): pp. 40–68.

Government of Canada, Department of Finance, *The Road to Balance: Creating Jobs and Opportunities* (F1-23/3-2014E2, 2014), p. 81, online http://www.budget.gc.ca/2014/docs/plan/pdf/budget2014-eng.pdf.

Hammar, Tomas, *Democracy and the Nation State: Aliens, Denizens and Citizens in a World of International Migration* (Aldershot: Ashgate, 1990).

Harrington, Brooke, *Capital without Borders: Wealth Managers and the One Percent* (Cambridge, MA: Harvard University Press, 2016).

Harvey, David, *A Brief History of Neoliberalism* (Oxford: Oxford University Press, 2005).

Heather, Derek, *A Brief History of Citizenship* (New York: NYU Press, 2004).

Henley and Partners, 'Citizenship-by-Investment', online https://www.henleyglobal.com/citizenship-by-investment/.

Joppke, Christian, 'Transformation of Citizenship: Status, Rights, Identity', *Citizenship Studies 11* (2007): pp. 37–48, doi: dx.doi.org/10.1080/13621020601099831.

Jordan, Bill and Frank Düvell, *Migration: The Boundaries of Equality and Justice* (Cambridge: Polity, 2003).

Ley, David, *Millionaire Migrants: Trans-Pacific Life Lines* (Malden: Wiley-Blackwell, 2010).

Migration Advisory Committee, *The Economic Impact of the Tier 1 (Investor) Route* (London: Migration Advisory Committee, 2013).

Morris, Christopher W., 'The State', in George Kolsko, ed., *Oxford Handbook of the History of Political Philosophy* (Oxford: Oxford University Press, 2012), pp. 544–560.

Neumayer, Eric, 'Unequal Access to Foreign Spaces: How States Use Visa Restrictions to Regulate Mobility in a Globalized World', *Transactions of the Institute of British Geographers 31* (2006): pp. 72–84.

Ong, Aihwa, *Flexible Citizenship: The Cultural Logic of Transnationality* (Durham: Duke University Press, 1999).

Radin, Margaret J., 'Market-Inalienability', *Harvard Law Review 100* (1987): pp. 1849–1937.

Sadiq, Kamal, *Paper Citizens: How Illegal Immigrants Acquire Citizenship in Developing Countries* (Oxford: Oxford University Press, 2008).

Sandel, Michael J., *What Money Can't Buy: The Moral Limits of Markets* (New York: Farrar, Straus and Giroux, 2012).

Satz, Debra, *Why Some Things Should Not Be for Sale: The Moral Limits of Markets* (Oxford: Oxford University Press, 2010).

Shachar, Ayelet, 'The Race for Talent: Highly Skilled Migrants and Competitive Immigration Regimes', *NYU Law Review 81* (2006): pp. 148–206.

Shachar, Ayelet, *The Birthright Lottery: Citizenship and Global Inequality* (Cambridge, MA: Harvard University Press, 2009).

Shachar, Ayelet, 'Earned Citizenship: Property Lessons for Immigration Reform', *Yale Journal of Law & the Humanities 23* (2011): pp. 110–158.

Shachar, Ayelet, *Olympic Citizenship: Migration and the Global Race for Talent* (Oxford: Oxford University Press, forthcoming 2018).

Shachar, Ayelet and Ran Hirschl, 'On Citizenship, States, and Markets', *Journal of Political Philosophy 22* (2014): pp. 231–257.

Smith, Rogers, 'Citizenship: Political', in Neil J. Smelser and Paul B. Baltes, eds., *International Encyclopedia of the Social & Behavioral Studies* (Oxford: Elsevier, 2001), pp. 1857–1860.

Somers, Margaret R., *Genealogies of Citizenship: Markets, Statelessness, and the Right to Have Rights* (Cambridge: Cambridge University Press, 2008).

Stiglitz, Joseph, 'Moving Beyond Market Fundamentalism to a More Balanced Economy', *Annals of Public and Cooperative Economics 80* (2009): pp. 345–360.

Sumption, Madeline and Kate Hooper, *Selling Visas and Citizenship: Policy Questions from the Global Boom in Investor Immigration* (Washington: Migration Policy Institute, 2014).

Sunstein, Cass R., 'Incommensurability and Valuation in Law', *Michigan Law Review 92* (1994): pp. 779–861.

Sunstein, Cass R., 'On the Expressive Function of Law', *University of Pennsylvania Law Review 144* (1996): pp. 2021–2053.

Tanasoca, Ana, 'Citizenship for Sale: Neomedieval, Not Just Neoliberal?', *European Journal of Sociology 57* (2016): pp. 169–195.

Titmuss, Richard M., *The Gift Relationship: From Human Blood to Social Policy* (New York: New Press, 1970).

Torpey, John, 'Coming and Going: On the State Monoplization of the Legitimate "Means of Movement"', *Sociological Theory 16* (1998): pp. 235–259.

Triadafilopoulos, Triadafilos, ed., *Wanted and Welcome? Policies for Highly Skilled Immigrants in Comparative Perspective* (New York: Springer, 2013).

United Nations Office on Drug and Crime, 'Migrant Smuggling', online https://www.unodc.org/unodc/en/human-trafficking/smuggling-of-migrants.html.

United States Department of Treasury, Financial Crimes Enforcement Network. FIN-2014-A004, *Advisory: Abuse of Citizenship-by-Investment Program Sponsored by the Federation of St. Kitts and Nevis* (20 May 2014), online: https://www.fincen.gov/resources/advisories/fincen-advisory-fin-2014-a004.

Vujnovic, Marina, 'Marketization', in George Ritzer, ed., *Wiley-Blackwell Encyclopedia of Globalization* (Blackwell Publishing, 2012).

Walzer, Michael, *Spheres of Justice: A Defense of Pluralism and Equality* (New York: Basic Books, 1983).

Zelizer, Viviana A., *Morals and Markets: The Development of Life Insurance in the United States* (New York: Columbia University Press, 1979).

Legal Sources

Judgment of 2 March 2010, *Janko Rotmann v. Freistaat of Bayren* C-135/08, E.C.R. I-01449, EU:C:2010:104.

Nottebohm Case (Liechtenstein v. Guatemala) [1955] I.C.J. 1.

CHAPTER 36

CITIZENSHIP AND MEMBERSHIP DUTIES TOWARD QUASI-CITIZENS

ROGERS M. SMITH

Two debates form the starting points for this chapter. The first is the disputation, beginning in the 1990s, over whether nation-states and nation-state citizenships are declining in significance in comparison to other forms of political community and membership. The second is contestation over what, in any case, the obligations of existing state governments are to various groups that are not officially their resident citizens—especially alien residents; the residents of other states with whom a government has treaty alliances or regional association memberships; the residents of states with which a particular government was formerly associated, often as a colonizer or colony; and residents of other states with whom a nation-state believes it shares an ethnocultural or ideological identity. Analysts have classified as 'quasi-citizens' those persons who possess some rights and duties of membership in states that do not recognize them as full citizens.[1] Many in all these categories claim at least such status. Though the debate over the decline of nation-states has itself declined somewhat in recent years, it has not ended. Debates over the rights and duties of those who claim at least to be 'quasi-citizens' of various states are central to many of the most important issues in world politics today.

The main arguments advanced here are that, although the end of the global political era in which nation-states have been the dominant form of political community is not yet in sight, significant transformations are under way. These transformations are primarily enabled by new forms of communication and transportation in tandem with economic, security, and cultural interests. The changes both reflect and create moral obligations on the part of states to various groups of 'quasi-citizens', including duties resting in part on past and present coercive uses of governmental powers. Those obligations should over time be better fulfilled; and seeking to do so will in all likelihood work to lessen further the primacy of sovereign, exclusionary nation-states in the structuring of politics and political communities around the globe.

THE 'END OF NATION-STATES' DEBATE

In 1995, when the new World Trade Organization replaced the post-World War II General Agreement on Trade and Tariffs, two different books appeared in English bearing the same title: the Japanese management consultant and soon-to-be UCLA public affairs professor Kenichi Ohmae's *The End of the Nation-State: The Rise of Regional Economies*, and the French diplomat Jean-Marie Guéhenno's *The End of the Nation-State*.[2] That same year, Canadian political scientist David Elkins published *Beyond Sovereignty: Territory and Political Economy in the 21st Century*, and the next year the cosmopolitan sociologist Saskia Sassen added *Losing Control? Sovereignty in an Age of Globalization*.[3] By then Turkish sociologist Yasemin Soysal had spurred wide discussion by publishing *The Limits of Citizenship*, which proclaimed that a

---

[1] Quasi-citizens are sometimes contrasted with 'semi-citizens', who do possess official citizenship but lack certain rights and duties. See Bauböck in this volume; Elizabeth F. Cohen, *Semi-Citizenship in Democratic Politics* (New York: Cambridge University Press, 2009).

[2] Kenichi Ohmae, *The End of the Nation-State: The Rise of Regional Economies* (New York: Free Press, 1995); Jean-Marie Guéhenno, *The End of the Nation-State*, translated by Victoria Elliott (Minneapolis: University of Minnesota Press, 1995).

[3] David Elkins, *Beyond Sovereignty: Territory and Political Economy in the 21st Century* (Toronto: University of Toronto Press 1995); Saskia Sassen, *Losing Control? Sovereignty in an Age of Globalization* (New York: Columbia University Press, 1996).

'new and more universal concept of citizenship has unfolded in the post-war era, one whose organizing and legitimating principles are based on universal person-hood rather than national belonging.'[4] These and kindred works precipitated controversies in many countries and in many disciplines, including political science, law, international relations, sociology, economics, philosophy, cultural studies, and more, about whether economic globalization, the Internet and other new systems of communication and transportation, heightened immigration, multiplying international human rights and trade agreements, along with international economic institutions like the WTO and transnational associations of all sorts, were actually making nation-states obsolete.

For a time, the trending answer appeared to be yes. Even if a world state of cosmopolitan citizens still seemed to most a remote utopia or dystopia, the European Union created a supra-national form of European citizenship via the Maastricht Treaty of 1992, helping to propel kindred efforts in Africa and South America.[5] The world's most powerful nation, the U.S., promised to subject its economy to regional dispute resolution processes when it signed the North American Free Trade Agreement that same year; and after ratifications, NAFTA became a reality in 1994. And nation-states not only acceded to the development of new international and regional authorities: simultaneously, new pressures for devolution arose within many regimes. Even long-established states like Great Britain and Spain felt compelled to grant greater measures of autonomy to regions, including Scotland and Catalonia, which saw themselves as distinct nations.[6] For these and many other reasons, scholars and commentators thought the predominance of nation-states might indeed be ending.

Then most leading nation-states heightened their efforts at border control after the September 11, 2001 attacks. Subsequent terrorist assaults, as well as a series of refugee crises sparked by warfare and disasters tied to climate change, which only seemed to mount as the twenty-first century proceeded, reinforced these initiatives. Nationalist movements that included protests against immigration, international trade agreements, and transnational economic institutions also surged in many parts of the world, especially northern and central Europe, but with important counterparts in the U.S., Russia, South and East Asia, and elsewhere. In light of these and other developments, many—probably most—analysts came to argue, as Rogers Brubaker did in 2015, that nation-states were displaying 'persisting significance,' with powers that were 'in some respects increasing rather than declining.'[7]

---

[4] Yasemin Soysal, *The Limits of Citizenship: Migrants and Postnational Membership in Europe* (Chicago: University of Chicago Press, 1994), p. 1.

[5] Willem Maas, *Creating European Citizens* (Lanham: Rowman & Littlefield, 2007); Maas in this volume; Strumia in this volume.

[6] Scott L. Greer, *Nationalism and Self-Government: The Politics of Autonomy in Scotland and Catalonia* (Albany: State University of New York Press, 2007); Jaime Lluch, *Visions of Sovereignty: Nationalism and Accommodation in Multinational Democracies* (Philadelphia: University of Pennsylvania Press, 2014).

[7] Rogers Brubaker, *Grounds for Difference* (Cambridge: Harvard University Press, 2015), pp. 7, 126.

At the same time, however, Brubaker conceded that 'the exclusive claims of the nation-state' to governmental authority 'have been eroded,' and that the world was witnessing 'an expansion and strengthening of states' ties to transborder populations and of transborder populations' claims on "homeland" states.'[8] Those ties are both formal and informal and greatly varied, as are the rights and claims to which they give rise. As David Cook-Martín has shown, the number of states formally permitting dual nationality 'quintupled between 1959 and 2005,' largely out of efforts by states to maintain or establish connections with highly desirable potential immigrants.[9] Since the fall of the Soviet Union, many central and eastern European states have also adopted policies that provide easier access to repatriation, as well as dual nationality and various economic benefits, to those they deem their ethnocultural 'compatriots.'[10] Increasingly, states are in fact granting such 'diaspora' populations voting rights, even when they have not been resident in their 'homelands' for many years, if at all, a practice that predictably has defenders and critics.[11] These developments have not by any means shown that nation-states are on the way out, since they are often devices for existing states to strengthen themselves through attracting new constituents and resources. Still, they have added to the already considerable complexities of the second debate with which this chapter is concerned, the obligations of states to various classes of non-citizens.

THE 'SPECIAL OBLIGATIONS' DEBATE

For many years most normative disputes over the significance of political memberships focused primarily on the opposition between obligations owed to fellow

[8] Ibid., pp. 126, 142.

[9] David Cook-Martín, *The Scramble for Citizens: Dual Nationality and State Competition for Immigrants* (Stanford: Stanford University Press, 2013), pp. 154, 159. Cf. Randal Hansen and Patrick Weil, eds., *Dual Nationality, Social Rights and Federal Citizenship in the U.S. and Europe* (New York: Berghahn Books, 2002); Spiro in this volume.

[10] Osuma Ieda, ed., *Beyond Sovereignty: From Status Law to Transnational Citizenship?* (Sapporo: Slavic Research Center, Hokkaido University, 2006); Myra Waterbury, 'From Irredentism to Diaspora Politics: States and Transborder Ethnic Groups in Eastern Europe,' Global Migration and Transnational Politics Working Paper no. 6 (July 2009), online https://www.gmu.edu/centers/globalstudies/publications/gmtpwp/gmtp_wp_6.pdf; Aleksandra Maatsch, *Ethnic Citizenship Regimes: Europeanization, Post-War Migration, and Redressing Past Wrongs* (Basingstoke, New York: Palgrave Macmillan, 2011).

[11] David Owen, 'Transnational Membership and the Democratic State: Modes of Membership and Voting Rights,' *Critical Review of Social and International Philosophy* 14, no. 5 (2011): pp. 641–663, doi: 10.1080/13698230.2011.617123; Jean-Michel Lafleur, *Transnational Politics and the State: The External Voting Rights of Diasporas* (New York: Routledge, 2013); Collyer in this volume.

national citizens versus obligations to humanity at large; and much valuable writing still does.[12] But the growth of non-citizen immigrant populations in many advanced industrial societies, and more recently the multiplication of different forms of transnational affiliations as just described, have turned attention to the normative claims of an internally variegated intermediate class: those with whom a nation-state has 'special' relationships that it does not have to all humankind, but who are still not its formal, legal citizens.[13] Some 'special' obligations, to be sure, are explicitly undertaken by states when they sign international agreements, treaties, and conventions that govern their treatment of refugees, asylum seekers, immigrants, environmental, energy, and labor policies, trade relations, joint security, humanitarian, educational, and cultural endeavors, and much more. Others are imposed by their own domestic statutes. But debates over the content of those 'positive law' obligations often invoke broader moral claims. Against longstanding legal and political assertions that states have obligations only to their own citizens, many contend that a variety of moral standards impose special obligations on some or all states even in the absence of formally adopted laws or agreements. Arguments about what nation-states owe to these various types of 'quasi-citizens' have proliferated in recent years. A far from definitive categorization of them is as follows:

All Affected Interests Arguments. The eminent democratic theorist Robert Dahl long stressed that there is a strong case for including in democratic decision-making all minimally competent persons whose basic interests are affected by the decisions in question—though his concern that democracies not be too large for viable participation made him stress this view only in regard to those who already resided within a political society, not transients or those living elsewhere.[14] With qualifications, Ian Shapiro and Robert Goodin have gone further, contending that a 'principle of affected interests' argues for restructuring decision-making processes in ways that often do not map onto existing boundaries.[15] Like Dahl, however, many

[12] E.g. Christopher Heath Wellman, 'Friends, Compatriots, and Special Obligations,' *Political Theory* 29, no. 1 (2001): pp. 217–236, online http://www.jstor.org/stable/3072510; David Miller, *National Responsibility and Global Justice* (Oxford: Oxford University Press, 2007); Nils Holtug, 'The Cosmopolitan Strikes Back,' *Ethics and Global Politics* 4, no. 3 (2011): pp. 147–163, doi: 10.3402/egp. v4i3.5873.

[13] E.g. Veit Bader, 'Reasonable Impartiality and Priority for Compatriots: A Criticism of Liberal Nationalism's Main Flaws,' *Ethical Theory and Moral Practice* 8, no. 1–2 (2005): pp. 83–103, doi: 10.1007/s10677-005-3292-6; Robert E. Goodin, 'Enfranchising All Affected Interests, and Its Alternatives,' *Philosophy and Public Affairs* 35, no. 1 (2009): pp. 40–68, doi: 10.1111/j.1088-4963.2007.00098.x; Rainer Bauböck, 'The Rights and Duties of External Citizenship,' *Citizenship Studies* 13, no. 5 (2009): pp. 475–499, doi: 10.1080/13621020903174647; Arish Abizadeh, 'Democratic Theory and Border Coercion: No Right to Unilaterally Control Your Own Borders,' *Political Theory* 36, no. 1 (2008): pp. 37–65, doi: 10.1177/0090591707310090.

[14] E.g. Robert A. Dahl, *After the Revolution? Authority in a Good Society*, revised edition (New Haven: Yale University Press, 1990) [1970], p. 51; Robert A. Dahl, *Democracy and Its Critics* (New Haven: Yale University Press, 1989), pp. 146–148.

[15] Ian Shapiro, *Democratic Justice* (New Haven: Yale University Press,1999), pp. 38–39; Goodin (n 13).

recent critics have expressed concern that this principle creates too many obligations to non-citizens, including extensions of voting rights and perhaps citizenship itself, thereby creating huge political communities, perhaps even a world state,
which would inevitably lack many vital features of democratic self-governance.[16]
Shapiro himself contends that the principle requires not a world state but rather the
construction of different electorates for different topics, 'disaggregating the demos
decision by decision'—clearly a complex challenge.[17]

   Social Membership Arguments. Many writers have also long contended that the
sociological reality of residing over time within a political community, so that persons' interests, attachments, and aspirations are all bound up with that society, create virtually irrefutable claims to recognition and rights as full members of that
political community—a case that Joseph Carens has made most thoroughly.[18] Citing
the seminal 1955 *Nottebohm* ruling of the International Court of Justice, Ayelet
Shachar has called for legal systems to adopt these arguments formally as a rule of
jus nexi membership, defined as giving 'legal recognition' for 'real and genuine ties
fostered on the ground.'[19] A subset of these analysts maintain that social memberships should be understood to include social networks that link persons to communities outside the borders of the countries in which they reside, including their
ancestral homelands or other nations to which they have close ties.[20] Usually these
multiple social memberships are understood to justify dual or multiple citizenships.[21] Yet even though almost all normative theorists agree that significant moral
weight should be given to the empirical facts of social membership, some contend
that, precisely because today transnational associations of many sorts are so ubiquitous, the sociological realities of interconnections alone cannot provide much
guidance as to what kinds of relationships with non-residents should be understood
to justify particular rights or forms of citizenship, or what those rights should be.[22]

   Stakeholder Arguments. One of the leading expositors of that concern, Rainer
Bauböck, has argued in an influential series of works for an alternative 'stakeholder
principle,' which would extend citizenship and political rights in particular communities to those who '(a) depend on that community for long-term protection of their
basic rights (*dependency criterion*) or (b) are or have been subjected to that community's political authorities for a significant period over the course of their lives

---

[16] E.g. Sarah Song, 'The Boundary Problem in Democratic Theory: Why the Demos Should Be
Bounded by the State,' *International Theory* 4, no. 1 (2012): pp. 39–68, doi: 10.1017/S1752971911000248,
at p. 41; Bauböck (n 1).

[17] Ian Shapiro, *Politics against Domination* (Cambridge: Harvard University Press, 2016), p. 115.

[18] E.g. Joseph H. Carens, *The Ethics of Immigration* (New York: Oxford University Press, 2013).
Donaldson and Kymlicka, in this volume, argue that membership concerns should extend to recognition of more extensive citizenship rights for animals, as well as children and cognitively disabled
persons.

[19] Ayelet Shachar, *The Birthright Lottery: Citizenship and Global Inequality* (Cambridge: Harvard
University Press, 2009), p. 169.

[20] Owen (n 11), p. 649.   [21] Spiro (n 9).   [22] Bauböck (n 13), p. 482; Bauböck (n 1).

(*biographical subjection criterion*).[23] Bauböck views his principle as less expansive, and so as more politically feasible as well as more morally defensible, than the 'all affected' principle or even 'social membership' views. For that very reason, he has been criticized for defining the rights of 'external citizens' too narrowly. Bauböck resists, for example, extending voting rights to second-generation expatriates, who may still have strong social ties to their homeland but who are neither dependent on it for protection nor substantially subjected to its authority. Others see the social ties as sufficient to justify enfranchisement.[24]

All Subjected or Coerced Persons Arguments. A final class of arguments resembles the second part of Bauböck's stakeholder principle, with its concern for those subjected to a political community's authority. But they modify that concern by shifting from the obligations of states to populations over whom the states claim *authority*, to populations over whom the states have actually exercised *coercion*. Though different scholars interpret 'coercion' more and less expansively, for all it includes a state's threatened or actual use of physical force to constrain behavior. And for proponents of many political traditions, a state's use of force creates at least one obligation: whether out of respect for the value of autonomy, personhood, human dignity, human moral capabilities, human basic needs, human well-being, membership in a global human community, equal rights to life, liberty, and the pursuit of happiness, or some other core political commitment, when states coerce persons, they must justify their coercion, certainly to themselves, and as far as possible to those they coerce.[25] Doing so requires in the first place reflecting on what their own moral commitments demand of them. And in the course of such reflections, the leaders and citizens of nation-states may decide they are morally compelled to recognize other obligations beyond merely seeking to justify their coercive acts.

Although Robert Dahl was probably the first to advance the 'principle of all affected interests' as a guide to the proper boundaries for democratic membership, David Owen argues convincingly that Dahl's real focus was on persons 'subject to the binding decisions' of a political community, so that we should attribute to him an 'all subjected persons principle'.[26] This principle is less inclusive than the 'all affected interests' position, since more persons may be significantly 'affected' by a governmental decision than can strictly be said to be 'bound' by it. Concentrating on those 'bound' by a state's decisions means, however, that the principle is (and is designed to be) far more a guide to the rights of persons already being governed within existing political societies than it is a formula for determining who should count as members or citizens of various societies.[27]

---

[23] Bauböck (n 13), p. 479; Bauböck (n 1).   [24] Owen (n 11), p. 660.

[25] See the related discussion by Owen in this volume.

[26] Dahl, *Democracy and Its Critics* (n 14), p. 129; Owen (n 11), p. 645. See also Bauböck (n 1) (arguing similarly and identifying other 'coercion' accounts).

[27] Dahl, *Democracy and Its Critics* (n 14), p. 148.

But because being 'subject to the binding decisions' of a state inescapably invokes the possibility of being coerced by that state, whenever it seeks to insure that its decisions *are* binding, this 'all subjected persons' principle can be interpreted to rest in part on the intuition that persons coerced by a state presumptively have moral claims against it. For Dahl, those claims arose from a right to 'personal autonomy' that all minimally competent adults equally deserve.[28] Sharing this value, Arash Abizadeh and others note that many coercive policies such as immigration restrictions are enforced, if not actively against everyone in the world, at least against everyone who seeks entry in violation of them, not only and indeed not primarily against the current citizens of a particular state.[29] So if 'all subjected persons' arguments are taken to require the provision of democratic voice to all persons coerced by a state's decisions, many millions if not billions worldwide have claims to voting rights on state policies like immigration. Again, critics contend that these arguments call for political communities too vast to be meaningfully democratic, among other concerns.[30]

It would take more space and knowledge than I have to explore comprehensively all the variants of these four general approaches to defining 'special' obligations to different categories of non-citizens or 'quasi-citizens,' much less the arguments for, against, and between them. It is also not plausible to think that any state can, will, or should define its obligations by choosing once and for all among these alternatives and then adhering strictly to its choice. Each set of arguments has genuine claims to serious moral consideration. And though those claims, along with the official recognition of special obligations to some outsiders that many states now accept on many grounds, speak against contentions that states have no obligations to anyone other than their own citizens, those contentions, too, have significant moral as well as political force. Political debates in most states will probably include appeals to some version of all these positions and more. Governmental decisions will in most instances rest on a politically potent combination of reasons that can attract support from adherents of different views.

I have previously argued for a certain kind of 'coercion' position, termed 'the principle of coercively constituted identities,' and in the remainder of this chapter I further develop that view, elaborating some of its implications for the obligations of states toward several categories of non-citizens with whom the states have special relationships.[31] But I do not contend that this focus on coercion is the only appropriate moral focus, nor that the obligations it indicates are the only or, always, the weightiest obligations a state can have. I do think they are obligations that have real

---

[28] Ibid., pp. 100, 129.   [29] Abizadeh (n 13), pp. 44–48.

[30] Song (n 16), pp. 49–52; Bauböck (n 1).

[31] Rogers M. Smith, *Political Peoplehood: The Role of Values, Interests, and Identities* (Chicago: University of Chicago Press, 2015), pp. 219–264.

weight, and that they argue for important changes in many state policies, including those defining state borders and state claims to sovereignty.

THE PRINCIPLE OF COERCIVELY CONSTITUTED IDENTITIES

The position defended here is narrower than many kindred coercion arguments, because it does not apply to all governmental exercises of coercive power. Somewhat like Bauböck's 'biographical subjection criterion,' it applies only to governmental coercive measures that can credibly be assigned substantial roles in the constitution of persons' identities, interests, and aspirations. It also employs a limited but undeniable definition of coercion as the actual or threatened use of imminent physical force. Though obligations may also arise from coercion more broadly defined, they surely arise from coercion in this least subtle form. Admittedly, judging what contributions to persons' identities are 'substantial' and when communications amount to coercive threats can be difficult. But the fact that precision is elusive does not mean that rough but reliable judgments cannot be made.

The principle of coercively constituted identities rests on appeals to the moral traditions that states already profess, although in most cases those traditions in turn invoke some sort of transcending authority, such as the will of God, standards of natural right, or universal, rational human morality. The case for the principle begins with the recognition that most modern states, certainly all those professing to be constitutional democracies or republics, officially affirm, albeit on varying grounds, that all human beings equally have some minimum of moral worth and are entitled to respect for their dignity and their capacities to lead relatively free, autonomous lives. Those are the commitments whose implications they must reflect on in deciding on their obligations. The principle does not apply per se to regimes that officially refuse to recognize all human lives as having worth; but in the modern world those cases are rare, and even then there may be elements in their moral traditions that would support obligations to those they coerce.

The next step invokes Will Kymlicka's contention that although people are generally shaped by multiple internally diverse, evolving, and overlapping cultures that are often transnational, the coercively enforced policies of governments often mean that persons have had their identities and values substantially constituted, albeit not determined, by specific nation-states. In consequence, many find it hard to conceive of normatively meaningful lives for themselves without engagement in, often membership in, those nation-states.[32] Whether they consider their nation-state's role in constituting their identities as a boon or a burden, or a mix of both, for most people those state-shaped identities remain their starting points in formulating their notions of the sorts of free, meaningful lives available to them. When governments define—as all do—a particular range of educational systems, religious practices, cultural practices, economic activities, recreations, marital and familial structures, modes of association and expression, and processes of governance as permissible, even valorized, even as they coercively punish people whose conduct falls outside that range, they have a profound impact on the core values, affiliations, and senses of self of many, if not most, persons subject to their policies.

The pervasiveness of these coercively enforced state regulations can be overlooked because they are so familiar. Most modern states do not permit school curricula proclaiming white supremacy, or religions practicing ritual human sacrifices, or slavery, or death-match gladiator contests, or incestuous marriages, or racial, gender, religious, and class disfranchisements. Yet all those examples have been permitted by regimes in the past. Most have been publicly celebrated. All still have adherents today. The fact that they are unacceptable to most persons now is dramatic evidence of how deeply and morally constitutive state restrictions on these practices, and alternative socializing institutions and policies, have been. We should expect that many, if not most, of the people thus constituted by modern states will feel they can best lead meaningful lives if they pursue endeavors that express their socialization—sometimes through compliance, sometimes through resistance, sometimes through modification, but usually through engagement with the populations and institutions of the state that has done so much to make them who they are. States professing to place moral value on human autonomy, personhood, dignity, well-being, capabilities, basic needs, rights and liberties, and kindred norms are therefore obligated by their own commitments to adopt policies that permit, and indeed aid, the persons they have coercively constituted to pursue those engagements in the ways those persons wish to do, insofar as possible.

POLICY IMPLICATIONS

While reiterating the caveat that this cannot and should not be the only factor policymakers consider, let us turn next to what this principle of coercively constituted identities implies for the construction of different forms of legal citizenship, and

---

[32] Will Kymlicka, *Multicultural Citizenship: A Liberal Theory of Minority Rights* (Oxford: Oxford University Press, 1995), pp. 82–83.

particularly for the various types of 'quasi-citizenships' that have proliferated in recent years.

Birthright Citizenship. Most directly, the principle provides a strong foundation for requiring states professing these values to extend citizenship automatically to all persons born and raised within the bounds of the territories they govern. Having coercively shaped native-born residents to be persons who are likely to feel their well-being and freely chosen pursuits of happiness are profoundly connected to holding citizenship in their native lands, states cannot deny persons that right and opportunity without betraying their own commitments. To be sure, the principle does not answer all the concerns that scholars, including Peter Schuck and me, have raised about *jus soli* birthright citizenship policies.[33] Persons born on the soil of a nation-state who reside there only in the initial days or weeks after their birth, before growing up elsewhere, may not have had their identities coercively constituted by that state to any substantial degree. As many have argued, including advocates of 'social membership' approaches, the claims of long-term residents to citizenship are much stronger.[34] It is obviously difficult to judge how long 'long-term' should be in this regard, and the principle advanced here provides no certain guide. It suggests only that policymakers should use their discretionary judgment to write rules insuring that persons whose identities *have* been coercively constituted by the state of their birth are not denied its citizenship, should those persons desire it.

Citizens of Current and Former Colonies and Territories. The principle of coercively constituted identities does, however, constrain policymakers' discretion in some important particulars. For twenty-first century states that commanded empires well into the twentieth century, or that still do today, there are groups of persons that those states may now deem to have been born outside their borders, or in territories they control but to which they do not extend birthright citizenship, who have special claims to consideration, assistance, and affiliation from, and sometimes full citizenship in, those former or current imperial states. The principle is clearly pertinent whenever states have forced a current population, or their recent ancestors, to become its subjects and have imposed policies shaping their constitutive experiences and prospects, their political, economic, educational, cultural, religious, marital, and familial lives. Determining how recent the 'recent ancestors' should be is made difficult because, as Daniel Butt has observed, the generations that make up any nation-state overlap, and descendants benefit from policies that perpetuate the consequences of past coercive actions of their governments.[35] Yet it is

---

[33] Peter H. Schuck and Rogers M. Smith, *Citizenship without Consent: The Illegal Alien in the American Polity* (New Haven: Yale University Press, 1985).

[34] Ibid., pp. 98–99; Carens (n 18), p. 36.

[35] Daniel Butt, 'Nations, Overlapping Generations, and Historical Injustice,' *American Philosophical Quarterly* 43, no. 4 (2006): pp. 357–367, online http://www.jstor.org/stable/20010258.

not plausible to treat the duties incurred by coercive colonial rule as unending: after more than 230 years of U.S. independence, it is unpersuasive to say Britain is obligated to offer special opportunities for British citizenship to modern Americans, even though Britain's coercive policies deeply shaped the U.S. in ways that undeniably persist today. As a rule of thumb, we might judge states to have obligations to their former colonial populations for three generations after the end of colonial rule, roughly two-thirds to three-quarters of a century.

Many of the world's leading nations openly practiced imperialism up through World War II. Some retain colonies. A number have coercively shaped the destinies of their former colonies in ensuing decades. These current and recent imperial powers can credibly be assigned special obligations to the populations of their colonies and ex-colonies. What is required to fulfill those obligations—whether granting independence, or greater powers of autonomous self-determination; or offering trade, tax, development aid, or other economic benefits; or offering opportunities for political voice, legal protection, and contestation of hostile decisions; or permitting full citizenship in the imperial or formerly imperial nation-state—depends on the degree and character of that state's past and present coercive measures, and, always, on the wishes of the populations coercively shaped.[36] Though other moral considerations may point to different conclusions, the principle of coercively constituted identities never justifies further coercive measures toward those whose identities an imperial state has shaped, only the extension of more or less expansive types of aid and opportunities.

As examples of the range of obligations that flow from imperial coercive policies: the U.S. acquired several overseas colonies in the Spanish American War, including Puerto Rico and Guam, which remain U.S. territories today; the Philippines, which was a U.S. territory until 1946 and then had to host an intimidating U.S. military presence for almost a half century more; and Cuba, which was briefly occupied, then granted independence in 1902, though the U.S. imposed a contract to occupy Guantanamo Bay for ninety-nine years, renewable as long as the U.S. (or Cuba) so desires.[37] The U.S. has since acquired other overseas territories, sometimes through military actions, sometimes through negotiations with other colonial powers who initially gained through force the territories they later bargained away.

Currently, the U.S. does not recognize constitutional birthright citizenship for any of these territorial inhabitants, only more easily revocable statutory citizenship or nationality. And though it has granted all of them greater measures of autonomy over time, none has votes in U.S. national elections or voting representatives in

---

[36] Bauböck, (n 1), contends that being subjected to coercion grounds only claims to equal protection and a right of contestation of coercion, not citizenship. But if unequal, coercive exclusion from citizenship is what is being justly contested, a right to citizenship follows.

[37] Lisa García Bedolla, *Latino Politics* (Cambridge: Polity Press, 2009), pp. 95–100, 121–126.

the U.S. Congress.[38] The principle of coercively constituted identities implies that America's territorial residents should *all* be held to possess constitutional birthright citizenship, which they can renounce if they choose while remaining citizens of their territories. It also suggests that as political communities, the territories should be given choices to become full and equal states in the U.S., with full voting rights; or to retain an affiliated autonomous status; or to gain independence, as they wish. Filipinos in particular should receive, at a minimum, expedited opportunities for naturalized U.S. citizenship, and those born when the Philippines was still a U.S. territory should be recognized as already having constitutional birthright citizenship, so that their children are children of U.S. citizen parents.[39]

And though apart from Puerto Rico, no population in the Americas that is not now part of the U.S. was ever officially a U.S. colony, U.S. coercive policies massively shaped the development of Mexico, which lost half its territory in the Mexican-American War and experienced various forms of coercion in ensuing decades; Haiti, subjected to a crippling U.S. trade embargo when it first gained independence, and then occupied by the U.S. from 1915 until 1934, with economic oversight continuing until 1942; and Nicaragua, occupied by the U.S. from 1912 to 1933. The U.S. also has repeatedly undertaken briefer military interventions into all those countries as well as the Dominican Republic, while maintaining its naval base in Cuba and adding a large terrorist detention center there in 2002.[40] These coercive measures cannot be judged to have shaped the populations of these societies so extensively as to warrant granting them birthright U.S. citizenship, as in the case of the U.S. territories. But the obligations incurred by those measures do make a strong case for giving their residents priority in U.S. immigration and naturalization policies, if they desire those options, as well as for at least some of the forms of economic and national security assistance that they may seek.

Like the U.S. if not to even greater degrees, the major European powers all openly practiced imperialism up through World War II, and many have since coercively intervened in their former colonies. As a result, the principle of coercively constituted identities also justifies assigning to those states special obligations to aid their former colonial populations, in many cases including special access to citizenship for those who desire it. That imperative is pertinent to the residents of the former African colonies that the French subjected to the culturally assimilationist impositions of their *mission civilisatrice*, and also to many residents of Britain's former colonies whom it now deems 'overseas' citizens, possessed of some special rights but not permission to reside in the United Kingdom.[41] Like Britain, many European

---

[38] Rogers M. Smith, 'The Insular Cases, Differentiated Citizenship, and Territorial Statuses in the Twenty-First Century,' in Gerald L. Neuman and Tomiko Brown-Nagin, eds., *Reconsidering the Insular Cases: The Past and Future of the American Empire* (Cambridge: Harvard University Press, 2015), pp. 103–128, pp. 125–127.

[39] Smith (n 31), pp. 250–251.   [40] Ibid., pp. 252–253.

[41] Marc Morjé Howard, *The Politics of Citizenship in Europe* (New York: Cambridge University Press, 2009), pp. 41, 159–160; Collyer (n 11).

states do in fact now recognize some special obligations to the populations of their former colonies, occasionally including forms of birthright citizenship or dual citizenship.[42] These policies suggest that the moral obligations implied by the principle of coercively constituted identities already have intuitive appeal to adherents of many moral and political traditions. But it is likely that these measures would be augmented and adopted much more widely if the principle came to be more generally accepted and applied in state policymaking.

Other Immigrants, Authorized and Unauthorized. The most familiar controversies regarding the status of non-citizens or 'quasi-citizens' involve state policies structuring opportunities for full and equal legal citizenship for their alien residents. These residents are either present in accordance with the state's immigration laws, or in violation of them. The principle of coercively constituted identities adds to this familiar dichotomy of authorized/unauthorized status a further distinction: one between those immigrants who are present in large measure because their identities have been coercively constituted in ways that have fostered their desires to reside in a particular state, and those immigrants who may wish passionately to reside in the state, but whose aspirations have *not* been shaped by any coercive measures undertaken by the state.

In regard to all resident aliens, the core implication of the coercively constituted identities principle is that the more pervasively immigrants' interests, attachments, and values have been shaped by a state's coercive actions, the stronger their claims to citizenship within it.[43] Such coercive shaping almost inevitably increases the longer immigrants reside in a state's territory, experiencing its coercively enforced policies, institutions, and practices on an everyday basis (frequently to their benefit, but still in ways that are consequential for their identities and aspirations, and for state obligations). Consequently, like social membership views, the principle elaborated here implies that long-term resident aliens have very strong claims to citizenship indeed. Again, just how long 'long-term' must be in order to justify assigning the state an obligation to confer citizenship, should it be desired, is a matter of judgment. But it is reasonable to hold that those resident half a decade or more have weighty claims, particularly if much of their youthful socialization has taken place during those years.

Because the principle of coercively constituted identities means that a state has obligations to aid all residents, who are all subject to its coercive governance, to achieve their aspirations, it does give great moral weight to the desires of current citizens for effective collective self-governance. Consequently, the principle supports the power and right of states to restrict immigration in ways that reflect their citizens' desires, so long as they do so with due recognition of their other obligations. Ordinarily, it is also appropriate for states to give priority in access to citizenship to

---

[42] Howard (n 41), pp. 42, 89, 108, 151; Spiro (n 9), pp. 21–23.
[43] See also Owen (n 25), p. 15.

resident aliens who are present in compliance with a nation's immigrations laws, over those whose residency has not been authorized. Not only does this priority help to realize the citizenry's self-determination. A state's admission of immigrants to residency represents a positive commitment by the state to use its coercive powers to provide certain kinds of protections, and therefore opportunities, for those new immigrants. States do not make the same promises to those who enter and reside without their permission.

Nonetheless, *ceteris paribus*, the longer unauthorized immigrants reside in a state, the greater the degree that they are likely to be shaped by its coercively enforced ways of life, making it more and more difficult for many to believe they can find fulfillment if they are forced to leave their families, friends, and occupations and move to another country. Consequently, the principle of coercively constituted identities implies that long-term unauthorized resident aliens have claims to access to citizenship like those of authorized ones—albeit lesser claims, unreinforced by the state's commitments to its current citizens or the commitments states make to new immigrants, explicitly and implicitly, when welcoming them as residents.

Moreover, if unauthorized immigrants are present in large measure because a state's coercive policies, past and present, have shaped populations outside its official borders in ways that make them feel their best, perhaps only, opportunities for fulfilling lives are to cross borders illegally, then their claims to do so and to gain access to citizenship are, at a minimum, greater than those of unauthorized immigrants who cannot claim that the state has ever coercively constituted their identities, interests, and aspirations. I have argued for example that the long history of the U.S. directly coercing Mexican populations, and assisting in their coercion by various Mexican governments and private industries, justifies granting Mexicans special access to immigration to the U.S. and U.S. citizenship today—including some form of amnesty for long-resident unauthorized Mexican immigrants, as well as priority for Mexicans in U.S. immigration and naturalization queues. Though the U.S. has stationed large number of troops in New Zealand during wars in which the nations were allied, especially World War II, and their presence undoubtedly influenced New Zealand, it did so with New Zealand's consent. Consequently, New Zealanders cannot claim special treatment from the U.S.[44]

Similar contextual inquiries into other states' historical and contemporary policies and practices are necessary to determine what relevance their past and present coercive measures have for their immigration and naturalization policies. But the principle of coercively constituted identities suggests a guiding framework for all such analyses. Three factors: lengths of residence, legal admission statuses, *and* histories of being subject to coercive state policies, should be weighed in assessing the moral claims for access to citizenship for all resident immigrants (along with

[44] Smith (n 31), pp. 224–246.

consideration of the state's other interests and duties). These criteria suggest that opportunities for citizenship should be provided most robustly, and generally as a matter of right, to long-term, legally resident immigrants whose identities have been coercively constituted by a state both before and after their immigration. It is less obvious what policy priorities are appropriate when a state confronts immigrants with other combinations of these morally weighty factors, such as shorter lengths of residency, lesser histories of coercion, and/or absence of legal status. But it is not appropriate for states to fail to take all three factors into account in their immigration and naturalization laws.

Citizens of Regional Partners. Parallel considerations apply to the obligations of states to the citizens of other states with whom they have formed certain sorts of regional partnerships—economic, military, political, or some mix thereof. Because regional associations like the European Union, NAFTA (the North American Free Trade Agreement), NATO (the North Atlantic Treaty Organization), the Cooperation Council for the Arab States of the Gulf, the African Union, the Caribbean Community, the Andean Community, Mercosur (Mercado Común del Sur), and UNASUR (Unión de Naciones-Suramericanas), as well as the more broad-ranging British Commonwealth, are all authorized by treaties and mutually agreed upon international conventions, to a significant measure they explicitly prescribe the legal obligations that states owe toward the citizens and residents of their regional partners.[45] But those obligations are generally coercively enforced by the regional partnership's institutions, by a citizen's own state, and/or by the institutions of other member states. This means that the regional partnership's policies coercively shape all the residents of the member states to greater or lesser degrees, depending on those policies' scope, duration, and degree of actual enforcement.

The leading example of such partnerships, the European Union, was formally created by the Maastricht Treaty in 1992, but it built on predecessors that went back to the European Coal and Steel Community's creation in 1951. The EU is equipped with an extended set of governing institutions, and it formally confers European citizenship on its members, in addition to their citizenships within their nation-states.[46] In short, the EU has been coercively shaping the lives and identities of its residents for decades. Its member states therefore have strong moral obligations in addition to positive ones to recognize all the residents of the European Union as their fellow citizens. Though insistence on these obligations, like advocacy for unauthorized Mexican immigrants in the U.S., will predictably be met with strong opposition that can and has spurred resurgent anti-regional nationalisms and even Brexit, this political reality does not mean that the obligations can be dismissed. The opposition certainly generates daunting tasks of political prudence in deciding how

---

[45] See Bauböck (n 1), p. 5; Maas in this volume (n 5); Strumia (n 5).
[46] See sources cited in n 5.

those obligations may best be discharged, but again, on the principle of coercively constituted identities, it is not appropriate to fail to give them weight.

The obligations that flow from regional partnerships that are restricted to certain limited economic or military purposes, like NAFTA and NATO, and from regional partnerships that are far less consolidated and coercively implemented than the EU, like UNASUR and the African Union, are less wide and deep. But at least in some instances, they may well become more so over time. And from the outset, it is important for states who enter into such regional partnerships to consider not only what responsibilities they are explicitly assuming by doing so, but what moral obligations they will incur as they contribute to the coercive enforcement of the policies of those regional partnerships during the years in which they endure.

Ethnocultural and Ideological Compatriots. The last category of quasi-citizens considered here arises from policies that states adopt either in response to persons and communities living outside their borders who see themselves as sharing a national, ethnic, religious, cultural, or ideological identity with the states' populations and wish to establish special relationships with them; or they are policies that the states themselves initiate in hopes of gaining various sorts of material, political, and social benefits. These special relationships include the extension of dual citizenship, sometimes carrying voting rights. But as Myra Waterbury has noted, they also involve 'financial and logistical support for diaspora cultural, educational, and economic organizations; support for parents sending their children to mother-tongue schools; preferential access to homeland state educational institutions; and subsidies on travel to the homeland and entrance to cultural institutions there. Some legislation extends these benefits to temporary work permits,' and sometimes other special rights to welfare aid, property ownership, and tax privileges are provided.[47] Although these policies often represent humane efforts to assist populations who desire greater connections with what they see as their ethnocultural or ideological allies, indeed their homelands, and they also can be instruments through which states recruit new sources of human capital, they also have domestic political impacts. They strengthen conceptions of national identities that feature the ethnocultural and ideological traits that are the basis for privileged treatment of certain outside groups.

Consequently, these policies create moral complexities from the standpoint of the principle of coercively constituted identities. In some, perhaps many cases, the principle provides no support for them. Although 'diaspora' populations may see themselves as sharing an ethnocultural or ideological identity with what they judge to be their 'homeland' states, sometimes those perceptions are not credibly attributable to their coercive shaping by those states, where they may never have resided. If their senses of diaspora identity primarily arise from communications and

---

[47] Waterbury (n 10), pp. 5–8. See also Collyer (n 11).

social interactions with people in a state whom they see as their kin or ethnocultural or ideological compatriots, then the 'diaspora' members may well have claims grounded on social membership views for asserting claims to special treatment in the state's policies. The citizens of those 'homeland' states may also choose to provide 'diaspora' populations with special treatment as an exercise of their own rights and powers of collective self-governance. But absent the element of a state's coercive constituting of their senses of ethnocultural identity, the state's *duties* to extend such treatment receive no reinforcement from the principle advanced here.

Yet in other, perhaps many situations, it may instead be plausible to assert that, just as many residents of former colonies may be significantly constituted by the impacts of the policies of their imperial colonizer for many decades after colonization has ended, diaspora communities may have had their conceptions of their identity profoundly shaped on an enduring basis by the policies, institutions, and practices their homeland states coercively enforced when their ancestors resided there. In a much more limited set of cases, some members of self-perceived diasporas may be able to claim credibly that, even living abroad, they are still being coercively shaped by their ancestral states. If so, the principle of coercively constituted identities *would* provide a ground for their claims on those states, just as it does for the states' current populations whose senses of their identities and values feature ethnocultural and ideological themes due in large part to the states' policies. There is nothing in the principle that inherently implies or favors ethnoculturally or ideologically preferential policies. But if states enact them and the policies come to affect persons' senses of who they are, who they most want to be, who they wish to affiliate with, and how they want to live, those state actions matter morally. Because the principle *does* suggest that states have obligations to help the people they have shaped to fulfill their aspirations, in those circumstances it supports the propriety of special ethnocultural and ideological 'compatriot' policies which favor some populations residing abroad. It is likely, however, that in most instances, social membership approaches will provide the strongest support for such measures. All such policies, moreover, must be considered alongside other pertinent moral concerns, including human rights claims.

Conclusion

It should be clear that, even as the varied statuses here grouped together as kinds of 'quasi-citizens' are continuing to multiply, questions concerning the distinctive moral obligations of states toward the persons occupying these statuses are also becoming more complex. There are a number of credible moral standpoints from which to assess those obligations, including concerns for all persons affected or coerced by state policies, and social membership and stakeholder views, as well as strongly nationalist denials that any such special obligations exist at all. Most of those moral standpoints make certain empirical inquiries critical before any confident judgments can be reached: are different communities really so thickly interwoven that they can be said to share a social membership? Have states coercively constituted the identities of various groups, and if so, how and when? Whose interests do state policies actually affect, and in regard to what interests? What populations can truly be said to be dependent on a state, or subject to its authority? Even if we can obtain credible empirical answers to such questions, we will still be confronted by difficult judgment calls when we seek to create policies informed by our findings. How long must persons reside in a state before we say that either the realities of social membership or of coercively constituted identities mean that it should provide them with the option of citizenship? For overseas populations, what degrees of social memberships, or of coercive constituting, or of stakeholding justify some forms of recognition, assistance, and accommodation, and what should those forms be? When do obligations to former colonial populations, or coercively constituted ethnic compatriots, fade?

Precisely because they suggest, indeed demand, such a wide range of empirical and normative analyses, issues of special obligations to quasi-citizens provide a rich field both for scholarly research and for moral and political argumentation. But it is because they are issues of fundamental importance to the lives of so very many persons, residing within or outside the boundaries of the states they wish to regard as their own, that these issues merit rigorous exploration now, as the remarkable transformations of the twenty-first century continue. And if more states find it in their interests to establish new transnational associations and organizations, many with coercive authority; if more members of populations that states have coercively constituted continue to move away, while still seeking to enjoy special relationships with their homelands; and if more states also feel compelled to provide some accommodations to those claims—then current transformations shifting global political life away from the preeminence of nation-states are likely to increase. It will then be up to many citizens of many types in many regions to determine whether we will see the emergence of a political world that is better, worse, or simply strange and new.

Bibliography

Abizadeh, Arash, 'Democratic Theory and Border Coercion: No Right to Unilaterally Control Your Own Borders', *Political Theory* 36, no. 1 (2008): pp. 37–65, doi: 10.1177/0090591707310090.

Bader, Veit, 'Reasonable Impartiality and Priority for Compatriots: A Criticism of Liberal Nationalism's Main Flaws,' *Ethical Theory and Moral Practice 8*, no. 1–2 (2005): pp. 83–103, doi: 10.1007/s10677-005-3292-6.

Bauböck, Rainer, 'The Rights and Duties of External Citizenship,' *Citizenship Studies 13*, no. 5 (2009): pp. 475–499, doi: 10.1080/13621020903174647.

Brubaker, Rogers, *Grounds for Difference* (Cambridge: Harvard University Press, 2015).

Butt, Daniel, 'Nations, Overlapping Generations, and Historical Injustice,' *American Philosophical Quarterly 43*, no. 4 (2006): pp. 357–367, online http://www.jstor.org/stable/20010258.

Carens, Joseph H., *The Ethics of Immigration* (New York: Oxford University Press, 2013).

Cohen, Elizabeth F., *Semi-Citizenship in Democratic Politics* (New York: Cambridge University Press, 2009).

Cook-Martín, David, *The Scramble for Citizens: Dual Nationality and State Competition for Immigrants* (Stanford: Stanford University Press, 2013).

Dahl, Robert A., *After the Revolution? Authority in a Good Society*, revised edition (New Haven: Yale University Press, 1990) [1970].

Dahl, Robert A., *Democracy and Its Critics* (New Haven: Yale University Press, 1989).

Elkins, David J., *Beyond Sovereignty: Territory and Political Economy in the Twenty-First Century* (Toronto: University of Toronto Press, 1995).

García Bedolla, Lisa, *Latino Politics* (Cambridge: Polity Press, 2009).

Goodin, Robert E., 'Enfranchising All Affected Interests, and Its Alternatives,' *Philosophy and Public Affairs 35*, no. 1 (2007): pp. 40–68, doi: 10.1111/j.1088-4963.2007.00098.x.

Greer, Scott L., *Nationalism and Self-Government: The Politics of Autonomy in Scotland and Catalonia* (Albany: State University of New York Press, 2007).

Guéhenno, Jean-Marie, *The End of the Nation-State*, translated by Victoria Elliott (Minneapolis: University of Minnesota Press, 1995).

Hansen, Randall and Patrick Weil, eds., *Dual Nationality, Social Rights and Federal Citizenship in the U.S. and Europe* (New York: Berghahn Books, 2002).

Holtug, Nils, 'The Cosmopolitan Strikes Back,' *Ethics and Global Politics 4*, no. 3 (2011): pp. 147–163, doi: 10.3402/egp.v4i3.5873.

Howard, Marc Morjé, *The Politics of Citizenship in Europe* (New York: Cambridge University Press, 2009).

Ieda, Osuma, ed., *Beyond Sovereignty: From Status Law to Transnational Citizenship?* (Sapporo: Slavic Research Center, Hokkaido University, 2006).

Kymlicka, Will, *Multicultural Citizenship: A Liberal Theory of Minority Rights* (Oxford: Oxford University Press, 1995).

Lafleur, Jean-Michel, *Transnational Politics and the State: The External Voting Rights of Diasporas* (New York: Routledge, 2013).

Lluch, Jaime, *Visions of Sovereignty: Nationalism and Accommodation in Multinational Democracies* (Philadelphia: University of Pennsylvania Press, 2014).

Maas, Willem, *Creating European Citizens* (Lanham: Rowman & Littlefield, 2007).

Maatsch, Aleksandra, *Ethnic Citizenship Regimes: Europeanization, Post-War Migration, and Redressing Past Wrongs* (Basingstoke, New York: Palgrave Macmillan, 2011).

Miller, David, *National Responsibility and Global Justice* (Oxford: Oxford University Press, 2007).

Ohmae, Kenichi, *The End of the Nation-State: The Rise of Regional Economies* (New York: Free Press, 1995).

Owen, David, 'Transnational Membership and the Democratic State: Modes of Membership and Voting Rights,' *Critical Review of Social and International Philosophy 14*, no. 5 (2011): pp. 641–663, doi: 10.1080/13698230.2011.617123.

Sassen, Saskia, *Losing Control? Sovereignty in an Age of Globalization* (New York: Columbia University Press, 1996).

Schuck, Peter H. and Rogers M. Smith, *Citizenship without Consent: The Illegal Alien in the American Polity* (New Haven: Yale University Press, 1985).

Shachar, Ayelet, *The Birthright Lottery: Citizenship and Global Inequality* (Cambridge: Harvard University Press, 2009).

Shapiro, Ian, *Democratic Justice* (New Haven: Yale University Press, 1999).

Shapiro, Ian, *Politics against Domination* (Cambridge: Harvard University Press, 2016).

Smith, Rogers M., *Political Peoplehood: The Roles of Values, Interests, and Identities* (Chicago: University of Chicago Press, 2015).

Smith, Rogers M., 'The Insular Cases, Differentiated Citizenship, and Territorial Statuses in the Twenty-First Century,' in Gerald L. Neuman and Tomiko Brown-Nagin, eds., *Reconsidering the Insular Cases: The Past and Future of the American Empire* (Cambridge: Harvard University Press, 2015), pp. 103–128.

Song, Sarah, 'The Boundary Problem in Democratic Theory: Why the Demos Should Be Bounded by the State,' *International Theory 4*, no. 1 (2012): pp. 39–68, doi: 10.1017/S1752971911000248.

Soysal, Yasemin, *The Limits of Citizenship: Migrants and Postnational Membership in Europe* (Chicago: University of Chicago Press, 1994).

Waterbury, Myra, 'From Irredentism to Diaspora Politics: States and Transborder Ethnic Groups in Eastern Europe,' Center for Global Studies, George Mason University, Global Migration and Transnational Politics Working Paper no. 6 (July 2009), online https://www.gmu.edu/centers/globalstudies/publications/gmtpwp/gmtp_wp_6.pdf.

Wellman, Christopher Heath, 'Friends, Compatriots, and Special Obligations,' *Political Theory 29*, no. 1 (2001): pp. 217–236, doi: 10.1177/0090591701029002003.

CHAPTER 37

INCLUSIVE CITIZENSHIP BEYOND THE CAPACITY CONTRACT

SUE DONALDSON AND WILL KYMLICKA[*]

CITIZENSHIP in the modern era is usually territorially bounded, both vertically and horizontally: vertically, to be a citizen is to have a certain legal and political status vis-à-vis a territorially bounded state; and horizontally, to be a citizen is to be a member of a territorially bounded 'society', 'people', or 'nation'. This territorial definition of citizenship has come under scrutiny given the increasing interdependence of our globalized world, and this has led to calls to expand citizenship beyond territorial boundaries to include a transnational or cosmopolitan dimension.

Debates about the outward expansion of citizenship are discussed elsewhere in this volume. Our chapter, however, focuses on the challenge of expanding

[*] We are grateful to Ayelet Shachar, Rainer Bauböck, and Iseult Honohan for helpful comments on this chapter.

citizenship relationships *within* bounded polities, to all members of society. The scale of this internal challenge is often underestimated. Everyone acknowledges the long history of internal exclusions by which women, racialized castes, property-less workers, and others were deemed unable and unworthy of being equal participants in political decision-making. They were treated as subjects to be ruled paternalistically and coercively rather than as citizens sharing in self-rule through democratic co-authoring of the laws.

These internal exclusions are now discredited, at least formally. Most commentators assume that Western democracies have achieved something like universal citizenship for all members of society, and thereby exemplify what we might call the membership model (whether conceived as a social contract or cooperative scheme answerable to all members; or as the legitimate exercise of power answerable to all who are subject to the law; or as the meaningful participation of all stakeholders or all who belong).[1] While differing on the details of how to draw the external boundaries of citizenship, theorists presume that modern citizenship is democratic and egalitarian, committed to recognizing equal belonging, an equal right of all members to contribute to and benefit from social cooperation, and an equal right to influence the norms of shared society.

In reality, however, many members of society are still relegated, both de facto and de jure, to the status of passive subjects, not active citizens. Consider children, who form around one-third of the population of any given society. Or consider people with cognitive disabilities, who number in the millions in some countries. They are born into society, participate in its social relationships, share in the benefits and burdens of social cooperation, and live their lives within its territorial boundaries. And this fact of social membership is acknowledged in nationality law: children and people with cognitive disabilities have the formal status of citizenship or nationality by birth. They are not foreigners or stateless. Yet these members of society are disenfranchised, and precluded from enacting substantive citizenship. They are typically accorded certain rights to protection (against harm) and provision (of public services) as members of society, but denied the right to participate in democratic shared rule which defines modern ideals of citizenship.

An even more striking case of internal exclusion concerns domesticated animals. They too are members of society, at least according to most sociological definitions of sociality (participating in forms of intersubjective recognition, communication, trust, cooperation, and compliance with shared norms). Domesticated animals share a social world with us, and play a vital role in our schemes of economic production

---

[1] Stakeholders are those who have a 'real and effective link' to the political community (Ayelet Shachar, *The Birthright Lottery: Citizenship and Global Inequality* (Cambridge: Harvard University Press, 2009); Rainer Bauböck, 'Stakeholder Citizenship: An Idea Whose Time Has Come?', in *Delivering Citizenship: The Transatlantic Council on Migration* (Gütersloh: Verlag Bertelsmann Stiftung, 2008), pp. 31–48. On citizenship and 'belonging', see Joseph Carens, *The Ethics of Immigration* (Oxford: Oxford University Press, 2013).

and social cooperation, a reality which is now widely acknowledged (and studied) by sociologists and anthropologists.[2] Domesticated animals are governed by society's laws, and shaped by its institutions. They should qualify for citizenship under a membership model that ties citizenship to being a member of society, a stakeholder, or a subject of the law.[3] Yet, virtually without exception, theorists of citizenship exclude animals, often in the very same sentence that excludes children and people with cognitive disabilities.[4]

These internal exclusions sit awkwardly with modern discourses of universal citizenship, and highlight a fundamental dilemma for citizenship theory, not just about who qualifies for citizenship, but also about the very nature and purposes of citizenship. They reveal the ongoing existence of what Stacy Clifford calls a 'capacity contract', by which some members of society are deemed to be naturally governed by others.[5] According to the capacity contract, citizenship should be limited to those who are by nature capable of ruling, while all others are relegated to some subaltern status, such as wardship. As we will see, this capacity contract runs deep in the Western tradition, although its application has evolved over time. Perceptions of who is naturally governed by whom have changed, in part due to the citizenship struggles over the past century by women, workers, racialized minorities, people with physical disabilities, and indigenous communities. These groups have challenged assumptions of unruliness, dependency or incompetence invoked to justify coercive and paternalistic rule over them. James Tully uses the term 'citizenization' to describe this ongoing process in which prevailing hierarchies are identified and challenged, and new norms of inter-subjective recognition and participation come into being, replacing older hierarchical and coercive relations with relations based on equality and consent.[6]

However, while these citizenization struggles have challenged inherited assumptions about who is appropriately excluded by the capacity contract, they have rarely

---

[2] See Kay Peggs, *Animals and Sociology* (New York: Palgrave Macmillan, 2012).

[3] We develop this argument in *Zoopolis: A Political Theory of Animal Rights* (Oxford: Oxford University Press, 2011). We also discuss wild animals and how they raise issues of sovereignty, territorial rights, and international justice.

[4] For example, see Hobbes: 'Over natural fools, children, or madmen there is no law, no more than over brute beasts; nor are they capable of the title of just or unjust, because they had never power to make any covenant or to understand the consequences thereof' (*Leviathan* II.xxvi.12).

[5] Stacy Clifford, 'The Capacity Contract: Locke, Disability, and the Political Exclusion of "Idiots"', *Politics, Groups, and Identities* 2, no. 1 (2014): pp. 90–103. The language of contract is used here, not in the sense of a voluntary agreement, but in the sense that theorists talk of the 'racial contract', 'sexual contract', or 'settler contract': as a deeply embedded social logic that structures our institutions in hierarchical terms, subordinating some to the rule of others (Charles Mills, *The Racial Contract* (Ithaca: Cornell University Press, 2007); Carole Pateman, *The Sexual Contract* (Cambridge: Polity, 1988); Robert Nichols, 'Indigeneity and the Settler Contract Today', *Philosophy & Social Criticism* 39, no. 2 (2013): pp. 165–186.

[6] James Tully, 'Struggles over Recognition and Distribution', *Constellations* 7, no. 4 (2000): pp. 469–482, p. 473.

challenged the capacity contract itself. They have left intact the assumption that citizenship requires not only social membership, but also some further set of capacities, such as political speech or intellectual independence, and that possession of these capacities provides the basis on which we legitimately divide society into first-class participating citizens and second-class wards. The process of citizenization has challenged biases and arbitrariness in the way the capacity contract has been applied, but has not questioned the very need for a capacity contract. Indeed, struggles for the inclusion of women and other groups have arguably reinforced the capacity contract, by distancing these claimants from mistaken placement amongst the politically immature, childish, or unruly beasts properly excluded from participation.[7]

Our aim in this chapter is to rethink the relationship between the membership model and the capacity contract. Both run deep in the Western tradition, and indeed it is not uncommon for political philosophers to invoke both. In one sentence, they invoke the language of 'all affected' to define the demos, insisting that a legitimate state must be responsive to all those who are members of society or all who are subject to its rule. Yet in the very next sentence, they restrict the demos to neurotypical adults, thereby unilaterally evicting large numbers of members of society from the demos. Too often, this self-contradiction is ignored or dismissed in a footnote. We will argue, however, that the capacity contract is flatly inconsistent with the membership model, and that we must choose between them. Indeed this poses one of the most 'intractable problems in political theory',[8] even if contemporary political theory has largely ignored or evaded it.[9]

To foreshadow the discussion, we will argue that the capacity contract should be rejected. The fundamental purpose of citizenship is to ensure that all members of the community have a chance to realize their own understanding of their subjective good, to exercise meaningful forms of control in their lives, and to participate in shaping the social norms by which they are governed. There is no need or justification for qualifying this imperative by a capacity contract: the commitment to citizenship should apply to all members of society, wherever they stand on the spectra of linguistic or cognitive capacities, and regardless of differences in manner and degree concerning how they enact their citizenship.

---

[7] Andrew Rehfeld, 'The Child as Democratic Citizen', *Annals of the American Academy of Political and Social Science* 633, no. 1 (2011): pp. 141–166, p. 155.

[8] Toby Rollo, 'Feral Children: Settler Colonialism, Progress, and the Figure of the Child', *Settler Colonial Studies* (forthcoming), p. 1.

[9] Childhood and disability theorists have challenged the capacity contract in citizenship theory, but their work has been largely ignored by mainstream political theorists. See Kate Bacon and Sam Frankel, 'Rethinking Children's Citizenship', *International Journal of Children's Rights* 22, no. 1 (2014): pp. 21–42, p. 25; Barbara Arneil, 'Disability, Self-Image, and Modern Political Theory', *Political Theory* 37, no. 2 (2009): pp. 218–242.

To be sure, citizenization for these groups poses a deep challenge to traditional conceptions of the rights, responsibilities, and practices of citizens. Their inclusion is not just more *theoretically* destabilizing (due to the unique way in which they challenge the capacity contract) than the inclusion of women and racialized minorities; it is also more *politically* challenging, because people with cognitive disabilities, children, and domesticated animals are limited in their ability to self-organize and to fight for political power. They can engage in acts of individual resistance, but when it comes to organized resistance and political claims-making they are significantly dependent on neurotypical human adults to help articulate, represent, and fight for those claims.[10] To make good the promise of inclusive citizenship, we therefore need to rethink not just who is recognized as a citizen, but also what it means to claim, enact or 'perform' citizenship.[11]

We begin with an overview of how the capacity contract operates to exclude many members of society. We then explore how children, people with cognitive disabilities, and domesticated animals are oppressed rather than protected by the persistence of the capacity contract. Defenders of the capacity contract argue that wardship should not be seen as a subaltern status, but as a respected form of social membership that fits the needs and interests of those who do not qualify for citizenship. We raise doubts about this. We then sketch the parameters of a more inclusive conception of 'difference-centred' citizenship.[12] We close by considering how a more inclusive model of citizenship can inject new life into our democratic practices more generally.

THE CAPACITY CONTRACT

Children and people with cognitive disabilities are recognized as members of society, and as such are accorded the formal status of nationality. They are not foreigners or stateless. But they lack substantive citizenship with rights to participate in co-authoring social norms. All democracies disenfranchise children (until the age of 16 or 18), and most disenfranchise some people on the basis of intellectual disability or

---

[10] Older children/youth and people with moderate intellectual impairments are often powerful and articulate self-advocates.

[11] See Isin in this volume for an analysis of citizenship as performative claims-making.

[12] See Mehmoona Moosa-Mitha, 'A Difference-Centred Alternative to Theorization of Children's Citizenship Rights', *Citizenship Studies* 9, no. 4 (2005): pp. 369–388.

mental illness.[13] Nor are members of these groups provided with alternative mechanisms for influencing or holding to account the exercise of political power.

Only individuals with sophisticated cognitive capacities for political speech,
rational reflection, and moral responsibility are accorded substantive citizenship,
while other members of society are relegated to the status of 'semi-citizens' or 'partial citizens'.[14] They remain political wards unless and until they demonstrate that
they 'deserve' citizenship, and can be trusted to act in the public good through possession of what Andrew Rehfeld calls 'that bundle of cognitive, emotional, communicative and agency capability that justifies a claim to citizenship rights within any
democratic society'.[15]

Versions of this capacity contract can be found throughout the history of political philosophy, from Aristotle through Hobbes and Locke to Rawls, although the
details vary from thinker to thinker.[16] Rational speech (or linguistic agency, or *logos*)
is central to this contract. To be a citizen you must be able to articulate, understand,
evaluate, negotiate, and commit to linguistic propositions regarding the terms of
social cooperation with your fellow citizens.

The capacity contract remains largely untouched in modern conceptions of citizenship, and indeed is integral to prevailing images of democratic politics. Toby
Rollo argues that 'concepts related to childhood and democratic politics emerged as
conceptually coeval and mutually exclusive'—that is, democratic politics is conceptualized precisely as the outcome of a progression out of childhood/animality into
fully human agency.[17] To claim democratic citizenship, individuals, groups (e.g.,
women), or indeed entire societies (e.g. colonized peoples) needed to show that
they had progressed from 'the feral child's non-linguistic deficiency of humanity' to
a fully human state which 'venerates logos, language, and reason as the definitively
human form of relating to the world and to others'.[18]

The persistence within contemporary political theory of this view of citizenship
as the antithesis to childhood/animality is puzzling, given its perfectionist philosophical origins. For Aristotle, rational speech is what distinguishes humans from
other species and thereby defines human excellence; politics should be organized
to enable humans to maximally express their species' uniqueness; and so politics
should be organized around rational speech. This species perfectionism (or, if you

---

[13] Ludvig Beckman, *The Frontiers of Democracy: The Right to Vote and its Limits* (New York: Palgrave
Macmillan, 2009), p. 146. Some states have recently removed provisions disenfranchising those with
cognitive disabilities. For an up-to-date overview in EU states, see the EUDO database, http://eudo-
citizenship.eu/electoral-rights.

[14] On semi-citizenship, see Elizabeth Cohen, *Semi-Citizenship in Democratic Politics*
(New York: Cambridge University Press, 2009).

[15] Rehfeld (n 7), pp. 146, 149.   [16] Rollo (n 8); Bacon and Frankel (n 9), pp. 23–25.

[17] Rollo (n 8), p. 2.

[18] Ibid., p. 15. Rollo argues that the subjection of children and of colonial peoples rested on homolo-
gous processes of conceptualizing development from immaturity to full humanity.

prefer, species narcissism) is an incongruous inheritance within contemporary political theory. For most contemporary theorists, the function of politics is not to express species essences but to ensure that the distribution of the benefits and burdens of social cooperation is just, and that the exercise of political power over the governed is legitimate. And both justice and legitimacy would seem to push us in the direction of the membership model of citizenship. Children, people with cognitive disabilities, and domesticated animals may not engage in the forms of rational speech traditionally viewed as 'definitively human', but they share in the benefits and burdens of social cooperation, and they are subject to the exercise of political power. If our concern is with justice and legitimacy rather than with exalting species essences, then these facts of social participation and political subjection should generate rights to participate. Indeed, as we will see, excluding these groups from participation invites, and perhaps even guarantees, unjust social norms and illegitimate exercises of power.

What then explains the persistence of the capacity contract in contemporary citizenship theories? We suggest two factors are at work. On the one hand, there is unwarranted optimism that the status of passive wardship can secure justice and prevent oppression. On the other hand, there is unwarranted pessimism about the prospects of developing feasible models of political participation for those who lack rational speech. We will consider these two factors in turn.

THE PROBLEM WITH WARDSHIP

Contemporary citizenship theory has displayed remarkable indifference to the fate of those excluded by the capacity contract and relegated to the status of passive wards. Children under 16/18 constitute up to a third of the population of many democracies, and if we add people with cognitive disabilities (a growing proportion of the population)—not to mention domesticated animals—then our allegedly 'universal' theories of citizenship turn out to be offering citizenship to a quite restricted club. It would seem incumbent on these theories to say something about how wards are to be governed, how their interests are to be identified and taken into account, and how criteria of justice and legitimacy are to be applied to decisions that affect them, all without any participation from the affected themselves.

Yet one searches in vain for any extended discussion of the normative logic and political functioning of wardship. Defenders of the capacity contract assume that children, people with cognitive disabilities, and domesticated animals don't need participation rights because their interests can be adequately realized through passive representation.[19] This presupposes that the fundamental values of democratic citizenship do not apply to those classed as wards; they do not need to exercise meaningful control over their own lives, nor do they possess any epistemic privilege when it comes to understanding their own good and how it can be realized in the community. They can be adequately provided for and protected by parents, guardians, or trustees who 'know better' and represent their interests accordingly. They do not need to be empowered to shape society, or to hold to account those who exercise power over them.

We do not deny that guardians are often in the best position to identify and protect the long-term interests of the vulnerable, and some degree of paternalism is both inevitable and appropriate. But the fact that long-term interests may sometimes require overriding current preferences does not justify the failure to create mechanisms to solicit those preferences, and accord them weight. Nor does it justify the endless deferral of present interests, or indeed the erasure of children's interests qua children in favour of the adults they will become.

Optimism concerning the efficacy of passive representation is puzzling, given the historic track record of political wardship for other groups. For women, slaves, servants, indigenous and other colonized peoples, wardship has been a recipe for violent exploitation and disregard, which is why all of these groups have struggled for substantive citizenship. The problem was not simply the insult of being deemed politically incompetent or immature, but the profound failure of guardians and trustees, even those with the best intentions, to recognize, understand, or adequately represent, the interests of those classed as wards.

One might respond that the case of children and people with cognitive disabilities is different and that neurotypical adults (and parents in particular) are motivated to adequately represent the interests of these vulnerable members of society.[20] This comfortable assumption is belied by evidence of the ongoing failure of passive representation in modern states. Children and people with disabilities are significantly over-represented amongst the poor, and receive fewer state resources than vulnerable but enfranchised groups such as seniors.[21] They are disproportionately victims of sexual violence. And their interests in mobility and a safe environment are substantially ignored.[22] For example, human adults typically have weaker interests than children (or domesticated animals) in roaming outdoors in a car-free,

---

[19] See, e.g., Christopher Hinchcliffe, 'Animals and the Limits of Citizenship', *Journal of Political Philosophy* 23, no. 3 (2015): pp. 302–320.

[20] Indeed some call for additional empowerment of parents through proxy voting—giving adults who have children extra votes—on the assumption that this will lead to better representation of children. As Rehfeld notes, this is just to double down on passive representation, and does nothing to empower children to advance their own interests (Rehfeld (n 7), pp. 155–157).

[21] Ibid., p. 156.

[22] Alex Zakaras, 'Democracy, Children, and the Environment: A Case for Common Trusts', *Critical Review of International Social and Political Philosophy* 19, no. 2 (2016): pp. 141–162.

accessible, unpolluted environment, and can tolerate much higher exposures to environmental toxins. In what is described as the 'new pediatric morbidity', the five major illnesses affecting children in industrialized societies are all environmentally related, and yet adult interests in wealth creation and the convenience of car culture have consistently trumped efforts to act on these crucial interests.[23]

Work is another sphere where the interests of children and people with cognitive disabilities have been subordinated. Neurotypical adults have often acted to protect their own preferential access to employment (and its economic and social benefits) by calling for the exclusion of child or disabled workers, rather than heeding demands by these groups for transformation of workplaces to accommodate their participation. (We return to the issue of work below.) And adult demands for compliant workforce-ready graduates have generally held sway over child-centred curricula beyond the early education years.[24]

These ongoing failures of passive representation help to explain why children, people with cognitive disabilities and their advocates have pressed for genuine participation rights and a move towards full citizenship, just as previous casualties of wardship have done.[25] And these demands have been affirmed in recent United Nations Conventions. The UN Convention on the Rights of the Child (UNCRC) recognizes children's right to 'have a say' in matters that affect them, and for their input to be attended to in light of their evolving capacities—rights to participation, not just provision and protection (the '3P model').[26] There is considerable debate about the implications of the participation rights affirmed by the UNCRC, and some would argue that the results to date are tokenistic. But the UNCRC has undoubtedly spawned a range of experiments in childhood political participation.

The more recent 2008 Convention on the Rights of Persons with Disabilities (UNCRPD) goes further, guaranteeing to all people with disabilities (including cognitive disabilities) the right to full and effective participation in society, and full enjoyment of all fundamental rights. Article 12 guarantees the right 'to enjoy legal capacity on an equal basis with others in all aspects of life'. Article 29 guarantees

---

[23] Leonardo Trasande et. al., 'The Environment in Pediatric Practice', *Journal of Urban Health 83*, no. 4 (2006): pp. 760–772. Animal companions are also increasingly affected by neurodevelopmental disorders, cancers, and poisoning if allowed to roam free; and obesity and diabetes if kept 'safely' indoors.

[24] James Dwyer, 'No Place for Children', *Alabama Law Review 62*, no. 5 (2011): pp. 887–961.

[25] The treatment of domesticated animals offers further evidence for the limits of wardship. Farmers and researchers invoke the language of guardianship and stewardship, claiming to know and to respect the interests of those in their 'care', despite overwhelming evidence of violence, deprivation, and extreme exploitation. Of course, unlike children or people with cognitive disability, domesticated animals lack even basic rights of personhood, which dramatically exacerbates the risks of a failed wardship model. When wardship fails, as it always does, there is no backstop to the potential harm in the case of animals.

[26] On the 3P model, see Ann Quennerstedt, 'Children, But Not Really Humans? Critical Reflections on the Hampering Effect of the "3Ps"', *International Journal of Children's Rights 18*, no. 4 (2010): pp. 619–635.

'political rights and the opportunity to enjoy them on an equal basis with others'. These developments fundamentally challenge the idea that passive representation is adequate for any citizen.

In short, political wardship has been, and remains, an inadequate model of representation, and wherever possible, people try to escape its confines and seek respect and opportunities for participation. No doubt, some of these failures could be addressed by improving our models of wardship, perhaps with better oversight. For example, neurotypical adult representatives could be appointed under a fiduciary duty to act in wards' interests, a duty subject to multiple forms of incentive, oversight, and enforcement.[27] This kind of strict guardianship, in conjunction with other 'hand-tying' mechanisms like constitutionally protected trusts to constrain the decisions of neurotypical adults, could help represent the interests of the vulnerable, and limit the negative impact of decisions over which they have no control, without directly empowering them as political actors.

But how do we know what these interests are? Political wardship assumes that neurotypical adults (whether parents, guardians, experts) are best placed to understand the interests of wards, because the latter lack sophisticated capacities to reflectively scrutinize their own good and the public good. We believe this assumption overestimates the impartiality of guardians, and underestimates the distorting effects of standpoint, self-interest, and hierarchy. We will briefly discuss three ways in which wardship has systematically distorting effects: i) it masks the exercise of coercive power; ii) it masks the distribution of burdens and contributions; and iii) it unduly limits freedom.

Power: Wardship creates an image of pastoral care, in which wards are cared for by guardians, unlike regular citizens who are governed by laws and institutions. The implicit and sometimes explicit corollary is that 'caring for wards' does not need the same sort of checks and balances and accountability as 'governing of citizens'. Citizens need democratic protections from coercive state power, but wards do not need comparable protections from caregivers. This image masks the ways in which members of vulnerable groups are directly subjected to coercive state power. The state can remove children and people with cognitive disabilities from their families, compel them to live in institutions and/or to attend school, deny them equal protection of the law (e.g. the opportunity to testify or to bring suit), deny them the right to control property, deny them labour rights and social security benefits, limit their association rights (e.g. through curfews, zoning laws). Whether at home, school, work, or in public space, children and people with cognitive disabilities are subject to unaccountable power—by state authorities or guardians empowered by the state. So too for domesticated animals in homes, workplaces, farms, and laboratories.

---

[27] See Dwyer (n 24) concerning possible enhancements of legal guardianship.

848 SUE DONALDSON AND WILL KYMLICKA

These are the spaces and places where they need to be empowered as citizens, with the right to a say, and opportunities to contest their treatment.

Contribution: Some theorists worry that extending citizenship to children would in effect deny them their right to childhood. After all, citizenship involves not just rights and freedoms, but also duties—duties to participate, to contribute, and to take responsibility. Adults shouldn't burden children, but rather, should draw a protective bubble around childhood.[28] On this view, wardship secures a right of children to innocence and to play, free from adult responsibilities.

It is indeed crucial to protect a child's right to be a child (including unique developmental requirements for play), but a grave mistake to claim that respect for difference must come at the cost of political participation. The rhetoric of a responsibility-free childhood is as misleading as the image of a power-free childhood. It obscures the ways in which children do contribute—by undergoing education (which is usually framed as a benefit they receive, but which is also work which they undertake for society's benefit), and by performing various kinds of labour which is often ignored or trivialized. Children 'help out' in the home, including onerous work caring for sick relatives, but this 'help' is not recognized by society as work that requires recognition or compensation.[29]

The image of a responsibility-free childhood is even more unrealistic for those who don't enjoy a Western middle class existence. Children around the world perform huge amounts of work in and outside the home, bearing significant responsibility for the health and economic welfare of their families. The dominant attitude of Western organizations is to say that these children need to be brought into protective status, spared from work and responsibility. But this is often not what children themselves want. When asked, children indicate that empowerment is what they want—including better compensation and safer working conditions (consistent with their interests in education and other developmental needs)[30]—not restriction to an (allegedly) protective bubble. The fact is that children and people with cognitive disabilities, like the rest of us, see themselves as contributing members of society, and want to be respected for this.[31]

---

[28] Rehfeld (n 7); Beckman (n 13).

[29] Ruth Lister, 'Why Citizenship: Where, When and How Children?', *Theoretical Inquiries in Law 8*, no. 2 (2007): pp. 693–718, p. 707.

[30] Antonella Invernizzi, 'Everyday Lives of Working Children and Notions of Citizenship', in Antonella Invernizzi and Jane Williams, eds., *Children and Citizenship* (Thousand Oaks: Sage, 2008), pp. 131–141.

[31] Elizabeth Such and Robert Walker, 'Young Citizens or Policy Objects? Children in the "Rights and Responsibilities" Debate', *Journal of Social Policy 34*, no. 1 (2005): pp. 39–57. Regarding workplace attitudes of people with intellectual disabilities see Noelia Flores et al., 'Understanding Quality of Working Life of Workers with Intellectual Disabilities', *Journal of Applied Research in Intellectual Disabilities* 24 (2011): pp. 133–141. On the recognition of contribution as the key to recognition of membership, see Judith Shklar, *American Citizenship: The Quest for Inclusion* (Cambridge: Harvard University Press, 1991).

This pattern of, on the one hand identifying a group as incapable of or unsuited to work, while on the other hand discounting the extensive ways in which they do in fact contribute or work (and thereby evading duties of fair compensation and working conditions), aptly describes the situation of billions of working animals around the world.[32]

That wardship systematically obscures the reality of both power and contribution is unsurprising, since these are the bases of claims to citizenship on the membership model. Since the membership model says that individuals are owed citizenship in virtue of being subject to power and in virtue of participating in schemes of social cooperation, defenders of the capacity contract and wardship are compelled to deny or trivialize the extent to which children, people with cognitive disabilities, and domesticated animals are subject to power or engage in contribution.

Freedom: Wardship suffers from a third deficiency: it entails excessive paternalism because guardians are prone—perhaps even legally required—to be maximally risk-averse towards wards. This inevitably limits opportunities for mobility, exploration, choice, learning, challenge—all potentially crucial to wellbeing. The problem here is not that guardians are uncaring: just the opposite. The problem is that we all 'want autonomy for ourselves and safety for those we love'.[33] And the prioritizing of safety and security over choice and agency under wardship inevitably leads to what Goffman called 'curtailments of the self'.[34]

For example, there has been a striking reduction in the mobility and association rights of Western, middle class children in recent decades. The standard justification is protection (from cars, sexual predators, bullies, dangerous environments, etc.). Whereas children fifty years ago spent many unsupervised hours exploring their worlds, acquiring experience, developing skills and independence, now they are much more supervised and physically constrained.[35] This is not what children want. When asked, they express a strong desire for safe environments (and workplaces, and homes), but not at the cost of curbing their freedom and opportunities to control important dimensions of their lives. They don't want to be isolated from the world; they want the world to be re-structured to accommodate them—by restrictions on cars, removal of pollutants from the places they want to play, creation of safe workplaces with fair compensation and labour rights, opportunities to have meaningful input into decisions at home, work, and school.[36] So the issue is not whether protection is important and legitimate. The real issue is whether individuals are able to participate in decisions about *how* protection is provided, and

---

[32] On domesticated animals as workers and contributors, see Kendra Coulter, *Animals, Work, and the Promise of Interspecies Solidarity* (New York: Palgrave Macmillan, 2016).

[33] Atul Gawande, *Being Mortal* (New York: Metropolitan, 2014), p. 96.

[34] Erving Goffman, *Asylums* (Garden City: Anchor, 1961), p. 14.   [35] Lister (n 29), p. 714.

[36] Priscilla Alderson, *Young Children's Rights* (London: Jessica Kingsley, 2008). Michael Bourdillon, Ben White, and William Myers, 'Re-Assessing Minimum-Age Standards for Children's Work', *International Journal of Sociology and Social Policy* 29, no. 3 (2009): pp. 106–117; Flores et al. (n 31).

if children are given a say, they express a clear preference that protection not be pursued primarily by restricting their freedom.

The Western idea of protected childhood is becoming a self-fulfilling prophecy—delaying children's opportunities to develop capabilities, autonomy, and responsibility.[37] Children have started to internalize the idea that they are incompetent, vulnerable, and irresponsible.[38] As children grow up, adults start to fear these irresponsible not-yet-citizens (not just fear for them), resulting in attempts to restrict movement and association through public policies like curfews, zoning laws, extension of compulsory schooling age, stricter car licensing laws, and so on.[39]

This pattern of establishing a highly restrictive and paternalistic framework, motivated either by the desire to protect or the desire to control, is familiar from treatment of people with cognitive disabilities, and is precisely the paradigm being challenged by the UNCRPD. It can also be seen in all contexts concerning domesticated animals, even in farmed animal sanctuaries, which are, in most cases, dedicated to rescue and protection, not empowerment, and which are therefore prone to excessive paternalism.[40]

We are not disputing that paternalistic decisions are sometimes appropriate. The problem with political wardship is not that some people are entrusted to speak on behalf of, or to decide for, others in particular contexts, for particular purposes. Such relations are endemic in contemporary societies. All citizens, at some time or other, rely on trustees to act in our interests when we are temporarily incapacitated, when we lack relevant expertise, or as part of a division of labour. But wardship is qualitatively different: it involves a comprehensive political status, leaving individuals subject to paternalistic decision-making power across all dimensions of life, regardless of their capacities, interests, and desires—in perpetuity (or until age sixteen/eighteen). Wards in this sense are defined as a class in opposition to competent citizens. The latter may be subject to paternalistic protections, but these are understood to be provisional and purpose-specific departures from a baseline of respect for freedom. Someone may, for example, be judged unable to give informed consent to a particular medical or financial procedure, yet still be assumed competent to make decisions about friends, work, and politics. (In legal terms, wards are subject to 'plenary guardianship', as opposed to more specific forms of 'tailored guardianship' or 'assisted decision-making' in which citizens may need the assistance of others

---

[37] Alderson (n 36). Regarding the cost of excessive paternalism for people with intellectual disabilities, see Hill Walker et. al., 'A Social-Ecological Approach to Promote Self-Determination', *Exceptionality* 19 (2011): pp. 86–100.

[38] Allison James, 'To Be (Come) or Not Be (Come): Understanding Children's Citizenship', *Annals of the American Academy of Political and Social Science* 633 (2011): pp. 167–179.

[39] Lister (n 29), p. 706.

[40] Donaldson and Kymlicka, 'Farmed Animal Sanctuaries: The Heart of the Movement? A Socio-Political Perspective', *Politics and Animals* 1 (2015): pp. 50–74.

when making certain types of decisions in certain contexts[41]). In other words, political wardship is a status held *in lieu of* citizenship, and should not be confused with forms of tailored guardianship that enable and support the exercise of citizenship.

In short, the wardship model is inherently deficient in its denial of meaningful participation by vulnerable individuals, and its failure to check the partial and self-serving knowledge of the powerful. It offers a myth of benign pastoral care which is at odds with the empirical record, and which obscures the realities of power and contribution that generate the need for citizenship. The inevitable result is unaccountable power, unrecognized burdens, and excess paternalism.

Rethinking Political Agency

But how can those who lack linguistic agency participate politically? For many commentators, there is no alternative to the status of passive wards: some individuals simply are by nature incapable of political voice. As we noted earlier, this pessimistic assumption about the prospects of enabling political participation for those who lack rational speech is the flipside of the optimistic assumption about the prospects of developing feasible models of wardship, and the two assumptions together underpin the capacity contract.

We discuss below some ways of enabling political voice and participation by those who lack linguistic agency. But it may help to begin by exploring why contemporary theories of citizenship have so hastily dismissed the possibility of political agency for young children, people with cognitive disability, and domesticated animals. After all, it is quite clear that the members of these groups have experience and knowledge about their lives; they have preferences about what sorts of activities and relationships they want to engage in, and the kind of world they want to inhabit; they are communicative in any number of ways. What then is the obstacle to including their will in politics?

The answer, we would suggest, lies in the specific way that political agency is conceptualized within both the liberal and republican traditions as an *internal and self-asserted individual capacity*, rather than a social or relational achievement. Liberals emphasize individual autonomy, while republicans put greater emphasis on citizen engagement, participation, and co-creation of the public good.[42] Both, however,

---

[41] For these distinctions, and the necessity of replacing plenary guardianship/wardship with assisted decision-making, see Alexander A. Boni-Saenz, 'Sexuality and Incapacity', *Ohio State Law Journal 76*, no. 6 (2015): pp. 1201–1255.

[42] See Honohan in this volume for a helpful overview of these traditions.

envision citizens as self-sufficient reasoning and discursive agents. Society fills up children with the appropriate civic ideas, dispositions, and virtues, and churns out adults, each 'in a position where he or she can live in resilient, self-asserted freedom'.[43] Whether the focus is on conceiving and revising a subjective conception of the good; or on deliberating and articulating judgments in the democratic realm; or on responsibly fulfilling one's citizenship duties; or on holding power to account, citizens are conceived as independently able to initiate and perform the relevant thought processes, discursive acts, and forms of participation. Rational speech is the essential glue that links these self-sufficient, independent political agents into a political community, enabling communication, negotiation, commitment, and accountability.

This reification of intellectual independence, and of self-sufficiency in judgment and deliberation, entails that children can be conceived only as 'citizens-in-waiting' or 'apprentice citizens'.[44] People with cognitive disabilities are positioned as failing to develop or graduate into citizenship. Domesticated animals are positioned as never having the chance. All of these groups must be content with passive representation by neurotypical adults, just as women once enjoyed passive representation via their fathers and husbands.[45]

This generates a profound asymmetry in contemporary citizenship theory. Individuals' capacities for communication, reasoning, understanding, empathy, responsibility, and self-restraint fall along a spectrum, and the extent to which these capacities can be effectively exercised depends on a wide range of social conditions. Yet, under the capacity contract, citizenship theory draws a sharp dividing line, and applies completely different criteria to those who fall above or below that line. Neurotypical adults who fall above the line are granted unconditional political rights, even if they vote in ignorance, in poor judgment, in narrow self-interest or from a range of more dubious motivations. Indeed, society recognizes a duty to facilitate the exercise of their political rights, for example, by providing translation services, or help in accessing information or the voting booth. So long as individuals can assert their political claims as linguistic agents, we accept a strong duty to remove potential barriers to their equal and effective participation. But if someone falls below the threshold of linguistic agency, we renounce any obligation to solicit

[43] Knud Haakonssen, 'Republicanism', in Robert Goodin and Philip Pettit, eds., *A Companion to Contemporary Political Philosophy* (Oxford, Cambridge: Blackwell, 1993), pp. 568–574, p. 572.

[44] Lister (n 29), p. 696. Some liberal and republican accounts of citizenship education allow children to exercise carefully circumscribed political rights, but this is justified on instrumental grounds of producing competent future citizens, not on the basis of their own inherent right to political agency (Rehfeld (n 7)). As many scholars have noted, society (and political theory) tends to view children as 'becomings' not 'beings': children have claims in virtue of what they might become as adults, not in virtue of their lives as children (Jens Qvortrup, 'Childhood as a Social Phenomenon', *Eurosocial Reports* 36 (Vienna: European Centre, 1990)). All citizens might better be viewed as inhabiting variable states of 'becoming' and 'being'—as both 'learning *and* empowered actors' (Bacon and Frankel (n 9), p. 39).

[45] Rehfeld (n 7), pp. 154–156.

their input or to facilitate their participation, and indeed in many cases legally prohibit their participation, and consign them to the status of passive wardship.

This asymmetry is theoretically arbitrary, and democratically unjustified.[46] Some might argue that restricting citizenship to those with a capacity for linguistic agency is essential for preserving relations of political equality amongst members of the self-governing demos. How can we be political equals if some depend on others for support in exercising their political rights and responsibilities? But no matter where the threshold of linguistic agency is set, the capacity for independent political action will still be unequally distributed amongst members of the demos: the capacity contract does not remove the challenge of building an egalitarian ethos amongst members with varying capacities and dependencies. More importantly, preserving political equality by excluding members of society is a contradiction in terms. After all, those who are excluded from citizenship are still subject to political rule: those who exercise 'self-government' are not just exercising power over themselves, but over all members of society. The capacity contract does not enable self-government by equal citizens: rather, it gives some the right to rule over themselves and others. This is a Procrustean solution, preserving an appearance of equality by expelling all members who do not fit a pre-ordained vision of citizenship that was defined by and for some subset of members.

We need a different model of equal citizenship based on the idea of interdependent agency rather than (or in addition to) self-sufficient individual agency. Developing and revising one's script of the good life can be an interdependent process that occurs not solely inside one's head, but through trial and error (doing and re-doing, rather than thinking and re-thinking) in the context of trusting and supportive relationships with others.[47] And this subjective good can then be brought into the process of public deliberation, not just by the rational speech capacities of the individual, but through other modes of effective representation. Representatives can rely on careful observation, non-linguistic communication, trial and error feedback loops, creative projection, and inherited institutional and cultural knowledge.[48] Norms about the benefits and burdens of social life need not be rationally endorsed and discursively negotiated, but can be learned and internalized through unconscious, embodied, and habitual processes, and then renegotiated through structured choice situations.[49] And finally, it is not necessary that every individual

---

[46] Given that the political rights of neurotypical adults are not conditional on their knowledge or virtue, the exclusion of individuals lacking linguistic agency can't be justified on the basis of the quality of the decisions they might make. (See Claudio Lopez-Guerra, *Democracy and Disenfranchisement* (Oxford: Oxford University Press, 2014). The evidence concerning the quality of decision-making when children are empowered is in fact quite positive (Lister n 29), p. 702.)

[47] Leslie Francis and Anita Silvers, 'Liberalism and Individually Scripted Ideas of the Good: Meeting the Challenge of Dependent Agency', *Social Theory and Practice 33*, no. 2 (2007): pp. 311–334.

[48] Kim Smith, *Governing Animals* (New York: Oxford University Press, 2012), chapter 4.

[49] Sue Donaldson and Will Kymlicka, 'Unruly Beasts: Animal Citizens and the Threat of Tyranny', *Canadian Journal of Political Science 47*, no. 1 (2014): pp. 23–45.

citizen be able to hold distant power to account (e.g. by voting, expressing dissent, and other discursive mechanisms). The exercise of power can be held accountable through collective and third party mechanisms, including the forms of fiduciary guardianship discussed earlier.[50] Drawing on these mechanisms of learning, voice, socialization, choice, and accountability, we can construct new spaces and places of citizenship that allow all members to have a say in the norms that govern our shared life.[51]

Indeed, this sort of interdependent agency is central to how substantive citizenship is enacted for all of us, much of the time, whether or not we are capable of rational speech. The idealization of political agency as rational speech misses key dimensions of real-world democratic citizenship. We all rely on trust, greeting, rhetoric, embodied pro-social dispositions, and phatic communication to establish norms of civility, cooperation, and democratic community, and to establish spaces of democratic resistance and experimentation.[52] Ignoring these dimensions of political agency is pernicious even for those who are linguistic agents, given the unequal ways citizens may be situated with respect to dominant discourses and modes of participation.[53] For members of society who aren't capable of rational speech, this truncated conception is a disaster, leaving them completely disenfranchised.

To paraphrase Catherine Mackinnon, the idealization of citizenship functions as an affirmative action program for the members of society with the greatest access to rational speech. Access to rational speech, and the freedoms it creates, is, like many resources of 'public' life, dependent on silent armies of women, children, and animals performing invisible and unacknowledged reproductive and social labour.[54] Feminist and disability critiques of liberal and republican citizenship have challenged the idea that free and equal citizens must be materially independent, and liberated from the day-to-day activities of social and material reproduction. But we still lack a sustained critique of the view that political communication is an inherent self-asserted capacity of individuals, rather than a socially created public good to

---

[50] Laura Montanaro, 'The Democratic Legitimacy of Self-Appointed Representatives', *Journal of Politics* 74, no. 4 (2012): pp. 1094–1107; Jennifer Rubenstein, 'Accountability in an Unequal World', *Journal of Politics* 69, no. 3 (2007): pp. 616–632; Michael Saward, 'Authorization and Authenticity: Representation and the Unelected', *Journal of Political Philosophy* 17, no. 1 (2009): pp. 1–22.

[51] We explore these ideas in Sue Donaldson and Will Kymlicka, 'Rethinking Membership and Participation in an Inclusive Democracy: Cognitive Disability, Children, and Animals', in Barbara Arneil and Nancy Hirschmann, eds., *Disability and Political Theory* (Cambridge University Press, 2016), pp. 168–197; and in 'Farmed Animal Sanctuaries' (n 40).

[52] On the importance of non-standard communication see Iris Marion Young, *Inclusion and Democracy* (Oxford, New York: Oxford University Press, 2000). On application to relations with animals, see Eva Meijer, 'Political Communication with Animals', *Humanimalia* 5, no. 1 (2013): pp. 1–25. On the importance of phatic rituals to establishing citizenship relations, see James Slotta, 'Phatic Rituals of the Liberal Democratic Polity', *Comparative Studies in Society and History* 57, no. 1 (2015): pp. 130–160.

[53] Toby Rollo, 'Everyday Deeds: Enactive Protest, Exit, and Silence in Deliberative Systems', *Political Theory* (forthcoming).

[54] See Volpp in this volume for a related discussion.

which some individuals have privileged access. Unequal access to this public good is re-described as individual capacity, and used to rationalize the exclusion that creates the unequal access in the first place.

It should not surprise us that the inherited mechanisms of substantive citizenship reflect the capacities and interests of those who designed those mechanisms: citizenship has historically been defined by and for linguistic agents, to suit their particular interests and capacities. But it is circular to use these mechanisms as a basis for evaluating new claims for citizenship recognition.

CONCLUSION: TOWARDS INCLUSIVE CITIZENSHIP

Contemporary citizenship theory remains burdened by an age-old commitment to a capacity contract, according to which independent political agency via rational speech is both the *precondition* and the *purpose* of citizenship. We have argued it is time to renounce this capacity contract, and its underlying view of political agency. Linguistic agency is one particular mechanism for realizing citizenship, but it only works for some members of society, and relying on it exclusively generates arbitrary and illegitimate internal exclusions. Moreover, these exclusions cannot be compensated by naïve and discredited models of wardship, which systematically overestimate the willingness and capacity of guardians to act in the interests of the vulnerable, and systematically underestimate wards' capacities and contributions.

Instead, our first step should be to revisit the underlying moral purpose of citizenship. That moral purpose, we have argued, is to ensure that all members of the community have a chance to act on their own understanding of their subjective good, to exercise meaningful forms of control in their lives, and to participate in shaping the society and laws by which they are governed. This is the fundamental moral impulse underlying membership models of citizenship. If we accept this membership model, the next step is to ask whether all members of society can access existing mechanisms for realizing their citizenship, or whether we need to create new mechanisms to achieve these moral purposes.

For children and people with cognitive disabilities, this process of developing new practices is already under way. While much citizenship theory still ignores these groups as an intractable 'problem' for citizenship, real-world experiments in citizenship are proliferating, inspired in part by UN Conventions. Moreover, we believe that many of the practices being developed for these groups can provide a starting point for thinking about how to draw domesticated animals into citizenship. For all of these groups, however, we should expect that the more empowered they become as citizens, the more they will change how democratic citizenship is realized for all of us. This is not a development to be feared, but a welcome source of creative democratic renewal.

As we've noted, some people worry that substantive citizenship for children, people with cognitive disabilities, and domesticated animals would come at a cost to members of these groups, by denying the unique features of their situation, and imposing burdens of contribution, responsibility, and decision-making that they cannot handle, and should not be expected to handle. But a 'difference-centred' conception of citizenship is not about flattening differences, and imposing a one-size-fits-all model of how to enact citizenship. Rather, the aim is to be responsive to everyone's desire to control and shape their world in meaningful ways, and supporting them in the development of their competence and responsibility. This doesn't mean burdening children with a lot of questions and decisions (prompted by our sense of what is important). It doesn't mean abdicating our role in setting authoritative limits (on the contrary, limits are crucial to the development of competence and confidence). It does mean spending more time observing them, listening to them, understanding their perspectives and needs, developing mechanisms for contesting these interpretations, and most importantly, implementing mechanisms which ensure that these perspectives and expressions actually shape society. In other words, it is about providing avenues for excluded individuals' concerns to get onto the political agenda, not about conscripting them into our pre-set agenda. When, as a society, we ask: what *matters* to this person? what is she concerned about? what does she want to exercise control over? how does she want to live?—we are not thereby imposing an agenda on her, but enabling her to impose an agenda on us.

The tremendous challenges of this approach must be acknowledged. The problem of finding adequate mechanisms to restrain the power of neurotypical adults, and ensuring that the views of vulnerable groups are not simply consulted but actually shape decision-making, are formidable. However, we can't begin this process until we acknowledge the hollowness of universal citizenship, the failures of political wardship, and the illegitimacy of denying political agency to vulnerable groups. This must be our starting point.

In closing, it is worth looking further down the road. Who might be the next group in the citizenization process, demanding equal membership, not caste or ward status? One speculative possibility concerns the development of sentient robots. We are highly doubtful that such a development is possible, but it may be worth asking how our model of inclusive citizenship would apply to them. On the membership model we defend, the first question to ask is: are they members of the community? By the time artificial sentience emerges, if it does, robots, like domesticated animals now, would almost certainly be widely integrated into our societies—present in our homes, our workplaces, our public spaces, our cultural imaginaries, living and working alongside us. And so their subjectivity would emerge within our social world: they would be involved in intersubjective relationships with us, social norm negotiation, cooperation and contribution. They would be 'born' into society, governed by its rules, with a 'real and effective link' and a 'permanent interest in membership'. And so if robots evolve to become sentient beings with a subjective good, an interest in exercising meaningful control over their lives and in participating in shaping the society and laws by which they are governed, then they will be owed citizenship. And this will mean re-evaluating the mechanisms of substantive citizenship to see if they are workable for sentient robots, and if not, creating new mechanisms of citizenship to empower them.

This membership perspective on sentient robots differs from views which would ground our obligations to robots in their intelligence, or our causal role in creating them.[55] It also suggests how duties to sentient robots emerging within our society might differ from our duties to aliens arriving from outer space. The key question regarding robots would be the internal citizenship question of how we recognize their de facto membership and include them in substantive citizenship. The key question regarding aliens would be the external citizenship question—do we want to form a shared society with them? Can we live together? But for children, people with cognitive disability, and domesticated animals, that question is settled: they are already members, and we owe them inclusive citizenship.

BIBLIOGRAPHY

Alderson, Priscilla, *Young Children's Rights* (London: Jessica Kingsley, 2008).
Arneil, Barbara, 'Disability, Self-Image, and Modern Political Theory', *Political Theory 37*, no. 2 (2009): pp. 218–242.
Bacon, Kate and Sam Frankel, 'Rethinking Children's Citizenship: Negotiating Structure, Shaping Meanings', *The International Journal of Children's Rights 22*, no. 1 (2014): pp. 21–42.
Bauböck, Rainer, 'Stakeholder Citizenship: An Idea Whose Time Has Come?', in Bertelsmann Stiftung (ed.), *Delivering Citizenship: The Transatlantic Council on Migration* (Gütersloh: Verlag Bertelsmann Stiftung, 2008), pp. 31–48.
Beckman, Ludvig, *The Frontiers of Democracy: The Right to Vote and its Limits* (Basingstoke: Palgrave Macmillan, 2009).
Boni-Saenz, Alexander A., 'Sexuality and Incapacity', *Ohio State Law Journal 76*, no. 6 (2015): pp. 1201–1255.
Bourdillon, Michael, Ben White, and William Myers, 'Re-Assessing Minimum-Age Standards for Children's Work', *International Journal of Sociology and Social Policy 29*, no. 3 (2009): pp. 106–117.
Carens, Joseph, *The Ethics of Immigration* (Oxford: Oxford University Press, 2013).

---

[55] Eric Schwitzgebel, 'We Have Greater Moral Obligations to Robots than to Humans', *Aeon* (12 November 2015), online https://aeon.co/opinions/we-have-greater-moral-obligations-to-robots-than-to-humans.

Clifford, Stacy, 'The Capacity Contract: Locke, Disability, and the Political Exclusion of "Idiots"', *Politics, Groups, and Identities 2*, no. 1 (2014): pp. 90–103.

Cohen, Elizabeth, *Semi-Citizenship in Democratic Politics* (Cambridge: Cambridge University Press, 2009).

Coulter, Kendra, *Animals, Work, and the Promise of Interspecies Solidarity* (Basingstoke: Palgrave Macmillan, 2016).

Donaldson, Sue and Will Kymlicka, *Zoopolis: A Political Theory of Animal Rights* (Oxford: Oxford University Press, 2011).

Donaldson, Sue and Will Kymlicka, 'Unruly Beasts: Animal Citizens and the Threat of Tyranny', *Canadian Journal of Political Science 47*, no. 1 (2014): pp. 23–45.

Donaldson, Sue and Will Kymlicka, 'Farmed Animal Sanctuaries: The Heart of the Movement? A Socio-Political Perspective', *Politics and Animals 1* (2015): pp. 50–74.

Donaldson, Sue and Will Kymlicka, 'Rethinking Membership and Participation in an Inclusive Democracy: Cognitive Disability, Children, and Animals', in Barbara Arneil and Nancy Hirschmann, eds., *Disability and Political Theory* (Cambridge University Press, 2016), pp. 168–197.

Dwyer, James, 'No Place for Children', *Alabama Law Review 62*, no. 5 (2011): pp. 887–961.

Flores, Noelia, Cristina Jenaro, M. Begoña Orgaz, and M. Victoria Martín, 'Understanding Quality of Working Life of Workers with Intellectual Disabilities', *Journal of Applied Research in Intellectual Disabilities 24* (2011): pp. 133–141.

Francis, Leslie and Anita Silvers, 'Liberalism and Individually Scripted Ideas of the Good: Meeting the Challenge of Dependent Agency', *Social Theory and Practice 33*, no. 2 (2007): pp. 311–334.

Gawande, Atul, *Being Mortal* (New York: Metropolitan, 2014).

Goffman, Erving, *Asylums* (New York: Anchor, 1961).

Haakonssen, Knud, 'Republicanism', in Robert Goodin and Philip Pettit, eds., *A Companion to Contemporary Political Philosophy* (Oxford: Blackwell, 1993), pp. 568–574.

Hinchcliffe, Christopher, 'Animals and the Limits of Citizenship', *Journal of Political Philosophy 23*, no. 3 (2015): pp. 302–320.

Hobbes, Thomas, *Leviathan* II.xxvi.12.

Invernizzi, Antonella, 'Everyday Lives of Working Children and Notions of Citizenship', in Antonella Invernizzi and Jane Williams, eds., *Children and Citizenship* (Thousand Oaks: Sage, 2008), pp. 131–141.

James, Allison, 'To Be (Come) or Not Be (Come): Understanding Children's Citizenship', *Annals of the American Academy of Political and Social Science 633* (2011): pp. 167–179.

Lister, Ruth, 'Why Citizenship: Where, When and How Children?', *Theoretical Inquiries in Law 8*, no. 2 (2007): pp. 693–718.

Lopez-Guerra, Claudio, *Democracy and Disenfranchisement* (Oxford: Oxford University Press, 2014).

Meijer, Eva, 'Political Communication with Animals', *Humanimalia 5*, no. 1 (2013): pp. 1–25.

Mills, Charles, *The Racial Contract* (Ithaca: Cornell University Press, 1999).

Montanaro, Laura, 'The Democratic Legitimacy of Self-Appointed Representatives', *Journal of Politics 74*, no. 4 (2012): pp. 1094–1107.

Moosa-Mitha, Mehmoona, 'A Difference-Centred Alternative to Theorization of Children's Citizenship Rights', *Citizenship Studies 9*, no. 4 (2005): pp. 369–388.

Nichols, Robert, 'Indigeneity and the Settler Contract Today', *Philosophy & Social Criticism 39*, no. 2 (2013): pp. 165–186.

Pateman, Carole, *The Sexual Contract* (Cambridge: Polity Press, 1988).

Peggs, Kay, *Animals and Sociology* (Basingstoke: Palgrave Macmillan, 2012).

Quennerstedt, Ann, 'Children, But Not Really Humans? Critical Reflections on the Hampering Effect of the "3Ps"', *International Journal of Children's Rights 18*, no. 4 (2010): pp. 619–635.

Qvortrup, Jens, 'Childhood as a Social Phenomenon', *Eurosocial Reports 36* (Vienna: European Centre, 1990).

Rehfeld, Andrew, 'The Child as Democratic Citizen', *Annals of the American Academy of Political and Social Science 633* (2011): pp. 141–166.

Rollo, Toby, 'Feral Children: Settler Colonialism, Progress, and the Figure of the Child', *Settler Colonial Studies* (29 June 2016), online http://dx.doi.org/10.1080/2201473X.2016.1199826.

Rollo, Toby, 'Everyday Deeds: Enactive Protest, Exit, and Silence in Deliberative Systems', *Political Theory* (forthcoming. Published online 28 July 2016), doi: 10.1177/0090591716661222.

Rubenstein, Jennifer, 'Accountability in an Unequal World', *Journal of Politics 69*, no. 3 (2007): pp. 616–632.

Saward, Michael, 'Authorization and Authenticity: Representation and the Unelected', *Journal of Political Philosophy 17*, no. 1 (2009): pp. 1–22.

Schwitzgebel, Eric, 'We Have Greater Moral Obligations to Robots than to Humans', *Aeon* (12 November, 2015), online https://aeon.co/opinions/we-have-greater- moral-obligations-to-robots-than-to-humans.

Shachar, Ayelet, *The Birthright Lottery: Citizenship and Global Inequality* (Cambridge: Harvard University Press, 2009).

Shklar, Judith, *American Citizenship: The Quest for Inclusion* (Cambridge: Harvard University Press, 1991).

Slotta, James, 'Phatic Rituals of the Liberal Democratic Polity', *Comparative Studies in Society and History 57*, no. 1 (2015): pp. 130–160.

Smith, Kimberly K., *Governing Animals* (New York: Oxford University Press, 2012).

Such, Elizabeth and Robert Walker, 'Young Citizens or Policy Objects? Children in the "Rights and Responsibilities" Debate', *Journal of Social Policy 34*, no. 1 (2005): pp. 39–57.

Trasande, Leonardo et. al., 'The Environment in Pediatric Practice', *Journal of Urban Health 83*, no. 4 (2006): pp. 760–772.

Tully, James, 'Struggles over Recognition and Distribution', *Constellations 7*, no. 4 (2000): pp. 469–482.

Walker, Hill et. al., 'A Social-Ecological Approach to Promote Self-Determination', *Exceptionality 19* (2011): pp. 86–100.

Young, Iris Marion, *Inclusion and Democracy* (Oxford: Oxford University Press, 2000).

Zakaras, Alex, 'Democracy, Children, and the Environment: A Case for Common Trusts', *Critical Review of International Social and Political Philosophy 19*, no. 2 (2016): pp. 141–162.

INDEX

....

9 780198 805861